Praise for the first edition of *A Reader in the Anthropology of Religion*

"[A] reader that ambitiously attempts to represent the full breadth, depth, and complexity of anthropology's investigations into religion . . . The masterly general introduction situates this anthology within the long and often difficult anthropological engagement with this most mystified and powerful realm of social action. . . . [A]n excellent text."

International Social Science Review

Blackwell Anthologies in Social & Cultural Anthropology (ASCA)

Series Editor: Parker Shipton, Boston University

Drawing from some of the most significant scholarly work of the 19th and 20th centuries, the *Blackwell Anthologies in Social and Cultural Anthropology* series offers a comprehensive and unique perspective on the ever-changing field of anthropology. It represents both a collection of classic readers and an exciting challenge to the norms that have shaped this discipline over the past century.

Each edited volume is devoted to a traditional subdiscipline of the field such as the anthropology of religion, linguistic anthropology, or medical anthropology; and provides a foundation in the canonical readings of the selected area. Aware that such subdisciplinary definitions are still widely recognized and useful - but increasingly problematic - these volumes are crafted to include a rare and invaluable perspective on social and cultural anthropology at the onset of the 21st century. Each text provides a selection of classic readings together with contemporary works that underscore the artificiality of subdisciplinary definitions and point students, researchers, and general readers in the new directions in which anthropology is moving.

Series Board

Fredrik Barth, University of Oslo and Boston University
Stephen Gudeman, University of Minnesota
Jane Guyer, Northwestern University
Caroline Humphrey, University of Cambridge
Tim Ingold, University of Aberdeen
Emily Martin, Princeton University
John Middleton, Yale Emeritus
Sally Falk Moore, Harvard Emerita
Marshall Sahlins, University of Chicago Emeritus
Joan Vincent, Columbia University and Barnard College Emerita

Published Volumes:

1. *Linguistic Anthropology: A Reader, Second Edition*
Edited by Alessandro Duranti

2. *A Reader in the Anthropology of Religion, Second Edition*
Edited by Michael Lambek

3. *The Anthropology of Politics: A Reader in Ethnography, Theory, and Critique*
Edited by Joan Vincent

4. *Kinship and Family: An Anthropological Reader*
Edited by Robert Parkin and Linda Stone

5. *Law and Anthropology: A Reader*
Edited by Sally Falk Moore

6. *The Anthropology of Development and Globalization: From Classical Political Economy to Contemporary Neoliberalism*
Edited by Marc Edelman and Angelique Haugerud

7. *The Anthropology of Art: A Reader*
Edited by Howard Morphy and Morgan Perkins

8. *Feminist Anthropology: A Reader*
Edited by Ellen Lewin

9. *Ethnographic Fieldwork: An Anthropological Reader*
Edited by Antonius C. G. M. Robben and Jeffrey A. Sluka

10. *Environmental Anthropology: A Historical Reader*
Edited by Michael R. Dove and Carol Carpenter

11. Anthropology and Child Development: A Cross-Cultural Reader
Edited by Robert A. LeVine and Rebecca S. New

A Reader in the Anthropology of Religion

Edited by
Michael Lambek

Second Edition

Blackwell
Publishing

Editorial material and organization © 2008 by Blackwell Publishing Ltd

BLACKWELL PUBLISHING
350 Main Street, Malden, MA 02148-5020, USA
9600 Garsington Road, Oxford OX4 2DQ, UK
550 Swanston Street, Carlton, Victoria 3053, Australia

The right of Michael Lambek to be identified as the author of the editorial material in this work has been asserted in accordance with the UK Copyright, Designs, and Patents Act 1988.

Designations used by companies to distinguish their products are often claimed as trademarks. All brand names and product names used in this book are trade names, service marks, trademarks, or registered trademarks of their respective owners. The publisher is not associated with any product or vendor mentioned in this book.

This publication is designed to provide accurate and authoritative information in regard to the subject matter covered. It is sold on the understanding that the publisher is not engaged in rendering professional services. If professional advice or other expert assistance is required, the services of a competent professional should be sought.

First published 2002 by Blackwell Publishing Ltd
Second edition 2008

5   2012

Library of Congress Cataloging-in-Publication Data

A reader in the anthropology of religion / edited by Michael Lambek. – 2nd ed.
    p. cm. – (Blackwell anthologies in social & cultural anthropology ; 12)
    Includes bibliographical references (p.) and index.
    ISBN 978-1-4051-3615-0 (hardcover : alk. paper) – ISBN 978-1-4051-3614-3 (pbk. : alk. paper)   1. Ethnology–Religious aspects.   2. Religion.   I. Lambek, Michael.
    BL256.R43 2007
    306.6–dc22

                                2007011995

A catalogue record for this title is available from the British Library.

Set in 9 on 11 pt Sabon
by SNP Best-set Typesetter Ltd., Hong Kong
Printed and bound in Singapore
by Markono Print Media Pte Ltd

For further information on
Blackwell Publishing, visit our website at
www.blackwellpublishing.com

for Nadia and Simon

Contents

Preface to Second Edition

I have used the opportunity of an expanded second edition to redress certain omissions from the first. These include the entries by Burridge, Harding, Humphrey, Myerhoff and Pouillon. I have also added some newer work – essays by De Boeck, Hasan-Rokem, Palmié, and van de Port. I have tried in particular to strengthen the sections on religious change and the relationship of religion to politics as well as to add some coverage of gender, Judaism, north Asia, the Caribbean, and Latin America. I realize that large gaps in these and other areas remain but also that there is a limit to the weight of books students can be expected to shoulder in their knap-sacks. In making my selections I was assisted by a readers' survey conducted by Blackwell, by my very able research assistants Nina Nguyen and Shirley Yeung, and by the comments of a number of discerning readers, including Maurice Bloch, Fenella Cannell, Rodney Needham, Todd Sanders, Nicolas Sihle, and doubtless others – although in most cases I was not able to follow their advice. One excellent recommendation was Igor Kopytoff's classic essay "Ancestors as Elders in Africa" (*Africa* 41, 129–42, 1971, followed by the discussion in *Man* 17, 546–8, 1982); this is easily accessed on line.

Shirley Yeung is largely responsible for the upgraded bibliography and regional and topical indexes and is now co-author of this section. Unfortunately, given the timing of the editing and production process, we have not been able to comprehensively cover books published from 2005 onwards. I have made a few minor improvements and updates to the introductions.

Jane Huber initiated the second edition; Emily Martin, Deirdre Ilkson, and others at Blackwell ably guided me through it. Helen Gray was an efficient and reassuring copy-editor while Shirley Yeung assisted with proofing and updated the index. Jackie Solway once again provided invaluable judgment and a keen eye for the cover.

A recent useful overview of the field is by Rosalind Hackett, "Anthropology of Religion," in *Companion to the Study of Religion*, edited by John Hinnells (London: Routledge), pp. 144–63, 2005. I have also published a short analysis of

"Anthropology and Religion" in the *Oxford Handbook of Religion and Science* (2006), edited by Philip Clayton, pp. 440–73.

Since the appearance of the first edition political events and social circumstances have encouraged two trends that remain under-represented in the second edition. The first concerns the politicization both of Islam and of the reception of Muslims in Europe and North America. One site of the latter concerns *l'affair du foulard* (the headscarf controversy) and subsequent events in France (Bowen 2004a, b, 2006; cf. Asad 2003, Mahmood 2006). Secondly, in response to developments in the cognitive and neurosciences there is the growth of cognitive approaches to religion, of which some of the most interesting work is Astuti (in press), Bloch (2005), and Whitehouse (2004). Partly in reaction to biblical literalism, perhaps, there is also enthusiasm in some quarters for a related "neo-Darwinian" school (Atran 2004, Boyer 1994, 2001). See Berliner and Sarró, eds. (2006), for more broadly based discussions on learning religion as well as de Vries, ed. (in press), for contemporary interdisciplinary takes on religion at large.

Acknowledgments to the First Edition

Heartfelt thanks to the following people for specific advice, suggestions, and in some cases course syllabi: Paul Antze, Ellen Badone, Sandra Bamford, Sarah Caldwell, Fenella Cannell, Hilary Cunningham, Filip De Boeck, Paul Hanson, Keith Hart, Bob Hefner, Jack Kugelmass, John Leavitt, Bruce Lincoln, Anne Meneley, Birgit Meyer, Peter Pels, Parker Shipton, Jackie Solway, Jonathan Spencer, Charles Stafford, Anne Vallely, Andrew Walsh, Nireka Weeratunge, Brad Weiss, Dick Werbner, Aram Yengoyan, and a remaining anonymous referee of the original table of contents. My apologies if I have missed someone. Paul Antze, Sam Bamford, Janice Boddy, Anne Meneley, and Andrew Walsh provided very useful feedback on a penultimate version of the table of contents and introductory material. Their comments have improved the book. The contributors responded to my request for verification of abridgments with good humor and advice (which I could not always follow). Sarah Gould served as an efficient assistant at my end, as did Sarah Coleman at Blackwell. Juanita Bullough (copy editor), Deirdre Rose (index), Annette Chan, and Audrey Glasbergen provided outstanding assistance. The reader would not have been conceived or produced without Jane Huber's steely editorial persistence, so well sheathed in charm and diplomacy. Her advice, enthusiasm, and lunches have been critical. Jackie Solway provided even more advice, encouragement, and meals, and Nadia and Simon Lambek urged me enthusiastically to get on with it.

M. L.

General Introduction

This anthology demonstrates the strength and vibrancy of the anthropological study of religion across the 20th century. The collection is neither purely historical in orientation, nor a survey of contemporary work, and is not a comprehensive coverage of the broad variety of topics anthropologists of religion address. Rather, it views the anthropology of religion as a live tradition of intellectual inquiry and attempts to show broad connections within a body of work. It charts the recurrence or perdurance of certain central questions, even if, as Geertz pithily put it, "Anthropology . . . is a science whose progress is marked less by a perfection of consensus than by a refinement of debate. What gets better is the precision with which we vex each other" (1973a: 29).

The anthropological tradition in the study of religion is an "extended conversation," now dating back well over a century. It is difficult to fully understand contemporary interventions without tracing back the roots of debate. Yet the conversation has been long and complex, and the essays included in the anthology simply provide some of the highlights of that conversation. They are essays significant for the originality, elegance, or clarity with which the authors develop their positions or the rich ethnography with which they illuminate particular aspects of religious practice. Most of them have long been recognized as such and thus are widely cited. Conversely, much significant work has had to be omitted for considerations of space.

The anthology is addressed to readers both within and outside anthropology who seek a direct entry to what anthropologists have (had) to say about religion. It is suitable for students at various levels; the contributions are scholarly and vary in their difficulty. Their sequence in the volume is based on the application of several criteria: the time at which they were written, the order in which they made an impact, and the theme or topic. The contributions can, of course, be read in any order.

The Anthropological Tradition

Anthropology as a field has long been open to interdisciplinary work and, indeed, may even be conceptualized as a kind of transdiscipline. As the contents of this volume reflect, not all of the most significant contributions have come from people identified as anthropologists. Nevertheless, participants in the anthropological conversation on religion can be said to share a certain broad and evolving outlook with respect to the kinds of questions they find useful or interesting to ask, the methods appropriate to address them, and the frameworks through which contributions are received. This outlook overlaps with, but is distinct from, that found in alternate approaches to religion characterized as theological, philosophical, sociological, historical, and so on.

The specifically anthropological conversation on religion, which, to be sure, has comprised many strands, heated arguments, and rich digressions, can be broadly characterized by the following features (which are often ascribed to the field of anthropology as a whole). An anthropological approach comprehends arguments that are variously holistic, universalistic, ethnographic, comparative, contextual, historical, dialogical, and critical. By holism is meant that anthropologists see "religious" facts as parts or dimensions of larger social and cultural wholes, do not begin by immediately demarcating a "religious" sphere from that of the nonreligious (or one religion from another), and understand the presence or production of such distinctions as problematic, hence as part of their subject matter. A holistic approach examines the inextricable links among religion and, for example, the social reproduction of families, gender hierarchy, political organization, and modernity.

Anthropology is universalistic in that it takes the whole range of human societies, past and present, as its subject matter and attempts not to privilege the western tradition or literate societies. Thus, along with universalistic coverage comes the continuous attempt to address ethnocentric bias and the need to produce models that make sense both of diversity and unity. In practice, anthropology's universalism has meant it was the only discipline to take seriously the existence of small-scale societies without traditions of literacy.

Anthropology's ethnographic perspective means that our analyses are usually developed through the study of specific societies and even of smaller units – individual communities, congregations, religious experts, particular events, etc. – within them. The view is often "up close and personal," or draws from data collected by means of intensive and intimate fieldwork that aims, in the first instance, to understand a local way of seeing and doing things. The result is often a book-length narrative portrait (an ethnography).

Yet anthropology is also resolutely comparative, insofar as the particularistic ethnographic accounts must be made to speak to each other and to a developing (and frequently debated) analytic language so that we can think, at least provisionally, by means of such concepts as "deities," "the sacred," "ritual," "sacrifice," and so on. These terms come to take on particular meanings within the anthropological conversation that they do not necessarily hold outside it. Overall, anthropology must walk a fine line between exoticizing or idealizing, on the one hand, and banalizing, on the other, the statements, practices, and experiences that exercise those whom we study.

The approach is contextual in that anthropological "facts" are always understood relative to their contexts. The elaboration of context – linguistic, cultural, social, political, etc. – is a central feature of anthropological interpretation, yet the relative weight given to specific aspects of context – e.g., the structural versus the pragmatic – has often been the location of our most vigorously contested arguments.

Increasingly, context has been understood in terms that have been called histori-cal; in particular, this temporal (and spatial) locatedness has meant understanding personal and collective agency with respect to past and present political and eco-nomic forces, notably those of colonialism, capitalism, and emergent globalization. Our approach is also historical insofar as we attend to local (cultural) forms of historical consciousness and of making and addressing change; frequently these are couched in religious idioms and practices.

The anthropological perspective is dialogical in that our method is rooted in conversation with, and especially in listening to, those whose practices, knowledge, and experience we attempt to understand. Questions of how far to privilege which kinds of voice and how to comprehend diversity, including contextually muted voices, have become increasingly significant. More abstractly, anthropology is dialogical insofar as foreign concepts and practices need to be described in terms of concepts and practices available to the broader community of anthropologists (including resources from philosophy and other fields). The foreign, in turn, con-tributes to the elaboration and sophistication of anthropological language.

Finally, the anthropological conversation can be characterized as critical, meaning by this both "critical" in the sense of literary critical and "critical" in the political sense of concern with power and its subterfuges and abuses. The best anthropology is also self-critical; here our concern with overcoming the various and multiple forms of ethnocentrism and intellectual narrowness remains a characteristic feature of any contribution that wishes seriously to be taken as anthropological. This is not to assert that we have overcome our biases and constraints, and especially not to assume that we are somehow more advanced along the slope of enlightenment than either our interlocutors or our intellectual forebears. As philosopher David Hoy has put it, "Reflection on the partiality of past interpretations demands reflection on the partiality of the present" (1978: 167).

Anthropologists have also, over time, variously emphasized evolutionist, rational-ist, functionalist, social structural, structuralist, symbolic, interpretive, political, Marxist, social constructionist, phenomenological, psychoanalytic, poststructural-ist, cognitive, aesthetic, and ethical approaches or modes of understanding. As an intellectual tradition, anthropology is marked less by consensus than by the way such arguments have taken account of each other.

Anthropology on Religion

Questions of religion have been central to anthropology since its beginnings, whether we place these in the 19th century with thinkers like Tylor or Robertson-Smith, or in the 18th century with Vico. Indeed, these are among anthropology's hardest and most enduring questions – questions about difference, rationality, community, modernity, symbolization, meaning, relativism, mimesis, projection, mediation, power, order, hierarchy, harmony, conflict, alienation, love, well-being, dignity, aesthetic coherence, creativity, playfulness, reproduction, fertility, maturation, death, tedium, excitement, motivation, suffering, and redemption. The anthropology of religion points to the unique conjunctions of morality, desire, and power, of subjection and freedom, of worldliness and asceticism, of ideal and violence, of imagination and embodiment, immanence and transcendence, inwardness and outwardness, origins and ends, order and chaos, structure and practice, cosmos and history, that have constituted distinctive human worlds.

Contemporary anthropology of religion draws from a number of sources. From the Americanist (Boasian) tradition it draws a sense of the intimate connection between religion, language, and poetics, and the importance of consulting and understanding the experience of gifted individual practitioners (e.g., the entries by Radin and Tedlock, chapters 19 and 31). From Durkheim (chapter 2) comes the understanding of religious phenomena as social, as well as the intimate connection between function and meaning in religious ritual and representation, and between religion and social order (e.g., the selections by Turner and Rappaport, chapters 26 and 33). From the evolutionists comes the question of the rationality of primitive thought, a question that, while now moot in and of itself, continues to inform discussion about the logic and legitimation of any particular form of religious declaration or practice (e.g., the essays by Douglas and Tambiah, chapters 16 and 25). From the evolutionists as well, and variously mediated by phenomenologists and psychoanalytic thinkers, come questions concerning the relative weight of thought and experience, the intellectual and the practical, the rational and the nonrational, the conscious and the unconscious in the religious sphere (e.g., the essays by Gell and Obeyesekere, chapters 22 and 29). From Marx comes attention to power, alienation, fetishism, and mystification (e.g., Bloch and Taussig, chapters 32 and 35). From Weber (chapter 3) comes attention to the comparative aspects of the text-based religions, to the place of religion in transitions to modernity, to the links between religion and the wellsprings of both political and economic action, and finally to the question of theodicy, the puzzle of locating meaning in the givenness of the world, suffering, and death (e.g., Geertz and Hirschkind, chapters 4 and 42). All these questions, in turn, have roots in ancient thought, in Plato's distinction between mimesis and philosophy, in Aristotle's discussions of ethics and poetics, and in the portrayals in texts like Oedipus and Job (to draw from the title of chapter 28 by Fortes) of fate and justice.

Most vital of all has been the stream of ideas emanating from the variety of religious traditions (including those of the West) that anthropologists have studied. Not only have they supplied some of the key terms with which we have routinely worked – totem, taboo, mana, karma – but our experiences in the field and the lessons we have learned from our interlocutors have shaped the way we ask and answer questions, and have had enormous impact on the nature of our reception of the various theoretical currents mentioned above.

The anthropological tradition understands religious worlds as neither fully objective nor fully subjective phenomena, but as poised in the mediating space of culture or the social and as participating in a dialectic that both objectifies and subjectifies. Good anthropology understands that religious worlds are real, vivid, and significant to those who construct and inhabit them and it tries, as artfully as it can, to render those realities for others, in their sensory richness, philosophic depth, emotional range, and moral complexity. In acknowledging the value and power of such worlds, but also their variety and competition, anthropology must understand them as so many means for acting, asking, shaping, and thinking, rather than as a set of fixed answers whose validity either can be independently assessed (objectivism) or must be accepted as such (relativism).[1]

With respect to the ultimate truth of religion (or specific religious traditions), anthropologists have offered a variety of answers; perhaps the most popular has been the phenomenological one of simply bracketing the question as outside of the scope of discussion. Another has been to accept the social reality of religious phenomena for those who adhere to them. Anthropologists do ask how religious truths become socially realized and confirmed, and also recognize that flourishing symbolic worlds contain the means to reflect back on themselves, to dwell on paradox, and to enable internal debate, skepticism, and relativity. The anthropology of religion does not shy away from recognizing the human constitution of any given religious formation, nor from elucidating the particular mystifications necessary to the construction or enactment of religion. Anthropology explores the ways religious practices are embedded in, or complicit with, specific forms of sociality, regimes of power, historical struggles, and modes of production. In sum, the anthropology of religion engages with politics and history yet refuses to reduce religion to either of these.

Anthropology has sometimes been seen as poised between idealism and materialism, although few contributors can be said to fall into either form of reductionism. Ideas are formed within and therefore with respect to specific material conditions, but at the same time, material conditions can only be grasped and evaluated within or with respect to a specific system of ideas, semiotic code, or way of looking at the world. Symbolic and material forms, practices, and contexts change at different rates; no religion worth the name is epiphenomenal. At the same time, such dynamic systems and their proponents are often, but not always, in active competition with each other. The nuances of how all this works out in practice or how it is to be understood in theory have been the object of much debate – hardly any two of the contributors to this volume take precisely the same stand on the issues – but the recognition of some kind of dialectical relationship is central. The dialectic may be phrased as base and superstructure, mind and body, structure and practical reason, nature and culture, myth and history, imagination and reality, sacred and profane, ritual and common-sense knowledge. As the word "dialectic" suggests, these terms are not simply opposed to one another; we attempt to work through the successive interrelationships, contradictions, and mediations to which they give rise.

This leads further into the question of how such relations are understood within any given cultural tradition and how we, in turn, are to interpret that understanding. Are sacred and profane, myth and history, etc., locally distinguished from one another, or is the universe grasped in more holistic terms? Thus Lévi-Strauss, for example, argued that totemism is a structure in which can be seen the play of nature and culture, and attempts to both mediate between them and to think through each domain by means of metaphors drawn from the other.

A persistent theme in the anthropological conversation has concerned the logic of religious thought and practice. If many of the 19th-century thinkers saw members of smaller-scale societies mired in superstition, ignorance, bliss, or folly, the personal connections forged in decent ethnographic fieldwork immediately deprived westerners of any illusions of intellectual or moral superiority. Concomitantly, theorists began to realize that rather than compare nonwestern systems of thought directly to western science, it was much more sensible both to compare religion, common sense, and specialized knowledge about the world *within* any given society (and hence how categories and hierarchies of knowledge are formed and function in the first place), and to compare western *religious* practices with nonwestern ones. Thus the problem shifted from explaining the ostensibly irrational religious practices of others to understanding the nature of religious practice anywhere.

But things are more complex than this sounds, since the very distinction between religion and science, or for that matter the natural and the supernatural, does not characterize all societies. Nor does it characterize consistently the attitudes of all members of any given society. Many anthropologists thus begin with a more holistic picture, or one in which the religious cosmos provides the place of the whole or the grounds for truth that among secular thinkers has come to be replaced by such concepts as "nature," "society," or "mind." Hence the need to grasp beliefs and practices relative to the universes in which people live, whatever the specific references to gods, prayer, and the like. It follows from this that the anthropologist's own cosmos is but one among many; our position is possibly an epistemologically privileged one, but it is not located in some neutral space outside of culture. Thus objectivism, in the sense of assuming such a privileged "Archimedean" position, must be abandoned.

To leave things here, however, may be to give too much to relativism, since it is clear both that all humans do have much in common and that we can learn to understand each other or meet each other halfway. Cultural worlds are open to each other, not closed. Moreover, we can ask how particular worldviews are constituted and explore their underlying structure (whether conceived as grammatical, propositional, projective, tropic, or performative and rhetorical). We can also ask how such world "views" are composed, produced, and legitimated; that is, how and in what respects they come to be realized as "worlds," taken as real, as "natural" rather than socially constructed, as true rather than contingent. Indeed, following Rappaport (1999; chapter 33 below), we ask how certain religious acts and utterances become the ground against which social acts and cultural facts can themselves be established, validated, or, to use a religious word, sanctified (as happens, for example, under oath); and how they relate to forms and distributions of political power, to changing social, material, and economic constraints and opportunities, as well as to psychic processes both rational, nonrational, and irrational. We can also recognize that cultural and religious worlds, including our own, are not necessarily internally consistent but may juxtapose both contradictory and incommensurable concepts, practices, and traditions. The epistemological stance that encompasses this diverse range of questions and that approximates the location of many thoughtful contemporary anthropologists might be referred to very broadly as *critical hermeneutics*.

Clifford Geertz, in the 1966 essay abridged as chapter 4 below, complained that mid-20th-century anthropology of religion had not been theoretically adventurous enough. Freud, of course, was in vogue at the time and anthropologists continue to draw on him as well as on the subsequent, if at present somewhat rocky, career of psychoanalytic thought. But Geertz had in mind the philosophers. If Geertz drew from Langer (see chapter 10) and Ryle, subsequent writers have found greater interest in the work of Ryle's colleague, Austin, on the performative dimension of speech (see chapters 25 and 33). Lévi-Strauss (chapter 17) was also on Geertz's horizon. Lévi-Straussian structuralism may be seen as a philosophical transformation of Durkheim by way of Saussurean linguistics. Others have been more influenced by the version of semiotics initiated by Peirce or by the hermeneutic critique (and perhaps appropriation) of structuralism elucidated by Ricoeur. More recently, some anthropologists have discovered continental phenomenology (Merleau-Ponty), existentialism (Heidegger), or Lacanian psychoanalysis (chapters 38, 45), while others have drawn from the Marxist tradition, notably from Gramsci and Raymond Williams, or from Foucault and the poststructuralists (see chapters 9 and 35). Other philosophers have a longer reach; Aristotle is a figure addressed, to quite different ends, in the contributions by Becker and Taussig (chapters 18 and 35).

Since the 1950s, literary criticism has been in dialogue with anthropological structuralism; anthropologists then benefited from the new energy released by the discovery of Bakhtin and Benjamin. The former connection is represented in the selection from Stallybrass and White (chapter 21), the latter in that of Hirschkind (chapter 42). Yet other anthropologists have been increasingly attracted to the insights of cognitive psychology in the ambitious attempt to build a universal (objectivist) theory of human knowledge that would incorporate religious ideation. In sum, if the parochialism of which Geertz complained has not been entirely superseded, it is now complemented by attention to a wide range of theory.

Contemporary anthropology is also engaged with globalism and with the effects of the expansion of the West under mercantilism, colonialism, and present-day, "late" capitalism. With respect to religion this concerns confrontations between so-called "world" or universalizing religions like Christianity and more localized forms, as well as the perceived competition among universalizing traditions. Some anthropologists have seen small-scale societies gladly replacing their parochialism with broader cosmologies, while others have emphasized the coercive and hegemonic effects of missionary activity or processes of religious rationalization. Today, in many parts of the world, people are switching from older forms of missionary Christianity to Pentecostalism and anthropologists are engaged in trying to figure out why (van Dijk 1998, Martin 1990, Meyer 1998, 1999). Given the geopolitical situation and the demonization of Islam in the western press, other anthropologists have attempted to present more informed accounts of Muslim versions of modernity (Eickelman and Piscatori 1996, Hefner 1998, 2000). Yet others compare secularizing and religious social movements, examine ethnic, regional, or class conflicts that come to be expressed in religious terms, or try to understand the increasing ethnicization or hardening of religious boundaries in places once known for more open, tolerant, holistic or incorporative social fields (James, ed. 1995). Thus, where anthropological accounts of religious diversity in South Asia were once shaped by the Redfieldian contrast between "big" and "little" traditions (Singer 1972, Fuller 1992), they now attend to political mobilization, nationalism, and collective violence (Tambiah 1992, 1996, Hansen 1999; Van der Veer 1994).

Religion has also been understood as a form of social protest, as evident in the literature on cargo cults and millenarian movements (Burridge 1969, Worsley 1957; chapter 34 below). Some anthropologists examine the place of religion in rationalized political interventions, such as the Sanctuary movement on the Mexican/US border (Cunningham 2000), Latin American liberation theology, Gandhiism, and environmentalism (see chapters 43, 44). Anthropologists have also been concerned with the relationship between state policy and the formation of religious institutions and boundaries, with the cult of political figures, and with the impact of religious interests and differences on national and transnational politics. The continuing vitality of religion as a social and political force is amply illustrated by events and activities such as the Iranian revolution, the rise of the religious right in the United States (chapter 37), the increasing success of Pentecostalism in Africa and Latin America, the role of Buddhism in Sri Lankan and Tibetan national struggles, and the growth of saint cults in Israel.

Yet this anthology emphasizes the religious and symbolic construction *of* the world more than the way such constructions form responses *to* it. This is one of the things that anthropologists study particularly well and whose elucidation is almost exclusively in the hands of anthropology as a discipline. The anthropological perspective here is neither that of the theologian, whether as interested insider or outsider, nor that of the distanced observer who finds any particular local set of practices simply wrong, superficial, or epiphenomenal, whether on epistemological, practical, or political grounds. To grasp the attraction and power of religion, or its motivating force in political and economic affairs, one must, as Weber put it so well, understand the world it proposes and in which it situates its actors. A world in which it can be stated that "time is money" (see chapter 3) is of a very different order from one where it can be stated with equal matter-of-factness that "men are parrots" (Crocker 1977).

While it would be absurd to deny that politics and economics affect religious realities and actions, a view of religion as merely superstructural is disturbingly close to the dominant ideology of bourgeois capitalism. Rather than accepting that view with undue complacency (whether from a liberal or a Marxian perspective), it too must be understood in complex relationship with the political and economic circumstances that inform it and that it informs.

There is also the question of how tightly sealed or inevitable one finds such connections. Anthropologists vary from positions of rather strict determinism, whether of Marxian, Durkheimian, Freudian, or culturalist roots, to positions of Weberian elective affinities or ones that emphasize contingency, ambiguity, and imagination. And historically, one can note contrasts between societies or sectors of society that readily gave up particular religious structures and practices in the face of more powerful social realities, and those that tried to hang on steadfastly.

Religion Itself?

Insofar as religion forms the cultural "ground" (or "worldview") of a society or serves to articulate its major concerns, it is intimately linked to such matters as human conception, kinship, and the life cycle, to the environment, ideas of human sociality, affinity, and exchange, conceptions of and conditions for human dignity, justice, creativity, and general well-being. Hence we are led to ask both how subjects are constituted and how agents are motivated. The study of religion directs us to daily observance of prayer and dietary and cleanliness taboos, to judicious moral action in the face of specific events and toward the collective good (practices that Aristotle called phronesis), and to the adventures of sacrifice, pilgrimage, spirit possession, devotion, study, vision quest, prophecy, and the like. Religion also anticipates failures, omissions, inversions, and distortions; these are imagined in myth, liminality, pollution, sorcery and witchcraft, demons and spirits, and sometimes in the gods themselves.

But just what is religion? The prevalence, significance, and apparent universality of religion, and hence the scope of any field devoted to its study, depend on how we define it. Yet such a definition is by no means obvious. Few other than the writers of introductory textbooks would be satisfied with a concrete and narrow definition (derived from Tylor's account of animism, chapter 1 below) such as "belief in supernatural beings." This sort of definition begs many questions: What is "supernatural" except relative to someone's idea of the "natural," a concept surely of rather recent European vintage? Why a specifically dualist model? Why "beings" and only "beings" (or spirit, soul, God, or whatever the substantive part of the definition)? What is meant by "belief" (chapters 7, 8)? How would religious belief differ from ordinary knowledge or other forms of conviction?

Durkheim long ago moved well beyond "intellectualist" definitions that depend not only on a dubious concept of belief but on the assumption of an individual rational thinker at the source. He offered instead a definition that is structural, "relative to sacred things." The sacred was defined as that which was set apart and therefore could vary in substance from one social order to another, the particular content not being especially relevant for understanding the form. Durkheim also demonstrated the collective rather than the individual basis of symbolic classification, of which sacred/profane is a central opposition (chapter 2 below). More recently Rappaport has developed a model of the sacred as "a property of discourse" (1999: 281) and elaborated formal properties of sanctification (chapter 33 below).

"Belief in supernatural beings" would hardly warrant Susanne Langer's portentous description of religion as "the most typical and fundamental edifice of the human mind" (1948: 33). Indeed, it was a minimalist definition which enabled certain 19th-century thinkers to look with disdain upon "primitive societies" whose religions were assumed to be made up of little more than primary feelings of fear or awe towards the spiritual beings in whom they so bluntly and naively "believed." Of course, broader definitions that encompass the moral have not been lacking either. Valeri, for one, sums up religion as "the objectified system of ideas of a community," a Hegelian idea found not only in Feuerbach and Marx, but in

Robertson-Smith and Durkheim (Valeri 1985: x). Writers such as Geertz, Douglas, and Lévi-Strauss offer variants of such an approach. In this collection perhaps Stanner (chapter 6) offers the most robust substantive depiction of religion. A particular twist is to be found in the lineage from Mauss to Dumont and Schneider, who note that the separation of religion from politics or economics or more broadly of "cosmos from society" (de Coppet and Iteanu, eds., 1995) may be specific to the West.

The most interesting attempts at defining or modeling religion emphasize meaning and order. They thereby both identify religion with other domains of thought or symbolic practice (that is, with culture understood in symbolic, semiotic, or discursive terms) and distinguish its place relative to these domains. The distinction is on logical, structural, or functional grounds rather than content. Thinkers like Geertz, Rappaport, Bloch, and Asad variously enquire how conditions of meaning, meaningfulness, truth, and certainty are produced, guaranteed, and underpinned. Those mechanisms which most strongly establish, anchor, contextualize, and regulate meaningful order and orderly meaning may be called "religious." Emphasis is placed on world construction, entailing an imaginative poiesis by means of symbols, tropes, and performative rituals, and on locating and orienting people as subjects and agents within such worlds. Meaning and order are thus to be discovered simultaneously at both the conceptual and moral levels and questions of cosmos, eschatology, power, authority, motivation, and discipline are closely connected. Meaningful order becomes all the more clearly marked as anthropologists adopt theories that emphasize the fluidity, divisiveness, and creativity of culture and acknowledge the fragmentation, shallowness, uncertainty, and speed that characterize capital-driven postmodernity.

Characteristic of late-20th-century thought has also been a reaction against producing definitions for heuristic purposes and a move toward reviewing the genealogies of terms. Genealogists ask how particular definitions emerge and come to objectify their referents, how a concept like "religion" comes to appear as either an ostensibly "natural" category of thought or the referent of a naturally existing "organ" of human society. In doing so it becomes apparent that any definition is relative to the concerns of its time. Thus, in a trenchant essay, religious studies scholar Jonathan Z. Smith documents the shift from a "Catholic" conception of religion close to ritual to a "Protestant" one close to piety (1998: 271) and argues moreover that, "'Religion' is not a native category . . . It is a category imposed from the outside on some aspect of native culture" (ibid.: 269) (cf. Asad, chapter 9 this volume).

Edward Sapir early made the point that "a very useful distinction can be made between 'a religion' and 'religion.' The former appears only in a highly developed society in which religious behavior has been organized by tradition [a Weberian point]; the latter is universal" (1956 [1928]: 120). Nevertheless, as Smith remarks, the very distinction produces such questions as whether "the diverse 'religions' [form] species of a generic 'religion'?" (1998: 275).

Smith concludes that Melford Spiro's (1966: 96) definition of religion as "an institution consisting of culturally patterned interaction with culturally postulated superhuman beings" (a much more sophisticated version of the intellectualist definition I presented above) has gained the widest assent among scholars of religion. But he remarks astutely that it "places human cultural activities or institutions as the *summum genus* and religion as a subordinate taxon" (1998: 281). Spiro, of course, is an American cultural anthropologist.

If some early anthropologists saw Christianity as the only "true" religion, the response that other religions could be equal or equivalent carried its own ethnocentric bias – namely the assumption that religions were to be recognized by their similarities, substantive or analogical, to Christianity, which continued to serve implicitly as the prototype religion. And yet, of course, the very nature of Christianity, defined through its relation to larger cosmological and social wholes, has changed over time – from its origins as a rebellious millenarian movement in a Roman colony, to the days when it anchored medieval society, to the rise of Protestant sectarianism, and then the subsumption of religion within capitalist modernity (compare Cannell 2006).

The conception of religions as distinct, bounded entities closely follows Christian ideas that religions are mutually exclusive, that one can commit to only one at a time, and that commitment occurs through a form of inner "belief" or "faith" (see the essays by Ruel and Asad, here chapters 8 and 9, respectively). Yet in many parts of the world religious ideas have diffused and been accepted or rejected in whole or part much as any other elements of culture; inner conviction is not privileged over outer observance; and conversion is not a salient category. Indeed, it is hard to see how it could be otherwise in contexts where religions are not objectified entities but simply dimensions of ways of life. Syncretism, transformation, and pluralism are all more likely responses. Analysts such as Werbner (1977), Ranger (1993a, b), and Wiessner and Tumu (1998) have noted the spread of precolonial regional cults and in much of the world today we see the presence of incommensurable discourses without the idea of mutual exclusion, competition, or conflict. One may note the multiple forms of religious practice (Buddhist, Shinto, etc.) in Japan, the copresence of Confucian and Taoist temples in Vietnam, or the jostling of Islam and spirit possession in places as distinct as Morocco, Sudan, and Madagascar. The same has been noted for Buddhism and spirit cults in Burma and Thailand and for Catholicism and voodoo in Haiti. The Indian subcontinent has provided its own forms of open pluralism, despite the emergence and sectarian quarrels of Buddhists, Jains, and Sikhs, the rise of "communalism," and the complicity of Islam, Hinduism, and Buddhism with nationalism. In the United States one can see the conjunction of Christianity with civil religion, though the two have become perhaps all too closely linked in the time since Bellah wrote his essay (chapter 39). Similarly for Roman Catholicism and nationalism in France, although there the former has had a strong opponent in rationalism (*laicité*).

The prevalent conjunctions of such incommensurable or even contradictory sets of ideas and practices suggest that the Dumontian unity of cosmos and society may be too tightly conceived and that structuralist accounts are often a good deal tidier than the phenomena they claim to model. Nevertheless, structuralism serves the highly salutary function of moving us away from the naiveté of simple behaviorism and often reveals alternate forms of ordering the world and profound levels of connection and relation which strictly empiricist comparison would certainly miss.

In sum, we can see that anthropology is caught between, on the one hand, scrutinizing, relativizing, and in effect deconstructing the general, dominant, and ostensibly universal categories by which it begins its inquiry and, on the other, seeking more general categories by which it can carry out comparison and describe conclusions. Some of our best work has been deconstructionist *avant la lettre*: Steiner's *Taboo* (1956), Evans-Pritchard's *Theories of Primitive Religion* (1965), and Lévi-Strauss's *Totemism* (1963e) spring immediately to mind. Conversely, other significant essays have found new ways to generalize across cases: van Gennep, *The Rites of Passage* (1960 [1908]), Hertz, *Death and the Right Hand* (1960 [1909]), Mauss, *The Gift* (1990 [1925]), Douglas, *Purity and Danger* (1966), Burridge, *New Heaven New Earth* (1969), Turner, *The Ritual Process* (1969), and Bloch and Parry, eds., *Death and The Regeneration of Life* (1982) are among the most notable.

The ethnographic literature invites theoretical comprehension of such evident similarities as the attention given to ancestors in East Asia and Africa or to men's houses and sacred flutes in Amazonia and Papua New Guinea – not to mention the near universality or family resemblance of things we can call sacrifice, taboo, prayer, or initiation – without apparently excessive violence to the individual cases. To be sure, some concepts have proved less durable than others, and the deconstructions of previously dominant and reified terms such as totemism have been critical. The structuralist movement attempted to replace reified categories with structures of relations, and Needham (1975) usefully drew attention to the idea of polythetic classification (classes in which each member shares something in common with at least one other member but in which there may be nothing shared by all members). These are lessons that anthropology should have internalized and can still draw from productively. What anthropology cannot do (and has not done) is take an exclusively genealogical or deconstructive position.

This is so for two reasons. First, with respect to the ideas and practices of those we study, we can be skeptical about specific religious objects or arguments, but not about the idioms and acts through which they are evidently constructed. And we have no business taking the missionary position, even when the creed we advocate is secular rationalism (or postmodern irrationalism). Second, with respect to our own field of study, we continue to need a language into which to translate our findings and in which to speak.

In any case, this book has been conceived on the edge of this dilemma, begun with the notion that compiling a set of articles under the rubric "religion" was a valuable exercise, while recognizing equally the danger of reifying its subject. Definitions, contents, and boundaries should be held in question and the frame should be understood always as only one among many through which any particular set of human phenomena can be viewed. What is advocated is not the discovery of more precise definitions but the acknowledgment of the contingency, provisionality, and implications of any definitions we choose to deploy. In particular, we need to be intellectually self-conscious of how we might talk about "religion" in those societies that do not have a discrete field that maps onto the contemporary western notion of the religious, or that cannot be judged by norms established via the monotheistic Judeo-Christian-Islamic lineage. And we need to be more open and creative in imagining "religion" in societies that do and can.

While outsiders look to anthropology for generalizations, anthropologists them-selves, some notable exceptions aside, remain happier exhibiting differences, explor-ing particularities, following connections, tracing patterns, elaborating context, demonstrating complexity, illuminating paradoxes, or simply poking holes in the universalizing theories of other disciplines. Our craft is one of recognizing incom-mensurabilities and their limits; hence we remain more comfortable with raising questions than with answering them.

In Sum

The problems religion raises have been central to anthropological thought from its origins in the 19th century through to the present. As religious belief began to weaken in their own societies, Victorian thinkers focused ever more closely on its presence elsewhere. Early writers wrote about peoples who seemed to have too much belief or not enough, and well into the 20th century they were obsessed with defining religion and discriminating between it and its lesser cousins – magic, super-stition, etc. Definitional questions also pervaded discussions of myth and ritual until they were rendered less consequential by the structuralist revolution. But we still scratch our heads over the boundaries of phenomena – the relationship of "limin-oid" activities like nightclubbing, drama, or camp reunions to the "liminal" phases characteristic of rites of passage or pilgrimage; of purity and pollution activities and the relationships between bodily discipline or healing and religion; of political ideology or scientific authority and religious dogma; of concepts of spirit or soul and concepts of self or mind; even the question of "belief" itself and whether it can demarcate religious from ordinary cognition. Definitive answers to these sorts of questions are unlikely to be found; indeed, many people would say the only defen-sible positions are heuristic. But what is clear is that religion, especially that of "others," has proved, in Lévi-Strauss's famous phrase, "good to think."

At the same time, the anthropology of religion has made great strides in its enqui-ries. We are not, on the whole, nearly so ethnocentric as we once were. We have learned to appreciate the intellectual complexity, aesthetic richness, and moral depth of other peoples' constructions and practices; learned to understand how certain ideas and practices come to seem natural and inevitable to those who follow them; learned to see the intricate connections between ideology and power, from the grand myths of state to the minute capillary action of habitual disciplinary practices; learned to recognize generally recurring means and idioms of representing (through myth) or enabling (through ritual) creation, transition, transformation, order, and disorder; learned to appreciate the open-ended, edifying, world-building, life-enriching, and subversive qualities of much symbolic practice. We have a good general idea of better and worse ways to go about trying to understand, compare, and explain symbolic and social phenomena; and we have learned that the social and symbolic are inextricably connected: all that is social signifies, and signifying practices are simultaneously socializing.[2]

Perhaps, as Lévi-Strauss found for myth, it is from music that we can best draw the metaphors for what we produce – odes, variations, and so on. Among our greatest achievements, then, are the ethnographies like *Nuer Religion* (Evans-Pritchard 1956), *Divinity and Experience* (Lienhardt 1961), and *Bwiti* (Fernandez 1983) – to take only three superb Anglophone accounts of African religions – that are the closest we come to symphonies.

It is under the rubric of the "Anthropology of Religion" that fundamental questions of human difference have been addressed. These are often posed in dualist form – West versus rest, history versus myth, science versus religion, modern versus traditional, civilized versus primitive, and so on. It is extraordinarily difficult to escape from the pervasive strength of such dualisms. Some people would argue (dualistically) that the difference between the West and the rest is precisely the former's commitment to dualism and the latter's freedom from it; others have seen dualism as central to human thought. But whatever the case, the history of anthropological conversation on these topics is largely the increasing sophistication with which these dualisms have been explored, mediated, and partially transcended. On the one hand, we do not want to exoticize and to exaggerate difference; on the other, we do not want to homogenize, an enterprise in which everyone inevitably comes across as pale versions of ourselves. The anthropological position is one that precisely straddles this dilemma, not ignoring it, not wishing it away, not reducing the answer to one side or the other.

From Tradition to Anthology

Reducing a long, healthy, and complex intellectual tradition to some 600 pages entails some hard choices and a good deal of violence. It was all too easy to find good articles to include in this reader. The anthropology of religion is blessed with riches and the field is a very broad one; structural analyses are appropriate to every domain, symbols and rituals are ubiquitous. If the selection is to be done well there needs to be an overall vision, yet one that is not overly narrow. I shall try briefly to indicate the grounds on which I have made my selections.

The primary aim has been to include a substantial body of significant work of relatively lasting significance. The temporal scope ranges from the 19th century to the contemporary period. Yet the anthology does not comprise a systematic history of anthropological approaches to religion so much as a number of significant interventions across that history. At some moments it captures the density of intertextual references, the cooperative building and also the *agon* characteristic of an intellectual tradition, while at other moments the selections are simply too widespread for direct mutual citation. I try to evoke some of the density via the order of presentation and the accompanying commentary. Thus Part I is constituted by a section setting out several contrasting orientations to religion followed by a section comprising skeptical rejoinders.

With respect to intellectual breadth, I have endeavored to avoid setting obvious boundaries. I take the anthropological tradition to be constituted in dialogue not only with the religious ideas and practices it has encountered, but with the broader western tradition out of which it has grown and to which (along with postcolonial scholarship) it must continue to speak. Hence I have not hesitated to include pieces by authors who are not anthropologists by profession. Likewise I include both work whose theme is "religion" in a straightforward and obvious sense and work that expands the horizons of what we might mean by "religion," approaching it sideways, as it were, and thereby linking it to broader questions of culture and politics.

A guiding principle has been to avoid the reification of both "religion" and of the various categories and topics – "prayer," "spirits," "Hinduism," etc. – often subsumed within it. Indeed, a major contribution by anthropologists has been to challenge these kinds of categories, and I include several essays that take an explicitly skeptical and reflexive approach (e.g., Humphrey, chapter 40, on 'shamanism'). I have selected pieces in the first instance on the basis of their contributions to general intellectual debate about religion in the broad sense, and only secondarily with an eye to systematic coverage of the range of topics generally included within religion as a field. However, I have attempted to include a broad range of approaches as well as a sample of religious practices from diverse social contexts and cultural traditions.

Similarly, I have looked for a way to organize the sections and chapters that would not simply reproduce older forms of classification (myth, ritual, etc.). I have not, of course, either wished or been able to dispense with classification entirely. Parts II and III are distinguished very loosely according to the Aristotelian categories of making (poiesis) and doing (praxis), which I have found useful both to overcome more stubborn dualities of reason and unreason (Lambek 2000a) and to articulate observations in my own ethnographic work (Lambek 1998, 2002a, b). While each inevitably implies and overlaps with the other, together they form a productive way to conceptualize religion (the production of worlds and the activities within them) and to comprehend the range of emphases that a variety of anthropologists have brought to the subject. I conclude with Part IV under the rubric of history, which is simply a matter of different emphasis rather than of topic. These essays emphasize the historicity and dynamism of religion and the political and economic impingements on, and entailments of, both poiesis and praxis at specific historical locations, including, of course, the present.

Homage to the Missing

If the most obvious function of an anthology is to introduce new readers to a field of study, it introduces them to old (relatively speaking) authors. This implies that a second function is commemorative. An anthology produces a record of what has transpired. This record is necessarily selective. It is one of the tasks of memory work to forget in a principled way. I have tried to be principled but it has been a cause of grief that I have had to "forget" – to put aside, to cut, to disregard – so much.

When I began I had the idea that if I consulted widely I could discover some sort of consensus as to what should be included, but of course, the more people I asked, the more suggestions I received. All were interesting and some I have adopted, but overall consultation made the process of selection harder. I became resigned to the fact that the choice would have to be mine and that any selection would be to some degree idiosyncratic. The result is a combination of "classic" essays that have already been inscribed in institutional memory, pieces that I was taught or that I have used in teaching, works that have stayed in mind because of their place in the development of my thinking and ethnographic work, and pieces that I have discovered in the process of asking advice and sampling the literature. The result is the product less of a systematic search or clearly elaborated plan than a somewhat tortuous hermeneutic circling around and through its object.

In compiling the anthology I have felt that there were many obligations to be met and that in trying to meet them all I have not done proper service to any. To begin with, there is the debt to the ancestors. Much excellent work written on religion over the course of the 20th century and before is now too rarely cited or read. It was exciting to rediscover, for example, Lowie and Sapir, but they did not make the cut. Second, is the parental obligation. My selection is weighted toward things that were new when I was in graduate school and I can only say that the early 1970s were genuinely a high point in the anthropology of religion in North America, vibrant with the work of Turner, Geertz, and their students and the local reception of structuralism and hermeneutics. Then there are my peers, to whom I apologize for slighting, and my chronological juniors, where my authority is perhaps weakest.

Some of the other things I thought to balance in the process: theory relative to ethnography; small-scale societies relative to "world religions;" "West" to "rest;" world-building relative to "hermeneutics of suspicion;" thought or reason relative to emotion or performance; complex, multistranded, lengthy interpretation that best exemplifies ethnographic method relative to short, punchy, polemical articulation; historical, topical, and regional representation; mainstream or canonical relative to shaking up the consensus with ignored, idiosyncratic, or original pieces.

The cuts have been ruthless and the omissions are glaring. No specialist in the field (not even the contributors) is likely to be completely satisfied with the selection and it will replicate no instructor's ideal course. But the anthology can serve as a core text to be supplemented as desired. I have also provided suggestions for further reading, but am all too aware that even these merely skim the surface.

In order to maximize inclusion I stuck to one principle and gave way on another. Each author receives only one entry. But although I attempted to select short pieces, I also, after much hesitation, engaged in abridging. The abridgments have been checked with the authors where possible and are clearly marked by [...]. The individual acknowledgments and some footnotes have been deleted without notation. The individual selections are not meant to be "representative" of their authors' work nor necessarily either their "best piece" or "last word." Rather, each entry was selected to fit as part of the emerging whole and thus at times to serve several ends at once.

The entries must thus be seen as invitations: invitations to seek the unabridged originals and to read more of each author's work, invitations to read more on the topics or themes each entry represents, and invitations, via the bibliographic index, to read on topics, regions, and traditions omitted from the selections. Finally, the quintessence of anthropological insight is necessarily absent from this anthology; it can only be grasped by reading full monographs, and ideally more than one, by a given author or on a given society.

Recent introductory texts on the anthropology of religion include Bowen (1998b), Bowie (1999), Klass (1995), and Morris (1987). Wallace (1966) was particularly original for its time. Lessa and Vogt, eds. (in various editions, most recently 1979) is the classic anthology and has served as an inspiration for the present work; Dolgin, Kemnitzer, and Schneider, eds. (1977) anthologizes symbolic anthropology. Bowen ed. (1998a) and Klass and Weisgrau, eds. (1999) provide collections of recent articles; Glazier, ed. (1999) and Scupin, ed. (2000) offer handbooks. A good advanced introduction to the rationality debate is Tambiah (1990), while Firth (1996) is a lively and accessible collection of essays on religion by a senior scholar.

NOTES

1   See the important discussion in Bernstein 1988.
2   I regret having forgotten the source of this pithy remark.

Part I

The Context of Understanding and Debate

Opening Frameworks

Introduction

We begin with four classic and profound statements on the nature of religion which take us from one of the ablest evolutionists (Tylor), through the two greatest sociologists on the subject (Durkheim and Weber), to the anthropologist who has been, if not the most influential, at least the most talked about theoretician in the latter decades of the 20th century (Geertz). The first three figures present what came (along with a Freudian model) to be seen as the main alternative approaches to the understanding of religion. Through the mid-20th century the choice was particularly between Durkheim and Tylor. Then, in part through the writing of Geertz, Weber became of great interest to anthropology.

Tylor and Durkheim both seek the origins or foundations of religion. For Tylor they lie in individual reasoning, hence his position is often referred to as rationalist or intellectualist, whereas for Durkheim they lie in the collective consciousness that society has of itself. Durkheim's position is therefore social. Both men seek the clearest exemplification of religion's foundations in what they consider to be the simplest known societies. Tylor's method is one of comparison, derived from ostensible facts gleaned from a voluminous number of travelers' reports of varying quality, while Durkheim begins with the analysis of what he takes to be a single case, namely Aboriginal Australia. For Tylor the presence of religion could be explained as a reasonable, albeit mistaken, attempt to solve intellectual problems, whereas Durkheim took a more symbolic approach and argued that religious ideas and rituals both express and regenerate society.

Weber's concerns were not with the origins of religion per se so much as with the role of religion in the origins of modernity. He was concerned not with small-scale societies but with states, especially when comparing Asia with Europe. His approach was also distinctly historical, in contrast to the synchronic structure-functionalism to which Durkheimian ideas gave rise. He was interested, like Tylor, in what motivated people to think and act as they did, but he understood action in the context of collective systems of meaning. Where Tylor saw religious ideation as the product of direct and universal human concerns, Weber emphasized how such concerns are themselves shaped by diverse religious traditions. Likewise, where Tylor operated with an ostensibly universal and unequivocally positive idea of rationality, Weber was concerned with alternate kinds of means–ends relations, and especially with the emergence of various forms of what he called rationalization, which he viewed with some unease. In Weber the narrative of unequivocal progress assumed by the Victorians is replaced by distinct ambivalence.

This is not the place to rehearse the complex elements of either Durkheim's or Weber's analyses of religion, nor to chart a history of the respective traditions they founded or the way they twine through anthropological work (see O'Toole 1984 for a good sociological introduction). But it is to note that most contemporary anthropological analyses are informed by both these thinkers, whether in affirmation or resistance, tacitly or explicitly, and whether leavened by doses of Marx and Freud. Marx and Freud do belong here as well, and would have been represented by excerpts from *Capital* on commodity fetishism and from *Totem and Taboo*. Certain Freudian and Marxist arguments are presented in the selections from Obeyesekere and Taussig, respectively. All these interpretations of religion are prefigured by Feuerbach's analysis of religion as a human product (1975).

Geertz is present in this section not as a founding ancestor but as one of the strongest attempts within modern anthropology to compose a definition of religion and hence a model for subsequent research. Moreover, Geertz attempts a kind of implicit synthesis of previous approaches. We can see threads of both Tylor and Durkheim, while the overriding interest is Weberian. Geertz's roots are also Boasian, via Ruth Benedict, in that he is interested in portraying distinctive cultural worlds by means of ethnographic particulars.

Few other anthropologists have been able to develop original and powerful definitions of religion or to model its relationships to culture and society. A theoretical synthesis by sociologist Peter Berger, *The Sacred Canopy* (1967; see also Berger and Luckmann 1966), has strong parallels with Geertz. Rappaport (1999) is a magisterial anthropological attempt to understand religion's place in nature and, like Durkheim, its place at the foundations of social life.

1

Religion in Primitive Culture

Edward Burnett Tylor

"The growth of religious ideas is environed with such intrinsic difficulties that it may never receive a perfectly satisfactory exposition. Religion deals so largely with the imaginative and emotional nature, and consequently with such uncertain elements of knowledge, that all primitive religions are grotesque and to some extent unintelligible." Such was the opinion of Lewis Henry Morgan (1877: 5, as cited by Guenther 1999: 58), a contemporary of Tylor's. While Tylor (1832–1917) and Morgan are considered the leading figures of 19th-century evolutionary anthropology, and certainly among the very few who are still read today, Tylor's view of religion could not have departed further from Morgan's statement. Tylor, holder of the first chair in anthropology at the University of Oxford, found primitive religions neither grotesque nor unintelligible, and he thought he had developed a model of their development. Nor did he empha-size their "imaginative and emotional" side. Tylor was a rationalist and departed from many of his contemporaries in finding this quality in so-called "primitive man" as well. However, he felt equally that despite the rationality of their thought, the conclusions reached by members of small-scale societies were in error.

If Tylor is the only 19th-century writer to be included here, it is not only because he was among the more sensible, but because the core of his definition of religion as "the belief in Spiritual Beings" remains congenial to many contemporary thinkers and is indeed almost a part of western "common sense" on the subject. His characterization of animism remains fruitful and does serve as one means to generalize about religious phenomena of all kinds. Animism speaks today to reflections on the mind/body problem and conceptualizations of the person, to the relations between humans and other species, especially in hunting societies, and to conceptualizations of death and the centrality of both mortuary ritual and sacrifice in human societies. (See the essay by Viveiros de Castro, chapter 23 below.)

Tylor's main successor was Sir James Frazer, who developed a stronger contrast between magic, religion, and science as forms of reasoning (1890). It was Lucien Lévy-Bruhl (1985 [1910], 1966 [1923]) who provided the most direct alternative to rationalism. He is associated with the view that "natives" lived in some mystical connection with the world that transcends or evades the rational. It is easy to criticize Lévy-Bruhl (and he eventually criticized himself – 1949), but his argument looks rather more sophisticated if we see it as the complete inverse of Tylor, namely that if primitives are not rational, neither can they be said to be in error with respect to their conclusions. For Lévy-Bruhl, at least, the relation to the world was a rich and powerful one.

The criticisms of Tylor have been well rehearsed. The evolutionism entails value judgments and assumes a static quality to the thought of small-scale societies, as if they had been frozen in time; the comparative method decontextualizes ethnographic facts whose meaning is thereby reduced and distorted; the rationalism ignores the emotional side of religion; and the intellectualism ignores the collective, symbolic, representational dimension. The fact that Tylor sees religion grounded in error has appeared to many subsequent thinkers to debase and reduce the subject. Moreover, despite his concern for accurate empirical evidence, Tylor's approach is characterized by his own excessive speculation. Tylor's errors were compounded in Frazer.

Both Tylor and Lévy-Bruhl present one-sided and therefore impoverished pictures. Members of small-scale societies are far more sophisticated thinkers than either gave them credit for. They have far greater knowledge of the human condition and far richer, more variegated, and complex religious lives than Tylor recognized. They are also capable of much greater critical distance and abstract reasoning than Lévy-Bruhl imagined. Moreover, it is a mistake to generalize about small-scale societies; there are great differences among them and over time. A comprehensive critique of Tylor, Lévy-Bruhl, and other evolutionists is to be found in Evans-Pritchard (1965).

Nevertheless, there are kernels of thought here that subsequent anthropologists have found of interest. There has been a stream of self-conscious "Neo-Tyloreanism" (notably Horton 1993) in response to an overly structure-functionalist approach to religion. This school draws particular inspiration from the fact that whatever his ethnocentrism, Tylor begins with the rational and questioning nature of all people to try to understand the human situation and our place in the world, and that religious ideas are adequate to the worlds they describe and shift as the horizons of those worlds shift, as Horton put it, from microcosm to macrocosm. In reading Tylor today it is striking to see behind the evolutionary language a basic concern with universals in human thought and experience and the continuity of religious thought between small-scale societies and his own; in this respect Tylor forms a precursor to contemporary cognitivist approaches. Moreover, although some of the language used appears highly problematic, Tylor's basic argument was against those who saw in smaller-scale societies either a degeneration or a borrowing from large-scale ones. What Tylor staunchly defends is the rationalism and creativity of all humans. Conversely, authors such as Devisch (1993) and Jackson (1989) (see also Leenhardt 1979 [1947]) suggestively reimagine aspects of mystical participation through ideas of embodied knowledge and experience. However, neither mental nor bodily relationships are unmediated; on both counts Durkheimian or culturalist understandings of the way society and language shape collective representations and individual experiences are critical.

[. . .]

The first requisite in a systematic study of the religions of the lower races, is to lay down a rudimentary definition of religion. By requiring in this definition the belief in a supreme deity or of judgment after death, the adoration of idols or the practice of sacrifice, or other partially-diffused doctrines or rites, no doubt many tribes may be excluded from the category of religious. But such narrow definition has the fault of identifying religion rather with particular developments than with the deeper motive which underlies them. It seems best to fall back at once on this essential source, and simply to claim, as a minimum definition of Religion, the belief in Spiritual Beings. If this standard be applied to the descriptions of low races as to religion, the following results will appear. It cannot be positively asserted that every existing tribe recognizes the belief in spiritual beings, for the native condition of a considerable number is obscure in this respect, and from the rapid change or extinction they are undergoing, may ever remain so. It would be yet more unwarranted to set down every tribe mentioned in history, or known to us by the discovery of antiquarian relics, as necessarily having passed the defined minimum of religion. Greater still would be the unwisdom of declaring such a rudimentary belief natural or instinctive in all human tribes of all times; for no evidence justifies the opinion that man, known to be capable of so vast an intellectual development, cannot have emerged from a nonreligious condition, previous to that religious condition in which he happens at present to come with sufficient clearness within our range of knowledge. It is desirable, however, to take our basis of enquiry in observation rather than from speculation. Here, so far as I can judge from the immense mass of accessible

evidence, we have to admit that the belief in spiritual beings appears among all low races with whom we have attained to thoroughly intimate acquaintance; whereas the assertion of absence of such belief must apply either to ancient tribes, or to more or less imperfectly described modern ones. The exact bearing of this state of things on the problem of the origin of religion may be thus briefly stated. Were it distinctly proved that non-religious savages exist or have existed, these might be at least plausibly claimed as representatives of the condition of Man before he arrived at the religious state of culture. It is not desirable, however, that this argument should be put forward, for the asserted existence of the non-religious tribes in question rests . . . on evidence often mistaken and never conclusive. The argument for the natural evolution of religious ideas among mankind is not invalidated by the rejection of an ally too weak at present to give effectual help. Non-religious tribes may not exist in our day, but the fact bears no more decisively on the development of religion, than the impossibility of finding a modern English village without scissors or books or lucifer-matches bears on the fact that there was a time when no such things existed in the land.

I propose here, under the name of Animism, to investigate the deep-lying doctrine of Spiritual Beings, which embodies the very essence of Spiritualistic as opposed to Materialistic philosophy. Animism is not a new technical term, though now seldom used. From its special relation to the doctrine of the soul, it will be seen to have a peculiar appropriateness to the view here taken of the mode in which theological ideas have been developed among mankind. The word Spiritualism, though it may be, and sometimes is, used in a general sense, has this obvious defect to us, that it has become the designation of a particular modern sect, who indeed hold extreme spiritualistic views, but cannot be taken as typical representatives of these views in the world at large. The sense of Spiritualism in its wider acceptation, the general belief in spiritual beings, is here given to Animism.

Animism characterizes tribes very low in the scale of humanity, and thence ascends, deeply modified in its transmission, but from first to last preserving an unbroken continuity, into the midst of high modern culture. Doctrines adverse to it, so largely held by individuals or schools, are usually due not to early lowness of civilization, but to later changes in the intellectual course, to divergence from, or rejection of, ancestral faiths; and such newer developments do not affect the present enquiry as to the fundamental religious condition of mankind. Animism is, in fact, the groundwork of the Philosophy of Religion, from that of savages up to that of civilized men. And although it may at first sight seem to afford but a bare and meagre definition of a minimum of religion, it will be found practically sufficient; for where the root is, the branches will generally be produced. It is habitually found that the theory of Animism divides into two great dogmas, forming parts of one consistent doctrine; first, concerning souls of individual creatures, capable of continued existence after the death or destruction of the body; second, concerning other spirits, upward to the rank of powerful deities. Spiritual beings are held to affect or control the events of the material world, and man's life here and hereafter; and it being considered that they hold intercourse with men, and receive pleasure or displeasure from human actions, the belief in their existence leads naturally, and it might almost be said inevitably, sooner or later to active reverence and propitiation. Thus Animism in its full development, includes the belief in souls and in a future state, in controlling deities and subordinate spirits, these doctrines practically resulting in some kind of active worship.

One great element of religion, that moral element which among the higher nations forms its most vital part, is indeed little represented in the religion of the lower races. It is not that these races have no moral sense or no moral standard, for both are strongly marked among them, if not in formal precept, at least in that traditional consensus of society which we call public opinion, according to which certain actions are held to be good or bad, right or wrong. It is that the conjunction of ethics and Animistic philosophy, so intimate and powerful in the higher culture, seems scarcely yet to have begun in the lower. I propose here hardly to touch upon the purely moral aspects of religion, but rather to study the animism of the world so far as it constitutes, as unquestionably it does constitute, an ancient and worldwide philosophy, of which belief is the theory and worship is the practice.

Endeavouring to shape the materials for an enquiry hitherto strangely undervalued and neglected, it will now be my task to bring as clearly as may be into view the fundamental animism of the lower races, and in some slight and broken outline to trace its course into higher regions of civilization. Here let me state once for all two principal conditions under which the present research is carried on. First, as to the religious doctrines and practices examined, these are treated as belonging to theological systems devised by human reason, without supernatural aid or revelation; in other words, as being developments of Natural Religion. Second, as to the connexion between similar ideas and rites in the religions of the savage and the civilized world. While dwelling at some length on doctrines and ceremonies of the lower races, and sometimes particularizing for special reasons the related doctrines and ceremonies of the higher nations, it has not seemed my proper task to work out in detail the problems thus suggested among the philosophies and creeds of Christendom. Such applications, extending farthest from the direct scope of a work on primitive culture, are briefly stated in general terms, or touched in slight allusion, or taken for granted without remark. Educated readers possess the information required to work out their general bearing on theology, while more technical discussion is left to philosophers and theologians specially occupied with such arguments.

The first branch of the subject to be considered is the doctrine of human and other Souls, an examination of which will occupy the rest of the present chapter. What the doctrine of the soul is among the lower races, may be explained in stating the animistic theory of its development. It seems as though thinking men, as yet at a low level of culture, were deeply impressed by two groups of biological problems. In the first place, what is it that makes the difference between a living body and a dead one; what causes waking, sleep, trance, disease, death? In the second place, what are those human shapes which appear in dreams and visions? Looking at these two groups of phenomena, the ancient savage philosophers probably made their first step by the obvious inference that every man has two things belonging to him, namely, a life and a phantom. These two are evidently in close connexion with the body, the life as enabling it to feel and think and act, the phantom as being its image or second self; both, also, are perceived to be things separable from the body, the life as able to go away and leave it insensible or dead, the phantom as appearing to people at a distance from it.

The second step would seem also easy for savages to make, seeing how extremely difficult civilized men have found it to unmake. It is merely to combine the life and the phantom. As both belong to the body, why should they not also belong to one another, and be manifestations of one and the same soul? Let them then be considered as united, and the result is that well-known conception which may be described as an apparitional-soul, a ghost-soul. This, at any rate, corresponds with the actual conception of the personal soul or spirit among the lower races, which may be defined as follows: It is a thin unsubstantial human image, in its nature a sort of vapour, film, or shadow; the cause of life and thought in the individual it animates; independently possessing the personal consciousness and volition of its corporeal owner, past or present; capable of leaving the body far behind, to flash swiftly from place to place; mostly impalpable and invisible, yet also manifesting physical power, and especially appearing to men waking or asleep as phantasm separate from the body of which it bears the likeness; continuing to exist and appear to men after the death of that body; able to enter into, possess, and act in the bodies

of other men, of animals, and even of things. Though this definition is by no means of universal application, it has sufficient generality to be taken as a standard, modified by more or less divergence among any particular people.

Far from these world-wide opinions being arbitrary or conventional products, it is seldom even justifiable to consider their uniformity among distant races as proving communication of any sort. They are doctrines answering in the most forcible way to the plain evidence of men's senses, as interpreted by a fairly consistent and rational primitive philosophy. So well, indeed, does primitive animism account for the facts of nature, that it has held its place into the higher levels of education. Though classic and mediæval philosophy modified it much, and modern philosophy has handled it yet more unsparingly, it has so far retained the traces of its original character, that heirlooms of primitive ages may be claimed in the existing psychology of the civilized world. Out of the vast mass of evidence, collected among the most various and distant races of mankind, typical details may now be selected to display the earlier theory of the soul, the relation of the parts of this theory, and the manner in which these parts have been abandoned, modified, or kept up, along the course of culture.

To understand the popular conceptions of the human soul or spirit, it is instructive to notice the words which have been found suitable to express it. The ghost or phantasm seen by the dreamer or the visionary is an unsubstantial form, like a shadow or reflexion, and thus the familiar term of the *shade* comes in to express the soul. Thus the Tasmanian word for the shadow is also that for the spirit; the Algonquins describe a man's soul as *otahchuk*, "his shadow;" the Quiché language uses *natub* for "shadow, soul;" the Arawak *ueja* means "shadow, soul, image;" the Abipones made the one word *loákal* serve for "shadow, soul, echo, image." The Zulus not only use the word *tunzi* for "shadow, spirit, ghost," but they consider that at death the shadow of a man will in some way depart from the corpse, to become an ancestral spirit. The Basutos not only call the spirit remaining after death the *seriti* or "shadow," but they think that if a man walks on the river bank, a crocodile may seize his shadow in the water and draw him in; while in Old Calabar there is found the same identification of the spirit with the *ukpon* or "shadow," for a man to lose which is fatal. There are thus found among the lower races not only the types of those familiar classic terms, the *skia* and *umbra*, but also what seems the fundamental thought of the stories of shadowless men still current in the folklore of Europe, and familiar to modern readers in Chamisso's tale of Peter Schlemihl. Thus the dead in Purgatory knew that Dante was alive when they saw that, unlike theirs, his figure cast a shadow on the ground.

Other attributes are taken into the notion of soul or spirit, with especial regard to its being the cause of life. Thus the Caribs, connecting the pulses with spiritual beings, and especially considering that in the heart dwells man's chief soul, destined to a future heavenly life, could reasonably use the one word *iouanni* for "soul, life, heart." The Tongans supposed the soul to exist throughout the whole extension of the body, but particularly in the heart. On one occasion, the natives were declaring to a European that a man buried months ago was nevertheless still alive. "And one, endeavouring to make me understand what he meant, took hold of my hand, and squeezing it, said, 'This will die, but the life that is within you will never die;' with his other hand pointing to my heart." So the Basutos say of a dead man that his heart is gone out, and of one recovering from sickness that his heart is coming back. This corresponds to the familiar Old World view of the heart as the prime mover in life, thought, and passion. The connexion of soul and blood, familiar to the Karens and Papuas, appears prominently in Jewish and Arabic philosophy. To educated moderns the idea of the Macusi Indians of Guiana may seem quaint, that although the body will decay, "the man in our eyes" will not die, but wander about. Yet the association of personal animation with the pupil of the eye is familiar to European folklore, which not unreasonably discerned a sign of bewitchment or approaching death in the disappearance of the image, pupil, or baby, from the dim eyeballs of the sick man.

The act of breathing, so characteristic of the higher animals during life, and coinciding so closely with life in its departure, has been repeatedly and naturally identified with the life or soul itself. Laura Bridgman showed in her instructive way the analogy between the effects of restricted sense and restricted civilization, when one day she made the gesture of taking something away from her mouth: "I dreamed," she explained in words, "that God took away my breath to heaven." It is thus that West Australians used one word *waug* for "breath, spirit, soul;" that in the Netela language of California, *piuts* means "life, breath, soul;" that certain Greenlanders reckoned two souls to man, namely his shadow and his breath; that the Malays say the soul of the dying man escapes through his nostrils, and in Java use the same word *ñawa* for "breath, life, soul." How the notions of life, heart, breath, and phantom unite in the one conception of a soul or spirit, and at the same time how loose and vague such ideas are among barbaric races, is well brought into view in the answers to a religious inquest held in 1528 among the natives of Nicaragua. "When they die, there comes out of their mouth something that resembles a person, and is called *julio* [Aztec *yuli* = to live]. This being goes to the place where the man and woman are. It is like a person, but does not die, and the body remains here." *Question.* "Do those who go up on high keep the same body, the same face, and the same limbs, as here below?" *Answer.* "No; there is only the heart." *Question.* "But since they tear out their hearts [i.e. when a captive was sacrificed], what happens then?" *Answer.* "It is not precisely the heart, but that in them which makes them live, and that quits the body when they die." Or, as stated in another interrogatory, "It is not their heart that goes up above, but what makes them live, that is to say, the breath that issues from their mouth and is called *julio.*"

The conception of the soul as breath may be followed up through Semitic and Aryan etymology, and thus into the main streams of the philosophy of the world. Hebrew shows *nephesh*, "breath," passing into all the meanings of "life, soul, mind, animal," while *ruach* and *neshamah* make the like transition from "breath" to "spirit"; and to these the Arabic *nefs* and *ruh* correspond. The same is the history of Sanskrit *âtman* and *prâna*, of Greek *psychē* and *pneuma*, of Latin *animus, anima, spiritus*. So Slavonic *duch* has developed the meaning of "breath" into that of soul or spirit; and the dialects of the Gypsies have this word *dūk* with the meanings of "breath, spirit, ghost," whether these pariahs brought the word from India as part of their inheritance of Aryan speech, or whether they adopted it in their migration across Slavonic lands. German *geist* and English *ghost*, too, may possibly have the same original sense of breath. And if any should think such expressions due to mere metaphor, they may judge the strength of the implied connexion between breath and spirit by cases of most unequivocal significance. Among the Seminoles of Florida, when a woman died in childbirth, the infant was held over her face to receive her parting spirit, and thus acquire strength and knowledge for its future use. These Indians could have well understood why at the death-bed of an ancient Roman, the nearest kinsman leant over to inhale the last breath of the departing (et excipies hanc animam ore pio). Their state of mind is kept up to this day among Tyrolese peasants, who can still fancy a good man's soul to issue from his mouth at death like a little white cloud.

It will be shown that men, in their composite and confused notions of the soul, have brought into connexion a list of manifestations of life and thought even more multifarious than this. But also, seeking to avoid such perplexity of combination, they have sometimes endeavored to define and classify more closely, especially by the theory that man has a combination of several kinds of spirit, soul, or image, to which different functions belong. Already in the barbaric world such classification has been invented or adopted. Thus the Fijians distinguished between man's "dark spirit" or shadow, which goes to Hades, and his "light spirit" or reflexion in water or a mirror, which stays near where he dies. The Malagasy say that the *saina* or mind vanishes at death, the *aina* or life becomes mere air, but the *matoatoa* or ghost hovers round the tomb. In North America, the duality of the soul is a strongly

marked Algonquin belief; one soul goes out and sees dreams while the other remains behind; at death one of the two abides with the body, and for this the survivors leave offerings of food, while the other departs to the land of the dead. A division into three souls is also known, and the Dakotas say that man has four souls, one remaining with the corpse, one staying in the village, one going in the air, and one to the land of spirits. The Karens distinguish between the "là" or "kelah," the personal life-phantom, and the "thah," the responsible moral soul. More or less under Hindu influence, the Khonds have a fourfold division, as follows: the first soul is that capable of beatification or restoration to Boora the Good Deity; the second is attached to a Khond tribe on earth and is reborn generation after generation, so that at the birth of each child the priest asks who has returned; the third goes out to hold spiritual intercourse, leaving the body in a languid state, and it is this soul which can pass for a time into a tiger, and transmigrates for punishment after death; the fourth dies on the dissolution of the body. Such classifications resemble those of higher nations, . . .

[. . .]

Having thus surveyed at large the theory of spirits or souls of objects, it remains to point out what, to general students, may seem the most important consideration belonging to it, namely, its close relation to one of the most influential doctrines of civilized philosophy. The savage thinker, though occupying himself so much with the phenomena of life, sleep, disease, and death, seems to have taken for granted, as a matter of course, the ordinary operations of his own mind. It hardly occurred to him to think about the machinery of thinking. Metaphysics is a study which first assumes clear shape at a comparatively high level of intellectual culture. The metaphysical philosophy of thought taught in our modern European lecture-rooms is historically traced back to the speculative psychology of classic Greece. Now one doctrine which there comes into view is especially associated with the name of Democritus, the philosopher of Abdera, in the fifth century BC. When Democritus propounded the great problem of metaphysics,

"How do we perceive external things?" – thus making, as Lewes says, an era in the history of philosophy – he put forth, in answer to the question, a theory of thought. He explained the fact of perception by declaring that things are always throwing off images (εἴδωλα) of themselves, which images, assimilating to themselves the surrounding air, enter a recipient soul, and are thus perceived.

Now, supposing Democritus to have been really the originator of this famed theory of ideas, how far is he to be considered its inventor? Writers on the history of philosophy are accustomed to treat the doctrine as actually made by the philosophical school which taught it. Yet the evidence here brought forward shows it to be really the savage doctrine of object-souls, turned to a new purpose as a method of explaining the phenomena of thought. Nor is the correspondence a mere coincidence, for at this point of junction between classic religion and classic philosophy the traces of historical continuity may be still discerned. To say that Democritus was an ancient Greek is to say that from his childhood he had looked on at the funeral ceremonies of his country, beholding the funeral sacrifices of garments and jewels and money and food and drink, rites which his mother and his nurse could tell him were performed in order that the phantasmal images of these objects might pass into the possession of forms shadowy like themselves, the souls of dead men. Thus Democritus, seeking a solution of his great problem of the nature of thought, found it by simply decanting into his metaphysics a surviving doctrine of primitive savage animism. This thought of the phantoms or souls of things, if simply modified to form a philosophical theory of perception, would then and there become his doctrine of Ideas. Nor does even this fully represent the closeness of union which connects the savage doctrine of flitting object-souls with the Epicurean philosophy. Lucretius actually makes the theory of film-like images of things (simulacra, membranæ) account both for the apparitions which come to men in dreams, and the images which impress their minds in thinking. So unbroken is the continuity of philosophic speculation from savage to cultured thought. Such are the debts which civilized philosophy owes to primitive animism.

The doctrine of ideas, thus developed in the classic world, has, indeed, by no means held its course thenceforth unchanged through metaphysics, but has undergone transition somewhat like that of the doctrine of the soul itself. Ideas, fined down to the abstract forms or species of material objects, and applied to other than visible qualities, have at last come merely to denote subjects of thought. Yet to this day the old theory has not utterly died out, and the retention of the significant term "idea" (ἰδέα, visible form) is accompanied by a similar retention of original meaning. It is still one of the tasks of the metaphysician to display and refute the old notion of ideas as being real images, and to replace it by more abstract conceptions. It is a striking instance that Dugald Stewart can cite from the works of Sir Isaac Newton the following distinct recognition of "sensible species:" "Is not the sensorium of animals, the place where the sentient substance is present; and to which the sensible species of things are brought, through the nerves and brain, that there they may be perceived by the mind present in that place?" Again, Dr. Reid states the original theory of ideas, while declaring that he conceives it

to have no solid foundation, though it has been adopted very generally by philosophers. ... This notion of our perceiving external objects, not immediately, but in certain images or species of them conveyed by the senses, seems to be the most ancient philosophical hypothesis we have on the subject of perception, and to have, with small variations, retained its authority to this day.

Granted that Dr. Reid exaggerated the extent to which metaphysicians have kept up the notion of ideas as real images of things, few will deny that it does linger much in modern minds, and that people who talk of ideas do often, in some hazy metaphorical way, think of sensible images. One of the shrewdest things ever said about either ideas or ghosts was Bishop Berkeley's retort upon Halley, who bantered him about his idealism. The bishop claimed the mathematician as an idealist also, his ultimate ratios being ghosts of departed quantities, appearing when the terms that produced them vanished.

It remains to sum up in few words the doctrine of souls, in the various phases it has assumed from first to last among mankind. In the attempt to trace its main course through the successive grades of man's intellectual history, the evidence seems to accord best with a theory of its development, somewhat to the following effect. At the lowest levels of culture of which we have clear knowledge, the notion of a ghost-soul animating man while in the body, and appearing in dream and vision out of the body, is found deeply ingrained. There is no reason to think that this belief was learnt by savage tribes from contact with higher races, nor that it is a relic of higher culture from which the savage tribes have degenerated; for what is here treated as the primitive animistic doctrine is thoroughly at home among savages, who appear to hold it on the very evidence of their senses, interpreted on the biological principle which seems to them most reasonable. We may now and then hear the savage doctrines and practices concerning souls claimed as relics of a high religious culture pervading the primeval race of man. They are said to be traces of remote ancestral religion, kept up in scanty and perverted memory by tribes degraded from a nobler state. It is easy to see that such an explanation of some few facts, sundered from their connexion with the general array, may seem plausible to certain minds. But a large view of the subject can hardly leave such argument in possession. The animism of savages stands for and by itself; it explains its own origin. The animism of civilized men, while more appropriate to advanced knowledge, is in great measure only explicable as a developed product of the older and ruder system. It is the doctrines and rites of the lower races which are, according to their philosophy, results of point-blank natural evidence and acts of straightforward practical purpose. It is the doctrines and rites of the higher races which show survival of the old in the midst of the new, modification of the old to bring it into conformity with the new, abandonment of the old because it is no longer compatible with the new.

Let us see at a glance in what general relation the doctrine of souls among savage tribes stands to the doctrine of souls among barbaric and cultured nations. Among races within the limits of savagery, the general doctrine of souls is found worked out with remarkable breadth and consistency. The souls of animals are recognized by a natural extension from the theory of human souls; the souls of trees and plants follow in some vague partial way; and the souls of inanimate objects expand the general category to its extremest boundary. Thenceforth, as we explore human thought onward from savage into barbarian and civilized life, we find a state of theory more conformed to positive science, but in itself less complete and consistent. Far on into civilization, men still act as though in some half-meant way they believed in souls or ghosts of objects, while nevertheless their knowledge of physical science is beyond so crude a philosophy. As to the doctrine of souls of plants, fragmentary evidence of the history of its breaking down in Asia has reached us.

In our own day and country, the notion of souls of beasts is to be seen dying out. Animism, indeed, seems to be drawing in its outposts, and concentrating itself on its first and main position, the doctrine of the human soul. This doctrine has undergone extreme modification in the course of culture. It has outlived the almost total loss of one great argument attached to it – the objective reality of apparitional souls or ghosts seen in dreams and visions. The soul has given up its ethereal substance, and become an immaterial entity, "the shadow of a shade." Its theory is becoming separated from the investigations of biology and mental science, which now discuss the phenomena of life and thought, the senses and the intellect, the emotions and the will, on a groundwork of pure experience. There has arisen an intellectual product whose very existence is of the deepest significance, a "psychology" which has no longer anything to do with "soul." The soul's place in modern thought is in the metaphysics of religion, and its especial office there is that of furnishing an intellectual side to the religious doctrine of the future life.

Such are the alterations which have differenced the fundamental animistic belief in its course through successive periods of the world's culture. Yet it is evident that, notwithstanding all this profound change, the conception of the human soul is, as to its most essential nature, continuous from the philosophy of the savage thinker to that of the modern professor of theology. Its definition has remained from the first that of an animating, separable, surviving entity, the vehicle of individual personal existence. The theory of the soul is one principal part of a system of religious philosophy which unites, in an unbroken line of mental connexion, the savage fetish-worshipper and the civilized Christian. The divisions which have separated the great religions of the world into intolerant and hostile sects are for the most part superficial in comparison with the deepest of all religious schisms, that which divides Animism from Materialism.

[. . .]

Lastly, a few words of explanation may be offered as to the topics which this survey has included and excluded. To those who have been accustomed to find theological subjects dealt with on a dogmatic, emotional, and ethical, rather than an ethnographic scheme, the present investigation may seem misleading, because one-sided. This one-sided treatment, however, has been adopted with full consideration. Thus, though the doctrines here examined bear not only on the development but the actual truth of religious systems, I have felt neither able nor willing to enter into this great argument fully and satisfactorily, while experience has shown that to dispose of such questions by an occasional dictatorial phrase is one of the most serious of errors. The scientific value of descriptions of savage and barbarous religions, drawn up by travellers and especially by missionaries, is often lowered by their controversial tone, and by the affectation of infallibility with which their relation to the absolutely true is settled. There is something pathetic in the simplicity with which a narrow student will judge the doctrines of a foreign religion by their antagonism or conformity to his own orthodoxy, on points where utter difference of opinion exists among the most learned and enlightened scholars.

The systematization of the lower religions, the reduction of their multifarious details to the few and simple ideas of primitive philosophy which form the common groundwork of them all, appeared to me an urgently needed contribution to the science of religion. This work I have carried out to the utmost of my power, and I can now only leave the result in the hands of other students, whose province it is to deal with such evidence in wider schemes of argument.

Again, the intellectual rather than the emotional side of religion has here been kept in view. Even in the life of the rudest savage, religious belief is associated with intense emotion, with awful reverence, with agonizing terror, with rapt ecstasy when sense and thought utterly transcend the common level of daily life. How much the more in faiths where not only does the believer experience such enthusiasm, but where his utmost feelings of love and hope, of justice and mercy, of fortitude and tenderness and self-sacrificing devotion, of unutterable misery and dazzling happiness, twine and clasp round the fabric of religion. Language, dropping at times from such words as soul and spirit their mere philosophic meaning, can use them in full conformity with this tendency of the religious mind, as phrases to convey a mystic sense of transcendent emotion. Yet of all this religion, the religion of vision and of passion, little indeed has been said in these pages, and even that little rather in incidental touches than with purpose. Those to whom religion means above all things religious feeling, may say of my argument that I have written soullessly of the soul, and unspiritually of spiritual things.

Be it so: I accept the phrase not as needing an apology, but as expressing a plan. Scientific progress is at times most furthered by working along a distinct intellectual line, without being tempted to diverge from the main object to what lies beyond, in however intimate connexion. The anatomist does well to discuss bodily structure independently of the world of happiness and misery which depends upon it. It would be thought a mere impertinence for a strategist to preface a dissertation on the science of war, by an enquiry how far it is lawful for a Christian man to bear weapons and serve in the wars. My task has been here not to discuss Religion in all its bearings, but to portray in outline the great doctrine of Animism, as found in what I conceive to be its earliest stages among the lower races of mankind, and to show its transmission along the lines of religious thought.

The almost entire exclusion of ethical questions from this investigation has more than a mere reason of arrangement. It is due to the very nature of the subject. To some the statement may seem startling, yet the evidence seems to justify it, that the relation of morality to religion is one that only belongs in its rudiments, or not at all, to rudimentary civilization. The comparison of savage and civilized religions brings into view, by the side of a deep-lying resemblance in their philosophy, a deep-lying contrast in their practical action on human life. So far as savage religion can stand as representing natural religion, the popular idea that the moral government of the universe is an essential tenet of natural religion simply falls to the ground. Savage animism is almost devoid of that ethical element which to the educated modern mind is the very mainspring of practical religion. Not, as I have said, that morality is absent from the life of the lower races. Without a code of morals, the very existence of the rudest tribe would be impossible; and indeed the moral standards of even savage races are to no small extent well-defined and praiseworthy. But these ethical laws stand on their own ground of tradition and public opinion, comparatively independent of the animistic belief and rites which exist beside them. The lower animism is not immoral, it is unmoral. For this plain reason, it has seemed desirable to keep the discussion of animism, as far as might be, separate from that of ethics. The general problem of the relation of morality to religion is difficult, intricate, and requiring an immense array of evidence, and may be perhaps more profitably discussed in connexion with the ethnography of morals . . .

The essential connexion of theology and morality is a fixed idea in many minds. But it is one of the lessons of history that subjects may maintain themselves independently for ages, till the event of coalescence takes place. In the course of history, religion has in various ways attached to itself matters small and great outside its central scheme, such as prohibition of special meats, observance of special days, regulation of marriage as to kinship, division of society into castes, ordinance of social law and civil government. Looking at religion from a political point of view, as a practical influence on human society, it is clear that among its greatest powers have been its divine sanction of ethical laws, its theological enforcement of morality, its teaching of moral government of the universe, its supplanting the "continuance-doctrine" of a future life by the "retribution-doctrine" supplying moral motive in the present. But such alliance belongs almost or wholly to religions above the savage level, not to the earlier and lower creeds. It will aid us to see how much more the fruit of religion belongs to ethical influence than to philosophical dogma, if we consider how the introduction of the moral element separates the religions of the world, united as they are throughout by one animistic principle, into two great classes, those lower systems whose best result is to supply a crude childlike natural philosophy, and those higher faiths which implant on this the law of righteousness and of holiness, the inspiration of duty and of love.

2

The Elementary Forms of Religious Life

Emile Durkheim

Emile Durkheim (1858–1917) was a sociologist of Jewish background concerned primarily with questions of social solidarity, vitality, and malaise in modernity, especially in his native France. If Tylor ended by arguing that primitive religions are characterized by their amoral quality, one of the central aims for Durkheim is to show the intrinsic connection of the moral and the religious. The excerpt here is inevitably composed of small portions of a large and hugely influential body of work. Like Tylor, Durkheim was an evolutionist and, like Tylor, he sought the origins of religion. But he was much clearer than Tylor (or Freud) that one could not trace social phenomena to some moment of sheer beginning, and so restates the question of origins in a structural manner as a quest for "the ever-present causes upon which the most essential forms of religious thought and practice depend" (1915 [1912]: 20). His strategy is also radically different from Tylor's. Where Tylor progresses by citing a vast sample of material to support his generalizations, Durkheim turns a slow and careful eye on what he considered a single case, namely the Aborigines of central Australia, that he thought could show the "elementary forms" of religion most directly. Durkheim also departs from Tylor by proposing an original way in which a nonbeliever can yet understand any and every religion as not being in error. Furthermore, the core of his definition of religion lies not with any specific belief or kind of belief but with a system of classification.

By defining the sacred as that which is set apart, Durkheim deftly evades having to give it any substantive content, a strategy that has enabled subsequent scholars to move beyond trite definitions. This is vastly superior to something like "belief in the supernatural," where, as noted in the General Intro-

From Emile Durkheim, *The Elementary Forms of Religious Life*, ed. and trans. Karen Fields (New York: The Free Press, 1995 [1912]), pp. 1–13, 35–44, 419–23. Abridged, most footnotes removed.

duction, both "belief" and "super-natural" beg a good many questions. (But see Collier and Yanagisako 1989 for a feminist critique of the sacred/profane dichotomy.) A system of classification is also collective and no longer to be derived from individual psychology or experience or from Kantian innate categories of understanding. With respect to the social, Durkheim makes a number of significant arguments. First is the strong idea that religion is a natural expression of society, society's moment of reflecting on its own transcendent power. Second is the functionalist notion that religion provides a form of social cohesion, the glue of mechanical solidarity. These are actually inversions of one another: the first can be captured in the phrase that "the family that stays together prays together" and the second, to quote from a billboard from my youth, that "the family that prays together stays together." Perhaps what is most interesting about the latter is less the functionalism than the attention given to ritual as a form of action.

Durkheim's most infamous argument is that all religions can be understood as true once it is seen that what they represent is actually society. His position is thus one that recognizes the essentially symbolic quality of religion. If totems or gods symbolize society, this is not as reductive as it sounds, since Durkheim's understanding of society is itself so high-minded. Durkheim accepted and drew upon the dualism present at the time (in Freud as well) between the biological or natural individual and the social and moral collective. For Durkheim society enables humanity to transcend itself, both to overcome selfish and violent urges and to seek, via the categories of understanding it provides, higher and ennobling paths. Society seen in this light does in fact approximate the view of religion as understood by many non-Durkheimians.

Durkheim influenced a subsequent line of French thinkers, including his nephew Marcel Mauss, who published in the *Année Sociologique*. Among the significant essays of the Durkheim school (translated into English by Evans-Pritchard and his Oxford colleagues) are those by Durkheim and Mauss on symbolic classification (1963 [1903]), Hubert and Mauss on sacrifice (1964 [1898]), Mauss on the gift (1990 [1925]), on bodily habitus (1973 [1935]), and on the concept of the person (1985 [1938]), and Hertz on death and on the right hand (1960 [1909]; cf. Needham, ed. 1973). Important collections of Durkheim's own essays (1973, 1974, 1992) include useful modern introductions. Lévi-Strauss was also interested in problems of symbolic classification but, as it is often said, he turned Durkheim on his head. If there are correspondences between society and ideational patterns, for Lévi-Strauss this is because both of these stem from the same source, namely the mind, rather than from society. Insofar as Durkheim depicted totemism as the elementary form of religion, Lévi-Strauss's book deconstructing totemism may also be seen as an attack on his intellectual ancestor.

In describing the northwest American potlatch as a "total" phenomenon, Mauss (1990 [1925]) makes the shattering observation that attempting to distinguish the religious from the economic or the political makes little sense in certain kinds of societies, and may provide quite distorted images. These categories – religion, economy, etc. – are conceptual tools emerging from the social experience of modern western societies (based on organic solidarity). The ethnographic facts from other times and places are not tailored to fit them. Moreover, the lesson that the study of other societies may bring back to us is the arbitrariness of our own systems of classification and division into discrete social institutions. And thus mana itself, which was the essence of religion in the theories of the proponents of animatism (who succeeded Tylor and the concept of animism), is revealed by Mauss to mean wealth or authority as much as sacred power and, indeed, to refer to a world in which these are not understood as discrete and autonomous. Since Durkheim's and Mauss's work on the categories of thought, one of the effects of the anthropological study of "religion" has thus been to immensely complicate the issue by seeing things of "religious" or "symbolic" import in domains of life that western society has tried to argue are quite distinct and built up entirely on practical, secular, or rational grounds. Conversely, where religion is not separated from other social institutions, so it does not stand opposed to them as some morally distinct and distinctively moral realm. (The analogy here is to the argument that the gift in such societies cannot take on the connotations of pure generosity that it has for us. See the important discussion by Parry (1986).)

Another element of Mauss's thought that has had a profound influence on the anthropology of religion and is more fully worked out in his essay on the person (1985 [1938]) is that the chiefs taking part in the potlatch were understood as incarnations of the gods and ancestors (cf. Mauzé 1994). Indeed, the concept of the "individual" no less than that of "religion" is revealed as ethnographically and historically specific. This, in turn, would challenge theories like Tylor's that tend to assume a universal individuality. These points have been particularly well developed by Dumont (1970, 1986).

Finally, it may be mentioned that in his discussion of honor, Mauss makes questions of morality central. Honor, dignity, self-worth, and the virtuous comportment and action they suppose are as critical to human consciousness as the puzzlement, awe, and fear attributed to humans by some thinkers or the instrumental concerns with food, sex, or power attributed to them by others. Elsewhere, in his essay on the body (1973 [1935]), Mauss sets out the notion of the habitus, subsequently developed by Bourdieu (1977), in which moral comportment is understood as rooted in embodied habit. In these respects Mauss and Bourdieu draw on Aristotelian conceptions of virtuous disposition and practice (Lambek 2000a).

The other major locus of Durkheim's influence was on the structural-functionalism that developed in British anthropology with Radcliffe-Brown (1964 [1952]) and produced a number of major studies of religion in specific societies (e.g., Warner 1959, Middleton 1987 [1960]). The British also drew on Durkheim's predecessors Robertson Smith (1894) and Fustel de Coulanges (1956 [1864]). For all these thinkers, society or the social group was understood as primary, and among the British it was the representational and functional sides of Durkheim's approach that were developed and elaborated, often making very good sense of aspects of the lineage-based societies of Africa, although not of all aspects (as Evans-Pritchard, in particular, was quick to note). Durkheim's conception of the sacred and his concerns with symbolic classification are most systematically pursued by Douglas, who is perhaps the most Durkheimian of the generation of symbolic anthropologists (see chapter 16 below). Durkheim's emphasis on the moral remains extremely significant while his chief weakness, as has often been noted, lies with the inability to address historical change. Weber is much more attuned to history.

I propose in this book to study the simplest and most primitive religion that is known at present, to discover its principles and attempt an explanation of it. A religious system is said to be the most primitive that is available for observation when it meets the two following conditions: First, it must be found in societies the simplicity of whose organization is nowhere exceeded;[1] second, it must be explainable without the introduction of any element from a predecessor religion.

I will make every effort to describe the organization of this system with all the care and precision that an ethnographer or a historian would bring to the task. But my task will not stop at description. Sociology sets itself different problems from those of history or ethnography. It does not seek to become acquainted with bygone forms of civilization for the sole purpose of being acquainted with and reconstructing them. Instead, like any positive science, its purpose above all is to explain a present reality that is near to us and thus capable of affecting our ideas and actions. That reality is man. More especially, it is present-day man, for there is none other that we have a greater interest in knowing well. Therefore, my study of a very archaic religion will not be for the sheer pleasure of recounting the bizarre and the eccentric. I have made a very archaic religion the subject of my research because it seems better suited than any other to help us comprehend the religious nature of man, that is, to reveal a fundamental and permanent aspect of humanity.

This proposition is bound to provoke strong objections. It may be thought strange that, to arrive at an understanding of present-day humanity, we should have to turn away from it so as to travel back to the beginning of history. In the matter at hand, that procedure seems especially unorthodox. Religions are held to be of unequal value and standing; it is commonly said that not all contain the same measure of truth. Thus it would seem that the higher forms of religious thought cannot be compared with the lower without bringing the higher forms down to the lower level. To grant that the crude cults of Australian tribes might help us understand Christianity, for example, is to assume – is it not? – that Christianity

proceeds from the same mentality, in other words, that it is made up of the same superstitions and rests on the same errors. The theoretical importance sometimes accorded to primitive religions could therefore be taken as evidence of a systematic irreligion that invalidated the results of research by prejudging them.

I need not go into the question here whether scholars can be found who were guilty of this and who have made history and the ethnography of religion a means of making war against religion. In any event, such could not possibly be a sociologist's point of view. Indeed, it is a fundamental postulate of sociology that a human institution cannot rest upon error and falsehood. If it did, it could not endure. If it had not been grounded in the nature of things, in those very things it would have met resistance that it could not have overcome. Therefore, when I approach the study of primitive religions, it is with the certainty that they are grounded in and express the real. In the course of the analyses and discussions that follow, we will see this principle coming up again and again. What I criticize in the schools I part company with is precisely that they have failed to recognize it. No doubt, when all we do is consider the formulas literally, these religious beliefs and practices appear disconcerting, and our inclination might be to write them off to some sort of inborn aberration. But we must know how to reach beneath the symbol to grasp the reality it represents and that gives the symbol its true meaning. The most bizarre or barbarous rites and the strangest myths translate some human need and some aspect of life, whether social or individual. The reasons the faithful settle for in justifying those rites and myths may be mistaken, and most often are; but the true reasons exist nonetheless, and it is the business of science to uncover them.

Fundamentally, then, there are no religions that are false. All are true after their own fashion: All fulfill given conditions of human existence, though in different ways. Granted, it is not impossible to rank them hierarchically. Some can be said to be superior to others, in the sense that they bring higher mental faculties into play, that they are richer in ideas and feelings, that they contain proportionately more concepts than sensations and images, and that they are more elaborately systematized. But the greater complexity and higher ideal content, however real, are not sufficient to place the corresponding religions into separate genera. All are equally religious, just as all living beings are equally living beings, from the humblest plastid to man. If I address myself to primitive religions, then, it is not with any ulterior motive of disparaging religion in general: These religions are to be respected no less than the others. They fulfill the same needs, play the same role, and proceed from the same causes; therefore, they can serve just as well to elucidate the nature of religious life and, it follows, to solve the problem I wish to treat.

[. . .]

My research is not solely of interest to the science of religions. There is an aspect of every religion that transcends the realm of specifically religious ideas. Through it, the study of religious phenomena provides a means of revisiting problems that until now have been debated only among philosophers.

It has long been known that the first systems of representations that man made of the world and himself were of religious origin. There is no religion that is not both a cosmology and a speculation about the divine. If philosophy and the sciences were born in religion, it is because religion itself began by serving as science and philosophy. Further, and less often noted, religion has not merely enriched a human intellect already formed but in fact has helped to form it. Men owe to religion not only the content of their knowledge, in significant part, but also the form in which that knowledge is elaborated.

At the root of our judgments, there are certain fundamental notions that dominate our entire intellectual life. It is these ideas that philosophers, beginning with Aristotle, have called the categories of understanding: notions of time, space, number, cause, substance, personality. They correspond to the most universal properties of things. They are like solid frames that confine thought. Thought does not seem to be able to break out of them without destroying itself, since it seems we cannot think of objects that are not in time or space,

that cannot be counted, and so forth. The other ideas are contingent and changing, and we can conceive of a man, a society, or an epoch that lacks them; but these fundamental notions seem to us as almost inseparable from the normal functioning of the intellect. They are, as it were, the skeleton of thought. Now, when one analyzes primitive religious beliefs methodically, one naturally finds the principal categories among them. They are born in and from religion; they are a product of religious thought. This is a point that I will make again and again in the course of this book.

Even now that point has a certain interest of its own, but here is what gives it its true significance.

The general conclusion of the chapters to follow is that religion is an eminently social thing. Religious representations are collective representations that express collective realities; rites are ways of acting that are born only in the midst of assembled groups and whose purpose is to evoke, maintain, or re-create certain mental states of those groups. But if the categories are of religious origin, then they must participate in what is common to all religion: They, too, must be social things, products of collective thought. At the very least – since with our present understanding of these matters, radical and exclusive theses are to be guarded against – it is legitimate to say that they are rich in social elements.

This, it must be added, is something one can begin to see even now for certain of the categories. For example, what if one tried to imagine what the notion of time would be in the absence of the methods we use to divide, measure, and express it with objective signs, a time that was not a succession of years, months, weeks, days, and hours? It would be nearly impossible to conceive of. We can conceive of time only if we differentiate between moments. Now, what is the origin of that differentiation? Undoubtedly, states of consciousness that we have already experienced can be reproduced in us in the same order in which they originally occurred; and, in this way, bits of our past become immediate again, even while spontaneously distinguishing themselves from the present. But however important this distinction might be for our private experience, it is far from sufficient to constitute the notion or category of time. The category of time is not simply a partial or complete commemoration of our lived life. It is an abstract and impersonal framework that contains not only our individual existence but also that of humanity. It is like an endless canvas on which all duration is spread out before the mind's eye and on which all possible events are located in relation to points of reference that are fixed and specified. It is not *my time* that is organized in this way; it is time that is conceived of objectively by all men of the same civilization. This by itself is enough to make us begin to see that any such organization would have to be collective. And indeed, observation establishes that these indispensable points, in reference to which all things are arranged temporally, are taken from social life. The division into days, weeks, months, years, etc., corresponds to the recurrence of rites, festivals, and public ceremonies at regular intervals. A calendar expresses the rhythm of collective activity while ensuring that regularity.

The same applies to space. As Hamelin has shown, space is not the vague and indeterminate medium that Kant imagined. If purely and absolutely homogeneous, it would be of no use and would offer nothing for thought to hold on to. Spatial representation essentially consists in a primary coordination of given sense experience. But this coordination would be impossible if the parts of space were qualitatively equivalent, if they really were mutually interchangeable. To have a spatial ordering of things is to be able to situate them differently: to place some on the right, others on the left, these above, those below, north or south, east or west, and so forth, just as, to arrange states of consciousness temporally, it must be possible to locate them at definite dates. That is, space would not be itself if, like time, it was not divided and differentiated. But where do these divisions that are essential to space come from? In itself it has no right, no left, no high or low, no north or south, etc. All these distinctions evidently arise from the fact that different affective colorings have been assigned to regions. And since all men of the same civilization conceive of space in the same manner, it is evidently necessary that these affective color-

ings and the distinctions that arise from them also be held in common – which implies almost necessarily that they are of social origin.

Besides, in some instances this social character is made manifest. There are societies in Australia and North America in which space is conceived in the form of an immense circle, because the camp itself is circular; and the spatial circle is divided in exactly the same way as the tribal circle and in its image. As many regions are distinguished as there are clans in the tribe, and it is the place the clans occupy in the encampment that determines the orientation of the regions. Each region is defined by the totem of the clan to which it is assigned. Among the Zuñi, for example, the pueblo is made up of seven sections; each of these sections is a group of clans that has acquired its own unity. In all likelihood, it was originally a single clan that later subdivided. Space similarly contains seven regions, and each of these seven sections of the world is in intimate relationship with a section of the pueblo, that is, with a group of clans. "Thus," says Cushing, "one division is considered to be in relation with the north; another represents the west, another the south, etc." Each section of the pueblo has its distinctive color, which symbolizes it; each region has its own color, which is that of the corresponding section. Over the course of history, the number of basic clans has varied, and the number of regions has varied in the same way. Thus, spatial organization was modeled on social organization and replicates it. Far from being built into human nature, no idea exists, up to and including the distinction between right and left, that is not, in all probability, the product of religious, hence collective, representations.

Analogous demonstrations concerning the notions of genus, force, personality, and efficacy will be found below. One might even ask whether the notion of contradiction does not also arise from social conditions. What tends to make this plausible is the fact that the hold the notion of contradiction has had over thought has varied with times and societies. Today the principle of identity governs scientific thought; but there are vast systems of representation that have played a major role in the history of ideas, in which it is commonly ignored: These systems are the mythologies, from the crudest to the most sophisticated. Mythologies deal with beings that have the most contradictory attributes at the same time, that are one and many, material and spiritual, and capable of subdividing themselves indefinitely without losing that which makes them what they are. These historical variations of the rule that seems to govern our present logic show that, far from being encoded from eternity in the mental constitution of man, the rule depends at least in part upon historical, hence social, factors. We do not know exactly what these factors are, but we can presume that they exist.

Once this hypothesis is accepted, the problem of knowledge can be framed in new terms. [. . .]

Religious phenomena fall into two basic categories: beliefs and rites. The first are states of opinion and consist of representations; the second are particular modes of action. Between these two categories of phenomena lies all that separates thinking from doing.

The rites can be distinguished from other human practices – for example, moral practices – only by the special nature of their object. Like a rite, a moral rule prescribes ways of behaving to us, but those ways of behaving address objects of a different kind. It is the object of the rite that must be characterized, in order to characterize the rite itself. The special nature of that object is expressed in the belief. Therefore, only after having defined the belief can we define the rite.

Whether simple or complex, all known religious beliefs display a common feature: They presuppose a classification of the real or ideal things that men conceive of into two classes – two opposite genera – that are widely designated by two distinct terms, which the words *profane* and *sacred* translate fairly well. The division of the world into two domains, one containing all that is sacred and the other all that is profane – such is the distinctive trait of religious thought. Beliefs, myths, dogmas, and legends are either representations or systems of representations that express the nature of sacred things, the virtues and powers attributed to them, their history, and their relationships with one another as well as with profane

things. Sacred things are not simply those personal beings that are called gods or spirits. A rock, a tree, a spring, a pebble, a piece of wood, a house, in a word anything, can be sacred. A rite can have sacredness; indeed there is no rite that does not have it to some degree. There are words, phrases, and formulas that can be said only by consecrated personages; there are gestures and movements that cannot be executed by just anyone. If Vedic sacrifice has had such great efficacy – if, indeed, sacrifice was far from being a method of gaining the gods' favor but, according to mythology, actually generated the gods – that is because the virtue it possessed was comparable to that of the most sacred beings. The circle of sacred objects cannot be fixed once and for all; its scope can vary infinitely from one religion to another. What makes Buddhism a religion is that, in the absence of gods, it accepts the existence of sacred things, namely, the Four Noble Truths and the practices that are derived from them.

But I have confined myself thus far to enumerating various sacred things as examples: I must now indicate the general characteristics by which they are distinguished from profane things.

One might be tempted to define sacred things by the rank that is ordinarily assigned to them in the hierarchy of beings. They tend to be regarded as superior in dignity and power to profane things, and particularly to man, in no way sacred when he is only a man. Indeed, he is portrayed as occupying a rank inferior to and dependent upon them. While that portrayal is certainly not without truth, nothing about it is truly characteristic of the sacred. Subordination of one thing to another is not enough to make one sacred and the other not. Slaves are subordinate to their masters, subjects to their king, soldiers to their leaders, lower classes to ruling classes, the miser to his gold, and the power seeker to the power holders. If a man is sometimes said to have the religion of beings or things in which he recognizes an eminent value and a kind of superiority to him, it is obvious that, in all such cases, the word is taken in a metaphorical sense, and there is nothing in those relations that is religious in a strict sense.

On the other hand, we should bear in mind that there are things with which man feels relatively at ease, even though they are sacred to the highest degree. An amulet has sacredness, and yet there is nothing extraordinary about the respect it inspires. Even face to face with his gods, man is not always in such a marked state of inferiority, for he very often uses physical coercion on them to get what he wants. He beats the fetish when he is displeased, only to be reconciled with it if, in the end, it becomes more amenable to the wishes of its worshipper. To get rain, stones are thrown into the spring or the sacred lake where the god of the rain is presumed to reside; it is believed that he is forced by this means to come out and show himself. Furthermore, while it is true that man is a dependent of his gods, this dependence is mutual. The gods also need man; without offerings and sacrifices, they would die. I will have occasion to show that this dependence of gods on their faithful is found even in the most idealistic religions.

However, if the criterion of a purely hierarchical distinction is at once too general and too imprecise, nothing but their heterogeneity is left to define the relation between the sacred and the profane. But what makes this heterogeneity sufficient to characterize that classification of things and to distinguish it from any other is that it has a very particular feature: *It is absolute.* In the history of human thought, there is no other example of two categories of things as profoundly differentiated or as radically opposed to one another. The traditional opposition between good and evil is nothing beside this one: Good and evil are two opposed species of the same genus, namely morals, just as health and illness are nothing more than two different aspects of the same order of facts, life; by contrast, the sacred and the profane are always and everywhere conceived by the human intellect as separate genera, as two worlds with nothing in common. The energies at play in one are not merely those encountered in the other, but raised to a higher degree; they are different in kind. This opposition has been conceived differently in different religions. Here, localizing the two kinds of things in different regions of the physical universe has appeared sufficient to separate them;

there, the sacred is thrown into an ideal and transcendent milieu, while the residuum is abandoned as the property of the material world. But while the forms of the contrast are variable, the fact of it is universal.

This is not to say that a being can never pass from one of these worlds to the other. But when this passage occurs, the manner in which it occurs demonstrates the fundamental duality of the two realms, for it implies a true metamorphosis. Rites of initiation, which are practiced by a great many peoples, demonstrate this especially well. Initiation is a long series of rites to introduce the young man into religious life. For the first time, he comes out of the purely profane world, where he has passed his childhood, and enters into the circle of sacred things. This change of status is conceived not as a mere development of preexisting seeds but as a transformation *totius substantiae.*[2] At that moment, the young man is said to die, and the existence of the particular person he was, to cease – instantaneously to be replaced by another. He is born again in a new form. Appropriate ceremonies are held to bring about the death and the rebirth, which are taken not merely in a symbolic sense but literally. Is this not proof that there is a rupture between the profane being that he was and the religious being that he becomes?

Indeed, this heterogeneity is such that it degenerates into real antagonism. The two worlds are conceived of not only as separate but also as hostile and jealous rivals. Since the condition of belonging fully to one is fully to have left the other, man is exhorted to retire completely from the profane in order to live an exclusively religious life. From thence comes monasticism, which artificially organizes a milieu that is apart from, outside of, and closed to the natural milieu where ordinary men live a secular life, and that tends almost to be its antagonist. From thence as well comes mystic asceticism, which seeks to uproot all that may remain of man's attachment to the world. Finally, from thence come all forms of religious suicide, the crowning logical step of this asceticism, since the only means of escaping profane life fully and finally is escaping life altogether.

The opposition of these two genera is expressed outwardly by a visible sign that permits ready recognition of this very special classification, wherever it exists. The mind experiences deep repugnance about mingling, even simple contact, between the corresponding things, because the notion of the sacred is always and everywhere separate from the notion of the profane in man's mind, and because we imagine a kind of logical void between them. The state of dissociation in which the ideas are found in consciousness is too strongly contradicted by such mingling, or even by their being too close to one another. The sacred thing is, par excellence, that which the profane must not and cannot touch with impunity. To be sure, this prohibition cannot go so far as to make all communication between the two worlds impossible, for if the profane could in no way enter into relations with the sacred, the sacred would be of no use. This placing in relationship in itself is always a delicate operation that requires precautions and a more or less complex initiation. Yet such an operation is impossible if the profane does not lose its specific traits, and if it does not become sacred itself in some measure and to some degree. The two genera cannot, at the same time, both come close to one another and remain what they were.

Now we have a first criterion of religious beliefs. No doubt, within these two fundamental genera, there are secondary species that are themselves more or less incompatible with each other. But characteristically, the religious phenomenon is such that it always assumes a bipartite division of the universe, known and knowable, into two genera that include all that exists but radically exclude one another. Sacred things are things protected and isolated by prohibitions; profane things are those things to which the prohibitions are applied and that must keep at a distance from what is sacred. Religious beliefs are those representations that express the nature of sacred things and the relations they have with other sacred things or with profane things. Finally, rites are rules of conduct that prescribe how man must conduct himself with sacred things.

When a certain number of sacred things have relations of coordination and subordination with one another, so as to form a system that has a certain coherence and does not belong to any other system of the same sort, then the beliefs and rites, taken together, constitute a religion. By this definition, a religion is not necessarily contained within a single idea and does not derive from a single principle that may vary with the circumstances it deals with, while remaining basically the same everywhere. Instead, it is a whole formed of separate and relatively distinct parts. Each homogeneous group of sacred things, or indeed each sacred thing of any importance, constitutes an organizational center around which gravitates a set of beliefs and rites, a cult of its own. There is no religion, however unified it may be, that does not acknowledge a plurality of sacred things. Even Christianity, at least in its Catholic form, accepts the Virgin, the angels, the saints, the souls of the dead, etc. – above and beyond the divine personality (who, besides, is both three and one). As a rule, furthermore, religion is not merely a single cult either but is made up of a system of cults that possess a certain autonomy. This autonomy is also variable. Sometimes the cults are ranked and subordinated to some dominant cult into which they are eventually absorbed; but sometimes as well they simply exist side by side in confederation. The religion to be studied in this book will provide an example of this confederate organization.

At the same time, we can explain why groups of religious phenomena that belong to no constituted religion can exist: because they are not or are no longer integrated into a religious system. If, for specific reasons, one of those cults just mentioned should manage to survive while the whole to which it belonged has disappeared, it will survive only in fragments. This is what has happened to so many agrarian cults that live on in folklore. In certain cases, what persists in that form is not even a cult, but a mere ceremony or a particular rite.

Although this definition is merely preliminary, it indicates the terms in which the problem that dominates the science of religions must be posed. If sacred beings are believed to be distinguished from the others solely by the greater intensity of the powers attributed to them, the question of how men could have imagined them is rather simple: Nothing more is needed than to identify those forces that, through their exceptional energy, have managed to impress the human mind forcefully enough to inspire religious feelings. But if, as I have tried to establish, sacred things are different in nature from profane things, if they are different in their essence, the problem is far more complex. In that case, one must ask what led man to see the world as two heterogeneous and incomparable worlds, even though nothing in sense experience seems likely to have suggested the idea of such a radical duality.

Even so, this definition is not yet complete, for it fits equally well two orders of things that must be distinguished even though they are akin: magic and religion.

Magic, too, is made up of beliefs and rites. Like religion, it has its own myths and dogmas, but these are less well developed, probably because, given its pursuit of technical and utilitarian ends, magic does not waste time in pure speculation. Magic also has its ceremonies, sacrifices, purifications, prayers, songs, and dances. Those beings whom the magician invokes and the forces he puts to work are not only of the same nature as the forces addressed by religion but very often are the same forces. In the most primitive societies, the souls of the dead are in essence sacred things and objects of religious rites, but at the same time, they have played a major role in magic. In Australia as well as in Melanesia, in ancient Greece as well as among Christian peoples, the souls, bones, and hair of the dead figure among the tools most often used by the magician. Demons are also a common instrument of magical influence. Now, demons are also surrounded by prohibitions; they too are separated and live in a world apart. Indeed, it is often difficult to distinguish them from gods proper. Besides, even in Christianity, is not the devil a fallen god? And apart from his origins, does he not have a religious character, simply because the hell of which he is the keeper is an indispensable part in the machinery of the Christian religion? The magician can invoke regular and official deities. Sometimes these are gods of a foreign people: For example, the Greek magicians called upon Egyptian, Assyrian, or Jewish gods. Sometimes they are even national gods:

Hecate and Diana were objects of a magic cult. The Virgin, the Christ, and the saints were used in the same manner by Christian magicians.

Must we therefore say that magic cannot be rigorously differentiated from religion – that magic is full of religion and religion full of magic and, consequently, that it is impossible to separate them and define the one without the other? What makes that thesis hard to sustain is the marked repugnance of religion for magic and the hostility of magic to religion in return. Magic takes a kind of professional pleasure in profaning holy things, inverting religious ceremonies in its rites. On the other hand, while religion has not always condemned and prohibited magic rites, it has generally regarded them with disfavor. As messieurs Hubert and Mauss point out, there is something inherently antireligious about the maneuvers of the magician. So it is difficult for these two institutions not to oppose one another at some point, whatever the relations between them. Since my intention is to limit my research to religion and stop where magic begins, discovering what distinguishes them is all the more important.

Here is how a line of demarcation can be drawn between these two domains.

Religious beliefs proper are always shared by a definite group that professes them and that practices the corresponding rites. Not only are they individually accepted by all members of that group, but they also belong to the group and unify it. The individuals who comprise the group feel joined to one another by the fact of common faith. A society whose members are united because they imagine the sacred world and its relations with the profane world in the same way, and because they translate this common representation into identical practices, is what is called a Church. In history we do not find religion without Church. Sometimes the Church is narrowly national; sometimes it extends beyond frontiers; sometimes it encompasses an entire people (Rome, Athens, the Hebrews); sometimes it encompasses only a fraction (Christian denominations since the coming of Protestantism); sometimes it is led by a body of priests; sometimes it is more or less without any official directing body. But wherever we observe religious life, it has a definite group as its basis. Even so-called private cults, like the domestic cult or a corporate cult, satisfy this condition: They are always celebrated by a group, the family or the corporation. And, furthermore, even these private religions often are merely special forms of a broader religion that embraces the totality of life. These small Churches are in reality only chapels in a larger Church and, because of this very scope, deserve all the more to be called by that name.

Magic is an entirely different matter. Granted, magic beliefs are never without a certain currency. They are often widespread among broad strata of the population, and there are even peoples where they count no fewer active followers than religion proper. But they do not bind men who believe in them to one another and unite them into the same group, living the same life. *There is no Church of magic.* Between the magician and the individuals who consult him, there are no durable ties that make them members of a single moral body, comparable to the ties that join the faithful of the same god or the adherents of the same cult. The magician has a clientele, not a Church, and his clients may have no mutual relations, and may even be unknown to one another. Indeed, the relations they have with him are generally accidental and transient, analogous to those of a sick man with his doctor. The official and public character with which the magician is sometimes invested makes no difference. That he functions in broad daylight does not join him in a more regular and lasting manner with those who make use of his services. . . .

By contrast, religion is inseparable from the idea of Church. In this first regard, there is already a fundamental difference between magic and religion. Furthermore, and above all, when magic societies of this sort are formed, they never encompass all the adherents of magic. Far from it. They encompass only the magicians. Excluded from them are the laity, as it were – that is, those for whose benefit the rites are conducted, which is to say those who are the adherents of regular cults. Now, the magician is to magic what the priest is to religion. But a college of priests is no more

a religion than a religious congregation that worships a certain saint in the shadows of the cloister is a private cult. A Church is not simply a priestly brotherhood; it is a moral community made up of all the faithful, both laity and priests. Magic ordinarily has no community of this sort.

But if one includes the notion of Church in the definition of religion, does one not by the same stroke exclude the individual religions that the individual institutes for himself and celebrates for himself alone? There is scarcely any society in which this is not to be found. As will be seen below, every Ojibway has his personal *manitou* that he chooses himself and to which he bears specific religious obligations; the Melanesian of the Banks Islands has his *tamaniu*; the Roman has his *genius*; the Christian has his patron saint and his guardian angel, and so forth. All these cults seem, by definition, to be independent of the group. And not only are these individual religions very common throughout history, but some people today pose the question whether such religions are not destined to become the dominant form of religious life – whether a day will not come when the only cult will be the one that each person freely practices in his innermost self.

But, let us put aside these speculations about the future for a moment. If we confine our discussion to religions as they are in the present and as they have been in the past, it becomes obvious that these individual cults are not distinct and autonomous religious systems but simply aspects of the religion common to the whole Church of which the individuals are part. The patron saint of the Christian is chosen from the official list of saints recognized by the Catholic Church, and there are canonical laws that prescribe how each believer must conduct this private cult. In the same way, the idea that every man necessarily has a protective genie is, in different forms, at the basis of a large number of American religions, as well as of Roman religion (to cite only these two examples). As will be seen below, that idea is tightly bound up with the idea of soul, and the idea of soul is not among those things that can be left entirely to individual choice. In a word, it is the Church of which he is a member that teaches the individual what these personal gods are, what their role is, how he must enter into relations with them, and how he must honor them. When one analyzes the doctrines of that Church systematically, sooner or later one comes across the doctrines that concern these special cults. Thus there are not two religions of different types, turned in opposite directions, but the same ideas and principles applied in both cases – here, to circumstances that concern the group as a whole, and there, to the life of the individual. Indeed, this unity is so close that, among certain peoples, the ceremonies during which the believer first enters into communication with his protective genie are combined with rites whose public character is incontestable, namely, rites of initiation.

What remains are the present-day aspirations toward a religion that would consist entirely of interior and subjective states and be freely constructed by each one of us. But no matter how real those aspirations, they cannot affect our definition: This definition can be applied only to real, accomplished facts, not to uncertain possibilities. Religions can be defined as they are now or as they have been, not as they may be tending more or less vaguely to become. It is possible that this religious individualism is destined to become fact; but to be able to say in what measure, we must first know what religion is, of what elements it is made, from what causes it results, and what function it performs – all questions whose answers cannot be preordained, for we have not crossed the threshold of research. Only at the end of this study will I try to look into the future.

We arrive thus at the following definition: *A religion is a unified system of beliefs and practices relative to sacred things, that is to say, things set apart and forbidden – beliefs and practices which unite into one single moral community called a Church, all those who adhere to them.* The second element thus holds a place in my definition that is no less essential than the first: In showing that the idea of religion is inseparable from the idea of a Church, it conveys the notion that religion must be an eminently collective thing.

[. . .]

＊

Most often, the theorists who have set out to express religion in rational terms have regarded it as being, first and foremost, a system of ideas that correspond to a definite object. That object has been conceived in different ways – nature, the infinite, the unknowable, the ideal, and so forth – but these differences are of little importance. In every case, the representations – that is, the beliefs – were considered the essential element of religion. For their part, rites appeared from this standpoint to be no more than an external, contingent, and physical translation of those inward states that alone were deemed to have intrinsic value. This notion is so widespread that most of the time debates on the topic of religion turn around and about on the question of whether religion can or cannot be reconciled with science – that is, whether there is room alongside scientific knowledge for another form of thought held to be specifically religious.

But the believers – the men who, living a religious life, have a direct sense of what constitutes religion – object that, in terms of their day-to-day experience, this way of seeing does not ring true. Indeed, they sense that the true function of religion is not to make us think, enrich our knowledge, or add representations of a different sort and source to those we owe to science. Its true function is to make us act and to help us live. The believer who has communed with his god is not simply a man who sees new truths that the unbeliever knows not; he is a man who *is stronger*. Within himself, he feels more strength to endure the trials of existence or to overcome them. He is as though lifted above the human miseries, because he is lifted above his human condition. He believes he is delivered from evil – whatever the form in which he conceives of evil. The first article of any faith is belief in salvation by faith.

But it is hard to see how a mere idea could have that power. In fact, an idea is but one element of ourselves. How could it confer on us powers that are superior to those given us in our natural makeup? As rich in emotive power as an idea may be, it cannot add anything to our natural vitality; it can only release emotive forces that are already within us, neither creating nor increasing them. From the fact that we imagine an object as worthy of being loved and sought after, it does not follow that we should feel stronger. Energies greater than those at our disposal must come from the object, and, more than that, we must have some means of making them enter into us and blend into our inner life. To achieve this, it is not enough that we think about them; it is indispensable that we place ourselves under their influence, that we turn ourselves in the direction from which we can best feel that influence. In short, we must act; and so we must repeat the necessary acts as often as is necessary to renew their effects. From this standpoint, it becomes apparent that the set of regularly repeated actions that make up the cult regains all its importance. In fact, anyone who has truly practiced a religion knows very well that it is the cult that stimulates the feelings of joy, inner peace, serenity, and enthusiasm that, for the faithful, stand as experimental proof of their beliefs. The cult is not merely a system of signs by which the faith is outwardly expressed; it is the sum total of means by which that faith is created and re-created periodically. Whether the cult consists of physical operations or mental ones, it is always the cult that is efficacious.

This entire study rests on the postulate that the unanimous feeling of believers down the ages cannot be mere illusion. Therefore, like a recent apologist of faith,[3] I accept that religious belief rests on a definite experience, whose demonstrative value is, in a sense, not inferior to that of scientific experiments, though it is different. I too think "that a tree is known by its fruits,"[4] and that its fertility is the best proof of what its roots are worth. But merely because there exists a "religious experience," if you will, that is grounded in some manner (is there, by the way, any experience that is not?), it by no means follows that the reality which grounds it should conform objectively with the idea the believers have of it. The very fact that the way in which this reality has been conceived has varied infinitely in different times is enough to prove that none of these conceptions expresses it adequately. If the scientist sets it down as axiomatic that the sensations of heat and light that men have correspond to some objective cause, he does not thereby conclude that this cause is the same as it appears to the senses. Likewise, even if the

feelings the faithful have are not imaginary, they still do not constitute privileged intuitions; there is no reason whatever to think that they inform us better about the nature of their object than ordinary sensations do about the nature of bodies and their properties. To discover what that object consists of, then, we must apply to those sensations an analysis similar to the one that has replaced the senses' representation of the world with a scientific and conceptual one.

This is precisely what I have tried to do. We have seen that this reality – which mythologies have represented in so many different forms, but which is the objective, universal, and eternal cause of those *sui generis* sensations of which religious experience is made – is society. I have shown what moral forces it develops and how it awakens that feeling of support, safety, and protective guidance which binds the man of faith to his cult. It is this reality that makes him rise above himself. Indeed, this is the reality that makes him, for what makes man is that set of intellectual goods which is civilization, and civilization is the work of society. In this way is explained the preeminent role of the cult in all religions, whatever they are. This is so because society cannot make its influence felt unless it is in action, and it is in action only if the individuals who comprise it are assembled and acting in common. It is through common action that society becomes conscious of and affirms itself; society is above all an active cooperation. As I have shown, even collective ideas and feelings are possible only through the overt movements that symbolize them. Thus it is action that dominates religious life, for the very reason that society is its source.

To all the reasons adduced to justify this conception, a final one can be added that emerges from this book as a whole. Along the way, I have established that the fundamental categories of thought, and thus science itself, have religious origins. The same has been shown to be true of magic, and thus of the various techniques derived from magic. Besides, it has long been known that, until a relatively advanced moment in evolution, the rules of morality and law were not distinct from ritual prescriptions. In short, then, we can say that nearly all the great social institutions were born in religion. For the principal features of collective life to have begun as none other than various features of religious life, it is evident that religious life must necessarily have been the eminent form and, as it were, the epitome of collective life. If religion gave birth to all that is essential in society, that is so because the idea of society is the soul of religion.

Thus religious forces are human forces, moral forces. Probably because collective feelings become conscious of themselves only by settling upon external objects, those very forces could not organize themselves without taking some of their traits from things. In this way, they took on a kind of physical nature; they came to mingle as such with the life of the physical world, and through them it was thought possible to explain events in that world. But when they are considered only from this standpoint and in this role, we see only what is most superficial about them. In reality, the essential elements out of which they are made are borrowed from consciousness. Ordinarily, they do not seem to have a human character except when they are thought of in human form, but even the most impersonal and most anonymous are nothing other than objectified feelings.

Only by seeing religions in this way does it become possible to detect their real meaning. If we rely on appearances, the rites often seem to be purely manual operations – anointings, purifications, meals. To consecrate a thing, one places it in contact with a source of religious energy, just as today a body is placed in contact with a source of heat or electricity in order to heat or electrify it. The procedures used in the two cases are not essentially different. Understood in this way, religious technique seems to be a kind of mystical mechanics. But these physical operations are but the outer envelope in which mental operations lie hidden. In the end, the point is not to exert a kind of physical constraint upon blind and, more than that, imaginary forces but to reach, fortify, and discipline consciousnesses. The lower religions have sometimes been called materialistic. That term is incorrect. All religions, even the crudest, are in a sense spiritualistic. The powers they bring into play are, above all, spiritual, and their primary function is to act upon moral life. In this way, we understand that what was done in the name of religion cannot have been done in vain, for it is necessarily the society of men, it is humanity, that has reaped the fruits.

[. . .]

NOTES

1 I will call those societies and the men of those societies primitive in the same sense. This term certainly lacks precision, but it is hard to avoid; if care is taken to specify its meaning, however, it can safely be used.

2 Of the whole essence.

3 William James, *The Varieties of Religious Experience* [London, Longmans, 1902].

4 Ibid. (p. 19 of the French translation).

3

The Protestant Ethic and the Spirit of Capitalism

Max Weber

A large question addressed by the anthropology of religion has concerned the emergence of secular modernity. What is to be meant by modernity, and how does it differ from other social forms? What has been the role of religion in its formation? Here the most suggestive thinker has been German sociologist Max Weber (1864–1920), whose concepts of rationalization and the disenchantment of the world, no less than the elective affinity between certain forms of religious thought and certain kinds of economic structures and activities, notably between Protestantism and capitalism, have led to rich analyses and enormous debate (e.g., Lehmann and Roth, eds., 1993).

Although they were first published in 1904–5 I have placed these excerpts from *The Protestant Ethic and the Spirit of Capitalism* after those of Durkheim for two reasons. The first is that Weber's contribution is in a fundamental sense more contemporary than Durkheim's.

With Weber there is no recourse to universalistic evolutionary, functional, or determinist schemes; he is historical through and through. Furthermore, he no longer takes religion as an essence to be uncovered and defined from the bottom up, as it were, but is rather concerned with the relationships between religious factors (ideas, practices, institutions, and forms of authority) and economic and political processes. Second, Weber came to be appreciated by most anthropologists after Durkheim. If during the first half of the 20th century Durkheim was the central figure, the second half was Weber's. This is precisely because his central concern lies with social change and specifically with the transitions to capitalism and modernity. I pluralize transitions because Weber's approach is always rigorously comparative. As Weber himself put it, he "always underscored those features in the total picture of a religion which have been decisive for the fashioning of

From Max Weber, *The Protestant Ethic and the Spirit of Capitalism*, trans. Talcott Parsons (New York: Charles Scribner & Sons, 1958 [1904–5]), pp. 47–56, 87–92, 180–3. Reprinted by permission of Simon & Schuster, Inc., New York. Abridged, references and most notes removed.

the practical way of life, as well as those which distinguish one religion from another" (1946b [1915]: 294).

Weber is interested in historical contingency and, specifically, the way certain religious formulations and class or status positions within particular sociopolitical orders have an affinity with one another such that their conjunction forms the basis for transformative social action. This is a nondeterminist approach to historical generalization. Where the Durkheimians look to the relationship between thought and ritual, Weber asks what a given religious formulation establishes as ethical and practical outlooks for its adherents, and conversely, which class is likely to accept and advocate such a view of the world. Ritual is only of interest insofar as a priestly group practices excessive ritualism by contrast to another status group that emphasizes intellectual rationalization, ecstatic experience, contemplation, or whatever. Weber was particularly interested in the rise of what he called worldly asceticism or a calling, as in the Protestant work ethic, and its relationship to processes of economic and political rationalization, as well as what he memorably referred to as the "disenchantment of the world."

All of this would be enough to justify Weber's importance, but our selection indicates another reason for Weber's inspirational quality, namely his careful and lucid depiction of meaningful and ethical action specific to a highly particular ethos. He is a master of the art of interpretation and the elucidation of cultural difference; his use of Benjamin Franklin as an exemplary "cultural text" anticipates both interpretive anthropology and cultural studies, and does so both in its method and its unblinking ability to see the cultural basis of his own time. Weber's depictions of various types of religious institutions and in particular his discussion of charisma and its routinization have also been extremely influential. Weber's interest in theodicy is developed in the selection by Geertz (chapter 4). Finally, it should be mentioned that the applications of Weber to economically naive and politically conservative versions of modernization theory run counter to both his relativism and skepticism with respect to modernity and his own careful balancing of political and economic with cultural factors. Weber should be understood as complementary rather than opposed to Marx. Readers eager for more Weber should turn first to the three magnificent essays on religion published in *From Max Weber* (Gerth and Mills, eds., 1946). An essay that develops an evolutionary model of several stages from Weber's scheme is Bellah (1964), which was subsequently developed into an insightful textbook on the anthropology of religion by Peacock and Kirsch (1980).

In the title of this study is used the somewhat pretentious phrase, the *spirit* of capitalism. What is to be understood by it? The attempt to give anything like a definition of it brings out certain difficulties which are in the very nature of this type of investigation.

If any object can be found to which this term can be applied with any understandable meaning, it can only be an historical individual, i.e. a complex of elements associated in historical reality which we unite into a conceptual whole from the standpoint of their cultural significance.

Such an historical concept, however, since it refers in its content to a phenomenon significant for its unique individuality, cannot be defined according to the formula *genus proximum, differentia specifica*, but it must be gradually put together out of the individual parts which are taken from historical reality to make it up. Thus the final and definitive concept cannot stand at the beginning of the investigation, but must come at the end. We must, in other words, work out in the course of the discussion, as its most important result, the best conceptual formulation of what we here understand by the spirit of capitalism, that is the best from the point of view which interests us here. This point of view (the one of which we shall speak later) is, further, by no means the only possible one from which the historical phenomena we are investigating can be analyzed. Other standpoints would, for this as for every historical phenomenon, yield other characteristics as the essential ones. The result is that it is by no means necessary to understand by the spirit of capitalism only what it will come to mean to *us* for the purposes of our analysis. This is a necessary result of the nature of historical concepts which attempt for their methodological purposes not to grasp historical reality in abstract general formulæ, but in concrete genetic sets of relations which are inevitably of a specifically unique and individual character.

Thus, if we try to determine the object, the analysis and historical explanation of which we are attempting, it cannot be in the form of a conceptual definition, but at least in the beginning only a provisional description of what is here meant by the spirit of capitalism. Such a description is, however, indispensable in order clearly to understand the object of the investigation. For this purpose we turn to a document of that spirit which contains what we are looking for in almost classical purity, and at the same time has the advantage of being free from all direct relationship to religion, being thus, for our purposes, free of preconceptions.

Remember, that *time* is money. He that can earn ten shillings a day by his labour, and goes abroad, or sits idle, one half of that day, though he spends but sixpence during his diversion or idleness, ought not to reckon *that* the only expense; he has really spent, or rather thrown away, five shillings besides.

Remember, that *credit* is money. If a man lets his money lie in my hands after it is due, he gives me the interest, or so much as I can make of it during that time. This amounts to a considerable sum where a man has good and large credit, and makes good use of it.

Remember, that money is of the prolific, generating nature. Money can beget money, and its offspring can beget more, and so on. Five shillings turned is six, turned again it is seven and threepence, and so on, till it becomes a hundred pounds. The more there is of it, the more it produces every turning, so that the profits rise quicker and quicker. He that kills a breeding-sow, destroys all her offspring to the thousandth generation. He that murders a crown, destroys all that it might have produced, even scores of pounds.

Remember this saying, *The good paymaster is lord of another man's purse.* He that is known to pay punctually and exactly to the time he promises, may at any time, and on any occasion, raise all the money his friends can spare. This is sometimes of great use. After industry and frugality, nothing contributes more to the raising of a young man in the world than punctuality and justice in all his dealings; therefore never keep borrowed money an hour beyond the time you promised, lest a disappointment shut up your friend's purse for ever.

The most trifling actions that affect a man's credit are to be regarded. The sound of your hammer at five in the morning, or eight at night, heard by a creditor, makes him easy six months longer; but if he sees you at a billiard-table, or hears your voice at a tavern, when you should be at work, he sends for his money the next day; demands it, before he can receive it, in a lump.

It shows, besides, that you are mindful of what you owe; it makes you appear a careful as well as an honest man, and that still increases your credit.

Beware of thinking all your own that you possess, and of living accordingly. It is a mistake that many people who have credit fall into. To prevent this, keep an exact account for some time both of your expenses and your income. If you take the pains at first to mention particulars, it will have this good effect: you will discover how wonderfully small, trifling expenses mount up to large sums, and will discern what might have been, and may for the future be saved, without occasioning any great inconvenience.

For six pounds a year you may have the use of one hundred pounds, provided you are a man of known prudence and honesty.

He that spends a groat a day idly, spends idly above six pounds a year, which is the price for the use of one hundred pounds.

He that wastes idly a groat's worth of his time per day, one day with another, wastes the privilege of using one hundred pounds each day.

He that idly loses five shillings' worth of time, loses five shillings, and might as prudently throw five shillings into the sea.

He that loses five shillings, not only loses that sum, but all the advantage that might be made by turning it in dealing, which by the time that a young man becomes old, will amount to a considerable sum of money.

It is Benjamin Franklin who preaches to us in these sentences, the same which Ferdinand Kürnberger satirizes in his clever and malicious *Picture of American Culture* as the supposed confession of faith of the Yankee. That it is the spirit of capitalism which here speaks in characteristic fashion, no one will doubt, however little we may wish to claim that everything which could be understood as pertaining to that spirit is contained in it. Let us pause a moment to consider this passage, the philosophy of which Kürnberger sums up in the words, "They make tallow out of cattle and money out of men." The peculiarity of this philosophy of avarice appears to be the ideal of the honest man of recognized credit, and above all the idea of a duty of the individual toward the increase of his capital, which is assumed as an end in itself. Truly what is here preached is not simply a means of making one's way in the world, but a peculiar ethic. The infraction of its rules is treated not as foolishness but as forgetfulness of duty. That is the essence of the matter. It is not mere business astuteness, that sort of thing is common enough, it is an ethos. *This* is the quality which interests us.

When Jacob Fugger, in speaking to a business associate who had retired and who wanted to persuade him to do the same, since he had made enough money and should let others have a chance, rejected that as pusillanimity and answered that "he [Fugger] thought otherwise, he wanted to make money as long as he could", the spirit of his statement is evidently quite different from that of Franklin. What in the former case was an expression of commercial daring and a personal inclination morally neutral, in the latter takes on the character of an ethically coloured maxim for the conduct of life. The concept spirit of capitalism is here used in this specific sense, it is the spirit of modern capitalism. For that we are here dealing only with Western European and American capitalism is obvious from the way in which the problem was stated. Capitalism existed in China, India, Babylon, in the classic world, and in the Middle Ages. But in all these cases, as we shall see, this particular ethos was lacking.

Now, all Franklin's moral attitudes are coloured with utilitarianism. Honesty is useful, because it assures credit; so are punctuality, industry, frugality, and that is the reason they are virtues. A logical deducation from this would be that where, for instance, the appearance of honesty serves the same purpose, that would suffice, and an unnecessary surplus of this virtue would evidently appear to Franklin's eyes as unproductive waste. And as a matter of fact, the story in his autobiography of his conversion to those virtues, or the discussion of the value of a strict maintenance of the appearance of modesty, the assiduous belittlement of one's own deserts in order to gain general recognition later, confirms this impression. According to Franklin, those virtues, like all others, are only in so far virtues as they are actually useful to the individual, and the surrogate of mere appearance is always sufficient when it accomplishes the end in view. It is a conclusion which is inevitable for strict utilitarianism. The impression of many Germans that the virtues professed by Americanism are pure hypocrisy seems to have been confirmed by this striking case. But in fact the matter is not by any means so simple. Benjamin Franklin's own character, as it appears in the really unusual candidness of his autobiography, belies that suspicion. The circumstance that he ascribes his recognition of the utility of virtue to a divine revelation which was intended to lead him in the path of righteousness, shows that something more than mere garnishing for purely egocentric motives is involved.

In fact, the *summum bonum* of this ethic, the earning of more and more money, combined with the strict avoidance of all spontaneous enjoyment of life, is above all completely devoid of any eudaemonistic, not to say hedonistic, admixture. It is thought of so purely as an end in itself, that from the point of view of the happiness of, or utility to, the single individual, it appears entirely transcendental and absolutely irrational. Man is dominated by the making of money, by acquisition as the ultimate purpose of his life. Economic acquisition is no longer subordinated to man as the means for the satisfaction of his material needs. This reversal of what we should call the natural relationship, so irrational from a naïve point of view, is evidently as definitely a leading principle of capitalism as it is foreign to all peoples not under capitalistic influence. At the same time it expresses a type of feeling which is closely connected with certain religious ideas. If we thus ask, *why* should "money be made out of men", Benjamin Franklin himself, although he was a colourless deist, answers in his autobiography with a quotation from the Bible, which his strict Calvinistic father drummed into him again and again in his youth: "Seest thou a man diligent in his business? He shall stand before kings" (Prov. xxii. 29). The earning of money within the modern economic order is, so long as it is done legally, the result and the expression of virtue and proficiency in a calling; and this virtue and proficiency are, as it is now not difficult to see, the real Alpha and Omega of Franklin's ethic, as expressed in the passages we have quoted, as well as in all his works without exception.

And in truth this peculiar idea, so familiar to us today, but in reality so little a matter of course, of one's duty in a calling, is what is most characteristic of the social ethic of capitalistic culture, and is in a sense the fundamental basis of it. It is an obligation which the individual is supposed to feel and does feel towards the content of his professional activity, no matter in what it consists, in particular no matter whether it appears on the surface as a utilization of his personal powers, or only of his material possessions (as capital).

Of course, this conception has not appeared only under capitalistic conditions. On the contrary, we shall later trace its origins back to a time previous to the advent of capitalism. Still less, naturally, do we maintain that a conscious acceptance of these ethical maxims on the part of the individuals, entrepreneurs or labourers, in modern capitalistic enterprises, is a condition of the further existence of present-day capitalism. The capitalistic economy of the present day is an immense cosmos into which the individual is born, and which presents itself to him, at least as an individual, as an unalterable order of things in which he must live. It forces the individual, in so far as he is involved in the system of market relationships, to conform to capitalistic rules of action. The manufacturer who in the long run acts counter to these norms, will just as inevitably be eliminated from the economic scene as the worker who cannot or will not adapt himself to them will be thrown into the streets without a job.

Thus the capitalism of today, which has come to dominate economic life, educates and selects the economic subjects which it needs through a process of economic survival of the fittest. But here one can easily see the limits of the concept of selection as a means of historical explanation. In order that a manner of life so well adapted to the peculiarities of capitalism could be selected at all, i.e. should come to dominate others, it had to originate somewhere, and not in isolated individuals alone, but as a way of life common to whole groups of men. This origin is what really needs explanation. Concerning the doctrine of the more naïve historical materialism, that such ideas originate as a reflection or superstructure of economic situations, we shall speak more in detail below. At this point it will suffice for our purpose to call attention to the fact that without doubt, in the country of Benjamin Franklin's birth (Massachusetts), the spirit of capitalism (in the sense we have attached to it) was present before the capitalistic order. There were complaints of a peculiarly calculating sort of profit-seeking in New England, as distinguished from other parts of America, as early as 1632. It is further undoubted that capitalism remained far less developed in some of the neighbouring colonies, the later Southern States of the United States of America, in spite of the fact that these latter were founded by large capitalists for business motives, while the New England colonies were founded by preachers and seminary graduates with the help of small bourgeois, craftsmen and yeomen, for religious reasons. In this case the causal relation is certainly the reverse of that suggested by the materialistic standpoint.

But the origin and history of such ideas is much more complex than the theorists of the superstructure suppose. The spirit of capitalism, in the sense in which we are using the term, had to fight its way to supremacy against a whole world of hostile forces. A state of mind such as that expressed in the passages we have quoted from Franklin, and which called forth the applause of a whole people, would both in ancient times and in the Middle Ages have been proscribed as the lowest sort of avarice and as an attitude entirely lacking in self-respect. It is, in fact, still regularly thus looked upon by all those social groups which are least involved in or adapted to modern capitalistic conditions. This is not wholly because the instinct of acquisition was in those times unknown or undeveloped, as has often been said. Nor because the *auri sacra fames*, the greed for gold, was then, or now, less powerful outside of bourgeois capitalism than within its peculiar sphere, as the illusions of modern romanticists are wont to believe. The difference between the capitalistic and precapitalistic spirits is not to be found at this point. The greed of the Chinese Mandarin, the old Roman aristocrat, or the modern peasant, can stand up to any comparison. And the *auri sacra fames* of a Neapolitan cab-driver or *barcaiuolo*, and certainly of Asiatic representatives of similar trades, as well as of the craftsmen of southern European or Asiatic countries, is, as anyone can find out for himself, very much more intense, and especially more unscrupulous than that of, say, an Englishman in similar circumstances.
[. . .]

Luther's Conception of the Calling

. . . Although the Reformation is unthinkable without Luther's own personal religious development, and was spiritually long influenced by his personality, without Calvinism his work could not have had permanent concrete success. Nevertheless, the reason for this common repugnance of Catholics and Lutherans lies, at least partly, in the ethical peculiarities of Calvinism. A purely superficial glance shows that there is here quite a different relationship between the religious life and earthly activity than in either Catholicism or Lutheranism. Even in literature motivated purely by religious factors that is evident. Take for instance the end of the *Divine Comedy*, where the poet in Paradise stands speechless in his passive contemplation of the secrets of God, and compare it with the poem which has come to be called the *Divine Comedy of Puritanism*. Milton closes the last song of *Paradise Lost* after describing the *expulsion* from paradise as follows: –

They, looking back, all the eastern side
  beheld
Of paradise, so late their happy seat,
Waved over by that flaming brand; the gate
With dreadful faces thronged and fiery arms.
Some natural tears they dropped, but wiped
  them soon:
The world was all before them, there to
  choose
Their place of rest, and Providence their
  guide.

And only a little before Michael had said to Adam:

           . . . Only add
Deeds to thy knowledge answerable; add
  faith;
Add virtue, patience, temperance; add love,
By name to come called Charity, the soul
Of all the rest: then wilt thou not be loth
To leave this Paradise, but shall possess
A Paradise within thee, happier far.

One feels at once that this powerful expression of the Puritan's serious attention to this world, his acceptance of his life in the world as a task, could not possibly have come from the pen of a mediaeval writer. But it is just as uncongenial to Lutheranism, as expressed for instance in Luther's and Paul Gerhard's chorales. It is now our task to replace this vague feeling by a somewhat more precise logical formulation, and to investigate the fundamental basis of these differences. The appeal to national character is generally a mere confession of ignorance, and in this case it is entirely untenable. To ascribe a unified national character to the Englishmen of the seventeenth century would be simply to falsify history. Cavaliers and Roundheads did not appeal to each other simply as two parties, but as radically distinct species of men, and whoever looks into the matter carefully must agree with them. On the other hand, a difference of character between the English merchant adventurers and the old Hanseatic merchants is not to be found; nor can any other fundamental difference between the English and German characters at the end of the Middle Ages, which cannot easily be explained by the differences of their political history. It was the power of religious influence, not alone, but more than anything else, which created the differences of which we are conscious to-day.

We thus take as our starting-point in the investigation of the relationship between the old Protestant ethic and the spirit of capitalism the works of Calvin, of Calvinism, and the other Puritan sects. But it is not to be understood that we expect to find any of the founders or representatives of these religious movements considering the promotion of what we have called the spirit of capitalism as in any sense the end of his life-work. We cannot well maintain that the pursuit of worldly goods, conceived as an end in itself, was to any of them of positive ethical value. Once and for all it must be remembered that programmes of ethical reform never were at the centre of interest for any of the religious reformers (among whom, for our purposes, we must include men like Menno, George Fox, and Wesley). They were not the founders of societies for ethical culture nor the proponents of humanitarian projects for social reform or cultural ideals. The salvation of the soul and that alone was the centre of their life and work. Their ethical ideals and the practical results of their doctrines were all based on that alone, and were the consequences of purely religious motives. We shall thus have to admit that the cultural consequences of the Reformation were to a great extent, perhaps in the particular aspects with which we are dealing predominantly, unforeseen and even unwished-for results of the labours of the reformers. They were often far removed from or even in contradiction to all that they themselves thought to attain.

The following study may thus perhaps in a modest way form a contribution to the understanding of the manner in which ideas become effective forces in history. In order, however, to avoid any misunderstanding of the sense in which any such effectiveness of purely ideal motives is claimed at all, I may perhaps be permitted a few remarks in conclusion to this introductory discussion.

In such a study, it may at once be definitely stated, no attempt is made to evaluate the ideas of the Reformation in any sense, whether it concern their social or their religious worth. We have continually to deal with aspects of the Reformation which must appear to the truly religious consciousness as incidental and even superficial. For we are merely attempting to clarify the part which religious forces have played in forming the developing web of our specifically worldly modern culture, in the complex interaction of innumerable different historical factors. We are thus inquiring only to what extent certain characteristic features of this culture can be imputed to the influence of the Reformation. At the same time we must free ourselves from the idea that it is possible to deduce the Reformation, as a historically necessary result, from certain economic changes. Countless historical circumstances, which cannot be reduced to any economic law, and are not susceptible of economic explanation of any sort, especially purely political processes, had to concur in order that the newly created Churches should survive at all.

On the other hand, however, we have no intention whatever of maintaining such a foolish and doctrinaire thesis[1] as that the spirit of capitalism (in the provisional sense of the term explained above) could only have arisen as the result of certain effects of the Reformation, or even that capitalism as an economic system is a creation of the Reformation. In itself, the fact that certain important forms of capitalistic business organization are known to be considerably older than the Reformation is a sufficient refutation of such a claim. On the contrary, we only wish to ascertain whether and to what extent religious forces have taken part in the qualitative formation and the quantitative expansion of that spirit over the world. Furthermore, what concrete aspects of our capitalistic culture can be traced to them. In view of the tremendous confusion of interdependent influences between the material basis, the forms of social and political organization, and the ideas current in the time of the Reformation, we can only proceed by investigating whether and at what points certain correlations between forms of religious belief and practical ethics can be worked out. At the same time we shall as far as possible clarify the manner and the general *direction* in which, by virtue of those relationships, the religious movements have influenced the development of material culture. Only when this has been determined with reasonable accuracy can the attempt be made to estimate to what extent the historical development of modern culture can be attributed to those religious forces and to what extent to others.

[. . .]

One of the fundamental elements of the spirit of modern capitalism, and not only of that but of all modern culture: rational conduct on the basis of the idea of the calling, was born – that is what this discussion has sought to demonstrate – from the spirit of Christian asceticism. One has only to re-read the passage from Franklin, quoted at the beginning of this essay, in order to see that the essential elements of the attitude which was there called the spirit of capitalism are the same as what we have just shown to be the content of the Puritan worldly asceticism, only without the religious basis, which by Franklin's time had died away. The idea that modern labour has an ascetic character is of course not new. Limitation to specialized work, with a renunciation of the Faustian universality of man which it involves, is a condition of any valuable work in the

modern world; hence deeds and renunciation inevitably condition each other today. This fundamentally ascetic trait of middle-class life, if it attempts to be a way of life at all, and not simply the absence of any, was what Goethe wanted to teach, at the height of his wisdom, in the *Wanderjahren,* and in the end which he gave to the life of his *Faust.* For him the realization meant a renunciation, a departure from an age of full and beautiful humanity, which can no more be repeated in the course of our cultural development than can the flower of the Athenian culture of antiquity.

The Puritan wanted to work in a calling; we are forced to do so. For when asceticism was carried out of monastic cells into everyday life, and began to dominate worldly morality, it did its part in building the tremendous cosmos of the modern economic order. This order is now bound to the technical and economic conditions of machine production which today determine the lives of all the individuals who are born into this mechanism, not only those directly concerned with economic acquisition, with irresistible force. Perhaps it will so determine them until the last ton of fossilized coal is burnt. In Baxter's view the care for external goods should only lie on the shoulders of the "saint like a light cloak, which can be thrown aside at any moment". But fate decreed that the cloak should become an iron cage.

Since asceticism undertook to remodel the world and to work out its ideals in the world, material goods have gained an increasing and finally an inexorable power over the lives of men as at no previous period in history. Today the spirit of religious asceticism – whether finally, who knows? – has escaped from the cage. But victorious capitalism, since it rests on mechanical foundations, needs its support no longer. The rosy blush of its laughing heir, the Enlightenment, seems also to be irretrievably fading, and the idea of duty in one's calling prowls about in our lives like the ghost of dead religious beliefs. Where the fulfilment of the calling cannot directly be related to the highest spiritual and cultural values, or when, on the other hand, it need not be felt simply as economic compulsion, the individual generally abandons the attempt to justify it at all. In the field of its highest development, in the

United States, the pursuit of wealth, stripped of its religious and ethical meaning, tends to become associated with purely mundane passions, which often actually give it the character of sport.

No one knows who will live in this cage in the future, or whether at the end of this tremendous development entirely new prophets will arise, or there will be a great rebirth of old ideas and ideals, or, if neither, mechanized petrification, embellished with a sort of convulsive self-importance. For of the last stage of this cultural development, it might well be truly said: "Specialists without spirit, sensualists without heart; this nullity imagines that it has attained a level of civilization never before achieved."

But this brings us to the world of judgments of value and of faith, with which this purely historical discussion need not be burdened. The next task would be rather to show the significance of ascetic rationalism, which has only been touched in the foregoing sketch, for the content of practical social ethics, thus for the types of organization and the functions of social groups from the conventicle to the State. Then its relations to humanistic rationalism, its ideals of life and cultural influence; further to the development of philosophical and scientific empiricism, to technical development and to spiritual ideals would have to be analyzed. Then its historical development from the mediaeval beginnings of worldly asceticism to its dissolution into pure utilitarianism would have to be traced out through all the areas of ascetic religion. Only then could the quantitative cultural significance of ascetic Protestantism in its relation to the other plastic elements of modern culture be estimated.

Here we have only attempted to trace the fact and the direction of its influence to their motives in one, though a very important point. But it would also further be necessary to investigate how Protestant Asceticism was in turn influenced in its development and its character by the totality of social conditions, especially economic. The modern man is in general, even with the best will, unable to give religious ideas a significance for culture and national character which they deserve. But it is, of course, not my aim to substitute for a one-sided materialistic an equally one-sided spiritualistic causal interpretation of culture and of history. Each is equally possible,[2] but each, if it does not serve as the preparation, but as the conclusion of an investigation, accomplishes equally little in the interest of historical truth.

NOTES

1   In spite of this and the following remarks, which in my opinion are clear enough, and have never been changed, I have again and again been accused of this.

2   For the above sketch has deliberately taken up only the relations in which an influence of religious ideas on the material culture is really beyond doubt. It would have been easy to proceed beyond that to a regular construction which logically deduced everything characteristic of modern culture from Protestant rationalism. But that sort of thing may be left to the type of dilettante who believes in the unity of the group mind and its reduceability to a single formula. . . .

4

Religion as a Cultural System

Clifford Geertz

Clifford Geertz (1926–2006) was an American anthropologist trained at Harvard University who, after teaching for several years at the University of Chicago, served as Professor at the Institute for Advanced Study in Princeton, New Jersey.

Geertz's essay is among the most interesting and influential of mid-20th-century attempts to develop a general depiction of religion. If Weber notoriously postponed defining religion, Geertz steps in on his behalf, but in a manner that effortlessly incorporates insights from both the Durkheimian and Boasian traditions. Geertz's approach has even been referred to as neo-Tylorean. In fact, Geertz draws from the synthesis of Durkheim and Weber developed by the sociologist Talcott Parsons and is able to render Parsons' rather ponderous thought in a much more readable language, in part because of his wonderful way with anecdote and quota-

tion and his finely wrought ethnographic descriptions.

Geertz has been the major exponent of a Weber-inspired interpretive anthropology which attempts to understand religion within a broadly cultural/symbolic domain, but also with reference to public circumstances in all their historical messiness. In this essay Geertz describes how religions constitute the worlds their adherents inhabit and provide guides for their action within them. Such worlds must provide assurances that they are ultimately comprehensive and comprehensible. When the power to do so breaks down, new religious movements may arise.

Geertz is at his best when he does what he advocates and weaves his theoretical insights from ethnographic material, often by means of contrasting cases. Hence, in addition to turning to the unabridged version of this essay, I recommend readers examine a parallel exposition of the argument as worked

From Clifford Geertz, "Religion as a Cultural System," in *Anthropological Approaches to the Study of Religion* (London: Tavistock, 1966), pp. 1–46. Abridged.

out in a discussion of *Islam Observed* (1968, especially chapter 4). Geertz's preferred vehicle is the extended essay. *The Interpretation of Cultures* (1973a) collects some of the best, including the one reprinted here. The first three essays of the book provide the theoretical underpinnings, while "Person, Time, and Conduct in Bali" (originally 1966) provides a superb exemplification of his approach to culture, and the concluding essay on the Balinese cockfight is where he most famously and explicitly compares cultural analysis to the interpretation of texts. Other essays relevant to religion include *Negara* (1980), on the precolonial Balinese "theater state," *Local Knowledge* (1983), and *Available Light* (2000).

Despite, or perhaps because of, Geertz's staunch rejection of French structuralism, his work has found tremendous resonance in the humanities. Equally, it has drawn more than its share of criticism from within anthropology, often due to a false identification on the part of critics of Geertz's hermeneutic methodology with philosophical idealism and subjectivism (both of which Geertz is at pains to reject). "Person, Time, and Conduct in Bali" provoked a response from Bloch (1989b [1977]) that nicely illustrates the contrast between a Boasian/Weberian approach, on the one hand, and a Durkheimian/Marxian approach on the other. While Geertz is sometimes criticized for painting overly consistent portraits of other peoples' religions, in fact, his first book, *The Religion of Java* (1960), emphasized the internal diversity of tradition. Scholarly appraisal of Geertz can be found in Ortner, ed. (1999) and Schweder and Good (2005).

Any attempt to speak without speaking any particular language is not more hopeless than the attempt to have a religion that shall be no religion in particular. . . . Thus every living and healthy religion has a marked idiosyncrasy. Its power consists in its special and surprising message and in the bias which that revelation gives to life. The vistas it opens and the mysteries it propounds are another world to live in; and another world to live in – whether we expect ever to pass wholly over into it or no – is what we mean by having a religion.

SANTAYANA, Reason in Religion

[. . .]

As we are to deal with meaning, let us begin with a paradigm: viz., that sacred symbols function to synthesize a people's ethos – the tone, character, and quality of their life, its moral and aesthetic style and mood – and their world view – the picture they have of the way things in sheer actuality are, their most comprehensive ideas of order. In religious belief and practice a group's ethos is rendered intellectually reasonable by being shown to represent a way of life ideally adapted to the actual state of affairs the world view describes, while the world view is rendered emotionally convincing by being presented as an image of an actual state of affairs peculiarly well-arranged to accommodate such a way of life. This confrontation and mutual confirmation has two fundamental effects. On the one hand, it objectivizes moral and aesthetic preferences by depicting them as the imposed conditions of life implicit in a world with a particular structure, as mere common sense given the unalterable shape of reality. On the other, it supports these received beliefs about the world's body by invoking deeply felt moral and aesthetic sentiments as experimental evidence for their truth. Religious symbols formulate a basic congruence between a particular style of life and a specific (if, most often, implicit) metaphysic, and in so doing sustain each with the borrowed authority of the other.

Phrasing aside, this much may perhaps be granted. The notion that religion tunes human actions to an envisaged cosmic order and projects images of cosmic order onto the plane of human experience is hardly novel. But it is hardly investigated either, so that we have very little idea of how, in empirical terms, this particular miracle is accomplished. We just know that it is done, annually, weekly, daily, for some people almost hourly; and we have an enormous ethnographic literature to demonstrate it. But the theoretical framework which would enable us to provide an analytic account of it, an account of the sort we can provide for lineage segmentation, political succession, labor exchange, or the socialization of the child, does not exist.

Let us, therefore, reduce our paradigm to a definition, for, although it is notorious that definitions establish nothing, in themselves they do, if they are carefully enough constructed, provide a useful orientation, or reorientation, of thought, such that an extended unpacking of them can be an effective way of developing and controlling a novel line of inquiry. They have the useful virtue of explicitness: they commit themselves in a way discursive prose, which, in this field especially, is always liable to substitute rhetoric for argument, does not. Without further ado, then, a *religion* is:

(1) a system of symbols which acts to (2) establish powerful, pervasive, and long-lasting moods and motivations in men by (3) formulating conceptions of a general order of existence and (4) clothing these conceptions with such an aura of factuality that (5) the moods and motivations seem uniquely realistic.

a system of symbols which acts to . . .

Such a tremendous weight is being put on the term "symbol" here that our first move must be to decide with some precision what we are going to mean by it. This is no easy task, for, rather like "culture," "symbol" has been used to refer to a great variety of things, often a number of them at the same time.

In some hands it is used for anything which signifies something else to someone: dark clouds are the symbolic precursors of an oncoming rain. In others it is used only for explicitly conventional signs of one sort or another: a red flag is a symbol of danger, a white of surrender. In others it is confined to something which expresses in an oblique and figurative manner that which cannot be stated in a direct and literal one, so that there are symbols in poetry but not in science, and symbolic logic is misnamed. In yet others, however, it is used for any object, act, event, quality, or relation which serves as a vehicle for a conception – the conception is the symbol's "meaning" – and that is the approach I shall follow here.[1] The number 6, written, imagined, laid out as a row of stones, or even punched into the program tapes of a computer, is a symbol. But so also is the Cross, talked about, visualized, shaped worriedly in air or fondly fingered at the neck, the expanse of painted canvas called "Guernica" or the bit of painted stone called a churinga, the word "reality," or even the morpheme "-ing." They are all symbols, or at least symbolic elements, because they are tangible formulations of notions, abstractions from experience fixed in perceptible forms, concrete embodiments of ideas, attitudes, judgments, longings, or beliefs. To undertake the study of cultural activity – activity in which symbolism forms the positive content – is thus not to abandon social analysis for a Platonic cave of shadows, to enter into a mentalistic world of introspective psychology or, worse, speculative philosophy, and wander there forever in a haze of "Cognitions," "Affections," "Conations," and other elusive entities. Cultural acts, the construction, apprehension, and utilization of symbolic forms, are social events like any other; they are as public as marriage and as observable as agriculture.

They are not, however, exactly the same thing; or, more precisely, the symbolic dimension of social events is, like the psychological, itself theoretically abstractable from those events as empirical totalities. There is still, to paraphrase a remark of Kenneth Burke's, a difference between building a house and drawing up a plan for building a house, and reading a poem about having children by marriage is not quite the same thing as having children by marriage.[2] Even though the building of the house may proceed under the guidance of the plan or – a less likely occurrence – the having of children may be motivated by a reading of the poem, there is something to be said for not confusing our traffic with symbols with our traffic with objects or human beings, for these latter are not in themselves symbols, however often they may function as such.[3] No matter how deeply interfused the cultural, the social, and the psychological may be in the everyday life of houses, farms, poems, and marriages, it is useful to distinguish them in analysis, and, so doing, to isolate the generic traits of each against the normalized background of the other two.

So far as culture patterns, that is, systems or complexes of symbols, are concerned, the generic trait which is of first importance for us here is that they are extrinsic sources of information. By "extrinsic," I mean only that – unlike genes, for example – they lie outside the boundaries of the individual organism as such in that inter-subjective world of common understandings into which all human individuals are born, in which they pursue their separate careers, and which they leave persisting behind them after they die. By "sources of information," I mean only that – like genes – they provide a blueprint or template in terms of which processes external to themselves can be given a definite form. As the order of bases in a strand of DNA forms a coded program, a set of instructions, or a recipe, for the synthesis of the structurally complex proteins which shape organic functioning, so culture patterns provide such programs for the institution of the social and psychological processes which shape public behavior. Though the sort of information and the mode of its transmission are vastly different in the two cases, this comparison of gene and symbol is more than a strained analogy of the familiar "social heredity" sort. It is actually a substantial relationship, for it is precisely because of the fact that genetically programmed processes are so highly generalized in men, as compared with lower animals, that culturally programmed ones are so important; only because human behavior is so loosely determined by intrinsic sources of information that extrinsic sources are so vital.

To build a dam a beaver needs only an appropriate site and the proper materials – his mode of procedure is shaped by his physiology. But man, whose genes are silent on the building trades, needs also a conception of what it is to build a dam, a conception he can get only from some symbolic source – a blueprint, a textbook, or a string of speech by someone who already knows how dams are built – or, of course, from manipulating graphic or linguistic elements in such a way as to attain for himself a conception of what dams are and how they are built.

This point is sometimes put in the form of an argument that cultural patterns are "models," that they are sets of symbols whose relations to one another "model" relations among entities, processes or what-have-you in physical, organic, social, or psychological systems by "paralleling," "imitating," or "simulating" them.[4] The term "model" has, however, two senses – an "of" sense and a "for" sense – and though these are but aspects of the same basic concept they are very much worth distinguishing for analytic purposes. In the first, what is stressed is the manipulation of symbol structures so as to bring them, more or less closely, into parallel with the pre-established nonsymbolic system, as when we grasp how dams work by developing a theory of hydraulics or constructing a flow chart. The theory or chart models physical relationships in such a way – that is, by expressing their structure in synoptic form – as to render them apprehensible; it is a model of "reality." In the second, what is stressed is the manipulation of the nonsymbolic systems in terms of the relationships expressed in the symbolic, as when we construct a dam according to the specifications implied in an hydraulic theory or the conclusions drawn from a flow chart. Here, the theory is a model under whose guidance physical relationships are organized: it is a model for "reality." For psychological and social systems, and for cultural models that we would not ordinarily refer to as "theories," but rather as "doctrines," "melodies," or "rites," the case is in no way different. Unlike genes, and other nonsymbolic information sources, which are only models for, not models of, culture patterns have an intrinsic double aspect: they give meaning, that is, objective conceptual form, to social and psychological reality both by shaping themselves to it and by shaping it to themselves.

It is, in fact, this double aspect which sets true symbols off from other sorts of significative forms. Models *for* are found, as the gene example suggests, through the whole order of nature; for wherever there is a communication of pattern, such programs are, in simple logic, required. Among animals, imprint learning is perhaps the most striking example, because what such learning involves is the automatic presentation of an appropriate sequence of behavior by a model animal in the presence of a learning animal which serves, equally automatically, to call out and stabilize a certain set of responses genetically built into the learning animal.[5] The communicative dance of two bees, one of which has found nectar and the other of which seeks it, is another, somewhat different, more complexly coded, example.[6] Craik has even suggested that the thin trickle of water which first finds its way down from a mountain spring to the sea and smooths a little channel for the greater volume of water that follows after it plays a sort of model *for* function.[7] But models *of* – linguistic, graphic, mechanical, natural, etc., processes which function not to provide sources of information in terms of which other processes can be patterned, but to represent those patterned processes as such, to express their structure in an alternative medium – are much rarer and may perhaps be confined, among living animals, to man. The perception of the structural congruence between one set of processes, activities, relations, entities, and so on, and another set for which it acts as a program, so that the program can be taken as a representation, or conception – a symbol – of the programmed, is the essence of human thought. The intertransposability of models *for* and models *of* which symbolic formulation makes possible is the distinctive characteristic of our mentality.

. . . to establish powerful, pervasive, and long-lasting moods and motivations in men by . . .

So far as religious symbols and symbol systems are concerned this intertransposability

is clear. The endurance, courage, independence, perseverance, and passionate willfulness in which the vision quest practices the Plains Indian are the same flamboyant virtues by which he attempts to live: while achieving a sense of revelation he stabilizes a sense of direction.[8] The consciousness of defaulted obligation, secreted guilt, and, when a confession is obtained, public shame in which Manus' seance rehearses him are the same sentiments that underlie the sort of duty ethic by which his property-conscious society is maintained: the gaining of an absolution involves the forging of a conscience.[9] And the same self-discipline which rewards a Javanese mystic staring fixedly into the flame of a lamp with what he takes to be an intimation of divinity drills him in that rigorous control of emotional expression which is necessary to a man who would follow a quietistic style of life.[10] Whether one sees the conception of a personal guardian spirit, a family tutelary, or an immanent God as synoptic formulations of the character of reality or as templates for producing reality seems largely arbitrary, a matter of which aspect, the model *of* or model *for*, one wants for the moment to bring into focus. The concrete symbols involved – one or another mythological figure materializing in the wilderness, the skull of the deceased household head hanging censoriously in the rafters, or a disembodied "voice in the stillness" soundlessly chanting enigmatic classical poetry – point in either direction. They both express the world's climate and shape it.

They shape it by inducing in the worshipper a certain distinctive set of dispositions (tendencies, capacities, propensities, skills, habits, liabilities, pronenesses) which lend a chronic character to the flow of his activity and the quality of his experience. A disposition describes not an activity or an occurrence but a probability of an activity being performed or an occurrence occurring in certain circumstances: "When a cow is said to be a ruminant, or a man is said to be a cigarette-smoker, it is not being said that the cow is ruminating now or that the man is smoking a cigarette now. To be a ruminant is to tend to ruminate from time to time, and to be a cigarette-smoker is to be in the habit of smoking cigarettes."[11] Similarly, to be pious is not to be performing something we would call an act of piety, but to be liable to perform such acts. So, too, with the Plains Indian's bravura, the Manus' compunctiousness, or the Javanese's quietism, which, in their contexts, form the substance of piety. The virtue of this sort of view of what are usually called "mental traits" or, if the Cartesianism is unavowed, "psychological forces" (both unobjectionable enough terms in themselves) is that it gets them out of any dim and inaccessible realm of private sensation into that same well-lit world of observables in which reside the brittleness of glass, the inflammability of paper, and, to return to the metaphor, the dampness of England.

So far as religious activities are concerned (and learning a myth by heart is as much a religious activity as detaching one's finger at the knuckle), two somewhat different sorts of disposition are induced by them: moods and motivations.

A motivation is a persisting tendency, a chronic inclination to perform certain sorts of acts and experience certain sorts of feeling in certain sorts of situations, the "sorts" being commonly very heterogenous and rather ill-defined classes in all three cases. . . .

As a motive, "flamboyant courage" consists in such enduring propensities as to fast in the wilderness, to conduct solitary raids on enemy camps, and to thrill to the thought of counting coup. "Moral circumspection" consists in such ingrained tendencies as to honor onerous promises, to confess secret sins in the face of severe public disapproval, and to feel guilty when vague and generalized accusations are made at seances. And "dispassionate tranquility" consists in such persistent inclinations as to maintain one's poise come hell or high water, to experience distaste in the presence of even moderate emotional displays, and to indulge in contentless contemplations of featureless objects. Motives are thus neither acts (that is, intentional behaviors) nor feelings, but liabilities to perform particular classes of act or have particular classes of feeling. And when we say that a man is religious, that is, motivated by religion, this is at least part – though only part – of what we mean.

Another part of what we mean is that he has, when properly stimulated, a susceptibility to fall into certain moods, moods we sometimes lump together under such covering terms as "reverential," "solemn," or "worshipful." Such generalized rubrics actually conceal, however, the enormous empirical variousness of the dispositions involved, and, in fact, tend to assimilate them to the unusually grave tone of most of our own religious life. The moods that sacred symbols induce, at different times and in different places, range from exultation to melancholy, from self-confidence to self-pity, from an incorrigible playfulness to a bland listlessness – to say nothing of the erogenous power of so many of the world's myths and rituals. No more than there is a single sort of motivation one can call piety is there a single sort of mood one can call worshipful.

The major difference between moods and motivations is that where the latter are, so to speak, vectorial qualities, the former are merely scalar. Motives have a directional cast, they describe a certain overall course, gravitate toward certain, usually temporary, consummations. But moods vary only as to intensity: they go nowhere. They spring from certain circumstances but they are responsive to no ends. Like fogs, they just settle and lift; like scents, suffuse and evaporate. When present they are totalistic: if one is sad everything and everybody seems dreary; if one is gay, everything and everybody seems splendid. Thus, though a man can be vain, brave, willful, and independent at the same time, he can't very well be playful and listless, or exultant and melancholy, at the same time.[12] Further, where motives persist for more or less extended periods of time, moods merely recur with greater or lesser frequency, coming and going for what are often quite unfathomable reasons. But perhaps the most important difference, so far as we are concerned, between moods and motivations is that motivations are "made meaningful" with reference to the ends toward which they are conceived to conduce, whereas moods are "made meaningful" with reference to the conditions from which they are conceived to spring. We interpret motives in terms of their consummations, but we interpret moods in terms of their sources. We say that a person is industrious because he wishes to succeed; we say that a person is worried because he is conscious of the hanging threat of nuclear holocaust. And this is no less the case when the interpretations are ultimate. Charity becomes Christian charity when it is enclosed in a conception of God's purposes; optimism is Christian optimism when it is grounded in a particular conception of God's nature. The assiduity of the Navaho finds its rationale in a belief that, since "reality" operates mechanically, it is coercible; their chronic fearfulness finds its rationale in a conviction that, however "reality" operates, it is both enormously powerful and terribly dangerous.[13]

... by formulating conceptions of a general order of existence and ...

That the symbols or symbol systems which induce and define dispositions we set off as religious and those which place those dispositions in a cosmic framework are the same symbols ought to occasion no surprise. For what else do we mean by saying that a particular mood of awe is religious and not secular, except that it springs from entertaining a conception of all-pervading vitality like mana and not from a visit to the Grand Canyon? Or that a particular case of asceticism is an example of a religious motivation, except that it is directed toward the achievement of an unconditioned end like nirvana and not a conditioned one like weight-reduction? If sacred symbols did not at one and the same time induce dispositions in human beings and formulate, however obliquely, inarticulately, or unsystematically, general ideas of order, then the empirical differentia of religious activity or religious experience would not exist. A man can indeed be said to be "religious" about golf, but not merely if he pursues it with passion and plays it on Sundays: he must also see it as symbolic of some transcendent truths. And the pubescent boy gazing soulfully into the eyes of the pubescent girl in a William Steig cartoon and murmuring "There is something about you, Ethel, which gives me a sort of religious feeling," is, like most adolescents, confused. What any particular religion affirms about the fundamental nature of reality may be obscure, shallow, or, all too often, perverse; but it must, if it is not to consist of the mere collection of received practices and conventional sentiments we usually refer to as moralism, affirm something. If one were to essay a minimal definition of religion today, it would perhaps not be Tylor's famous "belief in spiritual beings," to which Goody, wearied of theoretical subtleties, has lately urged us to return, but rather what Salvador de Madariaga has called "the relatively modest dogma that God is not mad."[14]

Usually, of course, religions affirm very much more than this: we believe, as James remarked, all that we can and would believe everything if we only could.[15] The thing we seem least able to tolerate is a threat to our powers of conception, a suggestion that our ability to create, grasp, and use symbols may fail us, for were this to happen, we would be more helpless, as I have already pointed out, than the beavers. The extreme generality, diffuseness, and variability of man's innate (that is, genetically programmed) response capacities means that without the assistance of cultural patterns he would be functionally incomplete, not merely a talented ape who had, like some underprivileged child, unfortunately been prevented from realizing his full potentialities, but a kind of formless monster with neither sense of direction nor power of self-control, a chaos of spasmodic impulses and vague emotions. Man depends upon symbols and symbol systems with a dependence so great as to be decisive for his creatural viability and, as a result, his sensitivity to even the remotest indication that they may prove unable to cope with one or another aspect of experience raises within him the gravest sort of anxiety. . . .

There are at least three points where chaos – a tumult of events which lack not just interpretations but *interpretability* – threatens to break in upon man: at the limits of his analytic capacities, at the limits of his powers of endurance, and at the limits of his moral insight. Bafflement, suffering, and a sense of intractable ethical paradox are all, if they become intense enough or are sustained long enough, radical challenges to the proposition that life is comprehensible and that we can, by taking thought, orient ourselves effectively within it – challenges with which any religion, however "primitive," which hopes to persist must attempt somehow to cope.

Of the three issues, it is the first which has been least investigated by modern social anthropologists (though Evans-Pritchard's classic discussion of why granaries fall on some Azande and not on others, is a notable exception)....[16] Any chronic failure of one's explanatory apparatus, the complex of received culture patterns (common sense, science, philosophical speculation, myth) one has for mapping the empirical world, to explain things which cry out for explanation tends to lead to a deep disquiet – a tendency rather more widespread and a disquiet rather deeper than we have sometimes supposed since the pseudoscience view of religious belief was, quite rightfully, deposed. After all, even that high priest of heroic atheism, Lord Russell, once remarked that although the problem of the existence of God had never bothered him, the ambiguity of certain mathematical axioms had threatened to unhinge his mind. And Einstein's profound dissatisfaction with quantum mechanics was based on a – surely religious – inability to believe that, as he put it, God plays dice with the universe.

But this quest for lucidity and the rush of metaphysical anxiety that occurs when empirical phenomena threaten to remain intransigently opaque is found on much humbler intellectual levels. Certainly, I was struck in my own work, much more than I had at all expected to be, by the degree to which my more animistically inclined informants behaved like true Tyloreans. They seemed to be constantly using their beliefs to "explain" phenomena: or, more accurately, to convince themselves that the phenomena were explainable within the accepted scheme of things, for they commonly had only a minimal attachment to the particular soul possession, emotional disequilibrium, taboo infringement, or bewitchment hypothesis they advanced and were all too ready to abandon it for some other, in the same genre, which struck them as more plausible given the facts of the case. What they were *not* ready to do was abandon

it for no other hypothesis at all; to leave events to themselves.

And what is more, they adopted this nervous cognitive stance with respect to phenomena which had no immediate practical bearing on their own lives, or for that matter on anyone's. When a peculiarly shaped, rather large toadstool grew up in a carpenter's house in the short space of a few days (or, some said, a few hours), people came from miles around to see it, and everyone had some sort of explanation – some animist, some animatist, some not quite either – for it. Yet it would be hard to argue that the toadstool had any social value in Radcliffe-Brown's sense, or was connected in any way with anything which did and for which it could have been standing proxy, like the Andaman cicada....[17]

Nor is this to argue that it is only, or even mainly, sudden eruptions of extraordinary events which engender in man the disquieting sense that his cognitive resources may prove unavailing or that this intuition appears only in its acute form. More commonly it is a persistent, constantly re-experienced difficulty in grasping certain aspects of nature, self, and society, in bringing certain elusive phenomena within the sphere of culturally formulatable fact, which renders man chronically uneasy and toward which a more equable flow of diagnostic symbols is consequently directed. It is what lies beyond a relatively fixed frontier of accredited knowledge that, looming as a constant background to the daily round of practical life, sets ordinary human experience in a permanent context of metaphysical concern and raises the dim, back-of-the-mind suspicions that one may be adrift in an absurd world:

Another subject which is matter for this characteristic intellectual enquiry [among the Iatmul] is the nature of ripples and waves on the surface of water. It is said secretly that men, pigs, trees, grass – all the objects in the world – are only patterns of waves.... On one occasion I took some Iatmul natives down to the coast and found one of them sitting by himself gazing with rapt attention at the sea. It was a windless day, but a slow swell was breaking on the beach. Among the totemic ancestors of his clan he counted a personified slit gong who had floated down the river to the sea and who was believed to cause the waves. He was gazing at the waves which were heaving and breaking when no wind was blowing, demonstrating the truth of his clan myth.[18]

The second experiential challenge in whose face the meaningfulness of a particular pattern of life threatens to dissolve into a chaos of thingless names and nameless things – the problem of suffering – has been rather more investigated, or at least described, mainly because of the great amount of attention given in works on tribal religion to what are perhaps its two main loci: illness and mourning. Yet for all the fascinated interest in the emotional aura that surrounds these extreme situations, there has been, with a few exceptions such as Lienhardt's recent discussion of Dinka divining, little conceptual advance over the sort of crude confidence-type theory set forth by Malinowski: viz., that religion helps one to endure "situations of emotional stress" by "open [ing] up escapes from such situations and such impasses as offer no empirical way out except by ritual and belief into the domain of the supernatural."[19] The inadequacy of this "theology of optimism," as Nadel rather dryly called it, is, of course, radical.[20] Over its career religion has probably disturbed men as much as it has cheered them; forced them into a head-on, unblinking confrontation of the fact that they are born to trouble as often as it has enabled them to avoid such a confrontation by projecting them into sort of infantile fairy-tale worlds where – Malinowski again – "hope cannot fail nor desire deceive."[21] With the possible exception of Christian Science, there are few if any religious traditions, "great" or "little," in which the proposition that life hurts is not strenuously affirmed, and in some it is virtually glorified:

She was an old [Ba-Ila] woman of a family with a long genealogy. Leza, "the Besetting One", stretched out his hand against the family. He slew her mother and father while she was yet a child, and in the course of years all connected with her perished. She said to herself, "Surely I shall keep those who sit on my thighs." But no, even they, the children of her children, were taken from her . . . Then came into her heart a desperate resolution to find God and to ask the meaning of it all . . . So she began to travel, going through country after country, always with the thought in her mind: "I shall come to where the earth ends and there I shall find a road to God and I shall ask him: 'What have I done to thee that thou afflictest me in this manner?'" She never found where the earth ends, but though disappointed she did not give up her search, and as she passed through the different countries they asked her, "What have you come for, old woman?" And the answer would be, "I am seeking Leza." "Seeking Leza! For what?" "My brothers, you ask me! Here in the nations is there one who suffers as I have suffered?" And they would ask again, "How have you suffered?" "In this way. I am alone. As you see me, a solitary old woman; that is how I am!" And they answered, "Yes, we see. That is how you are! Bereaved of friends and husband? In what do you differ from others? The Besetting-One sits on the back of every one of us and we cannot shake him off." She never obtained her desire; she died of a broken heart.[22]

As a religious problem, the problem of suffering is, paradoxically, not how to avoid suffering but how to suffer, how to make of physical pain, personal loss, wordly defeat, or the helpless contemplation of others' agony something bearable, supportable – something, as we say, sufferable. It was in this effort that the Ba-Ila woman – perhaps necessarily, perhaps not – failed and, literally not knowing how to feel about what had happened to her, how to suffer, perished in confusion and despair. Where the more intellective aspects of what Weber called the Problem of Meaning are a matter of affirming the ultimate explicability of experience, the more affective aspects are a matter of affirming its ultimate sufferableness. As religion on one side anchors the power of our symbolic resources for formulating analytic ideas in an authoritative conception of the overall shape of reality, so on another side it anchors the power of our, also symbolic, resources for expressing emotions – moods, sentiments, passions, affections, feelings – in a similar conception of its pervasive tenor, its inherent tone and temper. For those able to embrace them, and for so long as they are able to embrace them, religious symbols provide a cosmic guarantee not only for their ability to comprehend the world, but also, comprehending it, to give a precision to their feeling, a definition to their emotions which enables them, morosely or joyfully, grimly or cavalierly, to endure it.

Consider in this light the well-known Navaho curing rites usually referred to as "sings."[23] A sing – the Navaho have about sixty different ones for different purposes, but virtually all of them are dedicated to removing some sort of physical or mental illness – is a kind of religious psychodrama in which there are three main actors: the "singer" or curer, the patient, and, as a kind of antiphonal chorus, the patient's family and friends. The structure of all the sings, the drama's plot, is quite similar. There are three main acts: a purification of the patient and audience; a statement, by means of repetitive chants and ritual manipulations, of the wish to restore well-being ("harmony") in the patient; an identification of the patient with the Holy People and his consequent "cure." The purification rites involve forced sweating, induced vomiting, and so on, to expel the sickness from the patient physically. The chants, which are numberless, consist mainly of simple optative phrases ("may the patient be well," "I am getting better all over," etc.). And, finally, the identification of the patient with the Holy People, and thus with cosmic order generally, is accomplished through the agency of a sand painting depicting the Holy People in one or another appropriate mythic setting. The singer places the patient on the painting, touching the feet, hands, knees, shoulders, breast, back, and head of the divine figures and then the corresponding parts of the patient, performing thus what is essentially a bodily identification of the human and the divine.[24] This is the climax of the sing: the whole curing process may be likened, Reichard says, to a spiritual osmosis in which the illness in man and the power of the deity penetrate the ceremonial membrane in both directions, the former being neutralized by the latter. Sickness seeps out in the sweat, vomit, and other purification rites;

health seeps in as the Navaho patient touches, through the medium of the singer, the sacred sand painting. Clearly, the symbolism of the sing focuses upon the problem of human suffering and attempts to cope with it by placing it in a meaningful context, providing a mode of action through which it can be expressed, being expressed, understood, and being understood, endured. The sustaining effect of the sing (and since the commonest disease is tuberculosis, it can in most cases be only sustaining) rests ultimately on its ability to give the stricken person a vocabulary in terms of which to grasp the nature of his distress and relate it to the wider world. Like a calvary, a recitation of Buddha's emergence from his father's palace, or a performance of *Oedipus Tyrannos* in other religious traditions, a sing is mainly concerned with the presentation of a specific and concrete image of truly human, and so endurable, suffering powerful enough to resist the challenge of emotional meaninglessness raised by the existence of intense and unremovable brute pain.

The problem of suffering passes easily into the problem of evil, for if suffering is severe enough it usually, though not always, seems morally undeserved as well, at least to the sufferer. But they are not, however, exactly the same thing – a fact I think Weber, too influenced by the biases of a monotheistic tradition in which, as the various aspects of human experience must be conceived to proceed from a single, voluntaristic source, man's pain reflects directly on God's goodness, did not fully recognize in his generalization of the dilemmas of Christian theodicy Eastward. For where the problem of suffering is concerned with threats to our ability to put our "undisciplined squads of emotion" into some sort of soldierly order, the problem of evil is concerned with threats to our ability to make sound moral judgments. What is involved in the problem of evil is not the adequacy of our symbolic resources to govern our affective life, but the adequacy of those resources to provide a workable set of ethical criteria, normative guides to govern our action. The vexation here is the gap between things as they are and as they ought to be if our conceptions of right and wrong make sense, the gap between what we deem various individuals deserve and what we see that they get – a phenomenon summed up in that profound quatrain:

The rain falls on the just
And on the unjust fella;
But mainly upon the just,
Because the unjust has the just's umbrella.

[. . .]

Nor is it necessary to be theologically self-conscious to be religiously sophisticated. The concern with intractable ethical paradox, the disquieting sense that one's moral insight is inadequate to one's moral experience, is as alive on the level of so-called primitive religion as it is on that of the so-called civilized. The set of notions about "division in the world" that Lienhardt describes for the Dinka is a useful case in point.[25] Like so many peoples, the Dinka believe that the sky, where "Divinity" is located, and earth, where man dwells, were at one time contiguous, the sky lying just above the earth and being connected to it by a rope, so that men could move at will between the two realms. There was no death and the first man and woman were permitted but a single grain of millet a day, which was all that they at that time required. One day, the woman – of course – decided, out of greed, to plant more than the permitted grain of millet, and in her avid haste and industry accidentally struck Divinity with the handle of the hoe. Offended, he severed the rope, withdrew into the distant sky of today, and left man to labor for his food, to suffer sickness and death, and to experience separation from the source of his being, his Creator. Yet the meaning of this strangely familiar story to the Dinka is, as indeed is Genesis to Jews and Christians, not homiletic but descriptive:

Those [Dinka] who have commented on these stories have sometimes made it clear that their sympathies lie with Man in his plight, and draw attention to the smallness of the fault for which Divinity withdrew the benefits of his closeness. The image of striking Divinity with a hoe . . . often evokes a certain amusement, almost as though the story were indulgently being treated as too childish to explain the consequences attributed to the event. But it is clear that the point of the story of Divinity's

withdrawal from men is not to suggest an improving moral judgment on human behaviour. It is to represent a total situation known to the Dinka today. Men now are – as the first man and woman then became – active, self-assertive, inquiring, acquisitive. Yet they are also subject to suffering and death, ineffective, ignorant and poor. Life is insecure; human calculations often prove erroneous, and men must often learn by experience that the consequences of their acts are quite other than they may have anticipated or consider equitable. Divinity's withdrawal from Man as the result of a comparatively trifling offence, by human standards, presents the contrast between equitable human judgments and the action of the Power which are held ultimately to control what happens in Dinka life. . . . To the Dinka, the moral order is ultimately constituted according to principles which often elude men, which experience and tradition in part reveal, and which human action cannot change. . . . The myth of Divinity's withdrawal then reflects the facts of existence as they are known. The Dinka are in a universe which is largely beyond their control, and where events may contradict the most reasonable human expectations.[26]

Thus the problem of evil, or perhaps one should say the problem *about* evil, is in essence the same sort of problem of or about bafflement and the problem of or about suffering. The strange opacity of certain empirical events, the dumb senselessness of intense or inexorable pain, and the enigmatic unaccountability of gross iniquity all raise the uncomfortable suspicion that perhaps the world, and hence man's life in the world, has no genuine order at all – no empirical regularity, no emotional form, no moral coherence. And the religious response to this suspicion is in each case the same: the formulation, by means of symbols, of an image of such a genuine order of the world which will account for, and even celebrate, the perceived ambiguities, puzzles, and paradoxes in human experience. The effort is not to deny the undeniable – that there are unexplained events, that life hurts, or that rain falls upon the just – but to deny that there are inexplicable events, that life is unendurable, and that justice is a mirage. The principles which constitute the moral order may indeed often elude men, as Lienhardt puts it, in the same way as fully satisfactory explanations of anomalous events or effective forms for the expression of feeling often elude them. What is important, to a religious man at least, is that this elusiveness be accounted for, that it be not the result of the fact that there are no such principles, explanations, or forms, that life is absurd and the attempt to make moral, intellectual, or emotional sense out of experience is bootless. The Dinka can admit, in fact insist upon, the moral ambiguities and contradictions of life as they live it because these ambiguities and contradictions are seen not as ultimate, but as the "rational," "natural," "logical" (one may choose one's own adjective here, for none of them is truly adequate) outcome of the moral structure of reality which the myth of the withdrawn "Divinity" depicts, or as Lienhardt says, "images."

The Problem of Meaning in each of its intergrading aspects (how these aspects in fact intergrade in each particular case, what sort of interplay there is between the sense of analytic, emotional, and moral impotence, seems to me one of the outstanding, and except for Weber untouched, problems for comparative research in this whole field) is a matter of affirming, or at least recognizing, the inescapability of ignorance, pain, and injustice on the human plane while simultaneously denying that these irrationalities are characteristic of the world as a whole. And it is in terms of religious symbolism, a symbolism relating man's sphere of existence to a wider sphere within which it is conceived to rest, that both the affirmation and the denial are made.[27]

... and clothing those conceptions with such an aura of factuality that ...

There arises here, however, a more profound question: how is it that this denial comes to be believed? How is it that the religious man moves from a troubled perception of experienced disorder to a more or less settled conviction of fundamental order? Just what does "belief" mean in a religious context? Of all the problems surrounding attempts to conduct anthropological analysis of religion this is the one that has perhaps been most troublesome

and therefore the most often avoided.... But the problem will not go away, it is not "merely" psychological (nothing social is), and no anthropological theory of religion which fails to attack it is worthy of the name. We have been trying to stage Hamlet without the Prince quite long enough.

It seems to me that it is best to begin any approach to this issue with frank recognition that religious belief involves not a Baconian induction from everyday experience – for then we should all be agnostics – but rather a prior acceptance of authority which transforms that experience. The existence of bafflement, pain, and moral paradox – of The Problem of Meaning – is one of the things that drives men toward belief in gods, devils, spirits, totemic principles, or the spiritual efficacy of cannibalism (an enfolding sense of beauty or a dazzling perception of power are others), but it is not the basis upon which those beliefs rest, but rather their most important field of application:

> We point to the state of the world as illustrative of doctrine, but never as evidence for it. So Belsen illustrates a world of original sin, but original sin is not an hypothesis to account for happenings like Belsen. We justify a particular religious belief by showing its place in the total religious conception; we justify a religious belief as a whole by referring to authority. We accept authority because we discover it at some point in the world at which we worship, at which we accept the lordship of something not ourselves. We do not worship authority, but we accept authority as defining the worshipful. So someone may discover the possibility of worship in the life of the Reformed Churches and accept the Bible as authoritative; or in the Roman Church and accept papal authority.[28]

This is, of course, a Christian statement of the matter; but it is not to be despised on that account. In tribal religions authority lies in the persuasive power of traditional imagery; in mystical ones in the apodictic force of supersensible experience; in charismatic ones in the hypnotic attraction of an extraordinary personality. But the priority of the acceptance of an authoritative criterion in religious matters over the revelation which is conceived to flow from that acceptance is not less complete than in scriptural or hieratic ones. The basic axiom underlying what we may perhaps call "the religious perspective" is everywhere the same: he who would know must first believe.

But to speak of "the religious perspective" is, by implication, to speak of one perspective among others. A perspective is a mode of seeing, in that extended sense of "see" in which it means "discern," "apprehend," "understand," or "grasp." It is a particular way of looking at life, a particular manner of construing the world, as when we speak of an historical perspective, a scientific perspective, an aesthetic perspective, a common-sense perspective, or even the bizarre perspective embodied in dreams and in hallucinations. The question then comes down to, first, what is "the religious perspective" generically considered, as differentiated from other perspectives; and second, how do men come to adopt it.

If we place the religious perspective against the background of three of the other major perspectives in terms of which men construe the world – the common-sensical, the scientific, and the aesthetic – its special character emerges more sharply. What distinguishes common sense as a mode of "seeing" is, as Schutz has pointed out, a simple acceptance of the world, its objects, and its processes as being just what they seem to be – what is sometimes called naive realism – and the pragmatic motive, the wish to act upon that world so as to bend it to one's practical purposes, to master it, or so far as that proves impossible, to adjust to it.[29] The world of everyday life, itself, of course, a cultural product, for it is framed in terms of the symbolic conceptions of "stubborn fact" handed down from generation to generation, is the established scene and given object of our actions. Like Mt. Everest it is just there, and the thing to do with it, if one feels the need to do anything with it at all, is to climb it. In the scientific perspective it is precisely this givenness which disappears.[30] Deliberate doubt and systematic inquiry, the suspension of the pragmatic motive in favor of disinterested observation, the attempt to analyze the world in terms of formal concepts whose relationship to the informal conceptions of common sense become increasingly problematic – there are the hallmarks of the attempt to grasp the world scientifically. And as for the aesthetic perspective, which under the rubric of "the aesthetic attitude" has been perhaps most exquisitely examined, it involves a different sort of suspension of naive realism and practical interest, in that instead of questioning the credentials of everyday experience, one merely ignores that experience in favor of an eager dwelling upon appearances, an engrossment in surfaces, an absorption in things, as we say, "in themselves": "The function of artistic illusion is not 'make-believe' ... but the very opposite, disengagement from belief – the contemplation of sensory qualities without their usual meanings of 'here's that chair', 'that's my telephone' ... etc. The knowledge that what is before us has no practical significance in the world is what enables us to give attention to its appearance as such."[31] And like the common sensical and the scientific (or the historical, the philosophical, and the artistic), this perspective, this "way of seeing" is not the product of some mysterious Cartesian chemistry, but is induced, mediated, and in fact created by means of curious quasi objects – poems, dramas, sculptures, symphonies – which, dissociating themselves from the solid world of common sense, take on the special sort of eloquence only sheer appearances can achieve.

The religious perspective differs from the common-sensical in that, as already pointed out, it moves beyond the realities of everyday life to wider ones which correct and complete them, and its defining concern is not action upon those wider realities but acceptance of them, faith in them. It differs from the scientific perspective in that it questions the realities of everyday life not out of an institutionalized skepticism which dissolves the world's givenness into a swirl of probabilistic hypotheses, but in terms of what it takes to be wider, nonhypothetical truths. Rather than detachment, its watchword is commitment; rather than analysis, encounter. And it differs from art in that instead of effecting a disengagement from the whole question of factuality, deliberately manufacturing an air of semblance and illusion, it deepens the concern with fact and seeks to create an aura of utter actuality. It is this sense of the "really real" upon which the religious perspective rests and which the symbolic activities of religion as a cultural system are devoted to producing, intensifying, and, so far as possible, rendering inviolable by the discordant revelations of secular experience. It is, again, the imbuing of a certain specific complex of symbols – of the metaphysic they formulate and the style of life they recommend – with a persuasive authority which, from an analytic point of view, is the essence of religious action.

Which brings us, at length, to ritual. For it is in ritual – that is, consecrated behavior – that this conviction that religious conceptions are veridical and that religious directives are sound is somehow generated. It is in some sort of ceremonial form – even if that form be hardly more than the recitation of a myth, the consultation of an oracle, or the decoration of a grave – that the moods and motivations which sacred symbols induce in men and the general conceptions of the order of existence which they formulate for men meet and reinforce one another. In a ritual, the world as lived and the world as imagined, fused under the agency of a single set of symbolic forms, turn out to be the same world, producing thus that idiosyncratic transformation in one's sense of reality to which Santayana refers in my epigraph. Whatever role divine intervention may or may not play in the creation of faith – and it is not the business of the scientist to pronounce upon such matters one way or the other – it is, primarily at least, out of the context of concrete acts of religious observance that religious conviction emerges on the human plane.

However, though any religious ritual, . . . involves this symbolic fusion of ethos and world view, it is mainly certain more elaborate and usually more public ones, ones in which a broad range of moods and motivations on the one hand and of metaphysical conceptions on the other are caught up, which shape the spiritual consciousness of a people. Employing a useful term introduced by Singer, we may call these full-blown ceremonies "cultural performances" and note that they represent

not only the point at which the dispositional and conceptual aspects of religious life converge for the believer, but also the point at which the interaction between them can be most readily examined by the detached observer. . . .[32]

Of course, all cultural performances are not religious performances, and the line between those that are and artistic, or even political, ones is often not so easy to draw in practice, for, like social forms, symbolic forms can serve multiple purposes. But the point is that, paraphrasing slightly, Indians – "and perhaps all peoples" – seem to think of their religion "as encapsulated in these discrete performances which they [can] exhibit to visitors and to themselves."[33] The mode of exhibition is however radically different for the two sorts of witness, a fact seemingly overlooked by those who would argue that "religion is a form of human art."[34] Where for "visitors" religious performances can, in the nature of the case, only be presentations of a particular religious perspective, and thus aesthetically appreciated or scientifically dissected, for participants they are in addition enactments, materializations, realizations of it – not only models of what they believe, but also models *for* the believing of it. In these plastic dramas men attain their faith as they portray it.

As a case in point, let me take a spectacularly theatrical cultural performance from Bali – that in which a terrible witch called Rangda engages in a ritual combat with an endearing monster called Barong.[35] . . . the drama consists of a masked dance in which the witch – depicted as a wasted old widow, prostitute, and eater of infants – comes to spread plague and death upon the land and is opposed by the monster – depicted as a kind of cross between a clumsy bear, a silly puppy, and a strutting Chinese dragon. Rangda, danced by a single male, is a hideous figure. Her eyes bulge from her forehead like swollen boils. Her teeth become tusks curving up over her cheeks and fangs protruding down over her chin. Her yellowed hair falls down around her in a matted tangle. Her breasts are dry and pendulous dugs edged with hair, between which hang, like so many sausages, strings of colored entrails. Her long red tongue is a stream of fire. And as she dances she splays her dead-white hands, from which protrude ten-inch clawlike fingernails, out in front of her and utters unnerving shrieks of metallic laughter. Barong, danced by two men fore-and-aft in vaudeville horse fashion, is another matter. His shaggy sheepdog coat is hung with gold and mica ornaments that glitter in the half-light. He is adorned with flowers, sashes, feathers, mirrors, and a comical beard made from human hair. And though a demon too, his eyes also pop and he snaps his fanged jaws with seemly fierceness when faced with Rangda or other affronts to his dignity; the cluster of tinkling bells which hang from his absurdly arching tail somehow contrives to take most of the edge off his fearfulness. If Rangda is a satanic image, Barong is a farcical one, and their clash is a clash (an inconclusive one) between the malignant and the ludicrous.

This odd counterpoint of implacable malice and low comedy pervades the whole performance. Rangda, clutching her magical white cloth, moves around in a slow stagger, now pausing immobile in thought or uncertainty, now lurching suddenly forward. The moment of her entry (one sees those terrible long-nailed hands first as she emerges through the split gateway at the top of a short flight of stone stairs) is one of terrific tension when it seems, to a "visitor" at least, that everyone is about to break and run in panic. She herself seems insane with fear and hatred as she screams deprecations at Barong amid the wild clanging of the gamelan. She may in fact go amok. I have myself seen Rangdas hurl themselves headlong into the gamelan or run frantically about in total confusion, being subdued and reoriented only by the combined force of a half-dozen spectators; and one hears many tales of amok Rangdas holding a whole village in terror for hours and of impersonators becoming permanently deranged by their experiences. But Barong, though he is charged with the same mana-like sacred power (*sakti* in Balinese) as Rangda, and his impersonators are also entranced, seems to have very great difficulty in being serious. He frolics with his retinue of demons (who add to the gaiety by indelicate pranks of their own), lies down on a metallaphone while it is being played or

beats on a drum with his legs, moves in one direction in his front half and another in his rear or bends his segmented body into foolish contortions, brushes flies from his body or sniffs aromas in the air, and generally prances about in paroxysms of narcissistic vanity. The contrast is not absolute, for Rangda is sometimes momentarily comic as when she pretends to polish the mirrors on Barong's coat, and Barong becomes rather more serious after Rangda appears, nervously clacking his jaws at her and ultimately attacking her directly. Nor are the humorous and the horrible always kept rigidly separated, as in that strange scene in one section of the cycle in which several minor witches (disciples of Rangda) toss the corpse of a stillborn child around to the wild amusement of the audience; or another, no less strange, in which the sight of a pregnant woman alternating hysterically between tears and laughter while being knocked about by a group of gravediggers, seems for some reason excruciatingly funny. The twin themes of horror and hilarity find their purest expression in the two protagonists and their endless, indecisive struggle for dominance, but they are woven with deliberate intricacy through the whole texture of the drama. They – or rather the relations between them – are what it is about.

It is unnecessary to attempt a thoroughgoing description of a Rangda–Barong performance here. Such performances vary widely in detail, consist of several not too closely integrated parts, and in any case are so complex in structure as to defy easy summary. For our purposes, the main point to be stressed is that the drama is, for the Balinese, not merely a spectacle to be watched but a ritual to be enacted. There is no aesthetic distance here separating actors from audience and placing the depicted events in an unenterable world of illusion, and by the time a full-scale Rangda–Barong encounter has been concluded a majority, often nearly all, of the members of the group sponsoring it will have become caught up in it not just imaginatively but bodily. . . . As a performance, the drama is like a high mass, not like a presentation of *Murder in the Cathedral*: it is a drawing near, not a standing back. [. . .]

It is in the direct encounter with the two figures in the context of the actual performance that the villager comes to know them as, so far as he is concerned, genuine realities. They are, then, not representations of anything, but presences. And when the villagers go into trance they become – *nadi* – themselves part of the realm in which those presences exist. To ask, as I once did, a man who has *been* Rangda whether he thinks she is real is to leave oneself open to the suspicion of idiocy.

The acceptance of authority that underlies the religious perspective that the ritual embodies thus flows from the enactment of the ritual itself. By inducing a set of moods and motivations – an ethos – and defining an image of cosmic order – a world view – by means of a single set of symbols, the performance makes the model *for* and model *of* aspects of religious belief mere transpositions of one another. Rangda evokes fear (as well as hatred, disgust, cruelty, horror, and, though I have not been able to treat the sexual aspects of the performance here, lust); but she also depicts it:

> The fascination which the figure of the Witch holds for the Balinese imagination can only be explained when it is recognized that the Witch is not only a fear inspiring figure, but that she is Fear. Her hands with their long menacing finger-nails do not clutch and claw at her victims, although children who play at being witches do curl their hands in such gestures. But the Witch herself spreads her arms with palms out and her finger flexed backward, in the gesture the Balinese call *kapar*, a term which they apply to the sudden startled reaction of a man who falls from a tree. . . . Only when we see the Witch as herself afraid, as well as frightening, is it possible to explain her appeal, and the pathos which surrounds her as she dances, hairy, forbidding, tusked and alone, giving her occasional high eerie laugh.[36]

And on his side Barong not only induces laughter, he incarnates the Balinese version of the comic spirit – a distinctive combination of playfulness, exhibitionism, and extravagant love of elegance, which, along with fear, is perhaps the dominant motive in their life. The constantly recurring struggle of Rangda and

Barong to an inevitable draw is thus – for the believing Balinese – both the formulation of a general religious conception and the authoritative experience which justifies, even compels, its acceptance.

. . . that the moods and motivations seem uniquely realistic

But no one, not even a saint, lives in the world religious symbols formulate all of the time, and the majority of men live in it only at moments. The everyday world of common-sense objects and practical acts is, as Schutz says, the paramount reality in human experience – paramount in the sense that it is the world in which we are most solidly rooted, whose inherent actuality we can hardly question (however much we may question certain portions of it), and from whose pressures and requirements we can least escape.[37] A man, even large groups of men, may be aesthetically insensitive, religiously unconcerned, and unequipped to pursue formal scientific analysis, but he cannot be completely lacking in common sense and survive. The dispositions which religious rituals induce thus have their most important impact – from a human point of view – outside the boundaries of the ritual itself as they reflect back to color the individual's conception of the established world of bare fact. The peculiar tone that marks the Plains vision quest, the Manus confession, or the Javanese mystical exercise pervades areas of the life of these peoples far beyond the immediately religious, impressing upon them a distinctive style in the sense both of a dominant mood and a characteristic movement. The interweaving of the malignant and the comic, which the Rangda–Barong combat depicts, animates a very wide range of everyday Balinese behavior, much of which, like the ritual itself, has an air of candid fear narrowly contained by obsessive playfulness. Religion is sociologically interesting not because, as vulgar positivism would have it, it describes the social order (which, in so far as it does, it does not only very obliquely but very incompletely), but because, like environment, political power, wealth, jural obligation, personal affection, and a sense of beauty, it shapes it.

The movement back and forth between the religious perspective and the common-sense perspective is actually one of the more obvious empirical occurrences on the social scene, though, again, one of the most neglected by social anthropologists, virtually all of whom have seen it happen countless times. Religious belief has usually been presented as a homogeneous characteristic of an individual, like his place of residence, his occupational role, his kinship position, and so on. But religious belief in the midst of ritual, where it engulfs the total person, transporting him, so far as he is concerned, into another mode of existence, and religious belief as the pale, remembered reflection of that experience in the midst of everyday life are not precisely the same thing, and the failure to realize this has led to some confusion, most especially in connection with the so-called primitive-mentality problem. Much of the difficulty between Lévy-Bruhl and Malinowski on the nature of "native thought," for example, arises from a lack of full recognition of this distinction; for where the French philosopher was concerned with the view of reality savages adopted when taking a specifically religious perspective, the Polish-English ethnographer was concerned with that which they adopted when taking a strictly common-sense one.[38] Both perhaps vaguely sensed that they were not talking about exactly the same thing, but where they went astray was in failing to give a specific accounting of the way in which these two forms of "thought" – or, as I would rather say, these two modes of symbolic formulations – interacted, so that where Lévy-Bruhl's savages tended to live, despite his postludial disclaimers, in a world composed entirely of mystical encounters, Malinowski's tended to live, despite his stress on the functional importance of religion, in a world composed entirely of practical actions. They became reductionists (an idealist is as much of a reductionist as a materialist) in spite of themselves because they failed to see man as moving more or less easily, and very frequently, between radically contrasting ways of looking at the world, ways which are not continuous with one another but separated by cultural gaps across which Kierkegaardian leaps must be made in both directions.

[. . .]

Having ritually "lept" (the image is perhaps a bit too athletic for the actual facts – "slipped" might be more accurate) into the framework of meaning which religious conceptions define, and the ritual ended, returned again to the common-sense world, a man is – unless, as sometimes happens, the experience fails to register – changed. And as he is changed, so also is the common-sense world, for it is now seen as but the partial form of a wider reality which corrects and completes it.

But this correction and completion is not, as some students of "comparative religion" would have it, everywhere the same in content. The nature of the bias religion gives to ordinary life varies with the religion involved, with the particular dispositions induced in the believer by the specific conceptions of cosmic order he has come to accept. On the level of the "great" religions, organic distinctiveness is usually recognized, at times insisted upon to the point of zealotry. But even at its simplest folk and tribal levels – where the individuality of religious traditions has so often been dissolved into such desiccated types as "animism," "animatism," "totemism," "shamanism," "ancestor worship," and all the other insipid categories by means of which ethnographers of religion devitalize their data – the idiosyncratic character of how various groups of men behave because of what they believe they have experienced is clear. A tranquil Javanese would be no more at home in guilt-ridden Manus than an activist Crow would be in passionless Java. And for all the witches and ritual clowns in the world, Rangda and Barong are not generalized but thoroughly singular figurations of fear and gaiety. What men believe is as various as what they are – a proposition that holds with equal force when it is inverted.

It is this particularity of the impact of religious systems upon social systems (and upon personality systems) which renders general assessments of the value of religion in either moral or functional terms impossible. The sorts of moods and motivations which characterize a man who has just come from an Aztec human sacrifice are rather different from those of one who has just put off his Kachina mask. Even within the same society, what one "learns" about the essential pattern of life from a sorcery rite and from a commensal meal will have rather diverse effects on social and psychological functioning. One of the main methodological problems in writing about religion scientifically is to put aside at once the tone of the village atheist and that of the village preacher, as well as their more sophisticated equivalents, so that the social and psychological implications of particular religious beliefs can emerge in a clear and neutral light. And when that is done, overall questions about whether religion is "good" or "bad," "functional" or "dysfunctional," "ego strengthening" or "anxiety producing," disappear like the chimeras they are, and one is left with particular evaluations, assessments, and diagnoses in particular cases. . . .

[. . .]

The anthropological study of religion is therefore a two-stage operation: first, an analysis of the system of meanings embodied in the symbols which make up the religion proper, and, second, the relating of these systems to social-structural and psychological processes. My dissatisfaction with so much of contemporary social anthropological work in religion is not that it concerns itself with the second stage, but that it neglects the first, and in so doing takes for granted what most needs to be elucidated. To discuss the role of ancestor worship in regulating political succession, of sacrificial feasts in defining kinship obligations, of spirit worship in scheduling agricultural practices, of divination in reinforcing social control, or of initiation rites in propelling personality maturation, are in no sense unimportant endeavors, and I am not recommending they be abandoned for the kind of jejune cabalism into which symbolic analysis of exotic faiths can so easily fall. But to attempt them with but the most general, common-sense view of what ancestor worship, animal sacrifice, spirit worship, divination, or initiation rites are as religious patterns seems to me not particularly promising. Only when we have a theoretical analysis of symbolic action comparable in sophistication to what we now have for social and psychological action, will we be able to cope effectively with those aspects of social and psychological life in which religion (or art, or science, or ideology) plays a determinant role.

NOTES

1 S. Langer, *Philosophy in a New Key*, 4th ed. (Cambridge, Mass., 1960).

2 K. Burke, *The Philosophy of Literary Form* (Baton Rouge, La.: Louisiana State University Press, 1941), p. 9.

3 The reverse mistake, especially common among neo-Kantians such as Cassirer, of taking symbols to be identical with, or "constitutive of," their referents is equally pernicious. [Cf. E. Cassirer, *The Philosophy of Symbolic Forms* (New Haven: 1953–7), 3 vols.] "One can point to the moon with one's finger," some, probably well-invented, Zen Master is supposed to have said, "but to take one's finger for the moon is to be a fool."

4 K. Craik, *The Nature of Explanation* (Cambridge, 1952).

5 K. Lorenz, *King Solomon's Ring* (London, 1952).

6 K. von Frisch, "Dialects in the Language of the Bees," *Scientific American*, August 1962.

7 Craik, *Nature of Explanation*.

8 R. H. Lowie, *Primitive Religion* (New York, 1924).

9 R. F. Fortune, *Manus Religion* (Philadelphia, 1935).

10 C. Geertz, *The Religion of Java* (Glencoe, Ill., 1960).

11 G. Ryle, *The Concept of Mind* (London and New York, 1949).

12 Ibid., p. 99.

13 C. Kluckhohn, "The Philosophy of the Navaho Indians," in *Ideological Differences and World Order*, ed. F. S. C. Northrop (New Haven, 1949), pp. 356–84.

14 J. Goody, "Religion and Ritual: The Definition Problem," *British Journal of Psychology* (1961): 143–64.

15 W. James, *The Principles of Psychology*, 2 vols. (New York, 1904).

16 E. Evans-Pritchard, *Witchcraft, Oracles and Magic Among the Azande* (Oxford, 1937).

17 A. R. Radcliffe-Brown, *Structure and Function in Primitive Society* (Glencoe, Ill., 1952).

18 G. Bateson, *Naven*, 2nd ed. (Stanford, 1958).

19 G. Lienhardt, *Divinity and Experience* (Oxford, 1961), p. 151ff; B. Malinowski, *Magic, Science and Religion* (Boston, 1948), p. 67.

20 S. F Nadel, "Malinowski on Magic and Religion," in *Man and Culture*, ed. R. Firth (London, 1957), pp. 189–208.

21 Malinowski, *Magic, Science and Religion*, p. 67.

22 C. W. Smith and A. M. Dale, *The Ila-Speaking Peoples of Northern Rhodesia* (London, 1920), p. 197ff.; quoted in P. Radin, *Primitive Man as a Philosopher* (New York, 1957), pp. 100–1.

23 C. Kluckhohn and D. Leighton. *The Navaho* (Cambridge, Mass., 1946); G. Reichard, *Navaho Religion*, 2 vols. (New York, 1950).

24 Reichard, *Navaho Religion*.

25 Lienhardt, *Divinity and Experience*, pp. 28–55.

26 Ibid.

27 This is *not*, however, to say that everyone in every society does this; for as the immortal Don Marquis once remarked, you don't have to have a soul unless you really want one. The oft-heard generalization that religion is a human universal embodies a confusion between the probably true (though on present evidence unprovable) proposition that there is no human society in which cultural patterns that we can, under the present definition or one like it, call religious are totally lacking, and the surely untrue proposition that all men in all societies are, in any meaningful sense of the term, religious. But if the anthropological study of religious commitment is underdeveloped, the anthropological study of religious noncommitment is nonexistent. The anthropology of religion will have come of age when some more subtle Malinowski writes a book called "Belief and Unbelief (or even 'Faith and Hypocrisy') in a Savage Society."

28 A. MacIntyre, "The Logical Status of Religious Belief," in *Metaphysical Beliefs*, ed. A. MacIntyre (London, 1957), pp. 167–211.

29 A. Schutz, *The Problem of Social Reality*, vol. 1 of *Collected Papers* (The Hague, 1962).

30 Ibid.

31 S. Langer, *Feeling and Form* (New York, 1953), p. 49.

32 M. Singer, "The Cultural Pattern of Indian Civilization," *Far Eastern Quarterly* 15 (1955): 23–6.

33 M. Singer, "The Great Tradition in a Metropolitan Center: Madras," in *Traditional India*, ed. M. Singer (Philadelphia, 1958), pp. 140–82.

34 R. Firth, *Elements of Social Organization* (London and New York, 1951), p. 250.

35 The Rangda–Barong complex has been extensively described and analyzed by a series of unusually gifted ethnographers and I shall make no attempt to present it here in more than schematic form. [See, for example, J. Belo, *Bali: Rangda and Barong* (New York, 1949); J. Belo, *Trance in Bali* (New York, 1960); B. DeZoete and W. Spies, *Dance and Drama in Bali* (London, 1938); G. Bateson and M. Mead, *Balinese Character* (New York, 1942); M. Covarrubias, *The Island of Bali* (New York, 1937).] Much of my interpretation of the complex rests on personal observations made in Bali during 1957–8.

36 G. Bateson and M. Mead, *Balinese Character*, p. 36.

37 Schutz, *The Problem of Social Reality*, p. 226ff.

38 Malinowski, *Magic, Science and Religion*; L. Lévy-Bruhl, *How Natives Think* (New York, 1926).

Skeptical Rejoinders

Introduction

"Religion" is not a given in the world, not the referent for a discrete species, but the product of a particular kind of discursive stance that distinguishes some things (e.g., "religion") from others (e.g., "economy"), and unites some things with others within the category of "religion." A book like this cannot help doing the same, but the essays here do try to problematize the categories whereof they speak. Although many anthropologists in the first half of the 20th century gave a good deal of attention to definitional problems concerning religion, ritual, myth, primitive society, and so on, a working skepticism at the resulting objectifications has also always been a part of the anthropological tradition. Contemporary skepticism is not the product of some radical "postmodern" break so much as ongoing investment in an intellectual practice intrinsic to the anthropological craft. What is perhaps new is the specifically Nietzschean strain that sees intellectual discourses as inevitably derivative of, and hence contributory to, larger schemes of power.

In any case, this section includes five strong skeptical responses to the various frameworks established or evoked in the previous one. They are, in turn, the product of diverse standpoints. It is worth drawing attention to three additional powerful works of skeptical "deconstruction" written within the anthropological mainstream. The first is that of Franz Steiner who, in a posthumous publication of a course of lectures, entitled *Taboo* (1956; Adler and Fardon, eds., 1999), systematically demolishes the model of "primitive religion" that was built up around the term, querying not only the objectification of "taboo" as a kind of religion but its status as a general concept, thereby throwing the entire comparative method into question. Steiner showed how authors like Robertson, Smith, and Frazer used the category of taboo to claim that so-called primitive religions lacked adequate concepts of morality. For more positive accounts of taboos, see van Gennep (1904), Douglas (1966), Gell (1979) and Lambek (1992).

The implications of Steiner's critique have been expanded by philosopher Alasdair MacIntyre as part of his program to show the inadequacy of an objectivist (or what he calls encyclopaedist) approach to moral inquiry (1990). For MacIntyre, the approach of Frazer et al. was symptomatic of the incoherence of liberal modernist culture with respect to its own (and therefore our) moral concerns. The breakdown of traditional social orders like those of precolonial Hawaii or the European Christian Middle Ages simultaneously produces false abstractions like "taboo" or "obligation" and confuses the means by which to actually learn to live a moral life. Steiner, MacIntyre, and Douglas speak from what is ultimately a conservative perspective that values hierarchy, for the holism it provides. The holism comprises social cohesion embedded in political hierarchy that is in turn encompassed by religion. MacIntyre's implicit nostalgia for the age of Aquinas can be contrasted to Marx's forthright critique of feudalism (1961 [1887]), or the depiction of medieval Christianity provided by Asad (1993).

Lévi-Strauss accomplished the same feat for and in *Totemism* (1963e [1962]) that Steiner did for and in *Taboo*. His argument there is that what is relevant about so-called totemic practices (such as animals serving as symbols for social groups) is less the intrinsic qualities of individual species of animals than the system of analogies they establish. A given Native American group is less interested in the intrinsic properties of "bears" or "deer" than the contrast that can be set up by means of them. Totemism is thus to be understood as a system of classification or naming rather than as a religious phase or institution.

Finally, Evans-Pritchard pursued the question of rationality through both a sustained critical demolition of the theories of the evolutionists and a positive exposition of the logic of ostensibly irrational beliefs in an African society. The critiques first appeared in a pair of powerful essays published in Egypt in 1933 and 1934 and were later incorporated in revised form in *Theories of Primitive Religion* (1965). They formed the prolegomena to his masterly *Witchcraft, Oracles, and Magic among the Azande* (1937; 1976 for a condensed version), which set a new standard for thinking ethnographically about rationality that few other works have met. Evans-Pritchard showed, among other things, why it was reasonable for Azande to continue to believe in witchcraft as an explanation for misfortune and, indeed, how difficult it is to escape from its terms; how witchcraft does not preclude, but rather complements, a materialist explanation for events; and how the practices associated with witchcraft provide a guide for orderly action. His account of the workings of a relatively "closed" system of thought was not unlike philosopher Thomas Kuhn's model of successive paradigms in the history of western science (1970), and influenced philosophers (Polanyi 1970; cf. Gluckman 1970). What Evans-Pritchard perhaps failed to fully acknowledge was how the witchcraft system operated in the interests of the local system of power (McLeod 1972).

For reasons of copyright, the excerpt by Wittgenstein that was found in the first edition of this Reader has had to be cut back. Readers are encouraged to turn to the original for the full text.

5

Remarks on Frazer's *Golden Bough*

Ludwig Wittgenstein

An Austrian who spent much of his professional life in England, Ludwig Wittgenstein (1889–1951) was among the most profound philosophers of the 20th century. His brilliance is evident in these incisive remarks on Frazer. In fact, they skewer not only Frazer but the entire intellectualist tradition that sees ritual and religious practices as primarily a form of explanation, and a simple-minded and mistaken one. But Wittgenstein's remarks also effectively counter any reductionist account. "Man," he says simply, "is a ceremonious animal." Wittgenstein anticipates many developments in anthropology, which generally proceeded without benefit of these remarks. These insights are evident in works such as those of Lienhardt (chapter 24), Fernandez, or Tambiah (chapter 25), who see ritual shaping experience; in those like Langer (chapter 10) and Ortner (chapter 12), who take seriously the symbolic dimension of culture and religion; and in those who explore the nature and effects of language as something at once simpler and more complex than a direct representation of reality (as variously, Becker, Bloch, and Rappaport, chapters 18, 32 and 33 below). But perhaps Wittgenstein would go further in sweeping away all preconceptions and refusing to generalize.

These aphorisms speak for themselves and resist explication. As Wittgenstein famously said, "Whereof we cannot speak, thereof we must be silent." Nevertheless, readers may find the extended commentary in "Remarks on Wittgenstein and Ritual" (in Needham 1985) useful. Rodney Needham has been the earliest and strongest champion of Wittgenstein in anthropology (1972, 1975) as well as authoring a number of other intriguing essays on religion, notably "Characteristics of Religion" (in Needham 1981). Wittgenstein is also invoked in an intriguing analysis of mortuary ritual (Metcalf 1987), while a recent overview of anthropology whose Wittgensteinian influence is evident in its title is *The Ceremonial Animal* (James 2004).

From Ludwig Wittgenstein, *Remarks on Frazer's Golden Bough*, trans. A. C. Miles, rev. and ed. Rush Rhees (Nottingham: Brynmill Press Ltd., 1979 [c.1931]), pp. 1e–7e. Footnotes deleted.

Frazer's account of the magical and religious notions of men is unsatisfactory: it makes these notions appear as *mistakes*.

Was Augustine mistaken, then, when he called on God on every page of the *Confessions?*

Well – one might say – if he was not mistaken, then the Buddhist holy-man, or some other, whose religion expresses quite different notions, surely was. But *none* of them was making a mistake except where he was putting forward a theory.

Even the idea of trying to explain the practice – say the killing of the priest-king – seems to me wrong-headed. All that Frazer does is to make this practice plausible to people who think as he does. It is very queer that all these practices are finally presented, so to speak, as stupid actions.

But it never does become plausible that people do all this out of sheer stupidity.

When he explains to us, for example, that the king must be killed in his prime because, according to the notions of the savages, his soul would not be kept fresh otherwise, we can only say: where that practice and these views go together, the practice does not spring from the view, but both of them are there.

It may happen, as it often does today, that someone will give up a practice when he has seen that something on which it depended is an error. But this happens only in cases where you can make a man change his way of doing things simply by calling his attention to his error. This is not how it is in connexion with the religious practices of a people; and what we have here is *not* an error.

Frazer says it is very difficult to discover the error in magic and this is why it persists for so long – because, for example, a ceremony which is supposed to bring rain is sure to appear effective sooner or later.

But then it is queer that people do not notice sooner that it does rain sooner or later anyway.

I think one reason why the attempt to find an explanation is wrong is that we have only to put together in the right way what we *know*, without adding anything, and the satisfaction we are trying to get from the explanation comes of itself.

And here the explanation is not what satisfies us anyway. When Frazer begins by telling the story of the King of the Wood at Nemi, he does this in a tone which shows that something strange and terrible is happening here. And that is the answer to the question "why is this happening?": Because it is terrible. In other words, what strikes us in this course of events as terrible, impressive, horrible, tragic, &c., anything but trivial and insignificant, *that* is what gave birth to them.

We can only *describe* and say, human life is like that.

Compared with the impression that what is described here makes on us, the explanation is too uncertain.

Every explanation is an hypothesis.

But for someone broken up by love an explanatory hypothesis won't help much. – It will not bring peace.

The crush of thoughts that do not get out because they all try to push forward and are wedged in the door.

Put that account of the King of the Wood at Nemi together with the phrase "the majesty of death", and you see that they are one.

The life of the priest-king shows what is meant by that phrase.

If someone is gripped by the majesty of death, then through such a life he can give expression to it. – Of course this is not an explanation: it puts one symbol in place of another. Or one ceremony in place of another.

A religious symbol does not rest on any *opinion*.

And error belongs only with opinion.

One would like to say: This is what took place here; laugh, if you can.

The religious actions or the religious life of the priest-king are not different in kind from any genuinely religious action today, say a confession of sins. This also can be "explained" (made clear) and cannot be explained.

Burning in effigy. Kissing the picture of a loved one. This is obviously *not* based on a belief that it will have a definite effect on the object which the picture represents. It aims at some satisfaction and it achieves it. Or rather, it does not *aim* at anything; we act in this way and then feel satisfied.

[. . .]

We could almost say, man is a ceremonious animal. This is partly false, partly nonsensical, but there is also something in it.

In other words, one might begin a book on anthropology in this way: When we watch the life and behaviour of men all over the earth we see that apart from what we might call animal activities, taking food &c., &c., men also carry out actions that bear a peculiar character and might be called ritualistic.

But then it is nonsense if we go on to say that the characteristic feature of *these* actions is that they spring from wrong ideas about the physics of things. [. . .]

6

Religion, Totemism and Symbolism

W. E. H. Stanner

W. E. H. Stanner (1905–81) taught at the Australian National University and was a leading figure in the study of Aboriginal religion and the initiation of land rights. What Wittgenstein does to the intellectuals, Stanner does to Durkheim. But Stanner's standpoint is very different. He writes as someone with extensive ethnographic experience among the people of whom he speaks.

Australian Aboriginal culture has played a particularly significant role in the development of anthropological thought. Having suffered tremendous violence and massive appropriation at the hands of white Australian settlers, and deploying a fairly simple material technology, the Aborigines were thought in the 19th century to be among the simplest societies on the planet. It was for this reason that Durkheim looked to Australia for the fundamental aspects of religion. However, anthropologists who subsequently worked with still viable communities have been universally impressed by the depth and complexity of Aboriginal thought as well as by the manner in which their philosophy was able to encompass their social structure and way of life, providing a uniquely holistic and comprehensive world.

Stanner provides a wonderful rejoinder to the ethnocentric work that preceded him. He offers a lucid criticism of Frazer and the evolutionists and an equally strong critique of the model of elementary religion as totemism, which Durkheim had constructed from written material on Australia. Here Stanner's critique is not on empirical grounds alone. He faults Durkheim and others for ignoring the grounds of Aboriginal ontology and hence for seeing religion as derivative of the social. There are numerous other critiques of an overly sociological approach to religion and, as noted, Lévi-Strauss's short book, *Totemism*, is perhaps the most comprehensive

From W. E. H. Stanner, "Religion, Totemism and Symbolism," in *White Man Got No Dreaming, Essays 1938–73* (Canberra: Australian National University Press, 1979 [1962]), pp. 111–25. © W. E. H. Stanner, 1979. Abridged.

deconstruction of that false subject – "a mentity, not an entity," as Stanner pithily puts it (1979 [1962]: 126). But Stanner's critique is simultaneously a superb introduction to the positive features of Aboriginal religion – indeed, he provides a forceful and one might even say "religiously musical" account of it. His observation concerning "the absence from [Aboriginal] religious thought and practice of any life-compensatory themes" might be compared to Sahlins's analysis of western cosmology (1996).

Stanner's essay provides an example of one of the many critiques launched by the generations of solid fieldworkers against the reified abstractions like animism and totemism that were central to the preceding generations of "armchair" thinkers who speculated about the religious lives of peoples whom they had never encountered. The importance of sympathetic, firsthand understanding is clear from Stanner's account. Indeed, although he stays at the general and continental level, Stanner's appreciation is a *tour de force* of anthropological interpretation. Readers may appreciate that this essay of 1962 presages several subsequent developments in anthropological thought, including even an allusion to initiation as a form of discipline. Readers interested in Stanner should turn to the original text and supplement it with Stanner (1963). Another powerful and influential essay on ontology written about the same time as Stanner and equally from the sympathetic perspective of a master ethnographer is that by Hallowell (1960) on the Ojibwa of Canada.

[. . .]

Modern anthropologists criticize their nineteenth-century predecessors for many faults, and the force of the criticisms is reflected in many abandoned positions. No one now supposes that natural science is free of metaphysic, or assumes that if the method of natural science is followed then human facts under study have to be treated as if they too are non-human. Not many now hold to the idea that historical explanation is, intrinsically, the only right explanation of co-existent human facts. The grandiose sweep of theory, the "ineffable parochialism" (Lowie) of definitions and assumptions, and the pejorative use of rationalistic concepts, are much less common. But a cardinal fault – the invincible ignorance about Aboriginal religion – has not been criticized sufficiently. I have already mentioned the superficial causes – unimaginative observation, preconception and bigotry. But there were also a lack of detachment toward the intellectual foundations of the new discipline; a certain sycophancy toward fashionable vogues in science (especially biology) and philosophy;

and an unwillingness to risk being thought guilty of writing devotional exercises. A desire to free study from emotion became a fear of emotion, and a drying out of true sensibility. The lack of sensibility certainly strikes forcibly a modern reader of their works. Even Sir James Frazer, in unconscious paraphrase of Ridley half a century earlier – and, of course, of Goethe long before – came very near to saying so in addressing the Ernest Renan Society: ". . . without tenderness, without poetry, one cannot understand man or his creations." (Needless to say, he was not thinking of the Aborigines: as late as 1937 he still referred to them as "these savages".)
[. . .]

The scholars who wrote as if religion *did* not exist, and the men of religion who worked as if it *could* not exist, among so barbarous a people, were not in even distant collusion with authorities who had no motive of credibility to think or act beyond a vague and ill-policed policy of protection. But the nineteenth-century pages echo with a tacit compact to underwrite a negativism to which ugliness and ignobility were added in every decade down to the 1930s.

Under the Australian law of charity, sympathy for racial injustice had come to vary inversely with nearness to the evil.

There must have been a score of causes contributing to Aboriginal misery. But from the early nineteenth century, none had a more devastating effect than the pervasive doctrine of Aboriginal worthlessness. That depended to a decisive extent on the specific blindness to which I have referred. Yet, as R. M. Berndt has rightly said: traditional Aboriginal religion was "a living faith, something quite inseparable from the pattern of everyday life and thought". The connection was so intimate that "there is no sharp demarcation between secular and sacred life". In the words of Father E. A. Worms, Aboriginal religion "penetrates all facets of life and has little to fear from distinctions which are both abstract and disunitive and which we, with our philosophical education, often make".

I shall sketch as briefly as possible the positive character of the religion as we now understand it. (1) The Aborigines thought the world full of signs to men; they transformed the signs into assurances of mystical providence; and they conceived life's design as fixed by a founding drama. (2) At its best the religion put a high worth on the human person, both as flesh and as spirit. (3) It magnified the value of life by making its conservation and renewal into a cult. (4) It acknowledged the material domain as being under spiritual authority. (5) Religious practice included a discipline to subdue egotistical man to a sacred, continuing purpose. (6) Religious belief expressed a philosophy of assent to life's terms. (7) The major cults inculcated a sense of mystery through the use of symbolisms pointing to ultimate or metaphysical realities which were known by their signs. Each proposition rests on well-established facts, which have often been recorded and left, uninterpreted, as mere "custom". To deny them what seem their plain implications is now unjustifiable. I shall discuss each of the main statements in turn. It will then be clear, I hope, that what prevented their earlier recognition were the unexamined assumptions of scholars who were either not interested in religion as such, or had too

narrow a conception of it, or misunderstood their task.

1.   The Aborigines' positive knowledge has been well appreciated, especially that involved in their techniques of subsistence and in their manipulation of the segmentary forms of social organization. In those fields of life they were masterfully confident. What may be called their religious confidence has been left rather understated. They lived as though sure of their power, through ritual observances, to sustain their being in a world which, though grounded on mystery, had no real problem of futurity. The nomadic life of hunting and foraging must have had its fair share, perhaps more, of vicissitudes. But their religion had a notably strong theurgic component which expressed itself everywhere in the continent, at least in all the regions about which we have good knowledge, in the conception of a great founding drama. That drama was marked by a climax in which everything – including man, and his whole condition of life – came to be as it is. Form, style, and function became determinate. Consequently, the types of tension between past, present, and future that characterize so many systems of religion were entirely absent from theirs. The given condition of life was one in which the typical preoccupations of many other religious faiths could have had no function. A full understanding of the Aboriginal view of life and the world requires a careful study of the whole body of doctrine about The Dream Time (*altjira, bugari*), which is the common but not universal way of referring to the time of the founding drama. It has not yet been appraised at all adequately. But it represents an immense store of meanings, variably drawn on by different cult-groups, yet evidently never fully explored or used by any of them because subtle (and probably important) variations occurred in different regions. The religious tone was certainly affected. In Cape York Ursula McConnel found that many myths dealing with the founding drama had a quality of "self-dedication"; in the Northern Territory the quality seemed to me rather that of "sad finality". Those were not wholly subjective impressions. One would expect that, within a continent of so many contrasting environments, many qualitative differences

would occur. Had there been a higher rate of social change in Aboriginal life than was evidently the case, many elements which were subliminal would probably have developed. A foundation existed for a systematic belief in gods and for institutions of priesthood, prayer, and sacrifice. Once observers were able to cease identifying religion with theism, a perception of those foundations drew them on to many false attributions. That error in turn has to be rectified. The central problem of study is to stay within the actual evidence but at the same time to draw from it the legitimate religious implications. Widely, two complementary emphases stood out in the doctrine of The Dream Time: the fixation or instituting of things in an enduring form, and the simultaneous endowment of all things – including man, and his condition of life – with their good and/or bad properties. The central meaning was clear. Men were to live always under that foundation.

When the myths about the drama of The Dream Time are studied with care it becomes clear that the Aborigines had taken, indeed had gone far beyond, the longest and most difficult step toward the formation of a truly religious outlook. They had found in the world about them what they took to be signs of intent toward men, and they had transformed those signs into *assurances* of life under mystical nurture. Their symbolic observances toward the signs, in rites of several kinds, were in essence acts of faith toward the ground of that assurance.

It is not yet possible to bring together under that principle all the ritualized cults of which we have heard, but those that fit within the trilogy suggested many years ago by A. P. Elkin – historical rites, initiation rites, and "increase" rites (*talu, inticbiuma*) intended to maintain and renew the life of natural species – appeared in some sense to recapitulate some feature or aspect of the founding drama. One could doubtless speak of "imitation" and thus cast all ritual into a mould of "magic," but that really will not do. The aetiology is obviously too profound. If the word "religion" means, as its etymology probably suggests, two dispositions in man – to ponder on the foundations of human life in history, and to

unite or reconcile oneself with the design incorporated in those foundations – then the Aborigines were a very religious-minded people. The motive of their strong sense of religious duty and the purpose of their rites become more understandable if approached from that viewpoint. So do the intellectual, emotional, psychological, and social components of their religious thought and life. *If* life has a mystical foundation, and *if* its design was fixed once-for-all, what else should rational men do but maintain and renew that design? Most anthropologists familiar with the Aborigines would testify to their apparent inability to grasp that life can have any other rationale as satisfying and conclusive as that on which their religion is founded.

If one can judge from contemporary and recent Aboriginal life, what must have fascinated them – it still does – was the apparent evidence of *design* in the world; design in the sense of pattern, shape, form, structure; *given* design that seemed to them to point to *intent*. It would be tedious to list the facts of that kind of which they take sharp note, but the proofs that they always did so are contained in their language categories. It is to those facts, not to the imaginary phenomena with which Herbert Spencer, Tylor, and Frazer made so much play, that a theorist of the origins of Aboriginal religion should turn. Pattern, shape, form, and structure, occurring in what we call "nature", constituted for them a world of signs to men. Part of their religion seems to be like a return of equivalent or compensatory signs to the mysterious domain whence they came. There cannot have been many primitive rites which so strongly suggested a conscious attempt by men to bind themselves to the design in things they saw about them, and to the enduring plan of life as they experienced it.

2. The worth attached to the person was shown in a striking manner by the high ritualization of the life-cycle of males. Always a particular person, or a very small group of equivalent persons, was thus honoured; and the community, not a clique or set, paid the honour. Each individual, at his due times, was brought to the first place in public life. For days or weeks he was made the focus of elaborate efforts of the imaginative and material

arts. The effect was to dignify and in some sense sanctify each person so honoured. One is impelled to conclude that the rites had a plain meaning: *man is of value in himself and for others.* The relative value of initiates at such times was the highest that society could contrive for them. The meaning "man has value" was also implied by the respect for totems, totem-places, and insignia and emblems standing for persons; by the restraints against the use of names, or other extensions of personality such as shadows and tracks, in a dangerous or disrespectful way; by the unde-monstrative care of the sick, blind, halt, and mentally afflicted; and by the dutiful obsequies to the body, the spirit/soul/ghost/shade, and the social memory of the dead. Such acts, atti-tudes, and beliefs are deeply inconsonant with a low valuation of human life and personality. One could not rightly say that in themselves they amounted to a religious view of man. But there was a further fact that, added to them, warrants such a conclusion. In several parts of Aboriginal Australia one met the fundamental belief that great guardian-spirits (Baiame, Kunmanggur) existed – whether as ancestral or as self-subsistent beings – to "look after" living men. Elsewhere, lesser spirits did so. The conception thus deepens: man is of value in himself and for others, and *there are spirits who care.* That, by any test, is a religious view of man. But the generalization must be given its true measure in the light of certain negative facts. The religious valuation was qualified by a secular valuation both within, and especially between, clans and tribes. The worth of infants and the very old was notoriously held of small account: in desperate circumstances, both were left to die. On occasions, individuals acted toward others with intense cruelty, disregard, and selfishness within small kin-groups and, outside – except in respect of close cognates and affines – without restraint other than that induced by fear of consequences. Almost uni-versally, the valuation of women was low in respect of their personal as distinct from their functional worth. They were usually held in low regard ritually, too, but not always in all circumstances. Their blood-making and child-giving powers were thought both mysterious and dangerous, but there was nothing elevated

in their sex or marriage. It may be suggested that those negative facts were the products of pragmatic, egotistic, and politic conditions, the concomitants of any religious system in practice. Aboriginal religion was not alone in being infiltrated and, in some respects, made part-prisoner by expediency, power, and vested interest. But all that only qualified Aboriginal man's dignity. It flawed, but did not destroy, the estate into which he came in The Dream Time.

3. What I have called the "magnification of life" was shown by the intense, one could almost say obsessive, preoccupation with the signs, symbols, means, portents, tokens, and evidences of vitality. The whole religious corpus vibrated with an expressed aspiration for life, abundant life. Vitality, fertility and growth; the conservation, production, protection, and rescue of life: themes such as these seem to have been widely implicit and, in some notable regional cases, quite explicit. Vitalistic things obtruded throughout the myths and rites – water, blood, fat, hair, excrements; the sex organs, semen, sexuality in all its phases, the quickening in the womb; child-spirits, mystical impregnation and reincarnation; the develop-ment of the body from birth to death; the tran-sitions of the human spirit from before organic assumption until after physical dissolution; apparently animated phenomena such as green leaves, rain and the seasons, lightning, whirl-winds, shooting stars and the heavenly bodies; or things of unexplained origin, unusual appearance and giant size. Poor descriptions of rites, and bad or over-literal translations of myths, have often left such stresses latent or obscure. But the careful studies by Warner, Elkin, and R. M. and C. H. Berndt in Arnhem Land, by E. A. Worms more widely, and the skilful linguistic work by A. Capell and T. G. H. Strehlow, to choose a few examples only, make clear what must have been commonly the case. The known evidence suggests that Aborig-inal religion was probably one of the least material-minded, and most life-minded, of any of which we have knowledge. It may not have "magnified goodness", as Bacon said of Chris-tianity, but it did magnify life.

4. The overrule of the material dimension by spiritual authority was not complete. By

"spiritual authority" I mean the rule of all invisible potencies, however imagined, that were believed to have effects on men's lives, effects not possible by unaided means in the hands of ordinary men. We have evidence that the *whole* of materiality was not thought to be influenced in that way, so that runaway doctrines of animatism and animism are unjustified. No *one* spirit or potency had authority over *all* the materiality that was so influenced. Not all spirits were thought of as man-like; some were supposed to have quasi-animal forms, or even to be indescribable. Of those that were man-like only some were thought ancestral; others were considered to be "self-finding" (self-existent, self-subsistent). But there were many things in the environment that were just things, themselves only and no more, without import, standing for nothing. And the authority of spirits and other potencies, as understood by the Aborigines, was only vaguely a moral-ethical authority. Those reservations having been stated, one really need point only to *two* well-known classes of fact to justify the main proposition, though of course many more could be cited. The first is the class of beliefs concerning the impregnation of women by pre-existing child-spirits that *act under their own volition*. The second is the class of beliefs concerning the dependence of men on a *potential* of life (for example, of humans, animals, and plants) *pre-existing* in totem-places. Men could – should – help the child-spirits to do their work, and could – indeed, must – ritually facilitate the release of the potential. But they did not create that store and without it were helpless. The *manifestation* of life on a visible, material plane was thus a spiritual function. So was the power of humans to *subsist* on that plane. Those postulates were fundamental to Aboriginal social existence as a form of being-as-it-is. (The question whether we are dealing with "magic" or "religion" does not arise in the case of the first set of beliefs and, in the second, concerns only the mode of releasing the potential.)

5. The myths contain much of the "human-all-too-human" character of man. A certain image of *original* man emerges as though with two faces, one well drawn, the other less so. The first face has on it the marks of egotism,

always wayward and self-willed, sometimes wanton: greed, envy, bad faith, anger, selfishness, pride, disobedience, and the like are common themes in the myths. To complete the features of the other (let us think of it for the time being as *one* face, though we will probably find many when the matter is studied with care) one has to do two things: elicit the conventions of understanding within which the myths were told and heard, and interpret the climax of each myth. Both are dangerous procedures since it is easy to slip beyond the evidence. Many myths, one cannot say all, had a homiletic effect; perhaps the Aborigines drew a moral lesson from them; but to all appearances a strong, explicit religious ethic was absent, probably for the same reasons that a religious creed was absent. Three vital preconditions were missing – a tradition of intellectual detachment; a class of interpreters who had the prerogative or duty to codify principle; and a challenge that would have forced morals and beliefs to find anatomies.

All this made the moral aspect of the religion rather amorphous, although what was there was consistent. But a study of the ritual practices now suggests a possible need to modify that rather unfavourable judgement. Until recently, to know how to investigate the problem more adequately seemed peculiarly difficult. But it now appears possible to compare fruitfully two things that did not seem comparable – the structural anatomies of myths and rites. Many myths reveal a mounting of incidents to a crisis or culmination that exhibits a cluster of meanings with a distinct moral quality. The initiatory rites all rose to a tense crisis that brought about, or was supposed to bring about, a physical-moral-spiritual change in the initiates. The two types of crisis appear to have been symbolic paramorphs. In myth, an imagined crisis was dealt with by a spoken imagery. In rite, an actual crisis was dealt with by a gestural-visual imagery. In such cases the myths, although a sort of allegorical poesy, may have served as the implicit moral "theory" of the rites. How far that approach will stand up to test, and how far the morphological likenesses can be traced through the symbolic systems, remain to be seen. It is too soon to say certainly that the funerary rites contained the same symbolic pattern, or one comparable, or whether all variants of the trilogy studied so formatively by Elkin did so. But even a partial success in demonstrating that that was the case will reinforce what we already know. All the evidence collected since Collins's time [1798] establishes that the rites of initiation existed as *disciplines*. They both *fashioned* uncompleted man, and *transformed* him into a being of higher worth.

The moral and mystical content of the rites varied regionally. It may have varied too over time as one cult replaced or mixed with another. But the canon of the rites was invariable: to subdue refractory, unfinished personalities to a purpose held to be sacred and timeless. They put on the body, mentality, and social personality of initiates ineffaceable signs designating stages in the socialization of man. It is a plausible hypothesis that the outward signs were thought of as having inward counterparts; that the rites were held to put on initiates a moral-spiritual mark as well. The crude vehicles of that purpose – tooth-avulsion, depilation, scarification, circumcision, subincision – have been stumbling-blocks of European understanding. It is most necessary here to look beyond the symbol to the symbolized. But it is also necessary to take more account of the experiential and creative aspects of Aboriginal religion. The convention followed for so long that the study of a religion is to be equated with the study of its beliefs and actions (myths and rites) is plainly too restrictive. Aboriginal religion drew on a human experience of life, and had a creative purpose in life. The four categories of experience, belief, action and purpose were co-ordinate. If any is neglected a study may be *about* religion but not *of* it.

6. There were no Aboriginal philosophers and one can thus speak of "philosophy" only metaphorically. But there is ground for saying that they lived – and therefore thought – by axioms, which were "objective" in that they related to a supposed nature of man and condition of human life. Myths presented the axioms in an intuitive-contemplative aspect. Rites presented them in a passionist-activist aspect. No Aboriginal put the axioms into words but the existence and efficacy of anything – including intuitional awarenesses and insights – do not depend on someone's formal affirmation of them in words. Myths would not be stories, and rites would not have an invariant structure, if axioms could not subsist by other than formalized means. I shall not try to do more than state what I believe to have been the principle of Aboriginal philosophy in the metaphorical sense. I propose to call it a principle of assent to the disclosed terms of life. Anthropologists who have worked with Aborigines commonly note that a supposed past – the whole doctrine of The Dream Time – was said to, and to all appearances did, weigh on the present with overmastering authority. But as far as one can tell, the human response to that situation was not tragic, pessimistic, fatalistic or even quietistic on the one hand, or rebellious and complaining on the other. I have remarked elsewhere that the Aborigines seemed either to have stopped short of, or gone beyond, a true quarrel with the terms of life. They appeared to assent to a reality-as-it-is-and-must-be. Hence, I suggest, three things: the "human-all-too-human" quality postulated as true of men and life's condition in The Dream Time; the constancy of the ritual motive to memorialize the culminating events of that mythical time; and the absence from religious thought and practice of any life-compensatory themes. But within that larger equipoise they evidently sought to make the physical and social life-process of man a process of moral development as well.

Any such construction must take into account a number of facts which, though not new, are now coming into better perspective among anthropologists. There is no doubt that cultural influences, including religious influences, coming from beyond the continent (especially but not only to Arnhem Land – and thence, who knows how far?) had powerful effects before European settlement. It is also certain that the dynamic of development within Australia was higher, and diffused its products more widely, than was once supposed. Thirdly, cults recently and now under study give some evidence – as yet indirect; but to my mind very suggestive – of a process of religious discovery. Conceivably, all those things were causally connected. That possibility remains to be investigated. But taking, as far as one can at this stage, a continental view, it is difficult to resist a conclusion that both the religious and the social cultures were in a dynamic state when Europeans came. We shall undoubtedly learn much more by deeper analyses of the surviving regional cults, no less in their steady phases than in the fervour of their rise and the possible degenerations of their fall. One may end with a question. If the philosophy was one of assent, why the *creative* effort of *new* cult?

7. In several respects the known cults suggest a classification with the mystery-religions. With remarkable theatrical skill, they used mystagogy to inculcate an attitude – an *archaist* attitude – to things of *this* world. Whether the cultists taught or learnt anything of moral or spiritual significance is perhaps open to doubt. The fact may be, as Aristotle said of the Greek mysteries, that "the initiated do not learn anything so much as feel certain emotions and are put in a certain frame of mind". Most anthropologists who have seen the cults practised would agree that there were probably deep effects on both mind and personality. But the ritual symbolisms were also treasured for their own sakes. In some sense, the Aborigines may have been imprisoned by them through the aesthetic pleasure of taking part. One need not hesitate to speak of "mystical participation" in the sense of taking part in evocative dramas having to do with mysteries. But any suggestion of mere traditionalism or mindless automatism would be wrong. Effort, treasure, and enthusiasm were spent far too freely.

Contemporary study is weakened by the fact that there is so much bias in the old printed record. One cannot turn very hopefully to it for test or confirmation of new insights. Far too much of the information was the product of minds caught up with special pleadings of one kind or another. The Parson Thwackums: "When I mention religion, I mean the Christian religion; and not only the Christian religion, but the Protestant religion; and not only the Protestant religion, but the Church of England." The Ernest Crawleys: "Magic being simply the superstitious or religious *method* as

opposed to the scientific." The sceptics: all those influenced by the succession from Comte and Spencer, through Tylor and Frazer to Freud, who appeared to suppose that a disdain, ironical or hostile, of *all* religion should be part of a scientific attitude to *any* religion, even if unknown. Anthropology became what it is within, and in a definite sense because of, the great historical dissent from religion. Its debt to scepticism is profound. Take away the influence of the men listed above and the discipline would be unrecognizable. Even the formulation of problems for study retains much of their outlook. But the dissent in the first place was from particular religion – Christianity over an historical phase – and in respect of some only of its theological formulations and institutional practices. That did not make a warrant for the critique of all religion or the contempt of any. Again far too much of our old information bears the influence of men who wrote, as it were, with their left hands *about* religion but not of it while, with their right, they were mystery-mongering about Magic, Totemism, and an imaginary Childhood of Man.

[. . .]

If any of the early scholars had found Aboriginal ontology of interest, the history of study would read less dismally. It is preposterous that something like a century of study, because of rationalism, positivism, and materialism, should have produced two options: that Aboriginal religion is either (to follow Durkheim) what someone called "the mirage of society" or (to follow Freud) the neurosis of society. The fault goes deeper than concepts and categories. It is due to the imposition of a philosophy of understanding. A philosopher of religion may feel entitled to make such an imposition but not, I suggest, an anthropologist of religion.

But be all that as it may. The primary duty now is to avoid mishandling what opportunities of study remain. The Aboriginal religions must be described and analysed as significant in their own right, as expressions of human experience of life; as essays of passion, imagination, and striving among people to whom our historical dissents, clear and blurred, have meant . . . nothing.

7

Remarks on the Verb "To Believe"

Jean Pouillon

Jean Pouillon (1916–2002) was one of the great intellectuals of 20th-century France. His work embraces an engagement with ethnology, philosophy, literature, politics, and psychoanalysis. Pouillon wrote on literature, film and politics in *Les Temps Modernes*, beginning with the first volume in 1945 and moving on to anthropological subjects by the mid-1950s. He carried out fieldwork among the Hadjeraï of Chad and in Ethiopia, and was editor of *L'Homme* from 1960 to 1996. Some of his best essays are collected in *Fétiches sans Fétichisme*, Paris, Maspero, 1975, and *Le Cru et le Su*, Paris, le Seuil, 1993.

The essay here, reprinted in virtual entirety, is elegant and to the point, incisively demonstrating the paradoxical and culturally specific nature of the verb "to believe." Together with the following essay by Malcolm Ruel it successfully dismantles what is often taken as the key term in definitions or descriptions of religion. Although the article was described as "structuralist," the approach has strong affinities to the school of ordinary language philosophy associated with Austin and the later portion of Wittgenstein's thought in that it begins by looking at the ways in which words are actually used in everyday speech ("parole" rather than "langue"). As Pouillon implies, this complicates the translation problem; we have first the difficult task of exploring language use (rather than simply definition in the abstract) in our field settings and second the problem of mapping uses from one linguistic community to another. Pouillon offers the suggestion of two kinds of religion, one based on faith and the other on local knowledge. But this in turn might lead us to inquire about the presence of what would then be a kind of philosophical skepticism (rather than theological doubt) in the latter context.

From Remarks on the Verb "To Believe" in Michel Izard and Pierre Smith, eds, John Leavitt, trans. *Between Belief and Transgression: Structural Essays in Religion, History, and Myth* (University of Chicago Press, 1982 [1979]) pp. 1–8. Slightly abridged.

The French verb *croire* ("to believe")[1] is paradoxical in that it expresses doubt as well as assurance. To believe (*croire*) is to state a conviction; it is also to add a nuance to that conviction: "I believe" (*je crois*) often signifies "I'm not sure." This ambiguity involves the subjective side of belief (*croyance*). As regards its object, the situation is no less equivocal, since the complement of the verb can be produced in two ways: direct or indirect. What is more, the indirect construction itself has two forms: *croire à . . .* ("to believe in," "to think of") is not the same thing as *croire en . . .* ("to believe in," in the sense of being willing to rely on), which both differ from *croire* + direct object or *croire que . . .* ("to believe that . . ."). Finally, the meaning of the verb and the construction of the complement can vary depending on the nature of the object: man, god, fact, value, statement. . . .

This suggests two questions (at least): is it possible to order this diversity of usages? If so, is this order universal or does it characterize only a certain type of culture, and in this case what is the basis for the word's unity? In other words: how is it that multiple meanings do not require diverse expressions?[2] But since this is apparently the case, is a translation of the verb in all its senses possible in other languages, using a single term?

Croire à . . . is to state that something exists; *croire en . . .* is to have confidence; *croire que . . .* is for something to be represented in a certain way. Although the difference between the two indirect constructions may appear slight, it is undeniable, as the following example shows: a person believes in (*croire en*, "trusts in") God, while one believes in (*croire à*) the Devil, that is, one recognizes that he exists without, by definition, putting one's faith in him: one cannot *croire en* the Devil. *Croyance en* ("belief in, trust in") God does imply *croyance à* ("belief in") his existence, but implication is not identity. On the other hand, this implication seems so obvious that it often goes unformulated: a believer believes in (*croire en*, "trusts in") God, he feels no need to say that he believes in (*croire à*) God's reality; he believes in (*croire à*) it, one would say, implicitly. But is this certain? In fact, the believer not only need not say that he believes

in (*croire à*) the existence of God, but he need not even believe in (*croire à*) it; precisely because in his eyes there can be no doubt about it: the existence of God is not believed in (*crue*), but perceived. On the contrary, to make God's existence an object of belief, to state this belief, is to open up the possibility of doubt – which begins to clarify the ambiguity with which we started. So one could say that it is the unbeliever who believes that the believer believes in (*croire à*) the existence of God. One could call this a play upon words; but these words do lend themselves to it, and it is precisely this possibility that must be explored, if not elucidated, in trying to organize the field of their usages. Besides, what I have just said will appear much simpler if we leave the religious domain. If I have confidence in a friend, if I believe in (*croire en*, "have faith in") him, will I say that I believe in (*croire à*) his existence? Certainly not; that existence is, simply, undeniable. It is only if it were not unquestionable that I would have to believe in (*croire à*) it, and believe in it explicitly. Again, it will probably be said that this is playing on words, this time on the word "existence," for man's existence, by definition, is not on the same level as that of the deity. By definition, yes, but by cultural definition: the distinction between a cultural world and a natural world, or between a "this world" and a "beyond," is widespread, but it is not universal. It is this distinction between two modes of existence that leads to a distinction between two ways of apprehending what exists: perception and knowledge on one side, belief (*croyance*) on the other. From this kind of perspective, the existence of supernatural beings can only be an object of belief, and this is why wherever this distinction is made the phenomon of belief as the affirmation of existence takes on this ambiguous aspect, between the certain and the questionable.

This is not the only reason. Let us now consider the relations between *croire à . . .* ("to believe in (a fact)") and *croire que . . .* ("to believe that . . ."). To believe in (*croire à*) the existence of X – "god, table, or washbasin" – can be expressed in a direct construction: to believe that (*croire que*) X exists. But this is a statement of a peculiar type – the existence of a god or of a hundred thalers is not an attribute – and is different from the statement that endows X with certain characteristics which permit X to be represented to oneself. The representation, the content of belief, is accompanied by an affirmation of existence but is separable from this affirmation; the affirmation can be bracketed – the Husserlian *epoché* – and this is what makes possible studies of beliefs as such: one need not believe in (*croire à*) what one believes in order to analyze it. The "I believe" (*je crois*) which precedes so many statements of the most diverse kinds, is the mark of a distancing and not of an adhesion.

These two movements, which a single verb is able to express, appear radically opposed, or else completely unrelated. Belief as representation, as statement, pertains to what is also called ideology; there is no isolated belief, every representation is part of a global system which is more or less clearly, more or less consciously articulated, a system which may be religious but may also be philosophical, political. . . . Belief as faith (*confiance*) is the conviction that he to whom one has given something will reciprocate in the form of support or protection; it calls forth a relationship of exchange, of which the relationship between the believer and his god is only a particular case, even if a frequently privileged one. One puts one's faith (*confiance*) to the same end, whether in an individual, in a party, in an institution. It is significant in this regard that Benveniste, in his *Indo-European Language and Society* (1969; English edition, London, 1973), discusses belief (*la croyance*) not in the section on "religion" but in that on "economic obligations." For he sees the original meaning of belief in this credit which has been accorded and should be returned. Must we then see belief-as-representation as a derivative meaning? Or else as a meaning that has been added on, and which would turn the verb "to believe" into a conglomerate without unity?

This derivation is certainly a possible one: to believe in (*croire en*) someone, to give him credit, is, among other things, to believe (*croire*) what he says, and in this way one goes from the trust to the statement that it allows

one to take as established fact. This is especially evident when the belief appears in the form of religious faith: trust in (*croyance en*) a god is usually the basis of what we call a *credo*, a group of statements which become the direct object of belief. The same is true in many other domains. For political examples, there is an over-abundance of choices. But it is also possible (more often than is usually . . . believed!) to accept a proposition that is said to be scientific just as one accepts a dogma or even the possibly fantastic assertion of a man who is judged worthy of trust; I believe it not because I am able to prove it, but because I have faith in those who say they have proven it, for example, in Einstein when, following him, I write $E = mc^2$. But we would miss the essential part of belief-as-representation if we reduced it to this sole case in which it is based on the argument of authority. The specific trait of a representation is to appear obvious, to be self-evident, and the fact that it is always possible to bracket the judgment or the feeling of obviousness changes nothing: the obvious is replaced by the arbitrary, but both simply mean that this form of belief is based on nothing but itself or the cultural system within which it finds its meaning.

So it seems impossible to overcome the polysemy of the word. Its religious usage does allow us to unify the verb's three constructions, but it does not eliminate the other usages; over and above this, it only unites the three constructions in religions of a certain type. This observation leads us to question its anthropological usage, now well established and apparently unproblematic.[3] What anthropologist would deny that he seeks to uncover the beliefs of those whom he studies, to compare them with our own beliefs or those of other peoples, as if this object of study and its designation presented no a priori problem, as if it were obvious that every human being "believes" (*croire*) – this being one of our beliefs – in the same way, if not, of course, in the same things? The danger in this situation is not simply the well-known if not always foreseen one of inappropriately applying a category that may have meaning only in our own culture; it has to do with the fact that this category may not be a single, unified one at all, even for us, or at the least that it is a shattered category, whose fragmentation is, precisely, a singular cultural phenomenon. What is more, anthropological usage reduplicates the paradox I emphasized above when I said that it is the unbeliever who believes that the believer believes. If for example I say that the Dangaleat[4] believe in (*croire à*) the existence of *margaï*, this is because I do not believe in their existence and, not believing in it, I think that they can only be believing in (*croire à*) it in the same way that I imagine I could, if I did. But how can one tell whether they believe (*croire*) and in what way? What question can one ask them, using what word of their language, in what context? Or, inversely, how is it possible to translate into French the word or words they use to talk about what is to our eyes an object of belief?

In J. Fédry's *Dictionnaire dangaleat*, we find the verb *àbidé* "to perform the rites faithfully." It comes from the local Arabic *abada*, "to adore God," adoration being understood as a ritualized activity. It is a matter of worship (*du culte*), of faith in action, and not of the representation of a being whose existence must also be affirmed. This verb is used with a direct-object complement: this being, God for converts to Christianity or Islam, or the *margaï* for others. The best way to translate it is thus "to serve," in the biblical sense of the term: to worship (*rendre un culte à*). *No abday maragi,* "I serve the *margaï*." Another verb, *àmniyé,* signifies "to bestow one's trust on," "to rest on," "to believe in" (*croire en*). It is constructed with an indirect-object complement, introduced by the preposition *ku: no amnay ku marigo,* "I have faith in the *margaï*," "I give my faith to the *margaï*"; this is the verb that Christians use to say "I believe in (*croire en*) God," *no amnay ku bungir.* In contrast to the foregoing, this verb is not used exclusively in religious contexts: one can evidently, as in French, put one's faith in another person. The first sense given by the dictionary, besides this, is "to be used to, familiar with . . . ," and one will say, for example: *no amniyiy-g pisò,* "I am used to horses." This too is a word of Arabic origin whose Semitic root has given us the "amen" of Christian liturgy which, as Fédry points out, marks adhesion to a person more

than to a conceptual "truth." As this author notes, "one may wonder about the fact that both of these verbs come from Arabic, whose linguistic influence is very strong in Dangaleat, as in other Hadjeraï languages. But this should not make us doubt that what the Dangaleat have taken in has become an integral part of themselves." I will add in turn that from the language of a religion with a *credo* (an affirmation of existence and a set of statements and representations) the Dangaleat have taken what fits their own way of "believing" (*croire*): the terms that designate a specific behavior and mental attitude – worshipping (*rendre un culte*) and trusting in the addressee of the worship – and not terms that are based on definite representations or propositions.

One may thus translate our "believe in" (*croire en*) into Dangaleat, and the fact that the Hadjeraï took the word from Arabic suggests that for them it expresses the essential aspect of belief (and of religious faith in general, says Fédry, who belongs to the Society of Jesus and should know whereof he speaks): faith (*la confiance*). But in this case, how can we translate "to believe (that)" (*croire que*)? To find out, to know, to know about something, is *ibiné*; *pakkine* serves to render: think, suppose, figure out, foresee. These two verbs are pure Dangaleat. The first will be used to mark certainty and so translates "to believe" (*croire*) in cases where the French verb is more or less equivalent with "to know," when for instance Don Juan says to Sganarelle, who is questioning him about belief, "I believe that two and two make four." The second verb covers the doubtful usages of our verb, all those in which the speaker takes a certain distance with regard to what he is talking about.

In sum, we can translate all aspects of the verb "to believe" . . . except the verb itself. What we have been able to translate has been the French equivalent of "to believe" in each of its particular usages, but in Dangaleat there is no single term that serves as the basis of their unification. In other words, we can translate everything except the ambiguity. We must therefore return to the reasons for this ambiguity. Ambiguity is not simply polysemy, the fact that a verb sometimes has one meaning and sometimes another, each of them unequivocal;

it is, rather, that all of these meanings, even the contradictory ones, are intrinsically linked; that, above all, there is always doubt at the heart of the conviction, and that the affirmation itself indicates that it could always be suspended. But why condense this paradoxical liaison into a single word instead of sorting out its elements, as the Hadjeraï do? The answer, "I believe," lies in the comparison between a religion like Christianity and a religion like that of the Dangaleat.

It is not so much the believer, I would say, who affirms his belief as such, it is rather the unbeliever who reduces to mere believing what, for the believer, is more like knowing. Nevertheless, the Christian cannot avoid expressing his faith not only as trust in God (*confiance en*), but also as belief in (*croyance à*) his existence and belief that (*croyance que*) God possesses such and such attributes, that the world was created, and so forth. He states this as a belief, even though he knows it – but also because he knows that by this very fact it is contestable and contested. Above all he knows that there are other beliefs, on the one hand because his religion has a history and was constituted against the "false" gods, on the other because this history is not over yet and there are still idols to be eliminated; and there can be *other* beliefs only because his own belief is one among others. Next, he knows – it is even an essential point in his *credo* – that the object of his belief is in a "reality" of a different order than the realities of the world of creation, which are the object of a permanently revisable scientific knowledge, or of calculations, of predictions that can be proven wrong; and he also knows that this possibility of revision lies in the demonstrable or verifiable character of the knowledge or the hypothesis, a character whose legitimacy he challenges in the case of his belief, but which, inversely, challenges the legitimacy of his belief. Thus he must simultaneously assume both his affirmation and the challenge to it, a challenge that belief is, nonetheless, supposed to make impossible on its own level. In other words, the contradiction is inside his faith, and that is what it is "to believe."[5]

This situation is the result of the distinction made between two worlds: the Kingdom of God and this world. In our culture such a distinction seems so characteristic of religion, to those who reject it as much as to its adherents, that religion in general and so-called "primitive" religions in particular are usually defined by a belief in supernatural powers and by their worship. There is even a tendency to think that the extent and importance of the supernatural world are much greater for "primitives" than for "moderns," that super-nature is not only the domain of gods and spirits but also, for example, the domain in which the power of the magician and the sorcerer operates. I certainly do not mean to deny that at any latitudes one can find people who believe in (*croire à*) the supernatural, but one equally finds people for whom such an affirmation is completely meaningless – without them being, for all that, areligious – far from it. For here we have a major misunderstanding: because we have constructed the concept of natural law, we are ready to admit the supernatural (whether as illusion or as other reality hardly matters) as a place to put whatever contravenes, or seems to contravene, natural law; but this is our own notion, whether we judge it well grounded or not, and not that of the people to whom we abusively attribute it. As Evans-Pritchard remarks, "many peoples are convinced that deaths are caused by witchcraft. To speak of witchcraft being for these peoples a supernatural agency hardly reflects their own view of the matter, since from their point of view nothing could be more natural."[6] For his part, Claude Lévi-Strauss has stressed the realist, materialist character of magic, its monistic, not dualistic, conception of the world.[7]

The *margaï*, these spirits who have such an important place in the individual and social lives of the Hadjeraï, are invisible, nonhuman powers; they act unpredictably, and are the cause of whatever disturbs the natural course of things. But they are no less a part of the same world as human beings. The latter believe in (*croire à*) the existence of the *margaï* like they believe in their own existence, in that of animals things, atmospheric phenomena. . . . Or rather they do not believe in (*croire à*) it: this existence is simply a fact of experience:[8] there is no more need to believe in (*croire à*) the *margaï* than to believe that if you throw a stone it will fall. One fears and/or trusts in them, one gets to know them, one gets used to them, one performs the special sacrifices that please each *margaï*, and one is careful to make no mistakes, for fear of getting sick or being affected in some unpleasant way. If we can speak of a Dangaleat religion – another untranslatable expression – it is not in the sense in which the faithful share a single elaborated body of beliefs about supernatural beings, but rather in the etymological sense, according to Benveniste, of the Latin *religio*:[9] that of a meticulous concern for the proper carrying out of the cult, without, however, being able to define the necessary correctives in advance; at every occasion, one takes aim within uncertainty. One can only estimate what each *margaï* desires. The four verbs mentioned above define these behaviors equivocally and without contradictions: one serves the *margaï*, one trusts in them (that is, in the mutually fruitful nature of the exchange inaugurated by the sacrifice), one knows from experience that they exist, and one tries to guess their intentions. All this does presuppose a particular representation of the world, but one which excludes the possibility of its explanation in the form of "belief," of an assertion that in spite of itself is doubtful, relativized. The Dangaleat certainly know that others think differently, and it happens that many of them convert to Islam or to Christianity. But this situation cannot surprise them: one does not believe in (*croire à*) the *margaï*; one experiences them, and this experience is first of all a local one; such spirits do not necessarily exist everywhere. While the encounter with otherness relativizes Christian belief in an other-worldly absolute, it confirms the Dangaleat experience of the world, which is relative from the beginning and so cannot be disturbed by diversity. This is why religions of the Dangaleat type are without the proselytizing inherent in religions founded on beliefs whose vulnerability impels their formidable dynamism.[10]

If the Dangaleat have no need of the verb "to believe" this is not solely because of their monism, as opposed to Christian dualism. Equally in play is another opposition, one between the historicism of the Christian religion and the empiricism of Dangaleat religion. This empiricism assures everyone of the presence of the *margaï*, and has no need of an intercessor. Every man performs his own sacrifices and will have recourse to the diviner only to know what animal, of what sex and what color, he should kill and on what day. A religion like Christianity or Islam is based, on the contrary, on a revelation, testimony, a transmission whose fidelity is guaranteed by a church or specialized experts. This revelation is, precisely, that another world exists; the revelation is a unique historical event, its content is constituted by the words of its protagonist, God incarnate or prophet. So everything rests on a faith, which is simultaneously a trust and a specific *credo*. All the meanings of the verb "to believe" should then come together, but this necessity is nothing more or less than a cultural necessity. It is only in this perspective, in my opinion, that we can speak of "religious belief," and it is only when it is understood that this notion does not have universal value that we can appreciate how difficult the problem of a general definition of religion really is; but this may also be the point from which we can try to resolve the problem.

NOTES

1 TN: The author's distinctions among different meanings of the verbs *croire*, *croire en*, *croire à*, etc., bear on the semantics of the word, not directly on its morphology. For this reason I have not followed the inflections of the French verb in my bracketed clarifications, but have usually put the infinitive form, whatever the tense, person, etc. of the verb in the text. For example, when the French text says *il croit* I have put "he believes" [*croire*], to make clear the opposition with, say, *il croit en*, which I translate "he believes in."

2 Diverse expressions do exist, however: credit (*créance*), confidence, trust (*confiance*), faith (*foi*). . . . But while one might turn to these for the sake of precision, they are not required by usage.

3   Rodney Needham has done this (*Belief, Language, and Experience*), in a perspective different from my own. The two do overlap, however: the themes are necessarily the same, but they are put together in different ways.

4   The Dangaleat are one of the groups called Hadjeraï, who live in the central region of the Republic of Chad, Department of Guera. They worship (*rendent un culte à*) what one could summarily call local spirits: the *margaï*.

5   It would be easy to show that today many "political believers" find themselves in an analogous situation. But they are not always as aware of it as Saint Augustine was when, according to Tertullian, he said: *credo quia absurdum*.

6   *Theories of Primitive Religion* (Oxford, 1965), pp. 109–10.

7   Lévi-Strauss, *The Savage Mind*, English translation (Chicago, 1966), pp. 221–2.

8   In the same way, among the Nuer the expression *Kwoth a thin* ("God is present") "does not mean 'there is a God.' That would be for the Nuer a pointless remark. God's existence is taken for granted by everybody. Consequently, when we say, as we can do, that all Nuer have faith in God, the word 'faith' must be understood in the Old Testament sense of trust (the Nuer *Ngath*). . . . There is in any case, I think, no word in the Nuer language which could stand for 'I believe'." Evans-Pritchard, *Nuer Religion* (Oxford, 1956), p. 9.

9   Benveniste, *Indo-European Language and Society*.

10   I do not mean to say that some beliefs are vulnerable and others are not. Any belief, in the fact of its communication, makes itself, and knows itself to be, vulnerable.

8

Christians as Believers

Malcolm Ruel

Malcolm Ruel is a British anthropologist (trained at the University of Oxford, taught at the University of Cambridge) who has carried out fieldwork in both West Africa (1969) and among the Kuria of Kenya, East Africa (1997). The collection of essays on the Kuria (in which this essay was reprinted as chapter 2) contain some particularly fine reflections on the nature of religion and the means to comprehend it. The thrust of Ruel's argument is that one may need to dispense with western, Christian-inspired notions of belief and deity and that, indeed, the primary inclinations of Kuria religion may be described without recourse to metaphysical concepts. Ruel concludes that "religion is possible without the supernatural and that the supernatural figures only peripherally in Kuria religion" (1997: 237). What concerns the Kuria in the conduct of their rituals is "ordered growth" and "the securing of life."

Ruel's essay is important for several reasons. First, it addresses the Christian tradition anthropologically and thereby forces us to become aware of how much of the anthropological framework on religion has been compromised by that tradition. Ruel's essay also shows the importance of historical accounts of key terms whose meaning and use shift over time. In effect, he provides us with a multilayered genealogy of a key term of both Christianity and anthropology. Ruel also shows the connection between the history of the term and the political developments within the church. In so doing, he questions the value of "belief" as a concept for the anthropology of religion, not, like Needham (1972), for reasons of philosophical or psychological precision, nor, like Pouillon, for problems of comparability, but because of the very different meanings it has held within even one historical tradition. Ruel offers independent confirmation

From Malcolm Ruel, "Christians as Believers," in John Davis, ed., *Religious Organization and Religious Experience* (London: Academic Press, 1982), pp. 9–31. Abridged.

of Pouillon's argument that in many societies the relations that people hold to the concepts they use or the ideas they express may be radically distorted by the application of the term "belief," thereby leading in turn to a whole series of false problems such as how such "beliefs" can be justified.

For further elaboration readers should turn to *Belief, Ritual, and the Securing of Life: Reflexive Essays on a Bantu Religion* (Ruel 1997). The arguments there are developed by means of an apprecia-

tion of Kuria religion, but in fact have relevance for much of Africa and beyond. Although Ruel is directly and deeply indebted to Evans-Pritchard, it is instructive to contrast Ruel's conclusions with those of Evans-Pritchard with respect to the East African Nuer (chapter 11). On the Christian bias underlying anthropology and the paradoxical consequence that this has obscured the anthropological analysis of Christianity in particular, see Cannell (2005, 2006).

The argument of my paper is summed up in an early observation of Wilfred Cantwell Smith:

The peculiarity of the place given to belief in Christian history is a monumental matter, whose importance and relative uniqueness must be appreciated. So characteristic has it been that unsuspecting Westerners have . . . been liable to ask about a religious group other than their own as well, "What do they believe?" as though this were the primary question, and certainly were a legitimate one. (1978, p. 180. But see also Smith, 1977, 1979)

"Unsuspecting Westerners" must of course include unsuspecting western anthropologists who, as many texts will show (e.g. Evans-Pritchard, 1937, p. 21), give primacy to what people "believe" without fully declaring what that word means, nor recognizing, it would seem, just how rooted the concept is in our own cultural religious tradition, Christian and post-Christian, and thus how loaded any statement concerning "belief" easily becomes.

This then is one reason why an anthropologist may be excused if he moves so far from his last as to attempt, however incompetently, to sketch in outline the monumental peculiarity of Christian "belief". At a time when anthropology has turned more and more to give an account of the cognitive aspects of culture it is as well for us to be aware of the complexity of the concepts that we draw from

our own culture, which have a history and contextual compulsion of their own which often ill-match the ideas and actions they are used to interpret. The need for critical reflection becomes even greater when, as in the case of "believing", there has been a radical shift in the use of a term whilst something of its force has been retained. "Believing" in the sense of being committed to some definable set of values has become secularized, detached from Christian believing but not demoted as a concept, so that in a post-Christian, secular culture the phrase "I believe . . ." (e.g. in the title of Forster's essay, 1939) still gives promise of a personal statement of some significance, a declaration of moral identity.

There is here another reason why it is appropriate for an anthropologist to attempt the task of ethnographic placing, for it is part of the anthropologist's trade to look hard and long at certain key concepts and to explore how use and meaning, context and idea, are constantly engaged in an interplay in which concepts link situations while situations qualify (and thus help to define) concepts. Now "belief" is essentially a word that relates and defines: it relates people, situations and ideas; but in its turn, as I shall argue, it is also in very important ways defined by the context of its use. In this, function and meaning come almost (but never entirely) to coincide; consider, for example, the phrase "the community of believers" that runs like a thematic passacaglia through Hans Küng's *The Church* (1968). If only to keep for some short time the philosophers at bay (to whom the cognitive promise contained in the word "belief" comes, as it were, as a gift from heaven) let us assert resolutely, at least for the present, that the (Christian) concept of belief is as it does and proceed to consider it situationally and behaviourally.

To narrow somewhat the vastness of the topic, four periods have been selected from the history of the church in which to discuss the idea of belief and how it is involved in any definition, corporate or personal, of Christian identity. They are: (1) the critical, initial phase in which Christians, the Nazarene sect, emerged as a distinctive religious movement, a community of believers; (2) the immediately succeeding period leading to the Council of Nicaea (325) that witnessed both the developing formal organization of the Church and the establishment of orthodox creeds, sanctioned by the Church councils; (3) the Reformation and in particular Luther's reformulation of what it means to believe (i.e. to have faith); and finally, since we cannot leave ourselves out, (4) the present period, which might be characterized in both Christian and secular contexts as belief diffused – "beyond belief" in the phrase of one (diffusely) believing anthropologist. In this section I use the word "belief" only with its Christian reference and where at all possible I keep to this one word, assuming a sufficient continuity and overlap in meaning between "faith" and "belief" to allow "belief" to do duty for both, except where there is particular need to distinguish them. This usage has the advantage of permitting a single word correspondence between *belief* in English, *pistis* in Greek and the root *'mn* in Hebrew; this does not imply that these words have (collectively) the same meaning nor that they have (singly) a constant meaning, only that their range of meaning is historically and semantically continuous. (On this issue my usage is radically at variance with that of Wilfred Cantwell Smith.)

The detailed scholarly writings on the terminology of belief, *pistis*, in the New Testament books make it possible to offer a number of summary points. (I rely chiefly on Bultmann and Weiser, 1961; Hatch, 1917; Michel, 1975;

and Moule, unpublished.) In its various forms, *pistis* (belief), *pisteuo* (believe), *pistos* (faithful, trustworthy), *apistia* (unbelief), form a key and much used set of terms in the New Testament. The meaning of the word-group does not (with some qualification) depart from its general meaning, or set of meanings, in Greek, but its New Testament use also carries certain connotations derived from that fact that *pisteuo*, to believe, was the term consistently used to translate the Hebrew *he'min*, from the root *'mn* (meaning to be true, reliable or faithful) in the Septuagint. One needs here to distinguish between the meanings of words and the religious ideas they express, for although the two may coincide, they do not always do so, and changes in meaning follow often from the development of pre-existing ideas. Thus both the original Greek use of *pisteuo* and the Hebrew term *'mn* express centrally the notion of trust or confidence. Originally the Greek word-group "denoted conduct that honoured an agreement or bond. It had a social orientation, and its use indicated misconduct by implication" (Michel, 1975, p. 594). In classical Greek literature *pistis* means the trust that a man may place in other men, or gods; credibility, credit in business, guarantee, proof or something to be trusted. Similarly, *pisteuo* means to trust something or someone (ibid.). The word acquired a religious use at an early date, when to "believe" (*pisteuo*) the gods or an oracle expressed on the one hand confidence in them (their veracity or ability to promote welfare) and on the other obedience to them, an acknowledgement of their power to determine human fate. The Hebrew term *'mn* denotes even more directly a quality of relationship: it was used of the reliability or trustworthiness of a servant, a witness, messenger, or a prophet, but it also served to characterize the relationship between God and his people, reciprocally trusted and trusting, bound by covenant to each other (Michel, 1975, pp. 595–6). In the New Testament the word *pistis* and its related forms still carry the ideas of trust and confidence. In a citation that rings reverberatively through the theology of the centuries, Paul refers to the belief (*pistis*) that Abraham had in God's promise that he would become "the father of many nations" (the story is told in Genesis 15) as an exemplar for the kind of belief (*pistis*) shared by the early Christians. As the belief (i.e. trust) of Abraham was reckoned as righteousness for him, so "Faith is to be reckoned as righteousness to us also, who believe in Him Who raised from the dead our Lord Jesus Christ, who was delivered to death for our sins and raised again to secure our justification" (Romans 4: 13–25).

Yet in spite of this continuity between the Hebrew and the Greek, the Old and the New Testament, the word *pistis* does come to acquire a special twist in the apostolic writings of the New Testament. One might say that it acquires a technical use. Thus the verb *pisteuo*, to believe, is often used in the sense of to be converted, to become a Christian: "they heard the message and believed" is a formula that repeatedly occurs in the narrative of the expanding church in the Acts of the Apostles; Paul writes of "when we were first believed" (Romans 13:11) in the sense of "when we were first converted"; and there are other examples. Similarly, the nominal form "believers" (either *hoi pisteuontes*, "those believing", or *hoi pistoi*, "those of the belief") refers to the converted, the "brothers" or the "saints" as they are also called. We should note that the word "Christian" is itself rarely used (three times in the New Testament) and then always in the context of what others – the people the Christians called unbelievers – were calling them. Finally, the noun *pistis* denotes the "belief" held collectively by the early Christians as a common conviction, a shared confidence that both distinguished and united them as a community. Paul lists these identifying features explicitly and succinctly in Ephesians 4:4–5 in which the central elements are "one Lord, one belief, one baptism".

We need to look more closely at the substance of this shared belief in the last sense above, for it is in relation to this that the concept gains added depth and range. Essentially what these early converts believed was what theologians have come to call (using another technical term) the *kerygma* or proclamation of the Christian message (Bultmann and Weiser, 1961, p. 69; Michel, 1975, pp. 601, 605; Hatch, 1917, pp. 33–4). Now this does not mean just the teaching *of* Jesus, but rather the teaching *about* Jesus, and the crucial fact about Jesus, which summed up all the rest, was his resurrection: this fact is expressed clearly in the passage from Paul, quoted above, and throughout the epistles (and we should recall that these are the earliest Christian documents that we have; the gospels were written later). Christian *belief* now begins to part company from Hebrew *trust*. Both refer to relationship – the confidence that people have in God, and in the case of the Christians in God through Christ – but for Christians there is the added confidence or conviction about an event (the resurrection and all that that signifies) that had actually taken place. The belief is not just open-ended, oriented to what God may or can do: it is rooted firmly in what God has done, which to deny is to deny the Word of God, that is, the action of God in the world. (On this point see especially Bultmann and Weiser, 1961, p. 82 *et seq.*) This development was to have enormous consequences for the later use of the concept for it is but a short step from *belief* as accepting as a fact (i.e. the event of the resurrection) to *belief* as asserting as a proposition. A distinction made frequently today is between "belief in" (trust in) and "belief that" (propositional belief). The distinction may clear our minds today but it confuses history, for the point about Christian belief, reiterated by theologians (e.g. Lampe, 1976; Moule, unpublished), is that it was both at once.

The creeds, which we must now consider, both reflect and perpetuate this particular notion of Christian belief, that concerns a complex person-event, not least in their reiterated verbal formula: "I believe in – who did –": Person + Event, the two reciprocally defining (Lampe, 1976). Yet if the kernel of the creeds is the recognition of this person-event, their history is one of growing elaboration and formalization, a development that takes place in relation to the developing organization of the Christian body: the shared conviction of a scattered community of Christians becomes the confirmed orthodoxy of the conciliar church.

Brief credal phrases are common in the New Testament and there are occasional longer summaries (as in the passage by Paul) when the writer evidently felt something more explicit was required. In either case they serve as summary statements of the teaching or *kerygma* concerning Christ. The formulary phrase, *Kurios Iesous*, "Jesus [is] Lord", is common and there are many variants. It is clear moreover that such phrases served as conventional declarations of religious allegiance of a symbolic kind. Thus Paul: "If with your mouth you confess *Kurios Iesous* and believe in your heart that God has raised him from the dead, you will be saved" (Romans 10:9) and in another passage (1 Corinthians 12:3) Paul contrasts this confessional formula of affirmation with its opposite, that of denial or denunciation (*Kurios Iesous* v. *Anatheina Iesous*, "Cursed be Jesus"), declaring that only the former can be spoken by the Holy Spirit, i.e. that a Christian should be unable to deny Christ. There is some evidence that suspected members of the Christian sect were tested by being asked to make just such a formal denial (Lampe, 1976, p. 54; Kelly, 1972, p. 15) and in the gospels the story of Peter's thrice denial of Christ assumes its significance against the importance of thus "confessing Christ" in the early church (and indeed thereafter). Belief in this context becomes then a badge, a symbol, something that is explicitly affirmed where the act of affirmation has its own functional value.

Such formulary statements were not however creeds in the usual sense of extended declarations of belief. These were to develop in the period up to the fourth century. They emerged in the first place in the context of baptism and then, it would seem, began to be used as statements of the received teaching first for regional congregations and then, in a more self-consciously developed form, as the conciliar creeds prepared for and affirmed by councils representing the whole church or large sections of it. The fact that the earliest creeds were baptismal (on this all authorities are agreed) leads us to note the important post-Easter development of this rite, which acts as a ritual counterpart to the "believing" we have already spoken of as denoting conversion. Jesus's religious career was initiated by baptism from St. John the Baptist but he himself did not baptize people and (except in the case of Jesus) the

baptism of St. John was specifically a "baptism of repentance" (i.e. a cleansing rite) and not an initiation. (St. John's message was similarly one of repentance, not of belief.) From the time of the early church, however, baptism came to be used to mark the transition to membership that is so characteristic of Christianity and which in this clear-cut, boundary-marking way is absent from all other world religions. Baptism and belief have parallels in other ways too, for baptism re-enacts symbolically the basic postulate of the belief: as Christ died and rose again so too (it is held) the person being baptized dies and rises again "in Christ". Baptism acts therefore not only as a rite of passage for individual Christians but also as the act by which the church, identified with the risen Christ, is perpetually re-constituted. For it should be understood that the church, although pre-figured in Christ's life, was not in fact founded until after his death and resurrection by those who "believed", i.e. accepted the *kerygma*. (On this point see Küng, 1968, pp. 70–9.) "Belief" here has theologically and sociologically a critical function in establishing the organic relationship between Christ, the risen Lord, and the church as the community who believe in his resurrection and in this way perpetuate it. Hence the importance of conversion (believing) as a break, a passage from the old life to the new life, a kind of resurrection, comparable for the community of believers to the passage through the Red Sea for the Israelites (the Old Testament analogue for Christian baptism). All this is implicit in Paul's "one Lord, one belief, one baptism".

In their relation to baptism the earliest creeds had a dual function: first, and as part of the ritual, candidates were required to respond affirmatively to certain questions about their belief put to them; second, and by extension of the first, statements of belief in the form of a condensed, continuous declaration were used for the instruction of the candidate. (Here and throughout my account of the creeds I rely heavily on Kelly, 1972.) It was the latter form that was to be adopted by the later conciliar creeds but it would seem that even before that happened their use was influenced by the recognition that the received teaching they embodied should be uniform, subject to what Irenaeus in the second century defined as a common "rule of truth", and such credal declarations grew in length and elaborateness because of this. Emerging as "a by-product of the Church's fully developed catechetical system" (Kelly, 1972, p. 64) such creeds were in fact ancillary to the interrogatory baptismal creeds. Thus, a fourth-century treatise recalls and comments on the questions asked at baptism that date in this form from at least the second century:

> You were questioned, "Dost thou believe in God the Father almighty?" You said, "I believe", and were immersed, that is were buried. Again you were asked, "Dost thou believe in our Lord Jesus Christ and His cross?" You said, "I believe", and were immersed. Thus you were buried along with Christ; for he who is buried along with Christ rises again with Him. A third time you were asked, "Dost thou believe also in the Holy Spirit?" You said, "I believe", and a third time were immersed, so that your threefold confession wiped out the manifold failings of your earlier life. (*De Sacramentis* 2, 7 quoted in Kelly, 1972, p. 37)

The triadic structure of this interrogatory form was carried over into the declaratory baptismal creeds and thence all the later creeds.

The baptismal creeds summarized the received teaching, but their local use in the widely scattered Christian communities, headed as each was by their bishop, was subject to variation and reformulation. By the end of the third century there is evidence of certain baptismal creeds being cited to test the acceptability of the teaching of a local community, which is to say the teaching of the bishop. There was here a shift in the use of creeds which was critical. It was no longer the catechumen's belief that was at issue (and thus individual membership of the Christian community) but rather the orthodoxy of the bishop (and thus his and his congregation's valid membership of the Christian body). The major, decisive step was taken with the Council of Nicaea (325) when the assembled bishops were asked to accept a statement of teaching, which was set out in the form of a declaratory creed. (This was not the "Nicene creed" of the prayer books but it laid the basis for it.) A major preoccupation in the drafting of this statement was to exclude the teaching of Arius and his followers who (as it happened) had themselves drawn up a creed-like summary of their position (Kelly, 1972, p. 206). Two hundred and eighteen out of 220 bishops attending the Council did sign their acceptance and an indication of the change in function of this, the first of the conciliar creeds, is the fact that the document drawn up states not only what is the received belief, but also what is not: *anathema* is pronounced on those who hold certain propositions (i.e. those held by Arius and his supporters). "Belief" now comes to define, not merely the Christian from the non-Christian (the believer from the non-believer), but the true Christian from the false (the true believer from the heretic). Moreover, the latter function assumes an organized authority: bishops in council and not just in their sees.

Two important circumstances are associated with the Council of Nicaea (Kelly, 1972; Chadwick, 1967). The first is the patronage of Constantine, who had recently adopted the Christian cause and who was concerned to bring the scattered Christian communities into some kind of common organization. Nicaea was the first of the church councils and its establishment of an overall church authority is evidenced not only by the bishops' formal acceptance of the creed but also by their agreement to a number of other liturgical and disciplinary measures (the latter concerning not least the actions of bishops). The second circumstance has already been mentioned: the teachings of Arius who, in emphasizing the absolute perfection of the Godhead, was led to accord a lower, unequal place to Christ. The Council of Nicaea did not resolve the Arian controversy (nor indeed the underlying issue of how to interpret a trinitarian God) and the fluctuating fortunes of the Arian and anti-Arian (or Nicene) camps dominated the church until the Council and creed of Constantinople (381) formulated what was to become the basic doctrine of the Trinity. Any account of this period (e.g. Chadwick, 1967, Chapter 9) makes it clear that, whatever the merits of the intellectual issue, community loyalties and identities were also very closely involved: the major cleavage between Greek East and Latin West; the dominance of certain key bishoprics and their sees; the fortunes of individual bishops who were promoted or ousted according to their spiritual (and human) loyalties; the relationship of the church to the foundering Roman empire; all have a part to play in the story. Out of this time and out of this general debate also (but not directly out of Arianism) emerged the one doctrinal and credal point that separates the Roman from the Orthodox churches, the West from the East. This concerns the phrase *filioque*, "from the Son", which found its way into the Western creeds after the Constantinopolitan creed and has been consistently rejected by the Eastern churches. The issue bears, like Arianism, on the relative status of God the Father and the Son: the Western church, concerned for their equality of status, has come to hold that the Holy Spirit emanates equally "from the Father *and from the Son*" whilst the Orthodox churches hold that the phrase both is an interpolation and makes little theological sense (cf. Ware, 1964, pp. 58–60). In all these issues belief as doctrine has become embedded in the authority-structure of the church.

The conciliar creeds did not replace the baptismal creeds, nor were they intended to do so. The so-called "Athanasian" creed (composed in Latin and unrecognized as a statement of belief in the East) is really a hymn that uses the credal form (and, uniquely, embodies the anathemas also) to make an act of worship. The Apostles' creed entered the liturgical tradition by a later and yet different route; I return to it below. Such developments in the credal form were paralleled by an ever-extending use of creeds in the liturgy. Always important in baptism, creeds were later adopted for general use in the eucharist, first in the East (from at least the sixth century) and later in the West (formally, from the early eleventh century; Jungmann, 1959, pp. 295–8). The Orthodox, Roman, Anglican and (in lesser measure) Nonconformist churches all continue to give central place to the singing or saying of the creed in their services. The point to make here is that this performance of the creeds is as complex, symbolic and condensed an act of ritual as any

other liturgical act and is consequently as much subject to the categories developed, for example, by Turner (1967) for the analysis of ritual symbolism. (On the variable meaning of the creed for different persons saying it see the chapter on the creeds in Doctrine Commission of the Church of England, 1976.)

[. . .]

There is no simple formula to describe what happened at the Reformation; the processes that are distinguished by that term were already in train before the period usually covered by it and they certainly continued beyond it. In describing the nature and effects of the Reformation it becomes necessary to resort to the term "faith" which, although by no means new, acquired an extra dimension of significance that gave it (like the *pisteuo* word-group before it) a quasi-technical use. Deriving from the Latin *fides* (itself cognate with the Greek *pistis*, which it normally translated in the Bible), "faith" carries by semantic origin very much the same range of meanings as did originally "belief"/*pistis*, that is, trust or confidence; and, as alternative translations of the Bible show, the two words in English often serve as synonyms, with "faith" becoming religiously the more specialized (see OED under "Belief"); the fact that "faith" has no verbal form has also produced the asymmetrical situation in which the verb "to believe" is often matched with the noun "faith". This linguistic variation is more confusing however than the broad semantic situation would seem to warrant. Augustine in his treatise on the creed, *De Fide et Symbolo*, uses the term faith/*fides* precisely in the sense of orthodox belief as it is expressed in the creeds, "the Catholic faith" as the received teaching of the church. We may contrast this sense with the meaning the word more readily has in many Protestant writings, where what is at issue is less the substance of belief (although that is not unimportant) than how such belief (often expressed as the Gospel or the Word) has been subjectively appropriated. The difference between "faith" in the two senses – "the Catholic faith" and a person's own "faith" – is thus less a matter of the difference between church authority and individual reason (which anyway much exercised medieval theologians) than of the difference between belief as declaration and belief as commitment. This extra dimension to the notion of belief had organizational implications but its immediate thrust was psychological.

Luther's role in helping to effect this shift was crucial but complex. Some would see Luther as simply re-expressing the personal commitment already implicit in the Pauline explication of belief (and Paul's Epistles were of vital importance in Luther's own spiritual biography); others would see his account of belief as an appeal ultimately to unreason, a faith that is given by God's grace, no-one can know how. But however one interprets Luther's life and work, a characteristic theme of both is his stress on the inward totality of Christian belief, the faith of the believer. Thus his so-momentous reaction to the spurious hawking of indulgences (the very first of the Ninety-Five Theses sets the tone by insisting that when "Jesus Christ said 'Repent . . .', he meant that the whole life of believers should be one of penitence"); thus his contrast between the (external) Theology of Glory (that of the Church to date) and the (inwardly experienced) Theology of the Cross (Luther's own preferred theology); thus his distinction between law, a matter of outward performance, and the Gospel, Word or Grace, that works inwardly (the point is made by one of the Heidelberg theses: "The law says 'Do this' and it is never done. Grace says 'Believe this' and everything is done"); and thus, not least, the governing principle of justification by faith, which while proffering intellectually an objective view of God's grace in fact locates faith in the intensity and totality of a person's experience of it. (On these various points see Rupp, 1975; von Loewenich, 1976; Rupp and Drewery, 1970.) Luther stands in history not only as a thinker and writer but also as a paradigm of the person who achieves a fully realized belief only after an intense inward struggle, who possesses belief by being possessed by it: such is the "faith" that comes from without but signifies a subjective transition from disorganized doubt to clarity, conviction and a certain kind of personal freedom.

Two recent representations of Luther that have something of this paradigmatic aura

provide a useful bridge to the present. Erikson's psychoanalytic study (1959) grants all of Luther's theological importance (e.g. p. 250) but focuses especially on the concern Luther showed in his own biographical struggle with the intensity and expressiveness of the experience of belief. The title of the key chapter in the book, "The meaning of 'meaning it'", states the issue succinctly: as Erikson writes, "To Luther, the preaching and the praying man, the measure in depth of the perceived presence of the Word was the reaction with a total affect which leaves no doubt that one 'means it'" (1959, p. 203). But, Erikson goes on to point out, what Luther had to fight to secure, comes to us as the easy convention of our age:

> [Luther's] formulations, once revolutionary, are the commonplaces of today's pulpits. They are the bases of that most inflated of all oratorical currency, credal protestations in church and lecture hall, in political propaganda and oral advertisement: the protestation, made to order of the occasion, that truth is only that which one means with one's whole being, and lives every moment. We, the heirs of Protestantism, have made convention and pretence out of the very sound of meaning it. . . . (ibid.)

John Osborne's play (1961), which is based on Erikson's study, points a different but related message. If – to paraphrase Erikson – we are all sincere believers now, Osborne's *Luther* hints that we should beware of being too convinced, too secure in our righteous convictions. The point is made most clearly in the two final scenes, most notably when "Martin" admits to his longstanding friend and advisor (Staupitz) that his delay under interrogation at the Diet of Worms (when his career and even his life were in jeopardy and he is said by tradition to have declared "Here I stand. I can do no other") was in fact the result of his uncertainty, of his doubt. Left alone on the stage, he confesses "Oh Lord, I believe. I do believe. Only help my unbelief."

In our age we seem then to believe in belief, but with not too exclusive a conviction. This note of diffuse belief is struck quite remarkably by two books that are in their separate ways both revealing and authoritative. *The Culture of Unbelief* publishes "studies and proceedings from the First International Symposium on Belief held in Rome, March 22–27, 1969" under the sponsorship, amongst others, of the Vatican Secretariat for Non-believers, which was set up following Vatican II. The Symposium gathered a highly distinguished group of social scientists, mainly sociologists, specializing in the study of religion, without regard to their personal religious position, together with and including a number of notable churchmen. It was not, however, the intention of the Symposium to produce "dialogue" – we are told that "in a number of cases the organizers would have been hard put to identify a participant as either a 'believer' or a 'non-believer'" – but rather that of "study in preparation for dialogue" (Caporale and Grumelli, 1971, p. ix). One must break off at this point to comment on the crucial word "unbelief". The idea itself is as old as its positive counterpart "belief": *apistia* means lack of trust, non-confidence in its general sense and specifically lack of trust in God or non-belief in Christ in a religious context. Thus the remark of Osborne's Luther quoted above recalls the outburst of the father of the convulsed boy in Mark 9:24, "Immediately the father of the child cried out and said, 'I believe; help my unbelief!'" There is then nothing new, or especially contemporary, in the idea of unbelief, although it has no doubt a contemporary twist. Pope Paul in his address to the Symposium certainly knew what he meant – the rejection of the Christian religion (see p. 302, op. cit.). Yet one of the features of the Symposium is the very indeterminate value that the terms "belief" and "unbelief" come to acquire in it. Berger in his foreword refers to this "ambiguity in the definition of the problem" and notes the "rather remarkable" fact that "the theoretical position papers, each in its own way, tend to deny the very existence of the phenomenon under scrutiny [i.e. unbelief]" (ibid., p. xiii). The remark covers papers by both Luckmann and Parsons but is nowhere so pertinent as in its reference to Bellah's paper, "The historical background of unbelief". Starting with an account of the Greek concept, the paper sets "belief" in an institu-

tional, church context and associates it with "an effort to maintain authority" on the part of the church, "part of a whole hierarchical way of thinking about social control" (p. 44). Belief (which in Bellah's discussion has become very rapidly intellectualized, a matter of doctrine and dogma) is thus distinguished from religion, the former tied to an institutional (church) structure, the latter more diffusely present in shared values. Against then this narrowly defined, historical view of "belief" Bellah contrasts what he sees as an "emergent religion of humanity" (p. 50). Nevertheless, by the end of the paper he is so carried away in his enthusiasm for the latter that all distinctions have disappeared and Christians and non-Christians, belief and religion, the Church and humanity are all rolling together in a single glorious banner:

> The modern world is as alive with religious possibility as any epoch in human history. It is no longer possible to divide mankind into believers and non-believers. All believe something and the lukewarm and those of little faith are to be found inside as well as outside the churches. . . . Christians, along with other men, are called to build the boundaryless community, the body of man identified with the body of Christ, although all men are free to symbolize it in their own way. (p. 52)

There *can* be no unbelief in such a world and the word "believe" has become so generalized as to have lost most of its content. Like Forster's "What I believe", it is a muffled (but not so muted) cry.

Christian Believing (1976), as a book, is an altogether less grandiose affair. It is the report of the Doctrine Commission of the Church of England, who were asked by the Archbishop of Canterbury to examine "the nature of the Christian faith and its expression in holy scripture and creeds". The very striking thing about the report is its lack of dogmatism, tolerance of even opposed views, concern to respect both tradition and the right to criticize and re-evaluate it. The emphasis once again is on existential belief, *believing* as the adventure of faith rather than *belief* as a body of doctrine. The most singular feature of the report is, however, the fact that over half of it consists of eight individual essays by members of the Commission, each in effect outlining his personal view of the nature of the Christian faith. The implication throughout is that each "believer" must find his own way, respecting traditional truths but respecting also other people's right to hold different views from his own. Belief as doctrine has *almost* become the honest opinion of anyone who declares himself to be a Christian.

There is both continuity and change in the notion of belief that I have sketched above at four phases of its history: trust become conviction about an event (the "Christ-event" of history); become an initiatory declaration; become a corporately declared orthodoxy; become an inwardly organizing experience; become values common to all men (even though different). Yet throughout the concept remains central to Christianity, which is clear from the way it reflects so much of the Church's organizational and intellectual history. Moreover much of the word's meaning in non-Christian use can only be drawn from the particular significance that it has acquired in Christianity – else why attach any importance at all to having or not having beliefs? In the remainder of this chapter I write Belief with a capital letter to signify this multilayered, complex yet condensed range of use and meaning that the concept has acquired in this its long career in Christianity.

Negative demonstrations are always difficult and usually lengthy and for this reason I argue the comparative case only summarily. I find little evidence that there is anything equivalent to Christian Belief in other world religions although there are other comparable organizing or nodal concepts. The contrast is greatest with Judaism (as one would expect, historically and sociologically), the similarities (as one would also expect) closest with Islam. The teaching of the law, the *Torah*, stands at the centre of Judaism in a way functionally comparable – but with different practical implications – to Belief in Christianity; and there are comparable differences in the identity-markers of the two religions. With Islam the parallel is closer: the first of the "five pillars" of Islam – witness to God and his prophet – comes close

to being a credo; there is some concern for orthodoxy of belief and there are even formal creeds (although the ordinary Muslim is unlikely to know them). Islam – submission to the one God – can be identified with having belief, *iman*; a Muslim is also a believer, *mu'min*. Yet, as these words' shared root with the Hebrew *'mn* testifies, their reference is essentially to the quality of a relationship, that of keeping faith, having trust. Correspondingly, it is less the content of belief that has become elaborated in Islam than the duties of relationship: the practice of ritual, the following of Islamic custom, the observance of Islamic law.

Gombrich, writing about Buddhism, struggles awkwardly for two pages to find an equivalent to the verb "to believe" or "to believe in" before moving directly to the term ("best not translated at all") *dharma* (1971, p. 60). For Hinduism the parallels are even more indirect and fragmented.

The absence of any self-conscious credal or doctrinal component forms a commonplace observation of most, if not all, traditional or community religions. Should one attempt to distinguish for them, as one can perhaps for other world religions, any organizing concept, comparable to that of Belief in Christianity? I can answer only for the two cultures I know at first-hand, and in both cases I find the question relevant and revealing. For Banyang the idea of truth (*tetup*) has a central significance, in part as an attribute of God but more particularly as a touchstone in people's relationships, where the possibility of duplicity is obsessively elaborated by Banyang witchcraft beliefs. On a less cognitive level, the Kuria category of *inyangi*, which I am forced to translate summarily as "ritual", although it means something less, and more, serves also as touchstone ordering their own relationships (kin and generational) so as to accord with what Kuria see as the natural principles of growth. Both concepts have content but also operate functionally in the organization and determination of relationships.

[. . .]

Clearly it is not possible, nor even desirable, to limit the word "belief" to its specifically

Christian use. Yet at the same time we should be clear that it has a Christian use and that this use must affect its connotations in contexts other than Christian. It is surely plain naive to pluck the word from the linguistic planisphere (the OED Guide to the Galaxy conveniently at hand) and to use it then as though it were a given, something that just happened to be around, which had incidentally been made some use of by Christians. Let me be clear: in ordinary speech there are many uses of the word "believe" that are straightforward and unambiguous. On the whole these have a relatively weak set of connotations, implying usually (of oneself) presupposition or expectation, or (of others) assumption. There are advantages, as Needham indicates, in avoiding "believe" altogether, but the word is current English and in this its weak sense it is not likely to be misunderstood. It is when the word is given a strong sense that it may well mislead: for example, when it forms part of a definition or categorization or is used in posing a problem. Here I would argue that it is almost impossible not to draw on connotations from its Christian use. Moreover, these connotations, contextually transposed, create false assumptions that then lead to fallacies. I speak of these contextually transposed assumptions as "shadow fallacies" and for the non-Christian use of the term "belief" identify four:

(1)   That belief is central to all religions in the same way as it is to Christianity. That this is a fallacy is the major argument of my paper and Sections I and II of the paper are concerned with its demonstration. It is, however, very easy for a Western writer to slip from talking about religion to talking about Christianity, and back again, without clear distinction. For example, Needham in considering spiritual commitment as a possible criterion of religious belief (1972, p. 86–9) appears to do just this: he moves from a specifically Christian view of belief as commitment to Christ (ibid., p. 86), then argues that other people can be similarly "committed" to particular enterprises or persons (pp. 87–8) and then concludes that there is no discriminable difference between religious and non-religious commitment (ibid.,

p. 88). But it is not commitment *per se* that identifies Christianity but commitment to Christ: Christianity cannot be treated as a type-case of religious commitment; it is a specific case of a particular commitment to a single historical person. The same fallacy can be detected I think in a somewhat different way in Martin Southwold's thoughtful paper on "Religious belief". Much of Southwold's critical commentary is highly relevant to any discussion of religion but why focus the discussion on the nature of belief? And does not the framing of the question thus itself determine the kind of answer that will be obtained? Namely, that "basic religious tenets are 1) empirically indeterminate 2) axiomatic 3) symbolic, and 4) collective" (1979, p. 633). Christian Belief is historically and conceptually more precise in its references than this, but take belief (the shadow idea) to apply to other religions (as one might take Judaic *torah* or a shadow extension of it) and one may well find the correspondence to be indeterminate and indirect (symbolic).

(2)   That the belief of a person or a people forms the ground of his or their behaviour and can be cited therefore as a sufficient explanation for it. For an example of this fallacy I would draw on my own teaching experience. Along no doubt with many others, I regularly set my first-year students in social anthropology an essay on Zande witchcraft usually in the first few weeks of the course. One topic I commonly use runs: since Zande oracles must often give false answers, why then do Azande continue to believe in witchcraft? and, all being well, the essay that is returned duly rehearses Evans-Pritchard's situational analysis of Zande reasoning. But, not infrequently, all is not well and my (I think now misguided) weak use of "believe" is turned into a strong use: the evidence in the book for individual Zande scepticism is ignored, as is much else, to present Azande with such unalterable firmness of conviction as would make a Calvinist jealous. Nor does the matter stop there, for make belief fundamental to the behaviour of a person or a people and the issue in relation to others is then relativized. That is what Azande believe: finish: there can be no further discussion of the substance of their belief in terms

that do not bracket it off as something to do with *them* (rather than their experience of the world) and thus hinder its discussion in comparative terms (i.e. what we too experience of the world). The insidiousness of this process of relativization must be emphasized. "We all have our beliefs: all peoples have their beliefs." It is a way of setting people into cultural compartments.

(3)   That belief is fundamentally an interior state, a psychological condition. The fallacy once again is to transpose what some have emphasized as the inwardness of Christian belief (faith) to the non-Christian context and use of the word. I would argue that Needham does just this, to the enormous detriment of his discussion, in adopting Evans-Pritchard's assertion concerning Nuer religion and generalizing it to all belief. Yet as Alan Ryan points out (1973), over-insistence on the privacy of what goes on in people's minds distracts from the primary task of construing the sense or reality of what it is they believe, and it is one of the skills of anthropology to do precisely this by contextual explication. Is the meaning of words interior to the words? That belief was a psychological state for Luther does not imply that it must be a psychological state for everyone, or even that it was *only* that for Luther. It does not make much sense to call the belief subscribed to by the Council of Nicaea a psychological state. Southwold's criticism of Leach on the "inner psychological" aspect of belief is here much to the point (1979, p. 631). We should recall that the notion of "belief" gains much of its significance in Christianity from the first person use of the verb: I believe. . . . But anthropologists necessarily use the verb in the third person: Azande believe. . . . To assume that *our* presentation of their belief carries the same force as though *they* said "We believe . . ." is to misunderstand the semantic conjugation of the verb and to transpose Christian assumptions unwarrantably (cf. Southwold, 1979, p. 630; Smith, 1977, p. 52 et seq.).

(4)   That the determination of belief is more important than the determination of the status of what it is that is the object of the belief. In Christianity to be a believer is to acknowledge an allegiance and to declare an identity: the person does not always have to be clear about the full content of his belief. The same circumstance transposed to non-Christian religions makes much less sense. To say that a people "believe" in this, that or other abstraction (witchcraft, God, spirits of the ancestors, humanism) tends to bracket off ideas that they hold about the world from the world itself, treating their "beliefs" as peculiar to them, a badge of their distinctiveness, and all knowledge of the world our privileged monopoly. The shadow cast by the Christian respect-for-belief obscures what really it is that people see or think they see. If we are to converse with each other (and I assume that social anthropology is a kind of conversation between cultures) we need fewer such shadows, cast by the contextual transposition of inappropriate categories, and a clearer, steadier gaze on to the world we share. Or, at least, a clearer admission as to what we think, or assume or presuppose, or understand about the world we share.

REFERENCES

Bultmann, R. and Weiser, A., 1961: *Faith*. Bible Key Words from G. Kittel's *Theologisches Wörterbuch zum Neuen Testament*. London (Adam and Charles Black).

Caporale, R. and Grumelli, A. (eds.) 1971: *The Culture of Unbelief*. Berkeley (University of California Press).

Chadwick, H., 1967: *The Early Church*. The Pelican History of the Church Vol. 1. Harmondsworth (Penguin Books).

Doctrine Commission of the Church of England, 1976: *Christian Believing*. London (SPCK).

Erikson, E. H., 1959: *Young Man Luther*. London (Faber and Faber).

Evans-Pritchard, E. E., 1937: *Witchcraft, Oracles and Magic among the Azande*. Oxford (Clarendon).

Forster, E. M., 1939: *What I Believe*. Hogarth Sixpenny Pamphlets 1. London (Hogarth Press).

Gombrich, R. F., 1971: *Precept and Practice*. Oxford (Clarendon).

Hatch, W. H. P., 1917: *The Pauline Idea of Faith*. Harvard Theological Studies Vol. 2. Cambridge, Mass. (Harvard University Press).

Jungmann, J. A., 1959: *The Mass of the Roman Rite*. Trans. from the German by F. A. Brunner and C. K. Riepe. London (Burns and Oates).

Kelly, J. N. D., 1972: *Early Christian Creeds*. London (Longman). (3rd edition).

Küng, H., 1968: *The Church*. Translated from the German by R. and R. Ockenden. London (Burns and Oates).

Lampe, G. W. H., 1976: The origins of the creeds. In *Christian Believing*, Doctrine Commission of the Church of England. London (SPCK).

Loewenich, W. von., 1976: *Luther's Theology of the Cross*. Belfast (Christian Journals Ltd).

Michel, O., 1975: Faith, Persuade, Belief, Unbelief. In *The New International Dictionary of New Testament Theology*, ed. C. Brown. Exeter (Paternoster Press).

Moule, C. F. D., unpublished: Belief and trust in the New Testament vocabulary. Paper given to the Cambridge "D" Society, manuscript.

Needham, R., 1972: *Belief, Language and Experience*. Oxford (Blackwell).

Osborne, J., 1961: *Luther*. London (Faber and Faber).

Rupp, E. G., 1975: Luther and the German Reformation to 1529. In *The Reformation* (G. R. Elton, ed.). The New Cambridge Modern History Vol. 2. Cambridge (Cambridge University Press).

Rupp, E. G. and Drewery, B., 1970: *Martin Luther*. Documents of Modern History series. London (Edward Arnold).

Ryan, A., 1973: By-ways of belief. Review of Needham (1972). *New Society*, 11th January.

Smith, W. C., 1978 (1962): *The Meaning and End of Religion*. London (SPCK).

——, 1977: *Belief and History*. Charlottesville (University Press Virginia).

——, 1979: *Faith and Belief*. Princeton, N. J. (Princeton University Press).

Southwold, M., 1979: Religious belief. *Man* 14(4) December.

Turner, V., 1967: *The Forest of Symbols*. Ithaca (Cornell University Press).

Ware, T., 1964: *The Orthodox Church*. Harmondsworth (Penguin).

9

The Construction of Religion as an Anthropological Category

Talal Asad

Talal Asad is an anthropologist trained in the United Kingdom and currently distinguished professor at the graduate center of the City University of New York. Asad's provocative account, like that of Ruel, grounds its critique of anthropological predecessors in its account of the history of Christianity, but here the critique is even stronger, challenging not only the category of belief but of religion itself. Asad rejects essentialist definitions of religion, arguing that the very idea of such a definition "is itself the historical product of discursive processes," i.e., within the cultural location of secular modernity. Thus his argument is not merely about the use of language but advocates an entirely different conceptual and methodological framework from that developed in the essay by Geertz. Asad's account is indicative of a shift away from a symbolic anthropology toward a poststructuralist one that is more centrally concerned with power and discipline and with the way that religious subjects (i.e., practitioners) are formed. Indeed, his essay forms one of the major statements from within the anthropology of religion (there have been many critiques from materialist anthropologists outside the subfield) to offer an alternative to the symbolic approach. The latter, broadly defined, is characteristic not only of Geertz but of many of the authors who follow in this anthology.

Asad's account also demonstrates the effects a change in perspective can bring. He begins with a Muslim assumption that religion and power cannot be separated. In addition, he draws explicitly on Vygotsky and implicitly on Foucault and Bourdieu in this bracing account. But even more interestingly, the argument is worked out in part through Asad's own historical anthropological work on medieval European Christianity. Unfortunately, for reasons

From "Anthropological Conceptions of Religion: Reflections on Geertz," in *Man*, New Series, Vol. 18, No. 2 (June, 1983), pp. 237–59.

of space, I have had to exclude many of Asad's learned footnotes that help to bring this home. The essay reprinted here is followed in his *Genealogies of Religion* (Asad 1993) by "Toward a Genealogy of the Concept of Ritual," which pursues the medieval angle more directly. The book also contains a number of important essays on Islam and the contemporary politics of religion. More recently Asad (2003) has published a series of trenchant essays about secularism as an integral part of modernity and its relation to the politics of Islam both in the Middle East and in Europe. Recent discussion of his work can be found in Hirschkind and Scott (2006).

In much nineteenth-century evolutionary thought, religion was considered to be an early human condition from which modern law, science, and politics emerged and became detached.[1] In this [twentieth] century most anthropologists have abandoned Victorian evolutionary ideas, and many have challenged the rationalist notion that religion is simply a primitive and therefore outmoded form of the institutions we now encounter in truer form (law, politics, science) in modern life. For these twentieth-century anthropologists, religion is not an archaic mode of scientific thinking, nor of any other secular endeavor we value today; it is, on the contrary, a distinctive space of human practice and belief which cannot be reduced to any other. From this it seems to follow that the essence of religion is not to be confused with, say, the essence of politics, although in many societies the two may overlap and be intertwined.

In a characteristically subtle passage, Louis Dumont has told us that medieval Christendom was one such composite society:

I shall take it for granted that a change in relations entails a change in whatever is related. If throughout our history religion has developed (to a large extent, with some other influences at play) a revolution in social values and has given birth by scissiparity, as it were, to an autonomous world of political institutions and speculations, then surely religion itself will have changed in the process. Of some important and visible changes we are all aware, but, I submit, we are not aware of the change in the very nature of religion as lived by any given individual, say a Catholic. Everyone knows that religion was formerly a matter of the group and has become a matter of the individual (in principle, and in practice at least in many environments and situations). But if we go on to assert that this change is correlated with the birth of the modern State, the proposition is not such a commonplace as the previous one. Let us go a little further: medieval-religion was a great cloak – I am thinking of the Mantle of Our Lady of Mercy. Once it became an individual affair, it lost its all-embracing capacity and became one among other apparently equal considerations, of which the political was the first born. Each individual may, of course, and perhaps even will, recognize religion (or philosophy), as the same all-embracing consideration as it used to be *socially*. Yet on the level of social consensus or ideology, the same person will switch to a different configuration of values in which autonomous values (religious, political, etc.) are seemingly juxtaposed, much as individuals are juxtaposed in society. (1971, 32; emphasis in original)

According to this view, medieval religion, pervading or encompassing other categories, is nevertheless *analytically* identifiable. It is this fact that makes it possible to say that religion has the same essence today as it had in the Middle Ages, although its social extension and function were different in the two epochs. Yet the insistence that religion has an autonomous essence – not to be confused with the essence of science, or of politics, or of common sense – invites us to define religion (like any essence) as a transhistorical and transcultural phenomenon. It may be a happy accident that this effort of defining religion converges with the liberal demand in our time that it be kept quite separate from politics, law, and science – spaces in which varieties of power and reason articulate our distinctively modern life. This definition is at once part of a strategy (for secular liberals) of the confinement, and (for liberal Christians) of the defense of religion.

Yet this separation of religion from power is a modern Western norm, the product of a unique post-Reformation history. The attempt to understand Muslim traditions by insisting that in them religion and politics (two essences modern society tries to keep conceptually and practically apart) are coupled must, in my view, lead to failure. At its most dubious, such attempts encourage us to take up an a priori position in which religious discourse in the political arena is seen as a disguise for political power.

In what follows I want to examine the ways in which the theoretical search for an essence of religion invites us to separate it conceptually from the domain of power. I shall do this by exploring a universalist definition of religion offered by an eminent anthropologist: Clifford Geertz's "Religion as a Cultural System" [reprinted in his widely acclaimed *The Interpretation of Cultures* (1973)]. I stress that this is not primarily a critical review of Geertz's ideas on religion – if that had been my aim I would have addressed myself to the entire corpus of his writings on religion in Indonesia and Morocco. My intention in this chapter is to try to identify some of the historical shifts that have produced our concept of religion as the concept of a transhistorical essence – and Geertz's article is merely my starting point.

It is part of my basic argument that socially identifiable forms, preconditions, and effects of what was regarded as religion in the medieval Christian epoch were quite different from those so considered in modern society. I want to get at this well-known fact while trying to avoid a simple nominalism. What we call religious power was differently distributed and had a different thrust. There were different ways in which it created and worked through legal institutions, different selves that it shaped and responded to, and different categories of knowledge which it authorized and made available. Nevertheless, what the anthropologist is confronted with, as a consequence, is not merely an arbitrary collection of elements and processes that we happen to call "religion." For the entire phenomenon is to be seen in large measure in the context of Christian attempts to achieve a coherence in doctrines and practices, rules and regulations, even if that was a state never fully attained. My argument is that there cannot be a universal definition of religion, not only because its constituent elements and relationships are historically specific, but because that definition is itself the historical product of discursive processes.

A universal (i.e., anthropological) definition is, however, precisely what Geertz aims at: A *religion*, he proposes, is "(1) a system of symbols which act to (2) establish powerful, pervasive, and long-lasting moods and motivations in men by (3) formulating conceptions of a general order of existence and (4) clothing these conceptions with such an aura of factuality that (5) the moods and motivations seem uniquely realistic" (90). In what follows I shall examine this definition, not only in order to test its interlinked assertions, but also to flesh out the counterclaim that a transhistorical definition of religion is not viable.

The Concept of Symbol as a Clue to the Essence of Religion

Geertz sees his first task as the definition of symbol: "any object, act, event, quality, or relation which serves as a vehicle for a conception – the conception is the symbol's 'meaning'" (91). But this simple, clear statement – in which *symbol* (any object, etc.) is differentiated from but linked to *conception* (its meaning) – is later supplemented by others not entirely consistent with it, for it turns out that the symbol is not an object that serves as a vehicle for a conception, *it is itself the conception*. Thus, in the statement "The number 6, written, imagined, laid out as a row of stones, or even punched into the program tapes of a computer, is a symbol" (91), what constitutes all these diverse representations as versions of the same symbol ("the number 6") is of course *a conception.* Furthermore, Geertz sometimes seems to suggest that even as a conception a symbol has an intrinsic connection with empirical events from which it is merely "theoretically" separable: "the symbolic dimension of social events is, like the psychological, itself theoretically abstractable from these events as empirical totalities" (91). At other times, however, he stresses the importance of keeping symbols and empirical objects quite separate: "there is something to be said for not confusing our traffic with symbols with our traffic with objects or human beings, for these latter are not in themselves symbols, however often they may function as such" (92). Thus, "symbol" is sometimes an aspect of reality, sometimes of its representation.[2]

These divergencies are symptoms of the fact that cognitive questions are mixed up in this account with communicative ones, and this makes it difficult to inquire into the ways in which discourse and understanding are connected in social practice. To begin with we might say, as a number of writers have done, that a symbol is not an object or event that serves to carry a meaning but a set of relationships between objects or events uniquely brought together as complexes or as concepts,[3] having at once an intellectual, instrumental, and emotional significance. If we define symbol along these lines,[4] a number of questions can be raised about the conditions that explain how such complexes and concepts come to be formed, and in particular how their formation is related to varieties of practice. Half a century ago, Vygotsky was able to show how the development of children's intellect is dependent on the internalization of social speech. This means that the formation of what we have here called "symbols" (complexes, concepts) is conditioned by the social relations in which the growing child is involved – by the social activities that he or she is permitted or encouraged or obliged to undertake – in which other symbols (speech and significant movements) are crucial. The conditions (discursive and nondiscursive) that explain how symbols come to be constructed, and how some of them are established as natural or authoritative as opposed to others, then become an important object of anthropological inquiry. It must be stressed that this is not a matter of

urging the study of the origin and function of symbols in addition to their meaning – such a distinction is not relevant here. What is being argued is that the authoritative status of representations/discourses is dependent on the appropriate production of other representations/discourses; the two are intrinsically and not just temporally connected.

Systems of symbols, says Geertz, are also *culture patterns*, and they constitute "extrinsic sources of information" (92). Extrinsic, because "they lie outside the boundaries of the individual organism as such in that inter-subjective world of common understandings into which all human individuals are born" (92). And sources of information in the sense that "they provide a blueprint or template in terms of which processes external to themselves can be given a definite form" (92). Thus, culture patterns, we are told, may be thought of as "models *for* reality" as well as "models *of* reality."[5]

This part of the discussion does open up possibilities by speaking of modeling: that is, it allows for the possibility of conceptualizing discourses in the process of elaboration, modification, testing, and so forth. Unfortunately, Geertz quickly regresses to his earlier position: "culture patterns have an intrinsic double aspect," he writes; "they give meaning, that is objective conceptual form, to social and psychological reality both by shaping themselves to it and by shaping it to themselves" (1973, 93). This alleged dialectical tendency toward isomorphism, incidentally, makes it difficult to understand how social change can ever occur. The basic problem, however, is not with the idea of mirror images as such but with the assumption that there are two separate levels – the cultural, on the one side (consisting of symbols) and the social and psychological, on the other – which interact. This resort to Parsonian theory creates a logical space for defining the essence of religion. By adopting it, Geertz moves away from a notion of symbols that are intrinsic to signifying and organizing practices, and back to a notion of symbols as meaning-carrying objects external to social conditions and states of the self ("social and psychological reality").

This is not to say that Geertz doesn't think of symbols as "doing" something. In a way that recalls older anthropological approaches to ritual,[6] he states that religious symbols act "by inducing in the worshipper a certain distinctive set of dispositions (tendencies, capacities, propensities, skills, habits, liabilities, proneness) which lend a chronic character to the flow of his activity and the quality of his experience" (95). And here again, symbols are set apart from mental states. But how plausible are these propositions? Can we, for example, predict the "distinctive" set of dispositions for a Christian worshiper in modern, industrial society? Alternatively, can we say of someone with a "distinctive" set of dispositions that he is or is not a Christian? The answer to both questions must surely be no. The reason, of course, is that it is not simply worship but social, political, and economic institutions in general, within which individual biographies are lived out, that lend a stable character to the flow of a Christian's activity and to the quality of her experience.

Religious symbols, Geertz elaborates, produce two kinds of dispositions, *moods* and *motivations*: "motivations are 'made meaningful' with reference to the ends towards which they are conceived to conduce, whereas moods are 'made meaningful' with reference to the conditions from which they are conceived to spring" (97). Now, a Christian might say that this is not their essence, because religious symbols, even when failing to produce moods and motivations, are still religious (i.e., true) symbols – that religious symbols possess a truth independent of their effectiveness. Yet surely even a committed Christian cannot be unconcerned at the existence of truthful symbols that appear to be largely powerless in modern society. He will rightly want to ask: What are the conditions in which religious symbols can actually produce religious dispositions? Or, as a nonbeliver would put it: How does (religious) power create (religious) truth?

The relation between power and truth is an ancient theme, and no one has dealt with it more impressively in Christian thought than St. Augustine. Augustine developed his views on the creative religious function of power after his experience with the Donatist heresy, insisting that coercion was a condition for the realization of truth, and discipline essential to its maintenance.

For a Donatist, Augustine's attitude to coercion was a blatant denial of Christian teaching: God had made men free to choose good or evil; a policy which forced this choice was plainly irreligious. The Donatist writers quoted the same passages from the Bible in favour of free will, as Pelagius would later quote. In his reply, Augustine already gave them the same answer as he would give to the Pelagians: the final, individual act of choice must be spontaneous; but this act of choice could be prepared by a long process, which men did not necessarily choose for themselves, but which was often imposed on them, against their will, by God. This was a corrective process of "teaching," *eruditio*, and warning, *admonitio*, which might even include fear, constraint, and external inconveniences: "Let constraint be found outside; it is inside that the will is born."

Augustine had become convinced that men needed such firm handling. He summed up his attitude in one word: *disciplina*. He thought of this *disciplina*, not as many of his more traditional Roman contemporaries did, as the static preservation of a "Roman way of life." For him it was an essentially active process of corrective punishment, "a softening-up process," a "teaching by inconveniences" – *a per molestias eruditio*. In the Old Testament, God had taught his wayward Chosen People through just such a process of *disciplina*, checking and punishing their evil tendencies by a whole series of divinely-ordained disasters. The persecution of the Donatists was another "controlled catastrophe" imposed by God, mediated, on this occasion, by the laws of the Christian Emperors. . . .

Augustine's view of the Fall of mankind determined his attitude to society. Fallen men had come to need restraint. Even man's greatest achievements had been made possible only by a "straight-jacket" of unremitting harshness. Augustine was a great intellect, with a healthy respect for the achievements of human reason. Yet he was obsessed by the difficulties of thought, and by the long, coercive processes, reaching back into the horrors of his own schooldays, that had made this intellectual activity possible; so "ready to lie down" was the fallen human mind. He said he would rather die than become a child again. Nonetheless, the terrors of that time had been strictly necessary; for they were part of the awesome discipline of God, "from the school-masters' canes to the agonies of the martyrs," by which human beings were recalled, by suffering, from their own disastrous inclinations. (Brown 1967, 236–8)

Isn't Geertz's formula too simple to accommodate the force of this religious symbolism? Note that here it is not mere symbols that implant true Christian dispositions, but power – ranging all the way from laws (imperial and ecclesiastical) and other sanctions (hellfire, death, salvation, good repute, peace) to the disciplinary activities of social institutions (family, school, city, church) and of human bodies (fasting, prayer, obedience, penance). Augustine was quite clear that power, the effect of an entire network of motivated practices, assumes a religious form because of the end to which it is directed, for human events are the instruments of God. It was not the mind that moved spontaneously to religious truth, but power that created the conditions for experiencing that truth. Particular discourses and practices were to be systematically excluded, forbidden, denounced – made as much as possible unthinkable; others were to be included, allowed, praised, and drawn into the narrative of sacred truth. The configurations of power in this sense have, of course, varied profoundly in Christendom from one epoch to another – from Augustine's time, through the Middle Ages, to the industrial capitalist West of today. The patterns of religious moods and motivations, the possibilities for religious knowledge and truth, have all varied with them and been conditioned by them. Even Augustine held that although religious truth was eternal, the means for securing human access to it were not.

From Reading Symbols to Analyzing Practices

One consequence of assuming a symbolic system separate from practices is that important distinctions are sometimes obscured, or even explicitly denied. "That the symbols or symbol systems which induce and define dispositions we set off as religious and those

which place these dispositions in a cosmic framework are the same symbols ought to occasion no surprise" (Geertz, 98). But it does surprise! Let us grant that religious dispositions are crucially dependent on certain religious symbols, that such symbols operate in a way integral to religious motivation and religious mood. Even so, the symbolic process by which the concepts of religious motivation and mood are placed within "a cosmic framework" is surely quite a different operation, and therefore the signs involved are quite different. Put another way, theological discourse is not identical with either moral attitudes or liturgical discourses – of which, among other things, theology speaks. Thoughtful Christians will concede that, although theology has an essential function, theological discourse does not necessarily induce religious dispositions and that, conversely, having religious dispositions does not necessarily depend on a clear-cut conception of the cosmic framework on the part of a religious actor. Discourse involved in practice is not the same as that involved in speaking about practice. It is a modern idea that a practitioner cannot know how to live religiously without being able to articulate that knowledge.

Geertz's reason for merging the two kinds of discursive process seems to spring from a wish to distinguish in general between religious and secular dispositions. The statement quoted above is elaborated as follows:

For what else do we mean by saying that a particular mood of awe is religious and not secular, except that it springs from entertaining a conception of all-pervading vitality like mana and not from a visit to the Grand Canyon? Or that a particular case of asceticism is an example of a religious motivation except that it is directed toward the achievement of an unconditioned end like nirvana and not a conditioned one like weight-reduction? If sacred symbols did not at one and the same time induce dispositions in human beings and formulate . . . general ideas of order, then the empirical differentia of religious activity or religious experience would not exist. (98)

The argument that a particular disposition is religious partly because it occupies a conceptual place within a cosmic framework appears plausible, but only because it presupposes a question that must be made explicit: how do authorizing processes represent practices, utterances, or dispositions so that they can be discursively related to general (cosmic) ideas of order? In short, the question pertains to the authorizing process by which "religion" is created.

The ways in which authorizing discourses, presupposing and expounding a cosmology, systematically redefined religious spaces have been of profound importance in the history of Western society. In the Middle Ages, such discourses ranged over an enormous domain, defining and creating religion: rejecting "pagan" practices or accepting them;[7] authenticating particular miracles and relics (the two confirmed each other); authorizing shrines; compiling saints' lives, both as a model of and as a model for the Truth; requiring the regular telling of sinful thoughts, words, and deeds to a priestly confessor and giving absolution to a penitent; regularizing popular social movements into Rule-following Orders (for example, the Franciscans), or denouncing them for heresy or for verging on the heretical (for example, the Beguines). The medieval Church did not attempt to establish absolute uniformity of practice; on the contrary, its authoritative discourse was always concerned to specify differences, gradations, exceptions. What it sought was the subjection of all practice to a unified authority, to a single authentic source that could tell truth from falsehood. It was the early Christian Fathers who established the principle that only a single Church could become the source of authenticating discourse. They knew that the "symbols" embodied in the practice of self-confessed Christians are not always identical with the theory of the "one true Church," that religion requires authorized practice and authorizing doctrine, and that there is always tension between them – sometimes breaking into heresy, the subversion of Truth – which underlines the creative role of institutional power.[8]

The medieval Church was always clear about why there was a continuous need to distinguish knowledge from falsehood (religion from what sought to subvert it), as well

as the sacred from the profane (religion from what was outside it), distinctions for which the authoritative discourses, the teachings and practices of the Church, not the convictions of the practitioner, were the final test.[9] Several times before the Reformation, the boundary between the religious and the secular was redrawn, but always the formal authority of the Church remained preeminent. In later centuries, with the triumphant rise of modern science, modern production, and the modern state, the churches would also be clear about the need to distinguish the religious from the secular, shifting, as they did so, the weight of religion more and more onto the moods and motivations of the individual believer. Discipline (intellectual and social) would, in this period, gradually abandon religious space, letting "belief," "conscience," and "sensibility" take its place. *But theory would still be needed to define religion.*

The Construction of Religion in Early Modern Europe

It was in the seventeenth century, following the fragmentation of the unity and authority of the Roman church and the consequent wars of religion, which tore European principalities apart, that the earliest systematic attempts at producing a universal definition of religion were made. . . . Herbert produced a substantive definition of what later came to be formulated as Natural Religion – in terms of beliefs (about a supreme power), practices (its ordered worship), and ethics (a code of conduct based on rewards and punishments after this life) – said to exist in all societies.[10] This emphasis on belief meant that henceforth religion could be conceived as a set of propositions to which believers gave assent, and which could therefore be judged and compared as between different religions and as against natural science (Harrison 1990).

The idea of scripture (a divinely produced/ interpreted text) was not essential to this "common denominator" of religions partly because Christians had become more familiar, through trade and colonization, with societies that lacked writing. But a more important reason lies in the shift in attention that occurred in the seventeenth century from God's words to God's works. "Nature" became the real space of divine writing, and eventually the indisputable authority for the truth of all sacred texts written in merely human language (the Old Testament and the New). . . . In this way, Natural Religion not only became a universal phenomenon but began to be demarcated from, and was also supportive of, a newly emerging domain of natural science. I want to emphasize that the idea of Natural Religion was a crucial step in the formation of the modern concept of religious belief, experience, and practice, and that it was an idea developed in response to problems specific to Christian theology at a particular historical juncture.

By 1795, Kant was able to produce a fully essentialized idea of religion which could be counterposed to its phenomenal forms: "There may certainly be different historical *confessions*," he wrote,

> although these have nothing to do with religion itself but only with changes in the means used to further religion, and are thus the province of historical research. And there may be just as many religious *books* (the Zend-Avesta, the Vedas, the Koran, etc.). But there can only be *one religion* which is valid for all men and at all times. Thus the different confessions can scarcely be more than the vehicles of religion; these are fortuitous, and may vary with differences in time or place. (Kant 1991, 114)

From here, the classification of historical confessions into lower and higher religions became an increasingly popular option for philosophers, theologians, missionaries, and anthropologists in the nineteenth and twentieth centuries. As to whether any particular tribe has existed without any form of religion whatever was often raised as a question,[11] but this was recognized as an empirical matter not affecting the essence of religion itself.

Thus, what appears to anthropologists today to be self-evident, namely that religion is essentially a matter of symbolic meanings linked to ideas of general order (expressed through either or both rite and doctrine), that it has

generic functions/features, and that it must not be confused with any of its particular historical or cultural forms, is in fact a view that has a specific Christian history. From being a concrete set of practical rules attached to specific processes of power and knowledge, religion has come to be abstracted and universalized. In this movement we have not merely an increase in religious toleration, certainly not merely a new scientific discovery, but the mutation of a concept and a range of social practices which is itself part of a wider change in the modern landscape of power and knowledge. That change included a new kind of state, a new kind of science, a new kind of legal and moral subject. To understand this mutation it is essential to keep clearly distinct that which theology tends to obscure: the occurrence of events (utterances, practices, dispositions) and the authorizing processes that give those events meaning and embody that meaning in concrete institutions.

Religion as Meaning and Religious Meanings

The equation between two levels of discourse (symbols that induce dispositions and those that place the idea of those dispositions discursively in a cosmic framework) is not the only problematic thing in this part of Geertz's discussion. He also appears, inadvertently, to be taking up the standpoint of theology. This happens when he insists on the primacy of meaning without regard to the processes by which meanings are constructed. "What any particular religion affirms about the fundamental nature of reality may be obscure, shallow, or, all too often, perverse," he writes, "but it must, if it is not to consist of the mere collection of received practices and conventional sentiments we usually refer to as moralism, affirm something" (98–9).

The requirement of affirmation is apparently innocent and logical, but through it the entire field of evangelism was historically opened up, in particular the work of European missionaries in Asia, Africa, and Latin America. The demand that the received practices must *affirm something about the fundamental nature of reality*, that it should therefore always be possible to state meanings for them which are not plain nonsense, is the first condition for determining whether they belong to "religion." The unevangelized come to be seen typically either as those who have practices but affirm nothing, in which case meaning can be attributed to their practices (thus making them vulnerable), or as those who do affirm something (probably "obscure, shallow, or perverse"), an affirmation that can therefore be dismissed. In the one case, religious theory becomes necessary for a correct reading of the mute ritual hieroglyphics of others, for reducing their practices to texts; in the other, it is essential for judging the validity of their cosmological utterances. But always, there must be something that exists beyond the observed practices, the heard utterances, the written words, and it is the function of religious theory to reach into, and to bring out, that background by giving them meaning.

Geertz is thus right to make a connection between religious theory and practice, but wrong to see it as essentially cognitive, as a means by which a disembodied mind can identify religion from an Archimedean point. The connection between religious theory and practice is fundamentally a matter of intervention – or constructing religion in the world (not in the mind) through definitional discourses, interpreting true meanings, excluding some utterances and practices and including others. Hence my repeated question: how does theoretical discourse actually define religion? What are the historical conditions in which it can act effectively as a demand for the imitation, or the prohibition, or the authentication of truthful utterances and practices? How does power create religion?

What kinds of affirmation, of meaning, must be identified with practice in order for it to qualify as religion? According to Geertz, it is because all human beings have a profound need for a general order of existence that religious symbols function to fulfill that need. It follows that human beings have a deep dread of disorder. "There are at least three points where chaos – a tumult of events which lack not just interpretations but *interpretability* –

threatens to break in upon man: at the limits of his analytic capabilities, at the limits of his powers of endurance, and at the limits of his moral insight" (100). It is the function of religious symbols to meet perceived threats to order at each of these points (intellectual, physical, and moral):

> The Problem of Meaning in each of its intergrading aspects . . . is a matter of affirming, or at least recognizing, the inescapability of ignorance, pain, and injustice on the human plane while simultaneously denying that these irrationalities are characteristic of the world as a whole. And it is in terms of religious symbolism, a symbolism relating man's sphere of existence to a wider sphere within which it is conceived to rest, that both the affirmation and the denial are made. (108)

Notice how the reasoning seems now to have shifted its ground from the claim that religion must affirm something specific about the nature of reality (however obscure, shallow, or perverse) to the bland suggestion that religion is ultimately a matter of having a positive attitude toward the problem of disorder, of affirming simply that in some sense or other the world as a whole is explicable, justifiable, bearable. This modest view of religion (which would have horrified the early Christian Fathers or medieval churchmen)[12] is a product of the only legitimate space allowed to Christianity by post-Enlightenment society, the right to individual *belief*: the human condition is full of ignorance, pain, and injustice, and religious symbols are a means of coming positively to terms with that condition. One consequence is that this view would in principle render any philosophy that performs such a function into religion (to the annoyance of the nineteenth-century rationalist), or alternatively, make it possible to think of religion as a more primitive, a less adult mode of coming to terms with the human condition (to the annoyance of the modern Christian). In either case, the suggestion that religion has a universal function in belief is one indication of how marginal religion has become in modern industrial society as the site for producing disciplined knowledge and personal discipline. As such it comes to resemble the conception Marx had of religion as ideology – that is, as a mode of consciousness which is other than consciousness of reality, external to the relations of production, producing no knowledge, but expressing at once the anguish of the oppressed and a spurious consolation.

Geertz has much more to say, however, on the elusive question of religious meaning: not only do religious symbols formulate conceptions or a general order of existence, they also clothe those conceptions with an aura of factuality. This, we are told, is "the problem of belief." *Religious belief* always involves "the prior acceptance of authority," which transforms experience:

> The existence of bafflement, pain, and moral paradox – of the Problem of Meaning – is one of the things that drives men toward belief in gods, devils, spirits, totemic principles, or the spiritual efficacy of cannibalism, . . . but it is not the basis upon which those beliefs rest, but rather their most important field of application. (109)

This seems to imply that religious belief stands independently of the worldly conditions that produce bafflement, pain, and moral paradox, although that belief is primarily a way of coming to terms with them. But surely this is mistaken, on logical grounds as well as historical, for changes in the object of belief change that belief; and as the world changes, so do the objects of belief and the specific forms of bafflement and moral paradox that are a part of that world. What the Christian believes today about God, life after death, the universe, is not what he believed a millennium ago – nor is the way he responds to ignorance, pain, and injustice the same now as it was then. The medieval valorization of pain as the mode of participating in Christ's suffering contrasts sharply with the modern Catholic perception of pain as an evil to be fought against and overcome as Christ the Healer did. That difference is clearly related to the post-Enlightenment secularization of Western society and to the moral language which that society now authorizes.

Geertz's treatment of religious belief, which lies at the core of his conception of religion, is a modern, privatized Christian one because and to the extent that it emphasizes the priority of belief as a state of mind rather than as constituting activity in the world: "The basic axiom underlying what we may perhaps call 'the religious perspective' is everywhere the same: he who would know must first believe" (110). In modern society, where knowledge is rooted either in an a-Christian everyday life or in an a-religious science, the Christian apologist tends not to regard belief as the conclusion to a knowledge process but as its precondition. However, the knowledge that he promises will not pass (nor, in fairness, does he claim that it will pass) for knowledge of social life, still less for the systematic knowledge of objects that natural science provides. Her claim is to a particular state of mind, a sense of conviction, not to a corpus of practical knowledge. But the reversal of belief and knowledge she demands was not a basic axiom to, say, pious learned Christians of the twelfth century, for whom knowledge and belief were not so clearly at odds. On the contrary, Christian belief would then have been built on knowledge – knowledge of theological doctrine, of canon law and Church courts, of the details of clerical liberties, of the powers of ecclesiastical office (over souls, bodies, properties), of the preconditions and effects of confession, of the rules of religious orders, of the locations and virtues of shrines, of the lives of the saints, and so forth. Familiarity with all such (religious) knowledge was a precondition for normal social life, and belief (embodied in practice and discourse) an orientation for effective activity in it – whether on the part of the religious clergy, the secular clergy, or the laity. Because of this, the form and texture and function of their beliefs would have been different from the form and texture and function of contemporary belief – and so too of their doubts and their disbelief.

The assumption that belief is a distinctive mental state characteristic of all religions has been the subject of discussion by contemporary scholars. Thus, Needham (1972) has interestingly argued that belief is nowhere a distinct mode of consciousness, nor a necessary institution for the conduct of social life. Southwold (1979) takes an almost diametrically opposed view, asserting that questions of belief do relate to distinctive mental states and that they are relevant in any and every society, since "to believe" always designates a relation between a believer and a proposition and through it to reality. Harré (1981, 82), in a criticism of Needham, makes the more persuasive case that "belief is a mental state, a grounded disposition, but it is confined to people who have certain social institutions and practices."

At any rate, I think it is not too unreasonable to maintain that "the basic axiom" underlying what Geertz calls "the religious perspective" is *not* everywhere the same. It is preeminently the Christian church that has occupied itself with identifying, cultivating, and testing belief as a verbalizable inner condition of true religion (Asad 1986b).

Religion as a Perspective

The phenomenological vocabulary that Geertz employs raises two interesting questions, one regarding its coherence and the other concerning its adequacy to a modern cognitivist notion of religion. I want to suggest that although this vocabulary is theoretically incoherent, it is socially quite compatible with the privatized idea of religion in modern society.

Thus, "the religious perspective," we are told, is one among several – common-sense, scientific, aesthetic – and it differs from these as follows. It differs from the *common-sense* perspective, because it "moves beyond the realities of everyday life to wider ones which correct and complete them, and [because] its defining concern is not action upon those wider realities but acceptance of them, faith in them." It is unlike the *scientific* perspective, because "it questions the realities of everyday life not out of an institutionalized scepticism which dissolves the world's givenness into a swirl of probabilistic hypotheses, but in terms of what it takes to be wider, non-hypothetical truths." And it is distinguished from the *aesthetic* perspective, because "instead of effecting a disengagement from the whole question of factuality, deliberately manufacturing an air of semblance and illusion, it deepens the concern with fact and seeks to create an aura of utter actuality" (112). In other words,

although the religious perspective is not exactly rational, it is not irrational either.

It would not be difficult to state one's disagreement with this summary of what common sense, science, and aesthetics are about. But my point is that the optional flavor conveyed by the term *perspective* is surely misleading when it is applied equally to science and to religion in modern society: religion is indeed now optional in a way that science is not. Scientific practices, techniques, knowledges, permeate and create the very fibers of social life in ways that religion no longer does. In that sense, religion today *is* a perspective (or an "attitude," as Geertz sometimes calls it), but science is not. In that sense, too, science is not to be found in every society, past and present. We shall see in a moment the difficulties that Geertz's perspectivism gets him into, but before that I need to examine his analysis of the mechanics of reality maintenance at work in religion.

Consistent with previous arguments about the functions of religious symbols is Geertz's remark that "it is in ritual – that is, consecrated behavior – that this conviction that religious conceptions are veridical and that religious directives are sound is somehow generated" (112). The long passage from which this is taken swings back and forth between arbitrary speculations about what goes on in the consciousness of officiants and unfounded assertions about ritual as imprinting. At first sight, this seems a curious combination of introspectionist psychology with a behaviorist one – but as Vygotsky (1978, 58–9) argued long ago, the two are by no means inconsistent, insofar as both assume that psychological phenomena consist essentially in the consequence of various stimulating environments.

Geertz postulates the function of rituals in generating religious conviction ("In these plastic dramas men attain their faith as they portray it" [114]), but how or why this happens is nowhere explained. Indeed, he concedes that such a religious state is not always achieved in religious ritual: "Of course, all cultural performances are not religious performances, and the line between those that are, and artistic, or even political, ones is often not so easy to draw in practice, for, like social forms, symbolic forms can serve multiple purposes" (113). But the question remains: What is it that ensures the participant's taking the symbolic forms in the way that leads to faith if the line between religious and nonreligious perspectives is not so easy to draw? Mustn't the ability and the will to adopt a religious standpoint be present prior to the ritual performance? That is precisely why a simple stimulus-response model of how ritual works will not do. And if that is the case, then ritual in the sense of a sacred performance cannot be the place where religious faith is attained, but the manner in which it is (literally) played out. If we are to understand how this happens, we must examine not only the sacred performance itself but also the entire range of available disciplinary activities, of institutional forms of knowledge and practice, within which dispositions are formed and sustained and through which the possibilities of attaining the truth are marked out – as Augustine clearly saw.

I have noted more than once Geertz's concern to define religious symbols according to universal, cognitive criteria, to distinguish the religious perspective clearly from nonreligious ones. The separation of religion from science, common sense, aesthetics, politics, and so on, allows him to defend it against charges of irrationality. If religion has a distinctive perspective (its own truth, as Durkheim would have said) and performs an indispensable function, it does not in essence compete with others and cannot, therefore, be accused of generating false consciousness. Yet in a way this defense is equivocal. Religious symbols create dispositions, Geertz observes, which seem uniquely realistic. Is this the point of view of a reasonably confident agent (who must always operate within the denseness of historically given probabilities) or that of a skeptical observer (who can see through the representations of reality to the reality itself)? It is never clear. And it is never clear because this kind of phenomenological approach doesn't make it easy to examine whether, and if so to what extent and in what ways, religious experience relates to something in the real world that believers inhabit. This is partly because religious symbols are treated, in circular fashion, as the precondition for religious

experience (which, like any experience, must, by definition, be genuine), rather than as one condition for engaging with life.

Toward the end of his essay, Geertz attempts to connect, instead of separating, the religious perspective and the common-sense one – and the result reveals an ambiguity basic to his entire approach. First, invoking Schutz, Geertz states that the everyday world of common-sense objects and practical acts is common to all human beings because their survival depends on it: "A man, even large groups of men, may be aesthetically insensitive, religiously unconcerned, and unequipped to pursue formal scientific analysis, but he cannot be completely lacking in common sense and survive" (119). Next, he informs us that individuals move "back and forth between the religious perspective and the common-sense perspective" (119). These perspectives are so utterly different, he declares, that only "Kierkegaardian leaps" (120) can cover the cultural gaps that separate them. Then, the phenomenological conclusion:

> Having ritually "leapt" . . . into the framework of meaning which religious conceptions define, and the ritual ended, returned again to the common-sense world, man is – unless, as sometimes happens, the experience fails to register – changed. *And as he is changed, so also is the common-sense world*, for it is now seen as but the partial form of a wider reality which corrects and completes it. (122; emphasis added)

This curious account of shifting perspectives and changing worlds is puzzling – as indeed it is in Schutz himself. It is not clear, for example, whether the religious framework and the common-sense world, between which the individual moves, are independent of him or not. Most of what Geertz has said at the beginning of his essay would imply that they are independent (cf. 92), and his remark about common sense being vital to every man's survival also enforces this reading. Yet it is also suggested that as the believer changes his perspective, so he himself changes; and that as he changes, so too is his common-sense world changed and corrected. So the latter, at any rate, is not independent of his moves. But it would appear from the account that the religious world *is* independent, since it is the source of distinctive experience for the believer, and through that experience, a source of change in the common-sense world: there is no suggestion anywhere that the religious world (or perspective) is ever affected by experience in the common-sense world.

This last point is consistent with the phenomenological approach in which religious symbols are sui generis, marking out an independent religious domain. But in the present context it presents the reader with a paradox: the world of common sense is always common to all human beings, and quite distinct from the religious world, which in turn differs from one group to another, as one culture differs from another; but experience of the religious world affects the common-sense world, and so the distinctiveness of the two kinds of world is modified, and the common-sense world comes to differ, from one group to another, as one culture differs from another. The paradox results from an ambiguous phenomenology in which reality is at once the distance of an agent's social perspective from the truth, measurable only by the privileged observer, and also the substantive knowledge of a socially constructed world available to both agent and observer, but to the latter only through the former.[13]

Conclusion

Perhaps we can learn something from this paradox which will help us evaluate Geertz's confident conclusion: "The anthropological study of religion is therefore a two-stage operation: first, an analysis of the system of meanings embodied in the symbols which make up *the religion proper*, and, second, the relating of these systems to social-structural and psychological processes" (125; emphasis added). How sensible this sounds, yet how mistaken, surely, it is. If religious symbols are understood, on the analogy with words, as vehicles for meaning, can such meanings be established independently of the form of life in which they are used? If religious symbols are to be taken as the signatures of a sacred text, can we know

what they mean without regard to the social disciplines by which their correct reading is secured? If religious symbols are to be thought of as the concepts by which experiences are organized, can we say much about them without considering how they come to be authorized? Even if it be claimed that what is experienced through religious symbols is not, in essence, the social world but the spiritual,[14] is it possible to assert that conditions in the social world have nothing to do with making that kind of experience accessible? Is the concept of religious training entirely vacuous?

The two stages that Geertz proposes are, I would suggest, one. Religious symbols – whether one thinks of them in terms of communication or of cognition, of guiding action or of expressing emotion – cannot be understood independently of their historical relations with nonreligious symbols or of their articulations in and of social life, in which work and power are always crucial. My argument, I must stress, is not just that religious symbols are intimately linked to social life (and so change with it), or that they usually support dominant political power (and occasionally oppose it). It is that different kinds of practice and discourse are intrinsic to the field in which religious representations (like any representation) acquire their identity and their truthfulness. From this it does not follow that the meanings of religious practices and utterances are to be sought in social phenomena, but only that their possibility and their authoritative status are to be explained as products of historically distinctive disciplines and forces. The anthropological student of *particular* religions should therefore begin from this point, in a sense unpacking the comprehensive concept which he or she translates as "religion" into heterogeneous elements according to its historical character.

A final word of caution. Hasty readers might conclude that my discussion of the Christian religion is skewed towards an authoritarian, centralized, elite perspective, and that consequently it fails to take into account the religions of heterodox believers, of resistant peasantries, of all those who cannot be completely controlled by the orthodox church. Or, worse still, that my discussion has no bearing on nondisciplinarian, voluntaristic, localized cults of noncentralized religions such as Hinduism. But that conclusion would be a misunderstanding of this chapter, seeing in it an attempt to advocate a better anthropological definition of religion than Geertz has done. Nothing could be farther from my intention. If my effort reads in large part like a brief sketch of transmutations in Christianity from the Middle Ages until today, then that is not because I have arbitrarily confined my ethnographic examples to one religion. My aim has been to problematize the idea of an anthropological definition of religion by assigning that endeavor to a particular history of knowledge and power (including a particular understanding of our legitimate past and future) out of which the modern world has been constructed.

NOTES

1 Thus, Fustel de Coulanges 1873. Originally published in French in 1864, this was an influential work in the history of several overlapping disciplines – anthropology, biblical studies, and classics.

2 Compare Peirce's more rigorous account of *representations*.

> A representation is an object which stands for another so that an experience of the former affords us a knowledge of the latter. There must be three essential conditions to which every representation must conform. It must in the first place like any other object have qualities independent of its meaning ... In the 2nd place a representation must have a real causal connection with its object. . . . In the third place, every representation addresses itself to a mind. It is only in so far as it does this that it is a representation. (Peirce 1986, 62)

3 Vygotsky (1962) makes crucial analytical distinctions in the development of conceptual thought: heaps, complexes, pseudoconcepts, and true concepts. Although, according to Vygotsky, these represent stages in the development of children's use of language, the earlier stages persist into adult life.

4 The argument that symbols *organize practice*, and consequently the structure of cognition, is central to Vygotsky's genetic psychology – see especially "Tool and Symbol in Child Development," in Vygotsky 1978. A cognitive conception of symbols has recently been revived by Sperber (1975). A similar view was taken much earlier by Lienhardt (1961).

5 Or, as Kroeber and Kluckhohn (1952, 181) put it much earlier, "Culture consists of patterns, explicit and implicit, of and for behaviour acquired and transmitted by symbols."

6 If we set aside Radcliffe-Brown's well-known preoccupation with social cohesion, we may recall that he too was concerned to specify certain kinds of psychological states said to be induced by religious symbols: "Rites can be seen to be the regulated symbolic expressions of certain sentiments (which control the behaviour of the individual in his relation to others). Rites can therefore be shown to have a specific social function when, and to the extent that, they have for their effect to regulate, maintain and transmit from one generation to another sentiments on which the constitution of society depends" (1952, 157).

7 The series of booklets known as penitential manuals, with the aid of which Christian discipline was imposed on Western Europe from roughly the fifth to the tenth centuries, contains much material on pagan practices penalized as unChristian. So, for example, "The taking of vows or releasing from them by springs or trees or lattices, anywhere except in a church, and partaking of food or drink in these places sacred to the folk-deities, are offenses condemned" (quoted in McNeill 1933, 456). . . .

8 The Church always exercised the authority to read Christian *practice* for its

religious truth. In this context, it is interesting that the word *heresy* at first designated all kinds of errors, including errors "unconsciously" involved in some activity (*simoniaca haersis*), and it acquired its specific modern meaning (the verbal formulation of denial or doubt of any defined doctrine of the Catholic church) only in the course of the methodological controversies of the sixteenth century (Chenu 1968, 276).

9 In the early Middle Ages, monastic discipline was the principal basis of religiosity. Knowles (1963, 3) observes that from roughly the sixth to the twelfth centuries, "monastic life based on the Rule of St. Benedict was everywhere the norm and exercised from time to time a paramount influence on the spiritual, intellectual, liturgical and apostolic life of the Western Church. . . . the only type of religious life available in the countries concerned was monastic, and the only monastic code was the Rule of St. Benedict." During the period the very term *religious* was therefore reserved for those living in monastic communities; with the later emergence of nonmonastic orders, the term came to be used for all who had taken lifelong vows by which they were set apart from the ordinary members of the Church (Southern 1970, 214). The extension and simultaneous transformation of the religious disciplines to lay sections of society from the twelfth century onward (Chenu 1968) contributed to the Church's authority becoming more pervasive, more complex, and more contradictory than before – and so too the articulation of the concept and practice of lay religion.

10 When Christian missionaries found themselves in culturally unfamiliar territory, the problem of identifying "religion" became a matter of considerable theoretical difficulty and practical importance. For example,

> The Jesuits in China contended that the reverence for ancestors was a social, not a religious, act, or that if religious, it was hardly different from Catholic prayers

for the dead. They wished the Chinese to regard Christianity, not as a replacement, not as a new religion, but as the highest fulfillment of their finest aspirations. But to their opponents the Jesuits appeared to be merely lax. In 1631 a Franciscan and a Dominican from the Spanish zone of Manila travelled (illegally, from the Portuguese viewpoint) to Peking and found that to translate the word *mass*, the Jesuit catechism used the character *tsi*, which was the Chinese description of the ceremonies of ancestor-worship. One night they went in disguise to such a ceremony, observed Chinese Christians participating and were scandalized at what they saw. So began the quarrel of "the rites," which plagued the eastern missions for a century and more. (Chadwick 1964, 338)

11 For example, by Tylor in the chapter "Animism" in part 2 of *Primitive Culture* [see chapter 1].

12 When the fifth-century bishop of Javols spread Christianity into the Auvergne, he found the peasants "celebrating a three-day festival with offerings on the edge of a marsh. . . . 'Nulla est religio in stagno,' he said: There can be no religion in a swamp" (Brown 1981, 125). For medieval Christians, religion was not a universal phenomenon: religion was a site on which universal truth was produced, and it was clear to them that truth was not produced universally.

13 In the introduction to his 1983 collection of essays, Geertz seems to want to abandon this perspectival approach. . . .

14 Cf. the final chapter in Evans-Pritchard 1956, and also the conclusion to Evans-Pritchard 1965.

REFERENCES

Asad, T. 1986b. "Medieval Heresy: An Anthropological View." *Social History* II, no. 3.

Brown, P. 1967. *Augustine of Hippo*. London: Faber and Faber.

——. 1981. *The Cult of the Saints: Its Rise and Function in Latin Christianity*. London: SCM.

Burckhardt, J. 1950 [1860]. *The Civilization of the Renaissance in Italy*. London: Phaidon.

Burling, R. 1977. Review of *Political Language and Oratory in Traditional Society*, by Maurice Bloch. *American Anthropologist 79*.

Burns, E. 1990. *Character: Acting and Being on the Pre-Modern Stage*. New York: St. Martin's.

Butler, C. 1924. *Benedictine Monasticism*. Cambridge: Cambridge Univ. Press.

Butterfield, H. 1931. *The Whig Interpretation of History*. London: Bell.

Bynum, C. W. 1980. "Did the Twelfth Century Discover the Individual?" *Journal of Ecclesiastical History 31*, no. 1.

Caenegem, R. C. van. 1965. "La preuve dans le droit du moyen âge occidental." *La Preuve*, Recueils de la société Jean Bodin pour l'histoire comparative des institutions, vol. 17. Brussels.

Chadwick, O. 1964. *The Reformation*. Harmondsworth, Middlesex: Penguin.

Chenu, M-D. 1968. *Nature, Man, and Society in the Twelfth Century: Essays on Theological Perspectives in the Latin West*. Chicago: Univ. of Chicago Press.

Coulanges, Fustel de. 1873. *The Ancient City: A Study on the Religion, Laws, and Institutions of Greece and Rome*. Boston: Lothrop, Lee and Shepherd.

Dumont, L. 1971. "Religion, Politics, and Society in the Individualistic Universe." *Proceedings of the Royal Anthropological Institute for 1970*.

Evans-Pritchard, E. E. 1956. *Nuer Religion*. Oxford: Clarendon.

——. 1965. *Theories of Primitive Religion*. Oxford: Clarendon.

Geertz, C. 1973. *The Interpretation of Cultures*. New York: Basic Books.

——. 1983. *Local Knowledge: Further Essays in Interpretive Anthropology*. New York: Basic Books.

Harré, R. 1981. "Psychological Variety." In *Indigenous Psychologies*, edited by P. Heelas and A. Lock. London: Academic Press.

Harrison, P. 1990. *"Religion" and the Religions in the English Enlightenment*. Cambridge: Cambridge Univ. Press.

Kant, I. 1991. *Kant: Political Writings*. Edited by H. Reiss. Cambridge: Cambridge Univ. Press.

Knowles, M. D., ed. 1963. *The Monastic Order in England: 940–1216*. 2d ed. Cambridge: Cambridge Univ. Press.

Kroeber, A. L., and C. Kluckhohn. 1952. *Culture: A Critical Review of Concepts and Definitions*. Papers of the Peabody Museum, vol. 47, no. 1. Cambridge, Mass.: Peabody Museum.

Lea, H. C. 1896. *A History of Auricular Confession and Indulgences in the Latin Church*. 3 vols. Philadelphia: Lea Bros.

Leach, E. R. 1954. *Political Systems of Highland Burma*. London: Bell.

——. 1973. "Ourselves and Others." *Times Literary Supplement*, 6 July.

Leavitt, J. 1986. "Strategies for the Interpretation of Affect." Manuscript.

Leclercq, J. 1957. "Disciplina." In *Dictionnaire de Spiritualité*, 3. Paris: Beauchesne.

——. 1966. "The Intentions of the Founders of the Cistercian Order." *Cistercian Studies 4*.

——. 1971. "Le cloître est-il une prison?" *Revue d'ascétique et de mystique 47*.

——. 1977. *The Love of Learning and the Desire for God: A Study of Monastic Culture*. 2d ed. New York: Fordham Univ. Press.

——. 1979. *Monks and Love in Twelfth-Century France*. Oxford: Oxford Univ. Press.

Leclercq, J., and G. Gärtner. 1965. "S. Bernard dans l'histoire de l'obéissance monastique." *Annuario De Estudios Médiévales 2*.

Le Goff, J. 1980. *Time, Work, and Culture in the Middle Ages*. Chicago: Univ. of Chicago Press.

Lekai, L. J. 1977. *The Cistercians: Ideals and Reality*. Kent, Ohio: Kent State Univ. Press.

Lerner, D. 1958. *The Passing of Traditional Society: Modernizing the Middle East*. New York: Free Press.

Levi, A. 1964. *French Moralists: The Theory of the Passions, 1585 to 1649*. Oxford: Clarendon.

Lienhardt, G. 1961. *Divinity and Experience.* Oxford: Clarendon.

McNeill, J. T. 1933. "Folk-Paganism in the Penitentials." *Journal of Religion* 13.

Needham, R. 1972. *Belief, Language, and Experience.* Oxford: Basil Blackwell.

Peirce, C. S. 1986. *Writings of C. S. Peirce.* Vol. 3. Bloomington: Indiana Univ. Press.

Radcliffe-Brown, A. R. 1952 [1939]. "Taboo." In *Structure and Function in Primitive Society.* London: Cohen and West.

Southern, R. W. 1970. *Western Society and the Church in the Middle Ages.* Harmondsworth, Middlesex: Penguin.

Southwold, M. 1979. "Religious Belief." *Man,* n.s. 14.

Sperber, D. 1975. *Rethinking Symbolism.* Cambridge: Cambridge Univ. Press.

Tylor, E. B. 1871. *Primitive Culture.* London: J. Murray.

Vygotsky, L. S. 1962 [1934]. *Thought and Language.* Cambridge, Mass.: MIT Press.

———. 1978. *Mind in Society.* Cambridge, Mass.: Harvard Univ. Press.

Part II

Poiesis: The Composition of Religious Worlds

Signs and Symbols

Introduction

Over the next few chapters we examine the way religion can be understood as something crafted or made. Following Aristotle, we can name this creative process *poiesis*. Poiesis is a useful concept in part because it does not distinguish the ideal from the material. Indeed, the notion is not all that different from Marx's idea of productive work and the sense that it is through labor that humans express their species being (cf Arendt 1999). Unfortunately, anthropology has long been caught in a duality that distinguishes the realm of creation of and by means of ideas from that of material creation (physical labor and its tools and products). Hence (despite some notable exceptions) we have tended to separate and distinguish the study of religion from the study of such things as the means of gaining a livelihood or reproducing family and collective life. However, at the root of cultural anthropology has been the idea of the symbol as both the primary human product and the primary human tool. Symbols are understood as the building blocks not only of religion but of language, culture, and social practice more broadly. As many American anthropologists have argued, symbols mediate our relations to the world. Linked together by means of poiesis, creative production, they ultimately shape particular understandings of the world and orientations to it, as Geertz argued in his essay (chapter 4).

If we take religious worlds to be crafted or made, and if we take as one of our tasks the comprehension and interpretation of such cosmologies (meaningful worlds or worlds of meaning), then the way to begin is through examining processes of signification, produced by means of signs or symbols, and of rhetoric, elaborated by means of tropes. Philosopher Susanne Langer's book is one place in which the argument concerning symbols has been clearly laid out; another is in the work of Leslie White (1949). These have formed the basis for much American symbolic anthropology.

There are several approaches to the production of meaning: semiotics is inspired by American philosopher Charles Peirce's extensive discussion of signification (1960), while structuralism draws from Swiss linguist Ferdinand de Saussure (1959). Symbolic anthropology, semiotics, and structuralism all see their subject as systems of signs, meaning, or signification, and hence more broadly than what is generally subsumed under "religion." Conversely, it is questionable whether any of these approaches are sufficient to fully account for "religion," and in particular to comprehend ritual, religious experience, or religious action.

10

The Logic of Signs
and Symbols

Susanne K. Langer

Susanne Langer (1895–1985) was an American philosopher whose book *Philosophy in a New Key* was a particularly incisive and influential account of the turn to meaning. Langer managed to synthesize work in anthropology, linguistics, psychology, and aesthetics as well as philosophy. In the chapter before the one presented here, Langer emphasizes the direct origins of religion in human mental functioning. She provides a vigorous rejection of utilitarian accounts of symbol and ritual, arguing instead that the mind's need to emit a continuous stream of symbolic expression is as strong as any practical interest: "The fact that the human brain is constantly carrying on a process of symbolic transformation of the experiential data that come to it causes it to be a veritable fountain of more or less spontaneous ideas" (1948 [1942]: 34). She also deftly shows the limitations of an ethological model (a model drawn from the study of animal behavior) for understanding humans.

Langer distinguishes sign and symbol, providing a simpler model than that of Peirce (in whose terminology, now more widely used than Langer's, the symbol is one category of sign). Although the debate over meaning – and over the usefulness of terms like "denotation," "connotation," and the very "meaning of 'meaning'" – has continued vigorously since Langer's day, she provides a particularly clear exposition of some of the main issues. Langer emphasizes how symbols are critical for thought. Unlike animals, humans do not simply respond to the world, but must interpret it. In subsequent chapters she distinguishes the effects of discursive forms of symbolism (by means of language) from presentational (nonlinguistic, simultaneous, integral) ones,

Reprinted by permission of the publisher from "The Logic of Signs and Symbols," in *Philosophy in a New Key: A Study in the Symbolism of Reason, Rite and Art* by Susanne K. Langer, (Cambridge, MA: Harvard University Press), pp. 53–67. Copyright © 1942, 1951, 1957 by the President and Fellows of Harvard College, Renewed 1970, 1979 by Susanne K. Langer, 1985 by Leonard C. R. Langer. Abridged.

addressing questions of meaning in art and music.

These insights have been developed in a variety of ways by subsequent thinkers. They lie behind Geertz's profound argument concerning the evolutionary dependence of the brain on the process of symbolic transformation ("culture" in his vocabulary) in order to function (1973c [1962]) as well as behind Sahlins's sustained accounts of the mediation of all human practice by symbolic transformation ("culture" or "structure") (1976). And they anticipate the kind of argument made by Lévi-Strauss concerning the continuous production of "undomesticated" thought in myth (see chapter 17), while recognizing the Freudian account of symbolic transformation in dreams.

Although all three main approaches to meaning – structuralism, semiotics, and symbolic (interpretive) anthropology – share much common philosophical ground, they apportion things differently. Structuralism begins with a concept of the linguistic sign which, like Langer's concept of "symbol" (and confusingly, unlike her concept of "sign"), is arbitrary. Structuralists deploy the binary distinction between signifier and signified and examine sets of signs constructed through relations of minimal contrasts, on the model of phonemes. Semiotics, which is based more faithfully on Peirce's extensive elaboration, begins with a distinction among index, icon, and symbol as the three main categories of signs and emphasizes the key concept of the interpretant. Peirce is deployed to great effect in Valentine Daniel's *Fluid Signs: Being a Person the Tamil Way* (1984), which includes an unforgettable description of a South Indian pilgrimage. What Langer calls the psychological dimension of meaning might today be referred to as the intentional or pragmatic dimension. Semiotics more easily accommodates pragmatics and so has generally taken precedence in technical accounts of meaning. Lee (1997) offers an advanced interdisciplinary synthesis.

. . . Meaning has both a logical and a psychological aspect. Psychologically, any item that is to have meaning must be *employed* as a sign or a symbol; that is to say, it must be a sign or a symbol *to* someone. Logically, it must be *capable* of conveying a meaning, it must be the sort of item that can be thus employed. In some meaning-relations this logical requirement is trivial, and tacitly accepted; in others it is of the utmost importance, and may even lead us a merry chase through the labyrinths of nonsense. These two aspects, the logical and the psychological, are thoroughly confounded by the ambiguous verb "to mean"; for sometimes it is proper to say "*it* means," and sometimes "*I* mean." Obviously, a word – say, "London" – does not "mean" a city in just the same sense that a person employing the word "means" the place.

Both aspects, the logical and the psychological, are always present, and their interplay produces the great variety of meaning-relations over which philosophers have puzzled and fought for the last fifty years. The analysis of "meaning" has had a peculiarly difficult history; the word is used in many different ways, and a good deal of controversy has been wasted on the subject of *the* correct way, *the* meaning of "meaning." Whenever people find several species of a genus, they look for the prime form, the archetype that is supposed to be differently disguised in each special case; so, for a long time, philosophers hoped to find the true quality of meaning by collecting all its various manifestations and looking for a common ingredient. They talked more and more generally about "symbol-situations," believing that by generalization they might attain to the essential quality which all such situations had in common. But generalizing from vague and muddled special theories can never give us a clear general theory. The sort of generalization that merely substitutes "symbol-situation" for "denotation-or-connotation-or-signification-or-association-etc." is scientifically useless; for the whole purpose of general concepts is to make the distinctions between special classes clear, to relate all subspecies to each other in definite ways; but if such general concepts are simply composite photographs of all known types of meaning, they can only blur, not clarify, the relations that obtain among specialized senses of the word.

Charles Peirce, who was probably the first person to concern himself seriously with semantics, began by making an inventory of all "symbol-situations," in the hope that when all possible meanings of "meaning" were herded together, they would show empirical differentia whereby one could divide the sheep from the goats. But the obstreperous flock, instead of falling neatly into a few classes, each according to its kind, divided and subdivided into the most terrifying order of icons, qualisigns, legisigns, semes, phemes, and delomes, and there is but cold comfort in his assurance that his orginal 59,049 types can really be boiled down to a mere sixty-six.[1]

A few further attempts were made to grasp the essential quality of meaning by empirical methods, but the more varieties could be found, the less did they promise to reveal a common essence. Husserl, distinguishing each type of meaning as a special notion, ended with as many theories as there are "meanings."[2] But we have still the sheep and the goats and all their several relatives, and are still left wondering why one family name, Meaning, should apply where no family likeness can be detected.

There is in fact no quality of meaning; its essence lies in the realm of logic, where one does not deal with qualities, but only with relations. It is not fair to say: "Meaning is a relation," for that suggests too simple a business. Most people think of a relation as a two-termed affair – "A-in-relation-to-B"; but meaning involves several terms, and different

types of meaning consist of different types and degrees of relationship. It is better, perhaps, to say: "Meaning is not a quality, but a *function* of a term." A function is a *pattern* viewed with reference to one special term round which it centers; this pattern emerges when we look at the given term *in its total relation to the other terms about it*. The total may be quite complicated. For instance, a musical chord may be treated as a function of one note, known as the "written bass," by writing this one note and indicating its relation to all the other notes that are to go above it. In old organ music, the

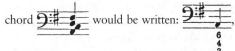

which means: "The A-chord with the sixth, the fourth and the third notes above A." The chord is treated as *a pattern surrounding and including* A. It is expressed as a function of A.

The meaning of a term is, likewise, a function; it rests on pattern, in which the term itself holds the key-position. Even in the simplest kinds of meaning there must be at least two other things related to the term that "means" – an object that is "meant," and a subject who uses the term; just as in a chord there must be at least two notes besides the "written bass" to determine what the chord is (one of these may be merely "understood" by musicians, but without it the combination would not be a determinate chord). The same may be said for a term with a meaning; the existence of a subject is often tacitly accepted, but if there is not at least one thing meant and one mind for which it is meant, then there is not a complete meaning – only a partial pattern which might be completed in different ways.

Any term in a pattern may be taken as a key-term to which the others are related. For instance, the chord ♪ may be regarded as a function of its lowest note, and expressed by the description ♪; or it may be treated with reference to the note on which it is built harmonically, which happens to be D. A musician analyzing the harmony would call this chord "the second inversion of the seventh-chord on the dominant, in the key of G." The "dominant" of that key is D, not A. He would treat the whole pattern as *a function of D*; that sounds more complicated than the other treatment, which fixed the notes from the A upward, but of course it is not really so, because it comes to just the same pattern.

Similarly, we may view a meaning-pattern from the point of view of any term in it, and our descriptions of the same pattern will differ accordingly. We may say that a certain symbol "means" an object to a person, or that the person "means" the object by the symbol. The first description treats meaning in the logical sense, the second in the psychological sense. The former takes the symbol as the key, and the latter the subject.[3] So, the two most controversial kinds of meaning – the logical and the psychological – are distinguished and at the same time related to each other, by the general principle of viewing meaning *as a function, not a property, of terms.*

In the further analyses that follow, "meaning" will be taken in the objective sense, unless some other is specified; that is to say, I shall speak of terms (such as words) as "meaning" something, not of people as "meaning" this or that. Later we shall have to distinguish various subjective functions; but at present let us consider the *relations of terms to their objects.* What *relates* the terms to their objects is, of course, a subject; that is always to be understood.

There are, first of all, two distinct functions of terms, which have both a perfectly good right to the name "meaning": for a significant sound, gesture, thing, event (e.g. a flash, an image), may be either a *sign* or a *symbol.*

A sign indicates the existence – past, present, or future – of a thing, event, or condition. Wet streets are a sign that it has rained. A patter on the roof is a sign that it is raining. A fall of the barometer or a ring round the moon is a sign that it is going to rain. In an unirrigated place, abundant verdure is a sign that it often rains there. A smell of smoke signifies the presence of fire. A scar is a sign of a past accident.

Dawn is a herald of sunrise. Sleekness is a sign of frequent and plentiful food.

All the examples here adduced are *natural signs.* A natural sign is a part of a greater event, or of a complex condition, and to an experienced observer it signifies the rest of that situation of which it is a notable feature. It is a *symptom* of a state of affairs.

The logical relation between a sign and its object is a very simple one: they are associated, somehow, to form a *pair*; that is to say, they stand in a one-to-one correlation. To each sign there corresponds one definite item which is its object, the thing (or event, or condition) signified. All the rest of that important function, signification, involves the third term, the subject, which *uses* the pair of items; and the relation of the subject to the other two terms is much more interesting than their own bare logical coupling. The subject is related, essentially, to the other two terms *as a pair.* What characterizes them is the fact that they are paired. Thus, a white bump on a person's arm, as a mere sense-datum, would probably not be interesting enough even to have a name, but such a datum *in its relation to the past* is noted and called a "scar." Note, however, that although the subject's relation is to the *pair* of other terms, he has also a relation to each one of them individually, which makes one of them the sign and the other the object. What is the difference between a sign and its object, by virtue of which they are not interchangeable? Two terms merely associated as a pair, like two socks, two balances of a scale, two ends of a stick, etc., could be interchanged without any harm.

The difference is, that the subject for which they constitute a pair must *find one more interesting than the other, and the latter more easily available than the former.* If we are interested in tomorrow's weather, the events now present, if coupled with tomorrow's weather-phenomena, are signs for us. A ring round the moon, or "mares' tails" in the sky, are not important in themselves; but as visible, present items coupled with something important but not yet present, they have "meaning." If it were not for the subject, or *interpretant*, sign and object would be interchangeable. Thunder may just as well be a sign that there has been lightning, as lightning may signify that there will be thunder. In themselves they are merely correlated. It is only where one is perceptible and the other (harder or impossible to perceive) is interesting, that we actually have a case of *signification belonging to term.*[4]

Now, just as in nature certain events are correlated, so that the less important may be taken as signs of the more important, so we may also *produce* arbitrary events purposely correlated with important ones that are to be their meanings. A whistle means that the train is about to start. A gunshot means that the sun is just setting. A crêpe on the door means someone has just died. These are artificial signs, for they are not part of a condition of which they naturally signify the remainder or something in the remainder. Their logical relation to their objects, however, is the same as that of natural signs – a one-to-one correspondence of sign and object, by virtue of which the interpretant, who is interested in the latter and perceives the former, may apprehend the existence of the term that interests him.

The interpretation of signs is the basis of animal intelligence. Animals presumably do not distinguish between natural signs and artificial or fortuitous signs; but they use both kinds to guide their practical activities. We do the same thing all day long. We answer bells, watch the clock, obey warning signals, follow arrows, take off the kettle when it whistles, come at the baby's cry, close the windows when we hear thunder. The logical basis of all these interpretations, the mere correlation of trivial events with important ones, is really very simple and common; so much so that there is no limit to what a sign may mean. This is even more obviously true of artificial signs than of natural ones. A shot may mean the beginning of a race, the rise of the sun, the sighting of danger, the commencement of a parade. As for bells, the world is mad with their messages. Somebody at the front door, the back door, the side door, the telephone – toast is ready – typewriter line is ended – school begins, work begins, church begins, church is over – street car starts – cashbox registers – knife grinder passes – time for dinner, time to get up – fire in town!

Because a sign may mean so may things, we are very apt to misinterpret it, especially when it is artificial. Bell signals, of course, may be either wrongly associated with their objects, or the sound of one bell may actually be confused with that of another. But natural signs, too, may be misunderstood. Wet streets are not a reliable sign of recent rain if the sprinkler wagon has passed by. The misinterpretation of signs is the simplest form of *mistake*. It is the most important form, for purposes of practical life, and the easiest to detect; for its normal manifestation is the experience called *disappointment.*

Where we find the simplest form of error, we may expect to find also, as its correlate, the simplest form of knowledge. This is, indeed, the interpretation of signs. It is the most elementary and most tangible sort of intellection; the kind of knowledge that we share with animals, that we acquire entirely by experience, that has obvious biological uses, and equally obvious criteria of truth and falsehood. Its mechanism may be conceived as an elaboration of the conditioned-reflex arc, with the brain doing switchboard duty, and getting the right or the wrong number for the sense organ that called up the musculature and expects an answer in terms of altered sensations. It has all those virtues of simplicity, componability, and intelligibility that recommend a concept for scientific purposes. So it is not surprising that students of genetic psychology have seized upon sign interpretation as the archetype of all knowledge, that they regard *signs* as the original bearers of meaning, and treat all other terms with semantic properties as subspecies – "substitute signs," which act as proxy for their objects and evoke conduct appropriate to the latter instead of to themselves. . . . However, the characteristics of symbols in general, and their essential difference from signs, must go on record.

A term which is used symbolically and not signally does *not* evoke action appropriate to the presence of its object. If I say: "Napoleon," you do not bow to the conqueror of Europe as though I had introduced him, but merely think of him. If I mention a Mr. Smith of our common acquaintance, you may be led to tell me something about him "behind his back," which is just what you would *not* do in his presence. Thus the symbol for Mr. Smith – his name – may very well initiate an act appropriate peculiarly to his absence. Raised eyebrows and a look at the door, interpreted as a *sign* that he is coming, would stop you in the midst of your narrative; *that* action would be directed toward Mr. Smith in person.

Symbols are not proxy for their objects, but are *vehicles for the conception of objects*. To conceive a thing or a situation is not the same thing as to "react toward it" overtly, or to be aware of its presence. In talking *about* things we have conceptions of them, not the things themselves; and *it is the conceptions, not the things, that symbols directly "mean."* Behavior toward conceptions is what words normally evoke; this is the typical process of thinking.

Of course a word may be used as a sign, but that is not its primary role. Its signific character has to be indicated by some special modification – by a tone of voice, a gesture (such as pointing or staring), or the location of a placard bearing the word. In itself it is a symbol, associated with a conception, not directly with a public object or event. The fundamental difference between signs and symbols is this difference of association, and consequently of their *use* by the third party to the meaning function, the subject; signs *announce* their objects to him, whereas symbols *lead him to conceive* their objects. The fact that the same item – say, the little mouthy noise we call a "word" – may serve in either capacity, does not obliterate the cardinal distinction between the two functions it may assume.

The simplest kind of symbolistic meaning is probably that which belongs to proper names. A personal name evokes a conception of something given as a unit in the subject's experience, something concrete and therefore easy to recall in imagination. Because the name belongs to a notion so obviously and unequivocally derived from an individual object, it is often supposed to "mean" that object as a sign would "mean" it. This belief is reinforced by the fact that a name borne by a living person always is at once a symbol by which we think of the person, and a call-name by which we

signal him. Through a confusion of these two functions, the proper name is often deemed the bridge from animal semantic, or sign-using, to human language, which is symbol-using. Dogs, we are told, understand names – not only their own, but their masters'. So they do, indeed; but they understand them *only in the capacity of call-names*. If you say "James" to a dog whose master bears that name, the dog will interpret the sound as a sign, and *look for* James. Say it to a person who knows someone called thus, and he will ask: "What about James?" That simple question is forever beyond the dog; signification is the only meaning a name can have for him – a meaning which the master's name shares with the master's smell, with his footfall, and his characteristic ring of the doorbell. In a human being, however, the name evokes the *conception* of a certain man so called, and prepares the mind for further conceptions in which the notion of that man figures; therefore the human being naturally asks: "What about James?"

There is a famous passage in the autobiography of Helen Keller, in which this remarkable woman describes the dawn of Language upon her mind. Of course she had used signs before, formed associations, learned to expect things and identify people or places; but there was a great day when all sign-meaning was eclipsed and dwarfed by the discovery that a certain datum in her limited sense-world had a *denotation*, that a particular act of her fingers constituted a *word*. This event had required a long preparation; the child had learned many finger acts, but they were as yet a meaningless play. Then, one day, her teacher took her out to walk – and there the great advent of Language occurred.

"She brought me my hat," the memoir reads,

and I knew I was going out into the warm sunshine. This thought, if a wordless sensation may be called a thought, made me hop and skip with pleasure.

We walked down the path to the well-house, attracted by the fragrance of the honeysuckle with which it was covered. Some one was drawing water and my teacher placed my hand under the spout. As the cool stream gushed over my hand she spelled into the other the word *water*, first slowly, then rapidly. I stood still, my whole attention fixed upon the motion of her fingers. Suddenly I felt a misty consciousness as of something forgotten – a thrill of returning thought; and somehow the mystery of language was revealed to me. I knew then that w-a-t-e-r meant the wonderful cool something that was flowing over my hand. That living word awakened my soul, gave it light, hope, joy, set it free! There were barriers still, it is true, but barriers that in time could be swept away.

I left the well-house eager to learn. Everything had a name, and each name gave birth to a new thought. As we returned to the house every object which I touched seemed to quiver with life. That was because I saw everything with the strange, new sight that had come to me.[5]

This passage is the best affidavit we could hope to find for the genuine difference between sign and symbol. The sign is something to act upon, or a means to command action; the symbol is an instrument of thought. Note how Miss Keller qualifies the mental process just preceding her discovery of words – "This thought, *if a wordless sensation may be called a thought.*" Real thinking is possible only in the light of genuine language, no matter how limited, how primitive; in her case, it became possible with the discovery that "w-a-t-e-r" was not necessarily a sign that water was wanted or expected, but was the *name* of this substance, by which it could be mentioned, conceived, remembered.

Since a name, the simplest type of symbol, is directly associated with a conception, and is employed by a subject to realize the conception, one is easily led to treat a name as a "conceptual sign," an artifical sign which announces the presence of a certain idea. In a sense this is quite justified; yet it strikes a strained and unnatural note, which is usually a fair warning that the attempted interpretation misses the most important feature in its material. In the present case, it misses *the relation of conceptions to the concrete world*, which is so close and so important that it enters into the very structure of "names." A name, above all, *denotes* something. "James" may represent a conception, but it *names* a

certain person. In the case of proper nouns this relation of the symbol to what it denotes is so striking that denotation has been confused with the direct relation of sign and object, signification. As a matter of fact, "James" does not, without further ado, *signify* a person; it *denotes* him – it is associated with a conception which "fits" the actual person. The relation between a symbol and an object, usually expressed by "S denotes O," is not a simple two-termed relation which S has to O; it is a complex affair: S is coupled, for a certain subject, with a conception that fits O, i.e. with a notion which O satisfies.

In an ordinary sign-function, there are three essential terms: subject, sign, and object. In denotation, which is the commonest kind of symbol-function, there have to be four: subject, symbol, conception, and object. The radical difference between sign-meaning and symbol-meaning can therefore be logically exhibited, for it rests on a difference of pattern, it is strictly a different function.[6]

Denotation is, then, the complex relationship which a name has to an object which bears it; but what shall the more direct relation of the name, or symbol, to its associated *concept* be called? It shall be called by its traditional name, *connotation*. The connotation of a word is the conception it conveys. Because the connotation remains with the symbol when the object of its denotation is neither present nor looked for, we are able to *think about* the object without reacting to it overtly at all.

Here, then, are the three most familiar meanings of the one word, "meaning": signification, denotation, and connotation. All three are equally and perfectly legitimate, but in no possible way interchangeable. [. . .]

So much, then, for the venerable "logic of terms." It appears a little more complicated than in the medieval books, since we must add to the long-recognized functions, connotation and denotation, a third one, signification, which is fundamentally different from the other two; and since, moreover, in discussing the semantic functions of terms we have made the rare discovery that they really are *functions*, not powers or mysterious properties or what-not, and have treated them accordingly. The traditional "logic of terms" is really a metaphysic of meaning; the new philosophy of meaning is first of all a logic of terms – of signs and symbols – an analysis of the relational patterns in which "meaning" may be sought.

But a semantic of separate symbols is only a rudimentary foundation for a more interesting aspect of meaning. Everything is mere propaedeutic until we come to *discourse*. It is in discursive thinking that truth and falsehood are born. Before terms are built into propositions, they assert nothing, preclude nothing; in fact, although they may *name* things, and convey ideas of such things, they *say* nothing. I have discussed them at such great length simply because most logicians have given them such cavalier treatment that even so obvious a distinction as that between sign-functions and symbol-functions passed unnoticed; so that careless philosophers have been guilty of letting ambitious genetic psychologists argue them from the conditioned reflex to the wisdom of G. Bernard Shaw, all in one skyrocketing generalization.

[. . .]

NOTES

1 From two letters to Lady Welby, 1904 and 1908 respectively, first cited by Ogden and Richards in *The Meaning of Meaning* (App. D, pp. 435–44), and now published in *The Collected Papers of Charles S. Peirce* (1932), II, 330.
2 Edmund Husserl, *Logische Untersuchungen*, 2 vols. (1913 and 1921), vol. II, part I, *passim*.
3 Where the object is taken as the key, the resulting description begins with the "knowledge-content" postulated in some epistemologies.

4 Cf. Whitehead, *Symbolism* [1927], pp. 9–13.
5 Helen Keller, *The Story of My Life* (1936; 1st ed. 1902), pp. 23–4.
6 If a symbol could be said normally to "signify" anything, its object would be the occurrence of an act of conception. But such a function of a symbol is casual, and crosses with its use *as a symbol*. In the latter function it is not the act of conception, but *what is conceived*, that enters into the meaning-pattern. We shall avoid much confusion and quibbling by recognizing that signification does not figure in symbolization at all.

11

The Problem of Symbols

E. E. Evans-Pritchard

E. E. Evans-Pritchard (1902–73), or "E.-P.," as he was known, was arguably the most important anthropologist of his generation, certainly in the United Kingdom (he was professor at the University of Oxford). He was a superb fieldworker and theoretician and his theory is often implicit in his ethnographic exposition. Trained by Malinowski and influenced by Radcliffe-Brown, he was an original and independent thinker who shifted from a primarily structure-functionalist to a more historical and humanistic position.

While many anthropologists have taken religious symbols as complex variants of ordinary symbols as defined by Langer, thus as "packets" of meaning that could be unpacked (see chapters 12 and 13, respectively, as well as Turner 1967, for notable unpackings), Evans-Pritchard is unusual in following more clearly the point made by Langer that

the relevant question is one of predication. In the selection from *Nuer Religion* reprinted here, Evans-Pritchard looks less at the content of the symbol (for which see the profound analysis in his preceding chapter on the refractional nature of Nuer deity, *Kwoth*) than on the meaning of the verb that establishes it as a predicate. He is concerned, then, with what it means for Nuer to *say* that twins are birds or what it means when Nuer *replace* cattle with cucumbers in their sacrifices. The question is thus not the meaning of twins, birds, oxen, or cucumbers qua symbols but what the Nuer mean when they say and do certain things about and with twins, birds, oxen, and cucumbers. In this very subtle essay Evans-Pritchard thus takes us to the complexities of religious meaning and the intricate gradations between literal and metaphorical predication.

It is sometimes remarked that Evans-Pritchard portrays Nuer religion in a

From E. E. Evans-Pritchard, "The Problem of Symbols," in *Nuer Religion* (Oxford: Clarendon Press, 1956), pp. 123–43. Reprinted by permission of Oxford University Press. Abridged.

manner not entirely dissimilar to Roman Catholicism, or rather that the arguments he makes to explain Nuer refractions of spirit or the material symbolism of spirit are not altogether different from the ways in which Catholic theologians might defend the concept of the Trinity or the Communion. This is not necessarily a criticism; some people have gone on to suggest that anthropologists who practice religion can have a better appreciation of the religion of their subjects than the agnostic majority. While this may be true in the case of Evans-Pritchard, I doubt the general validity of the argument. Moreover, while a religious sensibility is certainly evident in this essay, more to the point is Evans-Pritchard's philosophical acuity and ethnographic precision. I would, however, make the broader hermeneutic point that *any* anthropological interpretation will be informed by the position of the anthropologist, not only by the ethnographer's own religious formation but by the context of the debate over religious, philosophical, or political issues in which the anthropologist is immersed within his or her own time and tradition. Evans-Pritchard's professional debate, as we glimpse toward the end of his essay, was with Tylor, Lévy-Bruhl, and others who made arguments that denigrated either the conclusions or the very rationality of "primitive thought." As discussed above, Evans-Pritchard's *oeuvre* on religion is a masterly refutation of these arguments.

In the last chapter I discussed how the Nuer conception of Spirit is figured in different ways to different persons and categories and groups. In this chapter I consider the material forms in which Spirit manifests itself or is represented. God is, properly speaking, not figured in any material representations, nor are almost all the spirits of the above, though both God and his supra-terrestrial refractions may reveal themselves in signs. But the spirits of the below are represented in creatures and things. Our problem chiefly concerns these spirits of the below. It can be simply stated by the question: What meaning are we to attach to Nuer statements that such-and-such a thing is *kwoth*, spirit? The answer is not so simple.

There are several ways in which what we would render as "is" is indicated in the Nuer language. The one which concerns us here is the particle *e*. It is used to tell the listener that something belongs to a certain class or category and hence about some character or quality it has, as "*e dit*", "it is a bird", "*gat nath e car*", "the Nuer is black", and "*Duob e ram me goagh*", "Duob is a good man.' The question we are asking is what meaning or meanings it has for Nuer when they say of something

"*e kwoth*", "it is Spirit" (in the sense either of God or of a divine refraction).

Nuer do not claim to see God, nor do they think that anyone can know what he is like in himself. When they speak about his nature they do so by adjectives which refer to attributes, such as "great" and "good", or in metaphors taken from the world around them, likening his invisibility and ubiquity to wind and air, his greatness to the universe he has created, and his grandeur to an ox with widespread horns. They are no more than metaphors for Nuer, who do not say that any of these things is God, but only that he is like (*cere*) them. They express in these poetic images as best they can what they think must be some of his attributes.

Nevertheless, certain things are said, or may be said, "to be" God – rain, lightning, and various other natural – in the Nuer way of speech, created – things which are of common interest. There is here an ambiguity, or an obscurity, to be elucidated, for Nuer are not now saying that God or Spirit is like this or that, but that this or that "is" God or Spirit. Elucidation here does not, however, present great difficulties.

God being conceived of as in the sky, those celestial phenomena which are of particular significance for Nuer, rain and lightning, are said, in a sense we have to determine, to be him. There is no noun denoting either phenomenon and they can only be spoken of by verbs indicating a function of the sky, as "*ce nhial deam*", "the sky rained", and "*ce nhial mar*", "the sky thundered". Also pestilences, murrains, death, and indeed almost any natural phenomenon significant for men are commonly regarded by Nuer as manifestations from above, activities of divine being. Even the earthly totems are conceived of as a relationship deriving from some singular intervention of Spirit from above in human affairs. It is chiefly by these signs that Nuer have knowledge of God. It might be held, therefore, that the Nuer conception of God is a conceptualization of events which, on account of their strangeness or variability as well as on account of their potentiality for fortune or misfortune, are said to be his activities or his activities in one or other of his hypostases or refractions. Support for such a view might be found in the way Nuer sometimes speak of one or other of these effects. They may say of rain or lightning or pestilence "*e kwoth*", "it is God", and in storms they pray to God to come to earth gently and not in fury – to come gently, it will be noted, not to make the rain come gently.

I do not discuss this ontological question here beyond saying that were we to suppose that such phenomena are in themselves regarded as God we would misunderstand and misrepresent Nuer religious thought, which is pre-eminently dualistic. It is true that for them there is no abstract duality of natural and supernatural, but there is such a duality between *kwoth*, Spirit, which is immaterial rather than supernatural, and *cak*, creation, the material world known to the senses. Rain and lightning and pestilences and murrains belong to this created world and are referred to by Nuer as *nyin kwoth*, instruments of God.

Nevertheless, they and other effects of significance for men are διοσημία, signs or manifestations of divine activity; and since Nuer apprehend divine activity in these signs, in God's revelation of himself to them in material forms, the signs are, in a lower medium, what they signify, so that Nuer may say of them "*e kwoth*", "it is God". Rain and pestilence come from God and are therefore manifestations of him, and in this sense rain and pestilence are God, in the sense that he reveals himself in their falling. But though one can say of rain or pestilence that it is God one cannot say of God that he is rain or pestilence. This would make no sense for a number of reasons. In the first place, the situation could scarcely arise, God not being an observable object, in which Nuer would require or desire to say about him that he is anything. In the second place, the word *kwoth* does not here refer to a particular refraction of Spirit, a spirit, but to Spirit in its oneness, God, and he could not be in any way identified with any one of his manifestations to the exclusion of all the others. A third, and the most cogent, reason is that rain is water which falls from the sky and pestilence is a bodily condition and they are therefore in their nature material things and not Spirit. Indeed, as a rule, rain is only thought of in connexion with Spirit, and is therefore only said to be Spirit, when it does not fall in due season or falls too much or too violently with storm and lightning – when, that is, the rain has some special significance for human affairs. This gives us a clue to what is meant when Nuer say of something that it is God or that it is a spirit of the air, as thunder may be said to be the spirit *wiu* or a prophet of the spirit *deng* may be said to be *deng* – especially as Nuer readily expand such statements by adding that thunder, rain, and pestilence are all instruments (*nyin*) of God or that they are sent by (*jak*) God, and that the spirit *deng* has filled (*gwang*) the prophet through whom it speaks. In the statement here that something is Spirit or a spirit the particle *e*, which we translate "is", cannot therefore have the meaning of identity in substantial sense. Indeed, it is because Spirit is conceived of in itself, as the creator and the one, and quite apart from any of its material manifestations, that phenomena can be said to be sent by it or to be its instruments. When Nuer say of rain or lightning that it is God they are making an elliptical statement. What is understood is not that the thing in itself is Spirit but that it is what we would call a medium or manifestation or sign of divine activity in relation to men and of significance for them. What precisely is posited by the hearer of any such elliptical statement depends on the nature of the situation by reference to which it is made. A vulture is not thought of as being in itself Spirit; it is a bird. But if it perches on the crown of a byre or hut Nuer may say "*e kwoth*", "it is Spirit", meaning that its doing so is a spiritual signal presaging disaster. A lion is not thought of as being in itself Spirit; it is a beast. But it may, on account of some event which brings it into a peculiar relation to man, such as being born, as Nuer think sometimes happens, as twin to a human child, be regarded as a revelation of Spirit for a particular family and lineage. Likewise, diseases, or rather their symptoms, are not thought of as being in themselves Spirit, but their appearance in individuals may be regarded as manifestations of Spirit for those individuals. Spirit acts, and thereby reveals itself, through these creatures. This distinction between the nature of a thing and what it may signify in certain situations or for certain persons is very evident in totemic relationships. A crocodile is Spirit for certain persons, but it is not thought to be in its nature Spirit, for others kill and eat it. It is because Nuer separate, and quite explicitly when questioned about the matter, spiritual conceptions from such material things as may nevertheless be said "to be" the conceptions, that they are able to maintain the unity and autonomy of Spirit in spite of a great diversity of accidents and are able to speak of Spirit without reference to any of its material manifestations.

So far I have been mostly speaking of the conception of God and of those of his refractions which belong to the category of the sky or of the above. With two possible exceptions,[1] we cannot say that the things said "to be" these spirits are material symbols or representations of them; at any rate not in the same sense as we can speak of things being symbols of those lesser refractions of Spirit Nuer call spirits of the earth or of the below, in which God stands in a special relationship to lineages and individuals – such diverse things as beasts, birds, reptiles, trees, phosphorescent objects, and pieces of wood. These lesser refractions of Spirit, regarded as distinct spirits in relation to each other, cannot, unlike the spirits of the air, easily be thought of except in relation to the things by reference to which they derive their individuality, and which are said "to be" them.

When, therefore, Nuer say that the pied crow is the spirit *buk* or that a snake is Spirit, the word "is" has a different sense from what it has in the statement that rain is Spirit. The difference does not merely lie in the fact that *kwoth* has here a more restricted connotation, being spoken of in reference to a particular and exclusive refraction – a spirit – rather than comprehensively as God or Spirit in its oneness. It lies also in the relation understood in the statement between its subject (snake or crow) and its predicate (Spirit or a spirit). The snake in itself is not divine activity whereas rain and lightning are. The story accounting for a totemic relationship may present it as arising from a revelation of divine activity, but once it has become an established relationship between a lineage and a natural species, the species is a representation or symbol of Spirit to the lineage. What then is here meant when it is said that the pied crow "is" *buk* or that a snake "is" Spirit: that the symbol "is" what it symbolizes? Clearly Nuer do not mean that the crow is the same as *buk*, for *buk* is also conceived of as being in the sky and also in rivers, which the pied crow certainly is not; nor that a snake is the same as some spiritual refraction, for they say that the snake just crawls on the earth while the spirit it is said to be is in the sky. What then is being predicated about the crow or snake in the statement that either is Spirit or a spirit?

It will be simpler to discuss this question in the first place in relation to a totemic relationship. When a Nuer says of a creature "*e nyang*", "it is a crocodile", he is saying that it is a crocodile and not some other creature, but when he says, to explain why a person behaves in an unusual manner towards crocodiles "*e kwothdien*", "it (the crocodile) is their spirit", he is obviously making a different sort of statement. He is not saying what kind of creature it is (for it is understood that he is referring to the crocodile) but that what he refers to is Spirit for certain people. But he is also not saying that the crocodile is Spirit – it is not so for him – but that certain people so regard it. Therefore a Nuer would not make a general statement that *"nyang e kwoth"*, "crocodile is Spirit", but would only say, in referring to the crocodile, *"e kwoth"*, "it is Spirit", the distinction between the two statements being that the first would mean that the crocodile is Spirit for everyone whereas the second, being made in a special context of situation, means that it is Spirit for certain persons who are being discussed, or are understood, in that context. Likewise, whilst it can be said of the crocodile that it is Spirit, it cannot be said of Spirit that it is the crocodile, or rather, if a statement is framed in this form it can only be made when the word *kwoth* has a pronominal suffix which gives it the meaning of "his spirit", "their spirit", and so forth; in other words, where the statement makes it clear that what is being spoken of is Spirit conceived of in relation to particular persons only. We still have to ask, however, in what sense the crocodile is Spirit for these persons.

Since it is difficult to discuss a statement that something which can be observed, crocodile, is something more than what is appears to be when this something more, Spirit, cannot be observed, it is helpful first to consider two examples of Nuer statements that things are something more than they appear to be when both the subject term and the predicate term refer to observable phenomena.

When a cucumber is used as a sacrificial victim Nuer speak of it as an ox. In doing so they are asserting something rather more than that it takes the place of an ox. They do not, of course, say that cucumbers are oxen, and in speaking of a particular cucumber as an ox in a sacrificial situation they are only indicating that it may be thought of as an ox in that particular situation; and they act accordingly by performing the sacrificial rites as closely as possible to what happens when the victim is an ox. The resemblance is conceptual, not perceptual. The "is" rests on qualitative analogy. And the expression is asymmetrical, a cucumber is an ox, but an ox is not a cucumber.

A rather different example of this way of speaking is the Nuer assertion that twins are one person and that they are birds.[2] When they say "twins are not two persons, they are one person" they are not saying that they are one individual but that they have a single personality. It is significant that in speaking of the unity of twins they only use the word *ran*, which, like our word "person", leaves sex, age, and other distinguishing qualities of individuals undefined. They would not say that twins of the same sex were one *dhol*, boy, or one *nyal*, girl, but they do say, whether they are of the same sex or not, that they are one *ran*, person. Their single social personality is something over and above their physical duality, a duality which is evident to the senses and is indicated by the plural form used when speaking of twins and by their treatment in all respects in ordinary social life as two quite distinct individuals. It is only in certain ritual situations, and symbolically, that the unity of twins is expressed, particularly in ceremonies connected with marriage and death, in which the personality undergoes a change. Thus, when the senior of male twins marries, the junior acts with him in the ritual acts he has to perform; female twins ought to be married on the same day; and no mortuary ceremonies are held for twins because, for one reason, one of them cannot be cut off from the living without the other. A woman whose twin brother had died some time before said to Miss Soule, to whom I am indebted for the information, "Is not his soul still living? I am alive, and we are really children of God."

There is no mortuary ceremony even when the second twin dies, and I was told that twins do not attend the mortuary ceremonies held for their dead kinsfolk, nor mourn them, because a twin is a *ran nhial*, a person of the sky or of the above. He is also spoken of as *gat kwoth*, a child of God. These dioscuric descriptions of twins are common to many peoples, but the Nuer are peculiar in holding also that they are birds. They say "a twin is not a person (*ran*), he is a bird (*dit*)", although, as we have just seen, they assert, in another sense, that twins are one person (*ran*). Here they are using the word *ran* in the sense of a human being as distinct from any other creature. The dogma is expressed in various ways. Very often a twin is given the proper name *Dit*, bird, *Gwong*, guineafowl, or *Ngec*, francolin.[3]

All Nuer consider it shameful, at any rate for adults, to eat any sort of bird or its eggs, but were a twin to do this it would be much more than shameful. It would be *nueer*, a grave sin, for twins respect (*thek*) birds, because, Nuer say, birds are also twins, and they avoid any sort of contact with them. The equivalence of twins and birds is expressed particularly in connexion with death. When an infant twin dies people say "*ce par*", "he has flown away", using the word denoting the flight of birds. Infant twins who die, as so often happens, are not buried, as other infants are, but are covered in a reed basket or winnowing-tray and placed in the fork of a tree, because birds rest in trees. I was told that birds which feed on carrion would not molest the bodies but would look at their dead kinsmen – twins and birds are also said to be kin, though the usage may be regarded as metaphorical – and fly away again. When I asked a Nuer whether adult twins would be buried like other people he replied "no, of course not, they are birds and their souls go up into the air". A platform, not used in the normal mode of burial, is erected in the grave and a hide placed over it. The body is laid on this hide and covered with a second hide. Earth is then carefully patted over the upper hide instead of being shovelled in quickly, as in the burial of an ordinary person. I was told that the corpse is covered with earth lest a hyena eat it and afterwards drink at a pool, for men might drink at the same pool and die from contamination (*nueer*).

It is understandable that Nuer draw an analogy between the multiple hatching of eggs and the dual birth of twins. The analogy is explicit, and, through an extension of it, the flesh of crocodiles and turtles is also forbidden to twins on the ground that these creatures too, like birds, lay eggs. Miss Soule once had a girl twin in her household who refused fish for the same reason – the only case of its kind known to either of us. But the analogy between multiple births in birds and men does not adequately explain why it is with birds that human twins are equated when there are many other creatures which habitually bear several young at the same time and in a manner more closely resembling human parturition. It cannot be just multiple birth which leads Nuer to

say that twins are birds, for these other creatures are not respected by twins on that account. The prohibition on eating eggs is clearly secondary, and it is extended to include crocodiles and turtles – and by Miss Soule's girl fish also – not because they lay eggs but because their laying eggs makes them like birds. Moreover, it is difficult to understand why a resemblance of the kind should in any case be made so much of. The multiple hatching of chicks is doubtless a resemblance which greatly strengthens the idea of twins being birds, but it is only part of a more complex analogical representation which requires to be explained in more general terms of Nuer religious thought. A twin, on account of his peculiar manner of conception is, though not Spirit himself, a special creation, and, therefore, manifestation of Spirit; and when he dies his soul goes into the air, to which things associated with Spirit belong. He is a *ran nhial*, a person of the above, whereas an ordinary person is a *ran piny*, a person of the below. A bird, though also not in itself Spirit, belongs by nature to the above and is also what Nuer call, using "person" metaphorically, a *ran nhial*, a person of the above, and being such is therefore also associated with Spirit. It cannot, of course, be determined for certain whether a twin is said to be a person of the above because he is a bird or whether he is said to be a bird because he is a person of the above, but the connexion in thought between twins and birds is certainly not simply derived from the multiple birth similitude but also, and in my view primarily, from both birds and twins being classed *by* Nuer as *gaat kwoth*, children of God. Birds are children of God on account of their being in the air, and twins belong to the air on account of their being children of God by the manner of their conception and birth.

It seems odd, if not absurd, to a European when he is told that a twin is a bird as though it were an obvious fact, for Nuer are not saying that a twin is like a bird but that he is a bird. There seems to be a complete contradiction in the statement; and it was precisely on statements of this kind recorded by observers of primitive peoples that Lévy-Bruhl based his theory of the prelogical mentality of these peoples, its chief characteristic being, in his view, that it permits such evident contradictions – that a thing can be what it is and at the same time something altogether different. But, in fact, no contradiction is involved in the statement, which, on the contrary, appears quite sensible, and even true, to one who presents the idea to himself in the Nuer language and within their system of religious thought. He does not then take their statements about twins any more literally than they make and understand them themselves. They are not saying that a twin has a beak, feathers, and so forth. Nor in their everyday relations with twins do Nuer speak of them as birds or act towards them as though they were birds. They treat them as what they are, men and women. But in addition to being men and women they are of a twin-birth, and a twin-birth is a special revelation of Spirit; and Nuer express this special character of twins in the "twins are birds" formula because twins and birds, though for different reasons, are both associated with Spirit and this makes twins, like birds, "people of the above" and "children of God", and hence a bird a suitable symbol in which to express the special relationship in which a twin stands to God. When, therefore, Nuer say that a twin is a bird they are not speaking of either as it appears in the flesh. They are speaking of the *anima* of the twin, what they call his *tie*, a concept which includes both what we call the personality and the soul; and they are speaking of the association birds have with Spirit through their ability to enter the realm to which Spirit is likened in metaphor and where Nuer think it chiefly is, or may be. The formula does not express a dyadic relationship between twins and birds but a triadic relationship between twins, birds, and God. In respect to God twins and birds have a similar character.

It is because Nuer do not make, or take, the statement that twins are birds in any ordinary sense that they are fully aware that in ritual relating to twins the actions are a kind of miming. This is shown in their treatment of the corpse of a twin, for, according to what they themselves say, what is a bird, the *tie* or *anima*, has gone up into the air and what is left and treated – in the case of adults platform burial being a convenient alternative to disposal in trees – as though it might be a bird is only the *ring*, the flesh. It is shown also in the convention that should one of a pair of twins die, the child who comes after them takes his place, counting as one of them in the various ceremonies twins have to perform and respecting birds as rigorously as if he were himself a twin, which he is not. The ceremonies have to be performed for the benefit of the living twin and their structure and purpose are such that there have to be two persons to perform them, so a brother or sister acts in the place of the dead.

This discussion of what is meant by the statement that a twin is a bird is not so far away from the subject of totemism as it might seem to be, for the stock explanation among the Nuer of a totemic relationship is that the ancestor of a lineage and a member of a natural species were born twins. The relationship of lineage to species is thereby made to derive not only from the closest of all possible relationships but also from a special act of divine revelation; and since the link between a lineage and its totem is the tutelary spirit of the lineage associated with the totem it is appropriate that the relationship should be thought of as having come about by an event which is a direct manifestation of Spirit.

However, an examination of the Nuer dogma that twins are birds was made not on account of totemic relationships commonly being explained in terms of twinship but because it was hoped that it would be easier to understand, in the light of any conclusions reached about what is meant by the statement that a twin is a bird, what Nuer mean when they say that some totemic creature, such as the crocodile, is Spirit. Certainly there is here neither the sort of metaphor nor the sort of ellipsis we found in earlier statements. Nor can Nuer be understood to mean that the creature is identical with Spirit, or even with a spirit, Spirit conceived of in a particular totemic refraction. They say quite definitely themselves that it is not; and it is also evident, for Nuer as well as for us, that a material symbol of Spirit cannot, by its very nature, be that which it symbolizes. Nevertheless, though crocodile and Spirit are quite different and unconnected ideas, when the crocodile is for a certain lineage a symbol of their special relationship to God, then in the context of that relationship symbol and what it symbolizes are fused. As in the case of the "twins are birds" formula, the relation is a triadic one, between a lineage and a natural species and God.

There are obvious and significant differences between the creature-Spirit expression and the cucumber-ox and bird-twin expressions. Cucumber, ox, man, and bird are all things which can be known by the senses; but where Spirit is experienced other than in thought it is only in its effects or through material representations of it. We can, therefore, easily see how Nuer regard it as being in, or behind, the crocodile. The subject and predicate terms of the statement that something is Spirit are here no longer held apart by two sets of visible properties. Consequently, while Nuer say that totemic spirits and totems are not the same they sometimes not only speak of, but act towards, a totem as if the spirit were in it. Thus they give some meat of sacrifice to the lion-spirit to lions, and when they sacrifice to the durra-bird-spirit they address also the birds themselves and tell them that the victim is for them. Nevertheless, they make it clear in talking about their totems that what respect they show for them is on account of their representing the spirits associated with them and not for their own sake.

Another difference is that whereas in the cases of the cucumber-ox and twin-bird expressions the equivalence rests on analogies which are quite obvious even to us once they are pointed out – the cucumber being treated in the ritual of sacrifice as an ox is, and twins and birds both being "children of God" and also multiple births – analogy is lacking in the creature-Spirit expression. There is no resemblance between the idea of Spirit and that of crocodile. There is nothing in the nature of crocodiles which evokes the idea of Spirit for Nuer, and even for those who respect crocodiles the idea of Spirit is evoked by these creatures because the crocodiles are a representation of Spirit in relation to their lineage and not because there is anything crocodile-like about Spirit or Spirit-like about crocodiles. We have passed from observation of resemblances to thought by means of symbols in the sort of

way that the crocodile is used as a symbol for Spirit.

We are here faced with the same problem we have been considering earlier, but in what, in the absence of analogical guidance to help us, is a more difficult form. The difficulty is increased by Nuer symbols being taken from an environment unfamiliar to us and one which, even when we familiarize ourselves with it, we experience and evaluate differently. We find it hard to think in terms of crocodiles, snakes, and fig-trees. But reflection shows us that this problem is common to all religious thought, including our own; that a religious symbol has always an intimate association with what it represents, that which brings to the mind with what it brings to the mind. Nuer know that what they see is a crocodile, but since it represents Spirit to some of them it is for those people, when thought of in that way, also what it stands for. The relationship of members of a Nuer lineage to Spirit is represented by a material symbol by which it can be thought of concretely, and therefore as a relationship distinct from the relationships of other lineages to Spirit. What the symbols stand for is the same thing. It is they, and not what they stand for, which differentiate the relationships. There results, when what acts as a symbol is regarded in this way, a fusion between Spirit, as so represented, and its material representation. I would say that then Nuer regard Spirit as being in some way in, or behind, the creature in which in a sense it is beholden.

The problem is even more difficult and complex than I have stated it, because we might say that what are fused are not so much the idea of Spirit and its material representation as the idea of Spirit and the idea of its material representation. It is rather the idea of crocodile than the saurian creatures themselves which stands for Spirit to a lineage. If a Nuer cannot see Spirit he likewise in some cases seldom, if ever, sees his totem; so that it is no longer a question of a material object symbolizing an idea but of one idea symbolizing another. I doubt whether those who respect monorchid bulls or waterbuck often see a member of the class or species, and children in these and other cases must often be told about their totemic attachments before they have seen their totems. There must also be Nuer who respect dom palms who live in parts of Nuerland to the east of the Nile where this tree does not grow.[4] Indeed, I feel confident that one totem, the *lou* serpent, a kind of Loch Ness monster, does not exist, and if this is so, a totem can be purely imaginary. As this point has some theoretical importance for a study of totemism I draw attention to a further significant fact. Nuer do not speak of the spirit of crocodiles, lions, tamarind-trees, and so on, but always of the spirit of crocodile, lion, and tamarind-tree, and they would never say that crocodiles, lions, and tamarind-trees were somebody's spirit but always that crocodile, lion, and tamarind-tree, was his spirit. The difference in meaning between the plural and singular usage is not, perhaps, very obvious in English but it is both clear and vital in Nuer. It is the difference between crocodiles thought of as they are seen in rivers and crocodiles thought of as crocodile or as the crocodile, as a type of creature, crocodile as a conception. The point I am making is exemplified by the story already recorded (p. 65) of a man who gave up respecting lions because they killed his cattle. He still regarded lion-spirit, Spirit in the representation of lion, as a spirit connected with his family. But if a totemic relationship may be an ideal one, and has always something of the ideal in it, I would still say that Nuer regard Spirit as being in some way in, or behind, totemic creatures when they think of them as representations of Spirit.

[. . .]

. . . The more Spirit is thought to be bound to visible forms the less it is thought of as Spirit and the more it is thought of in terms of what it is bound to. In other words, there are gradations of the conception of Spirit from pure unattached Spirit to Spirit associated with human, animal, and lifeless objects and more and more closely bound to what it is associated with the farther down the scale one goes. This scale of Spirit, as I have explained earlier, is related to segmentation of the social order and is represented by Nuer by levels of space as well as by levels and degrees of immanence. So when Nuer say of something that it is Spirit

we have to consider not only what "is" means but also what "Spirit" means. Nevertheless, though the sense of "*kwoth*" varies with the context, the word refers always to something of the same essence; and what is being said, directly or indirectly, in the statements is always the same, that something is that essence.

We can make some contribution towards a solution of the problem in the light of this discussion. When Nuer say of something "*e kwoth*", "it is Spirit", or give it a name of which it can be further said "that is Spirit", the "is" does not in all instances have the same connotation. It may be an elliptical statement, signifying that the thing referred to is a manifestation of Spirit in the sense of God revealing himself in instruments or effects. Or it may be a symbolical statement, signifying that what in itself is not Spirit but represents Spirit to certain persons is for these persons Spirit in such contexts as direct attention to the symbolic character of an object to the exclusion of whatever other qualities it may possess. Or it may be a statement signifying something closer to identity of the thing spoken of with what it is said to be, Spirit. The statements never, however, signify complete identity of anything with Spirit, because Nuer think of Spirit as something more than any of its modes, signs, effects, representations, and so forth, and also as something of a different nature from the created things which they are. They are not able to define what it is, but when it acts within the phenomenal world they say it has come from above, where it is conceived to be and whence it is thought to descend. Consequently Spirit in any form can be detached in the mind from the things said to be it, even if they cannot always be so easily detached from the idea of Spirit.

I can take the analysis no farther; but if it is inconclusive it at least shows, if it is correct, how wide of the mark have been anthropological attempts to explain the kind of statements we have been considering. Anthropological explanations display two main errors. The first, best exemplified in the writings of Lévy-Bruhl, is that when a people say that something is something else which is different they are contravening the Law of Contradiction and substituting for it a law of their own pre-logical way of thinking, that of mystical participation.[5] I hope at least to have shown that Nuer do not assert identity between the two things. They may say that one is the other and in certain situations act towards it as though it were that other, or something like it, but they are aware, no doubt with varying degrees of awareness, and readily say, though with varying degrees of clarity and emphasis, that the two things are different. Moreover, it will have been noted that in the seemingly equivocal statements we have considered, with perhaps one exception, the terms cannot be reversed. The exception is the statement that twins are birds, because it can also be said that birds are twins. That a hatch of birds are twins is a statement, to which we also can give assent, which does not derive logically from the statement that twins are birds but from a perception independent of that proposition; so it does not concern our problem. Rain may be said to be God but God cannot be said to be rain; a cucumber may be called an ox but an ox cannot be called a cucumber; and the crocodile may be said to be Spirit but Spirit cannot be said to be the crocodile. Consequently these are not statements of identity. They are statements not that something is other than it is but that in a certain sense and in particular contexts something has some extra quality which does not belong to it in its own nature; and this quality is not contrary to, or incompatible with, its nature but something added to it which does not alter what it was but makes it something more, in respect to this quality, than it was. Consequently, no contradiction, it seems to me, is involved in the statements.

Whether the predicate refers to a conception or to a visible object the addition makes the subject equivalent to it in respect to the quality which both now have in common in such contexts as focus the attention on that quality alone. The things referred to are not the same as each other but they are the same in that one respect, and the equivalence, denoted by the copula, is not one of substance but of quality. Consequently we cannot speak here, as Lévy-Bruhl does, of mystical participation, or at any rate not in his sense of the words, because the two things are not thought to be linked by a mystical bond but simply by a symbolic nexus. Therefore, what is done to birds is not thought to affect twins, and if a totem is harmed the spirit of that totem may be offended but it is not harmed by the harm done to the totemic creature.

That the relation between the thing said to be something else and that something else it is said to be is an ideal one is indeed obvious, but anthropological explanations of modes of primitive thought as wide apart as those of Tylor, Max Müller, and Lévy-Bruhl, are based on the assumption that though for us the relation is an ideal one primitive peoples mistake it for a real one; and those anthropologists who sponsor psychological explanations often make the same assumption. This is the second error. If my interpretation is correct, Nuer know very well when they say that a crocodile is Spirit that it is only Spirit in the sense that Spirit is represented to some people by that symbol just as they know very well that a cucumber is only an ox in the sense that they treat it as one in sacrifice. That they do not mistake idea relations for real ones is shown by many examples in this book: the identification of a sacrificial spear with that of the ancestor . . ., the identification of man with ox in sacrifice . . ., the identification of a man's herd with that of the ancestor of his clan . . ., the identification of sickness and sin in a sacrificial context . . ., and the identification of the left hand with death and evil. . . . It is shown also in the symbolism of many of their rites, where their purpose is expressed in mimicry. . . .

I think that one reason why it was not readily perceived that statements that something is something else should not be taken as matter-of-fact statements is that it was not recognized that they are made in relation to a third term not mentioned in them but understood. They are statements, as far as the Nuer are concerned, not that A is B, but that A and B have something in common in relation to C. This is evident when we give some thought to the matter. A cucumber is equivalent to an ox in respect to God who accepts it in the place of an ox. A crocodile is equivalent to Spirit only when conceived of as a representation of God to a lineage. Consequently, though Nuer do not mistake ideal relations for real ones, an ideal equivalence is none the less true for them, because within their system of religious thought things are not just what they appear to be but as they are conceived of in relation to God.

This implies experience on an imaginative level of thought where the mind moves in figures, symbols, metaphors, analogies, and many an elaboration of poetic fancy and language; and another reason why there has been misunderstanding is that the poetic sense of primitive peoples has not been sufficiently allowed for, so that it has not been appreciated that what they say is often to be understood in that sense and not in any ordinary sense. This is certainly the case with the Nuer, as we see in this chapter and in many places elsewhere in this book, for example, in their hymns. In all their poems and songs also they play on words and images to such an extent that no European can translate them without commentary from Nuer, and even Nuer themselves cannot always say what meaning they had for their authors. It is the same with their cattle- and dance-names, which are chosen both for euphony and to express analogies. How Nuer delight in playing with words is also seen in the fun they have in making up tongue-twisters, sentences which are difficult to pronounce without a mistake, and slips of the tongue, usually slips in the presence of mothers-in-law, which turn quite ordinary remarks into obscenities. Lacking plastic and visual arts, the imagination of this sensitive people finds its sole expression in ideas, images, and words.

In this and the last chapter I have attempted to lay bare some features of the Nuer conception of Spirit. We are not asking what Spirit is but what is the Nuer conception of *kwoth*, which we translate "Spirit". Since it is a conception that we are inquiring into, our inquiry is an exploration of ideas. In the course of it we have found that whilst Nuer conceive of Spirit as creator and father in the heavens they also think of it in many different representations (what I have called refractions of Spirit) in relation to social groups, categories, and persons. The conception of Spirit has, we found, a social dimension (we can also say, since the statement can be reversed, that the social structure has a spiritual dimension). We found also that Spirit, in the Nuer conception of it, is experienced in signs, media, and symbols through which it is manifested to the senses. Fundamentally, however, this is not a relation of Spirit to things but a relation of Spirit to persons through things, so that, here again, we are ultimately concerned with the relation of God and man, and we have to consider not only what is the God-to-man side of the relationship, to which attention has so far mostly been given, but also the man-to-God side of it, to which I now turn.

NOTES

1 The spear *wiu* may be said to stand for the spirit *wiu*, and the pied crow may be said to stand for the spirit *buk* which is the most terrestrially conceived of among the greater spirits.

2 I have given a more detailed account in "Customs and Beliefs Relating to Twins among the Nilotic Nuer", *Uganda Journal*, 1936.

3 That the names, at least all those I have heard, are taken from birds lowest in the scale of Nuer reckoning requires comment, especially in view of the argument I later develop. It may be due to the Nuer habit of speaking of their relation to God – the birth of twins constitutes such a context – by comparing themselves with lowly things. On the other hand, it may be simply in keeping with the logic of the analogy. Twins belong to the class of the above but are below; just as guineafowl and francolin belong to the class of birds, which as a class is in the category of the above, but are almost earthbound.

4 Dr. Lienhardt tells me that a number of lineages in western Dinkaland respect creatures which no longer exist there. A Dinka who travelled with him to other parts of the Southern Sudan was astonished when he first saw his totem, an elephant. Nana

Kobina Nketsia IV of Sekondi permits me to say that the first time he saw his totem, the buffalo, was last year in a film at Oxford. Professor I. Schapera tells me that the ruling family of the senior tribe in the Bechuanaland Protectorate, the Kwena, have been living for a hundred years in a region where their totem, the crocodile, is unknown (see also what he says in *The Tswana* (International African Institute), 1953, p. 35, and Hugh Ashton, *The Basuto*, 1952, p. 14). Other examples could be cited. It may help us to appreciate the point better if we consider the nearest parallels in our own country. When we think of the lion as our national symbol we do not think of the mangy creatures of the African bush or in zoos. Nor does it incommode us that there are no unicorns and never have been any.

5   I refer to his earlier writings, in particular *Les Fonctions mentales dans les sociétés inférieures* (1910) and *La mentalité primitive* (1922). The second part of his last book, *L'Expérience mystique et les symboles chez les primitifs* (1938), which took account of modern research, is a brilliant discourse on the problems we have been discussing.

12

On Key Symbols

Sherry B. Ortner

Sherry Ortner is an American anthropologist, who trained at Chicago and taught at Michigan and Columbia before moving to UCLA. She is renowned for the clarity of her synthetic appraisals of theory, of which this is an early one (see also 1984, 1995), her contributions to gender theory and feminist anthropology (1974, 1996a; Ortner and Whitehead 1981), and her ethnographies of Sherpa Buddhism (1978, 1989, 1999b) as well as class in the USA. Ortner was a student of Geertz who, despite her interest in seeking broader and more "muscular" forms of social explanation than he provides (Dirks, Eley, and Ortner, eds., 1994), has remained one of the most articulate spokespersons for the significance of culture in social theory.

If Langer and White established the symbolic ground of culture, there was a trend in American anthropology to go further and seek the symbols that could sum up the particular focus, ethos, character, or worldview of a given cultural system. In this essay Ortner captures a particularly exciting moment in the discipline as symbolic anthropology emerged into prominence, and usefully articulates the various ways anthropologists have conceived, derived, or applied dominant symbols and how the symbols operate. Ortner suggests both the ways systems of meaning are organized and the ways different kinds of symbols work to condense, produce, or invite meaning. Whether or not such symbols work effectively in the ethnographic portraits constructed by anthropologists, they often do appear to serve such ends for the groups in which they are found. What Ortner offers is a series of Weberian "ideal types," not species of symbols. This essay represents the state of the art in the early 1970s; Ortner has since moved well beyond it in an attempt to fully historicize cultural accounts. For

From Sherry B. Ortner, "On Key Symbols," *American Anthropologist* 75 (1973): 1338–46. Reprinted by permission of the American Anthropological Association. Notes deleted.

a later essay that links meaning with power, see Ortner (1999a).

Victor Turner (1967) provides several great essays on religious symbols from a Durkheimian perspective. Douglas (1975) offers a classic analysis of a central symbol, the Lele pangolin, while De Boeck (1994) gives a more recent intricate symbolic interpretation from the same Central African culture area as Turner and Douglas. A general account of symbols is to be found in Firth (1973), while Munn (1973; cf. 1986, 1990) is an excellent discussion of the transformative properties of ritual symbols. Schneider moves away from individual symbols to account for the symbolic constitution of persons and the conceptions underlying such cultural domains as kinship and religion (1977 [1969], 1980 [1968]). The notion of cultural scenarios is well developed in Schieffelin (1976). Both Pepper (1942) and White (1973) offer suggestive accounts of the power of underlying metaphors. In addition to the essay by Tambiah (chapter 25, below), the best anthropological work on metaphor is by Fernandez (1986b; ed. 1991) and Sapir and Crocker, eds. (1977). For a more directly linguistic account illustrating the prevalence of metaphor in ordinary language, see Lakoff and Johnson (1980).

This paper reviews the use of the notion of "key symbol" in anthropological analysis. It analyzes phenomena which have been or might be accorded the status of key symbol in cultural analyses, categorizing them according to their primary modes of operating on thought and action.

It is by no means a novel idea that each culture has certain key elements which, in an ill-defined way, are crucial to its distinctive organization. Since the publication of Benedict's *Patterns of Culture* in 1934, the notion of such key elements has persisted in American anthropology under a variety of rubrics: "themes" (e.g., Opler 1945; Cohen 1948), "focal values" (Albert 1956), "dominant values" (DuBois 1955), "integrative concepts" (DuBois 1936), "dominant orientations" (F. Kluckhohn 1950), and so forth. We can also find this idea sneaking namelessly into British social anthropological writing; the best example of this is Lienhardt's (1961) discussion of cattle in Dinka culture (and I say culture rather than society advisedly). Even Evans-Pritchard has said, "as every experienced field-worker knows, the most difficult task in social anthropological field work is to determine the meanings of a few key words, upon an understanding of which the success of the whole investigation depends" (1962:80). Recently, as the focus in the study of meaning systems has shifted to the symbolic units which formulate meaning, the interest in these key elements of cultures has become specified as the interest in key symbols. Schneider (1968) calls them "core symbols" in his study of American kinship; Turner (1967) calls them "dominant symbols" in his study of Ndembu ritual; I called them "key symbols" in my study of Sherpa social relations (Ortner 1970).

The primary question of course is what do we mean by "key"? But I will postpone considering this problem until I have discussed the various usages of the notion of key symbols in the literature of symbolic analysis.

Two methodological approaches to establishing certain symbols as "core" or "key" to a cultural system have been employed. The first approach, less commonly used, involves analyzing the system (or domains thereof) for its underlying elements – cognitive distinctions, value orientations, etc. – then looking about in the culture for some figure or image which seems to formulate, in relatively pure form, the underlying orientations exposed in the analysis. The best example of this approach in the current literature is David Schneider's (1968) analysis of American kinship; Schneider first analyzes the kinship system for its basic components – nature and law – and then decides that conjugal sexual intercourse is the form which, given its meaning in the culture, expresses this opposition most succinctly and meaningfully. Schneider expresses his debt to Ruth Benedict, and this debt turns out to be quite specific, since the other major work which embodies this method is Benedict's *The Chrysanthemum and the Sword* (1967). The sword and the chrysanthemum were chosen by Benedict from the repertoire of Japanese symbols as most succinctly, or perhaps most poetically, representing the tension in the Japanese value system which she postulated. She did not arrive at this tension through an analysis of the meanings of chrysanthemums and swords in the culture; she first established the tension in Japanese culture through analysis of various symbolic systems, then chose these two items from the repertoire of Japanese symbols to sum up the opposition.

In the second, more commonly employed approach, the investigator observes something which seems to be an object of cultural interest, and analyzes it for its meanings. The observation that some symbol is a focus of cultural interest need not be very mysterious or intuitive. I offer here five reasonably reliable indicators of cultural interest, and there are probably more. Most key symbols, I venture to suggest, will be signaled by more than one of these indicators:

(1)   The natives tell us that X is culturally important.
(2)   The natives seem positively or negatively aroused about X, rather than indifferent.
(3)   X comes up in many different contexts. These contexts may be behavioral or systemic: X comes up in many different kinds of action situation or conversation, or X comes up in many different symbolic domains (myth, ritual, art, formal rhetoric, etc.).
(4)   There is greater cultural elaboration surrounding X, e.g., elaboration of vocabulary, or elaboration of details of X's nature, compared with similar phenomena in the culture.
(5)   There are greater cultural restrictions surrounding X, either in sheer number of rules, or severity of sanctions regarding its misuse.

As I said, there may be more indicators even than these of the key status of a symbol in a culture, but any of these should be enough to point even the most insensitive fieldworker in the right direction. I should also add that I am not assuming that there is only one key symbol to every culture; cultures are of course a product of the interplay of many basic orientations, some quite conflicting. But all of them will be expressed somewhere in the public system, because the public symbol system is ultimately the only source from which the natives themselves discover, rediscover, and transform their own culture, generation after generation.

It remains for us now to sort out the bewildering array of phenomena to which various investigators have been led to assign implicitly or explicitly the status of key cultural symbol. Anything by definition can be a symbol, i.e., a vehicle for cultural meaning, and it seems from a survey of the literature that almost anything can be key. Omitting the symbols established by the first approach cited above, which have a different epistemological status, we can cite from the anthropological literature such things as cattle among the Dinka and Nuer, the Naven ritual of the Iatmul, the Australian churinga, the slametan of the Javanese, the potlatch of the northwest coast, the forked stick of Ndembu rituals, and from my own research, the wheel-image in Tibet and food among the Sherpas. We could also add such intuitive examples as the cross of Christianity, the American flag, the motorcycle for the Hell's Angels, "work" in the Protestant ethic, and so on.

The list is a jumble – things and abstractions, nouns and verbs, single items and whole events. I should like to propose a way of subdividing and ordering the set, in terms of the ways in which the symbols operate in relation to cultural thought and action.

The first major breakdown among the various types of symbols is along a continuum whose two ends I call "summarizing" *vs.* "elaborating." I stress that it is a continuum, but I work with the ideal types at the two ends.

Summarizing symbols, first, are those symbols which are seen as summing up, expressing, representing for the participants in an emotionally powerful and relatively undifferentiated way, what the system means to them. This category is essentially the category of sacred symbols in the broadest sense, and includes all those items which are objects of reverence and/or catalysts of emotion – the flag, the cross, the churinga, the forked stick, the motorcycle, etc. The American flag, for example, for certain Americans, stands for something called "the American way," a conglomerate of ideas and feelings including (theoretically) democracy, free enterprise, hard work, competition, progress, national superiority, freedom, etc. And it stands for them all at once. It does not encourage reflection on the logical relations among these ideas, nor on the logical consequences of them as they are played out in social actuality, over time and history. On the contrary, the flag encourages a sort of all-or-nothing allegiance to the whole package, best summed up on a billboard I saw recently: "Our flag, love it or leave." And this is the point about summarizing symbols in general – they operate to compound and synthesize a complex system of ideas, to "summarize" them under a unitary form which, in an old-fashioned way, "stands for" the system as a whole.

Elaborating symbols, on the other hand, work in the opposite direction, providing vehicles for sorting out complex and undifferentiated feelings and ideas, making them comprehensible to oneself, communicable to others, and translatable into orderly action. Elaborating symbols are accorded central status in the culture on the basis of their capacity to order experience; they are essentially analytic. Rarely are these symbols sacred in the conventional sense of being objects of respect or foci of emotion; their key status is indicated primarily by their recurrence in cultural behavior or cultural symbolic systems.

Symbols can be seen as having elaborating power in two modes. They may have primarily conceptual elaborating power, that is, they are valued as a source of categories for conceptu-

alizing the order of the world. Or they may have primarily action elaborating power; that is, they are valued as implying mechanisms for successful social action. These two modes reflect what I see as the two basic and of course interrelated functions of culture in general: to provide for its members "orientations," i.e., cognitive and affective categories; and "strategies," i.e., programs for orderly social action in relation to culturally defined goals.

Symbols with great conceptual elaborating power are what Stephen Pepper (1942) has called "root metaphors," and indeed in this realm the basic mechanism is the metaphor. It is felt in the culture that many aspects of experience can be likened to, and illuminated by the comparison with, the symbol itself. In Pepper's terms, the symbol provides a set of categories for conceptualizing other aspects of experience, or, if this point is stated too uni-directionally for some tastes, we may say that the root metaphor formulates the unity of cultural orientation underlying many aspects of experience, by virtue of the fact that those many aspects of experience can be likened to it.

One of the best examples of a cultural root metaphor in the anthropological literature is found in Godfrey Lienhardt's discussion of the role of cattle in Dinka thought. Cows provide for the Dinka an almost endless set of categories for conceptualizing and responding to the subtleties of experience. For example: "The Dinkas' very perception of colour, light, and shade in the world around them is . . . inextricably connected with their recognition of colour-configurations in their cattle. If their cattle-colour vocabulary were taken away, they would have scarcely any way of describing visual experience in terms of colour, light and darkness" (1961:13). More important for Lienhardt's thesis is the Dinka conceptualization of the structure of their own society on analogy with the physical structure of the bull. "'The people are put together, as a bull is put together,' said a Dinka chief on one occasion" (ibid.: 23), and indeed the formally prescribed division of the meat of a sacrificed bull is a most graphic representation of the statuses, functions, and interrelationships of the major social categories of Dinka society, as the Dinka themselves represent the situation.

In fact, as Mary Douglas points out, the living organism in one form or another functions as a root metaphor in many cultures, as a source of categories for conceptualizing social phenomena (1966). In mechanized society, on the other hand, one root metaphor for the social process is the machine, and in recent times the computer represents a crucial modification upon this root metaphor. But the social is not the only aspect of experience which root-metaphor type symbols are used to illuminate; for example, much of greater Indo-Tibetan cosmology – the forms and processes of life, space, and time – is developed on analogy with the quite simple image of the wheel (Ortner 1966).

A root metaphor, then, is one type of key symbol in the elaborating mode, i.e., a symbol which operates to sort out experience, to place it in cultural categories, and to help us think about how it all hangs together. They are symbols which are "good to think," not exactly in the Lévi-Straussian sense, but in that one can conceptualize the interrelationships among phenomena by analogy to the interrelations among the parts of the root metaphor.

The other major type of elaborating symbol is valued primarily because it implies clear-cut modes of action appropriate to correct and successful living in the culture. Every culture, of course, embodies some vision of success, or the good life, but the cultural variation occurs in how success is defined, and, given that, what are considered the best ways of achieving it. "Key scenarios," as I call the type of key symbol in this category, are culturally valued in that they formulate the culture's basic means-ends relationships in actable forms.

An example of a key scenario from American culture would be the Horatio Alger myth. The scenario runs: poor boy of low status, but with total faith in the American system, works very hard and ultimately becomes rich and powerful. The myth formulates both the American conception of success – wealth and power – and suggests that there is a simple (but not easy) way of achieving them – singleminded hard work. This scenario may be contrasted with ones from other cultures which present other actions as the most effective means of achieving wealth and power, or which formulate wealth and power as appropriate goals only for certain segments of the society, or, of course, those which do not define cultural success in terms of wealth and power at all. In any case, the point is that every culture has a number of such key scenarios which both formulate appropriate goals and suggest effective action for achieving them; which formulate, in other words, key cultural strategies.

This category of key symbols may also include rituals; Singer seems to be making the point of rituals as scenarios when he writes of "cultural performances" (1958), in which both valued end states and effective means for achieving them are dramatized for all to see. Thus this category would include naven, the slametan, the potlatch, and others. The category could also include individual elements of rituals – objects, roles, action sequences – insofar as they refer to or epitomize the ritual as a whole, which is why one can have actions, objects, and whole events in the same category.

Further, scenarios as key symbols may include not only formal, usually named events, but also all those cultural sequences of action which we can observe enacted and reenacted according to unarticulated formulae in the normal course of daily life. An example of such a scenario from Sherpa culture would be the hospitality scenario, in which any individual in the role of host feeds a guest and thereby renders him voluntarily cooperative vis-à-vis oneself. The scenario formulates both the ideally valued (though infrequently attained) mode of social relations in the culture – voluntary cooperation – and, given certain cultural assumptions about the effects of food on people, the most effective way of establishing those kinds of relations. Once again then, the scenario is culturally valued – indicated in this case by the fact that it is played and replayed in the most diverse sorts of social contexts – because it suggests a clear-cut strategy for arriving at culturally defined success.

I have been discussing the category of key symbols which I called "elaborating" symbols, symbols valued for their contribution to the sorting out of experience. This class includes both root metaphors which provide categories for the ordering of conceptual experience, and key scenarios which provide strategies for organizing action experience. While for purposes of this discussion I have been led by the data to separate thought from action, I must hasten to put the pieces back together again. For my view is that ultimately both kinds of symbols have both types of referents. Root metaphors, by establishing a certain view of the world, implicitly suggest certain valid and effective ways of acting upon it; key scenarios, by prescribing certain culturally effective courses of action, embody and rest upon certain assumptions about the nature of reality. Even summarizing symbols, while primarily functioning to compound rather than sort out experience, are seen as both formulating basic orientations and implying, though much less systematically than scenarios, certain modes of action.

One question which might be raised at this point is how we are to understand the logical relationships among the types of key symbols I have distinguished. As the scheme stands now, it has the following unbalanced structure:

summarizing   vs.   elaborating
                          /   \
                        /   \
                    root   key
                  metaphor   scenario

I would argue that this asymmetry follows from the content of the types: the meaning-content of summarizing or sacred symbols is by definition clustered, condensed, relatively undifferentiated, "thick," while the meaning-content of elaborating symbols is by definition relatively clear, orderly, differentiated, articulate. Thus it is possible to make distinctions among the different ordering functions of elaborating symbols, while the denseness of meaning of summarizing symbols renders them relatively resistant to subdivision and ordering by types. Nonetheless, in the interest of systematic analysis, we may raise the question of whether such subdivisions are possible, and in particular whether the thought/action distinction which subdivides elaborating symbols (into root metaphors and key scenarios)

also crosscuts and subdivides summarizing symbols.

The important mode of operation of summarizing symbols, it will be recalled, is its focusing power, its drawing-together, intensifying, catalyzing impact upon the respondent. Thus we must ask whether some summarizing symbols primarily operate to catalyze thought or in any case internal states of the actor, while others primarily operate to catalyze overt action on the part of the actor. Now it does seem possible, for example, to see the cross or some other religious symbol as primarily focusing and intensifying inner attitude, with no particular implied public action, while the flag or some other political symbol is primarily geared to focusing and catalyzing overt action in the public world. Yet, intuitively at least, this distinction seems relatively weak and unconvincing compared to the easily formulated and grasped distinction between the two types of elaborating symbols: static formal images serving metaphor functions for thought (root metaphors), and dramatic, phased action sequences serving scenario functions for action (key scenarios). Of course, as I said, root metaphors may imply particular modes of, or at least a restricted set of possible modes of, action; and key scenarios presuppose certain orderly assumptions of thought. But the distinction – the former geared primarily to thought, the latter to action – remains sharp.

Summarizing symbols, on the other hand, speak primarily to attitudes, to a crystallization of commitment. And, in the mode of commitment, the thought/action distinction is not particularly relevant. There may certainly be consequences for thought and action as a result of a crystallized commitment, but commitment itself is neither thought nor action. The point perhaps illuminates the generally sacred status of summarizing symbols, for they are speaking to a more diffuse mode of orientation in the actor, a broader context of attitude within which particular modes of thinking and acting are formulated.

This is not to say that nothing analytic may be said about summarizing symbols beyond the fact that they catalyze feeling; there are a number of possible ways of subdividing the catalog of sacred symbols in the world, some no doubt more useful or illuminated than others. My point is merely that the particular factor which subdivides elaborating symbols – the thought/action distinction – does not serve very powerfully to subdivide the category of summarizing symbols, since the summarizing symbol is speaking to a different level of response, the level of attitude and commitment.

We are now in a position to return to the question of "key" or central status. Why are we justified in calling a particular symbol "key"? The indicators provided earlier for at least provisionally regarding certain symbols as key to a particular culture were all based on the assumption that keyness has public (though not necessarily conscious) manifestation in the culture itself, available to the observer in the field, or at least available when one reflects upon one's observations. But the fact of public cultural concern or focus of interest is not *why* a symbol is key; it is only a *signal* that the symbol is playing some key role in relation to other elements of the cultural system of thought. The issue of keyness, in short, has to do with the internal organization of the system of cultural meaning, as that system functions for actors leading their lives in the culture.

Broadly speaking, the two types of key symbols distinguished above, defined in terms of how they act upon or are manipulated by cultural actors, also indicate the two broad modes of "keyness" from a systemic point of view, defined in terms of the role such symbols are playing in the system; that is, a given summarizing symbol is "key" to the system insofar as the meanings which it formulates are logically or affectively prior to other meanings of the system. By "logically or affectively prior" I mean simply that many other cultural ideas and attitudes presuppose, and make sense only in the context of, those meanings formulated by the symbol. The key role of an elaborating symbol, by contrast, derives not so much from the status of its particular substantive meanings, but from its formal or organizational role in relation to the system; that is, we say such a symbol is "key" to the system insofar as it extensively and systematically formulates relationships – parallels, isomorphisms, complementarities, and so forth – between a wide range of diverse cultural elements.

This contrast between the two modes of "keyness" may be summed up in various ways, all of which oversimplify to some extent, but which nonetheless give perspective on the point. (1) "Content versus form": The keyness of a summarizing symbol derives from its particular substantive meanings (content) and their logical priority in relation to other meanings of the system. The keyness of an elaborating symbol derives from its formal properties, and their culturally postulated power to formulate widely applicable modes of organizing cultural phenomena. (2) "Quality versus quantity": The keyness of a summarizing symbol derives from the relative fundamentality (or ultimacy) of the meanings which it formulates, relative to other meanings of the system. The keyness of an elaborating symbol derives from the broadness of its scope, the extent to which it systematically draws relationships between a wide range of diverse cultural elements. (3) "Vertical versus lateral": The keyness of a summarizing symbol derives from its ability to relate lower-order meanings to higher-order assumptions, or to "ground" more surface-level meanings to their deeper bases. (The issue here is degree of generality of meaning. Whether more general meanings are termed "higher" or "deeper," "ultimate" or "fundamental," by a particular cultural analyst seems a matter of personal preference.) The keyness of an elaborating symbol by contrast derives from its ability to interconnect disparate elements at essentially the same level, by virtue of its ability to manifest (or bring into relief) their formal similarities.

All of these terminological contrasts – form/content, quantity/quality, lateral/vertical – are really perspectives upon the same basic contrast, for which we have no more general term; that is, when we say a summarizing symbol is "key" to the system, we mean that its substantive meanings have certain kinds of priority relative to other meanings of the system. When we say an elaborating symbol is key to the system, we refer to the power of its formal or organizational role in relation to the system.

But at this point we must stop short of reifying the distinctions, for, in practice, the contrast between the two broad types of key symbols and the two modes of "keyness" may break down. It seems empirically to be the case that an elaborating symbol which is accorded wide-ranging applicability in the culture – played in many contexts, or applied to many different sorts of forms – is generally not only formally apt but also substantively referential to high-level values, ideas, cognitive assertions, and so forth. Indeed, insofar as such high level formulations are made, a key elaborating symbol of a culture may move into the sacred mode and operate in much the same way as does a summarizing symbol. And, on the other hand, some summarizing symbols may play important ordering functions, as when they relate the respondent not merely to a cluster of high-level assumptions and values, but to a particular scenario which may be replayed in ongoing life. (One may think, for example, of the Christian cross evoking, among other things, not only a general sense of God's purpose and support, but also the particular scenario of Christ's martyrdom.)

Thus we are brought to an important point, namely, that we are distinguishing not only types of symbols, but types of symbolic functions. These functions may be performed by any given symbol – at different times, or in different contexts, or even simultaneously by different "levels" of its meaning. While there are many examples of summarizing and elaborating symbols in their relatively pure forms, the kinds of functions or operations these symbols perform may also be seen as aspects of any given symbols.

To summarize the original scheme briefly, key symbols may be discovered by virtue of a number of reliable indicators which point to cultural focus of interest. They are of two broad types – summarizing and elaborating. Summarizing symbols are primarily objects of attention and cultural respect; they synthesize or "collapse" complex experience, and relate the respondent to the grounds of the system as a whole. They include most importantly sacred symbols in the traditional sense. Elaborating symbols, on the other hand, are symbols valued for their contribution to the ordering or "sorting out" of experience. Within this are symbols valued primarily for the ordering of conceptual experience, i.e., for providing cultural "orientations," and those valued primarily for the ordering of action, i.e., for providing cultural "strategies." The former includes what Pepper calls "root metaphors," the latter includes key scenarios, or elements of scenarios which are crucial to the means-end relationship postulated in the complete scenario.

This scheme also suggests, at least by the choices of terms, the modes of symbolic analysis relevant to the different types of key symbols. The first type (summarizing symbols) suggests a range of questions pertaining to the cultural conversion of complex ideas into various kinds of relatively undifferentiated commitment – patriotism, for example, or faith. The second type (root metaphors) suggests questions applicable to the analysis of metaphor in the broadest sense – questions of how thought proceeds and organizes itself through analogies, models, images, and so forth. And the third type (key scenarios) suggests dramatistic modes of analysis, in which one raises questions concerning the restructuring of attitudes and relationships as a result of enacting particular culturally provided sequences of stylized actions.

This article has been frankly programmatic; I am in the process of implementing some of its ideas in a monograph on Sherpa social and religious relations. Here I have simply been concerned to show that, although a method of cultural analysis via key symbols has been for the most part unarticulated, there is at least incipiently method in such analysis. It is worth our while to try to systematize this method, for it may be our most powerful entree to the distinctiveness and variability of human cultures.

REFERENCES CITED

Albert, Ethel. 1956. The Classification of Values: A Method and Illustration. *American Anthropologist* 58: 221–48.

Benedict, Ruth. 1934. *Patterns of Culture.* Boston: Houghton-Mifflin.

——.1967. *The Chrysanthemum and the Sword.* Cleveland and New York: World.

Cohen, A. K. 1948. On the Place of "Themes" and Kindred Concepts in Social Theory. *American Anthropologist* 50: 436–43.

Douglas, Mary. 1966. *Purity and Danger.* New York: Praeger.

DuBois, Cora. 1936. The Wealth Concept as an Integrative Factor in Tolowa-Tututni Culture. *In Essays in Anthropology Presented to A. L. Kroeber.* Robert Lowie, Ed. Berkeley: University of California Press.

——.1955. The Dominant Value Profile of American Culture. *American Anthropologist* 57: 1232–9.

Evans-Pritchard, E. E. 1962. *Social Anthropology and Other Essays.* New York: Free Press.

Kluckhohn, Florence. 1950. Dominant and Substitute Profiles of Cultural Orientation. *Social Forces* 28: 376–93.

Lienhardt, Godfrey. 1961. *Divinity and Experience.* Oxford: Clarendon Press.

Opler, Morris E. 1945. Themes as Dynamic Forces in Culture. *American Journal of Sociology* 51: 198–206.

Ortner, Sherry B. (Sherry O. Paul). 1966. Tibetan Circles. M.A. thesis, University of Chicago.

——.1970. Food for Thought: A Key Symbol in Sherpa Culture. Ph.D. thesis, University of Chicago.

Pepper, Stephen. 1942. *World Hypotheses.* Berkeley and Los Angeles: University of California Press.

Schneider, David M. 1968. *American Kinship.* Englewood Cliffs, N.J.: Prentice-Hall.

Singer, Milton. 1958. The Great Tradition in a Metropolitan Center: Madras. In *Traditional India: Structure and Change.* Milton Singer, Ed. Philadelphia: American Folklore Society.

Turner, Victor. 1967. *The Forest of Symbols.* Ithaca: Cornell University Press.

13

The Virgin of Guadalupe:
A Mexican National Symbol

Eric R. Wolf

Eric Wolf (1923–99) was one of the most significant American anthropologists of the 20th century, serving as a leading advocate and clear expositor of a scholarly, politically accountable historical materialist approach and advancing the study of peasant or agrarian societies. He conducted fieldwork in both Latin America and Europe. Wolf gives central place to power (1999) and to historicizing (rather than abstracting or idealizing) culture; his book on the consequences for "the people without history" of European expansion (1982) has been particularly influential. Wolf's approach is evident already in this early interpretation of a master symbol (in Ortner's terms, a summarizing key symbol) that gained national importance in Mexico. The essay illuminates both the nature of such a symbol and the process of syncretism (cultural mixing). Wolf suggests how the imposition of Christianity was "localized" to provide continuity with pre-Hispanic (Aztec) religion, yet in such a manner as to conceal the continuity from the conquerors. He thus draws close links between religious practices, social change, resistance, and state power – themes to be pursued in Part IV.

Wolf also provides an insightful analysis of the Virgin as a mother-figure, thus implicitly illustrating that symbols can become especially powerful when they draw on both deep psychological and social structural dimensions (a point explicitly articulated in Turner 1967). Interestingly, Wolf draws on two kinds of mother-images which figure longing and rebellion, respectively. The Guadalupe symbol links the psychological sources with the struggle for class and national deliverance and dignity. For a powerful psychoanalytic interpretation of the Virgin in a different cultural context (Italy), see Parsons (1969), as well as subsequent work by Carroll (1986).

Eric R. Wolf, "The Virgin of Guadalupe: A Mexican National Symbol," *Journal of American Folklore* LXXI (1958): 34–9. Reprinted by permission of the American Anthropological Association.

There is much work from a theological and missionary perspective on what is called "inculturation", i.e., the adaptation of Christianity to local understandings. Anthropologists are more likely to look at the way symbols and symbolic practices provide foci and means of struggle and resistance to the hegemony of colonizers and other dominant groups, or play a role in addressing moral problems produced by rapid social change, abjection, class formation, and divergent economic opportunities.

Hunt (1977) offers a structural analysis of pre-Columbian Mesoamerican religion; for Mexican Christianity see Ingham (1986) and Eiss (2002). A thoughtful collection on syncretism is Stewart and Shaw (1994) and see also Gellner (2001). Finally, Wolf has an excellent essay on Santa Claus (1964).

Occasionally, we encounter a symbol which seems to enshrine the major hopes and aspirations of an entire society. Such a master symbol is represented by the Virgin of Guadalupe, Mexico's patron saint. During the Mexican War of Independence against Spain, her image preceded the insurgents into battle.[1] Emiliano Zapata and his agrarian rebels fought under her emblem in the Great Revolution of 1910.[2] Today, her image adorns house fronts and interiors, churches and home altars, bull rings and gambling dens, taxis and buses, restaurants and houses of ill repute. She is celebrated in popular song and verse. Her shrine at Tepeyac, immediately north of Mexico City, is visited each year by hundreds of thousands of pilgrims, ranging from the inhabitants of far-off Indian villages to the members of socialist trade union locals. "Nothing to be seen in Canada or Europe," says F. S. C. Northrop, "equals it in the volume or the vitality of its moving quality or in the depth of its spirit of religious devotion."[3]

In this paper, I should like to discuss this Mexican master symbol, and the ideology which surrounds it. In making use of the term "master symbol," I do not wish to imply that belief in the symbol is common to all Mexicans. We are not dealing here with an element of a putative national character, defined as a common denominator of all Mexican nationals. It is no longer legitimate to assume "that any member of the [national] group will exhibit certain regularities of behavior which are common in high degree among the other members of the society."[4] Nations, like other complex societies, must, however, "possess cultural forms or mechanisms which groups involved in the same over-all web of relationships can use in their formal and informal dealings with each other."[5] Such forms develop historically, hand in hand with other processes which lead to the formation of nations, and social groups which are caught up in these processes must become "acculturated" to their usage.[6] Only where such forms exist, can communication and coordinated behavior be established among the constituent groups of such a society. They provide the cultural idiom of behavior and ideal representations through which different groups of the same society can pursue and manipulate their different fates within a coordinated framework. This paper, then, deals with one such cultural form, operating on the symbolic level. The study of this symbol seems particularly rewarding, since it is not restricted to one set of social ties, but refers to a very wide range of social relationships.

The image of the Guadalupe and her shrine at Tepeyac are surrounded by an origin myth.[7] According to this myth, the Virgin Mary appeared to Juan Diego, a Christianized Indian of commoner status, and addressed him in Nahuatl. The encounter took place on the Hill of Tepeyac in the year 1531, ten years after the Spanish Conquest of Tenochtitlan. The Virgin commanded Juan Diego to seek out the archbishop of Mexico and to inform him of her desire to see a church built in her honor on Tepeyac Hill. After Juan Diego was twice unsuccessful in his efforts to carry out her

order, the Virgin wrought a miracle. She bade
Juan Diego pick roses in a sterile spot where
normally only desert plants could grow, gathered the roses into the Indian's cloak, and told
him to present cloak and roses to the incredu-
lous archbishop. When Juan Diego unfolded
his cloak before the bishop, the image of the
Virgin was miraculously stamped upon it. The
bishop acknowledged the miracle, and ordered
a shrine built where Mary had appeared to her
humble servant.

The shrine, rebuilt several times in centuries
to follow, is today a basilica, the third highest
kind of church in Western Christendom.
Above the central altar hangs Juan Diego's
cloak with the miraculous image. It shows a
young woman without child, her head lowered
demurely in her shawl. She wears an open
crown and flowing gown, and stands upon a
half moon symbolizing the Immaculate
Conception.

The shrine of Guadalupe was, however, not
the first religious structure built on Tepeyac;
nor was Guadalupe the first female supernatural associated with the hill. In pre-Hispanic
times, Tepeyac had housed a temple to the
earth and fertility goddess Tonantzin, Our
Lady Mother, who – like the Guadalupe – was
associated with the moon. Temple, like basilica, was the center of large-scale pilgrimages.
That the veneration accorded the Guadalupe
drew inspiration from the earlier worship of
Tonantzin is attested by several Spanish friars.
F. Bernardino de Sahagún, writing fifty years
after the Conquest, says:

> Now that the Church of Our Lady of Guada-
> lupe has been built there, they call her
> Tonantzin too. . . . The term refers . . . to that
> ancient Tonantzin and this state of affairs
> should be remedied, because the proper name
> of the Mother of God is not Tonantzin, but
> Dios and Nantzin. It seems to be a satanic
> device to mask idolatry . . . and they come
> from far away to visit that Tonantzin, as much
> as before; a devotion which is also suspect
> because there are many churches of Our Lady
> everywhere and they do not go to them; and
> they come from faraway lands to this
> Tonantzin as of old.[8]

F. Martín de León wrote in a similar vein:

> On the hill where Our Lady of Guadalupe is
> they adored the idol of a goddess they called
> Tonantzin, which means Our Mother, and this
> is also the name they give Our Lady and they
> always say they are going to Tonantzin or they
> are celebrating Tonantzin and many of them
> understand this in the old way and not in the
> modern way. . . .[9]

The syncretism was still alive in the seventeenth century. F. Jacinto de la Serna, in discussing the pilgrimages to the Guadalupe at
Tepeyac, noted: ". . . it is the purpose of the
wicked to [worship] the goddess and not the
Most Holy Virgin, or both together."[10]

Increasingly popular during the sixteenth
century, the Guadalupe cult gathered emotional impetus during the seventeenth. During
this century appear the first known pictorial
representations of the Guadalupe, apart from
the miraculous original; the first poems are
written in her honor; and the first sermons
announce the transcendental implications of
her supernatural appearance in Mexico and
among Mexicans.[11] Historians have long
tended to neglect the seventeenth century
which seemed "a kind of Dark Age in Mexico."
Yet "this quiet time was of the utmost importance in the development of Mexican Society."[12]
During this century, the institution of the haci-
enda comes to dominate Mexican life.[13] During
this century, also, "New Spain is ceasing to be
'new' and to be 'Spain.'"[14] These new experiences require a new cultural idiom, and in the
Guadalupe cult, the component segments of
Mexican colonial society encountered cultural
forms in which they could express their parallel interests and longings.

The primary purpose of this paper is not,
however, to trace the history of the Guadalupe
symbol. It is concerned rather with its functional aspects, its roots and reference to the
major social relationships of Mexican society.

The first set of relationships which I would
like to single out for consideration are the ties
of kinship, and the emotions generated in the
play of relationships within families. I want
to suggest that some of the meanings of the
Virgin symbol in general, and of the Guadalupe symbol in particular, derive from these
emotions. I say "some meanings" and I use the

term "derive" rather than "originate," because the form and function of the family in any given society are themselves determined by other social factors: technology, economy, residence, political power. The family is but one relay in the circuit within which symbols are generated in complex societies. Also, I used the plural "families" rather than "family," because there are demonstrably more than one kind of family in Mexico.[15] I shall simplify the available information on Mexican family life, and discuss the material in terms of two major types of families.[16] The first kind of family is congruent with the closed and static life of the Indian village. It may be called the Indian family. In this kind of family, the husband is ideally dominant, but in reality labor and authority are shared equally among both marriage partners. Exploitation of one sex by the other is atypical; sexual feats do not add to a person's status in the eyes of others. Physical punishment and authoritarian treatment of children are rare. The second kind of family is congruent with the much more open, mobile, manipulative life in communities which are actively geared to the life of the nation, a life in which power relationships between individuals and groups are of great moment. This kind of family may be called the Mexican family. Here, the father's authority is unquestioned on both the real and the ideal plane. Double sex standards prevail, and male sexuality is charged with a desire to exercise domination. Children are ruled with a heavy hand; physical punishment is frequent.

The Indian family pattern is consistent with the behaviour towards the Guadalupe noted by John Bushnell in the Matlazinca-speaking community of San Juan Atzingo in the Valley of Toluca.[17] There, the image of the Virgin is addressed in passionate terms as a source of warmth and love, and the *pulque* or century plant beer drunk on ceremonial occasions is identified with her milk. Bushnell postulates that here the Guadalupe is identified with the mother as a source of early satisfactions, never again experienced after separation from the mother and emergence into social adulthood. As such, the Guadalupe embodies a longing to return to the pristine state in which hunger and unsatisfactory social relations are minimized.

The second family pattern is also consistent with a symbolic identification of Virgin and mother, yet this time within a context of adult male dominance and sexual assertion, discharged against submissive females and children. In this second context, the Guadalupe symbol is charged with the energy of rebellion against the father. Her image is the embodiment of hope in a victorious outcome of the struggle between generations.

This struggle leads to a further extension of the symbolism. Successful rebellion against power figures is equated with the promise of life; defeat with the promise of death. As John A. Mackay has suggested, there thus takes place a further symbolic identification of the Virgin with life; of defeat and death with the crucified Christ. In Mexican artistic tradition, as in Hispanic artistic tradition in general,[18] Christ is never depicted as an adult man, but always either as a helpless child, or more often as a figure beaten, tortured, defeated and killed. In this symbolic equation we are touching upon some of the roots both of the passionate affirmation of faith in the Virgin, and of the fascination with death which characterizes Baroque Christianity in general, and Mexican Catholicism in particular. The Guadalupe stands for life, for hope, for health; Christ on the cross, for despair and for death.

Supernatural mother and natural mother are thus equated symbolically, as are earthly and otherworldly hopes and desires. These hopes center on the provision of food and emotional warmth in the first case, in the successful waging of the Oedipal struggle in the other.

Family relations are, however, only one element in the formation of the Guadalupe symbol. Their analysis does little to explain the Guadalupe as such. They merely illuminate the female and maternal attributes of the more widespread Virgin symbol. The Guadalupe is important to Mexicans not only because she is a supernatural mother, but also because she embodies their major political and religious aspirations.

To the Indian groups, the symbol is more than an embodiment of life and hope; it restores to them the hopes of salvation. We must not forget that the Spanish Conquest signified not only military defeat, but the defeat also of the old gods and the decline of the old ritual. The apparition of the Guadalupe to an Indian commoner thus represents on one level the return of Tonantzin. As Tannenbaum has well said, "The Church . . . gave the Indian an opportunity not merely to save his life, but also to save his faith in his own gods."[19] On another level, the myth of the apparition served as a symbolic testimony that the Indian, as much as the Spaniard, was capable of being saved, capable of receiving Christianity. This must be understood against the background of the bitter theological and political argument which followed the Conquest and divided churchmen, officials, and conquerors into those who held that the Indian was incapable of conversion, thus inhuman, and therefore a fit subject of political and economic exploitation; and those who held that the Indian was human, capable of conversion and that this exploitation had to be tempered by the demands of the Catholic faith and of orderly civil processes of government.[20] The myth of the Guadalupe thus validates the Indian's right to legal defense, orderly government, to citizenship; to supernatural salvation, but also to salvation from random oppression.

But if the Guadalupe guaranteed a rightful place to the Indians in the new social system of New Spain, the myth also held appeal to the large group of disinherited who arose in New Spain as illegitimate offspring of Spanish fathers and Indian mothers, or through impoverishment, acculturation or loss of status within the Indian or Spanish group.[21] For such people, there was for a long time no proper place in the social order. Their very right to exist was questioned in their inability to command the full rights of citizenship and legal protection. Where Spaniard and Indian stood squarely within the law, they inhabited the interstices and margins of constituted society. These groups acquired influence and wealth in the seventeenth and eighteenth centuries, but were yet barred from social recognition and power by the prevailing economic, social and political order.[22] To them, the Guadalupe myth came to represent not merely the guarantee of their assured place in heaven, but the guarantee of their place in society here and now. On the political plane, the wish for a return to a

paradise of early satisfactions of food and warmth, a life without defeat, sickness or death, gave rise to a political wish for a Mexican paradise, in which the illegitimate sons would possess the country, and the irresponsible Spanish overlords, who never acknowledged the social responsibilities of their paternity, would be driven from the land.

In the writings of seventeenth century ecclesiastics, the Guadalupe becomes the harbinger of this new order. In the book by Miguel Sánchez, published in 1648, the Spanish Conquest of New Spain is justified solely on the grounds that it allowed the Virgin to become manifest in her chosen country, and to found in Mexico a new paradise. Just as Israel had been chosen to produce Christ, so Mexico had been chosen to produce Guadalupe. Sánchez equates her with the apocalyptic woman of the Revelation of John (12:1), "arrayed with the sun, and the moon under her feet, and upon her head a crown of twelve stars" who is to realize the prophecy of Deuteronomy 8:7–10 and lead the Mexicans into the Promised Land. Colonial Mexico thus becomes the desert of Sinai; Independent Mexico the land of milk and honey. F. Francisco de Florencia, writing in 1688, coined the slogan which made Mexico not merely another chosen nation, but the Chosen Nation: *non fecit taliter omni nationi*,[23] words which still adorn the portals of the basilica, and shine forth in electric light bulbs at night. And on the eve of Mexican independence, Servando Teresa de Mier elaborates still further the Guadalupan myth by claiming that Mexico had been converted to Christianity long before the Spanish Conquest. The apostle Saint Thomas had brought the image of Guadalupe-Tonantzin to the New World as a symbol of his mission, just as Saint James had converted Spain with the image of the Virgin of the Pillar. The Spanish Conquest was therefore historically unnecessary, and should be erased from the annals of history.[24] In this perspective, the Mexican War of Independence marks the final realization of the apocalyptic promise. The banner of the Guadalupe leads the insurgents; and their cause is referred to as "her law."[25] In this ultimate extension of the symbol, the promise of life held out by the supernatural mother has become the promise of an independent Mexico, liberated from the irrational authority of the Spanish father-oppressors and restored to the Chosen Nation whose election had been manifest in the apparition of the Virgin on Tepeyac. The land of the supernatural mother is finally possessed by her rightful heirs. The symbolic circuit is closed. Mother; food, hope, health, life; supernatural salvation and salvation from oppression; Chosen People and national independence – all find expression in a single master symbol.

The Guadalupe symbol thus links together family, politics and religion; colonial past and independent present; Indian and Mexican. It reflects the salient social relationships of Mexican life, and embodies the emotions which they generate. It provides a cultural idiom through which the tenor and emotions of these relationships can be expressed. It is, ultimately, a way of talking about Mexico: a "collective representation" of Mexican society.

NOTES

1 Niceto de Zamacois, *Historia de México* (Barcelona-Mexico, 1878–82), VI, 253.

2 Antonio Pompa y Pompa, *Album del IV centenario guadalupano* (Mexico, 1938), p. 173.

3 F. S. C. Northrop, *The Meeting of East and West* (New York, 1946), p. 25.

4 David G. Mandelbaum, "On the Study of National Character," *American Anthropologist*, LV (1953), 185.

5 Eric R. Wolf, "Aspects of Group Relations in a Complex Society: Mexico," *American Anthropologist*, LVII (1956), 1065–78.

6 Eric R. Wolf, "La formación de la nación," *Ciencias Sociales,* IV, 50–1.

7 Ernest Gruening, *Mexico and Its Heritage* (New York, 1928), p. 235.

8 Bernardino de Sahagún, *Historia general de las cosas de nueva españa* (Mexico, 1938), I, lib. 6.

9 Quoted in Carlos A. Echánove Trujillo, *Sociología mexicana* (Mexico, 1948), p. 105.

10 Quoted in Jesús Amaya, *La madre de Dios: genesis e historia de nuestra señora de Guadalupe* (Mexico, 1931), p. 230.

11 Francisco de la Maza, *El guadalupismo mexicano* (Mexico, 1953), pp. 12–14, 143, 30, 33, 82.

12 Lesley B. Simpson, "Mexico's Forgotten Century," *Pacific Historical Review,* XXII (1953), 115, 114.

13 François Chevalier, *La formation des grands domaines au Mexique* (Paris, 1952), p. xii.

14 de la Maza, p. 41.

15 María Elvira Bermúdez, *La vida familiar del mexicano* (Mexico, 1955), chapters 2 and 3.

16 For relevant material, see: Bermúdez; John Gillin, "Ethos and Cultural Aspects of Personality," and Robert Redfield and Sol Tax, "General Characteristics of Present-Day Mesoamerican Indian Society," in Sol Tax, ed., *Heritage of Conquest* (Glencoe, 1952), pp. 193–212, 31–9; Gordon W. Hewes, "Mexicans in Search of the 'Mexican'," *American Journal of Economics and Sociology,* XIII (1954), 209–23; Octavio Paz, *El laberinto de la soledad* (Mexico, 1947), pp. 71–89.

17 John Bushnell, "La Virgen de Guadalupe as Surrogate Mother in San Juan Atzingo," paper read before the 54th Annual Meeting of the American Anthropological Association, 18 November 1955.

18 John A. Mackay, *The Other Spanish Christ* (New York, 1933), pp. 110–17.

19 Frank Tannenbaum, *Peace by Revolution* (New York, 1933), p. 39.

20 Silvio Zavala, *La filosofía en la conquista de America* (Mexico, 1947).

21 Nicolas León, *Las castas del México colonial o Nueva España* (Mexico, 1924); C. E. Marshall, "The Birth of the Mestizo in New Spain," *Hispanic American Historical Review,* XIX (1939), 161–84; Wolf, "La formación de la nación," pp. 103–6.

22 Gregorio Torres Quintero, *México hacía el fin del virreinato español* (Mexico, 1921); Eric R. Wolf, "The Mexican Bajío in the Eighteenth Century," *Middle American Research Institute Publication* XVII (1955), 180–99; Wolf, "Aspects of Group Relations in a Complex Society: Mexico."

23 de la Maza, pp. 39–40, 43–9, 64.

24 Luis Villoro, *Los grandes momentos del indigenismo en México* (Mexico, 1950), pp. 131–38.

25 Luis González y González, "El optimismo nacionalista como factor en la independencia de México," *Estudios de historiografía americana* (Mexico, 1948), p. 194.

Structure, Function, and Interpretation

Introduction

It is one thing to recognize symbols as the building blocks of religious worlds and another thing to know how to go about analyzing symbolic constructions. Anthropologists have been in some disagreement over the correct manner to investigate such symbolic phenomena as myths, ideology, systems of classification, ritual injunctions, and aesthetic productions and performances. Should one focus on structure or content, surface or depth, figure or ground? Should explanation lie with pragmatic interests, social function, meaningful texture, unconscious conflicts, or cognitive processes? This section highlights some of the forms of explanation or interpretation to which anthropologists have turned, and debates among them. This is a large topic and a rich field. I have selected a few forceful statements by well-known figures.

14

Myth in Primitive Psychology

Bronislaw Malinowski

Bronislaw Malinowski (1884–1942) is one of the founders of modern anthropology. In a series of remarkable works written largely in the 1920s, he demonstrated the importance of rich ethnographic observation. Born in Poland, he spent most of his teaching career at the London School of Economics, where he influenced a large cohort of students, many of whom made their own important contributions to the ethnographic corpus on religion (notably Firth 1940, 1967, and Richards 1956, among many others).

From this entry readers may glimpse how Malinowski was able to capture the imagination of earlier generations of audiences, both professional and public. Malinowski invites us to share his romantic and pleasurable field odyssey in the Trobriand Islands of Melanesia while making no bones about the superiority of his approach over preceding ones. This essay is famous for developing the argument of myth as "charter" but it can be seen, I think, that Malinowski escapes the narrowly functionalist interpretations that are often placed on his ideas. Among other things, he emphasizes the immediacy and "living reality" of myth as well as its discursive and pragmatic (hence dialogical) qualities (that is, the recitation of myths as speech events). While it would be wrong to suggest either that all myths have political functions or that the interest or value of any given myth can be reduced to its instrumental political function, Malinowski was undoubtedly correct to look at the place of myth in legitimating particular forms of social organization and loci of power or interest and the contestation this inevitably brings. Myth becomes a language of legal argument.

Useful developments and exemplifications of Malinowski's approach include Leach's discussion of "myth as a justifica-

From Bronislaw Malinowski, "Myth in Primitive Psychology," in *Magic, Science and Religion and Other Essays* (Garden City, NY: Doubleday & Co., Inc., 1954 [1926]), pp. 100–26, 145. Reprinted by permission of Macmillan Publishers, Inc. Abridged.

tion for faction and social change" in highland Burma (1964: Chapter IX) and Andriolo's essay on genealogy in the Old Testament (1973). Leach himself later turned to structuralist (Lévi-Straussian) analyses of the Old Testament (1969). Whereas Malinowski claims the meaning of myth is on the surface, many writers would disagree. Marx and Freud are both noted for arguing that meaning is concealed and needs to be recovered, while structuralists see the issue as one of revealing the codes or grammar by which meaning is produced.

[. . .]

Myth as it exists in a savage community, that is, in its living primitive form, is not merely a story told but a reality lived. It is not of the nature of fiction, such as we read today in a novel, but it is a living reality, believed to have once happened in primeval times, and continuing ever since to influence the world and human destinies. This myth is to the savage what, to a fully believing Christian, is the Biblical story of Creation, of the Fall, of the Redemption by Christ's Sacrifice on the Cross. As our sacred story lives in our ritual, in our morality, as it governs our faith and controls our conduct, even so does his myth for the savage.

The limitation of the study of myth to the mere examination of texts has been fatal to a proper understanding of its nature. The forms of myth which come to us from classical antiquity and from the ancient sacred books of the East and other similar sources have come down to us without the context of living faith, without the possibility of obtaining comments from true believers, without the concomitant knowledge of their social organization, their practiced morals, and their popular customs – at least without the full information which the modern fieldworker can easily obtain. Moreover, there is no doubt that in their present literary form these tales have suffered a very considerable transformation at the hands of scribes, commentators, learned priests, and theologians. It is necessary to go back to primitive mythology in order to learn the secret of its life in the study of a myth which is still alive – before, mummified in priestly wisdom, it has been enshrined in the indestructible but lifeless repository of dead religions.

Studied alive, myth, as we shall see, is not symbolic, but a direct expression of its subject matter; it is not an explanation in satisfaction of a scientific interest, but a narrative resurrection of a primeval reality, told in satisfaction of deep religious wants, moral cravings, social submissions, assertions, even practical requirements. Myth fulfills in primitive culture an indispensable function: it expresses, enhances, and codifies belief; it safeguards and enforces morality; it vouches for the efficiency of ritual and contains practical rules for the guidance of man. Myth is thus a vital ingredient of human civilization; it is not an idle tale, but a hard-worked active force; it is not an intellectual explanation or an artistic imagery, but a pragmatic charter of primitive faith and moral wisdom.

[. . .]

In the subsequent chapters of this book we will examine a number of myths in detail, but for the moment let us glance at the subjects of some typical myths [from the Trobriand Islands]. Take, for instance, the annual feast of the return of the dead. Elaborate arrangements are made for it, especially an enormous display of food. When this feast approaches, tales are told of how death began to chastise man, and how the power of eternal rejuvenation was lost. It is told why the spirits have to leave the village and do not remain at the fireside, finally why they return once in a year. Again, at certain seasons in preparation for an overseas expedition, canoes are overhauled and new ones built to the accompaniment of a special magic. In this there are mythological allusions in the spells, and even the sacred acts contain elements which are only comprehensible when the story of the flying canoe, its ritual, and its magic are told. In connection with ceremonial trading, the rules, the magic, even the geographical routes are associated with corresponding mythology. There is no important magic, no ceremony, no ritual without belief; and the belief is spun out into accounts of concrete precedent. The union is very intimate, for myth is not only looked upon as a commentary of additional information, but it is a warrant, a charter, and often even a practical guide to the activities with which it is connected. On the other hand the rituals, ceremonies, customs, and social organization contain at times direct references to myth, and they are regarded as the results of mythical event. The cultural fact is a monument in which the myth is embodied; while the myth is believed to be the real cause which has brought about the moral rule, the social grouping, the rite, or the custom. Thus these stories form an integral part of culture. Their existence and influence not merely transcend the act of telling the narrative, not only do they draw their substance from life and its interests – they govern and control many cultural features, they form the dogmatic backbone of primitive civilization.

This is perhaps the most important point of the thesis which I am urging: I maintain that there exists a special class of stories, regarded as sacred, embodied in ritual, morals, and social organization, and which form an integral and active part of primitive culture. These stories live not by idle interest, not as fictitious or even as true narratives; but are to the natives a statement of a primeval, greater, and more relevant reality, by which the present life, fates, and activities of mankind are determined, the knowledge of which supplies man with the motive for ritual and moral actions, as well as with indications as to how to perform them.

In order to make the point at issue quite clear, let us once more compare our conclusions with the current views of modern anthropology, not in order idly to criticize other opinions, but so that we may link our results to the present state of knowledge, give due acknowledgment for what we have received, and state where we have to differ clearly and precisely.

It will be best to quote a condensed and authoritative statement, and I shall choose for this purpose of definition an analysis given in *Notes and Queries on Anthropology*, by the late Miss C. S. Burne and Professor J. L. Myres. Under the heading "Stories, Sayings, and Songs," we are informed that "this section includes many *intellectual* efforts of peoples" which "represent the earliest attempt to exercise reason, imagination, and memory." With some apprehension we ask where is left the emotion, the interest, and ambition, the social role of all the stories, and the deep connection with cultural values of the more serious ones? After a brief classification of stories in the usual manner we read about the sacred tales: "*Myths* are stories which, however marvelous and improbable to us, are nevertheless related in all good faith, because they are intended, or believed by the teller, to explain by means of something concrete and intelligible an abstract idea or such vague and difficult conceptions as Creation, Death, distinctions of race or animal species, the different occupations of men and women; the origins of rites and customs, or striking natural objects or prehistoric monuments; the meaning of the names of persons or places. Such stories are sometimes described as *etiological*, because their purpose is to explain why something exists or happens."[1]

Here we have in a nutshell all that modern science at its best has to say upon the subject. Would our Melanesians agree, however, with this opinion? Certainly not. They do not want to "explain," to make "intelligible" anything which happens in their myths – above all not an abstract idea. Of that there can be found to my knowledge no instance either in Melanesia or in any other savage community. The few abstract ideas which the natives possess carry their concrete commentary in the very word which expresses them. When being is described by verbs to lie, to sit, to stand, when cause and effect are expressed by words signifying foundation and the past standing upon it, when various concrete nouns tend towards the meaning of space, the word and the relation to concrete reality make the abstract idea sufficiently "intelligible." Nor would a Trobriander or any other native agree with the view that "Creation, Death, distinctions of race or animal species, the different occupations of men and women" are "vague and difficult conceptions." Nothing is more familiar to the native than the different occupations of the male and female sex; there is nothing to be *explained* about it. But though familiar, such differences are at times irksome, unpleasant, or at least limiting, and there is the need to justify them, to vouch for their antiquity and reality, in short to buttress their validity. Death, alas, is not vague, or abstract, or difficult to grasp for any human being. It is only too hauntingly real, too concrete, too easy to comprehend for anyone who has had an experience affecting his near relatives or a personal foreboding. If it were vague or unreal, man would have no desire so much as to mention it; but the idea of death is fraught with horror, with a desire to remove its threat, with the vague hope that it may be, not explained, but rather explained away, made unreal, and actually denied. Myth, warranting the belief in immortality, in eternal youth, in a life beyond the grave, is not an intellectual reaction upon a puzzle, but an explicit act of faith born from the innermost instinctive and emotional reaction to the most formidable and haunting idea. Nor are the stories about "the origins of rites and customs" told in mere explanation of them. They never explain in any sense of the word; they always state a precedent which constitutes an ideal and a warrant for its continuance, and sometimes practical directions for the procedure.

We have, therefore, to disagree on every point with this excellent though concise statement of present-day mythological opinion. This definition would create an imaginary, non-existent class of narrative, the etiological myth, corresponding to a non-existent desire to explain, leading a futile existence as an "intellectual effort," and remaining outside native culture and social organization with their pragmatic interests. The whole treatment appears to us faulty, because myths are treated as mere stories, because they are regarded as a primitive intellectual armchair occupation, because they are torn out of their life context, and studied from what they look like on paper, and not from what they do in life. Such a definition would make it impossible either to see clearly the nature of myth or to reach a satisfactory classification of folk tales. In fact we would also have to disagree with the definition of legend and of fairy tale given

subsequently by the writers in *Notes and Queries on Anthropology.*

But above all, this point of view would be fatal to efficient field work, for it would make the observer satisfied with the mere writing down of narratives. The intellectual nature of a story is exhausted with its text, but the functional, cultural, and pragmatic aspect of any native tale is manifested as much in its enactment, embodiment, and contextual relations as in the text. It is easier to write down the story than to observe the diffuse, complex ways in which it enters into life, or to study its function by the observation of the vast social and cultural realities into which it enters. And this is the reason why we have so many texts and why we know so little about the very nature of myth.

We may, therefore, learn an important lesson from the Trobrianders, and to them let us now return. We will survey some of their myths in detail, so that we can confirm our conclusions inductively, yet precisely.

Myths of Origin

We may best start with the beginning of things, and examine some of the myths of origin. The world, say the natives, was originally peopled from underground. Humanity had there led an existence similar in all respects to the present life on earth. Underground, men were organized in villages, clans, districts; they had distinctions of rank, they knew privileges and had claims, they owned property, and were versed in magic lore. Endowed with all this, they emerged, establishing by this very act certain rights in land and citizenship, in economic prerogative and magical pursuit. They brought with them all their culture to continue it upon this earth.

There are a number of special spots – grottoes, clumps of trees, stone heaps, coral outcrops, springs, heads of creeks – called "holes" or "houses" by the natives. From such "holes" the first couples (a sister as the head of the family and the brother as her guardian) came and took possession of the lands, and gave the totemic, industrial, magical, and sociological character to the communities thus begun.

The problem of rank which plays a great role in their sociology was settled by the emergence from one special hole, called Obukula, near the village of Laba'i. This event was notable in that, contrary to the usual course (which is: one original "hole," one lineage), from this hole of Laba'i there emerged representatives of the four main clans one after the other. Their arrival, moreover, was followed by an apparently trivial but, in mythical reality, a most important event. First there came the *Kaylavasi* (iguana), the animal of the Lukulabuta clan, which scratched its way through the earth as iguanas do, then climbed a tree, and remained there as a mere onlooker, following subsequent events. Soon there came out the Dog, totem of the Lukuba clan, who originally had the highest rank. As a third came the Pig, representative of the Malasi clan, which now holds the highest rank. Last came the Lukwasisiga totem, represented in some versions by the Crocodile, in others by the Snake, in others by the Opossum, and sometimes completely ignored. The Dog and Pig ran round, and the Dog, seeing the fruit of the *noku* plant, nosed it, then ate it. Said the Pig: "Thou eatest *noku*, thou eatest dirt; thou art a low-bred, a commoner; the chief, the *guya'u*, shall be I." And ever since, the highest subclan of the Malasi clan, the Tabalu, have been the real chiefs.

In order to understand this myth, it is not enough to follow the dialogue between the Dog and the Pig which might appear pointless or even trivial. Once you know the native sociology, the extreme importance of rank, the fact that food and its limitations (the taboos of rank and clan) are the main index of man's social nature, and finally the psychology of totemic identification – you begin to understand how this incident, happening as it did when humanity was *in statu nascendi*, settled once for all the relation between the two rival clans. To understand this myth you must have a good knowledge of their sociology, religion, customs, and outlook. Then, and only then, can you appreciate what this story means to the natives and how it can live in their life. If you stayed among them and learned the language you would constantly find it active in discussion and squabbles in reference to the relative superiority of the various clans, and in

the discussions about the various food taboos which frequently raise fine questions of casuistry. Above all, if you were brought into contact with communities where the historical process of the spread of influence of the Malasi clan is still in evolution, you would be brought face to face with this myth as an active force.

Remarkably enough the first and last animals to come out, the iguana and the Lukwasisiga totem, have been from the beginning left in the cold: thus the numerical principle and the logic of events is not very strictly observed in the reasoning of the myth.

If the main myth of Laba'i about the relative superiority of the four clans is very often alluded to throughout the tribe, the minor local myths are not less alive and active, each in its own community. When a party arrives at some distant village they will be told not only the legendary historical tales, but above all the mythological charter of that community, its magical proficiencies, its occupational character, its rank and place in totemic organization. Should there arise land quarrels, encroachment in magical matters, fishing rights, or other privileges the testimony of myth would be referred to.

Let me show concretely the way in which a typical myth of local origins would be retailed in the normal run of native life. Let us watch a party of visitors arriving in one or the other of the Trobriand villages. They would seat themselves in front of the headman's house, in the central place of the locality. As likely as not the spot of origins is nearby, marked by a coral outcrop or a heap of stones. This spot would be pointed out, the names of the brother and sister ancestors mentioned, and perhaps it would be said that the man built his house on the spot of the present headman's dwelling. The native listeners would know, of course, that the sister lived in a different house nearby, for she could never reside within the same walls as her brother.

As additional information, the visitors might be told that the ancestors had brought with them the substances and paraphernalia and methods of local industry. In the village of Yalaka, for instance, it would be the processes for burning lime from shells. In Okobobo, Obweria, and Obowada the ancestors brought the knowledge and the implements for polishing hard stone. In Bwoytalu the carver's tool, the hafted shark tooth, and the knowledge of the art came out from underground with the original ancestors. In most places the economic monopolies are thus traced to the autochthonous emergence. In villages of higher rank the insignia of hereditary dignity were brought; in others some animal associated with the local subclan came out. Some communities started on their political career of standing hostility to one another from the very beginning. The most important gift to this world carried from the one below is always magic; but this will have to be treated later on and more fully.

If a European bystander were there and heard nothing but the information given from one native to the other, it would mean very little to him. In fact, it might lead him into serious misunderstandings. Thus the simultaneous emergence of brother and sister might make him suspicious either of a mythological allusion to incest, or else would make him look for the original matrimonial pair and inquire about the sister's husband. The first suspicion would be entirely erroneous, and would shed a false light over the specific relation between brother and sister, in which the former is the indispensable guardian, and the second, equally indispensable, is responsible for the transmission of the line. Only a full knowledge of the matrilineal ideas and institutions gives body and meaning to the bare mention of the two ancestral names, so significant to a native listener. If the European were to inquire who was the sister's husband and how she came to have children, he would soon find himself once more confronted by an entirely foreign set of ideas – the sociological irrelevance of the father, the absence of any ideas about physiological procreation, and the strange and complicated system of marriage, matrilineal and patrilocal at the same time.

The sociological relevance of these accounts of origins would become clear only to a European inquirer who had grasped the native legal ideas about local citizenship and the hereditary rights to territory, fishing grounds, and local pursuits. For according to the legal principles of the tribe all such rights are the monopolies of the local community, and only people descendent in the female line from the original ancestress are entitled to them. If the European were told further that, besides the first place of emergence, there are several other "holes" in the same village, he would become still more baffled until, by a careful study of concrete details and the principles of native sociology, he became acquainted with the idea of compound village communities, i.e., communities in which several subclans have merged.

It is clear, then, that the myth conveys much more to the native than is contained in the mere story; that the story gives only the really relevant concrete local differences; that the real meaning, in fact the full account, is contained in the traditional foundations of social organization; and that this the native learns, not by listening to the fragmentary mythical stories, but by living within the social texture of his tribe. In other words, it is the context of social life, it is the gradual realization by the native of how everything which he is told to do has its precedent and pattern in bygone times, which brings home to him the full account and the full meaning of his myths of origin.

For an observer, therefore, it is necessary to become fully acquainted with the social organization of the natives if he wants really to grasp its traditional aspect. The short accounts, such as those which are given about local origins, will then become perfectly plain to him. He will also clearly see that each of them is only a part, and a rather insignificant one, of a much bigger story, which cannot be read except from native life. What really matters about such a story is its social function. It conveys, expresses, and strengthens the fundamental fact of the local unity and of the kinship unity of the group of people descendent from a common ancestress. Combined with the conviction that only common descent and emergence from the soil give full rights to it, the story of origin literally contains the legal charter of the community. Thus, even when the people of a vanquished community were driven from their grounds by a hostile neighbor their territory always remained intact for them; and they were always, after a lapse of time and when their peace ceremony had been concluded, allowed to return to the original site, rebuild their village, and cultivate their gardens once more. The traditional feeling of a real and intimate connection with the land; the concrete reality of seeing the actual spot of emergence in the middle of the scenes of daily life; the historical continuity of privileges, occupations, and distinctive characters running back into the mythological first beginnings – all this obviously makes for cohesion, for local patriotism, for a feeling of union and kinship in the community. But although the narrative of original emergence integrates and welds together the historical tradition, the legal principles, and the various customs, it must also be clearly kept in mind that the original myth is but a small part of the whole complex of traditional ideas. Thus on the one hand the reality of myth lies in its social function; on the other hand, once we begin to study the social function of myth, and so to reconstruct its full meaning, we are gradually led to build up the full theory of native social organization.

One of the most interesting phenomena connected with traditional precedent and charter is the adjustment of myth and mythological principle to cases in which the very foundation of such mythology is flagrantly violated. This violation always takes place when the local claims of an autochthonous clan, i.e., a clan which has emerged on the spot, are overridden by an immigrant clan. Then a conflict of principles is created, for obviously the principle that land and authority belong to those who are literally born out of it does not leave room for any newcomers. On the other hand, members of a subclan of high rank who choose to settle down in a new locality cannot very well be resisted by the autochthons – using this word again in the literal native mythological sense. The result is that there come into existence a special class of mythological stories which justify and account for the anomalous state of affairs. The strength of the various mythological and legal principles is manifested in that the myths of justification still contain the antagonistic and logically irreconcilable facts and points of view, and only try to cover them by facile reconciliatory incident, obviously manufactured *ad hoc*. The study of such stories is extremely interesting, both because it gives us a deep insight into the native psychology of tradition, and because it tempts us to reconstruct the past history of the tribe, though we must yield to the temptation with due caution and scepticism.

[. . .]

As far as the sociological theory of these legends goes the historical reconstruction is irrelevant. Whatever the hidden reality of their unrecorded past may be, myths serve to cover certain inconsistencies created by historical events, rather than to record these events exactly. The myths associated with the spread of the powerful subclans show on certain points a fidelity to life in that they record facts inconsistent with one another. The incidents by which this inconsistency is obliterated, if not hidden, are most likely fictitious; we have seen certain myths vary according to the locality in which they are told. In other cases the incidents bolster up non-existent claims and rights.

The historical consideration of myth is interesting, therefore, in that it shows that myth, taken as a whole, cannot be sober dispassionate history, since it is always made *ad hoc* to fulfill a certain sociological function, to glorify a certain group, or to justify an anomalous status. These considerations show us also that to the native mind immediate history, semi-historic legend, and unmixed myth flow into one another, form a continuous sequence, and fulfill really the same sociological function.

And this brings us once more to our original contention that the really important thing about the myth is its character of a retrospective, ever-present, live actuality. It is to a native neither a fictitious story, nor an account of a dead past; it is a statement of a bigger reality still partially alive. It is alive in that its precedent, its law, its moral, still rule the social life of the natives. It is clear that myth functions especially where there is a sociological strain, such as in matters of great difference in rank and power, matters of precedence and subordination, and unquestionably where profound historical changes have taken place. So much can be asserted as a fact, though it must always remain doubtful how far we can carry out historical reconstruction from the myth.

We can certainly discard all explanatory as well as all symbolic interpretations of these myths of origin. The personages and beings which we find in them are what they appear to be on the surface, and not symbols of hidden realities. As to any explanatory function of these myths, there is no problem which they cover, no curiosity which they satisfy, no theory which they contain.

[...]

The science of myth in living higher cultures, such as the present civilization of India, Japan, China, and last but not least, our own, might well be inspired by the comparative study of primitive folklore; and in its turn civilized culture could furnish important additions and explanations to savage mythology. This subject is very much beyond the scope of the present study. I do, however, want to emphasize the fact that anthropology should be not only the study of savage custom in the light of our mentality and our culture, but also the study of our own mentality in the distant perspective borrowed from Stone Age man. By dwelling mentally for some time among people of a much simpler culture than our own, we may be able to see ourselves from a distance, we may be able to gain a new sense of proportion with regard to our own institutions, beliefs, and customs. If anthropology could thus inspire us with some sense of proportion, and supply us with a finer sense of humor, it might justly claim to be a very great science.

[...]

NOTE

1 Quoted from *Notes and Queries on Anthropology,* pp. 210 and 211.

15

Folk Dialectics of
Nature and Culture

Marshall Sahlins

Marshall Sahlins is one of the most intellectually imaginative and acute of North American anthropologists, known for his sharp wit and powerful theoretical arguments. He has carried out fieldwork on Fiji and engaged in the study of precolonial Hawaii. Sahlins is Professor Emeritus at the University of Chicago.

In this brief analysis Sahlins takes us to the heart of some of the West's most cherished discourses in political philosophy and biological science concerning human nature and the individual. This entry follows perfectly from Malinowski because, while Sahlins illustrates Malinowski's idea of myth as charter with respect to the relations of biology and capitalism, he also inverts much of Malinowski's logic. For Sahlins, myth, religion, or culture are not simply products of interest or practice but shape or mediate practice. In this essay he speaks usefully of a dialectic. While the nature/culture dialectic he describes is particu-

lar to the modern (capitalist) West, the broader argument might fit all societies – the way in which social logic is authorized by something that is supposedly outside its reach but whose content (as it is understood locally) is actually shaped by that very logic. The use of "nature" in this dialectic provides echoes both of Marx's analysis of commodity fetishism in *Capital* (1961 [1887]) and Lévi-Strauss's reworking of "totemism" in *The Savage Mind* (1966 [1962]; (see also chapters 23 and 43, below, for alternate cultural approaches to nature). This dialectic is mystified to those who are caught up in it. Although Sahlins speaks of sociobiology as ideology, contemporary readers might prefer to apply Gramsci's conception of hegemony (1971, Comaroff and Comaroff 1991), since what Sahlins describes has been so largely taken for granted as authoritative rather than remarked and contested. There is an important methodological lesson in the

From Marshall Sahlins, "Folk Dialectics of Nature and Culture," in *The Use and Abuse of Biology: An Anthropological Critique of Sociobiology* (Ann Arbor: University of Michigan Press, 1976), pp. 93–107.

fact that the "myth" in this analysis is hardly what the natives would classify as such.

Sahlins has a superb essay on western cosmology that surveys the entire history of western philosophy (1996). Among many other works, particularly instructive are his discussions of the relation of structure to practice and event, both in the abstract (1976) and in specific relation to the history of Hawaii and the Hawaiian reception of Captain Cook (1985; cf. the controversy raised in Obeyesekere 1992, and Sahlins 1995). A comprehensive collection of his essays appeared in 2000 while the most recent is 2004.

So that in the first place, I put for a generall inclination of all mankind, a perpetuall and restlesse desire of Power after power, that ceaseth onely in Death.

THOMAS HOBBES, Leviathan

To discover the lineaments of the larger society in the concepts of its biology is not altogether a "Modern Synthesis." In Euro-American society this integration has been going on in a particular dialectic way since the seventeenth century. Since Hobbes, at least, the competitive and acquisitive characteristics of Western man have been confounded with Nature, and the Nature thus fashioned in the human image has been in turn reapplied to the explanation of Western man. The effect of this dialectic has been to anchor the properties of human social action, as we conceive them, in Nature, and the laws of Nature in our conceptions of human social action. Human society is natural, and natural societies are curiously human. Adam Smith produces a social version of Thomas Hobbes, Charles Darwin a naturalized version of Adam Smith; William Graham Sumner thereupon reinvents Darwin as society, and Edward O. Wilson reinvents Sumner as nature. Since Darwin, the movement of the conceptual pendulum has accelerated. Every decade, it seems, we are presented with a more refined notion of man as species, and a more refined species of "natural selection" as man.

In the opening chapters of *Leviathan* there is presented a picture of man as a self-moving and self-directing machine. C. B. Macpherson, whose reading of Hobbes and explication of "possessive individualism" I here follow very closely, describes the Hobbesian natural man as an "automated machine," having built into it "equipment by which it alters its motion in response to differences in the material it uses, and to the impact and even the expected impact of other matter on it" (1962, p. 31). The machine is part of the informational system of the world in which it moves, as nothing is present to its mind that was not first present to its senses – "there is no conception in a man's mind, which hath not at first, totally, or by parts, been begotten by the organs of sense" (Hobbes, part 1, chap. 1; all citations of *Leviathan* are from the Everyman paperback edition [1950]). Language introduces the potentiality of error into this sensory epistemology, as also a greater capacity for right movements, but it cannot transcend the intrinsic values of sensory experience. In chapters 5 through 11, the general direction of the machine is indicated. "Felicity of this life," Hobbes says, "consisteth not in the repose of a mind satisfied. . . . Nor can a man any more live, whose Desires are at an end. . . . Felicity is a continuall progresse of the desire" (chap. 11). The machine acts to continue its own motion by approaching things that sustain that motion and avoiding things inimical. Motion toward is "desire" (or "appetite") and its objects are "good." Motion away is "aversion" and its objects are "evil." Each human machine "endeavoureth to secure himself against the evill he feares, and procure the good he desireth" (chap. 12). As the abstract positive and negative of human action, these two motions are comprehensive. They exhaust all particular motivations which are just so many circumstantial modalities of motion toward or motion away. Appetite with the opinion it will be satisfied is "hope"; without this opinion "despair." Aversion with the anticipation of hurt from the object is "fear"; with the hope of resisting hurt, it is "courage." And so for anger, confidence, diffidence, indignation, benevolence, covetousness, pusil-lanimity and magnanimity, liberality and par-simony, kindness, lust or jealousy – they are products of a single-minded concern for one's own good.

In the eighth chapter, however, Hobbes states the relativity of the calculus of good. Insofar as it is social, it is a differential good. Hobbes argues that the good men value is determined by whatever other men already have. Virtue and worth are only realizable as a differential success, as preeminence, and "consisteth in comparison. For if all things were equally in all men, nothing would be prized" (chap. 8). The success of men in secur-ing their own good thus depends on the strength of their desires and their respective abilities. But then, the pursuit of one's own good cannot remain at the level of independent production. For the power of one man to obtain his own good is opposed by the powers of others. "The power of one man resisteth and hindereth the effects of the power of another" (cf. Macpherson 1962, pp. 35–6). There is an opposition of powers. And in the end, success turns on the competitive appro-priation of the powers of others. A man secures his own good to the extent he can harness the powers of other men. There is a net transfer of powers. The means are all such things as riches, reputation, love, and fear.

> Riches joyned with liberality, is Power; because it procureth friends, and servants. . . . Reputa-tion of Power, is Power; because it draweth with it the adhearence of those that need pro tection. . . . Also, what quality soever maketh a man beloved, or feared of many, or the repu-tation of such quality, is Power; because it is the means to have the assistance, and service of many. (chap. 10)

Macpherson notes that in Hobbes's scheme, men actually enter into a market for the exchange of powers. Men find their worth as

the price others will pay for the use of their powers. It is in this mode, as *acquisition*, that Hobbes put as the "generall inclination of all mankind, a perpetuall and restlesse desire of Power after power, that ceaseth onely in Death" (chap. 11). As all men are so inclined, no one man can rest secure in his own powers without engaging "by force, or wiles, to master the persons of all men he can, so long, till he see no other power great enough to endanger him" (chap. 13). Hence the famous struggle among men in a state of nature, the "Warre" of every man against every man, enduring so long as they do not agree to surrender their force to a Common Power (the State) that will "keep them all in awe."

Writing in an era of transition to a devel-oped market society, Hobbes reproduces the historical sequence as a logic of human nature. The expropriation of man by man at which Hobbes arrives in the end is, as Macpherson explains, the theory of action in a fully com-petitive economy. It differs from a mere strug-gle for preeminence, as would occur in transitional phases of simple commodity pro-duction, because in the model of the latter each man has access to his own means of livelihood and need not convey his powers to other men. Producers may maximize their own position in market exchange; they remain, however, independent proprietors and their labor power as such is not a commodity. The full market system also differs from exploitative structures such as feudalism and slavery, since in the latter conditions, the rights to power, although they may yield a net transfer, are relatively fixed among the classes. No one is free to convey his powers as he will, for none can escape his definition as a social being, defini-tion that presupposes his position in the circu-lation of powers. Men are slaves and serfs, others are lords and masters, but the system is not competitive such that it would be neces-sary to struggle after more power just to con-serve the amount one has, or else lose out to those stronger in desire or capacity. The full market system refers to the historical time when men do become free to alienate their powers for a price, as some are compelled to do because they lack the productive means to independently realize their own good. This is a very distinctive type of society as well as a particular period of history. It is marked by what Macpherson styles "possessive individualism." Possessive individualism entails the unique notion – counterpart to the liberation from feudal relations – that men own their own bodies, the use of which they have both the freedom and necessity to sell to those who control their own capital. (It was Marx, of course, who penetrated the inequities of this exchange, that is, the net transfer, since the value produced by labor power is greater than its price.) In such a condition, every man confronts every man as an owner. Indeed, society itself is generated through the acts of exchange by which each seeks the greatest possible benefits in others' powers at the least possible cost to his own.

It was, Macpherson explains,

a conception of the individual as essentially the proprietor of his own person or capacities, owing nothing to society for them. The individual was seen neither as a moral whole, nor as part of a larger social whole, but as owner of himself. The relation of ownership, having become for more and more men the critically important relation in determining their actual freedom and actual prospect of realizing their full potentialities, was read back into the nature of the individual. . . . Society becomes a lot of free individuals related to each other as proprietors of their own capacities and of what they have acquired by their exercise. *Society consists of relations of exchange between proprietors.* (1962, p. 3; italics added)

Social scientists will recognize in this description the "utilitarianism" that has beset their own disciplines since Spencer and before (cf. Parsons 1968; Sahlins 1976). It is precisely a perspective in which the individual is seen "neither as a moral whole, nor as part of a larger social whole, but as owner of himself." In the social sciences, as in sociobiology, the homebred economizing of the market place is then all too easily transposed from the analysis of capitalist society to the explication of society *tout court*. The analytic place thus left to the social fact has been well described by Louis Dumont:

In modern society . . . the Human Being is regarded as the indivisible, "elementary" man, both a biological being and a thinking subject. Each particular man in a sense incarnates the whole of mankind. He is the measure of all things (in a full and novel sense). The kingdom of ends coincides with each man's legitimate ends, so the values are turned upside down. What is still called "society" is the means, the life of each man is the end. Ontologically, the society no longer exists, it is no more than an irreducible datum, which must in no way thwart the demands of liberty and equality. Of course, the above is a description of values, a view of mind. . . . A society as conceived by individualism has never existed anywhere for the reason we have given, namely, that the individual lives on social ideas. (1970, pp. 9–10)

I underscore Dumont's observations on the indivisibility of the human being in the perspective of the sociological utilitarianism: man as a thinking subject is also the same man as a biological being. Hence society may be derived from the rational action of individuals seeking to satisfy their needs – a project in which "thought" serves merely as the means and the representation of inherent ends. Sociobiology operates on exactly the same premise. Hobbes provided the original basis for this subordination of the symbolic to the natural by situating the society he knew in the state of nature. Man was seen as a wolf to man. Again one can say that the objective of sociobiologists is very similar so far as it concerns human society. But it goes further. Since they would now extend the same folk conception of capitalism to the animal kingdom as a whole, for sociobiologists it is also true that the wolf is a man to other wolves. Actually, however, I compress a long cycle of reciprocal interpretations of nature and culture that has been characteristic of the Western consciousness, both as science and as ideology. I can briefly describe this cycle by making two further points.

First, it is clear that the Hobbesian vision of man in a natural state is the origin myth of Western capitalism. In modern social practice, the story of Genesis pales by comparison. Yet it is also clear that in this comparison, and indeed in comparison with the origin myths of all other societies, the Hobbesian myth has a very peculiar structure, one that continues to attend our understandings of ourselves. So far as I am aware, we are the only society on earth that thinks of itself as having risen from savagery, identified with a ruthless nature. Everyone else believes they are descended from gods. Even if these gods have natural representations, they nonetheless have supernatural attributes. Judging from social behavior, this contrast may well be a fair statement of the differences between ourselves and the rest of the world. In any case we make both a folklore and a science of our brutish origins, sometimes with precious little to distinguish between them. And just as Hobbes believed that the institution of society or the Commonwealth did not abolish the nature of man as wolf to other men but merely permitted its expression in relative safety, so we continue to believe in the savage within us – of which we are slightly ashamed. At an earlier period it was *Homo economicus*, with a natural propensity to truck and barter, an idea that rationalized the developing capitalist society to itself. It took but two centuries to evolve another species, *Homo bellicosus*, or so one might classify that contentious ape popularized by Ardrey and other recent writers. Now comes sociobiology, and with it apparently a reversion to economic type, programmed in the natural propensity of DNA to maximize itself at the expense of whom it may concern.

Hence the response by men of the Left becomes intelligible, as does the interest of the public at large. What is inscribed in the theory of sociobiology is the entrenched ideology of Western society: the assurance of its naturalness, and the claim of its inevitability.

The second point concerns the ideological dialectic to which I previously alluded. Since the seventeenth century we seem to have been caught up in this vicious cycle, alternately applying the model of capitalist society to the animal kingdom, then reapplying this bourgeoisfied animal kingdom to the interpretation of human society. My intent in adopting the Macpherson reading of Hobbes was just to imply that most of the elements and stages of the biological theory of natural selection – from differential success to the competitive

struggle to reproduce one's stock and the transfer of powers – already existed in the *Leviathan*. As a critic of this capitalist conception, it was left to Marx to discern its realization in Darwinian theory. In a letter to Engels, Marx wrote:

> It is remarkable how Darwin recognizes among beasts and plants his English society with its division of labour [read, diversification], competition, opening up of new markets [niches], "inventions" [variations], and the Malthusian "struggle for existence." It is Hobbes's "bellum omnium contra omnes," and one is reminded of Hegel's *Phenomenology* where civil society is described as a "spiritual animal kingdom," while in Darwin the animal kingdom figures as civil society. (Marx in Schmidt 1971, p. 46)

The same point was to be made later by Hofstadter:

> A parallel can be drawn between the patterns of natural selection and classical economics, suggesting that Darwinism involved an addition to the vocabulary rather than to the substance of conventional economic theory. Both assumed the fundamentally self-interested animal pursuing, in the classical pattern, pleasure or, in the Darwinian pattern, survival. Both assumed the normality of competition in the exercise of the hedonistic, or survival, impulse; and in both it was the "fittest," usually in a eulogistic sense, who survived or prospered – either the organism most satisfactorily adapted to his environment, or the most efficient and economic producer, the most frugal and temperate worker. (1959, p. 144)

In a letter to Lavrov, Engels described the ensuing dialectical return, the representation of culture to itself in the form of a capitalist nature:

> The whole Darwinist teaching of the struggle for existence is simply a transference from society to living nature of Hobbes's doctrine of "bellum omnium contra omnes" and of the bourgeois-economic doctrine of competition together with Malthus's theory of population. When this conjurer's trick has been performed . . . the same theories are transferred back again from organic nature into history and now it is claimed that their validity as

eternal laws of human society has been proved. (Engels in Schmidt 1971, p. 47)

It might be noted that Darwin was not altogether happy with this reciprocal reflection of the animal kingdom as his own English society. "I have received in a Manchester newspaper rather a good squib," he wrote to Sir Charles Lyell, "showing that I have proved 'might is right,' and therefore that Napoleon is right, and every cheating tradesman is also right" (cited in Hofstadter 1959, p. 85).

But no such reserve would inhibit William Graham Sumner – to take the outstanding American example – from transferring the Darwinian teaching back to its original social source. "The truth is that the social order is fixed by laws of nature precisely analogous to those of the physical order" (Sumner 1934, vol. 2, p. 107). Hofstadter succinctly summarizes Sumner's inspiration:

In the Spencerian intellectual atmosphere of the 1870s and 1880s it was natural for conservatives to see the economic contest in competitive society as a reflection of the struggle in the animal world. It was easy to argue by analogy from natural selection of fitter organisms to social selection of fitter men, from organic forms with superior adaptability to citizens with a greater store of economic virtues. ... The progress of civilization, according to Sumner, depends on the selection process; and that in turn depends upon the workings of unrestricted competition. Competition is a law of nature which "can no more be done away with than gravitation," and which men can ignore only to their sorrow. (Hofstadter 1959, p. 57)

One aspect of Sumner's biologism deserves special comment. It concerns the motivation which Sumner frequently alleged for the accumulation of wealth in a ruthless competitive struggle. This is exactly the same motivation adduced by sociobiology for the parallel struggle in nature – "inheritance" (by the offspring of the fittest). The double service of the term is not unusual. From the late Middle Ages onward, Western society has gone to considerable effort to encode its economic activity within a pervasive metaphor of improvement of the stock. Terms for animal reproduction have been appropriated for economic categories and vice versa, at first figuratively, but then so consistently that metaphor dies and it becomes impossible to distinguish the original reference from the derived. The peculiarity of a native category that refers interchangeably to the social reproduction of economic goods and the natural reproduction of animate beings then goes unnoticed, banished from consciousness as well as memory. On the contrary, the category becomes a basis for scientific or popular reflections on the essential identity of the two processes. These reflections accordingly take the form of a folk etymology. They recapitulate, for example, the derivation of the English terms "capital" and "chattel" from an older "cattle," which precisely as the movable and increasable "livestock" was distinguished from the dead stock of fixed farm equipment. (Indeed the common origin of the concepts of transactable wealth and cattle in the Indo-European *peku*, together with the appearance of a cognate category of *pasū viru* in Avestan including men and their domestic animals, suggests a primitive integration of the economic, the social and the natural; modern usage would merely represent cognitive homology [cf. Benveniste 1969; and relevant entries of the *OED*].) It is the same with "inheritance," which initially referred to the continuity of goods over generations of people, only to denote at a later date the continuity of the generational "stock" itself. W. G. Sumner was thus empowered by the folk wisdom to find cause for the economic competition over resources in a genetic transmission – just as E. O. Wilson would later describe the natural process of genetic transmission as a struggle for resources:

The socialist assails particularly the institution of bequest or hereditary property. ... The right of bequest rests on no other grounds than those of expediency. The love of children is the strongest motive to frugality and to the accumulation of capital. The state guarantees the power of bequest only because it thereby encourages the accumulation of capital on which the welfare of society depends ... hereditary wealth transmitted from generation to generation is the strongest instrument by which we keep up a steadily advancing civilization. (Sumner 1934, vol. 2, pp. 112–13)

We seem unable to escape from this perpetual movement, back and forth between the culturalization of nature and the naturalization of culture. It frustrates our understanding at once of society and of the organic world. In the social sciences we exhaust our own symbolic capacities in an endless reproduction of utilitarian theorizing, some of it economic, some ecologic. In the natural sciences, it is the vulgar and scientific sociobiologies. All these efforts taken together represent the modern encompassment of the sciences, both of culture and of life, by the dominant ideology of possessive individualism.

The net effect is a curious form of totemism of which scientific sociobiology is the latest incarnation. For if totemism is, as Lévi-Strauss says, the explication of differences between human groups by reference to the distinctions between natural species, such that clan *A* is related to and distinct from clan *B* as the eagle hawk is to the crow, then sociobiology merits classification as the highest form of the totemic philosophy. For its sophistication and advance over the primitive varieties, both in the West and abroad, it does seem to merit a special name, one in keeping with its own synthetic pretensions as the latest branch of the sciences and the principal hope of civilization. Give it its due: sociobiology is a Scientific Totemism.

But with all respects to the *pensée sauvage*, this reliance on the deep structure of Western thought, with its assimilation of the reproduction of people to the reproduction of goods as a kinship of substance, cannot do for the science to which we now aspire. The confusion of categories is too immoderate. It puts us all, biological and social scientists alike, in the state known all too well to the practitioners of totemism: of mess and "dirt," as Mary Douglas has taught us, of pollution and tabu. Beyond all the politics, it is of course this descent into the kingdom of tabu that ultimately makes sociobiology so fascinating. But we pay a heavy penalty in knowledge for the distinctions we are forced to surrender. "The most serious harm to science that I see in the present fashion of applying ethnological terms to animals," Susanne Langer writes, "is that – odd as it may seem – it is really based on the assumption that the two studies, ethnology and what is called 'ethology' . . . will never become true integral parts of biological science. If they should ever do so, the use of words literally in one context and figuratively in another would cause havoc" (1971, p. 328). Yet we stand to lose even more than our science. We should have to abandon all understanding of the human world as meaningfully constituted, and so the one best hope of knowing ourselves.

REFERENCES

Benveniste, Emile. 1969. *Le vocabulaire des institutions indo-européennes; vol. 1: Economie, parenté, société*. Paris: Editions de Minuit.

Dumont, Louis. 1970. *Homo Hierarchicus*. Chicago: University of Chicago Press.

Hobbes, Thomas. 1950 [1651]. *Leviathan*. New York: E. P. Dutton.

Hofstadter, Richard. 1959. *Social Darwinism in American thought*. Revised edition. New York: Braziller.

Langer, Susanne K. 1971. The great shift: Instinct to intuition. In *Man and beast: Comparative social behavior*, ed. J. F. Eisenberg,

and W. S. Dillon. Washington, DC: Smithsonian Institution Press, pp. 314–32.

Macpherson, C. B. 1962. *The political theory of possessive individualism*. London: Oxford University Press.

Parsons, Talcott. 1968. *The structure of social action*. 2 vols. New York: The Free Press.

Sahlins, Marshall. 1976. *Culture and practical reason*. Chicago: University of Chicago Press.

Schmidt, Alfred. 1971. *The concept of nature in Marx*. London: NLB.

Sumner, William Graham. 1934. *Essays of William Graham Sumner*. 2 vols. Ed. A. G. Keller, and M. R. Davie. New Haven: Yale University Press.

16

Land Animals,
Pure and Impure

Mary Douglas

Mary Douglas (1921–2007) was a most distinguished British anthropologist who trained at the University of Oxford and taught at University College London and elsewhere. She is the author of many works, of which the key ones with respect to religion include *Purity and Danger* (1966), *Natural Symbols* (1970), and the essays in *Implicit Meanings* (1975, cf. 1996). She conducted research among the Lele of Central Africa, on contemporary British and American society, and on the Old Testament (1993, 1999). Her work has been the subject of an extensive study by Fardon (1999).

The present essay is taken from a recent interpretation of the biblical book of Leviticus. As Douglas explains, its origins lie in her much earlier analysis of "The Abominations of Leviticus" in *Purity and Danger*. That work, in turn, owed its immediate inspiration to Steiner's essay on taboo (1956), which in some respects paralleled Durkheim on

the sacred and Lévi-Strauss on totemism in showing its subject as relationally rather than substantively constituted. In an enormously influential analysis Douglas argued that systems of classification and the anomalies they inevitably produce are central objects of religious concern in *any* society. "Dirt," she famously stated, is simply "matter out of place" and hence always relative to a particular system of classification. Rather than explaining systems of purity and taboos in terms of biological germ theory (as though, somehow, the ancient Israelites had known about the dangers of trichinosis in uncooked pork), Douglas reverses the prevalent argument and sees modern concerns with hygiene as another instance of symbolic ordering. *Purity and Danger* thus helped develop a radical shift in the way that symbolic systems of small- and large-scale societies could be compared to one another, and was also inspirational for establish-

From Mary Douglas, "Preface" and "Land Animals, Pure and Impure," in *Leviticus as Literature* (Oxford: Oxford University Press, 1999), pp. v–viii, 134–51. Reprinted by permission of Oxford University Press. Abridged.

ing the significance of the metaphoric properties of the body and food within cultural systems. Douglas provides a forthright critique of the all-too prevalent perspective she calls (after William James) "medical materialism," which is not distinct from the ideology that Sahlins critiques in the preceding essay. This form of argument which reduces symbol to function is evident in Harris's popular explanations for the refusal to eat pigs in the Middle East or cows in South Asia (1985), and subject to lively refutation in Sahlins (1976). However, Douglas differs from Sahlins in that while she has embraced new directions in structuralism and phenomenology, she remains true to her Durkheimian roots in seeing symbolic practice as emerging from and addressing social boundaries and relations.

In *Leviticus as Literature* Douglas revisits the question of symbolic classification in the Bible. Her account is no longer merely a very clever piece of analysis but an interpretation that is grounded in a deep and emergent understanding of the religion of ancient Judaism and the styles of reasoning and writing used by the authors of the different books of the Torah (Pentateuch). Remaining rigorously opposed to piecemeal moralizing and materialist explanations of individual food taboos, in this chapter she explains the rules of impurity in terms of the logic of the whole. The argument now attends to the positive meaning of ritual purity and the rules of sacrifice rather than the ostensible disgust or puzzlement at anomalies. It also draws on the model developed elsewhere in the book of a system of analogies between Mount Sinai, the tabernacle, animal offerings, and the bodies of the people of Israel. Somewhat to Douglas's own puzzlement, and much to her credit, the interpretation moves beyond her inclination to seek direct correspondences between the social and symbolic orders. For other work on symbolic classification see Needham, ed. (1973); for an additional anthropological foray into the Bible, Leach (1969).

... To study the book of Leviticus as an anthropologist has been a project very dear to my heart. It seemed far beyond my reach. Yet not to do it would be to leave dangling a number of threads from early work. Let me explain some things about my training which have influenced my attitude to the Bible. Young anthropologists in Oxford in the late 1940s and 1950s were heirs to an old debate about human rationality, a debate provoked by the experience of science and biased by the experience of empire. Nineteenth-century rationalists centred on what they thought of as the natives' intellectual problems. Gross superstitions, naive magic, and immoral gods, were explained by reference to moral evolutionism. The mind of the primitive in aeons past had been hampered by illogical mental habits and proneness to letting emotions govern reason, and the same handicaps were thought to afflict present-day backward peoples. However, in reaction, for the students of my generation the main text was Evans-Pritchard's *Witchcraft, Oracles and Magic* (1937). From this we learnt that people from alien traditions, trusting in their gods and ancestors and fearing their witches, were every bit as logical as we (or just as illogical). It is actually no more "logical" to believe in a divinely created moral universe than to believe in an amoral self-generating universe. Foundational beliefs stand beyond the operations of logic. Our researches were framed by an interest in the moral construction of the universe and the nature of belief.

In those days it was axiomatic for anthropologists that, however peculiar they might seem to us, the strange beliefs of a foreign tradition make sense. Explanations of other minds based on mystery, mystique, native credulity or mysticism, were out. Moral evolution was replaced by a down-to-earth approach to alternative ways of living and dying. We took on a hardy skepticism and a nuts-and-bolts demand for evidence. The point about doing fieldwork was to learn how a world-view was adapted to what the people were trying to achieve, especially to what they were doing towards living together in society. Hence our attention to ritual and symbolism. Rain rites, for example, would be a collective act of affirmation. The rite did not attempt to prove the priests' control of meteorology, it was done to affirm publicly the moral aspect of the natural order. Spectacular ceremonials to appease the gods were also performed for the sake of influencing each other's minds.

I would never have felt impelled to attempt an anthropological reading of Leviticus if during African fieldwork I had not been confronted by local dietary rules, and so thought of looking up the passage in chapter 11 on the forbidden animals. I actually cited Leviticus and the parallel passage in Deuteronomy in my "Animals in Lele religious symbolism" (1957). What I wrote ten years later about uncleanness and pollution in *Purity and Danger* (1966) was driven by fieldwork experience, stiffened by training in Oxford anthropology and enriched with some reading about the psychology of perception. But before looking up those baffling chapters, I had never read the Bible, either at school or at university or subsequently. When I came eventually to read the scholarly commentaries on the Mosaic dietary laws I was surprised to find so much disagreement on such an important subject. Though with some minor variations scholars almost unanimously associated the forbidden animals with unpleasant characteristics, there was no agreement and no satisfactory explanation either in the book or outside it about why each particular species should have been selected and not others which might equally be abominated.

Reflecting on these animals I was drawn to focus on the class of unclassifiable things. The forbidden land animals were certainly described as such a class, and I extended it with some confidence to water creatures and speculatively to those in the air that could not be identified. I proposed a theory of anomaly, a universal feeling of disquiet (even of disgust) on confrontation with unclassifiables. Taking the Levitical classification system as it revealed itself, the said abominable species failed to show the taxonomic requirements of inhabitants of the three environmental classes, land, air, water, and the abominability of species that "go upon the belly" in all environments went by the same rule: the forbidden animals were species that escaped being classified. Consistently with the main thrust of social anthropology of my period, the argument explained abominability, but denied magicality and favoured the rationality of the Mosaic dietary code. It was gratifying to find that some Bible scholars accepted the idea that the puzzles of the abominable animals in Leviticus and Deuteronomy could be laid to rest, the prohibitions being part of the process of tidying up the classifications of the environment (see Levines *FPS Commentary, Leviticus* (1989), 243). But a puzzle remained.

The central argument of *Purity and Danger* was that classifications are not otiose. They do something, they are necessary in organization. The pollution theory that I have seen develop over the last thirty years shows that where lines of abominability are drawn heavy stakes are at issue. The classification of the universe is part and parcel of social organization, and the categories are useful in defining who can be admitted where, and who comes first and who comes second or nowhere at all. This works so effectively elsewhere that I was implicitly waiting for it to be found true of biblical pollution (see my "Sacred contagion" (1996)). It applies well enough, in fairly obvious ways, for the cult of the tabernacle and the dignity of the priesthood, but for the organization of society the doctrine of pollution did nothing except draw a boundary round the people of Israel against outsiders. Nothing happens at the level of action to explain the selection of forbidden animals. Against everything I believe, the cognitive scheme which left these creatures unclassified hung in the air uselessly. If chapter 11 of Leviticus was a case for pollution theory the classifying of the animals should correspond to some important classifying for the internal organization of society. But the more that pollution theory developed, and the more that pollution was seen as the vehicle of accusations and downgradings, the more I was bound to acknowledge that it does not apply to the most famous instance of the Western tradition, the Pentateuch. All of this volume is an attempt to explain why. General pollution theory still stands, but its application to the Bible is limited. The forbidden animals turn out to have a much more interesting role than ever I imagined. [. . .]

> Behold, I establish my covenant with you and your descendants after you, and with every living creature that is with you, the birds, the cattle, and every beast of the earth with you, as many as came out of the ark. (Gen 9: 9–10)

> For thou lovest all things that exist, and hast loathing for none of the things which thou hast made, for thou wouldst not have made anything if thou hadst hated it. (Wisdom 11:24)

God met his people on Mount Sinai and continues to meet them in the tabernacle. In sacrifice the body of the sacrificial animal becomes another microcosm in its own right, corresponding to the tabernacle and the holy mountain. Then the sequence of cultic laws is interrupted by the narrative in chapters 8–10. When the law-giving is resumed it develops a different bodily microcosm. This time the body of the worshipper is made analogous to the sanctuary and the altar. Whatever will render the altar impure will do the same for the Israelite's body. The laws of impurity sketch out the parallel in meticulous detail over chapters 11–15. The animal that is taken into the body by eating corresponds to that which is offered on the altar by fire; what is disallowed for the one is disallowed for the other; what harms the one harms the other. One thing that the book never says is that it is bad for the health of the body to eat any of the forbidden animals.

Land Animals under the Covenant

Chapter 11 is probably the best known in Leviticus because it deals with the Mosaic dietary laws. It has been taken to imply that the forbidden animal meats are abominable, detestable, or unedifying in one way or another. Taking account of the full context, which is the rest of the Pentateuch, it would be difficult to overlook one biblical principle: God is compassionate for all living things; not only to the humans, he is good to all his creatures (Psalm 145: 8–9). So if he himself does not detest them, why should he tell humans to detest any of his animals? This is a serious and central doctrinal problem.

Two kinds of covenant are the basis of chapter 11. First the covenant with Noah and his descendants in which God said he would never again punish the land and the living things on it for the evil things done by mankind, and made the rainbow its sign. It is emphatically also a covenant with the animals: "This is the sign of the covenant which I make between me and you and every living creature that is with you, for all future generations" (Gen 9: 12) . . . I will remember my covenant which is between me and you and every living creature of all flesh . . ." (Gen 9: 15, repeated in vv. 16 and 17). A few verses earlier in the same chapter God has required a reckoning for the life-blood of humans. "Only you shall not eat flesh with its life, that is, its blood. For your life-blood I will surely require a reckoning; of every beast I will require it and of man" (Gen 9: 4,5). In Genesis God gave man dominion over animals. Robert Murray[1] has argued persuasively that dominion for Genesis always entails responsibility. Leviticus presents the further implications of human dominion over animals. A one-sided pledge from God cannot quite be called a covenant: the animals are not bound by any counter-obligations, unless by a stretch of the imagination the command to them at the creation to go forth and multiply counts as such.

Later, the covenant with Abraham is a promise of fertility to his descendants. It does not mention the animals, but extravagantly it says that his descendants will be as innumerable as the dust (Gen 13: 16). It echoes the blessing of Genesis to Noah and his sons, "Be fruitful and multiply, and fill the earth" (Gen 9: 1), and "Be fruitful and multiply, bring forth abundantly on the earth and multiply in it" (Gen 9: 7), the very words used for his blessing on the creatures of the water and the air after they had been created (Gen 1: 22). There is no doubt that this God is concerned with fertility, and that his promise is linked with their obedience.

The covenant with Moses on Sinai is the explicit assertion of God's overlordship over the people of Israel and their livestock. It specifically includes the servants and the cattle in the sabbath observance (Exod 20: 8). From householder to children, to servants, to cattle, the animals come under the lines of authority drawn by the Sinai covenant. Sabbath observance only affects the work animals, the ox that treads the husks off the grain, that draws the cart, that turns the water-wheel.[2] Exodus also makes the point strongly by requiring that the male first-born of the domestic animals be offered to the Lord just as the first-born of humans. "Consecrate to me all the first-born; whatever is the first to open the womb among the people of Israel, both of man and of beast, is mine" (Exod 13: 2). "You shall set apart to the Lord all that first opens the womb. All the firstlings of your cattle that are males shall be the Lord's" (Exod 13: 12). The rule for land animals which always sounds so complicated is quite simple when the covenant is seen to be its guiding principle. God is the feudal Lord. From this it follows that no one is allowed to harm God's people or use God's things, nor must his followers harm each other, or harm the other living beings on his territory without his express permission. This he gives for the killing of herd animals in sacrifice, and use of their carcasses.

The question of whether they do or do not come under the covenant is paramount. Leviticus divides land animals into two categories, first, the herds and flocks which share the lives of their owners, travel with them, and provide their sustenance, and second, all the rest. The pure animals come under the terms of the covenant of their masters, and their treatment is strictly regulated. The feudal relationship extends from God to his people and to their livestock.

The teaching about the sanctity of blood derives from this feudal relationship. God protects the people of Israel, his rites give them

covering, sacrifice is the means he has given to them for expiation. Sacrifice protects them from the consequences of their own behaviour, even from his just anger. They are never, ever, allowed to eat blood, but he has given them the right to consecrate the lives of their herd animals, to use their blood to make atonement to him for their sins, and to eat the blood-free flesh for their own nourishment (Lev 17: 11). This solemn injunction teaches the sanctity of life (the life is in the blood). In religious terms, the mosaic dietary code is an invitation to Israel to join in the divine work of creation by living a life that honours the way God made the world and the covenants God has made with his people.

The Two Texts

The two texts in Leviticus and Deuteronomy start by running in close parallel. They give a perfectly logical classification which echoes the opening chapters 1–7 on sacrifice with a description of the domesticated ruminants of their herds, cattle, sheep, goats, which may be consecrated for offering on the altar. Then follows in both texts a careful set of rules to discriminate near-misses, candidates for entry into the class of domestic ruminants which fail because they show one but not both the required criteria.

Marching in step, the two texts say that the unclean animals are only "unclean for you". Because the dietary rules about land animals derive from the covenant, they only apply to the people of Israel. Deuteronomy seems to say by its prefatory remark that abominable things are the things forbidden as unclean in 14: 7–8. The equation of unclean with abominable in Deuteronomy is the source of the idea that the forbidden animals have some detestable characteristic, the focus of so much scholarly ingenuity. But in Leviticus the unclean animals are not abominable.

The microcosm is based on the body of anyone of the congregation of Israel about to take nourishment; the body is equivalent to the altar and so is his hospitable board round which he gathers his family and friends. Way back in the time of the Leviticus writer the

Table 1 Land animals, pure and impure, Deuteronomy 14: 3–8 and Leviticus 11: 2–8

Deuteronomy	*Leviticus*
3. You shall not eat any abominable thing.	2. These are the living things which you may eat among all the beasts that are on the earth.
4. These are the animals you may eat: the ox, the sheep, the goat,	
5. the hart, the gazelle, the roebuck, the wild goat, the ibex, the antelope, and the mountain-sheep.	3. Whatever parts the hoof and is cloven-footed and chews the cud, among the animals, you may eat.
6. Every animal that parts the hoof and has the hoof cloven in two, and chews the cud, among the animals, you may eat.	4. Nevertheless among those that chew the cud or part the hoof, you shall not eat these: The camel, because it chews the cud but does not part the hoof, is unclean to you.
7. Yet of those that chew the cud or have the foot cloven you shall not eat these: The camel, the hare and the rock badger, because they chew the cud but do not part the hoof, are unclean for you.	5. And the rock badger, because it chews the cud but does not part the hoof, is unclean to you.
8. And the swine, because it parts the hoof but does not chew the cud, is unclean for you. Their flesh you shall not eat and their carcasses you shall not touch.	6. And the hare, because it chews the cud but does not part the hoof, is unclean to you.
	7. And the swine, because it parts the hoof and is cloven-footed but does not chew the cud, is unclean to you.
	8. Of their flesh you shall not eat and their carcasses you shall not touch.

body was already the analogue of the altar. Not a secular analogue, for in a total religious system (such as that of Leviticus) the word secular does not have much meaning. The table, and all who eat at it, and everything that has been cooked for them to eat, are under the same law of holiness.[3] Body for altar, altar for body, the rules which protect the purity of the tabernacle are paralleled by rules which protect the worshipper. What he can eat without contracting impurity and what can be offered to God in sacrifice are the same.

An interesting difference between the texts of Deuteronomy 14 and Leviticus 11 is that the Leviticus opening, with its reference to living beings on the earth (Lev 11: 2), recalls the account of the creation in Genesis, "Let the earth bring forth living creatures according to their kinds: cattle and creeping things and beasts of the earth, according to their kinds" (Gen 1: 24). The opening verses of Leviticus II are only the beginning of a larger survey of land animals (the beasts of the earth) which is not featured in Deuteronomy.

When Leviticus has listed the different types of land animals that are impure and must not be eaten, look round and see what is left –

nothing! All these land animals are either clean or unclean, pure or impure. Now that verse 26 is taken to refer to animals with solid hoofs, we can use the following comprehensive typology of the land animals:

(i)   animals of the flocks and herds, ruminants, split hooves;
(ii)   ruminants without split hoofs, e.g. camel, rock badger, hare;
(iii) non-ruminant with split hoofs, pig;
(iv)   solid hooves, e.g. asses, horses;
(v)   paws, e.g. lion, civet cat, dog, hyena;
(vi)   list of eight land animals that go on their belly: the mole, the mouse, the great lizards, the gecko, the land crocodile, the lizard, the sand lizard, and the chameleon.

The zoological criteria are good enough to make an exhaustive list of land animals. By the end of the chapter everything living on the land has been included: going on hoofs, going on paws, gliding on the belly – what else is there? Everything has been accounted for. . . .

The first set are under the covenant, and clean. All other land animals, excluding the first set, are unclean or impure, and their dead

Table 2 Living beings on the earth

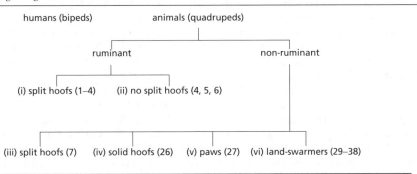

humans (bipeds)   animals (quadrupeds)

ruminant   non-ruminant

(i) split hoofs (1–4)   (ii) no split hoofs (4, 5, 6)

(iii) split hoofs (7)   (iv) solid hoofs (26)   (v) paws (27)   (vi) land-swarmers (29–38)

bodies not to be touched or eaten. Deuteronomy makes a point of allowing the killing and eating of wild counterparts of domestic herds (Deut 13: 5), of which Leviticus does not speak. Were Leviticus explicitly to permit secular slaughter, it would undermine the covenant basis of the Levitical rules constraining humans from eating animals that they have not reared. A similar silence covers what is to be done with blemished animals from their flocks and herds which are not allowed to be sacrificed. Presumably they are quietly eaten.

Many four-footed animals are not specifically mentioned in the catalogue; for instance, rodents such as squirrel, rabbit, rat, cat, do not need to be listed since they are covered by the rules for animals that go on their paws. Finally, not on the chart above, there are other land-dwellers indicated as "swarming things that go on the belly, go on all fours, or with many feet" (Lev 11: 42), including land-dwelling insects, snakes, worms, spiders, centipedes. Leviticus calls these by a word that is translated as abominable, but Leviticus uses a different word from that used by Deuteronomy and also translated the same way. Leviticus also confuses the issues by applying a general defilement term for land-swarmers: the people must not "defile" themselves by contact with their carcasses (Lev 11: 43–4). The sanction for infringing the rule is not severe. Though uncleanness is very contaminating, the sanction is just to wait till sundown (Lev 11: 31, 39). If someone has gone further than just touching an unclean corpse, the sanction is still mild, he must wash his clothes and remain

unclean until evening; and anyone who carries its carcass shall wash his hands and remain unclean until evening (Lev 11: 40). We should not exaggerate the penalties or the severity of the rules.

The rule of uncleanness only affects contact with the dead carcass. In this respect contact with the carcasses of land animals are accorded a similar, though lesser, impurity as contact with human corpses. The people of Israel are enjoined to have towards their livestock some of the responsibilities of a feudal lord to his followers. Both humans and livestock are called to be separate and pure in the interior circle of a world of unclean nations or unclean animals. Milgrom says that the effect of the criteria for edible quadrupeds (Lev 11: 3) is to limit Israel to three domestic species: sheep, goats, and cattle.[4] But there is more to it than just not eating. Notice some of the tacit restrictions that follow from these rules. All land animals have been classified within the system. They can all be touched alive, but the only ones that can be touched after death are the classified ruminants. This means that only the latter can be killed for sacrifice. While they are alive camels and asses can be harnessed, loaded, ridden, dogs can be beaten, cats can be kicked, mice can be trapped, without incurring impurity, but once they are dead they convey uncleanness.

In effect the rule against touching a dead animal protects it in its lifetime. Since its carcass cannot be skinned or dismembered, most of the ways in which it could be exploited are ruled out, so it is not worth breeding, hunting, or trapping. These unclean animals are safe from the secular as also from the sacred kitchen. The rule is a comprehensive command to respect the dead body of every land animal. If anyone were to take it seriously it would be very restrictive. The verb to touch has also the idea of harming, damaging, laying hands upon as if to steal or strike. An example is in Genesis when Abimelech commands his followers not to harm Isaac: "Whoever touches this man or his wife shall be put to death" (Gen 26: 11), and says to Isaac: "We have not touched you and have done to you nothing but good" (Gen 26: 29). The rule of not touching the corpse makes the skins useless for fur coats or fur blankets, no leather waistcoats or bags, no shoe leather or wine-skins. Their bones and teeth cannot be carved for combs, buttons, containers, dice, jewellery, utensils. Their gut cannot be used for stringed instruments, or their stomachs or bladders for bags, or their sinews for sewing. In practice the penalty is so light that the rule would hardly prevent a taxidermist or tanner from pursuing his trade, so long as he purified his clothes and himself before approaching the tabernacle. Nonetheless it is still unequivocally forbidden to touch these creatures when dead. The tremendous domestic complications entailed by the high degree of contagiousness might deter the furrier, and it would be awkward for the wearer of a mink coat to have to keep washing, and no one else could so much as shake hands with the wearer without afterwards performing the same ablutions. To be classified unclean ought to be an advantage for the survival of the species.

Interpretations of Uncleanness/Impurity

Though Moses admonished Aaron and his sons to distinguish between the holy and the common and between the clean and the unclean (Lev 10), he did not explain what is meant by unclean, or holy. The sages did not make much sense of it at all. Why pig is counted unclean in the Bible has been the subject of much speculation. Changing the word to "impure" does not really help. Why

ever should a non-ruminant with cloven hoofs be counted impure?

Some scholars favour the idea that pig has to do with cults of the dead in Egypt or Canaan, but this does not explain the uncleanness of the other three animals named with it. When the classification is so comprehensive it cannot be sound to take the animals as if they were separate items in a catalogue without headings or subheadings. If some of the rules have the effect of banning predators, or blood, or carrion-eaters, it is not a comprehensive explanation. It is also too Hellenistic, too oriented to feelings, for this book. The same for the idea of Philo, the first-century CE Jewish philosopher,[5] that the forbidden species each signifies vice or virtue. In a long, rambling homily he takes each forbidden animal separately and explains its prohibition in terms of symbols. His fanciful allegories are not rooted anywhere in the Bible text, only in the imagination of the philosopher, and so inevitably his moral preoccupations dominate the reading. He derives from Leviticus 11 a lesson to control gluttony, passions, and desire. The animals that go on the belly are forbidden so as to teach the people not to pay attention to their bellies. It is not a naturalist explanation, he does not consider the forbidden animals to be bad in themselves, rather the contrary:

> All the animals of land, sea or air whose flesh is the finest and fattest, thus titillating and exciting the malignant for pleasure, he sternly forbade them to eat, knowing that they set a trap for the most slavish of the senses, the taste, and produce gluttony, an evil very dangerous both to soul and body.

Philo was not working from any tradition that was close to the writing of the text, for he does not draw on the rest of Leviticus or Deuteronomy to construct his sermons.

Some moralizing interpreters have regarded the laws as oblique commands that will restrain human "omnivorousness and ferocity";[6] others again as arbitrary commands to test obedience.[7] Others give up on interpreting at all, treating the rules as inexplicable, though deriving from an ancient time when they presumably once made some kind of sense. Some treat the Levitical scheme as a relic of a pastoral way of life.[8] For this to be serious there would need to be a theory of why some relics remain strong when their supporting context has passed away, while others are forgotten. In default of such a theory it can still be argued that the Leviticus writer could not betray all the pastoral tradition. His commitment to the idea of the ancient covenant would preserve rules about herd animals. However, the general disarray among rival interpretations testifies to the lost tradition. Not surprisingly the general public is ready to believe that there is something abhorrent about the creatures which the book tells them to abhor. To this day it is common to hear distinguished scholars explain ritual purity by natural reactions:

Many people wince at having to pick up a dead animal; most people (except two-year-olds) try to avoid touching defecation; corpses inspire a natural feeling of awe, and we hesitate to touch them; washing off semen and blood is almost natural, and certainly not hard to remember. Even gnat-impurity, which sounds picky, is not hard to understand. Who wants a fly in one's soup?[9]

Most of the discussion is based on the Deuteronomy formula, not on Leviticus. The first mistake in this quotation is to have used lines from Deuteronomy as if they came from Leviticus and as if they all meant the same thing. Deuteronomy says that winged insects are unclean, but not Leviticus. Humans are constantly under their attack, flies feast on babies' eyes, they breed their maggots in the larder, walk contemptuously over food, they suck blood and sting to frenzy. It is plausible that invasive insects and creepy-crawlies might be disliked universally. Another mistake is to use supposedly natural or "almost natural" reactions to justify all the uncleanness rules. The nuisance value of insects makes this explanation plausible, but the rules are not mostly about insects. Why revile shy animals like hares and useful animals like camels by classifying them with the naturally dislikeable? The naturalist explanation must be wrong for a book so sophisticated as Leviticus, and for anthropologists it is always wrong to take natural as a universal category, forgetting that nature is culturally defined.

Again, the text itself specifically says that these are rules made for the people of Israel; what is designated as unclean for them is not unclean for the whole of humanity. Thus the rules of impurity are not a way of promoting a universal hygienic principle or pronouncing a general health warning. The only explanation will be in the rest of the rule system. Many civilizations have been built on camel meat, or pork, and though hyrax is hard to get, there is nothing bad for you in adding hyrax or hare to your diet; some people habitually eat blood, and the dietary value of suet fat can be underestimated. One popular explanation for the banning of the water-swarmers (which in Leviticus are not unclean) is that they are scavengers: pigs will eat carrion; shrimps and crabs feed upon dead fish; so dirty feeders are forbidden. This explanation is weak because a lot of animals would opportunistically consume carrion if they found it, and anyway the text says nothing about carrion-feeding animals.

The concept of dirtiness has contaminated the conceptual field; the idea of disgust at eating unclean things dominates interpretation. The kitchen, medical, and bathroom senses intrude. Leviticus certainly plays upon disgust at bodily exudations in its long disquisition on uncleanness of bleeding and leprosy in chapters 12–15. If impure was not originally a term of vilification it certainly has become one. Appeals to medical and aesthetic principles are not the way to interpret an enigmatic law in Leviticus: the only safe path is to trace the contrast sets and parallels the book itself develops. The impurity of an animal kind is part of the technical meaning of ritual purity.

In itself the idea of impurity is not difficult to translate. The word is well chosen from secular contexts where unclean, defiled, impure, dirty correspond to a situation which calls for an act of cancellation. But washing, polishing, burnishing, are too superficial to carry all the meanings of purification. In Christianity impure is used for the defilement of sin, with frequent reference to the parallel with a soiled garment, it is taught that the repentant soul requires a cleansing rite. But the listed uncleannesses of Leviticus are not sin in general, they are a separate set of sins, they depend on physical contact only, and the central principle is that the contaminated body has contagious power, which entails that all its future physical contacts convey contamination. The rules prescribe how the object spreading defilement must be washed, destroyed, or somehow stopped, according to the gravity of the defilement.

The word for impure, *tame*, is worked very heavily in Leviticus and used sparsely elsewhere in the Bible.[10] We may ask why it became such a favourite word for the priestly writer, but the first question is how it relates to holiness. Once again, the most illuminating passage to explain what it is about is the warning that God gave to Moses about the sanctity of Mount Sinai. In Exodus 19: 10–24 he tells Moses to make a fence round the mountain and to prevent the people from approaching the mountain, not even to touch the edge of it. He tells Moses to tell them to purify themselves, to wash their clothes and be ready for the day when he will appear to them, but to wait until they are summoned by trumpet: "Go down and warn the people, lest they break through to the Lord to gaze, and many of them perish. And also let the priests who come near to the Lord consecrate themselves, lest the Lord break out upon them" (Exod 19: 21–2). The danger is two-edged: the people might break through or the Lord might break out, and in either case, people will die. This is the effect of holiness. The holy thing that is not correctly guarded and fenced will break out and kill, and the impure person not correctly prepared for contact with the holy will be killed. Furthermore, a person who has had the misfortune to "contract" holiness, to use Milgrom's term, may inadvertently contaminate other unprotected things or persons, merely by contact.[11]

The nearest usage in European languages for the idea of contagion is in the discourse of honour, especially with reference to the virtue of women or the honour of a knight. The taint of dishonour gives a fair idea of impurity and violation. In Mediterranean cultures a woman's honour must be protected at all costs; if she is defiled her violator must be killed; if her father or brothers fail to cancel the offence they will be dishonoured too, and the whole family. It is not a metaphor, it is a concept about behaviour that has practical consequences: none of her sisters will be able to marry, no respectable person will do business on equal terms with the menfolk, they will not be able to hold up their heads at a meeting, the contaminated family is ruined.[12]

Israel had a patronal society in which the patron-client relation is expressed by the client's respect for the honour of the patron. At meetings between lord and vassals the latter bring specified gifts of food to be ceremoniously shared. Leviticus says that the cereal offering must expressly be given with the "salt of the covenant" (Lev 2: 13), which suggests that the terminology and values of covenant would have been current and easily interpretable for the people for whom the book was written. Defilement as a violation of holiness is a particularly apt expression for an attack on the honour of God perceived as a feudal lord. The word for holy has the sense of "consecrated", "pledged", "betrothed", as "sacrosanct" in modern English, something forbidden for others,[13] not to be encroached upon, diluted, or attacked. A key text for understanding impurity in Leviticus would be: "For you are people holy to the Lord your God; the Lord your God has chosen you to be a people for his own possession, out of all the peoples that are on the face of the earth" (Deut 7: 6). This is followed by a reference to the principle of requital on which the covenant rests (Deut 7: 9–10). A few verses later the same text goes on to say what being holy or reserved to the Lord entails in terms of behaviour. It corresponds to the requirements of chastity and fidelity in the discourse of honour and betrothal, which is similar to, or rather, modelled upon the discourse of alliance and covenant. "You shall therefore be careful to do the commandment, and the statutes, and the ordinances, which I command you this day" (Deut 7: 11).

In addition to obedience the covenant with the overlord requires protecting his honour, or abstaining from insult. His power protects his people or his things and places, and to insult any of them is an insult to his honour. The parallel with the discourse of honour explains why sins cause uncleanness to adhere to the sanctuary and to the altar. Jacob Milgrom is curious to know why the altar should need atonement when the altar has not sinned. He develops a convincing theory of contagion from sin clustering on and around the holy places until it is washed off by the rite of atonement.[14] His analysis of contagious impurity is impeccable, but one can notice that the language of dirt and ablution is unnecessarily materialist. In the courts of chivalry a warrior would recognize that his armour is dishonoured if he himself is impeached: as well as his children, and father and mother, his helmet, his coat of arms, his house, all are tainted and made worthless by the contagious dishonor. Blood washes off the major taint, a noble gift cancels a minor fault. In the same way, bringing uncleanness into the Lord God's sanctuary makes it impure since the place shares in the insult to God.

Leviticus has first described the pure animals as ruminant hoof-cleavers, and then has gone on to exclude "ruminants" which do not cleave the hoof and the one non-ruminant species which does (the pig). This order of listing gives the impression of excluded animals trying to get into the privileged enclosure so that they too could be consecrated and share in the Lord's cult. There would have been pressure from enterprising cooks seeking to alleviate the monotony of the menu. The sense of pressure to be included adds to the meaning of the animals excluded for having only one but not both defining features.

In the midrash the image of a reclining pig stretching out its cloven hoofs and saying: "Look, I'm pure," while concealing the fact that it does not chew the cud, is used to characterize the hypocrisy of the Roman empire, which posed as being dedicated to law and justice, while actually oppressing the peoples it ruled.[15]

Frivolously one can ask why pig or any other animal would seek to be accounted pure when the pure animals are destined for early death and the fire of the altar. On a secular view, having one but not both the criteria for purity would be a saving blessing, but the context is religious.

The meaning of purity depends on the sense of God's awful majesty, manifest in his creation. Exodus describes it in a narrative of volcanic explosion, thunder, fire. Deuteronomy describes it with words about God's power, and with verbal warnings of disaster. Leviticus conveys it by double, triple, multiple microcosms. The people, with their children and their servants and their domestic animals too, benefit from his covenant. As vassals of God their unworthiness is immeasurable, but yet they are invited to eat at his table, and may eat the food that is offered to him. Sacrifice is a communal feast. Theoretically the people of Israel never eat meat except in God's company, in his house and with his blessing. They have been singled out for the honour of being consecrated to God, to be his people. The height and the depth of this honour is inexpressible. At another level it is a parallel honour for their flocks and herds, the cloven-hoofed ruminants, to be singled out of all animal kinds to be consecrated to God. This paradigm turns the covenant animals into vassals in relation to the people of Israel, as are the people of Israel the vassals of God.

Sacred Contagion

We still can ask what interest Leviticus could have had in elaborating the concept of holiness and impurity in these ways. The full answer must relate to the fact that belief in the maleficent power of demons has been demolished. The theodicy has to be changed: his friends will no longer be able to tell a sick man that he has been seized by a leprosy demon or a woman that her child has died because a female demon took it. Suffering and sorrow still remain, and death. The priests are expected to explain, give comfort, and help. This is what the doctrine of purity does. If you fall sick, it could be that God has broken out on you because you unknowingly incurred holiness or impurity. This is a close parallel to the superseded idea that a demon might have caught you. A sacrifice will put it right, or a wash and waiting till evening, according to the gravity of the transgression. The word "unclean" is particularly apt for relating the field of demonological medicine to the new regime, it affords a theory of pain and suffering free of demons and affords an alternative explanation for bodily afflictions.

So why should touching unclean animals provoke a dangerous breaking-out of this kind? The insult to God is to have come into his sacred place after profane and contagious contact with the corpse of one of his creatures. Taken together the food purity rules and the touch purity rules are part of a unified doctrine in which corpse pollution, bloodshed, and unsanctified death are classed as breaches of covenant.

It has been a puzzlement to Christian readers that Leviticus puts unclean contact into the same bracket as breaches of the moral code. However, there is nothing puzzling about both kinds of disobedience to the Lord's command being treated together. To touch an unclean thing and then to approach the tabernacle puts the person in need of atonement. Leviticus in chapter 5 begins the topic of uncleanness:

> Or if anyone touches an unclean thing, whether the carcass of an unclean beast or a carcass of unclean cattle, or a carcass of unclean swarming things, and it is hidden from him, and he has become unclean, he shall become guilty (Lev 5: 2). When a man is guilty in any of these, he shall confess the sin he has committed and he shall bring his guilt offering to the Lord for the sin he has committed . . . and the priest shall make atonement for him for his sin. (Lev 5: 5–6)

And again in the summing up, chapter 7 emphasizes the contagions principle:

> Flesh that touches any unclean thing shall not be eaten; it shall be burned with fire. All who are clean may eat flesh, but the person who eats of the flesh of the sacrifice of the Lord's peace offerings while an uncleanness is upon him, that person shall be cut off from his people. And if anyone touches an unclean thing, whether the uncleanness of man or an unclean beast or any unclean abomination, and then eats of the flesh of the sacrifice of the

Lord's peace offerings, that person shall be cut off from his people. (Lev 7: 19–21)

This is very emphatic language, repetitive, classificatory, and redolent of mythopoetic analogy. Such a statement from an archaic thought style cannot be decoded into modern terms. The interpreter must not read emotional quality into language which is primarily cast in a spatio-temporal mode. The contact has been forbidden, and the person who has become contagious shall not carry the contagion sacrilegiously to defile the holy place or to eat the flesh of the Lord's peace offerings; he will be punished. A domestic ruminant is the designated medium of atonement and the priest following the instructions for a sin offering in chapters 4 and 5 will make atonement for a sinner and he will be forgiven. He can live his ordinary life in this contagious state, but because of the contagion he and other persons he may contact will commit sacrilege if they take part in the cult of the tabernacle. He can expect to be criticized by his believing fellows and be made to take the blame for a community-wide disaster, and possibly expelled, like Jonah by the sailors.

Unclean is not a term of psychological horror and disgust, it is a technical term for the cult, as commentators have often pointed out. To import feelings into the translation falsifies, and creates more puzzles. The technique of delayed completion postpones the meanings until chapter 17. At that point Leviticus commands the people not to eat blood, not to eat an animal that has died an unconsecrated death, that is, an animal that has died of itself, or an animal torn by beasts, presumably with its blood still in it (Lev 17: 8–16; see also Deut 14: 21). The dietary laws thus support the law against unconsecrated killing. The Leviticus writer's reverential attitude to life, animal and human, explains the animal corpse pollution rules. "Thou shalt not stand upon [profit from] another's blood" (Lev 19: 16). The case of the animal's blood and the case of the human's blood are parallel. Ritual impurity imposes God's order on his creation.

NOTES

1 Murray 1992.
2 The ass that carries loads and persons is not mentioned here. A half-way category, it is given a half-way treatment when it comes to offering the first-born to the tabernacle: "Every firstling of an ass you shall redeem with a lamb . . ." (Exod 13: 13).
3 After the destruction of the temple when the Mishnah substituted the cleanness of the worshipper's body and food for that of the altar and sacrifice, they already had a strongly developed precedent in Leviticus, chapter 11. Neusner 1977.
4 Milgrom 1989.
5 Philo 1939: 99–102.
6 Kass 1994: 12.
7 Maimonides 1881.
8 Houston 1993.
9 Sanders 1990: 145.
10 *tame*, impure, occurs 89 times in the Bible; 47 times in Leviticus; 8 times in Deuteronomy, and not at all in Exodus.
11 Milgrom 1991: 443–56 argues that in Leviticus holy things do not transmit holiness to persons, but contact kills them, whereas Ezekiel following an older tradition taught that holy things could transmit holiness to persons as well as to objects.
12 Campbell 1964.
13 Tigay 1996: 86.
14 Milgrom 1983.
15 Tigay 1996: 139.

REFERENCES

Campbell, John, *Honour, Family and Patronage* (Oxford University Press, 1964).

Douglas, M., "Animals in Lele religous symbolism", *Africa* 27 (1957).

—— "Sacred Contagion", in John Sawyer (ed.), *Leviticus* (Sheffield Academic Press, 1996), 86–106.

—— *Purity and Danger: An Analysis of the Concepts of Pollution and Taboo* (London, Routledge & Kegan Paul, 1966).

Evans-Pritchard, E. E., *Witchcraft, Oracles, and Magic among the Azande* (Clarendon Press, 1937).

Houston, Walter, *Purity and Monotheism: Clean and Unclean Animals in Biblical Law* (JSOTS 140, Sheffield Academic Press, 1993).

Kass, L. R., *The Hungry Soul, Eating and the Perfection of Our Nature* (Free Press, 1994).

Levine, Baruch, *The FPS Commentary, Leviticus* (Jewish Publication Society, 1989).

Maimonides, Moses, *Guide for the Perplexed* (London, 1881).

Milgrom, Jacob, "Israel's sanctuary: the priestly 'Picture of Dorian Gray'". in *Studies in Cultic Theology and Terminology*, Studies in Judaism in Late Antiquity, ed. Jacob Neusner, 36 (Brill, 1983), 390–400.

—— "Rationale for cultic law: the case of impurity", *Semeia* 45 (1989), 103–9.

—— *Leviticus* 1–16, The Anchor Bible (Doubleday, 1991).

Murray, Robert, *The Cosmic Covenant*, Heythrop Monographs, 7 (Sheed and Ward, 1992).

Neusner, Jacob, "History and Structure, the Case of the Mishnah" FAAR 45/2 (1977), 161–92.

Philo, with English translation, ed. F. H. Colson, viii: *The Special Laws* (Harvard University Press, 1939).

Sanders, E. P., *Jewish Law from Jesus to the Mishnah, Five Studies* (SCM Press, 1990).

Tigay, J., *Deuteronomy, the People's Torah* (Jewish Publication Society, 1996).

17

A Jivaro Version of *Totem and Taboo*

Claude Lévi-Strauss

Professor emeritus at the Collège de France, Paris, Lévi-Strauss has been a towering figure in the intellectual debates of the 20th century. Apart from his reputation as a founder of structuralism, he has made profound contributions to anthropology with respect to kinship, symbolic classification, myth, and human thought more generally. Lévi-Strauss conducted fieldwork in Brazil (1970 [1955]) and it is from the rich mythology of Brazilian Amerindians that his analyses and explorations of mythical thought spiral outward to embrace the Americas as a whole.

This essay is a relatively late piece in Lévi-Strauss's long and distinguished career but it provides a succinct exemplification of his approach to myth, demonstrating both his ability to generate his own imaginative chain of connections and his sharply polemical style, here directed against Freudian interpretation. As usual, his intelligence, wit, and encyclopedic erudition are on display.

The deliberate pun in the title *La Pensée Sauvage* (1966 [1962]), "the wild pansy," poorly translated as *The Savage Mind*, provides a clue to Lévi-Strauss's pursuit. By "savage" he means undomesticated or relatively spontaneous thought (which is much the same as "unrationalized" in a Weberian framework). In that work Lévi-Strauss makes a strong case for the systematic observational knowledge within Amerindian societies, but he is less interested in the practical (material) consequences than in how signs drawn from the natural world are spontaneously taken up and reapplied to produce a rich mythological superstructure. For Lévi-Strauss, unlike Freud, it is never the intrinsic meaning of any given symbol or myth that is at issue; drawing from Saussure's account of the structure of phonemes (1959), as well as Jakobson's application

From Claude Lévi-Strauss, "A Jivaro Version of *Totem and Taboo*," in *The Jealous Potter*, trans. Bénédicte Chorier (Chicago: University of Chicago Press, 1988 [1985]), pp. 185–206. Abridged.

of Saussurian principles of syntagmatic and paradigmatic relations to poetics (1960), Lévi-Strauss understands signs as having meaning only in terms of their contrastive relations to other signs. Signs drawn from one semantic domain, or code, as he refers to it here, are in turn contrasted with sets of signs drawn from other codes to produce chains, analogies, and "double twists" (Maranda 2001). He argues that through myth primary oppositions (like life and death) are mediated by oppositions from other codes (e.g., day and night), and shows how neighboring myths play off against each other in complex patterns of metaphor, metonymy, repetition, inversion, and puns that, in another analogy, can best be compared to those of music. These patterns are not produced to any singular purpose or meaning (as music is not), but express the mind's continuous signifying activity.

Lévi-Strauss has had a tremendous if somewhat idiosyncratic influence, showing more vividly than anyone the richness of human creativity while rigorously evading subjectivism or humanism and challenging anthropologists to become philosophically and aesthetically more sophisticated in their approach to cultural phenomena. However, while some attempt to turn the arguments concerning human thought into mathematical formulae (Maranda 2001), others have grown impatient with the endless transformational play of signifiers and want to know what precisely people in given contexts are thinking about or trying to say, and which of their symbolic productions become relatively "fixed," entextualized, and authorized in dominant regimes of meaning. The hermeneutic critique has been best expressed in the debate between Ricoeur and Lévi-Strauss (1970), by Geertz (1973e [1967]), and by Douglas in her response to one of Lévi-Strauss's best short pieces of myth analysis, known as Asdiwal (in Leach, ed. 1967).

The essays in *Structural Anthropology I* (1963a) form a good introduction to Lévi-Strauss before tackling the four-volume *Mythologiques* (1964–71). The former work also contains a pair of outstanding essays on shamanic cure that are rather more sympathetic to psychoanalysis (1963a, b). The secondary literature on Lévi-Strauss is enormous. Leach, in particular, provided introductions to an Anglophone public (1970, 1976), and Culler (1975) is also very good.

Freud gave the following subtitle to *Totem and Taboo*: "Some Points of Agreement between the Mental Lives of Savages and Neurotics." In the preceding pages I have set out to show instead that there are points on which the mental lives of savages and psychoanalysts coincide. At almost every step we have encountered perfectly explicit notions and categories – such as oral character and anal character – that psychoanalysts will no longer be able to claim they have discovered. All they have done is to rediscover them.

Better yet: it is *Totem and Taboo* in its entirety that, well ahead of Freud, the Jivaro Indians anticipated in the myth that for them plays the part of a Genesis: societies arose when the primitive horde split into hostile clans after the murder of the father whose wife had committed incest with their son. From a psychological point of view the Jivaro myth offers an even richer and more subtle plot than *Totem and Taboo*.

Let us outline the plot again. While his father, Uñushi, was away on a long trip. Ahimbi, the Snake, slept with his mother, Mika, the Clay Pot. It is as if these two offenders – the snake and the vase – symbolized, respectively, the male and the female genitals, naturally destined to unite, notwithstanding the social rules that would restrain their freedom. And the patriarch – their father and grandfather – actually banished them. They remained vagrants and had many children. When the deceived husband returned and discovered his misfortune, his wrath was directed not against the offenders but against his own mother, whom he accused of having encouraged their crime. It would be tempting to say that he held her responsible for his own incestuous desire for *her* and that his son's crime was the enactment of his own secret wish. The offspring of the incestuous couple wanted to avenge their grandmother, so they beheaded their mother's husband in *Totem and Taboo* style. This triggered a series of conflicts. Mika killed her children, who had murdered her husband; her incestuous son then sided against her, and, from that point on, the three camps – the father's, the mother's, and the son's – engaged in a merciless fight. This is how Society came about.

Psychoanalytical theory cannot be credited with uncovering the latent meaning of myths. Myths were its precursors in this. The Jivaro Indians' theory on the origin of society may well be similar to Freud's – indeed, they did not wait for him to announce it. How wise are the Americans in calling psychoanalysts "headshrinkers," thus spontaneously associating them with the Jivaro!

Therefore, Freud cannot be credited with knowing what myths say better than the myths themselves do. Myths don't need any help when it comes to reasoning like a psychoanalyst. Freud's merit lies elsewhere; it is of the same order as the merit I have recognized in Max Müller's achievements (see *The Naked Man*, p. 44). Each of these great minds deciphered one of the codes – Müller, the code of astronomy; Freud, the psycho-organic code – that myths have always known how to use. But each of them made two mistakes.

First, they tried to decipher myths by means of a single and exclusive code, while a myth will always put several codes in play, and it is from this layering of codes, one on top of another, that rules of interpretation derive. The signification of a myth is always global; it cannot be reduced to the interpretation provided by one particular code. No language – astronomical, sexual, or other – conveys the "better," meaning. As I pointed out in *The Raw and the Cooked* (p. 240): "The truth of

the myth does not lie in any special content. It consists in logical relations which are devoid of content or, more precisely, whose invariant properties exhaust their operative value, since comparable relations can be established among the elements of a larger number of different contents." There is no more truth in one code than in any other. The essence of the myth (or its message, if one wants to call it that) is founded on the property inherent in all codes: that of being mutually convertible.

The second mistake lies in the belief that, among all the codes available to myths, one particular code is obligatorily employed. A myth always uses several codes, but it does not follow that all conceivable codes, or all the codes identified by comparative analysis, are simultaneously at work in all myths. One could certainly draw up a list of all the codes that mythic thought uses – or could use – and such a list would be helpful to mythologists in the same way as the periodic table of elements is helpful to chemists. But each myth or family of myths makes a choice among all these codes. The few at work in a specific myth are in no way representative of all of the inventoried codes and are not necessarily the same ones as another myth or family of myths would have selected for its own particular use.

In this book I have concentrated on one family of myths in which the psycho-organic code – the sexual code, if you will (but I will come back to that) – is pressed into service, along with others: the technological, the zoological, the cosmological, etc. One would be wrong to assume from this that the psycho-organic code will have the same operational value in any other myth or family of myths, which may use entirely different codes.

The following problem was raised by Freud in Lecture X of his *General Introduction to Psychoanalysis*: "Even if there were no dream-censorship, we should still find it difficult to interpret dreams, for we should then be confronted with the task of translating the symbolic language of dreams into the language of waking life" (Freud 1935: 150). In other words, the essence of dreams lies in the fact that they are coded. But how can it be that we have access to this code, that "we arrive . . . at constant substitutions for a series of dream-elements, just as in popular books on dreams we find translations for everything that occurs in dreams," even though, "when we employ the method of free association, such constant substitutions for dream-elements never make their appearance"? (ibid., p. 134). Fifteen years later, in his *New Introductory Lectures on Psycho-Analysis*, Freud, still preoccupied by the problem, formulated it in the same terms: the contents of dreams "are to be taken as symbols for something else.... Since we know how to translate these symbols, while the dreamer does not ..., the sense of the dream is immediately clear to us ..., while the dreamer himself is still puzzled by it" (Freud 1933: 23).

Here psychoanalysis and structural analysis diverge on an essential point. Throughout his works, Freud oscillates – and in fact never succeeded in choosing – between two conceptions of the symbol: realist and relative. A realist conception would attribute one and only one signification to each symbol. These significations could all be listed in a dictionary, which, as Freud suggested, would differ little from a "dream book," except for its greater size. The second conception admits that the signification of a symbol varies with each particular case, and, to discover the signification, it has recourse to the method of free association. So, in an elementary and unsophisticated fashion, it recognizes that the symbol draws its signification from the context, from the way it relates to other symbols, which themselves, in turn, find their meaning only in relation to it. This second conception can yield positive results, provided the simplistic method of free association finds its due place within a global attempt at understanding the individual by reconstructing his personal history and the history of his family, his social environment, his culture, and so on. One would thus seek to understand an individual in the way an ethnographer seeks to understand a society.

So, though Freud had taken the first steps in this direction, he went no further; instead, hoping to discover an absolute signification for symbols, he seems to have turned more and more to everyday language, etymology, and philology (at times building on some significant mistakes made in these fields, as

Benveniste has pointed out). Freud's purpose in this was identical to Jung's; they differed only in that Jung proceeded with great haste, while Freud lingered in the backwaters of scholarly research and the arduous pursuit of what he called "the original myth":

> Consequently [in a search for the absolute meaning of symbols] I hold that the surface versions of myths cannot be used uncritically for comparison with our psychoanalytical findings. We must find our way back to their latent, original forms by a comparative method that eliminates the distortions they have undergone in the course of their history. (Freud and Jung 1974: 472)

Freud is quite right in opposing his method to Jung's, for, "in his recent mythological studies, [Jung ...] uses any mythological material whatsoever ... without selection.... Now, mythological material can be used in this way only when it appears in its original form and not in its derivatives" (Nunberg and Federn 1962–74: III, 335).

This criticism is quite pertinent – and intriguing, too, for it can also be applied to its author. Under the pretense of going back to the original myth, all Freud did – all he ever did – was to produce a modern version even more recent than the ones Jung used, which he condemned for their inauthenticity. Psychoanalysis has never been able to prove that its interpretations re-create myths in their original form – if only for the simple reason that the original form (provided this notion means anything) is and remains forever elusive. However far back we may go, a myth is known only as something that has been heard and repeated.

In starting off on a search for the original form, and in believing that he has found it, the psychoanalyst finds in the myth only what he himself has introduced into it, as Freud himself has candidly confessed: "The material has been transmitted to us in a state that does not permit us to make use of it for the solution of our problems. On the contrary, it must first be subjected to psychoanalytic elucidation" (Nunberg and Federn 1962–74: III, 335). In a letter to Jung about the writing of *Totem and Taboo* and his difficulties, he sadly admitted, "Besides, my interest is diminished by the conviction that

I am already in possession of the truths I am trying to prove" (Freud and Jung 1974: 472). One could hardly say it better.

In a way, though, Freud is unfair to himself. His greatness lies partly in a gift he possesses in the highest degree: he can think the way myths do. Considering that the snake can take on a male or female connotation, he wrote: "This does not, however, mean that the symbol has two significations; it is simply employed in the inverse sense" (Nunberg and Federn 1962–74: III, 335). He also wrote that in dreams we often find "the procedure of reversal, of turning into the opposite, of inverting relationships" (Freud 1964: XXII, 188). Still, working in an indirect way, Freud here reaches a key notion: that of transformation, which is at the root of all his analyses. According to him, in order to understand the biblical myth of Genesis or the Greek myth of Prometheus, one needs to invert them. Eve becomes the mother who gives birth to Adam, and man, rather than woman, fecundates his spouse by giving her seeds (a pomegranate) to eat. The myth of Prometheus also becomes clearer if the fennel stalk containing fire becomes, through inversion, a penis, that is, a tube carrying water (urine), allowing men to destroy fire (instead of obtaining it). Likewise, by an inversion of container into content, the actual theme of the legend of the Labyrinth turns out to be an anal birth: the winding paths of the maze represent the intestines, and Ariadne's thread is the umbilical cord.

These are excellent variants. The way they relate to the myths they are based on is quite similar to the relationship the ethnologist observes between the myths of one population and those of another, which, in borrowing the myths, has inverted the terms or has transposed them into a new code. One can easily imagine the neighbors of the ancient Hebrews telling the myth of Adam and Eve in the Freudian fashion, or Hesiod's Boeotian contemporaries similarly giving their own version of the Promethean myth. The trouble is that they did not. But it is in part thanks to Freud that these myths are still present in our spiritual heritage. The Oedipus myth, to cite but one example, has retained its vividness, still has an impact on us, because of Freud's new interpretations of it and the interest they have aroused among all groups and levels of our society. That is why, as I said thirty years ago, we must not hesitate to place Freud after Sophocles among our sources for the Oedipus myth. The variants elaborated by Freud obey the laws of mythic thought; they respect the same constraints and apply the same transformational rules.

Freud himself was aware of this affinity between mythic thought and his own. I mentioned above (pp. 187–8) that throughout his life he was haunted by the same question: "How do we profess to arrive at the meaning of these dream-symbols, about which the dreamer himself can give us little or no information?" (Freud 1935: 141). If such a difficulty exists, it comes from Freud's strange conception of the way this information reaches the analyst: "Just as in primitive, grammarless speech, only the raw material of thought is expressed, and the abstract is merged again in the concrete from which it sprang" (Freud 1933: 32–3). The ethnologist and linguist will certainly be startled by the notion that primitive languages are grammarless; but, leaving that aside, we can see that Freud actually touched on the crux of the problem when he wrote: "The dream seems to be an abridged extract from the associations, which has been put together in accordance with rules which we have not yet understood" (ibid., p. 22). These rules are precisely those of a grammar he considered from the start to be nonexistent, as we have just seen.

In order to avoid this dead end, Freud makes a strategic move:

> We derive our knowledge [of the meaning of dream-symbols] from widely different sources: from fairy tales and myths, jokes and witticisms, from folklore, i.e., from what we know of the manners and customs, sayings and songs, of different peoples, and from poetic and colloquial usage of language. Everywhere in these various fields the same symbolism occurs, and in many of them we can understand it without being taught anything about it. (Freud 1935: 141)

It is true that in all languages there are more or less exactly matching expressions, based on similarities or contrasts that might be thought to issue from assonances or homophonies that are specific to each language but in fact are the emanation, in popular language, of thoughts that draw their substance from the very roots of the mind. Freud could have propped up his theory better by quoting from chapter three of Rousseau's *Essay on the Origin of Languages:* "Figurative language came first; literal meaning was discovered last. Men first spoke only in poetry; it was a long time before they invented reasoning."

But if we accept Freud's solution, can we consider psychoanalysis as anything more than a branch of comparative anthropology applied to the study of individual minds? Freud himself acknowledged more than once the dependence of psychoanalysis on the social sciences and the humanities: "The province of symbolism is extraordinarily wide: dream-symbolism is only a small part of it. . . . Psycho-analytic work is so closely intertwined with so many branches of science, the investigation of which gives promise of the most valuable conclusions: with mythology, philology, folk-lore, folk psychology, and the study of religion" (Freud 1935: 149–50). However, this recognition proved so embarrassing that he hastened to add: "In its relation with all these other subjects, psychoanalysis has in the first instance given rather than received" (ibid., p. 150) – a claim supported only by the assertion that "the mental life of the human individual yields, under psychoanalytical investigation, explanations which solve many a riddle in the life of the masses of mankind or at any rate can show these problems in their true light" (ibid.). But the whole lecture from which these quotations are drawn rests on the very opposite of this premise, namely, that various facts that are relevant to the mental life of the individual – facts for which he himself can find no explanation – can be understood only by relating them to "the life of the masses of mankind." Precisely.

His *New Introductory Lectures*, written later than the *General Introduction*, show more caution on this issue. They cast a cloud over the whole debate, simply saying that "any confirmation we could get from other sources, from philology, folklore, mythology or ritual, was particularly welcome" and that "very

often pictures and situations appear in the manifest content of the dream which remind one of well-known themes from fairy stories, legends and myths" (Freud 1933: 38–9). But precedence is no longer an issue.

In *The Raw and the Cooked* (p. 338) I myself pointed out that the interpretation of myths from distant regions, myths that appear extremely obscure at first, is sometimes similar to the very obvious analogies we make in our native tongue, whatever it may be. But to understand the phenomenon we need to define symbolism as more than mere comparison. Neither figurative language nor its most common means of expression, metaphor, can be reduced to a transfer of meaning from one term to another. For these terms do not start out jumbled together in an indiscriminate mass; they are not contained in a common pool from which one could draw, at will, just any term and associate it or oppose it to just any other. Meaning is transferred not from term to term but from code to code – that is, from a category or class of terms to another category or class. It would be especially wrong to assume that one of these classes or categories naturally pertains to literal meaning, the other to figurative meaning; for these functions are interchangeable and relative to each other. As in the sex life of snails, the function of each class, literal or figurative, starts out as undetermined; then, according to the role that it will be called upon to play in a global structure of signification, it induces the opposite function in the other class.

In order to show that dream work translates abstract ideas into visual images, Freud cites an observation made by Silberer: "I think that I intend to smooth out an uneven passage in an essay I am writing. Visual image: I see myself planing a piece of wood" (Freud 1933: 37). However, the image of a writer sitting at his desk and bending over his manuscript to cross out a word would be no less visual than the image of the carpenter. This example is remarkable (note that it bears no trace of repression or sexuality), not because of the passage from the abstract to the concrete, but because an expression that in waking life is used in a figurative way is metaphorically transposed by the discourse of the dream into its literal meaning. It might be objected that the adjective "uneven," properly speaking, can refer only to a material surface, but in everyday life none of us thinks in the categories of the grammarian. To the writer, the work of the carpenter is an image of his own work, just as the writer's work might remind a carpenter of his own activity. A metaphor always works both ways; if I may use a rough simile, it is like a two-way street. In switching terms that belong to different codes, the metaphor rests on an intuition that these terms connote the same semantic field when seen from a more global perspective. The metaphor restores this semantic field, notwithstanding the efforts made by analytic thought to subdivide it. In Silberer's dream the metaphor does not replace an abstract element with a concrete one. Like all metaphors, it restores the full meaning of a notion that, whether used in its literal or its figurative meaning, is bound to be impoverished in everyday language. In other words, the metaphorical process is a regression effected by the savage mind, a momentary suppression of the synecdoches that are the operative mode of the domesticated mind. Vico, and Rousseau after him, were well aware of this. They came short in only one thing: they saw figurative or metaphorical language as issuing directly from passions and feelings. (Voltaire held the same belief, saying that metaphor, when it comes naturally, pertains to passions, whereas comparisons pertain solely to the mind.) They failed to see that it is, rather, the primitive apprehension of a global structure of signification – and *that* is an act of the understanding.

Vico, Rousseau, and Voltaire were on the wrong track, and Freud followed them in claiming that, for dream symbols, there is an unlimited number of signifiers, while the signifieds remain always the same – matters concerning sexuality. What was Freud's real stand on this issue? There is no doubt that any true disciple could provide a brilliant demonstration that, in his *New Introductory Lectures*, Freud was not contradicting himself when he repudiated a few formulas "which we have never put forward, such as the thesis that all dreams are of a sexual nature" (Freud 1933:

17), and then declared, only a few pages later, "Our work of interpretation uncovers what one might call the raw material, which often enough may be regarded as sexual" (ibid., p. 39); or, again, when he broadened his conception of sexuality, defining it as an "unconscious impulse, . . . the real motive force of the dream" (ibid., p. 35), and when he reproached Pfister for disputing "the splitting up of the sex instinct into its component parts" (Freud 1963: 62); for, as he had clearly stated in the *New Introductory Lectures*, "It is one of the tasks of psycho-analysis to lift the veil of amnesia which shrouds the earliest years of childhood and to bring the expressions of infantile sexual life which are hidden behind it into conscious memory" (Freud 1933: 44), adding that "all imperishable and unrealizable desires that provide the energy for the formation of dreams throughout one's whole life are bound up with the same childish experiences" (ibid.) – these childish experiences being of a sexual nature, as he has just stated. Besides, dream formation is not the only thing at stake: "The world of myths and fairy tales first became intelligible through the understanding of children's sexual life. . . . That has been achieved as a beneficial by-product of psychoanalytical studies" (Freud 1950: 60).

Such statements, oscillating between explicitness and ambiguity, leave one puzzled. It is not that sexuality is shocking to a mythographer: the tales told by American Indians and other peoples have put him into the swing of things, so to speak. But isn't it becoming increasingly clear that, even though dreams that can be interpreted as emanating from repressed sexual desires do indeed constitute a real, even an important, category of dreams, they remain just that: one special category among others? The dreamer uses a much more complex material in elaborating his dream. He doubtless draws on conscious or repressed desires; but he also vaguely perceives noises around him, his movements may be restrained by the presence of a foreign object in the bed, he may be physically indisposed, he may be worried about his work or his career, etc. Freud agrees that "the condition of repose without stimuli . . . is threatened . . . in a chance fashion by external stimuli during sleep, by interests of the day before which have not yet abated, and . . . by the unsatisfied repressed impulses, which are ready to seize on any opportunity for expression" (Freud 1933: 28). For him, however, these stimuli and interests constitute raw materials used by the repressed impulses to code a message that remains their property from start to finish. Couldn't one rather say that all these disparate elements are offered to the dreamer's subconscious as the scattered pieces of a puzzle and that, since their heterogeneity is intellectually discomforting, the subconscious will be obliged in the dream (dream-work also being a form of "bricolage"), by piecing them together into a syntagmatic sequence, to give them, if not coherence (certainly not all dreams are coherent), at least some sort of organized framework? According to Freud, "the real motive force of the dream always finds its outlet in a wish-fulfillment" (Freud 1933: 35). But wish-fulfillment presupposes desire, which is one of the most obscure notions in the whole field of psychology, and there are other motives at play, upstream from desire, so to speak: appetites and needs; and the universal need motivating dream-work is, contrary to what Freud sometimes appeared to think (see above), a need to impose a grammatical order on a mass of random elements.

It is not my purpose here to replace sexual symbolism with a symbolism of a linguistic or philosophical nature; that would bring us dangerously close to Jung, who, as Freud rightly pointed out, "attempted to give to the facts of analysis a fresh interpretation of an abstract, impersonal, and ahistorical character" (Freud 1948: 96). We will not attempt to find the "true" signification of myths or dreams. Myths, and perhaps also dreams, bring a variety of symbols into play, none of which signifies anything by itself. They acquire a signification only to the degree that relations are established among them. Their signification is not absolute; it hinges on their position.

To make a simplistic comparison, the analysis of myths is faced with something reminiscent of Japanese script or, rather, scripts. Japanese uses two syllabaries, which differ only in the way they are written; it also uses, in addition, a set of ideograms derived from

Chinese. These scripts are not independent but complementary. Each of the two *kana* syllabaries gives an unambiguous phonetic rendition of words but an ambiguous semantic one because of the great number of homonyms in Japanese; for example, the words *kan*, *kô*, and *shô* are each given no less than fifteen homonyms in a dictionary of everyday language. The Chinese characters, or *kanji*, work in the opposite way: most include a key or root that indicates the semantic field to which the transcribed word or words belong, whether in their noun or verbal forms. In Japanese one character can refer to more than ten words that are semantically related but sometimes completely different phonetically. The sound of the word is indicated by one or more *kana*, written above or next to the *kanji*; the meaning is mainly provided by the *kanji*. Japanese writing thus uses two codes at once (and even three, though nowadays one of the two syllabaries tends to be reserved for the transcription of foreign words not yet integrated into the language). The meaning of a text cannot be drawn from one or the other code, since each of them, taken alone, leaves ambiguities; it is the combination of the two that provides complete understanding. Myths work in a similar way, except that a greater number of codes are brought into play.

[. . .]

I will perhaps be charged with reducing the life of the mind to an abstract game, replacing the human soul and its passions with a clinical formula. I do not contest the existence of impulses, emotions, or the tumultuous realm of affectivity, but I do not accord primacy to these torrential forces; they irrupt upon a structure already in place, formed by the architecture of the mind. If we were to ignore these mental constraints, we would regress to the illusions of a naive empiricism, with one difference: the mind would appear passive before internal rather than external stimuli, a *tabula rasa* transposed from the realm of cognition to that of emotional life. A primitive schematism is always there to impose a form on the turmoil of emotions. In its most spontaneous impulses, affectivity tries to break through obstacles that also act as landmarks: these mental obstacles restrain affectivity while leading it along a limited number of possible paths, each with required halting-places.

[. . .]

We know that the meaning of a word is doubly determined: by the words that precede or follow it in the sentence and by the words that could be substituted for it to convey the same idea. Sequences of the first type are called syntagmatic chains by linguists; they are articulated in time. The second type are called paradigmatic sets; they are made up of words that could be mobilized at the moment a speaker chooses one in preference to others that he might also have used.

Now, what are the processes involved in defining a word, in shifting it into a figurative sense, and in choosing a symbol to represent the notion it stands for? Defining a word is replacing it with another word or phrase drawn from the same paradigmatic set. Using a metaphor is taking a word or phrase from one syntagmatic chain and placing it in another syntagmatic chain. The symbol, for its part, is an entity that entertains within a given conceptual realm the same syntagmatic relations with its context as, within a different conceptual realm, the thing symbolized has with its context. Symbolic thought thus brings together into the same paradigmatic set homologous terms each of which belongs to its own syntagmatic chain.

But the signification, or added signification, that one is aiming at does not belong per se to the new word, the new syntagmatic chain, or the new paradigmatic set. Signification is the product of the relations established between them and the other word, chain, or set, which they supplement rather than replace, so that they will enrich or nuance the semantic field to which they belong or will define its limits more precisely. Signifying is nothing but establishing a relation between terms. Even rigorous lexicographers, aware of the dangers of circular definitions, know that, in their efforts to avoid them, they often do no more than widen the circle. Definitions are bound to be circular: words are defined by other words that are ultimately defined by the very words they were defining. The vocabulary of a given language may be made up of tens or hundreds of thousands of words; nevertheless, ideally at least, at a given point in time it constitutes a closed system.

Thus the reciprocity of perspectives that I have seen as the specific character of mythic thought can claim a much wider range of applications. It is inherent in the workings of the mind every time it tries to delve into meaning. The only difference lies in the dimensions of the semantic units to which the mind applies itself. Free from the concern of anchoring itself to an outside, absolute reference, independent of all context, mythic thought should not thereby be opposed to analytical reason. With an authority that cannot be denied, it arises from the depths of time, setting before us a magnifying mirror that reflects, in the massive form of concrete images, certain mechanisms by which the exercise of thought is ruled.

REFERENCES

Benveniste, E. 1966. *Problèmes de linguistique générale.* 2 vols. Paris: Gallimard.

Freud, S. 1933. *New Introductory Lectures on Psycho-Analysis.* Transtated by W. J. H. Sprott. New York: Norton.

——. 1935. *A General Introduction to Psycho-Analysis.* Authorized English translation of the revised edition by Joan Rivière. New York: Liveright.

——. 1948. *An Autobiographical Study.* Translated by James Strachey. London: Hogarth Press and the Institute for Psycho-Analysis.

——. 1950. *The Question of Lay Analysis.* Translated by Nancy Prater-Greg. New York: Norton.

——. 1962. *Totem and Taboo.* Translated by James Strachey. New York: Norton.

——. 1963. *Psychoanalysis and Faith: The Letters of Sigmund Freud and Oskar Pfister.* Edited by Heinrich Meng and Ernst L. Freud. Translated by Eric Mosbacher. London: Hogarth Press and the Institute for Psycho-Analysis.

——. 1964. "The Acquisition and Control of Fire." Translated by James Strachey. Pp. 187–93 in *The Standard Edition of the Complete Psychological Works of Sigmund Freud*, vol. 22. London: Hogarth Press and the Institute for Psycho-Analysis.

Freud, S., and Jung, C. G. 1974. *The Freud–Jung Letters: The Correspondence between Sigmund Freud and C. G. Jung*. Edited by William McGuire. Translated by Ralph Manheim and R. F. C. Hull. Bollingen Series XCIV. Princeton: Princeton University Press.

Lévi-Strauss, C. 1969. *The Raw and the Cooked*. Vol. 1 of *Introduction to a Science of Mythology*. [*Mythologiques*.] Translated by John and Doreen Weightman. Chicago: University of Chicago Press.

——. 1981. *The Naked Man*. Vol. 4 of *Introduction to a Science of Mythology*. [*Mythologiques*.] Translated by John and Doreen Weightman. New York: Harper & Row.

Nunberg, H., and Federn, E., eds. 1962–74. *Minutes of the Vienna Psychoanalytic Society*. 4 vols. Translated by M. Nunberg. New York: International Universities Press.

18

Text-Building, Epistemology, and Aesthetics in Javanese Shadow Theatre

Alton L. Becker

Alton (Pete) Becker taught in Linguistics and the Centre for Southeast Asian Studies at the University of Michigan, where he also played in the gamelan orchestra conducted by his wife, ethnomusicologist Judith Becker. He is renowned for his unique, culturally informed approach to linguistic texts. Becker approaches ritual and religion from the direction of language, practicing what he calls philology (1995). His interests lie in the ways in which languages build worlds, and conversely, the world that can be seen contained within a single sentence or, in this case, a text. Becker invites us to see many subtle things about the relationship of language to religion and aesthetics in Southeast Asia and the differences between Javanese and western conceptions of textual coherence.

Becker elaborates an exemplary multileveled method for the interpretation of cultural texts. The Javanese shadow theater performances can be understood to be drawn from literal texts of the Ramayana, but Becker's method applies to a far broader understanding of cultural texts. Ricoeur (1971, 1976) provided a basic model for understanding the way speech or action becomes text and made a strong argument for interpretation with respect to changing context. Geertz (1973a) applied the textual metaphor to cultural interpretation. Geertz's critics often took this too literally; in fact, it can be fruitfully and flexibly applied to such open-ended, never written phenomena as spirit possession (Lambek 1981, Boddy 1989). The approach may be called structural – hermeneutic insofar as it draws from both structural linguistics and poetics and seeks both interpretive meaning and cultural grammar. For a more extensive discussion of shadow theater in its cultural context see Keeler (1987).

From A. L. Becker, "Text-Building, Epistemology, and Aesthetics in Javanese Shadow Theatre," in A. L. Becker and Aram A. Yengoyan, eds., *The Imagination of Reality: Essays in Southeast Asian Coherence Systems* (Norwood, NJ: Ablex Publishing Corp., 1979), pp. 211–43. Abridged.

*If aesthetics is ever to be more than a specula-
tive play, of the genus philosophical, it will
have to get down to the very arduous business
of studying the concrete process of artistic
production and appreciation.*

EDWARD SAPIR

Introduction: Speaking
the Past and Speaking
the Present

In this essay I would like to describe some of
the constraints on text-building in a language
quite different from our own. The language is
Javanese, the kind of text the Javanese shadow
play, *wayang kulit*, as I learned to perform it
from an East Javanese puppeteer, or *dalang*,
Ki Soedjathi Djathikoesoemo, in daily lessons
and in watching performances and discussing
them together over a period of two years,
1969–71. My goal there was not to become a
dalang myself – though that was necessary
in order to discover what *not* to do – but to
discover how to build a text in Javanese, to
explore what text-building revealed about
Javanese epistemology, and to learn how to
respond aesthetically to a very different artistic
medium. I have studied these things and shall
describe them within a particular, evolving set
of assumptions about what a text is and how
it can be said to be meaningful. These assumptions have their roots in traditional philology,
modified and expanded by the insights of
modern linguistics, ethnography, psychology,
and Javanese aesthetic theory itself into what
might be called a *modern philology*. These
assumptions form a partial epistemography[1] –
a specification of *what* it is important to write
about concerning Javanese shadow theater,
and how one achieves coherence and completeness in writing about it.

As an intellectual discipline, *philology* can
be defined as the text-centered study of language. Philologists have traditionally set themselves the task of making ancient and foreign
texts readable. Only part of this task is simple
translation, since any careful philologist knows
that few foreign words have translations.

Words and phrases must be described, often in
great detail, not merely mapped onto a foreign
term. This description traditionally takes the
form of masses of footnotes which explain
the contextual relations of words, phrases,
sentences, and larger units of the text. These
relations ideally include the following:

1. The relations of textual units to each other
   within the text, which establishes hierarchy and coherence in the text.
2. The relations of textual units to other
   texts, since part of the context of any text
   is, more or less, all previous texts in a
   particular culture, especially texts considered to be in the same genre; readable
   literature is structurally coherent with its
   own ancestors.
3. The relations of the units in the text to the
   intention of the creators of the text, with
   intention defined as the relations of the
   creator to the content of the text, the
   medium, and to the hearers or readers.
4. The relation of textual units to nonliterary
   events with which units in the text establish relations of the sort usually called
   reference.

The *meaning* of a text, then, is a set of relations, by no means all of which are listed
above. The information necessary to describe
the kinds of relations just listed must be known,
discovered, or reconstructed before one can
know the essential meaning of a text, any text.
For contemporary English works – except for
the most esoteric or specialized literature –
contextual relations have been presumed not
to require philological explication for English-
speaking readers. However, texts whose contexts (or epistemologies) are distant from the
best-trained readers require philological notes
as an essential foundation for interpretation.
In a multi-cultured world, a world of multiple
epistemologies, there is need for a new philologist – a specialist in contextual relations – in
all areas of knowledge in which text-building
(written or oral) is a central activity: literature,
history, law, music, politics, psychology, trade,
even war and peace.

The specific activity of the philologist is
contextualizing conceptually distant texts. For
many philologists in the past that was the only

goal, an annotated edition of a written or oral text. Some philologists, however, in the course of this activity and based upon it, have sought generalizations about the major constraints on text-building itself, the laws of grammar, poetics, narration, etc. Nowadays philology has been partitioned and distributed among various specialists. In the study of literature, there has developed a gulf between those who study particular texts (especially written texts) and those who study constraints on the activity of creating texts: the former is usually part of the humanities (literary scholarship), the latter a science (linguistics).

In the study of texts, however, these two activities correct each other, since any meaningful activity is a conjunction of preexisting constraints (or rules, or structures, or laws, or myths) with the present, the unpredictable, particular *now*. In this way a text always – but to varying degrees – contextualizes the present in the past.[2]

One can roughly specify for any language activity the degree to which the speaker/writer is speaking the past or the present. Repeating is almost entirely speaking the past, whether it be repeating something said a moment ago, or written a millennium ago – a repeated remark, a prayer, a song. Yet in these activities there is always something of the present, some variable of the communicative act which is free to express the *now*, be it only the voice quality of the speaker, the variations of tempo and pitch and resonance that express the repeater's attitude about what he is repeating. Furthermore, each repetition of a text (or bit of a text) is in a new context and takes new meaning from its context. One can never wholly speak the past. Even in those ritual repetitions when we speak the past as intently as possible in a kind of temporary trance, there is always something of the present communicated.

Likewise, one can never wholly speak the present. Even everyday language is highly conventional, far more constrained than we normally recognize. Consider how small talk varies from language to language in both content and form. Most conversations begin with repeated conventional content which is not meant to be discussed truthfully (i.e., in the present): How are you? (English); Where

are you going? (Javanese); Have you eaten yet? (Burmese), etc. At this point in a conversation relationships are being established, between speaker and hearer first, then between speaker and other – the people or things referred to. Some conversations never get beyond this stage, and the pace at which one moves conversationally from the conventional, predictable past to the present varies widely from language to language.

Notice that language, in these instances and always, communicates on at least two levels, the actual surface content of the message (the proposition being asserted, requested, questioned, etc.) and the relational statements that are conveyed simultaneously, more often by intonation, posture, facial expression, and the like, than by direct statement. This relational communication has been called *metacommunication* by Gregory Bateson and others – communication about relationships, about the context of the message. Hence in speaking the past, in prayer or small talk, too, we are communicating our relations to the hearer and the people or things referred to in the lexically expressed message. Ritual language speaks the past on the surface, but conveys the present at the metalinguistic level.

[. . .]

All language activity, including literature, involves, then, variation between spontaneity (present) and repetition (past) and communicates on at least two levels, the lexically expressed message (L) and the relational message (Lm). Of course the lexically expressed message may be about the relationship, in which case a new relational communication is conveyed, leading, if repeated, to the sorts of linguistic involutions exposed by R. D. Laing (1970).

[. . .]

To summarize, then, the analysis of a text requires, minimally, that the modern philologist describe several kinds of relations in order to re-create a conceptually distant context. A minimal set of these relations includes:

1.   The relation of words, phrases, sentences, and larger units of the text to each other (i.e., the coherence of the text),

2. The relation of this text to other texts; the extent that it is repetition or new (speaking the present or the past),

3. The relation of the author to both the text and the hearers/readers of the text – seen from the point of view of the author or from the points of view of the hearers/ readers (i.e., the intent of the text-builder),

4. The relation of units in the text to non-literary events (i.e., reference).

Context, then, includes coherence, degree of repetition/spontaneity, intent, and reference. Sorting out the *sources* of constraints on all these relations is a further task for the modern philologist: to what extent are the constraints on these relations human (i.e., universal to all texts)? Or are they operative only within a single language family or cultural tradition, or within a single language, or only in a specific genre, or only in the works of one author? Any work is constrained at all these levels.

The methodology of this essay will be to describe, in the order just stated, the various sorts of relations a particular kind of text, the Javanese shadow play, has with its context. I have been able to isolate some of the generic constraints on contextual relations, and some of these above the generic, particularly at the level of the Javanese language itself. By implication, too, I reveal something of that area of variation constrained only by the individual performer (the dalang) in a particular place and time (A. Becker, 1974; Young, Becker, and Pike, 1971).

Textual Coherence in a Wayang: Plot as Symbolic Action

Textual coherence can be examined at any level of structure in the hierarchy of structures that make up the text. One might examine the structure and categories of words in a wayang, isolating the special vocabulary and distinctive phonology of the language of the puppeteer (basa padalangan). At the level of sentences, and across sentences, there are kinds of coherence unexploited in most Western languages,

coherence based not on tense (which is the basis of Western narrative coherence) but upon a system of person (in its grammatical sense) elaborated far beyond similar systems in other languages. I have described this system elsewhere in relation to Old Javanese (Kawi) literature (A. Becker and Oka, 1976; Zurbuchen, 1976). These are constraints which are used in building many other kinds of Javanese texts as well. Here I would like to focus on a higher-level system of constraints, a level intermediate between the usual sentential (i.e., sentence-based) concerns of the linguist and the global concerns of the literary scholar, the level of plot.

The plot of a story or a play is a set of constraints on the selection and sequencing of dramatic episodes or motifs. These constraints are like the rules of a game, say tennis, which constrain the selection of possible acts in the game (i.e., defining illegal acts) and the arrangement of acts in the game (i.e., defining what may not be done at certain times within the context of the game). Plots, like tennis rules, do not allow one to predict – except in very general terms – what will happen in a play. Rather, plots tell us what cannot be done appropriately. They also, like scientific theories, tell us one other important thing; what the relevant variables are in the things one can do in the play. There is no rule in tennis against scratching my head as much as I want to in the course of a game. There is a rule, however, against serving with my feet across the base line. Head-scratching is, by implication, an irrelevant variable, but foot-faulting is constraint on position: it tells me where I may not stand, not where I must stand. Likewise, a set of constraints on a plot specifies what areas of variation are particularly relevant and what are insignificant. If I may borrow from a closely related medium, music, we may note that melodic variation is highly relevant to some kinds of Western music, but rather insignificant in some kinds of Javanese music. An American who is looking for melodic variation in gamelan music will be bored; a Javanese looking for dense musical texture in a symphony will also be bored. Likewise in drama, an American who seeks character development in wayang is going to be disappointed in all but a very few wayang stories, and a Javanese who seeks complex coincidences in all but a few American movies (those few being comedies, like the Marx Brothers' *Animal Crackers*) is also going to be disappointed. Plot (i.e., constraints on the selection and arrangement of dramatic episodes) includes constraints on the *kinds* of variation that are relevant.

For the most part, in most cultures, knowledge of plot constraints is unstated background knowledge, like the knowledge of grammar and syntax. It is learned indirectly, first through fairy tales and nursery rhymes (and their equivalents in other cultures), and then from the various media that have access to children. Some Greeks, however, were self-conscious about plots. Aristotle's *Poetics* includes a description of plot which still holds for most Western drama and narrative.

Aristotle calls plot *fable*: "The imitation of the action is the fable," he writes. "By fable I now mean the contexture of incidents, or the plot." He lists the six major variables in a drama:

1. fable or plot,
2. manners or character,
3. diction or metrical composition,
4. sentiments or speeches,
5. decoration,
6. music.

Aristotle continues, "Of all these parts the most important is the combination of incidents or the fable." Fable or plot is most important because it imitates what Aristotle held was the most important referential content of the drama, action (or imitation of action).

Among the constraints on plot which Aristotle lists are the following. Note that they are all phrased negatively – i.e., as constraints.

1. A proper fable must not be incomplete: "The poet who would construct his fable properly is not at liberty to begin and end where he pleases. . . ." A fable should, he explains, suppose nothing to precede it, and require nothing to follow it (book 2, chapter IV). Completeness here is completeness of linear (i.e., temporal) causality, a powerful constraint on selection *and* arrangement.

2. Coincidences are to be avoided. Sequences should follow as probable and necessary consequences. Nothing improbable should be admitted, or, if necessary, it should arise out of the fable. Perhaps Aristotle's most famous comment on plot makes just this point: "Impossibilities, rendered probable, are preferable to things improbable, though possible" (book 2, chapter VI; book 4, chapter VI).

3. No part of a proper fable may be transposed or omitted without destroying the whole. Anything that can be left out, should be (book 2, chapter V). Again there is emphasis on linear (temporal-causal) sequence.

4. The time in the text should not be more than a single day (book 1, chapter IX).

These basic constraints all have to do with unity and causality, above all with temporal unity and linear causality – two aspects of the same thing. All of them are rooted in the simple fact that intersentence coherence in Indo-European languages is achieved primarily by *tense*. Clarity and coherence *means* to speakers of these languages linear temporal/causal sequencing. Tense is seen as iconic: that is, past, present, and future are taken as facts about the world, rather than facts about language. Tense is not iconic in all language-cultures and hence temporal-causal linearity is not the major constraint on textual coherence in all languages.[3]

The linearity of Aristotle's constraints can be stated in another way. If meaning comes from temporal-causal sequences, then epistemologies do not, and cannot, change from episode to episode, or, as stated in a recent study of plot, "Semantically standard universes always have consistency in the interpretation of several connected ambiguous episodes" (Hahn, 1973:8). That is, Jay Gatsby, Godzilla, Agamemnon, John Wayne, and Charlie Chaplin do not and may not appear in the same plot.

What emerges in the episodes of Western serious drama are the disambiguating causes of actions. These causes are at base represented as character defects, often minor ones. The episodes lead to a catastrophe and a climax, a reversal of expectations, all of which leads on to the end of the causal chain.

Nearly all these constraints are violated by wayang plot structure. It is not that wayang plots may not have temporal unity, causal linear sequences, catastrophes, reversals and all the rest. These do appear in wayang plots, particularly in those plots most admired by Western viewers, such as the plot of *Dewa Ruci*, a linear search for the water of immortality, or the plot of the simplified and shortened versions of the Ramayana, a search for a stolen wife. These Aristotelian constraints, however, are not *necessary* to a good wayang plot, and to focus on, for instance, causal sequences and character development is to miss the area of relevant variation in wayang theater and to miss the subtlety and depth of good wayang.

Wayang plots are built primarily around coincidence, a word which we in the West use to explain away things of no meaning. "A mere coincidence" cannot, in the West, sustain prolonged scrutiny and analysis. In wayang theater coincidence motivates actions. There is no causal reason that Arjuna, the frail wayang hero, meets Cakil, a small demon, in the forest, as he (or a counterpart) does in each wayang. It is a coincidence; it happens (jadi), and because they are who they are, they fight and Cakil dies, but not forever; he will be killed over and over again in each wayang. When Arjuna and Cakil meet, two worlds, two epistemologies coincide for a moment, Cakil is purely physical. He attacks Arjuna because Arjuna makes him uncomfortable. Arjuna's meditation has raised the heat of the forest higher than the creatures who live there can bear. Cakil responds instinctively to this thermal pollution. On the other hand, Arjuna attacks Cakil because he recognizes him as evil (i.e., other), not because of anything he has done, but because he knows – by thought, not instinct – that it is his duty (dharma) to combat evil. He kills coolly, dispassionately, the passionate Cakil, who is defending his forest home against the intruder. Arjuna controls nature by killing it, but it renews itself again and again. There are other interpretations of this motif. Not every observer of wayang will agree with this interpretation of it. It does seem evident, however, that Arjuna and Cakil live in different conceptual worlds and that their meeting is not caused but is rather an accident, a coincidence of these worlds. Nothing in the prior events of the text nor in the succeeding events made it a necessary part of the plot in Aristotle's terms. Yet this motif is necessary (obligatory) within the constraints of wayang plot.

This is but one coincidence, one intersection in the interwoven, cyclic actions that inform a wayang plot – unmotivated, unresolved, meaningless within a chain of causes and effects, but symbolically very rich.

The name for a wayang plot derives from the root *laku* "step or act" plus the suffix *-an*, which normalizes the root, giving us, by vowel sandhi, *lakon* "an action, a way, an event, a plot." A lakon includes three major divisions, within each of which a certain range of voice pitches and a valuing of particular pitches is maintained, and within each of which there is a prescribed internal structure. These divisions, called *pathet*, include combinations of scenes called *jejer* (audience scenes, before a ruler or holy man), *adegan* (scenes outside the audience hall, e.g., *adegan wana* "forest adegan," *adegan gapuran* "gate adegan," *adegan gara-gara* "turmoil adegan," etc.), and *perang* (battle). The meanings of these names for the parts of a wayang are richly metaphoric. Understanding them as words helps to contextualize them within the Javanese semantic world. *Jejer* also means "what exists," "the subject of a sentence," and "the handle of a kris," as well as "an audience before the King." *Adegan*, the scenes outside the audience hall, means also, "propped up," "standing," "doorframe" and "the punctuation of a sentence" (two vertical, parallel lines). The linguistic metaphors suggest a paradigmatic, associational link between sentences and plays, within whose structures experience is shaped and expressed.

A wayang plot, then, is built hierarchically in structures made up of three basic units. A lakon (event) is divided into three *pathetan* or acts, each with the same internal structure. Each *pathet* is made of three basic scenes: (1) the *jejer* (static audience in a court or a hermitage where a problem arises and a plan is formed); followed by (2) two or more *adegan* derived from that audience, and always involving a journey away from the audience place; (3) a *perang* (battle) at the end of the journey.

Each scene, in turn, has three basic components: (1) description of a situation (either *janturan* "description of a place" or *carios* "description of prior action"); (2) dialogue (ginem); (3) action (sabetan). The *minimal* structure of a play – or an event is:

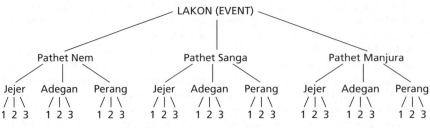

(Key: 1 = description, 2 = dialogue, 3 = action or motion)

Any given wayang allows for three basic operations on this minimal structure: permutation (reordering units below the level of *pathet*), conjunction (repeating units below *pathet*), and embedding (putting units within units below the level of *pathet*). *Pathet* structure was fixed in the tradition I studied.

[. . .]

As night goes on, different parts of the scenes are foregrounded, that is, some parts are shortened, others prolonged. In the first act (*pathet nem*) description usually takes more time than dialogue and action combined. In the second act, dialogue – mostly jokes, but also very heavy spiritual instruction from a holy man – is foregrounded. In the third and final act (*pathet manyura*), action – usually battle – predominates. When one part of a scene is dominant, however, the other two always appear, albeit often briefly.

One may notice that in describing the structure of a dramatic event, the words used are all Javanese not Sanskrit. Though stories are often imported into wayang, chiefly from Sanskrit epics, plots appear to be uniquely Javanese.

Having seen something of the sequencing of events or motifs in a wayang play, let us turn now to the paradigm of events themselves and the kinds of coherence that appear within the structure that has been described. It is often very difficult for the viewer, foreign or Javanese, to know just where he is in the story

being presented, i.e., in knowing that polarities between protagonists and antagonists are being established. One always knows, however, where one is in the plot – the structure defined earlier. The story may be very obscure, much of the action may take place off the screen or be assumed by the dalang to be well known, and there may be all sorts of loose ends left after the plot cycle has finished. It is primarily the clowns who try to tell the audience what is happening. Certainly little of the *motivation* for action appears in the plot. The clowns, using modern language, modern ideas, and modern behavior, step among the heroes and demons and gods like wideawake men in a dream world. They bring the present into the story (i.e., they always speak the present), and with the paradox of forethought, contextualize the present within the tradition, changing both, as usually seems to happen when epistemologies are allowed to coincide.

In the coincidence of epistemologies, as just noted, the real subtlety of wayang appears. The major epistemologies are (1) that of the demons, the direct sensual epistemology of raw nature, (2) that of the ancestor heroes, the stratified, feudal epistemology of traditional Java, (3) that of the ancient gods, a distant cosmological epistemology of pure power, (4) that of the clowns, a modern, pragmatic epistemology of personal survival. All these epistemologies coexist in a single wayang, and others may be added (most usually the epistemology of the

Islamic saints, that of the modern military, or that of some strange foreign land where one of the clowns goes to be king, like Gulliver among the Lilliputians). Between each of these epistemologies there may be – and usually is – a confrontation and a *perang*, a battle. No one ever wins conclusively, but rather a proper balance is restored. Each epistemology, each category of being, exists within a different concept of time, and all the times occur simultaneously. That is, nature time, ancestor time, god time, and the present are all equally relevant in an event, though for each the scope of an event is different. Throughout the wayang, each is kept distinct, even in language (which will be discussed later). The constraints on wayang plot sustain the notion of multiple time and multiple epistemology.

The differences with the Aristotelian notion of plot should now be apparent. What in the wayang plot are significant coincidences, in the Aristotelian plot are crudities, violations of the basic notions of unity and causality. In wayang, we might say that Gatsby, Godzilla, Agamemnon, John Wayne, and Charlie Chaplin – or their counterparts – do appear in the same plot, and that is what causes the excitement; that clash of conceptual universes is what impels the action.

As far as I know, the wayang tradition has no Aristotle, no one who has attempted to articulate the set of constraints which underlie the tradition. I cannot, as an outsider, do this with any depth or hope of adequacy. I am not even sure that in Javanese eyes it is worth doing, but the symmetry of this essay, the plot we are caught within at this moment, seems to demand it. A wayang plot, then, seems to be constrained in the following ways, all stated *by contrast* to Aristotelian constraints.

1. A wayang plot can begin at any point in a story. It has no temporal beginning, middle, or end. Indeed, a wayang plot is very similar to a piece of traditional Javanese music, in which a musical pattern is expanded from within, producing layer upon layer of pattern moving at different times.

    A wayang plot, however, must begin and end in certain *places*; it cannot begin and end anywhere, though it can begin and end anytime. It must also pass through a certain place in the middle. Thus wayang plot has a spatial, rather than temporal, beginning, middle, and end. It must begin and end in a court, the first the court of the antagonists, the last the court of the protagonists (to use the Greek *agon* terminology, which seems appropriate here). The middle section must be in nature, usually in the forest on a mountain, but sometimes, too, in or beside the sea. It is movement out and back, a trip. This structure may well reflect the origin of wayang as an instrument of communication with the dead via trance (Rassers, 1959).

    Like an Aristotelian plot, a wayang must not be incomplete, but incompleteness is not temporal or causal, but rather spatial.

2. Coincidences, far from being avoided, impel action, for they induce cognitive puzzles or paradoxes. Coincidences are the way things happen, and the way communication between unlikes occurs. In Javanese and Indonesian, the word used to describe what we call a coincidence (a causeless interaction) is *kebetulan* (or *kebenaran*), literally a "truth" (an abstract noun derived from the adjective *betul/benar* meaning "true"). There are many related terms (e.g., *dadi* "happen, become," *cocok* "come together, fit") which make up a semantic set used to describe events none of which imply linear causality. Likewise, a piece of music is structured by the coincidence of gongs occurring together, and a holy day by the coincidence of simultaneous calendrical cycles.

3. Any scene in a wayang plot may be transposed or omitted, except for the constraint that the plot begin in a court, have its center in nature, and return to the court. Transpositions and omissions of story material do not destroy or even change the whole. Almost anything can be left out or brought in.

    When something is brought in, however, it must follow the paradigmatic and syntagmatic constraints of the *lakon* structure described above. . . .

There are further constraints on the sets of characters (demons, heroes, gods, clowns) in relation to one another (e.g., how they speak and how they move) which will be described later. All of this makes up what might be called the *grammar* of a wayang plot.

4. Aristotle suggests that the time of a serious drama should not be more than a single day. He meant the time enacted within the plot on stage, not the whole story. Here is his most stringent constraint on temporal unity, one not always followed by Western playwrights but rather held as an ideal, even by such modern American dramatists as O'Neill, Miller, or Albee. Indeed, it may be one of the reasons for identifying these as good, serious playwrights in the Western tradition.

The *time* enacted within wayang is unconstrained, except that it must be multiple. Coincidences are timeless. But, the *performance* time of a wayang is *symbolically* a single day. It is necessary to explain this rather strange phenomenon. The division of scenes is marked by a large image of a tree (or a mountain) called a *kayon* (or *gunungan*). During the play, which is usually performed at night, the *kayon* marks the imaginary progression of the sun from east to west by the angle at which it is set against the screen (which is properly set up on an east-west axis, or if necessary, north-south, in which case north substitutes for east). The kayon is a dramatic clock which marks only the progression, of the *plot*, not the times in the story or the time on the wristwatches of the viewers.

These are but a few of the features which define the coherence of a wayang plot, particularly those few which contrast most sharply with Aristotle, whose writings about plot well define the unconscious constraints on plot that most of us in the West have absorbed since childhood. I now turn from discussion of the structure or coherence of a wayang to consideration of the relations of the text with its context, from inner to outer relations, with a full awareness that there is much more to be said, particularly at more technically linguistic levels of focus, about Javanese textual coherence in general, and wayang coherence in particular.

Text within Text: The Javanese Art of Invention

The distinction between story and plot is very important in studying the structure and development of a wayang text. The *plot* has been defined as a set of constraints on the selecting and ordering of episodes or motifs. The story is a prior text, fictitious or factual or both, which is the source of these episodes or motifs; it is a prior text to some degree known by the audience. Literature, in this sense, is mostly about prior literature. For example, in our own tradition any cowboy movie tells the story of the past more in the sense that it repeats episodes and characters of previous cowboy movies and novels than that it recounts "real" events that occurred in the American West. The "truth" of a cowboy movie is much more a matter of its correspondence with a mythology (a body of prior literature) than with any events recognizable by nonfiction cowboys in their own experiences.

Wayang has reference to a mythology accessible to us in Old Javanese or Sanskrit literature, primarily the two great epics, the Ramayana and the Mahabharata. Javanese, of course, have access to this mythology in many less literary ways: in names of people and places, in other theatrical performances and oral literature, in comics, in the very language itself (Resink, 1975; Anderson, 1965; Emmerson, forthcoming). A wayang plot, however, *need* not draw on this mythology, though it almost always does. That is, a dalang may well turn to Islamic or Christian or autocthonous Javanese mythology, wholly or in part, as a source of the motifs and characters for his performance, and he can do so without violating any of the plot constraints discussed earlier.

The story, whatever its source, provides *content* and *context* for the plot. To introduce Arjuna, the hero of the Mahabharata, as a character into a particular plot establishes as a context for that particular plot all the prior texts (mythology), oral or written, related to

Arjuna. Arjuna has done certain things, relates in certain ways to other characters, and is associated with many details of appearance, dress, behavior, speech, etc., which have been established in prior texts (Anderson, 1965; Hardjowirogo, 1968; Kats, 1923).

What happens to Arjuna in a particular plot may either repeat episodes from prior texts or it may be new, although consistent with prior texts. The new creation fills in more details of the growing text or mythology related to Arjuna, new episodes in his life, only hinted at previously, or a return to the world by Arjuna across time, into, for instance, an ancient Javanese court. The Arjuna mythology (or Rama mythology, or Hanuman mythology, etc.) is a living expanding text in Java. Two examples of this sort of text expansion may help to make this process of invention clearer.

During the Indonesian national elections in 1971, one dalang who supported the incumbent military government created a wayang in which Krishna, when he realizes that he must direct the Pandawa armies (the armies of Arjuna and his brothers Yudistira, Biam, Nakula, Sadewa, and their allies), in the great war of the Bharata, seeks out the old clown-servant Semar. Krishna asks Semar what he should do and how he should behave as a military leader. Then, in the center of the play, in the forest, Semar instructs Krishna in his duty, the common man in an era of democracy instructing the ruler. The text for these instructions was the *Sapta Marga*, the official Code of Behavior for modern Indonesian soldiers. This brilliant new story, *Bagawan Ismojo Sandi*, conceived by Ki Hari Puribadi, very deftly contextualizes past in present and present in past simultaneously; the Sapta Marga is sanctified as a modern Bhagavad Gita, and the ancient mythology is given rich current relevance.

Another kind of invention involves no overt innovation at all, but rather lets the audience infer the connection with current events. This second example was performed in 1971, too, but this time by a dalang opposed to the military government, a supporter of the PNI, the political party associated with former President Soekarno. This dalang performed the old text nearly without change, except that the clowns did say they were volunteer workers at the PNI party headquarters and made several jokes about campaign activities on a day-to-day level. The story was *Kangsa Adu Jago*, a traditional Sanskrit story of a powerful villain (Kangsa/Kamsa) who usurps Krishna's kingdom and drives Krishna into the forest. Krishna seeks the aid of his cousins, the Pandawas, particularly Bima, in defeating and driving out the powerful Kangsa. No one missed the political statement.

It is interesting to note that in those national elections the most powerful public statements against the government were made by dalangs, using just this technique. Every other medium of communication, including other forms of theater, was noncritical. It is also interesting that two sides, the government and the PNI, recognized the same mythological context; the difference lay in whether Krishna represented the modern Ksatria or the deposed king.

One of the most important differences between traditional artistic expression and modern individualistic artistic expression is that in a traditional medium the artist is consciously expanding a prior text, an open corpus of literature, art, or music, whereas an artist whose intent is self-expression creates and develops his own text, his own mythology, so far as he can and still communicate. When an artist can no longer work within the inherited mythology and plot constraints, he seeks new mythology and constraints, often from his own imagination, and he works in alienation from his own society. This same distinction appears to have been made by Lévi-Strauss, this time in distinguishing the shaman and the psychoanalyst:

... the shamanistic cure seems to be the exact counterpart to the psychoanalytic cure, but with an inversion of all the elements. Both cures aim at inducing an experience, and both succeed by recreating a myth which the patient has to live or relive. But in one case, the patient constructs an individual myth with elements drawn from his past; in the other case, the patient receives from the outside a social myth which does not correspond to a former personal state. To prepare for the abreaction, which then becomes an "adreaction," the psychoanalyst listens, whereas the shaman speaks. Better still: When a transference is established, the patient puts words into the mouth of the psychoanalyst by attributing to him alleged feelings and intentions; in the incantation, the shaman speaks for his patient. (Lévi-Strauss, 1963)

No dalang is in this sense a modern artist (or psychoanalyst). It is as if he were performing a new act of Hamlet, or relating a new episode from the Gospels, working on an expanding text which extends through space and time far beyond his own imagination. In this kind of traditional creation, the skill of the dalang is revealed in his ability to re-create the past, which he must do at the beginning of each wayang and at certain points throughout the performance, most particularly in singing short descriptive passages from Old Javanese (Kawi) texts. Here he speaks directly *to* the past of his own culture in words almost entirely unintelligible to the dalang or his audience. [. . .]

The art of invention for the dalang, working within the plot constraints of his medium, involves selection of motifs and characters from the body of mythology he believes in. This is not unlike the Aristotelian art of invention, which was primarily the selection of quotations and ideas from the classics – a kind of information retrieval – in order to interpret the present (Young and A. Becker, 1966).

A political change in Indonesia can be reflected in wayang as a change in mythology, as it has been described in the penetrating studies of Donald Emmerson (forthcoming), and Benedict Anderson (1965), and G. J. Resink (1975). One generation of heroes may replace another, or one set of gods may replace another, as was the case in a village wayang I saw in Lombok in which the Hindu gods were the villains who were defeated by Moslem heroes. This is, however, essentially new wine in old bottles, or what we might call *surface change*. Deep change, in terms of this essay, would be change in the plot, change in the constraints on selecting and ordering the characters and motifs. Deep change would be change in the Javanese conception of time and event, change of epistemology.[4]

Intentionality in a Text: The Uses of Texture

One of the first things a dalang learns is that not everyone will respond to a wayang in the same way. There is no assumption that everyone will be interested in the same things at the same time; someone will always be dozing. The setting for a wayang is noncompulsive, more like a Western sports event than serious theater. It is not shameful or embarrassing to sleep through what someone else is enjoying. Jokes, philosophy, action, poetic language, each has different appeal to different people, depending on their own mental makeup, which is often described in a way parallel to the Indian theory of rasa and guna (Coomaraswamy, 1957), a theory parallel, in turn, to the archaic theory of humors in the West. One responds according to his makeup. There can be no single, intended correct response to a play, no one complete interpretation. This multiplicity of events and perspectives builds the kind of thick texture that Javanese favor. As an old man responded when asked why he liked wayang, "Asalnya ramai!" ("Above all because it is bustling/complex/busy/beautiful!") *Ramai* < Old Javanese *ramia* < Sanskrit *ramya* "pleasing, beautiful." Notice the semantic change in Java from "beautiful" to "beautiful because bustling and complex." Sanskrit words, like Sanskrit stories, are recontextualized in Java.

Within the variety of responses – too thick to be untangled here – there are always two separate audiences at every wayang, an essential audience, without whom the play is pointless, and a nonessential audience, who may or may not be present and who in some sense overhear much of the drama. It is the nonessential audience that we have described so far, the various people who have various responses to a noncompulsive event, which is noncompulsive precisely because they are the nonessential audience.

The essential audience of a wayang is normally unseen: spirits, demons and creatures, gods, and ancestors. To whom does the dalang speak in Old Javanese and Sanskrit if not to those who understand these languages, which are unintelligible to the nonessential audience? Archaic language is not merely embellishment or mystification, else it would have been lost long ago. Rather it is essential language addressed to the essential audience, the ancients, the dead. All drama, as we have noted, speaks from the past, the unseen sources of power which are the widest context of the play.

The first words of a wayang – prior even to the *lakon* itself – are uttered softly to unseen hearers, "prayers" or mantra to the sources of power. Before the puppeteer arrives at the place of performance he establishes relations with this wider spiritual context, including his own, nonhuman brothers (kanda empat) who guard and extend his senses and provide buffers in an unpredictable, often hostile environment (Hooykaas, 1974). . . . This initial phrase of a wayang text is called the *manggala* in Old Javanese (Kawi) written literature. A *manggala* is anything – word, god, or person – which has the power to support the poet. The *manggala* is invoked, praised, and then relied upon to sustain the poet/dalang in his effort. Here is a point of choice, then, for the puppeteer, who is likely to turn his mind to several sources of support. For the dalang, unlike the poet in the kakawin (poetic literature of the Old Javanese period), it is a private act, invoking the widest context of the shadow play, the earth, the light, the wind, the mountains.

The language of the manggala-prayers is usually a single expanded sentence which includes a descriptive subject and an imperative predicate. The sentence is preceded by the original syllable, *Om*, which establishes the parameters of all language sounds, in Sanskrit linguistics. In structure, the *manggala* is very similar to a Vedic hymn:

Om. O' (insert name of the *manggala* and phrases describing him/her/it) + imperative predicate.

For example, as he adjusts the lamp (kerosene or oil), the dalang may softly say: "Om. Be there no hindrance. God of spirit, center of all, God of light – let the flame of this lamp illumine the world." The phrases of the prayer linguistically are parallel. All prayers follow the general pattern just given, except that the

phase "Be there no hindrance" is not always stated. The language is a blend of Sanskrit and Javanese, the subject in Sanskrit (the language of the gods, the remote past), and the predicate in modern Javanese (the language of the dalang himself, the immediate present). The words bridge past and present, and must be uttered with full attention.

Perhaps here is the place to note an extraordinary fact about the language of the wayang, a fact of great importance in understanding what is happening at any given moment. A wayang includes within it, in each performance, the entire history of the literary language, from Old Javanese, pre-Hindu incantation and mythology to the era of the Sanskrit gods and their language, blending with Javanese in the works of ancient poets (the suluks), adding Arabic and Colonial elements, changing with the power of Java to new locations and dialects, up to the present Bahasa Indonesia and even a bit of American English (in which one clown often instructs another). I do not just mean here what might be said of English, that it reflects its history in vocabulary, syntax, and phonological variation. That is also true of modern Javanese. The difference is that in the shadow play, the language of each of these different eras is separate in function from the others; certain *voices* speak only one or the other of these languages and dialects, and they are continually kept almost entirely separate from each other. One could even say that the content of the wayang is the languages of the past and the present, a means for contextualizing the past in the present, and the present in the past, hence preserving the expanding text that is the culture. I shall point out these different kinds of language as they appear, though we have already seen that the prayers (mantra) to the gods and other sources of power use Sanskrit and modern Javanese, the *suluk* use Old Javanese (Kawi), and the clowns use all modern languages, Javanese, Indonesian, Dutch, English, Japanese, French, neatly reflecting the context of modern Indonesia. Clowns speak the older languages only to mock them.

Like the manggala-prayers, the *suluk* speak to the ancients (not the gods but the Javanese ancestors) in their own language at the beginning of each scene. In many cases the chanted *suluk* are addressed to the individual characters represented by the puppets in the wayang. Like Vedic hymns they invoke the character in his own language by a kind of word magic, in which to state a thing properly and effectively, even without intent (as in a casual Brahmin's curse, which cannot be revoked), is to effect power in the world, bridging time and space.

It is here that wayang becomes an education in power. Wayang teaches men about their widest, most complete context, and it is itself the most effective way to learn about that context. There has been much written about the mystical communication in wayang, and its details are best left to Javanese themselves to write about. For us in the West it might be called *trance-communication*. The dalang is above all a man who can be "entered," a "medium," though to use our own terminology is to invoke all the wrong associations. *Trance speaking* can be defined as communication in which one of the variables of the speech act (I am speaking to you about x at time y in place z with intent a) is denied, most frequently the variable I is paradoxically both speaking and not speaking, or speaking involuntarily or nonintentionally. Trance is a kind of incongruence between statement and intent (I/not I am speaking to you/not you. . . .), and covers a wide spectrum of linguistic experiences, from the minor trance of singing the national anthem – or any song you *believe* – to the major trance of hypnosis and schizophrenia (Haley, 1963).

In any case, it is as trance communication as a means of relationship with an unseen, essential audience that wayang can be linked to the Barong drama of Bali, the autochthonous trance ritual of the other islands (e.g., the ma'bugi in Sulawesi), and the use of puppets and dolls as spirit media throughout Southeast Asia.

What is the use of communication with the ancients, besides preserving the text of the culture, which is probably not a primary goal but a constant effect of this communication? Two uses are implied in the instruction books for the dalang: to exorcise danger or potential danger, and to contextualize the present in the past. There are many well-known myths about the origin of wayang as a way of subduing or at least calming down dangerous power, the power of Siva amuck or the power of his demon son Kala (time) who formerly dealt out death indiscriminately.

How does wayang *control* power gone amuck, madness, demons, disease, and stupidity? By nature all these are sources of chain-reacting, linear power, which accelerates by repeating more and more of the same. Someone who is amuck kills and kills *without intent* until he in turn is killed. Likewise disease and madness feeds upon itself. The closest answer to the question of how wayang subdues power gone amuck came to me from a Balinese friend, who answered, "You know, it's like the doors in Bali." (NOTE: an entrance in Bali and traditional Java is backed by a flat wall or screen (Javanese *wrana*) a few feet behind the entrance gap in the outer wall, so that one cannot go straight in but must pass right or left. Demons and people possessed or amuck move in straight lines, not in curves like normal human beings.) My friend continued, after I looked mystified, "The demons can't get in. The music and shadow play move round and round and keep the demons out." Then he paused and laughed heartily, and added, "As you might say, demons think in straight lines!"

Clearly, from this point of view, it is not the story or the archaic words or the puppets but the whole thing, the *texture* itself, the maze of relations, that is most important. The structure of the medium itself subdues power gone amuck, inducing paradox and coincidence, anathema to those who think in straight lines.

In summary, then, the dalang speaks as himself and as the past through himself to an unseen, essential audience and to the immediate, nonessential audience, each containing a wide variety of perspectives on the action being performed. And he is playing with fire. If, for the immediate audience, the event is noncompulsive, for him, it is powerfully compulsive. Once begun, he may not for any reason (illness, storm, violence, power failure) stop until the play has finished. Hence, he must be careful not to begin anything he cannot end.[5]

Reference: On Language and Things of This World

[. . .]

In the dominant Western notion of reference (the one assumed in introductory and popular books about linguistics), there are three categories which can be labeled roughly *words* (language), *thoughts* (or concepts), and *things* (objects in the sensible world). These are assumed to be separable (though slightly overlapping) categories of being, since concepts appear to be stateable in different languages, and there appear to be different, unrelated names for the same things in different languages. The relations of language to concepts and things are therefore felt to be fundamentally arbitrary. If anything, natural language gets in the way of clearly seeing things as they *are* (Bacon's "idols of the market"), and gets in the way of clear, logical thought (based as it is for us now on measurable identities and differences). Thinkers in the West tend to give priority to concepts or things and treat language as a "tool" to be shaped to our ends, or discarded and replaced. Not for many centuries in the West (until recently in the works of Foucault and Lacan and with the development of modern linguistics) has language itself been given priority as a source of highly valued knowledge.

Opposed to this notion of the arbitrary nature of reference is one familiar in American thought in the work of Emerson, particularly in his essay "Language." In this earlier view, the relation of words, thoughts, and things is not arbitrary, though it has been confused by the multiplicity of languages. The laws of Nature govern thoughts, words, and things alike. Emerson could, therefore, make his essay "Language" a subsection of his larger work, *Nature*. *Signified* and *signifier* are constrained by the same laws. To know is to interpret either words or things or concepts. All three – signifier (words), signified (things), and the relations between them (concepts) – offer themselves to men to be deciphered in order to discover the "text" of the world. As Emerson wrote, "The world is emblematic. Parts of speech are metaphors, because the whole of nature is a metaphor of the human mind" (Emerson, 1948:18; A. Becker, 1975).

A favored form of discourse in this epistemology is the commentary or the essay, a decipherment or interpretation of language and nature. In commentary, etymology is an important strategy, not as an attempt to discover the original meaning of words, but rather as an attempt to discover the "intrinsic 'properties' of the letters, syllables, and, finally, whole words." One of the things that strikes us about the text of a Javanese shadow play is the pervasiveness of etymologizing as an explanatory strategy. Javanese call this etymologizing *djarwa dhosok* or "forced" (imposed) interpretation. My own first impulse was to dismiss etymological commentary in wayang as "folk" linguistics, rooted in ignorance about the true history of the words explained, for many of which I knew the Sanskrit etymons. I dismissed etymologizing, in spite of its frequency and obvious importance as a text-building strategy, since it did not give the "true" origin of words. Even more, it appeared to me as an embarrassing and silly aspect of wayang. What I failed to see then was that, since the meanings of words constantly change, etymologies must be reformulated (like genealogies), based upon what one now, in the present, sees as the "intrinsic" meaning of the word under consideration. A brief example: etymology A of the word *history* traces it to French *histoire*, then to Latin *historia* "a narrative of past events" to Greek *istoria* "Learning by inquiry" and back to *istor* "arbiter, judge" and hence back in time to a possible Indo-European root. Etymology B of the same word divides it into "his" and "story," and interprets the elements of the word in the present. "His-story" is also an account of past events, but an account relating primarily to men, with women in a secondary role. Which etymology is correct? It is impossible to answer, for the question is wrong in insisting that we reject one or the other conceptual strategy, etymology A or etymology B. Certainly etymology B tells us more that is relevant and true to current thought than etymology A. In traditional Javanese discourse, including wayang, but also including history and commentary, the strategy we have called *etymology B* is held to be serious and an important part of a text, a basic way of deciphering this world.

Etymologizing of this second sort is known to us, in part, as *explicating*, and the object to be explicated is usually a text clearly recognized as literary or religious or legal, and we have specialists who explicate each of these kinds of text. What they do is relate the words of the text (and the phrases and sentences, etc.) to the current context. Precisely in this sense, though less specialized, the dalang relates the old words to the current context. What differentiates the dalang from the explicators of texts in our society is that he explicates primarily proper nouns, names for things, whereas we tend to feel that names are the most arbitrary words of all, given to people and places before they really "are." Etymologizing about names is not unknown in our culture, of course, but it is not particularly highly valued as a way of understanding people and places. What can we know by explaining the name "Detroit," via etymological strategy A or B?

There are two structural points in a lakon when etymologizing, as a text-building strategy, is appropriate: in description or dialogue. (It never occurs in *suluks*, where it is most needed.) Etymologizing is the descriptive part of a scene (either *janturan*, "description of a place," or *carios*, "description of prior action") is done by the dalang directly and it is serious. Etymologizing in a dialogue is done by one of the characters, and may be serious and "academic," if spoken by Krishna or Abiasa, or only half-serious, if spoken by a clown. A major skill in puppetry is the ability to etymologize in all these ways. Let us examine a few instances.

After the mantra and a set musical interlude, the dalang brings out the puppets for the first scene, and begins the description of the first scene of the first *pathet* of the lakon, using fixed phrases:

Once there was a land. Many are god's creatures that walk the earth or fly the air or swim in the water. Many are the beauties of the world. Yet none can equal those of this land, Manikmantaka (here the name of the particular place in the particular story is inserted). Among a hundred there are not two, among a thousand not ten like Manikmantaka. . . .

Then the dalang describes the kingdom following the strategy of moving from widest physical context to narrowest, from the place of the kingdom among all kingdoms, the mountains around it, the sea, the town itself, the houses, the people, narrowing to a specific person, the king and those about him. All this is set language, though phrases can be left out or reordered slightly. In these passages, the skill of the dalang in controlling the rhythm and pitch contours of his voice in relation to the gamelan is established (or not).[6] In speaking the past almost entirely his legitimacy as a dalang is being proved in one area. At some point in the description, usually as a transition from the description of the kingdom to the description of the king, the dalang begins his first etymology, either on the name of the country or on the name of the king, or both. Here another skill is brought to the foreground, for the etymologies are not set, although one may borrow them from wayang promptbooks called *pakem* (at the risk of being known, condescendingly, as a "book" dalang). The dalang displays his skill at explication; he must be authoritative and informative. He does not, however, explain words by consulting a dictionary of Sanskrit roots, but interprets the elements of the words as Javanese words:

The king who ruled this land is called Maha Prabu Niwata Kawaca. And his name means "one who wears armor that may never be pierced" which, in our time, means "one who could not be defeated," for he and all his people believed that, and acted as if that were true. His name is made of three words: Ni, Wata, and Kawaca. Ni or nir is from the word *nirwana*. Nirwana means freedom from desires, freedom from the past, freedom from the future, something which cannot be likened to anything. In other words, the Great God. *Wata* means blind, without vision. Kawata comes from *Kaca*, which means mirror. Hence, his name, Niwatakawaca, means a mirror that is broken, a mirror which has lost its ability to reflect the truth, the Great God. When he was young he was called Nirbito, which comes from Nir and bito. Nir is, as was said, from *Nirwana*. Bito means afraid. For although all feared him, he was himself a coward and turned away from the Great God.

This is a version of the first etymology from the story, Arjuna Wiwaha, as I learned it. Notice that the name is explicated more than once, and that the meaning as a whole ("one who could not be defeated") is not the same as the meaning of the parts ("a mirror blind to nirwana"). Both are true and both, along with the childhood name of the king, tell us about him. If he had other names they would be interpreted here, too. Clearly, words here are not arbitrarily related to people and things.

I do not intend here to go into the ritual and magical potentialities of this language, chiefly because I only very dimly understand them. It is enough to say that the shadow play is a text nonarbitrarily related to the world outside the play, and that explication of the language is a means to cut through the hidden nature of things. The dalang is a skilled explicator, who demonstrates that complexity and obscurity can be unmasked and, hence, provides a model for understanding the world.

Others (Anderson, Resink, Emmerson) have described how the present world looks within this model. Events in Indonesia really are interpreted by some Javanese as lakon, the lakon plot does have psychological reality as a kind of meditation, names of political leaders are taken as revealing character and role, changes in stories or mythologies from which motifs are drawn to parallel social and religious changes. That is, each way that the text relates to its context (see the first section) is emblematic of the world and defines a way of interpreting the world, once one believes, knows, or pretends that reference is nonarbitrary.

Conclusion: Toward an Aesthetic Understanding of Communication

The methodology of this essay has been to describe the various sorts of relations a text (or a part of a text, a word, a sentence, a passage, an episode) has with its context. Parts of a text relate to the whole under the constraints of what we called *plot coherence*. The motifs or episodes of a text relate to their source in a cultural mythology under the constraints of

invention. The text and its parts relate to the participants in the linguistic act (direct or indirect speaker, direct or indirect hearer, direct or indirect beneficiary, etc.) under the constraints of intentionality. The text and its parts relate to the nontext world under the constraints of what we have called *reference* (either naming or metaphoric reference). In the previous sections of this commentary, these relations have been examined, not in terms of their specific content, but at the more general level of constraints on specific content.

[. . .]

The goal of the philologist is to guide outsiders (here non-Javanese) to what might be called an *aesthetic* understanding of a text. To achieve an aesthetic understanding it seems reasonable to say that in interpreting a text, the outsider must be aware of his own differences – particularly those most "natural" to him – and must learn to use new conventions of coherence, invention, intentionality, and reference. For an aesthetic response to be possible, a text must appear to be more or less coherent; the mythology it draws upon and presupposes must be more or less known; the conventional intent of the creator or speaker of the text in relation to one's own role as hearer/reader/interpreter must be relatively well understood; even the more basic assumptions about how words relate to thoughts and the things of the world need to be more or less shared. If any of these kinds of meaning is not understood, then one's responses to wayang are either incomplete or contradictory. Never fully to understand and constantly to misunderstand are linguistic pathologies that characterize a wide range of phenomena from the strategic understanding of the schizophrenic to the persistent confusion and uneasiness of one who is learning to use a foreign language; all these pathologies subject one to a world in which language and metalanguage are incoherent, where, to take an extreme case, people say "I love you" and at the same time reveal contradictory messages, even "I hate you," in a look or a slap.

The universal source of language pathology is that people appear to say one thing and "mean" another. It drives people mad (the closer it gets to home). An aesthetic response is quite simply the opposite of this pathology. It is opposite in the sense that the same constraints are relevant to both, but there is one difference. That is, opposites are things which are in the same class but differ in one feature (Hale, 1974). Schizophrenia, foreign language learning, and artistic expression in language all operate under the same set of linguistic variables, constraints on coherence, invention, intentionality, and reference. The difference is that in madness (and in the temporary madness of learning a new language or a new text) these constraints are misunderstood and often appear contradictory; whereas in an aesthetic response they are understood as a coherent integrated whole. Shadow theater, like any live art, presents a vision of the world and one's place in it which is whole and hale, where meaning is possible. The integration of communication (art) is, hence, as essential to a sane community as clean air, good food, and, to cure errors, medicine. In all its multiplicity of meaning, a well-performed wayang is a vision of sanity.[7]

NOTES

1 I owe this term, and much of my understanding of it, to Vern Carroll.

2 The notion of speaking the present and speaking the past came to me from Maurice Bloch. Speaking the past is a particular kind of speech act or mode of communication, which Bloch defines for the Merina of Madagascar, who themselves describe certain ritual speech making as "speaking the words of the ancestors" (Bloch, 1974). Bloch is wrong, I think, in contrasting formalized speech acts and everyday speech acts, on a scale of most to least formalized language. Everyday speech acts are also highly formalized. I feel that the poles of this scale range from repetition (most formal, speaking the past) to imagination or internal discourse (least formal, speaking the present), and I argue that neither pole is ultimately attainable. For an early view of wayang as "speaking the words of the ancestors," see W. H. Rassers (1959).

3 The notion of iconicity is derived from Kenneth Boulding (1961), a basic text in the study of comparative epistemography. The centrality of tense in establishing textual coherence in English narrative is demonstrated in William Labov, Transformation of experience in narrative syntax (1972).

4 Ironically, most attempts to "preserve" traditional drama require deep change. This "irony" is discussed in Becker (1974).

5 My teacher tells the story of his first wayang performance in which he insisted on performing a story which was too "heavy" (berat) for him. All the oil lamps died midperformance, so his grandfather pushed him aside and continued the performance, and all the lights came on again.

On Mount Kawi, near Malang, a wayang performance goes on every day and every night, nonstop year round, performing for the essential audience and preserving the spiritual texture, the ruwatan.

6 See Gregory Bateson, for further examples (chiefly Balinese) of the role of skill as a basic element in aesthetics: "Style, grace, and information in primitive art." Bateson writes, "Only the violinist who can control the quality of his notes can use variations of that quality for musical purposes" (1972:148).

7 This essay, taken together with Judith Becker's Time and Tune in Java [in the volume from which this extract comes, pp. 197–210], suggests the possibility of a single set of constraints running through the whole of the traditional Javanese epistemology, in music, calendars, texts, rituals, and social relations. Of course, this unity may be in part the oversimplification of an outsider, but if true, this unity is probably a rather rare situation in a culture, as it is in a person. In both it has great power. The complex of changes we call modernization necessarily fragments this unity. Social change alters one by one, and in no par-

ticular order, it seems, those relations of a text to its context which constitute its meaning. Modern single time (Greenwich Mean Time, manifest in the modern necessity of life, the wristwatch) thus strongly affects plot coherence by devaluing multiple time. If multiple time is devalued, coincidence ceases to be "truth" (kebetulan), and is replaced, usually, by narrative/causal "truth." ...

REFERENCES

Aristotle. *Politics and poetics* (B. Jowett and T. Twining, trans.). New York: Viking Press, 1969.

Anderson, Benedict R. O'G. *Mythology and the tolerance of the Javanese.* Data Paper No. 27. Ithaca: Cornell University Southeast Asia Program, 1965.

Bateson, Gregory. *Steps to an ecology of mind.* New York: Ballantine, 1972.

Becker, A. L. The journey through the night: Some reflections on Burmese traditional theatre. In Mohd. Taib Osman (Ed.), *Traditional drama and music of southeast Asia.* Kuala Lumpur: Dewan Bahasa dan Pustaka, 1974. (Also in *The drama review*, Winter 1970.)

Becker, Alton L. A linguistic image of nature: The Burmese numerative classifier system. *International Journal of the Sociology of Language.* 1975, *5*, 109–21.

Becker, Alton and I Gusti Ngurah Oka. Person in Kawi: Exploration of an elementary semantic dimension. *Oceanic linguistics,* 1976, *13*, 229–55.

Bloch, Maurice. Symbols, song, dance, and features of articulation. *European journal of sociology,* 1974, *XV*, 58.

Boulding, Kenneth. *The image.* Ann Arbor: University of Michigan Press, 1961.

Coomaraswamy, A. K. Hindu view of art: Theory of beauty. In *The dance of Shiva.* New York: Noonday Press, 1957.

Emerson, R. W. *Nature.* New York: Liberal Arts Press, 1948.

Emmerson, Donald. The Ramayana syndrome. Forthcoming.

Hahn, Edward. Finite-state models of plot complexity. *Poetics: International review for the theory of literature,* 1973, *8*.

Hale, Kenneth. A note on a Walbiri tradition of autonymy. In D. D. Steinberg and L. A. Jakobovits (Eds.), *Semantics: An interdisciplinary reader in philosophy, linguistics, and psychology.* New York: Cambridge University Press, 1974.

Haley, Jay. *Strategies of psychotherapy.* New York: Grove and Stratton, 1963.

Hardjowirogo. *Sedjarah Wajang Purwa.* Djakarta: Balai Pustaka, 1968.

Hooykaas, C. *Cosmology and creation in the Balinese tradition.* The Hague: M. Nijhoff, 1974.

Kats, J. *Het Javansche Jooneel I Wayang Poerwa.* Weltrveden, 1923.

Labov, William. *Language in the inner city.* Philadelphia: University of Pennsylvania Press, 1972.

Lacan, Jacques. *The language of self* (A. Wilden, trans.). Baltimore: Johns Hopkins Press, 1973.

Laing, R. D. *Knots.* New York: Vintage, 1970.

Lévi-Strauss, Claude. *Structural anthropology.* New York: Basic Books, 1963.

Rassers, W. H. On the origin of the Javanese theatre. In *Panji, the culture hero.* The Hague: Mouton, 1959.

Resink, G. J. From the old Mahabharata- to the new Ramayana-order. *Bijdragen tot de TaalLand en Volkenkunde,* DL 131 II/III, 1975, 214–35.

Young, R. E., and Becker, A. L. Toward a modern theory of rhetoric: A tagmemic contribution. In J. Emig, J. Fleming, and H. M. Popp (Eds.). *Language and learning.* New York: Harcourt, Brace and World, 1966.

Young, R. E., Becker, A. L., and Pike, K. L. *Rhetoric, discovery and change.* New York: Harcourt, Brace and World, 1971.

Zurbuchen, Mary. Kawi discourse structure: Cycle, event, and evaluation. *Rackham Literary Studies,* Winter 1976, 45–60.

Moral Inversions and Spaces of Disorder

Introduction

As Douglas argued, any structure will leave gaps and anomalies. In addition, any system of order will generate images of its inversion. Religion has to address disorder as well as order, anomaly as well as consistency, ambivalence as well as commitment, evil as well as good – and often does so by attempting to assimilate them. Indeed, religion draws on the rich imagery of the margins in order to make higher-level generalizations about the order it proposes. Often this happens in rituals of initiation (see the essay by Turner, chapter 26). In this section we draw on three different sources – myth, witchcraft, and carnival. These essays explore the prevalence of both the amoral and the immoral in the cultural imagination and in social practice. For further provocative ethnography that explores the social and historical consequences of a politics of the imaginary see, respectively, the essay by De Boeck (chapter 38) and van de Port (1998).

19

The Winnebago Trickster Figure

Paul Radin

Paul Radin (1883–1959) was an outstanding American anthropologist of the Boasian school noted for his close work with the Winnebago. As the present essay shows, Radin had tremendous appreciation for the insight conveyed in Amerindian narrative.

This excerpt from Radin's interpretive essay on the trickster myth of the Winnebago Indians is best read in conjunction with his record of the entire cycle set out earlier in his book. The trickster is an amoral yet essentially good-natured creature whose adventures as both duper and dupe express a kind of ontogeny, a coming into being of consciousness and differentiation that may be understood at both psychological and cosmological levels. The trickster cycle exemplifies the role of chaos and ambiguity in creation myth. Radin also points to the centrality of the comic. As Diamond (1972) indicates, the trickster personifies a frank recognition and acceptance of human ambivalence.

Trickster figures are known from many parts of the world. Individual trickster gods are found within the pantheon in polytheistic religions like those in ancient Greece or in West Africa. Tricksters are central to the storytelling of many Native American groups; I recommend Howard Norman's exquisite renderings of Swampy Cree versions (1976). A recent work on Southern African Bushmen emphasizes the role of trickster figures there and makes a number of useful connections with the literature on shamanism (Guenther 1999). Comedy and irony are also central to spirit possession and widespread in religious traditions, albeit rather absent from the sustained seriousness characteristic of most public or "official" rituals and representations of Christianity and Islam.

As a Boasian, Radin worked closely with gifted raconteurs in order to record

From Paul Radin, "The Nature and the Meaning of the Myth," in *The Trickster: A Study in American Indian Mythology* (reproduced by kind permission of the Philosophical Library, New York, 1972 [1956]), pp. 132–54.

cultural texts, and paid careful attention to what participants themselves said about the material and to the individual variants. In his classic accounts of *Primitive Man as Philosopher* (1957a [1927]) and *Primitive Religion* (1957b [1937]), Radin argued powerfully against the Lévy-Bruhlian view of a prelogical mentality and, indeed, against the entire evolutionist approach, the "fundamentally misleading doctrine that primitive peoples represent an early stage in the history of the evolution of culture" (1957a [1927]: x). For Radin there are always individuals holding more or less religious perspectives or who are more or less inclined to engage in philosophical speculation. Radin's portrait of intellectual and reflective speculation is far broader and richer than that portrayed by Tylor. Just as he demonstrates, in the chapter immediately following the ones presented here, the satirical dimension of the Trickster tales, so he locates "skepticism and critique" among certain thinkers in any "primitive" society (1957a: Chapter XIX). Other significant members of the Boasian school include Sapir (1956 [1928]), Lowie (1935, 1948), and Benedict (1934). They frequently emphasized the emotional dimension in religious expression and its relation to personality. For a lively rendition of the Americanist language-based tradition by contemporary practitioners see Valentine and Darnell (1999).

The Winnebago word for trickster is *wakdjunkaga*, which means *the tricky one*. The corresponding term for him in Ponca is *ishtinike*, in the kindred Osage, *itsike* and in Dakota-Sioux, *ikto-mi*. The meaning of the Ponca and Osage words is unknown, that of the Dakota is *spider*. Since all these three stems are clearly related etymologically, the question arises as to whether the Winnebago rendering, *the tricky one*, does not really mean simply *one-who-acts-like-Wakdjunkaga*, and is thus secondary. In no other Siouan language is the stem for *tricky* remotely like *wakdjunkaga*. It seems best, then, to regard the real etymology of *wakdjunkaga* as unknown.

The similarity of the exploits attributed to Wakdjunkaga and all other trickster-heroes in North America is quite astounding. The only possible inference to be drawn is that this myth-cycle is an old cultural possession of all the American Indians, which has remained, as far as the general plot is concerned, relatively unchanged. Just because of this fact the specific differences between the Winnebago myth-cycle and the others assume special importance and demand explanation. To do this adequately it will first be necessary to summarize the plot of the *Wakdjunkaga* myth-cycle in considerable detail.[1]

The cycle begins with an incident found in no other version, namely Wakdjunkaga pictured as the chief of the tribe, giving a warbundle feast on four different days. He, although host and consequently obligated to stay to the very end, is described as leaving the ceremony in order to cohabit with a woman, an act which is absolutely forbidden for those participating in a warbundle feast. On the fourth day he stays to the end and invites all the participants in the feast to accompany him by boat. Hardly has he left the shore when he returns and destroys his boat as useless. At this piece of stupidity some of his companions leave him. He then starts on foot, but after a short time destroys both his warbundle and his arrowbundle and finds himself eventually deserted by everyone and alone; alone, that is, as far as human beings and society are concerned. With the world of nature he is still in close contact. He calls all objects, so our text tells us, younger brothers. He understands them; they understand him.

This is clearly an introduction and its purpose is manifest. Wakdjunkaga is to be desocialized, to be represented as breaking all his ties with man and society. Why our raconteur began the cycle in this particular fashion it is impossible to say, but it is best to assume that it is a literary device. Presumably he has decided that Wakdjunkaga is to be depicted as completely unconnected with the world of man and as gradually evolving from an amorphous, instinctual and unintegrated being into one with the lineaments of man and one foreshadowing man's psychical traits. He has, in short, like many another epic writer, begun *in medias res*. What he seems to be saying is: "Here is Wakdjunkaga pretending to be thoroughly socialized and about to embark on a warparty. But let me tell you what he really is: an utter fool, a breaker of the most holy taboos, a destroyer of the most sacred objects!" And then he proceeds, in kaleidoscopic fashion, to reduce Wakdjunkaga to his primitive self.

The exploits that follow tell us precisely who Wakdjunkaga is. (See incidents 4–10 in text.) In the first he treacherously lures an old buffalo to destruction, kills him in most cruel fashion and butchers him. No ethical values exist for him. And how does he kill and butcher the buffalo? With only one hand, his right. The next incident shows why only one hand has been used. He is still living in his unconscious, mentally a child, and this is here symbolized by the struggle between his right and his left hands in which his left hand is badly cut up. He himself is hardly aware of why this has occurred. He can only ejaculate, "Why have I done this?" In contradistinction to Wakdjunkaga, the world of nature is represented as conscious, and the birds, in a language he cannot understand, exclaim, "Look, look! There is Wakdjunkaga. There he goes!"

In the next incident he is still Wakdjunkaga the undifferentiated and instinctual. He comes upon a being with four little children who must be fed in a certain manner and at a certain time lest they die. In short, the principle of order must be recognized. But he knows no such principle. The father warns him that if the children die because Wakdjunkaga has failed to follow his instructions, he will kill him. Yet Wakdjunkaga, because of his own hunger, disobeys the instructions given him and the children die. Immediately the father is upon him. Wakdjunkaga is pursued around the island world, that is the universe, and only by jumping into the ocean surrounding it does he escape death.

As he swims aimlessly in the water, not knowing where the shore is, if, indeed, one exists, completely without bearings, he asks fish after fish where he can find land. None of them knows. Finally he is told that he has been swimming along the shoreline all the time.

He has barely landed, that is, he has barely got his bearings, when he attempts to catch some fish. But all he can obtain is the water through which some fish have passed. Out of this he enthusiastically prepares a soup, and fills himself to his utmost capacity. As he lies there, practically incapacitated, his stomach shining from being distended, a dead fish drifts by. He seizes it, but he cannot eat any more and he buries it.

Here we find Wakdjunkaga completely unanchored. He is not only isolated from man and society but – temporarily at least – from the world of nature and from the universe as well. Small wonder, then, that he is described as thoroughly frightened and as saying to himself, "That such a thing should happen to Wakdjunkaga, the warrior! Why I almost came to grief." What the author intended here – the enraged father, the pursuit, the headlong flight and the submerging in the ocean – may well have been meant as a description of what can happen to anyone who leads the life instinctual.

However, there is also another point involved here. Being frightened is, in Winnebago symbolism, generally the indication of an awakening consciousness and sense of reality, indeed, the beginning of a conscience. And that seems to be borne out by the next incident (11 in text), where Wakdjunkaga is represented as imitating what he takes to be a man pointing at him but which turns out to be a tree stump with a protruding branch. The important point here is his reaction to his blunder and stupidity. "Yes, indeed," so he says, "*it is on this account that the people call me Wakdjunkaga, the foolish one! They are right.*" He has one of the necessary traits of an individualized being now, a name. In Winnebago society a child had no legal existence, no status, until he received a name.

The episode which follows (12 in text) is known throughout North America in a practically identical form. It describes how

Wakdjunkaga persuades some ducks to dance for him with eyes closed and how he wrings their necks as they dance, though most of them succeed in escaping. He roasts the few he has killed and, exhausted from his encounter, goes to sleep after instructing his anus to keep watch. His anus does its best to awaken him when foxes appear, but to no avail, and Wakdjunkaga awakens to find the ducks have been eaten. In anger he punishes his anus by burning it, and when he can endure the pain no longer, he exclaims, "Ouch! This is too much! . . . *Is it not for such things that I am called Wakdjunkaga? Indeed, they have talked me into doing this, just as if I had been doing something wrong!*" Important for our purpose is this exclamation, and also the one in incident 14, where Wakdjunkaga discovers that he has been devouring parts of his own intestines and commenting upon how delicious they taste: "*Correctly indeed am I named Wakdjunkaga, the foolish one! By being called thus I have actually been turned into a wakdjunkaga, a foolish one!*"

With these incidents (12, 13, 14 in text) we have reached a new stage in Wakdjunkaga's development. The emphasis is now upon defining him more precisely, psychically and physically. He is now to be shown emerging out of his complete isolation and lack of all identity, and as becoming aware of himself and the world around him. He has learned that both right and left hands belong to him, that both are to be used and that his anus is part of himself and cannot be treated as something independent of him. He realizes, too, that he is being singled out, even if only to be ridiculed, and he has begun to understand why he is called Wakdjunkaga. But he does not as yet accept responsibility for his actions. In fact, he holds other people, the world outside of himself, as compelling him to behave as he does.

It is only at this point that we are told anything specific about Wakdjunkaga's appearance. Every Winnebago, of course, knew what it was. Why then are we informed about it just here? The answer seems to be that his original appearance is now to be altered. He is now to be given the intestines and anus of the size and shape which man is to have.

That this episode has not been placed here just through accident is proved by the fact that in the episode which immediately follows we have the first mention of his penis, of its size and of his manner of carrying it in a box on his back. And for the first time are we made aware of his sexuality. In all other specifically trickster myths lust is his primary characteristic; in these all his adventures reek with sex. If in the Winnebago Wakdjunkaga cycle it is not mentioned until now, this is because the author or authors who gave this cycle its present shape wished to give us not a series of Trickster's adventures as such but the evolution of a Trickster from an undefined being to one with the physiognomy of man, from a being psychically undeveloped and a prey to his instincts, to an individual who is at least conscious of what he does and who attempts to become socialized. Sex is treated primarily in its relation to Wakdjunkaga's evolution. Sexual escapades do not really seem to interest our raconteurs as such.

It is not strange then that the first sexual episode related of Wakdjunkaga should consist of his waking from his sleep to find himself without a blanket. He sees it floating above him, and only gradually recognizes that it is resting on his huge penis erectus. Here we are brought back again to the Wakdjunkaga whose right hand fights with his left, who burns his anus and eats his own intestines, who endows the parts of his body with independent existence and who does not realize their proper functions, where everything takes place of its own accord, without his volition. "That is always happening to me," he tells his penis.

It is not an accident that this episode is placed just here. It belongs here for it is to serve as an introduction to giving Wakdjunkaga an understanding of what sex is. Quite properly, we first have the symbol for masculine sexuality and an example of how it is thought of socially, namely as analogous to the banner raised by the chief when the tribal feast is given, and that then there follows an example (incident 16 in text) of how it is used concretely and properly.

Incident 16, the sending of the penis across the water so that Wakdjunkaga can have intercourse with the chief's daughter, is as well known in North America as that of the hood-winked ducks. In most of the trickster cycles it is immaterial where it is placed. Here, clearly, this is not true. It belongs here, for it is to be used to indicate how meaningless and undifferentiated Wakdjunkaga's sex drive still is inherently; indeed, to show how meaningless it is for all those involved. Penis, cohabitation are only symbols here; no sense of concrete reality is attached to them. That Wakdjunkaga has as yet developed no sense of true sex differentiation is made still clearer by the episode where he transforms himself into a woman (incident 20 in text).

Immediately following incident 16 we find the well-known theme of how he begs the turkey-buzzard to carry him on his back and fly with him. Whatever may be its larger psychological implications, this incident seems to play no role in the drama of Wakdjunkaga's development and must be regarded as an interlude. His rescue by women, after turkey-buzzard has treacherously dropped him into a hollow tree, is part of the secondary satire on man and society that permeates the whole cycle and about which we will have more to say in the next section.

We have now reached the crucial episode where Wakdjunkaga changes his sex and marries the chief's son. The overt reason given for his doing this is that he and his companions have been overtaken by winter and are starving and that the chief and his son have plenty. This episode like the preceding ones is well known; no trickster cycle omits it. The reason generally given is that Trickster does it to avenge some insult. The change of sex is a trick played on an oversexed individual in order to show to what lengths such a person will go, what sacred things he will give up and sacrifice to satisfy his desires. Such is its role in one of the most famous of all North American Indian trickster cycles, that of *Wisaka* of the Fox tribe.[2] But here in the Winnebago cycle it is not to avenge an insult but ostensibly to obtain food that the transformation of sex has occurred.

Taken in conjunction with the sex episodes which have preceded and the two incidents that follow, its meaning becomes clear. It is part of Wakdjunkaga's sex education. This

must begin by sharply differentiating the two sexes. It is as if Wakdjunkaga were being told: this is the male; this, the penis; this is cohabitation; this is the female organ; this is pregnancy; this is how women bring children into the world. Yet how can Wakdjunkaga, with his generalized sexual organs, arranged in the wrong order and still living distinct from him in a receptacle on top of his body, how can he be expected to understand such matters? For that reason Wakdjunkaga's sex life, indeed, his whole physical life, is for him still something of a wild phantasmagoria. This phantasmagoria reaches its culmination point in incidents 20 and 21 of the text. Satire, Rabelaisian humour and grotesqueness are combined in these passages with amazing effect. Thrice, within very short intervals before the visit to the chief's son, the man-woman, Wakdjunkaga, is made pregnant; she, a woman, does her own courting; the man-woman becomes pregnant again. Whose are the children he brings forth? We are purposely left in ignorance in order to stress the fact that it makes no difference. Parenthood is immaterial, for they are born of a man-woman.

We have here reached a point where ordinary words and terms are indeed completely inadequate. Only symbols, only metaphors, can convey the meaning properly. As soon as the last child is born he begins to cry and nothing can stop him. A specialist at pacifying children, an old woman who has passed her climacteric, that is, one who is beyond sex, is called, but she is helpless. Finally the infant cries out, "*If I could but play with a piece of white cloud.*" To translate this into meaning then becomes the task of a special shaman. So it is with the child's other requests. They seem all unreasonable and unseasonable. What else can we expect in this phantasmagoria? Yet these requests are, at the same time, reasonable and have concrete non-symbolic significance. Not for the child, however, but for Wakdjunkaga, who is waiting for spring to come and for the time when he can obtain his food himself. Be it remembered: at no time is Wakdjunkaga represented as becoming a victim of this phantasmagoria. He always remains his old primordial self. He has as yet not learned very much and has forgotten even less.

The denouement arrives when Wakdjunkaga is chased around the fireplace by his mother-in-law, when his vulva drops from him and he is revealed as his true self. Ordinarily on such an occasion in the Wakdjunkaga cycle he is represented as laughing at the discomfiture of those on whom he has played a trick. But here he runs away. The reason is clear; the situation is fraught with too many difficulties. Too many taboos have been broken, the sensibilities of too many people have been outraged, too many individuals have been humiliated. It is serious enough for a chief's son to be indulging in what turns out to be homosexual practices, but far more serious is the situation in which the chief's wife, Wakdjunkaga's "mother-in-law", finds herself. Among the Winnebago the mother-in-law taboo was very strict, yet here she is openly associating with one who could have married her daughter and become her son-in-law and thus a person with whom she is not allowed to speak and with whom no joking is possible. The right to joke with and to tease an individual implies a very special relationship. It can only take place between a very restricted number of blood-relatives and a less restricted number of relatives-by-marriage. Joking between a mother-in-law and son-in-law is simply unthinkable. Apparently it was even unthinkable in this *Walpurgisnacht* atmosphere, for the narrator does not use the term *daughter-in-law* when he speaks of the chief's wife teasing Wakdjunkaga, but the term *hiciga*, brother's son's wife. The fact that Wakdjunkaga when functioning as the daughter-in-law could not possibly be *hiciga* a Winnebago audience, of course, would know, but, under the circumstances, any term was better than to call him daughter-in-law.

The shock of all these revelations to those participating in this comic-tragic drama is clear, and our raconteur has expressed this shock by bringing his narrative to a full stop. He apparently feels that one must get out of this insane atmosphere quickly. I think he has done this very astutely. He has Wakdjunkaga not only run away but suddenly come to some realization of what he was doing. Suddenly, and for the first time in the cycle, he is pictured as a normal man with a wife to whom he is legally married and a son for whom it is still necessary to provide. In short, he is suddenly represented as a good citizen, as a thoroughly socialized individual. And so he returns to his home, is received there with joy and stays with his family until his child is well able to take care of himself. The only indication that it is Wakdjunkaga with whom we are here dealing is found in the last three sentences of this episode. "I will now go around and visit people for I am tired of staying here. I used to wander around the world in peace but here I am just giving myself a lot of trouble." In these words we have his protest against domestication and society with all its obligations. Doubtless this also voices the protest of all Winnebago against the same things.

The biological education of Wakdjunkaga is now to be resumed. The next adventure is a utilization of a strictly Rabelaisian theme found throughout aboriginal America, the talking laxative bulb (incidents 23 and 24 in text). Although he now possesses intestines of normal human size he knows nothing about them. He comes upon a bulb which tells him that whoever chews it will defecate. Nature has never taunted him in this fashion before. So he takes the bulb and chews it to find that he does not defecate but only breaks wind. This expulsion of gas increases in intensity progressively. He sits on a log, but is propelled into the air with the log on top of him; he pulls up trees to which he clings, by their roots. In his helplessness he has the inhabitants of a village pile all their possessions upon him, their lodges, their dogs, and then they themselves climb upon him, for he tells them that a large warparty is about to attack them. And so the whole world of man is now on Wakdjunkaga's back. With a terrific expulsion of gas he scatters the people and all their possessions to the four quarters of the earth. And there, we are told, he stood laughing until his sides ached.

Apart from the grotesque humour and the obvious satire, is there anything else involved here? Yes. Broadly speaking, a Winnebago would say this is an illustration of what happens when one defies nature even in a minor fashion, that this is what happens when man climbs on Wakdjunkaga's back.

But this world to which he has fled to escape from society, the world where he could wander around in peace, has not finished its test with him. He now begins to defecate. The earth is covered with excrement. To escape it he takes refuge in a tree, but to no avail, and he falls into mountains of his own excrement. Blinded by the filth clinging to him he gropes helplessly for a path to water. The trees whom he asks for information mock and mislead him. Finally he reaches the water and can cleanse himself.

However, despite this reminder of ignorance, knowledge concerning himself and the outside world comes to him slowly. No sooner has he cleansed himself completely than he mistakes the reflection in the water of plums growing on a tree on the shore for the plums themselves.[3]

There now follows a series of incidents (27–46 in text) that have little bearing on the education of Wakdjunkaga. Apart from their manifest satiric implications they are more or less the typical adventures of all North American tricksters. They exemplify all the traits customarily attributed to him, the meaningless cruelty he inflicts upon others in order to obtain food, and how, at the last moment, he is always frustrated and cheated, cheated in fact, not only by others but by himself (see incidents 30, 31); how he comes to grief by trying to imitate others (incidents 32, 33, 41–4); and how occasionally he turns the tables on his tormentors (incidents 34, 45, 46). From a literary and psychological point of view our myth-cycle breaks down after incident 26, where Wakdjunkaga is knocked unconscious by diving after the reflection of plums in the water, although some of the threads are pulled together, albeit not too well, after incident 38.

What should have followed incident 26, I feel, is the episode where Wakdjunkaga, through the instrumentality of chipmunk, is taught where his genitals should be placed on his body and the proper order of penis and testicles. (See incidents 38 and 39 in text.)

The words of Wakdjunkaga in the dialogue between him and chipmunk are worth noting. They are meant to point out that Wakdjunkaga is at last to become aware concretely of his sex. "Is it not your penis you are carrying on your back?" chipmunk shouts at him, and Wakdjunkaga answers, "What an evil person it is who mentions that! He seems to have full knowledge of what I am carrying on my back." Again chipmunk shouts at him, "Your testicles together!" and Wakdjunkaga answers, "Why, this being must have been watching me closely." Throughout Wakdjunkaga acts bewildered and embarrassed. At first he behaves purely passively, although he follows the instruction. He becomes angry only when chipmunk finally shouts at him his last injunction – "Put the head of the penis on top, put it on top!" It is then, when his genitals are in their right place and correctly arranged, when he has really become aware of his sex and his masculinity, it is only then, that he pursues his tormentor. He attacks chipmunk with his penis, not, ostensibly, in order to cohabit with him but to punish and destroy him for making him aware of his genitals and of his sex. It is his final protest at becoming a mature male. Be it remembered that his penis is still of tremendous length. The farther he penetrates the hole in which chipmunk has sought refuge, the more of his penis the latter bites off until it finally has been reduced to human size. In such fashion does Wakdjunkaga become a male and attain sex consciousness.

A very important addendum now follows. In contrast to the manner in which he disposes of the sloughed-off portions of his intestines, namely, by eating them himself, the parts of the penis which chipmunk has bitten off are thrown into the water and transformed into food plants for man.

Wakdjunkaga's resistance to attaining sexual maturity has innumerable larger psychological and psychoanalytical implications the explanation of which, however, I must leave to others. What I would like to stress here are two questions: first, the fact that he cannot himself reduce his large and amorphous genitals to their normal human size, arrange them in their proper order or place them properly. This must be accomplished through some outside agency. Yet, on the other hand, he himself is represented as responsible for reducing the size of his intestines. Second, it might be asked, whether there is involved in the final act, where chipmunk in his hole bites off large parts of Wakdjunkaga's penis, some form of emasculation or some form of cohabitation. My own belief is that neither is involved, but that we are still dealing with Wakdjunkaga's biological evolution and that what is being implied here symbolically is his transition from a generalized natural and procreative force to a concrete heroic human being. This, I feel, is expressly stated in his exclamation, "Of what a wonderful organ have I been deprived! But why should I say this? I can make useful objects of all these pieces of my penis for human beings!" Thus from being an unconscious benefactor he has now become a conscious benefactor not only of mankind but of nature as well.

Having attained biological maturity one would have imagined that the narrative would then indicate how he attains full psychical and social-ethical maturity. But the incidents that follow show this very inadequately and inconsistently, if at all. It was perhaps actually an impossible thing to do, considering Wakdjunkaga's traditional associations. One of the reasons for this failure, at least from a literary-psychological point of view, lay probably in the fact that one basic exploit or rather, series of exploits, connected with Wakdjunkaga and without which in the minds of the Winnebago the Wakdjunkaga cycle was unthinkable, had still to be included, namely his visits to various animals, the manner in which he was entertained by them and the manner in which he attempts, quite unsuccessfully, to reciprocate their hospitality. (See incidents 41–4.) But these episodes could only with the greatest of difficulty be used to illustrate any progressive development in Wakdjunkaga's character. An attempt, however, seems clearly to have been made, at least in one direction, namely, to show him as developing some sense of social and moral responsibility.

In the incident immediately following the transformation of the gnawed-off pieces of his penis we are told of Wakdjunkaga's meeting with coyote and his attempt to compete with him as a keen scenter. Its only significance in our cycle is to serve as an introduction to the theme of his visits to the muskrat, snipe, woodpecker and polecat (incidents 41–4), and to motivate his turning the tables on coyote (inci-

dent 46). What we have in the coyote episode is a very abbreviated form of a competition between Wakdjunkaga and coyote which plays a much greater role in trickster myths in other parts of North America.

The most that our raconteur can do with the episode of the visits to the various animals is to credit Wakdjunkaga with wishing to provide his family with food, to present him as a harmless, vainglorious blunderer and fool, and as one who succeeds in finally obtaining revenge on those who have humiliated him or desire to do so, like mink and coyote. (See incidents 40 and 46.) This is all part of his socialization. Thus, for example, after polecat visits him and kills innumerable deer for his family we have the following idyllic scene. It is really best to quote it:

> "Well, wife, it is about time for us to go back to the village. Perhaps our relatives are lonesome for us especially for the children." "I was thinking of that myself," replied his wife.... Then they packed their possessions and began to carry them away.... After a while they got near their home and all the people in the village came out to greet him and help him with the packs. The people of the village were delighted. "Kunu, firstborn, is back," they shouted. The chief lived in the middle of the village and alongside of him they built a long lodge for Wakdjunkaga. There the young men would gather at night and he would entertain them for he was a good-natured fellow. The prodigal son has made good and returned!

This reads almost like an account of the return of a successful warleader, or at least a great hunter. Yet something of his old unregenerate self still adheres to him, as is seen in the delight he takes in humiliating mink and coyote. However, a Winnebago audience would have sympathized with this humiliation of mink and coyote. They would have agreed that Wakdjunkaga was a very good-natured person, a blundering fool, it is true, but more sinned against than sinning, one who really meant well but whose good intentions always went amiss. It is in this light that we must interpret the two episodes (incidents 47 and 48) which follow, Wakdjunkaga's removal of natural obstacles in the Mississippi River that would interfere with the free movement of human beings.

But before proceeding to the discussion of these, a few words about the implications of one of the points in the fourth of his visits, that to the polecat, seem in point. In that delightful and Rabelaisian episode polecat kills deer by shooting them with wind he expels from his anus. He "loads" Wakdjunkaga with four such shots to take home with him. Wakdjunkaga is now faced with a new situation. In the case of his visits to muskrat, snipe and woodpecker (41–3), all he had to do to get himself into difficulties and inflict pain upon himself was to imitate them. But now, provided with the means for really accomplishing what his host, polecat, had done, how was he to fail, for fail he must? The problem is simply solved: he must waste these provisions. So, without any reason, he persuades himself that polecat has deceived him, and he shoots at four objects in succession blowing them to pieces – at a knoll, at a tree, at an enormous rock and at a rocky precipitous hill, the last the symbol of a sacred precinct. It is his last act of defiance against the world of nature with which he had, until recently, been on such intimate terms. It is Caliban protesting against the civilization which had been forced upon him.

It would be quite erroneous to think that the author-raconteurs of our cycle were trying in incidents 47 and 48 to exhibit to us a Wakdjunkaga who had now become a wholly beneficent being, a semi-deity in fact. What we have here is a purely secondary addition with no actual connection with what has preceded. It represents largely the influence of the most sacred of all Winnebago narratives, the *Origin Myth of the Medicine Rite*. There, after Earthmaker has created the universe and all its inhabitants, animal and human, he discovers that evil beings[4] are about to exterminate man. In order to help them he sends Wakdjunkaga, the first being comparable to man he has created, down to earth. This is what is meant when we are told that Wakdjunkaga suddenly remembered the purpose for which he had been sent to the earth. In the *Origin Myth of the Medicine Rite* Wakdjunkaga is described

as failing completely. Not even Earthmaker apparently could properly "rehabilitate" him. But on earth Wakdjunkaga could accomplish nothing. As the myth phrases it, "Every variety of small evil animals began to play pranks on him and plague him and he finally sat himself down and admitted to himself that he was incapable of doing anything."[5] Yet in spite of all his trickster antecedents he has here, for a moment, been elevated to the rank of a true culture-hero, although the specific role he is being given belongs properly to an entirely different hero, or rather heroes, the *Twins*.

As I have indicated above, I think that a large part of this transformation of the character of Wakdjunkaga is due to the role he plays or was intended to play in the founding of the Medicine Rite. However, to judge from the fact that there seems to have been a difference of opinion among the Winnebago two generations ago, and one which was definitely not of recent origin, as to how he was to be evaluated, it may very well be that people always interpreted him and his activities in two ways. But to this we will return in the following section when we deal with the Winnebago attitude toward Wakdjunkaga in the first decade of this century.

In the last scene (incident 49) we get still another picture of him. We see him as a deity, an aspect of his nature completely neglected in our cycle, and as the elemental trickster, an ageing trickster, indeed almost a demiurg, taking his last meal on earth. He is pictured sitting on top of a rock with his stone kettle, eating. He perpetuates this last meal for all time, leaving in the rock the imprint of his kettle, of his buttocks and his testicles. He then departs and, since he is the symbol for the procreating power as such and the symbol for man in his relation to the whole universe, he first dives into the ocean and ascends to that island-world over which he presides, that lying immediately under the world of Earthmaker. . . .

The above summary should give the reader some idea of the composite nature of the Winnebago trickster cycle and the degree to which the various episodes composing it have been welded together into a new whole. To obtain a better conception of the success the Winnebago achieved in this regard one must read the trickster cycles of other American Indian tribes. Then it will become clear to what an extent in the Winnebago Wakdjunkaga episodes, incidents, themes and motifs have been integrated, and then the consummate literary ability with which this has been done will stand out sharply. That this literary remodelling and reinterpretation is secondary there can be no question. It is apparently due to special circumstances in Winnebago history and to the existence of a special literary tradition there. To form some idea of what the Wakdjunkaga cycle was originally we must, however, divest our version of all those features which have made it an aboriginal literary masterpiece. This we shall attempt to do in the concluding section of this introduction when we deal with the North American Indian trickster-cycle in general.

The Attitude of the Winnebago toward Wakdjunkaga

Much of the analysis given in [the previous] section is the analysis of an outsider, of a white man, and it goes without saying that such an analysis has its dangers and pitfalls, no matter how well such an outsider thinks he knows an aboriginal culture. It is always best to let members of the culture themselves speak, and I shall, therefore, attempt to present now in a few words what were the ideas and evaluations of contemporary Winnebago – I am speaking of 1908–18 – in regard to Wakdjunkaga and how he was pictured in Winnebago literature. In those years when the new Peyote religion was spreading throughout the tribe and many Winnebago began to make evaluations and re-evaluations of their culture, Wakdjunkaga found both defenders and antagonists. Let me commence with the statement of an old conservative which he prefaced to a myth not included in the cycle being given here:

"The person we call Wakdjunkaga," so he said, "was created by Earthmaker, and he was a genial and good-natured person. Earth-maker created him in this manner. He was likewise a chief. He went on innumerable adventures. It is true that he committed many sins. Some people have, for that reason, insisted that he really was the devil.[6] Yet, actually, when you come to think of it, he never committed any sin at all. Through him it was fulfilled that the earth was to retain for ever its present shape, to him is due the fact that nothing today interferes with its proper functioning. True it is that because of him men die, that because of him men steal, that because of him men abuse women, that they lie and are lazy and unreliable. Yes, he is responsible for all this. Yet one thing he never did: he never went on the warpath, he never waged war.

"Wakdjunkaga roamed about this world and loved all things. He called them all brothers and yet they all abused him. Never could he get the better of anyone. Everyone played tricks on him."

What this particular Winnebago is undoubtedly trying to say is that Wakdjunkaga represented the reality of things, that he was a positive force, a builder, not a destroyer. The reference to his not having gone on the warpath is very illuminating. It indicates that, for this particular individual, Wakdjunkaga's failure to help mankind by destroying those who were plaguing it was not a reprehensible thing because it would have meant violence, meant waging war. If Wakdjunkaga was thus useless after he had prepared the earth for man that is quite intelligible. That men do not understand him, that they misinterpret and laugh at his activities, this too is intelligible. He does not belong in the world of men but to a much older world.

In contrast to this sympathetic attitude we have that of the members of the Peyote rite. They used Wakdjunkaga and his cycle to point a moral. It would be quite erroneous to imagine that this was an entirely new attitude; it existed long before the Peyote rite came into existence. The attitude of the Peyote people is best illustrated in the following homily:

The older people often spoke to us of Wakdjunkaga. However, we never knew what they meant.[7] They told us how, on one occasion, he wrapped a racoon-skin blanket around himself and went to a place where there were many people dancing. There he danced until evening and then he stopped and turned around. There was no one to be seen anywhere, and then he realized that he had mistaken for people dancing the noise made by the wind blowing through the reeds.

So do we Winnebago act. We dance and make a lot of noise but in the end we accomplish nothing.

Once as Wakdjunkaga was going toward a creek he saw a man standing on the other side, dressed in a black suit and pointing his finger at him. He spoke to the man but the latter would not answer. Then he spoke again and again but without receiving any reply. Finally he got angry and said: "See here! I can do that too." So he put on a black coat and pointed his finger across the creek. Thus both of them stood all day. Toward evening, when he looked around again, he noticed that the man across the creek who had been pointing his finger at him was really a tree stump.

"O my! What have I been doing all this time? Why did I not look before I began? No wonder the people call me the Foolish-One!"

Wakdjunkaga was walking around with a pack on his back. As he walked along someone called to him. "Say, we want to sing." "All right," said he. "I am carrying songs in my pack and if you wish to dance, build a large lodge for me with a small hole at the end for an entrance." When it was finished they all went in and Wakdjunkaga followed them. Those who had spoken to him were birds. He told them that, while they were dancing, they were not to open their eyes for if they did their eyes would become red. Whenever a fat bird passed Wakdjunkaga would choke it to death, and if the bird squeaked he would say, "That's it! That's it! Give a whoop!"

After a while one of the birds got somewhat suspicious and opened its eyes just the least little bit. He saw that Wakdjunkaga was choking all the birds he caught to death, and he cried out, "Let all those who can run save themselves for he is killing us!" Then this bird flew out through the top of the house. Wakdjunkaga took the birds he had killed and roasted them. But he did not get a chance to eat them for they were taken away from him.

So are we Winnebago. We like all that is forbidden. We say that we like the Medicine Rite; we say that it is good and yet we keep it secret and forbid people to witness it. We tell members of the society not to speak about it until the world comes to an end. They are, in consequence, afraid to speak of it. We, the Winnebago, are the birds and Wakdjunkaga is Satan.

Once as Wakdjunkaga was going along the road someone spoke to him. He listened and he heard this person saying, "If anyone eats me, faeces will come out of him." Then Wakdjunkaga went up to the object that was talking and said, "What is your name?" "My name is Blows-himself-away." Wakdjunkaga would not believe it and so he ate this object. (It was a shrub.) After a while he blew himself away. He laughed. "O, pshaw! I suppose this is what it meant." As he went along it grew worse and worse, and it was really only after the greatest hardship that he succeeded in returning home.

So are we Winnebago. We travel on this earth all our lives and then, when one of us tastes something that makes him unconscious,[8] we look upon this very thing with suspicion upon regaining consciousness . . .

Here we have Wakdjunkaga as both the glorified image of man and as the tempter. The Winnebago term used for Satan here is Hereshguina. The latter is the great evil spirit who is believed to have existed from the beginning of time, who is as old as Earthmaker and always negating what Earthmaker creates. According to one etymology his name means "he-of-whose-existence-one-is-doubtful". That Wakdjunkaga should be equated with him by the members of the semi-Christian Peyote rite is not strange.

This insistence on Wakdjunkaga's purely negative side is very old attitude. We find it among the Dakota-Sioux and the Ponca. But equally old is the interpretation of his character and of his positive activities to which I have referred before and which finds its best expression in a very old myth, *The Two Boys*.[9] In this myth he is represented as actively helping Hare in his endeavours to secure the powers that are eventually to help one of the great spirits to victory over his enemy. In this myth

Wakdjunkaga is represented as addressing Earthmaker as follows:

Father, it is well. That which we desired, this you have given us precisely as we wished it and without any hesitation. It is my friend Hare who is to see that our purpose is attained. He is the only one who can accomplish it. All the spirits in the lodge from which we have come listen and obey what he says, for his are good thoughts. It is he who helped the human beings before, and he will do this for them too.

To this speech of Wakdjunkaga Earthmaker replies in the following fashion:

Firstborn, you are the oldest of all those I have created. I created you good natured: I made you a sacred person. I sent you to the earth to remain there so that human beings would listen to you, honour you and obey you and that you might teach them by what means they could secure a happy life. This was the purpose for which you were created. What happened to you after you reached the earth that you brought upon yourself alone. It is because of your own actions and activities that you became the butt of everyone's jest, that everyone took advantage of you, even the smallest of insects. How is it then that now you are presenting as a model to be followed that very individual, Hare, who did do what I told him to? You, although you were given the greatest of powers, made light of my creation. It was not anything I told you to do. It is therefore your own fault if people call you the Foolish-One. I created you to do what your friend Hare actually did. I did not create you to injure my creation.

This apparent bewilderment of the Winnebago supreme deity concerning the reasons for Wakdjunkaga's actions and this disavowal of responsibility for them, it will be important to keep in mind.

[. . .]

NOTES

1 The story is presented as "The Winnebago Trickster Cycle" in the volume from which this extract comes, pp. 3–60.
2 W. Jones, *Fox Texts*, Publications of the American Ethnological Society, Leyden, 1907, pp. 315 ff.
3 This incident is probably of European origin.
4 These are not represented as having been created by him.
5 Another version of the same myth states, "He was like a small child crawling about. . . . All one saw of him was his anus. He accomplished no good and in fact injured Earthmaker's creation."
6 He is referring to the followers of the Peyote rite.
7 That is, they did not understand the significance of Wakdjunkaga's actions. The following episode is not found in our version of the myth.
8 He is referring to the eating of the peyote.
9 Cf. Special Publications of Bollingen Foundation, No. 3, Basel, 1954.

20

Witchcraft and Sexual Relations: An Exploration in the Social and Semantic Implications of the Structure of Belief

Raymond C. Kelly

Raymond Kelly, who taught at the University of Michigan, is recognized for the precision with which he builds theoretical arguments from ethnographic material. Kelly's account of Etoro witchcraft is exemplary for the way it situates witchcraft as an integral part of a broader, coherent cultural cosmology. The demonstration draws on structuralist method with its emphasis on conceptual oppositions and analogies. For the Etoro of Papua New Guinea, these operate not simply in the realm of the imagination but are part of a consistent logic of reproduction embracing eating practices, nurturance, and sexual relations. They generate specific anxieties that lead surely to the uncovering of witches, and even the killing of plump infants assumed to be witches. While much of the earlier literature saw witch beliefs as a secondary symbolic expression of the social structure or as operating to maintain social cohesion or regulate conflict, Kelly shows the far deeper roots of witchcraft as an integral dimension of Etoro society. For further development of Kelly's ideas see his magisterial monograph on the Etoro (1993), especially the elaboration of the present essay in Chapter 3. Knauft provides a fine account of sorcery in a neighboring group (1985) and a synthesis of sexual culture in the region (1993).

Witchcraft can be broadly understood as an imaginative inversion of dominant norms and values, especially those associated with nurture, kindness, and reciprocity characteristic of kinship. In a famous phrase, Monica Wilson characterized witch-beliefs as the "standard-

From Raymond C. Kelly, "Witchcraft and Sexual Relations: An Exploration in the Social and Semantic Implications of the Structure of Belief," in Paula Brown and Georgeda Buchbinder, eds., *Man and Woman in the New Guinea Highlands* (Washington, DC: American Anthropological Association, 1976), pp. 36–53. Abridged.

ized nightmare of a group" (1970 [1951]: 263). Although the best early account, Evans-Pritchard's *Witchcraft, Oracles, and Magic among the Azande* (1937, 1976), emphasized the logic of practice and the self-sustaining quality of a belief system, most mid-century studies concerned themselves with the purported functions, either psychological or social, of witchcraft accusations. Historical accounts attempted to explain epidemics of accusations and why certain categories of people are targeted. Marwick (1970) is the standard collection from this period. Kapferer (1997) interprets the elaborate anti-sorcery rites of Sri Lanka through a phenomenological account of the experiences of suffering from sorcery and being released from it, while Schneider (1990) is a stimulating broader analysis of the decline in witchcraft in Europe. Recent Africanist work addresses witchcraft in relation to modernity, severe economic instability, rapid social change, and the excesses of the state (Comaroff and Comaroff, eds., 1993, Geschiere 1997, Weiss 1998). See also chapters 35 and 38 below by Taussig and De Boeck, respectively.

Students are often confused by the diverse referents of the term "witchcraft" (Wicca, the European and American witch trials, western folklore and media images of figures on broomsticks, and the various ethnographic examples), and there is no reason why they should all be lumped together. Nevertheless, contemporary moral panics in North America and northern Europe concerning such matters as child abuse can best be understood by drawing on an anthropological perspective informed by studies of witchcraft (La Fontaine 1998). On practicing, self-described "witches" in England see Luhrmann (1989).

This paper is directed to the general objectives of delineating the place of witchcraft within a larger system of belief and – more importantly – exploring the significance of interrelationships between spheres or domains of belief within such wider contexts. Both areas of inquiry are susceptible to quite extensive exposition and I here attempt to probe only a restricted segment of each. The specific objectives of the present effort are to analyze the relationship (within a New Guinea culture) between two discrete but interconnected domains of belief pertaining to witchcraft and sexual relations, respectively, and to elucidate the semantic interdependence between these domains which is derived from both their mutual embeddedness within a larger system of ideas and their analogous positions within this system. Etoro thought and cosmology are ordered by a central and fundamental concept: that life and death are complementary and reciprocal aspects of a larger process whereby a spiritual "life-force" is transmitted from one human being to another. Acts of witchcraft and acts of sexual intercourse are the two modes of interaction through which this transmission is effected. Moreover, "life" and "death" are the reciprocal terms of the transaction in each case. Relations between sexual partners are comparable to those between witch and victim by virtue of this analogic conjunction, and the idioms in which each sphere of interaction is (respectively) grounded therefore stand in a metaphoric relation to each other. The juxtaposition of witchcraft and sexual relations enriches the cultural meaning of each and also provides a mechanism for projecting the characteristics of actors in one domain upon their analogic counterparts in the other, thereby contributing to the cultural delineation of social positions and the relationships between social positions. These semantic and social definitions are not directly specified by identifications (i.e., that x *is* y), but are products of the structure of the belief system itself, viewed in a wider context, in terms of metaphoric relations between domains.

The Etoro, who number about 400, inhabit the southern slopes of Mt. Sisa which lies along the southern edge of the central cordillera of New Guinea facing onto the Great Papuan Plateau. The residential unit in Etoro society is a longhouse community (of 35 to 40 people) which is ideally composed of two patrilineage segments linked by sister exchange. The classificatory terminological system imposes this idealized organization on diverse empirical arrangements such that every community is constituted as two sets of "siblings" who have married each other's "sisters" and "brothers." The longhouse itself . . . is divided into a communal section (toward the front) and separately enclosed men's and women's sleeping quarters in the rear. Widows may sit only along the outer walls of the communal section and may enter the dwelling only by side doors. The bachelors' sleeping quarters transect the men's and women's sections at the rear of the longhouse. This spatial arrangement of social categories . . . is concordant with the semantic delineation of their interrelationships discussed herein.

The lineages which enter into local organization are small and of limited genealogical span, seldom encompassing agnates more distantly related than FFBSS. "Brother" relationships between these patrilines are based on matrilateral sibling-ship rather than descent (cf. Kelly 1973: 139–92). Each patriline possesses a number of associated *Sigisato* spirits who are connected to the descent group through co-ownership of a territory from which both the spirit group and agnatic group draw their sustenance. (The *Sigisatos* occupy the bodies of cassowaries by day and subsist on the fruits and nuts of lineage lands.) The souls of members of the agnatic group are implanted in them by their associated *Sigisatos*, and the latter also assist and protect lineage members in a number of ways, of which several relating to witchcraft may be mentioned. Acting through a medium, a *Sigisato* cures illness resulting from witchcraft, confirms the identity of the witch responsible for a death, and may also decide the witch's fate by proclaiming, "I give you this person to kill." (For amplification of this very brief outline of selected aspects of social organization relevant to my present concerns see

Kelly 1973; discussion of the role of witchcraft in social processes such as lineage fission and local group formation may also be found there.)

The Etoro believe every human being to be possessed of two discrete spiritual aspects: the *ausulubo*, an immaterial spirit double, and the *hame*, a life-force or animating principle. Both are imparted to a child (at and before birth, respectively) by a *Sigisato* spirit associated with his or her lineage, and both are (jointly) immortal, persisting beyond the grave in the form of a *Kesame* or spirit of the dead. These spiritual aspects are significant to the present analysis insofar as they are affected by witchcraft and sexual relations, and will be examined from that perspective.

The *ausulubo* replicates the possessor's physical body in form but lacks corporeal substance. The same term is employed with reference to an individual's shadow, reflected image, and the echo of his voice, and these may be conceived as visible (or aural) manifestations of the *ausulubo*. All three are characterized by qualities of duplication and separability which are essential attributes of this spiritual aspect.

The *ausulubo* is normally contained within the owner's physical body but possesses a capacity for conscious independent activity under certain circumstances. The average individual's spirit double may wander only in dreams; its movements tend to be restricted to the immediate vicinity, and it does not normally venture into the spirit realms frequented by mediums. In contrast, the *ausulubo* of a medium may go on extended excursions to a variety of spirit worlds while he sleeps, during a seance, or even while his body carries out a normal routine of daily activities (although in a somewhat distracted manner). A witch (*mugwabe*) is likewise capable of leading a double life, and acts of witchcraft are generally perpetrated by an *ausulubo* operating apart from the body of its owner. The spirit double is invisible to an individual in his normal state, and the witch can therefore carry out his nefarious activities without being seen or identified by his victim or others present at the time. However, objects employed by the *ausulubo* of a witch (e.g., an ax) can be seen, and the sound of twigs snapping as the invisible spirit double approaches through the forest are also audible. In addition, the witch's *ausulubo* (which differs from that of normal individuals) gives off a pale glow, or *moropa*, that betrays the presence of a witch without revealing his (or her) identity.

The commission of an act of witchcraft entails the infliction of some injury upon the spirit double of the victim. In the typical case, some foreign object is thrust or impelled into the *ausulubo* of an individual, causing illness. The witch may then proceed to dismember the *ausulubo* of the weakened victim, limb by limb, on successive nights. These parts are either consumed by the witch or hidden for later consumption. Removal of the heart and liver (of the *ausulubo*) causes the final demise (and this may occur without the intervening dismemberment).

When the spirit double is injured, illness afflicts the corresponding part of the corporeal body; this provision applies to witch as well as victim. Thus a witch whose *ausulubo* has been burned with a torch or firebrand in the course of an act of witchcraft can later be identified by the analogous burns on his physical body. An arrow shot into the heart of the witch's spirit double will likewise kill the witch himself. Events such as these occur only in myths and legends, but are nevertheless indicative of the perceived relationship between the soundness of the *ausulubo* and that of its corporeal counterpart. It is also important to note that acts of witchcraft are perpetrated upon the *ausulubo* of the victim by that of the witch, such that the entire transaction takes place on what may be called the *ausulubo* "plane of existence".

The *hame* is the second major component of an individual's spiritual constitution. The *hame* embodies the animating principle and vital energy of human existence. It is formless, like the wind, and is manifested in breath (designated by the same term) in much the same way that the *ausulubo* is manifested in a person's shadow or reflection. Strength, vigor, and vitality emanate from the *hame*. However, it lacks consciousness as well as form, and is incapable of operating as an independent entity apart from the corporeal body and

ausulubo which are mutually animated by it. This dual role is evident in accounts of witchcraft. When a witch dismembers the limbs of his victim's spirit double, the corporeal limbs are weakened by the loss of both their essence and their vitality (corresponding to elements of the *ausulubo* and *hame*, respectively). Although the *hame* is thereby diminished, it nevertheless continues to provide a reduced quantity of vital energy to the corporeal flesh which remains – for it is imminent in both the physical and spirit body.

A *sigisato* spirit animates a fetus by implanting a nascent *hame* within it (and, at birth, imparts an *ausulubo* to the child). At the moment of death, the residual *hame* is exhaled with the last breath and is subsequently merged with the *ausulubo* to form a single entity which persists as a *Kesame*, or spirit of the dead. The *ausulubo* – which has previously been maimed, dismembered, and consumed by a witch – is somehow reconstituted and united with the analogously traumatized *hame* through a mysterious supernatural process described by a special verb (*keketosa*), elucidated by the paraphrase "many things become one." However, the manner in which this is effected is said to be beyond human understanding (perhaps because it is contradictory to other articles of belief). The evil spiritual aspect of a witch that distinguishes him (or her) from normal individuals is segregated in this process and ascends to the heavens to become a star, glowing with the pale light of the *moropa*. Thus purified of evil, the witch's *hame-ausulubo* descends to the river and associated underworld which is the domain of the *Kesames*.

The degree of strength and vitality which emanates from the *hame* varies during the course of an individual's lifetime. The *hame* may be conceived, in this respect, as a reservoir of life-force which can be augmented or diminished. This occurs in two ways – through witchcraft and through sexual intercourse. When a witch removes a limb from an individual's *ausulubo* and consumes it, he incorporates a portion of the victim's life-force, and thereby augments the strength of his *hame*, while depleting that of his victim. The witch grows uncommonly large and acquires added physical strength and vigor through this appropriation. The children he (or she) begets "as a witch" are also physically large and are themselves identifiable as *kagomano* or witch-children by this quality. (This is one of two ways witchcraft is acquired, as is discussed further below.)[1]

The corresponding diminution of the victim's life-force is evident from the weakened condition accompanying illness and is also registered by labored breathing, short-windedness, coughing, chest pains, and the like. Breath is a physical manifestation of the *hame* which reflects its spiritual condition, and respiratory difficulties are taken to be indicative of depletion of the *hame*'s reservoir of life-force. Labored breathing and short-windedness are onomatopoetically referred to as *hame hah hah*, and this condition is generally recognized as the outward sign of a concomitant spiritual disability. It is, moreover, a consequence of sexual intercourse as well as a result of bewitchment.

Every adult male possesses a limited quantity of life-force which resides in his body as a whole, but is especially concentrated in his semen. A portion of this is expended in each act of sexual intercourse so that a man's reservoir of life-force is gradually depleted over the course of his lifetime. The vital energy which emanates from the *hame* is correspondingly diminished, rendering the subject enervated and enfeebled. An elderly man – who was once strong and vigorous – is thus short-winded and suffers *hame hah hah* when climbing hills or engaging in other strenuous activity. The Etoro also point out that this self-same shortness of breath is experienced upon completion of the sexual act itself; the temporary condition becomes general as semen is progressively lost.

The life-force which a man expends in sexual intercourse is transferred, through the process of conception, to the children he begets (or, in the absence of conception, is lost). This serves to augment the nascent *hame* implanted in each child by the *Sigisato* spirits, and contributes to their early growth. Pre-pubescent boys are inseminated by their elders so as to provide them with semen (which they lack), and also to supply the life-force or vital energy they require in order to grow, mature, and develop

manly strength. The *hame* of the youth is augmented by this acquisition (while that of his inseminator is depleted). The growth-inducing properties attributed to semen are clearly expressed in these beliefs.

It is evident here that witchcraft and sexual relations are mutually embedded in a single conceptual system insofar as they constitute the two modes of interaction through which life-force is transmitted from one human being to another. The interconnection is particularly well-illustrated by the aforementioned belief that the child of a witch will be physically large. This follows from the fact that the parent has appropriated the life-force of others through acts of witchcraft, and is thus capable of transmitting an enriched infusion of this to his offspring in the process of conception. The witch-child grows large in the womb as a consequence of this. To explain why a large infant is the child of a witch clearly requires an understanding of the ideology of sexual relations as well as the ideology of witchcraft, for the two interpenetrate. However, the relation goes deeper than this, insofar as acts of intercourse are in some respects equivalent to acts of witchcraft, such that each stands in a metaphoric relation to the other. The semantic implications of this will be elucidated after beliefs concerning sexual relations are more fully explored.

The association of sexual intercourse with impairment of the *hame* is expressed in a number of restrictions which govern male-female relations and circumscribe the post-copulatory interaction of a man with his fellows. A man who has had intercourse with a woman must refrain from offering food or tobacco smoke (from his bamboo pipe) to another man throughout the remainder of the day. Should an individual consume such food or inhale smoke from the pipe of a copulator, he will experience *hame hah hah* and, in the latter case, a coughing spell as well.

Women are at all times enjoined from stepping over men's personal possessions, pipes and tobacco, and especially food and the items employed in its cooking and consumption. Thus a woman must never step over split firewood or sit on the woodpiles at the front of the longhouse. If a man consumes a morsel of food cooked by such firewood (or smokes tobacco which has likewise been subjected to this negative influence), he will suffer *hame hah hah* and a general lack of strength while pursuing his daily activities. Should a woman step over his ax, it will become dull.

A man must avoid seeing or coming into contact with a newborn child for 17 days. If he fails to do so, he will suffer especially severe *hame hah hah* and may die as a consequence. In addition, the father of the child should not offer food or pipe to any male for seven days. The growth of a youth would be forestalled by consumption of such food or smoke; an adult man would experience *hame hah hah*. In all these above instances, the enjoined behavior is *tobi*, i.e., stringently forbidden or taboo.

The Etoro do not espouse any beliefs concerning female pollution or the contamination of objects through the addition of impure substances or essences which would account for the negative effects attributed to violation of these regulations, and I would suggest that they are best interpreted as extensions of the basic concept of depletion discussed above. When a woman steps over an object, it "passes between her thighs," and this is a symbolic equivalent of intercourse. An object such as an ax thus loses its cutting edge, or essential property, in the same way that a man loses the essential property of his masculinity in copulation, i.e., his semen. The pipe smoke of a man who has recently copulated, and food, firewood, etc., subjected to symbolic intercourse all have the same effect on a man who internalizes them as intercourse itself; they are capable of transmitting the depletion signified by *hame hah hah*. These objects are, in some sense, negatively charged with respect to masculinity, and they have the capacity to drain or negate the life-force of a male who consumes them. A newborn child has the most powerful antithetical effect as a consequence of having lain within the womb for such as extended period. It is an especially potent carrier of depletion which can be transmitted to males by the mere sight of it.

Retrospective analysis suggests an important corollary to these effects of the gestation period upon the child. The Etoro note that males attain physical maturity later than females, and are particularly concerned to promote and insure male growth and development through insemination. Although I did not grasp the association during my fieldwork, recorded conversations strongly suggest that the perceived cause of this retarded male development which so concerns the Etoro is the birth of men from women; late maturation is a consequence of the adverse effects upon males of close contact with the depleting powers of femininity in the womb – adverse effects which the early-maturing female offspring never experience. The fact that food received from the father of a newborn child forestalls the growth of boys (but not girls) is consistent with this notion. The cumulative depletion of the father is manifested in the event of birth itself, since a child possesses life-force as a direct consequence of his father's loss of it. The state of a male parent after birth is comparable in nature to that of a man after copulation (although intensified in degree).

Although women have a weakening influence upon men (directly or indirectly) under certain specific conditions of actual and symbolic intercourse, they are not a source of pollution and therefore do not pose a continuous threat to male well-being. The absence of any beliefs concerning menstrual pollution is significant in this respect. Women do not move to physically separate quarters during menstruation, although they do avoid the communal section of the longhouse (and generally remain in confinement within the women's section for several days). Men do not perform protective magic to counteract female contamination, and there are no group (or individual) purification rites for males such as those reported for other areas of Melanesia, particularly the New Guinea Highlands (cf. Meggitt 1964; Allen 1967).

While intercourse is depleting, the female persona is not contaminating, and men therefore need not avoid contact with women *per se*. It follows that the general tenor of male-female relations is neither constrained nor hedged with anxiety. Men and women mingle and interact freely in gardening, in sago working, and in the communal portion of the longhouse during the course of daily activities. Women are careful to observe the prohibitions on stepping over certain items (noted above), but this does not restrict or constrain their movements, since food is normally kept out of the way in net bags hung from walls or house posts, and men's possessions are similarly placed or are stored in the men's quarters. If a woman does accidentally step across food, men would refrain from eating it but would not be exercised by the incident (except perhaps in the case of highly valued game or pork). Should a man's pipe be affected, he would set it aside for several days (and borrow another) but would be unlikely to discard it unless particularly concerned about his health at the time. Although the owner of the pipe might express mild irritation, other men tend to regard the situation as a humorous one. Jests made in such contexts stem from the prevalent view that a man who is truly strong (*keloi*) can withstand the weakening influence of women without noticeable ill effects. This view is also relevant to the male attitude toward marriage and polygyny. A man who has two wives and nevertheless remains vigorous in spite of the resultant double dose of depletion (through intercourse) takes pride in his demonstrated strength and vitality, and is admired for this by others.

The male attitude toward heterosexual intercourse itself is charged with ambivalence and ambiguity. Men privately nurture variable degrees of anxiety concerning the debilitating effects of copulation. However, they can quite effectively alleviate such anxiety by engaging in the very act that they fear and not experiencing the negative consequences believed to follow from it. A man thereby develops self-confidence in his residual vitality which is at once comforting and highly precarious. His attitude will shift rapidly to one of deep concern if he feels enervated or develops a cough or other respiratory sign of depletion.

The opposite poles of male ambivalence are well-illustrated by the events of an adulterous liaison (as related to me by an informant). A young man in his early twenties was secretly trysting with his FBW. When this was discovered, he temporarily fled to another community to avoid his uncle's wrath, returning after several days when compensation (of one mother-of-pearl shell) had been arranged by his father. At the time this was publicly paid, the cuckolded husband made a speech in which he vividly described the depleting effects of intercourse to his BS and other young men present at the time. Toward the conclusion of this harangue, he dramatically lifted his wife's skirt and exposed her genitals for all to behold. Several young men (including my informant) retched forthwith and the adulterous youth himself became queasy and visibly discomfited. Older men turned their faces aside with expressions of disgust, while the chastened wife wept from shame and repudiation. The point of this tale is that the spontaneous vomiting clearly indicates a very real and deep-seated anxiety, while the adulterous liaison documents the capacity to disregard it, at least temporarily. (The parties to the transgression continued to co-reside without further incident.)

Men are protected from undue depletion (and anxiety pertaining to same) by prolonged periods of enjoined abstinence. Heterosexual relations are narrowly circumscribed with respect to permitted times (and places) of occurrence. In all, copulation is prohibited (*tobi*) for an estimated 205 to 260 days a year. The specific proscriptions and the imputed results of their violation are:

(1)   Throughout the period from the commencement of a new garden until the trees have been felled (at the end of the fourth month). If this taboo is violated, the crops will not mature properly, yields will be poor, and pigs will ravage the garden.

(2)   From the time a sago palm is cut until processing is completed (lest yields be poor).

(3)   Whenever deadfall traps or snares have been set for wild pigs, marsupials, or cassowaries (else little or nothing will be caught).

(4)   During any period when sago grubs are maturing in an unprocessed palm cut for this purpose. If this restriction is not observed, the growth of any youth who consumes the grubs will be stunted.

(5)   When a new longhouse is under construction (else the project will be beset with difficulties).

(6) While a trading party from the longhouse is carrying out an expedition and for four days prior to their departure (or little of what is sought will be obtained).

These prohibitions are linked to virtually all major aspects of the productive economy – gardening, sago processing, and trapping are nearly tantamount to subsistence. Exchange and construction are not omitted. Moreover, these activities tend to be segregated in time so that there is relatively little overlap between one proscribed period and another. This imposes very substantial limitations on the frequency of heterosexual relations and there is, moreover, indirect evidence of general adherence to the prohibitions. Eight of ten births which occurred within the tribe during a 15-month period took place over a short span of 3 1/2 months. Although the economic preoccupations of all ten pairs of parents at the times of conception are not precisely known, the distribution of births is predictable in terms of the seasonal cycle of subsistence activity. (The birth rate itself is also rather low.)

Heterosexual intercourse should take place only in the forest, never within a garden, in a garden dwelling, in the longhouse, or the general vicinity of the longhouse. (Even in the forest one cannot be entirely at ease, for the Etoro maintain that death adders are offended by the noxious odor of intercourse and are particularly likely to strike a couple thus engaged.) Violation of the prohibition on copulation in and around the longhouse is a serious offense which may provoke public rebuke and expulsion from the community. The following incident is a case in point.

A widow and an older bachelor (aged 28) had been carrying on an affair, sporadically, for over a year. This was a subject of gossip and private disapproval, but no public action. It is not uncommon for younger widows to solicit the attentions of marriageable bachelors; indeed, this is frequently a prelude to remarriage. However, when the couple was discovered violating the locational prohibitions by copulating at the spring near the longhouse, and subsequently within the men's section (!) of the longhouse, the community was outraged. The close kin of the transgres-

sors were impelled by public opinion to put a stop to this immoral behavior. When the community foregathered for the usual afternoon meal (several days after the latest offense), the widow and bachelor were set upon and pummeled by three close kinsmen to the accompaniment of a chorus of recriminations and verbal abuse from the remaining members of the longhouse. Both ran off to take refuge (separately) with kinsmen at other locations. The bachelor returned about three days later and resumed his residence at the community after a public statement of contrition; the widow remained elsewhere.

The prohibition of heterosexual relations in the environs of the longhouse is also enforced upon the canine population. On several different occasions, the members of the longhouse community where I resided spent the better part of the day throwing stones at a bitch in heat and her coterie of male admirers in order to drive them into the forest. The women were especially vigilant in this effort to ensure proper behavior on the part of the dogs. In the first incident described above, the women were also most adamant in demanding that strong measures be taken to reestablish moral behavior. These data are significant in that they connote female acceptance of and adherence to the norms described herein.

These locational restrictions emphasize the fact that heterosexuality has no place within the community (or in inhabited areas), and is properly conducted only in the wild. It is fundamentally antisocial behavior in the strict sense of the term. The post-partum and post-copulatory taboos noted above accentuate this theme inasmuch as they proscribe the customary sharing of food and tobacco which is one of the central moral values of community life. Heterosexuality segregates a man and places him outside of society and, especially, outside the social community of males.

The imputed effects which are said to follow from violation of the (activity-related) temporal prohibitions are also instructive. Copulation diminishes the yields of gardens, sago palms, traps, and trading expeditions, just as it diminishes a man's life-force and depletes his *hame*. The central belief which is (once again) expressed here is also explicitly enunciated with respect to the undesirable effects said to result from copulation in gardens. The Etoro maintain that heterosexual intercourse in a garden will cause the crops to wither and die. The general consequences of heterosexuality are death and depletion. However, this is only one component of a complementary opposition between heterosexuality and homosexuality, for the Etoro also maintain that homosexual relations in a garden will cause the crops to grow, flourish, and yield bountifully.

One of the conceptual cornerstones of Etoro cosmology is the view that accretion at one point in the system entails depletion elsewhere. Life cannot be created *ex nihilo*, and the birth (and growth) of one generation are inextricably linked to the senescence and death of its predecessor. Life and death are complementary and reciprocal aspects of a larger process. In the context of this general concept, the gradual depletion of life-force which men experience in heterosexual intercourse is, at the same time, a precondition for the perpetuation of life through birth. The transference of life-force is similarly a precondition for the growth and maturation of boys into men.

Boys differ most importantly from men in that they completely lack the most critical and essential attribute of manhood, i.e., semen. The Etoro believe, moreover, that semen does not occur naturally in boys and must be "planted" in them. If one does not plant sweet potato vines, then surely no sweet potatoes will come up in the garden and, similarly, semen must be planted in boys if they are to possess it as men. Moreover, all aspects of manliness are seen as consequences of this acquisition. A youth is continually inseminated from about age ten until he reaches his early to mid-twenties. This period is also marked by rapid growth in stature, increased physical strength and endurance, the sprouting of facial and body hair, and the development of masculine skills and characteristics such as hunting ability and courageousness in war. These empirically observable changes are uniformly regarded as the direct results of insemination. (This is accomplished orally. The boy manipulates the man to the point of ejaculation and consumes the semen. The above effects are only realized through ingestion, and therefore

are not applicable to heterosexual relations: women do not acquire strength, etc., in this way.)

The recipient of semen in homosexual intercourse experiences beneficial effects which are the exact converse of the negative effects suffered as a consequence of loss of semen in heterosexual intercourse. While the *hame* of a man is weakened and depleted by copulation, the *hame* of a youth is correspondingly strengthened by insemination. Prior to this, boys are short-winded and tire readily; afterwards they possess strength and endurance. These effects are thought to be cumulatively manifested over the maturation period but are also apparent on specific occasions. For example, young men say that they are able to fell trees in a new garden for hours on end without tiring after they have consumed semen.

These ... beliefs ... are all relatable to a general equation whereby receiving semen : life, growth, and vitality :: losing semen : weakness, senescence, and death. However, receiving semen is also culturally associated with homosexuality, and the loss of it with heterosexuality such that the former is to life as the latter is to death. This opposition is expressed in myth, and also in the previously cited beliefs that heterosexual relations in a garden will cause the crops to wither and die, while homosexual relations will cause them to flourish and yield bountifully. Although informants report that loss of semen in both types of intercourse is equally enervating, the negative effects adhere only to heterosexual relations in formal ideology. Thus there are no rules which prohibit a man from offering food or smoke to others after homosexual intercourse, and there are no prohibitions which circumscribe such relations with respect to time and place. Men and boys may properly engage in sexual relations in the men's section of the longhouse (and in gardens) on any day of the year. Indeed, this is essential if the youths are to grow and attain manhood.[2]

The personal characteristics which a youth develops as he matures are believed to correspond to those of his inseminator. If a man is strong (*keloi*), vigorous in his advanced years, a proficient hunter and trapper, and/or a courageous warrior, then his protege will possess identical qualities and abilities upon attaining manhood. Witchcraft is also transmitted in this manner. The semen of a witch is said to contain minute frogs and worms which are the seed of witchcraft. Acquisition of these predisposes the *ausulubo* of a witch to develop a mutant evil spiritual aspect: the *tohorora*. This distinguishes a witch from normal individuals and endows one with the extraordinary capabilities that enable him (or her) to perform acts of witchcraft. (Transmission of witchcraft between women is discussed below.) The *tohorora* is located or concentrated in the heart and liver, and gives off a cold, phosphorescent light (the *moropa*) that is sometimes visible when a witch is active at night. This can also be seen when the heart of an executed witch is cut out in order to confirm his (or her) guilt. The organ (which is displayed on a stake) is said to glow like an ember with the light of the *moropa*. The frogs and worms that are the seed of witchcraft are visibly present in the auricles and ventricles respectively. However, the acquisition of these frogs and worms is not sufficient, in itself, to engender the development of the *tohorora*; the seed of witchcraft must also be nurtured by the malice and ill-will in a person's heart. The individual thus bears the ultimate responsibility for the mutation of his soul that makes him a witch.[3]

Youths are initiated into manhood in their late teens or early twenties, when they are physically mature (although not fully bearded). At intervals of about three years, all young men who have reached this stage of development go into seclusion at a lodge which is especially constructed for this purpose in an isolated area near the margin of the primary forest on the upper slopes of Mt. Sisa . . .

A generalized insemination of the youths by older men . . . takes place at the seclusion lodge. This is important in that it makes it impossible to retrospectively determine who may have transmitted the seed of witchcraft to whom. If a young man is named as a witch, his principal inseminator is not necessarily implicated. Similarly, any attempt to identify a particular individual as the source of witchcraft in a specific instance implicates many young men, some of whom are likely to be close kinsmen of the individual drawing the inference. Attempts to trace lines of transmission are thus avoided by everyone. Confirmed witches are excluded from the seclusion lodge proceedings, and those who participate are presumed to be free of witchcraft. Young men who are subsequently accused are thought to have secretly consorted with witches outside this context.

Little information is available concerning the beliefs and activities of women, since it is impossible, in the context of Etoro culture, for a male anthropologist to develop an informant relationship with a female. Moreover, each sex is supposed to be totally ignorant of the private activities of the other, and men generally respond to inquiries by saying that "only the women know what the women do." However, women are thought to engage in some form of homosexual activities and to transmit the seed of witchcraft in this way. Men appear to be genuinely ignorant concerning the processes of female maturation, and do not know whether this occurs naturally or as a consequence of transmission of substance. Some informants thought it plausible that girls obtained menstrual blood from mature women in the same way that boys obtained semen from men; others pointed out that females possess blood from birth (even though they do not menstruate until later), while boys completely lack semen. The *Sigisato* spirits determine the sex of a child by implanting a male or female *ausulubo* within it. Sex is therefore an aspect of the soul, and males and females are spiritually differentiated. The female *hame* is considered to be weak and underdeveloped, so that women are always short-winded in comparison with men.

In the preceding discussion, I have attempted to establish and document the point that an array of Etoro beliefs concerning sexual relations may be interrelated through a general equation whereby receiving semen : life, growth, and vitality :: losing semen : weakness, senescence, and death. This formulation also constitutes the specific ideational content of a more general and fundamental conceptual orientation of Etoro cosmology, *viz.* the concept that the total system is closed and bounded such that accretion at one node necessarily entails a corresponding depletion at another (and vice versa). This general concept is also expressed in the domain of witchcraft belief as is evident from material adduced earlier. A witch consumes portions of the *ausulubo* and *hame* of his victim, and thus grows unusually large and vigorous, while the victim is weakened and enfeebled by the resultant illness. The *hame* of the victim is depleted (as evidenced by respiratory distress), while that of the witch is augmented such that he fathers children of exceptional size. After the victim's demise, the witch is thought to return to the burial platform by night to fatten himself on the flesh of the corpse. An executed witch (and external enemies killed in warfare) are subject to cannibalism, although other members of the Etoro tribe are not. The flesh of the witch is consumed just as he consumes the flesh of his deceased victims. (However, no spiritual elements or personal attributes are transferred in cannibalism, and this view is understandable insofar as the soul of a witch is inherently evil and his characteristics totally undesirable.)[4]

There is a further correspondence between these two domains of belief which follows from the structurally analogous position of witchcraft and sexual relations as alternate modes through which life-force is transmitted. This brings the two sets of belief into an immediate relation such that each is partially defined with reference to the other. This is evident when the equation noted above is reformulated at a more general level, *viz.* augmentation of the *hame* : life, growth, and vitality :: depletion of the *hame* : weakness, senescence, and death. Homosexual relations (from the standpoint of a youth), acts of witchcraft (from the perspective of the witch), and conception (*vis-à-vis* the child) are all interchangeable in terms of augmenting the *hame*, and are equally productive of life, growth, and vitality for the youth, witch, and child, respectively. Similarly, homosexual and heterosexual relations (for an adult man) and acts of witchcraft (from the perspective of the victim) are interchangeable with respect to depletion of the *hame* and the effects which follow from this. There is, moreover, a threefold identification of youth, witch, and woman as *agents* of depletion in addition to the

identification of child, youth, and witch as beneficiaries thereof. The logical derivatives of these identities are the oppositional equations:

child : father
protege : inseminator   ::   witch : victim
(youth)
woman : man
(wife)   (husband)

All these invidious comparisons are applicable to Etoro thought and behavior in some degree, although each is elaborated in a somewhat different way, and is thus modified in its final ramifications. This elaboration takes the form of internal differentiation by contrasts (and further similarities) among the four terms which are here identified (i.e., child, youth, woman, and witch).

A witch is the epitome of maliciousness and antisocial selfishness, for he (or she) feeds on the souls and bodies of others out of spite, and with full intent to cause harm; he sates his gluttony as well as his hate and grows large and vigorous at others' expense. A woman, on the other hand, does not augment her *hame* through heterosexual relations. The loss of life-force a man suffers in this context contributes to the conception and early growth of his children. A woman is thus an agent of depletion but not a beneficiary and, conversely, a child is beneficiary but not agent. Neither manifests the intentional maliciousness of the witch, and the diminution of a man's *hame* is here viewed as part of the essential tragedy of human existence that senescence and death are preconditions for the perpetuation of life through birth.

However, excessive copulation and sexual relations which are not productive of offspring deplete a man to no end. A woman who encourages, entices, or demands her husband to engage in needless copulation – from which he alone will suffer – thereby approaches the purely negative role of witch. She sates her sexual appetite selfishly, knowingly causing harm, and perhaps with malicious intent. (This connotation applies with double force to a woman who consorts with an immature youth whose growth and development will be permanently arrested by loss of semen.) The identification of woman and witch therefore refers in only a restricted sense to an inherent quality of womanhood while being fully applicable to the potential characteristics of aggressive and demanding feminity and unregulated feminine sexuality. The association thus contributes to a constraining delineation of the female role and is not merely a static negative characterization.

Witchcraft also has its primeval origin in the epitome of unregulated sexuality – the act of incest. Moreover, the myth which recounts the event emphasizes the responsibility of the woman for releasing this agent of death upon mankind.

> At a longhouse community of the distant past there lived a brother and sister (of about age 8 to 10). One day they went to the forest together and copulated secretly there. The girl became pregnant and grew large with the child. "What have you been doing?" an elder man asked here. But she didn't answer: she turned her head aside and said nothing. In due course she gave birth to a boy. Secretly, she suckled it at her breast. The elders did not know of this at first, but one day a man came upon her as she was nursing the child. As he drew near, she tried unsuccessfully to conceal the baby from him.
>
> They had become witches, these three, and the elders decided they must be killed. The men caught the brother and sister and struck them and they cried out in pain as they died. Then, for the first time, the men heard the (now characteristic) whistle of the witch from the other side of the longhouse. "Tua, tua" shrilled the witch-child as he slipped away. "Now we have witches and men will die," an old man lamented. "Before today there were none, but these two became witches and henceforth we will die."

According to Etoro exegesis, the precocious siblings were transformed into witches by their incestuous conjunction itself, and the first witch-child (or *kagomano*) was the fruit of their union. Thus incest begat witchcraft, and introduced sickness and death into the world. Before this time, men were immortal.

It is important to note that the agent of death is "of woman born." The girl refuses to confess her evil act when queried by her elders, and later conceals the child from them. Worst

of all, she suckles the witch-child rather than submitting it to infanticide (as would be expected under the circumstances). By not only bringing death into the world but nurturing it at her breast, she thus transfers to women the ultimate responsibility for mankind's lost immortality. It is also significant that the evil of unregulated sexuality (here represented in its most extreme form) is ontologically prior to the evil of witchcraft.

The widow and children of a deceased man have both contributed to his demise (as agent and beneficiary of his depletion) and are subject to additional food restrictions as a result. About 77 percent (65/83) of the edible native taxa of game animals may not be consumed by a widow, and 71 percent (59/83) are likewise prohibited to the sons and daughters of the deceased below the ages of 17 and 12, respectively. Only approximately 35 percent of the total animal protein in the diet is available to these two most heavily restricted social categories of individuals, while the wives and children of living men have access to 97 percent and 74 percent, respectively (cf. Kelly 1973: 56–9). These restrictions are not integral to the three-year mourning period for widows as they extend beyond it. They are maintained until a woman remarries, or indefinitely if she does not (with the exception of one taboo which is removed when she passes childbearing age). The children are relieved of their taboos at about the time they reach puberty.

These regulations are significant in that they follow from the joint responsibility of widow and child for a husband/father's death, and also impose disabilities consequent upon this responsibility. To be "eaten" is a euphemism for sexual intercourse (of either variety), and a man is indeed spiritually consumed by it. It is therefore appropriate that the consumption of those who have partaken of him be restricted after his demise. The food taboos also demonstrate the impact of the ideological features under consideration upon behavior outside their immediate domain.

The position of the uninitiated youth differs from that of a woman or child in that he is both agent and beneficiary of his inseminator's depletion. However, frequent homosexual intercourse within the context of this relationship is not negatively regarded, since a youth grows in size, strength, and prowess in direct proportion to his consumption of life-force (and is also thought to require a heavy dosage in order to attain full maturity). Here again we encounter the tragic necessities of human existence. The full association of youth with witch turns on unregulated sexuality in this instance as well, but concerns inappropriate liaisons (and not excess within sanctioned relationships). It is the youth who consorts with others in his age class – and enhances his own growth and vitality at their expense – that replicates the behavior of the witch. The immature young men from whom the culprit draws life-force will suffer arrested or retarded development at the least, and may well die young as a result. The youth who garners this additional life-force manifests precocious, preternatural maturation, and will not only reach puberty at the early age of 13 or 14 but will also possess a fairly well-developed beard shortly thereafter (more specifically, the beard of a man in his early to mid-twenties). Any individual who possesses this trait (i.e., early beardedness) is thought to have taken advantage of other immature young men, and is included within the cultural category *sa:go* which designates such transgressors. *Sa:gos* are not only like witches but are universally deemed to *be* witches, and especially vicious ones at that. As in the case of women, the association of uninitiated youth with witch is fully applicable only with respect to a potential characteristic, and thus serves to regulate and bound sexual behavior.

The category *sa:go* is a particularly important one inasmuch as it represents an intersection of the ideologies of witchcraft and sexual relations. A *sa:go* is deemed a witch as a consequence of his sexual transgressions. While all *sa:gos* are thought to be witches, the converse does not hold, and the category thus contributes in a unique way to the cultural specification of the defining qualities of the witch. A *sa:go* is the more despicable of the two. His essential depravity turns on the fact that he intervenes in and perverts the normal transmission of life-force prescribed by the "natural" order of the system, expropriating for himself that which would otherwise provide for the growth and maturation of others. Such behavior is not only evil (by virtue of its harmful effects upon the depleted victim) but also subversive; it is a crime against both "nature" and human society.

A witch (other than a *sa:go*) also intervenes in natural process by appropriating life-force that would otherwise be bestowed upon the next generation, but acquires only a portion of this, as his victims have typically reproduced themselves to some extent. He foreshortens the life-span of individuals who would otherwise expire from sexual depletion at an advanced age, but does not so severely threaten the perpetuation of life itself as does the *sa:go*. The *sa:go* embodies and most fully expresses the full range of dimensions which comprise the Etoro conception of evil.

Witchcraft and sexual relations occupy analogous structural positions within a larger conceptual system – a system in which life and death are complementary and reciprocal aspects of the transmission of life-force. The analogic relation engenders a semantic interplay between the two constellations of beliefs in which witchcraft and sexual intercourse are ideologically grounded. The semantic dimensions of each set of beliefs is enriched and expanded by their juxtaposition; the cultural meaning of witchcraft is informed by the idiom of sexual relations (and vice versa). Moreover, this juxtaposition establishes a metaphoric relation through which the attributes of actors in one domain are projected upon their counterparts in the other, such that social positions are also invested with added dimensions of meaning. More specifically, the analogic correspondence between acts of witchcraft and acts of sexual relations connotes a like relation between the characteristics of the (respective) actors. At the same time, both the actors and their interaction are delineated – in the domain of sexual relations – by social roles. The social positions of wife, protege, and (to a lesser extent) child thereby acquire a penumbra of negative attributes (derived from the characterization of the witch) that sharply demarcate the boundaries of acceptable behavior, particularly in the sexual sphere. Behavior which exceeds these bounds is not merely erroneous, ungrammatical, or transgressive; it replicates the behavior of the witch and is categorically "evil." The strongest negative sanction – the witchcraft accusation – may be marshalled against those who violate such norms.[5] It is instructive here to contrast the respective cultural evaluations of a man and wife who engage in excessive sexual relations. He is, at worst, foolhardy in his beneficent generosity with the gift of life-force, while his wife – party to the self-same acts – is thought to be a witch.

These cultural definitions of certain parameters of a set of social positions are the direct product of a specific structural arrangement within the larger belief system, *viz.* a meta-phoric relation between two domains of belief which are discrete and largely autonomous at the conscious level. This structural relation is, moreover, a mechanism for the production of an elementary system of inequality based on age and sex. (All mature women occupy the social position "wife," and all young men are likewise "proteges".) Relations of inequality between adult male and adult female, young man and child, are delineated by the relationship of these categories to the encompassing system of life-force transmission and by the structural relation between the idioms of witchcraft and sexual relations within this belief system.

NOTES

The data on which this paper is based were collected during a fieldwork period extending from April 1968 to July 1969.

1 The Etoro maintain that the child of a witch and non-witch will not normally possess this characteristic. The offspring of two witches are thought likely to be *kago-mano*, but are not necessarily so. These contingencies turn on the belief that a witch must copulate "as a witch" in order to beget a *kagomano*, and only a pair of them are likely to do so (perhaps because the lone witch would reveal his true identity to his "natural" spouse by such behavior). In addition, two natural parents may have a witch-child born to them if the woman is unknowingly raped by the *ausu-lubo* of a witch while she sleeps. The birth of a *kagomano* therefore does not necessarily implicate either parent. All physically large infants are presumed to be *kagomano,* and are submitted to infanticide. (Thirty percent – 3/10 – of all children born during the 15 month period of my fieldwork met this fate.) Only witches are thought to preserve such offspring.

2 Both types of sexual relations are uniformly regulated by kinship. Wives and young male protégés should be selected from among those individuals who are within the kinship category *aua* (m.s.); husbands and inseminators are found within the reciprocal category *naua* (m.s. and w.s.). (See Kelly 1973: 305–11 for discussion of this kin category.) The ideal inseminator (among those eligible by kinship) is a boy's true sister's husband or her betrothed; brother and sister will then receive semen from the same man (ideally a FMBS) and be, in a sense, co-spouses to him. The young man is inseminated by his ZH from about age ten until he is fully mature – as evidenced by a manly beard – in his early to mid-twenties. Upon reaching maturity he will in turn become the inseminator of his WB (or the brother of his wife-to-be). It is prohibited for a man to be both donor and recipient of semen during the same period of his life, and marriage therefore necessitates a transition to inseminator, although this may occur anytime after full maturity is attained (irrespective of marital status). Thus when the ego of our example is about 40, his WB makes this transition, and homosexual relations between them necessarily cease. At this time, ego's kinship obligations to act as inseminator are fulfilled. Subsequent relationships may be contracted in the event of polygyny, or if ego is especially vigorous and therefore asked to serve in this connection (He will, in any event, continue to serve as an inseminator in the context of initiation ceremo-

nies.) It should be noted that a father arranges his daughter's marriage (when she is about five years old) and thereby nominates his son's inseminator, since these are ideally one and the same. The entire transaction involves the exchange of women for women at one level, the exchange of boys for boys at another, the exchange of women for life-force at still another level, and finally, the exchange of life and death (for youth and inseminator, respectively). During the critical period of a boy's growth and development (in his early teens), he will reside in the same community as his homosexual partner. Men related as WF and DH frequently co-reside, and the boy's residence with ZH therefore does not normally entail separation from his father (F and ZH being related to each other as WF and DH). Residence patterns are extensively discussed in Kelly (1973).

3   A predisposition toward development of the desirable characteristics of one's inseminator is also transmitted in the semen itself (rather than by tutelage). Some young men thus thought it conceivable that they might acquire the capabilities possessed by persons of Western culture (and hence the associated material culture) by ingesting their semen, and they asked me to make arrangements for them to go to the coast as contract laborers so that this experiment might be tried.

4   The basic concept of a circular closed system entailing a reciprocal relation of life and death is manifested in other aspects of cosmology which are outside the scope of this paper but may be briefly mentioned.

The spirits of the dead occupy the bodies of a certain fish (*abaso*) and reside in the rivers. The *Sigisatos* are descended from a primordial crocodile (and culture hero), and at times take this form (although they characteristically reside in the bodies of cassowaries by day). The crocodiles feed on the *abaso*, and this symbolically closes the circle of life and death inasmuch as the *Sigisatos* also implant souls in men. In other words, the *Sigisatos* symbolically consume "death" and also bring forth life.

5   A witch named as responsible for one death is likely to be named again, and thrice-named witches are characteristically executed. The full range of social disabilities imposed upon a witch are too extensive to be enumerated here, although it may be noted that these also include ostracism for periods of up to a year.

REFERENCES CITED

Allen, W. R. 1967. *Male Cults and Secret Initiations in Melanesia.* Melbourne: Melbourne University Press.

Kelly, R. C. 1973. Etoro Social Structure: A Study in Structural Contradiction. Ph.D. dissertation. University of Michigan. Ann Arbor: University of Michigan Press (1977).

Meggitt, M. J. 1964. Male-Female Relationships in the Highlands of New Guinea. *In* New Guinea: The Central Highlands. J. B. Watson, ed. *American Anthropologist* 66(4, Pt. 2): 204–24.

21

The Politics and Poetics of Transgression

Peter Stallybrass and Allon White

Allon White (1951–88) was an original literary and cultural critic (see White 1993); Peter Stallybrass is professor in the humanities at the University of Pennsylvania. Among Stallybrass's subsequent work is an elegant essay on "Marx's coat" found in the intriguing collection *Border Fetishisms* (Spyer 1998).

Stallybrass and White illustrate the exciting conjunction of literary and historical studies with anthropology. They bridge the work of Bakhtin (1968) with anthropologists like Gluckman (1965), Moore and Myerhoff (1977), Babcock, ed. (1978), and Douglas (1966), on car-nival and forms of structural inversion and add a strong mix of Marx and Freud. Here they review the literature on rituals of rebellion – events that permit, encourage, or demand the inversion of social norms – and ask whether such carnivalesque spaces and images serve to energize or challenge dominant and hegemonic social and cultural orders. The issue is central to the study of popular culture as well as religion, and forces us to acknowledge the pervasiveness of the aesthetic and social coding of "high" and "low" (refinement and vulgarity) and the prevalence of bodily metaphor.

Amongst the many remarkable things to be found in Ernst Robert Curtius's *European Literature and the Later Middle Ages* is an account of how the idea of "the Classic author" was originally derived from ancient taxation categories. In a chapter discussing the idea of model authors and the attendant notion of canon-formation, Curtius explains how tax-bands, a social division of citizens according to property qualifications under the constitutions of Servius, were adopted by Aulus Gellius as a way of designating the prestige and rank of writers. Citizens of the first taxation category, the top rank, came to be known as

From Peter Stallybrass and Allon White, "Introduction," in *The Politics and Poetics of Transgression* (Ithaca, NY and London: Cornell University Press and Methuen Books, 1986), pp. 1–20. Abridged.

"*classici*". This development in the generic terminology of antiquity (Gellius fl. *c.* 123–*c.* 165) subsequently had an enduring influence on the European system of hierarchizing authors and works. It separated out a distinct élite set (the *classici*) from the commonality (the *proletarius*) and used this as a model for literary discriminations. Curtius remarks:

> But it was not until very late, and then only in a single instance, that the name *classicus* appears: in Aulus Gellius (*Noctes Atticae*, XIX, 8, 15) . . . The thing to do is to follow the usage of a model author: "e cohorte illa dumataxat antiquiore vel oratorum aliquis vel poetarum, id est classicus adsiduusque aliquis scriptor, non proletarius"; "some one of the orators or poets, who at least belongs to the older band, that is, a first class taxpaying author, not a proletarian" . . . The *proletarius*, whom Gellius mentions by way of comparison, belongs to *no* tax class. When Sainte-Beuve, in 1850, discussed the question What is a Classic?, he paraphrased this passage in Gellius: "un écrivain de valeur et de marque, un écrivain qui compte, qui a du bien au soleil, et qui n'est pas confondu dans la foule des prolétaires." (Curtius 1953: 249–50)

And Curtius adds wryly "What a titbit for a Marxist sociology of literature!"

It was not Curtius's inclination to follow up his own remark and indeed we can detect a certain amused astonishment when he realizes where his investigations have finally led him. From the first it seems that the ranking of types of author was modelled upon social rank according to property classifications and this interrelation was still being actively invoked in the nineteenth century. In recent times we have been inclined to forget this ancient and enduring link between social rank and the organizing of authors and works, including literary genres, although for the major part of European history it was a natural assumption for readers and writers alike. Ian Jack noted that precisely this habit of ranking "kinds in a hierarchy analogous to that of the state" has led to a contemporary distrust, particularly of Renaissance categories:

> Just as the social hierarchy was traced from the prince through the nobility down to the common people, so the realm of Poetry had its own "degrees", from Epic, the Prince of all the kinds, down to the lowest species of all, "from Homer to the *Anthologia*, from Virgil to Martial and Owen's Epigrams . . . that is from the top to the bottom of all poetry". (Jack 1942: 4)

It is the contention of the present book that cultural categories of high and low, social and aesthetic, like those mentioned above but also those of the physical body and geographical space, are never entirely separable. The ranking of literary genres or authors in a hierarchy analogous to social classes is a particularly clear example of a much broader and more complex cultural process whereby the human body, psychic forms, geographical space and the social formation are all constructed within interrelating and dependent hierarchies of high and low. This book is an attempt to map some of these interlinked hierarchies on the terrain of literary and cultural history. More particularly it attends both to the formation of these hierarchies and to the processes through which the low troubles the high. The high/low opposition in each of our four symbolic domains – psychic forms, the human body, geographical space and the social order – is a fundamental basis to mechanisms of ordering and sense-making in European cultures. Divisions and discriminations in one domain are continually structured, legitimated and dissolved by reference to the vertical symbolic hierarchy which operates in the other three domains. Cultures "think themselves" in the most immediate and affective ways through the combined symbolisms of these four hierarchies. Furthermore (and this is where the title of the book comes in) transgressing the rules of hierarchy and order in any one of the domains may have major consequences in the others.

Although there are all sorts of subtle degrees and gradations in a culture it is striking that the extremes of high and low have a special and often powerful symbolic charge. Thus, in the example given above from Curtius, Gellius (as also Cicero and Arnobius) immediately fixes upon the top and bottom, the *classicus* and the *proletarius*, even though the system has five different grades within it. This does not necessarily militate against subtlety since "above" and "below" may be inscribed within a minutely discriminatory system of classification, but it does foster a simplifying binaryism of high and low *within which* further classification will be made. In other words the vertical extremities frame all further discursive elaborations. If we can grasp the system of extremes which encode the body, the social order, psychic form and spatial location, we thereby lay bare a major framework of discourse within which any further "redress of balance" or judicious qualification must take place.

In our study therefore we have focused upon the symbolic extremities of the exalted and the base. We have followed the instruction of Boethius – "Look to the highest of the heights of heaven" – and we have also plumbed the depths of social classification, the lower bodily stratum, the sewers, the underworld – what one might call the rock bottom of symbolic form. We have tried to see how high discourses, with their lofty style, exalted aims and sublime ends, are structured in relation to the debasements and degradations of low discourse. We have tried to see how each extremity structures the other, depends upon and invades the other in certain historical moments, to carry political charge through aesthetic and moral polarities. Indeed, the oppositions, interpenetrations and transgressions of high and low bear such an enormous weight of cultural organization that one marvels at the sheer labour of transcoding, displacement and partition involved in the elaborate networks of *super-* and *sub-* in our cultural history.

It would be wrong to imply that "high" and "low" in this context are equal and symmetrical terms. When we talk of high discourses – literature, philosophy, statecraft, the languages of the Church and the University – and contrast them to the low discourses of a peasantry, the urban poor, subcultures, marginals, the lumpenproletariat, colonized peoples, we already have two "high" and two "lows". History seen from above and history seen from below are irreducibly different and they consequently impose radically different perspectives on the question of hierarchy.

Indeed they may and often do possess quite different symbolic hierarchies but because the higher discourses are normally associated with the most powerful socioeconomic groups existing at the centre of cultural power, it is they which generally gain the authority to designate what is to be taken as high and low in the society. This is what Raymond Williams calls the "inherent dominative mode" and it has the prestige and the access to power which enables it to create the dominant definitions of superior and inferior. Of course the "low" (defined as such by the high precisely to confirm itself as "high") may well see things differently and attempt to impose a counter-view through an inverted hierarchy.

There is a growing body of research devoted to the topic of hierarchy inversion, of "world upside down" (WUD), and we have much to say about this in the following pages. However the politics of hierarchy inversion as a ritual strategy on the part of subordinate groups is not our principal theme. We have chosen to concentrate rather on the contradictory nature of symbolic hierarchies within the dominant constructions of literature, the body and the social formation.

The primary site of contradiction, the site of conflicting desires and mutually incompatible representation, is undoubtedly the "low". Again and again we find a striking ambivalence to the representations of the lower strata (of the body, of literature, of society, of place) in which they are both reviled and desired. Repugnance and fascination are the twin poles of the process in which a *political* imperative to reject and eliminate the debasing "low" conflicts powerfully and unpredictably with a desire for this Other. Edward Said in his work on *Orientalism* – the myth of the Middle East constructed by Europe to legitimate its own authority – has convincingly shown this operative ambivalence in action. In political terms Orientalism "depends for its strategy on [a] flexible *positional* superiority, which puts the Westerner in a whole series of possible relationships with the Orient without ever losing him the upper hand". But at the same time Said notices that "European culture gained in strength and identity by setting itself off against the Orient as a sort of . . . underground self"

(Said 1979: 3, 7). "An underground self with the upper hand". This curious, almost oxymoronic formulation captures a nexus of power and desire which regularly reappears in the ideological construction of the low-Other. It is not only a phenomenon of colonial and neo-colonial representation. We find the same constitutive ambivalence around the slum and the domestic servant in the nineteenth century; around the disposal of "waste" products in the city (though not in pre-Renaissance rural culture); around the carnival festivity of popular culture; around the symbolically base and abject animals like the pig and the rat. These are the subjects of specific chapters which follow in which we explore the contradictory and unstable representation of low-Others.

A recurrent pattern emerges: the "top" attempts to reject and eliminate the "bottom" for reasons of prestige and status, only to discover, not only that it is in some way frequently dependent upon that low-Other (in the classic way that Hegel describes in the master–slave section of the *Phenomenology*), but also that the top *includes* that low symbolically, as a primary eroticized constituent of its own fantasy life. The result is a mobile, conflictual fusion of power, fear and desire in the construction of subjectivity: a psychological dependence upon precisely those Others which are being rigorously opposed and excluded at the social level. It is for this reason that what is *socially* peripheral is so frequently *symbolically* central (like long hair in the 1960s). The low-Other is despised and denied at the level of political organization and social being whilst it is instrumentally constitutive of the shared imaginary repertoires of the dominant culture. This is evidenced by the history of the representation of "low" entertainment and the carnivalesque, to which we now turn.

From Carnival to Transgression

The new historian, the genealogist, will know what to make of this masquerade. He will not be too serious to enjoy it; on the contrary, he will push the masquerade to its limits and prepare the great carnival of time where masks are constantly reappearing. Genealogy is history in the form of a concerted carnival. (Foucault 1977: 160–1)

In the world of carnival the awareness of the people's immortality combined with the realisation that established authority and truth are relative. (Bakhtin 1968: 10)

There is now a large and increasing body of writing which sees carnival not simply as a ritual feature of European culture but as a *mode of understanding*, a positivity, a cultural analytic. How is it that a festive ritual now virtually eliminated from most of the popular culture of Europe has gained such prominence as an epistemological category? Is there a connection between the fact of its elimination as a physical practice and its self-conscious emergence in the artistic and academic discourses of our time? For both Michel Foucault in the passage cited above and for Mikhail Bakhtin in his seminal study *Rabelais and his World*, the Nietzscheian study of history leads to the ideal of carnival. Everywhere in literary and cultural studies today we see carnival emerging as a model, as an ideal and as an analytic category in a way that, at first sight, seems puzzling.

Undoubtedly it was the translation of Mikhail Bakhtin's monumental study of Rabelais and the carnivalesque which initially catalyzed the interest of Western scholars (albeit slowly – the book was only translated into English in 1968) around the notion of carnival, marking it out as a site of special interest for the analysis of literature and symbolic practices. Since the 1970s there has been an increasing number of literary and historical studies devoted to the topic. In 1978 Krystyna Pomorska could write with every justification that "Mikhail Bakhtin is today one of the most popular, if not the most popular, figures in the domain of humanistic studies" (Pomorska 1978: 379). More recently Tony Bennett averred that Bakhtin's study of Rabelais should hold an exemplary place in materialist cultural criticism (Bennett 1979: 90–2). This is surely correct: *Rabelais and his World* is ostensibly a scholarly study of Rabelais's popular sources in carnivalesque folk-culture which shows how indebted Rabelais is to the popular, non-literary, "low" folk humor of the French Renaissance. His intention in the study was self-consciously iconoclastic. "No dogma, no authoritarianism, no narrow-minded seriousness can coexist with Rabelaisian images; these images are opposed to all that is finished and polished, to all pomposity, to every ready-made solution in the sphere of thought and world outlook" (Bakhtin 1968: 3). Naturally this reading of Rabelais has not gone unchallenged by conventionally learned scholars (Screech 1979: 1–14, 479; also 1984: 11–13, but in this latter article, "Homage to Rabelais", Screech is much closer in spirit to Bakhtin than in the earlier book). But although Bakhtin is deeply concerned to elucidate the sources of Rabelais's work, the main importance of his study is its broad development of the "carnivalesque" into a potent, populist, critical inversion of *all* official words and hierarchies in a way that has implications far beyond the specific realm of Rabelais studies. Carnival, for Bakhtin, is both a populist utopian vision of the world seen from below and a festive critique, through the inversion of hierarchy, of the "high" culture:

> As opposed to the official feast, one might say that carnival celebrates temporary liberation from the prevailing truth of the established order; it marks the suspension of all hierarchical rank, privileges, norms and prohibitions. Carnival was the true feast of time, the feast of becoming, change and renewal. It was hostile to all that was immortalized and complete. (Bakhtin 1968: 109)

Carnival in its widest, most general sense embraced ritual spectacles such as fairs, popular feasts and wakes, processions and competitions (Burke 1978: 178–204), comic shows, mummery and dancing, open-air amusement with costumes and masks, giants, dwarfs, monsters, trained animals and so forth; it included comic verbal compositions (oral and written) such as parodies, travesties and vulgar farce; and it included various genres of "Billingsgate", by which Bakhtin designated curses, oaths, slang, humour, popular tricks and jokes, scatological forms, in fact all the "low" and "dirty" sorts of folk humor. Carnival is presented by Bakhtin as a world of topsy-turvy, of heteroglot exuberance, of ceaseless overrunning and excess where all is mixed, hybrid, ritually degraded and defiled.

If there is a principle to this hotch-potch it resides in the spirit of carnivalesque laughter itself, to which Bakhtin ascribes great importance:

> Let us say a few initial words about the complex nature of carnivalesque laughter. It is, first of all, a festive laughter. Therefore it is not an individual reaction to some isolated "comic" event. Carnival laughter is the laughter of all the people. Second, it is universal in scope; it is directed at all and everyone, including the carnival's participants. The entire world is seen in its droll aspect, in its gay relativity. Third, this laughter is ambivalent: it is gay, triumphant, and at the same time mocking, deriding. It asserts and denies, it buries and revives. Such is the laughter of the carnival. (Bakhtin 1968: 11–12)

Carnival laughter, then, has a vulgar, "earthy" quality to it. With its oaths and profanities, its abusive language and its mocking words it was profoundly ambivalent. Whilst it humiliated and mortified it also revived and renewed. For Bakhtin ritual defilements went along with reinvigoration such that "it was precisely this ambivalent abuse which determined the genre of speech in carnival intercourse" (Bakhtin 1968: 16). The "coarse" and familiar speech of the fair and the marketplace provided a complex vital repertoire of speech patterns excluded from official discourse which could be used for parody, subversive humour and inversion. "Laughter degrades and materialises" (Bakhtin 1968: 20). Fundamental to the corporeal, collective nature of carnival laughter is what Bakhtin terms "grotesque realism". Grotesque realism uses the material body–flesh conceptualized as corpulent excess – to represent cosmic, social, topographical and linguistic elements of the world. Thus already in Bakhtin there is the germinal notion of *transcodings* and *displacements* effected between the high/low image of the physical body and other social domains. Grotesque realism images the human body as multiple, bulging, over- or under-sized, protuberant and incomplete. The openings and orifices of this carnival body are emphasized, not its closure and finish. It is an image of impure corporeal bulk with its orifices (mouth, flared nostrils, anus) yawning wide and its lower regions (belly, legs, feet, buttocks and genitals) given priority over its upper regions (head, "spirit", reason).

Bakhtin is self-consciously utopian and lyrical about carnival and grotesque realism. "The leading themes of these images of bodily life are fertility, growth and a brimming-over abundance. Manifestations of this life refer not to the isolated biological individual, not to the private, egoistic, 'economic man' but to the collective ancestral body of all the people" (Bakhtin 1968: 19). To complete the image of grotesque realism one must add that it is always in process, it is always *becoming*, it is a mobile and hybrid creature, disproportionate, exorbitant, outgrowing all limits, obscenely decentred and off-balance, a figural and symbolic resource for parodic exaggeration and inversion. All these grotesque qualities have a positive force in Bakhtin. It was only after the Renaissance, according to Bakhtin, that the principles of grotesque realism were subjected to a monologic reading. Stigmatized as the vulgar practices of a superstitious and crude populace, the carnivalesque was prettified, incorporated into commercial or civic display or regarded as a purely negative phenomenon. Bakhtin's optimistic populism is at its most insistent (and problematic) in those passages where he emphasizes the positivity of the grotesque bodily element.

The grotesque body was traditionally presented, Bakhtin argues,

not in a private, egotistic form, severed from the other spheres of life, but as something universal, representing all the people. As such it is opposed to the severance from the material and bodily roots of the world; it makes no pretense to renunciation of the earthy, or independence of the earthy and body. We repeat: the body and bodily life have here a cosmic and at the same time an all-people's character; this is not the body and its physiology in the modern sense of these words, because it is not individualised. The material

bodily principle is contained not in the biological individual, not in the bourgeois ego, but in the people, a people who are continually growing and renewed. This is why all that is bodily becomes grandiose, exaggerated, immeasurable. (Bakhtin 1968: 19)

It is difficult to disentangle the generous but willed idealism from the descriptively accurate in passages like these. Bakhtin constantly shifts between prescriptive and descriptive categories in his work. In this passage the cosmic populism, which seems to us rather wishful and finally unusable as an analytic tool, assorts with an acute perception about the historically variable nature of the body-image. . . .

In Bakhtin's schema grotesque realism in pre-capitalist Europe fulfilled three functions at once: it provided an image-ideal of and for popular community as an heterogeneous and boundless totality; it provided an imaginary repertoire of festive and comic elements which stood over against the serious and oppressive languages of the official culture; and it provided a thoroughly materialist metaphysics whereby the grotesque "bodied forth" the cosmos, the social formation and language itself. Even linguistic rules are played up by what Bakhtin calls a *grammatica jocosa* whereby grammatical order is transgressed to reveal erotic and obscene or merely materially satisfying counter-meaning.

[. . .]

Whilst almost every reader of Bakhtin admires his comprehensive and engaged generosity, his combination of festive populism and deep learning, and whilst few would deny the immediate appeal and the vitality of the notion of carnival, various writers have been sceptical of Bakhtin's overall project.

Terry Eagleton thinks that the weakness of Bakhtin's positive embrace of carnival is transparent:

Indeed carnival is so vivaciously celebrated that the necessary political criticism is almost too obvious to make. Carnival, after all, is a *licensed* affair in every sense, a permissible rupture of hegemony, a contained popular blow-off as disturbing and relatively ineffectual as a revolutionary work of art. As Shakespeare's Olivia remarks, there is no slander in an allowed fool. (Eagleton 1981: 148)

Most politically thoughtful commentators wonder, like Eagleton, whether the "licensed release" of carnival is not simply a form of social control of the low by the high and therefore serves the interests of that very official culture which it apparently opposes. The classic formulation of this is in Max Gluckman's now somewhat dated *Order and Rebellion in Tribal Africa* (1963) and *Custom and Conflict* (1965), in which he asserted that while these "rites of reversal obviously include a protest against the established order . . . they are intended to preserve and strengthen the established order" (Gluckman 1965: 109). Roger Sales amplifies both on this process of containment and its ambivalence:

There were two reasons why the fizzy, dizzy carnival spirit did not necessarily undermine authority. First of all, it was licensed or sanctioned by the authorities themselves. They removed the stopper to stop the bottle being smashed altogether. The release of emotions and grievances made them easier to police in the long term. Second, although the world might appear to be turned upside down during the carnival season, the fact that Kings and Queens were chosen and crowned actually reaffirmed the *status quo*. Carnival was, however, Janus-faced. Falstaff is both the merry old mimic of Eastcheap and the old corruptible who tries to undermine the authority, or rule, of the Lord Chief Justice. The carnival spirit, in early-nineteenth century England as well as in sixteenth century France, could therefore be a vehicle for social protest and the method for disciplining that protest. (Sales 1983: 169)

As Georges Balandier puts it succinctly in *Political Anthropology*: "The supreme ruse of power is to allow itself to be contested *ritually* in order to consolidate itself more effectively."

It actually makes little sense to fight out the issue of whether or not carnivals are *intrinsically* radical or conservative, for to do so automatically involves the false essentializing of carnivalesque transgression (White 1982: 60). The most that can be said in the abstract is

that for long periods carnival may be a stable and cyclical ritual with no noticeable politically transformative effects but that, given the presence of sharpened political antagonism, it may often act as *catalyst* and *site of actual and symbolic struggle*.

It is in fact striking how frequently violent social clashes apparently "coincided" with carnival. Le Roy Ladurie's *Carnival in Romans* (1981) has popularized one such incident when the 1580 festival at Romans in eastern France was turned into armed conflict and massacre. Other social historians have documented similar occurrences (Davis 1975; Burke 1978; Thompson 1972). However to call it a "coincidence" of social revolt and carnival is deeply misleading, for as Peter Burke has pointed out, it was only in the late eighteenth and early nineteenth centuries – and then only in certain areas – that one can reasonably talk of popular politics *dissociated* from the carnivalesque at all. John Brewer has described English politics in the eighteenth century as "essentially a calendrical market", by which he designates a deliberate commingling of holiday and political events (in this case organized by the Hanoverians for conservative motives):

Far too little attention had [sic] been paid to the emergence during the eighteenth century of a Hanoverian political calendar, designed to inculcate loyal values in the populace, and to emphasize and encourage the growth of a national political consensus. Nearly every English market town celebrated the dates which were considered the important political landmarks of the nation. They can be found in most almanacs of the period, barely distinguishable from the time-honoured dates of May Day, Plough Monday, Twelfth Night, Shrove Tuesday and the like . . . In the early eighteenth century, these dates, together with the occasion of the Pretender's birthday, were occasions of conflict. The year of the Jacobite Rebellion, 1715, was especially contentious, with Hanoverian Mug House clubs fighting it out in the streets with Jacobite apprentices and artisans. On October 30, frequenters of a Jacobite alehouse on Ludgate Hill were beaten up by members of the Loyal Society who were celebrating the birthday of the Prince of Wales, the future George II. A Jacobite attempt to burn William III in effigy on November 4 was thwarted by the same Whig clubmen who the next day tried to cremate effigies of the Pretender and his supporters. On 17 November further clashes ensued and two Jacobites were shot dead. (Brewer *et al.* 1983: 247)

Again this should act as a warning against the current tendency to essentialize carnival *and* politics. On the one hand carnival was a specific calendrical ritual: carnival proper, for instance, occurred around February each year, ineluctably followed by Lenten fasting and abstinence bound tightly to laws, structures and institutions which had briefly been denied during its reign. On the other hand carnival also refers to a mobile set of symbolic practices, images and discourses which were employed throughout social revolts and conflicts before the nineteenth century. . . .

In recent social histories of England there has been a considerable debate over the interrelationship between popular culture and class conflict (Yeo and Yeo 1981; Bushaway 1982; Walvin 1978; Cunningham 1980; Thompson 1972; Malcolmson 1973; Stedman Jones 1983). Most of these studies unearth evidence of a long battle (with occasional truces) waged by the State, ecclesiastical and bourgeois authorities against popular custom. It is a battle that goes back well beyond the Renaissance but which, from the Renaissance on, produced local festivities as sites of resistance to the extension of power by the propertied and the State. Bushaway remarks: "Custom and ceremony became a battleground in the struggle between the labouring poor and the increasingly wealthy landowners and proprietors over the defence of popular rights and the protection of a normative view of the structure of the community held by the labouring poor" (Bushaway 1982: 21–2). This seems an altogether more accurate way of conceiving the relationship. Carnivals, fairs, popular games and festivals were very swiftly "politicized" by the very attempts made on the part of local authorities to eliminate them. The dialectic of antagonism frequently *turned* rituals into resistance at the moment of intervention by the higher powers, even when no overt oppositional element had been present

before. . . . Here we are only underscoring the banal but often ignored truth that the politics of carnival cannot be resolved outside of a close historical examination of particular conjunctures: there is no a priori revolutionary vector to carnival and transgression.

In his research on the carnivalesque Bakhtin had substantially anticipated by some thirty years main lines of development in symbolic anthropology. In his exploration of the *relational* nature of festivity, its structural inversion of, and ambivalent dependence upon, "official culture", Bakhtin set out a model of culture in which a high/low binarism had a fundamental place. Bakhtin's use of carnival centres the concept upon its "doubleness . . . there is no unofficial expression without a prior official one or its possibility. Hence, in Bakhtin's analysis of carnival, the official and unofficial are locked together" (Wilson 1983: 320). Symbolic polarities of high and low, official and popular, grotesque and classical are mutually constructed and deformed in carnival. Two of the best general synopses of Bakhtin's work correctly perceive this to be the most significant aspect of *Rabelais and his World*. Ivanov (1976) links Bakhtin's discovery of the importance of binary oppositions with the work of Lévi-Strauss:

the books by Bakhtin and Lévi-Strauss have much in common in their treatment of the functioning of oppositions in the ritual or the carnival which can be traced back historically to ritual performance. For Lévi-Strauss the chief purpose of the ritual and the myth is the discovery of an intermediate link between the members of a binary opposition: a process known as *mediation*. The structural analysis of the ambivalence inherent in the "marketplace word" and its corresponding imagery led Bakhtin to the conclusion (made independently from and prior to structural mythology) that the "carnival image strives to embrace and unite in itself both terminal points of the process of becoming or both members of the antithesis: birth–death, youth–age, top–bottom, face–lower bodily stratum, praise–abuse" [Bakhtin 1968: 238]. From this standpoint, Bakhtin scrutinized various forms of inverted relations between top and bottom "a reversal of the hierarchy of top and bottom" [Bakhtin 1968: 81] which takes place during carnival. (Ivanov 1976: 35)

The convergence of Bakhtin's thinking and that of current symbolic anthropology is highly significant. Where Ivanov points to the kinship Bakhtin shares with Lévi-Strauss and Edmund Leach (particularly Leach's essay on carnival, "Time and false noses", 1961), Masao Yamaguchi suggests that Bakhtin's work significantly parallels that of Victor Turner, Barbara Babcock and Mary Douglas in their shared interest in cultural negations and symbolic inversions (Yamaguchi 1983). We may note, for instance, the similarity of Bakhtin's concept of carnivalesque high/low inversion to the concepts developed in *The Reversible World*, a collection of essays on anthropology and literature edited by Barbara Babcock. Although apparently unaware of Bakhtin's study she assembles a range of writing on "symbolic inversion and cultural negation" which puts carnival into a much wider perspective. She writes: "'Symbolic inversion' may be broadly defined as any act of expressive behaviour which inverts, contradicts, abrogates, or in some fashion presents an alternative to commonly held cultural codes, values and norms be they linguistic, literary or artistic, religious, social and political" (Babcock 1978: 14).

This is what we refer to in this book as "transgression" (though there is another, more complex use of the term which arises in connection with extremist practices of modern art and philosophy; these designate not just the infraction of binary structures, but movement into an absolutely negative space *beyond the structure of significance itself*). For the moment it is enough to suggest that, in our view, the current widespread adoption of the idea of carnival as an *analytic* category can only be fruitful if it is displaced into the broader concept of symbolic inversion and transgression.

This is not to deny the usefulness of the carnivalesque as a sort of "modelling", at once utopian and counter-hegemonic, whereby it is viewed, in Roberto da Matta's words, as a *privileged locus* of inversion. In his attempt to go beyond Bakhtin's nostalgic and over-optimistic view of carnival, Matta acknowledges the degree to which festivity is licensed release, but he also praises its deep modelling of a different, pleasurable and communal ideal "of the people", even if that ideal cannot immediately be acted upon. Victor Turner has similarly argued with respect to role reversal that carnival is "a moment when those being moved in accordance to a cultural script were liberated from normative demands, where they were ... betwixt and between successive lodgements in jural political systems". Carnival in this view has been defended as having a persistent *demystifying* potential (Jones 1983; Arthur 1982; Stamm 1982; Davis 1975). Even Terry Eagleton wants to salvage Bakhtin's carnivalesque by seeing it as a utopian modelling yoked to a glimpse through the ideological constructs of dominance, a "kind of fiction", a "temporary retextualizing of the social formation that exposes its 'fictive' foundations" (Eagleton 1981: 149).

In this perspective the carnivalesque becomes a resource of actions, images and roles which may be invoked both to model and legitimate desire and to "degrade all that is spiritual and abstract". "The cheerful vulgarity of the powerless is used as a weapon against the pretence and hypocrisy of the powerful" (Stamm 1982: 47). In a most engaging description of this utopian/critical role of carnival Stamm continues:

On the positive side, carnival suggests the joyful affirmation of becoming. It is ecstatic collectivity, the superseding of the individuating principle in what Nietzsche called "the glowing life of Dionysian revellers" ... On the negative, critical side, the carnivalesque suggests a demystificatory instrument for everything in the social formation which renders such collectivity difficult of access: class hierarchy, political manipulation, sexual repression, dogmatism and paranoia. Carnival in this sense implies an attitude of creative disrespect, a radical opposition to the illegitimately powerful, to the morose and monological. (Stamm 1982: 55)

Refreshingly iconoclastic, this nevertheless resolves none of the problems raised so far concerning the politics of carnival: its nostalgia; its uncritical populism (carnival often violently abuses and demonizes *weaker*, not stronger, social groups – women, ethnic and religious minorities, those who "don't belong" – in a process of *displaced abjection*); its failure to do away with the official dominant culture, its licensed complicity.

In fact those writers and critics who remain purely within the celebratory terms of Bakhtin's formulation are unable to resolve these key dilemmas. It is only by completely shifting the grounds of the debate, by transforming the "problematic" of carnival, that these issues can be solved. It is precisely such an intervention in the current surge of Bakhtin-inspired studies which we have attempted in this book.... We have chosen therefore to consider carnival as one instance of a generalized economy of transgression and of the recoding of high/low relations across the whole social structure. The symbolic categories of grotesque realism which Bakhtin located can be rediscovered as a governing dynamic of the body, the household, the city, the nation-state – indeed a vast range of interconnected domains....

By tracking the "grotesque body" and the "low-Other" through different symbolic domains of bourgeois society since the Renaissance we can attain an unusual perspective upon its inner dynamics, the inner complicity of disgust and desire which fuels its crises of value. For the classificatory body of a culture is always double, always structured in relation to its negation, its inverse. "All symbolic inversions define a culture's lineaments at the same time as they question the usefulness and the absoluteness of its ordering" (Babcock 1978: 29). Indeed by attending to the low and the marginal we vindicate, on the terrain of European literary and cultural history, the more general anthropological assertion that the process of symbolic inversion, "far from being a residual category of experience, is its very opposite. What is socially peripheral is often symbolically central, and if we ignore or minimize inversion and other forms of cultural negation, we often fail to understand the dynamics of symbolic processes generally" (Babcock 1978: 32).

This is a scrupulously accurate and indispensable formulation. The carnival, the circus, the gypsy, the lumpenproletariat, play a symbolic role in bourgeois culture out of all proportion to their actual social importance. The dominant features of the psycho-symbolic domain cannot be mapped one-to-one onto the social formation.

BIBLIOGRAPHY

MMB = *Mikhail Mikhailovich Bakhtin: His Circle, His Influence*. Papers presented at the International Colloquium, Queen's University, Kingston, Ontario, 7–9 October 1983.

Arthur, K. (1982) "Bakhtin, Kristeva and carnival", unpublished dissertation, Melbourne.

Babcock, B. (1978) *The Reversible World: Symbolic Inversion in Art and Society*, Ithaca, Cornell University Press.

Bakhtin, M. M. (1968) *Rabelais and his World* (tr. H. Iswolsky), Cambridge, Mass., MIT Press.

Bennett, T. (1979) *Formalism and Marxism*, London, Methuen.

Brewer, J., McKendrick, N. and Plumb, J. H. (1983) *The Birth of a Consumer Society: The Commercialization of Eighteenth-century England*, London, Hutchinson.

Burke, P. (1978) *Popular Culture in Early Modern Europe*, London, Temple Smith.

Bushaway, B. (1982) *By Rite: Custom, Ceremony and Community in England 1700–1880*, Studies in Popular Culture, London, Junction Books.

Cunningham, H. (1980) *Leisure in the Industrial Revolution*, London, Croom Helm.

Curtius, E. R. (1953) *European Literature and the Latin Middle Ages*, London, Routledge & Kegan Paul, 1979.

Davis, N. Z. (1975) *Society and Culture in Early Modern France*, Stanford, Stanford University Press.

Eagleton, T. (1981) *Walter Benjamin: Towards a Revolutionary Criticism*, London, Verso.

Foucault, M. (1977) *Language/Counter-memory/Practice* (ed. D. F. Bouchard, tr. D. F. Bouchard and S. Simon), Ithaca, Cornell University Press.

Gluckman, M. (1963) *Order and Rebellion in Tribal Africa: Collected Essays with an Autobiographical Introduction*, London, Cohen.

Gluckman, M. (1965) *Custom and Conflict in Africa*, Oxford, Blackwell.

Ivanov, V. V. (1976) "The significance of Bakhtin's ideas on sign, utterance and dialogue for modern semiotics", in *Papers on Poetics and Semiotics* 4, Tel Aviv, The Israeli Institute for Poetics and Semiotics, Tel Aviv University.

Jack, I. (1942) *Augustan Satire: Intention and Idiom in English Poetry 1660–1750*, Oxford, Clarendon Press.

Jones, A. R. (1983) "Inside the outsider: Nashe's 'Unfortunate traveller' and Bakhtin's polyphonic novel", *English Literary History*, 50, 1, 61–82.

Le Roy Ladurie, E. (1981) *Carnival in Romans* (tr. M. Feeney), Harmondsworth, Penguin.

Leach, E. (1961) "Time and false noses", in Leach, E. (ed.) *Rethinking Anthropology*, Monograph/Social Anthropology 22, London, Athlone Press, 132–6.

Malcolmson, R. W. (1973) *Popular Recreations in English Society* 1700–1850, Cambridge University Press.

Pomorska, K. (1978) "Mikhail Bakhtin and his verbal universe", *Poetics and Theory of Literature* (PTL), 3, 379–86.

Said, E. (1979) *Orientalism*, New York, Vintage Books.

Said, E. (1984) *The World, the Text and the Critic*, London, Faber & Faber.

Sales, R. (1983) *English Literature in History 1780–1830: Pastoral and Politics*, London, Hutchinson.

Screech, M. A. (1979) *Rabelais*, London, Duckworth.

Screech, M. A. (1984) "Homage to Rabelais", *London Review of Books*, 6, 17.

Stamm, R. (1982) "On the carnivalesque", *Wedge*, 1, 47–55.

Stedman Jones, G. (1983) *Languages of Class*, Cambridge, Cambridge University Press.

Thompson, E. P. (1972) "'Rough music': le charivari anglais", *Annales ESC*, 27.2, 285–312.

Walvin, J. (1978) *Leisure and Society 1830–1950*, London, Longman.

White, A. (1982) "Pigs and pierrots: politics of transgression in modern fiction", *Raritan*, II, 2 (Fall), 51–70. New Brunswick, New Jersey.

Wilson, R. (1983) "Carnival and play", MMB (Coll.), Kingston, Ontario, Queen's University, 318–21.

Yamaguchi, M. (1983) "Bakhtin and symbolic anthropology", MMB (Coll.), 323–39. Kingston, Ontario, Queen's University.

Yeo, E. and Yeo, S. (eds) (1981) *Popular Culture and Class Conflict*, Brighton, Harvester.

Conceptualizing the Cosmos

Introduction

By contrast to most of the previous essays, which have interpreted single parts, segments, or dimensions of cultural worlds, these essays on cosmology attempt to portray such worlds as wholes. They thus move to levels of greater abstraction, offering larger pictures in terms of which the specific details of Polynesian carving or tattooing, or of Amerindian myth or shamanism, make sense. Such analytic portraits are surely one of the goals of anthropology and usually only realized in full-length monographs. It will be seen that both Gell and Viveiros de Castro raise complex issues and draw, to a degree, on western philosophical literature in order to more clearly locate and refine their ethnographic descriptions. One of the values of such broad cosmological arguments is that they radically throw into question the "native" (western) cosmology from which anthropologists normally begin their analyses and which forms the common-sense ground for most readers. More forcefully than any other approach, they relativize our assumptions and make us see ourselves, i.e., "our culture," as simply "another other among others." To this end, I would have liked to include Sahlins (1996) on the cosmology of the West.

Cosmology is sometimes phrased in terms of the conjunction of space and time. Eliade (1959) is a famous if somewhat idealized picture of different constructions of cosmos and history, while Daniel (1996) provides a subtle account of different conceptions of history among Sinhalese and Tamil speakers (Buddhists and Hindus, respectively) in contemporary Sri Lanka. Evans-Pritchard (1940) and Leach (1961) are classic loci on time (cf. Gell 1992), while Basso (1996) offers a profound meditation on place. As Bourdieu's concept of habitus (1977) and Bakhtin's concept of chronotope (1981) suggest, space and time are inextricably connected. Lambek and Walsh (1999) and Lambek (2002) offer ethnographic examples. Questions of cosmology are often tied to accounts of transformations to modernity, itself implicitly a cosmology although increasingly come to be seen as either unraveling or intensifying and contracting time and space (Appadurai 1996, Jameson 1991).

The beauty of unitary cosmologies and the power of holistic analysis (Rappaport 1999) notwithstanding, cosmological accounts should be supplemented by those that emphasize local diversity, whether through the social organization of knowledge (James 1988, Lambek 1993a), "popular" religion contrasted to orthodoxy (Badone, ed. 1990, Gellner 2001), religious debate within societies (Fischer 1980, Fischer and Abedi 1990), gender divisions (Boddy 1989, Gillison 1993), conversion (Hefner, ed. 1993), or pluralism and contestation (Masquelier 2001).

22

Closure and Multiplication: An Essay on Polynesian Cosmology and Ritual

Alfred Gell

Alfred Gell (1945–97) was an outstanding iconoclastic thinker who taught at the London School of Economics and wrote on time and art, among many other subjects. Gell's essay is a powerful account of Polynesian cosmology that begins with the startling assertion that the Polynesian world is one of immanence rather than transcendence and that such immanence brings problems in its wake. Rather than the carefree life that Polynesians are often portrayed as having, Gell paints a picture of anxiety in which you had to "watch your back," not so much from personal enemies as from the pervasive effects of the sacred. Gell's aesthetic sensibility is evident in the acute analysis of Polynesian carving and tattooing, supplemented by his own drawings and those of earlier western visitors to Polynesia (only some of which are reproduced here). See also his longer study *Wrapping in Images* (1993). The anthropology of art is a rich field overlapping that of religion.

Gell's analysis is based entirely on secondary sources; his own fieldwork was carried out in Melanesia (1975) and tribal India. He is the author of a particularly fine essay on taboo (1979). Other essays on Oceanian cosmologies are to be found in de Coppet and Iteanu (1995); see also Strathern (1988) and Bamford ed. (1998), as well as many excellent ethnographies.

The main features of Polynesian cosmological beliefs show a high degree of consistency and have become reasonably well known, through the efforts of a host of nineteenth-century writers, mostly missionaries or government officials, and subsequent re-working by Polynesia specialists. The Central-Eastern Polynesian culture area, comprising the Society Islands (Tahiti), the Marquesas, New Zealand, and Hawaii to name only the larger sub-

From Alfred Gell, "Closure and Multiplication: An Essay on Polynesian Cosmology and Ritual," in Daniel de Coppet and André Iteanu, eds, *Cosmos and Society in Oceania* (Oxford: Berg Publishers, 1995), pp. 21–56. Abridged.

regional systems, all maintained broadly similar systems of ritual and belief, which were founded on the cosmological scheme in which the creation of the cosmos came about through conflict and separation (Hanson 1982). The cosmos was originally one but this afforded no scope of action to the creator god (*Ta'aroa, Tane,* etc.) whose initial act was to bring about the separation of sky and earth, night and day, thus creating the "bi-cameral world" of the Polynesians which was divided into the *po,* the other-world, the world of night (*po*), darkness, the original gods, the dead, etc. and the *ao,* the world of light, day (*ao*) life, human activity, and so forth. This original separation was subsequently elaborated differently in different places, and might become formidably complicated, as is suggested by Figure 1, which shows a diagram of the cosmos created by a Tuamotuan informant for an inquisitive missionary in the late nineteenth century. The cosmos as a whole takes the form of a nested arrangement of "shells" (*'apu*), each associated with a particular cosmogonic episode of separation; and pathways or ladders are indicated by means of which intercourse is possible between different cosmological levels.

Polynesian thought about the universe differed from Judaeo-Christian "creationist" thought in that it was predicated, not on the creation of the universe *ex nihilo,* by God, but on the initial existence of everything in an all-embracing plenum or tightly-bound continuum. The creative epoch occurred as a process of "differentiation" within this pre-existing plenum, undertaken by a God who made "cuts". The Tahitian creation chant, part of which I am about to cite, is really wrongly so called, because nothing whatsoever is "created" in it. Instead, what the God does is to articulate, or differentiate, the world into its distinct components and qualities, but the substance of

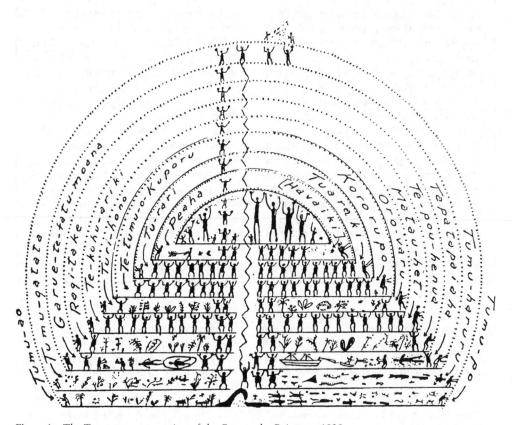

Figure 1   *The Tuamotuan conception of the Cosmos by Paiore, c. 1820*

the newly-articulated cosmos remains what it always was, nothing other than the God himself. The name borne by *Ta'aroa*, the Tahitian creator god, actually means "the severer". *Ta'aroa* is called thus because he made the initial severance between the *po* and the *ao*, and he created the various natural phenomena by rearranging his own body:

> So he overturned his shell and raised it up to form the sky . . . and he slipped out of another shell which covered him which he took for rock and sand. But his anger was not yet appeased, so he took his spine for a mountain range, his ribs for mountain slopes, his vitals for the broad fleeting clouds, his flesh for the fatness of the earth, his arms and legs for the strength of the earth, his finger-nails and toe-nails for scales and shells for the fishes, his feathers for trees, shrubs and creepers, to clothe the earth, his intestines for lobsters, shrimps and eels for the rivers and seas, and the blood of *Ta'aroa* got heated and drifted away for redness for the sky and the rainbows . . . *Ta'aroa* had crusts, that is, shells, so everything has a shell.
>
> The sky is a shell, that is, endless space in which the God placed the sun, the moon, the sporades [the scattered or individual stars], and the constellations of the gods. The earth is a shell to the stones, the water, the plants which spring from it. Man's shell is woman, because it is by her that he comes into the world, and woman's shell is woman, because she is born of woman. One cannot enumerate the shells of all the things the world produces. (Henry 1928: 339–40)

This projection of the body of the God into the phenomenal world, though developed in an exceedingly poetic way in the texts assembled by Teuira Henry, was not in itself an unorthodox conception of cosmogenesis. But it had profound consequences for the subsequent development and elaboration of indigenous religious thought. Because the *po* and the *ao* were originally emergent parts of a continuum, their separation had, for the Polynesians, only a provisional character, and they continually threatened to merge together again. Indeed the very instruments that kept them apart, kept them together and in communication. This was brought out most perspicuously in relation to the four props (*to'o*) which Ta'aroa positioned in order to keep the sky up and open a space (*atea*) for the *ao*, the world of light and of humanity. The props that separated the *po* and the *ao* also, by definition, joined them together, and thus became the exemplary prototypes of sacred objects, endowed with the power to communicate the divine presence. Society Islands politics revolved around rival claims to control certain ultra-sacred wooden billets, called *to'o*, which were counterparts of the "props" of the cosmos as a whole. But, being so sacred, these wooden billets had themselves to be separated from the world, whose continued existence/differentiation they guaranteed; so they were confined to an elaborate ark, and were massively bound around with sennit cordage, and other wrappings, and were only uncovered on the most sacred and propitious occasions, requiring many human sacrifices to allay the danger they presented to mortals, however sanctified by birth and ritual preparations (Henry 1928; Oliver 1974).

The cosmogonic scheme of differentiation rather than creation *ex nihilo* and of immanent rather than transcendent divinity was, I think, the source of certain ontological anxieties that played an enormous part in Polynesian life. For us, the immanent *deus sive natura* of Spinoza represents an optimistic rather than a pessimistic deism, a blessed relief from the angry and punishing Almighty God of traditional Christianity, set apart from His creation and judging it harshly. But that is because the idea of an immanent God was never really naturalized in Christian Europe, however much eighteenth-century intellectuals may have hankered after one. In Polynesia the situation was the precise opposite; the immanence of the Gods was the source of continuous anxiety (the proverbial hedonism of the South Sea Islanders was founded on a sense of acute and abiding hysteria) and the rapidity and enthusiasm with which the Polynesians accomplished their conversion to Christianity stemmed from their untold relief upon discovering that God was, after all, transcendent, not part of this world.

In this essay, the theme I want to address is Polynesian anxiety about immanence, about differentiation, and some of the ways in which this fundamental anxiety shaped the patterns of their cultural life. That is to say, I want to explore some of the ways in which the underlying conception of the creation of the world through a process of differentiation (splitting, separation) gave rise to countervailing pressure towards fusion, absorption, collapse, etc., which had to be continually held in check through ritual action. In particular I want to identify the symbolic strategies through which social individuals sought to keep immanence at bay, while, at the same time, acknowledging the fundamental fact that immanence pervaded the world and constituted it. The essential strategy of counter-immanence (averting the danger of being absorbed, de-differentiated, etc.) was the recapitulation, in one form or another, of the process of separation on which both the cosmos in general, and the being of the individual, were founded. In other words, the cosmogonic activities of *Ta'aroa* the severer had to be recapitulated at the level of the individual subject; not out of a vainglorious desire to emulate the God, but certainly for the same reasons that the creative gods engaged in the original splitting, i.e. in order to open a space, to establish a difference. And just as the original cosmogonic act was the opening up of a domain, within the plenum, which was relatively non-sacred (the *ao*, the world of light) so the means of ritually securing the subject was the opening of a space between the subject and the sacred domain whence he originated.

Most important Polynesian ritual operated in precisely the inverse sense to Christian communion, i.e. the intention was to cause the divinity to leave (some part of) the world, rather than to induce the divinity to enter (some part of) it. There were no rituals through which persons (e.g. kings) were consecrated, because they were already all-too-sacred, but action in the world was impossible for persons of high intrinsic sanctity, because they did not truly belong to it, belonging, instead, to the *po*. Thus, for instance, the non-executive sacred ruler of Tonga, the *Tu'i* Tonga, was not mourned when he died, and his funeral mound was covered with excrement rather than offerings, because he had never lived (Bott 1982). Instead of being sanctified, Polynesians of high

intrinsic (i.e. genealogically-based) rank had to be elaborately de-sanctified. Thus, the main passage-rites of the Society Islands were the *amo'a* or "head-releasing" rituals through which children, who were considered to be "little gods" (and highly *tapu*) were made "secular" by being offered blood drawn from the congregation, which replaced their sacred substance and freed them for ordinary worldly social interactions.

We can begin to consider the consequences of the cosmology of immanence for personal ontology by dwelling for a moment on the general Polynesian word for "god", *atua*. This word is based on the morpheme *tua*, which means "back", or the far, invisible, side of any object. The particularly sacred parts of a human being were the back (the spine) and the head – i.e. precisely those parts of the body that cannot normally be seen by their possessor. The *atua* (spiritual element) of the person was the *tua* (back) of the person. *Tua* also refers to elders and ancestors, the "back" portions of time, and these were also sacred. Immanent divinity was not a contingent presence, but a categorical, dimensional, feature of objects, spaces, times. Ordinary human intercourse was front to front, expressed in western Polynesia (and Fiji) in the fundamental social morality of "facing one another" (*fa'agaga*, cf. Shore 1982), while it was always strictly forbidden to move about behind some important person, invisibly to them. The back was the "individual" as opposed to the cosmological *po*, the inaccessible, threatening, but ever-present unseen. But it was possible also to intervene so as to protect this aspect of the person.

I think one can identify two basic strategies through which the integrity of the person could be maintained against cosmological collapse, to which I have attached the labels of "closure" and "multiplication". "Closure" is the provision of extra reinforcement, hardening the target of spiritual danger, while "multiplication" is the strategy of reduplicating the person in myriad forms. We can see both strategies at work in the cosmological myths referred to above: thus *Ta'aroa* multiplies himself by opening up the *ao*, assuming his myriad immanent forms; but also he closes it off with the "shells" (secured by the "props") so that it cannot fall in again. In fact, the entire cosmos consisted of such "shells", as Figure 1 shows. But, as the chant also specifies, people were also "shells", and so were their kin-groups. (In the eighteenth century, 'apu, "shell" was the standard Tahitian expression for the bilateral kindred, the basic unit of social organization, cf. Maori: hapu.) But rather than continue with these general observations, let me turn to consider some more specific imagery of closure and multiplication in the context of Polynesian art traditions.

Polynesian carving is particularly rich in Janiform images (Figure 2), which, though they occur elsewhere (particularly in India), nowhere assume the importance they have in this part of the globe. Figure 2, which we may take as a typical instance, is one of a small number of images of Siamese twin goddesses carved from whales' teeth, all of which were actually collected in Fiji, where they were regarded as the consorts of Ndeng'ei, the main god; but they are known to have been carved in Ha'apai (part of the Tongan group of islands), and they probably originally represented the Tongan Siamese twin culture heroines Nafanua and Tokupulu. The Tongan Siamese twin goddesses (Colocott 1921; Reiter 1907), who play an important role in the Tongan creation myth (and were responsible for assuring plentiful catches for Tongan fishermen), have Samoan counterparts in the form of the twins Taema and Tilafaega, also known as Nafanua the goddesses of tattooing and warfare respectively (Kraemer 1902). I do not want to expand on the mythological detail, but I would like to offer some suggestions as to why Janiform images of this type had so much ritual significance in the area.

The Siamese twin archetype combines closure and multiplication in their most elementary forms. The most outstanding feature of a Siamese twin is symmetry about the vertical axis, not only in one plane (left/right) but also about the other vertical plane (front/back). In other words, a Siamese twin has no "back", only a middle and a periphery. Such a being is protected, or encompassing, in a way in which no ordinary mortal can be. For merely one-dimensionally symmetric beings the back

Figure 2 *Tongan twin deities carved in whale ivory. Collected in Fiji by Gordon (Haddon Museum)*

always remains the most vulnerable area. . . . Siamese twins are immune from such dangers, and have therefore a kind of completeness which justifies their being considered among the immortals. Indeed, they seem to adumbrate creation (as splitting) itself, since their image seems to capture the moment at which the god created the world by splitting apart the plenum, which was himself. Siamese twins obviously qualify as "multiplied" beings, but at the same time they are closed in that their twofold symmetry closes off that part of the ordinary being which is open to assault from the back.

It would therefore be natural to expect that one of the strategies through which ordinary mortals might seek to recapitulate, in themselves original cosmogonic splitting, and thereby assure the integrity of their persons, might be to imitate the twins, and attach a secondary person to their backs. We are able to know that this possibility occurred to the minds of the inhabitants of Western Polynesia, from where the statuettes of the Siamese twin goddesses come, not because they practised artificial twinning, but because they were specifically disallowed from doing so. George Turner, a nineteenth-century missionary ethnographer, recorded that in Samoa it was forbidden for members of the family to sit leaning against one another back-to-back, on pain of immediate fatal, divine retribution (Turner 1884). I believe that in contemporary Christian Samoa it would still be thought very improper to adopt this posture. Turner also noted that all fruit or vegetables that grew together to form a fused pair (as happens sometimes with bananas, taro, yams, etc.) were immediately to be offered to the gods and might on no account be eaten. He makes both these observations in the same paragraph, and leaves one in no doubt that they were connected; but he offers no more specific explanation. In the light of what has been said so far, I think one can reasonably infer that the principle of the "sacredness of doubles" and the prohibition on back-to-back sitting relate to the image of divinities as protected, encompassing back-less beings who escape from the fundamental ontological deficit of ordinary mortals, i.e. an asymmetrical relationship with *tua*, the back. To become such a double being was to usurp a privilege afforded to the gods (or goddesses) alone. It was sacrilege, in other words.

But although overt doubling-up was not a feasible symbolic strategy, since it infringed too much on divine privilege (like eating "double" fruit or vegetables) there were other, more indirect means of achieving a similar result. At this point, multiplication and closure begin to diverge. Let me take multiplication first. Returning to the Siamese twin image, one possible reading of it is that it represents a mutual and symmetrical parturition (note that

the Western Polynesian mythic twins are all female). There is a direct connection between the idea of doubling and birth. Momentarily, at least, any woman giving birth is a Siamese twin, and indeed in the Marquesas (if not anywhere else, so far as I know) the word for "birth" (*fanau*) also referred to fused-double objects, such as double bananas, etc. (Dordillon 1934–5). It goes without saying that there is a strong relationship between cosmogony and birth, where cosmogony is specifically not conceptualized as creation *ex nihilo*: the God of the Old Testament does not noticeably "give birth" to the cosmos whereas the corresponding Polynesian texts, as has frequently been noticed, are permeated with procreative symbolism. Birth among mortals was also a process of cosmological significance recapitulating creation, in that children (in some places only the children of élite kindreds) were believed to come from the *po* and to be, in fact gods; exceptionally sacred, ranking higher than their parents (Oliver 1974). Because women were capable of recapitulating divine cosmogonic acts and were the means through which divinities entered the *ao*, it follows that women were not just more sacred, but also more protected against "defilement" (which I construe as de-differentiation) than men. Women were "naturally" *noa* (*me'ie*, etc.: various synonyms), i.e. "clear", non-sacred in the sense of being not endangered by other persons, though very capable of harming others, especially males, by infringing their *tapu* (Hanson 1982).

Tapu (Tahitian *ra'a*) was the general quality of personal, sacred distinctiveness, which was continually subject to dispersion. It is usually glossed as "sacredness", and so much has been written on the subject, that I hesitate to embark on a discussion of it here. But, as briefly as possible, here are the salient points. Objects and persons were *tapu* insofar as they were held to be invested with *po*-derived, *atua*-derived attributes and qualities. Because these sacred properties were immanent, they were liable to dispersion: any object, or person invested with *tapu* quality remained so only insofar as that object, or person did not lapse back or become merged, with the generality of things. Immanent sacredness can be localized and preserved only via isolation from non-sacred things: it is quite different from our kind of sacredness, which is transcendental in which the sacred object is secular until it has been consecrated by ritual action. With immanent sacredness it is the object, or the person which is sacred simply by virtue of being that object or person because, in some way, it is itself an *atua*. Broadly speaking, things and persons contained *tapu* in proportion to the extent to which their existence recapitulated cosmogonic acts. Persons (especially of the élite) were sacred because their coming-into-being recapitulated the birth of gods. Creative activities, such as carving, canoe-building or tattooing were sacred because the activity of craftsmen is godlike, they cut things, make lines, hollow things out, and so on. Another way of putting this is to say that *tapu* is "difference" in the sense that any thing or person that is non-substitutable, whose being there and then makes a difference, is characteristically *tapu*, and must be protected from indiscriminate contacts that diminish this difference. The effect of the philosophical attitude of immanence, just as is the case in India, is to place the whole weight of the religious system on the preservation of distinctions and boundaries (Dumont 1970). Where there is a god in everything, the need to keep things apart is overwhelming, because only this separation preserves essences, and essence precedes existence. Where boundaries are transgressed, annihilation follows.

To return to the question of the differential "sacredness" of males and females. Male *tapu* qualities were intrinsically vulnerable, though they also had their means of defence, which I will consider shortly. But women, though no less imbued with *tapu* than males (sometimes more) were not vulnerable to quite the same extent, because a woman is, so to speak, a complete system of differences in herself, a microcosm, whereas males were irreducibly incomplete beings, dependent on women for their presence in the world (and their departure from it). Women were containers and conductors of *tapu* quality, whereas men simply possessed *tapu* like a static electrical charge, and could be much more easily deprived of it. As the Tahitian chant says,

"woman is the shell of woman, because she is born of woman". On the surface this indicates a transitive relation

$$\text{woman (1)} \to \text{woman (2)} \to \text{(3)} \to \text{(n)}$$

in which one woman gives birth to another. But the phraseology suggests at the same time a recursive, self-referential relationship

$$\text{woman (1)} \to \text{woman (1)} \to \text{(1)} \to \ldots$$

i.e. a woman giving birth recapitulates her own birth, *ad infinitum*. Whereas the schemes, also given in the chant,

$$\text{woman} \to \text{man}$$

admits of no such interpretation. Hence, I would argue, the procreative powers of women make them *temporally* "symmetrical" beings (beings with no past and no future) in a way precisely analogous to the *spatial* symmetry of Siamese twins along the spatial axis front/back. They are thus, like the Siamese twins, both multiple and closed, their *tapu* not lessened by the fact that it is in no danger from without.

For males this solution does not exist: they faced an acute problem in becoming sufficiently *noa/me'ie* in order to carry on a normal existence, while not dispersing their *tapu* quality in such a fashion as to lose their distinctiveness. They had essentially two possibilities: they could find other means of imitating the natural characteristics of Siamese twins, women, etc., which enabled them to contain their sacredness so that it was not in danger from without, or they could disperse their sacredness under "controlled" conditions. I will consider instances of both of these.

One means that men could and did employ in order to convert themselves from mortals, with the fundamental ontological deficit that mortality implies, into "complete" beings, recapitulating cosmogony, was tattooing, which was widely practised in Polynesia, especially by men (almost exclusively by men in Western Polynesia). Tattooing was an obligatory passage rite of late adolescence for males, particularly in Samoa, which produced tattoo artists for the Tongan élite as well. As was noted above, tattooing was thought to have originated from the Siamese twin goddesses, *Tilafaenga* and *Teama* (who brought it from Fiji). This mythical association of tattooing with Siamese twins underlines the latent equivalence between the strategy of multiplication-twinning and the strategy of tattooing which was predicated mainly on "closure". One is able to know this by making a study of tattooing ritual and the nomenclature of tattoo designs. Figures 3, 4, and 5 show tattoo designs, two from Western Polynesia (Samoa), the other from Eastern Polynesia (the Marque-

sas). Of the three, the Samoan examples are the simpler, so I will discuss it first.

Samoan tattooing was a necessary preparation for war and for sexual life; untattooed males might not engage in either. Both of these were dangerous activities: it has already been made clear that women, by virtue of their position as mediators between the *po* and the *ao*, were a potent source of spiritual danger. Warfare was as well, indirectly, in that death in battle was never merely a matter of military incompetence, but would always be traced to spiritual debility. Tattooing strengthened young males and prepared them for warlike and amatory exploits. But how was tattooing conceptualized? To begin with, let us note that the area that was first tattooed was the lower part of the back, i.e. *tua*, and that over this vulnerable part were placed designs of a specifically protective nature (Buck 1930; Kraemer 1902; Stair 1897). The back-design as a whole was called *pe'a*, "flying fox", alluding, among other things, to the motto of the king-making descent-group of *Sava'i*, the *Tonumaipe'a*, descendants of *Nafanua*, which was "salvation comes from the flying fox". More generally, the flying fox was a well-protected animal;

Figure 3 *Samoan male tattooing (rear), by Kramer©*

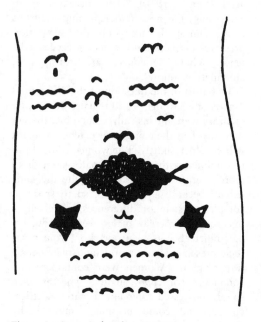

Figure 4 *Samoan female tattooing*

KAHI
HANAUPE

1 hope·vehine
2 ti'i pepehipu mit
   α matahoata
   β niho peata
3 ti'i pepehipu mit β &
   γ papua
4 ti'i kaokao mit α &
   δ Pohu
5 ti'i pii kohe mit α &
   ε opea
6· 6' kohe·ta mit ♂,
   η kofati &
   ι°· hiku·atu
7 vau
8 mataio
9 aniata
10 ama opea
11 paka hope
12 paka iti
13 paka nui
14 paka puha
15 papua
16 kake

Figure 5 *Marquesan tattooing (side), by Von den Steinen*©

anyone who has seen a flying fox securely wrapped in its enfolding wings will understand why. The design, which vaguely recalls the wing-shape of a flying fox, wrapped round the body. The back-design also has another name, *tapulu*, which means approximately "tattooed wrapping" (*ta + pulu*). Other motifs are "bindings" (*fusi*) "beams" (*aso*), etc., suggesting that the metaphor of tattooing is the construction of a housing or defensive screen covering the body. Finally, the last and ritually perhaps the most significant tattoo was applied to the navel (*pute*). Horatio Hale (1846) enquired about this, and was told the navel had to be tattooed out of "shame", because that was the part of the male body that was connected to the mother. One can certainly discount the idea that it was modesty as we would understand it that required the tattooing of the navel; everything suggests that it was the need to seal off the body, definitively, from the *po* and from the danger of dispersion via female "conductors" of *tapu* quality. The mark over the *pute* was called a *fusi*, a binding, making clear that this was indeed the idea.

The metaphoric basis of Samoan male tattoo was therefore biased towards closure rather than multiplication. But the implicit identity between the two (Milner 1969) is nonetheless suggested in the famous proverb

Tupu le tane, ta le tatau
Tupu fafine, fanafanau.

"The man grows up, he is tattooed,
The woman grows up, she gives birth."

But the imagery of multiplication could also be incorporated into the general anti-dispersive prophylaxis of tattooing. In order to see this one has to turn from the elegant restraint of Samoan tattoo, to the more florid style of the Marquesas. In the Marquesas, tattooing was called *pahu tikl*, literally, "wrapping in images" (*tiki*). It was obligatory for the same reasons as in Samoa, i.e. warfare and sexuality, and was applied in collective ceremonies which bear a strong resemblance to their Western Polynesian prototypes (W. Handy 1922).

The Marquesan tattooing style follows design principles which can be traced back 2,000 years to Lapitan pottery decoration, in that it consists of delimited "zones with decorative 'infills'" (Green 1979). Between the zones there are narrow undecorated strips, so that the form as a whole articulates into distinct segments (in Marquesan, *paka*, "crusts"). The effect of the zone-infill principle is to interfere with the perception of outlines, so that the body seems to dissolve into myriad fragments. This fragmentation, in turn corresponds to the non-unitary way in which the Marquesans treated their bodies conceptually, in that it was customary (for chiefs, especially) to have separate proper names for individual body-parts in addition to a personal name (Linton 1923). Thus a man (Roger, say) would have a head called Peter, a back called William, an arm called Charles and genitals called Henry, etc. Each of these separately-named members of the body would have its own life, be subject to its own *tapu* restrictions, and so on. The same principle applied to important artefacts, such as canoes, which also had separate proper names for all their different parts. In this, one perceives the passion for distinctiveness which, I have argued, is the corollary of the religious premises of immanence; difference, non-substitutability, is at a premium because it is only provisional, and can be annihilated at a stroke. . . .

The effects of tattooing was to de-totalize the body into distinct fragments, exaggerating differences and conserving *tapu* quality. But the fragments themselves, the "crusts", were a means of giving integrity to the body as a whole, by "wrapping" it. Often this is brought out in the nomenclature of individual motifs, which metaphorically evoke certain well-protected, enclosed creatures, objects and spaces (W. Handy 1922; Von den Steinen 1925). The most important animal motif was *honu* or *kea*, the generic name for testudinates, turtles and tortoises. These were particularly sacred creatures, which could only be eaten by chiefs, as a result of prestige conferred on them by their excellent armour, which corresponded to the ideal of "closure." Other "closure" motifs were shellfish motifs (*poi'i*), crab motifs (*karu*), enclosed garden motifs (*papua*), and a large class of motifs based on *ipu* (calabash, bowl, dish, etc.). But inspection of Figure 5 also reveals that, besides "enclosing" the body, Marquesan tattoo also protected it from immanence by multiplying it. The person was multiplied via an entourage of tattooed supernumeraries thronging his armoured integument. There are two types of such motifs: homunculi (*etua*, "gods") and tattooed "secondary faces", as Von den Steinen calls them. There is a clear structural relationship between the tattooing style of the Marquesas, in which the self was furnished with a collection of subsidiary selves to surround and protect it, and the type of Siamese twin image found in Figure 2, . . . The effect of the tattooing of "*etua*" motifs and secondary faces was to convert the body into such an *n*-tuplet. This is revealed particularly clearly in one Langsdorff's engravings of a young Marquesan Warrior sketched in 1801 by a Russian expedition (Figure 6). While mid-nineteenth-century Marquesan tattooing had become somewhat abstract, the more readable eighteenth-century style featured an important motif consisting of a death's-head positioned directly over the midline of the back. This design (*mata Komo'e*) had specifically military and protective functions, representing a dead (divinized) chief who was to be avenged. The Marquesan warrior, with his ghostly companion at his back, warding off harm, provides a striking

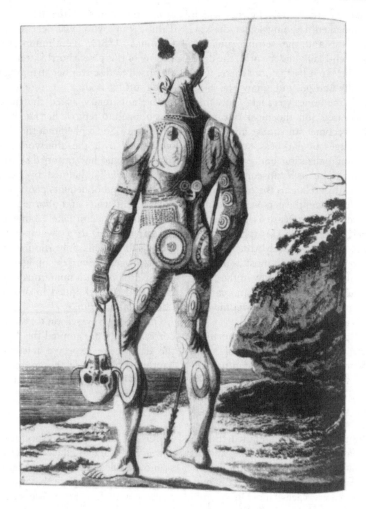

Figure 6 *Marquesan tattooing (incomplete), by Von den Steinen*©

male counterpart to the female Siamese twin images we considered earlier (cf. Figure 2). [. . .]

My general argument, up to now, has been that Polynesian cosmology is correlated with the religious attitude of immanence. The world is a space within the deity (the plenum of deity) that is kept apart through the preservation of difference. But everything in the *ao* has only a relative – one could say, "an embattled" – existence, and must eventually be consumed by the night, as the Maori culture-hero Maui was crushed within the grinding genitals of *Hine-nui-te-po*, in his vain attempt to confer immor-

tality on himself, and on mankind (to have achieved this he would have had to pass right through her, exiting through her mouth into the unimaginable country beyond the night). The Polynesians' refusal of transcendence explains both the extraordinary passion of their mourning ceremonies, and the unbounded relief, which I mentioned before, afforded them by Christian eschatology. What I want to turn to now is certain Polynesian mortuary practices that reflected the underlying religious attitudes to which I have referred.

The outcome of ordinary deaths, in most Polynesian belief systems, was that the dead person would return to the *po*, a journey which was usually imagined as going under the sea, towards the west and the setting sun. On arrival in the pitch-black underworld, the dead person would be eaten by the *atua* there, who would gradually scrape and gnaw the flesh away until only the bones were left. Only then would the deceased (on the most optimistic assumptions) become an *atua* himself or herself. The images of darkness, submersion, excoriation, cannibalization and extinction – not as punishment, but as a consequence of the mere fact of death – relate to the fundamental nemesis that must await the person in a cosmos pervaded by immanence. Death assumes a particularly terrifying shape in this type of intellectual milieu, and it is surely true that the Polynesians went further than most in increasing its terrors in the here and now in the treatment they meted out to the weak and captive whom they made into cannibal victims and human sacrifices.

The typical pattern of Polynesian mortuary practices (in Central and East Polynesia, anyway) was, first of all, exaggerated mourning, usually involving self-scarification by the bereaved, especially women, and the dispatching of funerary victims, in the case of great chiefs. There followed the exposure of the corpse and "mummification" (so called, though it was not really comparable to the ancient Egyptian variety), followed eventually by the final disposal of the dry remains, usually only the bones, in secret places, most frequently caves. Some bones were kept in family temples, and some were turned into ornaments, weapons and tools; but it would not be true to say that they ever became significant cult objects.

The only aspect of these mortuary practices that I propose to discuss here is the middle phase of the sequence, i.e. the desiccation or mummification of the corpse. And the point that I want to make about this phase of the mortuary sequence is that, once again, it reflects the basic cosmological scheme of immanence. Here I have one final illustration . . . of a scene witnessed, in 1844, by the missionary . . . Père Aimable Petithomme . . . (Williamson 1933). In this year died Iotete, in his hey-day called "le roi de *Tahuata*", a Marquesan chief of great stature, cunning, and renown, who sought to

attain the status of the *Pomare* "Kings" of Tahiti, but who was eventually humbled (Thomas 1986). Petithomme, visiting the widow of this chief shortly after his death, was surprised to discover her stripping the skin, bit by bit, off his body.

The missionary asked the queen why she was obliged to remove her late husband's skin in this way. She replied that the goddess *Oupu*, who ruled over the afterworld, had decreed that none who had tattooed skins might enter the "*Havaiki*" inhabited by the gods themselves, "a land of delights planted with all sorts of excellent fruits and adorned by the waters of a blue and calm lake", but would be consigned for ever to a swamp where the sun never shone. This obligation to excoriate the corpse (together with the obligation to feed the gods of the *po* with numerous mortuary sacrifices) had to be fulfilled in order to assure a "desirable" afterlife.

One can easily see that excoriation of the corpse simply pre-empted the "scraping" that the dead were expected to undergo at the hands of the *atua* in the *po* according to the standard conception of the afterlife in Polynesian religion.

[. . .]

But why did the queen specifically state that it was necessary to efface the tattooing on the skin of her dead consort in order to assure his place in paradise? Here the arguments of this paper comes full circle. We saw earlier that tattooing was conceptualized as "wrapping" (*pahu*) – wrapping that preserved the integrity of the self and prevented the diffusion of difference and *tapu*. Tattooing was a necessary part of worldly existence, part of a battery of essentially "defensive" structures that constituted the Polynesian ego – "character armour", to borrow a very apposite phrase from the ego-psychology of W. Reich (1950). But tattooing was incompatible with unmediated sacredness. For all the effort and inventiveness that the Marquesans lavished on the art of tattoo, they explicitly believed that their gods were *not* tattooed.

Finally, when the fragile defensive structures on which they depended caved in, and life was at an end, it was necessary to dismantle the defences bit by bit, in order fully to achieve the fusion and de-differentiation of absolute death. Not to attain a subsequent state of immortality, but an antecedent one: to make it as if the living individual had never been at all. Hence the mortuary sequence is essentially a playing out of the cosmogonic process in reverse, enacting gestation and birth in reverse (or "deconception": cf. Mosko 1983) at the hands of the female mourners/cannibals. The incremental logic of the passage through life's stages was replaced by a subtractive logic of remorseless exposure, desiccation and dissipation. This was not a "new birth" as Dante imagines it, in his famous lines on the flaying of Marsyas, who finds everlasting life "*Traeste dalla vagina delle membre sue*" – "dragged from the sheath (vagina) of his own limbs" – so much as birth undone, life stripped away, and a return to the *status quo ante*, in which the creation of the universe and all its consequent effects had been cancelled and annulled.

NOTE

Further discussion of the topics raised in this essay are continued in a book written by myself and published by Clarendon Press entitled *Wrapping in Images: Tattooing in Polynesia*.

REFERENCES

Bott, E. (1982). Tongan Society at the Time of Captain Cook's Visit. *Memoirs of the Polynesian Society*, 44. Wellington.

Buck, Sir P. (1930). Samoan Material Culture. *Bishop Museum Bulletin*, No. 75. Honolulu.

Colocott, V. (1921). Notes on Tongan Religion. *Journal of the Polynesian Society*, 30, 152–63, 227–40.

Dordillon (1934–5). *Dictionnaire de l'homme des îles Marquises*. Société des Océanistes, Paris.

Dumont, L. (1970). *Homo Hierachicus*. University of Chicago Press, Chicago.

Gell, A. (1993). *Wrapping in Images: Tattooing in Polynesia*. Clarendon Press, Oxford.

Green, R. (1979). Early Lapita Art. In: S. Mead (ed.), *Exploring the Visual Art of Oceania*. University of Hawaii Press, Honolulu.

Hale, H. (1846). *United States Exploring Expedition 1838–42 under the Command of Captain Wilkes . . . Ethnology and Philology*. Lea and Blanchard, Philadelphia.

Handy, E. (1923). Native Culture of the Marquesas. *Bishop Museum Bulletin*, 9. Honolulu.

Handy, W. (1922). Tattooing in the Marquesas. *Bishop Museum Bulletin*, 1. Honolulu.

Hanson, F. (1982). Female Pollution in Polynesia. *Journal of the Polynesian Society*, 91, 335–81.

Henry, T. (1928). Ancient Tahiti. *Bishop Museum Bulletin*, 48. Honolulu.

Kraemer, A. (1902). *Die Samoa-Inseln*. E. Schweizerbart, Stuttgart.

Linton, R. (1923). The Material Culture of the Marquesas. *Bishop Museum Memoirs*, No. 8, Part 5. Honolulu.

Milner, G. (1969). Siamese Twins, Birds and the Double Helix. *Man*, NS 4, 5–24.

Mosko, M. (1983). Conception, Deconception and Social Structure in Bush Mekeo culture. *Mankind*, 14, 24–32.

Oliver, D. (1974). *Ancient Tahitian Society*. University of Hawaii Press, Honolulu.

Reich, W. (1950). *Selected Writings*. Vision Press, London.

Reiter, F. (1907). Traditions Tonguiennes. *Anthropos*, 2, 743–54.

Shore, B. (1982). *Sala'ilua: A Samoan Mystery*. Columbia University Press, New York.

Stair, J. (1897). *Old Samoa*. Religious Tract Society, London.

Steinen, K. Von den (1925). *Die Marquesaner und ihre Kunst*. D. Reimer, Berlin.

Thomas, N. (1986). Le Roi de Tahuata. *Journal of Pacific History*, 21, 3–20.

—— (1990). *Marquesan Societies*. Oxford University Press, Oxford.

Turner, G. (1884). *Samoa 100 Years Ago and Long Before*. Macmillan, London.

Williamson, R. (1933). *The Religious and Cosmic Beliefs of Central Polynesia*. Cambridge University Press, Cambridge.

23

Cosmological Deixis and Amerindian Perspectivism

Eduardo Viveiros de Castro

Eduardo Viveiros de Castro is a Brazilian anthropologist who has taught in Rio de Janeiro, Paris, and Cambridge. Here he provides a brilliant and original account of Amerindian cosmology, situating it with respect to the literature on totemism, animism, and myth. He shows the lively fieldwork-inspired legacy of Lévi-Strauss in Brazilian anthropology and is also able to link his account of lowland (Amazonian) South American groups to people as far away as the Cree of northern Canada. He describes what he calls "perspectivism" and "multinaturalism": the ideas that humans, animals, and spirits see both themselves and one another differently from different kinds of bodies.

Viveiros de Castro's essay is also an intervention in the literature on shamanism, providing a particularly sharp account of what it is the shaman does

and linking shamanism in a fascinating but nonreductionist way to hunting. The discussion of body decoration can be instructively compared to Gell's account of Polynesian tattooing. Note also that whereas the thrust of Stallybrass and White's arguments might be to see universals in a practice like masking, Viveiros de Castro distinguishes very sharply between masking in Amerindian society and in the West. For a more complete picture, turn to his monograph (1992).

Further references to Amazonian and Northern North American cosmologies can be found in the essay. From a very rich field, excellent accounts include Descola (1994), Graham (1995), and Hugh-Jones (1979) from Amazonia, Hallowell (1960, 1967 [1955]) on Ojibwa, Witherspoon (1977) on Navajo, and Ortiz (1969) on Tewa from North America.

Eduardo Viveiros de Castro, "Cosmological Deixis and Amerindian Perspectivism," *Journal of the Royal Anthropological Institute*, n.s. 4 (3) (Oxford: Blackwell Publishers, 1998): 469–88.

This study discusses the meaning of Amerindian "perspectivism": the ideas in Amazonian cosmologies concerning the way in which humans, animals and spirits see both themselves and one another. Such ideas suggest the possibility of a redefinition of the classical categories of "nature", "culture" and "supernature" based on the concept of perspective or point of view. The study argues in particular that the antinomy between two characterizations of indigenous thought – on the one hand "ethnocentrism", which would deny the attributes of humanity to humans from other groups, and on the other hand "animism", which would extend such qualities to beings of other species – can be resolved if one considers the difference between the spiritual and corporal aspects of beings.

> ...la reciprocité de perspectives où j'ai vu le caractère propre de la pensée mythique...
>
> LÉVI-STRAUSS 1985: 268

Introduction

This article deals with that aspect of Amerindian thought which has been called its "perspectival quality" (Århem 1993): the conception, common to many peoples of the continent, according to which the world is inhabited by different sorts of subjects or persons, human and non-human, which apprehend reality from distinct points of view. This idea cannot be reduced to our current concept of relativism (Lima 1995; 1996), which at first it seems to call to mind. In fact, it is at right angles, so to speak, to the opposition between relativism and universalism. Such resistance by Amerindian perspectivism to the terms of our epistemological debates casts suspicion on the robustness and transportability of the ontological partitions which they presuppose. In particular, as many anthropologists have already concluded (albeit for other reasons), the classic distinction between Nature and Culture cannot be used to describe domains internal to non-Western cosmologies without

first undergoing a rigorous ethnographic critique.

Such a critique, in the present case, implies a redistribution of the predicates subsumed within the two paradigmatic sets that traditionally oppose one another under the headings of "Nature" and "Culture": universal and particular, objective and subjective, physical and social, fact and value, the given and the instituted, necessity and spontaneity, immanence and transcendence, body and mind, animality and humanity, among many more. Such an ethnographically-based reshuffling of our conceptual schemes leads me to suggest the expression, "multinaturalism", to designate one of the contrastive features of Amerindian thought in relation to Western "multiculturalist" cosmologies. Where the latter are founded on the mutual implication of the unity of nature and the plurality of cultures – the first guaranteed by the objective universality of body and substance, the second generated by the subjective particularity of spirit and meaning – the Amerindian conception would suppose a spiritual unity and a corporeal diversity. Here, culture or the subject would be the form of the universal, whilst nature or the object would be the form of the particular.

This inversion, perhaps too symmetrical to be more than speculative, must be developed by means of a plausible phenomenological interpretation of Amerindian cosmological categories, which determine the constitutive conditions of the relational contexts we can call "nature" and "culture". Clearly, then, I think that the distinction between Nature and Culture must be subjected to critique, but not in order to reach the conclusion that such a thing does not exist (there are already too many things which do not exist). The flourishing industry of criticisms of the Westernizing character of all dualisms has called for the abandonment of our conceptually dichotomous heritage, but to date the alternatives have not gone beyond the stage of wishful unthinking. I would prefer to gain a perspective on our own contrasts, contrasting them with the distinctions actually operating in Amerindian perspectivist cosmologies.

Perspectivism

The initial stimulus for the present reflections were the numerous references in Amazonian ethnography to an indigenous theory according to which the way humans perceive animals and other subjectivities that inhabit the world – gods, spirits, the dead, inhabitants of other cosmic levels, meteorological phenomena, plants, occasionally even objects and artefacts – differs profoundly from the way in which these beings see humans and see themselves.

Typically, in normal conditions, humans see humans as humans, animals as animals and spirits (if they see them) as spirits; however animals (predators) and spirits see humans as animals (as prey) to the same extent that animals (as prey) see humans as spirits or as animals (predators). By the same token, animals and spirits see themselves as humans: they perceive themselves as (or become) anthropomorphic beings when they are in their own houses or villages and they experience their own habits and characteristics in the form of culture – they see their food as human food (jaguars see blood as manioc beer, vultures see the maggots in rotting meat as grilled fish, etc.), they see their bodily attributes (fur, feathers, claws, beaks etc.) as body decorations or cultural instruments, they see their social system as organized in the same way as human institutions are (with chiefs, shamans, ceremonies, exogamous moieties, etc.). This "to see as" refers literally to percepts and not analogically to concepts, although in some cases the emphasis is placed more on the categorical rather than on the sensory aspect of the phenomenon.

In sum, animals are people, or see themselves as persons. Such a notion is virtually always associated with the idea that the manifest form of each species is a mere envelope (a "clothing") which conceals an internal human form, usually only visible to the eyes of the particular species or to certain trans-specific beings such as shamans. This internal form is the "soul" or "spirit" of the animal: an intentionality or subjectivity formally identical to human consciousness, materializable, let us say, in a human bodily schema concealed behind an animal mask. At first sight then, we would have a distinction between an anthropomorphic essence of a spiritual type, common to animate beings, and a variable bodily appearance, characteristic of each individual species but which rather than being a fixed attribute is instead a changeable and removable clothing. This notion of "clothing" is one of the privileged expressions of metamorphosis – spirits, the dead and shamans who assume animal form, beasts that turn into other beasts, humans that are inadvertently turned into animals – an omnipresent process in the "highly transformational world" (Rivière 1994: 256) proposed by Amazonian ontologies.[1]

This perspectivism and cosmological transformism can be seen in various South American ethnographies, but in general it is only the object of short commentaries and seems to be quite unevenly elaborated.[2] It can also be found, and maybe with even greater generative value, in the far north of North America and Asia, as well as amongst hunter-gatherer populations of other parts of the world.[3] In South America, the cosmologies of the Vaupés area are in this respect highly developed (see Århem 1993; 1996; Hugh-Jones 1996; Reichel-Dolmatoff 1985), but other Amazonian societies, such as the Wari' of Rondônia (Vilaça 1992) and the Juruna of the Middle Xingu (Lima 1995; 1996), also give equal emphasis to the theme.

Some general observations are necessary. Perspectivism does not usually involve all animal species (besides covering other beings); the emphasis seems to be on those species which perform a key symbolic and practical role such as the great predators and the principal species of prey for humans – one of the central dimensions, possibly even the fundamental dimension, of perspectival inversions refers to the relative and relational statuses of predator and prey (Århem 1993: 11–12; Vilaça 1992: 49–51). On the other hand, however, it is not always clear whether spirits or subjectivities are being attributed to each individual animal, and there are examples of cosmologies which deny consciousness to post-mythical animals (Overing 1985: 249 sqq.; 1986: 245–

6) or some other spiritual distinctiveness (Baer 1994: 89; Viveiros de Castro 1992*a*: 73–4). Nonetheless, as is well known, the notion of animal spirit "masters" ("mothers of the game animals", "masters of the white-lipped peccaries", etc.) is widespread throughout the continent. These spirit masters, clearly endowed with intentionality analogous to that of humans, function as hypostases of the animal species with which they are associated, thereby creating an intersubjective field for human-animal relations even where empirical animals are not spiritualized.

We must remember, above all, that if there is a virtually universal Amerindian notion, it is that of an original state of undifferentiation between humans and animals, described in mythology. Myths are filled with beings whose form, name and behaviour inextricably mix human and animal attributes in a common context of intercommunicability, identical to that which defines the present-day intra-human world. The differentiation between "culture" and "nature", which Lévi-Strauss showed to be the central theme of Amerindian mythology, is not process of differentiating the human from the animal, as in our own evolutionist mythology. The original common condition of both humans and animals is not animality but rather humanity. The great mythical separation reveals not so much culture distinguishing itself from nature but rather nature distancing itself from culture: the myths tell how animals lost the qualities inherited or retained by humans (Brightman 1993: 40, 160; Lévi-Strauss 1985: 14, 190; Weiss 1972: 169–70). Humans are those who continue as they have always been: animals are ex-humans, not humans ex-animals. In sum, "the common point of reference for all beings of nature is not humans as a species but rather humanity as a condition" (Descola 1986: 120).

This is a distinction – between the human species and the human condition – which should be retained. It has an evident connexion with the idea of animal clothing hiding a common spiritual "essence" and with the issue of the general meaning of perspectivism. For the moment, we may simply note one of its main corollaries: the past humanity of animals is added to their present-day spiritual-ity hidden by their visible form in order to produce that extended set of food restrictions or precautions which either declare inedible certain animals that were mythically cosubstantial with humans, or demand their desubjectivization by shamanistic means before they can be consumed (neutralizing the spirit, transubstantiating the meat into plant food, semantically reducing it to other animals less proximate to humans), under the threat of illness, conceived of as a cannibal counter-predation undertaken by the spirit of the prey turned predator, in a lethal inversion of perspectives which transforms the human into animal.[4]

It is worth pointing out that Amerindian perspectivism has an essential relation with shamanism and with the valorization of the hunt. The association between shamanism and this "venatic ideology" is a classic question (for Amazonia, see Chaumeil 1983: 231–2; Crocker 1985: 17–25). I stress that this is a matter of symbolic importance, not ecological necessity: horticulturists such as the Tukano or the Juruna (who in any case fish more than they hunt) do not differ much from circumpolar hunters in respect of the cosmological weight conferred on animal predation, spiritual subjectivation of animals and the theory according to which the universe is populated by extra-human intentionalities endowed with their own perspectives. In this sense, the spiritualization of plants, meteorological phenomena or artefacts seems to me to be secondary or derivative in comparison with the spiritualization of animals: the animal is the extra-human prototype of the Other, maintaining privileged relations with other prototypical figures of alterity, such as affines (Århem 1996; Descola 1986: 317–30; Erikson 1984: 110–12). This hunting ideology is also and above all an ideology of shamans, insofar as it is shamans who administer the relations between humans and the spiritual component of the extra-humans, since they alone are capable of assuming the point of view of such beings and, in particular, are capable of returning to tell the tale. If Western multiculturalism is relativism as public policy, then Amerindian perspectivist shamanism is multi-naturalism as cosmic politics.

Animism

The reader will have noticed that my "perspectivism" is reminiscent of the notion of "animism" recently recuperated by Descola (1992; 1996 [sic]). Stating that all conceptualizations of non-humans always refer to the social domain, Descola distinguishes three modes of objectifying nature: totemism, where the differences between natural species are used as a model for social distinctions; that is, where the relationship between nature and culture is metaphorical in character and marked by discontinuity (both within and between series); animism, where the "elementary categories structuring social life" organize the relations *between* humans and natural species, thus defining a social continuity between nature and culture, founded on the attribution of human dispositions and social characteristics to "natural beings" (Descola 1996 [sic]: 87–8); and naturalism, typical of Western cosmologies, which supposes an ontological duality between nature, the domain of necessity, and culture, the domain of spontaneity, areas separated by metonymic discontinuity. The "animic mode" is characteristic of societies in which animals are the "strategic focus of the objectification of nature and of its socialization" (1992: 115), as is the case amongst indigenous peoples of America, reigning supreme over those social morphologies lacking in elaborate internal segmentations. But this mode can also be found co-existing or combined with totemism, wherein such segmentations exist, the Bororo and their *aroe/bope* dualism being such a case.[5]

These ideas form part of a theory which I cannot discuss here as fully as it would merit. I merely comment on the contrast between animism and naturalism but from a somewhat different angle from the original one. (Totemism, as defined by Descola, seems to me to be a heterogeneous phenomenon, primarily classificatory rather than cosmological: it is not a system of *relations* between nature and culture as is the case in the other two modes, but rather of purely logical and differential *correlations*.)

Animism could be defined as an ontology which postulates the social character of relations between humans and non-humans: the space between nature and society is itself social. Naturalism is founded on the inverted axiom: relations between society and nature are themselves natural. Indeed, if in the animic mode the distinction "nature/culture" is internal to the social world, humans and animals being immersed in the same socio-cosmic medium (and in this sense "nature" is a part of an encompassing sociality), then in naturalist ontology, the distinction "nature/culture" is internal to nature (and in this sense, human society is one natural phenomenon amongst others). Animism has "society" as the unmarked pole, naturalism has "nature": these poles function, respectively and contrastively, as the universal dimension of each mode. Thus animism and naturalism are hierarchical and metonymical structures (this distinguishes them from totemism, which is based on a metaphoric correlation between equipollent opposites).

In Western naturalist ontology, the nature/society interface is natural: humans are organisms like the rest, body-objects in "ecological" interaction with other bodies and forces, all of them ruled by the necessary laws of biology and physics; "productive forces" harness, and thereby express, natural forces. Social relations, that is, contractual or instituted relations between subjects, can only exist internal to human society. But how alien to nature – this would be the problem of naturalism – are these relations? Given the universality of nature, the status of the human and social world is unstable and, as the history of Western thought shows, it perpetually oscillates between a naturalistic monism ("sociobiology" being one of its current avatars) and an ontological dualism of nature/culture ("culturalism" being its contemporary expression). The assertion of this latter dualism, for all that, only reinforces the final referential character of the notion of nature, by revealing itself to be the direct descendant of the opposition between Nature and Super*nature*. Culture is the modern name of Spirit – let us recall the distinction between *Naturwissenschaften* and *Geisteswissenschaften* – or at the least it is the name of the compromise between Nature and Grace. Of animism, we would be tempted to say that the instability is located in the opposite pole: there the problem is how to administer the mixture of humanity and animality constituting animals, and not, as is the case amongst ourselves, the combination of culture and nature which characterize humans; the point is to differentiate a "nature" out of the universal sociality.

However, can animism be defined as a projection of differences and qualities internal to the human world onto non-human worlds, as a "socio-centric" model in which categories and social relations are used to map the universe? This interpretation by analogy is explicit in some glosses on the theory: "if totemic systems model society after nature, then animic systems model nature after society" (Århem 1996: 185). The problem here, obviously, is to avoid any undesirable proximity with the traditional sense of "animism", or with the reduction of "primitive classifications" to emanations of social morphology; but equally the problem is to go beyond other classical characterizations of the relation between society and nature such as Radcliffe-Brown's.[6]

Ingold (1991; 1996) showed how schemes of analogical projection or social modelling of nature escape naturalist reductionism only to fall into a nature/culture dualism which by distinguishing "really natural" nature from "culturally constructed" nature reveals itself to be a typical cosmological antinomy faced with infinite regression. The notion of model or metaphor supposes a previous distinction between a domain wherein social relations are constitutive and literal and another where they are representational and metaphorical. Animism, interpreted as human sociality projected onto the non-human world, would be nothing but the metaphor of a metonymy.

Amongst the questions remaining to be resolved, therefore, is that of knowing whether animism can be described as a figurative use of categories pertaining to the human-social domain to conceptualize the domain of non-humans and their relations with the former. Another question: if animism depends on the attribution of human cognitive and sensory faculties to animals, and the same form of subjectivity, then what in the end is the difference between humans and animals? If animals are people, then why do they not see us as people? Why, to be precise, the perspectivism? Finally, if animism is a way of objectifying nature in which the dualism of nature/culture does not hold, then what is to be done with the abundant indications regarding the centrality of this opposition to South American cosmologies? Are we dealing with just another "totemic illusion", if not with an ingenuous projection of our Western dualism?

Ethnocentrism

In a well-known essay, Lévi-Strauss observed that for "savages" humanity ceases at the boundary of the group, a notion which is exemplified by the widespread autoethnonym meaning "real humans", which, in turn, implies a definition of strangers as somehow pertaining to the domain of the extra-human. Therefore, ethnocentrism would not be the privilege of the West but a natural ideological attitude, inherent to human collective life. Lévi-Strauss illustrates the universal reciprocity of this attitude with an anecdote:

> In the Greater Antilles, some years after the discovery of America, whilst the Spanish were dispatching inquisitional commissions to investigate whether the natives had a soul or not, these very natives were busy drowning the white people they had captured in order to find out, after lengthy observation, whether or not the corpses were subject to putrefaction. (1973: 384)

The general point of this parable (from which Lévi-Strauss derived the famous moral: "The barbarian is first and foremost the man who believes in barbarism") is quite simple: the Indians, like the European invaders, considered that only the group to which they belong incarnates humanity; strangers are on the other side of the border which separates humans from animals and spirits, culture from nature and supernature. As matrix and condition for the existence of ethnocentrism, the nature/culture opposition appears to be universal of social apperception.

At the time when Lévi-Strauss was writing these lines, the strategy of vindicating the full humanity of savages was to demonstrate that they made the same distinctions as we do: the proof that they were true humans is that they considered that they alone were the true humans. Like us, they distinguished culture from nature and they too believed that *Naturvölker* are always the others. The universality of the cultural distinction between Nature and Culture bore witness to the universality of culture as human nature. In sum, the answer to the question of the Spanish investigators (which can be read as a sixteenth-century version of the "problem of other minds") was positive: savages do have souls.

Now, everything has changed. The savages are no longer ethnocentric but rather cosmocentric; instead of having to prove that they are humans because they distinguish themselves from animals, we now have to recognize how *in*human *we* are for opposing humans to animals in a way they never did: for them nature and culture are part of the same sociocosmic field. Not only would Amerindians put a wide berth between themselves and the Great Cartesian Divide which separated humanity from animality, but their views anticipate the fundamental lessons of ecology which we are only now in a position to assimilate (Reichel-Dolmatoff 1976). Before, the Indians' refusal to concede predicates of humanity to other men was of note; now we stress that they extend such predicates far beyond the frontiers of their own species in a demonstration of "ecosophic" knowledge (Århem 1993) which we should emulate in as far as the limits of our objectivism permit. Formerly, it had been necessary to combat the assimilation of the savage mind to narcissistic animism, the infantile stage of naturalism, showing that totemism affirmed the cognitive distinction between culture and nature; now, neo-animism reveals itself as the recognition of the universal admixture of subjects and objects, humans and non-humans against modern *hubris,* the primitive and post-modern "hybrids", to borrow a term from Latour (1991).

Two antinomies then, which are, in fact, only one: either Amerindians are ethnocentrically "stingy" in the extension of their concept of humanity and they "totemically" oppose nature and culture; or they are cosmocentric and "animic" and do not profess to such a distinction, being models of relativist tolerance, postulating a multiplicity of points of view on the world.

I believe that the solution to these antinomies[7] lies not in favouring one branch over the other, sustaining, for example, the argument that the most recent characterization of American attitudes is the correct one and relegating the other to the outer darkness of pre-post-modernity. Rather, the point is to show that the "thesis" as well as the "anti-thesis" are true (both correspond to solid ethnographic intuitions), but that they apprehend the same phenomena from different angles; and also it is to show that both are false in that they refer to a substantivist conceptualization of the categories of Nature and Culture (whether it be to affirm or negate them) which is not applicable to Amerindian cosmologies.

The first point to be considered is that the Amerindian words which are usually translated as "human being" and which figure in those supposedly ethnocentric self-designations do not denote humanity as a natural species. They refer rather to the social condition of personhood, and they function (pragmatically when not syntactically) less as nouns than as pronouns. They indicate the position of the subject; they are enunciative markers, not names. Far from manifesting a semantic shrinking of a common name to a proper name (taking "people" to be the name of the tribe), these words move in the opposite direction, going from substantive to perspective (using "people" as a collective pronoun "we people/us"). For this very reason, indigenous categories of identity have that enormous contextual variability or scope that characterizes pronouns, marking contrastively Ego's immediate kin, his/her local group, all humans, or even all beings endowed with subjectivity: their coagulation as "ethnonyms" seems largely to be an artefact of interactions with ethnographers. Nor is it by chance that the majority of Amerindian ethnonyms which enter the literature are not self-designations, but rather names (frequently pejorative) conferred by other groups: ethnonymic objectivation is primordially applied to others, not to the ones in the position of subject. Ethnonyms are names of third parties; they belong to the category of "*they*" not to the category of "*we*". This, by the way, is consistent with a widespread avoidance of self-reference on the level of personal onomastics: names are not spoken by the bearers nor in their presence; to name is to externalize, to separate (from) the subject.

Thus self-references such as "people" mean "person", not "member of the human species", and they are personal pronouns registering the point of view of the subject talking, not proper names. To say, then, that animals and spirits are people is to say that they are persons, and to attribute to non-humans the capacities of conscious intentionality and agency which define the position of the subject. Such capacities are objectified as the soul or spirit with which these non-humans are endowed. Whatever possesses a soul is a subject, and whatever has a soul is capable of having a point of view. Amerindian souls, be they humans or animal, are thus indexical categories, cosmological deictics whose analysis calls not so much for an animist psychology or substantialist ontology as for a theory of the sign or perspectival pragmatics (Taylor 1993*a*; 1993*b*; Viveiros de Castro 1992*b*).

Thus, every being to whom a point of view is attributed would be a subject; or better, wherever there is a point of view there is a subject position. Whilst our constructionist epistemology can be summed up in the Saussurean formula: *the point of view creates the object* – the subject being the original, fixed condition whence the point of view emanates – Amerindian ontological perspectivism proceeds along the lines that the *point of view creates the subject*; whatever is activated or "agented" by the point of view will be a subject.[8] This is why terms such as *wari'* (Vilaça 1992), *dene* (McDonnell 1984) or *masa* (Århem 1993) mean "people", but they can be used for – and therefore used by – very different classes of beings: used by humans they denote human beings; but used by peccaries, howler monkeys or beavers they self-refer to peccaries, howler monkeys or beavers.

As it happens, however, these non-humans placed in the subject perspective do not merely "call" themselves "people"; they see themselves anatomically and culturally as *humans*. The symbolic spiritualization of animals would imply their imaginary hominization and culturalization; thus the anthropomorphic-anthropocentric character of indigenous thought would seem to be unquestionable. However, I believe that something totally different is at issue. Any being which vicariously occupies the point of view of reference, being in the position of subject, sees itself as a member of the human species. The human bodily form and human culture – the schemata of perception and action "embodied" in specific dispositions – are deictics of the same type as the self-designations discussed above. They are reflexive or apperceptive schematisms by which all subjects apprehend themselves, and not literal and constitutive human predicates projected metaphorically (i.e. improperly) onto non-humans. Such deictic "attributes" are immanent in the viewpoint, and move with it (Brightman 1993: 47). Human beings – naturally – enjoy the same prerogative and therefore see themselves as such.[9] It is not that animals are subjects because they are humans in disguise, but rather that they are human because they are potential subjects. This is to say *Culture is the Subject's nature*; it is the form in which every subject experiences its own nature. Animism is not a projection of substantive human *qualities* cast onto animals, but rather expresses the logical equivalence of the reflexive *relations* that humans and animals each have to themselves: salmon are to (see) salmon as humans are to (see) humans, namely, (as) human.[10] If, as we have observed, the common condition of humans and animals is humanity not animality, this is because "humanity" is the name for the general form taken by the Subject.

Multinaturalism

With this we may have discarded analogical anthropocentrism, but only apparently to adopt relativism.[11] For would this cosmology of multiple viewpoints not imply that "every perspective is equally valid and true" and that "a correct and true representation of the world does not exist" (Århem 1993: 124)?

But this is exactly the question: is the Amerindian perspectivist theory in fact asserting a multiplicity of representations of the same world? It is sufficient to consider ethnographic evidence to perceive that the opposite applies: all beings see ("represent") the world in the same way – what changes is the world that they see. Animals impose the same categories and values on reality as humans do: their worlds, like ours, revolve around hunting and fishing, cooking and fermented drinks, cross-cousins and war, initiation rituals, shamans, chiefs, spirits. "Everybody is involved in fishing and hunting; everybody is involved in feasts, social hierarchy, chiefs, war, and disease, all the way up and down" (Guédon 1984: 142). If the moon, snakes and jaguars see humans as tapirs or white-lipped peccaries (Baer 1994: 224), it is because they, like us, eat tapirs and peccaries, people's food. It could only be this way, since, being people in their own sphere, non-humans see things as "people" do. But the things that they see are different: what to us is blood, is maize beer to the jaguar; what to the souls of the dead is a rotting corpse, to us is soaking manioc; what we see as a muddy waterhole, the tapirs see as a great ceremonial house.

(Multi)cultural relativism supposes a diversity of subjective and partial representations, each striving to grasp an external and unified nature, which remains perfectly indifferent to those representations. Amerindian thought proposes the opposite: a representational or phenomenological unity which is purely pronominal or deictic, indifferently applied to a radically objective diversity. One single "culture", multiple "natures" – perspectivism is multinaturalist, for a perspective is not a representation.

A perspective is not a representation because representations are a property of the mind or spirit, whereas the point of view is located in the body.[12] The ability to adopt a point of view is undoubtedly a power of the soul, and non-humans are subjects in so far as they have (or are) spirit; but the differences between viewpoints (and a viewpoint is nothing if not a

difference) lies not in the soul. Since the soul is formally identical in all species, it can only see the same things everywhere – the difference is given in the specificity of bodies. This permits answers to be found for our questions: if non-humans are persons and have souls, then what distinguishes them from humans? And why, being people, do they not see us as people?

Animals see in the *same* way as we do *different* things because their bodies are different from ours. I am not referring to physiological differences – as far as that is concerned, Amerindians recognize a basic uniformity of bodies – but rather to affects, dispositions or capacities which render the body of every species unique: what it eats, how it communicates, where it lives, whether it is gregarious or solitary, and so forth. The visible shape of the body is a powerful sign of these differences in affect, although it can be deceptive since a human appearance could, for example, be concealing a jaguar-affect. Thus, what I call "body" is not a synonym for distinctive substance or fixed shape; it is an assemblage of affects or ways of being that constitute a *habitus*. Between the formal subjectivity of souls and the substantial materiality of organisms there is an intermediate plane which is occupied by the body as a bundle of affects and capacities and which is the origin of perspectives.

The difference between bodies, however, is only apprehendable from an exterior viewpoint, by an other, since, for itself, every type of being has the same form (the generic form of a human being): bodies are the way in which alterity is apprehended as such. In normal conditions we do not see animals as people, and vice-versa, because our respective bodies (and the perspectives which they allow) are different. Thus, if "culture" is a reflexive perspective of the subject, objectified through the concept of soul, it can be said that "nature" is the viewpoint which the subject takes of other body-affects; if Culture is the Subject's nature, then *Nature is the form of the Other as body*, that is, as the object for a subject. Culture takes the self-referential form of the pronoun "I"; nature is the form of the non-person or the object, indicated by the impersonal pronoun "it" (Benveniste 1966a: 256).

If, in the eyes of Amerindians, the body makes the difference, then it is easily understood why, in the anecdote told by Lévi-Strauss, the methods of investigation into the humanity of the other, employed by the Spanish and the inhabitants of the Antilles, showed such asymmetry. For the Europeans, the issue was to decide whether the others possessed a soul; for the Indians, the aim was to find out what kind of body the others had. For the Europeans the great diacritic, the marker of difference in perspective, is the soul (are Indians humans or animals?); for the Indians it is the body (are Europeans humans or spirits?). The Europeans never doubted that the Indians had bodies; the Indians never doubted that the Europeans had souls (animals and spirits have them too). What the Indians wanted to know was whether the bodies of those "souls" were capable of the same affects as their own – whether they had the bodies of humans or the bodies of spirits, non-putrescible and protean. In sum: European ethnocentrism consisted in doubting whether other bodies have the same souls as they themselves; Amerindian ethnocentrism in doubting whether other souls had the same bodies.

As Ingold has stressed (1994; 1996), the status of humans in Western thought is essentially ambiguous: on the one hand, humankind is an animal species amongst others, and animality is a domain that includes humans; on the other hand, humanity is a moral condition which excludes animals. These two statuses co-exist in the problematic and disjunctive notion of "human nature". In other words, our cosmology postulates a physical continuity and a metaphysical discontinuity between humans and animals, the former making of man an object for the natural sciences, the latter an object for the "humanities". Spirit or mind is our great differentiator: it raises us above animals and matter in general, it distinguishes cultures, it makes each person unique before his or her fellow beings. The body, in contrast, is the major integrator: it connects us to the rest of the living, united by a universal substrate (DNA, carbon chemistry) which, in turn, links up with the ultimate nature of all material bodies.[13] In contrast to this, Amerindians postulate a metaphysical continuity and

a physical discontinuity between the beings of the cosmos, the former resulting in animism, the latter in perspectivism: the spirit or soul (here not an immaterial substance but rather a reflexive form) integrates, while the body (not a material organism but a system of active affects) differentiates.

The Spirit's Many Bodies

The idea that the body appears to be the great differentiator in Amazonian cosmologies – that is, as that which unites beings of the same type, to the extent that it differentiates them from others – allows us to reconsider some of the classic questions of the ethnology of the region in a new light.

Thus, the now old theme of the importance of corporeality in Amazonian societies (a theme that much predates the current "embodiment" craze – see Seeger et al. 1979 [sic]) acquires firmer foundations. For example, it becomes possible to gain a better understanding of why the categories of identity – be they personal, social or cosmological – are so frequently expressed through bodily idioms, particularly through food practices and body decoration. The universal symbolic importance of food and cooking regimes in Amazonia – from the mythological "raw and the cooked" of Lévi-Strauss, to the Piro idea that what literally (i.e. naturally) makes them different from white people is "real food" (Gow 1991); from the food avoidances which define "groups of substance" in Central Brazil (Seeger 1980) to the basic classification of beings according to their eating habits (Baer 1994: 88); from the ontological productivity of commensality, similarity of diet and relative condition of prey-object and predator-subject (Vilaça 1992) to the ominipresence of cannibalism as the "predicative" horizon of all relations with the other, be they matrimonial, alimentary or bellicose (Viveiros de Castro 1993) – this universality demonstrates that the set of habits and processes that constitute bodies is precisely the location from which identity and difference emerge.

The same can be said of the intense semiotic use of the body in the definition of personal identities and in the circulation of social values (Mentore 1993; Turner 1995). The connexion between this overdetermination of the body (particularly of its visible surface) and the restricted recourse in the Amazonian *socius* to objects capable of supporting relations – that is, a situation wherein social exchange is not mediated by material objectifications such as those characteristic of gift and commodity economies – has been shrewdly pinpointed by Turner, who has shown how the human body therefore must appear as the prototypical social object. However, the Amerindian emphasis on the social construction of the body cannot be taken as the culturalization of a natural substrate but rather as the production of a distinctly human body, meaning *naturally* human. Such a process seems to be expressing not so much a wish to "de-animalize" the body through its cultural marking, but rather to particularize a body still too generic, differentiating it from the bodies of other human collectivities as well as from those of other species. The body, as the site of differentiating perspective, must be differentiated to the highest degree in order completely to express it.

The human body can be seen as the locus of the confrontation between humanity and animality, but not because it is essentially animal by nature and needs to be veiled and controlled by culture (Rivière 1994). The body is the subject's fundamental expressive instrument and at the same time the object *par excellence*, that which is presented to the sight of the other. It is no coincidence, then, that the maximum social objectification of bodies, their maximal particularization expressed in decoration and ritual exhibition is at the same time the moment of maximum animalization (Goldman 1975: 178; Turner 1991; 1995), when bodies are covered by feathers, colours, designs, masks and other animal prostheses. Man ritually clothed as an animal is the counterpart to the animal supernaturally naked. The former, transformed into an animal, reveals to himself the "natural" distinctiveness of his body; the latter, free of its exterior form and revealing itself as human, shows the "supernatural" similarity of spirit. The model of spirit is the human spirit, but the model of body is the bodies of animals; and if from the point of view of the subject culture takes the generic form of "I" and nature of "it/they", then the objectification of the subject to itself demands a singularization of bodies – which naturalizes culture, i.e. embodies it – whilst the subjectification of the object implies communication at the level of spirit – which culturalizes nature, i.e. supernaturalizes it. Put in these terms, the Amerindian distinction of Nature/Culture, before it is dissolved in the name of a common animic human-animal sociality, must be re-read in the light of somatic perspectivism.

It is important to note that these Amerindian bodies are not thought of as given but rather as made. Therefore, an emphasis on the methods for the continuous fabrication of the body (Viveiros de Castro 1979); a notion of kinship as a process of active assimilation of individuals (Gow 1989; 1991) through the sharing of bodily substances, sexual and alimentary – and not as passive inheritance of some substantial essence; the theory of memory which inscribes it in the flesh (Viveiros de Castro 1992a: 201–7), and more generally the theory which situates knowledge in the body (Kensinger 1995: ch. 22; McCallum 1996). The Amerindian *Bildung* happens in the body more than in the spirit: there is no "spiritual" change which is not a bodily transformation, a redefinition of its affects and capacities. Furthermore, while the distinction between body and soul is obviously pertinent to these cosmologies, it cannot be interpreted as an ontological discontinuity (Townsley 1993: 454–5). As bundles of affects and sites of perspective, rather than material organisms, bodies "are" souls, just, incidentally, as souls and spirits "are" bodies. The dual (or plural) conception of the human soul, widespread in indigenous Amazonia, distinguishes between the soul (or souls) of the body, reified register of an individual's history, site of memory and affect, and a "true soul", pure, formal subjective singularity, the abstract mark of a person (e.g. McCallum 1996; Viveiros de Castro 1992a: 201–14). On the other hand, the souls of the dead and the spirits which inhabit the universe are not immaterial entities, but equally types of bodies, endowed with properties – affects –

sui generis. Indeed, body and soul, just like nature and culture, do not correspond to substantives, self-subsistent entities or ontological provinces, but rather to pronouns or phenomenological perspectives.

The performative rather than given character of the body, a conception that requires it to differentiate itself "culturally" in order for it to be "naturally" different, has an obvious connexion with interspecific metamorphosis, a possibility suggested by Amerindian cosmologies. We need not be surprised by a way of thinking which posits bodies as the great differentiators yet at the same time states their transformability. Our cosmology supposes a singular distinctiveness of minds, but not even for this reason does it declare communication (albeit solipsism is a constant problem) to be impossible, or deny the mental/spiritual transformations induced by processes such as education and religious conversion; in truth, it is precisely because the spiritual is the locus of difference that conversion becomes necessary (the Europeans wanted to know whether Indians had souls in order to modify them). Bodily metamorphosis is the Amerindian counterpart to the European theme of spiritual conversion.[14] In the same way, if solipsism is the phantom that continuously threatens our cosmology – raising the fear of not recognizing ourselves in our "own kind" because they are not like us, given the potentially absolute singularity of minds – then the possibility of metamorphosis expresses the opposite fear, of no longer being able to differentiate between the human and the animal, and, in particular, the fear of seeing the human who lurks within the body of the animal one eats[15] – hence the importance of food prohibitions and precautions linked to the spiritual potency of animals, mentioned above. The phantom of cannibalism is the Amerindian equivalent to the problem of solipsism: if the latter derives from the uncertainty as to whether the natural similarity of bodies guarantees a real community of spirit, then the former suspects that the similarity of souls might prevail over the real differences of body and that all animals that are eaten might, despite the shamanistic efforts to de-subjectivize them, remain human. This, of course, does not prevent us having amongst ourselves more or less radical solipsists, such as the relativists, nor that various Amerindian societies be purposefully and more or less literally cannibalistic.[16]

The notion of metamorphosis is directly linked to the doctrine of animal "clothing", to which I have referred. How are we to reconcile the idea that the body is the site of differentiating perspectives with the theme of the "appearance" and "essence" which is always evoked to interpret animism and perspectivism (Århem 1993: 122; Descola 1986: 120; Hugh-Jones 1996; Rivière 1994)? Here seems to me to lie an important mistake, which is that of taking bodily "appearance" to be inert and false, whereas spiritual "essence" is active and real (see the definitive observations of Goldman 1975: 63). I argue that nothing could be further from the Indians' minds when they speak of bodies in terms of "clothing". It is not so much that the body is a clothing but rather that clothing is a body. We are dealing with societies which inscribe efficacious meanings onto the skin, and which use animal masks (or at least know their principle) endowed with the power metaphysically to transform the identities of those who wear them, if used in the appropriate ritual context. To put on mask-clothing is not so much to conceal a human essence beneath an animal appearance, but rather to activate the powers of a different body.[17] The animal clothes that shamans use to travel the cosmos are not fantasies but instruments: they are akin to diving equipment, or space suits, and not to carnival masks. The intention when donning a wet suit is to be able to function like a fish, to breathe underwater, not to conceal oneself under a strange covering. In the same way, the "clothing" which, amongst animals, covers an internal "essence" of a human type, is not a mere disguise but their distinctive equipment, endowed with the affects and capacities which define each animal.[18] It is true that appearances can be deceptive (Hallowell 1960; Rivière 1994); but my impression is that in Amerindian narratives which take as a theme animal "clothing" the interest lies more in what these clothes do rather than what they hide. Besides this, between a being and its appearance is its body, which is more than just that – and the very same narratives relate how appearances are always "unmasked" by bodily behaviour which is inconsistent with them. In short: there is no doubt that bodies are discardable and exchangeable and that "behind" them lie subjectivities which are formally identical to humans. But the idea is not similar to our opposition between appearance and essence; it merely manifests the objective permutability of bodies which is based in the subjective equivalence of souls.

Another classic theme in South American ethnology which could be interpreted within this framework is that of the sociological discontinuity between the living and the dead (Carneiro da Cunha 1978). The fundamental distinction between the living and the dead is made by the body and precisely not by the spirit; death is a bodily catastrophe which prevails as differentiator over the common "animation" of the living and the dead. Amerindian cosmologies dedicate equal or greater interest to the way in which the dead see reality as they do to the vision of animals, and as is the case for the latter, they underline the radical differences *vis-à-vis* the world of the living. To be precise, being definitively separated from their bodies, the dead are not human. As spirits defined by their disjunction from a human body, the dead are logically attracted to the bodies of animals; this is why to die is to transform into an animal (Pollock 1985: 95; Schwartzman 1988: 268; Turner 1995: 152; Vilaça 1992: 247–55), as it is to transform into other figures of bodily alterity, such as affines and enemies. In this manner, if animism affirms a subjective and social continuity between humans and animals, its somatic complement, perspectivism, establishes an objective discontinuity, equally social, between live humans and dead humans.[19]

Having examined the differentiating component of Amerindian perspectivism, it remains for me to attribute a cosmological "function" to the transspecific unity of the spirit. This is the point at which, I believe, a relational definition could be given for a category, Supernature, which nowadays has fallen into disrepute (actually, ever since Durkheim), but whose pertinence seems to me to be unquestionable. Apart from its use in labelling cosmographic

domains of a "hyper-uranian" type, or in defining a third type of intentional beings occurring in indigenous cosmologies, which are neither human nor animal (I refer to "spirits"), the notion of supernature may serve to designate a specific relational context and particular phenomenological quality, which is as distinct from the intersubjective relations that define the social world as from the "interobjective" relations with the bodies of animals.

Following the analogy with the pronominal set (Benveniste 1966a; 1966b) we can see that between the reflexive "I" of culture (the generator of the concepts of soul or spirit) and the impersonal "it" of nature (definer of the relation with somatic alterity), there is a position missing, the "you", the *second person*, or the other taken as other subject, whose point of view is the latent echo of that of the "I". I believe that this concept can aid in determining the supernatural context. An abnormal context wherein a subject is captured by another cosmologically dominant point of view, wherein he is the "you" of a non-human perspective, *Supernature is the form of the Other as Subject*, implying an objectification of the human I as a "you" for this Other. The typical "supernatural" situation in an Amerindian world is the meeting in the forest between a man – always on his own – and a being which is seen at first merely as an animal or a person, then reveals itself as a spirit or a dead person and speaks to the man (the dynamics of this communication are well analysed by Taylor 1993a).[20] These encounters can be lethal for the interlocutor who, overpowered by the non-human subjectivity, passes over to its side, transforming himself into a being of the same species as the speaker: dead, spirit or animal. He who responds to a "you" spoken by a non-human accepts the condition of being its "second person", and when assuming in his turn the position of "I" does so already as a non-human. The canonical form of these supernatural encounters, then, consists in suddenly finding out that the other is "human", that is, that *it* is the human, which automatically dehumanizes and alienates the interlocutor and transforms him into a prey object, that is, an animal. Only shamans, multinatural beings by definition and office, are always capable of transiting the various perspectives, calling and being called "you" by the animal subjectivities and spirits without losing their condition as human subjects.[21]

I would conclude by observing that Amerindian perspectivism has a vanishing point, as it were, where the differences between points of view are at the same time annulled and exacerbated: myth, which thus takes on the character of an absolute discourse. In myth, every species of being appears to others as it appears to itself (as human), while acting as if already showing its distinctive and definitive nature (as animal, plant or spirit). In a certain sense, all the beings which people mythology are shamans, which indeed is explicitly affirmed by some Amazonian cultures (Guss 1989: 52). Myth speaks of a state of being where bodies and names, souls and affects, the I and the Other interpenetrate, submerged in the same pre-subjective and pre-objective milieu – a milieu whose end is precisely what the mythology sets out to tell.

NOTES

1 This notion of the body as a "clothing" can be found amongst the Makuna (Århem 1993), the Yagua (Chaumeil 1983: 125–7), the Piro (Gow, pers. comm.), the Trio (Rivière 1994) and the Upper Xingu societies (Gregor 1977: 322). The notion is very likely pan-American, having considerable symbolic yield, for example, in North-west Coast cosmologies (see Goldman 1975 and Boelscher 1989), if not of much wider distribution, a question I cannot consider here.

2 For some examples see amongst many others: Weiss 1969: 158; 1972 (Campa); Baer 1994: 102, 119, 224; Renard-Casevitz 1991: 24–31 (Matsiguenga); Grenand 1980: 42 (Wayapi); Viveiros de Castro 1992a: 68 (Araweté); Osborn 1990: 151 (U'wa); Jara 1996: 68–73 (Akuriyo).

3 See for example, Saladin d'Anglure 1990; Fienup-Riordan 1994 (Eskimo); Nelson 1983; McDonnell 1984 (Koyukon, Kaska); Tanner 1979; Scott 1989; Brightman 1993 (Cree); Hallowell 1960 (Ojibwa); Goldman 1975 (Kwakiutl); Guédon 1984 (Tsimshian); Boelscher 1989 (Haida). See also Howell 1984; 1996; and Karim 1981, for the Chewong and Ma'Betisék of Malaysia; for Siberia, Hamayon 1990.

4 See Århem 1993; Crocker 1985; Hugh-Jones 1996; Overing 1985; 1986; Vilaça 1992.

5 Or, as we may add, the case of the Ojibwa, where the co-existence of the systems of totem and manido (Lévi-Strauss 1962a: 25–33) served as a matrix for the general opposition between totemism and sacrifice (Lévi-Strauss 1962b: 295–302) and can be directly interpreted within the framework of a distinction between totemism and animism.

6 See Radcliffe-Brown 1952: 130–1, who, amongst other interesting arguments, distinguishes processes of personification of species and natural phenomena (which "permits nature to be thought of as if it were a society of persons, and so makes of it a social or moral order"), like those found amongst the Eskimos and Andaman Islanders, from systems of classification of natural species, like those found in Australia and which compose a "system of social solidarities" between man and nature – this obviously calls to mind Descola's distinction of animism/totemism as well as the contrast of manido/totem explored by Lévi-Strauss.

7 The uncomfortable tension inherent in such antinomies can be gauged in Howell's article (1996) on Chewong cosmology, where the Chewong are described as being both "relativist" and "anthropocentric" – a double mischaracterization, I believe.

8 "Such is the foundation of perspectivism. It does not express a dependency on a predefined subject; on the contrary, whatever accedes to the point of view will be subject . . ." (Deleuze 1988: 27).

9 "Human beings see themselves as such; the Moon, the snakes, the jaguars and the Mother of Smallpox, however, see them as tapirs or peccaries, which they kill" (Baer 1994: 224).

10 If salmon look to salmon as humans to humans – and this is "animism" salmon do not look human to humans (they look like salmon), and neither do humans to salmon (they look like spirits, or maybe bears; see Guédon 1984: 141) – and this is "perspectivism". Ultimately, then, animism and perspectivism may have a deeper relationship to totemism than Descola's model allows for.

11 The attribution of human-like consciousness and intentionality (to say nothing of human bodily form and cultural habits) to non-human beings has been indifferently denominated "anthropocentrism" or "anthropomorphism". However, these two labels can be taken to denote radically opposed cosmological outlooks. Western popular evolutionism is very anthropocentric, but not particularly anthropomorphic. On the other hand, "primitive animism" may be characterized as anthropomorphic, but it is definitely not anthropocentric: if sundry other beings besides humans are "human", then we humans are not a special lot.

12 "The point of view is located in the body, says Leibniz" (Deleuze 1988: 16).

13 The counterproof of the singularity of the spirit in our cosmologies lies in the fact that when we try to universalize it, we are obliged – now that supernature is out of bounds – to identify it with the structure and function of the brain. The spirit can only be universal (natural) if it is (in) the body.

14 The rarity of unequivocal examples of spirit possession in the complex of Amerindian shamanism may derive from the prevalence of the theme of bodily metamorphosis. The classical problem of the religious conversion of Amerindians could also be further illuminated from this angle; indigenous conceptions of "acculturation" seem to focus more on the incorporation and embodiment of Western bodily practices (food, clothing, interethnic sex) rather than on spiritual assimilation (language, religion etc.).

15 The traditional problem of Western mainstream epistemology is how to connect and universalize (individual substances are given, relations have to be made); the problem in Amazonia is how to separate and particularize (relations are given, substances must be defined). See Brightman (1993: 177–85) and Fienup-Riordan (1994: 46–50) – both inspired by Wagner's (1977) ideas about the "innate" and the "constructed" – on this contrast.

16 In Amazonian cannibalism, what is intended is precisely the incorporation of the subject-aspect of the enemy (who is accordingly hyper-subjectivized, in very much the same way as that described by Harrison [1993: 121] for Melanesian warfare), not its desubjectivization as is the case with game animals. See Viveiros de Castro 1992a: 290–3; 1996: 98–102; Fausto 1997.

17 Peter Gow (pers. comm.) tells me that the Piro conceive of the act of putting on clothes as an animating of clothes. See also Goldman (1975: 183) on Kwakiutl masks: "Masks get 'excited' during Winter dances".

18 "'Clothing' in this sense does not mean merely a body covering but also refers to the skill and ability to carry out certain tasks" (Rivière in Koelewijn 1987: 306).

19 Religions based on the cult of the ancestors seem to postulate the inverse: spiritual identity goes beyond the bodily barrier of death, the living and the dead are similar in so far as they manifest the same spirit. We would accordingly have superhuman ancestrality and spiritual possession on one side, animalization of the dead and bodily metamorphosis on the other.

20 This would be the true significance of the "deceptiveness of appearances" theme: appearances deceive because one is never certain whose point of view is dominant,

that is, which world is in force when one interacts with other beings. The similarity of this idea to the familiar injunction not to "trust your senses" of Western epistemologies is, I fear, just another deceitful appearance.

21 As we have remarked, a good part of shamanistic work consists in de-subjectivizing animals, that is in transforming them into pure, natural bodies capable of being consumed without danger. In contrast, what defines spirits is precisely the fact that they are inedible; this transforms them into eaters *par excellence*, i.e. into anthropophagous beings. In this way, it is common for the great predators to be the preferred forms in which spirits manifest themselves, and it is understandable that game animals should see humans as spirits, that spirits and predator animals should see us as game animals and that animals taken to be inedible should be assimilated to spirits (Viveiros de Castro 1978). The scales of edibility of indigenous Amazonia (Hugh-Jones 1996) should therefore include spirits at their negative pole.

REFERENCES

Århem, K. 1993. Ecosofia makuna. In *La selva humanizada: ecologia aiternativa en el tròpico húmedo colombiano* (ed.) F. Correa. Bogotá: Instituto Colombiano de Antropología, Fondo FEN Colombia, Fondo Editorial CEREC.

——— 1996. The cosmic food web: human-nature relatedness in the northwest Amazon. In *Nature and society: anthropological perspectives* (eds) P. Descola & G. Pásson. London: Routledge.

Baer, G. 1994. *Cosmología y shamanismo de los Matsiguenga*. Quito: Abya-Yala.

Benveniste, E. 1966a. La nature des pronoms. In *Problèmes de linguistique générale*. Paris: Gallimard.

——— 1996b. De la subjectivité dans le langage. In *Problèmes de linguistique générale*. Paris: Gallimard.

Boelscher, M. 1989. *The curtain within: Haida social and mythical discourse*. Vancouver: Univ. of British Columbia Press.

Brightman, R. 1993. *Grateful prey: Rock Cree human-animal relationships*. Berkeley: Univ. of California Press.

Carneiro da Cunha, M.M. 1978. *Os mortos e os outros*. São Paulo: Hucitec.

Chaumeil, J.-P. 1983. *Voir, savoir, pouvoir: le chamanisme chez les Yagua du nord-est péruvien*. Paris: Ecole des Hautes Etudes en Sciences Sociales.

Crocker, J. C. 1985. *Vital souls: Bororo cosmology, natural symbolism, and shamanism*. Tucson: Univ. of Arizona Press.

Deleuze, G. 1988. *Le pli: Leibniz et le baroque*. Paris: Minuit.

Descola, P. 1986. *La nature domestique: symbolisme et praxis dans l'écologie des Achuar*. Paris: Maison des Sciences de l'Homme.

——— 1992. Societies of nature and the nature of society. In *Conceptualizing society* (ed.) A. Kuper. London: Routledge.

Erikson, P. 1984. De l'apprivoisement à l'approvisionnement: chasse, alliance et familiarisation en Amazonie amérindienne. *Techn. Cult.* **9**, 105–40.

Fausto, C. 1997. A dialética da predação e familiarização entre os Parakanã da Amazônia oriental. Thesis, Museu Nacional, Univ. of Rio de Janeiro.

Fienup-Riordan, A. 1994. *Boundaries and passages: rule and ritual in Yup'ik Eskimo oral tradition*. Norman: Univ. of Oklahoma Press.

Goldman, I. 1975. *The mouth of heaven: an introduction to Kwakiutl religious thought*. New York: Wiley-Interscience.

Gow, P. 1989. The perverse child: desire in a native Amazonian subsistence economy. *Man* (N.S.) 24, 567–82.

——— 1991. *Of mixed blood: kinship and history in Peruvian Amazonia*. Oxford: Clarendon Press.

Gregor, T. 1977. *Mehinaku: the drama of daily life in a Brazilian Indian village*. Chicago: Univ. of Chicago Press.

Grenand, P. 1980. *Introduction à l'étude de l'univers wayãpi: ethno-écologie des Indiens du Haut-Oyapock (Guyane Française)*. Paris: SELAF/CNRS.

Guédon, M.-F. 1984. An introduction to the Tsimshian world view and its practitioners. In *The Tsimshian: images of the past, views for the present* (ed.) M. Seguin. Vancouver: Univ. of British Columbia Press.

Guss, D. 1989. *To weave and to sing: art, symbol and narrative in the South American rain forest.* Berkeley: Univ. of California Press.

Hallowell, A. I. 1960. Ojibwa ontology, behavior, and world view. In *Culture in history: essays in honor of Paul Radin* (ed.) S. Diamond. New York: Columbia Univ. Press.

Hamayon, R. 1990. *La chasse à l'âme: esquisse d'une théorie du chamanisme sibérien.* Nanterre: Société d'Ethnologie.

Harrison, S. 1993. *The mask of war: violence, ritual and the self in Melanesia.* Manchester: Univ. Press.

Howell, S. 1984. *Society and cosmos: Chewong of peninsular Malaysia.* Oxford: Univ. Press.

—— 1996. Nature in culture or culture in nature? Chewong ideas of "humans" and other species. In *Nature and society: anthropological perspectives* (eds) P. Descola & G. Pálsson. London: Routledge.

Hugh-Jones, S. 1996. Bonnes raisons ou mauvaise conscience? De l'ambivalence de certains Amazoniens envers la consommation de viande. *Terrain* 26, 123–48.

Ingold, T. 1991. Becoming persons: consciousness and sociality in human evolution. *Cult. Dyn.* 4, 355–78.

—— 1994. Humanity and animality. In *Companion encyclopedia of anthropology: humanity, culture and social life* (ed.) T. Ingold. London: Routledge.

—— 1996. Hunting and gathering as ways of perceiving the environment. In *Redefining nature: ecology, culture and domestication* (eds) R.F. Ellen & K. Fukui. London: Berg.

Jara, F. 1996. *El camino del Kumu: ecología y ritual entre los Akuriyó de Surinam.* Quito: Abya-Yala.

Karim, W.-J. 1981. *Ma'betisék concepts of living things.* London: Athlone Press.

Kensinger, K. 1995. *How real people ought to live: the Cashinahua of eastern Peru.* Prospect Heights: Waveland Press.

Koelewijn, C. with P. Rivière 1987. *Oral literature of the Trio Indians of Surinam.* Dordrecht: Foris.

Latour, B. 1991. *Nous n'avons jamais été modernes.* Paris: Editions La Découverte.

Lévi-Strauss, C. 1962a. *Le totémisme aujourd'hui.* Paris: Presses Universitaires de France.

—— 1962b. *La pensée sauvage.* Paris: Plon.

—— 1973 [1952]. Race et histoire. In his *Anthropologie structurale deux.* Paris: Plon.

—— 1985. *La potière jalouse.* Paris: Plon.

Lima, T. S. 1995. A parte do cauim: etnografia juruna. Thesis, Museu Nacional, Univ. of Rio de Janeiro.

—— 1996. O dois e seu múltiplo: reflexões sobre o perspectivismo em uma cosmologia tupi. *Mana* 2:2, 21–47.

McCallum, C. 1996. The body that knows: from Cashinahua epistemology to a medical anthropology of lowland South America. *Med. Anthrop. Q.* 10:3, 1–26.

McDonnell, R. 1984. Symbolic orientations and systematic turmoil: centering on the Kaska symbol of *dene. Canad. J. Anthrop.* 4, 39–56.

Mentore, G. 1993. Tempering the social self: body adornment, vital substance, and knowledge among the Waiwai. *J. Archaeol. Anthrop.* 9, 22–34.

Nelson, R. 1983. *Make prayers to the Raven.* Chicago: Univ. of Chicago Press.

Osborn, A. 1990. Eat and be eaten: animals in U'wa (Tunebo) oral tradition. In *Signifying animals: human meaning in the natural world* (ed.) R. Willis. London: Unwin Hyman.

Overing, J. 1985. There is no end of evil: the guilty innocents and their fallible god. In *The anthropology of evil* (ed.) D. Parkin. London: Basil Blackwell.

—— 1986. Images of cannibalism, death and domination in a "non-violent" society. *J. Soc. Amer.* 72, 133–56.

Pollock, D. 1985. Personhood and illness among the Culina of western Brazil. Thesis, Univ. of Rochester.

Radcliffe-Brown, A. R. 1952 [1929]. The sociological theory of totemism. In *Structure and function in primitive society*. London: Routledge & Kegan Paul.

Reichel-Dolmatoff, G. 1976. Cosmology as ecological analysis: a view from the rain forest. *Man* (N.S.) **12**, 307–18.

—— 1985. Tapir avoidance in the Colombian northwest Amazon. In *Animal myths and metaphors in South America* (ed.) G. Urton. Salt Lake City: Univ. of Utah Press.

Renard-Casevitz, F.-M. 1991. *Le banquet masqué: une mythologie de l'étranger*. Paris: Lierre & Coudrier.

Rivière, P. 1994. WYSINWYG in Amazonia. *JASO* **25**, 255–62.

Saladin d'Anglure, B. 1990. Nanook, super-male; the polar bear in the imaginary space and social time of the Inuit of the Canadian Arctic. In *Signifying animals: human meaning in the natural world* (ed.) R. Willis. London: Unwin Hyman.

Schwartzman, S. 1988. The Panara of the Xingu National park. Thesis, Univ. of Chicago.

Scott, C. 1989. Knowledge construction among the Cree hunters: metaphors and literal understanding. *J. Soc. Amér.* **75**, 193–208.

Seeger, A. 1980. Corporação e corporalidade: ideologia de concepção e descendência. In his *Os índios e nós*. Rio de Janeiro: Campus.

Tanner, A. 1979. *Bringing home animals: religious ideology and mode of production of the Mistassini Cree hunters*. St John's Memorial Univ. of Newfoundland.

Taylor, A.-C. 1993a. Des fantômes stupéfiants: langage et croyance dans la pensée achuar. *L'Homme* **126–8**, 33/2–4, 429–47.

—— 1993b. Remembering to forget: identity, mourning and memory among the jivaro. *Man* (N.S.) **28**, 653–78.

Townsley, G. 1993. Song paths: the ways and means of Yaminahua shamanic knowledge. *L'Homme* **126–8**, 33:2–4, 449–68.

Turner, T. 1991. "We are parrots, twins are birds": play of tropes as operational struc-

ture. In *Beyond metaphor: the theory of tropes in anthropology* (ed.) J. Fernandez. Stanford: Stanford Univ. Press.

—— 1995. Social body and embodied subject: bodiliness, subjectivity, and sociality among the Kayapó. *Cult. Anthrop.* **10**, 143–70.

Vilaça, A. 1992. *Comendo como gente: formas do canibalismo Wari' (Pakaa-Nova)*. Rio de Janeiro: Editora da UFRJ.

Viveiros de Castro, E. 1978. Alguns aspectos do pensamento yawalpíti (Alto Xingu): classificaçõs e transformações. *Bol. Mus. nac.* **26**, 1–41.

—— 1979. A fabricação do corpo na sociedade xinguana. *Boi. Mus. nac.* **32**, 2–19.

—— 1992a. *From the enemy's point of view: humanity and divinity in an Amazonian society*. Chicago: Univ. of Chicago Press.

—— 1992b. Apresentação to A. Vilaça. In *Comendo como gente: formas do canibalismo Wari'*. Rio de Janeiro: Editoral da UFRJ.

—— 1993. Alguns aspectos da afinidade no dravidianato amazônico. In *Amazônia: etnologia e história indígena* (eds) E. Viveiros de Castro & M. Carneiro da Cunha. São Paulo: Núcleo de História Indígena e do Indigenismo (USP/FAPESP).

—— 1996. Le meurtrier et son double chez les Araweté: un exemple de fusion rituelle. *Syst. Pens. Afr. Noire* **14**, 77–104.

Wagner, R. 1977. Scientific and indigenous Papuan conceptualizations of the innate: a semiotic critique of the ecological perspective. In *Subsistence and survival: rural ecology in the Pacific* (eds) T. Bayliss-Smith & R.G. Feachem. London: Academic Press.

Weiss, G. 1969. The cosmology of the Campa Indians of eastern Peru. Thesis, Univ. of Michigan.

—— 1972. Campa cosmology. *Ethnology* **11**, 157–72.

Part III
Praxis: Religious Action

The Movement in Ritual: Emergence

Introduction

The Durkheimian and Tylorean traditions led to a lively debate as to whether ritual (and religion more generally) could best be seen as primarily expressive and aesthetic (symbolic) or intellectual and explanatory (proto-scientific) in nature (B. Wilson, ed. 1970, especially the essays by Horton and Beattie; Skorupski 1976). The polarization has been largely superseded by arguments that understand ritual as a form of action, as "doing" rather than simply "making" something. The essays in Part III all emphasize this active quality in various ways, but they build on the analyses of meaning presented in Part II rather than reverting to crude forms of functionalism or instrumentalism.

In this section we pick up from the critique made by Wittgenstein and follow the advice of the poet: "Where but in custom and in ceremony are innocence and beauty born?" (Yeats). Beauty and innocence are hardly the only consequences of ritual, but the point is to show ritual as a unique form of symbolic action which creates a state that can be described broadly as one of emergence. In addition to the essays here, readers are urged to turn to the work of James Fernandez, who provides compelling accounts of the transformations in experience enabled by ritual, and who manages to grasp precisely the quality of emergence as the "inchoate" is subjected to successive metaphoric predications (1983, 1986a [1985], 1986b). Kapferer (1983, 1997, 2000a) gives an equally powerful analysis of the aesthetics of ritual performance in the regenerative transformation of self and experience. Gilsenan (1973) offers an exquisite description of the religious experience generated in Sufi performances. The literature on the senses (Howes, ed. 1991) and the body (Csordas 1994; ed., 1994) is also relevant.

24

The Control of Experience: Symbolic Action

Godfrey Lienhardt

Godfrey Lienhardt was a close associate of Evans-Pritchard and taught at the University of Oxford. *Divinity and Experience* is one of the greatest and most respected ethnographic accounts of religion. It concerns Dinka, people of the southern Sudan closely related to Nuer, whose sacrificial practices are briefly described in the essay by Evans-Pritchard (chapter 11). Sacrifice is a central part of many religions and there have been many theories developed to explain its prevalence. In this excerpt Lienhardt's approach is different. He offers not a general explanation but a phase in a longer interpretive account that culminates in enabling the reader to comprehend the power and dignity realized in the Dinka practice of burying their spear masters alive. This voluntary death is an alternative to ritual regicide, the practice of killing an ailing ruler. Such "sacred kingship," in which the vitality of the ruler symbolized the health of the whole polity, was once found in many parts of Africa and elsewhere.

Lienhardt's particularly subtle discussion of sacrifice is couched in a more general model of what he calls symbolic action. Lienhardt shows how sacrifice provides a victory over death by placing its control in human hands. More generally, he argues that ritual can provide a means for humans to express control over, and hence shape, their experience. This control, as he says, is generally understood, to effect not physical circumstance, but what he calls the moral realm. This is a point we will see developed by Rappaport.

[. . .]

Animal sacrifice is the most complex, as it is the essential, symbolic act of the Dinka; and in order to reach an understanding of what it means in their life, it is necessary to consider it in the light of other acts which are simpler examples of symbolism. From the great variety of these, I choose four. The first is a small quasi-magical practice called in Dinka *thuic*, which may have no overtly religious signifi-

From Godfrey Lienhardt, "The Control of Experience: Symbolic Action," in *Divinity and Experience: The Religion of the Dinka* (Oxford: Clarendon Press, 1961), pp. 282–97. Reprinted by permission of Oxford University Press. Abridged.

cance. The second is the ceremony for cleansing people of incest, the third the ordinary mortuary ceremony, and the fourth the ceremony for concluding peace. In the light of an understanding of these, we may then turn to an analysis of the sacrificial rites earlier described.

The practice called *thuic* involves knotting a tuft of grass to indicate that the one who makes the knot hopes and intends to contrive some kind of constriction or delay. In one of the texts quoted, for example, an enemy is to be "knotted in grass", meaning that it is desired that his freedom of action, mental and physical, shall be restricted. One sometimes hears that masters of the fishing-spear whose people have been seriously troubled by lions will take a stone to represent the lion, and, before their people, enclose it in a knot of grass. This action is supposed to assist the people in their attempt to kill the lion with spears. Further, and most commonly, when Dinka are making a journey they often tie knots in the grass growing beside the path with the intention that the preparation of food at the end of the journey may be delayed until their arrival.[1]

This is a simple example of what has been called "imitative magic"; yet that expression does not adequately suggest the spirit in which the act is undertaken. No Dinka thinks that by performing such an action he has actually assured the result he hopes for. The framework of expectation within which such a symbolic act has meaning is not that appropriate for technical and practical acts. A Dinka who could send a message by the driver of some car going on ahead of him would not find it necessary to knot grass when hoping that supper might be kept for him. Further, the Dinka do not slacken their practical efforts to achieve their end because they have taken such "mystical" action. The tying of a stone representing the lion in a knot of grass is a prelude to serious hunting; the tying of knots of grass in the grass at the roadside is made as the traveller's mind, towards the end of his journey, dwells upon that end which his hastening footsteps bring rapidly nearer. This "mystical" action is not a substitute for practical or technical action, but a complement to it and preparation for it. The man who ties such a knot has made an external, physical representation of a well-formed mental intention. He has produced a model of his desires and hopes, upon which to base renewed practical endeavour.

This action of *thuic* is in itself trivial, and among the Dinka themselves is not regarded in any way as an important ceremony. The objects which the Dinka have in mind when knotting grass as we have described might, were their circumstances different, be achieved in some purely technical way. The principle involved, however, is similar to that which obtains in symbolic action in situations which, by their very nature, preclude the possibility of technical or practical action as a complete alternative. In the ceremonies for cleaning people of incest, for death, and for peacemaking which we now describe, what the symbolic action is intended to control is primarily a set of mental and moral dispositions, and hence in these ceremonies there is no purely technical alternative to the symbolic action taken.

In theory a Dinka may not marry any girl with whom he can trace cognatic relationship unless it is agreed that this relationship has become extremely remote. Even then, again in theory, a ceremony should be performed to permit such a marriage. Where large clans have branched out in many parts of Dinkaland, and where even in a single tribe there is a large group of agnates whose distinct main lineages are but remotely linked, intermarriage between members is permissible; but this is always justified on the grounds that, since the relationship had become remote, a ceremony was once performed in order to make the intermarriage legitimate and free its partners from the results of incest. In such cases the Dinka sometimes say cynically that "if a man has cattle, then he is my daughter's husband; if he has no cattle, then he is my clansman". The rules of exogamy can in fact be manipulated either to permit or exclude a particular marriage unless the partners are so clearly unrelated, or so clearly related, that no question of the fitness of the marriage is raised.

In sexual intercourse outside marriage, however, the Dinka judge of whether incest has been effectively committed by results. Incest, *akeeth*, is supposed to result automatically in a serious skin disease, also *keeth*. The offence is thus, in a sense, the same thing as the result experienced. Incestuous congress also results in sterility, and where a woman appears to be barren, or dies in child-birth, one of the reasons likely to be adduced is the possibility that she has had incestuous relations with someone. I heard of a case in which a girl, bearing a child, was according to the Dinka custom reciting the names of her lovers: "and she named ten of her father's clansmen, and ten of her mother's clansmen, and the child was not delivered. But she would not mention the last name, and so she died in childbirth." The implication in this particular case was probably that she had once been seduced by her father, which, for the Dinka, is a horror too appalling to name. It is incestuous also for a man's son to have congress with any of his father's wives (his own mother, of course, is in any case excluded) unless his father has deputed him to do so.

When people fear or experience the results of incest, they perform a ceremony for "separating" the partners to the incest and thus neutralizing the incest retroactively. I saw only one such ceremony, and it was for a comparatively minor case of incest, in which a man had slept with one of his father's junior wives and had for a time concealed the fact.[2] For serious cases a bull, or even a cow in calf, may have to be used to free the partners from the consequences of their sin. In this case only a ram was used. The ceremony was simple. A minor master of the fishing-spear made several short invocations with the guilty pair in front of him, and their kinsmen standing around, near a pool of rain-water. The ram was held near by. Then all went to the pool, and with a certain amount of joking and horseplay the partners to the incest were pulled into the water and ducked and washed by their kinsmen. While this was in progress the ram was also forced into the pool, and pushed under the water a few times. The intention of this, as is clear, was to cleanse the pair of their sin, and to transfer their condition to the ram. That this is conscious symbolism, and not a kind of materialist superstition that the sin in some way actually goes into the water, is shown by the fact that all the kin were also in the water. The sin was transferred only

to the ram, according to the Dinkas' symbolic intention.

After the washing the ram was taken from the pool, led away some little distance, and cut in half alive, longitudinally. The first cut of the spear in the throat probably killed it, but I did not watch this performance very closely. I was told, however, that what was particularly important, whether the victim was male or female, was that the sexual organs should be cut clearly apart in two longitudinal halves. In this case all the meat was carried away, presumably to be eaten, but it is said that sometimes a beast thus killed is not eaten, and sometimes only half of it used.

The important part of the symbolic act, however, is clearly the separation of the sexual organs, which obviously represent the single origin of the partners to the incest. This is negatively confirmed by those sacrifices in which it is particularly necessary that the sexual organs should *not* be divided or severed – sacrifices in which what is emphasized is the solidarity of the group of agnates performing the ceremony. . . . When it is thought that two branches of a clan have become remote enough to make intermarriage safe, a beast is longitudinally divided as we have described. The sin of incest and its consequences are thus controlled by symbolic action; and it could not be otherwise, for incest is a fact of the moral and not of the physical universe.

For a peace-making ceremony, which I did not see, I rely upon an account given by G. W. T. (Major G. W. Titherington), who witnessed such a ceremony,[3] and on texts collected by myself. Major Titherington described how the two parties who had come together to make peace sat about 20 yards apart, on opposite sides of a dry water-course. The killer was not present, but was represented by his kin. The cattle to be paid in compensation for the homicide (*puk*) were driven between the parties, together with a small bull provided by the family of the killer. According to Titherington, the man who directs the ceremony may be . . . either a master of the fishing-spear or a diviner or prophet – provided that he is not related to either party. When the leader of the ceremony indicated that they should do so, the people of the killer seized the forelegs of the bull, and the people of the killed man the hind legs. They turned it over on its back, and each side thrust a spear into its chest. The leader of the ceremony then at once cut the beast in half *across the belly*, the entrails were taken out and scattered over the two parties, and each party went off separately to divide its meat. After this the leader went to the spot where the bull had been slaughtered, and placed a spear among the remaining bits, thereafter taking some of the remains and throwing them over the two parties, who by this time had resumed their places. The parties then advanced in sixes, three from each side, and holding the spear between them in both hands bit into it, following this with spitting to the left, to the right, and downwards upon their own chests. They are said sometimes to spit upon each other. Ashes were then sprinkled over the knees of the parties, and this was the end of the ceremony. No form of words was spoken. It was believed that, after the conclusion of this ceremony, anyone who reopened the feud would surely die.

Here again the division of the beast is clearly made to represent the division of the relationship of feud between the parties, and it is significant that in this case the division of the animal, unlike that which takes place in incest ceremonies, should not involve the longitudinal division of the sexual organs which, in this situation, are not symbolically significant. The biting of the spear is almost certainly a form of oath to abide by the settlement, and (it is implied) involves the participants in crossing the watercourse which before (like the feud) had divided them. The spitting, scattering with entrails, and dusting with ashes, are all forms of purification and blessing. In this case it seems that gesture without speech was enough to confirm, in the external physical universe, an intention conceived interiorly in the moral.[4]

[. . .]

A final example of symbolic action, that which takes place at the death of ordinary people, emphasizes the special significance of those other mortuary rites which our concluding chapter describes. The Dinka do not talk much about death, and are not inclined to bring funeral ceremonies to one's attention.

Consequently, I saw only two burials in Dinkaland, and both of them took place in circumstances which prevented the normal procedure as some Dinka may be persuaded to describe it. This account, therefore, comes largely from a few Dinka informants.

When a man dies he is stripped of his decorations and ornaments. His shallow grave is then dug (it is in fact an oval hole about 4 or 5 ft. deep) and after that his head is shaved and his body first washed with water and then anointed with oil. A skin, or preferably a hide shield, is then placed in the grave for him to be laid on. He is then placed on his side in the grave, with his head facing to the west (the direction of death associated with the setting of the sun), his knees flexed and his hands under his head, in a position of sleep. His exposed ear is covered with a skin so that earth shall not enter it. The burial party crouch round the grave, facing away from it, and push the earth into it backwards with their hands. Then they wash off the earth from their knees on the grave, and a close kinsman stays to cover the grave with a mat.

After three days the family of the deceased bring a little ram, a twin, to the graveside. They take straw from the roof of the dead man's hut, throw it near the grave, and set it alight. The smoke blows over the people, and the people, and the senior member of the family, or master of the fishing-spear if he has been called in, walks round the people beating the living kid upon the ground. He finally holds the bleating kid over the fire a little, and then makes an incision in its belly and takes out the entrails. Their contents are sprinkled over the people, and the carcass is thrown away for the vultures. This "smoking" of the people is called *atol* (*tol* – smoke), and the kid is the *nyong atol*. The Dinka say that the offering is to please the deceased, and a twin animal is chosen because twins have a special relationship to Divinity.[5]

After another day a sheep or goat is sacrificed. This is called the *alok* (from *lok, lak*, "to wash"?) and it lifts the prohibition upon drinking milk from the dead man's family. Some time later a whole bull is sacrificed, and prayers are offered and invocations made by a master of the fishing-spear. This final sacrifice, called *apek*, propitiates the deceased, who without it would be likely to injure his people and kill their cattle.

There are some differences, though not large ones, between this ceremony and that for the death of a woman. A woman's skirts are placed about her, and tied up between her legs, for a woman's skirts are not ornaments. They are an essential part of her social personality. The period before "the kid of the smoke" is brought out is said to be four days for a woman. Four is the number associated with females, though the Dinka have no explanation of this and sometimes even reverse the three/male, four/female connexion. The *alok* sacrifice, when performed for a woman, is to release her cooking-utensils for use, and the *apek* sacrifice is a female goat instead of a whole bull. In both cases the eating of this final sacrifice finally "cleanses" the bereaved, who until that time still have the contamination of the dead about them.

The main principles behind these mortuary ceremonies we have described are easily understood. The mourners fill the grave without looking into it because they do not wish to experience the final interment. The suffering of "the kid of the smoke" (and it is particularly stressed that it must bleat) represents that of the mourners, transferred here again to an animal victim and expressed thus in separation from, and "outside", them. The other rites include *rites de séparation* and the eating of the final *apek* is also a *rite d'agrégation*. In suggesting that they represent and regulate the Dinka experience of death, we do not interpret them entirely differently from the Dinka themselves; for they assert that those who do not perform the mortuary ceremonies will be haunted by their dead. The ceremonies thus divide the dead from the living or (from our point of view) formally separate two different memories of the dead – the memory of them as they were in life, and the memory of them as dead. Hence, it is said, those killed in battle were left unburied, their presence above ground representing a reminder that they still claimed vengeance.

The symbolic actions described above thus re-create, and even dramatize, situations which they aim to control, and the experience of which they effectively modulate. If they do not change actual historical or physical events – as the Dinka in some cases believe them to do – they do change and regulate the Dinkas' experience of those events. Hence, in turning now to consider more generally animal sacrifice, the central symbolic act, we observe first that the objective of a sacrifice is achieved in the act itself, even though it may not at once, or at all, produce some change in external circumstances which the Dinka particularly hope for. For them also, a sacrifice involves *waiting* for some hoped-for amelioration in the condition which has occasioned it. They do not expect sacrifice automatically to achieve some specific result with the certainty of a well-tested technical procedure. So they will accept medical aid at the same time as performing sacrifices for the recovery of the sick. Medicine is not an alternative to sacrifice and prayer, but may complement it.

It is with this necessity for the symbolic as well as the technical act in mind that we end our discussion of symbolic action, and particularly the act of sacrifice which confirms and may accompany all other major symbolic acts. We ask ourselves what animal sacrifice may be observed to achieve for the Dinka, which technical action could not achieve. Why do they *both* sacrifice *and*, where possible, seek modern medical aid? And if sacrifice is made for the recovery of a sick man, for example, and he dies, why is sacrifice not regarded as ineffective, in the same way as a technical act which fails to produce its desired result?

The answer the Dinka give when faced with the failure of a sacrifice to produce the required result which is the proximate occasion of sacrifice is that "Divinity has refused" or, more likely, that the Power which was really the grounds of the man's sickness was not correctly identified. So, what is required is another sacrifice, and not alternative action.

But even if a sacrifice has manifestly failed to achieve a specific end which it was part of the intention of those making the sacrifice to achieve, it has not therefore been without effect altogether; for any sacrifice involves ends which go quite beyond any particular end which may be its special proximate occasion.

It is made not only and specifically for one sick man (to continue this example) and for his single sickness; it is made for and on behalf of the whole sacrificing community, for we have noted that the Dinka do not sacrifice individually, each for himself. A sick man does not make a sacrifice for his own recovery; his kin and community must be called together to sacrifice on behalf of their member. People provide the sacrificial victims for each other, and at the regular sacrificial ceremonies at the time of the harvest, members of different lineages take it in turn to provide for their masters of the fishing-spear the victims which he will sacrifice on behalf of and for the benefit of all.

No theory of sacrifice which neglects the fact that the act is primarily social can therefore be of service in interpreting the sacrifices of the Dinka. If sacrifice were merely, or essentially, a matter of exchanging the life of a beast for that of a man in a quasi-commercial traffic with supernatural persons, there would be no reason why a sick man should not take his own beast, kill it for himself, and ask divinities to accept its life in place of his. Such an act would be regarded as totally ineffective by the Dinka and, as I have pointed out, the importance of corporate action by a community of which the individual is really and traditionally a member is the reason for the fear which individual Dinka feel when they suffer misfortune away from home and kin. The individual whose sickness (in sacrifices for sickness) is the particular occasion of sacrifice derives benefit of some kind from his membership of the sacrificing community, whose sacrificial intention is partly, but only partly, focused upon him.

If we reduce to their main elements the actions which we have already described in our accounts of several sacrifices, they may be grouped consistently with the main elements of the oral rites as we have isolated them in the previous chapter. The victim is marked off from the other beasts of the herd by a special tethering or confinement (*mac*) and by invocations and gestures is made to stand in a special relationship to the human group which intends its death. To take a beast out of the herd and quickly kill it cannot be a sacrifice. The powerful gesturing with the spears in invocation, and the victimization of the beast first by a kind of imprisonment, which places it in human power, and then by the slapping, buffeting, and in some ceremonies more painful treatment to which it is subjected, are gestures complementary to what, in describing the oral rites, we referred to as statements of human power to prevail. The victim itself is made an object of displays of warlike hostility, which in gesture again complement the victimization of the oral rites, when the beast is made the vehicle of the *passiones* of men. This gesture, then, is correlative to the weakening of the victim which the oral part of the ceremony intends. Men manifest their strength in relation to the victim's weakness; and in this connexion it is interesting to note that the Dinka often show a theoretical preference for a strong victim, though they must often make the best of what they think they can afford. The stronger the victim, the more their own strength is emphasized by their ability to manipulate and finally kill it. For the young warriors, strength is primarily strength for battle with enemies; and hence their gestures of hostility at sacrifices represent at once the assertive repudiation of enemies, and of their own sufferings and misfortunes and sins which they have transferred to the victim. As we see in one set of invocations, the victim is to "go" and take away with it various sicknesses and dangers.

With these expressions of human strength are present also gestures by which weaknesses are admitted and then removed from the congregation. The effectiveness of a sacrifice requires, in fact, that those attending should already have disposed themselves in accordance with a part of the end which the sacrifice is intended to achieve. They intend that they shall be strong as a result of the sacrifice; they assert that they are so, both by claiming to wield the power which has enabled their ancestors to prevail in life and produce them, and by asserting, as they often do, the unity and peace of those attending. Quarrels weaken and divide the community. Hence, past quarrels are denied retroactively. Oaths falsely sworn create the confusion which the Dinka call *aliab*, and which particularly is singled out as destructive of the community itself. Hence, in some ceremonies, the "wether of the ashes" is symbolically washed to remove the effects of those false oaths. In the more generally intended act of asperging, less articulate conditions of weakness are washed away (in Dinka *wac wei*), and the strength which is derived from the victim is applied, in its chyme and urine, to human beings. These gestures are correlative to what we have seen to be admissions of human weakness in the oral rites; but like those admissions, their function is to detach weakening from strengthening elements within the situation of the rite and the consciousness of the participants. By recognizing their weakness, the Dinka are able symbolically to act upon it, in a way parallel to their attempts to recognize, and detach from, an individual patient, the Power to which his suffering may be attributed.

The assertions of human strength and confessions of weakness are accompanied by gestures honouring the victim, except in sacrifices to MACARDIT. Sometimes the beast's horns are anointed with butter, and beer is put in its mouth. Honour is rendered finally to the victim, and to Divinity and divinities, when the carcass is covered with leaves and lies for a while thus, as earlier described. The removal of the pizzle and testicles by the old women is carried out with every show of respect, and the covering of the haunches with a girl's skirt is also, as the Dinka say, "for respect". Thus the victim and the divinities to which it is offered are honoured together. By the end of the ceremony the victim has become identified with those divinities, as was originally intended in the dedication of the animal to them. In victimizing a bull or an ox the Dinka are aware of using or manipulating something physically more powerful than themselves; and through the identification of the victim with the divinities they also control something spiritually more powerful. From this comes the blend of supplication and command exhibited in the manual and oral rites.

The honour and respect showed to the victim are to be understood in the wider social context of the sacrifice. A sacrifice is a feast, to which guests are bidden, and where they should be treated with courtesy and generosity. As the guests arrive in the homestead where the sacrifice takes place, they are met by the womenfolk with songs and dance. This welcome, which honours the guests, is called *luor*, which I think is also a term used on occasions for the movement of those taking part in a sacrifice towards the victim in its death agonies. Mutual respect among members of the sacrificing community is thus connected with the respect shown to the divinities and their victims. This mutual regard is a condition of corporate life, and at sacrifices is strongly emphasized and reinforced. It is with this in mind that we can understand why, in Dinka tradition, the establishment of a new community – a new "cattle-camp" or section – is achieved by sacrifice, and the names of some Dinka subtribes today are explained as being derived from the colour-names of the beasts sacrificed to establish them. Similarly, the hymns sung in honour of clan-divinities and their victims evoke the notion of the communal strength of the clan. A good example is the following, sung in honour of the clan-divinity Gourd:

> . . . it is [for the enemy] bleeding of the belly
> It is coughing in the chest
> Bring these [upon the enemy]
> Come and work craftily
> Pray life from the container of seeds [the gourd]
> Great Gourd of my father will help me
> Even though I am left alone.
> A man who hates me, let him depart from me
> A man who loves me, let him come to me
> Great Gourd of my father will help me
> Great Gourd had filled the earth
> The cow of DENG is milked for libations
> The cow of my father is milked
> A huge gourd of milk
> Great Gourd of my father has filled the earth.

In such hymns the honouring of the clan-divinity is also an expression of the collective strength of the clansmen. The divinity is asked that enemies should depart, leaving only those who are bound together in mutual regard and who will help and not destroy each other.

It will have been obvious that the situation of sacrifice and the role of masters of the fishing-spear in it are in general prefigured in the myths of masters of the fishing-spear, and it is not necessary here to draw attention to such general correspondences between myth and rite, which a glance at the myths earlier recorded will make apparent. It remains, however, to make explicit the nature or the drama of life and death enacted in sacrificial rites, in relation to that drama as is represented in myths.

In some of the myths, it will be remembered, the fishing-spear of the prototype of spear-masters is darted at the heads of men in the situation of a river-crossing. Men are being killed, until the spear of Aiwel Longar is deflected from them. Then Aiwel shares his life-giving power among the founders of those clans which are spear-masters at the present day, and in some versions is represented as making a feast, or a sacrifice, with animal victims, from which comes the divinity Flesh shared among the spear-masters. With the provision of animal victims, that is, Aiwel Longar hands on to the people his gift of life, when previously it was against the people themselves that his energies had been directed.

The darting of the spear which, in the myths, originally brings death to human beings, is re-enacted in the sacrifical rites but directed against an animal victim. It is amply clear that this beast dies in place of men, and its fitness thus to represent men has been suggested earlier in the book. In the boldest terms, then, both myth and rite represent the conversion of a situation of death into a situation of life. In the myth the spear is deflected from men and handed on to them as a source of life. In the rite the death of the victim is explicitly the source of life to the people. This conversion of death into life is particularly clear in the details of the rites we have described, especially in the removal of the sexual organs of the sacrificial victim by women and their consumption as a source of fertility to the lineage.

It is clear, then, that an important feature of sacrifice is that the people for whom it is made enact the death of a victim which in important respects represents themselves, in order to survive that death. In relation to this we may draw attention to one curious and, to the Dinka, inexplicable, feature of Aiwel's behaviour in a version of the myth. There Aiwel places the carcass of an ox upon Adheou, and

fixes him to the ground with a fishing-spear, and prays that he may die. But the carcass putrefies around Adheou, and yet he lives. The picture here presented is of the living man within the carcass of an ox, which decays about him, and leaves him still alive.

Every sacrificial rite thus anticipates the death (with its Dinka associations of sterility and finality) which the Dinka expect and fear, and by doing so demonstrates their own power of survival. Hence, it is not necessary for the validation of belief in sacrifice that a particular sickness which sacrifice is intended to avert should be immediately cured, or even cured at all. For when sacrifice is made, the victim dies while the patient still lives, and his life, however weak, remains life in relation to the death of the victim. A Dinka sacrifice is in part, therefore, a drama of human survival.

In some of the versions of the myth the darting of the spear of Aiwel Longar into the heads of men is made in the setting of a river-crossing, and we have earlier pointed out that "to cross the river" means "to survive". This detail also has its parallel in the regular sacrificial rites of the autumn, for those rites are performed in anticipation of the movement to the dry-season pastures which is to come. Dinka giving a brief general account of the autumn sacrifices will often say something like "and then the master of the fishing-spear will kill something to Divinity, and the people will go to the dry-season pastures". As in some details of the myths, but with an animal victim, a death is a prelude to the river-crossing which ensures continued life.

I have pointed to the political significance of the fact that in some versions of the myth it is made explicit that the means by which Aiwel Longar's spear is deflected from men is a female symbol. In the sacrificial rites death is deflected from men by the provision of animal victims, ideally cattle. Cattle are in many ways substitutes for humans; but more specifically they are substitutes for women, who by the gift of cattle in bridewealth are brought into the families of their husbands and produce new life in bearing children there. So the victim which deflects death from the people in the sacrificial rites is in a special sense representative of women, as in the myths

Aiwel's death-dealing spear is deflected by female symbols. It will be remembered too that a girl's skirt is draped over the haunches of the victim. Again, though the Dinka do not normally sacrifice cows, the sacrifice of a cow, and even more of a cow-in-calf, is considered necessary to avert great calamities. Between the role of the female in the myths and in the sacrificial rites there are thus consistencies which, in a different account of the Dinka from that here attempted, might be examined more closely.

NOTES

1 This is a common Nilotic practice. The Anuak do it even more frequently than the Dinka, and their attitude towards it, at once hopeful and sceptical in a humorous Anuak way, may be conveyed by the statement made by one of them that if you want to be quite sure of not being disappointed, you ought to tie two knots – one for porridge and one for sauce.

2 An old father may permanently allot a junior wife to one of his sons, but without this understanding, it is possible that son and father may sleep with the same wife, and the father may further sleep with the mother of the son.

3 G. W. T., "Peace-Making Ceremony of Raik Dinka, Bahr-el-Ghazal Province", *S. N. & R.*, vol. vii, part 2, 1924, pp. 127–8.

4 Though perhaps Major Titherington means merely that no form of words was used to conclude the ceremony, as is more likely.

5 Twins, representing a divided unity, are particularly fitted to be closely associated with Divinity.

25

Form and Meaning of Magical Acts

Stanley Jeyaraja Tambiah

Stanley Tambiah is Research Professor of Anthropology at Harvard University. He has written a number of excellent books on Buddhism in Thailand (1970, 1976, 1984), and on politics in his native Sri Lanka (1992, 1996), as well as a lucid account of the rationality debate (1990). The piece here, drawn from a set of superb theoretical essays, critiques distinctions between magic and religion by combining arguments concerning symbolic action with ideas drawn from the theory of metaphor and the philosophy of language. The result is perhaps the clearest account we have of the logic of so-called "magic." It is thus of great relevance for understanding healing practices as well as popular religion more generally.

Like one of the proverbial blind men who probed different parts of the elephant's body, I shall investigate merely a fragmentary portion of the gigantic question: Is there a basic difference in the modes of thought of "traditional prescientific" and "modern science-oriented" societies? This was implicitly the theme of Evans-Pritchard's justly famous "dialogue" with Lévy-Bruhl. I shall attempt here only a mini-dialogue with Evans-Pritchard concerning the theoretical implications of his Zande data on magic.

My general thesis will be as follows. The *analogical* mode of thought has always been exploited by man generally. While both "magic" and "science" are characterized by analogical thought and action, they comprise differentiated varieties whose validity it would be inappropriate to measure and verify by the same standards. Magical acts, usually compounded of verbal utterance and object manipulation, constitute "performative" acts by which a property is imperatively transferred to a recipient object or person on an analogical

From Stanley Jeyaraja Tambiah, "Form and Meaning of Magical Acts," in *Culture, Thought, and Social Action: An Anthropological Perspective* (Cambridge, MA: Harvard University Press, 1985 [1973]), pp. 60–86. Abridged.

basis. Magical acts are ritual acts, and ritual acts are in turn performative acts whose positive and creative meaning is missed and whose persuasive validity is misjudged if they are subjected to that kind of empirical verification associated with scientific activity. Neither magic nor ritual constitutes applied science in the narrow sense.

In contrast, the exploitation of analogical thought in science consists in making the known or apprehended instance serve as a model for the incompletely known in the phenomenon to be explained. The model serves to generate a prediction concerning the *explicandum*, which is then subjected to observation and verification tests to ascertain the prediction's truth value.

"Performative" acts of a persuasive kind are by no means confined to the primitive; modern industrial societies also have their rites and ceremonies which achieve their effects by virtue of conventional normative understandings. However, science (strictly defined) is an achievement perhaps only of certain complex and literate civilizations. In the West at least, where it has attained its fullest development, science probably developed and differentiated out of certain forms of traditional and magical thought and activity; but this should not automatically serve as a universal linear scheme, nor should there be a retrospective and backward thrust by which the "rationality" of magic is pitted against the "rationality" of science, to the former's inevitable and foregone detriment. Indeed it is precisely because many Western anthropologists have approached the ritual performances of other societies from the perspective of their own historical experience and intellectual categories that they have misunderstood the semantic basis of magical acts.

I shall try to give flesh to these programmatic assertions by working through a body of concrete ethnographic data.

The Observer's Problem: The Example of the Azande

Although Evans-Pritchard in his book on the Azande (1937) and in an earlier article written in 1929 admitted that the spell was nearly always a part of and indeed essential to Zande magical rites, he emphasized over and over again (perhaps to drive home the difference between Zande and Trobriand magical systems) that it was "medicines" which played the major part. Mystical power, producing the desired end, resided in the material substance used, whereas spells, having no specific virtue by themselves, were merely words of direction uttered to the "medicines" linking them to the desired ends.

A major concern of Evans-Pritchard was to investigate the attributes and logic of selection of Zande "medicines," and their role in effecting the end sought by the rite. It is my view that in most of Evans-Pritchard's discussion of the potency of Zande "medicines" he was troubled by a theoretical framework whereby "magic" stood for effects automatically ensuing from the ritual operations alone (particularly the manipulation of material substances), and also whereby the efficacy of the ritual acts was sought to be seen within an observer's empirical "cause-effect" scheme.

At several points in his book Evans-Pritchard (1937) tried to apply the observer's distinction *ritual* (or *mystical*) versus *empirical* to the rites he was examining and found them difficult to apply consistently. This question of whether Zande medicines were mystical or empirical plagued him with recurring insistence in his final chapter, entitled "Leechcraft." It is instructive to summarize the findings of this chapter, for here at least where the subject matter was the etiology and cure of disease and the efficacy of Zande "drugs" and "pharmacopoeia" we might expect the discussion to be more concrete than that pertaining to the more elusive magical rites and witchcraft attacks. A propos his use of concepts which I have put in quotation marks above, Evans-Pritchard disarmingly states: "We can later decide to what extent their leech-craft is magic, their leeches magicians, and their drugs mere *materia medica* of magical ritual." I shall be concerned here with the implications of that postponed decision.

[. . .]

Evans-Pritchard's final attempt at sorting the data, in answer to the query: "To what extent are Zande medical practices 'empirical' as opposed to 'ritual'?" ran something like this. In acute and sudden illnesses the attribution of genesis may be to "mystical" causes like sorcery and witchcraft alone; in chronic and prolonged illnesses recourse is to a theory of *dual causation* in that there is the disease itself *plus* witchcraft, which conditions its occurrence and continuance. (This dual theory is paralleled by Evans-Pritchard's earlier elucidation of witchcraft: while the Zande are aware of the physical circumstances of accidents and disease, witchcraft explains why a particular sufferer and no other was the victim. "Witchcraft explains why events are harmful to man and not how they happen" – p. 72.) In both acute and chronic illness, in which mystical forces are at play, the drugs used are appropriately thought to have "mystical" efficacy, as seen in the notion of *mbisimo ngua*, "the soul of medicine" (corresponding to the notion "soul of witchcraft").

Mild illnesses, in contrast, bring to the fore, so Evans-Pritchard says, "natural" or organic causation, with the witchcraft allegation sinking into the background. But even here "the treatment may be just as useless in a slight as in a serious illness" (p. 505). It is not surprising then that Evans-Pritchard admits with a touch of bafflement: "There are many varieties of behaviour and opinion which defy rigid classification because they shade into one another in a complicated pattern of interconnexions" (p. 506).

Despite this confession, it is evident that Evans-Pritchard did sort things out after a fashion. With the benefit of hindsight it might seem that a greater attention to folk classification of disease and "medicines" and the native exegesis about them might have provided additional clarification. My thesis is that this lack itself is the concomitant of a certain theoretical perspective. Evans-Pritchard had clear clues that much of Zande magic was based on analogical thought and action, but rather than investigate its semantics deeply, he, being at this stage of his thought unable to liberate himself from the influence of the observer's distinction between things empirical and things mystical (and the like), simply subjected Zande magic and leechcraft to the Westerner's criteria

of induction and verification. The unstated assumption of such an intellectual exercise is that Zande practices had the same empirical purposes and objectives as those of Western science and that they, like science, were concerned with "causal" relations. This chapter is largely concerned with the consequences of (erroneously) submitting Zande analogical thought and action to Western scientific standards of induction and verification.

The Uses of Analogy

Evans-Pritchard's originality could not, of course, be confined for long within the bounds of limiting frameworks. Consequently, fresh insights break through here and there in the Zande book. One such is contained in the passing phrase "imitative symbolism," and another in the idea of "homeopathy," discussed briefly in two pages (pp. 449–50). Here we find the seeds of an approach to Zande magic (and indeed other magical systems) which I shall call "analogical action."

Apparently the Azande themselves recognized the analogical and metaphorical basis for the use of material substances in their rites. . . . Evans-Pritchard (1937) writes: "They [the Azande] say, 'We use such-and-such a plant because it is like such-and-such a thing,' naming the object towards which the rite is directed. Likewise they say, 'We do so-and-so in order that so-and-so may happen,' naming the action which they wish to follow. Often the similarity between medicine and desired happening is indicated in the spell" (p. 449). Evans-Pritchard proceeds to give the example . . . of the tall *bingba* grass, which is profuse in growth and has featherlike branches, being used by verbal direction and by direct action to make the oil-bearing melon (*kpagu*) flourish.

There are many examples of analogical action in word and deed scattered throughout the book. A systematic assembling and examination of these examples may provide an alternative interpretation to the one proposed by Evans-Pritchard.

Scrutinize these preliminary examples with this objective in view:

1. When the Azande prick the stalks of bananas with crocodiles' teeth they say, "Teeth of crocodile are you, I prick bananas with them, may bananas be prolific like crocodiles' teeth" (p. 450).

2. Azande tie *gbaga* (the fruit of a palm tree) to their girdles as medicine of masculinity and to secure sexual potency. When tying they say: "You are *gbaga*. May I be very potent sexually. May I not become sexually weak" (p. 455).

3. Here is an expressive example that could equally well come from Sri Lanka or Thailand. If a man is a victim of *menzere* (sorcery) medicine, he goes to a much-frequented crossroads, kneels there, and verbally disperses it: "If it is *menzere*, may it follow all paths and not return" (p. 394).

4. Finally, there is the celebrated case of the stone, placed in the fork of a tree to retard the sun: "You stone, may the sun not be quick to fall today. You, stone, retard the sun on high so that I can arrive first at that homestead to which I journey; then the sun may set" (p. 469).

Note here that the Azande refer to the stone used as *ngua uru*, which Evans-Pritchard translates as "sun-medicine."

It is my submission that, had Evans-Pritchard followed leads of this sort, he could have thrown more light on why within the range of plant life and arboreal substances (which form the major category of "medicines") used by the Azande, certain woods or roots or leaves rather than others were chosen to represent specialized ideas. Furthermore, the utterances and spells are in fact, as we have seen in these examples, critical for telling us which feature of an object-symbol is the focus of attention on an analogical basis. A shift of theoretical interest from "inherent potency" of medicines to "analogical transfer of their qualities" might have made the botanical enumeration of Zande medicines less tedious and unnecessary than Evans-Pritchard feared.

Here is a critical passage which I shall take as the text for my discussion. It encapsulates the "closed" system of Zande thought, a central theme of this book (and grist for the Popperian mill):

I do not know whether more than a verbal analogy is implied in the Zande name for mumps (the affected parts are massaged with an unguent): *imawirianzoro*, sickness of the little (*wiri*) *anzoro* birds (finches) which have lumps on their necks. But it may well be so, for we know that in primitive patterns of thought objects which have a superficial resemblance are often linked up by nomenclature and ritual and are connected in mystical patterns of thought. In Zande therapeutics this mystical connexion is found in notions about cause and cure. Ringworm resembles in appearance fowls' excrement, and fowls' excrement is at the same time both cause and cure of ringworm. Blepharoptosis resembles a hen's egg, and a hen's egg is its cure. Generally the logic of therapeutic treatment consists in the selection of the most prominent external symptoms, the naming of the disease after some object in nature which it resembles, and the utilization of the object as the principal ingredient in the drug administered to cure the disease. The circle may even be completed by belief that the symptoms not only yield to treatment by the object which resembles them but are caused by it as well. (1937: 486–7)

A number of words appear in this commentary that are worthy of "practical criticism." "Superficial resemblance" can get its meaning only by unstated comparison with the notion of deeper identity from a scientific causal viewpoint; "mystical connexion" can only mean unobservable and unknown connection by comparison with empirically observable connection. The backdrop then is the standards of verification of science.

[...]

Most historians of science begin with the Greeks, and one of the principles of thought attributed to early Greek natural philosophy is that "like attracts like," which in its application meant "that a relationship of similarity may sometimes constitute a magical bond between two things, so that what happens to one of them may influence what happens to the other" (Lloyd, 1966: 180). Thus, Hesse (1961) explains that one of the commonest analogies in "primitive" Greek thought was "the analogy of attraction": men apparently, having experienced sympathy and antipathy, attraction and repulsion, between themselves and other men, and between themselves and nature, therefore see these as forces which can produce effects in nature. Popular maxims based on ideas of attraction and repulsion provided, we are told, concepts of *motion* and *change* – thus, "like attracts like" was supplemented by other maxims such as "like nourishes like," "like affects like," "like perceives like." The doctrine of attraction explained why animals flock together with their kind, seeds of the same size seek each other when shaken in a sieve, and pebbles of like size are grouped on the seashore. In Plutarch is found the example of treating jaundice with the yellow eye of a stone curlew.

For the historian and philosopher of science, the analogy of attraction is principally of interest because the early Greek philosophers used it to explain the phenomenon of *action at a distance*, a perennial problem in scientific explanation. The Greek breakthrough from primitive analogy to "scientific" thinking, we are told, began to occur when two things happened: first, when a firm distinction was made between the animate and inanimate, and when it was recognized that phenomena of gravity and radiation were different in kind from the behavior of animals; second, when thereby a certain amount of "mechanization" of physics took place, with Aristotle and with the atomists. Indeed "action at a distance" became intellectually problematic only when this stage had been reached. "Part of the history of the problem of action at a distance is therefore that of the growth of a mechanical conception of matter, and the use of mechanical analogies in explaining natural processes" (Hesse, 1961:30). Thus, for example, it was the "atomists," we are told, who by virtue of their notion of atoms in motion introduced a purely mechanical theory of motion and change through contact.

Readers of the Azande book will have noticed that Evans-Pritchard was very concerned with this classical problem of "action at a distance," which was spelled out in terms of "mystical" ties, the "soul" of witchcraft or of "medicine" affecting a victim, and the like, all of which are adduced in an attempt to solve an "intellectual" problem which is not necessarily the Azande's.

How relevant are classical Greek scholarship and the writings of historians of science for illuminating the thought patterns of the Azande, Trobrianders, and other "prescientific" peoples? I cannot go into this matter at length here, but let me sound a note of caution. From a comparative point of view it is useful to bear in mind that many Western philosophers are concerned with how early Greek thought led by stages to the development of scientific thought wedded to experimental verification – in other words, how Greek thought was transformed from "magic" to "science," and how the seeds sown by the Greek philosophers ultimately flowered in the scientific revolution of the seventeenth century, when "the analogy of mechanism" alone was exploited with respect to events in nature and when nature's laws were sought in mechanical conceptions. Indeed, when later Newton's theory of gravity was propounded, the Cartesians attacked him for propounding a theory of "attraction" in the occult idiom – that is, action at a distance without contact. The linear evolution and transformation of Western thought from the sixth century B.C. to the present day in the field of science should not be taken as an intellectual model when investigating the societies anthropologists study, unless at the same time one is deeply conscious of the underlying intellectual interests of the scholars who formulated it. Their interests were the foundations of scientific thought and of formal logic in Greece and the unique (?) development by which Greek analogical thought became subject to empirical verification, falsification, and deductive-inductive reasoning. Must analogical thought of the Azande necessarily be examined and its form and meaning unraveled in relation to these intellectual preoccupations?

In order to answer this question, let us examine carefully the kinds of analogies that exist and their uses. First of all, what do we mean by "analogy"? Basically, analogy depends on the recognition of similarities between the instances compared, and, as many philosophers have recognized, analogy stands as a prototype of reasoning from experience. J. S. Mill's paradigm serves well as a definition: "Two things resemble each other in one or more respects; a certain proposition is true of the one; therefore it is true of the other." Lloyd elucidating Keynes's thinking on the subject (in *A Treatise on Probability*) remarks that "both Bacon's own inductive method, based on the use of 'exclusions and rejections,' and Mill's Methods of Agreement and Difference, aim at the determination of the resemblances and differences between particular instances, at the determination of what Keynes called the Positive and Negative Analogies" (1966:173).

Hesse in an instructive essay (1963), on which I draw, lists four kinds of analogies. For my purposes, I shall modify her examples, and elaborate in new directions fundamentally two types of analogy – the *scientific predictive* and the *conventional persuasive*. First, let us bear in mind that "positive analogy" relates to properties shared or points of similarity between the things compared, "negative analogy" to their points of difference or properties they do not share, and "neutral analogy" to properties of the things compared of which we do not yet know whether they are of positive or negative character.

Of the two fundamentally different types of analogies that can be distinguished, one serves as a model in science generating hypotheses and comparisons which are then subject to verification inductively. In this use, the known or apprehended instance serves as the "model" and the unknown or incompletely known is the *explicandum*, the phenomenon to be explained by means of a theory.

Figures 1 and 2 show examples of analogies that might be used in science. Following Hesse, I indicate in the figures two kinds of dyadic relations that should be recognized: the *horizontal* and *vertical* relations. If Figure 1 is to serve as a material analogy in science, the pairs of horizontal terms (echoes:reflection, and so forth) should be either identical or *similar*, and the vertical relations (between the properties of sound such as echoes, loudness) should be *causal*, which term given a wide interpretation should mean at least a tendency to *co-occurrence*, in that certain properties are necessary or sufficient conditions for the occurrence of other properties.

In the "looser" example given in Figure 2, the horizontal relation may show similarities of *structure* or of *function*, and the vertical relation that of whole to its parts depending on some theory of interrelation of parts, evolutionary or adaptive.

	SIMILARITY RELATIONS	
CAUSAL RELATIONS	*Properties of sound*	*Properties of light*
	echoes	reflection
	loudness	brightness
	pitch	color
	etc.	

Figure 1 *Examples of analogies that might be used in science, showing relations of similarity and causality*

	SIMILARITIES	
CO-OCCURRENCE	*Bird*	*Fish*
	wing	fin
	lungs	gill
	feathers	scales

Figure 2 *Examples of analogies that might be used in science, showing relations of similarity and co-occurrence*

It is essential to note that analogies can usefully serve as theoretical models only if the horizontal dyadic relations are relations of similarity (that is, judged by identities and differences), if the vertical relations of the model are *causal* in some scientifically acceptable sense and if those of the *explicandum* also promise relations of the same kind, and if the essential properties and causal relations of the model have not been shown to be part of the negative analogy between model and *explicandum*. If these conditions are satisfied, then predictions can legitimately be made from any set of known – say, three – terms to an unknown fourth. For example, in the case of the sound and light analogies in Figure 1, if we have established the similarity of "echoes" to "reflection," then from the known property of "loudness" in sound we may expect to find the "similar" property of "brightness" in light. Or in the bird and fish analogy, one can predict from the known parts of the bird skeleton to a "missing" part of the fish skeleton. To put it differently, the fun lies in extrapolating from the domain of positive analogy into the domain of neutral analogy, as these were defined above. Ultimately, of course, these predictions should be capable of verification or falsification in terms of observation statements.

There is another kind of traditional analogy used widely in human discourse that does not owe its genesis and use to the pursuit of "scientific" knowledge. It would therefore be ridiculous to weigh and measure its adequacy in terms of inductive verification. Consider the following analogy that may occur in political rhetoric: the employer is to his workers as a father is to his children.

$$\frac{father}{children} : \frac{employer}{workers}$$

Let us say that the purpose of this analogy is propagandist, that it is disseminated by employers in order to "evoke" attitudes in workers rather than to "predict" them.

It should be noted that in this example the vertical relations are not specifically causal; nor is it necessary that if three terms occur, the fourth also must. Even more important, there is not in this example any horizontal relation of similarity between the terms, except by virtue of the fact that the two pairs are up to a point *related by the same vertical relation*. (There may be other persuasive analogies in which, in spite of horizontal similarities between terms, the critical relation is still the vertical one.)

How must this analogy work if it is to succeed as political rhetoric? The relation of father to children bears some resemblance to the relation of employer to workers (positive analogy) in the sense, let us say, that just as the father provides for the material needs of his children so does the employer provide work and wages for his workers. Let us next say that the relation of children to father (and vice versa) is much more than this dependence; children should love their father, obey and respect him, and so on. These meanings are not necessarily implied in the employer-worker

relation (negative analogy). It is precisely this expansion of meaning or the transfer of these additional values to the employer-worker relation that is sought by invoking the father-children analogy. Since in this case the ultimate aim is to make workers believe that they are like "children," there is a sense in which we can say that the operation consists in "transferring" (rather than "predicting") from the postulated three terms the value of "children" to the fourth term, the "workers." It is for this reason that this analogy and its variants are labeled "persuasive," "rationalizing," or "evocative."

It is my thesis that in ritual operations by word and object manipulation, the analogical action conforms to the "persuasive" rather than the "scientific" model. I shall later illustrate the argument that in Zande rites (as well as those of many other societies) the operation rests on the explicit recognition of *both similarity* (positive analogy) *and difference* (negative analogy) *between the vertical relations of the paired terms*. And the rite consists in persuasively transferring the properties of the desired and desirable vertical relation to the other which is in an undesirable condition, or in attempting to convert a potential, not-yet-achieved state into an actualized one. The manipulation is made operationally realistic by directing the transfer not only by word but, as in the Zande case, by bringing a material piece of the object in the desirable-desired analogy into contact with the object in need of the transfer. There are nuances in this basic manipulation which are best illustrated when dealing with the concrete cases.

Thus, a vital difference exists between the use of "analogy" in science and its use in ritual. Barring a few instances, in most Zande magical rites (especially those considered important by the people concerned), the analogical relation or comparison and the wished-for effect are stated *verbally* simultaneously with or before the carrying out of the "homeopathic" act (of influencing certain objects by manipulating other objects which resemble them). Why must the analogy of attraction be stated in word and deed for it to be effective? No classical philosopher or historian of science appears to have asked this when propounding that the principle of "like attracts like" activated primitive thought and action. In a laboratory of today, the only time a scientist may be found to foretell and verbally explain his actions while simultaneously doing his experiment would be, for example, when he is teaching a class the procedure involved in conducting that experiment. (And of course he does not expect that his words will automatically make the experiment come out right, as we know from the failed experiments in science classes we have attended at school.) Outside some such situation, his sanity would be suspect if he gave instructions aloud to his apparatus to do his bidding.

Note also how extraordinary the magical operation must look in terms of the traditional explanation (of like attracts like) when placed in relation to the use of analogy made by a scientist. Supposing a scientist constructs an electronic brain-model to "simulate" in some ways a human biochemically structured brain. The former is useful as a predictive model only in those areas where the material makeup of the analogue is not essential to the model (that is, constitutes the innocuous negative analogy) but where the pattern of mutual relation of the parts and the behavioral relations expressed by it are the essential features. If, say, a man is weak in arithmetic the scientist does not bring a brain-model that can add and place it in contact with the head of the former so that his additions may be thus "caused" to be correct. But this is precisely what we are told the primitive magician might attempt to do! (On the other hand, the scientist may demonstrate the working of an adding machine to our hypothetical subject, and it is possible that after sufficient demonstration of its workings the subject's abilities might increase. This is a technique of "persuasion" through contact. Could it be that this is the logic of the magical operations as well?)

Some Zande Analogies

I have already noted that for the first time, well toward the end of the Azande book, Evans-Pritchard (1937) broached the question of the analogical basis of magical rites as seen by the

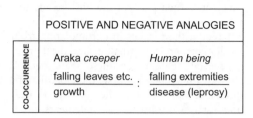

Figure 3 *Zande analogies between* araka *creeper and human being*

actors. It is, however, a pity that he did not compile a more thorough indigenous exegesis on why certain "medicines" were used, and what properties or features of the substance used were singled out as "similar" to those of the recipient of the rite. Hence, in the examples he cryptically cites, the logic of their use is open to an alternative interpretation that is as plausible as Evans-Pritchard's own implicitly theory-dictated view that the medicines and drugs, chosen on the basis of superficial resemblances and to which is given mystical significance, are empirically ineffective and scientifically false, although used as if they had automatic effects. Let us look at some Zande cases:

1. At a certain time of their growth the stems of the creeper *araka* lose their leaves. These are replaced by a double row of bands, joined to the stalks, which little by little dry, split, and fall in small pieces just as the extremities of the hands and feet disappear in "*la lèpre mutilante.*" This creeper is highly thought of as furnishing treatment for this kind of leprosy (p. 450).

    I suggest that the analogical reasoning in this example is more complex than is implied by a simplistic "like attracts like," in that it brings to view both similarities and differences, positive and negative analogies, in the *vertical relations* of the terms (see Figure 3). In the case of the creeper, the falling of its extremities is a *phase of its growth cycle*, whereas in the case of human beings the decay of limbs through leprosy is a *disease that leads to degeneration and death*. Thus, this comparison proceeds to use the *araka* creeper

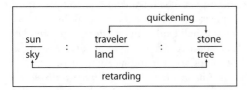

Figure 4 *Zande analogies describing a man on a journey*

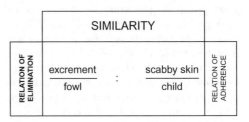

Figure 5 *Zande analogies for the treatment of ringworm*

in the rite as a vehicle or agent of life, the message being: may the leprosy disappear and health appear, just as the shedding process in the creeper stimulates growth. The rite expresses the wish that one "vertical" relation that is undesired be replaced by another desired one; it itself represents symbolic, not causal, action.

2. Let us next take the celebrated example already cited of a man indulging "in the action of placing a stone in the tree and relating by a few words this action to a desired end." We should bear in mind that the man is on a journey and wishes to arrive home before sunset (pp. 468–9).

We can plausibly say that here the initial comparison is between the sun "traveling" toward sunset (in the sky) and a man traveling (on land) to his homestead (see Figure 4). The sun and the man are therefore similar in their situations, but their interests are not identical (the difference that constitutes the negative analogy). The man wishes to travel faster than the sun. It is in this context that we must view the operation of putting a stone in the fork of a tree and thus wedging it. It represents the desired positive effect of retarding the sun and the implicit counter-effect (or negative analogy) of quickening his footsteps home, which in fact the traveler actually does by performing this rite.

3. A third example is a case of "homeopathic" treatment of a disease. Ringworm in children is called *imanduruakondo* (*ima* = sickness; *nduruakondo* = fowl house). It is so called because the scabby patches of the disease resemble fowls' excrement. Hence, they appear to consider the disease a result of the afflicted child's having eaten

food grown on a dung heap in the vicinity of a fowl house. Hence also they consider the remedy to consist in fowls' excrement dried and reduced to ashes and mixed into a paste with a little palm oil and applied to the ringworm (p. 485).

While the "like attracts like" argument would say that the fowls' excrement is (falsely) used to attract the scabs on the skin which it (falsely) resembles, I am tempted to say that the analogy is interesting and is capable of being acted upon creatively because, once again, of the positive and negative features it exhibits (see Figure 5). The relation of fowl to excrement is one of *elimination* of (unwanted) waste product, while that of scabby skin on child is one of (unwanted) *adherence* to body. Hence it is that the fowl's excrement can convey the desired idea of eliminating the scabs when applied to the body, because while in one sense similar to it, it is also essentially different.

[. . .]

How to Understand Ritual (Which Includes "Magic")?

I have perhaps so far only indicated negatively how "magic" should not be viewed, and not positively how it might be viewed in terms of a new perspective. I have argued that to view magic as an attempt at science that failed (or more crudely a "bastard science in the manner of Frazer, or more sophisticatedly as a "closed" system of thought that allows for no verification and falsification of its principles *à la* Popper) is to assert that in their magic and ritual the primitives tried to achieve results through "causal" reasoning and failed. I have also argued that while it is the case that much primitive magic is based on analogical thought and action as is Western science, the difference between them is that whereas in science the use of an analogy is closely linked to prediction and verification, and its adequacy judged in terms of inductive support, or of meeting standards of probability criteria, or of standing up to tests of falsifiability, and the like, the semantics of a magical rite are not necessarily to be judged in terms of such "true/false" criteria of science but on different standards and objectives. The corresponding objectives in (magical) ritual are "persuasion," "conceptualization," "expansion of meaning," and the like, and the criteria of adequacy are better conveyed by notions such as "validity," "correctness," "legitimacy," and "felicity" of the ceremony performed.

It is this latter assertion that I wish to elucidate now. In [my essay "The Magical Power of Words"] I took some steps toward understanding the form and meaning of ritual in terms of its inner semantic frame and outer pragmatic frame. My starting point with regard to the former was that most "magical rites" (as indeed most rituals) combine word and deed and that the rite is devoted to an "imperative transfer" of effects, which some might phrase as the "telic" and others as the "illocutionary" or "performative" nature of the rite (Austin, 1962; Finnegan, 1969). The semantics of the transfer itself, the logic of construction of the transfer, in the Trobriand case depend 1) on metaphorical and analogical transfers by word, mediated by realistic contact transfer through objects used as "transformers," and 2) on imperative verbal transfer of energy to a "whole" through the metonymic naming of the parts. One of the points I made was that the same laws of association that apply to ordinary language apply to magical language – I reiterate this because one reader at least has managed to misunderstand my effort and thinks I tried to deal with the special character of "magical" utterances (Finnegan, 1969: 349), thereby also not appreciating my critique of the theory of "magical" language held by Ogden and Richards, Malinowski,

and others. But fortunately, in compensation, Finnegan has led me to Austin (1962), whose ideas I shall exploit in an attempt to formulate a perspective, according to my own design, for viewing the form and meaning of ritual.

In Austin's *How To Do Things with Words* (1962), the chief topic of elaboration is what he calls the "performative" or "illocutionary" act, in which the uttering of the sentence cannot merely be described as saying something, but is, or is a part of, the *doing of an action*. When in a marriage ceremony the man says "I do take this woman to be my lawful wedded wife" (or some such formula), or the man says in a will "I give and bequeath . . . ," to utter these sentences in the appropriate circumstances "is not to *describe* my doing of what I should be said in so uttering to be doing or to state I am doing it: it is to do it" (p. 6).

What ultimately I think Austin arrives at toward the end of his exercise is a classification of speech acts, "the issuing of utterances in a speech situation," which makes any stating "performing an act." (This is close to Malinowski's approach of seeing speech as part of action; . . .) How many senses may there be in which to say something is to do something, or in saying something we do something, or even by saying something we do something? The following classification of speech acts may help answer the question:

1. To perform a *locutionary* act: To utter a sentence with a certain sense and reference (an assertion, a descriptive statement of fact) which is *true or false in a referential sense*.

2. To perform an *illocutionary* act: This relates to an utterance which has a *certain conventional force*, a performative act *which does something* (as implied in promising, ordering, apologizing, warning). Usually the explicit illocutionary utterance is reducible or analyzable into a form with a verb in the first person singular present indicative active (that is, the "I," the "active," and the "present" seem appropriate). These statements cannot be subject *to the true-false test*, but are *normatively judged* as "happy"/"unhappy,"

valid/invalid, correct/defective, and so forth.

3. To perform a *perlocutionary* act: This refers to what we bring about or achieve by *saying something* (as connoted by convincing, persuading, misleading). It refers to both the intended and unintended *consequence* upon the hearer of words uttered by the speaker. (By saying it I convinced him . . .)

These three are analytically separate but in reality not exclusive categories: both locutionary and illocutionary acts can have consequences listed as perlocutionary; and an illocutionary act can have referring and predicating elements together with the performative. We could perhaps say that an imperative illocutionary act attempts to get the world to conform to words, whereas "true" when ascribed to illocutions attributes success in getting words to conform to the world.

Adapting these ideas for our purposes, we can say that ritual acts and magical rites are of the "illocutionary" or "performative" sort, which simply by virtue of being enacted (under the appropriate conditions) achieve a change of state, or do something effective (for example, an installation ceremony undergone by the candidate makes him a "chief"). This performative aspect of the rite should be distinguished from its locutionary (referential, information-carrying) and perlocutionary (consequences for the participants) features.

It was quite evident to Austin that, while he focused on the role of speech in illocutionary acts, the utterance was not the sole thing necessary if the illocutionary act was to be deemed to have been performed, and also that *actions other than speech*, whether physical or mental, were entailed for the full realization of the performance. Indeed it is even possible at the other extreme to enact a performative act without uttering words at all – a hypothetical example would be the establishing of blood brotherhood by the physical exchange of blood (without an exchange of words).

The vast majority of ritual and magical acts combine word and deed. Hence, it is appropriate to say that they use words in a performative or illocutionary manner, just as the action (the manipulation of objects and persons) is correspondingly performative.

I shall attempt to formalize in a few words the essentials of what I see as the form and meaning of magical ritual acts. The rite usually consists of a close interweaving of *speech* (in the form of utterances and spells) and *action* (consisting of the manipulation of objects). The *utterance* can be analyzed with respect to its "predicative" and "illocutionary" frames. In terms of predication and reference the words exploit analogical associations, comparisons, and transfers (through simile, metaphor, metonym, and so forth). The illocutionary force and power by which the deed is directed and enacted are achieved through use of words commanding, ordering, persuading, and the like: "Whistle, whistle, I send you after a thief" – so commands a Zande spell. And a Trobriand spell combines both metaphor and illocutionary force by urging the *taytu* yam to throw out foliage like the spider spinning its web (Malinowski, 1965: 148):

The spider covers up, the spider covers
  up . . .
The open space, the open space between thy
  branches, O taytu
the spider covers up,
. . . Shoot up, O head of my taytu
. . . Make mop upon mop of leaves, O head of
  my taytu . . .

The action can be similarly analyzed. The objects manipulated are chosen analogically on the basis of similarity and difference to convey meaning. From the performative perspective, the action consists of an operation done on an object-symbol to make an imperative and realistic transfer of its properties to the recipient. Or to put it differently, two objects are seen as having resemblances and differences, and an attempt is made to transfer the desirable quality of one to the other, which is in a defective state.

It is clear that the words and action closely combine to form an amalgam which is the magical or ritual *act*. The interrelation between the two media – speech and object manipulation – can take different forms. What I want to emphasize here is that this way of looking at "magical art" breaks through the

Saussurean *langue/parole* distinction. On the one hand, the magical act bears predicative and referential *langue*-type meanings, and on the other it is a performative act. Both frames are coexistent, and it is as a *performative* or "illocutionary" act directed by analogical reasoning that magic acquires its distinctiveness.

It is *inappropriate* to subject these performative rites to verification, to test whether they are true or false in a referential or assertive sense or whether the act has effected a result in terms of the logic of "causation" as this is understood in science. Let me illustrate the point by considering the Thai rite in which a new house is blessed by Buddhist monks (so that evil spirits may be driven out and prosperity result) through the recitation of sacred verses and the performance of certain acts. Several conditions have to be satisfied if a performance of this rite is not, to use Austin's word, to become an "infelicity": there must exist a conventional procedure properly enacted only by authorized persons – for example, monks or householders; the monks who take part must be entitled to conduct the ceremony (as in this particular instance); and the actual ceremony must be executed both correctly and completely.

Quite another set of conditions relates to the *bona fides* of the actors. For example, the rite is intended for beneficiaries who expect to conduct themselves in certain ways and who have the right intentions. In fulfillment of this, it is necessary that the participants, in the actual rite performed, satisfy these expectations and actually so conduct themselves subsequently.

Now suppose that after the performance of the rite, it is found that one or more of these conditions were not fulfilled – the monks may have been bogus, the ceremony incorrectly performed, or the householder never intended to live in the house with his family but planned to use it for an illicit purpose. We cannot in these circumstances say that the rite itself was false or empirically ineffective in a causal sense. The ceremony *itself* cannot ever be said to have been proved to be false or untrue or ineffective; however, any particular enactment of it may be said to be void, unworthy, or defective. A bigamist who on false pretenses has gone through

a second marriage ceremony does not on that account make the institution of marriage false, wrong, or ineffective; what can be said is that he has undergone the ceremony in bad faith and that he has not properly "married" a second time.

The conclusions therefore are that 1) while to particular instances of ritual enactments of the illocutionary or performative type *normative* judgments of efficacy (legitimacy, defectiveness, propriety, and so forth) may be applied, it is inappropriate to judge their efficacy in terms of *verification statements* and inductive rules, and 2) while ritual in general as an institution cannot be declared to be defective, particular instances of it may be so declared, if the proper conditions of performance were not met. It is at this point that I wish to take issue with Evans-Pritchard and Robin Horton.

Evans-Pritchard in his classic study of Zande witchcraft, oracles, and magic, having elucidated the coherence and close linkage of these systems of belief, felt it necessary to ask how they fitted into the observer-imposed ritual/empirical categories and how they related to Zande "practical" day-to-day activity. More pointedly, Evans-Pritchard, naturally interested in a "European" intellectual problem, asked how magic, which was oriented to achieving effects, compared with Western empiricism based on canons of proof and experimentation. Evans-Pritchard gave various reasons why the Azande did not cease believing in magic even when the expected or wished-for magical effect did not materialize. His answer was that although Azande may be skeptical about the skills and knowledge of particular witch doctors or their poor medicines or the correct performance of particular performances, and the like, their belief in the efficacy of the system itself was not thereby assailed. Whereas Evans-Pritchard gave this as evidence of why Zande magic cannot be empirically proven wrong, he did not perhaps fully appreciate that the answers he received were appropriate to all conventional performative and illocutionary acts – particular performances may for various reasons be "unhappy" or "incorrect" and therefore inefficacious while the convention itself is unassailable.

Robin Horton (1967) compounds the "error" in his challenging essays, suggestively entitled "African Traditional Thought and Western Science." On the one hand, Horton argues that African traditional thought (with its supernatural entities couched in a personal idiom) and Western science (with its concepts couched in an impersonal idiom) are similar in that reference to theoretical entities is used to link events in the visible, tangible world (natural effects) to their antecedents in the same world (natural causes). On the other hand, however – and here is the sting – this same African thought-system whose aim is explanatory and predictive (just like science) refuses to subject itself (like good science) to falsifiability and other verification tests. Indeed, African traditional thought (just as Evans-Pritchard elucidated it) is a "closed system." The believer cannot get outside the web of his thought, he cannot be agnostic, there is no vision of alternatives. Furthermore, it portrays unreflective thinking – that is, traditional thought lacks logic and philosophy and reflection upon the rules of explanation. Evans-Pritchard's demonstration is driven home in traditional thought by a process of *secondary elaboration*; other current beliefs are utilized in such a way as to "excuse" each failure as it occurs, and thus the major theoretical assumptions are protected even in the face of negative evidence. By comparison, the collective memory of the European scientific community is littered with the wreckage of discarded theories. This is true, but Horton's enthusiasm for Popper's idealizations may benefit from some of Kuhn's skepticism.

I think it is possible to differ from Horton on the basic assumptions of the comparisons between traditional and scientific thought. One cannot deny that traditional societies reflect the patterns he enumerates. But I think it is fundamentally mistaken to say that African religion and ritual are concerned with the same intellectual tasks that science in Western society is concerned with: this is a case of analogy abused. The net result of such comparative pursuit is to land oneself where Frazer found himself – magical rituals are like science with the difference that they are mistaken and false.

My counterargument is that to view most ritual and magical acts as if they were directed to the purposes of scientific activity – to discover natural causes, predict empirical consequences in terms of a theory of causation – is inappropriate and not productive of maximum understanding. The analogical thought of Western science and that of primitive ritual have different implications. Like "illocutionary" and "performative" acts, ritual acts have consequences and effect changes; they structure situations not in the idiom of "Western science" and "rationality" but in terms of convention and normative judgment, and as solutions of existential problems and intellectual puzzles. These orders of thought and action after all are to be found in Western societies as well – they coexist with science and thrive outside its field of action or relevance. (It would be interesting to know what Horton thinks is the relation between science and religion in Western society.)

But returning to the problem of magic itself: Have I merely evaded answering what magic is by embedding it in ritual and seeing it as an analogical cum performative act? By and large I think this embedding is a correct representation of it. But I must also go on to say that insofar as magical rites try to effect a transfer, they are often geared to achieving practical results – such as cure of disease or production of a fine harvest – as much as they are geared to effecting social results. Although we should not judge their *raison d'être* in terms of applied science, we should however recognize that many (but not all) magical rites are elaborated and utilized precisely in those circumstances where non-Western man has not achieved that special kind of "advanced" scientific knowledge which can control and act upon reality to an extent that reaches beyond the realm of his own practical knowledge. Let us not forget what Evans-Pritchard's conclusion was. Zande rites were most "mystical" where the diseases they dealt with were the most acute and chronic. These rites, then, are on a different wavelength from scientific technology; or at least in primitive societies it is better to assimilate witchcraft and magic to "ritual" rather than to "applied science."

Let us also not forget one of Evans-Pritchard's most pregnant observations: the Zande belief in witchcraft does not exclude "empirical knowledge of cause and effect," but it provides a social and cultural method of acting upon the world. "In every case witchcraft is the socially relevant cause, since it is the only one which *allows intervention* and determines social behaviour" (1937: 73; italics added). Thus, through ritual man imposes meaning on the world, anticipates the future, retrospectively "rationalizes" the past, and effects results.

It is perhaps because magic and applied science are, so to say, on different wavelengths, yet may (partially) overlap on the ground they cover, that the results of the spread of modern science and technology in "traditional" societies are complex, inconsistent, and nonlinear. An effective pesticide may over time render a "magical rite" for killing pests redundant and unnecessary. But a sacrifice which creates the cosmos persists because it "creates" the world in a sense that is different from that known in the laboratory. How does one understand the Hindu theory of sacrifice, which asserts claims vaster than the causal act itself? And in the new urban communities of developing societies, "drugs" may replace traditional "medicines," but scientific "skepticism" and "prediction" do not replace astrology, or consulting of oracles or of diviners, for the guidance of human actions and for providing meaning in perplexing situations.

But what may be true of non-Western societies may not be true of Western civilization in its recent past. And hereby possibly hangs a tale.

The Relevance of European Experience

In certain respects the history and experience of Western civilization are unique. There is the possibility that, perhaps because the Western anthropologist himself is so naturally grounded in his own civilization, he may at times project it as a potentially universal experience. Let me clarify. If Western anthropologists faced with certain ritual procedures of non-Western societies view them as "magic" that is empirically false and doomed to concede to the claims of science, they are right as far as their own history is concerned, irrespective of the truth of the assertion elsewhere. There is no denying that in Europe there is some kind of developmental sequence by which out of more "primitive" notions and "magical" practices, more "scientific" notions and experimentation were born. The process was by no means linear, but it is true that alchemy gave way to chemistry, astrology to astronomy, leechcraft to medicine. It is also to be borne in mind that old concepts from Greek natural philosophy (such as "atoms," "species," "force," "attraction") and from Greek medicine (especially the Hippocratic corpus) still persist (in form), although they have been transformed (in meaning) in the process. Somewhere in the middle of the transition it is very plausible that science differentiated out of magic, while magic itself was at the same time making "empirical" claims. It may very well be that the Western experience is a *privileged* case of transition from "magic" to "science."

It is further possible that the outlines of similar transitions and developments can also be discerned in other great literate civilizations, such as China and India. For example, the relation between early Vedic ritual and cosmological ideas and the concepts of classical Indian medicine of later times is comparable to the development in Europe, although the trend may not have gone as far. Filliozat (1964), who has examined the question with great scholarship (and who is interesting in that he thinks Indian medical ideas may have influenced the Greeks rather than vice versa), came to the conclusion that between the ideas of Vedic times and those of later periods of Indian developments in the field of medicine there were both discontinuities and continuities.

Classical Indian medicine claims to explain by means of a coherent system the pathogeny and applies its therapeutics as a function of its theories; its design is entirely scientific, even though many of its doctrines are, in fact, erroneous. It cannot, therefore, have its bases in the pathology and the therapeutics of the Veda. It does not, however, follow that the classical medical texts are not rich in Vedic souvenirs. We have seen that a number of Vedic names of diseases are explained by naturally climbing back from their meaning in classical medicine to the sense possessed by them in the Veda. But in the Veda, we have not found the prefiguration of ulterior pathological doctrines. (p. 137)

Anthropologists should heed this warning in their comparative studies. By simply naming rituals of non-Western societies as "magic," and the substances they use as "medicines" and "drugs," one cannot thereby attribute to the phenomena so named, by virtue of that naming, characteristics that may be peculiar to one's own contemporary civilization. It is only a short step from here to go on to measure these same ritual practices and ideas as equivalent to, but of course misguided and falling short of, empirical science. It is not that such a perspective is wrong but that it may hide from view the positive, persuasive, and creative, though "nonscientific," features of analogical thought and action expressed in magical rites. The dangers of excessive historical universalization should be kept in view. The rise of industry, capitalism, and experimental science in Europe in recent centuries found its counterpart in sociological theorizing in Weber's doctrine of growing "rationality" and "rationalization" in Western civilization – an inevitable historical process toward efficiency of social forms like bureaucracy, toward pragmatic orientation whereby means were closely linked to ends, and toward the generation of context-free, neutral, and universal constructs and principles. I am merely indicating that this is a particular historical experience which need not and should not be universalized if it entails automatic projections of how things traditional inevitably become things rational.

REFERENCES

Austin, John L. 1962. *How To Do Things with Words.* Oxford: Clarendon.

Evans-Pritchard, Edward E. 1929. The morphology and function of magic: A comparative study of Trobriand and Zande ritual and spells. *American Anthropologist* 31: 619–41.

—— 1937. *Witchcraft, Oracles and Magic among the Azande.* Oxford: Clarendon.

Filliozat, Jean. 1964. *The Classical Doctrine in Indian Medicine: Its Origin and Greek Parallels.* Delhi: Munshiram Manoharlal.

Finnegan, Ruth. 1969. How to do things with words: Performative utterances among the Limba of Sierra Leone. *Man*, n.s., 4: 537–52.

Hesse, Mary B. 1961. *Forces and Fields: The Concept of Action at a Distance in the History of Physics.* London: Nelson.

—— 1963. *Models and Analogies in Science.* Newman History and Philosophy and Science Series, 14. London: Sheed and Ward.

Horton, Robin. 1967. African traditional thought and Western science. *Africa* 37: 50–71.

Lloyd, Geoffrey E. R. 1966. *Polarity and Analogy: Two Types of Argumentation in Early Greek Thought.* Cambridge: Cambridge University Press.

Malinowski, Bronislaw. 1965. *Coral Gardens and Their Magic.* Vol. 1. Bloomington: Indiana University Press.

26

Liminality and Communitas

Victor Turner

Victor Turner (1920–83), who taught at the universities of Manchester, Cornell, Chicago, and Virginia, is remembered as both a master ethnographer and one of the most creative minds in the field. He is almost singlehandedly responsible for transforming the anthropology of religion from dry social science into a humanistic field that could bring religious practices to life. He combined a rigorous approach to social process with an appreciation for the open-endedness of imagination. More than anyone else Turner was able to evoke the humanness of religion and the religious creativity of humankind. His work is rooted in a series of wonderful ethnographic studies on the Ndembu of Zambia (1957, 1962, 1967, 1969, 1981 [1968]), followed by essays on Christian pilgrimage (1974, 1979) and ritual as theater (1986). As he progressed, Turner widened his scope until his subject was virtually humanity as a whole. The essay here is both the clearest marker of the transition in his work and Turner at his illuminative best.

Turner builds on van Gennep's early tripartite model of rites of passage (1960 [1908]) and Gluckman's approach to social process to develop a rich account of the ways in which rituals manage transitions for individuals and collectivities. Such transitions are key to the shaping of both temporal and social experience. Turner's work is thus critical for studies of birth, initiation and death rites, calendrical rituals, political installations and secessions, pilgrimage, healing, and all forms of movement in social life. As such rituals work on and by means of the body, Turner can also be credited as one of the first to direct scholarly attention toward embodiment. Turner founded a lively school. Among the best explorations and elaborations of his ideas with respect to religious and ritual phenomena are Myerhoff (1974,

From Victor Turner, "Liminality and Communitas," in *The Ritual Process: Structure and Anti-Structure* (Chicago: Aldine Publishing, 1969), pp. 94–113, 125–30. Abridged.

1978), Handelman (1989), Kapferer (1983), and Werbner (1989). Turner's widow, Edith, has a very fine account of Ndembu women's initiation (E. Turner 1992). De Boeck (1991) and Devisch (1993) offer more advanced work on rituals of affliction in the central African region.

Form and Attributes of Rites of Passage

In this Chapter I take up a theme I have discussed briefly elsewhere (Turner, 1967, pp. 93–111), note some of its variations, and consider some of its further implications for the study of culture and society. This theme is in the first place represented by the nature and characteristics of what Arnold van Gennep (1960) has called the "liminal phase" of *rites de passage*. Van Gennep himself defined *rites de passage* as "rites which accompany every change of place, state, social position and age." To point up the contrast between "state" and "transition," I employ "state" to include all his other terms. It is a more inclusive concept than "status" or "office," and refers to any type of stable or recurrent condition that is culturally recognized. Van Gennep has shown that all rites of passage or "transition" are marked by three phases: separation, margin (or *limen*, signifying "threshold" in Latin), and aggregation. The first phase (of separation) comprises symbolic behavior signifying the detachment of the individual or group either from an earlier fixed point in the social structure, from a set of cultural conditions (a "state"), or from both. During the intervening "liminal" period, the characteristics of the ritual subject (the "passenger") are ambiguous; he passes through a cultural realm that has few or none of the attributes of the past or coming state. In the third phase (reaggregation or reincorporation), the passage is consummated. The ritual subject, individual or corporate, is in a relatively stable state once more and, by virtue of this, has rights and obligations vis-à-vis others of a clearly defined and "structural" type; he is expected to behave in accordance with certain customary norms and ethical standards binding on incumb-

ents of social position in a system of such positions.

Liminality

The attributes of liminality or of liminal *personae* ("threshold people") are necessarily ambiguous, since this condition and these persons elude or slip through the network of classifications that normally locate states and positions in cultural space. Liminal entities are neither here nor there; they are betwixt and between the positions assigned and arrayed by law, custom, convention, and ceremonial. As such; their ambiguous and indeterminate attributes are expressed by a rich variety of symbols in the many societies that ritualize social and cultural transitions. Thus, liminality is frequently likened to death, to being in the womb, to invisibility, to darkness, to bisexuality, to the wilderness, and to an eclipse of the sun or moon.

Liminal entities, such as neophytes in initiation or puberty rites, may be represented as possessing nothing. They may be disguised as monsters, wear only a strip of clothing, or even go naked, to demonstrate that as liminal beings they have no status, property, insignia, secular clothing indicating rank or role, position in a kinship system – in short, nothing that may distinguish them from their fellow neophytes or initiands. Their behavior is normally passive or humble; they must obey their instructors implicitly, and accept arbitrary punishment without complaint. It is as though they are being reduced or ground down to a uniform condition to be fashioned anew and endowed with additional powers to enable them to cope with their new station in life. Among themselves, neophytes tend to develop an intense comradeship and egalitarianism. Secular distinctions of rank and status disappear or are homogenized. The condition of the patient and her husband in *Isoma* had some of these attributes – passivity, humility, near-nakedness – in a symbolic milieu that represented both a grave and a womb. In initiations with a long period of seclusion, such as the circumcision rites of many tribal societies or induction into secret societies, there is often a rich proliferation of liminal symbols.

Communitas

What is interesting about liminal phenomena for our present purposes is the blend they offer of lowliness and sacredness, of homogeneity and comradeship. We are presented, in such rites, with a "moment in and out of time," and in and out of secular social structure, which reveals, however fleetingly, some recognition (in symbol if not always in language) of a generalized social bond that has ceased to be and has simultaneously yet to be fragmented into a multiplicity of structural ties. These are the ties organized in terms either of caste, class, or rank hierarchies or of segmentary oppositions in the stateless societies beloved of political anthropologists. It is as though there are here two major "models" for human interrelatedness, juxtaposed and alternating. The first is of society as a structured, differentiated, and often hierarchical system of politico-legal-economic positions with many types of evaluation, separating men in terms of "more" or "less." The second, which emerges recognizably in the liminal period, is of society as an unstructured or rudimentarily structured and relatively undifferentiated *comitatus*, community, or even communion of equal individuals who submit together to the general authority of the ritual elders.

I prefer the Latin term "communitas" to "community," to distinguish this modality of social relationship from an "area of common living." The distinction between structure and communitas is not simply the familiar one between "secular" and "sacred," or that, for example, between politics and religion. Certain fixed offices in tribal societies have *many* sacred attributes; indeed, every social position has *some* sacred characteristics. But this "sacred" component is acquired by the incumbents of positions during the *rites de passage*, through which they changed positions. Something of the sacredness of that transient humility and modelessness goes over, and tempers the pride of the incumbent of a higher position or office. This is not simply, as Fortes (1962, p. 86) has cogently argued, a matter of giving a general stamp of legitimacy to a society's structural positions. It is rather a matter of giving recognition to an essential and generic human bond, without which there could be *no* society. Liminality implies that the high could not be high unless the low existed, and he who is high must experience what it is like to be low. No doubt something of this thinking, a few years ago, lay behind Prince Philip's decision to send his son, the heir apparent to the British throne, to a bush school in Australia for a time, where he could learn how "to rough it."

Dialectic of the developmental cycle

From all this I infer that, for individuals and groups, social life is a type of dialectical process that involves successive experience of high and low, communitas and structure, homogeneity and differentiation, equality and inequality. The passage from lower to higher status is through a limbo of statuslessness. In such a process, the opposites, as it were, constitute one another and are mutually indispensable. Furthermore, since any concrete tribal society is made up of multiple personae, groups, and categories, each of which has its own developmental cycle, at a given moment many incumbencies of fixed positions coexist with many passages between positions. In other words, each individual's life experience contains alternating exposure to structure and communitas, and to states and transitions.

The Liminality of an Installation Rite

One brief example from the Ndembu of Zambia of a *rite de passage* that concerns the highest status in that tribe, that of the senior chief Kanongesha, will be useful here. It will also expand our knowledge of the way the Ndembu utilize and explain their ritual symbols. The position of senior or paramount chief among the Ndembu, as in many other African societies, is a paradoxical one, for he represents both the apex of the structured politico-legal hierarchy and the total community as an unstructured unit. He is, symbolically, also the tribal territory itself and all its resources. Its fertility and freedom from drought, famine, disease, and insect plagues are bound up with his office, and with both his physical and moral condition. Among the Ndembu, the ritual powers of the senior chief were limited by and combined with those held by a senior headman of the autochthonous Mbwela people, who made submission only after long struggle to their Lunda conquerors led by the first Kanongesha. An important right was vested in the headman named Kafwana, of the Humbu, a branch of the Mbwela. This was the right to confer and periodically to medicate the supreme symbol of chiefly status among tribes of Lunda origin, the *lukanu* bracelet, made from human genitalia and sinews and soaked in the sacrificial blood of male and female slaves at each installation. Kafwana's ritual title was Chivwikankanu, "the one who dresses with or puts on the *lukanu*." He also had the title *Mama yaKanongesha*, "mother of Kanongesha," because he gave symbolic birth to each new incumbent of that office. Kafwana was also said to teach each new Kanongesha the medicines of witchcraft, which made him feared by his rivals and subordinates – perhaps one indication of weak political centralization.

The *lukanu*, originally conferred by the head of all the Lunda, the Mwantiyanvwa, who ruled in the Katanga many miles to the north, was ritually treated by Kafwana and hidden by him during interregna. The mystical power of the *lukanu* and hence of the Kanongesha-ship, came jointly from Mwantiyanvwa, the political fountainhead and, Kafwana, the ritual source: its employment for the benefit of the land and the people was in the hands of a succession of individual incumbents of the chieftainship. Its origin in Mwantiyanvwa symbolized the historical unity of the Ndembu

people, and their political differentiation into subchiefdoms under Kanongesha; its periodic medication by Kafwana symbolized the *land* – of which Kafwana was the original "owner" – and the total community living on it. The daily invocations made to it by Kanongesha, at dawn and sunset, were for the fertility and continued health and strength of the land, of its animal and vegetable resources, and of the people – in short, for the commonweal and public good. But the *lukanu* had a negative aspect; it could be used by Kanongesha to curse. If he touched the earth with it and uttered a certain formula, it was believed that the person or group cursed would become barren, their land infertile and their game invisible. In the *lukanu*, finally, Lunda and Mbwela were united in the joint concept of Ndembu land and folk.

In the relationship between Lunda and Mbwela, and between Kanongesha and Kafwana, we find a distinction familiar in Africa between the politically or militarily strong and the subdued autochthonous people, who are nevertheless ritually potent. Iowan Lewis (1963) has described such structural inferiors as having "the power or powers of the weak" (p. III). One well-known example from the literature is to be found in Meyer Fortes's account of the Tallensi of northern Ghana, where the incoming Namoos brought chieftainship and a highly developed ancestral cult to the autochthonous Tale, who, for their part, are thought to have important ritual powers in connection with the earth and its caverns. In the great Golib Festival, held annually, the union of chiefly and priestly powers is symbolized by the mystical marriage between chief of Tongo, leader of the Namoos, and the great earth-priest, the Golibdaana, of the Tale, portrayed respectively as "husband" and "wife." Among Ndembu, Kafwana is also considered, as we have seen, symbolically feminine in relation to Kanongesha. I could multiply examples of this type of dichotomy many times from African sources alone, and its range is world-wide. The point I would like to stress here is that there is a certain homology between the "weakness" and "passivity" of liminality in diachronic transitions between states and statuses, and the "structural" or synchronic inferiority of certain personae, groups, and social categories in political, legal, and economic systems. The "liminal" and the "inferior" conditions are often associated with ritual powers and with the total community seen as undifferentiated.

To return to the installation rites of the Kanongesha of the Ndembu: The liminal component of such rites begins with the construction of a small shelter of leaves about a mile away from the capital village. This hut is known as *kafu* or *kafwi*, a term Ndembu derive from *ku-fwa*, "to die," for it is here that the chief-elect dies from his commoner state. Imagery of death abounds in Ndembu liminality. For example, the secret and sacred site where novices are circumcised is known as *ifwilu* or *chifwilu*, a term also derived from *ku-fwa*. The chief-elect, clad in nothing but a ragged waist-cloth, and a ritual wife, who is either his senior wife (*mwadyi*) or a special slave woman, known as *lukanu* (after the royal bracelet) for the occasion, similarly clad, are called by Kafwana to enter the *kafu* shelter just after sundown. The chief himself, incidentally, is also known as *mwadyi* or *lukanu* in these rites. The couple are led there as though they were infirm. There they sit crouched in a posture of shame (*nsonyi*) or modesty, while they are washed with medicines mixed with water brought from Katukang'onyi, the river site where the ancestral chiefs of the southern Lunda diaspora dwelt for a while on their journey from Mwantiyanvwa's capital before separating to carve out realms for themselves. The wood for this fire must not be cut by an ax but found lying on the ground. This means that it is the product of the earth itself and not an artifact. Once more we see the conjunction of ancestral Lundahood and the chthonic powers.

Next begins the rite of *Kumukindyila*, which means literally "to speak evil or insulting words against him"; we might call this rite "The Reviling of the Chief-Elect." It begins when Kafwana makes a cut on the underside of the chief's left arm – on which the *lukanu* bracelet will be drawn on the morrow – presses medicine into the incision, and presses a mat on the upper side of the arm. The chief and his wife are then forced rather roughly to sit on the mat. The wife must not be pregnant, for the rites that follow are held to destroy fertility. Moreover, the chiefly couple must have refrained from sexual congress for several days before the rites.

Kafwana now breaks into a homily, as follows:

Be silent! You are a mean and selfish fool, one who is bad-tempered! You do not love your fellows, you are only angry with them! Meanness and theft are all you have! Yet here we have called you and we say that you must succeed to the chieftainship. Put away meanness, put aside anger, give up adulterous intercourse, give them up immediately! We have granted you chieftainship. You must eat with your fellow men, you must live well with them. Do not prepare witchcraft medicines that you may devour your fellows in their huts – that is forbidden! We have desired you and you only for our chief. Let your wife prepare food for the people who come here to the capital village. Do not be selfish, do not keep the chieftainship to yourself! You must laugh with the people, you must abstain from witchcraft, if perchance you have been given it already! You must not be killing people! You must not be ungenerous to people!

But you, Chief Kanongesha, Chifwanakenu ["son who resembles his father"] of Mwantiyanvwa, you have danced for your chieftainship because your predecessor is dead [i.e., because you killed him]. But today you are born as a new chief. You must know the people, O Chifwanakenu. If you were mean, and used to eat your cassava mush alone, or your meat alone, today you are in the chieftainship. You must give up your selfish ways, you must welcome everyone, you are the chief! You must stop being adulterous and quarrelsome. You must not bring partial judgments to bear on any law case involving your people, especially where your own children are involved. You must say: "If someone has slept with my wife, or wronged me, today I must not judge his case unjustly. I must not keep resentment in my heart."

After this harangue, any person who considers that he has been wronged by the chief-elect in the past is entitled to revile him and most fully express his resentment, going into as much detail as he desires. The chief-elect, during all this, has to sit silently with downcast head, "the pattern of all patience" and humility. Kafwana meanwhile splashes the chief with medicine, at intervals striking his buttocks against him (*kumubayisha*) insultingly. Many informants have told me that "a chief is just like a slave (*ndung'u*) on the night before he succeeds." He is prevented from sleeping, partly as an ordeal, partly because it is said that if he dozes off he will have bad dreams about the shades of dead chiefs, "who will say that he is wrong to succeed them, for has he not killed them?" Kafwana, his assistants, and other important men, such as village headmen, manhandle the chief and his wife – who is similarly reviled – and order them to fetch firewood and perform other menial tasks. The chief may not resent any of this or hold it against the perpetrators in times to come.

Attributes of Liminal Entities

The phase of reaggregation in this case comprises the public installation of the Kanongesha with all pomp and ceremony. While this would be of the utmost interest in study of Ndembu chieftainship, and to an important trend in current British social anthropology, it does not concern us here. Our present focus is upon liminality and the ritual powers of the weak. These are shown under two aspects. First, Kafwana and the other Ndembu commoners are revealed as privileged to exert authority over the supreme authority figure of the tribe. In liminality, the underling comes uppermost. Second, the supreme political authority is portrayed "as a slave," recalling that aspect of the coronation of a pope in western Christendom when he is called upon to be the "*servus servorum Dei.*" Part of the rite has, of course, what Monica Wilson (1957, pp. 46–54) has called a "prophylactic function." The chief has to exert self-control in the rites that he may be able to have self-mastery thereafter in face of the temptations of power. But the role of the humbled chief is only an extreme example of a recurrent theme of liminal situations. This theme is the stripping off of preliminal and postliminal attributes.

Let us look at the main ingredients of the *Kumukindyila* rites. The chief and his wife are dressed identically in a ragged waist-cloth and share the same name – *mwadyi*. This term is also applied to boys undergoing initiation and to a man's first wife in chronological order of marriage. It is an index of the anonymous state of "initiand." These attributes of sexlessness and anonymity are highly characteristic of liminality. In many kinds of initiation where the neophytes are of both sexes, males and females are dressed alike and referred to by the same term. This is true, for example, of many baptismal ceremonies in Christian or syncretist sects in Africa: for example, those of the *Bwiti* cult in the Gabon (James Fernandez; personal communication). It is also true of initiation into the Ndembu funerary association of Chiwila. Symbolically, all attributes that distinguish categories and groups in the structured social order are here in abeyance; the neophytes are merely entities in transition, as yet without place or position.

Other characteristics are submissiveness and silence. Not only the chief in the rites under discussion, but also neophytes in many *rites de passage* have to submit to an authority that is nothing less than that of the total community. This community is the repository of the whole gamut of the culture's values, norms, attitudes, sentiments, and relationships. Its representatives in the specific rites – and these may vary from ritual to ritual – represent the generic authority of tradition. In tribal societies, too, speech is not merely communication but also power and wisdom. The wisdom (*mana*) that is imparted in sacred liminality is not just an aggregation of words and sentences; it has ontological value, it refashions the very being of the neophyte. That is why, in the *Chisungu* rites of the Bemba, so well described by Audrey Richards (1956), the secluded girl is said to be "grown into a woman" by the female elders – and she is so grown by the verbal and nonverbal instruction she receives in precept and symbol, especially by the revelation to her of tribal *sacra* in the form of pottery images.

The neophyte in liminality must be a *tabula rasa*, a blank slate, on which is inscribed the knowledge and wisdom of the group, in those respects that pertain to the new status. The ordeals and humiliations, often of a grossly physiological character, to which neophytes are submitted represent partly a destruction of the previous status and partly a tempering of their essence in order to prepare them to cope with their new responsibilities and restrain them in advance from abusing their new privileges. They have to be shown that in themselves they are clay or dust, mere matter, whose form is impressed upon them by society.

Another liminal theme exemplified in the Ndembu installation rites is sexual continence. This is a pervasive theme of Ndembu ritual. Indeed, the resumption of sexual relations is usually a ceremonial mark of the return to society as a structure of statuses. While this is a feature of certain types of religious behavior in almost all societies, in preindustrial society, with its strong stress on kinship as the basis of many types of group affiliation, sexual continence has additional religious force. For kinship, or relations shaped by the idiom of kinship, is one of the main factors in structural differentiation. The undifferentiated character of liminality is reflected by the discontinuance of sexual relations and the absence of marked sexual polarity.

It is instructive to analyze the homiletic of Kafwana, in seeking to grasp the meaning of liminality. The reader will remember that he chided the chief-elect for his selfishness, meanness, theft, anger, witchcraft, and greed. All these vices represent the desire to possess for oneself what ought to be shared for the common good. An incumbent of high status is peculiarly tempted to use the authority vested in him by society to satisfy these private and privative wishes. But he should regard his privileges as gifts of the whole community, which in the final issue has an overright over all his actions. Structure and the high offices provided by structure are thus seen as instrumentalities of the commonweal, not as means of personal aggrandizement. The chief must not "keep his chieftainship to himself." He "must laugh with the people," and laughter (*ku-seha*) is for the Ndembu a "white" quality, and enters into the definition of "whiteness" or "white things." Whiteness represents the seamless web of connection that ideally ought

to include both the living and the dead. It is right relation between people, merely as human beings, and its fruits are health, strength, and all good things. "White" laughter, for example, which is visibly manifested in the flashing of teeth, represents fellowship and good company. It is the reverse of pride (*winyi*), and the secret envies, lusts, and grudges that result behaviorally in witchcraft (*wuloji*), theft (*wukombi*), adultery (*kushimbana*), meanness (*chifwa*), and homicide (*wubanji*). Even when a man has become a chief, he must still be a member of the whole community of persons (*antu*), and show this by "laughing with them," respecting their rights, "welcoming everyone," and sharing food with them. The chastening function of liminality is not confined to this type of initiation but forms a component of many other types in many cultures. A well-known example is the medieval knight's vigil, during the night before he receives the acolade, when he has to pledge himself to serve the weak and the distressed and to meditate on his own unworthiness. His subsequent power is thought partially to spring from this profound immersion in humility.

The pedagogics of liminality, therefore, represent a condemnation of two kinds of separation from the generic bond of communitas. The first kind is to act only in terms of the rights conferred on one by the incumbency of office in the social structure. The second is to follow one's psychobiological urges at the expense of one's fellows. A mystical character is assigned to the sentiment of humankindness in most types of liminality, and in most cultures this stage of transition is brought closely in touch with beliefs in the protective and punitive powers of divine or preterhuman beings or powers. For example, when the Ndembu chief-elect emerges from seclusion, one of his subchiefs – who plays a priestly role at the installation rites – makes a ritual fence around the new chief's dwelling, and prays as follows to the shades of former chiefs, before the people who have assembled to witness the installation:

Listen, all you people, Kanongesha has come to be born into the chieftainship today. This white clay [*mpemba*], with which the chief, the ancestral shrines, and the officiants will be anointed, is for you, all the Kanongeshas of old gathered together here. [Here the ancient chiefs are mentioned by name.] And, therefore, all you who have died, look upon your friend who has succeeded [to the chiefly stool], that he may be strong. He must continue to pray well to you. He must look after the children, he must care for all the people, both men and women, that they may be strong and that he himself should be hale. Here is your white clay. I have enthroned you, O chief. You O people must give forth sounds of praise. The chieftainship has appeared.

The powers that shape the neophytes in liminality for the incumbency of new status are felt, in rites all over the world, to be more than human powers, they are invoked and channeled by the representatives of the community.

Liminality Contrasted with Status System

Let us now, rather in the fashion of Lévi-Strauss, express the difference between the properties of liminality and those of the status system in terms of a series of binary oppositions or discriminations. They can be ordered as follows:

Transition/state
Totality/partiality
Homogeneity/heterogeneity
Communitas/structure
Equality/inequality
Anonymity/systems of nomenclature
Absence of property/property
Absence of status/status
Nakedness or uniform clothing/distinctions of clothing
Sexual continence/sexuality
Minimization of sex distinctions/maximization of sex distinctions
Absence of rank/distinctions of rank
Humility/just pride of position
Disregard for personal appearance/care for personal appearance
No distinctions of wealth/distinctions of wealth

Unselfishness/selfishness
Total obedience/obedience only to superior rank
Sacredness/secularity
Sacred instruction/technical knowledge
Silence/speech
Suspension of kinship rights and obligations/kinship rights and obligations
Continuous reference to mystical powers/intermittent reference to mystical powers
Foolishness/sagacity
Simplicity/complexity
Acceptance of pain and suffering/avoidance of pain and suffering
Heteronomy/degrees of autonomy

This list could be considerably lengthened if we were to widen the span of liminal situations considered. Moreover, the symbols in which these properties are manifested and embodied are manifold and various, and often relate to the physiological processes of death and birth, anabolism and katabolism. The reader will have noticed immediately that many of these properties constitute what we think of as characteristics of the religious life in the Christian tradition. Undoubtedly, Muslims, Buddhists, Hindus, and Jews would number many of them among their religious characteristics, too. What appears to have happened is that with the increasing specialization of society and culture, with progressive complexity in the social division of labor, what was in tribal society principally a set of transitional qualities "betwixt and between" defined states of culture, and society has become itself an institutionalized state. But traces of the *passage* quality of the religious life remain in such formulations as: "The Christian is a stranger to the world, a pilgrim, a traveler, with no place to rest his head." Transition has here become a permanent condition. Nowhere has this institutionalization of liminality been more clearly marked and defined than in the monastic and mendicant states in the great world religions.

For example, the Western Christian Rule of St. Benedict

provides for the life of men who wish to live in *community* and devote themselves entirely to God's service by *self-discipline*, prayer, and *work*. They are to be essentially *families*, in the care and under the *absolute control* of a father (the abbot); individually they are bound to personal *poverty, abstention from marriage*, and *obedience to their superiors*, and by the vows of stability and conversion of manners [originally a synonym for "*common life*," "*monasticity*" as distinguished from secular life]; a moderate degree of austerity is imposed by the night office, fasting, abstinence from fleshmeat, and *restraint in conversation* (Attwater, 1962, p. 51 – my emphases)

I have stressed features that bear a remarkable similarity to the condition of the chief-elect during his transition to the public installation rites, when he enters his kingdom. The Ndembu circumcision rites (*Mukanda*) present further parallels between the neophytes and the monks of St. Benedict. Erving Goffman (*Asylums*, 1962) discusses what he calls the "characteristics of total institutions." Among these he includes monasteries, and devotes a good deal of attention to "the stripping and leveling processes which . . . directly cut across the various social distinctions with which the recruits enter." He then quotes from St. Benedict's advice to the abbot: "Let him make no distinction of persons in the monastery. Let not one be loved more than another, unless he be found to excel in good works or in obedience. Let not one of noble birth be raised above him who was formerly a slave, unless some other reasonable cause intervene" (p. 119).

Here parallels with *Mukanda* are striking. The novices are "stripped" of their secular clothing when they are passed beneath a symbolic gateway; they are "leveled" in that their former names are discarded and all are assigned the common designation *mwadyi*, or "novice," and treated alike. One of the songs sung by circumcisers to the mothers of the novices on the night before circumcision contains the following line: "Even if your child is a chief's son, tomorrow he will be like a slave" – just as a chief-elect is treated like a slave before *his* installation. Moreover, the senior instructor in the seclusion lodge is chosen partly because he is father of several boys undergoing the rites and becomes a father for the whole group, a

sort of "abbot," though his title *Mfumwa tubwiku*, means literally "husband of the novices," to emphasize their passive role.

Mystical Danger and the Powers of the Weak

One may well ask why it is that liminal situations and roles are almost everywhere attributed with magico-religious properties, or why these should so often be regarded as dangerous, inauspicious, or polluting to persons, objects, events, and relationships that have not been ritually incorporated into the liminal context. My view is briefly that from the perspectival viewpoint of those concerned with the maintenance of "structure," all sustained manifestations of communitas must appear as dangerous and anarchical, and have to be hedged around with prescriptions, prohibitions, and conditions. And, as Mary Douglas (1966) has recently argued, that which cannot be clearly classified in terms of traditional criteria of classification, or falls between classificatory boundaries, is almost everywhere regarded as "polluting" and "dangerous" (passim).

To repeat what I said earlier, liminality is not the only cultural manifestation of communitas. In most societies, there are other areas of manifestation to be readily recognized by the symbols that cluster around them and the beliefs that attach to them, such as "the powers of the weak," or, in other words, the permanently or transiently sacred attributes of low status or position. Within stable structural systems, there are many dimensions of organization. We have already noted that mystical and moral powers are wielded by subjugated autochthones over the total welfare of societies whose political frame is constituted by the lineage or territorial organization of incoming conquerors. In other societies – the Ndembu and Lamba of Zambia, for example – we can point to the cult associations whose members have gained entry through common misfortune and debilitating circumstances to therapeutic powers with regard to such common goods of mankind as health, fertility, and climate. These associations transect such important components of the secular political system as lineages, villages, subchiefdoms, and chiefdoms. We could also mention the role of structurally small and politically insignificant nations within systems of nations as upholders of religious and moral values, such as the Hebrews in the ancient Near East, the Irish in early medieval Christendom, and the Swiss in modern Europe.

Many writers have drawn attention to the role of the court jester. Max Gluckman (1965), for example, writes: "The court jester operated as a privileged arbiter of morals, given license to gibe at king and courtiers, or lord of the manor." Jesters were

> usually men of low class – sometimes on the Continent of Europe they were priests – who clearly moved out of their usual estate. . . . In a system where it was difficult for others to rebuke the head of a political unit, we might have here an institutionalized joker, operating at the highest point of the unit . . . a joker able to express feelings of outraged morality.

He further mentions how jesters attached to many African monarchs were "frequently dwarfs and other oddities." Similar in function to these were the drummers in the Barotse royal barge in which the king and his court moved from a capital in the Zambezi Flood Plain to one of its margins during the annual floods. They were privileged to throw into the water any of the great nobles "who had offended them and their sense of justice during the past year" (pp. 102–4). These figures, representing the poor and the deformed, appear to symbolize the moral values of communitas as against the coercive power of supreme political rulers.

Folk literature abounds in symbolic figures, such as "holy beggars," "third sons," "little tailors," and "simpletons," who strip off the pretensions of holders of high rank and office and reduce them to the level of common humanity and mortality. Again, in the traditional "Western," we have all read of the homeless and mysterious "stranger" without wealth or name who restores ethical and legal equilibrium to a local set of political power relations by eliminating the unjust

secular "bosses" who are oppressing the smallholders. Members of despised or outlawed ethnic and cultural groups play major roles in myths and popular tales as representatives or expressions of universal-human values. Famous among these are the good Samaritan, the Jewish fiddler Rothschild in Chekhov's tale "Rothschild's Fiddle," Mark Twain's fugitive Negro slave Jim in *Huckleberry Finn*, and Dostoevsky's Sonya, the prostitute who redeems the would-be Nietzschean "superman" Raskolnikov, in *Crime and Punishment*.

All these mythic types are structurally inferior or "marginal," yet represent what Henri Bergson would have called "open" as against "closed morality," the latter being essentially the normative system of bounded, structured, particularistic groups. Bergson speaks of how an in-group preserves its identity against members of out-groups, protects itself against threats to its way of life, and renews the will to maintain the norms on which the routine behavior necessary for its social life depends. In closed or structured societies, it is the marginal or "inferior" person or the "outsider" who often comes to symbolize what David Hume has called "the sentiment for humanity," which in its turn relates to the model we have termed "communitas."

Millenarian Movements

Among the more striking manifestations of communitas are to be found the so-called millenarian religious movements, which arise among what Norman Cohn (1961) has called "uprooted and desperate masses in town and countryside . . . living on the margin of society" (pp. 31–2) (i.e., structured society), or where formerly tribal societies are brought under the alien overlordship of complex, industrial societies. The attributes of such movements will be well known to most of my readers. Here I would merely recall some of the properties of liminality in tribal rituals that I mentioned earlier. Many of these correspond pretty closely with those of millenarian movements: homogeneity, equality, anonymity, absence of property (many movements actually enjoin on their members the destruction of what property they possess to bring nearer the coming of the perfect state of unison and communion they desire, for property rights are linked with structural distinctions both vertical and horizontal), reduction of all to the same status level, the wearing of uniform apparel (sometimes for both sexes), sexual continence (or its antithesis, sexual community, both continence and sexual community liquidate marriage and the family, which legitimate structural status), minimization of sex distinctions (all are "equal in the sight of God" or the ancestors), abolition of rank, humility, disregard for personal appearance, unselfishness, total obedience to the prophet or leader, sacred instruction, the maximization of religious, as opposed to secular, attitudes and behavior, suspension of kinship rights and obligations (all are siblings or comrades of one another regardless of previous secular ties), simplicity of speech and manners, sacred folly, acceptance of pain and suffering (even to the point of undergoing martyrdom), and so forth.

It is noteworthy that many of these movements cut right across tribal and national divisions during their initial momentum. Communitas, or the "open society," differs in this from structure, or the "closed society," in that it is potentially or ideally extensible to the limits of humanity. In practice, of course, the impetus soon becomes exhausted, and the "movement" becomes itself an institution among other institutions – often one more fanatical and militant than the rest, for the reason that it feels itself to be the unique bearer of universal-human truths. Mostly, such movements occur during phases of history that are in many respects "homologous" to the liminal periods of important rituals in stable and repetitive societies, when major groups or social categories in those societies are passing from one cultural state to another. They are essentially phenomena of transition. This is perhaps why in so many of these movements much of their mythology and symbolism is borrowed from those of traditional *rites de passage*, either in the cultures in which they originate or in the cultures with which they are in dramatic contact.

Hippies, Communitas, and the Powers of the Weak

In modern Western society, the values of communitas are strikingly present in the literature and behavior of what came to be known as the "beat generation," who were succeeded by the "hippies," who, in turn, have a junior division known as the "teeny-boppers." These are the "cool" members of the adolescent and young-adult categories – which do not have the advantages of national *rites de passage* – who "opt out" of the status-bound social order and acquire the stigmata of the lowly, dressing like "bums," itinerant in their habits, "folk" in their musical tastes, and menial in the casual employment they undertake. They stress personal relationships rather than social obligations, and regard sexuality as a polymorphic instrument of immediate communitas rather than as the basis for an enduring structured social tie. The poet Allen Ginsberg is particularly eloquent about the function of sexual freedom. The "sacred" properties often assigned to communitas are not lacking here, either: this can be seen in their frequent use of religious terms, such as "saint" and "angel," to describe their congeners and in their interest in Zen Buddhism. The Zen formulation "all is one, one is none, none is all" well expresses the global, unstructured character earlier applied to communitas. The hippie emphasis on spontaneity, immediacy, and "existence" throws into relief one of the senses in which communitas contrasts with structure. Communitas is of the now; structure is rooted in the past and extends into the future through language, law, and custom. While our focus here is on traditional preindustrial societies it becomes clear that the collective dimensions, communitas and structure, are to be found at all stages and levels of culture and society. [. . .]

Liminality, Low Status, and Communitas

The time has now come to make a careful review of a hypothesis that seeks to account for the attributes of such seemingly diverse phenomena as neophytes in the liminal phase of ritual, subjugated autochthones, small nations, court jesters, holy mendicants, good Samaritans, millenarian movements, "dharma bums," matrilaterality in patrilineal systems, patrilaterality in matrilineal systems, and monastic orders. Surely an ill-assorted bunch of social phenomena! Yet all have this common characteristic: they are persons or principles that (1) fall in the interstices of social structure, (2) are on its margins, or (3) occupy its lowest rungs. This leads us back to the problem of the definitions of social structure. One authoritative source of definitions is *A Dictionary of the Social Sciences* (Gould and Kolb, 1964), in which A. W. Eister reviews some major formulations of this conception. Spencer and many modern sociologists regard social structure as "a more or less distinctive arrangement (of which there may be more than one type) of specialized and mutually dependent *institutions* [Eister's emphasis] and the institutional organizations of positions and/or of actors which they imply, all evolved in the natural course of events, as groups of human beings, with given needs and capacities, have interacted with each other (in various types or modes of interaction) and sought to cope with their environment" (pp. 668–9). Raymond Firth's (1951) more analytical conception runs as follows:

> In the types of societies ordinarily studied by anthropologists, the social structure may include critical or basic relationships arising similarly from a class system based on relations with the soil. Other aspects of social structure arise through membership in other kinds of persistent groups, such as clans, castes, age-sets, or secret societies. Other basic relations again are due to position in a kinship system. (p. 32)

Most definitions contain the notion of an arrangement of positions or statuses. Most involve the institutionalization and perdurance of groups and relationships. Classical mechanics, the morphology and physiology of animals and plants, and, more recently, with Lévi-Strauss, structural linguistics have been ransacked for concepts, models, and homologous forms by social scientists. All share in common the notion of a superorganic arrangement of parts or positions that continues, with modifications more or less gradual, through time. The concept of "conflict" has come to be connected with the concept of "social structure," since the differentiation of parts becomes opposition between parts, and scarce status becomes the object of struggles between persons and groups who lay claim to it.

The other dimension of "society" with which I have been concerned is less easy to define. G. A. Hillery (1955) reviewed 94 definitions of the term "community" and reached the conclusion that "beyond the concept that people are involved in community, there is no complete agreement as to the nature of community" (p. 119). The field would, therefore, seem to be still open for new attempts! I have tried to eschew the notion that communitas has a specific territorial locus, often limited in character, which pervades many definitions. For me, communitas emerges where social structure is not. Perhaps the best way of putting this difficult concept into words is Martin Buber's – though I feel that perhaps he should be regarded as a gifted native informant rather than as a social scientist! Buber (1961) uses the term "community" for "communitas": "Community is the being no longer side by side (and, one might add, above and below) but *with* one another of a multitude of persons. And this multitude, though it moves towards one goal, yet experiences everywhere a turning to, a dynamic facing of, the others, a flowing from *I* to *Thou*. Community is where community happens" (p. 51).

Buber lays his finger on the spontaneous, immediate, concrete nature of communitas, as opposed to the norm-governed, institutionalized, abstract nature of social structure. Yet, communitas is made evident or accessible, so to speak, only through its juxtaposition to, or hybridization with, aspects of social structure. Just as in *Gestalt* psychology, figure and ground are mutually determinative, or, as some rare elements are never found in nature in their purity but only as components of chemical compounds, so communitas can be grasped only in some relation to structure. Just because the communitas component is elusive, hard to pin down, it is not unimportant. Here the story of Lao-tse's chariot wheel may be apposite. The spokes of the wheel and the nave (i.e., the central block of the wheel holding the axle and spokes) to which they are attached would be useless, he said, but for the hole, the gap, the emptiness at the center. Communitas, with its unstructured character, representing the "quick" of human interrelatedness, what Buber has called *das Zwischenmenschliche*, might well be represented by the "emptiness at the center," which is nevertheless indispensable to the functioning of the structure of the wheel.

It is neither by chance nor by lack of scientific precision that, along with others who have considered the conception of communitas, I find myself forced to have recourse to metaphor and analogy. For communitas has an existential quality; it involves the whole man in his relation to other whole men. Structure, on the other hand, has cognitive quality; as Lévi-Strauss has perceived, it is essentially a set of classifications, a model for thinking about culture and nature and ordering one's public life. Communitas has also an aspect of potentiality; it is often in the subjunctive mood. Relations between total beings are generative of symbols and metaphors and comparisons; art and religion are their products rather than legal and political structures. Bergson saw in the words and writings of prophets and great artists the creation of an "open morality," which was itself an expression of what he called the *élan vital*, or evolutionary "life-force." Prophets and artists tend to be liminal and marginal people, "edgemen," who strive with a passionate sincerity to rid themselves of the clichés associated with status incumbency and role-playing and to enter into vital relations with other men in fact or imagination. In their productions we may catch glimpses of that unused evolutionary potential in mankind which has not yet been externalized and fixed in structure.

Communitas breaks in through the interstices of structure, in liminality; at the edges of structure, in marginality; and from beneath structure, in inferiority. It is almost everywhere held to be sacred or "holy," possibly because it transgresses or dissolves the norms that govern structured and institutionalized relationships and is accompanied by experiences of unprecedented potency. The processes of "leveling" and "stripping," to which Goffman has drawn our attention, often appear to flood their subjects with affect. Instinctual energies are surely liberated by these processes, but I am now inclined to think that communitas is not solely the product of biologically inherited drives released from cultural constraints. Rather is it the product of peculiarly human faculties, which include rationality, volition, and memory, and which develop with experience of life in society. . . .

The notion that there is a generic bond between men, and its related sentiment of "humankindness," are not epiphenomena of some kind of herd instinct but are products of "men in their wholeness wholly attending." Liminality, marginality, and structural inferiority are conditions in which are frequently generated myths, symbols, rituals, philosophical systems, and works of art. These cultural forms provide men with a set of templates or models which are, at one level, periodical reclassifications of reality and man's relationship to society, nature, and culture. But they are more than classifications, since they incite men to action as well as to thought. Each of these productions has a multivocal character, having many meanings, and each is capable of moving people at many psychobiological levels simultaneously.

There is a dialectic here, for the immediacy of communitas gives way to the mediacy of structure, while, in *rites de passage*, men are released from structure into communitas only to return to structure revitalized by their experience of communitas. What is certain is that no society can function adequately without this dialectic. Exaggeration of structure may well lead to pathological manifestations of communitas outside or against "the law." Exaggeration of communitas, in certain religious or political movements of the leveling type, may be speedily followed by despotism, overbureaucratization, or other modes of structural rigidification. For, like the neophytes in the African circumcision lodge, or the Benedictine monks, or the members of a millenarian movement, those living in community seem to require, sooner or later, an absolute authority, whether this be a religious commandment, a divinely inspired leader, or a dictator. Communitas cannot stand alone if the material and organizational needs of human beings are to be adequately met. Maximization of communitas provokes maximixation of structure, which in its turn produces revolutionary strivings for renewed communitas. The history of any great society provides evidence at the political level for this oscillation.

[. . .]

But together they constitute the "human condition," as regards man's relations with his fellow man.

BIBLIOGRAPHY

Attwater, Donald (ed.). 1962. *A Catholic encyclopedia*. New York: Macmillan.

Buber, Martin. 1961. *Between man and man*. (Trans. by R. G. Smith). London and Glasgow: Fontana Library.

Cohn, Norman. 1961. *The pursuit of the millennium*. New York: Harper Torch Books.

Douglas, Mary. 1966. *Purity and danger*. London: Routledge and Kegan Paul.

Firth, Raymond. 1951. *Elements of social organization*. London: Watts.

Fortes, Meyer. 1962. Ritual and office. In Max Gluckman (ed.), *Essays on the ritual of social relations*. Manchester: Manchester University Press.

Gennep, Arnold Van. 1960. *The rites of passage*. (Trans. by Monika B. Vizedom and Gabrielle L. Caffee.) London: Routledge and Kegan Paul.

Goffman, Erving. 1962. *Asylums*. Chicago: Aldine Publishing Company.

Gould, J., and W. L. Kolb (eds.). 1964. *A Dictionary of the social sciences*. London: Tavistock.

Hillery, G. A. 1955. Definitions of community: areas of agreement. *Rural Sociology*, vol. 20.

Lewis, Iowan M. 1963. Dualism in Somali notions of power. *Journal of the Royal Anthropological Institute*, vol. 93, Part 1.

Richards, Audery I. 1956. *Chisungu*. London: Faber and Faber.

Turner, Victor W. 1967. *The forest of symbols*. Ithaca, N.Y.: Cornell University Press.

Wilson, Monica. 1957. *Rituals of kinship among the Nyakyusa*. London: Oxford University Press.

Gender, Subjectivity, and the Body

Introduction

The essays in this section address religious experience from multiple perspectives, but they are all notable for not objectifying it. They avoid reducing it to either a specific psychological property or to the sense of awe and fear that successive Christian writers (e.g., Otto 1923 [1917]) have posited as lying at the root of religion. Experience is culturally shaped or in dialectical relation to culture, society, power, and the body, not something that exists prior to or independent from them. The same can be said of gender and other attributes of subjectivity, self, and person that are explored in these essays.

27

"Jewish Comes Up in You from the Roots"

Barbara Myerhoff

Barbara Myerhoff (1935–1985) taught at the University of Southern California.

This entry consists of excerpts from chapter 7 of Myerhoff's wonderful book *Number Our Days*, an ethnography of a Jewish center for the elderly in Los Angeles, California. Born in eastern Europe and Yiddish speaking, her subjects are people whose emigration before World War II enabled them to avoid the shoah. Although trained at UCLA, Myerhoff was strongly influenced by Victor Turner and, like members of the Manchester School, worked by means of the extended case study and strove to show the way in which moments of ritual as well as disruptive events fit into the flow of actual life. Hence she develops her narrative by means of the situational analysis of critical events that took place at the center during her fieldwork. These include the struggles to produce meaningful rituals in radically changed social contexts. Although the members of the center are largely secular (contrasted in the episode presented here to an adjacent home for orthodox Jews) they nevertheless draw on ritual to maintain a sense of continuity with the past and a collective identity. Myerhoff's work thus addresses problems of memory and diaspora, as well as what, in a work edited with Sally Falk Moore, they called "secular ritual," that is the question of how meaningful rituals are produced and conducted in a post-religious modern context. In addition, Myerhoff pioneered what today is called "collaborative ethnography." She begins each chapter with transcriptions from discussion groups she held with her subjects and I have preserved a part of that here.

The excerpt addresses squarely the gendered nature of religious experience and perspective. Judaism, like many religious traditions, is patriarchal in its theology and its rules, but Myerhoff shows how different this looks when one begins with daily practice and experi-

From Barbara Myerhoff, "Jewish Comes Up in You from the Roots," in *Number Our Days* (New York: Simon and Schuster, 1978) pp. 232–61. Highly abridged.

ence, especially as it is laid down in childhood. In her evocative and literary way she thus anticipates the influence of Pierre Bourdieu's discussion of habitus. This kind of habitual memory can also be contrasted with the "flashbulb" memory inculcated through "rites of terror" as described by Whitehouse (2004) for Melanesian male initiation cults (and which form the basis for his development of a cognitive account of learning religion). In this excerpt Myerhoff also alludes to the distinction developed by Robert Redfield (1956) between great and little traditions, a model that has been best applied to the contrast between urban and rural Hindu practices in India (Singer 1972, cf. Fuller 1992) and that, I think, only partially overlaps with the distinction Myerhoff is making here between formal and domestic forms of religious practice.

An excellent complement to Myerhoff's ethnography is Kugelmass (1996).

See also his edited collection on American Jewry (1988).

One of the first and best practitioners of the reflexive (self-reflective) movement in anthropology, Myerhoff's writing vividly interlaces her own experience with that of her subjects. Subsequent to her research among relatively secular Jews, Myerhoff began exploring the practices of religious Hasidic Jews in California. The film *In Her Own Time* documents Myerhoff's fieldwork during serious personal illness. Her move from ethnographic skepticism to religious embrace of – and by – her subjects demonstrates vulnerability and religious awe that goes well beyond the portrait of Sylvia presented below. Myerhoff's work implicitly raises the question of a gendered dimension not only to religious practice but to empathic ethnography. Conversely, it leads us to ask whether theory might be a (masculine?) defence against attachment.

[. . .]

MOSHE: While we are talking about women we should bring in how important they were in keeping up Judaism. I would say the women had more to do with preserving Jewishness than the men. This is not maybe a popular opinion, but it is how I am seeing things. The father had the job to bring the boy to circumcision, then to cheder, then to Bar Mitzva. But it was the woman who was the guide. Always quietly, without a big fuss. Remember, it was the women who saved Moses and raised him up in secret. Always, it was the woman who gave the moments of life into the family, in the holidays, in the tragic moments. She could do this because she was allowed to express herself more than the men. She was more free with her emotions; and to a small child, this is the most important. A man's religious expression was in the crowd, in the shul. Uneducated she was, but the woman did the rituals. She had the wisdom. She knew how to live with all the men prayed and talked about.

BASHA: Barbara, darling, I will explain to you. You know Judaism is really what happens in the family, and this makes it something a woman knows best. A lot of these men aren't religious. We all overthrew a lot of that, especially the men, when they came to this country, even before. But what came into the family through the woman, you couldn't overthrow.

NATHAN: You see, that is something we don't know as children. All we hear is to follow the rules. When I was fifteen years old, I stopped going to synagogue altogether because we revolted against the praying. We threw out the good things with the bad.

RACHEL: I would like to come in on this. What the girls had is different from the boys. Now what ideas Moshe and Nate got, they come to through the schooling. We girls had another kind of a religion. We couldn't doubt too much because we didn't know enough. You could say, from this we were always in a positive way. You see, all this is from what's going on in the family.

That's the root of being Jewish. Jewish comes up in you from the roots.

Now you could say we girls were more superficial. We couldn't question things. "That's just how things are supposed to be." God said it. We girls had what you could call domestic religion, that means it comes into you through the rituals. I will explain to you. We had a grandmother who gathered us seven girls around. The two boys went off early in the morning to pray. For us, we had to say the morning prayers. I couldn't understand the Hebrew words, the meanings of it, because we were girls and we never went to school. But I understood the expression of the little grandmother. She was so beautiful, so tiny and white. And we gathered around her before we are going to have our breakfast.

Now I knew the Hebrew words already by heart, I knew about the washing of the hands, the prayer for the bread, keeping separate the meat and milk, all these things Grandmother taught us. But not what anything means. But it was our habit and it was beautiful. God wants it so, that's all. After breakfast comes the ritual of dividing up the work. This the grandmother does in Yiddish, because this we must understand. That speech she makes after breakfast also was the way God wanted us to do, made very carefully, as carefully as the prayers, so that one girl doesn't get more to do than the other, all arranged according to her age. That was her wisdom. And this wisdom, we are believing, comes to her through God. Grandmother made such a nice division, in such a beautiful way, not commanded, but just like she was a part of God, even though it wasn't in Hebrew.

Now I did not like to wipe the dishes because the towel was so rough, it didn't feel good, and I did not know how to explain this to Grandmother. The towel was thick, tough, because everything had to be sturdy, not refined like if it would be in a rich house where they got everything soft. So I rebelled against that. The job was not well done. I'll never forget that, how my grandmother, she took me aside one day. She did not reprimand me in front of everybody. She began first all around with praises. "Rucheleh," she says, "you know you are a beautiful girl" (and maybe I was), "Rucheleh, you know

you are carrying a holy name. And according to your name, you have to be perfect." Well, she gave me all that until when I looked at her, my spirit was rising and rising, higher and faster until I forgot all about that sturdy towel and my hatred for it. The towel, it was straight from the peasants, you could make rugs from it. But after that speech, I was transformed into a different person. The towel became soft as fine linen and I loved to wipe the dishes. And always before me, when I was wiping the dishes was the name of the holy mother Rachel, and I thought, "She's right. I am that woman." That, that is what I call domestic religion. It makes the adrenaline flow. It changes your entire view on things.

I think the boys didn't have it that way. They knew what the sacred words meant so they could argue and doubt. But with us girls, we couldn't doubt because what we knew came without understanding. These things were injected into you in childhood and chained together with that beautiful grandmother, so ever since infancy you can't know life without it. The boys in cheder could learn the words and forget them, but in this domestic religion, you could never get rid of it. This is not like with Nathan. You could not just put it aside when you don't agree anymore. When it goes in this way, I describe, Jewish comes up in you from the roots and it stays with you all your life.

[. . .]

The next day was Friday, the day the Sabbath was celebrated in the Center. It always seemed to me to belong especially to the women, even though the men dominated the ceremony and directed the women's participation for that event. Perhaps I had this impression because the Sabbath was so completely associated with home and family for the old people. After Yom Kippur, the Sabbath is the most sacred of Jewish holidays. On Sabbath, for one day, a Jew may enter Paradise. The *balebosteh*, in lighting the candles, brings the foretaste of Paradise into her home. When she offers the challah, her kitchen is the Temple, she is the priestess, and her ordinary oven the altar for her sacrifice. On Sabbath, some say, the Jew has an extra soul. Certainly something special was in the air on Fridays [. . .] Everyone was always especially excited, the women in particular.

The Oneg Shabbat ceremony was a perilous venture, the Center's most ambitious undertaking and the only regular, traditional, religious event attempted. Always, cynical and dissident voices were heard, complaining about variations pressed upon the people by necessity: The service was held midday instead of at twilight as was proper; it followed instead of preceded the meal; there was too much Hebrew for some, too little for others. Always there was the danger that the confusion and contentiousness that were normally acceptable, even functional in Center affairs could destroy the delicate mood and the event would collapse in a rubble of broken spirits and empty forms. But it never did. Somehow each week, for the space of less than an hour, the essential religious experience occurred in the Center – a true hierophany, when the sacred shows itself to us, breaking through the secular plane, and allows us a moment of contact with a wholly different reality. The Center folk never found the ideal Sabbath of peace, but they reached their religious climax in flashes of genuine and intense unity with each other and continuity with the past, most conspicuously when the women lit the candles.

Center people's memories of the Sabbath always returned to the theme of the Jewish homemaker. "We sat at the table with such dignity and happiness. No matter how poor, Mama always managed to find somehow a fish or a chicken, even if she had to hock her pearls. On this night only would she sit down with us to eat. Only this night, my father would not lose his temper, no matter what. Everything was transferred into a different realm. The papa was king, the mama was queen and we were the luckiest people in the world." This was Moshe's description of Sabbath in his childhood. He concluded sadly, "All this here beauty didn't do us any good. We could give to our American children nice clothes, good food, education, but we couldn't give them what our fathers and mothers gave us. It all went out from us, all that respect for the mama and the papa, the love of the home. American children didn't receive that memory."

Basha did not agree with him. "Whether you give it out or not, on Friday there's still something special in the air. Because American children don't take it in, don't mean it isn't still the Sabbath, like it always was."

Elderly women of the Center, without their own households had no access to the three religious duties enjoined on them. Postmenopausal, they did not attend the ritual bath. They no longer baked, so could not prepare or offer the Sabbath loaf. And having neither home nor family, they did not light candles, though technically it would have been possible to do so, alone in their rooms. But this was probably too painful a reminder of their isolation and none of the women lit candles outside of the Center. At the Oneg Shabbat on Friday, the Center became home and the members family. For all old people at the Center, memories of their mother fulfilling the blessed obligations of the Sabbath held the greatest personal and religious significance.

Every week, before a woman was called to the candles by the president, there was a hesitation in the ceremony. Which woman would receive the honor? Normally, only one woman lights the candles. In the Center the honor was shared by two or sometimes three women. In the silence before the names were called, there was a faint rustling in the room. It was the women who knew the prayer quietly fluttering their scarves in their lap, wordlessly signaling their readiness. This week Basha, Faegl, and Olga were named. They approached the table together. Olga began. In a strong alto voice, she sang a song of her own composition, a Yiddish blessing, belting it out like a torch singer, then stepped back. Faegl struck the match and lit the candles, then barely audible, Basha chanted the traditional Hebrew prayer, encircling the flames three times with open hands, drawing their holiness to her face, covering her eyes with her hands, finishing with her own private prayer as tears spread through her fingers down her cheeks. She removed her hands, looked about as though surprised, smiled fully and wished everyone a "Gut Shabbes," turned and kissed Olga and Faegl. Slowly, the women returned to their seats, stopping to shake hands, embrace their special friends, wishing everyone "a gute woch," a good week, while Moshe helplessly implored them to sit down so the ceremony could continue. Reluctantly they did so, still clasping the outstretched hands of their friends who thanked and complimented them.

Basha rarely said the blessing. She was very pleased that Moshe had honored her in recognition of her impending departure. She hadn't expected to be so moved. The candle blessing was a powerful and complex event in Basha's life, in which she experienced a unification with her mother, and with herself as a child. Such rare moments of personal integration may happen when early memories stored in the body are triggered by the enactment of ancient long-known ethnic ritual gestures. Later Basha said, "Do you know what it meant to me when I was called to the candles last Friday? I'll tell you. When I was a little girl, I would stand this way, beside my mother when she would light the candles for Shabbat. We were alone in the house, everything warm and clean and quiet with all the good smells of the cooking food coming in around us. We were still warm from the mikva. My braids very tight, to last through Shabbes, made with my best ribbons. Whatever we had, we wore our best. To this day, when the heat of the candles is on my face, I circle the flame and cover my eyes, and then I feel again my mother's hands on my smooth cheeks."

Basha's description of how the Sabbath ritual affected her and stayed with her, preserving intact with complete freshness the original context in which she acquired it, seemed to me a striking example of what Rachel had called "Domestic Religion." It had the same features she described, acquired in early childhood, completely associated with family and household, blending nurturance and ethnic specificities, and it was this blend that gave hearth-based religion such endurance and depth. Rachel's concept of Domestic Religion corresponded to what Shmuel called Jewish culture, distinguishing it from nationalism and religious doctrine, and it was what most Center people would have called Yiddishkeit if they were asked about it. Robert Redfield's distinction between Little and Great Traditions points to a similar interpretation. The latter, referring to

the abstract, eternal verities of a culture, are usually controlled by literati from a distance, interpreted and enforced by official institutions. The Little Tradition, in contrast, is a local, folk expression of a group's beliefs; unsystematized, not elaborately idealized, it is an oral tradition practiced constantly and often unconsciously by ordinary people without external enforcement or interference. Domestic Religion, Little Tradition, folk culture ethnicity – whatever term one prefers – have in common the potential of providing a sacredness that issues from its being thoroughly embedded in a culture. Its authority comes from the fact that it is completely internalized within the psyche of a people, permeating every institution and relationship. More a matter of customs than ideas, it is mostly enacted rather than discussed, it is often evoked by ritual, triggered by certain symbols that usually pertain to the family, the home, and the immediate community.

Indeed, in the shtetl the distinctions between Great and Little Tradition were exceptionally clear. Great scholars of Judaism represented the Great Tradition and in their practices the tradition was exalted, pure and perpetual. Their studies were devoted to systematizing, scrutinizing, reading, and writing about enormous ideas, in the language of the Great Tradition, Hebrew. But Yiddishkeit was a matter of everyday life and mundane concerns, no less authentically Jewish because more homely. The Jews were "One People" insofar as they participated in the Great Tradition, sharing the literate history and language, practicing scholarship and prayer, but most shtetl folk and almost all Center folk were not able to participate in the Great Tradition, fully or consistently. It was mediated to them through their leaders, teachers, and sages. The more direct version of Judaism, diffuse and concrete, came in the form of Yiddishkeit.

Victor Turner has suggested that sacred symbols have two opposite poles, one abstract, ideal, normative, the other concrete, physiological, affective. An exchange of these properties may occur in rituals, and then their abstract dimension fuses with the concrete, so that the abstract pole is made vital and personal, while the particular and physiological pole becomes ennobled and equated with the highest ideals of the collectivity. Thus does duty become desire. It is the physiological pole that is most basic, acquired earlier, in the preverbal experiences of the infant in relation to those who nurture him or her; it is survival, existence itself.

Survival comes in cultural inflections. The infant is fed particular foods, lulled with particular words and songs, wrapped in particular garments. Desire, appetite, fundamental feelings are inflected in local, household idioms that once acquired are not interchangeable. These forms precede ideas or words. They become expressible later in the child's life, and then their meanings may be overtly taught, but this teaching is an overlay that rarely penetrates the very ground of being in the same way that the first inexpressible meanings do. When sacred symbols are employed in rituals, when the poles fuse, a single experiential reality is created and the individual becomes the embodiment of certain of the collectivities' beliefs. The beliefs are laid upon and empowered by the original mixture of household odors, habits, gestures, sounds, tastes, and sentiments, the accumulation of historical moments – perhaps no longer consciously remembered but nonetheless effective. These first experiences of domestic life, transmuted into Domestic Religion, are permanent and powerful, for their roots have been set down in the deepest layers of the heart. It is no wonder then that Basha felt she could face any difficulty, bear any loss except that of no longer being able to speak to someone in Yiddish.

On leaving the Sabbath ceremony at the Center one afternoon not long after Rachel expounded her views about Domestic Religion, I stopped by the Ocean Beach Kosher Guest Home. What I encountered there might have been designed by her if she had wanted to provide proof for her theory. Services were held once a week at the Guest Home, begun by the devout old men who had been praying together for years. Previously it was their custom to circulate among the several small synagogues in the neighborhood. As the community had dwindled in size, all but four of

the shuls had closed, two on the boardwalk, and two within walking distance. A Jewish charitable organization had purchased the mortgages on those remaining and agreed that as long as a *minyon* (ten men required for prayer) held services in them once a week, the synagogues would be kept open. The shrinking circle of devout old men became known as the "marching minyon." Each Friday they strode along the boardwalk, picking up extra men whenever they could. Recently they had become too frail to continue making the circuit and had retrenched, using the lounge in the Guest Home instead. The home was a drab plaster one-story duplex converted into a facility for about sixty people, all of whom were Center members. Once a week, the "lounge" served as shul, and the television set became a bima. On Friday afternoons the broken Naugahyde chairs and ragged couches were pushed against the walls. The room smelled of mold and disinfectant. It reminded me of a bus station waiting room in northern Mexico. The women had moved into the corridor, where they leaned patiently against the walls, peering into the lounge. Many of the men were Orthodox and would not pray with women. About half the men wore fringed blue and white prayer shawls. All had covered their head in one way or another – with golf caps, berets, paper yarmulkes, jeweled and beaded yarmulkes, and one man had borrowed a woman's scarf that he had tied up like a turban. Two men stood before the bima leading the prayers. They were blind but preserved the appearance of reading, as required by Jewish law. A third man stood nearby and prompted them from time to time. Eighteen men were in the room, all praying with great *kavannah*,[*] swaying deeply, stepping forward and back, bowing, striking their chest with clenched fists. I had never seen the Center men so energetic and forceful. The faintest of them now seemed to fill up and throb with vitality, and their hymns rang out powerfully. Outside, the women moved their lips with the men's chants. I was sad and resentful watching them there, trying to follow the prayers. I remembered a

---

[*] Religious fervor; inner intention of a prayer.

story Basha once told me about how as a small girl she had been indignant at having to stay with her mother in the women's gallery over the main body of the synagogue where the men prayed. She had leaned out as far as she dared to try to catch a glimpse of her father and brothers below. She resented being cooped up with the women, some so ignorant they held their prayer book upside down. The gallery had been terribly hot and crowded. Basha thought she was going to faint and had to run outside, weeping in outrage and humiliation.

As I stood watching the women, I noticed Sylvia, standing apart in a dark, little niche in the hall. She was "on the other side," as people said about those they regarded as senile. Usually remote and disoriented, Sylvia seldom spoke. She did not wear glasses. Her eyes were bright but glazed and unseeing. She wore a faded cotton washdress and her feet bulged over her broken, shapeless shoes. I was puzzled seeing her now, for she was very animated. I could not hear her from where I stood, but I saw her lips moving. She bobbed up and down, from one foot to another, almost dancing, waving her hands upward, weeping, laughing, shaking her finger, head, and shoulders, seeming to scold or argue with an invisible antagonist. On her head was an odd white patch. So bizarre was her behavior that I wondered if she was hallucinating or if somehow she had had a head injury and the patch was a bandage. I moved closer and stood next to her. She was reciting the prayer for the dead, "El Moley Rachamim," engaged in an intense, prolonged debate with God, conducting her own private Sabbath service.

The white patch on her head was a piece of folded toilet paper, pinned precisely in place. Beneath it her hair was damp. She had combed it neatly with water. Following Orthodox custom, she had covered her head to say the prayers. I was very close to her, but she didn't see me. When she finished I said her name. She regarded me without expression and was silent. I took her hand and wished her a good Sabbath. The physical contact was startling. Something suddenly flew open, as though a window shade had snapped up. For a moment I felt as though I was standing inside a membrane with her. She smiled and clutched me so fervently that her hard, yellow nails raised red welts on my forearm.

"Look, darling, how beautiful it is today," she said. "I am rejoicing in the Sabbath, like always. This I must do because if you wouldn't rejoice in the Sabbath in this world, you wouldn't know what to do in the world to come. These are the same, 'Ot hi le olam, the Sabbath is a token of eternity.' So on Sabbath, I get all dressed up, the best what I can, and let my heart rise up, like in the psalm:

'Come forth from thy ruins,
Long enough have you dwelt in the vale of tears.
Shake off your dust. Arise
Put on your glorious garments, my people.
Be not ashamed.
Your God will rejoice over you
As a bridegroom rejoices over his bride.
Come my beloved, meet the Sabbath bride . . .'"

Sylvia reached her hand to her hair and shyly, vainly, smoothed it beneath the head covering. The gesture bespoke a sense of inner beauty on this Sabbath eve. Truly she had come forth from the ruins and put on glorious garments.

"On Sabbath, darling, there is only joy. You shouldn't cry." She reached up and with great gentleness wiped away my tears. "Shabbat shalom, you should have peace.

"You see, darling, I still know all my prayers. I still got all the sounds in my heart. It comes back to me every week like this, like the Sabbath soul, neshoma yetera. All the prayers, the psalms, the hymns. My Jewish heart is lasting long." Sylvia was here, on this side, connected and present, tied by a band of memory to God and the day, and for that instant, to me.

Driving home, I thought about the day and the praying of the afternoon. I remembered how often I had been utterly unmoved by beautiful temple services held in lavish halls, the women dressed in finery, fully included as participants in the ceremonies, sitting in dignity and comfort with the men, the rich sounds of well-trained choirs surrounding the sermons of erudite and subtle rabbis. I had avoided synagogues ever since adolescense, for I never found in them the kind of religious experience I wanted. But I would return to the Ocean Beach Kosher Guest Home on Friday after-noons as often as I could, even though as a woman I would have to stand outside. I had never been to so religious a service, nor had I ever beheld an object so sacred as the covering on Sylvia's head.

[. . .]

28

Fate in Relation to the Social Structure

Meyer Fortes

Meyer Fortes (1906–83) was professor of anthropology at the University of Cambridge. In the course of his distinguished career he made huge contributions to the study of kinship and descent and wrote major monographs on the Tallensi of northern Ghana. Fortes was one of the preeminent social structuralists, but his sociological approach is complemented by a Freudian outlook. In his classic essay on Tallensi religion (or Tallensi social psychology, as Robin Horton in his essay appended to the 1983 edition, calls it) from which this selection is taken, Fortes provides an incisive portrait of so-called ancestor worship in a lineage-based society in which the father–son bond is composed simultane-ously of filial piety and suppressed hostility. A person's ancestors help to articulate the social persona and life course, but Fortes complicates the picture further by exploring how the Tallensi explain lives that are somehow "spoiled" through a principle of personal destiny that stands apart from the ancestors and is rooted instead in something akin to the unconscious. Fortes's argument concerns the moral frameworks in terms of which interpretations of life events and life trajectories are inevitably set. Readers are urged to turn to the entire essay as well as his collection of related essays, suitably titled *Religion, Morality and the Person* (Fortes 1987).

[. . .]

Frazer derived ancestor-worship from a belief in the immortality of the soul, coupled with a fear of the dead, which he thought was virtually instinctive among mankind. Such an explanation would be a ludicrous oversimplification for the Tallensi, or any other West African people. The Tallensi have an ancestor cult not because they fear the dead – for they do not, in fact, do so – nor because they believe in the immortality of the soul – for they have no such notion – but because their social structure

From Meyer Fortes, "Fate in Relation to the Social Structure," from *Oedipus and Job in West African Religion* (Cambridge: Cambridge University Press, 1983 [1959]), pp. 32–40. Abridged.

demands it. To put it in other words, they have a complex and elaborate body of ritual beliefs and practices for perpetuating and regulating the significance of the dead in the lives of their descendants. They worship their ancestors because ancestry, and more particularly parenthood, is the critical and irreducible determinant of their whole social structure. Not fear, ignorance or superstition but the moral bonds of the filio-parental relationship are the springs of Tale ancestor-worship. The significant parallels with Oedipus and Job lie in this.

We have seen that Tale jural and ritual concepts distinguish with precision a number of elements in the social and individual constitution of a person by reference to the different domains of social structure in which they are effective. We have noted that the mere fact of being born alive and remaining alive is the primary element. This receives a specific ritual imprimatur in the institution of the spirit guardian. The spirit guardian serves both to identify and to give value to the fact of individual life and to show how it depends on parental care. It is because one owes one's life to one's parents, Tallensi say, that one has irrevocable and absolute bonds with them. First there are the affective and moral bonds which Tallensi derive from the relationship of upbringing. Parental discipline, authority, affection and care create reciprocal dependence, obedience, and respectful love on the part of the children. Then there is the jural component of status in one's lineage and locus in the web of kinship, acquired by birth, through one's parents, and forming an element in the continuity of the social structure through time. The ritual imprimatur for this is the conception of the ancestors as sovereign and eternal, mirroring the total system of kinship and descent which is seen as an everlasting and fixed framework for the individual's social existence. Lastly there are the bonds created by the succession of generations. Sons must succeed fathers and daughters mothers in the passage of the generations. This is jurally expressed in the facts of inheritance and succession and ritually demonstrated in the worship of the spirits of the dead parents.

In this context the critical fact is that the individual has no choice. Submission to his ancestors is symbolic of his encapsulation in a social order which permits of no voluntary alteration of his status and social capacities. It is the common interest, the collective purposes that prevail.

We can see that an individual who was incurably impeded from fitting into the social structure would be an anomaly. Hence the great importance of giving specific ritual recognition to the individuality of each life-history. It acknowledges the need for the realities of life to be accommodated to the fixity of structural norms; and it is easy to see how notions of luck, chance, destiny and even, in a more sophisticated idiom, election, could be used to reconcile the determinism of jural and ritual status imposed by the social structure with the variability and unpredictability of the individual life-cycle. If we imagine a graph of a person's life among the Tallensi, one axis would stand for his movement into and through the social structure, the other for his personal development, the origin being the fact of his being born alive of particular parents.

This is where Oedipal concepts come into evidence. They recognize forces in social and personal development that cannot be changed or regulated by society. The Tale notion of Prenatal Destiny designates what, in more abstract language, could best be described as an innate disposition that can be realized either for good or for ill. The Tallensi themselves do not, of course, have the cultural resources for analyzing their religious symbolism in this form. Indeed, if they were able to do so the symbols would be denuded of their affective and expressive force. It is only the outside investigator, viewing the symbolism in relation to the other religious institutions of those who live by them, and in its context of social structure, who can perceive its abstract meaning.

What strikes us then is the criteria by which a person's evil Prenatal Destiny are diagnosed. Proof that it is working itself out in an evil way is the victim's irremediable but involuntary failure to fulfil the roles and achieve the performance regarded as normal for his status in the social structure. It would not be going too far to say that the Tallensi define a person as being afflicted by an evil Prenatal Destiny if he turns out to be incapable of being or remaining incorporated in the social structure. If, on the other hand, he gains and holds his due place in it, this is credited to his Good Destiny.

Why, then, is the victim of an evil Prenatal Destiny dissociated from the social structure? Tale doctrine and ritual usage imply that it is because he has, from the moment of birth, rejected society, preferring death to incorporation in the network of fundamental family and kinship relations and turning his back on the basic moral norms. This is not a conscious or deliberate rejection, since the sufferer is not aware of his predisposition until he learns of it through divination. From the point of view of society, as expressed in Tale doctrine, the fault lies in his inescapable, inborn wishes. But from the sufferer's point of view, as shown in his attitudes and conduct, his condition is forced upon him by society. He sees himself as implicitly disowned by his kin and his ancestors, since all the resources of social organization, therapeutic skill, ritual, and parental devotion have failed to open a way to social normality for him. He is justified in this because the sovereign authority over his life so obviously resides in society and because the notion of Prenatal Destiny is a last-ditch defence. Those responsible for his well-being only fall back on it, with the sanction of a diviner's findings, when appeals to the ancestors to save him have come to naught. What is symbolized in the notion of evil Prenatal Destiny is, therefore, a failure in the relationship of belonging to society, which, for the Tallensi, means family, lineage and kin. In developmental terms this means a failure in the primary relationships of parents and children, since it is through these relationships that the individual is fitted into society and the norms and the demands of society are implanted in him.

These structural considerations suggest a number of parallels in the story of Oedipus. His Fate is evil; it enters into his life at the very beginning through his being rejected by his parents when they cast him away. He survives only because he is accepted by substitute parents, but he becomes an outcast again when his Fate catches up with him. He is finally overwhelmed by his Fate because he unknowingly violates the basic norms of the filial relationship. His tragedy can be described as that of a man blindly seeking to achieve his legitimate place in society, first as son, then as husband, father and citizen against the unconscious opposition of an inborn urge to avenge himself by repudiating his parents, his spouse, and his children. When, in the end, he succumbs to this Fate he shows his revulsion against himself by mutilating his own eyes and so blotting out his relationship with his kin and his society. Nor is he ever accepted back into society. He dies in exile, almost like a ghost departing from this world rather than like an ordinary man.

We must remember, however, that the notion of Prenatal Destiny is not merely a label for a class of persons definable in structural terms. It is a religious concept, associated with ritual procedures for disposing, by symbolic displacement, of the emotional and moral tensions generated in the structural antimonies in which the fated individual finds himself. We have seen how it serves to exonerate both society and the sufferer by fixing ultimate responsibility on the ancestors and on a prenatal, that is presocial, event. Thus the onus of the rejection is shifted on to the supernatural plane and the individual's feelings of helplessness and depression are made tolerable. In the case of Oedipus, too, the onus of guilt falls on Fate. Even his father and mother are victims of this hereditary determinism. Where the Oedipus story diverges most strikingly from the simpler Tale pattern is in the place assigned to human will. Laius and Jocasta thought they could thwart Fate by casting away their child. They failed; and the Tallensi would understand this, for they do not believe that hostile supernatural forces can be averted by human prudence. Only ritual measures can, in their scheme of thought, defend them against supernatural threats.

The reason lies in the Tale concept of mystical causation mentioned earlier in this essay. Its effect is seen in the beliefs and practices related to the process by which the innate potentiality of Destiny is turned to beneficial ends. The evidence for its beneficence is demonstrated capacity to achieve the economic, jural and social goals that are normal for a person's age, sex and status. But continued beneficence is only ensured if particular (ideally paternal) ancestors accept the supernatural responsibility for his Destiny. We can readily see that this is the expression, in religious symbols and sanctions, of the ideal of the parents (particularly the father) as beings who accept their child in order to care for him throughout his life. Since Destiny ancestors are the agents of the collective ancestors, their role is also the symbolic equivalent of incorporating him into the political and jural domain of the social structure in his character as a person with a unique life-cycle. Consequently, when a man submits to his ancestors he is accepting his dependence on his parents, particularly his father and, *a fortiori*, his incorporation in society. This is an absolute – that is, supernaturally sanctioned – relationship, in which the duty to abide by the basic moral axioms of society is appropriated by each person as a supreme value. It is the very opposite condition to that of a supposed victim of evil Prenatal Destiny. In the abstract terms we have been using, we would say that harnessing the individual's inborn potentialities to the needs and values of society prevents them from becoming destructive and turns them into capacities for productive social development and normal life in society.

To put the argument in a slightly different way, if parents fail in their task of upbringing, the latent hostility of their children in their relations with them and sentiments towards them gets the upper hand – or at least it is deemed to do so – and eventually destroys the bonds between them. Evil Prenatal Destiny conceptualizes this experience. On the other hand, if parents succeed in this task, it shows that they have used the powers and authority vested in them by society with benevolence – in religious terms, with the blessings of the ancestors. Conversely, it also shows that their children have responded to parental discipline, care and affection with growth to adulthood. This means that trustful acquiescence towards their parents has been more powerful than latent antagonism. The notion of the Good Destiny conceptualizes this experience and gives sanction and value to it as a lasting moral force in the individual's life. This is where Tale

beliefs are quite unlike the story of Oedipus. For him there was no way of changing his evil fate into a beneficent destiny. But it is reminiscent of Job.

Figuratively speaking, therefore, we might say that an Oedipal predisposition is in this way transformed into a Jobian fulfilment. The drama of Job's life springs from the circumstance that he is chosen by his god in order to put his fidelity to test. It is comparable to the way Destiny ancestors choose their ward among the Tallensi and continually try his faith by making demands on him. This is one indication among many that Job is never disowned, avowedly or implicitly, by either his fellows or his god. The tribulations he endures are of a quite different order from the catastrophes brought on Oedipus by irrevocable Fate. They can, as I suggested at the beginning, well be compared to a severe but just form of paternal correction, and that is why they are not tragic like those of Oedipus but simply pathetic though on a cosmic scale. They are, in fact, part of the total texture of a relationship with his fellows and his god in which he is cherished, despite appearances to the contrary, and which he never turns away from. Such a relationship is essential for God, the superior, to be in a position to chastise Job, and for Job, the inferior, to be in a position to defend himself by righteous conduct and argument. It is true that Job at first feels himself estranged from his fellows and persecuted unjustly by God. This is because he mistakes his status and believes himself entitled to recognition and reward in terms of his own standards of virtue and right. Tallensi would not fall into this error in relation to their ancestors.

Job's salvation comes when he recognizes his god's omnipotence as a phenomenon beyond human questioning. He perceives that submission to his god must be absolute, whether or not it corresponds to norms of righteous conduct among men. This is submission in the attitude of filial humility and faith towards all-powerful parents. In this relationship it is possible, and indeed inevitable, for the inferior to accept everything willed for him by his superior, whether it turns out to his advantage or not, as an act of justice. In Job's case it makes his tribulations appear as the means by which he was taught a true understanding of the nature of his dependence on God and of the services befitting to this relationship. It is appropriate that he is in the end restored not only to God's favour, but to health, status and rank. The Tallensi would understand this story very well by analogy with their ancestor cult; for Oedipus, such a road back to normality does not exist.

Recapitulation

To recapitulate, the notion of evil Prenatal Destiny among the Tallensi serves to identify the fact of irremediable failure in the development of the individual to full social capacity. More than that, it gives symbolic expression to the implicit structural meaning of such failure as an indication of abortive filio-parental relationships. The possibility of these relationships going wrong is a threat to fundamental moral and affective ties and sentiments. This is neutralized by ritual procedures based on the belief that evil Prenatal Destiny is in the last resort susceptible of control by the ancestors if they so will it. Thus the ill-fated are by implication those unfortunate people who are felt to be rejected by the parental institutions of society symbolized in the ancestor figures. The hostile component in the filio-parental relationship comes to the fore, and is given symbolic expression in the image of evil Prenatal Destiny which finally destroys its victim.

The notion of Good Destiny, on the other hand, symbolically identifies the fact of successful individual development along the road to full incorporation in society. It serves to make this fact comprehensible and to set a seal of religious value on it as implicitly significant of normal and successful filio-parental relationships. The symbolism utilized is the notion that Destiny operates in this way if it is absorbed and sanctioned by the ancestors. It thus accounts for the rewards that witness to successful development, and provides a basis for ritual procedures to neutralize the demoralizing effects, on fundamental moral and affective ties and sentiments, of the hazards

that accompany each person's progress through life. The well-fated are by implication those fortunate enough to be accepted by the parental institutions symbolized in the cult of the ancestors and endowed with the ability to maintain relationships of mutual trust and support with them. This means that the hostile component in the filio-parental relationship is overcome in the attribution of a predominantly benevolent character to the ancestors. In this context the punitive aspect of the ancestor figures has a disciplinary not a destructive function. It is the instrument of their justice and a measure of their sovereignty paralleling, on the religious plane, the usages and forms of family government we have previously described. It helps to drain away individual feelings of anxiety and guilt by canalizing them into customary rituals of placation and expiation; and these are effective simply because the ancestors are believed not only to exact punishment for wrong conduct but also to behave justly and benevolently in the long run.

What can we learn from this limited inquiry? Frazer's own work is a warning against drawing facile generalizations from parallels between the customs and beliefs of widely different societies. However, my aim in this essay has not been to find parallels but to elicit basic common elements in the religious conceptions I have described. And one common element is patent. All the concepts and beliefs we have examined are religious extrapolations of the experiences generated in the relationships between parents and children in societies with a social organization based on kinship and descent. They are magnified and disguised extrapolations; and their effect is to endow the critical components of filio-parental relationships with an external reality and representation that belongs to the whole society and not to the realm of individual thought and fantasy. The religious conceptions of the Tallensi show us this process in a direct form. We can uncover the roots of these beliefs in the family system and observe how their branches spread through the entire social structure. We can see how they bind the internal domain of the family, where children are reared, to the external domain of political society, where they eventually run their life-course; and we can see why parenthood, on the one hand, and the sovereignty of society, on the other, are invested with sacredness. Oedipus and Job dramatize the basic elements of this type of religious system. They, too, are reflexions, partly exact, partly distorted, of family and kinship institutions. If they appeal more to our imagination and emotions than do the unsophisticated facts of Tale religion, this is because they deck out the bare bones of belief and concept in the rich panoply of the ethical thought and metaphysical doctrines of literate cultures. The core of fundamental beliefs and attitudes is the same.

Here, then, are the areas of common human experience to which our data must be referred. Ever since Freud's bold speculations in *Totem and Taboo* and Durkheim's great work on *The Elementary Forms of the Religious Life*, anthropologists have known that the springs of religion and ritual lie in kinship and social organization. What I have tried to do has been to relate particular religious conceptions to the significance, for the society, of the process of taking its individual members into itself. Considered merely as superstition, beliefs in Fate and the Ancestors (or Job's God) seem to be antithetical. The first is amoral, the second is supremely moral. In fact, we have seen that in West African religions they are not opposed but rather supplement each other. For the Tallensi, at any rate, they can be described as supplementary conceptual moments in a religious apparatus for dealing with the commitments created for society collectively and for its members severally by the passage of the individual into and through society. They reconcile the two main alternatives in the hazardous progress of the individual from the state of unchecked dependence, as an infant at the mother's breast, to that of constrained independence, as an adult and citizen. It is a law of nature that some people must fail in the whole or in parts of the task of becoming and remaining social persons. The predicament this gives rise to is interpreted, given moral value, and brought under control in the interests of society and of the individual, by means of the beliefs and rituals focused in the notion of Predestiny, or Oedipal Fate. Most people will succeed; but they can do so only by coming to terms with unforeseeable hazards and precarious rewards. To give meaning and absolute moral value to this experience the Tallensi invoke personified supernatural figures cast in the mould of glorified parents who intervene justly in the life of the individual and of society. The image of the Good Destiny in which these ideas are focused is, in essentials, a simple version of Job's God.

In the ultimate sense, perhaps, the concept of Predestiny may be taken to designate tendencies that originate in organic sources and in the earliest experiences of infantile dependence. It is of profound interest that these tendencies appear to be intuitively recognized in many societies and are deemed to manifest themselves in unwitting resistance to the normal relationships of parenthood. Ancestor- or deity-worship, on the other hand, presupposes the triumph of parenthood. It recognizes the paramountcy of the moral norms emanating from society as a whole over the dangerous egotism of childhood.

29

Medusa's Hair: An Essay on Personal Symbols and Religious Experience

Gananath Obeyesekere

Gananath Obeyesekere is professor emeritus at Princeton University. The author of numerous works on land tenure, social change, and Buddhism in Sri Lanka, he is widely recognized for his contributions to psychoanalytic anthropology, including a major study of myths and ritual practices concerning the South Asian goddess Pattini (1984) and a theoretical essay conjoining Weberian and Freudian perspectives (1990). *Medusa's Hair* is probably the best known of his works. It is a marvelous study of a number of individual religious ascetics associated with the shrine of Kataragama in Sri Lanka who are notable for their matted locks of hair and their often painful devotional practices. At the same time as Obeyesekere connects the motivational histories of the ascetics to their specific signifying practices within the spectrum of Buddhist–Hindu worship, he develops an abstract account of the relationship between public and private symbols more generally. The book is also notable for its discussion of fantasy as a source of cultural enrichment and for the way it draws on psychoanalytic concepts of transference and counter-transference to illuminate the relationship between anthropologists and their subjects.

Freud himself made several contributions to religion and anthropology. In *Totem and Taboo* (1958 [1913]) he attempted to apply his account of the development of the individual by means of the Oedipus complex to the origins of human society as a whole. The historicity of Freud's account has been largely discounted (Kroeber 1979a [1920], 1979b [1939]) but it remains highly suggestive for understanding the prevalence of themes of desire and frustration in all human societies and in the cultural representations of myth and religion (Paul 1996). Freud made two rather different arguments concerning religion.

From Gananath Obeyesekere, Part One of *Medusa's Hair: An Essay on Personal Symbols and Religious Experience* (Chicago: University of Chicago Press, 1981), pp. 13–46. Abridged.

In *Totem and Taboo* he saw it functioning as a kind of external superego, an adaptation to the basic human personality that reinforces and sanctifies society's necessary control over the drives (sex and aggression). In *The Future of an Illusion* (1961 [1927]) religion becomes a realm of projection and immature wish-fulfillment. Freud recognized its creative and compensatory qualities but argued that religion could disappear with the progress of rationality. His analysis of the production of symbols in dreams (1953 [1900–30]) has been very fruitful for understanding symbolic processes more generally.

Obeyesekere here provides a nuanced articulation of Freudian theory with mainstream anthropological thought. For a more direct statement see Spiro (1979), which could be read as a useful rejoinder to Lévi-Strauss (chapter 17 above). Some analyses (Spiro 1982, Paul 1983, and Gillison 1993) continue to explore Oedipal and other sexual themes and representations in the production of culture, while others have provided Freudian interpretations of individual religious practitioners and practices (Crapanzano 1973, 1980). Few as yet have seriously embraced subsequent developments, such as relational theory, within psychoanalysis (Chodorow 1989, 1999, Lambek 2003(c), Trawick 1990).

Introduction

I will introduce the theme of this essay with a discussion of Leach's influential paper "Magical Hair," where he analyzes the matted hair and shaven heads of Indian ascetics, which he treats as public symbols. Leach argues that, contrary to psychoanalytic thinking, public cultural symbols have no unconscious motivational significance for the individual or the group. By contrast, private symbols may involve deep motivation, but they have no cultural significance. I take this to be the standard social anthropological position regarding symbols – an inadequate one, I believe, since there are grounds for assuming that custom and emotion are often interwoven. I will then present case studies of three female ecstatics to show how cultural meanings are articulated to personal experience. At this stage in my analysis I focus on one symbol – matted hair – and the relation of that symbol to critical personal life crises. The complex personal experiences of the individual are crystallized in the (public) symbol. Thus symbols like matted hair operate on the psychological and cultural levels simultaneously; ergo, a naive psychoanalytic position is as inadequate as a naive anthropological

one. Personal symbols must be related to the life experience of the individual and the larger institutional context in which they are embedded.

Thus, from a critique of the antipsychological stance of social anthropology, I move to a criticism of the anti-institutional stance of psychoanalysis. One weakness in the psychoanalytic theory of symbolism is its assumption that all psychological symbols have motivational significance. I argue that psychological symbols can be broken down into a minimum of two types: personal symbols where deep motivation is involved, and psychogenetic symbols where deep motivation does not occur. Psychogenetic symbols *originate* in the unconscious or are derived from the dream repertoire; but the origin of the symbols must be analytically separated from its ongoing operational significance. This is often the case in myths and rituals: symbols originating from unconscious sources are used to give expression to meanings that have nothing to do with their origin.

Hence it is wrong for us to assume, as psychoanalysts often do, that all psychological symbols are linked to deep motivation; psychogenetic symbols are not. I will deal with psychogenetic symbols only briefly, to contrast them with personal symbols. It is in relation to the latter that the distinction between private and public symbols makes no sense. There are obviously other areas in social life where this distinction does not hold, but I do not deal with them in this essay.

Private and Public Symbols

Let me begin with my criticism of Leach's influential paper "Magical Hair," where he argues with Berg, a psychoanalyst, about the symbolic significance of matted locks and the shaven heads of Hindu and Buddhist ascetics. The thrust of the debate has to do with the relationship between symbol and emotion, between public and private symbols. Leach argues, rightly, I think, that the essence of public symbolic behavior is communication; the actor and the audience share a common symbolic language or culture. The problematic question is not the logical status of public symbols as communication, but rather the *nature* of communication. For Leach all public symbolic communication is devoid of emotional meaning or psychological content. He clearly recognizes the importance of individual psychology; but he adopts the classic social anthropological position that individual psychology cannot have cultural significance or that publicly shared symbols cannot have individual psychological meaning. If public symbols are devoid of emotional meaning, this is not true of the radically different category of private symbols. "In contrast the characteristic quality of private symbolism is its psychological power to arouse emotion and alter the state of the individual. Emotion is aroused not by appeal to the rational faculties but by some kind of trigger action on the subconscious elements of the human personality" (Leach 1958, p. 148).

Note that Leach, unlike many British social anthropologists, does not deny the validity of psychological analysis; but he thinks it is relevant only for interpreting private symbolism, not for understanding public culture. This position introduces a radical hiatus between public and private symbols, as it does between culture and emotion. "Public ritual behavior

asserts something about the *social* status of the actor; private ritual behavior asserts something about the *psychological state* of the actor" (Leach 1958, p. 166).

Nevertheless, Leach says public symbols may originate as private ones. Thus, while a private symbol may originate in the individual psyche as a result of intrapsychic conflict, it somehow or other ceases to have emotional meaning once it becomes publicly accepted culture. Leach poses the *problem* of transformation of private into public symbols; but he does not explain how such a transformation occurs.

[. . .]

Leach's argument is based on a silly book by a psychoanalyst, Charles Berg, on the unconscious significance of hair (Berg 1951). Berg analyzes – to Leach, quite plausibly – the unconscious significance of hair for the individual: hair = penis. Thus cutting hair is symbolic castration. From here Berg goes on to assert that the meaning of hair-cutting in public symbols and ritual (e.g., tonsure, head-shaving by monks) has the identical unconscious meaning of castration. Even more preposterous is his assertion that when all of us shave or trim our beards we are expressing deep-rooted castration anxieties.

Leach quite rightly castigates this kind of analysis. However, his criticism is not a new one; anthropologists using psychoanalytic theory have stated this before, and some like Hallowell have done so in even more detailed and critical terms (Hallowell 1955). Furthermore, Leach deliberately ignores the fallacy of using one work in psychoanalysis to castigate the discipline as a whole. One bad book does not damn a whole discipline; a weakness or inadequacy in a theory does not render it totally worthless. If this were the case, practically all social science would be of little value.

If some psychoanalysts treat both public and private symbols as belonging to the same qualitative order, Leach commits the identical fallacy. He sees all public symbolic and ritual behavior (and culture in general) as "rational," devoid of psychological or intrapsychic significance. The handshake is for him the ideal-typical case. The meaning of the symbolic action here is, "We are of the same standing and can converse with one another without embarrassment" (1958, p. 157) (even though such a handshake may be at variance with the actual social reality, since enemies and unequals shake hands). We may invoke common sense (which Leach also does) to point out the obvious fallacies of this position – that public symbolic communication can evoke rage or hostility (in war, in race riots, in language conflicts); that the ethnographic literature has plenty of references to communal orgies, cathartic and expressive rituals where the emotional feel is obvious and readily apparent. Much of social anthropology assumes that all symbolic communication is of a piece, rational and abstract. It ignores the obvious fact that this is *one* type of communication; emotions also may be communicated. If we assume that emotional messages may be socially communicated, we may also legitimately infer that the public symbol used as a vehicle for communicating that message may become invested with an affective load.

Not only can group emotions be generated and sustained in this manner, but shared cultural symbols may have personal meaning to the individual. Weber pointed this out in his discussion of theodicy, as did Evans-Pritchard in exploring the meaning of witchcraft for the Azande. The process whereby a public symbol becomes infused with personal meaning seems relevant for anthropology. . . .

The Problem

The immediate problem I want to investigate pertains to the matted hair of the Hindu ascetic. Leach summarizes Iyer's argument:

> The *sanyasin*'s freedom from social obligation and his final renunciation of the sex life is symbolized by change of dress but above all by a change of hair style. According to the mode of asceticism he intends to pursue a *sanyasin* either shaves off his tuft of hair or else neglects it altogether, allowing it to grow matted and lousy. (Leach 1958, p. 156; Iyer 1928, 2:383; 1935, 1:332–4)

This statement is not as simple as it sounds, for the crucial phrase is *according to the mode of asceticism*. Some ascetic styles require a shaven head; some require the reverse: matted locks. The two kinds of symbols, as I shall show later, indicate two different modes of ascetic religiosity, on both the sociocultural and the psychological levels. For the moment, however, let us focus on the matted hair ascetic.

Berg interprets this cultural phenomenon thus: "Fakirs simply ignore altogether the very existence of their hair (cf. the ascetic tendency to ignore the existence of the genital organs). It grows into a matted, lice-inhabited mass and may almost be as much a source of unremitting torment as the neglected penis itself. Apparently it is not permitted to exist as far as *consciousness* is concerned" (Berg 1951, p. 71; Leach 1958, p. 156). Leach finds this an ethnocentric (psychoanalytic) and biased view, since the hair is a public, not a private, symbol.

> Dr. Berg's assumption is that the *sanyasin*'s behavior is a compulsive one, welling from some hidden springs in the individual unconscious. And no doubt if a European ascetic were to start behaving in this way it would be indicative of some complicated neurotic compulsion. But in the Indian context, the *sanyasin*'s detachment from sexual interests and the fact that the matted hair is a symbol of this detachment are both conscious elements in the same religious doctrine. The correct hair behavior – and also the correct sexual and excretory behavior of Indian ascetics was all laid down in the Naradaparivrajaka Upanishad over 2000 years ago. (1958, p. 156)

Leach goes on to say that the "matted hair means total detachment from the sexual passions because hair behavior and sex behavior are consciously associated from the start" (1958, p. 156).

In the case of the neurotic European pseudoascetic, the hair behavior has unconscious experimental significance: for the Hindu ascetic it is not so, because he performs a traditional customary form of behavior.

Both Berg and Leach are wrong, but in different ways. Both are wrong like many others who study symbols: we infer the meaning of the symbol from the symbol itself, rarely referring to the persons in the culture who employ the symbol. The bias is of course most apparent in semiological studies, including structuralism, which can analyze signs without reference to context, much as language may be analyzed without reference to the person, society, or culture in which it is embedded. This is theoretically a feasible thing to do (though it is one that is being increasingly questioned by anthropological linguists). Nevertheless, it would be futile to talk of the psychological significance, or lack thereof, of the symbol from this methodological perspective – in this case the matted hair of the ascetic – without reference to the ascetic himself and the group in which he lives, and to the people among whom he moves. I shall show that Berg is right when he deals with the unconscious emotional significance that hair has for the ascetic, though his statement about the tormented penis requires some qualification in my study of six *female* ascetics. Leach's view is that the symbols are publicly and overtly recognized; they are laid down in sacred books; therefore they cannot have unconscious significance. This seems to me an illogical inference, since there is no intrinsic contradiction between custom and emotion.

It is indeed true that in some instances the sexual significance of a symbol is explicitly and consciously recognized. Other parts of the human anatomy – right hand: left hand; head: foot – and the body as a whole are consciously and explicitly used in cultural symbolism. So with the genitals; penis and vagina are often, along with the act of intercourse itself, employed as obvious symbols of fertility or generation. But the *experience* of sex in human society is a complicated one; it is therefore likely that the experiential dimension of sexuality, with its strong emotional overlay, also appears in some of the symbols. The mere *existence* of a sexual symbol in the culture does not by itself warrant our making inferences regarding its personal or sociological significance. The operative context is crucial. When it involves inner experience, the significance of the symbol or symbolic sequence may elude the conscious thought of the members of the culture. Turner recognizes this when he says that a block in native exegesis may indicate that unconscious intrapsychic material is involved (Turner 1967, p. 38).

To come back to matted hair. Contrary to Leach, and in spite of the authority of the Upanishads, not one among my ordinary Sinhala Buddhist informants could consciously identify hair with sexuality. None of the six female ascetics interviewed could even remotely associate their matted hair with male or female genitalia. Suppose for argument's sake we agree with Leach and say that hair = genitals (or semen); but contra Leach we can document that this is not consciously recognized. May we not infer that there is a block in native exegesis at all levels and that unconscious perceptions and motivations are involved? If so, matted hair is locked into an emotional experience, which can be unraveled only through our knowledge of the ascetics themselves, not through a priori assumptions.

That ascetic experience is a complicated matter is easy to demonstrate. The person who in late life withdraws from the social world, forsaking family and friends, cutting himself loose from his social moorings, is not just any ordinary person consciously and rationally following the ancient Upanishadic instructions. If such withdrawal were an easy matter, the Indian world would be cluttered with ascetics. Fortunately, though ascetics are conspicuously visible, they are rare creatures. Leaving the world has not been for them a rationally calculated, deliberate act: it has been precipitated by complicated personal and social factors, often of a highly emotional sort. Thus one cannot agree with Leach's view that if a European pseudoascetic were to behave in this way it would indicate a complicated neurotic problem, but that the Hindu ascetic is exempt from this because of his reliance on old texts and customs. *Rather, both involve complicated experiences, but the Hindu's experiences are articulated in terms of traditional symbols. Furthermore, unlike the European ascetic, the Hindu's consciousness is already influenced by his culture, facilitating the expression of intrapsychic conflict in a cultural idiom.*

Female Ascetics and Matted Hair

In this section I shall initially describe the experiences of three female ascetics [only one here] so as to elucidate the experiential context in which their matted locks emerged. I shall then discuss the genesis of the symbol and interpret the meaning of matted locks for these ascetics. . . .

The case studies are presented from the informant's own point of view; many of the events have been filtered through later experiences and through a cultural sieve. Thus the past of these informants was often constituted of "filtered memories." I take these filtered experiences and memories seriously, since they are the experientially real ones for the informants and are critical to their identity. . . .

Female Ascetic-Ecstatics

Case 1: Karunavati Maniyo (Age 52)

I know very little of Karunavati's childhood. The information she volunteered was significant to her. The most serious early trauma she suffered was that her father deserted her mother when Karunavati was about five years old. She was brought up by her mother and her maternal grandfather, whom she loved dearly.

She married at about twenty in somewhat extraordinary circumstances. Her future husband was an overseer in the Public Works Department and was at that time supervising the construction of a road in her village (Haburugala). He fell in love with Karunavati's younger sister and wanted to marry her. (In this society it is considered unusual for the younger sister to marry while the older is unmarried.) Karunavati claims she had no real interest in her sister's boyfriend; she actually did not like him and objected to his marrying her sister. He was a loafer, a bad man, she said. One day she came from her aunt's house and saw her prospective brother-in-law and sister together in their house. She said for all to hear:

"What has my brother-in-law brought us?" "Then I took a mango seed from a dish [curry] and ate it, smacking my lips loudly . . . This was a joke. But I told my relatives that I was going to stop this marriage, as it was going to bring darkness to my sister's life." "Mother," I said, "you can take a coconut branch and cut out thousands, nay millions, of people like this." Karunavati said that this man resented her so much that he went to a sorcerer and gave her a love charm. "After this I had no interest in anything else: I simply wanted to go with this man." She eloped with him without the knowledge of her mother and sister. This, says Karunavati, is why her mother hated her. Apparently her mother was distraught by the incident and "cried and cried," she said. "That jealousy, that rage pursued me after her death."

Eventually her mother and relatives were reconciled and in fact had a formal wedding for her. "However," says Karunavati, her mother told her then, "'Daughter, this marriage of yours will never succeed; one day you'll be reduced to beggary.' You know that prophecy was fulfilled."

Her marriage, she claimed, was a disaster. Her husband used to drink heavily, gamble, smoke ganja, squander money. She enjoyed sexual intercourse with him, but she got "no pleasure out of living. If one goes on suffering, what pleasure is there?" She was also constantly beaten; she did not retaliate. They were often destitute, practically without clothes to wear; her two children were neglected. The husband lost his job as an overseer and became a day laborer. They drifted from place to place. Said Karunavati, "Had I had any foreknowledge of all this, I would have taken a vow of celibacy like our mother-Pattini."

Her mother died after Karunavati had spent seven to ten years of unhappy married life. She did not know of her death (her brother and sister did not inform her, since she was treated as a family outcast). She came to know of it much later. "I felt very sad about her death and about my not being able to be near her." "She apparently wanted to tell me something before she died but couldn't." Hence the punishment, the torture, her mother soon caused her by possessing her.

The initial possession occurred while Karunavati was living with her husband and children in a village near Navagamuva, site of the central shrine of the goddess Pattini, the ideal chaste and devoted mother and wife of Sinhala religion. "This was three months after my mother's death. The time was twelve noon [a demonic hour in Sinhala belief]. There was a noon ritual for the demon Mahasona [the great demon of the graveyard]. I heard the sound of drums: then I became possessed." It was her mother who had come after her. She had hung on a truck and come with the wind. This information was communicated by the mother, who spoke through the daughter.

The priests (*kattadiya*) who were summoned to cure her diagnosed it as *preta dosa*, misfortune caused by an evil ancestral spirit or *preta*. Several rituals were held to banish the evil spirit (the wrathful mother), but to no avail. The spirit did not allow the priests "to do their work" successfully. Karunavati was now considered *pissu* (mad) by her family and neighbors. She used to wander around, sometimes in and near cemeteries. During one of her attacks her mother spoke through her. "You cannot catch me or imprison me, since I come for your well-being [*yahapata*] after obtaining a warrant [*varama*] from the god."

Karunavati, like all the other ascetics described in this essay, then tried to convert the malevolent power into a force for good. She offered lamps and prayers for the Buddha and for the deity Huniyan, who is her personal guardian and protector. The latter also told her not to attempt to break the power (exorcise the spirit), but to use it for her own good and the welfare of others. Her family stopped the exorcisms and instead had a ritual for her of blessing by the goddess Pattini. During this ritual she became possessed and told a "real truth" to the village headman who was present there. This was her first *sastra*, and it proved accurate. Soon after she was possessed by two benevolent ancestors – her dead mother and grandmother. These departed spirits are mediators between Karunavati and the gods, conveying messages from the latter and helping her utter prophecies and cure the sick. She cemented the relationship between these now benevolent ancestors and herself by daily lighting a lamp for them in her house. She felt she had a *muka varam*, mouth boon, or *basa varam*, language boon, the power to utter prophecies, or *sastra*. However, she was still not sure whether this was truly a divine gift.

She initially interpreted her attack as revenge by the mother, who wanted to take her as a human sacrifice (*billa*). Later on, after her mother's admonition, she felt she was being punished as a kind of "test" of her ability to become a priestess. She said that her mother did not give her anything to eat or wear (she gave up rice but ate a few fruits and vegetables; during this period she compulsively ate bitter *kohomba* (margosa) leaves without even salt or chili pepper. She withered away and became skin and bone. "These noble ones [mother, grandmother, and the gods] wanted to test me to see whether I'd give up. I did not. I renounced everything for them; even my children, who were dispersed everywhere."

Then she went to Kataragama and obtained a formal warrant from the god Skanda to become a priestess. She walked the fire at Kataragama and thereby sealed her relationship with the god. There she was told by her mother in the presence of the god that her *muka varam* was a true gift given by the god. Soon afterward she went to the Visnu shrine at a Buddhist temple of Kande Vihara (near Beruwala), for she felt she had to have *avasara*, permission, from Visnu himself as the head of the pantheon. Then she was told to go to several pilgrimage centers – Alutnuvara, the seat of Dadimunda, the tamer of demons; Kaballava, the seat of Huniyan; and the Kali shrine at Munnesvaram. It was her mother who instructed her thus, either in person, through Karunavati's body, or in dreams. "She appears in dreams and manifests her form. 'I come for your welfare; do not get exorcists [to banish me]. Go to "places" and get the *vara prasada* [the gift of a boon] that is your due!'"

She now is a wanderer going from one sacred place to another, rarely in one place for long.

In many of these cases, increasing devotion to the god is accompanied by a movement away from family responsibility and by a renunciation of sex. The conflict between eros and agape comes out beautifully in her statement: "It is not me, it is the god who shoved my husband aside." She told me with some relish that she refused to let her husband have intercourse with her. This was on the god Huniyan's instructions. "I ran into the forest in the evenings"; that is, she went to visit others and avoided her husband. Sometimes he used force to make her comply.

One day she became possessed while worshiping at the central shrine of Huniyan at Kaballava. The god told me he would bestow on her seven matted locks if she totally renounced sex and obtained her husband's consent for this. According to Karunavati, Huniyan himself has seven locks, though standard iconography depicts him with five. Later she had a vision of the god in a dream; he repeated the same message and added that she should go with her husband to the mountain of Saman, wherein is embedded the sacred footprint (of the Buddha), and there formally obtain *vivarana*, permission, from her husband to renounce sex and be born as a male in her next birth.

The message from the dreaded god was enough to deter her husband. They went to the sacred mountain, and there she obtained from him her *pativrata balaya*, which she interpreted as "the power of celibacy." Sex is impure for the gods, she told him; they should live in purity, doing good. She also obtained permission from him to be born as a male in her next birth. "When I climbed up the sacred mountain I had combed and tied up my hair, but once I was there I was given seven matted locks as ordained by the divine lord Huniyan. Suddenly my hair became knotted into seven locks." She constantly affirmed her recollection of the event. Her husband gave her permission (*vivarana*) to refrain from sex and to achieve a male rebirth; then, lo and behold, seven matted locks appeared!

She claimed that she had an initial desire to cut off these locks. She went to Kataragama several times to ask the god Skanda's permission to cut them, but he refused to allow it; that is, the god spoke through her during her trance at Kataragama forbidding her to cut her hair. "At one time my matted locks were very

long, but when I get angry [*kopa venava*, i.e., shake my head in trance] or wander around cemeteries they break; or when they grow old they become brittle. I was told to deposit these relics in the Manik Ganga [the sacred river that flows past Kataragama]." Now she has only two matted locks left intact.

She says that her matted locks are her *ista devata*, her protector and guardian deity, and that they represent Huniyan himself. The hair was given to her to show the god's *sakti balaya*, the power of his *sakti* (strength, creative essence). She also refers to the locks as *dhatu*, relic or essence or life force. She is very protective of them and will not allow anyone to touch them or even come close to them, though she has lost some of them during her rapid changes of residence.

[. . .]

The Meaning of Hair

My analysis of the meaning of matted hair must deal with three interrelated problems, often confused in the analysis of symbols: the origin and genesis of the symbol; its personal meaning for the individual or group; and the social-cultural message it communicates to the group. It is in regard to the genesis of the symbol that psychological analysis is strongest. It can demonstrate that a certain class of experiences are so painful, complicated, and out of the reach of conscious awareness that the individual must express them in indirect representations and symbol formation. In the case of matted hair the symbol is a public one, but it is *recreated* each time by individuals. Moreover, the symbol would cease to exist (except in texts and nonliving icons) if individuals did not create it each time on the anvil of their personal anguish. For remember that, unlike the shaven head of the Buddhist monk, the matted hair is an *optional* tonsorial style. To be a Hindu ascetic you do not have to have matted hair, whereas a shaven head is an absolute role requisite for the monk.

The genesis of matted locks, or rather their re-creation by individuals, is linked with painful emotional experiences. In practically all cases three processes are noted.

1. Loss of sexual love – that is, the rejection of the husband's penis and an emotional-sexual relationship with him. The most dramatic representation of this process is Karunavati's (case 1) memory of the genesis of her matted locks: the husband vows to renounce sex and grant her a warrant to be reborn as a male when suddenly she is given seven matted locks.

2. Parallel with the movement away from the conjugal relationship is an intensification of an idealized relationship with a divine alter (an image of both husband and father). Always this relationship is established by "orgasmic" shaking of the body. The term orgasm is used advisedly; there is no technical term for orgasm in Sinhala, and many ecstatics have not experienced it in their ordinary sexual lives. The pleasure and release achieved through "shaking from within" is translated into religious language as a divine ecstasy.

3. The god's gift for having renounced eros for agape is matted hair. Psychologically, on the level of unconscious processes, the sublated penis emerges through the head. The matted hair, unlike the shaven head of the monk, does not represent castration for the ascetic, but rather stands for its very opposite: the denial of castration or loss of the penis. For in all of Hindu asceticism sexuality is not extinguished but suppressed. But why does it emerge from the head? Here we are dealing with the Hindu type of ascetics, not Leach's European pseudo ascetics. The consciousness of both may be similar in some fundamental ways, but the Hindu's consciousness has already been conditioned by his cultural heritage. The complex psychological experiences of the individual coalesce around the preexisting meanings imposed by his culture. In this case much of the thought is directly or indirectly derived from *yoga* and *tantra*. For example, in *kundalini yoga* the chief vein in the body is *susumna*, running along the spinal column. Situated along it are the six wheels, or *cakra*; these are centers of vital forces and psychic energy. At the top of this vein, beneath the skull, is *sahasrara*, a powerful psychic center symbol-

ized as the lotus (in turn a female-vaginal symbol). At the lowest *cakra* is *kundalini*, serpent power, which is generally quiescent. In *yoga* practice *kundalini* is aroused, it rises through the vein *susumna*, passes through all the *cakras*, and unites with the *sahasrara*, the lotus center. That some of these ideas exist in the minds of our informants is clear: Manci sees her matted hair as the vital breath that helps her turn her *cakras*. And of course we have Nandavati's matted lock that emerged from her head as a serpent (cobra). In my informants the vital forces are released with the *arude* or possession trance, in which the magnetism of the god infuses and suffuses the body of the priestess.

If the hair is the sublated penis emerging from the head, what kind of penis is it? Clearly it is no longer the husband's but the god's. But the relationship with the god is of a different order: eroticism is sublimated, idealized, and indirectly expressed. Gods, those idealized beings, cannot have penes like yours or mine; thus the matted hair is no ordinary penis but the god's *lingam*, the idealized penis, his *sakti*, the source of life and vitality. Hence on another level of meaning it is the life force itself, and its loss, according to Manci, heralds the death of its bearer. Thus the hair is a fusion of symptom and symbol. In some cases the hair emerges initially as a symptom . . . progressively it is transformed into symbol. In Karunavati (case 1) the symbol emerges full-fledged, obviating the necessity for symptom. The transformation of symptom into symbol is through the cultural patterning of consciousness, which in turn helps integrate and resolve the painful emotional experiences of the individual, converting eros into agape and patient into priest.

The god's gift establishes a contract, a close relationship between ecstatic and deity. This contract is expressed and sealed in several ways. The number of locks given is often the number possessed by a particular deity: six for Kataragama, seven or five for the god Huniyan, three for Huniyan as demon, and a hundred for Kali. Thus it is the god's own hair that is given, a manifestation of his grace, if one may use that word, and his love. The compact is sealed at Kataragama, generally by walking over the hot coals unscathed.

Personal meaning of (public) symbol

This must obviously be related to the genesis of the symbol but must not be confounded with it. The associations – personal and cultural – clustering around the symbol will help us unravel the personal meaning of the cultural symbol, primarily to the ascetics themselves and secondarily to members of the society.

To practically all ascetics the hair is smelly, dirty, lice-ridden, and uncomfortable, at least in its initial stages. Yet it is also something beautiful. . . .

The Sinhala term for matted hair is *hada palu*, meaning "beauty marks." The object that is held in fear and revulsion by the members of the society is called "beauty marks." I suspect that this semantic designation expresses the ascetics' point of view rather than the outsiders'.

From the public point of view the ascetics' matted locks contain a fleshy growth; practically every person described them as *mas dalu*, "buds of flesh," or "tender fleshy growths." Yet none of the ascetics claimed that their hair was entangled in fleshy growths, which of course is a realistic assessment. I suspect that the public reaction to the symbol is again related to the unconscious dimension of the symbol's origin: they are penes stuck on the head – fleshy growths.

The smelly associations of the symbol receive extra reinforcement from South Asian cultural beliefs pertaining to exuviae, most of which are viewed as polluting and dirty. Yet for these ascetics, as for some children, feces are also gold (Freud 1953).

Since the matted locks are a gift of the god, his sakti, there is power in them. They are religious objects, used for blessing audiences, holy relics that must be incensed and taken care of.

Cultural message and communication

Contrary to Leach, this aspect of the symbol is least amenable to analysis. Hence my view: There are (public) symbols and symbols; the handshake is different from matted locks in its meaning – its message. I shall develop this theme later; for the moment let us look at Leach's argument, which is one most social anthropologists would use. The meaning of matted hair is chastity: this meaning is laid down in texts. For them, nothing else is relevant. Yet note that to limit the meaning of this symbol to that one dimension is to deprive it of the rich symbolic associations presented earlier. Furthermore, are we sure that texts give us the correct information on such matters? Could not these texts, written by learned virtuosos, be rationalized explanations of observed ascetic behavior, or even be nothing but theological casuistry? If the message that is being communicated is a public conscious one – like the ideal typical handshake – then it would be easy enough to get the public reaction to the symbol and their explanations of it. Now here is the rub: not one member of the public that I interviewed at Kataragama could even vaguely associate matted hair with celibacy, except in an extremely indirect manner. They could state that ascetics ought to be celibate; but they need not have matted locks at all, and indeed most of them do not. "Penance" was closer to the public view. However, the most common reaction was emotional: fear, horror, disgust, revulsion. Practically all of them thought of matted hair as fleshy growths entangled in the hair as a result of neglect. Some believed the locks bled if wounded. Many, including educated informants, were puzzled when I explained that flesh does not grow from the head in that manner. Disgust with and fear of matted hair is inevitable, since it belongs to a larger class of polluted objects, exuviae. But beneath that it is likely that the symbol also evokes in some individuals deeper anxieties, such as those pertaining to castration anxiety.

Why is this the case? Because matted hair is a special type of symbol. It is manipulatory, that is, *used* by individuals. It is like other ritual symbols that are manipulated by the worshiper, but quite unlike a symbol that exists in a myth or story. Leach says, "the association between hair behavior and sex is not reestablished anew by each individual" (1958, p. 156). But he is wrong, for there is no obligation for the ascetic to adopt this hair style. Thus voluntarism or option is another characteristic of this type of symbol. I shall take up this theme later; here it is enough to assert that when choice exists the symbol may in fact be established anew by each individual and may be linked with complex personal experiences of the individual. Yet we noted that such experiences are orderly and, as we shall soon see, they are predictable: suppressed sexuality; transfer of a relationship from husband to god; the god's gift of grace. Underlying all is the core unconscious meaning of the sublated penis emerging via the head as the god's penis, his *lingam*, his *sakti*. That the symbol is related to the life experience of the ascetic does not mean that it is a private symbol: it only means that we have to reject the conventional wisdom that there is a radical hiatus between custom and emotion.

The matted hair of Leach's hypothetical pseudoascetic is a symptom, not a symbol. So is the matted hair of nonascetic beggars in Sri Lanka and India: they are simply dirty locks matted together through neglect. A symptom is a somatic manifestation of a psychic or physical malady. In my ascetics symptom is replaced by symbol. The symbol is generated primarily out of the unconscious; once generated, it exists on the public level as a cultural symbol. Through it the ascetics convey a public message: fear, revulsion. [One of the ascetics] Nandavati says people are afraid to look at her because of her matted locks. Socially the matted locks act as a marker to set aside their bearer as a special and redoubtable being. In this situation there is no need to draw a distinction between private and public symbols. All symbols are cultural and public; but a cultural symbol may exist on many levels – the personal and the social. It can communicate different messages, emotional and cognitive. The so-called private symbols are either symptoms (somatic signs) or fantasies, signs having ideational meaning only to the individual. Thus the oedipal father of psychopathology is not the real father: it is a fantasized image (Freud's imago) of the father, personal to the sufferer. It is not a symbol like god the father, which once again exists on both personal and cultural levels. A symbol, moreover, as many anthropologists have told us, does not exist by itself: it is part of a larger context. This can be

the personal-experiential context or an institutional context, . . .

Matted Hair and Shaven Head: Two Kinds of Psychological Symbolism

As I stated earlier, I prefer to define a symbol in cultural terms, and I qualify this view with the idea that there is no necessary contradiction between custom and emotion. It is entirely possible that such a contradiction may exist in some cultures. This depends on the relationship of emotion to public life. For example, in English elite culture, or in the academic culture of Western universities, there may in fact be a radical hiatus between culture and emotion; yet it is wrong to assume that this must be so in other societies. In the cults I describe, the underlying psychic conflict of the individual is permitted expression through public symbols, whereas in English elite life such conflict may be suppressed and not permitted cultural expression. In the latter situation a custom becomes purely formal, and like the ideal-typical handshake, a vehicle for the communication of a formal social message. Later on in this essay [see original] I shall discuss why this is the case, but for the moment let me get back to the discussion of matted hair as a symbol.

The communicative value of matted hair is, I have noted, not as important for ascetics as its personal meaning. Rather, it could best be explained in personal-experiential terms. I shall label the class of symbols to which matted hair belongs "personal symbols" – that is, cultural symbols whose primary significance and meaning lie in the personal life and experience of individuals. And individuals are also cultural beings or persons. There are only a few symbols that have exclusive personal meaning; hair has considerable social (interpersonal) meaning also, though it is vague and undifferentiated. Some symbols have both personal and interpersonal meaning, such as dress styles, where personal symbols are individually used and manipulated. Indeed, the looseness and ambiguity of such symbols are critical, since they facilitate manipulation. Even when symbols that have primary social and interpersonal significance are manipulated by individuals (in religious ritual, trance, and other emotional contexts), they become invested with personal experiential significance. Another feature of a personal symbol is option – choice or voluntariness involved in its use or manipulation. This is a basic difference between matted hair and shaven head. In the former there is choice, for there is no rule that says that an ascetic *must* have matted hair. The ascetic exercises an option, and that hair option is based on deep motivation. By contrast, the monk has no choice: all monks must shave their heads. In this case the link between motivation and symbol is never straightforward, and one finds people with a variety of motivations having little choice but to employ the symbol. In the latter case, the primary meaning of the symbol is interpersonal, intercommunicative. The symbol is part of a larger grammar; the shaven head is articulated with several symbols in a larger set: patched yellow robe, begging bowl, personal demeanor in public (eyes downcast, head bent). The articulation of a symbol in a larger set is true of all symbols used as cultural expressions. This is another reason why the matted hair of the beggar and the ascetic are different: the former is articulated to a set of symptoms, the latter to a larger set of symbols. In the case of shaven head, the primary psychological meaning of the symbol is *castration;* its further cultural meaning is *chastity;* its extended interpersonal message is *renunciation* when it is articulated with the larger grammar.

By the statement that the primary psychological meaning of the shaven head is castration, I mean that the shaven head is a *psychogenetic* symbol without being a personal one as is matted hair. Thus a psychological symbolism may be personal (matted hair); alternatively, it may be psychogenetic but not personal (shaven head). Psychogenetic symbols are also drawn from the imagery of dreams and the unconscious: both matted hair and shaven head are derived from the repertoire of the unconscious. But matted hair is personal in the sense that the symbol is re-created anew by the individual (option and manipulation), whereas the shaven head, though derived from the imagery of the unconscious, is not re-created anew (lack of choice, no manipulation). Thus a symbol can have psychogenetic meaning without having unconscious personal meaning; the symbol originating, as Leach says rightly, in the remote past has been given interpersonal, intercommunicative value (Leach 1958, p. 160). The personal symbol, by contrast, has unconscious, deep motivational and intracommunicative significance, for we know from G. H. Mead that symbolic communication can exist with one's own self (Mead 1934). The distinction between public and private symbols, between culture and emotion, is an artifact of Western culture. Other peoples can create (cultural) symbols that are also personal, a theme I shall develop later on in this essay.

[...]

REFERENCES

Berg, Charles. 1951. *The unconscious significance of hair.* London: George Allen and Unwin.

Freud, Sigmund. 1953. Character and anal eroticism. In *Collected Papers,* vol. 2, ed. Joan Rivière, pp. 45–50. London: Hogarth Press. Originally published 1908.

Hallowell, A. I. 1955. The recapitulation theory and culture. In *Culture and experience.* Philadelphia: University of Pennsylvania Press.

Iyer, L. K. Anantha Krishna. 1928, 1935. *The Mysore tribes and castes.* Mysore Government Press. (Vol. 2, 1928; vol. 1 1935.)

Leach, E. R. 1958. Magical hair. *Journal of the Royal Anthropological Institute* 88: 147–64.

Mead, G. H. 1934. *Mind, self and society,* ed. and with an introduction by Charles W. Morris. Chicago: University of Chicago Press.

Turner, Victor. 1967. Symbols in Ndembu ritual. In *Forest of symbols,* pp. 19–47. Ithaca: Cornell University Press.

30

Spirits and Selves in Northern Sudan: The Cultural Therapeutics of Possession and Trance

Janice Boddy

Janice Boddy is professor of anthropology at the University of Toronto. In addition to her acclaimed ethnography of women's culture in the northern Sudan (1989), she has edited a Somali life history (1994a) and completed a lengthy anthropological history of gender and the colonial encounter in the Sudan.

If time and space are culturally (symbolically) articulated, so too is the person and even, Boddy suggests, the self. Indeed, the problem for northern Sudanese village women, she avers, is that their selfhood is "culturally overdetermined." Boddy's essay is located on the border of religion and healing, a rich field that we only touch on in this anthology. She shows how practices like spirit possession are not merely reactions to problems – symptoms, indices, calculated strategies, etc. – but culturally shaped, meaningful acts and idioms that provide the space for the kinds of predication and reflection that we have seen invoked in previous essays. Also, where many studies of Islam represent exclusively male experience, Boddy turns to the other half of Muslim society. While most ethnographic accounts have portrayed homogeneous cultural realities that stem implicitly from the perspective of male elders, recent feminist work has demonstrated the internal diversity and contestability of religious perspectives and practices. Good feminist critique in the anthropology of religion includes Bamberger (1974) and Delaney (1986).

Boddy's essay unfolds in two movements. She first delineates the cultural formation of moral women and then shows how spirit possession provides an equally cultural alternative, at once distinct, different, and dialogical, a form of counter-hegemonic discourse (Boddy 1989) and its own font of creativity. Boddy is particularly deft in recognizing

From Janice Boddy, "Spirits and Selves in Northern Sudan: The Cultural Therapeutics of Possession and Trance," *American Ethnologist* 15(1) (1988): 4–27. Reprinted by permission of the American Anthropological Association. Abridged.

explanations for spirit possession based on relative social deprivation on the one side and psychoanalytic arguments on the other, while avoiding the reductive tendencies of both. Instead she opts for a more reflexive and phenomenological stance.

Spirit possession itself is fascinating for the way it combines an order of collective thought in the distinctions among the spirits as a semiotic system and a collective practice whereby spirits are provided with the spaces in which to perform. Possession thus provides a context in which contemporary experience can be actively mediated by past myth models, and vice versa. Second, it provides an instance in which the collective and personal clearly interpenetrate. Collective forms are internalized by individuals and, as Boddy shows, become self-transforming.

In Northern Arabic-speaking Sudan, numerous women – and very few men – are diagnosed to be suffering at some point in their lives from illness attributed to *zar*, a type of spirit possession. In Hofriyat, a village on the Nile some kilometers downstream from Khartoum, I found that in different years, 42 percent (1977) and 47 percent (1984) of women ever married and over the age of 15 have succumbed to this affliction.[1] Marital status is a significant factor in possession illness. *Zairan* (*zar* spirits), Hofriyati assert, rarely trouble themselves with the unwed – with women whose fertility has yet to be activated. Most affected are those between the ages of 35 and 55, among whom two-thirds acknowledge themselves to be possessed. The latter proportion is due to a cumulative effect: once possessed, a woman is always possessed thereafter.

This paper offers an interpretation, grounded in the Hofriyati world, of the *zar* cult and women's participation in it. My concern is to avoid viewing possession phenomena in terms that, though our culture finds them accessible, are foreign to Hofriyati – whether biochemical reactions to nutritional deficiency (cf. Kehoe and Giletti 1981), or women's instrumental efforts to assuage their subordinate status by acquiring goods or garnering attention (cf. Lewis 1971, 1986). Such approaches may prove fruitful in assessing and translating specific cases of possession illness, but since they neither account for possession forms, nor adequately credit the taken-for-grantedness of spirits in the everyday lives of the possessed, ultimately they distort and impoverish what they propose to understand. If the aim of the enterprise is to comprehend the scope of possession phenomena, to situate them in their cultural contexts, ethnographers must attend to their informants' experiences of possession and not seek merely to explain them away as something at once less dramatic and more clinical than they appear.

In what follows, I observe that, as others (for example, Bastide 1958; Crapanzano 1973, 1977, 1980; Lambek 1981, n.d.; Kapferer 1983; Kleinman 1980; Metraux 1959; Nelson 1971; Obeyesekere 1981) who have investigated such cults have found, spirit possession in Sudan is concerned with fundamental questions of identity and selfhood. Further, the preponderance of women among the possessed can be seen to derive from an interplay of factors, salient among them women's reproductive function as it is culturally constructed in Hofriyat. A major issue addressed by the *zar* is, I suggest, a problem of socialization: the cultural overdetermination of women's selves. And, although I agree that possession trance and ritual are legitimate psychotherapy, I would not stop short, as have others who pursue this approach (Bourguignon 1979: 290–1; Kennedy 1967: 191; Prince 1964: 115), of acknowledging their potential to foster insightful reflection in the possessed. The province of *zar* is meaning, and it is best addressed in that light.

The Cultural Context: Female Selves

Hofriyat is a village of some 500 Arabic-speaking Muslim residents and is similar in size, character, and composition to dozens of other farming settlements that cling to the Nile in the desert north of Khartoum. Hofriyati are loosely organized into a number of patrilineal, variably corporate, and putatively endogamous descent groups. Ideally, marriage takes place between patrilateral parallel cousins but in practice the majority of couples are close cognatic kin whose natal families reside in Hofriyat. The most important criterion of marriageability is that the families of prospective spouses be bound, prior to their wedding, by a thick net of moral obligation, the legacy of past intermarriages and generations of ramifying kinship. In Hofriyat, marriage is informed by an idiom or symbolic orientation I have elsewhere termed "interiority" (1982; 1989): an inward focus, a concern for limiting social and physical openings, which constitutes a general organizing paradigm and aesthetic standard of Hofriyat culture. "Interiority" expresses the defensive orientation of the village, an orientation sustained, in part, by a history of invasion, colonization, and exploitation from without, and similar to the stance of other peoples living in precarious social and physical environments (cf. Fans 1972; Isbell 1978).

The idiom of interiority or defense underwrites a range of other customs (ādāt), significant among them the genital operation performed on female children known as pharaonic circumcision (excision of the labia and clitoris followed by almost complete infibulation: intentional occlusion of the vulva entailing obliteration of the vaginal meatus). According to villagers, this operation complements the procedure of removing the penile prepuce for Hofriyati boys and, like it, is performed between the ages of 5 and 10. Prepubescent circumcision accomplishes the social definition of a child's sex by removing physical traits deemed appropriate to his or her opposite: external genitalia in the case of females, the covering or "veil" of the penis in the case

of males (cf. also Assaad 1980: 4). The socially salient reproductive organ of the male is established as such when exposed, and that of the female – the womb – when covered and enclosed. Genital surgery ritually initiates the process of genderization, and implicitly identifies neophytes with their gender-appropriate spheres of operation as adults: the interiors of houseyards enclosed by high mud walls in the case of females; the outside world of farmlands, markets, other villages, and cities in the case of males. Females are associated with enclosure, with the maintenance of life within the village; males are associated with the precarious outside world, with political and economic life. Following their operations children begin to perform gender-specific tasks and are increasingly segregated from their counterparts.

[...]

Although circumcision restrains female sexuality, this is not, [women] say, its purpose. The surgery, in that it is "hot" or "painful" (ḥārri), prepares a girl for womanhood; makes her body clean, smooth, and pure; renders her marriageable; confers on her the right to bear children; and invests her with fertility (cf. Boddy 1982). Fertility and sexuality are, of course, two sides of the same coin, yet each sex emphasizes one more than the other. Both point to a fundamental concern in Hofriyat with human reproduction, the responsibility for which rests principally with women. Only when physically transformed and shaped to the image of human morality can they be entrusted to reproduce.

Women's susceptibility to possession is, I submit, closely bound up with the implications of pharaonic circumcision for a female child's developing self-perception and is, I will argue below, indicative of women's problematic, socially overdetermined selfhood. I suggest that through this operation and ancillary procedures involving heat or pain – the two are equated here – appropriate feminine dispositions are being inculcated in young girls, dispositions which, following Bourdieu (1977: 15), are embedded in their bodies not only physically, but also cognitively and emotionally, in the form of mental inclinations, "schemes of perception and thought." The trauma of pharaonic circumcision alone is insufficient to cultivate a prescriptively feminine self: such acts must also be meaningful to those who undergo and reproduce them. For villagers, meaning is carefully built up through metaphors and associations that operate implicitly and overtly to establish an identification of circumcised women with morally appropriate fertility, thence to orient them subjectively toward their all-important generative and transformative roles in Hofriyati society.

[...]

Both men's and women's everyday experience is informed by the inward orientation of Hofriyat; yet the surgically altered bodies of women actively symbolize this cultural logic and their society's principal values. In this exist some additional implications for women's identity: (1) Hofriyati women bear the onus of maintaining those values, a responsibility amplified by increasing male labor emigration (cf. Hale 1985); (2) women, who are identified with the inside, are not only protected but also dependent; and (3) intrusions of powerful forces from without are more likely to be registered in female bodies than in male ones.

Taking these points in order, not only does a village woman's self-image rest squarely with her procreative ability, but also her sense of worth and social value. For only by giving birth, legitimately, to sons, might she achieve a position of respect and informal authority and, correspondingly, might her husband fulfill the ideal male role as founder of a lineage section. But more than this, the equation of femininity with socialized fertility and of the female marital role with reproduction means that responsibility for ensuring successful procreation – for giving men fitting, properly raised descendants and continuing society – belongs almost entirely to women. So, in the first stage of this process, if a woman fails to conceive within a year or two of her marriage, if she miscarries, bears a stillborn child, produces a daughter with her first pregnancy, or loses an unweaned infant, it is her ability to procreate that is called into question, not her husband's, and it is she who suffers as a result, through divorce or co-wifery. Such occurrences illuminate a fundamental contra-diction for women in Hofriyat: they are collectively indispensable to society while individually dispensable to men. At the very least, fertility problems place intense strain on a woman's self-image and often fragile marital relations.

As noted earlier, the sexes are segregated. Women are expected to spend most of their time within family compounds bounded by high mud-brick walls; men, on the other hand, have considerable mobility. The sexes rarely eat together, and never do so in public or before guests. In traditional households – the majority – they also sleep in separate quarters. In most respects there is a significant rift between men's and women's worlds, which is widened by labor emigration, entailing prolonged separations of husbands from their wives (cf. Kennedy 1978: 10 for Egyptian Nubians).

Within this polarized world, the sexes are conceived to be economically and productively interdependent: husbands and adult sons bear primary responsibility for production – they provide for their families through wage labor and/or farming – whereas wives and adult daughters consume and transform materials into items for consumption. Related to this, the essential dialectic between husband and wife, set in motion at their wedding, is that between producer and social reproducer. The dual role of a married woman, that of consumer and reproducer, is aptly expressed in symbols and metaphors that identify her with pigeons and livestock: domestic animals kept within family houseyards, fed on grain and fodder supplied by male labor, and valued – apart from their use as food – for their capacity to beget offspring.

In other matters, asymmetric gender complementarity extends to religion and, until recently, education. Men participate fully in the public rites of Islam and most, having learned the Qu'ran, are functionally literate. They belong with rare exception to one of the two religious fraternities in the area and regularly attend their ceremonies, called *zikrs*. On the other hand, women over the age of 25 are largely illiterate. They perform their daily prayers in private, if at all, and only the elderly among them attend mosque. Women are sometimes permitted to watch a *zikr* but are always barred from active participation, and whether at mosque or a *zikr*, they are segregated from men.

As these points demonstrate, neither sexual complementarity nor the symbolic value of femininity implies gender equivalence. A woman's life is subject to notable constraints in Hofriyat: she is forever a jural minor, morally and financially governed by her male kin, subordinate also to her husband. Moreover, since personal integrity, dignity, and emotional control are highly valued in both sexes, and displays of emotion considered vulgar – especially so in mixed company – a woman may be hard pressed to dispute her husband or brothers should she feel wronged.

However constrained their interactions, and however weighted the system would seem in favor of males, it must be remembered that both sexes participate in and reproduce Hofriyati culture. Both are subject to its pressures, though in different ways; for both there are advantages and disadvantages, if men are better able to cope with problems in a marriage by taking a second wife or divorcing the first, they are still under considerable obligation to conform to kinship values, masculine ideals, and the tenets of Islam. If women are more restricted than men in other ways, they are less constrained with regard to religion: they are neither expected to become familiar with matters of liturgy and doctrine, nor to have sufficient moral strength on their own to uphold them. Phrased positively, this means that women are relatively freer to embrace what men consider folk beliefs, those having so-called pagan elements and in whose company they place the *zar*. . . .

Although men publicly scorn the *zar*, privately they are not so intractable. For they, too, recognize the superior powers of *zairan*, and, feminine associations notwithstanding, a few told me they believe themselves to be possessed but would not openly admit to the affliction for fear of losing face. So, despite appearances of opposition, men tolerate women's involvement in the cult and are generally willing to provide for the spirits' demands. Few are inclined to doubt its efficacy.

Zairan and Zar Possession

In order to grasp what is involved in women's possession, we need to know something more about the spirits themselves. *Zairan* belong to a class of beings known as *jinn*, whose existence is substantiated in several verses of the Qu'ran. According to Hofriyati, jinn are the physical complementaries of humans in a holistic, quadripartite creation: where humans are composed of earth and water (Adam, the first human, is said to have been fashioned by Allah from moist clay), jinn are made up of fire and wind, or air. Humans are visible, substantial, and diurnal; jinn are normally invisible (though able to take human shape), formless, and nocturnal. Thus, jinn are natural beings – they are born, eventually they die – but their nature is such that they cannot wholly be confined by physical barriers like those (bodies, walls, and so forth) that contain human beings. They are therefore able to infiltrate humans and take possession of them at will. Once in possession, a jinn can influence the health and behavior of its human host; it does so either from within the body or by taking up a position above the head.

Most jinn are assimilated into three categories, coded by color. White jinn are benign; posession by one is not serious and in fact may go unnoticed. Black jinn or devils (*shawātīn*) bring grave disease and intractable mental illness; possession by one is a dire matter and curable, if at all, only by violent exorcism. Sickness caused by a black jinn might well result in death. Last, there are red jinn or *zairan*, whose color points to a characteristic association with blood and human fertility. These are pleasure-seeking, capricious, ambivalent beings that bring milder forms of illness which, though initially distressful, never result in death or severe mental dysfunction. Should someone who is *zar* possessed fall critically ill, then natural causes or sentient agents other than *zairan* are implicated. *Zairan* must be placated and do not respond kindly to attempted exorcism.

Zar possession is a lifelong, fundamentally incurable condition that is, however, manageable. Indeed, after its initial stages, it may be transformed out of all resemblance to what we might consider illness. The possessed can hope to gain some control over her symptoms first, by accepting – both subjectively and publicly – the possession diagnosis, then by undergoing a curing ceremony during which she enters, via trance, into a contractual relationship with the spirit(s) responsible for her lapse in health. During the ceremony chants are drummed invoking the schedule of named *zairan*. When the spirit that plagues her is summoned, the patient ideally enters trance; now identified, the intruder manifests itself through her body and makes known its demands, in return for which it should agree to restore, and refrain from further jeopardizing, her well-being.

Yet the successful conclusion of a woman's curing ceremony by no means ends her association – in or out of trance – with her *zar*. The spirit is said to remain above her, ready to enter her body at will. From a spirit's perspective, contracts with humans are infinitely renegotiable: if the possessed wishes to allay further attack from her *zar* she must mollify it continually. This requires her regular attendance at the *zar* ceremonies of others and performance of certain ritual acts on the spirit's behalf (for example, staining her hands or feet with henna in a particular [spirit] design). Should spirit or human neglect to uphold their agreement at any time, the latter may suffer relapse of her former illness. Yet the "cure" has opened communications between the two and any future difficulties can be dealt with expeditiously. If all goes well, what begins as an uneasy truce between a willful spirit and its reluctant host might graduate to positive symbiosis as their relationship stabilizes and matures.

One thing that the hedonistic *zar* hopes to gain by possessing a human being is a venue for access to the human world in ceremonial contexts where it can frolic and be entertained. Thus, when a spirit is ritually summoned by its chant, it simultaneously infiltrates each of its entranced hosts so as to interact with the human assembly through their bodies. Such rituals are always fraught with tension and surprise, for at any moment a woman might be "seized" by a spirit that Hofriyati did not before know existed, or she did not know she

had. One by one, throughout an evening's drumming, the spirits "descend" (*nazal*) into their hosts in the order that their chants are played. A spirit enters its host when called upon and, if well behaved, relinquishes her body when its chant is over and the rhythm shifts to that of another *zar*. Since an adept may be possessed by several different spirits at once, a woman might be in and out of trance all night as her various spirits descend and manifest themselves for up to 20 minutes each. When not entranced she participates in the drumming and chanting while observing other women who are.

Thus, in Hofriyat a woman is not considered to be possessed because she becomes entranced; rather, she becomes entranced because she is possessed. According to villagers, since possession trance fulfills their part of a bargain with the spirit world to restore and maintain human health, it is not pathological but therapeutic. Yet just how it might be therapeutic remains unresolved, and is an issue I will shortly address. On leaving trance women say they "see things differently" and they "feel well," statements that might be construed as affirming that the state itself has intrinsic remedial powers. But, even should this be the case, to limit the therapeutic value of *zar* to that of trance would be artificial and inadequate. The *zar* rite is a cultural therapy; its curative powers derive less from a virtual experience of trance than from the entire possession context that renders it, and countless other experiences, meaningful. Indeed, an individual's experience of trance is largely constructed by its context: in Hofriyat, possession provides her with a model of what trance is and should be like.

Still, if trance is an integral part of possession therapy and relapse prophylaxis, it is only one manifestation of possession, not consistently evinced by the possessed during ceremonies and, when evinced, variable in apparent depth and duration from one individual to the next. Not all who enter trance do so for immediate therapeutic motives; many who manifest their spirits do not feel sick at the time, though they are classed as ill. A *zar* rite is more than just a cure; it is also referred to as a "party" (*bafla*) (cf. Saunders 1977 on *zar* in Egypt). Despite its solemn aim to alleviate suffering, it can be a great deal of fun, mixing comedy, satire, and intellectual challenge in a heady atmosphere where nothing is quite as it seems. Possession trance is, I contend, therapeutic, but its therapeutic potential is broad, not confined to achieving a medical or psychological cure, and lies as much with observing it in others as experiencing it oneself. Even the experience of it is subordinate to an earlier acceptance of a possession diagnosis. In short, the relevant issue in the case of the *zar* is not trance per se, but trance firmly situated in a meaningful cultural context – possession – having medical, social, psychological, and often profound aesthetic implications. Before considering these, the nature of the illness that signals possession remains to be addressed.

Possession as Illness

Here I will begin to pull together the threads of my argument, indicating how possession is linked to what I consider is Hofriyati women's problematic selfhood. But on this issue, especially, I walk the ethnographer's unsteady line between keeping faith with informants' experience of their world and rendering that experience intelligible in the more familiar parlance of Western culture. In the attempt I must surely transgress realities on either side. For the *zar* in Hofriyat is a holistic phenomenon; it penetrates every facet of human existence. Consequently, it defies analytic reduction to a single constituent dimension: psychological, medical, or social, with which members of Western cultures might feel more at home (cf. Crapanzano 1977: 11). I have no doubt that in partially subjecting the possession idiom to an alien culture's constructs, some of its texture, richness, and cultural integrity will be lost. But similarly, in adapting concepts that have accepted meanings in our culture to aspects of another in which they do not exactly apply, the concepts – such as "illness," "person," or "self" – may be altered. The result is a partial distortion from either perspective. Yet, as the *zar* itself proposes, distortions can sometimes be instructive.

By now it is commonplace to say that a sociocultural system provides the stresses that

trigger the illnesses to which its members succumb, directs those members' coping responses, and furnishes an interpretive framework which renders their experiences meaningful, enables them to be expressed, and suggests possible therapeutic resolutions. Earlier I described some stresses and constraints to which Hofriyati women are exposed, and noted the strong identification they are implicitly and materially subjected, in the Foucaultian sense (Foucault 1980: 97), to feel with their fertility. When a woman's fertility mandate is impaired – for whatever reason – her self-image, social position, and ultimately general health are threatened. Women undergoing severe marital and/or fertility crises tend to phrase their experiences as illness or, less directly, to co-locate their difficulties with the onset of apparently unrelated physical symptoms. In thus complaining of illness, a woman avails herself of a culturally sanctioned medium for articulating her dysphoria (Constantinides 1977: 65; cf. Kleinman 1980: passim; with specific reference to complaints of possession illness, cf. Crapanzano 1977, Firth 1967, Lambek 1981, Obeyesekere 1970). Once this is done she can act upon her problems, where before she could not, by setting out to find a cure. The woman who claims to be ill but does not appear diseased does not feign sickness; her pain is real and may be attributed to what, from her perspective, are natural agents: *zairan.*

Hofriyati themselves link fertility problems and illness, although more subtly and obliquely than I have just proposed. A woman who is anxious or depressed is considered a prime target for *zairan* seeking entry to the human world; should such a spirit descend upon her it makes her feel "unwell." But, tautologically, *zairan* are able to create the very circumstances that make a woman anxious and prone to spirit assault. Their most common tactic is to "seize," "hold," or "steal" offspring, bringing about miscarriage, stillbirth, amenorrhea, or other problems affecting women's blood. Thus spirits can hold a woman's future and that of her husband for ransom, forcing both to acknowledge their presence and accede to their demands. *Zairan* have considerable leverage over human reproduction, and for this reason also are drawn to married women and unlikely to beset the unwed. However, not all possession incidents can be traced to uncertain fertility. . . .

[. . .]

. . . The demands of possessive spirits that their hosts eat "clean" foods; abstain from traditional mourning behavior such as sleeping on the ground; bathe with imported (Lux) soap; use henna and cologne; wear gold and clean clothing; and avoid overwork, anger, and frustration with kin, all have to do with the maintenance of feminine ideals. Combined with the link between possession and fertility, the above points suggest that for Hofriyati women, possession is intimately bound up with feminine self-image and standards of conduct. It is a condition perpetrated by capricious external agents, which demand preservation of a woman's ideal self, but may create or seize upon a situation in which these ideals are jeopardized in order to take control of her body, thus transforming it into a vessel of otherness. This they do so as ultimately to enjoy the earthly pleasure that upholding such ideals provides. But, more convoluted still, the spirits that so admire Hofriyati womanhood are themselves exemplars of its antithesis. This is really the crux of the possession phenomenon, and requires further explication.

Discussion: Spirits and Female Selves

[. . .]

Zairan inhabit a world parallel to our own and contiguous with it, yet imperceptible to humans except under certain conditions. Like us, they are divided into ethnic groups, families, occupations, and religions. They are either male or female (principally the former), and children, adults, or elders. They are neither wholly good nor wholly bad but, like humans, something of both. Their salient characteristics are ambivalence, amorality, and caprice, in all of which they differ from humans only by excess. Among their numbers are the spirit analogues of Muslim saints, Turkish administrators, "Europeans" (including North

Americans, Hindus, and Chinese), Ethiopians, Syrian gypsies, West Africans, nomadic Arabs, and Southern Sudanese, in short, of all human groups with whom Hofriyati have had contact over the past 150 years or more. Each spirit within these categories is named and has an individual history, typical behaviors when appearing in the human world, and relationships with other *zairan* that crosscut ethnic and religious lines.

Significantly, the spirits that possess Hofriyati belong only to foreign societies: villagers have no *zairan* that match themselves. Indeed, *zairan* epitomize all that is *not* Hofriyati in an integral, sentient universe; they are quintessential "others," at once physically, socially, and culturally alien to human villagers. This is especially true for Hofriyati women, since *zairan* represent extreme exteriority: they are powerful outsiders par excellence. Even Muslim *zairan*, exhibiting the positive traits of piety and self-control, ultimately subvert local values by being wed exogamously, to non-kin adherents of other faiths. Unlike circumcised, socialized women, who represent a victory of *aqel* over their naturally dominant *nafs* – of social concerns over self-interest – *zairan* are beings in whom *nafs* is permitted free rein.

Considering the qualities of *zairan* and villagers' cultural logic, it is unsurprising that women should be thought more vulnerable than men to spirit assault. Clearly this has broader implications than for diagnosing individual illness. This is so because for Hofriyati, who have a keen sense of who they are and how they differ from outsiders (cf. also Kennedy 1978), it is not only fertility but cultural identity that is vested in women's selves. In local thought the body is a virtual microcosm of village society (cf. Douglas 1966, 1973). Like village boundaries, body orifices are ambiguous, however necessary and inevitable. They are prone to a litany of dangers – spirit intrusion not least – and regulated by complex ritual procedures. They are considered best, both defensively and aesthetically, if kept as small as possible. The most ambiguous and problematic body opening is the vaginal meatus, for it is through women's bodies and uterine blood that village society can be renewed appropriately, from within itself, or inappropriately opened up to potentially destructive influences from without. So a woman's fertility must be defended, reserved and safeguarded first by pharaonic circumcision, then by endogamous marriage.

This brings us back to the issue of feminine self-image. I have discussed how through circumcision a woman's body is transformed into a living vessel of her culture's moral values, and she is thereafter exhorted to conduct herself accordingly. Female circumcision, plus the entire complex of associations and practices that express and realize femininity, strongly support the identification of the individual with her role – both social and symbolic – in Hofriyati culture.[2] This is the point: so tangibly socialized are women to this view of themselves that, for many, to experience the world otherwise is to experience it, quite literally, as a non-Hofriyati.

Thus reformulated, a central problem that possession addresses, in hundreds of idiosyncratic ways, is the cultural overdetermination of women's selfhood. To review the various concepts of "self" and "person" found in the literature is beyond the scope of this paper (see Carrithers, Collins, and Lukes 1985); however, let me clarify my analytical usage of these terms before giving closer consideration to the Hofriyati case. Drawing upon Burridge's argument in *Someone, No One: An Essay on Individuality* (1979), and, in a parallel vein, from Kegan's constructive-developmental psychology (1982), the self as a theoretical construct can be provisionally conceptualized, not as an entity, but as a creative energy or process, which actively engages the world, integrating the human biological organism with its physical and sociocultural environments, continually moving, becoming, maturing, making and organizing meaning (Burridge 1979: 5ff., 21; Kegan 1982: 2–15; cf. Elster 1986). Burridge writes, "the fact of integration – some sort of coherence or coordination of the parts of constituents of being – does not detach the integrative energy or self from its constituents, but still makes it more than the sum of the parts and, in that sense, conceptually and empirically distinct" [1979: 5]. In these terms, a self that is integrating in conformity with others realizes the "person": "[one] who, in repro-

ducing in word and deed the norms of a given traditional order, manifests the relations of that tradition" (1979: 5). In Hofriyat, the extreme identification of women with the cultural image of womanhood precipitates such a compression of the subjective self into an objective female person: a normative set of given roles and statuses, an entity in whom experience is continuously subordinated to cultural categories (Burridge 1979: 28, passim), a publicly confirmed social representation (La Fontaine 1985: 124). The projections of significant others – just as determined, perhaps, by feminine images and ideals – dominate her internal dialogue. She is compelled to personhood.

What the Hofriyati woman does not become or, better, is not at this stage given scope to become, is, in Burridge's terms, an "individual": a "moral critic who envisages another kind of social or moral order" (1979: 5).

> Becoming aware of a gap between the person's reproductions and the truth of things by seizing on or being seized by peculiarly significant events, the self is moved to a transcendance of the traditional categories, to a reintegration of the event in a new rationalization assigning new meaning and relevance. In this transcendance and reintegration, manifest in the new rationalization, the self realizes the individual. [1979: 7]

Burridge suggests that most people oscillate between these two integrative moments (p. 5); yet, given the close identification women are encouraged to feel with their fertility, the quotidian Hofriyati context actively conspires against such movement and the realization of "individuality" in their case. It effectively denies them the possibility to grow in self-awareness, to mature, to reflect on the categories of early socialization in which selfhood is enmeshed. Women's selfhood is, I submit, culturally overdetermined.

Why overdetermined? Because, paradoxically, the moral self-image women are enjoined to assume cannot always be sustained by experience. In this lies an ambiguity inherent to morality – between what is and what ought to be – which their continuous socialization may eventually fail to overcome: the woman who is, by definition, "morally appropriate fertility," may experience infertility or some other significant contravention of her feminine self-image.

The tension that the awareness of such untoward experience creates in her is first construed as a problem of internal disorder and registered as illness: in Hofriyat, body and person are not distinguished; hence, threats to one's sense of self and to the world in which one's self is located automatically jeopardize physical well-being. When this is coupled with the restriction on expressing emotion, the somatization of her dysphoria seems a normal, culturally appropriate response (cf. Kleinman 1980). It has the added effect of directing attention toward the one imperiled and away from a precipitating context likely to involve close superordinate kin, whom women, especially, feel powerless to rebuke or entreat. This leads to an important point: the feminine self in Hofriyat is constituted not only, as I have suggested, ideally, but also (among other ways) relationally. It is a virtual impossibility for a villager to think of himself or herself except in relation to kin. Thus illness, as an idiom for the expression of threatened selfhood, actually defends certain constituents of the self, notably, its formative relationships.

A great many villagers somatize negative affect, but not all go on to consider their illness a symptom of possession. Such admission signals a profound transformation of context, from one narrowly described by idioms of interiority that govern the commonsense world, to a broader one that places this orientation in relation to its converse: dysphoria for the possessed originates not within the self and its constituents, but outside them, indeed, outside the human world of Hofriyat. This, on the one hand, rationalizes the untoward event in a way which vehemently defends the socialized self, for the self's experience is again subordinated to "natural" categories – zairan – however extraordinary they might seem. From an observer's perspective, zairan symbolize and render concrete a woman's experiences of the world that conflict with her consensually validated view of what that experience should be like.

Thus, with acceptance of a possession diagnosis comes disassociation of the experience

from her self. Yet this not only supports her self-image, but also plants the seeds of its modification. First, by shifting the context of her illness from one of internal contradiction to external confrontation, of self or self-and-village-other to self-plus-alien-spirit, the potential for a negotiated resolution becomes apparent. More than this, zairan are representatives of non-Hofriyati cultures and by virtue of their extraordinariness, of their abilities and powers, of their failure to conform with local norms and rules even as they intervene in the course of village life, possession as a human condition allows for the possibility of ambiguity and otherness, otherwise lacking in the gender socialization process for women in Hofriyat. The context of the possessed's situation is now widened to incorporate the actions of beings from an alien yet parallel world. Both the entropy of well-being and location of its source in possession open up pathways for self-renewal, permitting a limited and, in this context, functional dissonance between person and self. In such cases illness itself may be therapeutic.

What I am describing is, I think, rather different from what appears to happen in emotional disorders common to Western cultures. If the self is truly a social construct and individual selves are constructed (cf. Berger and Luckmann 1967) or integrated (Burridge 1979) in the course of social interaction, the constituents and parameters of selfhood can be expected to vary from society to society. So, while parallels can be found between hysterical neurosis and Hofriyati possession, in that both conditions involve dissociation and may present initially as somatic complaints, these may be more obvious than real (cf. Ward 1982: 416). The two "illnesses" are grounded in disparate cultural contexts, based on rather different conceptualizations of the self. At the risk of simplification, perhaps one could characterize certain neuroses in Western cultures, where "self" is conceived as a bounded, individuated entity (cf. Geertz 1983: 59), as an overdetermination of selfhood whose symptoms are excessive subjectivity – a weakening of the ability to take the role of the "other" relative to one's self. In Hofriyat, where the essential feminine self is highly idealized, the problem seems to be one of excessive objectification: self is firmly identified with village "other" and identity emotionally realized in cultural symbolism to the point where any event perceived to negate that tenuous equation negates the woman's self. Thus, the most striking similarities occur between the normative process of curing or accommodating possession illness (that is, disengaging the self from its context) and the aberrant one of developing a neurosis – resulting in many an unfortunate lay observation that adepts are chronic hysterics. Despite thorough disassociation of the untoward event from the Hofriyati woman's self, she does not, like the textbook hysteric, unconsciously deny her experiences of otherness so much as embrace them, while consciously recognizing them as aspects of her being over which she has limited if potentially increasing control.

If we see spirits as symbolic of symptoms (cf. Obeyesekere 1981: 34–5), and symptoms as idiomatic of spirit intrusion (cf. Kapferer 983: 87; Lambek 1981: 53), we do not stray far from Hofriyati logic. But if we view spirits and symptoms as dissociated facets of the possessed woman's self, as our own psychology might direct us to do (cf. LaBarre 1975: 41; Bourguignon 1979: 286), we violate villagers' reality. We tacitly dismiss *zairan* as facts of Hofriyati existence and mistakenly employ a highly individualistic and compartmentalized concept of the self which has no basis in village culture. This, in turn, leads to an individualistic orientation to illness which, because it rarely addresses social context, misses the point of most illness in Hofriyat, including possession. Moreover, even the assumption that spirits represent projections of intolerable feelings is, as Crapanzano (1977: 12) notes, a debatable one: spirits, like the illnesses they cause, originate outside the human self, not within it. Unlike Western psychotherapy, which encourages the patient to accept and integrate previously dissociated feelings as part of herself, *zar* therapy works by convincing her to recognize them as separated from herself in the first place. Clearly, any attempt to merge such feelings and experiences with the Hofriyati woman's self – which I have described as idealized and relational, but is, after all, her

self – would be ethnopsychiatrically inappropriate. It could only deny her the validity of that self and potentially do more harm than good.

Again from an observer's perspective, one way to make sense of all this is by reference to the concept of framing. Following Elster (1986: 27), the Hofriyati woman's illness is "reframed" by a diagnosis of possession in such a way that the precipitating behavior or event – for example, infertility – becomes compatible with her self-image: she *is* fertile, for spirits have seen fit to usurp this most valuable asset. She generalizes that future untoward experiences do not undermine the equation of womanhood with fertility and all the rest; they signify the actions of *zairan*, who, unlike humans, are capricious and unpredictable. But for this there is a remedy. Thus, although dissociation may be psychologically adaptive for both Western neurotics and Hofriyati possessed, only for the former may it be symptomatic of pathology. For Hofriyati it is therapeutic. Most of those who acknowledge possession are competent, mentally healthy women who have responded in a culturally appropriate way to a stressful situation (cf. Crapanzano 1977: 14).

When a village woman who feels unwell but has identified no organic or mystical source for her complaint accepts that she is possessed, she can begin to recover. Her possessive spirit or spirits, soon to be revealed, gradually take shape as a part of her being which is not, so to speak, a part of her person, her Hofriyati self. It is during possession trance that the identity and characteristics of this non-kin, non-Hofriyati, non-human, but above all non-self-existent are publicly established, both for the woman and those who observe her. Once established, this veritable non-self is linked, inextricably, to her self; it is not, however, integrated with her person, a situation that possession rituals stress and seek to maintain. Still, though rarely manifest in her body, the spirit constituents of her non-self are in constant attendance, influencing her decisions and perceptions to the point where some of my informants spoke of themselves as if they were pluralities, substituting "we" (*nehna*) for "I" (*ānā*). Furthermore, since a spirit might possess any number of Hofriyati simultaneously, a woman's non-self, like her self, is unlikely to be individualistic: possession by a common spirit binds her to other Hofriyati selves and *zar* non-selves, yet in ways other than those specified by kinship, providing new ways to think about human relationships.

The felt presence of a "non-self" enhances, by opposition, a woman's sense of personhood, continuously affirming the integrity of what once might have been problematic. Though exogenous to her self, the non-self is, and becomes increasingly, essential to the self's comprehension (cf. Young 1975:578). Conversely, however, a woman's sense of self provides a negative ground by which to apprehend the parameters of her spirits. These two aspects of her being are maintained in contra-position throughout her life, neither reducing to its opposite, each becoming enriched in sympathy with the other, shifting, expanding, or contracting as their mutual situation changes over time.

In this way possession enables a woman to evolve, to recontextualize her experiences from a broadened perspective (cf. Kegan 1982). *Zairan* posit alternative sets of moral discriminations that are realized and displayed through her body and others' during trance. As detailed below, the observation and enactment of such episodes provides the possibility, by no means the assurance, that the integrating self will be "seized with a contrary or critical perception" (Burridge 1979:28) and empowered to alter her conditioning, to transcend the categories that have constrained her, to recognize them for what they are – cultural constructs, not immutable truths. The paradox of Hofriyati possession is that it defends the person while also enabling the self: it is at once a self-enhancing and self-maintaining condition.

Trance

It is through possession trance that the existence of her non-self becomes subjectively real to the possessed, or "introjected" (cf. Crapanzano 1977:13), and the culturally overdetermined self may be felicitously repositioned,

perhaps transcended. The experience of trance and its observation in others is the locus of possession's creativity, for in trance a woman becomes, legitimately if temporarily, a non-Hofriyati. In doing so she is indirectly cautioned that she and the symbolic constructs that define her sex are separate and distinct, however much the latter inform her image of self. Trance provides her the possibility of insight, of maturing, yet it does so obliquely, in a way that does not demand she take responsibility for her conclusions.

To begin with the notion of introjection, or the patient's subjective realization of a spirit's attachment and influence, the self of the possessed is not merely absent or repressed during trance in deference to that of the spirit, but, according to Hofriyati, actively engaged. Though she may be unaware of what her *zar* is doing while manifest to others, she is, villagers say, still aware, for when she and her spirit coalesce in her body they exchange experiential domains. With this the possessed transcends the visible world and "sees through the eyes of the spirit" into the normally invisible parallel universe. Thus she has, not a mystical experience, but an eminently social one. If possessed by a European spirit she experiences as a "European" would for the duration of its chant. My informants tell me they see and interact with other Europeans in European ways and perceive themselves to be surrounded by the trappings of European culture.[3] For that brief period, they say, a woman forgets who she is, her village, and family; she "knows nothing from her life." In having such a vision or, to use villagers' description, in briefly stepping outside the Hofriyati world and into another, a woman also briefly divests her self of its personhood, of its normative contents and constraints. In proportion to her subjective experience of otherness, her everyday reality is made to appear as one of many – less naturalized, less unquestionable, indeed, less subjectively real. The experience of trance is also, of course, a cultural one. Spirits are recognized entities; their social milieus are known, if incompletely understood. Yet despite this cultural patterning, or, in fact, because of it, trance is a liminal excursion. By the possessed's own admission the experience is one of tem-

porary isolation, of alienation from her Hofriyati world.

There is, I think, a subtle difference between
this situation and what Kapferer (1983, 1986)
suggests takes place during the complex Sinhalese exorcism ceremony, which it is instructive
to explore. There the demonic victim comes to
the ritual already in "an existential state of
solitude in the world" (1986:185) and it is the
purpose of the ceremony to reintegrate her
with society. This is accomplished in the structure of the performance where "the culturally
understood subjective world of the patient
finds external form" (1986:199); the demonic,
in all its chaos and terror, becomes temporarily
manifest and dominant in the human world.
Having drawn the victim's family and friends
– non-possessed participants – to experience
what is construed to be the subjective state of
the possessed, and thus linked their perceptions, the ritual then proceeds, via a subsequent comedic episode, to reassert cultural
order and bring both patient and audience
back into the world of shared understandings
(1986:201).

In Hofriyat it is not so much that shared
understandings are precipitately undermined
by a woman's untoward experience, but that
the rigidity of these understandings and her
emotional identification with them *prevents*
them from being undermined, prevents her
from being able to appreciate the distinction
between ideals and the exigencies of concrete
situations. If anything, she is too firmly
grounded in the social world. In the villagers'
view, spirits are attempting to subvert the
order of that world but she resists their influence – as she is exorted by Islam to do. Yet as
curers and adepts rightly observe, it is only
when she lets them in, when she loosens her
hold on her reality and enters an "existential
state of solitude," that she can start to
recover.

Recovery entails the experience and observation of trance in others. Like other such
ritual moments, the occasion is rife with ambiguities and potential ambivalences.[4] The qualities of spirits when juxtaposed to those of
humans give play to the imagination. It is
during such episodes that, as Burridge argues,
the would-be individual "perceives a hidden

message and accepts the invitation to explore"
(1979:145). Possession trance encourages
reflection, a limited dismantling of the taken-
for-granted world, enabling the possessed, in
its aftermath, to see her life in a very different
light. To take a mundane example: an orange
or a piece of bread, when eaten with knife and
fork by a Westerner *zar* during trance (which
normally Hofriyati would not do), becomes
something other than villagers' food, or
a metaphor for Hofriyati gender dialectics:
interior/exterior, fluid/substance, and so on. Its
"natural" associations are stripped away,
deconstructed.

A more protracted example further illustrates my point: it relates to the Hofriyati
wedding. The climax of that ceremony comes
near dawn of the third day when the virgin
bride is led out of seclusion. A bridal shawl of
red and gold silk, used also to cover girls at
their circumcisions and women during childbirth, is draped over her head, concealing all
of her body but her legs. She is positioned on
a red mat in the center of the courtyard, where
she stands, barefoot and immobile, until her
husband steps onto the mat and removes the
shawl. Now unveiled, she is seen in all her
finery and her family's gold, elaborately
hennaed hands covering her face in a gesture
of timidity. Gently the groom releases her arms
and she begins the exacting bridal dance – eyes
tightly shut, arms extended to the sides, back
arched, feet moving in mincing rhythmic steps
that barely leave the mat. Toward the end of
each song she breaks off her dance and shyly
recovers her face, then recommences with the
groom's signal, as before, repeating the
sequence until she has had enough and her
kinswomen lead her away. At no time ought
the bride to have seen her husband or the
gathering for whom her dance was the focus
of rapt attention and long anticipation. The
wedding dance is a poetic, crystalline demonstration of femininity in Hofriyat.

By contrast, in the *zar* realm, Luliya is
a female Ethiopian prostitute spirit which
demands that its human host obtain Sudanese
wedding incense, jewelry, and a bridal shawl
for its use during possession ceremonies. When
Luliya appears during a ritual, a bridal mat is
spread and the spirit, in the body of its host,

dances as a Hofriyati bride. When the silken veil is removed Luliya's host's hands cover her face; when these are pulled away she starts to dance with eyes closed, though in less inhibited manner than the bride and with obvious pretense at shyness.

What is happening here? On one level, a wanton, uncircumcised, nominally Christian alien presumes to dance as a chaste, circumcised, Muslim village woman. In the attempt the spirit tries to suppress its libertine disposition but overcompensates, exaggerating the controlled steps of a bride to the point where simulated Hofriyati drama becomes a spirit farce. Luliya is not by nature bashful; its timidity must be feigned. The spirit's real personality shows through the façade it erects with the aid of its host, illuminating the enacted Hofriyati behaviors against a background of patently non-Hofriyati traits.

But this is not all. What the audience actually observes is a normally restrained, circumcised Hofriyati woman in the role of a wanton, uncircumcised alien who in turn "plays" a village woman who is the epitome of restraint and self-control. In looking at the "other," Hofriyati see the other looking at them, while in looking at the woman entranced, they see themselves looking at the other looking at them. The multiple reflection is dramatically sustained . . . then suddenly shatters as Luliya peeks furtively over the hands of its host, giving itself away to the uproarious laughter of its human audience.

These and other densely convoluted episodes constitute more than a comic discourse on the ambiguities of gender and sexuality, for, as such, they raise them as issues in themselves and point to the somewhat subversive observation (in Hofriyat) that gender is not a natural attribute but a cultural construct and thus, perhaps, modifiable. Hence, categories that are largely unquestioned in the course of daily life become problematic in the *zar*. Through the accumulation of such episodes trance affords the participant an opportunity to mature: to grow, as Turner says, through antistructure (1982:114), to grasp not only her context, but the context of her context (cf. Bateson 1972). Possession is as much an aesthetic, a means to perceive new and rewarding

or possibly disturbing significances in what was formerly taken for granted, as it is therapy, a means to correct faulty perceptions, to cure.

Yet many who consider possession trance and ritual legitimate psychotherapy nonetheless disclaim their capacity to promote insightful reflection among the possessed (Bourguignon 1979: 290–91; Kennedy 1967: 191; Prince 1964: 115). Such "folk" therapies are generally considered to be effective in repatterning idiosyncratic conflicts and defenses in culturally appropriate ways, and furnishing a corrective emotional experience, the sanctioned release of negative affect (Bourguignon 1979: 274; Devereaux 1980: 17–18; Kennedy 1967: 189; Kleinman 1980:169–70). Here the patient's condition may be remedied, not cured, though her acknowledged vulnerability to relapse may be mitigated if she is incorporated into a cult providing group support for a healthful reorientation (Bourguignon 1979:291; Kennedy 1967: 191–2; Lewis 1971: passim; Messing 1958: 1125). Yet, despite the success of "folk" psychotherapies in securing symptom remission, and regardless of how culturally appropriate such techniques may be, they are often dismissed as inadequate when compared to Western psychoanalysis (Kiev 1964; for example, Derret 1979: 291 and Ozturk 1964: 361). They are judged deficient because apparently unable to provide the patient an opportunity for mature reflection, which constitutes the basis for a psychiatric cure (Devereaux 1980: 17–18).

None of these views does justice to the richness of the possession experience. In Hofriyat the context of possession carries within it the potential for insightful self-examination, however differently conceived from that of Western psychoanalysis. For what constitutes insight into the self is surely described by the cultural construction of an individual's selfhood. In cases of neurosis in Western cultures, psychotherapy provides a context in which the patient can learn to objectivate himself through conversation, to gain distance from an exaggerated "I." In Hofriyat, as we have seen, possession trance provides a context in which the patient is encouraged to achieve distance from her cultural context, the source of her over-objectification. Both therapies aim at replenishing the culturally specific constitution of the self by exploring and transcending former pitfalls: as individuals acquire insight into the process of self-construction, healthy, more appropriate dispositions of selfhood are suggested.

In the *zar*, dialogue takes place between a woman and her spirit(s) – her non-self – internally, through visions and dreams, and externally, through the reports of fellow villagers about her spirit's actions during trance (cf. Lambek 1980). Through such oblique discourse the possessed might work through her problems to achieve a greater understanding of herself and her society (Crapanzano 1977: 26). She is now given occasion to achieve a degree of detachment from the gender constructs that have so completely shaped her being, thus to establish a basis for the negotiation of her subordination. Possession, like anthropology, is a reflexive discourse: through it Hofriyati women can step outside their everyday world and gain perspective on their lives.

Trance is a significant factor in this process, whether experienced or observed. It has been defined as a temporary, subjectively felt change in an individual's reality orientation accompanied by a fading to abeyance of reflective, critical awareness (Deikman 1969: 45; Ludwig 1968; Shor 1969: 246; Van der Walde 1968). If we accept this view, the woman who sees into the spirit world during trance is in a state of heightened receptivity; she becomes, like the Ndembu initiand, a virtual tabula rasa (Turner 1969: 103). If her trance is deep enough and involving enough, she is thus presented with pure experience, vivid, unedited, emotionally real, and not just once, but several times, as throughout the ritual she takes on a sequence of other selves. It may not be during trance that she deepens her understanding of herself but afterwards, in remembering her trance experiences (cf. Kapferer 1986: 198) as she is expected to do. Such insights as are gleaned come indirectly, through witnessing several dimensions of what her self is not. Yet none of this is certain. The therapeutic efficacy of possession trance resists objective measurement, as does any aesthetic experience. For

some who say they see things differently, this may signal a real change in outlook, somatic disposition, and emotional balance. For others, it may not.

When discussing the therapeutics of possession trance, its potential effect on an unentranced audience is rarely considered. But possession trance is only part experience; it is also part performance (Leiris 1958). When the spirits manifest themselves in the bodies of their hosts a catalog of otherness comes to life. The spirits behave in ways appropriate to their respective ethnic groups, social roles, religions, and sex. They may be wanton and undignified, take on superior airs, beg piteously, dance about wildly, speak in brash or coy tones, exhibit any conduct fitting to their type. Spirits may be kings or slaves, prostitutes, nuns, male homosexuals, merchants, Coptic priests, or fierce tribal warriors. When a spirit's chant is sung and all whom it possesses ideally enter trance, it manifests itself in each simultaneously, sometimes presenting different aspects of its character, but always interacting with the audience in strange and sometimes terrifying ways.

To observe possession trance in another is to witness a paradox: woman who is not who she is – not human, not Hofriyati, not even, in most cases, female. Although the identities of the possessed and her intrusive *zar* are distinct, and it is the aim of the ceremony to cultivate awareness of their distinction in the possessed, for observers this separation of entities is not always easy to maintain. During trance the two are brought into intimate and often perplexing association, and those describing the episode often refer to the woman and her spirit interchangeably. Yet this risk of confusion, this ambiguity, is, I think, key to the aesthetics and therapeutics of *zar* in Hofriyat. Just as when one sees a play, the interpretation of a trance event is never wholly given in the event but must, in part, be constructed anew by each observer, who brings to the moment her own past experiences, present concerns, and critical awareness. But unlike the audience at a play, the Hofriyati observer of possession trance is utterly committed to the literal reality of what she sees. And what she sees is someone at once essential to her own construction of self and a symbol of it, who is also her own sheer antithesis. This thorough paradox, taken with the various properties of the entranced and her spirit, their individual traits and biographies, and the relations of parody, travesty, and inversion among elements of the episode, makes possible any number of interpretations, destructuring naturalized associations and temporarily freeing ideation from its moorings in the everyday world. In the course of a ceremony the possessed alternately observes and experiences trance; thus, for an entire evening she is given to see herself and those around her as in a hall of mirrors, the proportions of her selfhood shifting from moment to moment, context to context, now familiar, now alien, now frightening, now bizarre. In the course of her long association with the *zar* there are many such occasions, each affording her the possibility of new insights, refined understandings, and continued growth.

Zar (as both possession and performance) is a powerful medium for unchaining thought from the fetters of hegemonic cultural constructs and, to paraphrase Ricoeur (1976), for opening it up in different and possibly illuminating directions. In the possession context, of which trance is an integral part, the self becomes a pure issue, a subject for contemplation, negotiation, and, perhaps, felicitous regeneration.

NOTES

1   In 1977: $N = 129$, 54 possessed and 75 non-possessed; in 1984: $N = 135$, 63 possessed and 72 non-possessed.

2   ... An irony here is that female circumcision has a deleterious effect on fertility from a physiological standpoint. See the *Sudan Fertility Survey 1979* (Democratic Republic of Sudan 1982:56).

3   As Wallace (1959) has so ably demonstrated, how one experiences an altered state of consciousness is strongly influenced by cultural meanings and expectations.

4   Spirits are ambivalent figures, representing exaggerations of village values (for example, piety, dignity, or fertility), while also demonstrating their opposites: exogamous marriage or promiscuous sexuality. *Zairan* in their biographies are liminal: they "mediate between alternative and opposing contexts and are thus important in bringing about their transformation" (Turner 1982: 113). In the case of *zar*, transformation takes place in the consciousness of the possessed.

REFERENCES CITED

Assaad, Marie Bassili. 1980. Female Circumcision in Egypt. Social Implications, Current Research, and Prospects for Change. *Studies in Family Planning* 11 (1): 3–16.

Bastide, Roger. 1958. *Le Candomblé de Bahia.* Paris: Mouton.

Bateson, Gregory. 1972. *Steps to an Ecology of Mind.* New York: Ballantine Books.

Berger, Peter L., and Thomas Luckmann. 1967. *The Social Construction of Reality.* Garden City, NY: Doubleday.

Boddy, Janice. 1982. Womb as Oasis: The Symbolic Context of Pharaonic Circumcision in Rural Northern Sudan. *American Ethnologist* 9(4): 682–98.

——. 1989. *Wombs and Alien Spirits: Women, Men, and the Zar Cult in Northern Sudan.* Madison, WI: University of Wisconsin Press.

Bourdieu, Pierre. 1977. *Outline of a Theory of Practice.* Richard Nice, trans. London: Cambridge University Press.

Bourguignon, Erika. 1976. *Possession.* San Francisco: Chandler and Sharp.

——. 1979. *Psychological Anthropology.* New York: Holt, Rinehart and Winston.

Burridge, Kenelm. 1979. *Someone, No One: An Essay on Individuality.* Princeton, NJ: Princeton University Press.

Carrithers, Michael, Steven Collins, and Steven Lukes, eds. 1985. *The Category of the Person.* Cambridge: Cambridge University Press.

Constantinides, Pamela. 1977. "Ill at Ease and Sick at Heart." Symbolic Behavior in a

Sudanese Healing Cult. In *Symbols and Sentiments: Cross Cultural Studies in Symbolism*. I. M. Lewis, ed. pp. 61–83. New York: Academic Press.

Crapanzano, Vincent. 1973. *The Hamadsha: A Study in Moroccan Ethnopsychiatry*. Berkeley: University of California Press.

——. 1977. Introduction. In *Case Studies in Spirit Possession*. Vincent Crapanzano and Vivian Garrison, eds. pp. 1–39. New York: John Wiley.

——. 1980 *Tuhami: Portrait of a Moroccan*. Chicago: University of Chicago Press.

Deikman, Arthur J. 1969. Deautomatization and the Mystic Experience. In *Altered States of Consciousness*. Charles T. Tart, ed. pp. 25–46. New York: Anchor Books.

Democratic Republic of Sudan, Ministry of National Planning. 1982. *The Sudan Fertility Survey*, 1979. Vol. 1. Khartoum: Department of Statistics.

Derret, J. Duncan. 1979. Spirit Possession and the Gerasene Demoniac. *Man* 14(2): 286–93.

Devereaux, George. 1980. *Basic Problems of Ethnopsychiatry*. Basia Miller Gulati and George Devereaux, trans. Chicago: University of Chicago Press.

Douglas, Mary. 1966. *Purity and Danger: An Analysis of Concepts of Pollution and Taboo*. London: Routledge & Kegan Paul.

——. 1973. *Natural Symbols*. Harmondsworth: Penguin.

Elster, Jon. 1986. Introduction. In *The Multiple Self*. Jon Elster, ed. London: Cambridge University Press.

Fans, James. 1972. *Cat Harbour*. Newfoundland Social and Economic Studies No. 3. St. John's: Institute of Social and Economic Research, Memorial University of Newfoundland.

Firth, Raymond. 1967. *Tikopia Ritual and Belief*. Boston: Beacon.

Foucault, Michel. 1980. *Power/Knowledge*. Colin Gordon, ed. Colin Gordon et al., trans. New York: Pantheon.

Geertz, Clifford. 1983. *Local Knowledge: Further Essays in Interpretive Anthropology*. New York: Basic Books.

Hale, Sondra. 1985. Women, Work, and Islam: Sudanese Women in Crisis. Paper presented at the Annual Meeting of the American Anthropological Association, 3–8 December. Washington, DC.

Isbell, Billie-Jean. 1978. *To Defend Ourselves: Ecology and Ritual in an Andean Village*. Prospect Heights, IL: Waveland.

Kapferer, Bruce. 1983. *A Celebration of Demons: Exorcism and the Aesthetics of Healing in Sri Lanka*. Bloomington: Indiana University Press.

——. 1986. Performance and the Structure of Meaning and Experience. In *The Anthropology of Experience*. V. W. Turner and E. M. Bruner, eds. pp. 188–206. Chicago: University of Illinois Press.

Kegan, Robert. 1982. *The Evolving Self: Problem and Process in Human Development*. Cambridge, MA: Harvard University Press.

Kehoe, Alice B., and Dody H. Gilletti. 1981. Women's Preponderance in Possession Cults: The Calcium-Deficiency Hypothesis Extended. *American Anthropologist* 83(3): 549–61.

Kennedy, John G. 1967. Nubian *Zar* Ceremonies as Psychotherapy. *Human Organization* 26: 185–94.

Kennedy, John G., ed. 1978. *Nubian Ceremonial Life: Studies in Islamic Syncretism and Culture Change*. Los Angeles: University of California Press.

Kiev, Ari. 1964. The Study of Folk Psychiatry. In *Magic, Faith, and Healing*. Ari Kiev, ed. pp. 3–35. New York: Free Press.

Kleinman, Arthur. 1980. *Patients and Healers in the Context of Culture*. Berkeley: University of California Press.

La Barre, Weston. 1975. Anthropological Perspectives on Hallucination and Hallucinogens. In *Hallucination: Behavior, Experience, and Theory*. R. K. Siegel and L. J. West, eds. New York: John Wiley.

La Fontaine, J. S. 1985. Person and Individual: Some Anthropological Reflections. In *The Category of the Person*. M. Carrithers, S. Collins, and S. Lukes, eds. Cambridge: Cambridge University Press.

Lambek, Michael. 1980. Spirits and Spouses: Possession as a System of Communication among the Malagasy Speakers of Mayotte. *American Ethnologist* 7(2): 318–31.

——. 1981. *Human Spirits: A Cultural Account of Trance in Mayotte.* New York: Cambridge University Press.

——. n.d. *From Disease to Discourse: Remarks on the Conceptualization of Trance.*

Leiris, Michel. 1958. La possession et ses aspects théâtraux chez les Ethiopiens de Gondar. *L'homme: Cahiers d'ethnologie, de géographie et de linguistique.* Paris: Plon.

Lewis, I. M. 1971. *Ecstatic Religion: An Anthropological Study of Possession and Shamanism.* Harmondsworth: Penguin.

——. 1986 *Religion in Context: Cults and Charisma.* Cambridge: Cambridge University Press.

Ludwig, Arnold M. 1968. Altered States of Consciousness. In *Trance and Possession States.* Raymond Prince, ed. pp. 69–95. Montreal: R. M. Bucke Memorial Society.

Messing, Simon. 1958. Group Therapy and Social Status in the *Zar* Cult of Ethiopia. *American Anthropologist* 60: 1122–6.

Metraux, Alfred. 1959. *Voodoo in Haiti.* New York: Oxford University Press.

Nelson, Cynthia. 1971. Self, Spirit Possession, and World View: An Illustration from Egypt. *International Journal of Psychiatry* 17: 194–209.

Obeyesekere, Gananath. 1970. The Idiom of Possession. *Social Science and Medicine* 4: 97–111.

——. 1981. *Medusa's Hair.* Chicago: University of Chicago Press.

Ozturk, Orhan M. 1964. Folk Treatment of Mental Illness in Turkey. In *Magic, Faith, and Healing.* Ari Kiev, ed. pp. 343–63. New York: Free Press.

Prince, Raymond. 1964. Indigenous Yoruba Psychiatry. In *Magic, Faith, and Healing.* Ari Kiev, ed. pp. 84–120. New York: Free Press.

Ricoeur, Paul. 1976. *Interpretation Theory: Discourse and the Surplus of Meaning.* Fort Worth: Texas Christian University Press.

Saunders, Lucy Wood. 1977. Variants in *Zar* Experience in an Egyptian Village. In *Case Studies in Spirit Possession.* Vincent Crapanzano and Vivian Garrison, eds. pp. 177–91. New York: John Wiley.

Shor, Ronald E. 1969. Hypnosis and the Concept of Generalized Reality Orientation. In *Altered States of Consciousness.* Charles T. Tart, ed. pp. 239–67. New York: Anchor Books.

Turner, Victor. 1969. *The Ritual Process.* Chicago: Aldine.

——. 1982. *From Ritual to Theatre: The Human Seriousness of Play.* New York: Performing Arts Journal Publications.

Van der Walde, Peter H. 1968. Trance States and Ego Psychology. In *Trance and Possession States.* Raymond Prince, ed. pp. 57–68. Montreal: R. M. Bucke Memorial Society.

Wallace, Anthony. 1959. Cultural Determinants of Response to Hallucinatory Experiences. *A.M.A. Archives of General Psychiatry* 1:58–69.

Ward, Cohleen. 1982. A Transcultural Perspective on Women and Madness: The Case of the Mystical Affliction. *Women's International Journal Forum* 5(5): 411–18.

Young, Allan. 1975. Why Amhara Get Kureynya: Sickness and Possession in an Ethiopian *Zar* Cult. *American Ethnologist* 2(3): 567–84.

31

The Poetics of Time in Mayan Divination

Dennis Tedlock

Dennis Tedlock is professor of English and anthropology at the State University of New York at Buffalo, and is renowned for his translations of Zuni and Mayan religious texts and discussions of issues of translation and transcription (1983). Tedlock's essay illustrates a double turn to language. Double because it is attentive both to the language of religion – as it is expressed in such forms as prayer, sermons, divination, and the marvelous Mayan calendrical system – and attentive to the language of anthropologists who make a sustained effort to evoke the richness, subtlety, and complexity of religious worlds and the wholeness and polyvalence of experience. We see here what a difference attention to understanding and conveying speech forms can make.

Tedlock also provides the portrait of a religious practitioner at work. He describes a real event at which he was a central participant, ostensibly an apprentice being tested to perform as a diviner. The result is a beautiful evocation of a performance of divination, including a twist in the tail. Tedlock's essay thus also illustrates the approach that draws on anthropologists' own mimetic experience to understand that of their subjects. Too often naively ethnocentric, occasionally the anthropologist manages to pull it off. Here Tedlock's authority as diviner is evoked through the twitching of his own body. The essay also speaks indirectly to issues of sorcery and the allocation of responsibility. For further work on the Mayan calendar and daykeepers see Colby and Colby (1981), B. Tedlock (1992), and Wright (1990); on bodily experience see Csordas (ed. 1994).

From Dennis Tedlock, "The Poetics of Time in Mayan Divination," in John Leavitt, ed., *Poetry and Prophecy: The Anthropology of Inspiration* (Ann Arbor: University of Michigan Press, 1997), pp. 77–92.

The successive impressions of discourse, which strike a redoubled blow, produce a different feeling from that of the continuous presence of the same object, which can be taken in at a single glance.

JEAN-JACQUES ROUSSEAU

Mayans seem devoted to poetry in the sense Gaston Bachelard gave that term, which is to say that they have long been skilled at working against "the simple continuity of sequential time," having relatively little interest in what he called "time as duration that shatters echoes" (1988: 173). It is as if they would not allow time to move forward or backward without first listening for reverberations, and when it does move on they listen for the rhythms of its duration. A musical metaphor is an apt one, and so is the metaphor of a brocaded textile that complicates large patterns with variable details, the kind of textile the Quiché Maya produce in Guatemala (Tedlock and Tedlock 1985). Neither of these metaphors describes a circle, and they give us a way of thinking our way out of the naive dichotomy between lineal time, of which we in the West imagine ourselves to be the masters, and cyclical time, which keeps the Other outside of history as we define it – never mind the "wheels of progress."

When Mayan narrators run through a well-plotted action sequence, their language moves forward with very little reverberation, and indeed their stories are very short and fast moving when compared with those told by the indigenous peoples of the Amazon, for example, or those of southwestern or north-western North America. But when Mayans converse, pray, or make speeches, they tune in on time's echoes again and again. Their principal means is verse, parallel verse, in which the patterns of sound, syntax, and meaning work together to produce a paradigmatic pattern of sameness and difference, usually proceeding by pairs of phrases but sometimes by a group of three or four (D. Tedlock 1983: chap. 8). Verse passages within a longer discourse are usually introduced by words or phrases that stand alone, as if to locate small-scale rhythms within a larger system of widely spaced singular lines, implicitly parallel, that may or may not become manifest within a particular utterance. In the case of the Quiché Maya, these verse patterns are canonical, having been established, in the ancient book known as the Popol Vuh, by the gods themselves (D. Tedlock 1985: 78). The animals of the present-day world were demoted to their present status when they failed to learn the language lesson the gods gave them, a lesson that places a value not on the completion of a sentence but on the completion of verse patterns. Had the animals been able to learn, what the gods would have heard from them was the opening of a prayer:

Juraqan,
ch'ipa kaqulja, raxa kaqulja,
uk'ux kaj, uk'ux ulew,
tz'aqol, b'itol,
alom, k'ajolom

One of a Kind,
Newborn Thunderbolt, Raw Thunderbolt,
Heart of Sky, Heart of Earth,
Maker, Modeler,
Bearer, Begetter

After a singular opening, naming the only god who is not a member of a pair of gods, come four parallel couplets, each of them consisting of a grammatical paradigm in which one element is held constant while another is changed. In both the text and translation, the first pair of couplets is constructed at the lexical level, while the second is constructed at the morphological level. Shifting from the patterns of the signs themselves to their relationship with their objects, the first two couplets are actually reverberations of the opening singular line, giving two pairs of epithets for the singular god. The second pair of couplets shifts from the vertical lightning axis already established to the horizontal surface of the primordial sea, whose gods are sometimes called *uk'ux cho, uk'ux plo* "Heart of Lake, Heart of Sea". These gods have no definite number save that they are all in pairs, each consisting of a preparer of materials (Maker) and a shaper of those materials (Modeler), and/or a female (Bearer) and male (Begetter).

The point of interest here is that the words of the language lesson do not have an isomorphic, one-to-one relationship with a series of individual gods. The singular thunderbolt god gets a total of five names or epithets, while the other gods outnumber the words that happen to be addressed to them. Parallel verse has the effect of constantly shattering the notion that there is an essential connection between any particular word or phrase and any particular object in the world – a notion long dear to the Western mind, if only as a lost or as yet unattained ideal. Not even Mayan proper names can foster such an illusion, since there is scarcely a single god or human or place possessed of just one name. The language lesson could have given both the singular and dual gods more names and epithets or fewer without changing the basic rhythms of its sounds and meanings and without any need for an auxiliary lesson on the difference between objects and their representations.

For the Quiché, there is a level at which language does reflect the world, but this occurs at the level of structure rather than that of words. A clear and accurate discourse, right with itself and right with the world, is called *lemo tzij, cholo tzij, ajilan tzij* "mirror words, ordered [lined up] words, counted words," and there is textual evidence for a similar conception among the ancient lowland Maya (D. Tedlock 1988: 93). The language lesson "reflects" the gods by means of an iconicity that is more diagrammatic than imagistic, matching their singularity and duality with singular and dual words and phrases and positioning the singular god with respect to the cosmos and the others with respect to each other. Actual mirrors also reflect relationships among objects, but that is not the quality of mirrors that first occurs to the Western mind.

Bakhtin characterized poetry as monological and prose (prose fiction in particular) as dialogical (or polyphonic), but he didn't think about the poetics of parallelism. He writes of a force he calls "dialogism," which operates even at the level of individual words, since a given word exists in an environment of other words that could have been used with reference to the same object, words that may come to the mind of the hearer or reader (Bakhtin 1981: 326–30, 426). What happens in parallel verse is that one or more of these other words is actually given voice. Once the dialogic is on the surface of the poetry rather than hidden beneath it, the implication that still other words could have been used becomes obvious and verbatim reproduction from one occasion to another becomes a pointless essentialism. Some of the same phrases may be carried over, whether from one public inscription to another in the ancient temples at Palenque or from one speech to another by a contemporary Quiché prayer maker, but even when the objects of the signs remain the same we are unlikely to read or hear the exact reproduction of an entire sentence. At larger scales, there is nowhere an attempt to present or represent a complete discourse to which nothing should or could be added.

When Mayans use poetry as a means of elucidating events that are hidden from the present time of speakers and hearers, whether lost in the past or belonging to an uncertain future, they carry the dialogic beyond the juxtaposition of alternative words and phrases and let more than one person be heard – or at least what sounds like more than one person. When prophetic manuscripts are given public readings in a Yucatec village in Quintana Roo, two speakers take turns reading passages, improvising elaborations at the scale of parallel verse as they go (Burns 1983: 22–3). Among the Quiché Maya, it is said that when both members of a married couple are trained as diviners and they each seek an answer to a client's question at the same time, their combined pronouncements will shed more light than will those of a diviner working alone. Solo divinatory performances are far more common, but even then the client hears phrases that come from more than one source, spoken by what sounds like more than one voice. The voices in which the diviner addresses the gods and transmits their answers are poetic, highly versified, and thick with figures of speech. In contrast, the voice in which the diviner speaks directly to the client is relatively prosaic, taking shape as simple questions at first and later offering interpretations of divinatory poetry that fill gaps in the client's narrative understanding of the past or future.

It is along the path of narrative that I will approach Quiché divination here, letting the poetry be heard where it brings the story to a stop. Despite the development of the ethnography of speaking over the last twenty years, with all its attendant emphasis on placing texts in their sociocultural contexts, narrative accounts of particular speech events occurring at particular times and places remain surprisingly rare. The ethnography of speaking has in fact been written, for the most part, as an ethnology of speaking, which is to say that it represents a particular occurrence as if it typified an entire genre, recurring in a situation typical for that genre, and as if no outside observer had been present when it occurred. It is not only historical time that disappears in this process, but the echoes and reverberations that connect a particular event with others of the same kind – or, by way of a farther-reaching intertextuality, with events of different kinds, reaching even into the past experiences of the fieldworker. A narrative account has room for a fuller and richer temporality, one in which participant observation is not only a past methodology for the gathering of data for the writing of a present ethnology but continues to reverberate as the writer engages in "the observation of participation" (B. Tedlock 1991).

One of the earliest narrative ethnographies of speaking was Zora Neale Hurston's *Mules and Men* (1935), published long before arguments of the sort rehearsed here were formulated. She wrote an account of fieldwork among Florida and Louisiana blacks, with multiple instances of a full range of the verbal arts, including sayings, oratory, prayer, and song lyrics, all of them performed in the presence of Hurston herself. One of her contemporaries as a student of Franz Boas and Ruth Benedict at Columbia University was Ruth M. Underhill, who published accounts of the verbal arts of the Papago of Arizona. Underhill, like Hurston, was a skilled writer, but in her *Singing for Power* (1938) she proceeds genre by genre, describing what a Papago would typically sing when gathering salt, hunting for deer, and on other generic occasions. The difference between the two writers is only partly accountable to the fact that Hurston was a northern urban black returning to her own southern rural roots, whereas Underhill had to contend with the differences between urban white and rural Indian and between the English and Papago languages. Hurston became a writer as such, whereas Underhill finished her doctorate in anthropology and pursued an academic career. It has taken us a long time to reach the point where anthropology, no longer denying itself the full resources of writing, might no longer be a career separate from that of a writer. In this new anthropology, the verbal arts of the Others might at last play a full and central role in ethnography in general rather than being the object of an ancillary subcategory of ethnography.

Between Hurston's book and the 1980s there are very few narrative ethnographies of speaking to be found, but Georges Condominas's *We Have Eaten the Forest* (1977), first published in French in 1957, provides an outstanding exception. In this account of a Montagnard village in Vietnam, the ethnographic experience, the representation of village life, and the poetic voices of the villagers are all woven into a single narrative fabric. More recent books of this kind include William K. Powers's *Yuwipi* (1982), an account of a new religion among the Oglala Lakota; Steven Feld's *Sound and Sentiment* (1982), on poetry and song in the lives of the Kaluli of Papua New Guinea; Lila Abu-Lughod's *Veiled Sentiments* (1986), on the composition and recitation of lyric poetry among Bedouins in Egypt; *Yaqui Deer Songs/Maso Bwikam*, jointly authored by Larry Evers and Felipe S. Molina (1987); and *Haa Tuwunáagu Yís/For Healing Our Spirit*, an account of Tlingit oratory by Nora Marks Dauenhauer and Richard Dauenhauer (1990). These same authors may, in varying degrees, attempt such synchronic tasks as delineating genres and subgenres or categorizing tropes, but the poetry in their books remains connected with particular events and their reverberations in the lives of particular persons.

Like some of the authors just mentioned, I have found myself expected to learn, however imperfectly, some of the skills I was observing. This happened when Barbara Tedlock and I reached a point in our questions about divinatory practices where the only workable answer was an offer to teach us those practices (see B. Tedlock [1982] 1992: chaps. 1,3). In the episode presented here, I found myself called upon to put what I had learned into action and to do so not for a layperson but for another diviner, far from any possibility of prompting from my teacher. This happened without any warning and without the making of a tape recording, so that much of what I have written is a reconstruction rather than a direct transposition of field records. What I had to work from, in addition to my personal memory of that occasion and parallel occasions, was a general knowledge of divinatory procedure, a sketchy notebook entry that includes the date, and several photographs. The most useful images show the disposition of my divinatory paraphernalia at two different moments, revealing the results of the sortilege I performed. This information permitted me to rerun the divination in the very process of writing it. The result is certainly not an exact representation of what "really happened" on a mountaintop near Santa Cruz Quiché, Guatemala, on the afternoon of Eight Bird in the year Three Thought – or Sunday, December 5, 1976. There may even be a flat-out error of fact in the account, though I have remained strictly factual about every fact I imagine I still possess. My main effort has been to write an account whose own internal temporality retains not only the sequences but also the resonances of what particular persons said and did on a particular occasion – or what it seems, from here, they must have done.

As the scene opens, we are already on the mountaintop, in the company of a Quiché *ajq'ij*, or "daykeeper" (diviner), named Mateo Uz Abaj and two of his children. Like the man who taught us daykeeping, Don Mateo is *chuchkajaw*, or "motherfather," the head of his patrilineage. The date *Wajxaqib' Tz'ikin*, or "Eight Bird," belongs to the 260-day Mayan calendar that serves as the basis for divinatory investigations of time, consisting of all the permutations of 13 day numbers and 20 day names. Eight is good for visiting mountaintop shrines, while Bird is good for prayers, especially prayers for wealth in general and money in particular. We have already finished setting out offerings and saying prayers, and we have

already eaten the lunch we brought and sampled the bootleg liquor we used to anoint the shrine. Now we are simply relaxing before the shrine, an outdoor hearth created by rearranging the rubble of an ancient temple.

The voice written in *italics* is low and prayerful, loud enough to be heard by the humans present but not addressed to them. Another and lower voice, in SMALL CAPS, gives the divinatory meanings of the small muscle spasms or twitches that occur, unseen, in various parts of the diviner's body. Phrases that are ~~overscored~~ are unspoken but always on the tip of a diviner's tongue, ready for use whenever needed.

By this time the incense on the shrine was down to a mound of charcoal, sending up traces of white smoke. All that remained of the sticky tallow candles, given to the Holy World beneath our feet, was a large spot of grease, embedded with curled black lines of charcoal that had once been wicks. The smooth white candles, the tall wax tapers for the celestial gods, still had a long time to burn, but one of them was crooked now, bent by the heat while the incense was ablaze. Still laid out on one of the flat slabs of basalt in front of the hearth were our divining bundles, the large and lumpy one belonging to Don Mateo and the neat, fist-sized ones belonging to the ethnographers. Don Mateo looked at my bundle and then at me, and he said,

"I want to ask a question."

"A question?"

"Yes, I want you to count days for me."

"But where? There's no table here."

"That's all right. You can do it on that rock." And he reached out to tap the largest of slabs in front of the shrine, the one I was seated right next to.

"But there's no cloth to spread on it." Diviners always spread bright brocaded cotton cloth on their tables.

"That's all right, just do it right on the stone."

Diviners cannot refuse to answer a question, so long as the day on which they're asked has been kept. Today was a good time to ask, since the four of us with divining bundles wouldn't have come up here on this mountain in the first place unless we'd been keeping this day, unless we'd all been planning to abstain from sex and from anger for the whole day.

I felt awkward divining for a man who had been a diviner for who knows how many years, and speaking my lines with an accent, but I had no way out.

My bundle was on a rock beside Don Mateo, but I had to go and get it myself, since no one should handle a bundle that belongs to someone else. I sat back down on the ground, scrunching up as close as I could get to the large slab and setting my bundle down at the center of it, with the mouth, which was tied shut, pointing away from me. For a moment my fingers came in contact with the stone, and I could almost see the soft cloth I wished I had with me. Don Mateo moved closer for a better view, one knee on the ground and one folded up against his breast. With a table he would've been sitting across from me, but instead he was to the left of my work surface, and when I wasn't turning to address him I was facing the shrine. It was as if the Holy World were asking the question, or Don Mateo and the Holy World were asking it between them.

The motherfather who taught Barbara and myself how to divine often began by crossing himself and doing an Our Father and a Hail Mary and sometimes adding The Apostles' Creed, all in Spanish, before he prayed in Quiché and made his first move toward the bundle at the center of the table. I skipped all of this, which Don Mateo didn't mind in the slightest, and started in on the Quiché prayer I'd memorized – yes, memorized – from a text our teacher had dictated to us. He had composed it as he dictated, but then we studied it the only way we knew how, which was to commit it to memory word for word, like memorizing verse in school. Except that we'd made some small changes at the beginning, putting in a few words from the Popol Vuh.

Pardon my trespass, so go the opening words, but then, instead of saying Tiox, which is to say Dios, which is to say God, what I say is *Heart of Sky*, and then *pardon my trespass, Heart of Earth*, instead of Mundo, or World, and *pardon my trespass, grandmotherfathers*, all the human beings who once lived here on the face of the earth, just as I was taught, and I hold out my right hand with the cutting edge down, touching my bundle as if to divide into left and right halves, and then touch it again at right angles to make top and bottom halves,

the four quarters of the World. I can feel the small, hard things inside the cloth bag as I do this.

I'm taking hold of the yellow mixture, white mixture, and here I take up the bundle in my right hand, *dark beans, light beans, dark seeds, light seeds*, undo the bow in the thin string that keeps the bag shut, *cloudy crystals, clear crystals*, unwind the turns in the string, *yellow necklace, white necklace*, gently pour the red seeds and white crystals into a pile on the black basalt, *before you, Skyearth*, and I set the empty bag and its string to my left, near Don Mateo. While I mix and spread the pile, running the palm of my right hand over the seeds and crystals in circles, he finds a ten-cent piece in his pocket and places it on the bag, and the seeds and crystals click and clink as I stroke them.

I'm borrowing, just for a moment, your breath, and also what we have as our mountain, which is to say our body, and here I begin picking out the larger crystals from among the others, *I'm asking for the blessing, the favor*, place the largest crystal, not quite the length of a finger joint, on the far side of the pile, pointing away from me, this one is the mayor, the Mam, Old Man who bears the years, *for just this one clear light*, flank the mayor with a pair of aldermen, *for the sake of my work, my burden*, just one scribe, clearer than the other crystals, to the right of the right-hand alderman, and one treasurer, to the left, *my mixing, my pointing*, a pair of staff bearers flanking the left-hand alderman and the scribe, and another pair of staff bearers flanking them, and one more to the left.

With all ten presiding officials lined up in a tight row at the far side of my work surface, I depart from my set piece to address the longest crystal, the Mam, *Come hither, Old Man Deer, Old Man Wind*, the powerful lords of the days that bring in dangerous years, and then the next two crystals, *Old Man Tooth, Old Man Knowhow*, the lesser lords of the days that begin the calmer years, then *Secretary Net*, lord of the day of written records, *Treasurer Bird*, lord of the day of money, *do me a favor*, and then I pick up where I left off, *and also, dark clouds, light clouds, the mist, the cold, the wind, walking over mountains, over plains*, I'm running my hand over the seeds and small crystals again, *and also, the large hills, little hills, large flats, little flats, large volcanoes, little volcanoes, large plains, little plains, come out and talk! They'll speak for just a moment, for just this one light, for just this one question, in the chill, in the wind,* and here I look at Don Mateo, *they're speaking on this holy and precious day, in the chill, in the wind, they're speaking for a moment,* the clicking and clinking stops, *for just this one question, on the day Lord Eight Bird.*

"What is your question?" I ask Don Mateo.

"It's my pig. I want to know who killed my pig."

We heard him praying about this pig just a little while ago, asking that the person who killed it be delivered into the hands of the apostles and the Holy Quaternity, and to the mountains with gaping stones on top and the lightning archangels.

"What day did it die?"

"It was three days ago."

"Very well then, today is Eight Bird, so that would be, let's see, Seven Jaguar, Six Cane, Five Tooth. It happened on Five Tooth," I conclude, and go back to running my hand over the seeds and crystals.

Come hither, Lord Five Tooth, speak for a moment, for just this one light, just this one question, for Mateo Uz Abaj, by name. Then I hesitate, wondering just how to frame this question. He's already certain someone killed his pig, rather than wondering whether the pig just died, but I start off with the question I've been taught to ask.

Does his pain have an owner? Perhaps some neighbor, some companion, piled up words behind his legs, behind his arms, and again the clicking and clicking, *I'm taking hold of the yellow mixture, white mixture, dark beans, light beans,* the seeds and crystals that can move a question into a tinted light and then, for just a moment, into bright clarity, *and also, the grandmothers, the grandfathers, they talk, they speak, for a moment, for a while, concerning this one question,* and I stop for a moment. My eye is caught by the glint of the crystal scribe, I've almost forgotten to call the sheet lightning, the lightning that moves over distant horizons:

I'm borrowing the yellow lightning, white lightning that moves over the large lakes, the small lakes, from the place where the sun comes out, to the place where the sun goes down, four-cornered sky, four-cornered earth, may the lightning move over the horizon of my body, may I catch its reflection in my blood.

The hand stops moving. I raise it, cupped, to my mouth.

We're doing this right now, into my hand I blow a short breath, *pardon my trespass,* I grab a fistful of seeds and crystals, as many as I can tightly hold, and put them in a separate pile to the right. Then I push what's left of the original pile, the better part of it, off to the left, leaving a work space about the size of a large open book. From the right-hand pile, I take the seeds and crystals, in whatever combinations come to hand, and arrange them in clusters of four, making rows and files like those of a calendar, starting at upper left. If Don Mateo were doing this right now he'd be praying the whole time, but I'm just about out of words. At the end of the third row, I have one seed left over, which counts as a cluster but means the answer to the question will not be as certain as it would've been with an even number. Leaning back a little, I look the whole arrangement over. The mixing is done and it's time for the pointing.

Come hither, Lord Five Tooth, do me a favor, and I'm ready to count the clusters, starting at the upper left and moving across the rows, pointing with my first two fingers held together, but before I can even get started I feel lightning in my blood, a twitch moving up just under the skin of my left calf, and Don Mateo sees me withdraw my hand and glance down at the back of my pant leg.

"'THE WOMAN IS COMING,' it says," I say in the low but urgent voice of the blood, to no one in particular, and then in my normal voice, to Don Mateo, "There's a woman involved in this." No sooner do I turn back to the counting of days than the lightning moves across the base of the big toe on my right foot, and Don Mateo sees me glance at the toe of my shoe.

"'HE'S ILL,' it says," I say in the blood voice again, and then to Don Mateo, "Some old man, or some important man, is ill, or will be ill, but I don't know whether he'll die," and even as I speak the lightning darts into the crease behind my right knee, and this time

Don Mateo sees me move that leg a little, cocking my head to glance at the gathering of the pant leg behind my knee.

"'THE TOMB,', it says," I say, giving voice to my blood once again, and then, looking over at Don Mateo, "He's on his way to the grave, this old man." Again I look back to the rows of seeds, point at the upper left cluster, and this time the lightning holds back, the blood falls silent to hear the count. All the days come with auguries, but I speak only their names out loud:

Five Tooth, ~~the good road, the bad road,~~ Six Cane ~~in the house~~, Seven jaguar ~~before the Holy World~~, Eight Bird ~~praying, pleading, gold, silver~~, Nine Sinner ~~before God~~, Ten Knowhow ~~good thoughts, bad thoughts~~, Eleven Knife ~~lips that tremble~~, Twelve Rain ~~filling the bowl, setting the table~~, Thirteen Marksman – the lightning moves on the front of my right thigh – not in the middle, but off to one side – and Don Mateo sees me glancing there.

"'THE SHRINE,' it says," the blood says, and the count stops. To Don Mateo I say, "It's the shrine of your lineage, something's off center in your family. Or on your land. The table is not balanced on all four legs." Then I look back at the cluster I was pointing at when the lightning moved, repeating the name of the day, but this time I give voice to the augury that comes with it:

"This was Thirteen Marksman. 'Before the grandmotherfathers,' it says," and I add, looking at Don Mateo, "It's got something to do with the ancestors, and its been a long time." Just a trace of displeasure crosses his face. He serves as the motherfather for his lineage, and it's his responsibility to feed and pray to his ancestors for everyone else, but he says nothing. On with the count.

One Lefthanded ~~going mad~~, Two Wind ~~getting angry~~, Three Foredawn ~~opening, blaming~~, Four Net ~~a burden, a debt~~, Five Snake ~~the enemy~~, Six Death ~~bring good~~, Seven Deer ~~the motherfather~~, Eight Yellow ~~ripening~~, Nine Thunder ~~paying, suffering~~, Ten Dog ~~jealousy, uncertainty~~, Eleven Monkey ~~spinning thread~~, and here I reach the final, single seed, and announce the day in a louder voice, and the augury:

"Twelve Tooth. 'The good road, the bad road,' it says. Things are on the wrong track

because of what happened." There's more to this than just the incident of the pig. Don Mateo says nothing, and I continue with a second count clear through from the top, starting with the next day:

Thirteen Cane, One Jaguar, Two Bird, Three Sinner, Four Knowhow, Five Knife, Six Rain, Seven Marksman, Eight Lefthanded, the lightning moves under the edge of the heel of my right foot:

"'HE'S BEEN STEPPED ON,' it says," and then I tell Don Mateo why he's seen me glance at my shoe: "Whoever did this deed, you've almost got him, youve just –" the lightning interrupts me, ripples the blood at the edge of the palm of my right hand:

"'HE'S BEEN GRABBED,' it says. He's almost caught. Just this much is lacking," and I show Don Mateo my thumb and forefinger just a finger's breadth apart. Then I look at the cluster of seeds where I stopped counting:

"Eight Lefthanded. 'He's going mad,' it says. Whoever this is, he was crazy to kill your pig, but it's craziness that's going to grab him." And so on with the days:

Nine Wind, Ten Foredawn, the blood moves on the back of my left thigh:

"'IT ALREADY HAPPENED,' it says. The woman who's in this, I don't know, something happened between her and the man's lineage, some time ago. So says the blood." Don Mateo brightens, and I go on to take the day into account:

"Ten Foredawn. 'Blaming,' it says. Whatever happened, the man blames someone." Don Mateo gives just a trace of a nod. On with the count:

Eleven Net, Twelve Snake, Thirteen Death, One Deer, Two Yellow, Three Thunder, Four Dog, Five Monkey, Six Tooth, the lightning moves in my right testicle, I look straight down, and the only voice the blood has for this one is a chuckle.

"This woman had contact with a man," I tell Don Mateo, and then I reach the single seed at the end:

"Seven Cane. 'In the house, in the home,' it says. The man who killed the pig is in your own household. Or at least you're related to him in some way." Don Mateo looks excited now:

"Raimundo Sucac! Ask if it was Raimundo Sucac Awel!" That would be the father of his eldest son's wife. Maybe that man didn't really like giving his daughter in marriage to Don Mateo's son. But it's not mine to ask the questioner why he wants to test this name. I make a single pile of all the seeds and crystals again (except for the ones that serve as officials), mix again, grab a handful again, make clusters of four items each, posing the new question:

Raimundo Sucac Awel: is he the owner of this, the pain of my neighbor, my companion here? Don Mateo watches closely as I complete the last row, coming out to exactly four in the final cluster. A perfectly clear answer we'll get this time, I'm thinking, but as I reach to start the count, Don Mateo puts his hand on my arm:

"It's clear! Very clear! There's no need to count. The answer is yes. It's him."

"No need to count the days?"

"No. We already know very well who it is." So I give in, though I was taught otherwise. Don Mateo himself, who's not one to be fussy about the minute details of ritual, always dispenses with counting when all he wants is a yes/no answer. An odd number of seeds is no; an even number is yes. Four seeds at the end is an even better yes than two.

This time I bring the seeds and all the crystals together (officials included), rub them a few times, pick them up by handfuls, and funnel them into the bag, down to the last clicks and clinks. Don Mateo points out a seed that slipped off the slab at some point, properly leaving it to me to pick it up, and that goes in the bag, too, along with his ten-cent coin. When I've got the string wound tight and tied, I rub the whole bag between my palms a few times – it sounds like a rattle, but muffled – and then press it to my lips, putting it away in the big breast pocket of my wool shirt.

Nothing more was said about the pig that day, nor about Raimundo Sucac. But we later heard that the man had died two weeks after our visit to the mountain. That would have been on *Nine Thunder* ~~paying, suffering~~, which is to say Nine *Toj*, once the day of the god *Tojil*, the very god whose temple lies in ruins on that mountain.

When I heard the news, it came home to me that Don Mateo had tricked me into being a sorcerer's apprentice. I should have known it at the time. Whatever is said at a shrine, so long as incense is still smoking or candles are still burning, goes on the record with that mountain and with the Holy World, goes over the telegraph line that connects the mountains together, reaches Secretary Net, is written *in the First Book, in the Second Book, on the First Shelf, on the Second shelf*. Don Mateo had put the pig and its unnamed killer on record with his own prayers on the day *Eight Bird*, ~~praying, pleading~~ asking that the killer fall into the hands of the powers that be. Then he had set me in search of the man's identity – or else put me to work confirming a suspicion he already had. In the end, the name of the late Raimundo Sucac Awel had been uttered by both of us in the presence of the smoke and candlelight.

Don Mateo, as we already knew at the time, is the kind of person who knows how to *ask for justice*, as the matter is delicately put. That's the way he would put the matter, but there are other people who would call it by other names.

Itzb'al.

Brujería.

Witchcraft.

But he uses no scraps of clothing, no nail clippings, no locks of hair, nor toads, nor poisonous brews. Candles, incense, words, and names work well enough for him. And he gets a little help from a saint he has at home, the darkly clothed figure he keeps in the same room with his brightly painted Apostle John, but on the opposite side. It's the saint they call St. Simon, Simon Judas.

NOTE

Portions of this contribution have appeared in Dennis Tedlock, *Breath on the Mirror: Mythic Voices and Visions of the Living Maya* (San Francisco: Harper, 1993) and are reprinted here with permission of the author.

REFERENCES

Abu-Lughod, Lila. 1986. *Veiled Sentiments: Honor and Poetry in a Bedouin Society.* Berkeley: University of California Press.

Bachelard, Gaston. 1988. *The Right to Dream.* J. A. Underwood, trans. Dallas: Dallas Institute.

Bakhtin, M. M. 1981. *The Dialogic Imagination.* C. Emerson and M. Holquist, trans. Austin: University of Texas Press.

Burns, Alan F. 1983. *An Epoch of Miracles: Oral Literature of the Yucatec Maya.* Austin: University of Texas Press.

Condominas, Georges. 1977. *We Have Eaten the Forest: The Story of a Montagnard Village in the Central Highlands of Vietnam.* Adrienne Foulke, trans. New York: Hill and Wang.

Dauenhauer, Nora Marks, and Richard Dauenhauer. 1990. *Haa Tuwunáagu Yís/For Healing Our Spirit: Tlingit Oratory.* Seattle: University of Washington Press.

Evers, Larry, and Felipe S. Molina. 1987. *Yaqui Deer Songs/Maso Bwikam: A Native American Poetry.* Tucson: University of Arizona Press.

Feld, Steven. 1982. *Sound and Sentiment: Birds, Weeping, Poetics, and Song in Kaiuli Expression.* Philadelphia: University of Pennsylvania Press.

Hurston, Zora Neale. 1935. *Mules and Men.* Philadelphia: Lippincott.

Powers, William K. 1982. *Yuwipi: Vision and Experience in Oglala Ritual.* Lincoln: University of Nebraska Press.

Tedlock, Barbara. [1982] 1992. *Time and the Highland Maya.* Rev. ed. Albuquerque: University of New Mexico Press.

——. 1991. From Participant Observation to the Observation of Participation: The Emergence of Narrative Ethnography. *Journal of Anthropological Research* 47: 69–94.

——. and Dennis Tedlock. 1985. Text and Textile: Language and Technology in the Arts of the Quiché Maya. *Journal of Anthropological Research* 41: 121–46.

Tedlock, Dennis. 1983. *The Spoken Word and the Work of Interpretation.* Philadelphia: University of Pennsylvania Press.

——. 1985. *Popol Vuh: The Mayan Book of the Dawn of Life.* New York: Simon and Schuster.

——. 1988. Mayan Linguistic Ideology. In Paul V. Kroskrity, ed., *On the Ethnography of Communication: The Legacy of Sapir,* 55–108. Los Angeles: University of California at Los Angeles, Department of Anthropology.

Underhill, Ruth M. 1938. *Singing for Power: The Song Magic of the Papago Indians of Southern Arizona.* Berkeley: University of California Press.

What Ritual Does: The Foundations of Order

Introduction

Here we move to accounts that analyze ritual less in terms of the symbols it puts into play than in terms of its general effects. The structure of ritual is seen to enable a particular kind of action, one which carries significant consequences. Following Austin's analysis of speech acts (1962; introduced in Tambiah's essay, chapter 25), ritual is recognized not only to say something meaningful to those who participate in it, or to actively persuade them of something, but to institute change through its very performance, as when the correct enactment of a wedding ritual transforms two unmarried people into a married couple. How does this work, and why do people accept it? If the consequences are that people come to subscribe to larger orders of meaning and morality, ones that frequently entail their own subordination, what does this say for the relationship between ritual and religion, on the one hand, and society and politics, on the other? The essays here are selections from two of the most original and profound thinkers on these critical subjects. They should be rounded out with Tambiah's essay on performativity (1979).

32

The Disconnection between Power and Rank as a Process

Maurice Bloch

Maurice Bloch was professor of anthropology at the London School of Economics and visiting professor at the Collège de France. He is widely recognized for his incisive and provocative interjections in anthropological debate. His essay addresses the central issue of ideology or the relationship of the symbolic to the material, and hence of "rank" to "power." Refusing reductionist lines of either the idealist or the materialist variety, he develops a penetrating account of the way in which the production of rank through ritual has played a significant role in the evolution of political systems in highland Madagascar. In the full version Bloch develops a model for the rise of Merina and Betsileo kingdoms in central Madagascar and their organization into ranked demes (endogamous, landholding descent groups).

Bloch's essay also touches on the question of "sacred kingship," a topic of interest since Frazer and reinforced by the kinds of political systems anthropologists have described in Africa, Polynesia, and elsewhere. "Sacred kingship" conjoins the "religious" and the "political," and Bloch shows how this can come about. While Bloch's model does not account for all sides of ritual, he provides a compelling argument that attempts to address what is certainly a common feature of both political hierarchy and religion, namely mystification. It may be argued that in positing a transcendental order or sacred authority and a particular view of the world *any* religious system must work by concealing both the elements of its own devices and viable alternatives. This is not to suggest that any particular religious system is false, but rather that each must conceal something. While some might follow Marx to see this as a general critique of all religion, others (such as Rappaport in the essay that

From Maurice Bloch, "The Disconnection between Power and Rank as a Process: An Outline of the Development of Kingdoms in Central Madagascar," in *Ritual, History and Power: Selected Papers in Anthropology* (Oxford, Berg Publishers, 1989 [1979]), pp. 46–88. Abridged.

follows) argue that some mystification is necessary for the development of sacred authority that can stand as the guarantor of truth. A particularly intriguing look at Marxist demystification and the religious roots of the concept of ideology is Jarvis (2000).

Bloch has pursued the ideas developed in this early essay in a number of interesting directions, puzzling always over the distinction between everyday common sense or practical logic and the cultural/religious worlds established through ritual. See in particular his response to Geertz (Bloch 1989b [1977]), his attempt to follow Merina circumcision ritual historically (Bloch 1986), and his more general theory of sacrifice and the transcendent order (Bloch and Parry, eds., 1982, Bloch 1992). Most recently he has taken a cognitive approach to the problem (1998, 2005).

Introduction

The complex ranking systems of south Asia and Polynesia offer a special challenge and a special trap to the anthropologist or historian attempting to explain their development. He will inevitably trace the political and economic development of the state and link those to the appearance of new types of power groups and new structures of stratification. The trap lies in identifying and correlating directly the actors' concept of these groups, the distinctions and associations made in the emic system, with interest groups identified by analyses of the political or economic structures. This may be done consciously or by implication by translating actors' category terms by words such as "nobility", "ruling class", "bourgeoisie". This is likely to lead to gross ethnocentric assumptions and obscure the specific nature of the ethnographic example. The danger of such an approach has been explained well by Dumont and Pocock (1958; Dumont, 1966) for the most complex and the most famous of such hierarchical systems. They point out how the Indian caste system does not fit either in structural form or in ideological content models borrowed from feudal or class systems. Indeed such comparisons obscure the essentially religious aspect of Hindu ideology contained in the scheme. Similar criticisms would also be pertinent to the way the hierarchical systems of central Madagascar have been analysed, and for very similar reasons.

If the trap offered by the study of such systems has been brilliantly identified by Pocock and Dumont, the challenge on the other hand has been refused. The study of caste produced by these writers, however illuminating it is of the Indian case in separating power and religion and in pointing out that the latter cannot be reduced to the former, goes no further. However much the religious principle of purity is in practice reinterpreted in particular situations, it remains for them unaltered. Immaculately conceived in Indian theology, it has survived equally unsullied. There is, however, another legitimate and more ambitious way of handling such systems. It is the way suggested in part by Leach (1954; 1960; 1968). While Dumont sees the economic and political base as affected by the ideology of caste, the ideology itself is for them unaffected by the transformations in the base. By contrast with this approach, the case of central Madagascar will be examined here as a two-way relation where the economic base is not just being affected by the ideology but the ideology is being indirectly created by the base. Neither is reduced to the other since both transform themselves within their own logic, which because of their different nature is a different logic. The disconnection between rank or status and power is seen as a result of the evolution of states in central Madagascar, not as a reason to give ideology an existence and an origin of its own, or, in other words, to put it beyond explanation in material terms.

[. . .]

Hasina

Underlying both the notion of hierarchy and rank, as well as the notion of continuity and of the "natural" quality of power, is the concept of *hasina*. The best discussions of this for the Merina are to be found in the work of A. Delivré (1967: 177–88). . . . The word has proved to be one of the most difficult to translate from Malagasy. The first translation of *hasina* and of its adjectival form *masina* was "holy"; thus the earlier missionaries translated "Holy Spirit" by *fanahy* (spirit) *masina*. All notions of spirituality, of superiority as of essence, are describable as *masina*. However, the word also has a political aspect where it means legitimate or traditional authority. Thus, the hero kings of Madagascar are thought to be the epitome of the quality of *hasina*. The sites of their tombs and of their capitals are themselves *masina*. In this sense the word means power, vigour, fertility, efficacy or even sainthood. It is the essence of royalty and the essence of superiority of one person over another through "virtue" in the old sense. It is closely associated with the notion of power and virility, *mahery*, which is in fact the fetishized virility created by the circumcision ceremony and which is associated with descent and repetition of life channelled through the tombs (Delivré, 1967: 188).

Hasina is linked with the mystical power of nature, especially the power of reproduction, both in its human aspect and its aspect in relation to crops. In its human aspect the possession of *hasina* by the rulers and the *demes* is what ensures the passing on of life from generation to generation and the transcendence of death which can be seen as the kernel of Malagasy thought (Bloch, 1971: 222). In its agricultural aspect it is the presence of *hasina* which ensures fertility and climate; thus we see that those with *hasina* are able to bless crops in times of drought (Copalle, 1970: 52; Delivré, 1967: 182). The same can be said of the Betsileo notion of *hasina*. Dubois defines it as a "vertue inhérente à un être" and Edholm goes on to say that it is "given at birth – not acquired by political leadership. *Hasina* is quite widely possessed, although carefully maintained within the same group as a result of

stringent rules of exogamy . . ." (Edholm, 1971: 144). Dubois says that a man possessing *hasina* had a "nature supérieure et une authorité sacré" (Dubois, 1938: 99). Here again, therefore, *hasina* is inherent to certain people and its presence assures fertility. The pre-eminence of the ruler comes from his supreme possession of *hasina*: "He stands for the permanence and rightness of justice and authority and spiritual superiority" (Edholm, 1971: 153). *Hasina* is a supra-human quality and therefore although contained by certain *demes* in differing degrees it is not the result of their achievement but is given in their nature. The concern of the *hasina* holders should be to preserve it; creating *hasina* is out of the question. The concern of those who hold less or no *hasina* should be to preserve it in those who have it because they too benefit from it.

Thus the authority of the ruler is seen as a manifestation of something which has always existed, which is given in nature by the order of the world. The ideological picture could not be further removed from the short-lived, brutishly extortionate reality of traditional Merina and Betsileo power. This sort of notion is found associated with traditional authority in many parts of the world (Bloch, 1961; Chaney, 1970; de Heusch, 1966; Balandier, 1970). . . . We find the same concepts again and again: thus Southall referring to *Ker* among the Alur sees this notion as denoting power, beneficial domination and, in Balandier's words, an "organising and fertilising force" (Balandier, 1970: 104; Southall, 1956). Balandier, following Mauss, also points out another essential aspect of such concepts which is particularly relevant here: how the concepts of innate authority transcend and are a way of vanquishing the instability of real power. These concepts can, therefore, become agents of transformation in a conceptual alchemy where the achieved and therefore unstable turns into the permanent and therefore cosmic (Balandier, 1970: 110–13).

J. Pitt-Rivers goes further in associating such concepts especially in bringing together the notion of *mana*, which in its political manifestation for the Maori is similar to that of *hasina* for the Merina and Betsileo (Salmond, 1975), and the European concept of honour; in doing so he shows up the essential and necessary ambiguity of such notions. On the one hand honour and authority is unchallenged, given and religious; on the other, it is dependent on the actions of others since they must show their acceptance of the superiors' honour or *mana*. Thus the abstract word "honour" is dependent on the verb "to honour" – the actions of inferiors (Pitt-Rivers, 1974). In the same way we find that there is another side to the word *hasina* than the one of innate religious superiority with which we have been concerned so far. This side of *hasina* turns out not to be a *state* of superiors but an *action* of inferiors. For the sake of clarity I shall call that part of the semantic field which corresponds to the former idea *hasina* mark I, while that part of the semantic field which corresponds to the latter *hasina* mark II.

Hasina mark II manifests itself in the rendering of homage by somebody with lesser *hasina*. He gives *hasina* to the superior in the same way as the inferior renders honour to the honourable. This recognition on the part of somebody with lesser rank takes the form of the giving of gifts of respect and honour of a special kind, the use of certain greetings and the giving of precedence at such times as formal assemblies. Of particular relevance is the fact that the most significant gift which marks differential rank is the gift of an uncut silver coin; the coin is itself called *hasina* (Callet, 1908: 291; Delivré, 1967: 186). This coin is the Maria-Theresa Thaler which was in circulation throughout Madagascar for the period during which we are concerned. Its symbolical significance comes in part from the fact that it was *"tsy vaky"*, unbroken, while most thalers in circulation were cut to obtain smaller denomination. The coin therefore was the suitable gift to give to a superior to recognize his authority. At the important state rituals the differences in rank were marked by the giving of *hasina* mark II by subjects of differing *demes* to the ruler and by inferiors to superiors of any kind right down to fathers and sons (Ellis, 1838: 427).

The apparent contradiction between *hasina* in its mark I aspects and its mark II aspects is, however, not clear to the actors working within their own cultural system and mystified by its representation of power. To the analyst of the system the contradiction turns out to be of crucial significance for linking up the system of power described in the [omitted] section and the system of rank described in this one. What the ambiguity of the term *hasina* produces is the possibility of the representation of *hasina* as an innate quality possessed by superiors, which is a benefit and a blessing, to inferiors, while in fact this illusion is created by an act which is its opposite, the giving of a benefit, *hasina* mark II, by the inferior to the superior. *Hasina* mark II is thus doubly the opposite of *hasina* mark I: while the former is natural, the latter is supernatural; while the latter flows downwards, the former flows upwards. The difference is represented in Figure 1 which shows a ranked hierarchy of *demes* in the light of *hasina* mark I and mark II. In the light of the former, *hasina* is an essence which flows in the form of fertility from the superior to the inferiors; in the light of the second, *hasina* is gifts going the other way.

Thus, by the ambiguity of the term *hasina*, the supernatural gift of the superiors turns out to rest, as we know it must (hence the generality of this ambiguity) on the natural act of the inferior who, instead of receiving the blessing of *hasina*, creates it. Indeed, this reversal is still to be seen in family relations among the Merina and Betsileo to this day in the institution of the *tsodrano* (Bloch, 1971: 163). This word means the blowing of water and it is performed by elders for their juniors as a kind of blessing for fertility and success. The elder stands those he wants to bless in front of him and sprays them with water from a saucer he holds before his lips. Here we have the notion of *hasina* mark I transferring a blessing of fertility on the juniors because of the power of the holiness of the elders. However, in order that the elder may be able to do this he must be given coins, preferably the same coins as those used in the royal *hasina*-giving. The coin is placed in the water that is sprayed on those receiving the blessing, but it is pocketed by the elder as is the case for *hasina* mark II.

When Hasina is manifest

So far I have stressed the disconnection between power and rank and how a turbulent state

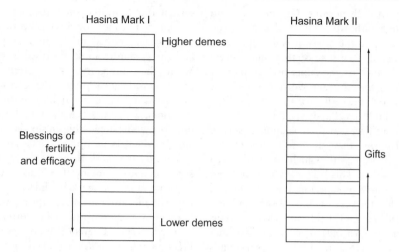

Figure 1

based on unscrupulous exploitation by a small minority of rulers of a large majority of ruled is misrepresented as an orderly harmonious system of fine gradation of rank which contains no sharp social breaks. We have seen how the representation of differential rank is seen in terms of a supernaturally given essence held in greater degree by those with high rank but which benefits all, an essence which not only comes from beyond men but has effect beyond men, since it accords with and stimulates the natural processes of reproduction. This cultural mystification is, however, more than just a veil over the eyes of the actors; by hiding the reality of exploitation and transforming it into an ideology which stresses the beneficent effect of the presence of the ruler, it serves to preserve the power of the rule, to facilitate its acceptance and thereby to maintain it. By drawing the line between rulers and ruled in the way that is done by the ranking system, the possibility of class consciousness on the part of the ruled is made much less likely and so here too the ideology preserves and indeed is an essential element of exploitation. The non-correspondence we have noted is, therefore, more than an ethnographic or a historical puzzle: it is one of the innermost mechanisms of the reproduction of the political system. This view of ideology is of course familiar in the social sciences through the

insight of Marx as well as several preceding and subsequent writers. Most recently one of its most elegant formulations has come in M. Godelier's analysis of the Inca state, where he shows how the transfer of surplus from inferior classes to superior classes is represented as a small return for the divine gift of fertility from the gods mediated by the Inca king and his collaborators (Godelier, 1973: 83).

If our task could be limited simply to demonstrating the function of ideology as a mechanism for the reproduction of social formations, this paper could end here. However, . . . if the ideology of Merina and Betsileo states obscures reality so as to reproduce it, the question of how this representation can have come about becomes of prime interest. The simplest answer, and one perhaps implied in Godelier's article, is that the false representation is a device on the part of the ruling class to maintain that which is plainly to their advantage. This, however, conjures up a totally unreal situation and is incompatible with the fact that all the evidence suggests that rulers were as mystified as ruled. The anthropologists must therefore do more and produce theories which account for the rise of ideologies maintaining certain social systems, without falling into the trap of thinking that these ideologies are either, on the one hand, actual reflections of reality, or on the other, conscious Machiavellian devices thought up by rulers to fool their subjects. The second half of this paper is an attempt to outline tentatively how a theory which avoids both these pitfalls can be constructed.

The first step in this case is to ask a question which should follow from the preceding section. If *hasina* is primarily a false mystical essence, what are the observable manifestations of this illusion and, secondly, when do they occur?

These manifestations are of two kinds: first, minor and frequent manifestations and, secondly, major infrequent manifestations. Of the minor manifestations the most important ones are greetings. People of differing rank should be greeted by different types of greeting, so *andrianas* [nobles], in the wide sense, in Imerina and to this day should be greeted by the phrase *Tsara va Tompoko* while other phrases should be used for non-*andrianas*. In a sense, *andrianas* have their rank at least at the beginning of conversations. Apart from this, in the past in both Betsileo and Merina kingdoms different ranks had rights to wear certain types of clothing, to speak at public assemblies in a certain order, and to be exempt from a few laws, none of great significance. For example, high *demes* in Imerina had the privilege of not having their blood spilt. So when they were condemned to death, instead of being killed in the usual ways they were either strangled or drowned. Also of significance were rights relating to tombs. Higher *demes* could have their tombs within the village walls, while lower *demes* could not, and the very highest *demes* had special shaped tombs, the topmost part of which were called *trano masina*: holy houses. (*Masina* in this case is the adjectival form of *hasina* (Callet, 1908: 301–74)).

Apart from these minor manifestations of differential *hasina* the demonstration of royal *hasina* from which all others sprang was focused on four major national rituals of outstanding importance: the circumcision ritual, the coronation ceremony, the ceremony of the royal bath, and royal funerals. Only a very brief outline of these can be given here.

The circumcision ceremony of the Merina and Betsileo is similar and it is the only one of the four which is still practised today, though

in a changed form. Every seven years or so, the ruler would declare the time for the circumcision come and for the following week or perhaps longer a series of rituals are performed. First, the whole kingdom is cleaned, both literally, and mystically in the case of witches, who are killed if they are discovered through the administering of a poison oracle to the whole population. Then *hasina* (mark II) is offered by all groups in ranking order to the ruler and also probably within the *demes* and between *demes* equally in order of rank. Then to mark the ritual state of the population, all plait their hair in a characteristic and complex way. The king as well as all the heads of *demes* go to the tombs of their predecessors and ancestors (assumed to be the same) and make offerings and prayers which in the case of the ruler are climaxed by the phrase "Ho masina anie", "Let me be *masina*". Then follows the ceremony of the fetching of the *rano masina*, holy water.

This water is fetched from several fixed places and its significance is that it increases the fertility of humans; thus through the agency of these with *hasina* the forces of nature are harnessed to be passed on in the increased fertility of the next generation which is the principal aim of the ceremony. Then the *hasina*-giving is repeated and all take part in a complex dance called *soratra* which is said to "*hampandroso hasina*", to "force *hasina* to enter", but which at the same time acts out the differential *hasina* of the various *demes* of the kingdom (Callet, 1908: 73–82).

The circumcision ceremony stresses very explicitly certain themes which we shall find again in the other ceremonies: 1) The king is associated by the ceremony with his royal predecessors and through contact with them he indirectly passes on fertility to the whole population. 2) The king is associated by the ceremony with the reproductive force of nature and because of his *hasina* he can canalize this to the rest of the population. 3) The king's and the *demes'* *hasina* is created by the giving of *hasina* mark II as well as by the dance; at the same time the relative amount of *hasina* is defined.

The second ceremony where the *hasina* of the ruler is stressed is the accession ceremony.

This takes place at a spot called Mahamasina (the place which renders *masina*; the present-day football stadium of Tananarive), where apart from receiving the *hasina* from his subjects in ranked order the king absorbed the *hasina* from his predecessors by drinking water containing earth drawn from the tombs of the previous kings which he claimed to be descended from (Ellis, 1838: vol. 1, p. 420). This ritual clearly demonstrates the incorporation by the present king of the *hasina* of his predecessors, which is seen as reproducing itself again and again from generation to generation channelled in one unchanging line. Of course, this type of material descent, contact with the corpses of predecessors, which is typical of central Madagascar (Bloch, 1971) is also highly manipulable, since it is not descent through any notion of filiation but descent through incorporation of predecessors which can be done by anybody irrespective of who his parents were.

[. . .]

Finally, and perhaps most interestingly, we have the yearly ceremony of the royal bath, the *fandroana*, . . . The best study available . . . is to be found in A. Delivré's *Interprétation d'une Tradition Orale* (1967). Delivré stresses how the royal ceremony, involving much singing and dancing and other ritual activity and lasting for anything up to a month, shows a clear pattern emerging: on the one hand the passage of the old year and the coming of the new, and on the other the repetition of kingship, not only within a reign, but beyond it from reign to reign.

The main rituals of the Fandroana are in order:

1. A moratorium on funerals.
2. Opening up of the tombs followed by a tidying up of the tomb of his predecessors by the king echoed in all *demes* by similar tidying up in *deme* tombs.
3. The ritual of the royal bath which gives the ceremony its name. The ruler, after receiving *hasina* in the form of the coin from his subjects in order of rank, takes a bath with much ritual. He then blesses the subjects by spraying them with the water of the bath. This increases their fertility and that

of the crops. On stepping out of the bath the ruler says: "Ho masina anie", "May I be *masina*". He then receives the gift of *hasina* again. This is echoed by gift-giving throughout the whole kingdom as inferiors give to superiors.[1] The night preceding the actual bath is marked by the whole population taking part in a torchlight procession and in the past by a period of sexual licence. The cause of both these is as much the royal bath as the fact that the royal bath coincides with the new year, the passage from the month of Alahotsy associated with death to the month of Alahamady associated with fertility. This is also the mid-point between harvest and the beginning of sowing the new crop of rice.
4. Forward-looking ceremonies at the royal tombs and closing of the tombs (echoed at *deme* tombs).

. . . The cycle of the year is linked with the actions of kinship. Then and by inevitable extension the fertility of the crops is linked with the *hasina* of the king and made dependent upon it. The giving of rank by the subjects to the king is linked to the giving of rank by all inferiors to all superiors, whether superior and inferior *demes*, or fathers and sons, or elder brothers and younger brothers, etc. In other words, the receiving of *hasina* by the king is seen as the final result of a wave of *hasina* giving throughout the society.

The recognition of rank by all is merged with the continuation of all, symbolized by the conquest over death, of which tombs are the symbol, as well as the fertility-giving blessing of the bath-water. This conquest over death for each *deme* and each family is seen as dependent on the conquest over death of the kingship. For this the present incumbent must be the rightful successor of other kings whose tombs are his tombs. . . . Material and essential succession is merged with a process which is in fact manipulable but which, when looked back upon, has all the appearance of biological descent, since it involves the transfer of material substance between generations of rulers.

The actual bathing also re-echoes central themes of both the circumcision ceremony and the royal funerals. The water for the bath should be obtained from the same places as the water for the *rano masina*, the holy water of the circumcision ceremony; by contact with the body of those with *hasina* it transforms natural fertility into social fertility, which is then used to bless the assembled multitude in the same way that the *rano masina* is poured by the elders on the penis of the child. This use of water also re-echoes the *tsodrano* discussed above. In all these ceremonies then we see the association of the power of nature and the power of men inextricably linked to become *hasina*. The substance which gives rank its legitimacy is as much of nature as of men; it is, therefore, beyond question and infinitely desirable since on it relies the life of all.

The passage from one year to the next and the promise of the future rice harvest is associated with the passage of kings from year to year through time, a passage which is continuous since the present king is the representative of the corpses inside the tombs where his predecessors have been buried which will contain him and his successors. The ritual associates the king and his bath with the renewal of human fertility through the water of the bath which, as in other ceremonies, symbolizes the continuity of human life. The whole ceremony is focused on the ritual at the palace but is re-echoed by many observances inside every Merina home. Its centre is marked by the bath, preceded by a night of unbridled sexual licence which has won it much fame among European writers but which often marks the turning-point in ceremonies of continuing fertility in Madagascar. The whole ceremony establishes, recognizes and differentiates between degrees of *hasina*. As the king comes out of his bath he utters the phrase: "Ho masina anie", "that I may be *masina*", and accompanying this, both immediately preceding and following the bath, he is given *hasina* mark II by the other high-ranking members of his entourage; a gesture repeated throughout the kingdom by those of lesser rank giving to those of higher rank, repeated inside every family by sons giving *hasina* to their fathers, younger brothers giving *hasina* to their older brothers, etc. At the very moment when the king manifests his supreme *hasina*, associating it with the recurring cycles of nature and reproduction, the whole hierarchical rank system of the kingdom is, so to speak, activated in order to mask the actual power situation. The masking process takes place in the transposition of political power, achieved by force against subjects and predecessors, to an aspect of the natural life-giving processes of nature and human sexuality; in other words, power is represented as beneficent nature – it is the transposition of unique achievement into repetitive and therefore infinite events and the transposition of a sharp break between rulers and ruled into a continuum of differential *hasina*.

The . . . royal rituals we have looked at so far carry the same message, an amazing message in the light of the reality of Merina and Betsileo history. The message is that political power is an aspect of a mystical power distributed throughout the population in differing degrees. This power is not primarily political but is an aspect of nature. Like nature it is repetitive but unending. Like nature it is life-giving. Like nature (by definition) it is not created by man but exists independently of man. The present ruler if he has *hasina* is, therefore, nothing but the continuation of his predecessors, the vessel of the *hasina* which they had. The life of the subjects and the produce of the earth is dependent on the communion with the religious forces of the universe which is achieved through him.

The analysis of the . . . royal rituals which has been outlined above shows when it is that the illusion of *hasina* and the rank are created. Apart from the minor manifestation of *hasina* and rank discussed above, it is during rituals that power is transformed into sainthood, that *hasina* mark II takes on the illusory appearance of *hasina* mark I. For periods of varying length, normal activity is suspended by rituals where the experience of exploitation and intimidation, implied by political rule most of the time, is transformed into a totally different picture, depersonalizing the relationships of oppression to relationships of protection by rulers who are vessels of universal beneficence in the form of fertility.

The fact that *hasina* and rank are illusions of certain times but not all times is what I believe can furnish us with an answer to the question posed above: how can a misrepresentation of political and economic reality come about without anybody working the system consciously so as to mislead others? The answer will come by looking at what is special about those times when *hasina* and rank appear to have reality, in other words by utilizing a theory of ritual.

The reason why a theory of ritual is relevant to the understanding of the relation between rank and power comes from the fact that when we are looking at power we are looking at unformalized (unritualized) action using ordinary language and physical force for its communication. We are looking at activities for which the manner in which things are done is secondary to what is done. When we are looking at rank, by contrast, we turn to rituals, whether religious or secular, whether large-scale extended affairs like the ceremony of the bath or very small-scale affairs like greetings.

These rituals use a type of communication different from other communication: formalized language, song, formalized bodily gestures, dance and communication by material symbols. When we are looking at power and rank we are therefore looking at *different* activities and *different* types of communication involving the *same* actors. From time to time life is "lifted up", so to speak, to another plane and we must understand the significance of this "lifting". It is important to stress that the difference between power and rank refers to different types of activities in which the actor is involved and not a move from the observer's to the actor's category (I believe this is a fairly common mistake in anthropology). Indeed, the perception of exaction in its unadorned form is just as much part of the experience of the actors as the experience of rank in rituals, but it occurs at different times and in a different mode of communication. The Merina peasant is sometimes faced by armed superiors who take away part of his crops but a few months later he is a singer and a dancer in the ceremonies of the bath.

Communication in Ritual

Only a very brief outline of a theory of ritual can be given here. The argument is presented in an article entitled "Symbols, song, dance and features of articulation: Is religion an extreme form of traditional authority?" ... [Bloch, 1974, reprinted as chapter 2 of the volume from which this extract comes]. The starting point of the argument is the observation that ritual, whether religious or not, is characterized by certain special (extraordinary) types of communication. These are mainly formalized speech and song, formalized bodily movement and dance and material symbols which replace words. All these media of communication share features in common in contradistinction to more ordinary communication, especially ordinary language. The first and most fundamental aspect of ritual communication is that although it appears richer in aesthetic and emotional values, it is poorer as to its semantic potential and its ability to carry a logical argument. This is because, as has been shown by generative semantics, the logical potential of communication is dependent on aspects of syntax, and these are weakened or destroyed in these media. Ordinary language depends for its ability to say new things within a given mould on the articulations which unite a continuous unit of communication. In ordinary language one bit of communication can be followed by any other bit. This is because syntax is a system which can link meaningfully practically any two propositions. In ordinary language one bit can be followed by a near infinity of other bits within a framework which gives this sequence meaning.

In the case of formalized language, and especially song and such non-linguistic communication as dance, this high flexibility in the articulation of communication is either greatly reduced or almost absent, and so the potential for saying new things within a given structure is equally reduced or absent. The articulation of communication becomes, so to speak, arthritic. While in ordinary language the suppleness of communication means that unit A can within the rule be followed by an infinity of units B, in ritual language or song A can, within the rule, be followed by very few or even only one B. Thus, while for ordinary language the only reason which links A and B is the nature and force of the argument, in ritual the link between A and B is partly given by the nature of the communication. Two points follow from this: 1) Communication is not easily or at all adjustable to the reality of a particular place or time because of its arthritic nature. 2) Reasoned contradiction or argument, which implies a supple form of link-up with previous utterances, is equally reduced or ruled out. As a result the communication of ritual is protected by its form from challenge, rapid modification, or evaluation against other statements or empirical data. Secondly, not only does ritual communication restrict the articulations between parts of the message, it also dramatically limits the range of words of larger units of communication which are appropriate. Particularly it reduces the range of possible illustrations which are thought suitable parallels to matter at hand. Often it specifies that any illustration must be drawn from a scriptural corpus or from a single historical tradition. The effect of this restriction on communication is particularly interesting: it means that any single ritual event is, in the perspective of ritual communication, going to be seen simply as a manifestation of an event which recurs or which is cyclic. Ritual communication makes the social world appear organized in a fixed order which recurs without beginning and without end. As a result the social is like the natural, even a part of nature, and so ritual communication projects the political, the social, the discontinuous, the cultural and the arbitrary into the image and the realm of repetitive nature. Since ritual cannot "come to grips" with reality this is transformed into something quite different.

The theory is relevant to what we have been looking at so far in the following way: it explains why the ritual representation of rank is apparently unchallenged by very different experiences of power. It also explains why rank and *hasina* are represented as cyclic and therefore permanent. It also makes clear why statements of power which are "given" in the universe (since they cannot be challenged) and repetitive, inevitably link up with the processes of nature and especially its beneficial cyclical aspects, fertility and reproduction. Putting statements into ritual language puts them outside society and into nature since the statements appear to have transcended the actions of men and are experienced as though from outside the individual (*pace* Durkheim).

The theory of ritual under discussion, however, has some more directly evolutionary implications. We should think of rituals less as given, more as part of the process of leadership. Political leaders have been divided between those with traditional authority and those with charismatic authority. It is clear that it is those with traditional authority who use rituals.

This was brilliantly analysed by Weber who stressed the processual side of this. Those who acquire power institutionalize it to make it less vulnerable from the attacks of rivals, they put this power "in the bank of ritual". They do this by creating an office of which they are the legitimate holders. But which has reality beyond them. This is done by gradual ritualization of the power-holder's communication with the rest of the world, especially his inferiors. As this ritualization process proceeds, communication loses the appearance of a creation on the part of the speaker, and appears like repeats of set roles specified by the office which appears to hold him. Reality is thus reversed and the creation of the power-holder appears to create him. This process means two things: power having become authority appears less and less challengeable, but at the same time it becomes less the power-holder's own. This results in the fact, also emphasized by Weber, that traditional authority is eminently transferable.

This is because as the leader puts his control "in the bank" he removes it from his own achievements by making it unrelated to history and part of nature (see above). Ritualizing power means that the achieved power is transformed into ritual rank by rituals, but it also means that in the process rank becomes separated from its origin, i.e. the acts of power, and any direct feedback is ruled out by the very process of rituals. In this way rank will inevitably become disconnected from power. Power produces rank through ritual but this gives rank independence, a "realism" which results in greater time persistence. Then power will change but the rank it has produced will stay.

The fact that ritualization removes authority from the person of power-holders has another evolutionary implication which we must touch on briefly, to return to it below. This removal is a problem for the ruler himself, in that it not only removes events from place and time and compels others by placing them in a repetitive and apparently external system, but it also depersonalizes him, removing from him the possibility of manipulation. If a ruler totally adopts the mode of communication of ritual for carrying out his will, he at the same time loses his ability to affect events for his own *personal* ends as opposed to the ends of his office. He must therefore continually switch from the mode of communication of ritual to a secular mode of communication, using the former for statements concerning his unchallenged role as "father of his people", the latter in order that he may play the astute politician (Bloch, 1975). In evolutionary terms one can see this whole process as one whereby rulers as they become accepted ritualize their communication with their subjects to protect themselves from short-term challenges, but as they do this they begin to need two alternative codes, playing one after the other, which correspond to two roles which they may well alternate, that of priest and politician, that of orator and patron. The superior who tries to avoid separating the contradictory roles of father of his people and politician is a successful ruler, but he is at all times facing the danger of being kicked upstairs as a priest or kicked aside by a successful rival who takes over the role he has created.

[. . .]

Conclusion

Dumont's characterization of the Indian caste system and his insistence on the disconnection between status and power gave us our starting point. While fully accepting the strictures on the danger of reducing one of these systems to the other I have tried to show that in an analogous case it is still possible to see the ideology of hierarchy as a product of political economic history. Of course, Malagasy history does not explain the specific form of the Indian system.

To use it in this way would be to fall again into the reductionism and ethnocentricism Dumont criticizes. What the study presented here does show is a system with striking similarities to the Indian caste system which can be accounted for. This is especially so since the similarities between the two systems, the gradual and all-encompassing nature of the hierarchy, the disconnection between religious and secular power, the continuity in the religious interpretation of human society and of nature are precisely those features of the Indian system particularly stressed by Dumont.

The method here has been to outline the existence of two systems. The first is the system of political economy evolving according to its own logic and affected by such things as the ecology of central Madagascar and the technology of what J. Goody has called the "means of destruction" (J. Goody, 1971).[2]

Then I have considered another system, the system of ideas held by the Merina and the Betsileo, and I have outlined the system as having two different kinds of relations to the first system. The system of ideas must, on the one hand, be in part congruent with the economic and political system, since it must offer a practical system of communication to operate it, in the same way as it must offer a practical system of communication to exploit nature and obtain a living from it. On the other hand, the system of ideas is in certain domains separated from the reality of life and feeds on itself to create another pseudo-reality. This is possible only because of the semantic implications of ritual communication which protect ideas from challenge by empirically generated knowledge, and which links up ideas in a way which is sub-logical. The system of ideas is therefore made up of two kinds of systems of communication which can never interact since they use different media. It is because of the existence of this second system of ideas that a disconnection occurs between ideas and reality, rank and power. Once this disconnection has occurred and the system of ideas in some matters gains a life of its own, its relation to such events as the growth and death of kingdoms becomes indirect, evolving within its own mystical rationality and creating further disconnections with the base.

It is because of this disconnection that most evolutionary theories, whether past or present, appear simple-minded or simply wrong. They all try to establish a direct and unique relation between the politico-economic base and ideology, while any study of a particular case shows this not to be valid. On the other hand, if we have to use much more complex theories in the future I hope I have shown, whatever the value of this particular case, that we need not give up.

NOTES

1 It should be noted that gift-giving in Madagascar is always a sign of inequality, while demands are a sign of equality.
2 See full version.

BIBLIOGRAPHY

Balandier, G. 1970. *Political Anthropology*. Translated from the French. London.

Bloch, Marc. 1961. *Les Rois Thaumaturges: Étude sur le Caractère Surnaturel attribué à la Puissance Royale particulièrement en France et en Angleterre*. Paris.

Bloch, Maurice. 1971. *Placing the Dead: Tombs, Ancestral Villages and Kinship Organisation among the Merina of Madagascar*. London, New York: Seminar Press.

—— 1974. Symbols, song, dance and features of articulation. *European Journal of Sociology*, vol. 15, pp. 55–81.

—— 1975. Introduction to M. Bloch (ed.), *Political Language and Oratory in Traditional Society*. London, New York: Academic Press.

Callet, R. P. 1908. *Tantaran ny Andriana eto Madagascar* 2nd edn, vol. 1, Tananarive: Académie Malgache.

Chaney, W. A. 1970. *The Cult of Kingship in Anglo-Saxon England*. Manchester.

Copalle, A. 1970. *Voyage à la Capitale du Roi Radama 1825–1826*. Documents anciens sur Madagascar, vol. 1, Association Malgache d'Archéologie.

Delivré, A. 1967. Interprétation d'une tradition orale. Unpublished thesis, Paris. Now published as Delivré 1974.

—— 1974. *Interprétation d'une Tradition Orale*. Paris: Klincksieck.

De Heusch, L. 1966. Pour une dialectique de la sacralité du pouvoir. *Le Pouvoir et le Sacré*. Annales du Centre d'Études des Religions. Brussels.

Dubois, H. M. 1938. *Monographie des Betsileo*, Travaux et Mémoires de l'Institut d'Ethnologie, vol. 34, Paris. Quoted in F. Edholm 1971.

Dumont, L. 1966. *Homo Hierarchus*. Paris.

—— and D. Pocock 1958. A. M. Hocart on caste: religion and power. *Contributions to Indian Sociology*, vol. 2.

Edholm, F. 1971. Royal funerary rituals among the Betsileo of Madagascar. Unpublished thesis, London School of Economics.

Ellis, W. 1838. *History of Madagascar*, vols 1 and 2. London.

Godelier, M. 1973. *Horizons, Trajets Marxistes en Anthropologie*. Paris: Maspéro.

Goody, J. 1971. *Technology, Tradition and the State in Africa*. London: Oxford University Press.

Leach, E. R. 1954. *Political Systems of Highland Burma*. London: Bell.

—— 1960. The frontiers of Burma. *Comparative Studies in Society and History*, vol. 3.

—— 1968. Introduction to E. R. Leach (ed.), *Dialectic in Practical Religion*. Cambridge: Cambridge University Press.

Pitt-Rivers, J. 1974. *Mana*. The London School of Economics and Political Science.

Salmond, A. 1975. Manners maketh man. In M. Bloch (ed.), *Political Language, Oratory and Traditional Society*. London, New York: Academic Press.

Southall, A. 1956. *Alur Society*. Cambridge.

33

Enactments of Meaning

Roy A. Rappaport

Roy Rappaport (1926–97) was professor of anthropology at the University of Michigan and one of the most distinguished theoretical and applied anthropologists of his generation. His work on the ritual regulation of a society in Papua New Guinea (1984) was a masterpiece of ecological analysis and he always retained an interest in understanding the whole.

Whereas Bloch emphasizes ritual's separation from – and mystification of – earthly power, Rappaport, like Durkheim, understands ritual lying at the root of all social connection. It is through ritual, Rappaport argues, that the bases of commitment and trust are forged. Although he does not mention it here, this reverses the preoccupation of earlier thinkers with the role of belief, as though it happened prior to action. For Rappaport, the act of performing ritual both brings into being moral states of affairs and entails commitment to their terms and to the order of which the ritual

forms a part. To engage in a marriage ceremony when one is eligible to do so is to get married and become obligated to live by its conditions – *whatever one's personal feelings in the matter*. Whether or not the parties intend to keep their commitments, the point about ritual is that it produces them.

This is an excerpt from a lengthy theoretical analysis and profound reflection on the nature of religion and its place in the life of the human species that deserves to be read in its entirety. Rappaport's discussion of the sacred and processes of sanctification (1999: Chapters 9 and 10) is especially important, and the trenchant last chapter on contemporary pathologies of religion is reminiscent of the final passages of Weber (1958). A preliminary version of the book's argument is to be found in Rappaport (1979, especially the essay "The Obvious Aspects of Ritual"), while Messer and Lambek (2001) offers some contextualization.

From Roy A. Rappaport, "Enactments of Meaning," in *Ritual and Religion in the Making of Humanity* (Cambridge: Cambridge University Press, 1999), pp. 104–38. Abridged.

[. . .]

The Physical and
the Meaningful

Both the occurrence of ritual and ritual's contents form and transform that upon which they are imposed, but . . . not primarily by force of energy or expenditure of matter. What is often called their "power" rests upon other means or principles. We may discern in nature two general classes of efficacy – the physical and the meaningful. The efficacy of what Leach calls "technique," achieving as it does its results through the deployment of matter and energy in accordance with the laws of physics and chemistry is, largely if not entirely, physical, but prayer is not, nor is ritual, nor are words. Their efficacy is grounded in principles of communication.

Bateson has noted some general differences between the two classes: when you enter the world of communication, of organization, etc., you leave behind the whole world in which effects are brought about by forces and impacts and energy exchange. You enter a world in which "effects" – and I am not sure one should still use the same word – are brought about by differences [bits of information]. . . .

> The whole energy relation is different. In the world of mind nothing – that which is not – can be a cause. In the hard sciences, we ask for causes and we expect them to exist and be "real." But remember that zero is different from one, and because zero is different from one, zero can be a cause in . . . the world of communication. The letter which you do not write can get an angry reply; the income tax form that you do not fill in can trigger the Internal Revenue boys into energetic action, because they, too, have had their breakfast, lunch, tea and dinner and can react with energy which they derive from their metabolism. The letter which never existed is no source of energy . . . what we mean by information, the elementary unit of information, is a difference which makes a difference, and it is able to make a difference because the neural pathways along which it travels and is continually transformed are themselves provided with energy. . . .

Because, in possible disagreement with Bateson, I take information to be no more than one form of meaning and because I do not think that all forms of meaning can be reduced to information in the strict sense, I designate the class into which ritual falls as that of "meaningful (rather than informational) acts."

To distinguish the meaningful and the physical as two distinct classes of efficacy, is not to propose that they are separate or separable in nature. That ritual achieves its effects through the communication of meanings does not imply that it does not both consume and mobilize energy and material, nor that technique proceeds in some mindless way without the guidance of meaning. Matter-energy devoid of information is necessarily devoid of life: information and other forms of meaning separated from matter-energy could be conceived as mathematical or formal abstraction, pure spirit or Platonic ideal, but the act of conceiving it as such, being a biological process like all other acts of conception, could not occur in the absence of matter and energy. Although there seems to be no direct relationship between the meaningfulness of messages and the amount of energy required to transmit them, the communication of meaning, both informational and of higher order, always requires energy and sometimes matter as well. Even speech is propelled by energy, and information is inscribed on paper, engraved on stone, combined in DNA and encoded on magnetized tape. Conversely, any change detected by an organism in the energy flux to which it is subjected, or any change it detects in its material environment conveys information to it, for information is, in one of its aspects, detected, or at least detectable, difference. Moreover, as Bateson observes, matter-energy and informational processes frequently cannot be separated from each other because the receipt of information leads organisms to expend their own energy to bring about effects that may include both material and informational elements. Matter-energy processes and informational processes, although they can be distinguished, are inseparable in nature, and it is of interest that the myths of many peoples, including both Australian aborigines and ancient Hebrews, describe creation, either in whole or in part, as an act or set of acts, imposing form upon an already existent but inchoate primordial matter (Bateson 1972a: xxiii ff.). Creation, this is to say, is conceived as the informing of substance and the substantiation of form. Higher-order meaning comes later.

Information and matter-energy processes may be inseparable in nature, but they, the objects they affect, and the ways in which they achieve their effects may be distinguished. Matter and energy, it seems clear, operate most effectively, that is with most predictable results, upon inert materials. The efficacy of information and other forms of meaning, on the other hand, rests not only upon the ability of senders to encode and transmit information, but upon the ability of others to receive those messages, that is to recognize, comprehend and take account of them.
[. . .]

That there are differences in what members of different human groups take to be meaningful is, of course, the *raison d'être* of comparative anthropology. Be this as it may, it is obvious that few Americans would be informed of much by a speech in Mongolian, and the same may be said of some of the non-verbal as well as verbal messages transmitted in rituals. Most American youths might be deeply impressed by being subincised, but none, it is probably safe to say, would be hastened on the road to sociological manhood by such an operation, as would young Walbiri or Arunta. The ritual form may be universal, but all human rituals include signs specific to the society, church, or congregation in which they are performed, and the arrangement of sign elements into liturgical orders is also in some degree socially and culturally specific. If the reception of the messages encoded in liturgical orders requires that they be in some sense "understood" (which is not to say that they may not at the same time be mysterious), then it is necessary that they be in some way learned, because the understanding of signs only conventionally related to their referents could not possibly be specified genetically. This is to say that participants must be trained, indoctrinated or otherwise prepared to receive the messages rituals transmit. The work of Campbell (1959), Erikson (1966), Turner

(1969) Wallace (1966) and Goodenough (1990) suggests that the ability to be informed by ritual is itself established in the individual, in part in the course of a series of rituals starting in early infancy and proceeding to maturity. Erikson (1966) has referred to this process of preparation as "ritualization," and we shall return to it in a later chapter. Here it is necessary to note only that the informative capacity of ritual, its ability to form and transform, rests not only upon its special mode of transmission but also upon its reception by specially prepared receivers.

The effects that can be achieved by the deployment of motion and energy on the one hand and meaning on the other are also obviously different. Physical effects – weights lifted, ditches dug, billiard balls knocked into pockets, acids neutralized, metals smelted, plants cultivated – must rely upon physical processes for their achievement. Conventional effects, on the other hand – princes transformed into kings and words into promises, the profane made sacred and truces declared – can *only* be achieved by meaningful acts. Whatever energy may have been required by a young man to fulfill the responsibilities of knighthood, or even required to complete his transformation to knighthood, did not flow into his shoulder from the sword with which he was dubbed, nor from the voice of whomever it was who dubbed him. It came, to recall Bateson, from his breakfast and dinner. Dubbing transformed him into a knight not by the force of its blow but by informing him of his knighthood, or better, informing him *with* knighthood. (In fact, according to the Oxford Unabridged Dictionary, a man is dubbed *to* knighthood, the transformative aspect of being informed being emphasized.) Although certain physical acts were performed with certain objects in dubbing, whatever transformation took place in the passage to knighthood was neither a physical alteration of the young man, nor was it effected by a process that can be comprehended as physical, chemical or biological. The transformation was, and could only be, effected by communicating meaning to whomever was the locus of the transformation, and to other concerned persons, in accordance with the conventions of the society in which it was occurring. The same may be said of the transformations in group membership and belligerency status effected by the planting of *rumbim* among the Maring, and even of those rituals in which the initiate is subjected to severe pain and by which he or she may be left physically marked for life: scarified, subincised, circumcized, canines removed, septum pierced, fingers lopped off. The significant transformations produced by such operations are obviously not physical, nor are they outcomes of the physical changes *per se* wrought by such operations but of the meanings those changes carry.

Ritual acts, such as body mutilation, planting *rumbim* and dubbing are, to use Van Neumann's term, "markers," that is "observable bundles, units or changes of matter-energy whose patterning bears or conveys the informational symbols from the ensemble" (James Miller 1965: 164). It is, of course, a matter of great interest that humans, who have a range of codes and markers to choose from, employ precise, subtle, energetically and materially inexpensive speech for the transmission of some messages and comparatively crude, expensive and sometimes painful physical acts for the transmission of others.

[. . .]

Speech Acts

There are important differences among the occurrences that have been rather casually included here in the class of meaningful acts. Events, such as dubbings, *rumbim* plantings and supercision must be distinguished from messages which simply inform receivers of conditions in their social or physical environments.

First, such rituals are more likely to inform the participants of changes in themselves or perhaps it would be better to say *with* changes in themselves, than they are of changes in their surroundings.

Secondly, whereas simple messages concerning environmental conditions leave the responses of receivers to their own devices, rituals specify their responses, often very precisely. When, in medieval Europe, a youth was dubbed he was not stripped of his status to become anything desire or imagination suggested to him. He became a knight and nothing but a knight. When an alien grasps the *rumbim* of a Maring local group he becomes a *de jure* member of that local group, and nothing else. When they uproot *rumbim*, Maring husbandmen become potential warriors. When they are supercised it is *t'aure'are'a*, and nothing else, that Tahitian boys become.

Thirdly, while a message concerning the state of the social or physical environment may lead us to undertake an action which will transform ourselves or the conditions surrounding us, at least some rituals themselves complete the transformations with which they are concerned. Dubbing, we have observed, does not tell a youth to be a knight, nor does it tell him how to be a knight. It makes him a knight.

Ritual is full of conventional utterances and acts which achieve conventional effects. "I dub thee to knighthood," "I name this ship the Queen Elizabeth," "I swear to tell the truth," "I promise to support you in warfare," "We find the defendant guilty." The importance of such utterances in the conduct of human affairs is so patent as to obviate the need to argue it, but philosophers, in the last few decades especially, have given considerable attention to their peculiar characteristics. J. L. Austin (1962) has called them "performative utterances" and "illocutionary acts," J. R. Searle (1969) includes them among what he calls "speech acts," F. O'Doherty (1973) refers to an important sub-class as "factitive" acts or utterances, J. Skorupski (1976) uses the term "operative acts" for a class resembling them closely.

It is important to make clear that the force of what I shall call "performatives," following Austin's earlier and simpler terminology, does not depend in any simple and direct way upon the effect of these acts and utterances upon the minds and hearts of those exposed to them. Whether or not he has reservations, planting *rumbim* joins a man to the group with whom he plants it. Regardless of what they may think or feel about it those who are excommunicated, outlawed, found guilty or demoted in rituals properly conducted by authorized persons are thereby excommunicated, outlawed, made felonious or degraded. If authorized persons declare peace in a proper manner, peace is declared whether or not the antagonists are persuaded to act accordingly. This is not to say that acts and utterances which are performative may not be persuasive, threatening, inspiring or otherwise affect the receiver in ways inducing him to act in particular ways. In the language of speech act theory they may have "perlocutionary" as well as "illocutionary" force.[1] It is to say that an action having a conventional effect is completed in the gesture or utterance itself.

Performatives differ in the scope of the action they complete. If an authorized person, following a proper procedure, names a ship the Queen Elizabeth, the ship is so named. Others may, if they like, call it "Hortense," but its name happens to be Queen Elizabeth, and that's really all there is to it. On the other hand, if a man has danced at another group's *kaiko*, thereby promising to help his hosts in warfare, that is *not* all there is to it, for it remains for him to fulfill his pledge and he may fail to do so. The naming, which not only constitutes an action but actually brings into being the state of affairs with which it is concerned, is of the class of performatives that we may call "factive." Whereas many actions completed in ritual – dubbings, declarations of peace, marriages, purification – are factive, it is obvious that all are not. Some – among which are those that Austin called "commissives" (1962: 150ff.) – do not bring into being the states of affairs with which they are concerned, but merely bring into being the commitment of those performing them to do so sometime in the future.[2]

The Special Relationship between Rituals and Performativeness

While many liturgies are performative, where some sort of performative act is the main point of the performance, transforming war into peace, restoring purity to that which has been polluted, joining men and women in wedlock,

performativeness is not confined to ritual. There is no advantage to be gained, for instance, in taking the publican's utterance "The bar is closed" to be ritual, but when he says "the bar is closed" it is thereby closed, and you are not likely to get another drink. Performatives are not confined to ritual, but there is a special relationship between ritual and performativeness.

First, the formal characteristics of ritual enhance the chances of success of the performatives they include. Like any other acts performatives can fail. If, for instance, I were to dub one of my junior colleagues Knight of the Garter he would not thereby become a Knight of the Garter, even if the conduct of the ritual were letter perfect. Conversely, if Queen Elizabeth dubbed Princess Anne's horse to knighthood it probably wouldn't make him a knight, even granted the well-known English tolerance of eccentricity. And if a befuddled cleric recited the funeral liturgy rather than the marriage service I doubt if the couple standing before him would thereby become objects of mourning (Austin 1962: *passim*). All of these instances of faulty performatives are of ritual performatives and ritual performatives can misfire. The ludicrous nature of these instances suggests, however, that they are less likely to do so than are other non-ritualized performatives because the formality of liturgical orders helps to insure that whatever performatives they incorporate are performed by authorized people with respect to eligible persons or entities under proper circumstances in accordance with proper procedures. Moreover, the formality of ritual makes very clear and explicit what it is that is being done. For instance, if one Maring casually said to another whom he happened to be visiting, "I'll help you when next you go to war" it would not be clear whether this was to be taken as a vague statement of intent, as a prediction of what he would be likely to do, or as a promise, nor would it necessarily be clear what might be meant by "help." To dance this message in a ritual, however, makes it clear to all concerned that a pledge to help is undertaken, and it is conventionally understood that that help entails fighting. Ritual, this is to say, not only ensures the correctness of the performative enactment, but also makes the performatives it carries explicit. It generally makes them weighty as well. If a message concerning the current states of participants is communicated by participation in ritual it will not be vague, and the formality, solemnity and decorum of ritual infuses whatever performatives the ritual incorporates with a gravity that they otherwise might not possess. In sum, simply by making their performatives explicit rituals make clear to their participants just what it is that they are doing and thus they specify, at least tacitly, what would constitute an abuse or violation of whatever obligations those performatives entail. Clear definition itself may reduce the likelihood of abuses and violations simply by leading people to "think twice" before acting. To put this a little differently, clear definition, which is intrinsic to the formality of ritual, itself possesses perlocutionary force, and so do the gravity, solemnity and decorum characteristic of many rituals. Reflexively, the perlocutionary force inhering in the formality of a ritual supports whatever performatives are enacted in that ritual.

There are two other closely related reasons for considering the performativeness of ritual. First, the association of the sacred and occult with performatives in magical and religious rituals may mystify their conventional nature, and this may enhance their chances of success. To take the state of affairs established by a king's enthronement to derive from the sacramental virtue of crown and chrism may be more effective with respect to the maintenance of the social order over which the king reigns than would be the recognition of enthronement as a naked performative, a mere conventional act, the effects of which could, for instance, in response to the short-run displeasure of his subjects, easily be reversed.

Second, as Ruth Finnegan (1969: 50) has suggested, albeit rather unspecifically, the "truth lying behind" assumptions concerning what is often called "the magical power of words" may be related to their illocutionary force or performativeness. It may be proposed, rather more specifically, that the magical power of some of the words and acts forming parts of liturgies derives from the relationships between them and the conventional states of affairs with which they are concerned. As we have already observed, the relationship of performatives to the states of affairs with which they are concerned is the inverse of that of statements. The facts, events or situations to which a statement refers presumably exist independent of and previous to the statement referring to them, and a statement is assessed true if it accords in some sufficient degree to those previously existing and independent states of affairs. Since performatives bring about the facts, events, situations. etc., with which they are concerned, these facts are subsequent to and contingent upon them. Performatives, and most unambiguous factives, are self-fulfilling: they make themselves true in the sense of standing in a relationship of conformity to the states of affairs with which they are concerned. In light of this it may be suggested that the performativeness, and more especially the factiveness of ritual acts and utterances provide a basis for occult efficacy in general, including the magical power of words in particular. Ritual's words do, after all, bring conventional states of affairs, or "institutional facts" into being, and having been brought into being they are as real as "brute facts" (Searle 1969: chapter 2, *passim*). It may also be that magical power is attributed to other words by extension of the principle of factiveness beyond the domain of the meaningful, in which it is clearly effective, into the physical, in which it is not, but we must be very careful about stipulating the limits of the effects ritual can accomplish. We have already argued in somewhat different terms that their illocutionary force may be augmented by perlocutionary force. The effectiveness of persuasion, threat, cajolery, inspiration and ecstasy may well thrust beyond the purely conventional, and beyond discursive consciousness into the organic, as in the cures of healing rituals and in the injuries of ensorcellment.

Ritual's First Fundamental Office

Performatives are not confined to ritual, and there seems to be more to some or even all liturgies than the performatives that they incorporate. Indeed, some liturgies may not seem to include performatives in any simple sense at all. Many religious rituals do not seem to be directed toward achieving simple conventional effects through conventional procedures. If, however, simple performatives is not criterial of ritual, something like it, but of higher order, may be. Although not all rituals are obviously and simply performative, performativeness itself may be made possible by ritual. We approach here the conjunction of formality and performance [. . .]. We come, this is to say, to what is intrinsic to the act of *performing* a liturgical order, and thus to the heart of the relationship between the self-referential and canonical.

The characteristic of liturgical orders salient here is the simple fact of their performance; that they must be performed. Without performance, there is no ritual, no liturgical order. Records or descriptions of liturgies performed in Ur and Thebes survive but they are merely *about* liturgies, not themselves liturgies. They are remains of the dead, for the liturgical orders they recall are no longer given life and voice by the bodies and breath of men. Performance is not merely one way to present or express liturgical orders but is itself a crucial aspect or component of the messages those orders carry. The following may seem involuted. The involution is intrinsic to the phenomenon, and not to my account of it. A liturgical order is a sequence of formal acts and utterances, and as such it is realized – made real, made into a *res* – only when those acts are performed and those utterances voiced. This relationship of the act of performance to that which is being performed – that it brings it into being – cannot help but specify as well the relationship of the performer to that which he is performing. He is not merely transmitting messages he finds encoded in the liturgy. He is participating in – that is, *becoming part of* – the order to which his own body and breath give life.

To *perform* a liturgical order, which is by definition a more or less *invariant* sequence of formal acts and utterances *encoded by someone other than the performer* himself, is *necessarily to conform to it*. Authority or directives, therefore, seem intrinsic to liturgical order (see

Maurice Bloch 1973). The account just offered suggests, however, something more intimate and perhaps more binding than whatever is connoted by terms like "authority" and "conformity." The general notion of communication minimally implies transmitters, receivers, messages, and channels through which messages are carried from transmitters to receivers. Sometimes, furthermore, as in the case of canonical messages, which ritual's performers find already inscribed in prayer books or prescribed by tradition, transmitters should be distinguished from encoders, whose identities may be lost in time and whose dicta are, in part for that very reason, timeless. We earlier noted a peculiarity of ritual communication, namely that in ritual the transmitter and receiver are often one and the same. At least the transmitter is always among the most important receivers. Now we note another of ritual's peculiarities. *To say that performers participate in or become parts of the orders they are realizing is to say that transmitter-receivers become fused with the messages they are transmitting and receiving. In conforming to the orders that their performances bring into being, and that come alive in their performance, performers become indistinguishable from those orders, parts of them, for the time being. Since this is the case, for performers to reject liturgical orders being realized by their own participation in them as they are participating in them is self-contradictory, and thus impossible. Therefore, by performing liturgical order the participants accept, and indicate to themselves and to others that they accept whatever is encoded in the canon of that order.*

This act of acceptance is the first of ritual's fundamental offices. The self-referential and the canonical are united in the acceptance of the canon. Acceptance is the self-referential message intrinsic to all liturgical performances, the indexical message without which liturgical orders and the canonical messages they encode would be without consequence, non-existent, or vacuous. It is not a trivial message because humans are not bound to acceptance of particular conventional orders by their genotypes. They are often free not to participate in rituals if they do not care to, and refusal to participate is always a possibility, at least logically conceivable, by potential actors. Participation, and thus acceptance, always rests in logic and in some degree in fact, upon choice. Such choices may sometimes be extremely costly, but are always possible.

Acceptance, Belief, and Conformity

The assertion that acceptance is intrinsic to liturgical performance may still seem to be either dubious or indubitable. It therefore requires some elaboration and clarification in this section and the next.

First, *acceptance is not belief*. The concept of belief is difficult to define and the occurrence of belief difficult to establish (see R. Needham 1972). Let us say that the term "belief" at least suggests a mental state concerning, or arising out of, the relationship between the cognitive processes of individuals and representations presented to them as possible candidates for the status of true. As such, "belief" is a second-order process, that is, one concerned with the relationship between a first order process and external reality. By this account, belief is an inward state, knowable subjectively if at all, and it would be entirely unwarranted either for us or for participants or witnesses to assume that participation in a ritual would necessarily indicate such a state.

Acceptance, in contrast, is not a private state, but a public act, visible both to witnesses and to performers themselves. People may accept because they believe, but acceptance not only is not itself belief; it doesn't even imply belief. Ritual performance often possesses perlocutionary force, and the private processes of individuals may often be persuaded by their ritual participation to come into conformity with their public acts, but this is not always the case. Belief is a cogent reason, but far from the only reason, for acceptance. Conversely, belief can provide grounds for refusals to accept. Reformers and heretics, for the very reason that they believe deeply in certain postulates concerning the divine, may refuse to participate in the rituals of religious institutions they take to have fallen into error or corruption.

This account suggests that although participation in liturgical performance may be highly visible it is not very profound, for it neither indicates nor does it necessarily produce an inward state conforming to it. Such a view is widely held by critics of religion who are inclined to take ritual participation to be nothing more than empty or even hypocritical formalism, a view reflected in one of the term's common modern meanings, formal behaviour devoid of substance or consequence. But, paradoxically, it may be, and it surely has been implied by religion's defenders, that the acceptance indicated by liturgical performance, being independent of belief can be more profound than conviction or sense of certainty, for it makes it possible for the performer to transcend his or her own doubt by accepting in defiance of it. Even the most devout, indeed especially the most devout, sometimes harbour doubts or even voice scepticism concerning propositions expressed in liturgies to which they scrupulously conform, and acceptance in this deep sense has much in common with certain Christian notions of faith. Fehean O'Doherty, a Catholic priest, writes "faith is neither subjective conviction nor experienced certitude, but may be at its best where doubt exists" (1973: 9), and Paul Tillich has said that faith *necessarily* includes an element of uncertainty or doubt (1957: 16 ff.). It is also of interest in this regard that Judaism does not require the devout to believe, for belief is not subject to command. It does, however, demand of them that they *accept* the law, and this acceptance is signalled by, and is intrinsic to, conformity to the ritual observances that pervade all of life.

Be this as it may, there may well be, and often are, disparities between the act of acceptance and the inward state associated with it. One can accept publicly not only that which one doubts but that which one privately despises or secretly denies. But if acceptance is intrinsic to performance it is not vitiated by secret denial. To recognize that secret denial may hide beneath the acceptance inhering in the act of performance is to recognize that the grounds of acceptance may vary widely, that acceptance is not necessarily founded upon belief, and that it does not even necessarily imply the subjective state termed "approval."

Acceptance, then, can be unconvinced and "insincere," *but insincerity does not nullify acceptance*. In what appears to be a flaw of sufficient seriousness to vitiate its meaningfulness lies the very virtue of acceptance through liturgical performance. Its social efficacy lies in its very lack of profundity, in the possibility of disparity between the outward act and the inward state. The distinction between belief and acceptance corresponds to the distinction made in the third chapter between the public and private. Participation in ritual demarcates a boundary, so to speak, between private and public processes. Liturgical orders, even those performed in solitude, are *public* orders and participation in them constitutes an acceptance of a public order *regardless* of the private state of belief of the performer. We may cite here Austin's views on a great range of performatives – promising, swearing, repudiating, commending, assessing – among which accepting is to be included:

> we must not suppose . . . that what is needed in addition to the saying of the words in such cases is the performance of some internal spiritual act, of which the words are then the report. It's very easy to slip into this view at least in difficult portentous cases . . . In the case of promising – for example, "I promise to be there tomorrow" – it's very easy to think that the utterance is simply the outward and visible . . . sign of the performance of some inward spiritual act of promising, and this view has been expressed in many classic places. There is the case of Euripedes' Hippolytus who said "My tongue swore to, but my heart did not" – perhaps it should be "mind" or "spirit" rather than "heart," but at any rate some kind of backstage artiste. (1970: 236)

It is gratifying to observe in this very example [that of Hippolytus] how excess of profundity, or rather solemnity, at once paves the way for immorality. For one who says "promising is not merely a matter of uttering words! It is an inward and spiritual act!" is apt to appear as a solid moralist standing out against a genera-

tion of theorizers: we see him as he sees himself, surveying the invisible depths of ethical space, with all the distinction of a specialist in the sui generis. Yet he provides Hippolytus with a let-out, the bigamist with an excuse for his "I do" and the welsher with a defence for his "I bet." Accuracy and morality alike are on the side of the plain saying that our word is our bond (Austin 1962: 10).

Acceptance in, or through, liturgical performance may reflect an inward state of conviction; it may also encourage "the mind," "the heart" and "the spirit" into agreement with itself. It does not necessarily do either, however, and therefore it does not eliminate all of the shenanigans of which the mind, the heart, the spirit, and other "backstage artistes" may be capable, but my argument, based on Austin's, proposes that although liturgical performance does not eliminate insincerity, it renders it publicly impotent. It is the visible, explicit, public act of acceptance, and not the invisible, ambiguous, private sentiment, which is socially and morally binding.

Because public and private processes are (and must be) related, but only loosely related, a range of what Austin (1962: 95ff., *passim*) called "infelicities" – insincerities and the like – are possible. But if, somehow, public orders could be required to depend upon the continuing belief, sincerity, goodwill, conviction or enthusiasm of those subject to them, the possibility of insincerity or deceit would surely be replaced by the high probability of non-order or disorder because of the near impossibility of meeting such a standard. This is not to say that the private processes may not be important in the dynamics of ritual. In a later chapter we shall take up belief and religious experience. It is simply to recognize that the private states of others are in their nature unknowable and even one's own attitudes may not always be easy to ascertain, for we are inclined to be ambivalent about matters of importance, like the conventions to which we are subordinate, and private states are likely to be volatile. "Common belief" cannot in itself provide a sufficiently firm ground upon which to establish public orders, even in very simple societies. We cannot know if a belief is common, for one thing, and whereas belief is vexed by ambivalence and clouded by ambiguity, acceptance is not. Liturgical orders are public, and participation in them constitutes a public acceptance of a public order, regardless of the private state of belief. Acceptance is not only public but clear. One either participates in a liturgy or one does not; the choice is binary and as such it is formally free of ambiguity. While ritual participation may not transform the private state of the performer from one of "disbelief" to "belief," our argument is that in it the ambiguity, ambivalence and volatility of the private processes are subordinated to a simple and unambiguous public act, sensible both to the performers themselves and to witnesses as well. Liturgical performance is, thus, a fundamental social act, for the acceptance intrinsic to it forms a basis for public orders which unknowable and volatile belief or conviction cannot.

That a liturgical order is accepted in its performance does not, furthermore, guarantee that the performer will abide by whatever rules or norms that order encodes. We all know that a man may participate in a liturgy in which commandments against adultery and thievery are pronounced, then pilfer from the poor box on his way out of church, or depart from communion to tryst with his neighbor's wife. To recognize such sordid realities is not to agree that liturgical acceptance is hypocritical, trivial or meaningless (Douglas 1973: 30), nor is it to dismiss claims for the social efficacy of acceptance through liturgical performance. It is, in fact, to affirm them, for such violations do not nullify acceptance, nor render it trivial. It is in such instances that the importance of ritual acceptance is most dramatically demonstrated. The primary function or metafunction of liturgical performances is not to control behavior directly, but rather to establish conventional understandings, rules and norms in accordance with which everyday behaviour is *supposed* to proceed. Participation in a ritual in which a prohibition against adultery is enunciated by, among others, himself may not prevent a man from committing adultery, but it does establish for him the prohibition of adultery as a rule that he himself has both enlivened and accepted. *Whether or not he abides by that rule, he has*

obligated himself to do so. If he does not, he has violated an obligation that he himself has avowed. The assertion here is similar to those of Austin (see above) and of the philosopher John Searle, who has argued that

when one enters an institutional activity by invoking the rules of that institution one necessarily commits oneself in such and such ways, regardless of whether one approves or disapproves of the institution. In the case of linguistic institutions like promising [and accepting] the serious utterance of words commits one in ways which are determined by the meaning of the words. In certain first person utterances the utterance is the undertaking of an obligation. (1969: 189)

Searle later notes that the notion of obligation is closely related to those of accepting, recognizing, acknowledging. This suggests that there is no obligation without acceptance, and perhaps that morality begins with acceptance. We may also note that while the acceptance of conventional undertakings, rules and procedures is possible outside of ritual, the formal and public nature of liturgical performance makes it very clear that an act of acceptance is taking place, that the acceptance is serious, and what it is that is being accepted. In Austin's terms (1962: *passim*) it is "explicitly performative." *In sum, it is not ritual's office to ensure compliance but to establish obligation.*

Performativeness, Metaperformativeness, and the Establishment of Convention

We may now return to the assertion that although all ritual may not include simple performatives – conventional procedures for achieving conventional effects – something formally similar to simple performativeness, but of higher order, is intrinsic to ritual's form, and that this characteristic of ritual makes performatives possible.

Austin (1962: 26ff.) listed six conditions that must be fulfilled if performatives are to be successful (see also Searle 1969: *passim*). These include a number of obvious stipulations already noted at least tacitly – that they be performed by properly authorized persons under proper circumstances, and that they be executed correctly and completely. We have observed that the formality of ritual goes a long way to assure that those conditions are met, but ritual's contribution to performativeness is not limited to its service as a protocol, conformity to which assures full and correct performance. Its significance is much more fundamental.

Austin states the first and most basic condition for performative success, that which he labels A.1, as follows: "There must *exist* an *accepted* conventional procedure having a certain conventional effect, the procedure to include the uttering of certain words [or the performance of certain symbolic acts] by certain persons in certain circumstances" (1962: 14) (emphasis mine). Conventional effects cannot be achieved without conventions for achieving them. If young men are to be transformed into knights there must be a procedure for doing so, and this procedure must be acceptable to the relevant public. We may also note, although Austin does not, that the acceptance of a procedure for dubbing knights tacitly but obviously entails an acceptance of the convention of knighthood itself. Yet further, if the young man is "armed as a knight for the service of Christ" by priests or bishops, an acceptance of Christ's divinity is also entailed (Marc Bloch 1961: ch. 33).

Austin's basic condition seems obvious, but it is not trivial because its violation is possible. A performative attempt could misfire because, for instance, no one but the performer recognized the procedure which it employed or the state of affairs it sought to achieve. An attempt by an American citizen living in the United States to win a divorce by repeating to his wife "I divorce you" three times would not rid him of matrimony's burdens, nor would any divorce procedure whatsoever succeed in a society not recognizing divorce at all (Austin 1962: 27). Conventional procedures and conventional states, or even entire conventional codes, may be accepted by some and not by others and there are surely changes in the conventions of any society through time, with the scope of their applicability expanding or contracting, some disappearing altogether while others appear. Conventions can cease to exist because they are no longer accepted (Austin 1962: 30), as, for instance, in the case of the code of honor of which duelling was a part. It is unlikely, to say the least, that in contemporary United States or Great Britain a slap of a glove across a cheek would lead to a duel. The conventions of which this ritual act was an element are no longer accepted. They are, as we say, "history."

Austin stipulated as requisite to the effectiveness of performatives that relevant conventions exist and be accepted, but he gave only scant attention to the ways in which this prerequisite might be fulfilled. The argument being presented here is that ritual may fulfill it. To establish a convention – a general public understanding, a regular procedure, an institution – is *both* to ascribe existence to it *and* to accept it. The two are hardly distinct, as Austin (1962: 26) understood, for the existence of a convention, given the meaning of the word, is a function of its acceptance (see Bateson 1951: 212ff.). To perform a liturgy is at one and the same time to conform to its order and to realize it or make it substantial. *Liturgical performance not only recognizes the authority of the conventions it represents, it gives them their very existence.* In the absence of performance liturgical orders are dead letters inscribed in curious volumes, or insubstantial forms evaporating into the forgotten. A ritual performance is an instance of the conventional order of which it conforms. Conversely, a ritual performance realizes the order of which it is an instance. Participants enliven the order that they are performing with the energy of their own bodies, and their own voices make it articulate. They thereby establish the existence of that order in this world of matter and energy; they *substantiate* the order as it *informs* them.

If performatives are to be understood as conventional procedures for achieving conventional effects, rituals are, by this account, more than simple performatives. We have already noted that a dubbing did more than transform a particular young man into a knight; it also repeatedly established (accepted the existence of) a conventional procedure for transforming young men into knights. It further established and re-established the conventions of knighthood itself, and of the divinity of the god in whose name and service knights were dubbed. The mass, in contrast, establishes a more general conventional understanding of the relationship of humans to the divine. The act of acceptance intrinsic to ritual performance is not simply performative, as are specific conventional acts occurring within rituals – crowning, marrying, dubbing, purifying – but *meta-performative*. Rituals do more than achieve conventional effects through conventional procedures. They establish the conventions in terms of which those effects are achieved.

The establishment of convention is the second of ritual's fundamental offices. It is fundamental because all of ritual's simple performative functions are founded upon, or presume it, and so may conventional procedures outside of ritual itself. It is fundamental, this is to say, because the establishment of convention is what might be called a "*meta*function" making possible the fulfillment of particular functions by the particular conventions established.

It is fundamental in a second, formal sense, because the establishment as convention of whatever is encoded in canon is intrinsic to the form of ritual, that is, to the performance of more or less invariant sequences of formal acts and utterances not encoded by the performer. We observe here the profound importance of invariance and formality. These are the features that maintain constant that which is accepted. In the absence of such constancy that which is accepted would not be conventional. Indeed, acceptance would be inconsequential, meaningless, or even logically impossible if the canon were made up afresh by each participant for each performance.

We note in passing that as one of "the realities" lying behind notions of the *magical* power of words may be simple performativeness or factiveness mystified, so may widespread notions concerning the *creative* power of *The Word* rest upon meta-performativeness or meta-factiveness mystified, upon the realiza-

tion of conventions through participation in invariant liturgical orders.

Ritual and Daily Practice in the Establishment of Convention

That the obligations clearly and explicitly accepted in liturgical performance are nullified by neither disbelief nor violation has a significance transcending the problems of insincerity and deceitfulness. We approach here a matter of profound importance, the relationship of convention to behavior and, more particularly, difficulties in establishing convention through ordinary usage. I have argued that one of ritual's fundamental offices is the establishment of convention, but no claim was made that convention is established only in ritual. It therefore may seem in this regard that ritual is no different from usage or practice in general. Convention, be it noted, may also be established by decree. There are important differences, however, between liturgical performance and other means for establishing convention.

First, we may contrast liturgical performance with quotidian practice. As Bateson (1951: 214) long ago remarked, "every statement in a given codification is an affirmation of that codification and is therefore in some degree metacommunicative (when I say 'I see the cat' I am implicitly affirming the proposition that the word 'cat' stands for what I see")." The core meaning of the term "code" is linguistic, in some usages it denotes vocabularies and the rules for combining their elements into larger meaningful units *without reference to or restriction upon what can or may be said*. While linguistic conventions may be taken to be paradigmatic of those established in ordinary practice, it should be kept in mind that the concept of code has been extended beyond language by some cognitive anthropologists, who tend to see cultures generally as complex codes made up of "shared finite cognitive set[s] of rules for the socially appropriate construction and interpretation of messages and behaviour" (Kernan 1972: 333, cf. Frake 1964). But a liturgy is not a code in this wide and semantically unspecifying sense. It is a more or less fixed sequence of stereotyped actions and utterances and as such what can be expressed in it is narrowly circumscribed. Permissible variations in some aspects of performance do allow or require the participants to encode indexical messages, but the content of the canon, the invariant aspect of the liturgy in respect to which the indexical messages may vary, is fixed, and therefore the range of indexical messages that may be transmitted in any liturgy is restricted. Moreover, as we have noted, the participants do not encode but only transmit the invariant messages the canon embodies. Since this is the case, the term "liturgical *order*" seems more appropriate than "liturgical *code*." It follows that the acceptance of an order, because it is in its nature highly restrictive, is therefore more socially consequential and significant than the affirmation of a more or less unrestrictive code. High valuation of the qualities of the consequential and the restrictive, as previous discussion suggests, invites the application of liturgical order, for liturgy tends to make explicit precisely what is being stipulated, it is in its very form constricting, and further, liturgical form and decorum tends to make its substance seem grave.

It would, of course, be mistaken to impose the simple dichotomous distinction of "codes" versus "orders" upon the conventions organizing social life. Linguistic codes and the conventional dogmatic understandings embodied in some liturgies stand at opposite ends of a continuum of constraint. Between them are stretched the conventions which organize not merely what people say to or about each other or the world, but what they do to and with each other and the world around them. Little is known about the order of this continuum, whether certain domains of culture are more likely to be subject to narrower or more rigorous constraints than others, or whether variation from one society to the next is wide. We shall return to this general question in a later chapter when we discuss sanctification. For now it may be noted that comparatively high degrees of constraint seem entailed by the invariant nature of liturgy, and it may further be suggested that the more highly motivated people are to violate a convention or the more

consequential its violation is deemed to be, the more likely it is to be established in liturgy than in daily practice, or the more closely and strongly will it be associated with conventional understandings that are so represented (see the discussion of sanctification in chapter 10 below). Be this as it may, certain conventions, for instance, those of speech, emerge out of ordinary usage and are maintained by ordinary usage in sufficient stability to allow meaningful and orderly social interaction. In such cases, "the norm is identical with the statistical average" (Leach 1972: 320). It may be suggested that variation with respect to such conventions can be comfortably tolerated and day-to-day usage may be allowed to establish, maintain or change them. But ordinary practice or usage is not in itself sufficient to establish all conventions, nor are statistical averages arising out of behavior always coextensive with conventions.

First, it is impossible for ordinary usage to establish conventions to which no ordinary usage corresponds. Such conventions include most importantly, and perhaps exclusively, the understandings upon which religions are founded, dogmas and mysteries concerning gods and the like which, being typically without material referents and always being taken to be extraordinary, cannot grow out of ordinary usage. The fundamental importance of these conventions will be discussed in later chapters.

Secondly, statistical averages arising out of usage represent no more than common practice, summations of behavior, and the utility of summations of behavior for guiding or assessing the behavior of which they are summations is limited, at best. They are particularly inadequate, first, in the case of conventions with moral import, for they tend to reduce the notion of immorality to deviation from a statistically average behavioral range – to that which "is not done," and the moral to that which "is done." Such a notion of morality and immorality is, on the one hand, descriptively erroneous – no society operates with such a conception of morality – and, on the other hand, operatively inadequate. No society could so operate, at least for long, because it would be without any means for assessing common practice itself, and a common practice may, even in terms of the moral code of the society in which it occurs, be vicious, antisocial or self-destructive. Common practice, statistical average, ordinary usage will have difficulty establishing conventions concerning aspects of social life that are obviously restrictive, obviously arbitrary, highly charged emotionally, especially dangerous, or require obedience conventions, this is to say, that demand of individuals that they subordinate their self-interests to the common good. Behavioral variation may be less tolerable with respect to these matters than with respect to linguistic usage, and uncertainty as to the precise nature of the conventions themselves, a different matter, may be even less tolerable than variations in the practices which they presumably direct. Ordinary usage always varies, and in ordinary usage rules and conventions are frequently violated. Leach was generally pointing in the right direction but did not go far enough when he suggested that "if anarchy is to be avoided, the individuals who make up a society must from time to time be reminded of the underlying order that is supposed to guide their social activities. Ritual performances have this function for the group as a whole. They momentarily make explicit what is otherwise fiction" (1954: 16). Although usage may not be faithful to it, that which is represented in a liturgical order is not a fiction, (except in the sense of being "made up," rather than given by non-human nature, see Geertz 1973: 15), and the performance does more than remind individuals of an underlying order.

It is well to make explicit an assumption tacit in our general argument. The orders of societies, like the order of the universe in general, tend to degenerate into disorder. Their material elements disintegrate or decay into non-functioning fragments if they are not maintained, and their meaningful elements, including conventional understandings and rules, dissolve into error, nonsense, ambiguity, vagueness, hypocrisy and meaninglessness unless continually clarified, corrected and reestablished. Far from clarifying and reasserting conventions, the vagaries of practice may tend to erode them. It is therefore necessary to establish at least some conventions in a manner which protects them from dissolution in the variations of day-to-day behavior and the violations in which history abounds. Liturgy does not simply remind people of the orders which usage – behavior and history – violates and dissolves. It establishes and ever again reestablishes those orders. *Liturgy preserves the conventions it encodes inviolate in defiance of the vagaries of ordinary practice, thereby providing them with existence independent of, and insulated against, the statistical averages which characterize behavior.* That "everyone does it" exonerates no one. For people of the Book adultery would remain a sin even if every married person indulged in it.

It should be noted, however, that the violation of convention is not always simply a matter of entropy, chaos or anarchy asserting itself against an ideal but not fully realized order. The constitution of some societies is such that the violation of some conventions is not only frequent but systematic, and yet the convention has a vital part to play in the life of the society. Gluckman long ago (1954) considered certain African rituals in this light, and we may note that among the Maring and other Highland New Guinea peoples, a strong patrilocal patrilineal ideology prevails. It is putatively patrilineal clans that hold territories and putatively patrilineal sub-clans that claim smaller tracts (Rappaport 1968: ch. 2). Rituals, addressed largely to patrilineal ancestors, are conducted by these groups at special places on the land which they and their deceased ancestors are said to occupy together. But the exigencies of life and death are such that the demographic fortunes of these small groups (sub-clans among the Tsembaga ran, in 1963, from almost none to about thirty-five persons, clans from sixteen to seventy persons), fluctuate widely, and fluctuations may lead to the violation of the patrilineal patrilocal ideal. Groups must maintain their strength *vis-à-vis* their neighbors, and when their numbers are low the members of a group will attempt to attract outsiders to settle among them. Their kinship terminology, which is Iroquois on ego's generation, but generational on all descending generations, as well as on the second ascending generation and above, seems well suited to the assimilation of strangers, obliterating as it does distinctions between agnates, other cognates and affines in two generations, and *rumbim* planting can be seen as the beginning of a process by which cognates are transformed into agnates. This ritual transformation of non-agnates into agnates is able to preserve the *conventions* of patrilocality and patrilineality, if not patrifiliation, inviolate in the face of continual violation in usage (see LiPuma 1990). This is of considerable adaptive importance. Densities sometimes become high in the New Guinea highlands and therefore it sometimes becomes necessary or desirable to exclude people who would like to immigrate (Meggitt 1965). Agnatic rules, necessarily violated by practice but preserved by ritual, provide a basis for such exclusion when there is need.

The formality definitive of ritual and distinguishing it from ordinary behavior is clearly of importance in preserving the conventions it encodes from the errors and trespasses of daily practice. Because preservation is virtually entailed by ritual's formality, and because the acceptance as well as the precise stipulation of convention is intrinsic to ritual's form, ritual may well be without functional, or metafunctional, equivalents.

Ritual, to be sure, is not altogether unique in establishing conventions at the same time that it insulates them from the variations and violations of behavior. Conventions may also be promulgated by decree and maintained by force. But the acceptance of those subject to a decree is not intrinsic to the promulgation of that decree. In contrast, it is one and the same ritual act that both realizes and accepts a liturgical order. Furthermore, the act of acceptance establishes an obligation with respect to the convention accepted, an obligation that is not specifically undertaken and may not be felt by those subject to decrees.

It is of interest in this regard that even in those instances in which conventions are self-consciously promulgated by kings or parliaments the act of promulgation and those participating in it are surrounded by ritual. Kings are crowned, public officers sworn into office, meetings of parliaments are ceremonially opened and closed, and their deliberations set within a more or less invariant procedure. Moreover, their decrees may be accepted, albeit indirectly and non-specifically, by those subject to them in such ritual acts as pledges of allegiance to the entities, or symbols thereof, from which the promulgators derive their authority. To accept an order is to ascribe legitimacy to its terms. To ascribe legitimacy to its terms is to oblige oneself to abide by them, or to put it a little differently, to agree to their application as a set of standards against which the acceptor's own actions are properly judged. Insofar as participation in a liturgical order is an acceptance of that order, it legitimizes that order. . . .

The Morality Intrinsic to Ritual's Structure

The performance of a liturgy not only brings conventions into being but invests them with morality. Moral dicta are not explicit in all liturgies, but morality, like social contract, is implicit in ritual's structure.

We have, following Searle, noted that obligation is entailed by the acceptance intrinsic to participation in ritual. Breach of obligation, it could be argued, is one of the few acts, if not, indeed, the only act that is always and everywhere held to be immoral. Homicide, for instance, is not. There are conditions, so common as to require no illustration, under which killing humans is laudable or even mandatory. What is immoral is, of course, killing someone whom there is an obligation, at least tacit, not to kill. A similar point can be made about most or possibly even all other specific acts generally taken to be immoral. Breach of obligation is of a higher order of generality than any such specific breach as murder, rape or robbery and it may be suggested that it is breach of obligation that transforms otherwise morally positive, neutral or empty acts into crimes such as murder or robbery. Breach of obligation may, then, be *the* fundamental immoral act, the element in the absence of which an act cannot be construed to be immoral, in the presence of which it is ipso facto immoral. The topic is a difficult one, and surely cannot be settled here. I will only emphasize that failure to abide by the terms of an obligation is universally stigmatized as immoral. To the extent, then, that obligation is entailed by the acceptance intrinsic to the performance of a liturgical order, ritual establishes morality as it establishes convention. The establishment of a convention and the establishment of its morality are inextricable, if they are not, in fact, one and the same.

We may refer again in this regard to the relationship of performatives to the states of affairs with which they are concerned. Austin initially tried to say that performatives differ from statements in that performatives are neither true nor false (1970: 233ff.) whereas statements are either true or false. Later he found this view to be questionable because certain performatives, notably verdictives, are supposed to stand in a relationship to states of affairs similar to that of true statements to states of affairs. Later he found this not always to be the case. Performatives do, however, differ from statements in a related way which he did not note but which does have to do with truth, and with the foundations of morality.

In discussing their indexical nature, we have observed that the relationship of performatives to the states of affairs with which they are concerned is the inverse of that of statements or descriptions. Statements *report* autonomously existing states of affairs. Performative acts *realize* states of affairs. The inverse nature of these relationships has obvious implications for assessment. The adequacy of a descriptive statement is assessed by the degree to which it conforms to the state of affairs that it purports to describe. If it is in sufficient conformity we say that it is true, accurate or correct. If it is not we say that it is false, erroneous, inaccurate or lying. *The state of affairs is the criterion by which the truth, accuracy or adequacy of a statement is assessed.* In the case of performatives there is an inversion. If, for instance, a man is properly dubbed to knighthood and then proceeds to violate all of the canons of chivalry, or if peace is declared in a properly conducted ritual but soon after one of the parties to the declaration attacks the other, we do not say that the dubbing or the peace declaration were faulty, but that the subsequent states of affairs are faulty. *We judge the state*

of affairs by the degree to which it conforms to the stipulations of the performative act. Liturgical orders provide criteria in terms of which events – behavior and history – may be judged. As such, liturgical orders are intrinsically correct or moral. Morality is inherent in the structure of liturgical performance prior to whatever its canons explicitly assert about morality in general or whatever in particular may be taken to be moral. Morality derives ultimately not from statements about what may be right and wrong but from what liturgy establishes as right or wrong. To put it a little differently, to establish a convention independent of usage is to establish an "ought" against which the "is" of behavior may be judged.

The establishment of morality is clearest in the case of simple factiveness and the commissive implications thereof. It is patently immoral to act incompatibly with the terms of a conventional state of affairs that one has ritually participated in bringing into being. My argument implies, however, that morality is also intrinsic to the metafactiveness of ritual, that is, to the establishment of particular conventions and conventional orders. One who violates not merely the terms of a conventional state of affairs, but of the conventional order defining such states of affairs is not guilty of a simple immoral act, but of apostasy. It is of interest here that in Zoroastrian Persia and Vedic India states of affairs that departed from the proper liturgically established order were designated by terms that also seem to have meant "lie," *druj* in Persia and *anrta* in India (Duchesne-Guillemin 1966: 26ff., N. Brown 1972: 252ff., Orlin 1976). What may be called "Vedic lies" or "Zoroastrian lies" (Rappaport 1979a), states of affairs that their perpetrators are aware do not conform to prevailing liturgically established orders, are the inverse of "vulgar lies," statements that their transmitters believe misrepresent the states of affairs which they purport to report.
[. . .]

Ritual as the Basic Social Act

To summarize, the existence of a conventional order is contingent upon its acceptance; in fact a rule or understanding cannot be said to be a convention unless it is accepted. In ritual, however, acceptance and existence entail each other, for a liturgical order is perforce accepted in its realization, in, that is to say, the performance which gives it substance. Since obligation is entailed by acceptance, and the breaking of obligation is *per se* immoral, the existence, acceptance, and morality of conventions are joined together indissolubly in rituals; they are, in fact, virtually one and the same. The same cannot be said of principles, rules, procedures or understandings established by proclamation, or legislation on the one hand or by daily practice on the other. This is to say that there is a logically necessary relationship between the form which is ritual, the performance of more or less invariant sequences of formal acts and utterances not encoded by the performers, and the messages rituals contain concerning both what is performed and the

relationship of the performer to what he performs. Ritual is not merely another way to "say things" or "do things" that can be said or done as well or better in other ways. The form which is ritual is surely without communicational equivalents and thus, possibly, without functional or metafunctional equivalents. That ritual's abilities are intrinsic to its form and in indissoluble association *only* with its form, goes far to account for its ubiquity.

In attending to ritual's form we must not lose sight of the fundamental nature of what it is that ritual does as a logically necessary outcome of its form. In enunciating, accepting and making conventions moral, ritual contains within itself not simply a symbolic representation of social contract, but tacit social contract itself. As such, ritual, which also establishes, guards, and bridges boundaries between public systems and private processes, is *the* basic social act.

NOTES

1 An act or utterance is said to have illocutionary force if it achieves its effect *in* its very utterance or enactment. An effect is intrinsic to an illocutionary act or performance; the concept of illocutionary force is a secular equivalent of the doctrine of *ex opera operato*, explicitly specifying the efficacy of the sacraments of Roman Catholicism, but implicit in the thought and practice of other religious traditions. In contrast, an act or utterance is said to have perlocutionary force if it achieves its result *through* its effect upon receivers. Its effect is not intrinsic to the act or utterance itself, but is realized only if the act or utterance persuades, threatens, cajoles (or whatever) some party into taking action. (Austin 1962, esp. Lecture VIII).

2 The identification of two classes of performative, factives and commissives, is sufficient for our purposes, but it does not conform to Austin's taxonomy. He identified five classes (1962: 150ff.).

  1 *Verdictives*, "typified by the giving of a verdict," but including also less formal

judgements, e.g., assessing, grading, ranking.
  2 *Exercitives*, "the exercising of powers, rights, or influence," e.g., appointing, voting, ordering.
  3 *Commissives*, "typified by promising; they commit you to do something."
  4 *Behabitives*, "a very miscellaneous group ... [having] to do with attitudes and *social behavior* ... apologizing, congratulating, commending, condoling, cursing and challenging" (emphasis in original).
  5 *Expositives*, "make plain how our utterances fit into an argument or conversation, how we are using words or are, in general, expository ... I argue, I concede, I illustrate ... I postulate."

These categories are obviously not mutually exclusive. Austin also notes that the distinction between performatives and statements, reports, and descriptions (the class of expressions he calls "constatives" (1962: 3)) is not always sharp and it is clear that illocutionary acts often possess perlocutionary force as well. Austin did not identify factives at all, but it is further clear that they cross-cut at least two of his categories, and that some (e.g., "we declare peace") have commissive entailments. All in all, it is better to regard Austin's categories, and the term "factive" as well, as designations of illocutionary *functions* rather than of distinct classes of expressions.

REFERENCES

Austin, J. L. 1962. *How to do Things with Words*. Oxford: Oxford University Press.

——. 1970. "Performative utterances," in J. Urmson and G. Warnock (eds.), *Philosophical Papers of J. L. Austin*. 2nd ed. Oxford: Oxford University Press.

Bateson, Gregory. 1951. "Conventions of communication: where validity depends upon belief," in J. Ruesch and G. Bateson, *Communication: The Social Matrix of Psychiatry*. New York: Norton.

——. 1972. *Steps to an Ecology of Mind*. New York: Ballantine.

——. 1972a. "The science of mind and order," in Bateson 1972.

——. 1972b. "Form, subsistence, and difference," in Bateson 1972. First published in *General Semantics Bulletin* no. 37 (1970).

Bloch, Marc. 1961. *Feudal Society*. Vols. 1 & 2. Trans. L. Manyon. Chicago: University of Chicago Press.

Bloch, Maurice. 1973. "Symbols, song, dance and features of articulation," *European Journal of Sociology* 15: 55–81.

Brown, Norman W. 1972. "Duty as truth," *Proceedings of the American Philosophical Society* 116 (3): 252–68.

Campbell, Joseph. 1959. *The Masks of God*. vol. 1, *Primitive Mythology*. New York: The Viking Press.

Douglas, Mary. 1973. *Natural Symbols: Explorations in Cosmology*. Harmondsworth: Penguin. First published by Barrie and Rocklift, 1970.

Duchesne-Guillemin, Jacques. 1966. *Symbols and Values in Zoroastrianism*. New York: Harper and Row.

Erikson, Erik. 1966. "Ontogeny of ritualization in man," in J. Huxley (convenor), *A Discussion of the Ritualisation of Behaviour in Animals and Man*. Philosophical Transactions of the Royal Society of London. Series B. Biological Sciences 251 (772).

Finnegan, Ruth. 1969. "How to do things with words: performative utterances among the Limba of Sierra Leone," *Man* 4: 537–51.

Frake, C. 1964. "A structural description of Subanun 'religious behavior'," in W. H. Goodenough (ed.), *Explorations in Cultural Anthropology: Essays in Honor of George Peter Murdock*. New York: McGraw-Hill.

Geertz, Clifford. 1973. *The Interpretation of Cultures*. New York: Basic Books.

Gluckman, Max. 1954. *Rituals of Rebellion in Southeast Africa*. The Frazer Lecture, 1952. Manchester: Manchester University Press.

Goodenough, Erwin Ramsdell. 1990. *Goodenough on the Beginning of Christianity*. Ed. A. T. Kraabel. Atlanta: Scholar's Press.

Leach, Edmund R. 1954. *Political Systems of Highland Burma. A Study of Kachin Social Structure*. Boston: Beacon Press.

——. 1972. "The influence of cultural context on non-verbal communication in Man," in R. Hinds (ed.), *Non-verbal communication*. Cambridge: Cambridge University Press.

LiPuma, Edward. 1990. "The terms of change: Linguistic mediation and reaffiliation among the Maring," *Journal of the Polynesian Society* 99: 93–121.

Meggitt, M. J. 1965b. *The Lineage System of the Mae Enga of New Guinea*. Edinburgh: Oliver and Boyd.

Miller, James. 1965. "Living systems: Basic concepts," *Behavioral Science* 10: 193–257.

Needham, Rodney. 1972. *Belief, Language, and Experience*. Oxford: Basil Blackwell.

O'Doherty, E. Fehean. 1973. Ritual as a second order language. Paper prepared for Burg-Wartenstein Conference, no. 59: Ritual and Reconciliation. M. C. Bateson and M. Mead (conveners). New York: Wenner-Gren Foundation.

Orlin, Louis L. 1976. "Athens and Persia ca. 507 B.C.: a neglected perspective," in L. Orlin (ed.), *Michigan Oriental Studies in Honor of George G. Cameron* Ann Arbor,

MI: Dept. of Near Eastern Studies, University of Michigan.

Rappaport, Roy A. 1968. *Pigs for the Ancestors: Ritual in the Ecology of a New Guinea People*. New Haven, CT: Yale University Press.

——. 1979. *Ecology, Meaning, and Religion*. Richmond CA: North Atlantic Books.

——. 1979a. "On cognized models," in Rappaport 1979.

——. 1979b. "Sanctity and lies in evolution," in Rappaport 1979.

Searle, J. 1969. *Speech Acts*. Cambridge: Cambridge University Press.

Skorupski, John. 1976. *Symbol and Theory: A Philosophical Study of Theories of Religion in Social Anthropology*. Cambridge: Cambridge University Press.

Tillich, Paul. 1957. *The Dynamics of Faith*. New York: Harper and Row.

Turner, Victor. 1969. *The Ritual Process*. Chicago: Aldine.

Wallace, Anthony F. C. 1966. *Religion: An Anthropological View*. New York: Random House.

Part IV

Historical Dynamics: Power, Modernity, and Change

Capitalism, Colonialism, Christianity, and Conflict

Introduction

From the 1960s anthropology became more politically self-conscious. In response to American engagement in the war in Vietnam and in observing the stark inadequacy of modernization theory as propounded by economists and other social scientists, anthropologists began to pay much greater attention to economic inequality and political oppression. There was a historical turn as the field began not only to examine the historical roots of particular structures of inequality but to recognize the fundamental historicity of all social formations, religion included. Thus began a lively discussion about the role of religion in the waves of colonial and capitalist expansion, the part played by missionaries, the transformations of the religious systems of colonized or rapidly changing societies, and the sometimes highly original religious responses they took. Of course, as the essay by Wolf (chapter 13) indicates, this interest had precedents. In particular one can point to discussions of revitalization and millenarian movements, of which the finest contributions include Burridge (1960, 1969), Wallace (1972), and Worsley (1957). Much of this tradition owes a more or less direct debt to Marx, but varies with respect to the role given to economic and political forces. Marx's passages on commodity fetishism (1961, 1977) have been particularly useful for making sense of the culture of capitalism.

34

New Heaven, New Earth

Kenelm Burridge

Kenelm Burridge, professor emeritus at the University of British Columbia, was trained at Oxford and the Australian National University (PhD 1953) and subsequently taught at the Universities of Baghdad, Oxford, and Western Australia, before settling at UBC in 1968. Burridge is the author of highly acclaimed work on Melanesian myth and religion, notably *Mambu: A Melanesian Millenium* (1960, reprinted 1995 and 2004) and *Tangu Traditions* (l969) and pioneered the study of indigenous forms of Christianity and of missionaries (1991).

New Heaven, New Earth (1969), from which these passages are taken, was a highly original look at what are sometimes called millenarian movements and what in the Pacific were described under the somewhat condescending label of "cargo cults" (Worsley 1957, Lindstrom 1993). The book addresses the source and course of radical religious change. The argument has a surprisingly contemporary ring. Burridge singles out redemption – in his definition, the means by which religious practitioners return the debts incurred in realizing their potential (thereby combining a notion of salvation with ethical goals) – as well as concerns with "the truth about power." Millenarian movements – new religions in the making – arise when assumptions about power are challenged, notably under colonial oppression, and when new avenues are needed to seek redemption, that is, to lead a dignified, responsible life. Burridge thus links religious perturbations to moral disquiet and political and economic processes. Here he was prescient in focussing on the significance of money in transforming systems of value and thus the conditions for social prestige, self-respect, and moral integrity.

In the book Burridge compares millenarian movements from a wide variety of sources; in addition to the Native

From Kenelm Burridge, *New Heaven, New Earth: A Study of Millenarian Activities* (Oxford: Blackwell, 1969), pp. 3–14, 41–46, 75–83. Abridged.

American case described here, these include European, South Asian, Melanesian and Polynesian examples. If Burridge's thinking owes much to Christianity, it could be argued that early Christianity, arising in a colonized province of the Roman empire, itself offers an elegant example of a millenarian movement.

To dream a dream and make it come true; to realize the shape of what can be seen only in the mind's eye; to feel compelled to bring about the seemingly impossible – these are the prerogatives of man. James Naylor was ploughing his fields when, in a blinding and timeless moment, he knew why he had been born. Like Saint Paul, who never wavered in his adherence to a truth revealed to him in a vision, James Naylor, despite the cruelties of parliament and a bigoted religious orthodoxy, remained steadfast in what his vision had revealed to him. Driven by her voices, a French peasant girl put new life into a dispirited army and routed the alien invader. She was burned at the stake as a heretic and witch; she was also canonized Saint Joan. Ann Lee claimed to be the new Christ; Joseph Smith had a vision of heavenly bliss to be realized in an earthly community life; and thousands of miles and moments away a Maori, a Papuan, an African, an Indian – each is impelled to tell his good news of a new way of life. Whether as fool, fraud, saint, respectable bourgeois, farmer or tycoon, the pain of the millennium belongs only to man. It is why he is man, why, when the time comes, he has to make a new man.

Some fifty years ago Haddon wrote:[1] "An awakening of religious activity is a frequent characteristic of periods of social unrest. The weakening or disruption of the old social order may stimulate new and often bizarre ideals, and these may give rise to religious movements that strive to sanction social and political aspirations. Communities that feel themselves oppressed anticipate the emergence of a hero who will restore their prosperity and prestige. And when the people are imbued with religious fervour the expected hero will be regarded as a Messiah. Phenomena of this kind are well known in history, and are not unknown at the present day among peoples in all stages of civilization."

A forceful and succinct enough statement. In the space of a paragraph Haddon describes the kind of activity we are setting out to examine. It is worthwhile going over it to make sure we know what we mean by some of the words Haddon uses.

Religion and Redemption

What we mean by "religious activity" is clearly of key importance. Writing at the time he did Haddon may have had in mind Tylor's minimal definition of religion: "the belief in spiritual beings".[2] Or, since it is more usual and puts more generally much the same point as Tylor made more specifically, it may be that Haddon thought of "religious activity" as essentially defined by a belief in the supernatural. But neither of these definitions is of much sociological value as they stand. For though we can observe rites and rituals and infer their symbolic references with some accuracy, the problem of belief begs the question, we cannot know what a spiritual being is without further qualification, and it is too often tempting to define a belief in the supernatural in terms that would scarcely apply to anybody anywhere.[3] We need a broader view, one that subsumes the variety of activities that may be religious.

Meditating on the infinite may be a religious activity, so may writing a cheque, eating corpses, copulating, listening to a thumping sermon on hell fire, examining one's conscience, painting a picture, growing a beard, licking leprous sores, tying the body into knots, a dogged faith in human rationality – there is no human activity which cannot assume religious significance. When it does so it has overriding importance. It points to that which permeates and informs a whole way of life, and, more crucially, it indicates sources or principles of power which are regarded as particularly creative or destructive.[4] Indeed, all religions are basically concerned with power. They are concerned with the discovery, identification, moral relevance and ordering of different kinds of power whether these manifest themselves as thunder, or lightning, atomic fission, untrammelled desire, arrogance, impulse, apparitions, visions, or persuasive words. Within these terms a spiritual being, whether thought of as a deity or ghost or human being or angel or goblin or fairy, becomes a named and identified source or principle of power with particular and often measurable attributes and ranges of power.[5] And all that is meant by a belief in the supernatural is the belief that there do exist kinds of power whose manifestations and effects are observable, but whose natures are not yet fully comprehended.

Religions, let us say, are concerned with the systematic ordering of different kinds of power, particularly those seen as significantly beneficial or dangerous. This entails a specific framework of rules. But because a religion is concerned with the truth of things, and reaches out to discover and identify those sorts of power which, though sensed and affective, are currently not wholly comprehended, its rules about the use and control of different kinds of powers are grounded in an interplay between experience, working assumptions, and those more rooted assumptions we call faith. As experience widens and deepens, some of the rules and assumptions will be qualified, and others abandoned altogether – a developmental process in which received truths or assumptions give way to new truths, and in which the new truths become in their turn the received assumptions of future generations. These assumptions are community truths, truths which command a consensus. From them are derived the sets of moral imperatives, obligations, and rules of conduct to which men, because they live in community, subject themselves. Yet though man governs his condition with explicit and articulate rules of this kind, they are rarely interconsistent. Concrete situations often involve selecting one rule at the expense of another, and individuals, whether selfishly or otherwise motivated, accord differing priorities to some obligations at the expense

of others. And here too we touch on the essence of religious activity. For, given a context determined by current assumptions about power, the process whereby individuals attempt to discharge their obligations in relation to the moral imperatives of the community is no less than a "redemptive process".

From the pen of a social scientist, "redemptive process" seems a curious phrase. But it is useful. The human condition appears as one of general indebtedness: a feature which we acknowledge in variations of the aphorism "paying our debt to society". For whether the capacities of a human being are given him by God and/or a particular combination of genes, his potential can only be realized after a long process of feeding, nurturing, teaching and training by parents and others. Society, moreover, prescribes the attitudes and activities by which its members can pay back or redeem the debt incurred in being nurtured, made morally aware, and enabled to exert and realize their potential. While these prescribed activities may be thought of as "redemptive media", the media through which the debt is repaid or redeemed, the process of engaging in the activities – activities which are ordered in terms of particular kinds of obligations – is, in our idiom, the redemptive process, a process which leads on to redemption itself. But this, the payment of the debt in full, can only be realized when a human being becomes in himself completely unobliged, without any obligation whatsoever – a free-mover in heaven, enjoying nirvana, or joined with the ancestors. For since existence in community, a moral order, necessarily entails existence within a network of obligations, redemption itself can only be realized at or after that appropriate death which brings to an end an appropriate mode of discharging one's obligations.

We may now move towards a working definition of religion and religious activity. Let us say that they refer to

The redemptive process indicated by the activities, moral rules, and assumptions about power which, pertinent to the moral order and taken on faith, not only enable a people to perceive the truth of things, but guarantee that they are indeed perceiving the truth of things.[6]

This definition has several advantages. Instead of tucking religion into an obscure and even almost irrelevant compartment of social life, we give it the overriding importance it actually seems to have. For not only are religions concerned with the truth about power, but the reverse also holds: a concern with the truth about power is a religious activity. Operationally, this concern is expressed in maintaining or challenging the rules which govern the use and control of power. And these rules assume the form of a set of moral discriminations which, in constricting animal man, also provide him with opportunities for realizing his moral nature and potential. The definition implies, and therefore leads us to expect – despite the conservatism of particular religious orthodoxies – that religious activities will change when the assumptions about the nature of power, and hence the rules which govern its use and control, can no longer guarantee the truth of things.

The use of this definition spares us unnecessary wrangling with distinctions between religion and magic. We are not led into the impasse of calling the religions of other peoples bundles of superstitions. We are insulated from the prejudgements contained in the dichotomies rational/irrational and secular/religious. If a general rationality and order among human beings and their affairs are not assumed from the start, sociological analysis must founder. The label "irrational" tends to become a portmanteau of ethnocentric prejudices, for faith is faith whether thought of as religious or secular. More positively, with this definition we can identify activities and movements of a generally millenarian type where the words "God", "deity", or "spiritual being" or their synonyms in other languages are not in evidence. Because politics, too, are concerned with power, it becomes clear and explicit that no religious movement lacks a political ideology. And, accepting the political significance, we are forced to look at the ways in which wealth is distributed, and we must take account of what powers are dependent on various kinds of wealth.

If it is not to become overly ethnocentric, anthropology or comparative sociology must, initially, use broad concepts capable of containing the varied arrangements offered by different cultures. The "redemptive process" is just such a concept. Not necessarily hedged with mystery, it is something we can observe, ask about, talk about. The rules which govern the use of power can be determined. Both emerge from the ways in which individuals discharge or evade their obligations, what they do to counter or meet the consequences of evasion, how they cope with a pledge redeemed, what they say the consequences will or might be. We can, too, identify preliminary or temporary states of redemption.[7] Finally, we can accept provisionally the crude formula, Salvation = Redemption = Unobligedness, or release from all obligations. For, by examining the kinds of redemption or releases from obligation that are offered by particular kinds of millenarian activity, we might be able to see more accurately what assumptions and rules are currently not revealing the truth of things, what kinds of redemptive process would be more in tune with an actual or desired distribution of power.

New Ideals

It will be clear from what has been said above that "periods of social unrest" and the "weakening or disruption of the old social order" refer to situations where the relevant assumptions about power are weakening and no longer enable individuals to perceive the truth of things. They cannot project a satisfactory redemptive process. Hence the "new and often bizarre ideals". These may be seen as attempts to reformulate assumptions about power so that they may account for the widening experiences of everyday life and provide the basis for a new mode of redemption. New ideals, new assumptions certainly. But whether or not they are bizarre is entirely subjective. No one, it may be assumed, does seriously what he himself thinks is bizarre. Just as other kinds of seeming strange and esoteric activities in foreign cultures have yielded their mystery to investigation, so again and again the apparently bizarre in millenarian movements has been shown to be unexceptionable in the circumstances, given the premises. The hypothesis that millenary activities predicate a new culture or social order coming into being – which is what Haddon implies when he speaks of these movements as sanctioning "social and political aspirations" – is a fair one. Certainly it is more scientific to regard these activities as new-cultures-in-the-making, or as attempts to make a new kind of society or moral community, rather than as oddities, diseases in the body social, or troublesome nuisances to efficient administration – though of course they may be all these as well.

Finally, of course, a millenarian movement is a new religion in the making. New assumptions are being ordered into what may become a new orthodoxy.

Oppression

Haddon wrote in the heyday of British Imperial and colonial power. Despite the purposeful widening of the problem in the last sentence – which is often left out when authors quote him – it is fair to say that most anthropologists have understood by "oppressed" simply the effects of the machinery of colonial expansion and government. The vast bulk of anthropological evidence has been drawn from the colonial situation: the effects of the activities of missionaries, traders, settlers, commercial enterprises and administrative bodies upon subject peoples; the whole business of a sophisticated, often greedy, and highly technological civilization imposing its rules and conventions and experience upon those who, hitherto, had led a relatively simple life in small communities based upon hunting, fishing, agriculture and handicrafts. Such evidence may well give a distorted impression, and it is useful to bear in mind that "oppression" does not necessarily come from outside a particular cultural boundary. A people or group may oppress themselves and may only afterwards direct their frustrations at outsiders. Hence perhaps Haddon's telling phrase: "Communities that *feel* [my italics] themselves oppressed ...". Further, it should not be thought that the word "oppressed" could refer to anything more than what we have identified already: traditional assumptions weakening, a moral order decay-

ing, a positive and active if not always apparently sober will to participate in wider or different categories of understanding whether these are phrased in economic or political or more mystical terms. "Feeling themselves oppressed" by current assumptions about power, participants in millenarian activities set themselves the task of reformulating their assumptions so as to create, or account for and explain, a new or changing material and moral environment within which a more satisfactory form of redemption will be obtained.

Heroes

The "emergence of a hero" touches the wellsprings of an abundant literature. We can afford to be brief. If he is to be accepted as such, a hero or prophet or messiah must make his presence known to the community that is expecting him; and in order to be recognized and enabled to communicate with his followers he must conform in some way to the popular image of a hero or prophet or messiah. Since existing authorities are quick to scent a challenge, it is only prudent to gain the support of respected leaders of the community without appearing as a rival to them; and this an emerging hero can only do if what he has to say expresses and articulates just those questions which the community feels disturbed and anxious about. Further, he should provide clear and acceptable answers or solutions to the questions being asked. Is acceptance really dependent on Haddon's rather vague "religious fervour"? Perhaps. But even if observers of the scene were competent to analyse effectively the hysteria and similar emotional disturbances which accompany many a millenarian movement, within the terms of our view of religion we can see that many other more accessible and as relevant features enter into the developing situation: differences in economic and political circumstances; variations in capacities and opportunities as between millenarian group and others; impasses of communication and understanding.

Nonetheless, providing that we understand by "religious fervour" not simply an emotional exhibition, but a state-of-being having sociological relevance, it is an important phrase. New assumptions which predicate the creation of a new man, a new culture, society or condition of being are being wrought. And these relate directly to "prosperity and prestige" – though not necessarily to a restoration of traditional kinds of prosperity and prestige. The new assumptions tend to meet in the hero and his (divine) revelation, and almost always refer to a "prosperity and prestige" that are consistent with, and even define, the new conditions of being, the new man. As we shall see, an adequate or more satisfactory way of gaining prestige, of defining the criteria by which the content of manhood is to be measured, stands at the very heart of a millenarian or messianic movement. And these criteria relate on the one hand to gaining or retaining self-respect, status, and that integrity which is implied in the approved retention of a particular status; and on the other hand to an acknowledged process whereby redemption may be won.

Logically, a messianic movement is one that requires a messiah. And so accustomed are we to a "movement" having a leader or hero or prophet that we tend to forget that some millenarian activities may take place without one. There must have been many episodes or occurrences in history, as there certainly have been in Oceania in recent times,[8] which, lacking one who could be identified as a leader, still evoke new assumptions and are otherwise of the same genre as those more coherently organized activities in which some kind of hero or prophet or messiah has been identified. In such cases, one may say, the new assumptions are implicit rather than explicit. The messiah or hero or prophet is but an emerging idea, unrealized as yet in the flesh.

Prophets

There is no need to say much about the words "messiah", "hero", "prophet", "chiliastic", "millenarian", "messianic", "cult", "movement", "activities". To think that each term refers to a distinct person or situation obscures rather than clarifies, closes rather than opens the sociological problem. Only when the activities have been made to yield to a general con-

ceptual framework may we go on to distinguish different types. Thus although outside the Judaeo-Christian-Islamic traditions there can in the strict sense be no prophets, messiahs or messianic traditions or expectations – though there may well be traditions of a messianic type, and many whom we could say were heroes – we shall use the word prophet to refer to the leader, prime mover, star or central personality in the kinds of activities we are discussing. Chiliastic, millenarian and messianic will be regarded as synonymous terms; and whether the activities constitute a cult or a movement the reader may decide for himself.[9] Such usage does not prejudge any useful distinctions there might be between these terms, but it does avoid argument as to whether a person was really a hero or messiah or false or true prophet before we are in a position to make the argument worthwhile. Being ourselves the children of a long-established tradition of messianic expectations there are advantages in using familiar terms, opportunities only for confusion in adding to the plethora of nomenclatures invented over recent years.

On the other hand, temptations to seize on similarities at the expense of differences should be resisted. As we shall see, there are pertinent differences between one kind of millenarian activity and another. There are also different kinds of prophet – a half-crazed woman obsessed with her visions, for example, or a sickly lad who dreams a dream upon which others act, but who himself is heard of no more; a shrewd man of stature with organizing ability; a visionary or seer given to trances; or a saintly man misled by his own piety. Further, at least in the preliminary stages before a movement has cohered, there may be no prophet at all – just a series of apparently impulsive activities accompanied by inchoate ideas, feelings and emotions. Only when the inchoate ideas have begun to cohere into new assumptions may a prophet emerge to articulate them, show them forth, make them explicit. This is the revelation which, thought of as divinely inspired, provides the basis for a new departure, a new mode of redemption.

Every millenarian movement for which we have evidence comes to us as a story, as a narration of historical or quasi-historical events. Often, too, we find either *ad hoc* or systematic attempts to relate the events of the story to events and features of social relationship which lie outside the confines of the story itself. This, in essence, is what is meant by "extracting the sociology from the history". The issue is how satisfactorily, completely and systematically it may best be done. What we have attempted in developing each brief excursus above in terms of the content of others is a movement towards defining particular kinds of social relations in terms of the content of other kinds of social relations. We have rejected religion as simply a belief in spiritual beings; oppression as necessarily connoting the colonial situation; the prophet as a particular personality type. Instead, we have tried to make some interrelated statements about millenarian activities which can be filled out with empirical fieldwork material.

To summarize:

(a) We are discussing assumptions about power which, whether or not investigator or people concerned think of them as pertaining to spiritual beings, predicate or entail a particular redemptive process.

(b) While the redemptive process is discoverable in discharges and evasions of obligation, redemption itself refers to complete release from obligation and is roughly equivalent to salvation.

(c) The redemptive process, and so redemption, bears significantly on the politico-economic process, particularly the prestige system.

(d) A prestige system is based upon particular measurements of manhood which relate to gaining or retaining self-respect and integrity, and which refer back to the politico-economic process, the redemptive process, and assumptions about power.

Accepting these points as a baseline, millenarian movements involve the adoption of new assumptions, a new redemptive process, a new politico-economic framework, a new mode of measuring the man, a new integrity, a new community: in short, a new man. A precondition of this regeneration is a dissatisfaction with the current system. But if we describe this precondition as "feeling oppressed", the "oppression" does not necessarily derive from an external political control: it may be rooted in internal dissatisfactions with present assumptions, rules and modes of redemption. Either way, we are interested in the patterns described when faith belies experience, when given assumptions about power no longer reveal the truth of things, when the redemptive process must change to accord with the new assumptions born of new experience. When, as may happen, the new assumptions and rules are implicit and unorganized, millenarian activities may take place without a prophet being identifiable. A prophet is he or she who organizes the new assumptions and articulates them; who is listened to and found acceptable; whose revelation is accorded authority for however brief a period. But a prophet cannot identify himself in terms of the community as it is: he identifies himself in an image of what might or should be.

[. . .]

Money

Millenarian activities, we have suggested, indicate competing sets of assumptions which, in turn, point to competing moral systems or social orders. Too much power on one side, however, makes competition impossible. While there may be attempts at millenarian activity, if the more powerful group actually exerts its power the development of millenarian thoughts into activities tends to be inhibited or snubbed out altogether. On the other hand, when the competing moral systems have some common ground in certain vital assumptions, then a millenarian movement is likely. Or, to put it in another way, millenarian activities are likely where, sharing or wanting to share a common set of assumptions which point to a particular redemptive process, one of the groups concerned is debarred from access to the rewards of the assumptions and cannot earn the kind of redemption implied. Female prophets are usefully appreciated in this light. For besides being prophets in the ordinary sense they also participate in an infrastructure of competition and privilege, that of men versus women in a world where men are privileged. Given this particular kind of competitive ambience, the relevant point of contract – through which we are enabled to recognize the existence of competing moral systems – lies in our ability to distinguish different ways of measuring the man, different kinds of redemptive process. In this the presence or absence of money is vital. Money goes along with particular moral and social relations.

Making a radical distinction between social orders which use money as a basic measure of man, and those which do not, is crucial. In the first case, a "complex economy", we have a highly differentiated division of labour; money; free exchange of goods and services through money and markets; generalized full-time specialization; conservation of wealth through the generations; and a basic measure of prestige and status by reference to money, though of course a variety of other qualities and capacities also enter the situation. In the second case, a "subsistence economy", we have a simple division of labour, a set of relations in which the tasks to be performed are basically determined by age and sex; a prescribed and specific use of treasure articles; specific and prescribed types of exchange; no money; part-time specialization; and a basic measure of prestige and status by reference to the subsistence activities which most or all undertake in common – though again, a variety of other capacities also enter into the situation. It is true that in some subsistence communities there are one or two magical, ritual, or even technological full-time specialists. But where these exist they are almost always found to have a prestige of their own; they are insulated from the requirements of the main prestige system. Further, while there are numerous examples of cash circulating in subsistence economies, whether or not this money has succeeded in becoming a basic measure of prestige and status is precisely the issue. We are not comparing standards of living, for many subsistence communities are richer and have higher standards of living than particular parts of a complex economy. We are distinguishing between two sets of social relations which seem, in principle, to be mutually exclusive. We are drawing the divide between one kind of moral system and another.

In any community the basic measure of prestige and status must refer either to the activities which all or most undertake in common, or to those assets to which all or most in the community have a common access, or both. In addition to these basic measures other more specific qualities and capacities are usually taken into account. In a subsistence community relative abilities in the main subsistence activities emerge as the basic measures. The possession, exchange and relative turnover of treasure articles reflect or measure industry, efficiency, cunning, shrewdness, foresight and a number of other qualities; further prestige may be gained or lost by the demonstration of virtues and vices – such as virility, courage, warrior capacities, envy, secretiveness – which may be, but are not necessarily, directly related to capacities in the subsistence activities. In the complex economy, on the other hand, where with a highly differentiated division of labour there can be no one set of activities engaged in common, the basic criterion for measuring farmer, smith, carpenter, wheelwright, teacher and others against each other must be that to which all have access, and by virtue of which they are enabled to specialize: money. And though one or more of a series of highly differentiated qualities and capacities are also usually taken into account, money remains the basic measure.

Succeeding to a large extent in measuring locally preferred and selected moral qualities, the treasure articles of a subsistence economy are, however, only wealth in themselves so far as, indicating particular qualities and capacities, they can be used to gain credit. For in order to get meaningful possession of such an article a man has to have been seen to do well, and in the prescribed way, the work that is required of him. Money may, but does not necessarily, measure the moral qualities. It keeps, may be banked for future use, *is* wealth in a way that the treasure articles of a subsistence economy are not. For whether gotten inside or outside the law, by good or evil acts, preferred or condemned kinds of procedures, money in a complex economy can command or buy labour, things, hearts, souls and even credit. As concrete as any could wish, susceptible to touch and handling, pieces of money yet refer to an entirely abstract system of quantitative and factorial relations which endure and remain what they are through all sorts of social vicissitudes. Banks, and the keeping qualities of money, owe their permanence more to the mathematical system to which they refer than to their material construction. Whereas the relative values of treasure articles depend on intrinsic qualities as well as social and historical associations, unless an old shilling is to become a treasure article it is worth as many pennies as a new one. More subtly, money is a factorial measure of man which entails quantifying his different capacities. It separates and differentiates qualities and capacities, and in doing so gives each a referent on a quantitative scale. Further, the handling of money is an exercise in unitary and factorial relations. But qualities can only be identified within a system of binary opposites (good/bad, strong/weak, skilled/unskilled, etc.); and the factorial nature of money introduces a hierarchy of quantitative values none of which can be said to have an opposite. The two schemes, binary opposites on the one hand, and what we may call the one-and-the-many on the other, are in principle mutually opposed.

A corresponding antithesis is encountered where the worth and stature of man are measured by money and clearly differentiated capacities on the one hand, and the quality of his performance in an agglutinated "package deal" of prescribed activities on the other. The problem is how to reconcile the antitheses. Though in practice the moneyed communities of a complex economy also use qualitative criteria, and most subsistence communities use some kind of quantitative criteria, far from detracting from the point at issue the antithesis is emphasized. A cursory glance at the millenarian activities which have taken place within the traditions of the great moneyed economies show that they turn significantly on money: on how access to money, and the uses to which money may be put, may be so prescribed and defined that this factorial and quantitative measure can accurately assess selected moral qualities. The poor man whose skills and honesty go unrecognized is as wretched as the richer whose acumen and thrift earn him nothing. Often obscured in the colonial situation by the more idealistic and humane relevances of different kinds of paternalism, this issue of quantifying and differentiating the qualities by reference to money is often ignored. Minted by the complex economy, by peoples who organize themselves into large, loose and highly differentiated entities, who engage in a multitude of specialized tasks and occupations, whose prestige systems, forms of organization and division of labour depend upon money, money quite naturally chases the stuffs its makers want, finds its way back into the pockets of those who know how to use it and make it work to advantage.

Despite attempts on the parts of colonial administrations to get money circulating amongst an indigenous people, they have always found difficulties in penetrating an indigenous prestige system based upon qualitative criteria, and then adapting or converting it to one based upon money. The indigenous qualitative criteria tend to persist. Prestige continues to depend upon competence in the subsistence activities, on turnover of exchanges, on the passage and exchange of treasure articles. The returned labourer with money in his pocket may enjoy a brief notoriety but, without a continuing access to money must needs put his hand to crook, goad, mattock, axe or adze. Such money as he may have tends to be buried, hoarded, used in *ad hoc* payments or as treasure articles.

If money is to circulate significantly, if an indigenous community is to have a satisfactory access to money, then the community must so adapt and alter its prestige system that money becomes a basic measure of worth. Unless and until money begins accurately to assess those qualities which a people or community finds meaningful, so long will they not be able to use money as it was meant to be used, so long will they not have a satisfactory access. Belonging to, and connoting, the complex social order of those who have minted it, use it, and bring it to foreign shores, money, particularly when of the more valuable or powerful currencies, demands acceptance of the kind of social ordering adopted by those who make it. Nevertheless, corrupted by a covetousness that is human, lured on by what seems to be a finer or more satisfactory means of realizing their potential, yet reluctant to abandon what tradition has hallowed, the dilemma is how to replace a current prestige system by another; how to further differentiate, factorialize and quantify the qualities; how to redefine the qualities so that they may be more satisfactorily quantified and differentiated. And both for those in a subsistence economy who want to make money a relevant measure of man, as well as for like-minded individuals within a complex economy who want to make money more accurately define the moral qualities, a millenarian movement is one way of resolving the dilemma.

To become it is first necessary to belong; and belonging makes it possible to define just who or what one is. Whether for participants or bystanders, millenarian activities provide the opportunity for becoming someone distinctive and worthwhile. And, because attitudes to money can so readily find out the man, define what is meant by integrity, millenial aspirations often find their focus in money.
[. . .]

Aspects of Integrity

All cultures and communities have particular criteria whereby members may measure relative prestige among themselves. As we have seen very briefly, among Polynesians a variety of criteria meet in the meaning of *mana*, command over the labour and allegiance of others, and competence in war. Other kinds of ability certainly contribute to the accumulation of *mana*: knowledge of protocol and myths, sexual competence, physical strength, handsome features, well-moulded muscular proportions, oratory, and skills in dancing, sports, sailing, fishing, hunting, agricultural activities and the manufacture of artifacts, to name but a few. But all these qualities tend to be subsumed in the required qualities of the political leader and warrior. And the basis of both these competences was control over land and its resources. A landless fellow, a man without any control over its resources, was necessarily a man without kin, or one whom others would not recognize as kin: scarcely a man at all. When Te Ua claimed to hold the

promise of a "redemption for his people, who had become forgetful, desolate and in doubt" his meaning in an objective sense must be related to the land question and to warfare. As accessible and useful lands began to shrink, and as traditional warfare began to become difficult or impossible within the context of a *Pax Britannica*, so the criteria of relative prestige became less and less clearly defined.

Not only that. For as the criteria of prestige become loose and ill-defined, so do the criteria of integrity become doubtful. The kinds of powers attached to a particular office or status become uncertain. There is no consensus as to the qualities required of those in positions of authority and responsibility. Further, traditional criteria of integrity tend to seem unimportant when compared with the apparently superior capacities of other peoples – in this case the European settlers. Whether we choose to regard the *Pai-marire* movement as one that attempted to capture a new integrity; or as one that attempted to recapture a traditional integrity; or as one that attempted to define an integrity compounded of both traditional and Christian or European features; the question of integrity emerges as paramount. This itself is bound up with the redemptive process, the programme of particular kinds of ways in which individuals are required to meet their obligations.

In a millenarian context both redemption and integrity are part and parcel of an overall developmental process – a movement from the more simple to the more complex, an increasing differentiation of the powers, statuses, qualities, jobs and techniques required to sustain community life. But we still have to show how varying aspects of integrity and redemption are related to different kinds of developmental process. Some examples from North America . . . will demonstrate my meaning.

The Plains Indians

For something over two hundred years until their final defeat by the white man, the cultures of the Plains Indians of North America had been based on possession of the horse, fighting, and hunting wild buffalo. Before the

Spanish brought their horses to North America, the indigenous peoples of the region had lived mainly on the edges of the plains, and comprised small hunting bands who followed the migrating herds of buffalo in the season on foot. They also practised some horticulture. But when they acquired horses they were able to take to the plains more or less permanently, relying for subsistence almost wholly on the buffalo. The population increased; the size of the effective political group increased. From being a motley collection of small hunting bands who could only have put up a token resistance to the white pioneers, they became the well-organized and formidable antagonists of an industrialized nation. They had neither artillery nor the means to manufacture guns and bullets. But they acquired guns and ammunition and fought for their plains and their buffalo until only a few remnants remained. Looking back, we can see that their fight against white men, who wanted the plains for farmland and range cattle, was doomed to failure. Yet they had fought according to the demands of their culture. And those who died bravely may be said to have earned a traditional redemption: they asked only that they should show themselves true to the prescriptions of their social order. But what of those who survived?

Of the many changes that possession of the horse initiated, the most crucial related to integrity and relative prestige. Horses became the new wealth. Gaining access to horses by taking them from enemies either by stealth or in open war became an important criterion of prestige. Getting horses by breeding them was tantamount to forgery. Warrior values became paramount. The dashing fighter who could get horses, count coups, gallop in amongst a herd of bewildered buffalo, and face extremes of physical pain in stoic silence, was well on the way to a position of high success. Add to these abilities qualities of wisdom, magnanimity, cunning, knowledge of the world and his people, and a certain ruthlessness, and the picture of the Plains Indian chief is complete in its outlines. At the other extreme, a male who could not show some competence in these matters was regarded as hardly a man at all. His alternatives were either to become a shaman, when again he would have to show himself able to face without flinching extremes of physical pain and deprivation; or become like a woman – dress in woman's clothes, do women's work, become a disposable part of a real man's household. Highly specialized, the prestige system was based on an intimate relationship between war, buffalo and horses. Death in war, fighting and dying bravely without asking for, or giving, quarter was thought a highly satisfactory redemption. To die peacefully having survived innumerable combats with a fully feathered war-bonnet and coups past counting; to have hunted successfully, fed dependants, and disposed of plenty of horses; to have fingers whose joints had been severed in attempts to gain visions of, and rapport with, a protector spirit; to bare a torso scarred with the hooks and skewers of voluntary torture – all these were tokens of a perhaps higher redemption.

What then was left for those remnants who lived through to the end of the Indian wars in reservations without horses, without buffalo, without war, dependent on the goodwill of an official agent, a trader with his store, and perhaps a missionary? Even as we look back with the advantage of hindsight it is not easy to suggest a realistic compromise for this brave but defeated people. To them defeat was a disgrace. But they had to live on in defeat and they were denied the opportunity of living and dying in the only fit ways they knew. In their own eyes rather less than men, despite assurances to the contrary their conquerors treated them with undisguised contumely. How and in what way could they overcome the irony of a glorious efflorescence based on the horse, a European import, and their ultimate defeat by Europeans? How and in what way could they find a new integrity, a new redemption?

In a sense there was no solution. Plains Indian culture was dead, could not develop into anything else. If in later years descendants of these folk could point to the fact that all the world plays at Cowboys and Indians, this simply reiterates the problem for the immediate survivors. Bereft of a traditional integrity, the scattered remnants of a once proud people could do little else but look back on their glories and, with the aid of some new symbols, screw hope and wishful thinking to the point where buffalo and horses might seem to be on the point of returning. For the Sioux, who were to suffer so dreadfully at the battle of Wounded Knee, one version of the many revelations contributed by numerous prophets to that complex of activities generally subsumed under the name "Ghost Dance Religion"[10] posited a general catastrophe as heralding the millennium. After a series of earthquakes, landslides, storms, whirlwinds and floods in which all the whites would be destroyed, the Indians would survive to see boundless prairies covered with wild grass and filled with great herds of buffalo and other game. Other prophets held that after the great catastrophe all race distinctions were to be obliterated, and that in the millennium that followed both whites and Indians would live amicably together. "You must not fight. Do not harm anyone. Do right always,"[11] said the prophet Wovoka.

A longer text from Wovoka's teaching reads as follows:

I found my children were bad, so I went back to heaven and left them. I told them that in so many hundred years I would come back to see my children. At the end of this time I was sent back to *try to teach them*. My father told me the earth was getting old and worn out and the people getting bad, and that I was to *renew everything as it used to be and make it better*.

He also told us that all our dead were to be resurrected; that they were all to come back to earth, and that, as the earth was too small for them and us, he would do away with heaven and make the earth itself large enough to contain us all; that we must tell all the people we met about these things. He spoke to us about *fighting*, and said *that was bad and we must keep from it*; that the earth was to be all good hereafter, and *we must all be friends with one another*. He said that in the fall of the year the youth of all good people would be renewed, so that nobody would be more than forty years old, and that if they behaved themselves well after this *the youth of everyone would be renewed* in the spring. He said if we were all good he would send people among us who could heal all our

wounds and sickness by mere touch and that we would *live forever*. He told us *not to quarrel or fight or strike each other, or shoot one another*; that the whites and Indians were to be *all one people*. He said if any man *disobeyed* what he ordered his tribe would be *wiped from the face of the earth*; that we must believe everything he said, and we must not doubt him or say he lied; that if we did, he would know it; *that he would know our thoughts and actions in no matter what part of the world we might be.*[12]

Here plainly is the attempt to excise the purely existential and apparently purposeless nature of the present by searching into the past in order to posit a viable future.

The Ghost Dance Religion spread from community to community in the plains area in much the same way as cargo cult activities have in more recent years spread from village to village in New Guinea. And in spite of Mooney's insistence on what was the 'true' or 'real' doctrine of the Ghost Dance Religion, it is probably wiser to accept that here (as in New Guinea and elsewhere) there were different versions; differently projected assumptions and aspirations turning on the central theme of a glorious past and a miserably uncertain future. On the other hand the rites of the Ghost Dance itself, which included singing, chanting, falling into trance, stripping naked, and the wearing of special shirts which would render the wearers invulnerable to the bullets of the white man, seem to have varied only slightly. Also, the overt purposes of the rites seem to have been much the same: attaining union with the glorious dead, enjoying now in trance what in the past had been fully realized. Moreover, if we look closely at the Ghost Dance we can discern certain themes – such as trance, self-torture, the excision of discordant ideas, the renewal and re-emphasis of community values, the reconciliation of disputants – which it had in common with the great Sun Dance: that vital political occasion when nomadic bands of Indians gathered together to dance, feast, resolve their disputes, compete in games and ritual exercises of self-torture, and, despite or because of their sectional exclusivisms, renew their common allegiance to an overall political order.[13] Thus the Ghost Dance was heir to the Sun Dance; the traditional gave authenticity to the new.

Here is Short Bull, with a message to the Sioux shortly before the battle of Wounded Knee:

My friends and relations: I will soon start this thing [the millennium] in running order. I have told you that this would come to pass in two seasons, but since the whites are interfering so much, I will advance the time from what my father above told me to do, so the time will be shorter. Therefore, you must not be afraid of anything. Some of my relations have no ears, so I will have them blown away.

Now there will be a tree sprout up, and there all the members of our religion and the tribe must gather together. That will be the place where we will see our dead relations. But before this time the earth will shiver very hard. Whenever this thing occurs, I will start the wind to blow. We are the ones who will then see our fathers, mothers, and everybody. We, the tribe of Indians, are the ones who are living a sacred life. God, our father himself, has told and commanded and shown me to do these things.

My father has shown me these things, therefore we must continue this dance [The Ghost Dance]. If the soldiers surround you four deep, three of you, *on whom I have put holy shirts* [supposedly bullet-proof], will sing a song, which I have taught you, around them, when some of them will drop dead. Then the rest will start to run, but their horses will sink into the earth. The riders will jump from their horses, but they will sink into the earth also. Then you can do as you desire with them. Now, you must know this, that all the soldiers and that race [the whites] will be dead. There will be only five thousand of them living on the earth. . . .

Now, we must gather at Pass Creek where the tree is sprouting. There we will go among our dead relations. You must not take any earthly things with you. Then the *men must take off all their clothing and the women must do the same.* No one shall be ashamed of exposing their persons. My father above has told us to do this, and we must do as he says. You must not be afraid of anything. The guns are the only things we are afraid of, but they belong to our father in heaven. He will see that they do no harm. Whatever white men may tell you, do not listen to them, my relations. That is all. I will now raise my hand up to my father and close what he has said to you through me.[14]

Is there not a note of desperation in that concluding "whatever white men may tell you, do not listen to them, my relations"? Here were people the reverse of "forgetful" but "desolate and in doubt" indeed – yet taking comfort in what a prophet had to say, and who took action because of what a prophet had to say. Perhaps one may be allowed to see the battle of Wounded Knee not as the horror that in fact it was, but rather as a final attempt to gain a traditional kind of redemption. For the battle was not overtly intended by either side. Starting as an inaugural for peace, during which the Sioux were to hand over their arms, an excited young Indian, losing control and composure in the tension accompanying the surrender, drew a rifle from under his blanket and fired at the white soldiers who were present in large numbers.[15] At this the whites too lost control, and three hundred and seventy Indian men, women and children were killed in the massacre that followed.

Dead men can be replaced. But here it was traditional Plains Indian culture itself which had been destroyed. The survivors had to find quite new principles and assumptions on which to base community life. Mere individuals with common traditions, they had to reintegrate themselves as communities based on quite different assumptions from those they had known in the past. But, unlike the more usual desert island "starting again", there was little material on which they could exercise their imaginations and traditional technical skills. First they had to become an organized community. A prophet could say, more positively, "Do right always". But what kinds of activities could be thought of as "right" now or in the future? Traditionally, the "right" thing to do always was to stand one's ground, defend one's honour and integrity, and fight. Yet they were being told not to do precisely this. What was a "right" thing to do – what the whites told them to do? Should they wait patiently in lodge or tipi doing no harm to anyone until a nervous Indian agent, afraid that his community might starve to death, handed out supplies from the trade store? Certainly they could plant a little tobacco. But few of these survivors knew how to grow corn or vegetables, or how to rear chickens and pigs so that there would be a "right" way of doing it which, through the productive and distributive process, would demonstrate ability, prestige and integrity. Wage labour in the towns? That meant being controlled and treated as a "naturally" inferior sort of person. With a future that could only be phrased in vague and general abstractions, it is hardly matter for surprise that such abstractions as might be realized, were in fact realized in terms of traditional activities. Those injunctions that could not be realized in terms of past activities could hardly be realized at all. As it was, those traditional activities which could be taken into the future – trance states, self-torture, the seeking of a guardian spirit by means of techniques calculated to induce a release from ordinary worldly and social cares, communication with the ancestors and so continuity with the cultural heritage – were contained within the rituals of the Ghost Dance itself. As in so many other instances over the world, the activity of the communal dance – in which participants might speak as with tongues, have visions, escape from the prisons of the body and formal modes of knowledge, gain inspiration – seems to have been the seed of such organizational forms as were to develop in the years that followed.

Faced with organizing themselves from virtually nothing into quite new kinds of communities, the Plains Indians could only realize new ways of behaving by using traditional sources of authority. That these traditional sources were sought through the communal dance and its accompanying trance-like states, takes the Plains Indians out of their purely cultural context and places them in a generally human setting.[16] For not only does the communal trance-dance appear as a generally human device for seeking inspiration and fresh initiatives, it is in itself the communal expression and analogue of just that experience whereby a prophet, a lone individual, comes to be inspired with the revelation that others afterwards discover they would like to make their own.

[. . .]

NOTES

1 Chinnery and Haddon, p. 455.
2 Tylor, p. 424.
3 If a "spiritual being" is expressly not human, it still must involve questions as to mass, visibility, and attributes of bilocation. Not to "believe in" phenomena such as trances, stigmata, possession, levitation, walking on hot coals without being burned, or skewering the cheeks without leaving a wound – which are all above or beyond the natural, not found in nature – is surely equivalent to being a "flat-earther".
4 When we say of a man that "art is his religion" we mean that he gives overriding importance to art, that he is particularly concerned with nurturing and developing his sources of inspiration, and guarding himself against those influences which might endanger his inspiration, betray his integrity as an artist, or nullify his ideas on what Art should be or do. The same applies to those of whom we might say "science is his religion", or "socialism is his religion", or "anthropology is his religion".
5 This holds even though it might be said that a "spiritual being" is but the rationalized projection of some internal impulse.
6 Cf. Lienhardt, pp. 327–9; Yinger, pp. 9, 71–2; Vernon, pp. 46–57; Horton.
7 See, for example, Burridge (1965), pp. 226–9, where a New Guinea people, after a series of reciprocal exchanges or discharges of obligation, attain to a state known as *mngwotngwotiki*, a word which connotes a particular field of relations in which the individuals concerned are temporarily unobliged to each other.

8 See Burridge (1960), pp. 1–4.
9 While "activity" is a general descriptive term, one may suggest that a cult, concerned with a particular source of power, is already organized, firm and static, whereas a movement seeks to impose its ideas and present organization upon a wider field.
10 Mooney.
11 Mooney, p. 19.
12 Mooney, pp. 26–7 (my italics).
13 See Hoebel (1941); (1960), pp. 11–16; and Ewers, pp. 174–84, 298ff.
14 Mooney, p. 31 (my italics. Cf. Mambu, p. 65).
15 Mooney, p. 118.
16 Cf. Burridge (1960), pp. 1–14.

REFERENCES CITED

Burridge, Kenelm (K.O.L.). *Mambu: A Melanesian Millennium*. London, 1960.

——. Tangu, Northern Madang District, in *Gods, Ghosts and Men in Melanesia* (eds. P. Lawrence and M. J. Meggitt), pp. 224–49. Oxford University Press, Melbourne, 1965.

Chinnery, E. W. P. and Haddon, A. C. Five New Religious Cults in British New Guinea, *The Hibbert Journal*, vol. XV, no. 3, 1917: 448–63.

Ekka, Philip. *The Tana Bhagats: A Study in Social Change* (Oxford). Unpublished D. Phil. thesis, 1966.

Ewers, John C. *The Blackfeet*. University of Oklahoma Press, 1961.

Fuchs, Stephen. *Rebellious Prophets*. Bombay, 1965.

Hoebel, E. A. The Comanche Sun Dance and Messianic Outbreak of 1873, *American Anthropologist*, vol. XLIII, 1941: 301–3.

——. *The Cheyennes*. New York, 1960.

Horton, Robin. A Definition of Religion, and its Uses, *Journal of the Royal Anthropological Institute*, vol. 90, Pt 2: 201–26.

Lienhardt, R. G. Religion, in *Man, Culture and Society* (ed. H. L. Shapiro). New York, 1956, pp. 310–29.

Mooney, James. *The Ghost Dance Religion and the Sioux Outbreak of 1890* (ed. Anthony F. Wallace). University of Chicago Press, London, 1965 (1896).

Roy, S. C. A New Religious Movement Among the Oraons, *Man in India*, vol. 1, no. 4, 1921: 267–324.

——. *Oraon Religion and Customs* (pp. 312–410). Ranchi and Calcutta, 1928.

Scholem, Gersholm G. *On the Kabbalah and its Symbolism*, London, 1965.

Serrin, O. The Bhagat Movement in Chota Nagpur, *Indian Academy*. Kurseny, 1917.

Tylor, Sir Edward Burnett. *Primitive Culture* (2 vols.). London, 1891.

Vernon, Glenn M. *Sociology of Religion*. McGraw Hill, New York, 1962.

Yinger, Milton. *Religion, Society and the Individual*. New York, 1957.

35

The Genesis of Capitalism amongst a South American Peasantry: Devil's Labor and the Baptism of Money

Michael Taussig

An Australian, trained first in medicine and then at the London School of Economics, Michael Taussig is currently professor at Columbia University, New York. He engages in a wonderful dialogue with Marx, Weber, and even Aristotle in this piece, which shows how certain "magical" practices found among plantation workers in Colombia emerge not only in response to capitalist exploitation but serve as an enlightened moral critique of its consequences. This might be seen as a late phase of the rationality debates, in which the tables are turned such that the rationality of the West comes under question from its victims and from the postcolonial world. Taussig argues that the plantation workers have an understanding of commodity fetishism akin to Marx. Commodity fetishism is a kind of inversion or transformation of totemism in which attention is placed on human products rather than natural species, but in which they are understood to have life, vitality, reproductive potential, and possibly even intentionality, while disguising the human labor entailed in their production.

Taussig's argument has stimulated much discussion; lively criticism as well as comparative material on the imagination of money can be found in Parry and Bloch (1989); cf. Burridge (chapter 34), De Boeck (1999). The local critique of forms of accumulation has formed the basis for many anthropological accounts, often with respect to witchcraft (Fisiy and Geschiere 1991, Solway 1998, Weiss 1998).

This essay was one of the first in a remarkable series of texts by Taussig that explore the creative responses to the horrendous impact of Europeans on Latin America and that serve, as in this essay, also as mirrors for modernity and meditations on materiality. The argu-

From Michael Taussig, "The Genesis of Capitalism amongst a South American Peasantry: Devil's Labor and the Baptism of Money," *Comparative Studies in Society and History* 19(2) (1977): 130–55. Abridged.

ment is expanded in his 1980 book, which adds an analysis of the practices of Bolivian tin miners well described by Nash (1979). Taussig then delved into surrealism and Frankfurt School theory to produce rich and stylistically experimental books on shamanism and violence (1987), colonial mimesis (1993; cf. Kramer 1993, Stoller 1995), and the state (1997). A powerful auto-critique of the functionalist inclinations of the original article – and that should be read in conjunction with it – is an essay that emphasizes the seductive qualities of transgression, danger, and sheer excess (1995, cf. 1999). Taussig (2006) is a recent collection of his essays.

What does wage labor and capital mean to a peasantry that is subjected to rapid rural proletarianization and what is the basis of that meaning?

I wish to discuss an aspect of this question in the light of certain ideological reactions manifested by a South American lowland peasantry as expanding sugar plantations absorb their lands and peasants are converted into landless wage laborers. In the southern extremities of the Cauca Valley, Colombia, it is commonly thought that male plantation workers can increase their output, and hence their wage, through entering into a secret contract with the devil. However, the local peasants, no matter how needy they may be, never make such a contract when working their own plots or those of their peasant neighbors for wages. It is also thought that by illicitly baptizing money instead of a child in the Catholic church, that money can become interest bearing capital, while the child will be deprived of its rightful chance of entering heaven.

Analysis of these beliefs in their social and historical context indicates that the lower classes' implicit understanding of the new mode of production is inherently critical and antagonistic and that the axiomatic basis of this antagonism rests on their conscious opposition of "use values" to "exchange values" – the opposition of the satisfaction of natural wants, on the one side, to the limitless search for profits and capital accumulation on the other. In making this distinction these people share a close affinity with the economic theorizing of the Schoolmen of the European Middle Ages, and with the economic philosophy of Aristotle, whose insights on this matter

were often quoted favorably by Karl Marx himself, since the opposition of use value to exchange value was basic to his entire system of analysis.

Further elucidation of this distinction leads to a discussion of the metaphysical and moral bases underlying the lower classes' understanding of capitalist relations of production and exchange, in which their folk mysticism is contrasted with that form of capitalist mystification to which Marx gave the name of "commodity fetishism." Evaluation of this contrast is enhanced by an analysis of the mode of reasoning utilized by the supporters of the use value economy. This reasoning appears to derive from a concept of the universe as an interrelated organism which is understood through the conscious application of animistic analogies, rather than by means of the atomistic causal paradigm which has gained ascendancy in the social sciences since the rise of Newtonian mechanics and the birth of the industrial revolution in the West.

Attitudes towards Wage Labor

A theme of constant interest to historians of the industrial revolution in Europe, as well as to sociologists concerned with socio-economic development in the Third World, is the attitude of workers who are new to the modern wage labor situations. The first reaction of peasants and artisans who become wage workers in modern business enterprises is frequently if not universally one of indifference to wage incentives. Regarded as a failure to maximize market opportunities, a lack of labor commitment, or a peculiar irrationality about complying with the postulates embodied in *homo oeconomicus*, this response has persistently frustrated capitalist entrepreneurs the world over.

Max Weber referred to this response as "primitive traditionalism," and much of his research was an attempt to explain its transcendence by the capitalist spirit and the capitalist work ethic.

> This traditionalism survives far down into the present; only a human lifetime in the past it was futile to double the wages of an agricultural laborer in Silesia who mowed a certain tract of land on a contract, in the hope of inducing him to increase his exertion. He would simply have reduced by half the work expended because with this half he would have been able to earn as much as before. (Weber, 1927: 335)

In a recent work, an anthropologist sums up some of his findings on this subject in terms of the persistence of use value practices rather than in terms of "primitive traditionalism":

> Recruited as plantation hands, they frequently showed themselves unwilling to work steadily. Induced to raise a cash crop, they would not react "appropriately" to market changes: as they were interested mainly in acquiring specific items of consumption, they produced that much less when crop prices rose, and that much more when prices fell off. And the introduction of new tools or plants that increased the productivity of indigenous labor might only then shorten the period of necessary work, the gains absorbed rather by an expansion of rest than of output. All these and similar responses express an enduring quality of traditional domestic production, that it is production of use values, definite in its aim, so discontinuous in its activity. (Sahlins, 1972: 86)

The exotic attitudes and beliefs which so-called traditional cultures exhibit towards the early stages of penetration by the modern capitalist economy often seem bizarre and irrational to Western eyes. Luther's identification of the devil with capitalism (Brown, 1959: 218–19; Tawney, 1954: 72–91), some Melanesian cargo cults, certain messianic movements, Weber's examples of "primitive traditionalism," as well as the beliefs we consider below, are but some of the numerous instances of such attitudes and concepts. Rather than dismissing these responses as "traditional" or irrational, the approach adopted in this essay is that it would seem to be more true to the facts as well as more enlightening to consider these reactions as outcomes of a clash between a use value orientation and an exchange value orientation, thus viewing them as the beginning of a potential critique of capitalism. They provide us with insights into the irrational basis of our own economy and stereotype of *homo oeconomicus*, and can be usefully considered as illustrative of form of "primitive Marxism."

This "primitive Marxism" was undoubtedly inherent in the outlook of the European proletariat in the early stages of the birth of the capitalist system, but has since been largely superseded by a new world view which regards the wage contract system, market pricing, and the institutionalization of profit and greed as natural and ethically commendable. In the light of this historical amnesia, which afflicts all social classes in a developed market economy, it is all the more important to dwell on the critique offered us by those neophytic proletarians in the Third World today, who are just entering the capitalist system with their goods and labor and who often appear to regard that system as anything but natural and good. In the Cauca Valley the sense given to the devil and his role in contracting wage labor is like the definition of the early Christian fathers as "he who resists the cosmic process," which in this context comes close to the idea of forcing things in the interest of private gain without regard to what are seen as their intrinsic principles (cf. Needham 1956: 69–71).

The destruction of the pre-capitalist metaphysics of production and exchange was considered by at least two influential social theorists as mandatory for the successful establishment of modern capitalism. Max Weber regarded the magical superstitions associated with production and trade to be one of the greatest obstacles to the rationalization of economic life (1927:355), and in his essay on *The*

Protestant Ethic and the Spirit of Capitalism often reiterated the point that

> Labor must . . . be performed as if it were an absolute end in itself, a calling. But such an attitude is *by no means a product of nature.* It cannot be evoked by low wages or high ones alone, but can only be the product of a long and arduous process of education. Today, capitalism once in the saddle, can recruit its laboring force in all industrial countries with comparative ease. In the past this was in every case an extremely difficult problem. (Weber, 1958: 62, my emphasis)

And as Karl Marx observed, the transition to the capitalist mode of production is only completed when direct force and external economic conditions, although still used, are only employed exceptionally. An entirely new set of traditions and habits have to be developed among the working class, to the point where common sense regards the new conditions as natural.

> It is not enough that the conditions of labor are concentrated in a mass, in the shape of capital, at the one pole of society, while at the other are grouped masses of men who have nothing to sell but their labor power. Neither is it enough that they are compelled to sell it voluntarily. The advance of capitalist production develops a working class, which by education, tradition, habit, looks upon the conditions of that mode of production *as self-evident laws of Nature.* (Marx, 1967, I:737, my emphasis)

However, the behavior and certain beliefs of the lower classes on whom this article focuses suggest strongly that the characteristics of the capitalist mode of production are there viewed neither as good nor as self-evident laws of Nature; in fact they are regarded as unnatural and even evil.

The lower classes are of Afro-American stock, and until 1955 or thereabouts most of them were smallholders owning parcels of land without legal title in the southern extremities of the Cauca Valley, an extremely fertile region in the southwest of Colombia. Since about 1955 the majority of these peasants have had little choice but to work full- or part-time as wage laborers for the surrounding

sugar plantations which have expropriated much of the peasant's land, often through direct physical force.

Historical sources amply demonstrate that ever since the abolition of slavery in 1851 the peasants have shown a marked aversion towards wage labor on the large estates of the rural elite. Until the early decades of the twentieth century they were able to retain their position as independent smallholders and formed a powerful political group capable of thwarting their previous owners who desperately needed labor to maintain the flagging estates and gold mines. However, with the opening of the valley to the international sea lanes in 1914, the influx of vast amounts of foreign capital at about the same time, and a sharp natural increase in local population, the large estate owners have been able to appropriate peasant lands and establish a flourishing plantation economy, a process accelerated by the *Violencia* of the early 1950s.[1]

Today no more than one-fifth of the population in the south of the valley lives in the countryside, while the remainder live in the rural slum towns, little more than impoverished barracks for plantation workers, bereft of clean drinking water and adequate sewerage. Few of the townspeople own land, and many of the peasants who still occupy farm land also work on the plantations. By any standards the bulk of the population is poor, and malnutrition is rife.

[. . .]

The workers themselves . . . feel that they are being constantly cheated, underpaid, and humiliated. They distrust and hate the plantations and generally resent the fact that the crops produced on the large estates are destined for export and not for local consumption. With their trade unions in ruin since the early 1960s, sabotage of mill machinery and tractors is common, and the plantation owners and managers travel the area in constant fear of assault and kidnapping. Police and soldiers are continually stationed in the mill compounds, and workers have been shot during scuffles on paydays. The mill owners always travel with an escort of armed guards, and all high-ranking personnel are equipped with two-way radios in communication with the

Defensa Civil and army located in the nearest city.

The Devil and Proletarian Labor

In the southern Cauca Valley today, it is commonly believed by local people – townspeople and country people, proletarians and peasants – that the male plantation workers sometimes make individual and secret contracts with the devil in order to increase individual output and hence their wage. Generally speaking, it is felt that output can be increased greatly by the individual worker only if he does make such a contract. The landless wage workers are widely supposed to sell their souls to the devil in order to maintain, or more commonly increase, productivity. Indian tin miners in highland Bolivia show similar patterns of behavior (Nash, 1972). But both groups of people do *not* do this as *peasants* working their own land. It is only when they become proletarianized that the devil enters the scene in this way. While the imagery of God and good, or the spirits of Nature and of ancestors, dominate the ethos of labor in the peasant mode of production, the devil and evil permeate the local metaphysics associated with the capitalist mode of production.

It is commonly thought that such a contract can increase a plantation worker's yield by two to three times. As a result of such a contract, however, the individual concerned will die prematurely and in agony, and while alive is soulless and a mere puppet in the hands of the devil. Furthermore, certain conditions attach to the money thus gained. This money cannot serve as productive "capital" but has to be spent immediately on what are considered to be luxury consumer items such as fine clothes, liquor, butter, and so on. To invest this money so as to produce more money – i.e., to use it as capital – is to invite ruin. For example, if one buys or rents land, that land will not produce, and if one buys a piglet to fatten for market, the animal will sicken or die. It is also believed that plantation sugar cane thus cut will not regrow. The ratoon or root will die, and the plantation land will not produce until plowed over and replanted.

It is crucial to realize that the local *peasantry* do *not* make contracts with the devil in order to augment or maintain productivity levels on their own plots. Neither do they make such a contract when working for wages on the plots of other peasants. People point out that such a practice would damage the peasant plot and that the money gained could not be used to maintain equipment or land. Despite the poverty that afflicts the majority of the local peasants, they are not therefore tempted by the monetary rewards that result from the devil contract, since those rewards are thought to diminish or curtail natural fertility. The notion of extracting more money from nature in the above way applies only to proletarians.[2]

The only magic allegedly used on the peasant plots is "good" magic worked through the Catholic saints and the *ánimas* – the souls of the ancestors – and such magic is aimed at curing the plot of malign influences in general and as a prophylaxis against thieving in particular. Petty retailers and middlemen also use magic to ensure success, but once again this is considered to be "good" magic and is worked through the medium of the Saints and the *ánimas*.[3]

Baptism of Money and the Secret of Interest-bearing Capital

According to the belief in *el bautizo del billete* (baptism of the bill), the Godparent-to-be conceals a peso note in his or her hand during the baptism of the child by the Catholic priest. The peso bill is thus believed to receive baptism instead of the child. When such a baptized bill enters into general monetary circulation it is believed that it will continually return to its owner with interest, enriching the owner and impoverishing the other parties to the deals transacted by the owner of the bill. The owner is now the Godparent of the peso bill. The child remains unbaptized, a cause of great concern since the child's soul is denied supernatural legitimacy and has no chance of escaping from Limbo or Purgatory, depending on when it dies. This practice is heavily penalized by the Church.

The baptized bill receives the name – the "Christian name" as we say in English – that the baptismal ritual was meant to bestow on the child and is now referred to by that name. It is then set to work as follows. The Godparent pays the bill over as part of a routine monetary transaction, as when one pays for goods in a store. The Godparent mutters the following type of refrain:

José	José
¿te vas o te quedas?	Are you going or staying?
¿te vas o te quedas?	Are you going or staying?
¿te vas o te quedas?	Are you going or staying?

The bill, referred to by its name, is asked three times whether it is going to return to its Godparent or not. If everything works as it should, then it will soon return to its Godparent, bringing a large amount of money with it. This transfer is accomplished invisibly.

A black middle-class family owned a corner store in the village. Halfway through the morning, when the wife was alone, she went out the back and then quickly returned because she thought she heard a noise in the till. Opening it she found all the cash gone. She then remembered that one of the customers had behaved peculiarly earlier that morning, and realized that someone had passed her a baptized bill. As soon as her back was turned, this bill had made off with all the money in the cash register.

In a busy supermarket in the large city nearby, a shop detective was startled to hear a woman standing near a cash register chanting under her breath: "Guillermo! ¿Te vas o te quedas? ¿Te vas o te quedas? ¿Te vas o te quedas?" He promptly concluded that she had passed a baptized bill and was waiting for it to return to her with the contents of the register, and he immediately arrested her. She was taken away and nobody knows what happened thereafter.

One of the few successful black store owners in the village was saved from a great loss only by a most unusual coincidence. Serving in his shop he was startled to hear a strange noise in

his cash register. Peering in he saw two bills fighting with each other for possession of the contents, and he realized that two customers, each with their own baptized bills, must have just paid them over and were awaiting their return. This strange coincidence allowed him to prevent the spiriting away of his cash.

Interpretation

Let us examine these beliefs with two questions in mind. What is the natural character attributed to monetary exchange and the productive process? What is the system of reasoning used to explain the exchange economy in a society geared to the production of use values? We will discuss the former in terms of commodity fetishism, and the latter in terms of analogical reasoning.

Commodity fetishism

Bizarre as the aforementioned beliefs may appear, in what way do they differ from our own? If we look at popular conceptions of capital in a developed capitalist society, we may note that elaborate metaphorical identifications of capital with the animate world are pervasive.

Take the financial section of the *New York Times* (April, 1974) for example. We read of the "economic climate," the "sagging dollar," of "earnings booming ahead," of "cash flows," of treasury bills "backing up," of runaway and galloping inflation, of "climbing interest rates," of "bear markets" and "bull markets," of factories referred to as "plants," of "money growing" in accordance with investment, of how "your investments can go to work for you," and so on. The active mood predominates: "Weakness in the market was widespread and reflected the performance of the 15 most active issues" and "Despite gasoline shortages and uncertain supplies, 10 of the 15 most active issues traded on Monday could be classed as travel-oriented." "Can the individual investor still find happiness in the market?" asks the muse, who on reflection answers, "today there are dozens of ways to put your capital to work." A Chicago banker is reported as saying, "A general feeling seems to persist that something had definitely gone wrong with what had come to be regarded as the natural order of economic, financial and commercial life." The price of copper bears no proportion to the value of the coins in which it is minted; one spokesman for an important producer said, "While our selling price is killing us, we do have contractual and other obligations to deliver, whether we like to or not." "Splitting his time between New York and his plant in Italy, Joe can't afford to waste time when he's dealing with his bank. That's where Bob comes in. 'As far as I'm concerned,' Joe says, 'Bob *is* Chemical Bank.'" Hence, "Our Man is your bank – Chemical Bank. The businessman, when his needs are financial, his reaction is chemical."

These are but commonplace manifestations of what Marx referred to as *commodity fetishism* occurring in a developed capitalist culture wherein capital and workers' products are spoken of in terms that are used for people and animate beings. It is money as interest-bearing capital that lends itself most readily to this type of fetishism. Capital appears to have an *innate* property of self-expansion, and this property diffuses into all economic life since in capitalism money is the universal equivalent and mediator between persons and all objects. Everything has to be paid for and everything has its price. "Cast in this role, money is said to have changed into a true God, for the intermediary reigns in real power over the things it mediates for me. Its cult becomes an end in itself" (Marx, cited in Ollman, 1971: 203).

The concept of commodity fetishism is meant to draw attention to the fact that capitalist society presents itself to consciousness as something other than it basically is, even though that consciousness does reflect the more or less superficial and hypostatized configuration of society. Fetishism denotes the attribution of life, autonomy, power, and even dominance to otherwise inanimate objects and presupposes the draining of these qualities from the human actors who bestow the attribution. Thus in the case of commodity fetishism, social relationships are dismembered and appear to dissolve into relationships between

things – the products of labor exchanged on the market – so that the sociology of exploitation masquerades as a natural relationship between systemic artifacts. Definite social relationships are reduced to the magical matrix of things. An ether of naturalness – fate and physicality – conceals and enshrouds human social organization and the historical human significance of the market and the development of a propertyless wage-earning class. Rather than man being the aim of production, production has become the aim of man and wealth the aim of production; rather than tools and the productive mechanism in general having liberated man from the slavery of toil, man has become the slave of tools and the instituted processes of production.

In surveying the opinions of eighteenth- and nineteenth-century British economists and statesmen on the question of capital and interest. Marx sarcastically pointed out that in their eyes it becomes "a property of money to generate value and yield interest, much as it is an attribute of pear trees to bear pears . . . Thus we get the fetish form of capital and the conception of fetish capital . . . a mystification of capital in its most flagrant form" (Marx, 1967, III:392). Elsewhere in the same chapter in *Capital* Marx quotes at length from economists like Price and Joshiah Child, and from economic journals of the mid-nineteenth century. He makes lavish use of the biological metaphors that their views of money so strongly suggest. "Money is now pregnant." "As the growing process is to trees, so generating money appears as innate in capital in its form as money-capital." . . .

Benjamin Franklin in his *Advice to a Young Tradesman* (1748) could just as well have been the target of Marx's irony.

Remember, that money is of the prolific, generating nature. Money can beget money, and its offspring can beget more, and so on. Five shillings turned is six, turned again it is seven and threepence, and so on, till it becomes a hundred pounds. The more there is of it, the more it produces every turning, so that the profits rise quicker and quicker. He that kills a breeding-sow, destroys all her offspring to the thousandth generation. (Franklin, cited in Weber, 1958:49)

At the same time these "fabulous fancies which outdid by far the fantasies of the alchemists" were systematically interwoven with the Weltanschauung of *homo economicus* – the supposed epitome of rationality. How could such an odd combination of rationality and fantasy so systematically coexist? What gave conviction to these biological metaphors? The answer lies in the peculiar and unique character of the social relations embodied both in capital and the commodities produced in the capitalist mode of production.

At great length and from a variety of viewpoints Marx argued that these social relations of production impressed themselves on everyday consciousness in such a way that the entire process of production and of the generation of surplus value is overlooked or slighted so that the social process of capital reproduction and expansion may easily appear as a property inherent in the thing itself, rather than the process of which it is part. This socially conditioned appearance is a mystification in which the entire social context conspires, so to speak, to mask itself. In this process of decontextualization, profit no longer appears to be the result of a social *relation*, but of a *thing*; i.e. reification.

Marx made his views on this clear when he compared the formula for interest bearing capital with what he called merchant's capital.

> The relations of capital assume their most externalised and most fetish-like form in interest bearing capital. We have here M-M′, money creating more money, self-expanding value, without the process that effectuates these two extremes. In merchant's capital, M-C-M′, there is at least the general form of the capitalist movement, although it confines itself solely to the sphere of circulation, so that profit appears merely as profit derived from alienation; but it is at least seen to be the product of social *relation*, not the product of a mere *thing*. (Marx, 1967, III:391)

The same point is made by Marx in many of his writings. For instance in the *Grundrisse*, in a passage where his antipathy to what he calls crude materialism is explained in terms of fetishism, he says:

> The crude materialism of the economists who regard as the *natural properties* of things what are social relations of production among people, and qualities which things obtain because they are subsumed under these relations, is at the same time just as crude an idealism, even fetishism, since it imputes social relations to things as inherent characteristics, and thus mystifies them. (Marx, 1973: 687)

Appealing to nature, to the paradoxical extreme wherein certain lifeless things are seen as animated, is merely one historically specific manifestation of that probably universal tendency whereby any culture externalizes its social categories onto nature, and then turns to nature in order to validate its social norms as "natural". Durkheim saw this attempt to invoke the principle of biological determinism in the ideology of "primitive" society, and Marx spotted the same phenomenon in the genesis, acceptance, and use of Darwinism.

> The whole Darwinist teaching of the struggle for existence is simply a transference from society to living nature of Hobbes' doctrine of "bellum omnium contra omnes" and of the bourgeois-economic doctrine of competition together with Malthus' theory of population. When this conjuror's trick has been performed . . . the same theories are transferred back again from organic nature into history and it is now claimed that their validity as eternal laws of human society has been proved. (cited in Schmidt, 1971: 47)

The same point can perhaps be made with regard to Newtonian physics and the role of human beings subordinated to the impersonal controls of the self-regulating market, the central institution if not the "solar system" of capitalist economy. E.A. Burtt draws our attention to the following characteristics of Newtonian metaphysics which have direct implications for our discussion of commodity fetishism and the philosophical roots of the ideology to be found in a market society.

> Here were those residual souls of men, irregularly scattered among the atoms of mass that swam mechanically among the etheral vapors in time and space, and still retaining vestiges of the Cartesian *res cogitans*. They too must be reduced to mechanical products and parts

of the self-regulating cosmic clock . . . Wherever it [the universal formula of gravitation], was taught as truth there was also insinuated as a nimbus of surrounding belief that man is but the puny and local spectator, nay irrelevant product of an infinite self-moving engine . . . which consists of raw masses wandering to no purpose in an undiscoverable time and space, and is in general wholly devoid of any qualities that might spell satisfaction for the major interests of human nature. . . . (Burtt, 1954: 300–1)

Thus, in the fetishism of commodities we encounter a more general formula guiding social awareness which can apply to capitalist culture as a whole. This formula, following Marx, is rooted in the relations of production and exchange as they impress themselves on consciousness in the workaday world. Briefly, this formula is none other than that the social relation is consummated in the relationship of a thing to itself, and that ontology lies not in a relational gestalt but squarely within the thing itself. Atomized, self-encapsulated things – what Burtt refers to as "raw masses" – become the prime object of analysis because their meaning and properties appear to lie within themselves alone. True explanation and understanding now seek to reduce whole phenomena to their simplest parts, and ultimate causality is to be found in the unchanging movement of elementary physical atoms. This dominance of "thinghood" (together with the logical conventions of identity and noncontradiction) tends to obliterate peoples' awareness and efface their capacity for moral evaluation of the bio-logic and socio-logic of relationships and process, particularly as regards their awareness of socio-economic activities and relationships. This is not to say that in this view things as such cannot be related to other such things and harmoniously related at that. Newton's scheme of the planets and Adam Smith's view of the self-regulating market are the outstanding examples of corpuscular interrelatedness forming an harmonious totality, much as modern Systems Theory is today. However, the relations that bind the things are viewed as *external* to the individuated things-in-themselves, whose identity and power is given in themselves alone.

But from another perspective this view is a gross deception since these apparently self-bounded and potent "things" are but the embodiments and concretizations of relationships which bind them to a larger whole. Their identity, existence, and natural properties spring from their *position* in an all-encompassing organic *pattern* of organization in which things are understood as but partial expressions of a self-organizing totality. The properties and activities of things will then be explained holistically and "structurally" in terms of their reticulate intelligibility as parts of an organic whole, and not in terms of mechanical causation and corpuscular collisions as separate bits of matter. If attention focuses on a single thing, as it must at some point in any analysis, then the thing is to be seen as containing its relational network and surrounding context within itself; the "thing" is a system of relationships.

On the other hand, if the atomistic view prevails, as it does in our culture, then the isolated thing-in-itself must inevitably tend to appear as animated because in reality it is part of an active process. If we "thingify" parts of a living system, close our eyes to the context of which they are part, and then observe that the things move, so to speak, it logically follows that the things may well be regarded or spoken of as though they were alive with their own autonomous powers. If regarded as mere things, they will appear as though they are indeed *animate* things – fetishes – so that capital, for instance, is regarded as analogous to a tree that bears fruit, and the thing itself is the source of its own increase. Hence, reification leads to fetishism.

Fetishism: pre-capitalist versus capitalist

In pre-capitalist societies, where commodity exchange and the market are absent, animism, magic, and various forms of fetishism flourish. But is this fetishism similar to the fetishism of commodities to be found in a capitalist mode of production, and is there anything to be gained by asking such a question? Marx, for one, was clearly of the opinion that there was a world of difference, and that in posing the question one was well on the way towards demystifying the illusions induced by the commodity form of exchange. "The whole mystery of commodities, all the magic and necromancy that surrounds the products of labor as long as they take the form of commodities," he wrote, "vanishes therefore so soon as we come to other forms of production" (1967:76).

Following this suggestion, we return to the belief in the baptism of money in the southern Cauca Valley. The belief is that through this illicit religious mechanism – illicit in that it deceives the parents, the child, and the priest, and spiritually mutilates the child, annihilating its acceptance into the citizenry of God – money shall breed money, or that money will grow. In other words, it is an exotic expression of the standard Marxist formula for capitalist circulation, M-C-M' (money-commodity-more money) or simply M-M', as opposed to the circulation associated with use value and the peasant mode of production, C-M-C (commodity A-money-Commodity B; selling in order to buy). The problem that Marx set himself, the mystery of capitalist economic growth and accumulation of capital whereby capital appeared to breed more of itself, is in this situation seen to occur as a result of the supernatural forces incurred by the Christian baptism of the money bill. Once activated in this way money becomes interest-bearing capital. An inert medium of exchange becomes a self-breeding quantity, and in this sense becomes a fetish, a thing with lifelike powers.

If this is a bizarre belief, then one has to consider that the system against which it is levelled is surely no less bizarre. We who have been accustomed to the laws of capitalist economics for several centuries have come to accept the manifestation of these laws as utterly natural and commonplace. The early prophets and analysts of capitalism, such as Benjamin Franklin, regarded the operations of the economy as completely natural to the degree that they could casually refer to interest as an inherent property of capital itself. The peasantry of the southern Cauca Valley, however, regard this as utterly unreal and

supernatural, and their belief in the baptism of money expresses this unreality.

Not only is it unreal, but it is done at the terrible cost of denying the child a legitimate place in rites of the life cycle and in the cosmological order, and hence bears the same profound stigma as does the wage workers' contract with the devil. This, in the second place, is what makes the difference with "pure" or capitalist commodity fetishism, because the baptism is seen as *immoral*.

Third, and, quite apart from this powerful value judgment, the sacrilegious baptism is still seen as the outcome of a chain of events *initiated by man*. It is true that the relationship is still "mystified," since *super*natural power is seen as necessary for the money to bear interest, yet it is clearly understood that the money would *not* do this *on its own*. The multiplication of money as capital is not seen as a power inherent in money. It is not *commodity* fetishism since these people do not consider it a *natural* property of money to reproduce more of itself. Indeed, it is so unnatural that supernatural power has to be obtained by devious and destructive means. And while the true relationship of capital to labor is mystified, there still remains the fact that Man is seen as necessary to trigger off the magical cycles, and this is in keeping with the fact that in a use value economy the regulations that men enter into in their work appear to them as direct, reciprocal, personal relations, and not as activities controlled by the relationships of their products. Indeed, it is precisely due to this consciousness of human interdependence and reciprocity in which both persons and their products are seen as forming a unity, that the specific forms of pre-capitalist fetishism that here concern us arise. When people are confronted by the early stages of penetration of the commodity market, it is the warping and imbalancing of that interdependence which casts the fetish into the realm of the unnatural and evil – the illicit baptism of money and the proletarians' devil contract. Until the spread of capitalist institutions has permeated most aspects of social life, the lower classes continue to perceive the bonds that unite people with their employers and with the fruits of their labor as mutual personal relations, albeit relations which are distorted, evil, and destructive, and not as the result of forces naturally inherent in things.

Analogical reason and the philosophy of use value

The principles underlying the belief in the baptized bill bear a striking resemblance to those concerning money and exchange in Aristotle's *Politics* and the economic theory of the late Middle Ages. Basic to this outlook was the distinction Aristotle drew between what are today called *use* value and *exchange* value, a distinction that occupies a central place in Marxist theory as well. In Book I of *The Politics* Aristotle writes:

> Every article or property has a double use; both uses are uses of the thing itself, but they are not similar uses; for one is the proper use of the article in question, the other is not. For example a shoe may be used either to put on your foot or to offer in exchange. Both are uses of the shoe; for even he that gives a shoe to someone who requires a shoe, and receives in exchange cash or food, is making use of the shoe as shoe, but not the use proper to it, for a shoe is not expressly made for exchange purposes. The same is the case with other articles of property. . . .

While the exchange function of any article could be utilized legitimately within a householding or subsistence economy, it was from this exchange function that money-making or capitalism arose to the detriment of the householding or "natural economy."

In accordance with the distinction between use value and exchange value, Aristotle distinguished between the natural and unnatural uses of money. As Eric Roll points out, this distinction between the two arts of money making,

> was not just an attempt to drive home an ethical distinction. It was also a true analysis of two different forms in which money acts in the economic process: as a medium of exchange whose function is completed by the acquisition of the good required for the satisfaction of a want; and in the shape of money capital leading men to the desire for limitless accumulation. (1973:33)

Roll gives emphasis in his discussion of Aristotle to the idea that money as used in the circulation of use values – Aristotle's householding, the natural economy – is *barren*. "Money is intended to be used in exchange, but not to increase at interest; it is by nature barren; through usury it breeds, and this must be the most unnatural of all the ways of making money" (1973:33). Table I shows this in tabular form.

From this set of contrasts several analogies clearly emerge. For instance:

Use Value of Money   Exchange Value of Money
    (money)   (capital)

$$\frac{natural}{barren} \quad : \quad \frac{unnatural}{fertile}$$

But in nature, in the biological world for example, things are naturally fertile, and Aristotle says on this score, "Money was intended to be a means of exchange, interest represents an increase in the money itself. We speak of it as a yield, as of a crop or a litter; for each animal produces its like, and interest is money produced out of money. Hence of all ways of getting wealth this is the most contrary to nature."

Table 1

Types of Value	Use Value	Exchange Value
Aim of Circulation	To satisfy natural wants	To gain money as an end in itself
Characteristics of Money	Means of exchange	Means to make more money (means as ends; capital)
	(C-M-C)	(M-C-M′)
	Natural	Unnatural
	Barren	Fertile

Following the method propounded by Hesse in her discussion of analogy (1963); this can be expressed as a set of positive and negative analogies, in which there is explicit recognition of *both* similarity and difference between the paired terms that constitute the analogy (see Table 2).

The analogy between animals and money as use value expresses a relationship of both similarity and of difference: they are similar because both are part of the natural world, and their properties function so as to ensure the original purpose of the ideal society ("to reestablish nature's own equilibrium of self-sufficiency," as Aristotle phrases it); and different because it is the natural property of animals to breed more of themselves, while money is by nature barren.

The analogy between animals and capital, or between money and capital, is also based on a set of similarities and differences. For instance capital exhibits the same properties as animals with regard to multiplication, but while one is natural, the other is unnatural. Similarly, money in the use value paradigm is similar to money as capital, but while the former is barren, the latter is fertile.

The task facing the inhabitants of the plantation zones in the southern Cauca Valley is how to explain and in some cases actually effect the transfer of properties of similarity into those of difference and those of difference into relationships of similarity. How to transmute the properties of animals, for example, into those of money, whose natural property is to remain barren? How to explain the transformation of money into interest-bearing capital? How to convert use values into exchange values?

This is done through the illicit rite of baptizing money. Unbaptized or natural money is not and should not be capital; it cannot and should not yield interest in the way capital or animals are seen to breed more of themselves. Money can achieve this unnatural property if it is acted on ritually through means of baptism. Barren money can become unnaturally fertile when transferred to God's domain and stamped with His life-giving properties.

The efficacy and rationality of the magical act would seem to be understood by means of a comparison between observed relationships of similarity and difference in separate spheres of existence, and the rite is utilized to manipulate and transmute relationships of difference into relationships of similarity.

$$\frac{\text{NATURAL}}{\text{animal}} : \frac{\text{UNNATURAL}}{\text{M}}$$

$$\frac{\text{animal}}{\text{litter}} : \frac{\text{M}}{\text{M}'}$$

The litter is the natural yield of the animal, whereas the increase of capital (M') is unnatural. The negative analogy (the comparison of difference) can be overcome and harnessed to the comparison of similarity (positive analogy) by means of the baptismal rite. Thus:

$$\frac{\text{baptism of child}}{\substack{\text{legitimation and}\\\text{growth}}} : \frac{\text{illicit baptism of money}}{\substack{\text{delegitimation and}\\\text{growth}}}$$

Nevertheless, that transfer is achieved by an *illicit* rite when applied to money, and is a sacrilege which deprives a human child of salvation and the endorsement necessary to the fulfillment of human potential. Thus although money can be converted into interest-bearing capital, this is seen as both supernatural and anti-natural. Capital is thus explained in terms which reveal it to be unnatural and immoral. The analogical paradigms based on a use value

Table 2 Positive and Negative Analogies

[biological realm] (natural)		[use value of money] (natural)		[exchange value of money] (unnatural)
$\dfrac{\text{animal}}{\text{litter}}$	:	$\dfrac{\text{M}}{\text{M}}$	:	$\dfrac{\text{M}}{\text{M}'}$

(Where M = Money, and M' = Money plus interest on that money; i.e. capital.)

orientation can be restructured through supernatural means, but for all the restructuring, the original meaning of use-value economics is still upheld.

The devil contract and the magic of capitalist production

In the case of the devil contract made by the plantation wage laborers in order to increase production, the money earned is understood to be barren. Thus, while the proletarian's production can increase, the money is not fertile; in fact it is redolent with infertility – the antithesis of baptized money. What is the meaning of this?

At one level this could be explained by the fact that as opposed to God, the contract is made with His antithesis – the devil. But one can dig deeper behind the symbols and explore Aristotle's and Marx's distinctions further. Aristotle makes the connection between production and the different forms of money in the following way:

> Hence we seek to define wealth and money-making in different ways; and we are right in doing so, for they *are* different; on the one hand true wealth, in accordance with nature, belonging to household management, productive; on the other money-making, with no place in nature, belonging to trade and not productive of goods in the full sense.

Here the antithesis between money as a mere means of exchange, and money as capital, is paralleled by the contrast between productive and non-productive goods and activities. Indeed, for Aristotle the contrast is even more stark than this, since "money-making" or capitalism is inherently *destructive* of the natural or house-holding economy, destructive of the reciprocal interplay of natural forces responsible for production and growth.

Thus the initial frame of reference which referred to the barren and fertile characteristics of money as a medium of *exchange*, is placed in the wider and more determinate context of *production* and a more profound sense of fertility. The analogy between animals and their offspring on the one side and money breeding money on the other is a totally unnatural one

in Aristotle's eyes; unnatural especially in the sense that the naturally barren form of money is grounded in productive activity – "in the full sense" – while the fertile form of money is not. Only in its naturally barren form does "money keep to its original purpose; to reestablish nature's own equilibrium of self-sufficiency." Hence use-values, money as a neutral mediator of exchange, nature's equilibrium of self-sufficiency, and productivity in the full sense, are all intrinsically related and necessary to one another.

A basic set of positive and negative analogies derived from this view is as follows:

$$\frac{money}{capital} : \frac{productive\ capacity}{destructive}$$

The problem facing the people in this culture is, therefore, how to explain and effect the inversion of these natural analogies, since it is empirically true that production can be maintained and increased within the sphere of capitalist production. On inversion:

$$\frac{money}{capital} : \frac{destructive}{productive}$$

This inversion is effected and explained in terms of the devil contract. Through the agency of this evil and destructive force, production within capitalist relations on the sugar plantations can be increased, and at the same time, as the analogy so neatly displays, the money wage gained is non-productive; it kills whatever it buys except for luxury articles consumed immediately. The natural set of relationships that should obtain according to the use-value paradigm can be transformed into capitalist relationships which defy the use-value analogies. But these capitalist relationships are viewed neither as natural nor as good since they necessitate the agency of the devil.

Conclusion

The "superstitions" we encountered in the Cauca Valley are thus revealed to be beliefs which systematically endorse the logic of the contradiction between use values and exchange values. In doing so, these beliefs are identical with the basic tenets of Aristotelian economics, the dominant doctrine of economics as postulated by Aquinas and others in the late Middle Ages, and one of the basic premises of Marxism. (Not for nothing did R. H. Tawney call Marx the last of the Schoolmen.) These "superstitions" are not confused vestiges deriving from a prior era when peasant life or Church influence was more intact, but are precise formulations which entail a systematic critique of the encroachment of the capitalist mode of production.

The sensitivity to the distinction between use values and exchange values as manifested by these beliefs is not merely the result of mummified ideals retained from the days when the peasant mode of production was flourishing. Nor would it seem solely due to the fact that some peasant production still coexists with the developing capitalist mode of production. It is also due to the fact that the "slum economy" of the recently urbanized peasants is similarly one based to a major degree on use value practices.

The paradigm of rationality entailed in these formulations is heavily dependent on analogical reason, examples of which are given above. Analogical explanations involve an account of the unfamiliar in terms of the familiar, and the analogical mode of reasoning at issue here is inherently holistic and dependent on identifying things in terms of their relationships to larger wholes. On the other hand, the causal paradigm which so thoroughly permeates modern Western social science and the mainstream of what is loosely called "Western thought" since the seventeenth century, is inherently atomistic and reductionist, defining identity in terms of the thing itself and not in relation to the context of which the thing is part. In light of this enormous epistemological difference it is obvious that the categories of contemporary sociology and classical economics tend to mystify peasant economics and to deny that peasant economic theory and behavior could be relevant to a critique of classical economics.

The mode of analogical reason outlined above would appear to be most prolific and consciously used in cultures which are guided by use value economics. As Tambiah has so elegantly shown in his interpretation of Zande magic, an awareness of its logic and systematization dispels the pejorative confusions entailed when such beliefs are subjected to the cannons of validity embodied in modern positivist methodology. Where Tambiah falls short, however, is in his failure to consider the underlying system of metaphysics from which the terms in such analogies draw their meaning. While it is a great service to have demonstrated how apparently weird connections and influences between phenomena can be postulated and upheld in terms of the purely *formal* properties of an analogical set, the indigenous ontology has to be considered as well. Placing the emphasis on the formal characteristics of analogical rationality gives us an understanding of the systematic precision entailed in modes of explanation which are not based on the cause-effect paradigm alone. Nevertheless, one still has to ask why certain properties and co-occurences are considered to be analogically related, and why those properties are thought to exist in the first place. While we can point to the analogical relationship between money and capital, for instance, and demonstrate the problem and solution such an analogy conveys, we are still doing no more than pointing to a set of givens whose meaning ultimately lies in a basis other than that given in the formal reasoning rules themselves. This basis is to be found in the metaphysics of nature and the indigenous social philosophy of the group concerned, and in this specific case a large aspect of that philosophy is conveyed by the paradigm of use value economics.

In a culture where Nature is regarded as animate, things which we consider as inert seem to be credited with mind, intelligence, and volition, in the same manner as we reserve those characteristics for the human being exclusively. Nature is seen as permeated with Mind, regulating some Grand Design. The human understanding of things in nature thus proceeds as much through a reckoning of the *meaning* and *intent* established by these things, as through their observable empirical characteristics. Furthermore, given this metaphysical scheme, the meaning and power of things depends on the *relational network* of which the thing is part, which is precisely what makes the analogical mode of reason so compelling.

The types of analogies considered in the examples taken from the Cauca Valley are exceedingly interesting in that the relationships of cause and similarity between the separate terms that make up any analogy depend upon the total set and are not given in the terms themselves. The concept of "cause" herein entailed is not that of mechanical causation, but rather that of "pattern," association, and purpose. In subjecting the latter to the mechanical paradigm of interacting forces akin to the percussion of rebounding billiard balls or interlocking cog wheels, nothing but confusion can result; hence the misguided attribution of irrationality by Western observers when presented with such forms of reason. In describing the properties of the following type of analogy, which is the same type as those considered above, Mary Hesse points out that the relations of similarity at the horizontal level are contingent upon the particular meaning established by the vertical relationships.

$$\frac{\text{father}}{\text{child}} : \frac{\text{state}}{\text{citizens}}$$

Moreover, the vertical relationships themselves are not causal in any specific sense, and furthermore, if the individual terms are considered apart from the total analogical set, they each possess a *variety* of connotations.

Thus the specific meaning of any of the terms within the total structure is dependent on the total set of relationships. This is surely what Lévi-Strauss in his analyses of the "savage mind" means by his obscure directive to look for meaning in relationships and not in the things themselves.

This is to say that the significance of the individual terms does *not* emerge when they are viewed as having meaning as isolates, disconnected from other isolates. Rather, as individual terms they are relational terms which embody the meaning established by the set of relationships of which any term is part. Things are relationships, and these relationships are ontological rather than logical.

The individual terms are not viewed atomistically. They are not conceived of by means of the Newtonian corpuscular paradigm or what A.N. Whitehead calls a philosophy of "external relations," but instead conform to a philosophy of "internal relations" in which each of the separate terms embodies the total set of relationships of which it is part (Whitehead, 1967: 111–18; Ollman, 1971: 27–42).

Put briefly, the metaphysical doctrine of external relations is the foundation of the analytic and reductive method by means of which explanation proceeds through analyzing any given phenomenon in terms of its supposedly irreducible atomistic constituents. The explanation is completed by illustrating the mathematical laws of cause and effect that supposedly hold between these atoms, which in sum constitute the whole phenomenon. This doctrine is central to the Cartesian tradition and the view of nature with which Galileo, Descartes, and Newton propelled modern science on its successful course. Modified in theoretical physics since the early twentieth century, it still seems to provide the basis of most of modern *social* science and popular Western ideologies concerning society. Two important properties concern us here. As Whitehead says, "The character of each of these ultimate things is thus conceived as its own private qualification. Such an existent is understandable in complete disconnection from any other such existent: the ultimate truth is that it requires nothing but itself in order to exist" (1967:113).

In other words, the meaning or identity of a thing is given in itself alone, rather than the "living" context of which it is part. Second, by virtue of such de-contextualization, relationships between things (and changes of things or their relationships), are conceived of "externally" to the things themselves, and suggest recourse to a certain type of Deism, which is how Newton, himself regarded the problem.

In light of this the Cauca Valley beliefs, which stem from a contrary metaphysic, are paradoxically similar insofar as they also make appeals to divine or "external" agencies. Despite this apparent similarity, the concept of nature and ontology in the Cauca Valley situation is one in which the identity or character of things is seen to lie in their being embodiments of relationships and process; hence the doctrine of "internal relations" and a natural science akin to the ancient Greek view of nature, based on the principle that the world of nature is saturated or permeated by mind.

To employ another usage, the peasant epistemology is such that individual terms are conceptualized like Hegel's "moments," constitutive of the totality which constitutes them, with each "moment" containing part of the whole within itself – "internally." The *identity* of the thing springs from its relation to the whole, and is not given in the properties of the thing seen as an isolated or isolable atom. Marxism itself rests on an acute appreciation of such a perspective (cf. Ollman), and Marx expressed this throughout his writing as the foregoing quotations from his works indicate.

Finally, it bears repeating that although the analogical forms can be inverted and that relationships can be transformed, the fact of the matter is that in the examples drawn from the Cauca Valley, where one mode of production is displacing another, the ethics and reason of use value are maintained. The metaphysics that underlie the analogical mode are not disowned despite the fact that the peasants now own little else but their abstract labor power. The analogies are not neutral, despite the neutralizing influence of the fact-value distinction intrinsic to modern science and economic theory in which it is held that ". . . Economics is entirely neutral between ends; that in so far as the achievement of any end is dependent on scarce means, it is germane to the preoccupations of the economist. Economics is not concerned with ends as such" (Robbins, 1935:24).

Nothing could be further from the economic theory and behavior of the peasants and field hands in the southern Cauca Valley for whom economics is totally "concerned with ends as such." Reason, whether it be economic or whatever, is for them far more than the narrow concern with the maximal coordination of scarce means to alternate ends. Rather, reason is that which embodies the conditions of objective existence.[4] Their understanding of capitalist reason and the praxis it embodies, is one which leads them to conclude that it is contrary to the laws of nature, evil, and ultimately destructive of the conditions of objective existence.

To subject their reason to the instrumentality of means and ends, and to the empty formality of analogies considered apart from their content and purpose, is to merely hasten the demise of the conditions embodied in that reason. A peasant society or community can be involved in commodity production – based on exchange value – but this need not be its total culture. A community can in many ways be affected and even controlled by the wider capitalist world, but this in itself does not necessarily make such a community a replica of the larger society and global economy. Attempts to interpret pre-capitalist social formations by means of what Polanyi called "our obsolete market mentality," are misguided exercises in an ingenuous ethnocentrism that in fact is not even applicable to the market society itself, but merely a replication of its appearance.

NOTES

1 Production of sugar in metric tons by plantations located south of the Desbaratado River in the southern region of the Cauca Valley, 1938–69 was as follows:

Year	Metric tons
1938	2,000
1963	13,220
1969	91,750

Source: Asocaña, Cali, Colombia (n.d.).

In the rural area of the southern Cauca Valley, the ratio of smallholders to landless day laborers was on the order of 53:10 in the year 1912 according to official census materials. By 1938 the ratio was around 9:10. Following the outbreak in 1948 of the so-called civil war, the *Violencia*, cash crops of the peasants were sprayed with herbicides by the plantations, reducing peasant production of cocoa by some 80 percent between 1950 and 1958, further accelerating the removal of peasants from the land.

2   The belief does not apply to all proletarians, but is restricted to *male* proletarians. Like peasants of both sexes, *female* wage laborers are *not* supposed to make a devil contract to increase their wages. The reason given for this is that since the "wages of the devil" are inherently destructive and barren, and since women assume almost all the obligation of raising children, it would be devastatingly counter-productive for them to try to raise a family with such money. An additional reason could be that short matrilines form the basis of the social structure, and that the souls of the deceased maternal ancestors are a very critical link to the rest of the supernatural world. Therefore, if a mother sells her soul to the devil, she deprives her descendants of their most crucial link with the spirit world of good ancestors, the Saints, and God.

3   These observations serve to emphasize that it is neither money per se, inequality, nor involvement in buying and selling activities which leads to the opprobrium of devil's work. The peasants spend most of their time in the cultivation of cash crops (cocoa and coffee) on their own plots or the plots of their neighbors, and of course retailers are almost exclusively involved in buying and selling. Furthermore, material inequalities abound within these social groups. The critical fact is that none of these activities is directly organized by capitalist relations of production, and that money is used only as a means of facilitating exchange, not as something to be maximized as an end in itself.

4   This formulation is the subject of intensive analysis by the "Frankfurt School" of Marxist scholars, especially Max Horkheimer in his work *The Eclipse of Reason*.

SELECTED BIBLIOGRAPHY

Asocaña (Asociación Nacional de Cultivadores de Caña de Azúcar) (1965) *Development of the Colombian Sugar Industry, 1967–1968.* Cali, Colombia.

Brown, Norman O. (1959) *Life Against Death*. Middletown, Conn.: Wesleyan University Press.

Burtt, Edwin Arthur (1954) *The Metaphysical Foundations of Modern Science*. New York: Anchor Books.

Hesse, Mary B. (1963) *Models and Analogies in Science*. London: Sheed and Ward.

Horkheimer, Max (1974) *The Eclipse of Reason*. New York: Seabury Press.

Marx, Karl (1967) *Capital*, 3 vols. New York: International Publishers.

—— (1973) *The Grundrisse*, M. Nicolaus (trans.), Middlesex, England: Penguin Books.

Nash, June (1972) "The Devil in Bolivia's Nationalised Tin Mines," *Science and Society*, XXVI, 2.

Needham, Joseph (1956) *Science and Civilisation in China*, vol. 2. Cambridge, England.

Ollman, Bertell (1971) *Alienation: Marx's Conception of Man in Capitalist Society*, Cambridge: Cambridge University Press.

Robbins, Lionel (1935) *An Essay on the Nature and Significance of Economic Science*, 2nd Edition. London: Macmillan.

Roll, Eric (1973) *A History of Economic Thought*, 4th Edition. London: Faber and Faber.

Sahlins, Marshall (1972) *Stone Age Economics*. Chicago & New York: Aldine Atherton.

Schmidt, Alfred (1971) *The Concept of Nature in Marx*. London: New Left Books.

Tambiah, S. J. (1973) "Form and Meaning of Magical Acts: A Point of View," in Robin Horton and Ruth Finnegan (eds.), *Modes of Thought*. London: Faber and Faber.

Tawney, R. H. (1954) *Religion and the Rise of Capitalism*. New York: Mentor.

Weber, Max (1927) *General Economic History*, Frank H. Knight trans., Greenberg, New York.

—— (1958) *The Protestant Ethic and the Spirit of Capitalism*, Talcott Parsons (trans.), New York: Charles Scribner's Sons.

Whitehead, Alfred North (1967) *Adventures of Ideas*. New York: Free Press.

36

The Colonization of Consciousness

John and Jean Comaroff

South Africans trained in the United Kingdom, Jean and John Comaroff are both professors of anthropology at the University of Chicago. They have sustained a remarkable intellectual partnership and are among the most powerful exponents of classical and contemporary social theory applied to ethnographically situated historical transformations. They write with great urgency and passion about large issues, but with close attention to specificity and nuance.

If, in the analysis of small-scale societies, religion is understood to be intimately connected to social relations, production, reproduction, and politics, so the Comaroffs demonstrate that the impact of Christian missionary activity on southern Africans, while ostensibly about purely "religious" matters, actually reshaped sociality, personhood, and

everyday practices, preparing Africans to be docile laborers at the bottom end of the emerging capitalist economy and docile citizens in the newly forming states. They show how modernity is cultural through and through and emphasize the role of Christianity in exporting and inculcating this culture, even if the missionaries themselves were not always aware of the connections. One of the effects of the missionaries, the Comaroffs point out, was that whether Africans were converted or not – and they problematize what such "conversion" could mean – Africans became drawn into conversations whose terms (central concepts and arguments) were set by Europeans. At the same time, the Comaroffs argue that the results are neither inevitable nor complete; elements of the new are synthesized with the old and form a space for resistance. Such

From John L. and Jean Comaroff, "The Colonization of Consciousness," in *Ethnography and the Historical Imagination* (Boulder, CO: Westview Press, 1992 [1989]), pp. 235–63. Copyright © 1992 by Westview Press, member of the Perseus Books Group. Reprinted by permission of Westview Press, a member of Perseus Books, LLC. Abridged.

resistance may be all the more powerful for being tacit, contained in signifying practices that themselves become quotidian.

The passages describing nondiscursive forms of response have been heavily abridged here, but they are the subject of beautiful exposition in Jean Comaroff's *Body of Power, Spirit of Resistance* (1985), as well as their joint two volumes on the encounter between missionaries and southern Africans (1991, 1997). Sundkler (1961) provides a superb earlier introduction to the creativity of southern African forms of Christianity. Recent work by the Comaroffs includes studies of what they strikingly call 'millenial capitalism' (2000) and the occult, citizenship and policing in contemporary South Africa.

Modern Southern Africa is built upon a long history of symbolic struggle, a bitter contest of conscience and consciousness. This is not to deny the coercive, violent bases of class antagonism and racial inequality here. Nor is it to underplay the brute material dimensions of the struggle; indeed, it is never possible simply to prize apart the cultural from the material in such processes. But, in the eyes of the Southern Tswana, the rural people with whom we shall be concerned in this essay, the past century and a half has been dominated by the effort of others to impose on them a particular way of seeing and being, to colonize their consciousness with the signs and practices, the axioms and aesthetics, of an alien culture. This alien culture is the culture of European capitalism in its various guises: capitalism as the direct extension of British commerce; capitalism, both agrarian and industrial, erected on the foundations of settler economy and society; capitalism matured in the systematic mold of the racist state. Capitalism, that is, refracted from an expanding global order into a myriad of local facets.

In the face of this assault, some black South Africans have succumbed, some have resisted, some have tried to recast the intrusive European forms in their own terms. And most have done all of these things, at one or another time, in the effort to formulate an awareness of, and gain a measure of mastery over, their changing world. It is no wonder, therefore, that any attempt to understand the Southern Tswana past and present keeps being drawn back to the colonization of their consciousness and their consciousness of colonization. Of course,

the dominant theme in the modern history of these peoples has been their incorporation into a colonial, and later postcolonial, state. But it is important to stress that this is a "state in both senses of the term: an institutional order of political regulation *and* a condition of being, a structure *and* a predicament. Consequently, the effort of the colonizer to impose it upon them has been as much a matter of the politics of experience as a matter of constitutional (and coercive) authority. So, too, with Tswana reactions: they have flowed well beyond the formal channels of political discourse and onto the diffuse terrains of everyday life. Nor is this unusual. Colonizers in most places and at most times try to gain control over both the material and semantic practices through which their would-be subjects produce and reproduce the very bases of their existence; no habit being too humble, no sign too insignificant to be implicated in the battle. And colonization everywhere gives rise to struggles – albeit often tragically unequal ones – over power and meaning on the moving frontiers of empire. It is a process of "challenge and riposte" (Harlow 1986: xi, after Bourdieu 1977: 12) often much too complex to be captured in mechanical equations of domination and resistance – or, for that matter, in grand models of the political economy of colonialism and the modern world system.

Among the Southern Tswana, any effort to document such processes – to analyze, that is, the colonization of consciousness and the consciousness of colonization – begins with the entry of evangelical Christianity onto the historical landscape. Not only were Nonconformist missionaries the vanguard of the British presence in this part of the South African interior; they were also the most ambitious ideological and cultural agents of Empire, bearing with them the explicit aim of reconstructing the native world in the name of God and Great Britain (Comaroff and Comaroff 1986). Of course, the chronicle of evangelical Protestantism does not tell us the whole story of the Tswana past. Nothing does, in and of itself. But it does hold one key to the symbolic and material processes involved in the colonial encounter – and to the modes of cultural transformation and ideological argument, of "challenge and riposte," to which it has given rise.

We should like, in this essay, to trace out an early chapter in the confrontation between the missions and the Tswana – and, with it, an early phase in the struggle over being and consciousness here. For this phase, partial and passing though it is in the broader history of Southern Africa, has some important lessons for the anthropology of colonialism in general, and for the history of consciousness in particular. In this respect, too, we offer our account with a general methodological point in mind: whether it be in the tradition of Durkheim, Marx, or Weber, anthropologists usually study consciousness and its transformations by examining its *effects* or its *expressions*. To be sure, modern anthropology has become highly skilled at describing the social and symbolic manifestations of the *conscience collective,* inferring the phenomenon, as it were, from the recurrent shadows it seems to cast upon the wall. Rarely, however, do we examine the nature of consciousness in the making – let alone in its own full historicity. Indeed, as a fashionable synonym for "culture," "ideology," "thought," or an ill-defined blend of all three, the notion of consciousness itself is seldom scrutinized. Sometimes it is regarded as the mere reflection of a reality beyond human awareness, sometimes as the site of creativity and agency. But, almost invariably, "consciousness" is treated as a substantive "model of" or "for" the world, as so much narrative content without form. Only specific historical analyses may force us to think beyond this inchoate preconception; to explore the relationship, in the making of human meaning, of form and content, sign and practice, intention and outcome.

The Nonconformist evangelists of the London Missionary Society (LMS) and the Wesleyan Methodist Missionary Society (WMMS) entered in the 1920s the world of the people whom we know today as the Tswana. We cannot describe that world in detail here . . . , [but] far from being closed communities or possessing "cold cultures," early nineteenth-century Tswana polities were dynamic structures that underwent complex transformations over space and time (see e.g. Legassick 1969; Comaroff and Comaroff 1990; J. Comaroff 1985; J. L. Comaroff 1973). What is more, they already had a long history of interaction; interaction, over considerable distances, through trade, raiding, and – most important here – the exchange of medical knowledge and cultural practices. For example, one of the earliest missionaries to visit the interior, the Reverend John Campbell (1822, 1: 307), tells how a party of Ngwaketse traveled for almost a year, far to the north of the Tswana world, to learn techniques and obtain preparations that might bring them rain and cause their enemies drought. Such odysseys, albeit usually on less grand a scale, seem to have been undertaken quite frequently.

Nor shall we go into the social origins of the British churchmen here; it, too, is a complex issue. . . . But it is necessary to stress that their mission was conditioned by an imperial vision conjured up in the fervent images of a triumphant bourgeoisie during the Age of Revolution (Hobsbawm 1962); that their position in the crevices of the changing class structure of industrial revolution Britain shaped their project, their own personal careers of upward mobility becoming an ideological mold for the moral future of Africa. In an epoch that celebrated hero-worship (indeed, as Carlyle [1842:1] asserts, almost made it into a theory of history) theirs was an epic quest, their emerging sense of "biography" as a "moral career" providing a model of and for a heroic history – their own as well as that of the heathen lands that would become colonies of God and the British monarch.

This quest took them far into the Southern African hinterland; far *beyond* the colonial frontier and the gaze of its administration, with which they had very uneasy relations from the first. In fact, as a "dominated fraction of the dominant class" and as the self-styled moral conscience of the civilized world, they were to come into frequent conflict with more powerful political and economic agents of colonialism for a long time to come (see Comaroff and Comaroff 1986). In this respect, their efforts to build a new Empire of the Spirit, and later of Great Britain, were driven by tensions inherent in a rapidly changing, secularizing Europe: they wished to recreate a romantically (and mythologically) conceived society, in which spiritual authority remained unquestioned; in which technical progress, itself much admired, did not cause the massive social upheaval it had sown among the working class in the north of England; in which the countryside was not disfigured, nor its free yeomanry dispossessed – as many of their own peasant fathers and grandfathers had been. They sought, in other words, a modern industrial capitalist world without its essential contradictions.

More immediately, they set about the task of "civilizing" the native by remaking his person and his context; by reconstructing his habit and his habitus; by taking back the savage mind from Satan, who had emptied it of all traces of spirituality and reason. Most of all, however, they wished to establish a viable peasantry – remaking, in Africa, the destroyed British yeomanry of their own imagined origins – tied at once to the soil and to an ethos of universal commerce. Remember that David Livingstone, perhaps the most popular missionary in the Victorian public consciousness (Jeal 1973), was to say, in a famous passage of his best selling *Missionary Travels and Researches* (1857: 34): "The promotion of commerce ought to be specially attended to . . . [I wish] to promote the preparation of the raw materials of European manufactures in Africa, for by that means we may not only put a stop to the slave-trade, but introduce the negro family into the body of corporate nations." In order to achieve these objectives, initially, the Protestants sought to hold up a mirror to the savage; a looking-glass in which he might gaze upon

himself and, in a revelatory moment of self-reflection, open his eyes and ears to the Good News, the narrative of Christianity. At the same time, in the same mirror, the heathen might also come to recognize the divided self of bourgeois individualism, the subject upon whom the edifice of modern European civilization was constructed.

Of course, this was all presented to the Tswana, and to the wider world, in the noncoercive rhetoric of rational argument and free choice. Again, take David Livingstone (1857: 21): "In our relations with this people we were simply strangers exercising no authority or control whatever. Our influence depended entirely on persuasion; [on teaching] them by kind *conversation* (our italics)."

As the first encounter between the Tswana and the evangelists gave way to a more sustained interaction, each tried to cast the other in his own image: the missionary, to portray the native as an unregenerate savage to be transformed; the Tswana, to draw on the power of the mission to protect a world endangered. Each, in other words, found the other indispensable in making real his own fantasy – although the Europeans were ultimately to prove better positioned to impose their construction on the reality they would come to share. For the Christians brought with them goods and knowledge – guns, wealth objects, technical skills, and the capacity to act as authoritative diplomatic agents – at a time when many chiefs were desperate for just such things in their struggle to maintain their autonomy in the face of *difaqane* and early settler advance.

Indeed, the fact that this was a period of great upheaval played into the hands of the missions, facilitating greatly their entry into the Tswana world. For, while many chiefs and royals saw the Europeans as potential rivals to their authority – some, it seems, even observed that their presence would "change the whole [social] system" – they became too valuable to pass up, and the various chiefdoms competed for their attentions (see e.g. Moffat 1842: 389f, 414). Seizing the opportunity, and showing great resourcefulness in making themselves indispensable, the evangelists soon entered into the conversation of which Livingstone wrote.

But the African rulers were as assiduous in trying to limit their influence. Here we explore three crucial registers in this long argument and the battle that ensued for control over its terms. For convenience, we refer to them as (i) the politics of water, (ii) the politics of production, and (iii) the politics of language.

The Politics of Water

As soon as they gained entry into Tswana communities, the evangelists set about establishing what we might think of as a mundane theater of industry; a site for the total reconstruction of the practical world of the natives. For example, the very first act of James Read, the earliest regular missionary among the Tlhaping, was to erect a square European house – even though he seems to have lived very comfortably in his wagon. He then built a smith's forge and began, before the "astonished" eyes of much of the local citizenry, to fashion the tools of peasant production. His account of these events indicates a keen awareness of their impact: "The people were struck with wonder," he wrote. "One of them said 'these men must be from God that can do such things'."

Here, then, was the matter-of-fact drama of Protestant fabrication, setting forth bit by bit the mode of rural production through which the missionaries hoped to shape the servants of Christ. Spanish Catholicism in seventeenth-century Mexico used ritual drama to impress pious submission on the natives (Trexler 1984), and colonizing Anglicanism in Rhodesia took hold of the Shona by making their landscape its own icon (Ranger 1987). But the Nonconformists in South Africa sought to reconstruct the inner being of the Tswana chiefly on the more humble ground of everyday life, of the routines of production and reproduction. Not only were they predisposed to such methods by their puritan creed and by their commitment to the bourgeois ideal of self-improvement through rational labor; their ritual parsimony also struck a chord with Setswana practice, which lacked symbolic or ceremonial elaboration. As Moffat (1842: 243–4) lamented early on:

The situation of the missionary among the Bechuanas is peculiar, differing . . . from any other among any nation on the face of the earth . . . He seeks in vain to find a temple, an altar, or a single emblem of heathen worship . . . Thus the missionary could make no appeals to legends, or to altars, or to an unknown God, or to ideas kindred to those he wished to impart.

Moffat was correct. Rather than proclaim itself to the European as overtly "religious," Tswana symbolic practice operated on another plane entirely. It saturated the ground of everyday activity, breathing life into the habitual forms of social existence. It was on this terrain that the missions had to battle for control over the salient signs of the world they wished to conquer (cf. Volosinov 1973) – a battle not for sacred sites, but for mastery of the mundane.

In their effort to engage the Tswana in just such a conversation about everyday life, the evangelists soon found themselves caught up in the politics and poetics of water. As it turns out, they were encouraged by both climes and times to conceive of themselves, in horticultural idiom, as the irrigators of the African desert. "Her vast moral wastes," wrote Moffat (1842: 614), a gardener by vocation in England, "must be watered by the streams of life." Such is the force of the poetic that this analogy, so good for the missionaries to think with, was to give particular form to their deeds in the "field." But the "wastes" of the Tswana world had already called forth a torrent of indigenous symbolic techniques to conserve this most precious and capricious resource. Furthermore, control over water was a vital aspect of chiefly power: the annual rains were held to be the inseminating force bestowed on the land and the people by a virile ruler, "made" (do dira) either by his own hand or by a rainmaker (moroka) of his choosing (Schapera 1971); without these royal rites the productive cycle could not begin. In fact, the political symbolism of rain, pula, was central in public life. Not only did chiefs open and close all assemblies by greeting their people "ka pula," with rain (Campbell 1822, 2: 157; Solomon 1855: 47), but the term itself was associated with the achievement of collective well-being. The word for water, *metse*, was the plural form of the vernacular for *town* – which, in Tswana cosmology, was the nucleus of all human life, and stood for the triumph of social order (metonymically represented in the chiefship) over the threatening, chaotic wild beyond the settlement.

The provision of a regular water supply was vital, too, in the Protestants' scheme of things. After all, they intended to create a Christian peasantry – to re-create, as we said, the lost British yeomanry – in the "desolate vineyard" of Africa (Moffat 1842: 330). They had also to grow enough for their own survival. To this end, they began to dig wells and trenches with which to irrigate their gardens, an activity that soon set them at odds with local values and interests. . . .

For Southern Tswana, water and land were given not by nature, but by the chief to households whose womenfolk, as primary producers, had direct control over them. In this dryland ecology, water was too scarce a domestic resource to be put to the irrigated cultivation of mission "gardens"; no wonder the women regarded the whole idea as unreasonable. These gardens – a term seldom used, incidentally, by the churchmen to refer to native horticulture – were a great source of pride to the Europeans. Laid out almost at once within neat fences, they were icons of the civilizing mission at large. Described in dispatches home as "examples to the natives of industry," it was in their cultivated shade that the few would-be converts who died in the early years were laid to rest. The Tlhaping, on the other hand, expressed their resentment by repeatedly stealing their fruits – and finally by destroying all efforts made to water them (Moffat 1842: 286). Indeed, Tswana resistance dates back to the very beginnings of the colonizing process and, from the first, involved women.

While the war with the women was waged over the productive deployment of water, another struggle raged over its ontology. In the absence of elaborate ritual or explicit iconography, the rites of rainmaking presented the Europeans with Tswana "superstition" in its most tangible form. In these revered rites, performed at the direction of the chief, the mis-

sionaries read the essence of savage unreason. "Rainmakers," said Moffat (1842: 305), "are our inveterate enemies, and uniformly oppose the introduction of Christianity amongst their countrymen to the utmost of their power." The evangelists became fairly obsessed with rainmaking and regarded its eradication, which they linked to the triumph of bourgeois reason, as a major measure of their success.

[. . .]

. . . The displacement of water from the domain of "ritual" to that of "technical management" created a legitimation crisis for the chiefship. But we concentrate, here, on the ontological rather than the temporal struggle. For there was a contradiction in the evangelical message – and an especially ironic one at that. On the one hand, the Christians introduced technical innovations and a "scientific" rationale into the production of water, seeking thereby to demystify its magicality. Yet, on the other hand, they tried to prove that the Christian God was the provenance of a superior water supply. And so they presented themselves as rainmakers of a competing power.

There was another, more subtle dimension to all this, however. Rainmakers might have known how to use the magic with which to activate the clouds and bring *pula*. But, for the Tswana, their power could only work when the community was in a state of moral balance, of "coolness" (*tsididi*). Any breach of that balance – through improper conflict among humans, or between them and the non-human realm – might pollute the cosmic order, and create the heat that dried up the rain. The rainmaker "made" the rain purely in so far as he ensured that the condition of the social world met the standards of ancestral beneficence. In this sense, he no more manufactured it than did a churchman praying to God, a point that was lost on the missionaries. As a result, most of them tried to convince indigenous practitioners, in "reasoned" argument, of the illogicality and dishonesty of their activity (Reyburn 1933). While a surprising number of them recorded their efforts, Livingstone (1857: 25f; also [ed. Schapera] 1960: 239f) alone described his debate with a Kwena practitioner in such a way as to suggest that there was little to choose between their positions:

[MEDICAL DOCTOR]: So you really believe that you can command the clouds? I think that can be done by God alone.

[RAIN DOCTOR]: We both believe the very same thing. It is God that makes the rain, but I pray to him by means of these medicines, and, the rain coming, of course it is then mine. It was I who made it for the Bakwains [Kwena] for many years . . . ; through my wisdom, too, their women became fat and shining. Ask them; they will tell you the same as I do.

M.D.: But we are distinctly told in the parting words of our Saviour that we can pray to God acceptably in his name alone, and not by means of medicines.

R.D.: Truly! but God told us differently. . . . God has given us one little thing, which you know nothing of. He has given us the knowledge of certain medicines by which we can make rain. We do not despise those things which you possess, though we are ignorant of them. We don't understand your book, yet we don't despise it. You ought not to despise our little knowledge, though you are ignorant of it. [Original italics.]

M.D.: I don't despise what I am ignorant of; I only think you are mistaken in saying that you have medicines which can influence the rain at all.

R.D.: That's just the way people speak when they talk on a subject of which they have no knowledge. When first we opened our eyes, we found our forefathers making rain, and we follow in their footsteps. You, who send to Kuruman for corn, and irrigate your garden, may do without rain; we can not manage in that way . . .

M.D.: I quite agree with you as to the value of the rain; but you can not charm the clouds by medicines. You wait till you see the clouds come, then you use your medicines, and take the credit which belongs to God only.

R.D.: I use my medicines, and you employ yours; we are both doctors, and doctors are not deceivers. You give a patient medicine. Sometimes God is pleased to heal him by means of your medicine; sometimes not – he dies. When he is cured, you take the credit of what God does. I do the same. Sometimes God grants us rain, sometimes not. When he

does, we take the credit of the charm. When a patient dies, you don't give up trust in your medicine, neither do I when rain fails. If you wish me to leave off my medicines, why continue your own?

In this carefully crafted dialogue, Livingstone presents himself as an uneasy spokesman for God and science, seeming to argue with himself over the logical impasse of the mission. The parallel use of the title "doctor," as much as the symmetry of the actual debate, implies the conviction that a contest is being waged on equal ontological ground. Thus he allows his opponent to suggest a functional correspondence between Tswana material icons and European verbal signs, and to cast reasoned doubt on the Christian distinction between the sacred and secular. In so doing, Livingstone anticipated by eighty years Evans-Pritchard's (1937) spirited defense of the rationality of African "magical" thought. But this did not deter him, or his brethren, from trying to persuade the Tswana to accept the Christian message on "rational grounds."
[. . .]
   It is hardly necessary to labor another of Evans-Pritchard's (1937) observations: given that criteria of technical efficacy are culturally specified, established knowledge is not falsified by evidence external to its (tauto)logical structure. What the evangelists took to be definitive proof of the "vain pretensions" of the natives in no way undermined Tswana cosmogonic assumptions. Instead, such events merely confirmed that the whites had introduced a distinct and competing power into the local world (see e.g. Hodgson [ed. Cope] 1977: 23). At the same time, everything pointed to the fact that this power was substantial. Their technological prowess and wealth, after all, must have come from somewhere, and the capacity to produce water from under the ground *was* impressive. It certainly seemed to many Tswana that it was worth pursuing the conversation with the Europeans – and trying to learn the techniques which held the key to their potency. Recall, here, the long-standing indigenous value placed on the exchange of cultural knowledge and practices.

Of course, as the participants on both sides searched for signs and symbols through which to communicate, they began also to recognize the distinctions between them. And so the speakers of each language came gradually to *objectify* their world in relation to a novel other, thereby inventing for themselves self-conscious coherence and distinctness – even while they accommodated to the new relationship that enclosed them. As is now well-known, the self-awareness of post-enlightenment Europe had long been sharpened in contrast to the non-European. The first generation of Protestant missionaries continued this reflexive process on the moral frontier with savage superstition. For the Tswana, the encounter with a people preoccupied with techniques of self-representation and rationalization brought forth a sense of opposition between *sekgoa* (European ways) and *setswana* (Tswana ways). The latter was perceived, for the first time, as a coherent body of knowledge and practice in relation to the former, which they had learned to see as a *system* of "belief" *(tumèlò,* lit. "agreement," itself a notion of doctrine as consensus; see Moffat 1842: 246f). In this moment of self-objectification, we suggest, lie the cultural origins of modern Tswana ethnicity. For, until this time, "the Bechuana" – who had no name for themselves, other than *batho,* human beings – were divided into political communities distinguished by their totemic affiliations, a quite different form of collective consciousness (J. L. Comaroff 1987).

Increasingly, then, the argument over such issues as rainmaking became a confrontation between two cultures, two social orders. For their part, the Tswana were motivated by a desire to appropriate the cultural and technical power of the whites without losing their autonomy. In the effort to harness that power to their own ends, however, they joined the conversation that was so profoundly to alter their sense of themselves and their world, the conversation of which David Livingstone had written (see above). And here is the point: in so doing, they were inducted into the *forms* of European discourse; into the ideological terms of rational argument and empirical reason. Who, indeed, *was* the better rainmaker? How

was it possible to decide the issue? The Tswana were not necessarily persuaded by the claims of the evangelists. Nor did this new mode of discourse simply take over their cultural universe. Still, they could not but begin slowly to internalize the terms through which they were being challenged. To be sure, in order even to respond to the arguments of *sekgoa*, it was necessary to use those terms. This, as we shall see in due course, was a critical moment in the colonizing process. But let us turn, secondly, to the politics of production.

The Politics of Production

The central role of agriculture in the evangelical vision of reconstruction has already been anticipated. Not only did many of the early Nonconformists have close ties with the recently marginalized British peasantry and a nostalgic sense of a lost rural world. They were also heirs to an idea of colonization that linked cultivation to salvation. Missionaries, wrote Moffat (1842:616–17), ought to "put their hand to the plough," preparing the stony African ground for "a rich harvest of souls." As agriculture flourished, so too would civilization. Given the African concern with cattle-keeping, it may seem curious that this imagery makes no mention of pastoralism. But the belief in the civilizing role of cultivation was as old as English colonialism itself. In the seventeenth century, Spenser had advocated a settled agrarian existence as the solution to the problem of the "wild Irish," whose barbarous and warlike state he ascribed to their semi-nomadic, pastoral pursuits (Muldoon 1975:275). Similar notions were carried to the new world and Africa, for they corresponded with what Europeans had come to regard as the natural evolution of their own superior world. Agriculture made men peaceful, law-abiding, and governable.

Agriculture, in short, would cultivate the worker as he cultivated the land: The production of new crops and the production of a new kind of selfhood went together in the evangelical imagination. Above all else, this new mode of production would encourage the would-be convert to yield enough of a surplus to tie him through trade with Christian Europe (Bundy 1979:39) – to a Kingdom of God, that is, which looked just like the imperial market-place. Blighted no more, the dark continent would become a "fruitful field," a rural periphery of the established centers of civilization (Broadbent 1865:204).

As we have already noted, the irrigated garden was an icon of the civilizing mission at large. Within its fenced confines, the churchmen enacted the principles of material individualism: the creation of value by means of self-possessed labor; the forceful domination of nature; the privatization of property; and the accumulation of surplus through an economy of effort.

[. . .]

The mission garden, clearly, was also meant as a lesson in the contrast of "labor" and "idleness" – and, no less, in the relative value of male and female work. For, to the churchmen, African production was "topsy-turvy" (Crisp 1896:16). The men, whose herds were tended by youths and serfs, appeared to be lazy "lords of creation" (Moffat 1842:505), their political and ritual exertions not signifying "work" to the missionary eye. Women, on the other hand, seemed to have been coerced into doing what was properly male labor, their desultory "scratching" on the face of the earth evoking the ineffectual efforts of mere "beasts of burden" (Kinsman 1983). There was no private property, no commerce, no sign of the "healthy, individualistic competition" or the maximization of time and effort that the Christians saw as righteous industry (Mackenzie quoted in Dachs 1972:652). As Reverend Willoughby (n.d.) put it, "The African lives a simple socialistic life, subordinating his individuality to the necessities of the tribe."

Determined to teach by example and compelled to become self-sufficient, then, the evangelist and his wife became metonyms of the European division of labor. Livingstone (1857:22) talks of "the accomplishments of a missionary in Central Africa, namely, the husband to be a jack-of-all-trades without doors, and the wife a maid-of-all-work within." Here lay another key to civilizing reform: the black woman was to be confined indoors to the sphere of domestic work – and a maid she

was indeed to become in the political economy of modern South Africa.

While the first reaction of the Tswana to the fertile mission garden was to steal its fruit (see below), the LMS station at Kuruman, with its drought-resistant crops, became a "comparative Goshen to the surrounding country" (Moffat, quoted in Northcott 1961:148). The heathen, however, did not immediately learn from it what the churchmen wished to teach; namely, that its fertility was the product of rationalized hard labor and "modern" methods of cultivation. In the early days at least, its bountiful harvest was seen to flow from the innate powers of the evangelists themselves, this expressing the Tswana sense of the continuity between persons and their capacities to act upon the world. Among the Seleka-Rolong, for instance, leading men vied to have their wives cultivate fields directly adjoining the obviously potent WMMS plots. But the Nonconformists persisted in offering their new techniques and, in time, the Tswana began to differentiate these forces of production from the personal potency of the whites – thereby also learning another lesson in European selfhood. First came the well and the irrigation ditch, next the plough, each being as critical to the construction of the Protestant worldview as it was to the material basis of the civilizing mission. Both were instruments that would transform the "fitful and disorderly" Tswana into settled communities founded on private property (Shillington 1985:17).

[. . .]

The churchmen were happy to report the steadily expanding reliance on plough agriculture (Mackenzie 1871:72). They were also glad to note some of its corollaries – the growing use of money from the sale of surpluses to purchase farm implements and consumer goods; the increasing signs of private property; and the reformation of the division of labor as women lost control over crop production. They were not so quick to record other, less palatable implications of their efforts: among them, the fact that drought and disease threatened the cattle economy; that, as more pasture was brought under cultivation, a few powerful families were gaining control of much of the land, including the best acreages around natural water sources (Shillington 1985:62). The material bases of inequality were being progressively – and, as it was to turn out, disastrously – reconstructed.

Here, then, is the origin of a fragmented peasantry caught up in an uneven transition to capitalism. As it was to turn out, Southern Tswana communities were to splinter along similar lines to those described by Lenin (1971:14f; see also Ferguson 1976) for the agrarian population of Russia. The upper peasantry was to give birth to a small rural black petty bourgeoisie; the lower peasantry, into which the vast majority were to be trapped, was to become South Africa's notorious reserve army of labor, its emergent class of peasant-proletarians; and, in the middle, was a class of producers who were to suffer all the contradictions associated with the rapid growth of commodity production within a world of non-capitalist relations (J. L. Comaroff 1977, 1982). It was a process of fragmentation that, over time, would lay the basis for emergent patterns of class distinction and consciousness. . . .

[. . .]

. . . While the technological innovations of the mission gave rise to a class of commercial farmers, in the longer term the plough brought the majority a harvest of hunger. It also served to mark the onset of an era in which *all* Tswana would have to turn toward the market, orienting themselves, at least to some degree, to the culture and practices of commodity production. Of course, an ever greater number would have to do so as laborers. Having come to recreate the lost British yeomanry, the Christians had begun to prepare the ground not for an independent peasantry but for an army of wage workers; or, more precisely, for a population of peasant-proletarians snared in a web of economic dependency. And all this well before coercive colonial policies sought to force the Tswana into perennial wage labor.

[. . .]

The evangelists could not take all the credit for this situation, of course. There were other forces at work in the dispossession and domination of the Southern Tswana. But they certainly could claim to have contributed, culturally and materially, to the entry of these peoples into a cycle of peasant (under-) production and wage labor. For they had toiled hard to introduce an appreciation of money, time, work discipline and the other essential features of industrial capitalism; in sum, the signs and practices of the commodity *form*. Again, the Tswana reacted differentially to the call of commerce, commodities, and cash crops. And they did so along the fault-lines of class distinction, whose symbolic markers had themselves been instilled by the churchmen – the small petty bourgeoisie, which came most fully to embody mission values, showing greatest enthusiasm. But gradually all alike were drawn into the purview of a world reconstructed according to the logic of the market. All alike began to internalize its terms and, hence, to reorder their own prior system of meanings accordingly. Once more, let us bear this in mind as we move on to the third register of the conversation between the Tswana and the mission, the politics of language.

The Politics of Language

For the Protestants, it was the Word, the literal message of God, that, more than anything else, bore the divine light into the dark recesses of heathen hearts and minds. Its dynamic force, they believed, could reach the inner core of being, penetrating the blindness of man in his "natural" state. A sermon given by Reverend Read captures this well: "I told the Bechuanas [Tswana] that when God's word began to work in their hearts that their tears would wash away all the red paint from their bodies." In this vivid image of conversion, outward signs of heathenism, themselves only skin deep, are dissolved by the internalized power of the word. Note also that such Christian rhetoric tended to braid together the themes of words and water, so that each chain of metaphors came to imply the other. Words conveyed reason to the mind as tears bore tangible witness to affected emotions. Water was distilled by the force of God's moving message, be it rain from the heavens or the weeping of the human heart. Evidence of this association is everywhere to hand in the poetics of the civilizing mission: the verbal "truth" was to

irrigate the desert of the native's mind as mois-
ture was to fructify his blighted habitat. In
1849, a LMS observer wrote: "It is a sight
worth travelling some distance to see – the
printing and binding operation at Kuruman.
The Fountains of Civilization so far up in the
interior of South Africa! And scores of men,
women and children having renounced
heathenism, intelligently reading the Word of
Life." The savage mind was indeed being
watered by the word of life, whose truth had
to be independently recognized and acknowledged by each self-willed citizen of God's
Kingdom.
[. . .]
   It is noteworthy . . . that, while the evangelists doubted the competence of Tswana speakers, they did not question the capacity of their
language to convey the meanings that civilization might demand of it. The heathen might
lack the reflective mentality with which to
analyze abstract terms. And he might be so
stupid as to confuse homonyms. But the
churchmen never doubted that Setswana
would yield to their meticulous efforts to
translate literally the English message they
bore. Thus Moffat (1842:302) was sure that,
while "a mass of rubbish . . . paralyze[d] the
mental powers of the natives," such detritus
was easily removed – whereupon their vacant
minds would be receptive to the biblical text
and all that it conveyed. In this spirit of optimism, he began a massive translation project.
As we might expect, Moffat's work had consequences far beyond his own intentions. Not
only did he hold up a Setswana mirror to the
English text. He created a counterpart of the
scriptures, as *he* read them, in the tongue of
the natives – as he had come to understand it.
In short, he transposed the Bible into a cultural
register true to neither, a hybrid creation born
of the colonial encounter itself.
   Hence, to take just one example, Moffat's
use of *badimo* ("ancestors") to denote
"demons" (Mathaio [Matthew] 7:22; 8:28,
32) did violence to both biblical and conventional Tswana usage. Nonetheless, it reflected
the mission ideology of the period, and was to
become standard church usage (Brown
1926:103), with long-term effects on indigenous consciousness. The Tswana did not

simply accept the revision of their key constructs, for the logic of a whole cultural scheme
intervened. Yet this logic itself was gradually
changing under the growing impact of another
order, and an obviously powerful one at that.
At the very least, they developed an awareness
of the relativity of meaning, and of the politics
of managing cultural distinctions. Thus all
Tswana, whether or not they entered the
church, were soon to learn that "ancestors"
were phenomena of different valence in
setswana and *sekgoa*. Within the European
dominated field of colonial culture, they were
signs of the "primitive."
   The subversion of native signs, then, was
part of the struggle that took place within the
speech field of the mission.
[. . .]
   Patently, there were major ontological differences between the linguistic worlds of
setswana and *sekgoa*. We cannot analyze these
in any detail here, save to emphasize the performative quality of the former; the axiom that
to talk and to name in this culture was to
create experience, to *construct* a reality. For,
while utterances bore the imprint of their
speakers, they also established tangible links
with their referents, a property that was taken
by Victorian scholars as evidence of "primitive
mentality." It was this property that Tambiah
(1968) was later to dub the "magical power of
words"; their power, as Horton (1967: 157)
put it of African thought, to "bring into being
the events or states they stand for." Such power
goes well beyond the scope of Western ideas
of the capacities of speech, further even than
the missionaries' belief in the potency of the
word. It implies verbal connections among
forces unwilled and inanimate (Turner 1967:
299f): words are enmeshed in dense fans of
association that might unwittingly be activated
by their mere mention. Thus Tswana have long
explained their reluctance to use the term
shupa ("seven") by observing that it also
means "to point out" (i.e. with the right index
finger, the digit that stands for the number
"seven"), a gesture which connotes "to curse"
(Willoughby 1932: 143).
   This notion of the continuity of word and
action, cause and effect, did not merely differ
from European conceptions. It violated the

empiricist epistemology inherent in the *sekgoa* of the nineteenth century, for which positive knowledge lay in the definitive separation of the construct from the concrete, the word from the thing or the act. It also makes clear why the evangelists saw the Tswana as unreasoning, magical thinkers – and why it was so crucial to them to reduce Setswana to (grammatical, conceptual) order. For the Christians, remaking African consciousness entailed freeing the native from this web of animist superstition, this epistemology of unreason. It was with reference to this epistemology, too, that the Tswana were to speak back to them, to give voice to their side of the conversation.

In so doing, they were to resist many of the distinctions introduced by the Christians – especially the attempt to sever man from matter, the abstract from the concrete, the word from the world.

[. . .]

There is also a clear message here for the anthropologist of colonialism. . . . the argument between colonizer and subject often escapes the register of reasoned verbal debate. History in the making, like ethnography, is not always reducible to a narrative or a text. Indeed, when the colonized respond in the genre of rational debate – at least as defined in European terms – the hegemony of the colonizing culture may be well on the way to instilling itself in its new subjects; that is why truly counter-hegemonic reactions so frequently seek out alternative modes of expression. Consequently, if we are to recover from the documentary record the riposte of the ruled, we have to move with them as they try, often by unexpected means, to shift the unequal encounter with Europe onto an entirely different plane; to acknowledge, that is, that this encounter may involve a struggle over the terms of representation, and is as likely to invoke the poetics of the concrete as it is to rely on a discourse of words. In this struggle, too, the politics of meaning go well beyond the appropriation of the signs of one culture to those of another. Their very essence lies in the shaping of new forms of signification to bear the transfigured images on which history insists.

In South Africa, for all the early resistance to the Christian message and the colonial impulse, the process of domination was to take its course, laying down a new hegemony of social forms – even though the surface planes of the world reconstructed in the colonial encounter were to become the site of a long and bitter political struggle.

This, in turn, leads to our more general conclusion. The colonization of South Africa – and many other parts of the world – began with an ideological onslaught on the part of Christian missionaries, self-styled bearers of European civilization. These men set out to "convert" heathens by persuading them of the content of their theological message and, even more profoundly, by reconstructing their everyday worlds. Modern Protestant conversion, of course, is itself an ideological construct framed in the bourgeois imagery of rational belief and the reflective self; of a moral economy of individual choice that echoes, on the spiritual plane, the material economics of the free market. It made little immediate sense along the South African frontier in the early nineteenth century. On the other hand, the *conversation* between the evangelists and the Tswana did have an enormous impact on the latter; in this respect, David Livingstone (above . . .) was to prove correct.

The everyday discourse of the mission, its theater of the mundane, was effective primarily because it enmeshed the Tswana in the *forms of sekgoa*: the commodity form, linguistic forms, kinship forms, rhetorical forms. The politics of water, production, and language – and we could equally have chosen to discuss architecture, clothing, or a number of other things – all tell the same story. The content of the civilizing mission, its substantive message, was debated and often rejected; increasingly, it would turn out later, along emerging class lines. But its forms were conveyed by the very structure of the conversation from the moment that the Tswana engaged in it. Thus, even to argue over the relative success of two kinds of rain medicine was unwittingly to concede a good deal to the ideology of rational empiricism; to adopt the plough was to redefine the division of labor along the lines of the bourgeois family and its engendered signs; to read a vernacular bible was to have Setswana poetics re-presented in the mode of a thin *sekgoa* narrative; and so on. In each sphere, the discourse presupposed a certain kind of subject, and a particular mode of knowing and being.

The colonization of consciousness, in other words, entailed two levels. At its most tangible, it involved an overt effort to *convert* the Tswana, an argument of images and messages intended to convince them of the ideological content of Christianity. Here the evangelists tried to disseminate, in the heart of darkness, the Good News, a persuasive narrative of biblical morality and "truth." At a deeper level, only partially distinguished from the first, they set their sights on the total *reformation* of the heathen world; i.e. on the inculcation of the hegemonic forms, the taken-for-granted signs and practices, of the colonizing culture. The Nonconformists, as we know, were sometimes quite explicit about working on both planes at once, since the really cultivated being had to be converted *and* reformed. And they seem to have been aware that the kind of personhood and consciousness they wished to instill did not arise from dogma and revelation alone; that it inhered as much in the practical and material forms of "civilization," those "outer things" at once devalued and yet tacitly encouraged by the church. Notwithstanding the intentions of these European colonizers, however, the two levels of transformation – conversion and reformation – do not necessarily occur together. Quite the opposite, the discontinuities between them often lie at the very heart of the history of consciousness and its struggles. That is why people who reject an ideological message may yet be reformed by its medium; why new hegemonies may arise amidst the most bitter of ideological battles.

This brings us, finally, to the reactions of people like the Tswana to the modern historical processes in which they find themselves caught up; that is, to their consciousness of colonization. There is much debate at present, among historians and anthropologists, about the nature of those reactions – in particular, about the nature of protest and the so-called "weapons of the weak" (Scott 1985). Does an act require explicit consciousness and articula-

tion to be properly called resistance? Should the term apply only to the intentions behind social and political acts, or may it refer equally to their consequences? When a people can be shown to express some measure of awareness of their predicament as victims of domination – and, better yet, can state the terms of their response – the matter is clear. Where they do not, defining and characterizing their reactions becomes an altogether more murky business. We would suggest, however, that there is an analytical lesson to be taken from the evident fact that most historical situations *are* extremely murky in just this respect.

Aside from organized protest – easily recognizable as "political action" by Western lights – much of what may be seen as the riposte of the colonized, as one or another form of (tacit, indirect) resistance, turns out to be a practical means of *producing* historical consciousness. Indeed, if anything is clear from our study, it is that much of the Tswana response to the mission encounter was an effort to fashion an awareness of, and gain conceptual mastery over, a changing world. This, it seems, is a very general phenomenon. Early on in the colonizing process, wherever it occurs, the assault on local societies and cultures is the subject of neither "consciousness" nor "unconsciousness" on the part of the victim, but something in between: recognition of varying degrees of inchoateness and clarity. Out of that recognition, and the creative tensions to which it may lead, there typically arise forms of experimental practice that seek, at once, techniques of empowerment and sources of new knowledge.

Such reactions, often seen as enough of a threat to the authority of the dominant to elicit coercive measures, seek to plumb the depths of the colonizing process. They search for the logic – and, sometimes, the *deus ex machina* – that lies behind its visible face. For the recently colonized generally believe that there *is* something invisible, something profound, happening to them; that their future may well depend on gaining control over it. Thus, for instance, many "Christianized" peoples the world over are, or once were, convinced that whites have a second, secret bible or set of rites (cricket? semaphore? tea parties?) on which their power depends. The whimsical "unreason" of such movements as cargo cults stems from precisely this conviction. These movements, as is now well known, are an early effort to grasp the bases of the colonial production of value, and to redirect it to the well-being of the dominated.

With time and historical experience, the colonized show greater discrimination, greater subtlety in interpreting the European embrace and its implications. Attempts to come to terms with it grow more diverse, and are ever more closely tied to processes of class formation. Among those drawn most fully into the forms of "modernity" – the petty bourgeoisies

and "new elites" scattered along the fringes of the world system – there occurs a gradual appropriation of the images, ideologies, and aesthetics of the post-enlightenment West. And these include orthodox styles of political discourse and protest. But, for the rest, modernity and its modes of resistance are by no means inevitable, or even likely consequences of the colonization of consciousness – or of the consciousness of colonization that follows. Indeed, the dynamics of cultural imperialism are such that, while the power structure of colonialism is everywhere clearly laid down, the colonizing process itself is rarely a simple dialectic of domination and resistance.

BIBLIOGRAPHY

Bourdieu, Pierre. 1977. *Outline of a Theory of Practice.* [Translated by R. Nice.] Cambridge: Cambridge University Press.

Broadbent, Samuel. 1865. *A Narrative of the First Introduction of Christianity Amongst the Barolong Tribe of Bechuanas, South Africa.* London: Wesleyan Mission House.

Brown, J. Tom. 1926. *Among the Bantu Nomads: A Record of Forty Years Spent Among the Bechuana.* London: Seeley Service.

Bundy, Cohn. 1979. *The Rise and Fall of the South African Peasantry.* Berkeley: University of California Press.

Campbell, John. 1822. *Travels in South Africa . . . Being a Narrative of a Second Journey,* 2 volumes. London: Westley. [Reprint, 1967. New York and London: Johnson Reprint Corporation.]

Carlyle, Thomas. 1842. *On Heroes, Hero-Worship, and the Heroic in History: Six Lectures.* New York: D. Appleton.

Comaroff, Jean. 1985. *Body of Power, Spirit of Resistance: The Culture and History of a South African People.* Chicago: University of Chicago Press.

Comaroff, Jean, and Comaroff, John L. 1986. Christianity and Colonialism in South Africa. *American Ethnologist* 13: 1–19.

——. 1990. Goodly Beasts, Beastly Goods: Cattle and Commodities in a South African

Context. *American Ethnologist* 17: 195–216; *infra,* Chapter 5.

Comaroff, John L. 1973. Competition for Office and Political Processes among the Barolong boo Ratshidi. Ph.D. dissertation, University of London.

——. 1977. *The Structure of Agricultural Transformation in Barolong.* Gaborone: Government Printer.

——. 1982. Dialectical Systems, History, and Anthropology: Units of Study and Questions of Theory. *Journal of Southern African Studies* 8: 143–172.

——. 1987. Of Totemism and Ethnicity: Consciousness, Practice, and the Signs of Inequality. *Ethnos* 52: 301–23; *infra,* Chapter 2.

Cope, Richard L. (ed.). 1977. *The Journals of the Rev. T.L. Hodgson, Missionary to the Seleka-Rolong and the Griquas, 1821–1831.* Johannesburg: Witwatersrand University Press.

Crisp, William. 1896. *The Bechuana of South Africa.* London: SPCK.

Dachs, Anthony J. 1972. Missionary Imperialism: The Case of Bechuanaland. *Journal of African History* 13: 647–658.

Evans-Pritchard, Edward E. 1937. *Witchcraft, Oracles, and Magic Among the Azande.* Oxford: Clarendon Press.

Ferguson, D. Frances. 1976. Rural/Urban Relations and Peasant Radicalism: A Preliminary Statement. *Comparative Studies in Society and History* 18: 106–118.

Harlow, Barbara. 1986. Introduction. In *The Colonial Harem*, (ed.) Malek Alloula. Minneapolis: University of Minnesota Press.

Hobsbawm, Eric J. 1962. *The Age of Revolution, 1789–1848*. New York: New American Library.

Horton, Robin. 1967. African Traditional Thought and Western Science. *Africa* 31: 50–71, 155–87.

Jeal, Tim. 1973. *Livingstone*. New York: Putnam.

Kinsman, Margaret. 1983. "Beasts of Burden": The Subordination of Southern Tswana Women, ca. 1800–1840. *Journal of Southern African Studies* 10: 39–54.

Legassick, Martin C. 1969. The Sotho-Tswana Peoples Before 1800. In *African Societies in Southern Africa*, (ed.) L. Thompson. London: Heinemann.

Lenin, Vladimir Ilyich. 1971. Selections from *The Development of Capitalism in Russia*. In *Essential Works of Lenin*, (ed.) H. Christman. New York: Bantam.

Livingstone, David 1857. *Missionary Travels and Researches in South Africa*. London: Murray.

Mackenzie, John. 1871. *Ten Years North of the Orange River: A Story of Everyday Life and Work Among the South African Tribes*. Edinburgh: Edmonston & Douglas.

Moffat, Robert. 1842. *Missionary Labours and Scenes in Southern Africa*. London: Snow. [Reprint, 1969. New York: Johnson Reprint Corporation.]

Muldoon, James. 1975. The Indian as Irishman. *Essex Institute Historical Collections* 3: 267–89.

Northcott, William Cecil. 1961. *Robert Moffat: Pioneer in Africa, 1817–1870*, London: Lutterworth.

Ranger, Terence O. 1987. Taking Hold of the Land: Holy Places and Pilgrimages in Twentieth-Century Zimbabwe. *Past and Present* 117: 158–94.

Reyburn, H.A. 1933. The Missionary as Rain Maker. *The Critic* 1: 146–53.

Schapera, Isaac. 1971. *Rainmaking Rites of Tswana Tribes*. Leiden: Afrikastudiecentrum.

Schapera, Isaac (ed.). 1960. *Livingstone's Private Journals, 1851–1853*. London: Chatto & Windus.

Scott, James C. 1985. *Weapons of the Weak: Everyday Forms of Peasant Resistance*. New Haven: Yale University Press.

Shillington, Kevin. 1985. *The Colonisation of the Southern Tswana, 1870–1900*. Johannesburg: Ravan Press.

Solomon, Edward S. 1855. *Two Lectures on the Native Tribes of the Interior*. Cape Town: Saul Solomon.

Tambiah, Stanley J. 1968. The Magical Power of Words. *Man* (n.s.) 3: 175–208.

Trexler, Richard C. 1984. We Think, They Act: Clerical Readings of Missionary Theatre in Sixteenth Century Spain. In *Understanding Popular Culture*, (ed.) S. Kaplan. Berlin: Mouton.

Turner, Victor W. 1967. *The Forest of Symbols: Aspects of Ndembu Ritual*. Ithaca: Cornell University Press.

Volosinov, Valentin N. 1973. *Marxism and the Philosophy of Language*. [Translated by L. Matejka and I. Titunik.] New York: Seminar Press.

Willoughby, William Charles. 1932. *Nature-Worship and Taboo: Further Studies in "The Soul of the Bantu."* Hartford: Hartford Seminary Press.

——. n.d. *Letter from Africa*. [Pamphlet.] London: London Missionary Society.

37

Convicted by the Holy Spirit: The Rhetoric of Fundamental Baptist Conversion

Susan F. Harding

Susan Harding teaches anthropology at the University of California at Santa Cruz. Trained at the University of Michigan, Harding's first fieldwork was carried out in Spain. The present article was followed by a series of compelling essays, including one that deconstructs the very category "fundamentalist" (1991) and culminating in a major monograph *The Book of Jerry Falwell: Fundamentalist Language and Politics* (2000).

The thesis that modernity entails secularization appears contradicted by the increasing popularity and ferment of religion towards the end of the 20th century. Harding turns away from causal explanations or recourse to mechanical models like deprivation theory and towards the poetic construction and practical experience of conversion itself. She implies that conversion entails learning to listen and eventually to speak in a new fashion. Her essay thus addresses several important issues: the role of language and rhetoric in religion; the nature and means of conversion; religious experience; and the attraction of evangelical Christianity in the US and elsewhere. Readers should consider how the use of "belief" in this essay might be specifically Christian (as described in the essays by Pouillon and Ruel; cf. Crapanzano 2000).

Where Rappaport's essay examined the illocutionary aspects of religious language, Harding addresses its perlocutionary or persuasive force. Her essay might be read alongside Geertz's account of the rhetorical power of ideology (1973f), Bloch's discussion of the way religious language brooks no argument (1989c), and especially Hirschkind's essay in this volume on Islamic sermons. Harding also emphasizes dialogue; unfortunately I have had to omit the passages where she draws inspiration from Bakhtin (1981). The Evangelicals' use of rhetoric provides a striking contrast to

From Susan F. Harding, "Convicted by the Holy Spirit: The Rhetoric of Fundamental Baptist Conversion," *American Ethnologist* 14: 167–81 (1987). Abridged.

the Puritans' emphasis on plain style, transparent language, and even silence, as described in Webb Keane's interesting discussion of sincerity (2002, 2006). If one version of Protestantism is connected to modernity and the rise of scientific objectivity, it is a kind of irony of history (perhaps a kind of contemporary counter-Reformation), that evangelical Christianity's inversion of this ideology of language also appears opposed to science, or at least to evolutionism (but compare Keller 2005, 2006).

Conversion, even to Christianity, does not always happen in the fashion described here. For further illustration see Hefner (1993), Meyer (1999), Robbins

(2004) and chapter 36 by the Comaroffs. Lambek (2000b, 2007b) argues that anthropological models of conversion are sometimes based too heavily on Christianity and that conversion itself may be a feature of the Abrahamic religions rather than a universal feature of religion.

Like Myerhoff, Harding raises profound questions about the religious subjectivity of the ethnographer. She draws on her own experience as a vehicle for anthropological knowledge, especially what she so strikingly describes as passing through the thin "membrane between disbelief and belief."

The Moral Majority and, more generally, the current political activism among fundamentalists are evidence of a deeper movement within American fundamentalism to abandon its historic separatism from "the world." Reverend Jerry Falwell and pastors allied with him are leading a faction of fundamentalists who are shifting the inner and outer boundaries that separate them from worldly culture.[1] They are breaking old taboos that constrained interactions with nonfundamentalists, claiming new cultural, political, and social territory, and refashioning themselves in church services, Sunday school, the family, in bed, on the air, in the political arena, in the news, in their literature, in Bible-study groups, classrooms, and daily interactions. In the process, they are transforming the fundamentalist mind and community, and altering what it means to be a fundamentalist.

It would seem a recipe for assimilation were it not for the fact that fundamentalists are primed – in a way, armed – for the confrontation. Their culture is premised on a commitment to assimilate "the world" on fundamentalist terms, and, indeed, fundamentalists routinely reproduce their cultural modes of interpretation through encountering, reconfiguring, and incorporating specimens of alien, worldly, culture. Most specifically, at the center

of the language of fundamentalism is a bundle of strategies – symbolic, narrative, poetic, and rhetorical – for confronting individuals, singly and in groups, stripping them of their cultural assumptions, and investing them with a fundamentalist mode of organizing and interpreting experience.

This bundle of strategies is the rhetoric of conversion, and my purpose here is to scrutinize a sample of that rhetoric to decipher its sources of efficacy. In particular, how does the language and performance of fundamental Baptist witnessing convict and convert the unsaved listener? Witnessing, and conversion talk more generally (testifying, evangelizing, gospel preaching, spreading the Word), is rhetorical in the sense that it is an *argument* about the transformation of self that lost souls must undergo, and a *method* of bringing about that change in those who listen to it. Fundamental Baptist witnessing is not just a monologue that constitutes its speaker as a culturally specific person; it is also a dialogue that reconstitutes its listeners. My focus is on this latter aspect, on witnessing as the practice, the rite, of conversion.

To be converted, to be regenerated, to receive grace, to experience religion, to gain assurance, are so many phrases which denote the process, gradual or sudden, by which a self hitherto divided, and consciously wrong, inferior and unhappy, becomes unified and consciously right, superior and happy, in consequence of its firmer hold upon religious realities. This at least is what conversion signifies in general terms, whether or not we believe that direct divine operation is needed to bring such a moral change about. (James 1906:160)

William James speculated that those who experienced dramatic conversions might have been born with a "melancholy disposition," a chronically "divided" mind, or else they had drunk "too deep of the cup of bitterness" (1906:158). Contemporary social scientists have also investigated "who" converts for some indication of "why" they convert. The notion is, apparently, that those who convert are somehow susceptible, vulnerable, in need, so the question is: "Why, what's wrong, what's unsettling them?" Or, "What's setting them up, how have they been predisposed to convert?" Social scientists scrutinize the external psychological and social conditions of converts looking for clues, patterns, and causes. They have found evidence in converts' lives of "psychological and social stress" (due to marriage problems, loss of a job, imprisonment, adolescence, dating, serious illness or accidents, encounters with death, "role" transitions, moving to a new city, going to college, and so on); "previous conditioning" (religious upbringing, education, class, gender); and "patterns of interpersonal influence" (by converted kin, friends, mentors). These correlations are not satisfying explanations, however, because, among other things, none of the circumstances have been found with enough regularity among converts, and the same circumstances have been found among nonconverts with too much regularity.[2]

There is also considerable literature, both popular and academic, on how various ritual practices and psychological techniques trigger experiences that result in a conversion from one worldview, or mind-set, to another.[3] Distinct conversion methods (social seclusion, dramatic enactments, bodily markings, physical stress or pain, fasting, interrogation, chanting, silence, immobility, and so on) certainly

pave the way for radical shifts in belief and commitment. What this approach, at least when plied by those who see conversion as a kind of brainwashing, tends to overlook is how persuasive in a quite unsensational way the recruiting rhetoric, the language of conversion as such, may be, how much it itself contributes to "dividing" the mind and bringing about conversion. The presumption that I think accounts for this oversight, and which in more muted form also guides many social scientific studies, is that "nobody in their right minds would believe this stuff." Since "belief" is irrational, some sort of suspension of normal thinking must have taken place and caused the convert to lose his or her grip on reality.

Social scientists through a variety of means generally do not let themselves get close enough to "belief" to understand it, or, for that matter, even to see what it is. Men and women convert to fundamental Christianity because they become convinced that supernatural reality is a fact, that Christ is the literal Son of God, that he did rise from the dead and is alive today, that the Holy Spirit is speaking to them, that Jesus will enter their hearts if they acknowledge their sins, that they will have eternal life, that God is really real. To continue to think otherwise would be irrational; it is disbelief that is false and unthinking. The appropriate question then is how does this supernatural order become real, known, experienced, absolutely irrefutable?

Among orthodox Protestants, and especially among fundamentalists, it is the Word, the gospel of Jesus Christ, written, spoken, heard, and read, that converts the unbeliever. The stresses, transitions, influences, conditioning, and techniques which social scientists scrutinize do not in themselves "explain," do not "cause," conversion to Christ. All they do is increase the likelihood that a person might listen to the gospel; they may "open" or "prepare a person's heart." It is the Word of God, the gospel, and, believers would add, the Holy Spirit, God himself, that converts, that "changes the heart."[4] We cannot understand fundamental Baptist conversion by looking only at what causes a person to listen to the gospel; the causes are innumerable. We must listen too, and we must explore the consequences of listening.

Witnessing and preaching are the two main situations in which believers "speak the gospel" most intensely. Preaching – the sermon – is a formal oration addressed to a body of believers and nonbelievers by an ordained or anointed speaker in church services and revivals. Sermons occur in the context of clear ritual format, of a collective, sanctifying scenario in which the mode of interpretation is enacted. Witnessing is more informal and often occurs in the course of what appears to be no more than a conversation between the witness, who is saved, and an unsaved listener. But it is no mere conversation. The witness and the unsaved "do not share a common understanding – either of the immediate situation or of reality more generally." Witnesses are "aware of this difference in understanding and self-consciously set out to change the views of those they address," and to create a "compelling religious reality completely at variance with their [listener's] experience" (Borker n.d.:1, 3).

Witnessing aims to separate novice listeners from their prior, given reality, to constitute a new, previously unperceived or indistinct, reality, and to impress that reality upon them; make it felt, heard, seen, known, undeniably real. The reality, or "truth," constituted in witnessing is, in part, a linguistic one: the supernatural is experienced as God's voice and his spirit is communicated and experienced through words. Much collective ritual among orthodox Protestants is likewise centered on words, on the Word. Especially among fundamentalists, church services and revivals are stripped of overt, imagistic, and sacramental material; relatively little happens visually, and spiritual realities are not communicated through sensuous, nonlinguistic means. In a way, witnessing is pure fundamentalist ritual, shorn of almost all distractions. It is the plainest, most concentrated method for revealing and transmitting the Word of God, one in which language is intensified, focused, and virtually shot at the unwashed listener.

Fundamentalists are by no means unique in their use of oratory to convert others. Their techniques and a good deal of the content of

their conversion rhetoric are broadly shared among conservative charismatics and evangelicals. Indeed, the principle of conversion, of one person insinuating his or her mode of interpretation into the mind of another, informs all dialogue. What distinguishes fundamental Baptists from the rest of us is the degree to which they have formalized rhetorical techniques for converting alien others, the precise and distinctly unconscious manner in which those techniques appropriate the listener's dialogic imagination, and the particular transformations of self evoked in the listener.

Preacher and Gospel

Dusk had fallen by the time I left Covenant Baptist Church, but I was bothered by the light as I looked around the parking lot for my car. It seemed as if everything had moved slightly. The church was on the outskirts of one of the poorer parts of Lynchburg, and I would have to zigzag across a half-dozen big streets that bisect the city to get back to my motel. I knew I was in some kind of daze after my long talk with Reverend Cantrell; I usually am after an interview, and this one had been especially intense. Halfway across town, I pulled my car up to a stop sign, stopped, started into the intersection, and was very nearly smashed by a car that seemed to come upon me from nowhere very fast. I slammed on the brakes, sat stunned for a split second, and asked myself "What is God trying to tell me?"

It was my voice, but not my language. I had been invaded by the fundamental Baptist tongue I was investigating. As Reverend Cantrell would have put it, the Holy Spirit was "dealing with me," "speaking to my heart," "bringing me under conviction." He was showing me that "life is a passing thing," that death could take me in an instant, no matter how much control I fancied I had over my life, and that I should put my life in the Lord's hands before it was too late.

If we conceive of conversion as a process of acquiring a specific religious language, I was initiated into fundamental Baptist conversion as I sat in my car that evening in Lynchburg, awash in apprehension and relief. The process starts when an unregenerate listener begins to appropriate in his or her inner speech the regenerate speaker's language and its attendant view of the world. The speaker's language, now in the listener's voice, converts the listener's mind into a contested terrain, a divided self. At the moment of salvation, which may come quickly and easily, or much later after great inward turmoil, the listener becomes a speaker. The Christian tongue locks into some kind of central, controlling, dominant place; it has gone beyond the point of invading the listener's mind to occupy the listener's identity. The Holy Spirit, the very Word of God, has come, as fundamental Baptists say, to "indwell the heart of the believer," who may now publicly display in speech and action a personal, which is to say, conversational, relationship with God.

It was quite specifically Reverend Cantrell's language and mode of interpretation that unfurled itself in my mind as I contemplated my near accident. I had intended to interview him that afternoon, but within the first few minutes of our talk Reverend Cantrell assumed control of the dialogue and reframed my appointment to interview him into his opportunity to witness to me for an hour and a half.

A witnessing session minimally includes the gospel story (an exegesis of the death, burial, and resurrection of Jesus Christ), and a confrontation between the witness and his or her listener in which the witness invites or exhorts the listener to receive Christ as his or her personal Savior. Witnesses may also tell how they and others came to know the Lord as Savior; they may testify (give accounts of encounters between themselves and God, and other narrative evidence of God's intervention in the natural world) and deliver other doctrinal exegeses (regarding, for example, heaven and hell, the origin and nature of sin, or the ways of Satan).

Witnessing, like evangelistic preaching, "is intended to create a spiritual crisis by calling to the fore one's desperate and lost condition, which one may have been totally unaware of" (Hill 1985:26). This crisis is the onset of the conversion process, what fundamentalists call "coming under conviction," and is based on a direct experience of the divine. You *know* when the Holy Spirit convicts you of, or "makes you see," your sins. Conviction effects a deep sensation of one's own impurity and separation from God, or one's "sinfulness," one's "sin nature," and a sense that "something has to be done about it." We shall see that the inner speech of "convicted sinners" is transformed as they are alienated from their previous voices ("the old self," "natural man"); cast into a limbo ("lost," "in need," "searching"), that is to say, somehow in a liminal state, a state of confusion and speechlessness; and begin to hear a new voice ("an inaudible voice," "the Holy Spirit").

It is a kind of inner rite of passage that is completed when sinners are "saved," or "born-again," "regenerated," "washed in the blood of Christ." Salvation is experienced as a release from the bondage of sin and a personal reconciliation with God. "A new self, "spiritual man," emerges and the supernatural imagination is cut loose as the newborn Christian "accepts the meaning of the gospel" and begins to speak the language of Christ. For many, as it was for Benetta Jules-Rosette (1976:135), who studied among, and joined, the Apostles of John Maranke in Africa, conversion is "a powerful clash resulting from the shift from one realm of thought and action to another, a moment of specific *shock*. Under this shock, the very terms of physical existence seem to alter."

The power of Reverend Cantrell's rhetoric to induce liminality was seconded in my case by several circumstances – I was on a number of margins. It was late afternoon, and his church was on the edge of town. We were in a corner of the church, in his study, alone, on the edge of propriety. I was beginning my fieldwork. And Reverend Cantrell seemed to me a peripheral character in my study. Having grown up with Jerry Falwell and trained to be a preacher at his Liberty Bible Institute, he was *in* but not quite *of* Falwell's empire. His congregation appeared to consist largely of white working class or unemployed men and women and their children. Covenant Baptist Church was, in his words, "a solid work," with about 350 members, and it sustained a number of outreaches, but Reverend Cantrell and his congregation were not engaged in any of the political or cultural activism that has earned Jerry Falwell a national reputation in the last few years.

Reverend Cantrell is a tall, trim, and muscular man, his silvery gray hair piled up from his forehead in waves an inch or two high. He sat at his desk, I to its side, and he looked me in the eye the entire time we talked. Later I realized that most people who sat in the chair I was sitting in came to Reverend Cantrell for spiritual help.

Born-again believers say that unbelievers cannot understand their faith. Jeanne Favret-Saada (1980:22) came to a similar conclusion while studying witchcraft in the Bocage region of France. "For anyone who wants to understand the meaning of [witchcraft] discourse, there is no other solution but to practice it oneself, to become one's informant." This is so, she tells us, because there are only two "positions" from which a person speaks or hears witchcraft talk, bewitched and unwitcher; if you are neither, you will never even hear others speaking the discourse (Favret-Saada 1980:16). The situation is, of course, quite different among fundamentalists. Gospel talk is public and targets outsiders, nonbelievers; but, as in witchcraft, there is no such thing as a neutral, "participant-observer" position, no place for an ethnographer who seeks "information." Either you are lost, or you are saved.

When I went to Lynchburg, I was naive enough to think I could be detached, that I could participate in the culture I was observing without partaking of it. I could come and stay for months, talk mainly to church people, attempt to "learn the language," ask questions based on respect and knowledge; and still remain outside, separate, obscure about what I believed and disbelieved. But there was no such ground. I might think there was, but they did not, no matter what I said. It was inconceivable to them that anyone with an appetite for the gospel as great as mine was simply "gathering information," was just there "to write a book." No, I was "searching." "God works in mysterious ways." In my case, he seemed to be letting me find my way to him through this book I said I was writing about

them. Several people told me as much; others just seemed amused when I told them what I was doing and gave me a look that indicated they knew better. My story about what I was doing there, instead of protecting me from going native (a kind of ethnographer's verbal fetish), located me in their world: I was a lost soul on the brink of salvation. And Reverend Cantrell spoke to me accordingly.

I asked him first how he became a pastor, and he took 15 minutes to answer me. I had expected to get something akin to "information" or "facts," and he gave me a long story of personal transformation, one that began with how he had been saved and had served the Lord before he was called to preach. He never acknowledged my academic project and seemed to speak to me as if I were what they call a "nominal Christian," someone who might think she was a Christian but who had never been saved. He could assume I was not born-again simply because I did not indicate I was, as believers do when they meet, if only by a turn of phrase. Certainly, he was aware of himself as witnessing to me, and he had been trained, formally and informally, in "soul-winning techniques," but his manner and his method seemed to draw more on unconscious intuition than deliberate design.

There are at least five distinct rhetorical movements in Reverend Cantrell's witnessing talk: equating his present listener with the listeners in his stories; defining the listener as lost; defining the speaker as saved; transforming his narrative listeners into speakers; exhorting his present listener to speak. I will trace these movements by exhibiting and expanding on sequential pieces of Cantrell's speech, hoping to show you, as much as tell you, what conversion and belief are among fundamental Baptists.

In this, his conversion narrative, Reverend Cantrell defined being "lost" and being "saved" and how he moved from one position to the other. Lostness, he indicated, is a position from which you listen, and salvation is one from which you speak. Note, too, how Cantrell began to pull me in and placed me into his narrative in the position of listener. Unfortunately, in words flattened out on a page, we may hear only suggestions of his southern, fundamental Baptist accent, his peculiar cadence, intonation, pausing, pitch, and stress.

I was saved when I was 15 years old. I was a member of a Methodist church all of my life as a child. At the age of 15 I still had not heard the gospel story of Jesus Christ and how that he died for our sins. I was instructed as a child coming up in the Methodist movement just to live a good life, to be morally good, and to maintain all of those particular statuses, and I would be okay. Now I was invited by a friend to visit a Baptist church. . . . And this was an independent fundamental Baptist church. And of course they had one of those hell-fire-and-damnation preachers in there, and he got down on my case that night. And I began to look at things and I realized there was something missing in my life. Because, though we've never seen God, we're still aware of the fact that he is present, we know he's there. And even though I wasn't saved I knew there was something bombarding my life that was beyond my power to see or to really understand at the time. And I couldn't understand why I wasn't receiving what I needed in the Methodist church. So after attending about three of their services [. . .] then the spirit of God began to convict me about my place in life and how that I was lost and had not yet turned my whole life over to Christ, so I was saved that week, I went forward and gave my heart to Christ. [. . .] And then after this, my life began to grow and materialize into something that was real, something that I could really identify with. That emptiness that was there before was now being replaced by something that had meaning and purpose in it. And I began to sense the need of telling others about what had happened to me. And basically I think perhaps the change could be detected in my life, as the Bible declares, that when a person is saved, the old man, the old person, or the character that they were passes away, and then they become a new creation in Christ Jesus. That is to say, they might be a character that may be drinking and cutting up and carrying on and a variety of other things that are ill toward God. All of these things began to dissolve away. I found that I had no desires for these things, but then I began to abhor them. I actu-

ally began to hate them. And this was in accordance with the Scriptures as I found out later. And then as my life began to mature in Christ I found that I too could win others to Christ the same way I was won: by simply telling them that there's a heaven to gain and a hell to shun.

Enlisting the Listener

Numerous poetic and performance features teem on the surface of Reverend Cantrell's speech. There are verse markers ("and" and "now"), special codes, figurative language, symbolic and metaphoric parallelism, and appeals to tradition. These features, according to Richard Bauman (1977:15–24), mark the text as an oral performance and indicate a special relationship between performer and listener, one in which the performer assumes responsibility for display of competence, indirectly instructs the listener about how to interpret messages, and invites, elicits, participation, binding the listener to the performer in a relationship of dependence and keeping the listener caught up in the display.

Reverend Cantrell also communicated my relationship to his speech more directly through his use of pronouns (emphasis added): "I still had not heard the gospel story of Jesus Christ and how that he died for *our* sins." "Because, though *we've* never seen God, *we're* still aware of the fact that he is present, *we* know he's there." Cantrell continued to place me in his narrative during the rest of the time we talked by using the "royal we," and he frequently shifted his pronouns and at times used "you" ambiguously, as a personal and impersonal pronoun. His listener by these means became the subject of a whole range of presuppositions posited in such a way that they were difficult to resist.

Reverend Cantrell at one point in this initial speech and at several points later on quite overtly identified me with his narrative listeners. The central, reiterated narrative structure in his witnessing was a dialogic encounter between person and God, or between a lost listener and a saved speaker. The context of his witnessing of course was also dialogic: Reverend Cantrell and I were engaged in a dialogue, one in which he, who was saved, was speaking, and I, who was not saved, was listening. Early in his conversion narrative, Reverend Cantrell began to collapse these parallel levels of dialogic structure and thereby place me in his stories, in his speech: "Now I was invited by a friend to visit a Baptist church . . . and of course this was an independent fundamental Baptist church. And of course they had one of those hell-fire-and-damnation preachers in there, and he got down on my case that night." In describing *his* context the night he was converted, Cantrell called attention to *our*, his and my, context. He too was a hell-fire-and-damnation preacher, and I, in effect, was informed that he would be getting down on my case and that I might be converted that afternoon. This is no mere innuendo: Cantrell was thus aligning me and my encounter with him with the listening persons and their encounters with God in his stories. Whenever a spiritualized speaker addressed a wayward listener, the speaker would also be addressing me. I too would be transfigured, if only by degrees, by the very act of listening to Milton Cantrell.

Reverend Cantrell reminded me of my position in his narrative several times. I heard it faintly when he said, "I found that I too could win others to Christ the same way I was won: by simply telling them that there's a heaven to gain and a hell to shun." He was more explicit later, when he told me how he was called to preach.

> Now when I had my calling at age 29, I was operating a service station. And I was in the station one afternoon, working on a car. And God did not speak to me with an audible voice, but he spoke to my heart. And there was a conversation going on much like the one that's here. I'm doing the talking and you're listening. And God was doing the talking and I was listening. I was down under the car, changing the oil, and . . . God was just dealing with me about doing this. And I said, "I can't do that." And much like Moses when the Word called him to do something, he said, "I can't even talk." And God said, "Well, I'll send your brother Aaron to help you." So every excuse I would come up with, he would

head me off by instructing me that he would do something to meet my shortcomings. So I finally surrendered in the sense of the word that afternoon.

If I had any doubt about where I belonged in Reverend Cantrell's talk, this passage dispelled it. God spoke to him under his car that afternoon just as Cantrell was speaking to me in his office. I am the listener; he is the speaker; that which transpires in his narrative dialogues shall somehow transpire between us. Reverend Cantrell also introduced, and located me within, another parallel level of dialogic structure, between God and Biblical figures, in this passage. I must listen to Cantrell as long ago Moses, and much later Cantrell, listened to God. Clues such as these inform, or, rather, persuade, the listener that the witness's words, though they appear to be about the witness and about other characters on the narrative surface, are on a deep level about the listener: You, too, are a character in these stories; these stories are about you.

Lostness

Keeping in mind that much of what Reverend Cantrell said about himself as he came under conviction also applied to his listener, let us examine how he fashioned the lost soul, the sinner, the person in need of salvation.

Young Cantrell realized there was something missing in his life. He needed something he wasn't getting; he was lost. He was carrying on in a variety of ways that were ill toward God. His life was empty and lacked meaning and purpose; it was not maturing or growing into something real. Yet he knew there was something bombarding his life beyond his power to see or really understand; though he had never seen God, he was still aware of his presence, he knew he was there. Cantrell was ostensibly describing himself here, but because he had put me in his narrative in his place, he was also describing me; indeed, he was refashioning me.

I am emptied, stripped of all vestiges of personality and uniqueness. My life is rendered meaningless, my past erased. I am primarily distinguished by what I lack, and, given my lacking, by what I need. I stand for absence, for void, yet I am aware of something more, something missing, unseen, hidden, and I come to need that, to desire it, perhaps to crave it, and am thus launched on a quest for affirmation and revelation which may be achieved only through conversion. All this is accomplished in me by implication and presupposition, not by direct argument. My consent is not sought; I am implicated, already enlisted as a collaborator, in my own metamorphosis.

Instilling the Spirit

As well as constituting the listener as a lost soul, Reverend Cantrell in his conversion story began to fashion the speaker, the saved soul, as he narratively moved himself, you could say, converted himself, from lost listener to a saved speaker of the Word of God.

The hell-fire-and-damnation speaker getting down on Cantrell's case shortly became the spirit of God convicting him about his place in life – that he was lost and had not yet given his whole life over to Christ. He was saved, and he went forward and gave his heart to Christ, and the spirit of God came to live in his heart. His life began to grow and materialize into something that was real, something that had meaning and purpose in it. His old character and its desires passed away. Then he began to sense the need of telling others about what had happened to him and found that he too could win others to Christ in the same way that he was won. The spirit of God first "worked on" Cantrell, then entered and transformed him, and finally spoke through him to bring others under conviction.

God's spirit, the Holy Spirit converts sinners, but he (the fundamental Baptist Holy Spirit is a male person) speaks through those who preach the gospel. Preachers speak the Word of God; God speaks through them. Reverend Cantrell started a church in a storefront after God called him, and on the first day of services, he wondered why anyone would come there to hear him preach. Later he realized "it was the Word of God they must come to hear, and not me. It's the Word of God that must

cause the change." The change is caused not by God as an external agent, but by the Word, the spirit, of God, which is internalized when a person accepts Christ. "By nature, Adam and Eve, you know, they caused the problem, but they invested into every one of us that would be borned a similar nature. Now this nature can be wiped clean, it can be changed by once again instilling the spirit of God within us."
[. . .]

Fundamental Baptists, especially preachers, are acutely aware of the power of witnessing and of the gospel, of the rhetoric of conversion in general. They attribute its transforming power to the workings of the Holy Spirit, that is, to supernatural agencies, but their glosses on those agencies invariably refer to words, to speaking and hearing and reading. In effect, in a coded way, they recognize language as a medium, even a subject, of religious experience, and they coach the unconverted in the linguistic dimension of conversion.

The Holy Spirit uses Reverend Cantrell's speech, as it were, to remodel his listeners' inner speech. The Holy Spirit impresses on Cantrell what to say and deals with the hearts of his listeners, bearing him up, after he's gone. "The heart" is contrasted with "the head," and seems to mark the difference between unconscious and conscious knowledge and belief. The Holy Spirit, the Word, "works on" the unconscious mind to bring the conscious mind "under conviction." As listeners appropriate the gospel, the Holy Spirit penetrates the conscious mind and becomes "another voice," "a real person," who begins to recast their inner speech. After salvation, the voice of the Holy Spirit "guides" converts, gives them "discernment," and seems to alter the very chemistry of desire.

Second Birth

Reverend Cantrell spelled out the moment of salvation elliptically in his own conversion narrative, and he elaborated it in his disquisition on Holy Spirit. He also posited the moment of salvation in highly charged symbolic terms, in Biblical exegeses on birth and death, flesh, spirit, blood, and sacrifice.

Cantrell drew on well-established parallels in evangelical culture between the narratives of Christ's death (the gospel story) and of personal conversion, between the cosmic order spelled out in the Bible from the Garden of Eden to Calvary and the epic of each individual in the face of inevitable death. The gospel story defines the movement, the passage that all believers must endure, from suffering and dying (coming under conviction), to burial (silence, absence, void), and resurrection (converting, being reborn). As God restored man to himself by sacrificing his son on the cross, so the unsaved may restore themselves to God by "dying" to their old selves and being born anew in Christ. All they need do is acknowledge their "sin nature," accept that Christ died for their sins, and ask him into their hearts. It is these words, once genuinely spoken, that resurrect a dead soul, that instill in the newborn believer the Holy Spirit, the very voice of God.

Reverend Cantrell began to elaborate the connection between the gospel story and salvation, as witnesses often do, by talking about Nicodemus, who came to visit Jesus one night and said to him, as Cantrell put it, "Now you've got something that we've missed."

Jesus said, "Nicodemus, I'm going to limit my words in talking to you. Listen carefully." He said, "Ye *must* be borned again. Ye *must* be borned again." And Nicodemus said, "How in the world can a man be born when he's old? Is it possible that I could enter again a second time into my mother's womb and be born?" Jesus said "No, you didn't listen. I'm going to repeat one more time. . . . You must be borned again. . . . That which is born of flesh is flesh. That which is born of spirit is spirit. Marvel not that I say, you've already had one birth, but you need more. You need the birth that's going to change you from the one you received from Adam, which is a sinful nature. You've already experienced that first birth and you're full of yourself. But now you need the second birth, the one that will give you this indwelling of the spirit of God." Now when I was born, I was born physically of my mother. Jesus said, "You must be borned of the water first, of the spirit second." When a child is about to be born, it's first enclosed in the

mother's womb. Is that true? [Yes.] That water must be broke before the child can be born. Now this is a representation of the first birth. He said, "You must be born of the water first, Nicodemus, you've already been born, you're here." But then he said, "Now you must be born by the spirit." Your mother birthed you the first time. And your mother cannot give you this spiritual birth. So this must come from above. Now God gives this second birth. [How does the second birth change a person?] Okay, Susan, you have the characteristics and the traits of your mother and your father. True? [Yes.] All right. Now the second birth will give you the characteristics or the traits of the Father that birthed you. Now the first time when you were born, you couldn't help your mother. If your life had depended on it, you had to depend upon her strength to bring you into this world. True? [Yes.] Now when we're saved, or borned again, this is absolutely and totally dependent upon God. Now where did the birth take place at? It had to be a birth of such a caliber that it had to take care of the whole world. And this was a place called Calvary. Jesus, when he was dying, was shedding his blood, and the Old Testament says that without the shedding of blood there is no remission, there can be no forgiveness for sin. So blood – the innocent – and God typified this in the animal sacrifices of the Old Testament. When Adam and Eve sinned, Genesis 3:21 said he slew innocent animals. And he took the skin off these animals, and he covered their nakedness, which is the type of giving them a covering which is representative of righteousness, and the blood was used to atone for their sins. . . . Atonement means to cover and the blood of the animals of the Old Testament typified one day that Christ would come, shed his blood, but then this blood, this blood being shed now, brings about redemption and not atonement which is a temporal covering. For thousands of years, the Jews under the Mosaic economy offered up sacrifice of animals – you've probably read that – and they did this because this was representative of one day a coming Savior. You remember the incident in Exodus, about Abraham went to offer his son Isaac on Mt. Moriah. And the Bible says that Isaac the son said, "Father" – he didn't know what was going on – he said, "Here's the altar, here's the wood, here's the knife, here's the fire, but where's the sacrifice? Where's the lamb?" And Abraham said, "My son, God himself shall provide a sacrifice. A lamb." Now we go down several thousand years into the future, and John the Baptist, when he saw Jesus Christ for the first time, he told the disciples that were with him, he said, "Behold, take a look, here is the lamb of God that will take away the sins of the world." And the lamb of God was Jesus Christ. Of course, Isaac was not slain. There was a ram caught in the thicket which was a type of substitution. So Jesus Christ died in my place as a substitution for me. . . . Now God so loved me that God himself died for me because Jesus Christ is a Very God.

"The conquest of death is the ultimate goal of Christianity" (Graham 1983:203), and victory is achieved when sinners are "borned again" and the spirit of God is instilled in them. Rebirth is totally dependent upon the grace of God, as a baby is totally dependent on its mother for its birth. Symbolically, Reverend Cantrell first moved his listener from the first birth, the mother, flesh, and water breaking, to the second birth, the Father, spirit, and blood shed. The second (spirit/male) birth takes over, subverts and cancels out the consequences of, the first (flesh/female), releasing the sinner from the wages of sin, death. The womb of the second birth was the cross at Calvary; Christ mediated between the first (flesh/female) and second (spirit/male) birth and created the possibility of reconciliation with God.
[. . .]

On a symbolic level, Cantrell argued that it was Christ's blood that made this transition possible. But narratively – looking at the form his argument took on the surface of his whole juxtaposition of tales, from Nicodemus to Abraham and Isaac to Christ on the cross – Cantrell emphasized the importance of spoken language, of dialogue, in making the passage from one world to the next. He repeatedly relied on dialogue (between Jesus and Nicodemus, himself and me, Isaac and Abraham, John the Baptist and the disciples) to set up the dilemma of human choice. In this respect, he was speaking as much within Old as New Testament tradition. Robert Alter points out

that Old Testament writers used "narration-through-dialogue" to highlight

> human will confronted with alternatives which it may choose on its own or submit to divine intervention. Articulated language provides the indispensable model for defining [the] rhythm of political or historical alternatives, question and response, creaturely uncertainty over against the Creator's intermittently revealed design, because in the biblical view of reality words underlie reality. (Alter 1981: 69)

And it is through spoken dialogue, through witnessing, that each sinner is confronted with and makes the choice to accept or reject Christ.

Do You Know Christ?

[. . .]

Reverend Cantrell then turned to me and asked, "Now Susan, let me ask you a question. Do you know Christ as your personal Savior?" He asked me several more questions. "Do you believe in God?" "What if you died today?" Then he told me a story of a man he buried a few weeks before who had choked to death on some food. "Had no idea he would be sent out into eternity." "Life is just an uncertain thing." He inquired again into my faith. "Have you ever sensed the presence of God?" Then he told me about a man who, at 40, lamented that he'd been "looking for a wife for so long." Cantrell told him "I think God has sent you the right woman, probably 20 times, and you turned her down." He said the man had overlooked the orchid and all the other beautiful flowers while looking for a rose. "Can you identify with that?"

Then Reverend Cantrell brought his exhortation to a rather stunning conclusion.

> Now if in this life, the Bible says, only we have hope, then we of all men are most miserable. But you see my life, my hope, is in the life to come, and I realize this life is a passing thing. Jeremiah says it's like a vapor. It appears but for a little while, and then vanishes. We know how uncertain life is. We're just not sure how long things are going to go. I went to work one

morning. I had some work to do on a Saturday morning. And one of my sons was 14 years old. And the other one was 15 years old. And we got up that morning. And I went in, and I rassled with my son and rassled him out of bed, the one that was 14. And we got up that morning and ate breakfast. We opened the Word of God. We read and we prayed together as a family, my wife, my two sons, and I. And I went on to do that work that morning. It was a Saturday. And I had something I wanted to move. And I was operating a crane. And I accidently killed him that morning. And I looked at God, and I said, "Lord, you told me in your Word that all things work together for good to those that love you, especially those that are called according to your purpose." And I said, "I've served you faithfully. And I've loved you. And I've given you my heart, my life, my soul, given you everything about me. And now I can't understand this, why you've taken my son." And God didn't speak with a voice that I heard with my ear but he spoke to my heart. He said, "Milton, you know maybe you don't understand what I've done at this particular time, but, can you accept it?" And I said, "Yes sir, I can accept it." And, Susan, when I made that statement, and I settled that in my own heart, and I said "Lord, I accept it though I don't understand it," I don't know where to say it came from other than that God gave it to me, but he gave me a peace in my soul. And I have not questioned it since. Now I went and shared it with my wife. I said, "Shirley," I said, "God said all things would work together for the good to us because we loved him." And she said basically the same thing I did, "Well, I don't understand. This isn't good." But I said, "Yeah, but God said it is good." And I shared with her, and when I shared this with her, she came of the same opinion. And we watched them close the casket on that little fellow and my, he was just super. I mean, he was almost my heartthrob, you know, that was my baby. And yet he died in my arms. And yet I looked at God and I said, "Lord, I'm going to love you if you take my other son. I'm going to love you if you take my wife. I'm going to love you if you take my health, if you strip me of everything I've got, I'm going to love you." Now I'm saying that because, Susan, he is real. This is not mythology. I'm 46 years old, and I'm no fool. God is

alive. And his son lives in my heart. And I'd love for him to live in your heart. Of all that I could give or think of ever giving over to you, I hope that what we've talked about here today will help you make that decision, to let him come into your heart, and then he will be your tutor. And he'll instruct you in things that perhaps I've stumbled over today. Sometimes the vocabulary may not be appropriate to really describe the depth and the detail the things that need to be said. But this is where the Holy Spirit can make intercession for us. The Bible says with groanings and utterings that we just cannot utter. I may miss something, but he'll bring it out. I may present something, and you don't understand it. But he will reveal it to you. This is what the whole thing is about.

Reverend Cantrell began his ultimate narrative on a note of wistful resignation. Life is a passing thing, a vapor; it's here for a little while and then vanishes. Without pause, he shifted into a homey story about getting his sons up one Saturday morning, opening and reading the Word of God, and going out to work in the yard. Then he delivered a split-second narrative shock: "And I accidently killed him that morning." The sentence disrupts, it stabs, but before it is absorbed Cantrell shifted to the real point – his conversation with God. God asked Milton to accept what he, God, had not asked Abraham to accept and what he, God himself, was willing to give: his son's death. And Milton obeyed: "Yes, sir. I can accept it." This sentence, in a moment as extreme and extraordinary as the tragic death of his son by his own hand, is what God asked of him to restore order in himself and in the world. By speaking his obedience, his submission to God's will, they were reconciled, and Cantrell received in return peace in his soul, an eager willingness to give still more. The same gifts, he concluded, awaited me, if only I too would accept Christ. "This is what the whole thing is about."

Conclusion

If conversion is a process of acquiring a specific religious language, and witnessing is an orthodox Protestant rite of conversion, then, if you are willing to be witnessed to, if you are seriously willing to listen to the gospel, you have begun to convert. Listening to the gospel initiates the unwashed into the Word, the language of God.

The single most important unconscious clue I gave Reverend Cantrell that I was "susceptible" to conversion was that I was willing to listen to the gospel. Crises, transitions, and upbringing as such do not lead you to convert; they may make you more likely to listen, and anything that makes you more likely to listen, including the work of ethnography, is actually what makes you susceptible.

"Susceptible" implies passivity, but I was not passively listening to Reverend Cantrell. I was struggling mightily against the grain of my ignorance and incredulity to make sense of what he was saying. His language was so intense and strange, yet deceptively plain and familiar, full of complex nuances and pushes and pulls, that I had no time, no spare inner speech, to "interpret" him, to rework what he said into my own words, as he talked. I just gripped my chair, as it were, and took it in straight. I was willfully uncritical as well, in the sense that I wanted to understand, as best I could, his words from his point of view, to assume his position, to make his speech mine. It was not exactly what Reverend Cantrell said that brought me under conviction; it is that I took it up, merely by listening to him actively and uncritically.

The membrane between disbelief and belief is much thinner than we think. All I had to do was to listen to my witness and to struggle to understand him. Just doing so did not make me a fundamental Baptist born-again believer, but it drew me across that membrane in tiny ways so that I began to acquire the knowledge and vision and sensibilities, to share the experience, of a believer.

Believers and disbelievers assert there is no middle ground: You are either one or the other. You cannot both believe and disbelieve. But that is precisely what it means to be under conviction. You do not believe in the sense of public declarations, but you gradually come to respond to, and interpret, and act in the world as if you were a believer. It is a state of unconscious belief, experienced with more or less turmoil and anxiety, depending on how strong your disbelieving voices are. It also depends for the ethnographer on how adamant your colleagues are about the "dangers" of doing "this kind of fieldwork." I was given to think my credibility depended on my resisting any experience of born-again belief. The irony is that this space between belief and disbelief, or rather the paradoxical space of overlap, is also the space of ethnography. We must enter it to do our work.

Reverend Cantrell's testimony was a hodgepodge of stories sewn together with "the scarlet thread of redemption," not a series of "logical" or "empirical" arguments. He persuaded me narratively. Disbelief is a conscious refusal to accept a particular version of reality, and believing involves the conscious acceptance of "doctrines," of particular claims about reality and one's relationship to it. But disbelief is also, in the case of evangelical Christianity at least, an unconscious refusal to participate in a particular narrative mode of knowing reality. Likewise, belief also involves an unconscious willingness to join a narrative tradition, a way of knowing and being through storytelling, through giving and taking stories. You cannot give born-again stories, you cannot fashion them, without acknowledging belief, but you can take them, you can absorb them, and that's how you "believe" when you are under conviction. You get caught up in the stories, no matter what your conscious beliefs and disbeliefs are.

I was caught up in Reverend Cantrell's stories – I had "caught" his language – enough to "hear God" when I almost collided with another car that afternoon. Indeed, the near accident did not seem like an accident at all, for there is no such thing as a coincidence in born-again culture; God's hand is everywhere. Gospel talk casts in your subliminal mind, your "heart," a Biblical rhythm of alternatives, a vibrating template, ready to fire God's speech given a context in which you seem to have a choice to submit to God's will or ply your own. Preachers construct such contexts verbally, and life presents them virtually every day – those apertures in the ordinary, when the seams split and you encounter the unknown, the unexpected, the uncontrollable, the irrational, the uncanny, the miraculous. These are moments ripe for supernatural harvesting, moments when fear or awe mutes your natural voices and God may speak, offering you the opportunity to speak back.

Coming under conviction (listening to gospel stories or voices) is easy compared to getting saved (speaking; telling stories). When you come under conviction, you cross through a membrane into belief; when you get saved, you cross another membrane out of disbelief. This passage is more problematic for some lost souls, for what outsiders would say were reasons of education, class, and intellect, insiders would say was hardness of the heart, ego or pride, the work of the devil. However you explain it, getting saved among fundamental Baptists involves giving up disbelief (not just suspending it, but disavowing it), accepting born-again belief (your conversational relationship to God) as the centering principle of your identity, your personal and public life, your view of human nature and history, and joining a particular narrative tradition to which you willingly submit your past, present, and future as a *speaker*.

One more reason Reverend Cantrell was a compelling witness was the extent to which, and eloquence with which, he gave his life to the language of Christ. This willingness to "submit one's life to God," to narrate one's experience and fashion stories out of it in dialogue with God's will and Biblical truths, makes God, and his Word, most real and known and irrefutable, to oneself and to one's listener. Reverend Cantrell understood this, at least intuitively, well enough to tell me about killing his son just before his final pitch for my

soul. The story disarmed me not only because he had killed his own son and because he so crisply gave up his grief and his guilt to God, but because he was telling me, a stranger, about it. He "sacrificed his own son" to his narrative tradition with a calm and assurance, a peace of heart, that I still find difficult to accept. Often that afternoon I found myself at a loss for words as Cantrell narratively generated what for me were novel grounds for knowing and for speaking, but the story of his son's death struck me dumb. He might as well have gone up in a puff of smoke.

A cynic, second-guessing Reverend Cantrell's motives, would say he was manipulative, that he used this painful story to "get to" his listener. But from within born-again culture, this telling was the ultimate evidence of belief, Cantrell's moment of maximum authenticity. If he told me the story for effect, it was to effect the reality of God in me. What God said to him and he said to God in that tragic moment meant that God is absolutely real. This was his own conclusion: "Now I'm saying that, Susan, because he is real. This is not mythology. I'm 46 years old, and I'm no fool. God is alive. And his Son lives in my heart."

Among fundamentalist Baptists, the Holy Spirit brings you under conviction by speaking to your heart. Once you are saved, the Holy Spirit assumes your voice, speaks through you, and begins to reword your life. Listening to the gospel enables you to experience belief, as it were, vicariously. But generative belief, belief that indisputably transfigures you and your reality, belief that becomes you, comes only through speech. Among fundamental Baptists, speaking is believing.

NOTES

1 All *evangelical Christians* have received Jesus Christ as their personal Savior and are "born-again." In 1982, Gallup (p. 31) estimated over 50 million adult Americans made this claim. Among them, those who call themselves *fundamentalists* are the most doctrinally strict, dispensationalist (their eschatology "raptures" them

before the tribulation), separatist, and politically conservative. There are no firm figures on how many evangelical Christians consider themselves fundamentalists; among Baptists perhaps 5 million would identify with the fundamentalist label (Wardin 1980: 27, 33; Ammerman 1986: 487). A recent poll (Kantzer 1980) estimated 29 million adult Americans identified themselves as *charismatics* or *pentecostals*. Many of them would agree with fundamentalists on most doctrinal and political questions, but they part company over the doctrine of charismas (the belief that the Holy Spirit manifests himself in the body of the believer through tongues, prophecy, and healing), which fundamentalists reject. A third major faction of born-again Christians, who are called *neo-evangelicals*, is more moderate or liberal politically, doctrinally, and socially than are fundamentalists. Finally, those who would simply describe themselves as *evangelicals* may be as doctrinally strict as fundamentalists but are more moderate in other respects. If Jerry Falwell is the emblematic fundamentalist preacher today, Jimmy Swaggert and Pat Robertson stand for the charismatics, at least the conservative ones; Jim Wallis for the neo-evangelicals; and Billy Graham for the evangelicals.

Jerry Falwell and most of the pastors allied with him are fundamental Baptists; they (but not all fundamental Baptists) are both evangelical (yet still in some respects Calvinist) and independent (nondenominational). They belong to the Baptist Bible Fellowship, a national network of preachers whose church members number about 1.5 million (Mead and Hill 1985: 44). The Moral Majority, insofar as it is a grass roots organization, rides piggyback on the BBF (Liebman 1983) but draws support from the wider range of fundamentalists and politically conservative charismatics and evangelicals.

2 I am here summarizing Heirich (1977).
3 Whitehead (1987) has an excellent, critical review of this literature in her study of conversion among Scientologists.
4 Evangelical social scientists and theologians have studied the secular literature on conversion and generated their own. Elmer Towns, Dean of Jerry Falwell's Liberty Baptist Seminary and a nationally known researcher in the "science of church growth," told me that the highest rate of conversion occurred among prisoners, the second highest among the bankrupt; he also emphasized the importance of personal networks and of reaching people while they are "in transition" of some kind. The difference between Towns and secular social scientists is that Towns would never suggest any of these factors really causes conversion; the Holy Spirit convicts sinners and Christ saves them.

REFERENCES CITED

Alter, Robert. 1981. *The Art of Biblical Narrative.* New York: Basic Books.
Ammerman, Nancy. 1986. The New South and the New Baptists. *The Christian Century*, 14 May: 486–8.
Bakhtin, Mikhail. 1981. Discourse in the Novel. In *The Dialogic Imagination: Four Essays* by M. M. Bakhtin. Michael Holquist ed, pp. 259–422. Austin: University of Texas Press.
Bauman, Richard. 1977. Verbal Art as Performance. In *Verbal Art as Performance.* Richard Bauman, ed., pp. 3–58. Prospect Heights IL: Waveland Press.
Borker, Ruth. n.d. The Presentation of the Gospel In Everyday Life. Unpublished manuscript.
Favret-Saada, Jeanne. 1980. *Deadly Words: Witchcraft in the Bocage.* Cambridge: Cambridge University Press.
Gallup, George. 1982. *The Gallup Report: Religion in America.* Princeton: Princeton Religion Research Center.
Graham, Billy. 1983. *Approaching Hoofbeats: The Four Horsemen of the Apocalypse.* Waco, TX: Word Books.
Heirich, Max. 1977. A Change of Heart: A Test of Some Widely Held Theories about Religious Conversion. *American Journal of Sociology* 83(3): 653–80.
Hill, Samuel S. 1985. *The South and the North in American Religion.* Athens: University of Georgia Press.
James, William. 1906. *Varieties of Religious Experience.* New York: Collier Books.
Jules-Rosette, Benetta. 1976. The Conversion Experience: The Apostles of John Maranke. *Journal of Religion in Africa* 7(2): 132–64.

Kantzer, Kenneth. 1980. The Charismatics Among Us. *Christianity Today* 24 (22 February): 25–9.

Liebman, Robert C. 1983. Mobilizing the Moral Majority. In *The New Christian Right: Mobilization and Legitimation*. Robert C. Liebman and Robert Wuthnow, eds, pp. 49–73, Hawthorne, NY: Aldine.

Mead, Frank S., and Samuel S. Hill. 1985. *Handbook of Denominations in the United States*. Nashville: Abington Press.

Myerhoff, Barbara, and Lynn Littman. 1986. *In Her Own Time*. Film.

Wardin, Albert W., Jr. 1980. *Baptist Atlas*. Nashville: Boardman Press.

Whitehead, Harriet. 1987. *Renunciation and Reformulation: A Study of Conversion in An American Sect*. Ithaca: Cornell University Press.

38

On Being Shege in Kinshasa: Children, the Occult and the Street

Filip De Boeck

Filip De Boeck is program director of the Africa Research Center and chair of the Department of Social and Cultural Anthropology at the Catholic University of Leuven in Belgium. He has carried out an extraordinary amount of fieldwork in Congo/Zaire, at the centre of the old Luunda kingdom (De Boeck 1994), among diamond miners on the Angolan frontier (1999), and as this entry indicates, in the city of Kinshasa. With Alcinda Honwana, he has edited *Makers and Breakers: Children and Youth in Postcolonial Africa* (Oxford: James Currey, 2005).

This entry is a much abridged selection from a chapter in the award-winning book which De Boeck composed together with photographer Marie-Françoise Plissart. If earlier work on African witchcraft attempted to demonstrate its logic (Evans-Pritchard 1937) or show its social function (Marwick 1970, Turner 1957), events have overtaken the possibility of making such arguments today. Where in the past witchcraft existed in some balance with the world of the everyday, De Boeck describes a scene in which it appears to have taken over, in which, he says, the distinctness between the real and the imaginary is no longer discernable. Not only are accusations of witchcraft widespread and their effects apparent everywhere, but in a collapse of the order of kinship and the logic of the gift, tragically it is young children and anyone who offers a spontaneous gift of food who are accused of witchcraft. In a drama of confession, in which the Christian churches play no little role, children are thereby turned out to live in the street and the cemeteries. De Boeck's work is notable for its integration of rich ethnographic description with continental theory. De Boeck is able to evoke the vibrant life of the city and especially the rich play of language, music and art. His portrait is

From Filip De Boeck, "On Being Shege in Kinshasa," in Filip De Boeck and Marie-Françoise Plissart, *Kinshasa: Tales of the Invisible City* (Gent-Amsterdam: Ludion, 2004), pp. 155–64, 168–71, 173–7. Abridged and photographs omitted.

acute and unsparing and yet not in the least condescending or judgmental.

The chapter should be compared with that of Kelly (chapter 20), where in a much more stable social setting than that described by De Boeck, young people and even infants can also be described as witches. Other work on the contemporary widespread salience of witchcraft and sorcery in Africa includes Ashforth (2000, 2005), Comaroff and Comaroff (1993, 1999), Fisiy and Geschiere (1990, 1991), Geschiere (1997), Meyer (1999), Moore and Sanders (2001), Weiss (1998), and West (2005).

Isn't the city of Kinshasa bewitched?
Bodo, painter and preacher, Kinshasa, May 2001

"Siting" the Imaginary

In Congo, as elsewhere in Africa, there has always lurked, in a rather unproblematic way, another reality underneath the surface of visible reality. Movement and stagnation, social or physical reproduction and death, the diurnal and the nocturnal, have always existed in and through each other. "More precisely," states Mbembe, "the invisible was not only the other side of the visible, its mask or its substitute. The invisible was in the visible, and vice versa, not as a matter of artifice, but as *one and the same* and as external reality simultaneously – as the image of the thing and the imagined thing, at the same time. In other words, the reverse of the world (the invisible) was supposed to be part and parcel of its obverse (the visible), and vice versa. And in this capacity to provide a basis for, and to state the inseparability of, the being and non-being of persons and things – that is, the radicality of their life and the violence of their death and their annihilation – lay the inexhaustible strength of the image."[1] Witchcraft is one of the mechanisms in which this inseparability and simultaneous multiplicity most clearly comes to the fore. "The efficacy of defensive fetishes and aggressive sorcery," notes Devisch, "relies on the principle of the subversive capacity of 'catastrophic retroflexion' (cf. *pli-catastrophe* [. . .]), otherwise described as the homeopathic reversal mobilized in the 'floating signifier' [. . .] proper to residue, detritus, or excretion. Maleficious sorcery is replete with imaginary exploits in a no-man's land of vertigo and fascination in which the forces of floating signifiers, reproduction and death, daring and delirium intersect [. . .]. Imprints, crushed leaves, ash, traces of blood, and feces all serve as the residual locus of delirious contamination or reversal between attack and immobility, between the eroticism of engendering life and the inebriation in the face of death and corruption."[2]

Setting out from a recent but widespread phenomenon, that of "witch-children" in the capital of Kinshasa, this chapter intends to discuss the changing nature – should we call it crisis? – of the imaginary, or better: of the qualities of junction and disjunction, of the equilibrium in the mechanisms of reversal between the imaginary and the symbolic, and, ultimately, of the epistemological breach that results from these alterations in Congo today. This breach is basically appearing in what is a growing indiscernibleness between the first and the second world, or between reality and its double.

In his insightful chapter on the "thing" and its double in Cameroonian cartoons, quoted from above, Achille Mbembe remarks upon exactly "the new experience of speech and things" which I have hinted at. He nevertheless assumes that despite the scale of the transformations and the discontinuities, an imaginary world has remained. More generally, the "imaginary," a notion with a complex genealogical tree which includes Lacan, Sartre, Barthes and Castoriadis, has become the social scientist's catchword to capture the ways in which a general subconsciousness, with its autochthonous networks of meaning, is related to the ruptures and constant alterations of a hybridized post-colonial urban (and increasingly also rural) landscape. Appadurai, for example, developed the concept of the imaginary, or more broadly, imagination, as an organized field of social practices in new global cultural processes. In the same vein Bayart, while discussing the cultural dimensions of political action, describes the imaginary as the dimension out of which emerges a continuous dialogue between tradition and innovation.[3] The imaginary is primarily, he adds, interaction: interaction between the past, the present and the projection of a future, but also interaction between social actors, or between societies, the relations of which are selectively shaped by their respective "imagining consciousnesses." The mediating qualities of the imaginary turn it into an institutionalizing social force through which a society confronts and absorbs changes and mutations, and thereby defines and authors itself anew. With the dissolution of more traditional anthropological locations for research, the imaginary, as an alternative field site, therefore presents novel opportunities for more detailed analytic scrutiny of the multiple transformations that African society is currently undergoing.

[. . .]

What happens if the very nature of the imaginary as a flexible but organized field of social practices has become disorganized and has lost, at least to some extent, its localizing force and its capacity for creating continuity, producing sociality? The imaginary is the dimension of the invisible, but what if the invisible becomes, or takes over, or pushes aside the visible? What if the imaginary is no longer the socially productive phantasmagoric but constantly crosses the boundaries and invades the real in an unmediated, non-symbolic way? What if the imaginary is no longer the *irréel* but, as Gilles Deleuze states, the *indiscernibility*, the incapacity to recognize the distinctness, between *réel* and *irréel*?[4] What, in other words, if the dual and therefore nonalienated relationship with the double which until recently certainly existed in local Congolese experience, most notably in relation to the witch, is becoming problematic and leads to alienation instead? If death, as the double of the living, belongs to the realm of the imaginary, and if the imaginary thus operates the disjunction between life and death, what then does it mean for a societal constellation when that distinction ceases to exist? Can we say that Congolese reality seems to be losing its capacity to dedouble itself easily into multiple others to (re)institutionalize itself through this act?

In dealing with the widespread phenomenon of witch-children in Kinshasa, I propose to tackle these questions by looking at the relationships between the growing presence of death, the notion of the double in the articulation between the imaginary and the symbolic level, and the forms in which continuity, exchange and gift are spelled out in Congolese towns and cities, and particularly in Kinshasa, today.[5] In these urban worlds the frenetic construction of local modernities goes hand in hand with the expectations and promises of a millennial capitalism that finds its sometimes fanatical expression in the thousands of independent churches operating and proliferating in the urban context of Congo and elsewhere in sub-Saharan Africa today. It is in these locations that the social and cultural imaginary in Bayart's sense, as interaction in time and space (between heritage and innovation, between past, present and future, between rural and urban realities, or between Congolese and the global world) is most strongly active. More and more, children and youngsters emerge as, and form the crucial sites of, identity, in which all of these interactions take place. Children and youngsters appear as the ultimate focal points of the contemporary Central African imaginary. Children, as *opus operatum* and as *modus operandi* of crisis and renewal, form the identity locations in which the ruptures and faultlines of an African world in transition become manifest. As part of a wider transformation of the sociocultural, political and economic architecture of the urban landscape, children and youngsters thus are at the heart, or better still, the *frontier* of the reconfiguration of geographies of inclusion and exclusion, or private and public. They have the capacity to fracture public space, and reinvent or even bypass it, [. . .]

Children of the street have always existed in Kinshasa, but in recent years their numbers have swollen dramatically. One phenomenon that has greatly contributed to the growing presence of the street child, variously referred to as *phaseur*, *moine* (monk), *moineau* (swallow) or *shege/chegue*, is the changing pattern of witchcraft accusations which may currently be observed in the capital. The incessant reinvention of the Central African urban lived environment is not at all marked by a Weberian *Entzauberung*. It is, on the contrary, enacted and produced most strongly, not only in the "enchanting" spaces of Christian fundamentalism, but also in the frenzied and often obsessional production of discourses and practices surrounding witchcraft. Both are, of course, intimately related. Overall, observers have remarked upon the general increase of witchcraft accusations in Congo over the last decades.[6] Although this remains to be proven, it is clear that the dynamics of witchcraft themselves have undergone some dramatic changes over the past years. One of the most disconcerting phenomena that highlights this evolution is the central role that children are nowadays given in these newly developing witchcraft discourses and practices. In contemporary Kinshasa, thousands of children are implicated in witchcraft accusations, and often end up in the street as a result of this.[7] Then, they find themselves at the heart of one of the most disturbing transformations in the Congolese societal *multi-crise* (*Le Potentiel* newspaper, 4/9/2000), namely the changing relationship between the world of the visible and the invisible, between life and death, or between reality and its double. Commonly described as a "dead society" (*société morte*), Kinshasa's street children, who to a large extent live during the night and often sleep, eat and live in places such as cemeteries, have come to embody the growing alienation of the order of the visible. They constitute a fulcrum between the processes of doubling and dedoubling and fully exemplify the permeability and interchangeableness of the borderlines between day and night, living and nonliving, public and private, or order and disorder.

Children and young adolescents have never before occupied a more central position in the public spaces of urban life, whether in the popular [. . .] music culture, the media, the churches, the army, the street, or the bed. Occupying such a prominent social position, children are not only victims but have also become active impact factors in and on Congolese society.

The newly generated, central but ambivalent, societal status of children seems to have crystallized most clearly around the figure of the witch, which is the materialization of a cultural imaginary of crisis [at] the intersection [. . .] [of] money, power, kinship and sexuality.

[. . .] "New situations demand new magic." Due to the increasing impact of global media and of globalization *tout court*, the newly arising tensions between traditions and modernities are being defined, and sometimes resolved most powerfully, in the field of witchcraft. First of all, the heritage of colonialist modernity as embodied by the postcolonial state is sometimes perceived to be a source of witchcraft and evil in and of itself. As one preacher of a healing church explained:

> The late Mobutu brought witchcraft from the village to the city. Now everything is destroyed in Congo, not because of the incapability of the Congolese, but because of witchcraft. Our country has been sold somewhere. It has been sold to a mysterious world (*monde mystérieux*), to museums abroad, even in France, Egypt, Morocco and the United States. These are strategic places of evil. And this witchcraft even brought us the war. All of this because our leaders and our government touched fetishes in India and elsewhere. (Interview, September 1999, Church of Beth Shalom, community of Masina, Kinshasa)

In this interpretation, the postindependence state, the heir and propagator of a certain colonialist model of modernity, but also the forces of globalization (from France to India) are at the origin of witchcraft. On the other hand, [. . .] there is not only the witchcraft of modernity. Witchcraft practices in Africa have also been reformulated gradually to come to represent one of the major gateways to "modernity," in a rapidly developing space of "expectations" and desire in which an "economy of the occult" has become the means to win the "war of dreams."[8] This nocturnal economy of power and desire, which forms the hyphen between a fast growing local economy of violence (including the violence of the new moral economy imposed by the churches) and the violence of a penetrating global economy, is also increasingly being accessed and shaped by the young. Children have started to occupy a more central position in the public realm. Here they appear also as major societal players with access to these new global economic fields, and often in direct opposition to the generations that precede them.

[. . .] The austere living conditions of Congolese urbanity have caused a profound transformation of existing idioms of witchcraft. The ever increasing poverty [. . .] is being accentuated by the war in the east of the country and adds to the pressure that existing structures of kin-based solidarity are currently undergoing in the urban context. Undoubtedly, the linkage between children and witches is related to a profound de- and restructuring of the notions of motherhood, gerontocracy, authority and, more generally, the field of kinship itself. These transformations are themselves grounded in an even more profound crisis that punctuates urban life: that of the logic of reciprocity and gift as the most constitutive part of the basal structure that underpins the field of kinship at large.

Finally, the crisis of the gift, in its Maussian sense as total social fact, also embodies the crisis of the symbolic, the increasing impossibility to "site" the imaginary in an unproblematic way. The crisis of the (structuring of the) symbolic, the capacity to symbolize, reveals itself in the unraveling and tearing of two interdependent levels: the level of the symbolic, the first world, the reality of reciprocity, contract and representation, and the level of the imaginary, to which the second world also belongs, and which informs the social logic and the symbolic as internalized social structure.[9] Because these two levels no longer operate as two sides of the same coin (hence the *mystique*-ness of the Congolese world, the awareness of "displacement," the experience of the world as dislocatory presence which evolves from a more general rupture between signifier and signified, or from a change in the ways in which the floating signifiers operate), the imaginary is no longer simultaneous with, no longer underpins and legitimates reality. Typical for the Congolese postcolonial reality, that is increasingly acquiring and marked by an oneiric dimension, ever larger chunks of the fields of kinship, reciprocity, money, market, sexuality, power and violence are thus pulled out of the symbolic realm back into the imaginary.

Witch-Children in the Streets of Kinshasa

[. . .]

My name is Mamuya. I am fourteen years old. I became a witch because of a boyfriend of mine, Komazulu. One day he gave me a mango. During the following night he came to visit me in my parents' house and threatened that he would kill me if I didn't offer him human meat in return for the mango he had given me earlier. From that moment I became his nocturnal companion and entered his group of witches. I didn't tell my mother. In our group we are three. At night we fly with our "airplane," which we make from the bark of a mango tree, to the houses of our victims. When we fly out at night, I transform myself into a cockroach. Komazulu is the pilot of our airplane. He is the one who kills. He gives me some meat and some blood and then I eat and drink. Sometimes he gives me an arm, at other times a leg. Personally I prefer to eat buttocks. I keep a part of the meat to give to my grandmother who is a witch too. Komazulu is a colonel in the second world, and he has offered me the grade of captain if I sacrifice a person. That's why I killed my baby brother. I gave him diarrhoea and he died. With our group we have already killed eight persons. Our victims haven't done any harm to us. Sometimes, though, we judge them. If they don't defend themselves well, we kill them. Sometimes when a man is buried in the cemetery, we go there and say a prayer. That prayer makes the dead person wake up and then we eat him. Now I have come out of the world of shadows thanks to the prayer of the preacher who treats me in church. But the others who are still in the second world keep pulling at me. They want to kill me now for fear that I betray them. (Interview in the

Church of the Holy Spirit, Selembao, Kinshasa, September 1999)

In 1994, I accidentally came into possession of a videotape which triggered my interest in witch-children. The videotape featured three Congolese children between the ages of eight and twelve. They were being cross-examined by a number of Congolese adults and two Belgian men, members of a Pentecostal prayer movement in the Congolese diaspora setting of Brussels, Belgium. The three children had recently left Kinshasa to come to Belgium. The tape shows how the three children are accused by the adults of the death of a number of their relatives in Kinshasa, one of whom is the mother of one of the accused boys. During the (at moments rather violent) cross-examination, of which the tape offers a one hour-long summary, the three kids acknowledge that they indeed "ate" a number of people in Kinshasa. [. . .] They explain in detail how they exited their bodies and flew to Congo in a "helicopter," which they had made out of a matchstick. In Kinshasa they had been helped by older witches and nocturnal friends, and most prominently among them the grandmother of one of the three boys. Finally, the three give a morbid account of how they killed their victims, chopped them up, and distributed the body parts amongst witch friends to "eat" during a nocturnal feast in which the grandmother participated, dancing naked around the victims' houses. The taped testimony was later sent to the boys' relatives in Kinshasa to corroborate the existing suspicions.

In 1999, such stories had become part and parcel of the daily life in a city like Kinshasa. [. . .] One immediate effect has been that the city streets have started to abound with ever growing groups of street children. [. . .]

Many of these children were forced to take to the street after being singled out by family members in a witchcraft accusation. Such accusations against children within one's own family have become a common occurrence that transcends all rank, class and ethnic divisions and differences that characterize Kinshasa's urban context. Increasingly, children between age four and eighteen are being accused of causing misfortunes and mishaps, as well as the illness or death of other children and adults in their family and neighborhood environment. The following is an account given by a thirty-year old AIDS patient, a mother of three children. At the time of my interview with her, she was being treated in a healing church together with her four-year-old daughter, Nuclette, accused of witchcraft:

I have suffered a lot in my life. I sold vegetables at the market. The father of Nuclette was deeply in love with me but now he has left me. I was responsible for this separation: All of a sudden I could not return his love anymore. One day, I noticed that my market money had disappeared. People told me that Nuclette had stolen it, but I wouldn't believe them. But then, Nuclette began to be suspected as a witch by our neighbors. Apparently, Nuclette had tried to bewitch a woman who lives in our neighborhood. Nuclette had changed herself and appeared like an adult woman when she went to harm this neighbor. One day, when I was out, that neighbor came over to our house and started complaining to my mother: "How can you accept to live together in one house with the same witch-child that has tried to bewitch and kill us in our home? We are no family of yours. We didn't know that this child is a witch. Why does she try to harm us?"

My mother and I decided to take the child to a prayer session at *pasteur* Norbert's. That evening I washed my two other kids, and we all went together to the "prayer control." The preacher started to prophesy and it was affirmed that Nuclette was a witch but that the two other children were not touched by this evil. Then the *pasteur* asked me where my husband was. I told him that he had left our neighborhood and was now living in a different area in the city. I didn't tell him my husband's name, but he cited it and said: "It was Nuclette who caused your marriage to break up. She made your husband leave. And when you were sleeping in your bed at night, she came with other witch-children and injected you by means of a diabolical needle with contaminated blood." This is how I started developing AIDS. I became very, very thin. People started saying that I had AIDS. Thanks to the preacher of this church, we now know that the AIDS is diabolical. I have been here in the church for over a month, and the preacher has purified me. I was dying when I arrived here, but now I am cured of AIDS. (Interview in Selembao, September 1999)

In other cases little girls are suspected of transforming themselves into stunningly beautiful women to lure their own fathers and uncles into their bed, to snatch away their testicles or penis, and to cause their impotence or even death. Illustrating the fact that Congo's current societal crisis is, to an important degree, also an etiological crisis [. . .] children are also believed to be at the origin of madness, cancer or heart attacks amongst their relatives and parents; other kids appear to be three or four year-olds in the first world, but in the nocturnal, second world they have themselves already given birth to many children. These in turn become witch-children roaming through the streets of Kinshasa. Others still are believed to transform themselves into "mystic" serpents, crocodiles or *mami wata* sirens. In each of these cases, the "real" self of these children is invisible to others. In the politics of invisibility that characterizes the second world, as product and as practice, the self has been separated from its external sign, the face.

Most of the time, all the hidden suspicions and open accusations erupt into a violent conflict within the accused child's family. Often the child in question is severely beaten, in some extreme cases even killed, by family members or neighbors:

[Field notes, Mombele, May 1997] A man frequently dreamed about the thirteen year old son of his landlord. The landlord and his family lived in a separate house in the same compound. In his dreams the boy harassed and threatened to strangle him. Soon everybody in the neighborhood was informed about these strange dreams. One morning some young men, all neighbors, gathered in the compound and started throwing stones on the corrugated iron roof of the owner's house. The boy was inside. When they started throwing the stones, the boy appeared. People started to stone him. A stone hit him on the head. The child fell down, bleeding profusely. Some men put a tire around his neck and set fire to it. When the boy's parents arrived, their child was already burning to death. The parents did not interfere for fear that they would undergo the same fate.

Although such forms of extreme violence are by no means the rule, most of these children, though, are disowned and repudiated. Displaced, disenfranchised, but feared by most, the alleged witch-children (called *sheta, tsor* or *tshor*, from French *sorcier*, witch) end up in the street, where they often team up after a while with other abandoned children. Children thus form their "stable" (*écurie*), usually a group of up to seven persons. These gangs have a varying life span (from some weeks to some months, rarely longer than a year). Often, several of these stables associate to form a larger, more loosely knit group. Witch-children are believed to adopt the same form of organization in the world of the night. Stables of witch-children also fashion themselves after a military army model. In their nocturnal army, witch-children accord grades to themselves, from sergeant to general, and one climbs in rank with every victim that one has killed and "eaten."

[. . .]

Due to the AIDS epidemic and other causes related to the poor living conditions in Congo, many of these children were orphaned at a very early age. Others were abandoned by their mothers, often teenagers themselves, and grew up amongst, sometimes distant, relatives: (classificatory) grandparents, uncles, aunts, cousins, or one of their father's co-wives. When one or both parents are still alive (and average life expectancy for the total population in R. D. Congo is less than fifty years and as low as forty-seven for men) they are often absent, an absence which is increasingly due to patterns of displacement, migration and diaspora under the pressure of economic factors, political instability and war.

Churches and Child-Witches

The spiral of violence that erupts in the kinship group because of the pattern of witchcraft accusations directed at children, is partly countered by the church and prayer movements that are flourishing everywhere. [. . .] Fundamentalist churches, and foremost amongst those the Pentecostal churches and apocalyptic movements that may be found throughout sub-Saharan Africa nowadays, devote a lot of attention to the figure of Satan, to demons, and the struggle between Good and Evil. Beyond any doubt the churches' contribution plays a crucial role in the ceaseless production and increasing centrality of the figure of the witch in the collective imaginary of Congolese society, which is itself being restructured in terms of an Armageddon, a second world in which demons have gathered in an all-out war against God (see the Book of Revelation, 16:16).

Paradoxically, then, [. . .] the figure of the witch in the discourse of these churches makes the witch itself more omnipresent in the social field. Therefore, the position of the churches in relation to evil, straightforward as it may seem at first sight, nevertheless produces contradictory tensions in the social field. The churches' role with regard to the child-witch phenomenon is an equally ambivalent one, which makes them both part of the witchcraft problem itself as well as of the local solution to this problem. On the one hand, the space of the churches is one of the most prominent sites in which the coincidence of the figure of the witch and the child is produced. During the masses and collective prayers, children are urged to make a public confession in order to reveal their true natures as witches and confess the number of victims they attacked [. . .]. Rather than being a perversion, the naming of the witch offers an opening to solve the crisis, as it has always done in more traditional settings. Before this public moment they have usually been sniffed out or recognized as witches by the church leaders and *pasteurs* during more private consultations. In these meetings more "traditional" divinatory models are often blended in with the church discourse to create a ritualized moment of witch-finding. As a consequence of these denunciations, however, international aid agencies and NGOs such as *Save the Children*, in their struggle against the marginalization of children, accuse the church leaders and *pasteurs* of child abuse. These organizations usually treat the problem of witch-children in Kinshasa as a humanitarian problem of street children, while choosing to totally disregard the cultural implications of the witchcraft aspect. And yet, one could argue that the churches, in providing and authorizing this type of diagnostic, offer an alternative to the violence and conflict that occur in the family as the result of a witchcraft accusation. The church leaders do not usually produce these accusations themselves, but merely confirm and thereby legitimate them. In doing so, the space of the "healing" church enables the relocation and reformulation of the sometimes extreme physical and psychological violence that the accused children have to undergo within their kin-group. The child is removed from the threatening family context in which its place has become highly problematic, and is left in the care of a *pasteur*. Here, the often equally tough treatment starts with an initial period of seclusion and quarantine, either individually or collectively with other child-witches. As I have observed myself in recent years, some churches take in up to a hundred children a week. The period of seclusion, during which these children usually live in rather poor conditions in terms of food and hygiene, may last from a couple of days to some weeks or even months, depending on the seriousness of the case in question.

During their seclusion, the children are subjected to a period of fasting and ritual purification. The lavish administration of laxatives and emetics aims at cleansing the witch-children's bodies from the meat of the victims that they ate. Undigested pieces of meat or bone, but also objects of all kinds which are found in the children's vomit and feces will be used as corroborants during their public confession before the assembled members of the church. During the period of seclusion, the children are regularly subjected to interrogations, sometimes alone, at other times in the presence of one or both of the child's parents or other related adults if the latter are willing to cooperate. Many adults, though, are too afraid of their children to maintain close contact with them. During these more private sessions that evolve between the child and the preacher or one of his or her assistants, there slowly emerges a narrative of disruption and descent into evil which will also help to structure the "outing ritual" of confession in the public space of the church later on. This period is a crucial point in a whole process of emplotment which helps to shape up the imaginative task of modeling an experience of crisis and drawing a rather standard and stereotypical narrative configuration out of a simple succession of illnesses and deaths. As part of a therapeutic narrative process, which eventually leads to the children's story of confession, the emplotment that takes shape here gives the experience of crisis a direction. It mediates disruption and promotes self-healing, even though the children themselves are not, or only in certain ways, free in their choices of how to plot their narratives.

During or after the moment of public confession, a relative of the accused child usually addresses the church gathering. In this way, Omba Shako's uncle asked permission to speak after his nephew's confession [. . .]:

My Brothers and Sisters in Christ! It is truly the Spirit of the Almighty which pushed me to bring this child here during the church's Evangelization Campaign! Praised be the Lord! This child is my sister's child. He lived in Kananga with his parents. He came to live with me in Kinshasa not longer than two months ago. But I am far from pleased with this child's behavior. He does everything with a jealous heart. It is easy to see that he is a sorcerer. I brought him to this church to make sure that I was not mistaken. At home he has already provoked numerous conflicts between my wife and me. One day, my wife and I had gone out. We had left our three year-old daughter, Rebecca, in the house. As soon as we had gone, Omba went into the house and opened the room where we store our food. He took a cooking pot which contained *pondu* [prepared cassava leaves] that my wife had made earlier that day. We would have eaten this upon our return home in the evening. Omba, however, took the cooking pot, opened it, looked left and right to see if nobody had seen him, and then he urinated in the pot. When we came home in the evening, my wife noticed that the pot was filled with a strange liquid. It smelled of urine. She wondered who could have done this. Little Rebecca informed us that Omba had urinated on the food. She said, "He took the cooking pot, opened it, looked around to see whether someone could observe him and urinated. He did not see me, but I could see him. Don't eat from this food, father!" This event caused me a lot of problems with my wife. We did not eat and everybody went to bed feeling hungry. Many people in the neighborhood had already told me that Omba was a witch. If we keep him with us any longer, he will kill either me or my wife. One of the children died recently. Omba is the one to blame. He gave my child to the witches. I have listened to everything he confessed today. I no longer want him in my house. Let him stay here in the church. Tell him that he abandons his witchcraft. Tell him to repent!

After his uncle had spoken, Omba fell down, got up again and started to cry, while singing: "They refuse to listen, they will not give up witchcraft" (*baboyaki koyoka, kindoki batika te*). Then he fell down again, got up and began to pray in a loud voice. Punctuated by biblical references to the story of Noah and his wife who were saved during the Great Flood, while all the sinners repented too late and perished, he prayed:

Oh Lord
I am your child
I come to you with all my heart
to you my Father
Oh Father of Love
Father, don't leave me behind in the hands of my enemies
I had forgotten you
I killed people
I ate the meat of my fellow brothers
I turned them into animals
They became like animals of the forest
But now I give myself to you
I am your image
Father, take my heart
You are the strongest

Some days after the crucial moment of such a public confession the preacher proceeds by organizing a number of exorcizing moments, referred to as *délivrance* (deliverance) or *cure d'âme* (soul healing). This ritualized exorcism is often carried out collectively in prayer groups under the guidance of female church members known as "interceptors" (*interces-seuses*). The child is placed in the middle of a circle of praying, often trancing, women who regularly lapse into speaking in tongues, a sign of the Holy Spirit's presence. The child, the focus of this powerful praying ritual, is then repeatedly subjected to exorcizing prayer and the laying on of hands. Usually one woman takes the lead in prayer while the others sustain her by regularly punctuating her preaching with religious songs and hymns. Depending on the type of church, these praying sessions unfold in collaboration with the child's mother or some other relative in the hope of facilitating a reintegration of the cleansed witch-child within its family. In many cases though, parents are not very collaborative and such reintegration remains problematic. The child's parents and other members of the kin group often remain too afraid to accept such a child again in their midst. It is usually in those all too frequent cases that the children are subsequently forced to take to the street.

[...]

NOTES

1 Mbembe, 2001 : 145.
2 Devisch, 2001 : 116.
3 See Appadurai, 1996; Bayart, 1996 : 143.
4 Deleuze, 1990.
5 The material presented here is based on several periods of field research in Kinshasa (1999–2004), and more particularly in the context of prayer movements and healing churches, most of which had links with Pentecostalism and other "fundamentalist" branches such as Watchtower and Jehovah's Witness, as well as Seventh Day Adventists. I frequented churches in the neighborhoods of Masina, Bandalungwa, Lemba, Selembao, Ndjili and Kintambo, and conducted interviews with children, church leaders, parents and other relatives of the children involved.
6 See for example Douglas, 1999.
7 The NGO *Save the Children* gives an estimate of 2000 children who are the subject of such accusations in Kinshasa. In my view the estimate is rather conservative in that it is based on an extrapolation of the number of children brought to the churches to be exorcized. However, it does not take into account the high turnover of children in those churches and the constant production of new child-witches. For the rest, the joining of children and witches is characteristic of all times and all places. While in Europe, before 1600, witches were mostly elderly people, children were increasingly accused of witchcraft after that date. Not only were children victims of bewitchment, [...] as in [...] seventeenth-century Salem, Massachusetts, but they were also accused of bewitching others. In seventeenth-century Europe, children were regularly burnt as witches, as attested by Midelfort's analysis of the Würzenberg witch trials of 1627–9, in which ten children between the ages of 6 and 20 were killed [...] (see Midelfort, 1972: 179ff). [...]
8 See Ferguson, 1999; Comaroff and Comaroff, 1999; Augé, 1999.
9 For an insightful treatment of these themes in relation to the gift see Baudrillard, 1976 and, more recently, Godelier, 1996.

REFERENCES

Appadurai, A. 1996 Disjuncture and Difference in the Global Cultural Economy. In *Modernity at Large. Cultural Dimensions of Globalization*. Minneapolis: University of Minnesota Press: 27–47.

Augé, M. 1999 *The War of Dreams. Studies in Ethno-Fiction*. London: Pluto Press.

Baudrillard, J. 1976 *L'échange symbolique et la mort*. Paris: Gallimard.

Bayart, J.-F. 1996 *L'illusion identitaire*. Paris: Fayard.

Comaroff, J. 1997 Consuming Passions: Child Abuse, Fetishism, and "The New World Order". *Culture* 17: 7–19.

Comaroff, J. and J. Comaroff. 1999 Occult Economies and the Violence of Abstraction:

Notes from the South African Postcolony. *American Ethnologist* 26 (2): 279–303.

Deleuze, G. 1990 *Pourparlers. 1972–1990*. Paris: Minuit.

Devisch, R. 2001 Sorcery Forces of Life and Death among the Yaka of Congo. In: G. C. Bond and D. Ciekawy (eds) *Witchraft Dialogues. Anthropological and Philosophical Exchanges*. Athens, Ohio: Ohio University Center for International Studies.

Douglas, M. 1999 Sorcery Accusations Unleashed: The Lele Revisited, 1987. *Africa* 69 (2): 177–93.

Ferguson, J. 1999 *Expectations of Modernity. Myths and Meanings of Urban Life in the Zambian Copperbelt*. Berkeley: University of California Press.

Geschiere, P. 1997 *The Modernity of Witchcraft. Politics and the Occult in Postcolonial Africa*. Charlottesville/London: University Press of Virginia.

Godelier, M. 1996 *L'enigme du don*. Paris: Fayard.

Mbembe, A. 2001 *On the Postcolony*. Berkeley: University of California Press.

Midelfort, E. 1972 *Witch-Hunting in Southwestern Germany 1562–1684*. Stanford: Stanford University Press.

Religious Ethics and Politics in the State, Public Sphere, and Transnational Scene

Introduction

The essays here address in various ways tensions in religious practice created by the pull between political demands and immediate social and material circumstances, on the one hand, and culturally informed ethical concerns on the other. Here Marxist analyses can be complemented by arguments concerning the impact of the state and other political forces on religious transformation. From Weber comes the suggestion to explore modernity with respect to increasing rationalization. Rationalization emerges from two directions: on the one hand, the role of the state and transnational institutions in shaping religion according to their own ends and more or less successfully appropriating it; on the other, the agency of individuals and communities engaged in relatively self-conscious reformation or secularization. These processes can lead to anomie or to sharp reaction, fueling various forms of intensified religious commitment and closure sometimes referred to as "fundamentalism" (James, ed. 1995), but also to new forms of ethical engagement such as the human rights movement or environmentalism. These diverse and at times contradictory processes must all be accounted for in the very large task of comprehending "modernity" (including "postmodernity"). However, as the essays show, similar processes can be discerned in religious struggles at other historical periods.

From a very rich field I would particularly recommend a few essays for additional reading. In her analysis of historical transformations within European religion (1990), Schneider examines the polarization of magic and religion, balancing the analysis of broad social forces with consideration of the ethical judgment of participants. Gombrich and Obeyesekere (1988) provide a particularly effective overview of comparable transformations within Sri Lankan Buddhism, developing the intriguing idea of the emergence of a "protestant" variant. Conversely, in a profound analysis of the forms of mythical and historical consciousness generated within

Buddhism and Hinduism, Daniel (1996) probes factors contributing to and emerging from the terrible violence that seized Sri Lanka. Appiah (1992) offers an engaging postcolonial intervention in the rationality debate that explores changing patterns of thought and ritual in Ghana, while Gellner (2001) provides insight into religious dynamics in Nepal and Japan. Willford and George (2005) is an excellent collection on the turbulent relationships among ethnicity, nationalism, and religion in colonial and postcolonial Southeast Asia. Hefner (1998) offers a particularly good overview of the main trends and issues.

39

Civil Religion in America

Robert N. Bellah

Robert Bellah is professor emeritus of sociology at the University of California, Berkeley. His Weberian concerns with transformation, interpretation, and ethics (Bellah et al. 1985) have made him among the most anthropological of sociologists. He is well known for his work on Japanese religion (1957) and American society (Bellah et al., 1985).

A useful introduction to civil religion runs as follows:

> Think of what is taught in state schools about the values and virtues of the state itself as the secular revelation of a "civil religion" (the term is Rousseau's). Except in the case of the deified emperor, this revelation is religious mostly by analogy, but the analogy is worth pursuing. For here, as the school example makes clear, is a "religion" that can't be separated from the state: it is the very creed of the state, crucial to its reproduction and stability over time. Civil religion consists of the full set of political doctrines, historical narratives, exemplary figures, celebratory occasions, and memorial rituals through which the state impresses itself on the minds of its members, especially its youngest or newest members. (Walzer 1997: 76)

Bellah's classic essay has spawned much secondary literature, including a book that reevaluates, develops, and applies the concept (Bellah 1975, Bellah and Hammond, eds, 1980). His model of civil religion might be compared with Malinowski on myth as charter, Hobsbawm and Ranger on invented traditions (1983), Anderson on imagined communities (1983), Cohn on colonial ceremony (1987) and, indeed, with the large literature that examines the role of history and memory in the ideological construction of the nation. Other work on state power and cults of leadership is influenced by sociologist Edward

From Robert N. Bellah, "Civil Religion in America," in *Beyond Belief: Essays on Religion in a Post-Traditional World* (New York: Harper & Row, 1970 [1967]), pp. 168–87. Copyright © 1991 The Regents of the University of California. Abridged.

Shils (1975; Geertz 1983). Not everyone refers to the subject as civil religion; indeed, one might think about the tensions between religion in the service of the state and religion as a basis for civil society and ethical conduct at arm's length from the state.

As Bellah put it, "the ubiquity of what can be called 'the religio-political problem' can hardly be doubted. In no society can religion and politics ignore each other" (Bellah and Hammond, eds, 1980: vii). Bellah is less cynical about this than many; he does not attempt to reduce religion to power. The passage continues (in what appears to be an American Christian phrasing), "Faith and power must always, however uneasily, take a stance toward one another. The polity, more than most realms of human action, deals obviously with ultimate things" (ibid.: vii). The various forms these connections can take are elaborated in his essay on religious evolution (1964), but Bellah's point, like Durkheim's (and subsequently Rappaport's), is that there is always a "noncontractual" element underlying any contract, i.e.,

something beyond mutual self-interest (Bellah and Hammond, eds., 1980: 202). This leads us to inquire about the bases for citizenship and civility in the present age, a topic that enjoins anthropologists to draw upon political philosophers from Plato and Aristotle through Arendt, Habermas, Rorty, and MacIntyre. See, for example, the innovative work on virtue ethics and popular piety in Egyptian Islam developed by Hirschkind (chapter 42) and Mahmood (2001, 2005).

Allen's (2005) journalistic but succinct and incisive discussion of the relationship between church and state at the founding of the American republic provides a very useful complement to Bellah's essay.

Robert Bellah has changed his views considerably since the original publication of this article and in fact no longer uses the term "civil religion." For his most recent thinking on this topic, as well as a variety of other significant essays on comparative and American religion, see *The Robert Bellah Reader*, edited by Robert Bellah and Steven Tipton, Duke University Press, 2006.

While some have argued that Christianity is the national faith, and others that church and synagogue celebrate only the generalized religion of "the American Way of Life," few have realized that there actually exists alongside of and rather clearly differentiated from the churches an elaborate and well-institutionalized civil religion in America. This article argues not only that there is such a thing, but also that this religion – or perhaps better, this religious dimension – has its own seriousness and integrity and requires the same care in understanding that any other religion does.[1]

The Kennedy Inaugural

John F. Kennedy's inaugural address of January 20, 1961, serves as an example and a clue with

which to introduce this complex subject. That address began:

> We observe today not a victory of party but a celebration of freedom – symbolizing an end as well as a beginning – signifying renewal as well as change. For I have sworn before you and Almighty God the same solemn oath our forebears prescribed nearly a century and three quarters ago.
>
> The world is very different now. For man holds in his mortal hands the power to abolish all forms of human poverty and to abolish all forms of human life. And yet the same revolutionary beliefs for which our forebears fought are still at issue around the globe – the belief that the rights of man come not from the generosity of the state but from the hand of God.

And it concluded:

Finally, whether you are citizens of America or of the world, ask of us the same high standards of strength and sacrifice that we shall ask of you. With a good conscience our only sure reward, with history the final judge of our deeds, let us go forth to lead the land we love, asking His blessing and His help, but knowing that here on earth God's work must truly be our own.

These are the three places in this brief address in which Kennedy mentioned the name of God. If we could understand why he mentioned God, the way in which he did it, and what he meant to say in those three references, we would understand much about American civil religion. But this is not a simple or obvious task, and American students of religion would probably differ widely in their interpretation of these passages.

Let us consider first the placing of the three references. They occur in the two opening paragraphs and in the closing paragraph, thus providing a sort of frame for the more concrete remarks that form the middle part of the speech. Looking beyond this particular speech, we would find that similar references to God are almost invariably to be found in the pronouncements of American presidents on solemn occasions, though usually not in the working messages that the President sends to Congress on various concrete issues. How, then, are we to interpret this placing of references to God?

It might be argued that the passages quoted reveal the essentially irrelevant role of religion in the very secular society that is America. The placing of the references in this speech as well as in public life generally indicates that religion has "only a ceremonial significance"; it gets only a sentimental nod that serves largely to placate the more unenlightened members of the community before a discussion of the really serious business with which religion has nothing whatever to do. A cynical observer might even say that an American President has to mention God or risk losing votes. A semblance of piety is merely one of the unwritten qualifications for the office, a bit more traditional than but not essentially different from the present-day requirement of a pleasing television personality.

But we know enough about the function of ceremonial and ritual in various societies to make us suspicious of dismissing something as unimportant because it is "only a ritual." What people say on solemn occasions need not be taken at face value, but it is often indicative of deep-seated values and commitments that are not made explicit in the course of everyday life. Following this line of argument, it is worth considering whether the very special placing of the references to God in Kennedy's address may not reveal something rather important and serious about religion in American life.

It might be countered that the very way in which Kennedy made his references reveals the essentially vestigial place of religion today. He did not refer to any religion in particular. He did not refer to Jesus Christ, or to Moses, or to the Christian church; certainly he did not refer to the Catholic Church. In fact, his only reference was to the concept of God, a word that almost all Americans can accept but that means so many different things to so many different people that it is almost an empty sign. Is this not just another indication that in America religion is considered vaguely to be a good thing, but that people care so little about it that it has lost any content whatever? Isn't Dwight Eisenhower reported to have said "Our government makes no sense unless it is founded in a deeply felt religious faith – and I don't care what it is," and isn't that a complete negation of any real religion?

These questions are worth pursuing because they raise the issue of how civil religion relates to the political society on the one hand and to private religious organization on the other. President Kennedy was a Christian, more specifically a Catholic Christian. Thus his general references to God do not mean that he lacked a specific religious commitment. But why, then, did he not include some remark to the effect that Christ is the Lord of the world or some indication of respect for the Catholic church? He did not because these are matters of his own private religious belief and of his relation to his own particular church; they are not matters relevant in any direct way to the conduct of his public office. Others with different religious views and commitments to different churches or denominations are equally qualified participants in the political process. The principle of separation of church and state guarantees the freedom of religious belief and association, but at the same time clearly segregates the religious sphere, which is considered to be essentially private, from the political one.

Considering the separation of church and state, how is a president justified in using the word "God" at all? The answer is that the separation of church and state has not denied the political realm a religious dimension. Although matters of personal religious belief, worship, and association are considered to be strictly private affairs, there are, at the same time, certain common elements of religious orientation that the great majority of Americans share. These have played a crucial role in the development of American institutions and still provide a religious dimension for the whole fabric of American life, including the political sphere. This public religious dimension is expressed in a set of beliefs, symbols, and rituals that I am calling the American civil religion. The inauguration of a president is an important ceremonial event in this religion. It reaffirms, among other things, the religious legitimation of the highest political authority.

Let us look more closely at what Kennedy actually said. First he said, "I have sworn before you and Almighty God the same solemn oath our forebears prescribed nearly a century and three quarters ago." The oath is the oath of office, including the acceptance of the obligation to uphold the Constitution. He swears it before the people (you) and God. Beyond the Constitution, then, the president's obligation extends not only to the people but to God. In American political theory, sovereignty rests, of course, with the people, but implicitly, and often explicitly, the ultimate sovereignty has been attributed to God. This is the meaning of the motto, "In God we trust," as well as the inclusion of the phrase "under God" in the pledge to the flag. What difference does it make that sovereignty belongs to God? Though the will of the people as expressed in majority vote is carefully institutionalized as the operative source of political authority, it is deprived of an ultimate significance. The will of the people is not itself the criterion of right and

wrong. There is a higher criterion in terms of which this will can be judged; it is possible that the people may be wrong. The president's obligation extends to the higher criterion.

When Kennedy says that "the rights of man come not from the generosity of the state but from the hand of God," he is stressing this point again. It does not matter whether the state is the expression of the will of an autocratic monarch or of the "people"; the rights of man are more basic than any political structure and provide a point of revolutionary leverage from which any state structure may be radically altered. That is the basis for his reassertion of the revolutionary significance of America.

But the religious dimension in political life as recognized by Kennedy not only provides a grounding for the rights of man that makes any form of political absolutism illegitimate, it also provides a transcendent goal for the political process. This is implied in his final words that "here on earth God's work must truly be our own." What he means here is, I think, more clearly spelled out in a previous paragraph, the wording of which, incidentally, has a distinctly biblical ring:

> Now the trumpet summons us again – not as a call to bear arms, though arms we need – not as a call to battle, though embattled we are – but a call to bear the burden of a long twilight struggle, year in and year out, "rejoicing in hope, patient in tribulation" – a struggle against the common enemies of man: tyranny, poverty, disease and war itself.

The whole address can be understood as only the most recent statement of a theme that lies very deep in the American tradition, namely the obligation, both collective and individual, to carry out God's will on earth. This was the motivating spirit of those who founded America, and it has been present in every generation since. Just below the surface throughout Kennedy's inaugural address, it becomes explicit in the closing statement that God's work must be our own. That this very activist and noncontemplative conception of the fundamental religious obligation, which has been historically associated with the Protestant position, should be enunciated so clearly in the first major statement of the first Catholic president seems to underline how deeply established it is in the American outlook. Let us now consider the form and history of the civil religious tradition in which Kennedy was speaking.

The Idea of a Civil Religion

The phrase "civil religion" is, of course, Rousseau's. In chapter 8, book 4 of *The Social Contract*, he outlines the simple dogmas of the civil religion: the existence of God the life to come, the reward of virtue and the punishment of vice, and the exclusion of religious intolerance. All other religious opinions are outside the cognizance of the state and may be freely held by citizens. While the phrase "civil religion" was not used, to the best of my knowledge, by the founding fathers, and I am certainly not arguing for the particular influence of Rousseau, it is clear that similar ideas, as part of the cultural climate of the late eighteenth century, were to be found among the Americans. For example, Benjamin Franklin writes in his autobiography.

I never was without some religious principles. I never doubted, for instance, the existence of the Deity; that he made the world and govern'd it by his Providence; that the most acceptable service of God was the doing of good to men; that our souls are immortal; and that all crime will be punished, and virtue rewarded either here or hereafter. These I esteemed the essentials of every religion; and, being to be found in all the religions we had in our country, I respected them all, tho' with different degrees of respect, as I found them more or less mix'd with other articles, which, without any tendency to inspire, promote or confirm morality, serv'd principally to divide us, and make us unfriendly to one another.

It is easy to dispose of this sort of position as essentially utilitarian in relation to religion. In Washington's Farewell Address (though the words may be Hamilton's) the utilitarian aspect is quite explicit:

Of all the dispositions and habits which lead to political prosperity, Religion and Morality are indispensable supports. . . . Let it simply be asked where is the security for property, for reputation, for life, if the sense of religious obligation *desert* the oaths, which are the instruments of investigation in Courts of Justice? And let us with caution indulge the supposition, that morality can be maintained without religion. Whatever may be conceded to the influence of refined education on minds of peculiar structure, reason and experience both forbid us to expect that National morality can prevail in exclusion of religious principle.

But there is every reason to believe that religion, particularly the idea of God, played a constitutive role in the thought of the early American statesmen.

Kennedy's inaugural pointed to the religious aspect of the Declaration of Independence, and it might be well to look at that document a bit more closely. There are four references to God. The first speaks of the "Laws of Nature and of Nature's God" that entitle any people to be independent. The second is the famous statement that all men "are endowed by their Creator with certain inalienable Rights." Here Jefferson is locating the fundamental legitimacy of the new nation in a conception of "higher law" that is itself based on both classical natural law and biblical religion. The third is an appeal to "the Supreme Judge of the world for the rectitude of our intentions," and the last indicates "a firm reliance on the protection of divine Providence." In these last two references, a biblical God of history who stands in judgment over the world is indicated.

The intimate relation of these religious notions with the self-conception of the new republic is indicated by the frequency of their appearance in early official documents.
[. . .]
Nor did these religious sentiments remain merely the personal expression of the President. At the request of both Houses of Congress, Washington proclaimed on October 3 of that same first year as President that November 26 should be "a day of public thanksgiving and prayer," the first Thanksgiving Day under the Constitution.

The words and acts of the founding fathers, especially the first few presidents, shaped the form and tone of the civil religion as it has been maintained ever since. Though much is selectively derived from Christianity, this religion is clearly not itself Christianity. For one thing, neither Washington nor Adams nor Jefferson mentions Christ in his inaugural address; nor do any of the subsequent presidents, although not one of them fails to mention God. The God of the civil religion is not only rather "unitarian," he is also on the austere side, much more related to order, law, and right than to salvation and love. Even though he is somewhat deist in cast, he is by no means simply a watchmaker God. He is actively interested and involved in history, with a special concern for America. Here the analogy has much less to do with natural law than with ancient Israel; the equation of America with Israel in the idea of the "American Israel" is not infrequent. What was implicit in the words of Washington . . . becomes explicit in Jefferson's second inaugural when he said: "I shall need, too, the favor of that Being in whose hands we are, who led our fathers, as Israel of old, from their native land and planted them in a country flowing with all the necessaries and comforts of life." Europe is Egypt; America, the promised land. God has led his people to establish a new sort of social order that shall be a light unto all the nations. . . .

What we have, then, from the earliest years of the republic is a collection of beliefs, symbols, and rituals with respect to sacred things and institutionalized in a collectivity. This religion – there seems no other word for it – while not antithetical to and indeed sharing much in common with Christianity, was neither sectarian nor in any specific sense Christian. At a time when the society was overwhelmingly Christian, it seems unlikely that this lack of Christian reference was meant to spare the feelings of the tiny non-Christian minority. Rather, the civil religion expressed what those who set the precedents felt was appropriate under the circumstances. It reflected their private as well as public views. Nor was the civil religion simply "religion in general." While generality was undoubtedly seen as a virtue by some, as in the quotation from Franklin above, the civil religion was specific

enough when it came to the topic of America. Precisely because of this specificity, the civil religion was saved from empty formalism and served as a genuine vehicle of national religious self-understanding.

But the civil religion was not, in the minds of Franklin, Washington, Jefferson, or other leaders, with the exception of a few radicals like Tom Paine, ever felt to be a substitute for Christianity. There was an implicit but quite clear division of function between the civil religion and Christianity. Under the doctrine of religious liberty, an exceptionally wide sphere of personal piety and voluntary social action was left to the churches. But the churches were neither to control the state nor to be controlled by it. The national magistrate, whatever his private religious views, operates under the rubrics of the civil religion as long as he is in his official capacity, as we have already seen in the case of Kennedy. This accommodation was undoubtedly the product of a particular historical moment and of a cultural background dominated by Protestantism of several varieties and by the Enlightenment, but it has survived despite subsequent changes in the cultural and religious climate.

Civil War and Civil Religion

Until the Civil War, the American civil religion focused above all on the event of the Revolution, which was seen as the final act of the Exodus from the old lands across the waters. The Declaration of Independence and the Constitution were the sacred scriptures and Washington the divinely appointed Moses who led his people out of the hands of tyranny. The Civil War, which Sidney Mead calls "the center of American history," was the second great event that involved the national self-understanding so deeply as to require expression in the civil religion.

[. . .]

The Civil War raised the deepest questions of national meaning. The man who not only formulated but in his own person embodied its meaning for Americans was Abraham Lincoln. For him the issue was not in the first instance slavery but "whether that nation, or any nation so conceived, and so dedicated, can long endure."

[. . .]

With the Civil War, a new theme of death, sacrifice, and rebirth enters the civil religion. It is symbolized in the life and death of Lincoln. Nowhere is it stated more vividly than in the Gettysburg Address, itself part of the Lincolnian "New Testament" among the civil scriptures. Robert Lowell has recently pointed out the "insistent use of birth images" in this speech explicitly devoted to "these honored dead": "brought forth," "conceived," "created," "a new birth of freedom." He goes on to say:

The Gettysburg Address is a symbolic and sacramental act. Its verbal quality is resonance combined with a logical, matter of fact, prosaic brevity. . . . In his words, Lincoln symbolically died, just as the Union soldiers really died – and as he himself was soon really to die. By his words, he gave the field of battle a symbolic significance that it had lacked. For us and our country, he left Jefferson's ideals of freedom and equality joined to the Christian sacrificial act of death and rebirth. I believe this is a meaning that goes beyond sect or religion and beyond peace and war, and is now part of our lives as a challenge, obstacle and hope.

Lowell is certainly right in pointing out the Christian quality of the symbolism here, but he is also right in quickly disavowing any sectarian implication. The earlier symbolism of the civil religion had been Hebraic without in any specific sense being Jewish. The Gettysburg symbolism (". . . those who here gave their lives, that that nation might live") is Christian without having anything to do with the Christian church.

The symbolic equation of Lincoln with Jesus was made relatively early. W. H. Herndon, who had been Lincoln's law partner, wrote:

For fifty years God rolled Abraham Lincoln through his fiery furnace. He did it to try Abraham and to purify him for his purposes. This made Mr. Lincoln humble, tender, forbearing, sympathetic to suffering, kind, sensitive, tolerant; broadening, deepening and widening his whole nature; making him the noblest and loveliest character since Jesus Christ. . . . I believe that Lincoln was God's chosen one.

With the Christian archetype in the background, Lincoln, "our martyred president," was linked to the war dead, those who "gave the last full measure of devotion." The theme of sacrifice was indelibly written into the civil religion.

The new symbolism soon found both physical and ritualistic expression. The great number of the war dead required the establishment of a number of national cemeteries. Of these, the Gettysburg National Cemetery, which Lincoln's famous address served to dedicate, has been overshadowed only by the Arlington National Cemetery. Begun somewhat vindictively on the Lee estate across the river from Washington, partly with the end that the Lee family could never reclaim it, it has subsequently become the most hallowed monument of the civil religion. Not only was a section set aside for the Confederate dead, but it has received the dead of each succeeding American war. It is the site of the one important new symbol to come out of World War I, the Tomb of the Unknown Soldier; more recently it has become the site of the tomb of another martyred President and its symbolic eternal flame.

Memorial Day, which grew out of the Civil War, gave ritual expression to the themes we have been discussing. As Lloyd Warner has so brilliantly analyzed it, the Memorial Day observance, especially in the towns and smaller cities of America, is a major event for the whole community involving a rededication to the martyred dead, to the spirit of sacrifice, and to the American vision. Just as Thanksgiving Day, which incidentally was securely institutionalized as an annual national holiday only under the presidency of Lincoln, serves to integrate the family into the civil religion, so Memorial Day has acted to integrate the local community into the national cult. Together with the less overtly religious Fourth of July and the more minor celebrations of Veterans Day and the birthdays of Washington and Lincoln, these two holidays provide an annual ritual calendar for the civil religion. The public school system serves as a particularly important context for the cultic celebration of the civil rituals.

The Civil Religion Today

In reifying and giving a name to something that, though pervasive enough when you look at it, has gone on only semiconsciously, there is risk of severely distorting the data. But the reification and the naming have already begun. The religious critics of "religion in general," or of the "religion of the 'American Way of Life,'" or of "American Shinto" have really been talking about the civil religion. As usual in religious polemic, they take as criteria the best in their own religious tradition and as typical the worst in the tradition of the civil religion. Against these critics, I would argue that the civil religion at its best is a genuine apprehension of universal and transcendent religious reality as seen in or, one could almost say, as revealed through the experience of the American people. Like all religions, it has suffered various deformations and demonic distortions. At its best, it has neither been so general that it has lacked incisive relevance to the American scene nor so particular that it has placed American society above universal human values. I am not at all convinced that the leaders of the churches have consistently represented a higher level of religious insight than the spokesmen of the civil religion. Reinhold Niebuhr has this to say of Lincoln, who never joined a church and who certainly represents civil religion at its best:

An analysis of the religion of Abraham Lincoln in the context of the traditional religion of his time and place and of its polemical use on the slavery issue, which corrupted religious life in the days before and during the Civil War, must lead to the conclusion that Lincoln's religious convictions were superior in depth and purity to those, not only of the political leaders of his day, but of the religious leaders of the era.

Perhaps the real animus of the religious critics has been not so much against the civil religion in itself but against its pervasive and dominating influence within the sphere of church religion. As S. M. Lipset has recently shown, American religion at least since the early nineteenth century has been predominantly activist, moralistic, and social rather than contemplative, theological, or innerly spiritual. De Tocqueville spoke of American church religion as "a political institution which powerfully contributes to the maintenance of a democratic republic among the Americans" by supplying a strong moral consensus amidst continuous political change. Henry Bargy in 1902 spoke of American church religion as "la poésie du civisme."

It is certainly true that the relation between religion and politics in America has been singularly smooth. This is in large part due to the dominant tradition. As de Tocqueville wrote:

The greatest part of British America was peopled by men who, after having shaken off the authority of the Pope, acknowledged no other religious supremacy: they brought with them into the New World a form of Christianity which I cannot better describe than by styling it a democratic and republican religion.

The churches opposed neither the Revolution nor the establishment of democratic institutions. Even when some of them opposed the full institutionalization of religious liberty, they accepted the final outcome with good grace and without nostalgia for an *ancien régime*. The American civil religion was never anticlerical or militantly secular. On the contrary, it borrowed selectively from the religious tradition in such a way that the average American saw no conflict between the two. In this way, the civil religion was able to build up without any bitter struggle with the church powerful symbols of national solidarity and to mobilize deep levels of personal motivation for the attainment of national goals.

Such an achievement is by no means to be taken for granted. It would seem that the problem of a civil religion is quite general in modern societies and that the way it is solved or not solved will have repercussions in many spheres. One need only to think of France to see how differently things can go. The French Revolution was anticlerical to the core and attempted to set up an anti-Christian civil religion. Throughout modern French history, the chasm between traditional Catholic symbols and the symbolism of 1789 has been immense.

[...]

The civil religion has not always been invoked in favor of worthy causes. On the domestic scene, an American-Legion type of ideology that fuses God, country, and flag has been used to attack nonconformist and liberal ideas and groups of all kinds. Still, it has been difficult to use the words of Jefferson and Lincoln to support special interests and undermine personal freedom. The defenders of slavery before the Civil War came to reject the thinking of the Declaration of Independence. Some of the most consistent of them turned against not only Jeffersonian democracy but Reformation religion; they dreamed of a South dominated by medieval chivalry and divine-right monarchy. For all the overt religiosity of the radical right today, their relation to the civil religious consensus is tenuous, as when the John Birch Society attacks the central American symbol of Democracy itself.

With respect to America's role in the world, the dangers of distortion are greater and the built-in safeguards of the tradition weaker. The theme of the American Israel was used, almost from the beginning, as a justification for the shameful treatment of the Indians so characteristic of our history. It can be overtly or implicitly linked to the idea of manifest destiny that has been used to legitimate several adventures in imperialism since the early nineteenth century. Never has the danger been greater than today. The issue is not so much one of imperial expansion, of which we are accused, as of the tendency to assimilate all governments or parties in the world that support our immediate policies or call upon our help by invoking the notion of free institutions and democratic values. Those nations that are for the moment "on our side" become "the free world." A repressive and unstable military dictatorship in South Vietnam becomes "the free people of South Vietnam and their government." It is then part of the role of America as the New Jerusalem and "the last best hope of earth" to defend such governments with treasure and eventually with blood. When our soldiers are actually dying, it becomes possible to consecrate the struggle further by invoking the great theme of sacrifice....

The civil religion is obviously involved in the most pressing moral and political issues of the day. But it is also caught in another kind of crisis, theoretical and theological, of which it is at the moment largely unaware. "God" has clearly been a central symbol in the civil religion from the beginning and remains so today. This symbol is just as central to the civil religion as it is to Judaism or Christianity. In the late eighteenth century this posed no problem; even Tom Paine, contrary to his detractors, was not an atheist. From left to right and regardless of church or sect, all could accept the idea of God. But today, as even *Time* has recognized, the meaning of "God" is by no means so clear or so obvious. There is no formal creed in the civil religion. We have had a Catholic president; it is conceivable that we could have a Jewish one. But could we have an agnostic president? Could a man with conscientious scruples about using the word "God" the way Kennedy and Johnson have used it be elected chief magistrate of our country? If the whole God symbolism requires reformulation, there will be obvious consequences for the civil religion, consequences perhaps of liberal alienation and of fundamentalist ossification that have not so far been prominent in this realm. The civil religion has been a point of articulation between the profoundest commitments of the Western religious and philosophical tradition and the common beliefs of ordinary Americans. It is not too soon to consider how the deepening theological crisis may affect the future of this articulation.

[...]

NOTE

This chapter was written for a *Daedalus* conference on American Religion in May 1966. It was reprinted with comments and a rejoinder in *The Religious Situation: 1968*, where I defend myself against the accusation of supporting an idolatrous worship of the American nation. I think it should be clear from the text that I conceive of the central tradition of the American civil religion not as a form of national self-worship but as the subordination of the nation to ethical principles that transcend it and in terms of which it should be judged. I am convinced that every nation and every people come to some form of religious self-understanding whether the critics like it or not. Rather than simply denounce what seems in any case inevitable, it seems more responsible to seek within the civil religious tradition for those critical principles which undercut the everpresent danger of national self-idolization.

1   Why something so obvious should have escaped serious analytical attention is in itself an interesting problem. Part of the reason is probably the controversial nature of the subject. From the earliest years of the nineteenth century, conservative religious and political groups have argued that Christianity is, in fact, the national religion. Some of them have from time to time and as recently as the 1950s proposed constitutional amendments that would explicitly recognize the sovereignty of Christ. In defending the doctrine of separation of church and state, opponents of such groups have denied that the national polity has, intrinsically, anything to do with religion at all. The moderates on this issue have insisted that the American state has taken a permissive and indeed supportive attitude toward religious groups (tax exemption, et cetera), thus favoring religion but still missing the positive institutionalization with which I am concerned. But part of the reason this issue has been left in obscurity is certainly due to the peculiarly Western concept of "religion" as denoting a single type of collectivity of which an individual can be a member of one and only one at a time. The Durkheimian notion that every group has a religious dimension, which would be seen as obvious in southern or eastern Asia, is foreign to us. This obscures the recognition of such dimensions in our society.

40

Shamanic Practices and the State in Northern Asia: Views from the Center and Periphery

Caroline Humphrey

Caroline Humphrey is a distinguished professor of anthropology at Cambridge University where she has founded and directed the Mongolia and Inner Asia Studies Unit. She has extensive research experience in Central Asia, among Buryats and Mongols especially, as well as in Nepal and Rajasthan. In addition to her contributions to religion (Humphrey 1996, Humphrey and Laidlaw 1994) she is the author of two books on a Siberian collective farm and the editor of many works on economic anthropology, the environment, and post-Soviet life in Asia.

In this essay Humphrey counters an old but still popular image of a supposedly "pure" version of shamans and shamanism with a much more dynamic picture. Humphrey shows the diverse historical manifestations of Central Asian and Siberian shamanism and links these closely to changing political contexts, especially to the ways in which shamanistic practice has both articu-lated with the rise of states and empires and continued long after their demise. Concomitantly, she analyzes the distinc-tive practices found at the centres and the peripheries of Asian states. She offers a sound rebuke to ahistorical, idealist, and essentializing portraits of shamans and provides insights into the workings of state power as well as its imagination in historical memory. Humphrey's essay offers a valuable example of the way the anthropological method and holistic vision can show dis-tinctive patterns across a vast span of space and time and yet remain true to particulars.

The original essay contains three sec-tions, covering, respectively, the found-ing of the Mongol state in the 13th century, events at the court of the Manchu (Qing) state (1644–1911), and recent practices among Daur Mongols. For reasons of space I have had to omit the middle section as well as many of the footnotes.

From Caroline Humphrey, "Shamanic Practices and the State in Northern Asia: Views from the Center and Periphery," in Nicholas Thomas and Caroline Humphrey, eds., *Shamanism, History, and the State* (Ann Arbor: University of Michigan Press, 1994), pp. 191–228. Abridged.

Northern Asia[1] is the region where it is generally supposed that "classic shamanism" used to exist, where shamans in elaborate costume went into trances, mastered spirits, journeyed to other worlds, and retrieved the souls of the dead. A compelling ideal type of Siberian shamanism, defined by the idea of ecstatic ascent to a celestial supreme being, was popularized by Eliade ([1951] 1964) and has been used by countless other authors as a point of comparison for their own regions. In constructing his concept of "shamanism in the strict and proper sense," Eliade turned the inspirational religious practices of north Asia into a timeless mystery. Peoples, of whom no description whatsoever is given, and at no particular date, are cited as providing examples of this or that aspect of shamanism, as though shamanism were some metaphysical entity making its presence felt despite history and societies; it was assumed that only a prototypical form of shamanism located in remote prehistorical antiquity was genuine. Eliade therefore wrote that "nowhere in the world or in history will a perfectly 'pure' and 'primordial' religious phenomenon be found" (1964: 11).

This chapter takes the view that, although shamanic practices are undoubtedly very ancient in north Asia, it is not helpful to search for some Eliadean original Ur-model, because inspirational religious practices have never been independent of context. Rather, they should be seen as reactive and constitutive in relation to other forms of power, and this may be a means by which we can understand, in a broad regional context, their character at given places and periods, and their transformations through history. Such a perspective implies at least two departures from earlier methodology. We should try to discover what shamans do and what powers they are thought to have, rather than crystallize out a context-free model derived from the images they may or may not use (mystic flight, a celestial supreme being, the world mountain, the cosmic tree, the bird-soul, and so on). Following from this, instead of defining only some specialists as true shamans, which is usually done on the basis of the ritual use of such imagery, it is necessary to look at the entire range of inspirational practice, including that of political leaders and ritual practitioners not usually considered to be shamans. Shamanic imagery does not form a coherent system, still less an ideology. It is a collection of representations, parts of which appear here and there in the cultures of the region, and these pieces can be used by anyone in a variety of ways (in rituals, songs, dreaming, prophesy, mythic genealogy, and clan and state ceremonial, as well as in the trance performances usually considered to be shamanic). The use of such imagery does not separate out a particular class of specialist shamans. Nor does it distinguish performative from liturgical ritual, or either of these from everyday contexts. In what follows, the term *shaman* is used for the specialists called by equivalent words in native languages, and *shamanism* refers to their practices and beliefs. But as I hope will become clear, this term is not meant to define a single category.

Leaving the category shaman rather open [. . .] is deliberate. It allows us to avoid focusing on one type of inspirational religious specialist in societies that have several and categorize them differently. More important, it is intended to signal a change in perspective, namely, the rejection of static models in favor of an understanding of shamanism as discourse.[2] This allows us to see shamanism as constitutive of social realities in contexts of power, and to anticipate, rather than be puzzled by, its multiplicities, contradictions, and changes of content, in different historical situations.

[. . .]

This chapter argues that shamanism has not always been in contradiction with the state: different manifestations of shamanic practice may support or undermine political authority and may even emerge from the core of the state. We need to know more about the purpose of shamanizing (the interests of its practitioners) and the forms of power at issue before useful generalizations can be made. I suggest here, using the example of twelfth- and thirteenth-century Mongols, that inspirational practices were deeply implicated in the formation of Inner Asian states.[3] Even after such states were bureaucratized and their ritual made liturgical, "the marginal" was still necessary for the legitimation and identity of the center, just as the imperial court was for the self-definition of the peoples on the periphery. Shamanic and inspirational practices were contexts for the making of such links. The example used here is the last of the inner Asian states that took power in China, the Manchu Qing Dynasty (1644–1911), in which the imperial family and court retained a quasi-shamanist cult until the twentieth century. This chapter is only a preliminary sketch in an area that requires more research, but I suggest here that the character and social importance of such shamanic practices may have varied, depending not only on stance or point of view of the actors (center, periphery) but on what one might call the political phase of the state (foundation, consolidation, decline).

Shamanism has changed over these centuries or, to be more precise, the aims of inspirational specialists and therefore the content of their practices have responded to the different configurations of power in changing historical circumstances. I suggest that during the formation of the Mongol state, when political power was very much up for grabs, shamanic practitioners entered the fray with a characteristic discourse of prophesy and interpreting omens, often using the imagery of natural events (hailstorms that would defeat an enemy and the like). After a state had been consolidated, taking the Manchus as an example, we find prophecy retreating in significance, to be replaced by discourse concerned primarily with interpersonal power and identity. In this kind of discourse, preoccupations with kinship, ancestry, and geography colored the traditional cosmic imagery of shamanism, and I will show that it had different registers in the center and periphery of the Manchu state. I do not suggest that there was a total transformation of shamanism over the centuries. Rather, these kinds of discourse represent possibilities, which were actualized in different circumstances as the energies and interests of shamans engaged with particular situations of power. Shamanism in north Asia seems to preserve memory traces of previously active discourse in the form of archaisms that might be revivified. Research on the history of shamanism in north Asia is exceedingly patchy. If more information emerges in the future, it may be possible

to investigate whether archaic and latent elements in shamanism can be related to the cyclical aspects of the sequence of polities in the hinterlands of China and Russia.

North Asia: States, Societies, and Religions

In the late nineteenth and early twentieth centuries, which is the period from which most of Eliade's materials derived, a synchronic picture of northern inner Asia would look as follows. Two great empires, the Russian and the Chinese, governed the entire region, using various forms of direct and indirect rule. The vast inner hinterland was occupied by peoples one could call in some sense marginalized: Xalx Mongols, Buryats, various Tungus groups, Daur, Barga, Manchu, Uriangxai, and many others. The Manchus, who had governed the Chinese Empire since the seventeenth century, were by this time socially divided. A sinicized elite lived in Peking and in various regimental Banner garrisons, and Manchu peasant farmers and hunters continued to live in the forested margins of the northeast. In the Russian and Manchu empires, there were a host of subpolities of various kinds, ranging from quite elaborate princedoms and monastic fiefdoms in Mongolia, through petty chiefdoms and tribal systems, to simple clan-based societies living by hunting, fishing, and reindeer herding. Buddhism of the Tibetan Lamaist monastic kind dominated in the princedoms. Institutionally, shamanic practice reached its heights of elaboration in the relatively wealthy, yet disunited, tribal societies of the steppe-forest borderlands, such as the western Buryats or the peoples of the Altai. By contrast, shamanism was simpler in hunter-fisher societies and in the princedoms dominated by Lamaism, where it was virtually eliminated in some places.

The geographical extent and social influence of Buddhism and shamanism varied through history. Put simply, the accepted picture is as follows. The Inner Asian states were built up in a context of shamanism. Once a ruling dynasty had been established, it introduced and propagated Buddhism (together with a cult of imperial ancestors). Shamanism was pushed to the margins and interstices. With the collapse of these states, Buddhism retreated, and shamanic practices, which had never entirely disappeared, reemerged. This accepted view requires some further thought if we accept that shamanism was not a particular kind of object to be pushed around but a fluid set of attitudes and practices that had a part in forming many different contexts of social life.

The devolution, or more accurately the disintegration, of Inner Asian states in this region is well documented. It is not always realized what follows from this, that many of the tribal peoples of Eliade's time had been imperial rulers some centuries before. The Mongols are the most famous of these. There also are the examples of the Khitans and Jurchens, the ruling elites of the Liao (tenth through twelfth centuries) and Jin (twelfth and thirteenth centuries) empires respectively, whose descendants became the impoverished peripheral tribes of early twentieth-century ethnography. Such imperial antecedents were not entirely forgotten. There were occasional attempts to revive past glories, and in the seventeenth century, the scattered Jurchen tribes of Manchuria succeeded. Their leader, Nurgaci, assembled a powerful union of tribes, which he declared to be a new dynasty, the Later Jin. His successor, Hong Taiji, renamed the Jurchens as Manchus and the dynasty as the Qing, but in the process of formalization of Manchu imperial legitimacy, there was insistence on reference to the ancestral Jin dynasty, even in the eighteenth century (Crossley 1987: 761–90).
[...]
Although the Chinese and the peoples of the hinterland were culturally very different, one idiom of the legitimation of political power linked them. This idiom was a concept of heaven (or more simply the sky) as the all-encompassing principle of cosmic order and human destiny. The various peoples under discussion had different understandings of heaven – it could be seen as a single whole, as a family, as two warring camps, and as a vertically layered series of skies – but every single group in the region at all periods had some idea of

this kind. The essential political idea was that of the ruler on earth who governed and succored his people by virtue of the destiny accorded by heaven. This is important in a heroic state organized by hierarchical solidarity: for the military hero's family to rule over every and any other people, it was required to have an all-encompassing divine legitimation. Inscriptions of the Eastern Turkic (seventh and eighth centuries) and Mongol (twelfth through fourteenth centuries) states refer to the "good fortune" of the emperor, and this good fortune was to be destined by heaven to rule, which was manifested by military victory.

A claim by shamans that they are able to ascend to the sky, or otherwise to know the will of heaven, is a politically highly charged matter. Eliade's concept of an Ur-shamanism, based on the idea of the shaman's ascent to celestial abodes, looks rather different when it is realized that this very ability was contested by political leaders. It seems that claims by shamans to communicate with the sky (or skies) occurred only in particular historical circumstances, because this was in effect a politically significant act giving access to information about the fate of human actions. After consolidation of the state, unsupervised shamans specializing in such a regular practice are found exclusively in safe backwaters, far from centers of imperial power.

Varieties of Shamanism

Everything I have written above would suggest that any particular instance of shamanism is not more than that and cannot be seen as characterizing shamanic discourse in general. However, it is possible to say something about the place of shamanism in the religious life of the region as a whole and to posit the existence of recurrent varieties of shamanism.

In no society of Inner Asia, including even the smallest tribe, was trance shamanism all that was going on in religious life. This fact is not always realized and the impression has been created by some authors using secondary or tertiary sources that there were many societies in the region where the shaman was the moral, spiritual, and ritual center of all religious life (see, for example, I. M. Lewis 1971). If we look more closely at the small peoples of south Siberia in the early twentieth century, we find that shamans took no part *as shamans* in several major rituals of social reproduction, and in many cases they were specifically excluded. For example, shamans were not allowed to attend the mountain cults of the Daur in the Hailar region, and they were excluded from the great bear-festivals of the Ul'chei, Nivkh, and Orochen. In the case of the Hailar Daurs, this can be explained by the fact that the mountain cult had been taken over by Buddhist lamas acting as priests for local political leaders, and lamas were notoriously jealous of shamans, but in other regions there was no trace of Lamaism, so we must look for some other explanation.

At this period in the Inner Asian hinterland, society, to be outrageously brief, was the object of two kinds of representation of social reproduction. One was focused on the continuation of patrilineal clans or feudal subpolities as ongoing, homogenous corporations, standing above the lives of the individuals comprising them at any one time. The second focused on biological reproduction, sexuality, and gender difference. The continuance of society was represented as a matter of achieving births and overcoming death, through metamorphosis and rebirth. Shamanism could be involved in both these kinds of representation, but it did not assume an exclusively dominant position in either of them. Both were contested areas where shamans (or more generally, inspirational practitioners) had to struggle for preeminence among other contenders.

The analyst can posit two varieties of shamanism that were engaged in the construction of these conflicting views of social reproduction (though it should be stressed that these varieties were not native categories and are introduced here only for explanatory purposes). One may be termed "patriarchal," because it concerned shamanic involvement in the symbolic reproduction of the patrilineal lineage, clan, or polity. The conceptual constructs and metaphors tended to be vertical or hierarchical, but not exclusively so. This version focused on sky-spirits (often called "father"), which were the cause of good

fortune, life-giving rain, and successful destinies. The cults were accompanied by games and festivities to promote virility and strength. Shamanic practices involved divination, offering, sacrifice, and prayer, and these forms of communication with supranatural forces meant that shamans did not transform themselves into other beings and that they used trance mainly to "call down" spirits to receive offerings. In this ritual arena, shamans were often subordinate to or replaced by elders of clans or Buddhist lamas. However, when chiefs and elders were politically weak and demoralized, as among the colonized Buryats in the nineteenth century, local leaders would hope to be recognized as shamans, too, because this would add to their efficacy in clan rituals.

The other variety of shamanism can be called "transformational." It operated by participation in all the forces thought to be immanent in the world (in natural physical entities, animals, humans, and manufactured things). Shamans were defined by their possession of some of these powers and their ability to become the vessel or embodiment of others. The trance was the means by which such manifestations of power took place. Gender and other kinds of difference were the separate sources of energies that had to be made manifest and that had to be negotiated and balanced to restore harmony to the world. Rituals were performance-centered, rather than liturgy-centered (see Atkinson 1989; Humphrey and Laidlaw, 1994). Shamanic practices included exorcism, substitution (of one energy by another), bribery, exchange, and the luring and entrapment of spirits. It might be thought that this context, which recognized biological difference, would be the undisputed terrain of shamanism, but this was not invariably so. Shamans could be undercut here by midwives, curers, casters-of-spells, and others attributed with magical powers. Furthermore, in northern Manchuria and eastern Mongolia, there were cults concerned with female fertility and child development that had their own special practitioners, who were not called by native terms for shaman, even though they often used trance. The cults may have had a Chinese origin, but they existed far beyond Han settlement areas. They became part of native cultures and took over aspects of religious activity that elsewhere were carried out by shamans.

The various inspirational practices called shamanism should be seen as intervening in religious life, as struggling to construct meaningful parts of it, rather than as simply being it. These contests were waged in different ways, from the parole of individual shamans in competition with one another, to what we may call registers of comparatively stable local discourse. I use the term *register* in an extended sense to include types of shamanic language, imagery, and practice manifest in particular contexts of political discourse. [. . .] Shamanic registers seem to be relatively short-lived, even if they contain archaic elements that might some day be revived. Nevertheless, these localized and time-specific registers of discourse can tell us something about how shamanism has interacted with the state and smaller polities.

Inspirational Practices and the Founding of the Mongol State

In the twelfth century in the region now called Mongolia, aristocratic warriors and their followers made sacrifices to heaven (*tenggri*), sending up animals' souls and praying for *tenggri's* blessing (Munkuyev 1975; Bese 1986). Exclusion from such rituals had political significance, as can be seen from the episode in the thirteenth-century *Secret History of the Mongols* (par. 70), in which Temujin's (the young Chinggis Khan's) mother was turned away from a sacrifice, which marked the start of the long-lasting war between her group and the Taychiut. Temujin started out as poverty-stricken and cold-shouldered by other Mongols, though he had illustrious forbears. With increasing power, the military leader became patron of sacrifices on behalf of ever-widening conglomerations of people. The will of heaven was evident from success, such as a military victory or accession to the khanship. Discovering heaven's will before an endeavor became a matter of crucial concern. It appears that certain people claimed privileged access to heaven and that others declared that they

received signs, but there is not clear evidence from Mongol sources of the existence of professional shamans at this early period. There are several Mongol accounts of the will of heaven being revealed by warriors, such as Qorchi, who exacted a price for his favorable omen.[4]

Because later, non-Mongol sources have described shamans among the Mongols, the literature on the period has generally identified some personages from the *Secret History* as shamans. The most famous of these is Kokochu, son of the military leader Munglig of the Qongqotan clan, a close ally who had saved Chinggis's life. The Persian historian Rashid-al-Din wrote of him:

> His habit was such that he uncovered secrets and fortold future events and he said, "God talks to me, and I visit the sky!" . . . In the heart of winter in Onan-Keluren, which is the coldest of those countries, it was his custom to sit naked in the middle of a frozen river, and from the heat of his body the ice would melt and steam would rise from the water. (Rashid-al-Din 1952, 1: 167)

Kokochu came to Chinggis Khan and told him, "God willed it that you be the master of the world," and he also gave Temujin the title Chinggis Khan, saying, "God willed it that you be called this" (Rashid-al-Din 1952, 1 (1): 167). According to a later Mongolian source, Chinggis invited this same Kokochu, now entitled *arsi*, "sage," to meet him on the southern slope of a snowy mountain, and Chinggis,

> having asked him the manner in which one might support and hold the government and how one might protect and support living beings, and having praised him approvingly, conferred upon him the title Teb Tenggri. [. . .] (quoted in Cleaves 1967: 254)

So the warrior-king Chinggis and the "shaman" Teb Tenggri respectfully conferred titles on one another. But soon they fell out. This is not surprising when we realize, from separate, non-Mongol sources, that Chinggis was able to discover the will of heaven himself. He seems to have been as inspirationally able as the legendary Teb Tenggri. An Islamic history records of Chinggis:

He was adept in magic and deception, and some of the devils were his friends. Every now and then he used to fall into a trance, and in that state of insensibility all sorts of things used to proceed from his tongue, and that state of trance used to be similar to that which happened to him at the onset of his rise, and the devils which had power over him foretold his victories. The tunic and clothes which he had on and wore on the first occasion were placed in a trunk and he was wont to take them along with him. Whenever this inspiration came over him, every circumstance – victories undertakings, the appearance of enemies, the defeat and reduction of countries – anything which he might desire, would all be uttered by his tongue. A person used to take the whole down in writing and enclose it in a bag and place a seal upon it, and when Chinggis Khan came to his senses again, they used to read his utterances over to him one by one, and according to these he would act, and more or less, indeed, the whole used to come true. (Boyle 1977, 22: 181)

[. . .]

In the end, Chinggis's desire for uncontrovertible control of the heroic polity necessitated a decisive defeat of Teb Tenggri. The final falling-out came when Teb Tenggri declared that heaven had willed that Chinggis's younger brother Qasar could well soon succeed him as khan. Upon hearing this, Chinggis immediately set out to capture Qasar, but he was stopped by his mother, who was outraged at this unbrotherly act. By this time, Teb Tenggri had attracted to his Qongqotan group a great many followers, including some of Chinggis's people, and furthermore, he insulted the emissary sent to get them back. For this, Chinggis had his stalwarts put Teb Tenggri to death by breaking his back.

With all the obfuscation of ecstasy and so on that surrounds the topic of shamanism, it is instructive to note the matter-of-factness of the Mongol account of Teb Tenggri in the *Secret History*. It is baldly recorded that he knew heaven's will, and that three days after his death, he ascended bodily through the smoke-hole of the tent in which his corpse had been left (*S.H.*, par. 246). Nothing is made of the supernatural aspect of these events. The

Mongols were practical people, and they wanted to know what really would happen. In the end the text indicates that Teb Tenggri was someone who made one prophecy too many. He and his Qongqotan group had attempted to destablize the khan's supremacy. Of the ascent through the smoke-hole, the classic shaman's move, Chinggis says flatly, "Because Teb Tenggri laid hands and feet on my brothers and spread baseless slander among my younger brothers, he was not loved by Heaven, and his life – as well as his body – has been taken and sent away." After Chinggis had disposed of Teb Tenggri, we read, "The morale of the Qongqotan was withered" (*S.H.*, par. 246; Onon 1990: 139–40).

All this suggests that at the turn of twelfth and thirteenth centuries, when Chinggis was in the process of building up his state, inspirational practices, particularly prophecy, were part of the activity of the war leaders themselves. The stakes were high and the activity dangerous. Get it right and the rewards could be great, as they were for Qorchi (see n. 4); but prophecies that went against the turn of power incurred the risk of death and political defeat. In the heroic polity, the psychological power of shamans over individuals at the center was refracted outward, through the familial structure of the state itself, so that it came to have incalculable influence at large. Other quasi-inspirational practices involved symbolizing the concept of the political center, as can be seen in the role of the "many-leaved tree," an image that recurs sporadically in patriarchal variants of shamanism. The *Secret History* is overwhelmingly practical in tone. It emphasizes Chinggis's military strength, justice, and respect for loyalty. It does not mention his prophetic trances. The will of heaven really appears in it only as another factor to be taken into account. This matter-of-factness perhaps also reflects the nature of the *Secret History* as a source: it was written in the mid-thirteenth century, after Chinggis's death, as a history of the Mongolian imperial line. By that time it would not have been appropriate to represent the emperors as themselves straining to know heaven's will, because by attaining their very status as world conquerors, they had proved it to be in their favor.

The confident assumption of acting by the mandate of heaven is written in numerous Mongol edicts of the generations subsequent to Chinggis. Not only is Chinggis presented in the *Secret History* as inevitably fulfilling the pursuit of pure power, but after he had removed the only rival who was both a shaman and a political leader, shamanic discourse could no longer be *the* discourse of the state. It was no longer appropriate to find out about something that had to seem evident (the imperial destiny).

Nevertheless, there is abundant evidence of a variety of shamanic involvement in lesser issues during subsequent reigns. Apparently the Mongol successors to Chinggis never set out on a campaign without consulting diviners, and they predicted lucky and unlucky days for all undertakings. The Persian historian Juvaini says that the Mongols would have returned to attack Hungary if the diviners had allowed it (Boyle 1977, 5: 340). Persian and European visitors mention shamanic healers, called *kam* (*shaman* in Turkic languages). The Mongols also made models as vessels for the spirits, which they kept in their tents (Vitebsky 1974), and used magical stones for producing rain and storms at strategic moments, both of which are practices known from later shamanism (Mikhailov 1987: 32–6). Mongol shamans held séances, closed to outsiders, at which they went into trances and invoked spirits. The *Secret History* contains many passages suggesting metaphorical thinking of the kind characteristic of transformational shamanism. A range of practices broadly similar to later shamanic activities were present in Mongol society during the Yuan dynasty, though they had less raw political import than at the time of the formation of the state.

[...] After the murder of Teb Tenggri, Chinggis avoided giving clear precedence to any particular religious practitioners. He toyed with the merits of various religions, inviting monks and priests to compete in disputations. However, in subsequent generations, the Mongol emperors mainly patronized Buddhism, as the rulers of earlier "barbarian" empires had done before them. A series of chosen high lamas, who came to be seen as giving religious legitimation to the ruler-patron, were given the title *bagshi*.

[...] I hope that I have provided enough evidence here to show that during the rise of the Mongol state, there was a distinct register of shamanic discourse, involving prophesy, omens, and other interventions that affected the outcome of political events. It seems to have been relatively spontaneous and unritualized. This high prophetic discourse may well have existed alongside other kinds of inspirational practice. After the empire was established, it seems to have been replaced by a very different register, which was ritualized, even liturgical, and backward-looking.

[...]

In the Manchu State: A View from the Periphery

The Manchu state, like the Mongol one before it, energetically promoted the Tibetan form of Buddhism, though in this case not so much for the court itself as for the Mongols and other people of the hinterland whom it was hoped to pacify. But many peoples on the periphery, including the Daurs, the various Tungus tribes, and the Manchus themselves in some rural areas, remained shamanist. How did they imagine the state? The following material comes from present-day Daurs of the older generation.

The Daurs are a Mongolian-speaking agriculturalist people, but they separated from other Mongol groups probably even before the Yuan dynasty. From Chinese sources, we know that the Daurs descend from people who were rulers in the Liao confederacy. But they do not remember this. They have stories about how they had writing and lost it, but historical memory goes back only as far as the seventeenth century, when they fled from Russian incursions on the Amur and were incorporated into the Manchu banners. In the early twentieth century, the localized banner units, which did not include all males, were crosscut by the still vital clans that mapped society. There were many ways in which such peoples related shamanically to the state. I do not want to give the impression that there was just one form of shamanic reaction to state power, or within one people just one way of thinking about it, but for reasons of space, only one case is given here.

Among the Daurs, as among the rural Manchus, the patriarchal kind of shamanism was regarded as secondary. It was centered on the *oboo*, the mountain cairn that was the site of propitiation of land spirits. These rituals were served by the *bagchi*, who was otherwise employed as a minor diviner and assistant to the main shaman. Each localized clan had its own *oboo*, where the clan chief ordered rituals at irregular intervals, when a drought threatened. There were also banner *oboos* set up by the state and banner authorities. This whole cult and its terminology was male (women and *yadgan* shamans were excluded). It was regarded as not very important: the Daurs were successful farmers, there was plenty of land, and the rains did not often fail.

Spiritual power was manifest in another kind of Daur shaman, the *yadgan* (or *shaman*). The *yadgan* could be either male or female, though most of them were men. They were regarded as infinitely more powerful than the *bagchis*. *Yadgans* were "chosen" by spirits; experienced initiatory death and rebirth; were capable of mastering spirits, transforming them from one kind to another, and renewing their powers; and were able to travel to the "other world" to rescue souls. Most of their activity was concerned with curing people of physical and psychological troubles, but they also held a complex ritual every few years for the revitalization of the relation between society and the entire range of spirits. There were two kinds of *yadgan*, those called clan shamans (that is, those whose helper spirits were clan ancestors), and those who were independent (that is, their spirits came to them nonlineally, through women, and in other ways). There were also female shamans called *otoshi* who had charge of a group of spirits concerned with childbirth, growth, and certain diseases. All these kinds of shaman were similar in that they operated in what I have called the transformational mode. On the periphery, when the empire had been long since bureacratized and distanced, the divinatory and patriarchal activities so important

when the state was being fought for and established, faded into relative insignificance, and the creative transformational variant of shamanism flourished even to the extent of taking over the sphere of clan ancestry.

The state was represented in two major ways in Daur shamanism. One can most simply be translated as "hell" – that is, as a cosmological vision, located underground, the world of the dead, which people called *ukel-un gurun* (the empire of death). This state was reachable by going down through the bottom of wells or through caves. When already underground, one had to cross a river, rowed by a lame boatman, and then to penetrate through the encircling walls, where the gatehouses were guarded by fearsome soldiers. Once inside, there were palaces and prisons, multistory buildings with glass windows, towers, barracks, and cities. The light was dim and yellowish. The state had a ruler, Ilmu-Khan, who was surrounded by numerous ministers and scribes. In the registers of Ilmu-Khan were written the destinies, the years of life, and the numbers of children of all people and animals in the living world. Ilmu-Khan was a just judge: he put the souls of the dead in prisons or gave them other punishments, or he allowed them to be reborn in the world. Animals and all living creatures could take their cases to him for judgment. From him or one of his subordinates, the shaman had to beg for renewed life for a dead soul.

This vision of the underworld as an urbanized state is undoubtedly influenced by Buddhism, particularly the idea of punishment for misdeeds in this world. It is part of a vertical cosmology, though one in which heaven is not visualized as a city or called *gurun* (state or empire). The sky (*tengger*) was imagined in layer after layer, vanishing into ethereal nothingness; it was personalized as one all-seeing, benevolent, universal "father"; or, at the most elaborate, it was seen as peopled by a kingly family of *tenggris*, with other sky-beings (*enduri*) floating on clouds and with dragons rippling in the far distance.

Stories about shamanism (for example, the epic of Nisan Saman, which was popular among all the rural peoples of Manchuria) often use this statelike image of the world of the dead. But as far as we can tell, Daur shamans did not operate with this vision, which was indeed explicitly repudiated by some people because of its alien preoccupation with cause and effect, whereby the soul becomes enmeshed in the results of previous actions. In shamanism, they maintained, action is free and is the manifestation of one's nature. In shamans' songs, which are not about shamanism but an active part of its practice, the "other world" seems to be the unseen powers of this world; the state is the Manchu dynasty in actions it never knew it undertook. This shift has the effect of horizontalizing the cosmology.[5] The "road" or "way" of the spirit becomes essential. The path between this world and the other is along a river or is represented as a transversal of real, named, geographical places. The spirits are envisaged not only, or even primarily, as ancestors: they include Tiger Spirit, Fox Spirit, birds, numerous female spirits, and Town Spirits (*xoton barkan*), who possessed soldiers in barracks. In the concept of ancestry, the Daurs were midway between the urban Manchus, who drew in diverse spiritual forces and had long since absorbed them with the human ancestors, and the Tungus peoples, who acknowledged the fleeting powers of the existential world in numberless spirits, among whom ancestors were relatively insignificant. This cosmological difference in emphasis may be related to the extent to which these peoples were actually engaged/disengaged with perpetuating state structures,[6] though it may just reflect the degree to which they were influenced by the Chinese cult of ancestors.

That a given spirit is called an ancestor tells us that the people see something of themselves in it, and we then need to know what this idea of ancestor contains. For the urban Manchus, ancestors were names on a written, though secret, list. For the nonliterate, rural Daurs, ancestry as imagined in shamanism had an extraordinary shattering violence. There were several multiple ancestor spirits. The main one, which was the earliest and therefore was ancestor to everyone, was Holieli, often called *Da Barkan* (the "great deity").[7] People made images of his spirit, which they kept in a box in their houses. It consisted, in the best known

example, of fifty-eight separate parts: bald monsters, nine-headed monsters, half-people, single legs, left-side cripples and right-side cripples, some different kinds of turtle and tortoise, a leather softener, nine fishes, a hunting gun, a dragon, and nine dancing boys and nine dancing girls.

There are many versions of the story of this spirit, and the components of the images also vary. In a *story* of the Nonni River Daurs, the Holieli ancestor is an antelope that emerged from a rock split asunder by lightning. It ran straight to Senyang, where it began to harass the people. The Manchu government had it seized, placed in a bag of cow leather, and thrown into the river. It drifted down the river till it met the flood dragon, where the bag burst on the dragon's horn. The antelope pushed its way out of the bag, gained the bank, and once more began to harass the people. The Manchu court again had it seized, placed in a bag, loaded on a horse, and sent off. The horse followed its nose to the Amur River, where it was captured by a tribe of strange Tungus. They thought there must be something very nice in the bag and opened it. The antelope leapt out and took to the forests. It was chased by the lightning, which struck and struck, and many creatures were killed, but the deer escaped by sheer luck. It got to the Nonni River, near the Eyiler and Bitai villages. A man was ploughing. When the antelope spirit ran beside the man, there was a great crash of thunder, and everything was smashed into ninety-nine pieces. Since then, the antelope's spirit and those of all the people and animals killed by lightning joined forces for haunting and possessing people. First, it was worshiped by the Tungus, and then it was recognized as a spirit by the Manchu court, people say (*Daur. Soc. Hist.* 244).

In a shaman's *song* for Holieli, the ancestor is smashed to pieces by lightning and becomes the half-people and crippled people. It starts from the end of the earth, which is at the source of the Ergune River. It is an old man, then it becomes a fish, traveling down the Jinchili River, gathering as it goes all the people of the clans and all kinds of animals. Its aim is the southern sea, the entourage of the Dalai Lama (*dalai* means ocean in Mongol). It raids the city of Peking and occupies the seat of orthodoxy. It is a loud voice yelling in the palace. It is given a jade throne, a pearl resting-place. From there it begins its journeys again, crossing all borders, passing through all boundaries; it reaches the Daur and becomes hidden in the plow-blade of the farmer. Again it is honored by the people. It is in its original place. It is given a two-dragon throne on the western wall of the house and offerings – all kinds of silks, damasks, and satins. In a robe of grass, it tramples on the clean satins. Again it seems to set out on its metamorphic journey. The song continues:

Where the rivers flow together
Where they flow down is a dug-out canoe,
The Tungus who live in the dense forest
Kill the boar and are skilfull master-hunters.
[It is] the tracks they do not find,
The footprints they do not see,
The gold-colored tortoise,
The silver-colored frog,
A buzzing biting wasp,
A creeping spider,
The wriggling lizards and snakes,
The sound of a shaken bell,
A cuckoo calling loudly,
The leopard growling,
The huge and fearless wild boar . . .
(*Daur. Soc. Hist.* 248–9)

The ancestor in a sense becomes the spirit-emperor, masterfully transcending the etiquette of the court and the boundaries of the empire. Effortlessly, it swims as a fish to the palace, where it yells; unhindered, it returns to the Daur. It cannot be pinned down: it is manifest both in the domestic sphere of the plough and the house and in the wilderness of the forests, where the best hunters cannot see it.

The ancestor Holieli has many powers because it has many transformations. It does not have all powers perhaps, because there are other spirits, with other metamorphoses. But specifically, it takes the power of the imperial ruler. Yet it seems that this is transcended by the idea of metamorphosis itself: the signs and marks of imperial rank are desecrated and abandoned as the spirit takes to the forest as a wasp, changes to a spider, and changes to the sound of a bell. In the practice of ordinary

Daurs, the pacification of this spirit, which caused very great harm and mental illness, involved furnishing its representation with imperial imagery (silk, dragons, special wood for the carved models, and so on). Shamans used to order people who had costly embroidered or damask clothing, the very means of imitating the courtly Manchus in real life, to offer them to this spirit. The spirit seems both a violent rejection of and a homage to the imperial state.

This spirit was considered a burden. Not all shamans could master it. The *bagchi* certainly could not, and he did no more than make small offerings. A *yadgan* was required for large sacrifices and the invocation of the spirit, and even so many felt themselves powerless before it. A story says that the people of the Dengteke clan near Hailar tried unsuccessfully to get rid of it because the sacrifices of cattle it demanded were so burdensome. They threw the box of images in the river, but it would not move, and soon the young men and women began to suffer nervous disorders.

My interpretation of this is that Holieli Barkan represents a forgotten and repressed imperial past. I am not borrowing the term repressed from psychoanalytic theory but using it in an attempt to explain a Daur idea. Perhaps punished would be a better term. The striking of the ancestor by lightning means, according to Daurs, the anger of heaven. This is the vision of those who know they are powerless, that they have not been born with the good fortune to rule. But in the semiforgotten past, the real ancestors of the Daurs were (or might have been) ruling peoples in the far off dynasties of the Liao and the Jin. The ancestor, or origin (Da *hujuur*, literally root), in Daur and Mongolian culture is a way of thinking about the self. There are many other spirits that are not thought of as ancestors. So in this case the Daurs in a sense are the smashed and dislocated people, half-people, monsters and limbs, and people who died and will take revenge unless placated, because those ancestors are what they came from. But at the same time, this spirit of Holieli Barkan survives and unites all the shattered parts. In the end, it is one spirit, not many, and it is like a wayward emperor and slips hither and thither and escapes from the bag in which the Manchu state tries to entrap it.

The imperial dynasty had recourse to the periphery in its attempt to define its identity and reaffirm its power. The people on the frontier, too, people who were not even Manchus, had at least one shamanic idiom of self-definition that spanned the distance between the village and the capital city in metaphors of effortless travel and self-transformation. It is a mistake to suppose that the practice of shamanism in face-to-face social groups limits its concerns to the local or restricts imagination.

Conclusion

Studies of north Asian shamanism have consistently ignored the ways in which it engages with politics, not simply politics in the narrow sense, but the power to have effect on the reproduction of particular forms of society. For millenia, north Asia has been a region of empires that ebbed and flowed over the land, but people here were not ignorant of hegemony, challenge, and independence, circumstances whose contours determined the kind of society in which one lived. For most of this history, the central interest was military, that is, war, not as an episode with a beginning and an end and interspersed with periods of peace, but as a permanent way of life necessary to reproduce the social group in the face of challenges from others. It is curious, therefore, that observers have noted how north Asian shamans dress like animals or birds but have generally ignored the more obvious ways in which the shaman is a warrior, wearing armor and bearing symbolic weapons. The shaman negotiates and fights with the spirit threats to the social group, even those conceived as ancestors. A shaman can do this in many ways: as an actor in the struggle for power, or, after the establishment of temporal powers, on their behalf, against them, or in some ambivalent relation to them.

In this chapter, I have tried to show how different aspects of shamanism took part in the rise and fall of north Asian states. It has not been possible to provide more than sketchy suggestions here, but my intention was to indicate a recognizably common stock of ritual activities, accompanied by a conglomeration of cosmological ideas, some of which are transmitted and acted out according to particular historical circumstances. Actual shamanism depends on the concerns of the participants, both patrons and shamans, and on the point of view from which they act. Although shamanism, being orally transmitted and performance-based, manifests its agency in small groups (the local clan, the village, the imperial court), there seems to be no justification for the idea that its interests or its view on the world are thereby confined or intrinsically archaic. It also does not seem right to attribute shamanism with one essential cosmological idea, such as the Eliadean ascent to celestial abodes, and then to say that this is distorted, hidden, or revealed according to the prevalence of outside influences. In shamanism, as the discussion has shown, "ancestry," "the other world," "the state," and indeed "heaven" (or "the sky"), are not invariant ideas; they do not take form or become concepts except from a particular standpoint. This is more the case for shamanism than with other religious phenomena, because shamanism is not so much reflection about the world as it is action on the world.

In the case of the rise of the Mongol state, we can perceive a visionary shamanism that denied or confirmed political action and whose interest and point of view was that of an actor and potential competitor. For this very reason, it had to be suppressed by the emergent supreme ruler. In the middle stages of the Manchu dynasty, the semipetrification of shamanic activity at the court did not prevent it from being deliberately sought as a solution for the regeneration of an empire in risky expansion. Just as the diverse spirits of nature were reassembled as "ancestors," the far-flung rituals of the "uncooked" peasants were diligently researched and brought to the capital as authentic links with all-powerful heaven. In the forested periphery of the empire, the Daurs enacted a shamanism that objectified and somehow made terrifying a historical sense of punishment, survival, and escape. Even here in the outback, the sense of self invoked in Daur ideas of ancestry was not localized and disengaged but vividly activated in the geographical distances and history of the state. Purists might say that only the last of these is "real shaman-ism," but it is more interesting to see it as one possibility, quite specific in time and place, and not unrelated to the others.

NOTES

1 This refers to Siberia, Mongolia, North-Western China, Manchuria, and the Altai.
2 I use this term in the broad sense of socially situated cultural practices employed by Foucault: "Discourses . . . [are] . . . practices that systematically form the objects of which they speak" (1972: 49).
3 This refers to the states that arose among the peoples of the inner Asian hinterland and later took power in China, not to the properly Han Chinese states. Thus, "inner Asian states" include the Liao Empire (946–1125) founded by the Khitan people, the Jin Empire (1115–1234) founded by the Jurchens, the Mongol Empire (1206–1368), and the Manchu Empire (1644–1911) [. . .]
4 In the *S.H.* (par. 121), when the quarrel between Temujin and Jamuqa threatened to split the confederacy, one of the commanders, Qorchi, made a prophesy. He said, "We would not have left Jamuqa, but a sign from heaven came to me." He reported that he had seen with his own eyes a yellowish-white ox harness itself to Temujin's tent-cart and pull it along, bellowing: "Heaven and Earth agree, let Temujin be the nation's master! Bearing the nation, I am bringing it to him!" Qorchi then asked Temujin what he would give for revealing this omen, and Temujin replied that if it really was like this and he became commander of the nation, he would give Qorchi ten thousand men. Qorchi replied that he wanted the freedom of the country's most beautiful women, too, and thirty of them to be made his wives. Later (par. 207), after Temujin has been made Chinggis Khan, he keeps his promise to Qorchi. This is a clear example of prophecy as politics by other means. Qorchi fixed the price of his allegiance, and the legitimacy provided by the omen may have significantly affected Temujin's chances.

5 More precisely, it had the effect of producing a horizontal version of the cosmology, which coexisted with the vertical one.
6 The Tungus hunters and reindeer-herders discussed by Shirokogoroff (1935) were outside the Manchu banner system and were called "wild" and "primitive" by such peoples as the Daurs. [. . .]
7 This spirit was also known among the various Tungus groups of northern Manchuria and south Siberia. Shirokogoroff classifies it as "non-ancestral" for the Tungus (1935: 150–53). It was known as Malu Burkan and was said to have come to its present worshipers from the Daurs, though it was of Tungus origin (the Daurs stole it from the Tungus and subsequently gave it back, but half of it did not want to leave and stayed with the Daurs). It is perhaps significant that the origin of Malu was thought to be the spirit of a specifically nonbannerman, "wild" Tungus. The separate parts of the spirit cause various diseases, including mental illness, listed by Shirokogoroff (1935: 151–52).

REFERENCES

Atkinson, J. 1989 *The Art and Politics of Wana Shamanship*. Berkeley: University of California Press.

Bese, Lajos. 1986 The shaman term *jukeli* in the *Secret History* of the Mongols, *Acta Orientalia* 40 (2–3): 241–8.

Boyle, J. A. 1977 *The Mongol World Empire: 1206–1370*. London: Variorum Reprints.

Cleaves, F. W. 1967 Teb Tenggeri. *Ural-Altaische Jahrbucher* 39.

Crossley, Pamela Kyle. 1987 Manzhou yuanliu kao and the formalization of the Manchu heritage. *Journal of Asian Studies* 46 (4): 761–90.

Eliade, Mircea. [1951] 1964 *Shamanism: Archaic Techniques of Ecstasy*. Trans.

William R. Trask. Reprint, Princeton, NJ: Princeton University Press.

Foucault, M. 1972 *The Archaeology of Knowledge and the Discourse on Language.* New York: Pantheon.

Humphrey, Caroline, and James Laidlaw. 1994 *The Archetypal Actions of Ritual.* Oxford: Oxford University Press.

Lewis, I. M. 1971 *Ecstatic Religion: An Anthropological Study of Spirit Possession and Shamanism.* Harmondsworth: Penguin Books.

Mikhailov, T. M. 1987 *Buryatskii Shamanizm: Istoriya, struktura i sotsial'nyye funktsii,* Novosibirsk: Nauka.

Munkuyev, N. Trans. 1975 *Men-Da Bei-Lu "Polnoye opisaniye mongolo-tatar."* Pamyatniki pis'mennosti vostoka 26. Moscow: Nauka.

Onon, Urgunge. 1990 *The History and the Life of Chinggis Khan.* Translation of *The Secret History of the Mongols.* Leiden: Brill.

Rashid-al-Din. 1952 *Sbornik letopisei,* I. Trans. O. I. Smirnova. Moscow-Leningrad: Akademiya Nauk.

—— 1954 *Sbornik letopisei,* I. Trans. L. A. Khetagurov. Moscow-Lenigrad: Akademiya Nauk.

Shirokogoroff, S. M. 1935 *The Psychomental Complex of the Tungus.* London: Kegan Paul, Trench, Trubner and Co.

Vitebsky, Piers. 1974 Some medieval European views on Mongolian shamanism. *Journal of the Anglo-Mongolian Society* 1 (1): 1–17.

41

"Using the Past to Negate the Present": Ritual Ethics and State Rationality in Ancient China

Mayfair Mei-hui Yang

Mayfair Yang is professor at the University of California, Santa Barbara. Her essay pursues the question of the relationship between state power, ritual, and public ethics. The excerpt is drawn from a larger and largely ethnographic study of China in the 1980s and 1990s, but usefully reminds us that historicity refers to far more than the colonial encounter and its aftermath and that the state's meddling in matters of ritual and ethics goes back to its origins several millennia ago. Yang provides a lucid account of aspects of Confucianism in historical and political context. Drawing implicitly on Weber's notion of ideal types, and illustrating what he called religious rationalization (here not as a feature of "modernity" but in the fifth and fourth centuries BCE!), she skillfully contrasts different relations of ritual or religion to the segmentary and bureaucratic state. Thus, where Bloch (chapter 32 above) emphasizes the mystification of the Merina state in contrast to an egalitarian nonstate society, Yang compares alternate models of the state as they succeeded each other in Chinese history, thereby helpfully showing that the relationship is not predetermined. She also illustrates how Confucianism has been used for different ends over the course of Chinese history as the tradition is reworked for successive political agendas – and yet always contains a residue of the past as a source of resistance to the present.

Ostensibly about ancient China, Yang's essay also draws its significance from more contemporary events and debate. Indeed, the subsequent chapter of her book provides a stimulating account of the Mao cult, drawing on recent theories of the subject as well as on Freud's arguments concerning mourning and melancholia.

From Mayfair Mei-hui Yang, "'Using the Past to Negate the Present': Ritual Ethics and State Rationality in Ancient China," in *Gifts, Favors and Banquets: The Art of Social Relationships in China* (Ithaca, NY: Cornell University Press, 1994 [1991]), pp. 216–44. Abridged.

A Reinterpretation of the Past

According to traditional Chinese historical sources, Confucius (ca. 550–479 B. C. E.) was born in the state of Lu in the Spring and Autumn period, an era that saw the beginnings of the collapse of an older sociopolitical order of hierarchical clan and lineage groupings and hereditary social strata. The emergence at this time of contending militaristic states, which no longer recognized the suzerainty of the royal Zhou clan, led directly to a period of turmoil later labeled appropriately, the Warring States period, and culminated in the unification of all China under a new centralized empire by the state of Qin, the most militaristic and powerful of the states. As a witness to the beginnings of these changes and social disorder, Confucius traveled from state to state as an itinerant philosopher preaching a way of life and a set of ethics to stem the tide of social disintegration. Several generations of his disciples helped record and transmit his teachings to posterity. Reference will be made here only to these early pre-Qin Rujia and not to the different Confucian traditions and commentaries of later imperial times.

Although the institution of written penal law codes can already be found toward the end of the sixth century B. C. E., the articulation of government by law and punishment did not become a coherent body of philosophy until later, with the emergence of Legalism in the Warring States. The Legalists themselves represented a very different response to that process of social disintegration and general state militarism which, although much more severe later on, had already begun in Confucius's lifetime. The implementation of Legalist doctrines and reforms were important, if not central, to the strengthening and ultimate victory of the state of Qin, which established the first unified imperial state system in China in 221 B. C. E. Although the Qin dynasty lasted only fifteen years, it laid the foundations for the centralized state system that operated in later dynasties all the way into the twentieth century. The two main Legalists referred to here are Shang Yang (390?–338 B.C.E.) and Han Feizi (280?–233? B.C.E.).

Government by kinship and government by the state

In the Rujia text *Analects* there is a passage in which Confucius is informed of the uprightness of a man who dutifully reported his father to the authorities for having stolen a sheep. Confucius replied, "Among us, in our part of the country, those who are upright are different from this. The father conceals the misconduct of the son, and the son conceals the misconduct of the father" (*Analects* 13.18; Legge 1961:270). A similar parable about another man who reported his father for stealing sheep is also found in the *Han Feizi*, a Legalist text, only in this version the man is executed by the authorities for being "loyal to the ruler but undutiful to his father." The Legalist response to the execution of this man, and Confucius's praise of the man who deserted the battlefield in order to take care of an old father, is to ask, "How can a state attain order and strength" when it upholds incompatible principles of filial piety and loyalty to the ruler (*Han Feizi* 1982: 670–1)? Although the examples here point to a line of disagreement between Confucian and Legalist discourses threaded throughout the texts of the two schools, their differences cannot be reduced to a mere matter of conflicting loyalties to one's father or to one's ruler. It will be more fruitful to examine the differences between them at the level of the general principles of government.

The early Rujia did not necessarily see the heavy stress they placed on kinship relations as being in opposition to loyalty to the state and the ruler, which they also upheld. Rather, they sought to improve government by realigning its principles of operation according to the correct roles, virtues, and mutual obligations of kinship relations, which include such elements as status distinction, affection, and obligation. Even the position of the dynastic ruler was to be embedded in kinship relations, to assume a paternal role with regard to the people, and that of a filial Son of Heaven (*tianzi*) who sacrifices to his ancestors and to

Heaven. Indeed, in Rujia discourse, the "state" was modeled on the family, and represented an extension of kinship principles, so that "[The rulers'] persons being cultivated, their families were regulated. Their families being regulated, their states were rightly governed. Their states being rightly governed, the whole kingdom was made tranquil and happy" (*The Great Learning* "Cha Yi," 5; Legge 1961: 359). Thus the Rujia tendency to favor the father rather than the ruler is not due to any championing of the family in opposition to the state, but is in keeping with the principles of kinship distance where one has a duty first to the closer kin.

The Rujia stress on interpersonal ethics, as seen in the virtues of filial piety (*xiao*), brotherhood (*di*), humaneness (*ren*), righteousness (*yi*), sincerity (*xin*), mutuality (*shu*), and reciprocity (*bao*), were to be applied not only within the family or clan, but also in government: "When those who are in high stations perform well all their duties to their relations, the people are aroused to virtue. When old friends are not neglected by them, the people are preserved from meanness" (*Analects* 8.2; Legge 1961: 208). Thus family, social life, and government were not distinct institutional spheres in Rujia discourse; rather, all three operated according to a single logic of the extension of kinship ethics....

Given the Rujia approach to government based on kinship ethics and kinship forms of power, it is appropriate that Confucius always looked back to the ancient past of the Three Dynasties (the Xia, Shang, and Western Zhou) for inspiration. Although all the features for the emergence of the state (urbanization, ceremonial and military centralization, systematic social stratification) can be found in these dynasties, the "state" in these periods was quite different from what started to develop in Eastern Zhou and imperial times. The "states" in the Three Dynasties period resembled what anthropologists call tribal federations and political kinship and ritual orders of agnatic clan and segmentary lineage systems (Chang 1983; Chang 1986: 364; Hsu and Linduff 1988: 147–85; Cooper 1982; Li 1962; Lewis 1990: 8–9, 28–36; He 1992; Savage 1985).

The royal house of each dynasty was actually a clan that had managed to dominate other, coexisting clans. Members of each clan traced descent to a common mythological paternal ancestor, practiced exogamy, and shared a common emblem (totem), which signified their common character. Within each clan, there was a system of stratified segmentary lineages and branch sublineages, comprising a genealogical system of differentiated degrees of political status in the social order. Thus it would seem that what crystallized into a stratified order of hereditary aristocracy in this period was the extension of a system of kinship-ranking derived from pre-state social systems....

The familial concept of the state meant that "the ruler reigned but did not rule" and the "sovereignty of rulers was not at all absolute," because respect to nobles and rulers was accorded to them personally as heads of families or clans, and not as institutionalized offices (Hsu 1965: 78–9). Therefore, the "state" of the Three Dynasties was not a purely political institution, but "resembled an enlarged household" in which the nominal king shared power with his brothers and close relatives, who were the nobles: "The Son of Heaven has his dukes; princes of states have their high ministers; ministers have [the heads of] their collateral families; great officers have the members of the secondary branches of their families; inferior officers have their friends; and the common people, mechanics, merchants, police runners, shepherds and grooms, all have their relatives and acquaintances to aid and assist them" (*Zuo Zhuan*; Legge 1872:466). Although there is relatively little information left to us about the social structure of the common people and the nature of their relationship with the nobles, this passage suggests that they too were integrated into the "state" order through kinship principles. These principles assigned them lowly kinship ranking and status, but they also may have prevented a clear line of demarcation from being drawn between rulers and subjects.

All this started to change in the Warring States period. As strong states tried to annex weaker states, the kinship ties that had held the sociopolitical order together began to dis-integrate. Seeking to protect itself in times of war, the new state formation came to treat the people's labor and wealth as material resources to be manipulated through systematized mea-sures of reward and punishment made possible through the introduction of written law.

In the school of Legalism, which arose during this period, the bifurcation of the Rujia ideal of a continuous kinship-state order is especially evident. The overriding concern of the Legalists was loyalty to the monarch and the state, which came to be seen as forming a single entity, whereas all other ethics of inter-personal relationship were interpreted as threats to the well-being of the state. This is evident in the repeated invocation of the oppo-sition between "private" and "public" as in this Legalists passage on etymology:

> In olden times, when [Cang Jie] invented the system of writing, he assigned the element "self-centered" [zihuan] to the character "private" [si]; and combined the elements, "opposite to" [bei] and "private," to form the character "public" [gong]. The contradiction between "public" and "private" was thus from the beginning well understood by [Cang Jie]. Today, to regard them both as serving an identical interest is a calamity born of neglect-ing to investigate. (Han Feizi 1982: 671; Liao 1959:286)[1]

Legalist discourse also sought to challenge the relational ethics of kinship and friendship:

> To perform private favors [xing si] for old friends, is called not neglecting [friendship]. To distribute alms with public funds [gong cai] is called being benevolent. To make light of [government] rewards and instead stress the [cultivation] of the self is called being a "superior person." To strain the law to shield one's relatives, is called having [good] conduct. To desert one's official post for cultivating personal friendships is called having a knightly sense of justice [you xia]. To keep aloof from the world and ignore one's superiors is called being high-minded. To be disputatious and disobey orders is called showing unswerving spirit. To pass out favors and gain a mass fol-lowing is called winning the people. (Han Feizi 1982:631–2; Liao 1959:248)*

For all these private virtues, the Legalists sub-stituted a public ethic, only in their discourse, "public" no longer meant simply the opposite of private, in the sense of a larger community, but came to be subsumed under the category of the ruler and the state. Thus by relegating all the ethics of interpersonal relationships of Rujia discourse into the category of the private, the Legalists set kinship up in opposition to the state.

In Rujia discourse, the "state" (guo) was only a part of the hierarchical kinship order; in Legalist discourse the strengthening of the state becomes the raison d'être of all social life.

[. . .]

Ritual power and the power of the law

Rujia discourse placed an inordinate emphasis on the significance and practice of ritual (li) and advocated a return to the rituals and music of Zhou. Yet however much they looked back to the rituals of the past, the way that the early Rujia talked about ritual marked a significant departure from previous times. It is evident that rituals were a constitutive component of ancient Chinese life. The archaeological record, resplendent with Shang and Zhou dynasty bronze ritual vessels of various shapes and pat-terns, shows the highly ritualistic nature of these clan-based state societies and the impor-tance of access to ritual for political authority (Chang 1983:40–1, 95; Chang 1980). Yet in pre-Rujia texts, the word for ritual was seldom used, and when it was, it usually referred merely to a specific rite or body of codes of conduct (Eno 1990:23, 212). The early Rujia were probably the first to thematize ritual as a general category of practices, to point out self-consciously its psychological impact on the person and its ethical and political effects on the social order.

The Chinese character for ritual, li, 禮, has a very interesting etymology. The oldest Chinese dictionary, the Shuowen Jiezi written by Xu Shen of the Han dynasty, defines li as "a step or act, that whereby we serve spiritual beings and attain happiness" (1959: juan I;

Legge, *The Li Ki* 1885:9–10). The radical *shi* 示 on the left originally referred to the suspended heavenly bodies (sun, moon, stars) that provided omens for humans and over time came to be associated with the affairs of spiritual beings, so that it is found in such characters as those for spirits 神 (*shen*), sacrifices 祭 (*ji*), and ancestor or origin 祖 (*zu*) (ibid.). The element on the right of the character is the phonetic *li* 豊, but it also has a semantic content of its own. It signifies "vessels used in performing [sacrificial] rites" and the lower half of this symbol refers to "vessels for food and meat in ancient times" (1959: *juan* 5). So from very early times, the notion of ritual was associated with the the cosmos and nature and with the sacrifice of food offerings to spiritual beings and ancestors in special vessels (see also He 1992:102), which by the Shang and Zhou dynasties had become the highly elaborate bronze ritual vessels prominent in the archaeological record until the early Han dynasty.

In Rujia discourse the notion of ritual attains a pivotal metaphoric status. "Ritual" comes to denote a whole range of philosophical as well as practical ethico-political tenets of life. The following quotation from the *Li Ji*, a Rujia-influenced text of the Han dynasty, with very archaic elements predating Confucius, gives an idea of the wide-ranging meanings of the Rujia notion of ritual. After some passages stating that ritual originates with the unity of the cosmos before it was divided and conforms to Heaven's constant principles of operation, the text goes on to say,

> [This cosmic principle to which ritual conforms] resides in the human world and can be called nurturance [the basis of human life]. Its realization is based on making offerings and laboring, and the [rituals] of declining and yielding, drinking ceremonies, feasting ceremonies, capping rites, marriage ceremonies, funeral rites, sacrificial rites, archery contests, chariot-driving, court audience ceremonies, and friendly missions [to other states]. (*Li Ji* 1987: 382)*

First, ritual signified the *cosmological order* or principle of operation that was embedded in nature. The practice of rituals according to the forms laid down in the past had the effect of enabling a person or the whole of social life itself to tap into or partake of this original cosmic order and unity. Second, ritual referred to *concrete and formal rites and ceremonies* performed by a community, such as various forms of sacrifice, capping (initiation for boys), marriage, funeral rites of passage, and other occasions for social gathering which adhered to sets of prescribed behavioral procedures and forms, and were hailed by the Rujia for promoting communal harmony and love (*Li Ji* 1987: 808). Third, through the extension of the rules of formal ceremonial performances to everyday life, ritual can also mean *propriety, custom, habits, and etiquette* in the conduct of social relationships. Such a meaning is suggested by the words "declining and yielding" (*ci rang*) above, postures of respect and politeness featured in banquet scenes, in which the guest initially declines the host's hospitality and both try to yield precedence of entering, seating, and eating to the other (*Li Ji* 1987:17, 28–31, 570).

Finally, the ancient usage of the word *li* also included the notion of "gift," in either the sense of a present given, an offering made, or a favor or hospitality rendered, as well as the ritual of a formal banquet (Morohashi 1955–60, 8:501). Among scholars and aristocrats, it was the etiquette that courtesy visits must always be accompanied by greeting gifts (Xu 1990:1–6). Ancient gifts often took the form of meat, wine, jade, or silk, which were also a kind of currency. Much etiquette was also prescribed to accompany the act of giving; there were rules concerning the kinds of gifts appropriate to each rank of people in each season of the year, how to hold and present each kind of gift, what deprecatory things to say about the gift being presented, how to receive a gift depending on the donor and recipients' relative social positions, and so forth (*Li Ji* 1987:568–70). In the *Book of Rites*, banquets and feasts were also guided by many ritual prescriptions.

In an encyclopedic examination of the history of Chinese gift-giving customs, Xu Ping notes that the polymorphic meanings of the word *li* in ancient Chinese "is definitely not a linguistic coincidence" (1990:9). Ritual in ancient China prescribed an ideal social order through different ritual acts, and these set the guidelines for the conduct of interpersonal and intergroup relations.

That the ritual form achieves its social ordering effects through "performance" and the positioning of the body was recognized by the Rujia, who "performed" their philosophy through music and dance and archery as part of their regimens of self-cultivation (Eno 1990). Many scholars have pointed out the absence of mind/body dualism in ancient Chinese notions of the "person" and "ritual" as integrated psychosomatic processes (Ames 1984; Tu 1983; Fingarette 1972; Zito 1994).

This early Rujia understanding of ritual coincides remarkably with the approach taken by Roy Rappaport in analyzing the "obvious aspects of ritual" (1979a). A symbolic, structuralist, or functional analysis of ritual does not take into account the special character of ritual in comparison to myth, poetry, and art, whereas an examination of the "surface" forms of ritual shows that "certain meanings and effects are intrinsic to the ritual form" (1979a:174). For Rappaport, the performer of ritual "is not merely transmitting messages encoded in the liturgy, he is also participating in – becoming part of – the order to which his own body and breath give life" (1979a:192).

The notion that ritual creates social order through bodily performance is illustrated in this marvelously suggestive passage about a country feasting ceremony held once every three years in early Zhou times:

The host honors the guest, therefore he seats the [principal] guest in the northwest and the accompanying guests in the southwest in order to assist the guest. The guest, whose demeanor toward [the host] is one of righteousness, sits in the northwest, [that he may imbibe of the force of righteousness]. The host, whose demeanor toward [the guests] is one of benevolence, virtue, and generosity, sits in the southeast, [that he may imbibe of the force of benevolence]. The host's attendant is seated in the northeast, in order to assist the host. [In this way,] as the forces of benevolence and righteousness come together, and guest and host each have their proper assignments, and the stands and dishes are presented in the proper numbers, then it is called [attain-

ing] the sacred. Having established [a state of] sanctity, and also treating [the occasion] with reverence, it is called propriety [li]. When ritual [li] embodies [ti] the distinction between elder and younger, it is called virtue [de]. Virtue is that which is obtained [de] through the body [shen]. That is why it is said: "The ancients who studied the arts of the Way sought thereby to moralize [de] the body." This, therefore, is the reason why the sages paid attention to the [practice of ritual]. (Li Ji 1987:974–5)*

My translation of the last three sentences differs markedly from that of Legge, who renders the third to the last sentence "Virtue is that which is the characteristic of the person" (Legge 1885, vol. 28:438). His translation of the word shen as "person" instead of "body," I believe, is not in keeping with passages earlier in the chapter describing the mutual bowing and yielding of precedence three times at the first meeting of host and guest. Nor does it adhere to the spirit of the rest of the passage above about the physical positioning of guests and host according to the directions of vital forces, and of the previous sentence about ritual "embodying" the distinction between elder and younger. Finally, the passage makes two word plays. There is a pun on the words "virtue" and "obtain," both pronounced de: virtue is "obtained"; and the way to obtain "virtue" is to somaticize it, or to "moralize" the body through ritual action. There is also an affinity drawn between the characters for "ritual" and "embody" (li 禮 and ti 體), since both characters have the same phonetic element, which means "ritual vessel." The implication that can be drawn from the linkage between the two characters is that the body is a ritual vessel for holding the virtues obtained through ritual practice.

This importance of ritual and music for Rujia lies not only in what can be called the regimens of "self-ritualization" followed by Rujia disciples in their study groups, such as those of ritual performance, music and dance, archery and charioteering, and the interpretation and discussion of ancient texts on ritual, history, and ethics (Eno 1990: 55–60). More pertinent for this history of the present is how the Rujia recognition of the performative effects of ritual led also to a discourse on what may be called the "reritualization of politics" or the will to recreate the social order and to conduct government through ritual.

> Zi Zhang asked about government. The Master said, "Zi, did I not speak to you on that subject before? The person of learning who understands ritual and music has only to take and apply them [in order to practice government], and that is all." (Li Ji 1987:813; Legge 1885; vol. 28:276)*

> Confucius said, "Lead the people with governmental measures and regulate them by law and punishment, and they will avoid wrongdoing but have no sense of honor and shame. Lead them with virtue and regulate them by the rules of propriety [li] and they will have a sense of shame, and, moreover, set themselves right." (Analects 2.3; Chan 1963:22)

What the Rujia proposed was to use the various forms of ritual as a system of "dikes" (fang) to shore up and channel human actions. The repeated performance of rituals serves to instill in the people customs and habits of daily life which are in accord with propriety (Li Ji 1987: 823–4; Li 1931:15). For instance, at the periodic rituals of sacrifice to the ancestors, the way that kin are physically arranged in order of precedence distinguishing between elder and younger, between male and female, and between more closely related and more distant kin, inculcates the principles of social ordering in the people and ritually assigns them roles and statuses (Li Ji 1987:782–6). The solemnity of the performances and the music inscribes in the participants (and simultaneously expresses) reverence and mourning for the deceased. The sharing of the sacrificial meats creates a sense of solidarity among all the living and deceased kin. The ritual of "declining and yielding" in greeting, visiting, and feasting serves to inculcate mutual consideration while damping tendencies for competition and self-gain. Ritual is all the more powerful as it relies not just on words, but on the involvement of the body.

There is much in the textual records to suggest that the Rujia discourse on ritual government did not arise in a vacuum, but was an elaboration on knowledge of the actual state of affairs in the Three Dynasties before Con-

fucius's time. The ancient usage of the word li also included that of "the system of governance of a state" (Morohashi 1955–60, vol. 8:501; Zhongwen Da Cidian 1967, vol. 24:95). A passage in the Zuo Zhuan describes how a Duke Zhuang wanted to go to another state to witness its sacrificial rite for the Spirits of the Land: "The ritual is conducted for the rectification of the people [zhengmin]. Hence there will be meetings of the princes to inculcate the [differential] duties of the high and low, and for determining each of their contributions of wealth. There will be court visiting rites to rectify the different ranks of nobility, and to arrange the order of the young and old" (Zuo Zhuan 10.2a; Legge 1872:105). It would seem that ritual in this society – like the display, symbolism, and drama of the nineteenth-century Balinese theater state described by Clifford Geertz (1980) – was not a mere extrinsic embellishment or legitimation of the proper workings of government, but an intrinsic component of government and an end in itself. This literal notion of government by ritual was lost or overshadowed very early in China by Legalistic notions of the workings of the state in terms of law, force, statecraft (shu), and administration, and in the West in the sixteenth century by a "command-and-obedience conception of political life," which reduced the state to matters of "regnancy, regime, dominion, mastery – statecraft" (Geertz 1980:121–2).

Since the Ruists lived amid the gathering storms of warfare and statism in the Eastern Zhou, for them, government through ritual and music must have presented an alternative to emerging new forms of government later favored by the Legalists, such as administrative bureaucracy, increasing military might, written law, and the meting out of punishments. For the Ruists, political and social order were to be brought about through ritual, and ritual was at the same time the conduct of politics: the two terms were regarded not as separate institutions, but as two aspects of one and the same thing. The order within ritual would serve as a vehicle to reproduce order in society. Furthermore, since the order found within ritual ultimately derived from the cosmic order and from the rhythms of nature, it meant that the principles of government were inextricably linked to the cosmic forces. This hearkening back to what was taken as an older mode of power can be seen as a way to resist the frightening new power order in which politics was beginning to cast off the encumbrances of ritual and kinship.

Let us examine how power exerted through ritual is different from what was to prove victorious during the Warring States period: a pure form of political rationality and an intensified state power. In ritual, power is *intrinsic* to the performance of ritual. According to Rappaport, there are two kinds of messages transmitted in ritual acts: (1) indexical messages, which transmit the current individual psychic and emotional states or roles of individual performers, and (2) canonical messages, which because they are concerned with enduring aspects of nature, society, and the cosmos, do not issue from participants but are already encoded in the prescribed sequential acts and utterrances of the ritual (1979a:179). Rujia discourse touched on both these aspects of ritual,[2] but it is with the latter that the present work will be concerned.

Canonical messages embedded in the arrangement of objects, bodies, and utterances in ritual are directives and elements of power carried from the past, and as they are reproduced, they exercise power on performers and witnesses. In the very act of performing a ritual, performers accept the directives encoded in the ritual, whether or not they believe them, because through their bodily enactments and utterances, they become fused with, and a part of, the messages they are transmitting and receiving. It is their performance, not their thought, which conforms with the prescribed ritual code and realizes and carries through the particular type of order and power implicit in the ritual (1979a: 192–4).

When ritual is employed as the primary means of establishing social order, it has certain implications for how power relations are arranged. The way that ritual exerts power from within itself is quite distinct from power imposed externally through decrees and commands backed by force or control over resources, as when power becomes crystallized in the machinery of a full-fledged state. When power is applied from without, through fixed laws and decrees, it means that the political function has attained an existence separate from the process of the reproduction of social order through ritual. When power acquires an autonomous base, the acceptance of the subordinated is not elicited through the very medium of the coded directives transmitted, but predicated on something external to the directives which can impose acceptance. *Therefore the implication of the Rujia discourse on government based on ritual is a society in which power is contained in the reproduction and conduct of social relations and not objectified and externalized in a universal state opposed to society.*

Instead of ritual government, the Legalists called for a system of objective laws (*fa*) and punishments drawn up by the monarch and made public for all to see. Just as a carpenter's various measuring tools are more accurate and objective than his unaided eyesight, so also the law provides an objective standard of judgment that does not discriminate between those of high and low intelligence or between ministers and commoners (*Han Feizi* 1982:50). This objectivity is the best way to control the wrongdoing of both the high and the low and to unify and standardize the behavioral norms of the people (ibid.). Thus law was understood not as a safeguard of the people's rights and privileges but as a way of strengthening the positions of the monarch and the state and insulating them from the threats posed by those of high rank or intelligence (ibid.).

The legal system required a new bureaucracy to supervise and execute the laws. Two complete sets of laws and mandates were to be kept in the capital, one in the palace of the Son of Heaven, one locked up in the Forbidden Archives, safe from tampering. These would serve as the absolute standards for the land. Three high-level law officials were to be designated by the Son of Heaven to officiate from the capital, and one of whom would be assigned to the palace, each of the other two to other centrally located state offices. One law officer and various law-enforcement officials would also be assigned to each commandary and prefecture throughout the empire, replicating the pattern of the capital. These officials were expected not only to apply the law but also to inform the people about the laws and to answer their questions, so that they would be deterred from violating the law themselves and at the same time would be able to prevent any wrong doing on the part of officials (*Shang Jun Shu* 1988: 194–6).

Besides a bureaucratic system, what also was to uphold the laws and to serve as its very strategy was a system of rewards and punishment (*shang xing*). . . . An example of reward for military merit in the law of Shang Yang was the stipulation that whoever cuts off one enemy head is given one degree in rank and those who desire to become officials will receive an office worth the price of 50 piculs or exemption from taxes (Duyvendak 1928:61, 297). Punishments fitting the crime were also written into the laws. No distinctions in punishment would be made on the basis of rank, kinship, or past good behavior. Shang Yang favored harsh punishments over light and also advocated that penalties be extended to three sets of kin related to the guilty (*Shang Jun Shu* 1988: 135–7).

The formulation and implementation of the law was intricately tied up with surveillance and mutual denunciation measures, both within the court bureaucracy and among the population. In Legalist discourse, the ruler becomes fully elevated above all in the realm, and the figure of what Gilles Deleuze and Felix Guattari called the "paranoid despot" (1987: 193) emerges.

[. . .]

. . . The Rujia texts are an amalgam of layers of different times and interpretations and contradictory passages: the segmentary state order, elements of which Confucius sought to revive, coexisted with the imperial state order, which found its way into the texts and which later commentaries tended to emphasize.

The character of the Rujia itself changed as it gained ascendancy in the Han court as state orthodox discourse. No longer was it an oppositional discourse outside the state; now it served the state and legitimated its rule by softening its impact on the people. The Han and later imperial dynasties preserved all the imperial state structures established by the Qin and inspired by Legalist discourse (such as the commandary-county system, the penal and surveillance system, and the bureaucracy), but replaced Legalist discourse with the moralism of Confucianism as its orthodoxy. Once the imperial state system was established, pre-Qin Rujia oppositional discourse became state Confucianism, which was predicated on and served as a cover for Legalism.

Rujia "employed the past to negate the present" (*yigu feijin*); Legalism "emphasized the present and denigrated the past" (*houjin bogu*); but except for occasional reformist attempts, state Confucianism under the empire used the past to strengthen the present of imperial power. According to early Rujia, the larger field of power, which invested the leader with the virtue and Mandate to rule and the social realm with order and regulation, was constructed as something dependent on ritual. Ritual practice, which involved the people, carved out and reproduced social order while bestowing sanctity on it. Under state Confucianism, the relationship between social institutions and ritual was reversed; ritual and the sanctity it produced became instruments of the state. Although the Han and later imperial orders revived the political role of ritual, once a systematic state administration appeared, ritual could never recover the importance it had had in the polity of the Three Dynasties. When the state relied mainly on its coercive institutions and resource extraction procedures, ritual power was neutralized, disconnected from the role envisioned for it by the early Rujia as the space in and through which the social order could be worked out involving the participants themselves.[3]

From the first traces of the imposition of the state onto primitive societies, through each successive historical upsurge or renewal of the state, older and more archaic elements were absorbed and integrated. The state "overcoded" its logic of centralized organization onto the segmentary kinship units of local communities so that they formed concentric circles revolving around the same central trunk of the state, all resonating with each other. The state, which Deleuze and Guattari call an "arborescent" structure because of its branches stemming from a singular, rooted, fixed, and rigid central trunk, becomes the "axis of rotation" for formerly independent kinship units (1987:208–13). It has been able to absorb older elements, such as ancestor worship, gift and kinship relations, clan and lineage organization, and reorient them to fit its own purposes of infiltrating into local communities.

At the same time, these remnants of another social order can also pose as centrifugal forces countering the centripetal project of the state. This alternative history of the present recognizes the now rarely conceded point that an appeal to the past is not always conservative or reactionary, but can be oppositional. If it is true that the early despotic state achieved a gathering of primitive kinship filiations into the direct filiation of the state machine (Deleuze and Guattari 1983:198), then it must also be true that within each new state order, the primitive past will always reappear and form oppositions to the present.

NOTES

1   Translation is modified. Hereafter, I will use the asterisk (*) to indicate that I have modified an original translation. If no translator is cited, the translation is my own and follows modern Chinese commentaries and annotations.

2   See *Xunzi Jinzhu*, Book 19, "On Ritual," for an eloquent assessment of how ritual transmits "indexical messages" to participants, bringing out deep emotions and appreciation for beauty (*Xunzi* 1975; Dubs 1928).

3   This argument on pre- and postimperial Confucianism parallels Rappaport's contrast between ritual as generative of social order and ritual as hypocritical lies (1979b:240).

BIBLIOGRAPHY

Ames, Roger T. 1984. "The Meaning of Body in Classical Chinese Thought." *International Philosophical Quarterly* 24, no. I: 39–53.

Chan Wing-tsit, ed. 1963. *A Source Book in Chinese Philosophy*. Princeton: Princeton University Press.

Chang Kwang-Chih. 1980. "The Chinese Bronze Age: A Modern Synthesis." In *The Great Bronze Age of China*, ed. Wen Fong. New York: Alfred A. Knopf and the Metropolitan Museum of Art.

——. 1983. *Art, Myth, and Ritual: The Path to Political Authority in Ancient China*. Cambridge: Harvard University Press.

——. 1986. *The Archaeology of Ancient China*. 4th ed. New Haven: Yale University Press.

Cooper, Eugene. 1982. "The Potlatch in Ancient China: Parallels in the Sociopolitical Structure of the Ancient Chinese and the American Indians of the Northwest Coast." *History of Religions* 22 (November): 103–28.

Deleuze, Gilles, and Félix Guattari. 1983. *Anti-Oedipus: Capitalism and Schizophrenia*. Translated by Robert Hurley. Minneapolis: University of Minnesota Press.

——. 1987. *A Thousand Plateaus: Capitalism and Schizophrenia*. Translated by Brian Massumi. Minneapolis: University of Minnesota Press.

Dubs, H. H., trans. 1928. *The Works of Hsuntze*. London: Probsthain.

Duyvendak, J. J. L., trans. 1928 *The Book of Lord Shang*. Chicago: University of Chicago Press. *See* Shang Jun Shu 1988.

Eno, Robert. 1990. *The Confucian Creation of Heaven: Philosophy and the Defense of Ritual Mastering*. Albany: State University of New York Press.

Fingarette, Herbert. 1972. *Confucius – The Secular as Sacred*. New York: Harper & Row.

Geertz, Clifford. 1980. *Negara: The Theatre State in Nineteenth-Century Bali*. Princeton: Princeton University Press.

Han Feizi xiaozhu 《韩非子校注》. 1982. The annotated *Han Feizi. Han Feizi xiaozhuzu* 《韩非子》校注组 (Annotating Group for the *Han Feizi*). Nanjing: Jiangsu Renmin chubanshe.

He Bingdi (Ho Ping-ti) 何炳棣. 1992. *Yuan Li*

《原礼》 (The origin of rites). *Ershiyi Shiji* 《二十一世纪》 (Twenty-first century), no. 11 (June).

Hsu Cho-yun. 1965. *Ancient China in Transition*. Stanford: Stanford University Press.

Hsu Cho-yun and Katherine M. Linduff. 1988. *Western Chou Civilization*. New Haven: Yale University Press.

Legge, James, trans. 1872. *The Ch'un Ts'ew with the Tso Chuen*. Vol. 5 of *The Chinese Classics*. Oxford: Clarendon Press.

——. 1885. *The Li Ki (Book of Rites)*. Vols. 27–28 of *The Sacred Books of the East*, ed. Max Muller. Oxford: Clarendon Press.

——. 1961. *The Analects*. Vol. I of *The Chinese Classics*. Hong Kong: Hong Kong University Press.

Lewis, Mark Edward. 1990. *Sanctioned Violence in Early China*. Albany: State University of New York Press.

Li Anzhai 李安宅. 1931. "*Yili*" yü "*Liji*" zhi shehuixue de yanjiu 《「仪礼」与「礼记」之社会学的研究》 (The sociological study of the *Yili* and the *Li Ji*). Shanghai: Shangwu Yinshuguan.

Li Ji Jinzhu Jinyi 《礼记今注今译》 1987. *The Book of Ritual, with Contemporary Annotation and Translation*. Translated by Wang Mengou 王梦鸥注译 Taibei: Taiwan Shangwu Yinshuguan.

Li Yanong 李亚农. 1962. *Zhouzu de shizuzhi yu tobazu de qian fengjianzhi* 《周族的氏族制与拓跋族的前封建制》 (The clan system of the Zhou people and the prefeudal system of the Toba people). In *Xinran zhai shi lunji* 《欣然斋史论集》 Shanghai: Renmin chubanshe.

Liao, W. K., trans. 1959. *The Complete Works of Han Fei Tzu*. Vol. 2., London: A. Probsthain.

Morohashi Tetsuji 诸桥辙次. 1955–60. *Dai kan-wa jiten* 《大汉和辞典》. Tokyo: Taishukan Shoten.

Rappaport, Roy A. 1979a. "The Obvious Aspects of Ritual." In *Ecology, Meaning, Religion*. Berkeley, Calif.: North Atlantic Books.

——. 1979b. "Sanctity and Lies in Evolution." In *Ecology, Meaning, Religion*. Berkeley, Calif.: North Atlantic Books.

Savage, William. 1985. *In the Tradition of Kings: The Gentleman in the Analects of Confucius*. Ph.D. diss., University of Michigan.

Shang Jun Shu 《商君书》 1988. The book of Lord Shang. Edited by Huo Lingxu 贺凌虚编. Taibei: Taiwan Shangwu Yinshuguan.

Tu Wei-ming. 1983. "The Idea of the Human in Mencian Thought: An Approach to Chinese Aesthetics." In *Theories of the Arts in China*. Princeton: Princeton University Press.

Xu Ping 许平. 1990. *Kuizeng Lisu* 《馈赠礼俗》 (The rituals and customs of gift-giving). Beijing: Zhongguo Huaqiao chuban gongsi.

Xu Shen 许慎. 1959. *Shuowen Jiezi* 《说文解字》 (Explanation of words and characters [in the Former Han dynasty]). Facsimile reprint of Song dynasty edition. Taibei: Si Ku Shanben Congshu.

Xunzi Jinzhu jinyi 《荀子今注今译》 1975. Translated and annotated by Xiong Gongzhe 熊公哲. Taibei: Shangwu yinshuguan.

Zhongwen Da Cidian 《中文大辞典》 1967. *Encyclopedic dictionary of the Chinese language*. Taibei: Zhongguo Wenhua Yanjiusuo.

Zito, Angela. 1994. "Ritualizing *Li*." Positions I, no. 2.

Zuo Zhuan 《左传》 1814. *Commentary on the Spring and Autumn annals*. In *Shisan Jing Zhushu* 《十三经注疏》 (The annotated Thirteen Classics). Nanchang.

42

Passional Preaching, Aural Sensibility, and the Islamic Revival in Cairo

Charles Hirschkind

Charles Hirschkind received his PhD in anthropology from Johns Hopkins University and now teaches at Berkeley. In this impressive contribution he amasses a range of theory, from Walter Benjamin's important essay on the impact of modern technology on experience through recent work on embodiment and the senses. What is unique is the way he combines this literature on perception and aesthetics with an interest in ethical practice and religious discipline. Developing ideas found in the work of his teacher, Talal Asad (see chapter 9, above), Hirschkind is able to show how pious Muslims reconstruct their sensibilities in accord with models of Islamic moral personhood. He thus brings his own anthropological sensibility to bear on practices and events that are systematically misunderstood in the West today. Hirschkind's analysis helps us both to grasp the meaningfulness and profundity of religious revival and to transcend simple oppositions between "tradition" and "modernity" or between power and morality (or subjection and agency). In showing the way religious practices cultivate virtuous dispositions and reflective citizenship, Hirschkind implicitly challenges the hegemony of doctrines of both rationalism and liberalism. For fuller argument see his book (2006a) as well as Mahmood (2005) for complementary and equally compelling work on pious women. For recent accounts of Islam and the state from other parts of the world see Hefner (2000) on Indonesia, Navaro-Yashin (2002) on Turkey, and Peletz (2002) on Malaysia. Casanova (1994) provides an important discussion of public religion more generally. Lively debate over secularism can be found in Bhargava, ed. (1998) and Connolly (1999).

From Charles Hirschkind, "The Ethics of Listening: Cassette Sermon Audition in Contemporary Cairo," *American Ethnologist* 28(2) (2001). Reprinted by permission of the American Anthropological Association. Abridged by the author.

Among the many lines of inquiry to which Walter Benjamin's rich *oeuvre* has given impetus, one of the most fruitful for anthropologists has been an interrogation into both the history of the senses and the structures of sensory perception that underline particular forms of historical experience. Benjamin's excavation of buried histories of sensory experience from within the outmoded objects of modernity, and in particular his work on the impact of modern media techniques on perception, have provided scholars less a set of theoretical formulations than a particular methodological sensibility – a feel for the historically discordant within the contemporary. Most influential, in this regard, has been his classic essay, "The Work of Art in the Age of Mechanical Reproduction" (1968 [1936]), in which he explored the impact of modern photographic and cinematic techniques on perception. In this essay, Benjamin argued that the particular experiential quality that grounded the uniqueness and authenticity of historical objects – what he called "aura" – had been all but effaced under the perceptual regime of modern technological culture. With the mechanical reproduction of works of art, not only does the idea of an authentic original lose all meaning; the traditions that were founded upon and upheld the knowledge of such authentic objects can no longer maintain the practical and perceptual conditions that sustained them. Benjamin further explored this process in "The Storyteller," written in the same year, where he argued that the traditional modes of knowledge and practice that grounded the art of storytelling had been rendered impracticable with the rise of information as the dominant communicative form.

In this essay, I want to take up Benjamin's interrogation of the relation between sensory experience and traditional practices, but from the standpoint of a question that Benjamin and those his work has inspired have rarely pursued. Specifically, I approach the question of the sensorium not from the side of the (modern) object and its impact on the possibilities of subjective experience, but rather from the perspective of a cultural practice through which the perceptual capacities of the subject are honed, and thus, through which the world those capacities inhabit is brought into being, rendered perceptible. In exploring such a practice, I hope to suggest how traditions not only presuppose, but actively seek to cultivate the particular sensory skills upon which the actions, objects, and knowledges that constitute these traditions depend. Such tradition-cultivated modes of perception and appraisal not only coexist within the space of the modern, but are even enabled in ways by the very conditions that constitute modernity. Thus, through an analysis of a particular cultural practice geared to this task, I hope to contribute to the important and ongoing task of rethinking our received – and decidedly stubborn – opposition between the traditional and the modern.

My specific focus here is on the practice of listening to tape-recorded sermons among contemporary Muslims in Egypt as an exercise of ethical self-discipline. During a period of a year and a half, I worked with a group of young men in Cairo for whom sermon audition was a regular activity.[1] I also took lessons throughout my stay in Cairo on the art of preaching from an experienced preacher. For all of these men, the cassette-sermon was a technology of self-improvement, one among a number of such technologies that have been popularized in recent decades with the gradual emergence of what is commonly referred to as the Islamic Revival (*al-Ṣaḥwa al-Islāmiyya*). In what follows, I explore the fashion of cassette-sermon audition as a disciplinary practice through which contemporary Egyptian Muslims hone an ethically responsive sensorium: the requisite sensibilities that they saw as enabling them to live as devout Muslims in a world increasingly ordered by secular rationalities. Notably, I use the terms "senses" and "sensibilities" here in a way that suggests their fundamental interdependency. Part of my argument is precisely to describe how emotions, capacities of aesthetic appreciation, and states of moral attunement or being – what we generally refer to as "sensibilities" – come to structure our most fundamental sensory experiences. It should be clear, therefore, that in referring to "senses," I am not indicating the object studied within the discipline of biology.

As I describe, among the men I worked with proper audition demanded a particular affective-volitional responsiveness – what I describe as an ethical performance – as a condition for "understanding" sermonic speech, while simultaneously deepening an individual's capacity to hear in this manner. To "hear with the heart," as those I worked with described this activity, was not strictly something cognitive in the usual sense but involved the body in its entirety, as a complex synthesis of disciplined moral reflexes. Indeed, the degree of benefit achievable through sermon audition was understood to be proportionate to the depth of moral sensibility the listener was able to bring to the act.

Cassette Discipline

Since the 1970s, cassette-recorded sermons of popular Islamic preachers (khuṭabāʾ, sing. khaṭīb) have increasingly become one of the most widely consumed media forms among lower-middle- and middle-class Egyptians (Hirschkind 2001; Salvatore 1998; Starrett 1995). Tapes are sold outside of mosques, on the sidewalks in front of train and bus stations, or in bookstores throughout the city. They may be listened to practically anywhere: while running a café or barbershop, while driving a bus or taxi, at home with one's family after returning from work.

At the time of my fieldwork, there were six licensed companies in operation in Cairo which produced and distributed taped sermons, the largest three of these having additional distribution centers outside of Cairo, primarily in the cities of Alexandria, Mansura, and Suez. Besides sermon tapes, many of these companies also sell other items often associated with Islamist social trends, such as headscarves and modest dress styles for women, the long white shirts (jalabiyya) commonly worn by Egyptian men, perfumes and scented oils, incense, as well as books and pamphlets from Islamist publishers. In addition to the commercially produced and marketed tapes, there are an equal or greater number which are recorded, copied, and sold by small-scale entrepreneurs

without commercial licenses, contracts with khuṭabāʾ, or the required permits from the Council on Islamic Research at the government-run al-Azhar mosque. Although the Egyptian police occasionally confiscate the merchandise of these vendors, most of the time they are left alone to sell their wares on the streets outside of mosques or bus stations. It should be noted, however, that the tapes sold within these commercial and informal markets do not reflect the number of people who participate in the practice of cassette-sermon audition today. This is due to the fact that the majority of tapes listened to in Egypt circulate outside of the structures of sales and marketing, and are obtained through informal practices of exchange and duplication among acquaintances, or from tape-lending libraries now offered by many mosques.

While the young men I worked with used cassette-sermons as a disciplinary technique to enhance their knowledge and ethical capacities, they seldom employed them in an exact or rigorous manner. Rarely, for example, would they listen at precise times of the day according to a fixed schedule. The one exception to this was in the case of mosque study groups, which would sometimes assign a certain number of tapes each member was to listen to in the course of a week. Usually, however, cassette sermon audition is a self-regulated activity, undertaken as a solitary exercise or in the company of a friend or family member. Among the sermon listeners I came to know, it was most often practiced in the evenings, after they had returned from work or school. As opposed to the communal sermon on Friday at the mosque, cassette audition takes place without the performance of ablutions (wudūʾ). Importantly, most tape-users attend the Friday mosque ceremony and consider the tapes to be an extension of it, not an alternative.[2]

Sermon tapes afford the listener a type of relaxation from which one can nonetheless expect an enriching of one's knowledge and a cathartic, purifying operation on the soul. As Ahmed, a recent university graduate now working in an aluminum plant, commented to me:

Remember when we were sitting at Muhammed's once and we played a tape of [the *khaṭīb*] Muhammed Hassan, you felt relaxed (*istirkhāʾ*)? This is what can happen, this is the opening of the heart [literally, "chest"] (*inshirāḥ al-ṣadr*), the tranquility (*itmiʾnān*), that makes you want to pray, read the Quran, makes you want to get closer to God, to think (*tafakkir*) more about religion (*dīn*). When you listen to a sermon, it helps you put aside all of your worries about work and money by reminding you of God. You remember that you will be judged and that fills you with fear (*khauf*) and makes you feel humility (*khushūʿ*) and repentance (*nadm*). The Shaykh teaches you about Islam, what it requires of you, so you won't make errors.

Another man I worked with, Husam, who worked in a small store that sold sermon tapes and religious literature, explained the utility of tape audition this way:

Tapes are always of benefit, whether on the torment of the grave (*ʿadhāb al-qabr*), Judgement Day (*yaum al-qiyāma*), death, on the most dangerous of sins (*kabāʾir*), or the headscarf. You learn things you didn't know, and this is useful. And they restore you to [moral] health (*biyashfūna*). Listening to a tape of a sermon you've already heard is a way of reinforcing what you've learned, strengthening the fear of God's punishments, so you won't commit a moral error (*maʿāṣī*). This leaves your heart calm (*muṭmaʾin*). There are some people who just do what they should. Many others, however, they realize that the devil has got into their heads (*yuwaswasu* [whispers to them]), and is making them think that what is evil (*ḥarām*) is actually good (*ḥalāl*). By listening, they strengthen themselves against this, as it gets them to pray and read the Quran. Then they begin to regret (*nadm*) what they have done, and ask God for forgiveness (*istighfār*). The tape, in other words, helps them to fight (*bijāhid*) against the devil.

Tapes thus enable a strengthening of the will, and what many people refer to as an ability to resist the devil's whispers (*waswās*). With repeated and attentive listening, they can also help lead a listener to change his or her ways. Ahmed put it this way:

My brother, who is religious but [does not belong to the] *Jamāʿa*,[3] heard this tape by [the popular preacher] Fawzi Saʿid and it really struck him. He immediately made me a copy. He decided he had to change his life, so he stopped smoking and using foul language, and started to go to the mosque and pray. Now he is always talking about religion, always trying to get his friends to comport themselves more piously. Many of his old friends don't want to be around him any more because they get tired of his talk. Every time I go to his house now, we listen to a tape. I'm not as into it as much as he is, but I do feel it makes me think about important things I would forget.

For sermon listeners, the regular practice of sermon audition serves as a constant reminder to monitor their behavior for vices and virtues. Even in the absence of a complete transformation of the kind Ahmed's brother went through, young men like Ahmed and Hussein relied on the tapes to maintain a level of self-scrutiny (*murāqaba*) in regard to their day-to-day activities and, when possible, to change or modify their behavior. Many of the young men I worked with in Egypt related their decision to become diligent in the performance of their Islamic duties to having been moved by a particularly powerful sermon, heard either on tape or live, at the mosque.

What renders tape audition a technique suitable for practices of ethical self-improvement lies in the capacity of speech to act on the heart and reform it (cf. Padwick 1996). For those I worked with, this was not a mechanical process. Simply putting on a sermon tape or listening to verses of the Quran does not cleanse a heart that has been corroded by sin. A person with a "rusted heart," as one man I had come to know put it, is precisely one whose ability to hear has been impaired. An author, writing in *al-Tauḥīd*, a popular religious digest often read and cited by the sermon listeners of my study, likens this to a short-circuit in the wiring which prevents an electrical current from reaching the lamp it is supposed to illuminate. Drawing out the metaphor, he suggests:

The Quran is effective in itself, just as the electrical current. If the Quran is present [to your ears], and *you have lost its effect*, then it is you yourself that you must blame. Maybe the conductive element is defective: your heart is damaged or flawed. Maybe a mist covers your heart, preventing it from benefiting (*intifaʿ*) from the Quran and being affected by it. Or maybe you are not listening well, or your heart is occupied with problems of money, and thinking about how to acquire and increase it. (Badawi 1996a: 13)

For the possessor of such a defective heart, the only solution according to the author lies in cleansing (*ṭahāra*) the heart, both by giving up the sinful acts that led to such a state, and by repeatedly listening, with intention and concentration, to sermons, exhortations, and Quranic verses. Such is the task that cassette-sermons are put to.

The Listening Body

The effect of sermon speech on the heart, however, is not just one of cleansing. As the above comments make evident, sermons evoke in the sensitive listener a particular set of ethical responses, foremost among them fear (*khauf*), humility (*khushūʿ*), regret (*nadm*), repentance (*tauba*), and tranquility (*iṭmīnān* or *sakīna*). As elaborated within classical Islamic moral doctrine, these are the affective dispositions that endow a believer's heart with the capacities of moral discrimination necessary for proper conduct.[4] In order to understand their usage by the men I worked with, however, it will be useful to draw on some of the contemporary writings that they themselves use and frequently refer to. The following discussion comes from an article published in the same journal I cited above, *al-Tauḥīd*. The article focuses on the effect of particular Quranic verses, when used by a *khaṭib*, on the moral condition of a faithful Muslim listener. Drawing from the exegetical works of classical scholars in regard to the interpretation of a verse from the Quranic chapter entitled *al-Zumar* (The Throngs), the author notes,

What is meant here is that when the true people of faith, the people of the eternal and deeply rooted doctrine (*al-ʿaqīda*) hear the

verses of warning (*al-waʿīd*) their flesh trembles in fear, their hearts are filled with despair (*inqabaḍat qulūbahum*), a violent angst shakes their backs (*irtaʿadat farāʾisuhum*), and their hearts become intoxicated with fear and dread. But if they then hear the verses of mercy (*al-raḥma*) and forgiveness (*istighfār*), their flesh becomes filled with delight (*inbasaṭ at julūdahum*), their chests are opened and relaxed (*insharaḥat ṣudūrahum*), and their hearts are left tranquil (*iṭmaʾnat qulūbahum*). (Badawi 1996b: 11–12)

What is described here is a kind of moral physiology, the emotional-kinesthetic experience of a body permeated by Islamic faith (*imān*) when listening to a *khaṭib*'s discourse. The description is derived directly from numerous verses of the Quran depicting the impact of godly speech on a rightly-disposed listener, as in the following verse from the chapter entitled *al-Anfāl* (Spoils of War): "Believers are only they whose hearts tremble whenever God is mentioned, and whose faith is strengthened whenever his messages are conveyed unto them" (*al-Anfāl*: 2).[5] This particular responsiveness constitutes what might be termed a Quranically-tuned body and soul. This attunement, according to the author, defines precisely the characteristic of a person who is close to God (Badawi 1996b: 11). For such a person, auditory reception involves the flesh, back, chest and heart, in short, the entire moral person as a unity of body and soul. To listen properly, we might say, is to engage in a performance, the articulated gestures of a dance.

The Task of the Khaṭib

In discussing the Islamic sermon and its role in the shaping of ethical dispositions, it is important to distinguish between a rhetorical practice of evoking or modulating the passions as a means to sway an audience toward a point of view, and one aimed at constructing the passions in accord with a certain model. In regard to the former, Aristotle dedicated considerable attention to the possibilities of rhetorically manipulating the passions, examining the means by which anger, fear, or pity might be intensified or attenuated by an orator to his advantage (1991). We also find in Augustine an emphasis on the utility of arousing the emotions as a means to move people to do what they know they should do but fail to. Such a technique is predicated on the instrumental use of emotions for purposes to which those emotions have no necessary relation. By contrast, in the practice of Islamic sermons, as I have noted, the objects of discourse and the emotions which are elicited in the context of their discussion are interdependent such that those emotions only achieve their proper formation through that relationship. The *khaṭīb*'s task, in other words, includes not just the modulation of emotional intensities but also the orienting of those emotions to their proper objects.

There is considerable debate among Egyptian *khuṭabāʾ* as well as their listeners today on this issue. One of the indications that many people take as evidence of a *khaṭīb*'s virtuosity is an ability to move an audience to tears. Weeping has an important place within Islamic devotional practices, as a kind of emotional response appropriate for both men and women when, with humility, fear, and love, they turn to God.[6] Many are concerned today, however, that people are crying during sermons for the wrong reasons. Note, for example, the following remark by the *khaṭīb* Fawzi Saʿid, in response to a question about why he didn't do more to evoke the passions of his listeners in his sermons:

Lots of people today just look forward to crying during sermons; they feel they are being cleansed, like Christians at baptism. But the sermon that just leads you to cry doesn't imprint upon the heart. It doesn't get people to change their actions. It is only through a careful engagement with the texts (*taʿaqqul maʿa al-nuṣūṣ*), reading the Quran and *sunna*, that knowledge gets rooted in the heart. Not that the sentiments are unimportant; but many people no longer know why they are crying.

One of the major concerns of the *khuṭabāʾ* I spoke with was that many cassette-sermon listeners today were engaging in the practice as a form of entertainment, for the pleasure of the emotional experience produced through audition. My preaching instructor, Muhammed Subhi, voiced this worry in a conversation on the problems with preaching today:

When people today listen, they hear about Judgment Day and the torment of hell and they feel relieved and exalted (*intishāʾ*). *Intishāʾ* is what you experience when you drink alcohol and feel that all of the pressures and difficulties of your life have been lifted. Or when you hear a really beautiful song, that touches all of your emotions (*ʿawāṭif wa mashāʾir*) and sensibilities (*iḥsās*). You feel a kind of comfort and relief (*tanfīs*), a calm (*rāḥā*), a kind of catharsis (*kathrasīs*): this is *intishāʾ*. If I am a Muslim, when I listen to the Quran I feel this relief (*nashwa*). But things must not stop at this feeling, as so often happens. It must be transformed into part of one's practical reality.

Subhi is concerned that sermons are being listened to for a momentary experience of catharsis, enthusiasm, and excitement which leaves no traces in the listener's behavior once the experience is over. As with Fawzi Saʿid above, Subhi is not advocating a rationalist, academic approach to preaching. In fact, he was quite critical of other *khuṭabāʾ*, whose intellectualist approaches succeeded neither in grabbing the attention of an audience nor in stirring their pious passions. Rather, he as well as most other *khuṭabāʾ* saw the problem as that of rooting (*raskh*) knowledge in the hearts of the listeners, binding their emotions to the appropriate objects, so as to move them toward pious comportment. Like many people I met, he worried that some contemporary preachers were playing on the emotions of their audience so as to bolster their own popularity, rather than sedimenting those emotions in their listeners in such a way as would incline them toward moral action. Knowledge of the events of Judgment Day, in other words, must not come to be assimilated to the categories of entertainment or information, the former linked to the wrong passions, the latter devoid of passions entirely. Rather, belief in these events, a requirement of Islam, must be passionately lived in one's daily actions.

Musical Emotions

The problem of affective attunement was
further elucidated for me through discussions
I had about the difference between listening to
cassette-sermons and listening to music. Many
of the people I spoke to invoked the example
of music in order to explain to me the kind of
relaxed feeling one felt when listening to a
sermon. One young man, Beha, described for
me the workings of *tarhīb* (the rhetorical style
geared toward inciting fear in listeners), and
then compared it to the experience of music:

> When you hear about the tortures in the
> grave, you get scared (*tikhāf*), you fear God,
> then you start to feel regret (*nadm*), between
> you and yourself, for what you've done wrong
> (*al-maʿāṣī*), so you ask God for forgiveness
> (*istighfār*), you repent (*tauba*) and then you
> remember his mercy (*raḥma*) and you feel
> calm (*rāḥā*), your chest opened (*munsharih
> al-ṣadr*), open to Islam, the Quran, God, and
> knowing that you will get close to him. When
> you listen to music, you also feel calm and
> relaxed (*rāḥā*), but that doesn't mean you're
> really close to God. With a sermon or Quran
> tape you can attain that closeness, so the
> feeling is better and greater than when you are
> just relaxed (*rāḥā*).

As noted above, many of the sermon-
listeners I spoke with in Egypt suggested that,
although they listened to taped sermons as a
means to ethical improvement, there were also
times when, feeling tired or tense, they might
choose a music tape over a sermon or Quran
recording. All three were understood to bring
one to a state of relaxation. Yet, as Beha's
comment begins to suggest, there is a key distinction to be drawn between the two experiences. As opposed to music, the sermon sets
in motion a moral (and, as I have suggested
above, bodily) progression from fear, to regret,
asking for forgiveness, repentance, and leading
eventually to a sense of closeness with God, an
experience that was described to me through
terms such as *inshirāḥ al-ṣadr* (opening of the
heart or chest), *iṭmīnān* (tranquility), and
sakīna (stillness). This progression constantly
reappeared in the comments of the people I
worked with in Cairo. Ahmed, for example,

told me: "If a Muslim sees hell close to him
[through a good *khaṭīb*], he won't find peace
until he asks forgiveness for his errors
(*dhunūb*), repents (*yatūb*), and returns humbly
and tearfully to God." Such is the movement
which a listener's body/soul, one learned in the
physiological dispositions I discussed above,
makes under the guidance of a skillful *khaṭīb*.
Importantly, this is not the *rāḥā* (calm) produced by soft music, but rather, a moral state
conceptually articulated within the traditions
of Islamic self-discipline. As I am suggesting,
such states have far more to do with embodied
capacities of gesture, feeling, and speech than
with obedience to rules or belief in doctrine.

The Dance of Words

The kind of attention and general attitude with
which people listen to taped sermons was a
frequent point of debate not only among the
khuṭabāʾ I discuss above but also among many
of those who listened to cassette-sermons.
Many people in Egypt listen to sermon tapes
while engaged in some other routine activity,
such as driving a taxi, working as a waiter at
a neighborhood café or cooking a meal, as was
common among the mothers and sisters of
the men I knew. Despite such styles of usage,
however, many argued that the degree of
ethical benefit a listener achieves through
sermon audition depended on the level of concentration he or she applied to the act. As
Ahmed, who I mentioned earlier, told me:
"When you listen with humility (*khushūʿ*), correctly and truly, and when you understand
each word, then you truly benefit (*fāida*). You
feel relieved, that your sins will be forgiven.
But if you listen as one would read a newspaper, distractedly or indifferently, which many
do, then the benefit is much less."

The fact that people listen with greater or
lesser degrees of attentiveness, while an important point empirically, tells us little in itself
about the kind of activity someone is engaged
in when listening to a sermon. For example,
people who attend the mosque on Friday also
listen to sermons with differing degrees and
modes of attention, some daydreaming, some
held by the murmuring sound of a *khaṭīb*'s

voice, some following with critical scrutiny the arguments being made. The fact that some of these ways of attending to a sermon would be recognized by many Muslims today as wrong points to the existence of a set of normative standards which define what a correct performance by a listener entails, and against which incorrect performances may be identified and measured (what J. L. Austin, referring to speech acts, describes as the act's "felicity conditions": the variable circumstances that secure the success of an utterance (1975 [1962]: 12–24)). An act, in other words, is not determined by what happens to be in someone's consciousness at the moment of its execution, though this may bear on the degree to which the act is successful. Rather, an act (such as "listening to a sermon") must be described in terms of the conventions which make it meaningful *as a particular kind of activity*, one enacted for certain reasons and in accord with certain standards of excellence and understood as such by those who perform and respond to it. This point was repeatedly stressed by the people I worked with: one may listen to a taped sermon as one would read a newspaper, watch television, or hear popular music, but the ethical benefit of such a listening will be correspondingly lower.

The men I worked with often made a distinction between the verb commonly used for "hearing," *sam'*, and two other terms that suggest a more deliberate act: *anṣat*, meaning to incline one's ear toward, or pay close attention, and *aṣghā*, to be silent in order to listen. Quranic recitation, as was often the case, provided the point of reference for explaining the meaning of these terms.[7] This is not surprising, given both the pervasive use of Quranic verses in the sermon, and the sermon's emphasis on acts of remembrance (*dhikr*), supplication (*du'a*), giving thanks (*shukr*), and expressing fearful and loving respect for God (*al-taqwā*). As it was described to me, "listening with close attention" (*al-inṣāt*) is a complex sensory skill, one opposed to mere hearing (*sam'*), understood as a passive and spontaneous receptivity. Such is the kind of attentiveness appropriate to those moments when one's heart is inclined toward God. Muhammed Subhi echoed this view from his perspective as a *khaṭīb* con-

cerned about the attention of his audience: "I may get you to focus on what I'm saying and comprehend it, but without getting you to feel emotionally disposed (*tata'aṭaf*) toward it. A *khuṭba* (sermon) must lead an audience beyond mere hearing (*al-sam'*) to where they pay close attention (*yunṣatu*), such that the words actually turn over (*tanqalab*) their behavior."

This skill of careful listening has been most fully elaborated in the large body of literature on the art of Quranic recitation. While these classical texts provide instruction in a particular tradition of vocal performance, the performance itself is understood to involve a kind of audition, insomuch as a skilled reciter should attempt to "hear the speech of God from God and not from [the voice of the reciter] himself" (al-Ghazali 1984:80). Among the demands of this audition cited by the eleventh-century theologian A. H. al-Ghazali are both practices of mental concentration and a variety of affective, gestural, and verbal responses whereby the reader or listener assumes the ethical dispositions corresponding to the recited or audited verses: humility, awe, regret, fear, and so on. In his manual on recitational technique, al-Ghazali writes:

During the Quran reading, when the Quran reader reads a verse on glorification of God, he will glorify Him and magnify Him. When he reads a verse on supplication [to God] and forgiveness [of Him], he will supplicate and seek forgiveness. If he reads a verse telling of any hopeful matter he will pray to God [for it]. But if he reads a verse on a frightening matter, he will seek the protection [of God]. (1984: 48)

In another section, al-Ghazali further elaborates this in terms of "fulfilling the right" (*al-ḥaqq*) of the verses:

When the Quran reader reads a verse necessitating prostration before God, he will prostrate himself. Likewise, if he hears [the recitation of] a verse of prostration by another person he will prostrate himself when the reciter prostrates. He will prostrate only when he is physically and ritually clean. . . . Its perfect form for him to utter *Allahu akbār* [God is Great!] and then prostrate himself and, while prostrate, supplicate with that supplication which is appropriate to the verse of prostration recited. (1984: 44–5)

The word of God, as we see from the instructions al-Ghazali provides, demands a kind of dialogue from the reciter/listener. The receiver must not only seek to understand God's message, in the cognitive sense, but must assume the attitudes and perform the acts that correspond to that understanding. As scholars of the contemporary practice of Quranic recitation have described, these principles still provide the basis for training in the art as it is taught today (Denny 1980, 1981; Nelson 1985). A recent rector of al-Azhar University, Abd al-Halim Mahmud, echoes this in a *fatwa* (non-binding legal opinion) advising people that while reading the Quran, "they pause and respond to words by enacting what is called for, asking forgiveness, regretting their misdeeds, imploring salvation when reading verses of warning or retribution (*'adhāb*), and so on" (al-Azhar 1988). It is this quite complex form of sensory engagement that also informs the practice of listening to sermons.

Importantly, the forms of comportment and concentration associated with Quranic audition and recitation are not simply transferred over into the sermon context as a set of guidelines or rules. More fundamentally, the cultivation of these skills stands as a necessary prerequisite for the sermon-listener to be able to follow, be moved by, and derive benefit from the sermon. Training in such skills begins in earliest infancy, insomuch as the interwoven practices of audition, memorization, and recitation are central to the ethical upbringing of children in Egypt. In addition, the Quran, as well as other traditional Islamic genres, such as *ahādīth*, *qasas* (Islamic stories), and *sīyār* (biographies of Muhammed and other early Muslim figures), are woven into much of daily life, with verses often punctuating the succession of devotional, ritual, public, and family activities occurring in the course of a day (Eickelman 1978; Graham 1987; Schimmel 1994). Moreover, just as individual Quranic verses invoke ethical responses, so also do ethical situations often give rise to the citation of verses, whether in acts of giving advice, instructing children, making decisions, or arguing a point, particularly among those Muslims more observant of the demands of piety.

Listening as Performance

The proper audition of a sermon on tape entails a complex variety of activities. To begin, the sermon necessitates a voiced or sub-vocal accompaniment, as listeners are repeatedly required to enact a range of illocutionary acts. The preamble is a collective utterance composed of acts of remembrance (*dhikr*), praise (*thanā'*), and supplication (*du'a*). While it is the *khatīb* who provides the guiding vocalization for these acts, it is incumbent on the audience to accompany him in this with their hearts, an act that often involves the mumbled or whispered utterance of the appropriate devotional formulas. Shaykh Kishk (d. 1996) – a widely popular Egyptian preacher during the 1970s and 1980s – on occasions called on his audience to repeat word for word the invocations he recited, or more frequently, had them repeat one phrase over and over (such as "I seek forgiveness from God"), exploiting the pathetic momentum such rhythmic repetitions evoke in an audience.

Listeners also must be ready to pronounce the *basmala* ("In the name of God, the compassionate, the merciful") each time the *khatīb* begins to recite a verse from the Quran, and call for prayers upon the Prophet ("God bless him and grant him salvation") each time his name is mentioned. Additionally, throughout a sermon listeners are frequently enjoined to vocalize a wide variety of supplicatory locutions, or *du'a*, that relate to the argument the *khat-īb* is making or the situation he is describing. For example, in warning his audience about the dangers of gossip (*ghība*) or backbiting (*namīma*), a *khatīb* will call on them to implore God for forgiveness from moral error (*istighfār*). When lecturing them on a topic such as proper burial technique, he will have them ask God to increase their knowledge, to lessen the agonies of dying, or to illuminate the darkness of their graves. While discussing the plight of Muslims in Bosnia, he will pause to have the audience ask protection for Muslims who face affliction elsewhere in the world, for the defeat of their enemies, for the strength to persevere the hardships they suffer. The popular *khaṭīb* Omar Abd al-Kafi punctuates his sermons at rapid-fire intervals with such enjoinders, continuously recruiting his listeners to vocally and morally participate in the oratory he performs. In the context of cassette audition, listeners may respond with clearly audible utterances, with whispers, or simply with a silent movement of the lips.

The final section of a sermon is composed solely of such acts of supplication (*duʿāʾ*), strung one after another by the *khaṭīb* in a rhythmic crescendo that gathers emotional momentum as it proceeds. During the live performance at the mosque, this is when the pathos of the audience reaches its peak, and it is not uncommon at this point for the entire assembly to weep without restraint. While a particularly moving *duʿāʾ* will also lead to tears among cassette-listeners and wet eyes are quite common, without the emotional dynamics put in play by a large crowd, the intensity of the experience is relatively less. Nonetheless, many of the men I worked with appreciated this section of the sermon for the ethical–emotional progression it could initiate, leaving them with a sense of closeness to God and the accompanying experience of relief and tranquility (*iṭmīnān, sakīna*).

As I have argued, this should not be thought of through a generic, psychophysiological model of catharsis, but as an experience of moral relief whose specific contours have been honed through practices of ethical discipline, such as sermon audition. The listener, for example, must have cultivated the capacity for humility (*khushuʿ*) and regret (*nadm*): these are both felicity conditions (in Austin's sense) for the act of supplication as well as conditions for the body's experience of *iṭmīnān*, the relief and kinesthetic relaxation that follows – via repentance (*nadm* and *istighfār*) – from such an act. If these conditions are not met, then the listener will not be able to adopt the attitudes and modes of concentration upon which successful and beneficial acts of audition revolve. One's listening, in short, will be impaired.

Much of the substance of sermons is drawn from those pieces of text which form the common stock of cultural wisdom: Quranic verses, *ahāadīth*, biographies of the Prophet, accounts of the lives of early Muslims, and various traditional story genres that have been elaborated on the basis of these primary sources. Knowledge of these Islamic narrative forms, as the sermon-listeners of my study visibly demonstrated in explaining the sermons to me, consists not simply in the ability to recite a given text, but also in performing its emotional, gestural, and kinesthetic contours, the bodily conditions of the text as memory. While listening to taped sermons with these men, they would often interrupt with comments and gestures intended to help me understand the particular *ḥadīth* or story being recounted by the *khaṭīb*, sometimes stopping the tape to elaborate in more detail or introduce relevant passages from the Quran or other traditional textual sources. They all brought a common expressive-gestural repertoire to their explanations. Thus, in the context of recounting a *ḥadīth*, the narrowness of the grave (a common sermon topic) is expressed by a drawing up of the shoulders; the exit of the soul from the neck of a good man is distinguished from that of an infidel by the smoothness of the hand movement tracing the passage, the relaxed muscles of the face and hand, tightened and contorted in the case of the infidel; encounters with respected Muslim figures in heaven are accompanied by the joyful relaxation of the chest, the upward glance of delight. The events surrounding Judgment Day, a very common sermon topic for which many *khuṭabāʾ* have produced extensive cassette series (drawn either from sermons or mosque lessons), all have a strong gestural component: grasping of the book of one's deeds from above the right or left shoulder, the testifying of the individual parts of one's body as to the deeds they have committed, the binding of the hands by the guards of hell. While these stories all have a striking visual intensity, insomuch as they are rarely given visual representation, their most visible aspect lies in the gestures and emotional expressions which accompany their verbal performance.

Sermon Reception and Ethical Sedimentation

As should now be clear, sermon oratory recruits the body of the listener in multiple ways. Beyond its referential content, the sermon can be seen as a technique for the training of the body's gestures and affects, its physiological textures and colorations, its rhythms and styles of expression. The stories impart not simply moral lessons but ethical habits, the organization of sensory and motor skills necessary for inhabiting the world in a manner considered by those I worked with to be appropriate for Muslims. In learning the many performances involved in a sermon, such as extracting the soul of a sinner with a labored and trembling gesture of the hand rising above the neck, one acquires the affective-gestural experiences that make possible – in the view of the sermon-listeners I knew – the practices, modes of sociability, and attitudinal repertoires underlying a devout Islamic community. The task is similar to that of an actor who, when playing the part of King Lear, must hone the strained gait, the movement of the hands, the manner of breathing, and the contortions of the face that express the tortured soul of one so betrayed. Note that I am not referring to the symbolic coding of the body, the attribution of meaning to its surfaces, movements, and speech. Rather, it is more like what rhetoricians called "attitude," a kind of "non self-referential mode of awareness" (Dreyfus 1994: 58) not reducible to mental states or symbolic processes.

Notably, the young men I knew in Cairo did not always agree with each other in regard to the truth-status of some of the accounts commonly found in sermons. It was common, for example, that one person would refer to a narrative element (such as the throne of God) as a symbol (*ramz* or *kināya*), while another would claim it as "literally real" (*ḥaqīqī, mish majāzi*) though unknowably so (*bila kaif*). A university student named Sayf, for instance, would often describe those parts of a sermon he understood to be somewhat far-fetched as "metaphors": for example, the writing of the word "infidel" on the forehead of the Antichrist, or the blackening of the heart that

follows from sin. Other men, on the other hand, as well as most of the *khuṭabā'* themselves, insisted that these were statements of literal truth. Yet, despite these differences of opinion and comprehension, all of the young men I worked with would mimetically represent the narratives from which these elements were drawn in more or less the same way, including the corresponding facial and postural expressions of fear, delight, or tranquility. Not to say that these differences of interpretation are insignificant. Indeed, arguments about the ontological status of Quranic references have been extremely consequential throughout Islamic history. What I am pointing to here is that, beneath the level of expressed belief and opinion, those I knew who participated in the fashion of sermon-listening shared a common substrate of embodied dispositions of the sort I have described as instrumental to the task of sermon audition. It is these ethical dispositions, I argue, more than a commitment to a normative rationality, that constitute the common ground upon which the discourses of tradition come to be articulated; the moral "reflexes" that make arguments about the status of Quranic references meaningful and worthy of engagement.

Of course, in the moment of listening to a sermon, one does not act out all of the gestures and movements corresponding to the particular account being narrated by the *khaṭīb*, nor vocalize each and every response solicited. Rather, and this an important part of my argument, an experiential knowledge of the gestural and emotive elements of the story constitute a condition for its ethical reception. That is to say, one is capable of hearing the sermon in its full ethical sense only to the extent one had cultivated the particular modes of sensory responsiveness that that discourse demands. The British philosopher R. G. Collingwood's description of the experience entailed in the reception of works of art is instructive here (1966 [1938]: 139–53). Collingwood argues that we hear the sounds, colors, movements, and emotions that a composer has written into her music only insofar as we have an ear – and a body – trained in the sensibilities the composer brought to bear on her work (1966: 146–51). One does not hear "the raw sound" and then elaborate upon it an imaginary experience of emotion and color. One simply "hears" the emotion and color. The sensibilities that allow one to do so are not something purely cognitive, but are rooted in the experience of the body as a whole, as a complex of culturally and historically honed sensory modalities.

Our common understanding of the kinds of synæsthetic experiences Collingwood is referring to here is that they are composed of two parts: an objective part, represented by the sensuous, audible element, and a subjective one, belonging not to the actual sounds but to something we create in our minds independently of what we hear. Collingwood argues that this distinction between a sensuous and an imaginary part is misleading. To become an object that can be retained and referred to, he argues, a sensation must be attended to by consciousness, an act that transforms that sensation into an idea, an object of the imagination. A person comes to consciously attend to particular stimuli in the course of becoming experienced or trained, and their reactions to those stimuli become patterned in accord with the particular form of life that training upholds, and subordinated to the practices and goals which define it. As Collingwood says, our sensations become "fitted into the fabric of our life instead of proceeding on their own way regardless of its structure" (1966 [1938]: 209). Thus, the "imaginary experience" of movement, color, touch, and emotion that occurs when we listen to music is not produced through the free creative activity of the mind, but rather, is grounded in the actual sensual experience of the body as a complex of culturally-honed perceptual capacities. Our sensory responses are similar to those of other listeners or viewers, and to those that the author of the work intended to produce in us, to the extent that our capacities of hearing or vision have been shaped within a shared disciplinary context. They possess a specific affective-volitional structure as a result of the practices by which we have been formed as a member of a specific community.

Collingwood's discussion of perception in terms of the integrated totality of the trained body has, despite obvious differences, certain parallels with recent anthropological work inspired in the phenomenology of Merleau Ponty (Csordas 1990, 1994, 1999; Jackson 1983a, 1983b, 1989). Thomas Csordas, in particular, has provided us with a rich body of ethnographic work that explores how the socially informed body, by placing us in a determinant and preobjective relation to the world, "orchestrates" the culturally-specific objectifications produced through reflective practice. Yet, despite this common concern for the embodied character of action and perception, the analysis I have presented here departs sharply from the phenomenological approach Csordas has elaborated. Specifically, while Csordas has focused on identifying the preobjective foundations, or *habitus*, upon which a religious discourse erects its particular architecture, my own work has been concerned with the practical techniques (such as sermon audition) by which the bodily dispositions that underlie virtuous conduct are inculcated. That is, I have given less attention to how those dispositions have been objectified within discourses of contemporary Islam and more to the techniques through which they have been inculcated both as sensory skills and moral habits.

Such an approach, for example, allows us to understand the distinction that cassette-sermon listeners would frequently make between a kind of hearing which only engages the mind (*al-'aql*) and one that stems from the heart (*al-qalb*). As we can now see, their use of this distinction is not simply grounded in a metaphorical conceit. Instead, they are pointing to two contrasting modes of sensory organization, one purely intellectual, the other ethical and grounded in Islamic disciplinary practices. To listen to an Islamic cassette-sermon with the heart means to bring to bear on it those sensory capacities honed within disciplinary contexts which allow one to "hear" (soulfully, emotionally, physically) what would escape a listener who applied only her "ear" or *al-'aql* (mind). At the same time, sermon audition is one of the means by which those capacities are developed and deepened.

The kind of ethical skills learned and deepened by the men I knew through taped-sermon audition (among other practices) are precisely of the kind that worried Plato in *The Republic*. In his view, those performances which engaged an audience in ways which bypassed a reflective, philosophical understanding – such as poetry, theater, or song (or, in this instance, sermons) – had a power to impact on and mold individuals which rendered such arts especially dangerous. As a contemporary interpreter of Plato recently noted:

> The problem with uncontrolled mimesis, as Plato sees it, is not just the character of the likenesses it brings into our presence. It is how these likenesses gradually insinuate themselves into the soul through the eyes and ears, without our being aware of it . . . It is as if eyes and ears offer painter and poet entry to a relatively independent cognitive apparatus, associated with the senses, through which mimetic images can bypass our knowledge and infiltrate the soul. (Burnyeat 1998: 8)

Recognizing the power of such arts to shape moral character, Plato advocated the prohibition of those performances which depicted human qualities not corresponding to the Athenian virtues he saw as foundational to the ideal city. Later Christian thinkers, in contrast, emphasized the positive contribution of such embodied forms of knowledge. Arguing along lines much closer to those suggested by the men I worked with, Christian theologians from Aquinas to Luther to John Henry Newman have asserted that a certain disposition of the passions was necessary in order to assess the validity of claims for the truth of scripture; that virtues such as gratitude, humility, and love of God have an epistemic value, allowing one to evaluate evidence for the authority of the Bible in the proper light (Wainwright 1995: 50–2).

Conclusion

In undertaking the practices of cassette-discipline I have described here, sermon-listeners sought to reconstruct their own knowledge, emotions, and sensibilities in accord with models of Islamic moral personhood. I have chosen to analyze this practice, less in terms of its ideological content – i.e., its

role in the dissemination of rules of conduct or the indoctrination of politico-religious subjects – than in its relation to the formation of a sensorium: the visceral substrate enabling of the particular form of life that those who undertook the practice aspired to. Practices of this kind do not impart mastery of a specific cultural activity, but perceptual habits that incline one toward certain acts, discourses, and gestures. As opposed to the sort of technical skills acquired in the course of learning, say, the game of chess – skills that inhabit a highly circumscribed arena of practice – the ethical capacities cultivated by the men I worked with were applicable across many contexts and social domains. In doing so, they opened up what Merleau-Ponty referred to as the "antepredicative unity of the world and of our life" (1962: xviii), rendering this world as a space of moral action and the actor as a moral being.

In light of the analysis presented here, I want to suggest we think about traditions, not simply in terms of doctrines or discourses, but as grounded upon perceptual skills – prediscursive modes of appraisal – shaped within practices for which language and discourse is essential, but not reducible to these. I do not refer here to a general model of enculturation – the idea that in inhabiting a culture or class position one acquires (as it were, unconsciously) the sensibilities that characterize that culture or socioeconomic location – but to self-reflexive practices specifically geared to the inculcation of perceptual habits. In speaking of such embodied capacities as grounded in and sustaining of the traditions of Islam, however, I am not suggesting that they constitute a universal and unchanging fundament beneath the actual historical and contemporary heterogeneity of Islamic societies. Clearly, the styles of narration and argument employed by *khuṭabā'* today, as well as the spaces and times within which the practice of audition occurs, have been shaped by social and political modernity – by the institutional structures and practices of national citizenship and global market capitalism. The perceptual capacities listeners seek to cultivate are mediated, on the one hand, by functional possibilities of cassette technology, such as mobility, replay, and discontinuous listening; and on the other, by the discursive conventions of the modern print and televisual-based public sphere. In this sense, the sensibilities honed through this practice do not inhabit and reproduce a static historical edifice, ever identical with itself. As Asad has argued, to conceive of tradition in this way is inadequate:

> An Islamic discursive tradition is simply a tradition of Muslim discourse that addresses itself to conceptions of the Islamic past and future, with reference to particular Islamic practice in the present . . . [I]t will be the practitioners' conceptions of what is *apt performance*, and of how the past is related to present practices, that will be crucial for tradition, not the apparent repetition of an old form. (1986: 14–15)

What makes the practice of cassette-sermon audition part of an Islamic tradition is not its exact conformity to a fixed model, but the fact that, in its contemporary organization, assessment, and performance, the practice relies on authoritative discourses and historical exemplars embedded in that tradition (Asad 1999: 189–90; 1993: 210–11).

My argument here is that, beyond the discursive practices of historical articulation emphasized in Asad's remark, we should interrogate traditions in terms of continuities of disciplined sensibility and the practices by which these are created and revised across changing historical contexts. My suggestion, in other words, is that Benjamin's analysis of how the perceptual regime ushered in by

modernity renders traditional worlds silent, invisible, in short, imperceptible, need be complemented by a recognition of the way in which practitioners of a tradition, through innovation and adaptation, attempt to cultivate and sustain the sensory conditions, the modes of attention and inattention, that make that tradition viable within modern contexts (see Seremetakis 1994: 1–22). As in the practice described here, the possibilities for such innovation are often rooted in modernity itself, in the social, political, economic, and technological elements that define the modern. Thus, to cite a rather obvious instance, cassette technology makes the acquisition of a kind of traditional knowledge possible within the times and spaces of modern urban existence, one where the sort of long-term study, immersion, and apprenticeship characteristic of Islamic pedagogical practices has become inaccessible and impractical to most people. To speak of "the modern" as an enabling condition for "traditional practices" in this way rubs against the grain of our (still) normative understandings of these concepts.[8] The idea of a distinct temporal structure that binds together the constellation of modern elements gives way to a fractured historical space composed of heterogeneous practices, objects, and structures of varying temporal determinations. As the example presented here suggests, this plurality need be explored not simply in terms of languages, discourses, or practices, but also through the disciplined sensibilities against which these become articulable.

NOTES

1   For an excellent discussion of women's participation in the Islamic Revival in Egypt, including the ways new Islamic media forms are being put to use by women, see Mahmood 2001.

2   The most interesting and comprehensive works on mosque sermons in the Middle East are those of Richard Antoun 1989 and Patrick Gaffney 1994.

3   The reference here is to the Islamic Group (*al-Jamāʿa al-Islāmiyya*), a militant Islamist organization in Egypt.

4   On Islamic moral philosophy see Izutsu 1966, 1985; Fakhry 1983; Sherif 1975.

5   All translations of the Quran are from Muhammad Asad 1980.

6   For two interesting discussions of emotion in relation to poetic practice in Arabic contexts, see Lila Abu-Lughod 1986 and Steve Caton 1990.

7   The most interesting works in English on the topic of Quranic recitation are Denny (1980, 1981), Nelson (1985), Graham (1985, 1987), and Gade (1999).

8   As should be clear, I do not refer here to the sort of historical sleight-of-hand by

which ancient roots are claimed for a practice that is actually of recent origin, what Hobsbawm and Ranger (1988) referred to as an "invented tradition."

REFERENCES

Abu-Lughod, Lila. 1986. *Veiled Sentiments: Honor and Poetry in a Bedouin Society*. Berkeley: University of California Press.

Antoun, Richard. 1989. *Muslim Preacher in the Modern World: A Jordanian Case Study in Contemporary Perspective*. Princeton: Princeton University Press.

Aristotle. 1991. *The Art of Rhetoric*. Hugh C. Lawson-Tancred, trans. London: Penguin Books.

Asad, Muhammad. 1980. *The Message of the Qu'ran*. Gibraltar: Dar al-Andalus.

Asad, Talal. 1986. *The Idea of an Anthropology of Islam*. Occasional Paper Series, Washington, DC: Georgetown University Center for Contemporary Arab Studies.

——. 1993. *Genealogies of Religion: Discipline and Reasons of Power in Christianity and Islam*. Baltimore: Johns Hopkins University Press.

——. 1999. Religion, Nation-State, Secularism. In *Nation and Religion: Perspectives on Europe and Asia*. P. Van der Veer, ed. pp. 178–96. Princeton: Princeton University Press.

Austin, J. L. 1975 [1962]. *How to Do Things with Words*. Cambridge: Harvard University Press.

al-Azhar. 1988. *Islamic Legal Opinions*. Cairo: al-Azhar University.

Badawi, Abdul Nazim. 1996a. Conditions for Benefit from the Qur'an. *al-Tauḥīd* 25(4): 10–13.

——. 1996b. The Quran and Its Effect on the Hearts. *al-Tauḥīd* 25(3): 9–12.

Benjamin, Walter. 1968 [1936]. The Work of Art in the Age of Mechanical Reproduction. In *Illuminations: Essays and Reflections*. H. Arendt, ed. pp. 217–51. New York: Schocken Books.

——. 1968 [1936]. The Storyteller. In *Illuminations: Essays and Reflections*. H. Arendt, ed. pp. 83–109. New York: Schocken Books.

Burnyeat, M. F. 1998. Art and Mimesis in Plato's "Republic." *London Review of Books* 20 (9), May 21: 3–9.

Cantwell, Robert. 1999. Habitus, Ethnomimesis: A Note on the Logic of Practice. *Journal of Folklore Research* 36 (2/3): 219–34.

Caton, Steven. 1990. *"Peaks of Yemen I Summon": Poetry as Cultural Practice in a North Yemeni Tribe*. Berkeley: University of California Press.

Collingwood, R. G. 1996 [1938]. *The Principles of Art*. New York: Oxford University Press.

Csordas, Thomas J. 1990. Embodiment as a Paradigm for Anthropology. *Ethos* 18: 4–47.

——. 1994. *Embodiment and Experience: The Existential Ground of Culture and Self*. Cambridge: Cambridge University Press.

——. 1999. Embodiment and Cultural Phenomenology. In *Perspectives on Embodiment: The Intersections of Nature and Culture*. G. Weiss and H. F. Haber, eds. pp. 143–62. New York: Routledge.

Denny, Frederick. 1980. Exegesis and Recitation: Their Development as Classical Forms of Quranic Piety. In *Transitions and Transformations in the History of Religions*. F. E. Reynolds and T. M. Ludwig, eds. Leiden: E. J. Brill.

——. 1981. The *Adab* of Quran Recitation: Text and Context. International Congress for the Study of Quran, Canberra: Australian National University.

Dreyfus, Hubert. 1994. *Being-in-the-World: A Commentary on Heidegger's Being and Time, Division 1*. Cambridge, MA: MIT Press.

Eickelman, Dale. 1978. The Art of Memory: Islamic Education and its Social Reproduction. *Comparative Studies in Society and History* 20: 485–516.

Fakhry, Majid. 1983 *A History of Islamic Philosophy*, 2nd edn. New York: Columbia University Press.

Gade, Anna M. 1999. An Envy of Goodness: Learning to Recite the Qur'an in Modern Indonesia. Ph. D. Dissertation, University of Chicago.

Gaffney, Patrick D. 1994. *The Prophet's Pulpit: Islamic Preaching in Contemporary Egypt*. Berkeley: University of California Press.

al-Ghazali, A. H. 1984. *The Recitation and Interpretation of the Quran*. Abul Quasem, Muhammad, trans. London: KPI Press.

Graham, William A. 1985. The Qur'an as Spoken Word: An Islamic Contribution to the Understanding of Scripture. In *Approaches to Islam in Religious Studies*. R. C. Martin, ed. Tucson: University of Arizona Press.

———. 1987. *Beyond the Written Word: Oral Aspects of Scripture in the History of Religion*. Cambridge: Cambridge University Press.

Hirschkind, Charles. 2001. Civic Virtue and Religious Reason. An Islamic Counter-republic. *Cultural Anthropology* 16(1): 3–34.

Hobsbawm, Eric and Terence Ranger, eds. 1988. *The Invention of Tradition*. Cambridge: Cambridge University Press.

Izutsu, Toshihiko. 1966 *Ethico-Religious Concepts in the Quran*. Montreal: McGill University Press.

———. 1985. *The Concept of Belief in Islamic Theology*. Salem: Ayer Co., Publishers, Inc.

Jackson, Michael. 1983a. Knowledge of the Body. *Man* 18(2): 327–45.

———. 1983b. Thinking Through the Body: An Essay on Understanding Metaphor. *Social Analysis* 14 (December): 127–49.

———. 1989. *Paths Toward a Clearing: Radical Empiricism and Ethnographic Inquiry*. Bloomington: Indiana University Press.

Mahmood, Saba. 2001. Feminist Theory, Embodiment, and the Docile Agent: Some Reflections on the Egyptian Islamic Revival. *Cultural Anthropology* 16(2): forthcoming.

Merleau-Ponty, Maurice. 1962. *Phenomenology of Perception*. James Edie, trans. Evanston, IL: Northwestern University Press.

Nelson, Kristina. 1985. *The Art of Reciting the Quran*. Austin: University of Texas Press.

Padwick, Constance. 1996. *Muslim Devotions: A Study of Prayer-Manuals in Common Use*. Oxford: Oneworld Publications.

Salvatore, Armando. 1998. Staging Virtue: The Disembodiment of Self-Correctness and the Making of Islam as a Public Norm. *Bielefeld Yearbook of the Sociology of Islam*: 187–217.

Schimmel, Annemarie. 1994. *Deciphering the Signs of God: A Phenomenological Approach to Islam*. Albany: State University of New York Press.

Seremátakis, C. Nadia, ed. 1994. *The Senses Still: Perception and Memory as Material Culture in Modernity*. Chicago: University of Chicago Press.

Sherif, Mohamed Ahmed. 1975. *Ghazali's Theory of Virtue*. Albany: State University of New York Press.

Starrett, Gregory. 1995. The Political Economy of Religious Commodities in Cairo. *American Anthropologist* 97(1): 51–68.

Wainwright, William. 1995. *Reason and the Heart: A Prolegomenon to a Critique of Passional Reason*. Ithaca: Cornell University Press.

43

Moral Landscapes: Ethical Discourses among Orthodox and Diaspora Jains

Anne Vallely

Anne Vallely received her PhD in anthropology at the University of Toronto and now teaches in the Department of Classics and Religious Studies at the University of Ottawa. In this fine essay Vallely both locates Jain practices within the South Asian cultural world more generally, and compares the subtle but profound transformations in moral outlook and sensibility that have taken place among migrants to North America. At the urging of her Toronto consultants, Vallely originally conducted fieldwork among Jain nuns in Rajasthan, about whom she has produced an engaging ethnography (Vallely 2002). Her work thus exemplifies the recent trend, following the logic of transnational movement, to practice multisited ethnography. In addition, Vallely problematizes easy distinctions between "other-worldly" and "this-worldly" forms of asceticism. Her essay is also a valuable contribution to the emerging body of work on religion and the environment. Such analyses do not always lead in the direction that environmental activists might suppose (Weeratunge-Starkloff 2000) but, subtly handled, they demonstrate both the incommensurability of culturally distinct ethical traditions and their adaptability. They also suggest that religion can remain a highly relevant and positive force in an ever-changing world. Vallely is currently engaged in further research in Rajasthan as well as among Digambar Jains in south India and editing a book on "Animal Others and the Human Imagination."

The Jain tradition has flourished on the Indian subcontinent since the sixth century BCE and, although numerically a minority, remains a thriving religion with a distinctive identity within the larger Hindu culture. Jainism's unique ethical system is centered on the ascetic ideal of world renunciation and of absolute non-violence. The tradition, commonly encap-

From Anne Vallely, "Moral Landscapes: Ethical Discourses among Orthodox and Diaspora Jains," 2001, previously unpublished.

sulated in the aphorism "Ahimsa Paramo Dharma" ("non-violence is the highest form of religion"), has devoted more attention to the theory and practice of non-violence than has any other religious philosophy. In India, the Jain ethical worldview is expressed through affiliation with a particular ascetic order (sect and ascetic lineage) which serves as the primary means through which identity, as well as social borders, are established and maintained.

Although Jainism has its own history, distinct convictions, and traditions, it shares with Hinduism certain core beliefs, such as reincarnation, karma, as well as the desirability of asceticism and world renunciation. In India, therefore, the dominant culture of Hinduism has, for the most part, accommodated rather than challenged the Jain worldview. The situation is, however, profoundly different in North America, where the dominant culture does not embrace these core beliefs.

In this essay, I set out to look at Jain ethics as they are traditionally understood and constituted in India, and at how they may be changing as they take root in North American soil.[1] Traditional orthodox Jain ethics are renunciatory and individualistic, and their central ethic of *ahimsa* (non-harm) reflects this ascetic orientation. However, within a growing segment of the diaspora community, Jain ethics no longer reflect the ascetic ideal. Rather than through the idiom of self-realization or the purification of the soul, ethics are being expressed through a discourse of environmentalism and animal rights. The shift from an orthodox liberation-centric ethos to a sociocentric (or "ecological") one is an important development among the immigrant Jain community. Equally striking, however, is that which has remained constant. The emphasis of Jain ethics has remained focused on individual ethics and on the non-human environment, reflecting an ontology whereby moral value is constituted, above all else, through interactions with "nature."

The actual number of Jains living outside of India is uncertain (see Israel, 1994). It has been variously estimated, from a low figure of 70,000–80,000 (Dundas, 1992), to as high as one million (Jain Centre of Toronto, 1998). Despite an insistence upon the exclusivity of their religion, Jains have often displayed a

degree of fluidity in religious identification (e.g., until recently – and only after considerable campaigning by Jain leadership – it was common for Jains to record themselves as "Jain-Hindu" on Indian census enumerations). That Jains have, in certain contexts, defined themselves as a sub-sect of Hinduism, or have emphasized caste over Jain identity, demonstrates the complex nature of religious identity, and has made the tradition difficult to pigeonhole (see Dundas, 1992).

Today the Jain diaspora comprises members from both the Svetambar and Digambar sects; from a wide number of *gacchas* (ascetic lineages) and castes; and also from all regions of India. At the turn of the twentieth century, however, the vast majority of immigrants, travelling mainly to East Africa, were Gujaratis and Svetambar image-worshipers (Dundas, 1992). Due to political instability in East Africa, Jains began emigrating to Britain and North America in the late 1960s. Banks (1991) estimates that as much as 80 percent of the Jain population of Britain today is Gujarati. In Canada, approximately 50 percent of the Jain population arrived via East Africa; the rest directly from India. Dundas writes that among the first wave of Jain immigrants to East Africa, caste connections were the basis of support networks and played a more important role in the successes of the migrants than did their identity as Jains (1992: 232–3). However, since the emergence of communities in Western Europe and North America, there has been a strong movement to establish an international Jain community and an inclusive religious identity across caste and sectarian lines.

Jains, like the larger Indian immigrant group of which they are a part, constitute a new community in Canada (see Israel, 1994). While Jains have been immigrating to Canada since the late nineteenth century, their numbers until recently were small. No self-perpetuating community existed until the 1970s when Canada's immigration laws (formerly restrictive to non-Europeans) opened up to Asians. Two-thirds of Canadian Jains are settled in Ontario, mirroring immigration patterns in general.

The geographical and cultural distance from India has led to changes in the beliefs and practices of what constitutes Jainism in Canada, but it has not diminished its significance as a potent source of identity. Rather, it may be argued that it has *increased* its importance. The extent to which Jains in India constitute a discrete social entity, transcending sectarian, caste, linguistic and regional differences, is a matter of debate (Carrithers & Humphrey, 1991). In North America, by contrast, there has been a major effort to create such a self-consciously distinct religious identity.

In the early 1980s, the Jain Society of Toronto was founded and the first Jain Center was established in that city. It replaced a home temple (a residence) that had served the community's needs since 1974. The Center houses a temple that is used jointly by members of the Svetambar Deravasi (idol-worshiping), Svetambar Sthanakvasi (non-idol-worshiping), and Digamabar sects. In addition, it publishes a newsletter and hosts a wide range of community activities and cultural events.

In North America, Jainism is being fostered in an environment where the standard markers of identity are either absent or altered. For instance – and importantly – there are no Jain ascetics in Canada. Ascetics act as powerful symbols of the tradition and are typically its central preceptors (see Babb, 1996). Their presence and interaction with the laity assures *gaccha* and sect loyalty, as well as the continuation of traditional, orthodox practices (viz., ritual, prayer, fasting, correct practice, scriptural knowledge, etc.). The absence in Canada of ascetic leadership appears to allow for the existence of a wider variety of religious belief as well as the development of a non-sectarian Jain socioreligious identity.

The absence of ascetic leadership is likely an important factor in a decline of sectarian affiliation, particularly for second-generation Jains. A number of the community's first-generation immigrants believe that Jainism as practiced in Canada is less "authentic" than that practiced in India, and readily attribute the perceived "degeneration" of Jainism outside of India to the absence of ascetics (this group was eager for me to conduct my doctoral research in India where I would encounter "real" Jainism). Others (especially, but by no means exclusively, second-generation Jains) consider orthodox Jainism to be overly tied to caste and sect, and essentially exclusive. They reject these "social"

dimensions of the tradition and espouse a universalistic, modern interpretation. They emphasize the values of vegetarianism, animal welfare, and meditation, and actively promote interfaith activities. The majority of the federation of Jain Associations in North America and the UK would fall under this latter category. Thus, for instance, the *Jain Study Circular* (published in New York), the *Jain Digest* (Ohio), *Jiv Daya* (California), and the new international journal *Jain Spirit* (UK) all champion a modern, scientific vision of Jainism.

The Moral Self in Orthodox Jainism

Through a brief description of a typical "day in the life" of an ascetic (based on my ethnographic experiences of living with a Jain ascetic order), I hope to elucidate the traditional Jain understanding of "nature" and the ideal role of human beings in nature.

It is three in the morning, and deep within the walls of the monastery, the *sadhvis* (nuns) begin to wake. The unruffled thin sheets covering their bodies indicate tranquil sleep, an auspicious sign. Completely motionless sleep is the objective because all movement is potentially dangerous to other living beings. Unkempt sheets would indicate reckless gestures, and thereby, sin. Spontaneous, unmonitored activity leads to the death of countless lives that surround us at all times. The *sadhvis* rise slowly from lying on their backs and settle into a lotus posture on the cardboard mat upon which they had slept. The *muhpatti* (or mouthshield) remains on. It is worn during the night for the same reasons it is worn during the day: viz., to prevent the harm to subtle living beings in the air, and is removed only when eating. Sitting tranquilly, the *sadhvis* begin their prayers and meditation, awaiting the rise of the sun. In the darkness, where the presence of tiny living beings are concealed, movement is folly.

After more than two hours the first hint of light sneaks in through a window. The countdown is on: 30, 20, 10, 5 more minutes . . . finally there is enough light to make out the fine lines in the palm of one's hand, and activity can begin. By insisting on sufficient light to read one's palm lines, the ascetics ensure their ability to be mindful of the living beings in their proximity. They begin the practice of *pratilekhna* (the meticulous inspection of one's clothes (and all items) for tiny life forms). Finally, with the sun high in the sky, there is a quick retreat from the building and we are off for the collection of alms. Consuming food is strictly prohibited when the sun goes down, so the items collected this morning will be the *sadhvis*' first bit of food and drink since before sunset the previous day.

As we move swiftly along the village paths in search of alms, we are mindful of each step. We walk only on sand and cement, for walking on grass would mean killing it; brushing against a bush would mean harming it. Jain ascetics cannot prepare their own food. Plants, water, fire, electricity – all the things necessary for cooking – are considered alive. By the time the ascetic consumes the food, it must be devoid of all life. By ingesting food and water that are no longer alive, the ascetic accrues no karma. Through the generosity of the pious householders, the ascetics remain karmically unaffected by violence inherent in the preparation of food. The householder, who has not renounced the world and is living "in" society, accepts that a certain amount of violence is necessary in order to survive, and is more than happy to provide ascetics with alms. By doing so she earns good karma.

We approach the home of a pious lay person. Her door is open and she beckons us in. We enter and the *sadhvi* examines the food before her. Importantly, she asks the woman for whom has she prepared the large quantity of food. The woman explains that it is made for her family – and certainly not with the expectation of giving it as alms to the ascetics. [Lay Jains, the householders, are not allowed to prepare food explicitly for ascetics and should not know in advance that the ascetic will be coming to beg. Instead the two are to meet by chance. To prepare food explicitly for the ascetics would involve them in violence.]

And how was it prepared?, asks the *sadhvi*. The woman of the house explains in detail that all the plants and fruits were boiled; that the water used in making porridge was first boiled. The nuns stand away from the small fridge in the centre of the room – for to brush against it would cause harm to fire-bodied beings in electricity. The *sadhvi* asks the woman if she washed her hands with "raw" water. No, the woman is emphatic, she only allows boiled (i.e., "dead") water to touch her. Satisfied, the *sadhvis* yield their alms bowls and collect a small quantity of food. Then we are off.

After visiting five or six homes, the *sadhvis* have collected enough food, and we head back to the monastery grounds. The food is distributed among their small group and consumed in its entirety. If any is left over (which doesn't happen often, but has happened), it must be buried. Discarded food would become the source of an orgy of violence – insects would swarm in it, dogs would eat the insects and would fight amongst themselves for it – and the ascetics would be implicated in the violence. After their meals, the ascetics depart again (in pairs) for "excretory purposes." Because water is alive, ascetics cannot use flush toilets, so they venture away from their dwellings to find a patch of land that is devoid of vegetation. Again, their refuse must be buried.

After sunset ascetics are prohibited from going outdoors because the night air is filled with dew which, like rain, is alive. If it is absolutely necessary to go outside, they must cover their heads with a cloth so that the falling dew or rain (water-bodied beings) will hit the fabric, and not die as a result of impacting directly against their bodies. Before sunset, they recite a prayer of *pratikraman* in which they repent for the sin of violence that may have occurred during the day; and perform *pratilekhna* again before changing into their night clothes. No food or medicines are consumed after sunset and, since ascetics cannot use electricity, they remain in the dark until a householder turns on a light. By 9 o'clock most have carefully lowered themselves onto cardboard mats (thoroughly examined for insects) and fallen fast asleep.

The entire logic of the ascetics' daily routine is dictated by the ethic of *ahimsa* or non-harm. It is in interactions with the non-human world that the ascetics are most highly attentive, observant, and mindful – this is, when they are most quintessentially ascetic. Interactions with "nature" – with the air, water, soil, and vegetation – define both lay and ascetic Jains, by determining the boundaries of their ethical being. The Jain scholar, James Laidlaw, insightfully describes *ahimsa* as an "ethic of quarantine." He argues that Jains' elaborate practices of non-violence are not so much about minimizing death or saving life, but about keeping life "at bay" and essentially amount to an attempt at the "avoidance of life" (1995).

Since all aspects of physical reality are imbued with life, harm done to any one of these lives results in karmic inflow. Violence against other human beings is, according to Jains, obvious wickedness. Such a gross violation would immediately condemn the culprit to countless future lives of suffering, and in an embodiment other than that of the human form. Since violence against human beings is universally condemned and relatively rare (in the sense that it is not something everyone engages in), the true cause of karmic bondage responsible for the cycle of death and rebirth (*samsar*) must lie elsewhere. For Jains, it is in the violence inherent in daily social life that is the cause of our bondage; simply existing leads to the unavoidable death of innumerable beings each day. In the most ancient of Jain texts, the Acarang Sutra of the fourth century BCE, it is written: "Action, whether done, caused or condoned by oneself, brings about rebirth, and the world is in a state of suffering caused by actions of ignorant people who do not know that they are surrounded by life-forms which exist in earth, water, air and fire" (Dundas, 1992).

Rather than being peripheral, interactions with the non-human world are at the very centre of the creation of the Jain moral self.[2] Jainism treats the whole of existence as part of its moral community. Moral worth is established, above all else, through interactions with the non-human world. Jains do not believe in a creator of the universe; they have no belief in a transcendent god, therefore salvation is not sought through a relationship with the divine. Instead nature becomes a *moral theatre*, within which one's ethical being is established, cultivated, and judged. This is a central feature of Jain ethical life. And, in spite of other profound differences, it is equally central for Jains in the diaspora as it is for Jains in India. I will return to this point in the discussion of the Jain immigrant community, but first it is necessary to provide an understanding of traditional, orthodox Jain ontology and its understanding of the ideal role of human beings in nature.

Traditional Jain Ontology

Jainism bases its teachings on a fundamental division of all existing things into two classes: *jiv* (that which has a soul), and its negation, *ajiv* (that which is devoid of soul). *Ajiv* represents physical matter, also called "karma" – as Jains understand karma to be a physical, material substance that sticks to the soul. The soul has no form, but during its worldly career it is vested with a body and becomes subject to an inflow of karmic "dust" *(asravas)*. These are subtle material particles that are drawn to a soul because of its worldly activities. All worldly souls – be they in the form of a worm, a blade of grass, a dewdrop, a clod of earth, or a human being – are in karmic bondage. The soul's association with karmic matter prevents it from realizing its true and omniscient nature, and it will go through a continuous cycle of death and rebirth until it attains *moksha* or spiritual liberation.

Ahimsa is the central practice in the quest for liberation because it defines – negatively – a state of purity and detachment within a violent, passionate world. It is an ethic of non-interference and a method of disconnecting or separating oneself from the violence of everyday life. And in so doing it establishes *difference*. *Ahimsa* makes the human incarnation unique among all living beings by making it moral. We see that in Jainism, the moral self is created through a retreat from the rest of nature. A central focus of all cultural life, cross-culturally, is devoted to establishing what it is to be properly human; the attempt to establish human uniqueness in contradistinction to the "otherness" of the environment is fundamental to human self-definition. The philosopher Charles Taylor (1989) argues that a moral reaction is an affirmation of a given "ontology of the human" – in other words, our morals reveal our notions of what it is to be truly human and why humans are worthy of respect.

In Jainism, human morality is established through restraint, stemming from a recognition that we share this world with a multitude of living beings, all of whom are now in bondage, but on the same path as we are to eventual liberation.

In the Judeo-Christian and secular western philosophical traditions, human dignity resides in that which *distinguishes* us from the non-human environment, in particular, that which *distinguishes* us from animals. Animals have always served as a contrast to illuminate human nature, and human worth is located in those areas that we believe we have a monopoly on – e.g., a soul, rationality, language, morality, etc. In Jainism, human dignity and moral consideration are not rooted in a nature–culture distinction. Value is not dependent on that which non-humans lack. Although Jains treat the human embodiment as a privileged and exalted one, they do not believe that humans possess anything *uniquely* or *exclusively* which should entitle them to their superior status. There exist five types of living beings in the Jain universe, each type having either one, two, three, four, or five senses. These beings are arranged according to the following schema:

Number and type of senses	Type of beings
1. One-sensed beings called *"nigodas"* (touch)	earth-, water-, fire-, air-, and plant bodied
2. Two-sensed beings (touch and taste)	worms, leeches, molluscs (oysters, mussels, snails, etc.)
3. Three-sensed beings (touch, taste, smell)	small insects, e.g., ants, fleas, centipedes
4. Four-sensed beings (touch, taste, smell, sight)	wasps, flies, mosquitoes, butterflies, moths, scorpions, etc.
5. Five-sensed beings, (touch, taste, smell, sight, hearing)	larger animals such as fish, birds, quadrupeds, humans

(*Umsvati – That which is*, 1994: 45)

It is the possession of a soul, and not the stage of development, nor number of senses a being possesses, that entitles one to a life of dignity and respect. Therefore, moral consideration does not hinge upon that which the human incarnation possesses alone, but on that which it shares with all other beings.

The greater the number of senses, the greater the self-awareness and, therefore, the greater the ability to understand worldly existence as a state of bondage in need of escape. But an increase in the number of senses does not mean greater moral worth. Consciousness is the inalienable characteristic of every *jiva*, however undeveloped it may be. It is present even in the *nigodas* (the least developed life form) and through its progressive development, the *nigoda* too may culminate in the supreme state of the soul, namely omniscience. Jains believe that the soul passes through an infinite number of embodiments as it progresses from the lowest to the highest state of spiritual development. These states have been classified into 14 stages called "*gunasthanas*," each of which is necessary to pass through to attain liberation.

In the Jain universe, plants and animals are not believed to have autonomous existences, but rather form part of the same tragic drama of bondage and liberation that humans do, albeit with fixed roles and characters. The whole of existence is assumed to be ordered in a hierarchical scale, moving up to the Tirthankaras (the revered teachers) and down from them, in what is regarded as diminishing degrees of perfection to ascetics, *shravaks* (or lay people), animals, plants, and single-sensed beings. Plants and animals are considered to be moral symbols of inherent pedagogic value, and are judged according to the same moral standards as are human beings. All things, animate and inanimate, are part of the same narrative.

In a moral cosmic order, where all beings are potent moral symbols, what makes humans worthy of their special status is not a unique possession of a soul, reason, or language: it is the display of moral superiority evidenced in their practices. In Jainism, human supremacy and distinction from the non-human environment is a matter of degree, not of kind; and importantly, it is established through ethical behavior. Since nature is a moral theater, and moral perfection is *demonstrable* only through its "acting out" (of which asceticism is the greatest performance), ethical behavior becomes a compelling and potent source of selfhood. Ethics are a resource, and represent the primary method through which Jains define and maintain the human domain. *Ahimsa* is the quintessential norm of Jain ethics – its application becomes the way to define

human beings at the centre of a universe full of similar souls. Voluntary restraint and ardent *ahimsa*, in a world characterized by meaningless activity and violence, establishes the uniqueness of the human incarnation. Therefore, the ideal moral self in Jainism is created through disengagement and withdrawal from nature.

Jain Ethics in Diaspora

The ascetic basis of Jainism – its traditional core – is decreasing in significance among a large segment of the Jain immigrant community, particularly the youth. A worldview which emphasizes quiescence and reunciation is commonly seen as "old-fashioned." As one young Jain put it, "Many youth are worried by the outdated and ascetic ideals that are presented to us by the form of Jainism that our parents practice" (Modi, 1993). Others consider ascetic practices to be irrelevant in the modern world. For instance, a Jain college student writes,

As for the discrepancy between the way of living in the West as opposed to the way that is shown in Jainism, timely changes need to be made. To live both ways of life requires a reinterpretation of the strict rules and outdated practices. For example, it was taught by our ancestors not to eat at night. Today, however, with parents working and daily activities extending into the late evening, it is not possible to eat early. In addition, health standards are safer here than they were hun-

dreds of years ago and hence, it seems acceptable that we eat late at night. Another example refers to the practice of boiling water before drinking it. Here, there is no need for that. The sanitation department already purifies it before we get it in our homes. Other practices such as these are no longer practical to this day and age. (Doshi, 1993).[3]

To a great number of Jains in North America, sect, *gaccha* (ascetic lineage), and caste are no longer significant markers of identity[4] as they are in India. There are simply too few Jains to maintain sect endogamy. Instead, in Toronto, all Jain sects are represented in a single Jain Center (in Etobicoke) and, unlike in India, intermarriage is common between sects and even outside the faith among strictly vegetarian Hindu families. In North America, *ahimsa* and, in particular, its dietary expression in terms of vegetarianism has, for many, become the only non-negotiable characteristic of being Jain.

Results from the survey that I am conducting within the Toronto Jain community (preliminary at this point, with responses from only approximately 10 percent), reveal a marked discrepancy between first- and second-generation Jains' understanding of the appropriate application of *ahimsa*. For most first-generation Jains, a life of non-violence (in particular, a vegetarian diet) is intrinsically tied up with ideas of purity and karma theory. *Ahimsa* is the practice that leads to spiritual liberation. While compassion for all living beings is an important part of their practice, violence (*himsa*) is avoided because it is an obstacle to self-realization. As the Jain scholar Padmanabh Jaini explains,

> for Jainas, [violence] refers primarily to injuring oneself – to behaviour which inhibits the soul's ability to attain *moksa*. Thus the killing of animals, for example, is reprehensible not only for the suffering produced in the victims, but even more so because it involves intense passions on the part of the killer, passions which bind him more firmly in the grip of *samsara* [cycle of death and rebirth]. (Jaini, 1990: 167)

For most Jain youths, however, violence refers principally to harm done to *others,* and *ahimsa* is primarily about alleviating the suffering of other living beings. Self-realization is subordinate to this overarching goal.

This socio-centric understanding of Jain ethics has led young Jains to "extend" the practices of non-violence to areas that the first generation (and orthodox Jainism more generally) has not ventured. For instance, the use of silk, leather, and dairy products poses an ethical problem for many young Jains that seems not to exist, for the most part, among older, first-generation Jains. The active promotion of a vegan lifestyle (i.e., one where no animal products whatsoever are used or consumed) is almost an exclusively second-generation effort.

The traditional Jain concern for the smallest of life forms (individual *nigodas*) has been transformed into a general concern for "the environment," and is expressed within a discourse of ecology – the need to preserve rain forests, green spaces, clean water, etc. And the traditional Jain concerns for animals, as fellow living beings in karmic bondage, is now commonly articulated within an animal rights discourse of rescue and protection. This socio-centric (or "ecological") interpretation of Jain ethics is the governing discourse on Jain websites and in Jain magazines (e.g., *Jain spirit; Jiv Daya*) and is widespread at Jain conventions.[5] And significantly, it is also commonly advocated at *pathshala* (schools for religious learning).[6]

Many Jain families in North America send their children to *pathshala*. It is one of the principal ways through which the community hopes to preserve and transmit Jain teachings within the diaspora community. A Toronto Jain Society booklet describes *pathshala* as "a place where children, youth and future generations receive a sound understanding of the Jain philosophy with an equal emphasis on practice of Jainism" (Jain Society of Toronto Souvenir). In addition to learning about Jainism's 24 revered teacher-ascetics (Tirthankaras), rituals, and vows, children are also encouraged to apply the principle of non-violence to remedy perceived social ills. For instance, at a *pathshala* class I attended in October 1999, the teacher asked the class (of about 15 young people between the ages of 12 and 16) to reflect on the following poem:

> Thanksgiving dinner's sad and thankless
> Christmas dinner's dark and blue
> When you stop and try to see it
> From the turkey's point-of-view
>
> Sunday dinner isn't funny
> Easter Feasts are just bad luck
> When you see it from the viewpoint
> Of a chicken or a duck
>
> Oh how I once loved tuna salad
> Pork and lobsters, lamb chops too
> Till I stopped and looked at dinner
> From the dinner's point of view (Silverstein, 1974)

The teacher asked: "What principles of Jainism does this poem convey?" The students called out: "*Ahimsa*" and "*Anekantvada*" (principle of multiple viewpoints). "Precisely," the teacher said, "The poem encourages us to practice nonviolence and to try to see reality from another perspective – in this case from the perspective of the animals."

A cursory examination of contemporary Jain activities within the diaspora reveals how *ahimsa* is being established as an ecological ethic. For example:

- A visit to the Toronto Jain Centre discloses this generational and cultural divide: side by side are the centre's permanent artwork depicting the Jain Tirthankaras (revered teacher-ascetics) and children's posters made at *pathshala* (schools for religious learning). The theme of many of the posters concerns human responsibility to the planet. One proclaims: "Don't Smoke; Don't Pollute: Don't Drink Alcohol." Another poster states: "Be Kind to Animals."
- The vast majority of Jain websites and journals published in the US, the UK, and Canada espouse a socio-centric interpretation of Jain ethics.
- Young British Jains recently organized two mass rallies in London (on Dec 31 1999) to highlight the world's growing environmental crisis and promote awareness of the vegetarian lifestyle, and the current plight of farm animals.
- "Mahavir Awards"[7] for work in non-violence were awarded to the following organizations: Compassion in World Farming, PETA (People for the Ethical Treatment of Animals), and the Green Party.
- In North America there has been a strong move by Jain groups to link up with animal rights and environmental organizations.

The reinterpretation of *ahimsa*, that I have been describing, reflects more than the inclusion of environmental and animal rights concerns: it reflects different understanding of "nature" and of the ideal role of human beings *in* nature. A socio-centric interpretation of Jain ethics estranges *ahimsa* from its liberation-centric, otherworldly ontology and, in addition, undermines its function in the creation of the Jain ascetic ideal. The differences between the liberation-centric and socio-centric worldviews can be nicely demonstrated by juxtaposing two versions of the same popular tale of the twenty-second "prophet" of Jainism – Tirthankara Neminath. The first story, told to me in India, reveals the liberation-centric focus

of orthodox Jainism; the second is a product of diaspora community, and reveals a distinctly sociocentric focus.

Orthodox "ascetic" version

Many years ago there was a handsome young prince called Nemi Kumar. He was to be married to a beautiful princess called Rajimati. On the arranged date the marriage procession started with Nemi Kumar riding the decorated king elephant. All the kings and princes of the Yadav clan joined the procession with their royal regalia and retinue. When the procession was approaching the destination, Nemi Kumar saw that on the side of the road there were large fenced-in areas with cages full of wailing animals and birds. Filled with sympathy and compassion, he asked the elephant driver why the animals and birds were being kept in bondage. The driver informed him that the creatures were collected to be butchered for meat for the large number of guests attending his marriage. Nemi Kumar was filled with despair and a feeling of detachment. He said to the elephant driver, "If I agree to be the cause of the butchering of so many living beings, my life and the one to come will be filled with pain and misery. Therefore, I will not marry. Immediately arrange for the release of all these creatures. Return home to Dwarka." The driver opened the gates of the cages. The animals ran away into the jungle. The driver came back and turned the elephant toward Dwarka. On the way Nemi Kumar took off all the valuables and ornaments on his body and handed them over to the elephant driver. The news spread panic in the marriage procession. All the seniors of the Yadav clan tried to change the mind of Nemi Kumar, but in vain. Nemi Kumar said to them, "As these animals were prisoners in iron cages, we all are prisoners in the cages of karma which is much stronger. See the feeling of joy evident in the animals released from the cages. Know that happiness is in freedom, not in bondage. I want to tread the path of breaking this bondage of karma and embrace eternal bliss." One day, not long afterward, he stood under an Ashoka tree before many onlookers. There he removed his clothes and pulled out five fistfuls of hair, initiating himself as an ascetic. He spent the next 54 days in deep spiritual practices, meditating and fasting without any attachment to his body. On the fifteenth day of the dark half of the month of Ashvin, while observing a two-day fast and mediating, he became an omniscient. He became the twenty-second *Tirthankara,* known as "*Arhat Neminath.*"

When Rajimati [Nemi Kumar's fiancée] recovered from her melancholy, she decided to follow the path taken by Nemi Kumar. When she learned that Nemi Kumar had become an omniscient, she took *diksa* (initiation). She lost herself in penance and other spiritual practices and in the end gained liberation.

Diaspora "ecological" version

Many years ago there was a handsome young prince called Nemi Kumar. He was to be married to a beautiful princess called Rajimati. On his wedding day Nemi Kumar led the procession of his family and friends, and his princely retinue, towards Princess Rajimati's palace. Everyone was in a festive mood. There was music in the air. The Prince was sitting calmly in his chariot, which his charioteer was driving. Suddenly Prince Nemi Kumar heard animal noises which got louder as they got nearer. They soon saw where the noises were coming from. Prince Nemi Kumar asked the procession to stop and listen. Hundreds of animals and birds were packed tightly in cages. There were fish in large tanks. The animals seemed frightened and restless. Their eyes were pleading. The Prince asked his friends why these animals and birds were captured. He was told they were for his wedding feast. This saddened the Prince, who was very kind and sensitive. The frightened sheep seemed to say, "We will be slaughtered for this prince's feast." A beautiful deer had his eyes full of tears, as if he were pleading, "I don't want to be killed, I want to go back to the forest and roam free." Beautiful green parrots were flying here and there in their cages trying to find a way out. A wise bull seemed to be saying, "These men are cruel. They cry when their children die, but how can they kill our children? Why can't they eat only plants and fruits, as we do? How can they claim to be superior to us when they kill us all the

time?" The kind Prince could bear it no longer. His heart was crying at the pain and fear the poor animals were suffering. He climbed down from his chariot and walked toward the cages. The animals quietened down, seeing such a stately but kind and loving figure walking toward them. They knew that they need no longer be frightened. The Prince opened the cages, and let the animals and birds out. He told his men to return the fish to the sea without harming them. The birds flew out happy and free. The animals ran into the forest. They all seemed to be thanking the Prince for saving them. Just then King Ugrasen, the Princess's father, came to meet the Prince. He saw the Prince releasing the animals and asked, "Why have you released these animals, O Prince?" The Prince replied, "How can we rejoice when so many animals are suffering? *How can we humans feast on these innocent animals and birds we are meant to protect?* What use is happiness if it is built on the suffering of so many? With this the Prince turned his chariot and went back. The wedding was called off. After some time, the Prince became a monk. Princess Rajimati followed in his footsteps and became a nun. The Prince Nemi Kumar was none other than the twenty-second Tirthankar Bhagvan Neminath. (Kapashi, Shah, & Desai, 1994: 16–17; emphasis added)

What is lost in the diaspora version is what is most meaningful to Jains in India, namely the ascetic values of detachment and renunciation. It estranges asceticism, and makes its connection with *ahimsa* or "non-violence" rather puzzling. Secondly, although it retains the centrality of the doctrine of *ahimsa,* it does so with an emphasis on the importance of suffering. A preoccupation with the avoidance of suffering betrays a this-worldly orientation, in that it assumes suffering is so wretched because it is so meaningless.

In the diaspora version, Nemi Kumar asks, "How can we humans feast on these innocent animals and birds we are meant to protect?" This idea of "protecting the innocent" implies that it is only humans who are endowed with moral judgment, which they should use to take care of "instinctual" beasts. But a central tenet of all Indian religio-traditions is that the universe is a moral order where all things are endowed with moral status (Jhingran, 1989: 33). Suffering may be abominable, but it is never meaningless. Moral law, and not the mechanical forces of nature, govern and control the world and all its processes. This is distinct from a "nature/culture" world-view which considers morality a human peculiarity in a passive, innocent nature and which, in turn, assumes an ethic of active support to be a uniquely human responsibility. Crusades to rid the world of suffering pre-suppose the human ability to do so; only humans with their "humanity" or "civiliza-tion" can bring morality to a profane, arbitrary "nature."

We conclude from the diaspora version of the story that Prince Nemi Kumar behaved righteously because he saved the lives of the animals. His reasons for renouncing the world and becoming a monk are not at all clear. If the alleviation of physical suffering was his motive, why should he not carry on doing this? Almost without exception, Jain stories end with the protagonist renouncing the world and embarking on the ascetic path. We do not learn about all the further austerities Nemi Kumar deliberately put himself through on his path of asceticism, perhaps because that would be dif-ficult to reconcile with a story first and fore-most about the avoidance of suffering. The original version, by contrast, does not stress the avoidance of suffering. Suffering has never been the primary concern of the Jain ethical system precisely because its existence can be rationalized within a moral cosmic order. The orthodox understanding of *ahimsa* is primarily concerned with the *avoidance* of behaviour that inhibits the soul's ability to attain *moksa*, not an injunction to alleviate suffering. The philosopher Charles Taylor argues that modern Westerners place an exceptional importance on avoiding suffering, far more now than even just a few centuries ago, and significantly, he attributes this to a decline in the West of the whole notion of a moral cosmic order which gave misfortune "meaning."

The orthodox version of the story places stress on detachment because *attachment* is the root of violence and the source of all bondage. The killing of animals is an extreme form of violence arising from attachment, but Nemi Kumar realizes that social life itself is inher-ently violent. Marriage, for example, as an attachment is also a form of violence. Asceti-cism, as a "stepping out" of society, becomes logical: the ascetic path is the best means to ensure a life of detachment. And while com-passion is a feature of the original story, it is not understood as emotional vicarious suffer-ing; instead it is presented as a respect for all living beings as equal souls. Every soul is entrapped in worldly bondage, and will one day have to break those bonds if liberation is to be attained. Compassion means recognizing that all living beings are essentially similar; that all deserve respect and that none should be injured. It means not interfering in another's spiritual journey.

Orthodox Jainism is intrinsically other-worldly; it problematizes nature and though it espouses a powerful ethos of respect and com-passion for all living beings, it is not a ethic of social activisim. The Jain ethic of non-harm *is* a powerful ecology in itself, but its teachings are not designed to remedy social ills so much as escape them. Orthodox Jain ethics reveal a perception of the world as inherently corrupt and in need of transcendence, and it leads to renunciation and to the desire to help individu-als out of *samsara*, not to active social involvement.

The understanding of "nature" that is being fostered in the North American context is pro-foundly different from that of traditional, orthodox Jainism. In a socio-centric ecological worldview, the ideal role for human beings is to become actively engaged with nature – to develop an ecology of love and enchantment in order to preserve it.

In conclusion, Jainism, as it is being consti-tuted in North America, reflects its new roots. Its traditional ethics of non-violence, self-control, and renunciation are being divorced from the traditional ontology, and redefined in ways that better reflect the concerns of the modern diaspora community. However, in spite of their divergences, the ethics of the orthodox and the diaspora communities both stress the centrality of "nature" in the consti-tution of the moral self. Both emphasize respect for individual living beings as subjects, and consider the human relations with the non-human to be of central importance. For both, "nature" is the moral theatre within which one's ethical being is established – a fact that may very well be the most important feature of Jain ethical life.

NOTES

The research for this essay was generously supported by a Rockefeller Foundation fellowship in the Humanities.

1   My Ph.D. research in the field of cultural anthropology was largely a study of Jain ethics. It was based on 13 months of field-work at a Jain monastery in the small town of Ladnun, Rajasthan. My initial point of entry into the community in India came from the Jain community in Toronto, with which I first made contact in 1994. My current research is in exploring the process of identity construction within the context of the Jain immigrant community. In particular, I am looking at the strategies of Jain identity formation and maintenance in the absence of ascetic leadership within multiethnic, religiously pluralistic metropolitan Toronto, home to nearly two-thirds of the Jain community in Canada (Israel, 1994; Jain Centre of Toronto, 1998).

2   The Jain concern with the tiniest of life forms – *nigodas* – has long been a source of mockery (ridiculed as a preoccupation with "insects" or with "bacteria"), puzzle-ment, and even frustration among those who would like to see greater Jain involve-ment in broader social issues (see Dundas, 1992; Jaini, 1990; O'Connell, 1998). The Jain concern with the simplest life forms must be understood within the context of its understanding of nature as a "moral theatre." Rather than being trivial, it is the harm done to these small life forms (each endowed with a soul) that is the primary cause of our karmic bondage.

3   This public health interpretation of tradi-tional ascetic practices ignores the original motivation underlying the restrictions, viz., the avoidance of harming minute living beings – in this case, fire-bodied and water-bodied beings (as an aside, these public health claims parallel those made by some "semi"-observant Jews, who insist that they do not need two sets of dishes (meat/dairy) because they have dishwashers to thoroughly clean them).

4   On a survey/questionnaire that I recently distributed among the community, a number of people expressed reservation in answering the question: "To which sect do you belong?" I was told that answering this seemed counter-productive to their efforts to eradicate sect-consciousness.

5   At the biannual Jain conventions, the orthodox "moksha-marg" (path to libera-tion) and ecologic worldview are equally represented. However, at the YJA (Youth Jain Association) meetings, a discourse of environmentalism and animal rights dominates.

6   This, however, largely depends on whether the teacher is a first- or second-generation immigrant.

7   Lord Mahavira is the revered twenty-fourth and final Tirthanakara of our present age.

REFERENCES

Babb, L. 1996. *Absent Lord: Ascetics and Kings in a Jain Ritual Culture*. Berkeley: University of California Press.

Banks, M. 1991. "Orthodoxy and Dissent: Varieties of Religious Belief Among Immi-grant Gujarati Jains in Britain." In *The Assembly of Listeners: Jains in Society*. Ed. M. Carrithers and C. Humphrey, pp. 241–59. Cambridge: Cambridge University Press.

——. 1992. *Organising Jainism in India and England*. Oxford: Clarendon Press.

Barth, F. 1969. *Ethnic Groups and Boundar-ies*. Boston: Little, Brown.

Carrithers, M. & C. Humphrey. 1991. *The Assembly of Listeners: Jains in Society*. Cambridge: Cambridge University Press.

Coward, H. & D. Goa. 1987. "Religious Experience of the South Asian Diaspora in Canada." In *The South Asian Diaspora in Canada: Six Essays*. Ed. M. Israel, pp. 73–86. Toronto: Multicultural History Society of Ontario.

Doshi, A. 1993. "The Future of Jainism in the West." Unpublished youth essay contest entry: Group 2, College Age, Jaina Convention, Pittsburgh.

Dundas, P. 1992. *The Jains*. London & New York: Routledge.

Israel, M. 1987. "Introduction." In *The South Asian Diaspora in Canada: Six Essays*. Ed. M. Israel, pp. 9–14. Toronto: Multicultural History Society of Ontario.

——. 1994. *In the Further Soil: A Social History of Indo-Canadians in Ontario*. Richmond Hill, Ontario: Organisation for the Promotion of Indian Culture.

Jain Centre of Toronto, 48 Rosemead Avenue, Etobicoke, Ontario. Personal communication.

Jain Society of Toronto souvenir booklet. 1995.

Jaini, P. 1990. "Ahimsa." Inaugural Roop Lal Jain Lecture, Center for South Asian Studies, University of Toronto.

Jhingran, S. 1989. *Aspects of Hindu Morality*. Delhi: Motilal Banarsidass.

Kapashi, V, A. Shah, & K. Desai. 1994. *Text Book of Jainism. Level 1*. Middlesex: Institute of Jainology.

Laidlaw, J. 1995. *Riches and Renunciation: Religion, Economy and Society among the Jains*. Oxford: Clarendon Press.

Modi, R. 1993. "Living a Jain Way of Life in the Western Environment." Unpublished youth essay contest entry: Group 2, College Age, Jaina Convention, Pittsburgh.

O'Connell, J. 1998. "Jain Contributions to Current Ethical Discourse." Roop Lal Jain Lecture, Center for South Asian Studies, University of Toronto.

Silverstein, S. 1974. "Point of View." In *Where the Sidewalk Ends: the Poems and Drawings of Shel Silverstein*. New York: HarperCollins Juvenile Books.

Taylor, C. 1989. *Sources of the Self*. Cambridge, MA: Harvard University Press.

Umasvati – That Which Is (Tattvartha Sutra). Trans. N. Tatia. Sacred Literature Series, London: HarperCollins, 1994.

44

Candomblé in Pink, Green, and Black: Re-scripting the Afro-Brazilian Religious Heritage in the Public Sphere of Salvador, Bahia

Mattijs van de Port

Mattijs van de Port is lecturer at the Research Centre on Religion and Society of the University of Amsterdam and the author of *Gypsies, Wars & Other Instances of the Wild: Civilization and its Discontents in a Serbian Town* (1998) a rather remarkable study of fantasy and violence in the Balkans. He brings what I would call his skepticism or even irreverence in the face of received pieties to his current work in Brazil, which is part of a large project under the directorship of Birgit Meyer on modern mass media, religion and the postcolonial state.

Brazil is home to a dynamic variety of religious practices that blend influences from indigenous, African, and European traditions. It is one place in the world where spirit possession, in the form of Umbanda (Brown 1994), finds a large following among an urban middle class. In this (heavily abridged) essay van de Port offers an account of a different Afro-Brazilian religion, Candomblé, centered in Bahia, that, as he shows, has been of much interest both to anthropologists and to Brazilians at large. Van de Port departs from most previous analyses in that instead of attending to Candomblé as a form of African heritage in the New World, or worrying about its ostensible religious depths or "authenticity," he takes heritage and authenticity as themselves contested symbols and products of modernity. What is of interest then is the way Candomblé is taken up in the wider Brazilian public sphere of the arts, entertainment, tourism, and politics, specifically by the gay, environmentalist, and black movements. Such an approach transcends the critique of the objectification of "religion" or specific religious symbols in capitalist modernity to examine the way religion becomes continuously transformed as it enters new discursive fields and is appropriated by or attempts to appropriate other social movements.

Van de Port's interest in circuits of ideas and images takes him from the temple to the street and from the urban to the national and ultimately the global scene. Here two points could be added. First, his account runs somewhat orthogonally to recent work on the Black diaspora and the production of a kind of transatlantic religious nexus, a public sphere in its own right. Second, the underplaying of specific and bounded "religions" in favor of a picture of the circulation of symbols in a "representational economy" is appropriate not only to (post)modernity but characteristic of other times and places, such as the Mediterranean in the Hellenistic age, or "popular" Chinese religion in the periods and places when it manages to evade the scrutiny of the state. Comparisons could readily be made with the other chapters in this section. A more direct analysis of religious innovations as social movements, which may be more advanced in the study of Latin America than in other regions, would certainly apply to such topics as liberation theology and Protestant evangelism, and perhaps to such phenomena as Falun Gong in China, "new age" practices in Europe and North America, and the so-called "new religions" in Japan.

A final virtue of van de Port's essay is the attention he pays to the role of anthropologists and other intellectuals in legitimating, reproducing and even transforming their objects of study; they (we) too form nodes in the circuits of public culture.

Candomblé, the Afro-Brazilian spirit-possession cult that will be discussed in this essay, has been intensively studied by anthropologists. From the first ethnographic explorations in late nineteenth-century Salvador by Nina Rodrigues (1935) to the post-modern musings of Muniz Sodré (2002) on the contemporary significance of candomblé, the tendency has been to highlight the African "genius" that animates the cult's rituals and practices. However, the focus is invariably placed on what is distinctive and singular about the cult, stressing how it differs from the world in which it operates rather than how it is part of that world. The temple (*terreiro*) is often portrayed as a universe on its own. In the pages that follow, I will argue that this approach obscures candomblé's thorough insertion into Bahian society, as well as the intricate ways in which Bahian society is involved in the making of the cult. To underline my proposition that a study of candomblé should no longer be confined to the temples of Salvador, I propose to start in an appropriately unconventional place: a fancy beauty parlour called *Beleza Pura* ("pure beauty") in a well-to-do neighborhood in Salvador.

It was there that Emerson had alerted me to an upcoming event in the famous terreiro of a priestess called Mãe Stella. Emerson was my hairdresser, a guy in his early thirties, born in the Bahian capital of Indian parents and raised in Madras, but happy to be back in Brazil. *Brazileiríssimo*[1] is how he liked to describe himself. At the occasion of my second haircut he had already confessed that he was "from candomblé". It struck me that he wasn't very secretive about his being an adept of the cult. He made no attempt to lower his voice, nor did he look around nervously, as is often the case when candomblé is talked about in public places.

[. . .]

[. . .] Emerson [. . .] gave me a newspaper, saying that I should read the announcement. "Come to the opening night", he said. It would

be "very interesting" for my research. Toninho would also be there, and I might get to know some of his other friends. At home, I read that there was going to be a *Semana Cultural da Herança Africana na Bahia* (Cultural Week of the African Heritage in Bahia), and that a host of national and international specialists in candomblé would be present. I clipped the announcement because it was such a typical example of the rather servile way in which Salvadorian journalists reproduce the discourse of the city's leading terreiros, copying and translating Yorubá terms, respectfully distinguishing between the religious traditions of the Angola, Jeje and Ketu "nations" so as to educate the general public, and stressing the solemnity and importance of all that happens in the candomblé universe.
[. . .]

[. . .] What must have been hundreds of cars were trying to make it to the opening night of the Semana Cultural da Herança Africana na Bahia, impatiently honking their horns, clogging up ill-lit roads and floodlighting street vendors, who ran from one car to the next selling cashew nuts, beer and silicone bra-strings. Policemen were all around, trying to control the traffic and monitoring the crowds, who entered the central square of the terreiro's compound in a steady stream.

The candomblé elite was there. I recognised some of the dreadlocked activists from Oxumaré, a candomblé house with an activist profile, chic ladies with expensive afro-print frocks and turbans and men dressed in Nigerian fashion, with wide, colourful pants, kaftan-like shirts and little hats in matching prints. I soon spotted some of the intellectuals and anthropologists who always show up at these events (the latter probably commenting on my eternal presence in their field-notes). I also identified some of the girls from the terreiro choir, who all boasted new, elaborately braided hair-dos and wore identical wine-red dresses. The rest of the audience must have been made up of a significant portion of the clients, members and affiliates of the Ilê Axé Opô Afonjá temple and – judging from their plastic *sandálias* – a great number of people from the local neighbourhood. As always, the place was full of gays [. . .]

On a raised platform behind a long table decorated with African fabrics, raffia, palm leaves and dried pumpkins on a string, sat Mãe Stella de Oxóssi, high priestess of Ilê Axé Opô Afonjá, with her honoured guests. The priestess was all dressed up for the occasion. Her white turban, many coloured necklaces and white crinoline dress sparkled in the spotlights – an exotic, queen-like figure, overshadowing the elderly gentlemen in ties and suits who sat to her right and left: Gilberto Gil, the minister of culture in the newly elected, leftist Lula government; Imbassahy, the mayor of Salvador; and two well known anthropologists, Julio Braga and Vivaldo da Costa Lima.

The latter was reading out loud an article he had written for the occasion: something about the Obás of Xangô, a council of twelve "ministers" – an honorary function this particular terreiro has introduced in the internal temple hierarchy. Da Costa Lima had made it his task to highlight the authenticity of that move with detailed ethnographic accounts from Africa. It went on and on and on, a stream of words that no one really listened to, but that, as a play of sounds – Portuguese mingling with "African" – sufficed to convey that Bahia's link with Yoruba culture was being celebrated here.

When Gilberto Gil finally took over the microphone, the chatting and muttering audience quietened down. The new minister in the Lula government – flown in by helicopter specially for the occasion, Emerson told me – reminded the audience that he too was an *obá*, a minister of Xangô. Accepting his new job in Brasília, he said, had been greatly facilitated by the fact that he had already been a minister "at this primary, that is, the spiritual level" [. . .] He praised Xangô, that "great saint", and expressed his deepest respect and the respect of all the ministers and members of parliament in Brasília to Mãe Stella, to the community of Axé, to the Roma Negra that is Salvador, to this Bahia, the "blessed land of the Orixás" [spiritual entities]. Time and again, he received a standing ovation from the audience. Television cameras pushed forward, trying to get as close as possible to the speaker. People in the audience took pictures as well. [. . .]

The opening of the Semana Cultural da Herança Africana na Bahia ended with a presentation of "Xangô Awards" to people whose outstanding support for the community of candomblé deserved to be highlighted. It turned out to be a veritable celebrity show as artists, scholars, actors and television personalities from within the community of Axé handed over the sculpted statues to artists, scholars, actors and television personalities from society at large.

[. . .] Amid the hollow phrases and worn out clichés that make up the soundscape of officialdom, Mãe Stella remained silent, a veritable queen of the sacred, radiating a power and potency that put ministers, mayors and academics in the shade.

I have tried to give a flavour of my research sites to introduce you to the topic I want to discuss: the circulation of candomblé (its symbols, aesthetics, rhythms, philosophies and cosmovisions) through various circuits of Salvador's public sphere. The fact that in present day Salvador candomblé has made it to the worlds of fancy hairdressers, politicians, entertainers, celebrities and intellectuals cries out for its history to be told: the story of how a "primitive" creed and worrisome reminder of the continuous presence of African culture in the state of Bahia became transformed into a highly esteemed part of the cultural heritage; how the solace and ultimate relief of the poor and desperate became a venue at which the high and mighty show off their dedication to Bahia's age-old traditions; and how an invisible presence that was whispered about in the shadowy corners of public life became a hyper-exposed phenomenon in the spotlight of public attention. That history will have to be told elsewhere, however. In this essay I want to focus on the consequences these transformations ought to have for the study of the cult.

My description of the events in the temple of Mãe Stella indicates that the boundaries between candomblé and society at large are highly permeable: in Salvador candomblé is "all over the place" and conversely, society at large is seeking and finding access to the temples. This observation is strikingly at odds with the way the cult is described in much anthropological work [. . .] Time and again one finds candomblé described as a closed uni-verse, shrouded in mystery, guarded by secrecy and accessible only through initiation. In line with this vision, the "classical" anthropological project is to study candomblé "in its own terms". [. . .] I argue that such a project is a highly problematic endeavour. As more and more groups have taken an interest in the cult, and more and more re-readings and re-interpretations of candomblé's cosmology and ritual practices have started to circulate, it is increasingly difficult to decide which terms could be labelled "candomblé's own". Likewise, as more and more groups claim to belong to the candomblé universe, and adopt practices and beliefs derived from the cult, it is increasingly difficult to argue that anthropologists should subscribe to the claims of the priesthood that they, and they alone, are to decide what qualifies as the "real" and "authentic" candomblé.

An alternative (or I should rather say complementary) approach [. . .] takes the absence of an "ultimate" or "essential" candomblé as a starting point for investigation. Keeping in mind Talal Asad's (1993: 31 ff.) warning never to lose sight of the fact that statements as to what constitutes the "essence" of a religion are inextricably tied up with, and work in the service of, specific configurations of power, I will take a sceptical stance towards any group that claims to represent the one-and-only candomblé. An exploration of the candomblé that figures in the discourses and practices of the Bahian gay movement, the green movement and the *movimento negro* allows for the suggestion that the cult can very well be approached as a set of symbols-and-practices-on-the-move, forever transforming and metamorphosing owing to its travels, defying all attempts at fixation, and at all times obstructing the classical project to study candomblé "in its own terms".

Working in Temples, Talking to Priests and Having Oneself Initiated

The suggestion that to study candomblé is to study the circulation of symbols and practices in new settings, implies a thorough break with the way the cult has been studied in the exemplary and highly influential work of anthropologists such as Ruth Landes (1947), Edison Carneiro (1948), Roger Bastide (1958), Pierre Verger (1981) and Juana Elbein dos Santos (1986). For these authors – and many of their followers – three methodological points of departure stand out as somehow indispensable for any successful research into the cult: (i) the designation of the temple as the prime locus of research; (ii) the designation of the priests as the prime exegetes of the cult and the prime interlocutors of the researcher; and (iii) the idea that a methodology akin to initiation itself is the *via regia* to knowledge about the cult. The pressure to adopt these methodological directives is considerable. Time and again, I was asked by colleagues in the field (as well as by priests and cult adepts) which particular temple I was studying, and whether or not I was on the initiation track already. My insistence on wanting to study the public appearances of candomblé elicited comments such as the one from the priest who said, "Oh, I see, you want to interview me about the superficial things!"

While I have no wish to discredit the merits of this particular approach (I am all too aware how much I depend on the "classic" monographs to make up for the many gaps in my knowledge), I do think that this tends to reproduce a very particular construction of the cult. And what is worse, if one is to remain within the methodological triangle temple–priest–initiation, one is very likely to reproduce the blind spots that come with this particular construction, hiding from view events such as the one described above or dismissing them as "superficial things". Allow me to elaborate my critique.

I'll begin with the fact that the temple is designated as the prime site of research in most studies. This terreiro is the place, the "universe", in which the anthropologist has to position him/herself in order to be able to study the cult "from within". It is not an easy accessible place as it is guarded by all the defence mechanisms of a cult with a long history of persecution. Much research energy therefore goes into finding one's way into the temple, overcoming resistance and building up rapport with the priests and cult adepts. This may count as one of the reasons why candomblé researchers who finally succeed in getting in tend to focus on the treasures they find "inside": that is, candomblé's rich mythology, its elaborate rituals, its highly complex rules and regulations, its use of Yorubá as a "liturgical" language and its particular cosmology. As a result of this focus, however, the cult is time and again portrayed as something wholly other, an encapsulated exotic world "on its own", a closed and somehow timeless religious universe within Bahian society. Curiously enough, the fact that syncretism has played (and continues to play) such a prominent role in the formation of the cult's practices and beliefs has been noticed by all researchers, but this has not diminished the "othering" of the cult. Roger Bastide, for example, while fully acknowledging the transformative impact that history, society and culture have had on the cult, announced in *O Candomblé da Bahia* that he purported to study candomblé "as an autonomous reality which certainly comprises elements from different origins, but which nevertheless forms a coherent whole that can be studied on its own" (Bastide 1958: 28).

In addition this "world-on-its-own" is often understood as essentially "African". Pierre Verger, in both his anthropological and photographic work, extensively highlighted "African survivals" in Bahia, and one only needs to open Juana Elbein dos Santos' classic *Os nagô e a morte* (1986) to get the message that one is about to study an African rather than a Brazilian phenomenon: all the cult terms – even names such as Xangô, Orixá and Exu, with which all Bahians are familiar – are written in italics and according to Yoruba spelling rules "as they have been laid down by specialised institutes in Nigeria" (1986: 26, note 1). Xangô, Orixá and Exu are thus transformed in exotic beings called Sango, òrìsà, and Èsù.

This focus on candomblé's separation and otherness has blinded many researchers about what we might call the "Brazilianness" or "Bahianness" of candomblé – that is, the striking similarities between this cult and the other religious denominations with which it has to compete in what Brazilian scholars refer to as the *mercado dos bens de salvação* ("market of salvation goods"). For example, [...] in the vast literature on candomblé, very little has been said about the baroque nature of its rituals and aesthetics (but see Montes 1998). Similarly, the famous "break with syncretism" by the aforementioned Mãe Stella and other leading priestesses in Salvador, made public in a manifesto in 1984, and the consequent re-africanisation of the cult is too often and too easily understood as a successful erasure of a catholic mindset in candomblé.

The second point to be commented upon is that, in the "classical" approach to the study of candomblé, the priests are the main interlocutors of any researcher.[2] This is not only because they are the obvious experts on religious matters. In candomblé, secrecy is a major concern and breaking secrets invites divine punishment, making many cult adepts very hesitant to talk. Priests are often the only people authorised to talk with outsiders. As will become clear, the candomblé priesthood has a political agenda of its own and priests tend to have very outspoken ideas about how candomblé should be represented to the outside world. For example, priests tend to support the idea of candomblé being a closed universe, governed by its own laws and rulings, and accessible only after long years of initiation. This particular representation links up well with their vested interest in making a clear distinction between the "real" or "authentic" candomblé of the temple and the "copied" forms, devoid of any religious significance, that are now circulating in the public sphere. Many priests also support – or at least pay lip service to – the "Africanisation" of the cult, tending to stress all that contributes to this particular image, and negating all that is in conflict with it. In addition, most priests want it recognised that their creed is a "religion" – not a "cult", or a "sect" or a religious "practice". Here too, one must conclude that the political agenda of the priest works against the anthropologist's instruction to keep in mind Talal Asad's (1993) well argued warning not to essentialise "religion" as a universal given.

Although the expertise and knowledge of the priesthood is clearly a crucial source of information, the work of the anthropologist is not in my opinion served well by going along with what priests deem "superficial" and "profound", or "real" and "copied" forms of candomblé. A preferable starting point for anthropological investigation should be the thought that nobody can claim to be representing "the real candomblé". The candomblé that figures in the imagination of clients and workers in an expensive beauty parlour (which takes on the aspect of astrological sign reading) is certainly not the same as the candomblé that figures in the imagination of a priest(ess) and his/her initiates in a temple on the outskirts of Salvador. Yet it is not up to the anthropologist to enter qualifications about which is the more "profound" or "authentic". The fact that priests do make such qualifications, and that some colleagues/anthropologists are in the business of legitimising them [...] are ethnographically interesting facts that ought to be studied. Yet these qualifications are certainly not to be adopted as one's own understanding.

A third recurrent characteristic of "classic" candomblé studies is that a methodology akin to initiation itself is the *via regia* to knowledge about the cult: the researcher needs to immerse him/herself in the daily practices of a chosen temple, submit him/herself to the religious regime and with time will begin to understand the ins and outs of the candomblé universe. Thus, Juana Elbein dos Santos wrote:

> Because the Nagô religion is constituted by the experience of initiation, during which knowledge is obtained through the lived experience of interpersonal and group relationships, through transmission and absorption of a force [*força*], and a gradual development of symbolical and complex knowledge about all the collective and individual elements of the system at all levels, it seems that the perspective that we call "an understanding from within" imposes itself almost inevitably. (dos Santos 1986: 17)

This methodological directive adopts the sacerdotal notion of a gradual and time-bound mystical revelation, as well as sacerdotal tropes of depth and superficiality. The description with which I have opened this article, however, has made clear that a research trajectory that urges one to dig deeper and deeper into the "inner world" of the temple tends to neglect the fact that on the surface candomblé is mutating in ever-newer forms and making its appearance at ever-newer places. In other words, a methodology akin to initiation is unable to capture the candomblé of Salvador's middle classes, the candomblé of the local newspapers, the candomblé of poor neighbourhoods, the candomblé of gays, black activists and politicians of all kinds and statures, the candomblé of the cultural scene and the entertainment industry, or the candomblé of the tourist. Such a methodology also leads one away from an investigation of all the myriad connections, exchanges and dialogues between these circuits and the temples.

Following my critique of the "classic" approach, I suggest that we expand our field of investigation to take in all those circuits in which candomblé is "doing its thing", rather than prioritise one particular circuit – the temple – as the site of the "real" or "authentic" candomblé, one particular voice – the priest or initiand – as the prime articulator of how one should understand the meanings of candomblé, and one particular method – initiation – as the preferred inroad to knowledge about the cult.

Obviously, I am not the first anthropologist to advocate an alternative approach to the study of candomblé. In an overview of Brazilian scholarship on the subject in the 1990s, Monique Augras lamented the ongoing production of "purely descriptive" studies of the cult. In her conclusion she noticed a new development, which is interested in the way candomblé is inserted in Brazilian society (Augras 1998: 100). Peter Fry (1982), Beatriz Goís Dantas (1988), Yvonne Maggy (1992), Patricia Birman (1995), Vagner Gonçalves da Silva (1995; 2001), Stephania Capone (2000), Rita Amaral (2002), Paul Christopher Johnson (2002) and Jocélio Teles dos Santos (2000) are just some of the anthropologists who have pointed out the permeable character of the temple walls.

My proposal is to radicalise the lines of thought that have been set out by these scholars. Rather than continue to think about candomblé as a religious cult, that needs to be described in its generic particularities, I would first and foremost think of it as an important "symbol bank" that enters into exchange relationships with ever wider circuits of Bahia's "economy of representation" (Keane 2002). These exchange relationships between candomblé and the worlds of literature, the arts, entertainment, science and politics can be traced back to the 1930s, when candomblé began to play an increasingly important role as a marker of Bahian identity. In the wake of an emergent Brazilian nationalism that sought to re-imagine the nation as a unique mix of the white, Indian and African races, a positive re-evaluation of the Afro-Brazilian heritage became possible. Afro-Brazilian cultural practices such as samba and capoeira became popular all over Brazil, and the beauty of Afro-Brazilian religious practices began to be appreciated. Bahia's (largely white) cultural elites were eager to profit from this renewed interest, and began to explore the rich cultural heritage of the overwhelmingly black population of their home state. Undoubtedly, one of their motives was to upgrade the image of Bahia, which at the time was considered a poor, decaying and utterly provincial outpost in the Brazilian federacy. Candomblé proved to be a sheer bottomless source of inspiration [. . .]

Stressing the circulation of items from the candomblé "symbol bank" and the transformations and re-evaluations that they undergo as they move from one setting to the next means that "religion" becomes one of the many gestalten in which candomblé makes its appearance, next to commodity, entertainment, art and tourist spectacle. This approach – fruitful examples of which I have found in the work of Armando Salvatore (1997) on the Muslim public sphere and Birgit Meyer (2004) on the "pentecostalisation" of the public sphere in Ghana – highlights the permeability of the boundaries between the temples of candomblé and society at large, and urges one to take notice of the continuing circular movements to which candomblé is liable: symbols, ideas and aesthetics migrate from the terreiro to the public arena, where they adapt to new formats and styles and find new publics. These publics then start to produce their own understandings (and fantasies) as to what the cult is all about and begin to interact with the religious community, taking their own particular interpretations back into the temple.

A further advantage of this approach is that it treats candomblé as forever in the making. It allows the researcher to stay away from those endless discussions about what is "pure", what is "degenerate", what is "real" and what is "fake" in candomblé. Instead, it urges one to consider these attempts at fixation as moves in a political field where several groups claim the truth. Understanding candomblé within an economy of representation also implies a reflexive move on the part of the researcher: candomblé research and studies are part and parcel of the circular movements in which candomblé is made and re-made, defined and re-defined, re-scripted and re-performed. Finally, this approach allows the study of candomblé to speak to larger issues, such as the changing role of religion and tradition in the emergent public sphere in Brazil and elsewhere.

To explore this alternative approach to the study of Bahian candomblé, and assess how it might further our understanding of the Afro-Brazilian religious heritage, I will limit my analysis in this article to three circuits in which items from the candomblé symbol bank can be found circulating: the gay scene, the discourse on ecology and the *movimento negro*. This focus allows me to give more detailed and ethnographically substantiated answers to the following questions. Why is it that groups with widely different political agendas have adopted elements of candomblé to articulate their cause? What is it that these adopted elements are supposed to "do" in their new settings? How are these elements moulded to serve the various projects in which they are now inserted? And how is it that these transformed elements, re-worked and re-signified in the public sphere, work their way back into the terreiro and link up with (or mess up) the political agendas of the candomblé priesthood?

Candomblé in Pink

I was alerted to the adoption of candomblé symbols by the emergent gay scene in Salvador during the Gay Pride Parade of 2003. This *Parada Gay* opened with an ode to Exu, god of the Afro-Brazilian pantheon. Surrounded by muscled go-go-boys in panther-print briefs, outrageously dressed transvestites, pink balloons and rainbow banners, a famous black singer sung his praise. Enormous loudspeakers blasted her voice over the many thousands that had gathered on Campo Grande in the centre of the Bahian capital. When I asked some friends whether the hymn was indeed sung in Yorubá – which was difficult to make out because the speakers distorted the sound considerably – they were somewhat irritated. What? Huh? Yes. They obviously felt I was bothering them with unimportant details, things only an anthropologist would want to know, on a jubilant and exciting moment for the gay community.

Nevertheless, someone had decided that the Parada Gay should begin with an ode to Exu. The more obvious reasons why this particular deity qualified to begin the march are not very hard to figure out. I have already argued that candomblé has become the dominant marker of Bahian identity. Highlighting the Bahia-ness of the parade would therefore mean including items from the candomblé symbol bank. More specifically, Exu is the messenger between human beings and gods, and in Afro-Brazilian thought his support is crucial to "open the roads" towards the realisation of one's goals. Pleasing the god with praise and offerings is the procedure required to obtain his blessings. Hence the hymn that marked the beginning of the march and the twenty-or-so priestesses that walked in front of the parade in full attire, scattering on the streets the traditional popcorn (*pipoca*) used to placate the Afro-Brazilian gods.

In addition, Exu has some particularities that resonate well with gay concerns. Being the messenger between human beings and orixás (the deities of the Afro-Brazilian pantheon), Exu is constantly being called upon to assist his worshippers in the pursuit of their dreams. He is therefore considered to be a genuine connoisseur of human desire – and that emphatically includes sexual desire. The fact that Exu is usually represented as a devilish figure with an impressive and lustfully erect cock (which seems the appropriate word here) is certainly no coincidence. In more fashionable readings, popular with contemporary artists and poets, Exu is made to symbolise the contradictions of modern urban life: he is lord of the city streets and the patron of the marginal and the powerless. Contradiction, marginality, streetlife: these too are concepts that resonate with the life experiences of many Bahian gays.

There is, however, more to the connection between homosexuals and candomblé. When afterwards I discussed the presence of candomblé imagery at a gay pride parade, none of my friends expressed any surprise. They took for granted the strong connections between the Afro-Brazilian cult and homosexuality. They would say things like "of course, all the priests are *bichas*" [effeminate, "passive" homosexuals] and that the temples are "*cheio de bichas*" ["full of *bichas*"]. The presence of homosexuals in the candomblé temples is hard to miss, and anthropologists have discussed their presence at length. Patricia Birman [. . .] highlighted an affinity between the desire to be bicha and the available spectrum of alternative gender roles within candomblé. Possession trance, she argued, offers an (often irresistible) opportunity for bichas to have their male bodies invaded by female orixás such as Iansá or Oxum or female spirits such as Maria Padilha or Cigana. Given the conviction in candomblé that possession implies the annihilation of self, which is subsequently replaced by the invading spirit, the practice allows bichas not just to dress up like women but to become the women of their dreams. In other words, she showed how bichas put a religious practice of divine possession at the service of the gender bending they were looking for (Birman 1995). In addition, Fry pointed out that once the terreiro got to be known as a place where bichas go, this designation became something of a self-fulfilling prophecy: "real men" started avoiding the temples for fear of being accused of being bichas, and gay men started frequenting the temples to realise themselves as bichas, to "hunt" other men or to hide from hostile families (Fry 1982).

What is interesting about the Parada Gay, however, is that it hardly qualifies as an example of bichas seeking refuge and the possibility of self-realisation in the sheltered confines of the candomblé temple. On the contrary, what we see here is the spectacle of gays moving into the public sphere, adorning themselves with the signs and symbols of candomblé. (The adoption of this English word "gay" is a significant move towards an identity label, as "bicha" primarily refers to sexual practice and, as such, seems a less totalising designation of self.)

[. . .]

Given the well established and long standing relations between gays and candomblé, it is hardly surprising that elements of the candomblé universe migrate to the localities of an emergent gay subculture. The presence of candomblé imagery and candomblé ritual at the Parada Gay, however, takes developments a step further. Consider the way the organiser, Marcello Cerqueira, looked back on the event:

> Our gay pride parade was blessed by the gods, those gods one calls for on a moment like this: Dionysus, Bacchus, Sappho, Logum-Edê, Exu. They descended and played with the crowds, and declared themselves in solidarity with us as they sent a rainbow to bless us all, one of the greatest symbols of nature that was like a punch in the stomach for all homophobes.

Here, a pre-existing affinity between bichas and the candomblé universe gets publicly translated into the idea that candomblé is an exemplary religion as far as "tolerance" towards sexual difference is concerned. The gods are with us, is what Cerqueira is saying. In other words, a local and particular discourse gets mapped on to a global discourse of gay rights and gay emancipation, and vice versa.

[. . .]

In sum, what we find in the public sphere is a re-reading of candomblé elements in terms of gay activism and a merging of candomblé imagery with a global gay iconography that somehow finds its way back into the cult.

Candomblé in Green

Not long before the Parada Gay, on the occasion of World Ecology Day (*Dia Mundial do*

Meio Ambiente), candomblé found another role to play in the public sphere. A Salvadorian newspaper reported that:

Heavy drumming was to be heard, yesterday, at World Ecology Day, in St Bartholomew Park, where a number of organisations from the Ferroviário district organised a forum to pay homage to the inquices, orixás, voduns and caboclos, who in the religions of African origin, are the primordial defenders of nature (*A Tarde*, 6 June 2003).

What we see here is how an assumed "inherent reverence for the forces of nature in candomblé" has been projected on to a global concern for environmental issues. This re-casting of orixás as environmental activists does not come out of the blue. Iconic elements of the cult lend themselves to ecological interpretation: the worshipping of trees; the association of each orixá with particular natural elements such as forests, waterfalls, seas, storms and fire; and the widely acclaimed knowledge of natural medicine. "Ossain", I read on a website, is not only "the orixá of leaves, herbs, vegetation and lord of medicine" but also "the patron of ecology". Another website presents the cult as an ecological movement *avant la lettre*, as it quotes a Bahian priestess who "as early as 1902" formulated the ecologist's dictum that the abuse of nature will always rebound on the abuser:

One does not take a dried leaf from a tree if it isn't necessary; that's like killing a person. Would anyone like to lose an arm, an eye or a foot? Why pick a flower and throw it away? Candomblé is living nature. There can be no worship of the orixá without earth, forest, river, sky, lightning, thunder, wind, sea . . . Violence towards nature is violence towards the orixá.

As in the case of the gay activists, there are a number of well-known intellectuals to spell out the links between ecology and candomblé. António Risério writes that the "sacralisation of nature" is one of the main sources of his fascination with candomblé, and praises "this cosmovision in which trees, lakes and rivers are understood as sites where the divine manifests itself" (Risério, in Pretto and Serpa 2002:

9–10). Muniz Sodré, a leading Brazilian scholar of candomblé who boasts degrees from the Sorbonne, argues that candomblé in fact preceded the environmentalist movement and can therefore be considered a kind of proto-ecological way of being in the world.
[. . .]
Another anthropologist, Reginaldo Prandi, launches the come-back of long forgotten orixá, called Onilé, Lady of the Earth:

In the present climate of a "return to the world of nature" and a concern with ecology, an orixá that had been almost completely forgotten is being gradually recovered. It is Onilé, Lady of the Earth, the orixá who represents our planet as a single whole, the world that we live in. . . . Discretely worshipped in the old terreiros from Bahia and in Africanised candomblés, Mother Earth raises the curiosity and interest of the followers of the orixás, above all those who belong to the more intellectual segment of the religion . . . For many followers of the religion of the orixás, interested in restoring the relation orixá-nature, the cult of Onilé thus represents the concern with the preservation of humanity itself, and all that is in its world.[3]

Here too, we might conclude that elements from candomblé lend themselves really well to emphasising the local in the global concern for the environment. And here too, I was confronted with instances where these re-readings of what candomblé is (and does) inform people's actions. A group of friends who wished to participate in the yearly offering to the sea goddess Iemanjá made an ecological *balaio*, which is the basket that is filled with presents for the goddess and then dropped into the ocean. This was not your regular basket full with the plastic combs, lipsticks, dolls, flowers, curling pins and perfume bottles that befit the vain goddess, but a wholly biodegradable balaio filled with food, real flowers and paper cuttings. I was assured that this ecological balaio would certainly please the sea goddess; folklore has it that gifts that return to the Bahian shores could not please Iemanjá, something more likely to happen to a plastic comb or Barbie doll than to organic matter.

As with the gay activist readings of candomblé, members of the priesthood show up in the circuits where the representational economy has taken the items of the candomblé symbol bank. For instance, priests appear on television in a programme called *Saude Alternativa* (*Alternative Health*), and the video production that every visitor to the little museum on the compound of Ilê Axé Opô Afonjá gets to see [. . .] is one endless sequence of images of nature (woods, animals, trees, plants and water); the voice-over explains that orixás are to be understood as "phenomena of nature, forces of life" ["*fenômenos da natureza, forças vitais*"].

Candomblé in Black

The black emancipation movement is a more obvious and logical example of a circuit in which candomblé gets translated and mapped on to the political projects of others. Jocélio Teles dos Santos, in his rich and detailed account of the progressive entanglement of candomblé and black emancipatory politics in Bahia, has shown that until the second half of the 1970s black movements actually demonstrated a striking reluctance to approach candomblé. Marxist ideology ruled the activist discourses at that time and propagated an understanding of candomblé as a "sect" and ultimately alienating institution, all the more so because of its veneration of Catholic saints and links with catholic institutions. Moreover, the way candomblé priests and priestesses sought protective ties with white power holders was repeatedly held against them (Santos 2000: 192).

By the early 1990s, however, candomblé had become something of a fetish, a cultural relic endowed with so much prestige and power that one comes under the impression that even the black movements could no longer resist its seductive spells. From the 1930s, Bahia's (white) cultural elites had been celebrating candomblé as the prime marker of the Bahian cultural heritage. First came a generation that included writer Jorge Amado, sculptor Carybé and song-writer Dorivall Caymmi; then the counterculture of the Tropicália movement in

the late 1960s (Dunn 2001). From the 1970s onwards this celebration of the Afro-Brazilian religious heritage received the full back-up of the Bahian state, as tourism boomed and Bahia sought to promote itself on the tourist market as an "exotic" and "mysterious" holiday destination (cf. Pinto 2001).

In addition, the work of Michel Agier (2000) on traditional black carnival organisations in Salvador shows that, parallel to this development, candomblé imagery was taken up in these circles as well. Radicalised by north American examples of black power and propagating the black-is-beautiful slogans of the era, they sought to reconstruct the aesthetics of negritude and glorified their African roots, finding in candomblé a rich reservoir of rituals and symbolic forms [. . .]

What these examples suggest is that, next to the occult powers for which candomblé has always been known (and feared), the cult accumulated so much prestige, coming from many different directions, that it became a powerful icon in itself. It seems reasonable to suggest that the political potential that candomblé had acquired could no longer be negated by black activists, who indeed started to undertake attempts to claim the cult as a somehow unalienable part of an Afro-Brazilian, rather than Bahian, heritage. Moreover, when leading terreiros in Salvador publicly broke with syncretism in order to restore their "true" African roots (which happened with the publication of a manifesto in 1984), a new [reading] of candomblé as a site of African resistance in a hostile environment becomes visible.

Risério writes that "in Brazil, candomblé functioned as a kind of peaceful and sacred Quilombo, a centre of cultural resistance and of the ethnic and social identity of blacks, saving them from total loss of their Africanness [*desafricanização total*]" (1981: 83). David Covin reports that in the early 1990s, the Bahian-based *Movimento Negro Unificado* included in its action programme the aim "to work for freedom of culture and religion for Afro-Brazilians" by restoring culture production to the "cultural and religious spaces" of the black population, and "systematically" fighting its commercialisation, folklorisation and distortion. (1996: 48). Santos gives many more examples of the rhetoric that now came to dominate the black emancipatory discourse:

> Both the Afro-Brazilian people and their religion were always victims of serious attacks over the centuries by the Catholic church and – ever more virulent in recent times – by the Protestant churches, with the objective – well known by the black community – of eradicating from its conscience the experience and the sacred world-view [of its African past]. (in Santos 2000: 76)

Impressionistic and all too brief as it may be, this description allows for the observation that the approximation of the black movements and candomblé came about through the manifold and complex exchanges between various circuits. And just as we have seen with the "pink" and "green" readings of candomblé, these "black" readings enter in circulation and move back into the temples.

In the rhetoric of the leading temples in Salvador that support the break with syncretism and embrace the re-africanisation of candomblé, elements of a black emancipatory discourse can certainly be pointed out. Some of these temples have initiated social programmes and neighbourhood schools aimed at the enhancement of the *auto-estima* (self-worth) and *conscientização* (consciousness-raising) of Afro-Brazilians. Jocélio Teles dos Santos, however, argues that the candomblé priesthood has certainly not adopted the political rhetoric of the black movements or is "racialising" its politics vis-à-vis society at large (2000: 120). If anything, says the author, the priesthood seeks to capitalise on the political support and legitimacy that the project of black emancipation has obtained over the last decades. It never loses sight, however, of the final aim, which is the further legitimation and reinforcement of their religion (2000: 198).

As the opening of this article shows, the venerable procedure of establishing relationships with power-holders (many of them white) to enhance power and prestige is still very much in use. This might be taken as another sign that there are clear limits to attempts by

the black movement to reclaim the terreiro as a site that somehow organically belongs to them. This tendency of the priesthood to establish links with, or even accommodate, whites also comes to the fore in an article [. . .] by Vagner Gonçalves da Silva and Rita Amaral (1993). The authors vividly describe the kind of tensions that may arise due to the simultaneous appearance of a racialised political discourse within the temple walls, and an increasing number of whites in temples and temple hierarchies. It is a somewhat sad story as, in conflicts over power, prestige and priestly favours, both groups can be found to stress the value of (stereotypical) characteristics attributed to them. Thus, black initiates claim to have more access to *axé*, the magical-religious life force of candomblé, and glorify their prowess in dancing and rhythm, whereas white initiates capitalize on their social standing, education and economic power. On the theological level, the authors notice the emergence of re-interpretations of candomblé cosmology and ritual practice that accommodate, explain or justify the presence of whites in candomblé. For example, in the new theological discourse, orixás – popularly thought of as "black" and "African" anthropomorphic figures – become abstract and universal "energies" (Gonçalves da Silva and Amaral 1993: 120). In a similar fashion, a white candomblé priest in Salvador told me that the orixás are so ancient that they precede the racial division of humankind. Such developments have far from crystallised, though. The theological difficulties arising from the ascendancy of whites in the temples, and the rhetorical acrobatics this fact necessitates, are well illustrated by Mãe Stella's words in an introduction to the life-history of a French anthropologist, Gisele Cossard, who became a priestess of candomblé and opened up a temple in Rio de Janeiro. In an obvious attempt to accommodate both Cossard and the project of re-africanising candomblé Mãe Stella highlights the fact that the anthropologist/priestess was a diplomat's daughter and born in Tangiers, Morocco:

> Gisele Cossard, this French girl, was called by the orixá from birth on, which is surprising, given the fact that she is a European woman

by birth and descent. Many other places could have served as her cradle due to the profession of her father. However, she was born on the very border of Europe and Africa: she saw the light, for the first time, in Morocco, a place where African culture is strong and active, first and foremost in its musical traditions. It is therefore only natural that this "*francesa africana*" was called for by the saints in their plenitude. (Mãe Stella, in Dion 1998: 7)

Conclusion. Scripts and Roles

I have given three examples of the circulation of candomblé imagery through various circuits in the public sphere. It is now time to conclude with a discussion of what is gained by studying candomblé as a set of symbols and practices on the move, rather than an enclosed universe in Bahian society.

What I have argued is that way beyond the temples of candomblé scripts are being written for (an imagined) candomblé community to perform, and that they are about topics as diverse as tolerance of gay life styles, black emancipation or ecological consciousness. The notion of a continuous re-scripting of the cult raises two sets of questions that need to be addressed. The first set pertains to the fact that so many different scriptwriters developed an interest in candomblé. For not only gays, ecologists and black activists have picked up candomblé as their "thing", but feminists, progressive Catholics, labour unionists, tourists, artists and conservative populist politicians are equally busy re-scripting the Afro-Brazilian religious heritage, making sure that their particular ideological outlook gets the star part. The very diversity of the scriptwriters suggests that an explanation of candomblé's appeal cannot be limited to the particularities of one or other circuit. Something in candomblé transcends these differences, and we need to ask what this "something" might be. A second set of questions relates to the fact that the candomblé priesthood actually gets involved in the performance of these scripts, begging the question why they would do so.

Let me start with candomblé's appeal to so many different groups. I suggest that the case of candomblé is a clear example of the new roles that have been designed for "tradition" in the post-modern world. As we have seen, in the representational economy of Bahia, candomblé has become an idiom of "autochthony" or "belonging" in a globalising world. As such, it provides Bahian gays, ecologists, black activists and others with a vocabulary that enables them to make the local global, and the global local. This is hardly a revolutionary research finding. I do want to stress, however, the importance of these local articulations of global concerns. Globalisation processes tend to bring about feelings of alienation. In Salvador, for example, adopting the identity-label "gay" implies a serious risk of becoming a stranger in one's social and cultural world. People increasingly take that risk, probably because an alternative gay scene is emerging, that promises a belonging to a global community. There is no denying the appeal of such a promise. This global community may show its contours at gay beaches where gay tourists mingle with local guys and even generate its "sentiments of belonging" in night hours at the discotheque. (I vividly recall crowds in a lower-class gay club singing along with Whitney Houston and Celine Dion at the tops of their voices, though none of them actually spoke a word of English). On the whole, however, the "global gay community" remains an abstract entity that for many is out of reach. Re-defining candomblé as a gay-friendly religion may offer a fantasy frame within which one may convince oneself (and others) that one is not "opting out" of Bahia, but one is acting squarely within the confines of *Baianidade*. Likewise, it is not very difficult to imagine how a Bahian scholar, trained at the Sorbonne in Paris, finds himself seduced into portraying candomblé as an ecological movement *avant-la-lettre* [. . .]

An appraisal of what candomblé "does" in the new circuits in which it appears also highlights just how much candomblé is in line with the role of Catholic and evangelical churches in the political field as it provides political activity with a religious frame. I want to stress that the quoted gay activists who praise the orixás for blessing the gay pride parade or ponder the possibility of founding a religious gay cult, as well as the black activists who praise the orixás, might be far more serious and far less ironic than a western reader might assume. Secularisation theories – whatever they are worth in the western world – are simply useless in Bahia, where one always performs in front of an audience of saints, spirits and gods. A political project that does not, in one way or the other, demonstrate its alliance with the saints and advertise its tap-roots into the sacred, will not add up to much in Bahia (hence the famous public statement of Fernando Henrique Cardoso, the former Brazilian president, that he considered himself "a Cartesian with a touch of voodoo"). The presence of so many politicians at the pompous ceremony that I described at the opening of this article, as well as Gilberto Gil's public confession that his ministry of Xangô was "of a spiritual, and therefore more important, level than his position in Brasília" are good examples. Yet the necessity of demonstrating one's connections with the sacred also showed up in a small gesture by UNEGRO[4] activists that I once saw: they had organised a public debate in a modern university building and began the session by publicly decorating the sterile laminate table-tops with leaves of the Sanseveria, a plant that in candomblé is known as the Sword-of-Ogum and is endowed with the power to chase away evil forces. Just by putting one leaf on each table, they managed completely to transform the frame of the occasion.

A third point [. . .] is that candomblé casts political projects in a frame of "victimhood". To opt for candomblé imagery is to invoke all kinds of emotions associated with slavery, persecution, historical injustice, the denial of a right of existence, the suffering of the weak, the poor and the miserable, which the history of candomblé (and of Afro-Brazilians in general) incorporates. Against this catalogue of tragedies, however, one can always point to the perseverance of the Afro-Brazilian faith, as well as the pride and self-esteem of the can-domblé community that has managed to survive all the hardships of its history. The appeal of this framing for counter-movements is evident ("their persecution is our persecution, their suffering is our suffering"). The populist politics of the Bahian elites, however,

are equally well served by the rhetorical possibilities of victimhood, be it in relation to sentiments regarding the federal state ("We Bahians are always discriminated against by those southern states"), or in attempts to create a populist image ("You may think we live in our golden towers, but we know of the people's suffering too").

As for the question of why it is that the priesthood has started to perform the novel scripts that have been written for their religious practices, it is instructive to go back to the opening of this article. The opening ceremony showed just how successful some temples have become at updating [. . .] the time-honoured politics of creating honorary functions for influential outsiders. While publicly maintaining an image of the religion of the oppressed (recall the peripheral location of Mãe Stella's temple, and Emerson saying that Mãe Stella was such a "humble" woman), Ilê Axé Opô Afonjá, the temple under discussion, manages to mobilise an impressive collection of powerful figures. In this particular temple, there is not only an "ogã-ship" on offer to outsiders – a function that does not require a long initiation and "receiving" of the spirits through possession – but also a chair in the "ministry of Xangô", an institution of twenty-four chair holders that was created in 1937 within this particular terreiro with the possible purpose (and definite effect) of allowing ever more influential outsiders into its ranks. The handing out of "Xangô awards" for celebrities who distinguish themselves as benefactors of the candomblé community during the ceremony that I have described might be seen as the new format in which this type of politics is cast.

Today, these politics seem to be motivated by a number of considerations. First, there is a deep concern over the booming of neo-Pentecostal churches that continuously attack candomblé, saying it is nothing less than the realm of the devil. In Bahia, a fear of outright persecution has somewhat diminished now that the cult has been officially and legally recognised as one of the religions in the state. Yet the priesthood is very much aware of the less favourable conditions of candomblé in other states such as São Paulo and Rio de

Janeiro, where Pentecostal churches demonise and marginalise the cult, as of old. The candomblé priesthood has therefore a vested interest in maintaining the framing of Bahia as "the blessed land of the orixás", just as a public display of the links with highly influential politicians and esteemed academics helps against the threat of neo-Pentecostal churches. The way that the community of candomblé has recently begun to stress its dedication to tolerance [tolerância] must also be understood against the threat of the Pentecostal churches, and might explain the ease with which priests pick up "liberal" issues such as gay rights, ecology or black emancipation.

Second, the creation of these honorary functions and the public demonstration of the alliances a temple manages to mobilise should be understood in relation to the attempts of the priesthood to enhance the respectability of the cult vis-à-vis a society that still has a lot of prejudice about candomblé [. . .] For all of its prestige, in the popular mind, candomblé is easily linked to black magic, occult forces and witchcraft [macumba]. The main temples seek to escape from these prejudices primarily by adopting the anthropological distinction between religion and magic, and positioning their beliefs in the former category (cf. Maggy 1986; Capone 2000). They have also launched a public-relations offensive to advance this understanding of candomblé as a religion – and seem to be quite successful. [. . .] It is stunning to see how the two main newspapers in Bahia seem to be under a very strict (self-) censorship, avoiding the kind of sensationalist reports about macumba that one finds elsewhere in Brazil, always going out of their way to educate the public with very orthodox visions of candomblé, and reproducing the solemn and sacred nature of Afro-Brazilian religion.

That there are limits to this playing along with the scripts that have been written elsewhere is evident. Especially in the field of entertainment, the priesthood tries to limit the use of candomblé imagery for fear of a "profanation" of the cult. As the opening night of the *Semana Cultural da Herança Africana na Bahia* illustrated so well, the priests from candomblé can hardly be described as putty in the hands of others: they are busy producing scenarios for a public form of candomblé, writing scripts to be enacted by politicians, activists and anthropologists.

The more general conclusion this article permits – and I dare say this has relevance beyond the study of candomblé – is that the well-established categories within which anthropologists have sought to delineate their objects of investigation are in need of revision. Candomblé is part of a world in which the forces of globalisation and the mass media operate: I have shown that the walls between the temple and society at large are highly permeable, and that at present "the whole world" is involved in the making and re-making of candomblé. In such a world, it makes little sense to try to contain candomblé within the bounded anthropological notion of a "cult".

My proposal to study candomblé as a symbol bank in Bahia's representational economy forces one to be aware of the multiple connections between the cult and the circuits through which its myths, its belief-tenets, its symbols, its aesthetics and its practices circulate. Above all, it urges one to be alert to the transformative work of the dialogues that take place thanks to these circulations: what happens when understandings pass through the endless communicative chains of priests talking to anthropologists, talking to gay activists, talking to politicians, talking to initiates, talking to talk-show hosts, and so on? Such a focus on circulation breaks with prioritising temples and priests as the preferred sites and exegetes of the cult. Instead, it urges one to analyse the fact that some people claim to represent the real candomblé, and that others support or contest those claims. It urges one to investigate what resources people have to substantiate their claims. It urges one to ponder the question of why some images of candomblé find support, while others that are equally present become obscured. Indeed, it urges one to consider the possibility that the continued representation of candomblé as a closed universe is part of an internal political strategy that seeks to deal with the permeability of the temple walls.

NOTES

1 The expression could be translated as "utterly Brazilian".

2 For an elaborate discussion and deconstruction of anthropological work in candomblé temples, see Vagner Gonçalves da Silva (2000).

3 Text found at the author's website: http://www.fflch.usp.br/sociologia/prandi/, last entered 20 September 2004.

4 União de Negros pela Igualdade (Union of Blacks for Equality).

REFERENCES

Agier, Michel. 2000. *Anthropologie du carnaval. La ville, la fête et l'Afrique à Bahia.* Paris: Éditions Parentheses.

Amaral, Rita. 2002. *Xirê! O modo de crer e de viver no candomblé.* Rio de Janeiro: Pallas.

Asad, Talal. 1993. *Genealogies of Religion. Discipline and Reasons of Power in Christianity and Islam.* Baltimore: Johns Hopkins University Press.

Augras, Monique. 1998. Tendances actuelles de la recherche sur les cultes afro-brésiliens, in Marion Aubrée (ed.), *Religions. Orthodoxie, heterodoxie et mysticisme*: 87–105. [= *Cahier du Brésil Contemporain* 35–6.]

Bastide, Roger. 2000 [1958]. *O candomblé da Bahia. Rito Nagô.* São Paulo: Editora Schwarz.

Birman, Patricia. 1995. *Fazer estilo, criando gêneros. Possessão e diferencas de gênero em terreiros de umbanda e candomblé no Rio de Janeiro.* Rio de Janeiro: EduERJ.

Capone, Stephania. 2000. *La quête de l'Afrique dans le candomblé. Pouvoir et tradition au Brésil.* Paris: Karthala.

Carneiro, Edson. 2002 [1948]. *Candomblés da Bahia.* Rio de Janeiro: Civilização Brasileira.

Connor, Randy P., and David H. Sparks. 2004. *Queering Creole Spiritual Traditions. Lesbian, Gay, Bisexual and Transgender Participation in African-inspired Traditions*

in the Americas. Binghamton: Harrington Park Press.

Covin, David. 1996. The role of culture in Brazil's unified black movement. Bahia in 1992, *Journal of Black Studies* 27: 39–55.

Dantas, Beatrice Góis. 1988. *Vovó nagô e papai branco. Usos e abusos da África no Brasil.* Rio de Janeiro: Editora Graal.

Dion, Michel. 1998. *Omindarewa. Uma francesa no candomblé. A busca de uma outra verdade.* Rio de Janeiro: Pallas.

Dunn, Christopher. 2001. *Brutality Garden. Tropicália and the Emergence of a Brazilian Counterculture.* Chapel Hill: University of North Carolina Press.

Fry, Peter. 1982. *Para inglês vet. Identidade e política na cultura brasileira.* Rio de Janeiro: Zahar Editores.

Hamilton, Russell G. 1967. Afro-Brazilian cults in the novels of Jorge Amado, *Hispania* 50: 242–52.

Johnson, Paul. 2002. *Secrets, Gossip and Gods. The Transformation of Brazilian Candomblé.* Oxford: Oxford University Press.

Keane, Webb. 2002. Sincerity, modernity and the Protestants, *Cultural Anthropology* 17: 65–92.

Landes, Ruth. 1947. *The City of Women.* New York: MacMillan.

Lipiani, José Luiz. 1999. *Orixás. Comportamento e personalidade de sues filhos. Comprehender melhor a si mesmo e a seus semelhantes através da umbanda.* Rio de Janeiro: Pallas.

Maggy, Yvonne. 1986. *Guerra de orixa. Um estudo de ritual e conflito.* Rio de Janeiro: Jorge Zahar.

——. 1992. *Medo do feitiço. Relações entre magia e poder no Brasil.* Rio de Janeiro: Arquivo Nacional.

Meyer, Birgit. 2004. "Praise the Lord". Popular cinema and Pentecostalite style in Ghana's new public sphere, *American Ethnologist* 31: 92–110.

Montes, Maria Lucia. 1998. As figuras do sagrado. Entre o publico e o privadoi, in Lilia Moritz Schwarcz (ed.), *História da vida privada no Brasil*, 63–173. São Paulo: Companhia das Letras.

Mott, Luis, and Marcello Cerqueira (eds.). 1998. *As religiões Afro-Brasileiras na luta contra a Aids*. Salvador: Editora CBAA.

Pinto. Roque. 2001. Como a cidade de Salvador empreende a produção do exótico atraves do texto da baianidade (Dissertação de mestrado EM sciences sociais, University of Salvador).

Prandi, Reginaldo. 1996. *Herdeiras do axé. Sociologia da religiões afro-brasileiras*. São Paulo: Editora HUCITEC.

Pretto, Nelson de Lucca, and Luiz Felippe Perret Serpa (eds.). 2002. *Expressões de Sabedoria. Educação, vida e sabers. Mãe stella de oxóssi, juvany viana*. Salvador: Edufba.

Risério, Antonio. 1981. *Carnaval ijexá*. Salvador: Corrupio.

Rodrigues, Nina. 1935 [1900]. *O animismo fetichista dos negros baianos*. Rio de Janeiro: Civilização Brasileira.

Salvatore, Armando. 1997. *Islam and the political discourse of modernity*. Reading, NY: Ithaca Press.

Santos, Juana Elbein dos. 1986 [1998]. *Os nâgô e a morte. Pàde, asèsè e o culto égun na Bahia*. Petrópolis: Editora Vozes.

Santos, Jocélio Teles dos. 1995. *O dono da terra. O caboclo nos candomblés da Bahia*. Salvador: Sarah Letras.

———. 2000. O poder da cultura e a cultura no poder. A disputa simbólica da herança cultural negra no Brasil (PhD dissertation, University of São Paulo).

Serra, Ordep. 1995. *Aguas do rei*. Rio de Janeiro: Vozes.

Silva, Vagner Gonçalves da. 1995. *Orixás da metrópole*. Petropolis: Vozes.

———. 2001. *O antropologo e sua magia. Trabalho de campo e texto etnográfico nas pesquisas antropológicas sobre religiões afro-brasileiras*. São Paulo: Editora USP.

Silva, Vagner Gonçalves da, and Rita Amaral. 1993. A cor do axé. Brancos e negros no candomblé de São Paulo, *Estudos Afro-Asiáticos* 25: 99–124.

Sodré, Muniz. 2002. *O terreiro e a cidade. A forma social negro-brasileira*. Salvador: Secretaria da Cultura e Turismo.

Trevisan, João Silvério. 2000. *Devassos no paraíso. A homossexualidade no Brasil, da colonia a atualidade*. São Paulo: Record.

Verger, Pierre. 1981. *Orixás, deuses Iorubás na África e no novo mundo*. Salvador: Corrupio.

Wafer, Jim. 1991. *The Taste of Blood. Spirit Possession in Brazilian Candomblé*. Philadelphia: University of Pennsylvania Press.

45

Martyr vs. Martyr: The Sacred Language of Violence

Galit Hasan-Rokem

Galit Hasan-Rokem is Professor of Hebrew Literature and Jewish and Comparative Folklore and Head of the Institute of Jewish Studies at the Hebrew University, Jerusalem. Trained as a folklorist in Finland and Israel, her work combines multilingual semiotic analysis, historical scholarship, and contemporary theory from the humanities to address the prevalence, perdurance, and meanings of religious motifs and images. She is the author of *Web of Life: Folklore and Midrash in Rabbinic Literature* and *Tales of the Neighborhood: Jewish Narrative Dialogues in Late Antiquity* as well as several works of poetry.

Hasan-Rokem here offers a stark and indelible account of the misappropriation of religious language in politics and indeed of the misappropriation of individual lives and deaths to the violence not only of bombs but of religious discourse. Starting from the funeral of a friend she reflects on "the growing usage of words from religious contexts

to legitimize violence and to attach powerful collective emotions to it" (quoting from her original abstract) and thus, indirectly, on the media and the mediated ways we come to assimilate current events and personal tragedies and possibly even to perpetuate cruelty. Like De Boeck, she thereby alludes to religion's possible complicity with fantasy and terror. Where most essays in this volume speak positively about subjects like communication and pollution rules, Hasan-Rokem writes of a "lethal dialogue" between related Jewish and Islamic concepts of martyrdom and of the potential – obviously not limited to the Middle East – for transforming defilement into religious violence. Her essay not only encourages us to attend more closely to our use of language, to listen more critically, but implicitly raises important questions about how religion can be kept at a proper distance from the political and what that distance ought to be.

From Galit Hasan-Rokem, "Martyr vs. Martyr: The Sacred Language of Violence," *Ethnologia Europaea* 33(2) (2003), pp. 99–104. Abridged.

The events of 9/11/01 in New York City heightened the awareness of human frailty and the limits of control of even great empires. They sharpened the general consciousness of the power of images and words to shape not only the concepts of individuals but also to instantly reshape the behavior of millions of individuals and a great number of governments, public agencies, and commercial corporations world-wide. In the following paper I wish to touch upon an aspect that is present in the specific media complex regarding those events in New York City, but that is even more visible and audible in the public discourse in the Middle East where the named events have deep roots. I shall trace the semiotics of one specific term, "martyr," that has played a fatal role in the molding of images between Israelis and Palestinians in their longtime strife over the territories of the Holy Land. The way the concept of martyr functions in the communication between these two identities infuses the [. . .] dialogue with a different tone than the positive value that most of us are used to attach to the term in the wake of European humanist and existentialist traditions represented by thinkers as different from each other as Martin Buber, Mikhail Bakhtin, and Hans Georg Gadamer.

The paper will not encompass the entire historical width and depth of the phenomenon of martyrdom. It has been part and parcel of religious phenomenology as long as we can trace it back, but was consolidated and institutionalized by Christianity and Judaism in the early centuries of the first millennium. It should, however, be mentioned that in the historical perspective it becomes very clear that the term martyr, derived from the Greek "witness," has always served in the generation of mutual relationships of entities contesting their legitimacy over a specific legacy, be it sacred texts or sacred territories. This fact as well as its phenomenal relationship to communication, and especially mass communication, may be illuminated by the following observation made by Daniel Boyarin on the "cooperative" emergence of martyrdom, under very different circumstances and power relations, in late antiquity:

Martyrdom, even more than tragedy, is *Thanatoi en tōi phanarōi*, "deaths that are seen," murders in public spaces. Insofar as martyrdom is, then by definition, a practice that takes place within the public, and therefore, shared space, *martyria* seem to be a particularly fertile site for the exploration of the permeability of the borders between so-called Judaism and so-called Christianity in late antiquity. (Boyarin 1999)[1]

I shall in the following resort to the tools of the ethnographer who uses herself as the source of information, thus appropriating the witnessing function from those who have used it in death to one who hopes to do it in the service of life.

[. . .]

I participated in the funeral of Daphna Shpruch. She had died [. . .] ten days after a bomb exploded at the Hebrew University Mount Scopus Cafeteria, [. . .] on July 31, 2002. Daphna died of a severe head injury caused by the explosion that destroyed the front part of her head.

Some secularized Jews in Israel today, to whom the form of the ceremonies of death are a matter of principle and of deep feelings, create an individually styled ceremony with music, poetry reading, etc. At Daphna's funeral it became clear that her stricken family had not made an extra effort to salvage the ceremony from the hands of the orthodox religious authorities. As a result, the raw pain of the family was laid bare by the harsh contradiction between the formality of the orthodox officials and the [. . .] lack of communication of the family members and close friends with the undertakers. The official cantor who recited the traditional texts of the Jewish funeral ceremony introduced Daphna Shpruch as a martyr, *qedosha*. Although the usage somewhat disturbingly alerted my attention, it was familiar enough from the prevalent public discourse so that no explanation was needed. The cantor obviously considered Daphna a martyr because her death had occurred within the context of the national conflict between Palestinians and Israelis. Her death was caused by a bomb in the current wave of terror.

In the original usage of martyrdom in early Christianity and rabbinic Judaism (*qiddush ha-shem*), the agency of the martyr who chooses death to witness her or his belief was reportedly of central significance. Political manipulation of individual agency seems to characterize the contemporary discourse of martyrdom. Perhaps we should not rule out the possibility that such manipulation lies also behind some of the martyrological discourse of earlier eras. However I cannot deal systematically with this last question in the context of the present paper, and will rather return to my short ethnographic account.

Upon hearing the word *qedosha*, I made an instant comment turning to one of Daphna's closest friends standing next to me. Incidentally the friend's father is one of the chief ideologues of the Canaanite movement that was especially active in Israel in the late forties and the early fifties of the twentieth century (Diamond 1986; Shavit 1987; Kuzar 2001). The major platform of this minuscule cultural movement, however of some consequence, was to diminish the influence of Jewishness and to ground Israeli identity in the territorial aspect of Canaan and the common heritage of the peoples of the land west of Jordan valley prior to the Moslems, Christians, and the Jews. The Canaanite ideology failed to incite the masses. However, its secularist, almost pagan, message infiltrated such enterprises as the reshaping of Jewish holiday traditions in the context of the agricultural life of kibbutzim. It is therefore noteworthy that the secularizing tendency of some parts of public language has with regard to the language of public mourning, especially concerning violence occurring in the context of national conflict, suffered a blatant failure. The way martyrs figure in public uses of language is a major example of this.

Let us return to Daphna. By the current language usage, applied for instance by the Rector of the Hebrew University (at least outwardly a perfectly secularized person) in his words of lament at the funeral, her name may or perhaps "should" be appended by the cliché *hashem yiqqom dammah* "may God revenge her blood" – routinely added to the names of victims of terror in speech as well as writing (obituaries, ads of mourning etc.). One could assume that the forwarding of the act of revenge to the Almighty in those words

expresses a belief in the governance that will restore some kind of moral balance into the grim reality experienced by mourners. Conceivably it could then serve to cancel any ideas about human revenge meted out by official agents of the state or others. There is, notwithstanding, a danger for another alternative to emerge, that will find some footing from biblical traditions onwards, that the collective "we" of the speaker envisages itself as the legitimate tool for the fulfillment of divine justice, dictated by internal group interests.

Since the religious language of the present quotes heavily from classical and medieval sources, I will now sketch some of the historical connotations emerging from the linguistic usages of *qedosha* (masc. *qadosh*) and *hashem yiqqom dammah* (masc. *dammo*).

The main usage of *qadosh* according to the dictionary of the Hebrew Bible concordance is "holy" as an attribute of God (translates into the *sanctus* of the Latin mass, according to Isaiah 6:3 *Qadosh, qadosh, qadosh adonai tsevaot*). Imparting the idea of emulation of the divine, anybody of great righteousness and adherence to God, and in special cases also Israel as a people (Exodus 19:6) may be described by the term. It also denotes places, objects, and persons who are not in any way defiled, and serves generally as the antonym for impure and secular.

In Rabbinical literature of late antiquity the connection between *qadosh* and martyrdom is created in complete dialogue with the emergence of martyrdom in Christianity as shown in the above mentioned work of Boyarin. The main semantic extension of the concept consists of an act of sacrificing one's life to testify (the Greek etymon of "martyr") to the existence of God, an act that sanctifies His name and elevates it. The expression in rabbinic literature is indeed the verbal compound "to sanctify His name", rather than an attribute of the martyrs themselves. The holiness of the martyrs is thus derived from their own act and from the holiness of its addressee, God, rather than from the atrocity meted out to them by others. This may be understood as intimately associated with the change in mentality occurring in late antique culture, first in the eastern part of the Mediterranean and later in most of the Roman Empire. This change may be best formulated as a new stage in the development of subjectivity and individual responsibility, expressed especially in the texts of Early Christianity and Rabbinic Judaism in parallel.

In medieval Jewish texts there is a slow but clear semantic shift that turns over the agency to create martyrs, qedoshim, to the executors. One could speculate on the transformation and varieties of Jewish identity, subjectivity, and agency in the transport from the land of origin, to first the Moslem, then the Christian Diaspora. Spanish-Jewish Maimonides (11th century Moslem Spain) in his essay on conversion calls those who prefer to die rather than embrace another religion "saints" (qedoshim) thus still retaining the exertion of a free will (Kellner 1991: 49–59). The chronicles describing the pogroms against the Jews of the Rhine valley (notably Speier, Worms and Metz), as a result of the zealotry of the crusaders on their way to the Holy Land, also apply the term for those who refused to Christianize, often in the context of cruel torture and desperate acts such as suicide and slaughtering their own children (Yuval 2000: 108–218; Einbinder 2000). From the fifteenth century onwards in Jewish texts from Germany (the emic term being Ashkenaz) qedoshim and qadosh have become standard usage for Jews being killed by non-Jews in a variety of contexts. Thus in the 17th-century autobiography of the remarkable woman Glikl Hamel, two Jewish thieves who were caught and repudiated the clemency of conversion are called by her "saints". In a number of epic poems of historical topics, for instance the victims of a great fire in Frankfurt are called qedoshim although there is no indication in the text that the fire was anything else but a calamity (Lowenthal 1977; Davis 1995).[2]

The earliest occurrence of the dictum hashem yiqqom dammo that I have been able to identify is the 13th-century Spanish poet and Bible interpreter [. . .] Moshe Ibn-Ezra's elaboration on Deuteronomy 32:43: "Rejoice, o you nations, with his people, for he will avenge the blood of his servants, and will render vengeance to his adversaries, and will be merciful to his land and to his people." This first half of the final verse of Moses' lengthy prophetic and didactic valediction (in which he outlines all the calamities that will befall Israel due to their disobedience before God will finally absolve them) is commented by Ibn-Ezra with the above mentioned exhortation, in plural: hashem yiqqom dammam.

In the twentieth century a completely new vocabulary for death, especially Jewish death, was created through the lethal industry of World War II and the Shoah. Ethical and political texts referring to the victims of Shoah often call them qedoshim. A forest of six million trees planted in the mountains close to Jerusalem, to commemorate the victims of Shoah, is consequently called "The Martyrs' Forest" – ya'ar ha-qedoshim. The very term "Holocaust" denotes a religious connection. This is a deplorable association to sacrifice, atonement, purgation. It constitutes a reply to the metaphor of defilement attached to the victims by the Nazis and thereby resumes it. This discursive act has aptly been critiqued by Giorgio Agamben:

> The wish to lend a sacrificial aura to the extermination of the Jews by means of the term "Holocaust" was, from this perspective, an irresponsible historiographical blindness. The Jew living under Nazism is the privileged negative referent of the new biopolitical sovereignty and is, as such, a flagrant case of *homo sacer* in the sense of a life that may be killed but not sacrificed. The truth – which is difficult for the victims to face, but which we must have the courage not to cover with sacrificial veils – is that the Jews were exterminated not in a mad and giant holocaust but exactly as Hitler had announced, "as lice," which is to say, as bare life. . . . If today there is no longer any one clear figure of the sacred man, it is perhaps because we are all virtually *homines sacri* (Agamben 1998: 114–115).[3]

The final sentence of this quote may be interpreted as a sinister description of the reality of terror of state, religious, political as well as individual nature.

I offer this all too concise historical excursus because it seems absolutely necessary to keep these facts in mind if we wish to even try to understand the complex resonance of the usage of qedosha for a woman like Daphna Shpruch.

What the performer of the funeral service (not a rabbi, by the way, but a member of the hevra qadisha, "the holy association" – an ancient institution responsible for the handling of the corpse and the funeral) did not know was that Daphna Shpruch was a fervent peace activist, one of the Women in Black of Jerusalem's Paris Square, women who in their body and presence have for fifteen years, since the beginning of the first Intifada, stood at the heart of Israel's capital, voicing (if mostly in silence) their resistance to and disagreement with the occupation and oppression of the Palestinians. Her death thus signals a double appropriation: that of her murderer who appropriated her as an enemy, as part of the occupation, a fact that no Israeli can avoid whatever the degree of her resistance to the majority politics is. The other appropriation is by the rhetoric of occupation, especially by applying on her the tag qedosha, communicating a rhetoric and state of mind fed and fueled by every act of terrorism.

The enormous impact of the peoples of the Middle East and especially the Holy Land for the religious history of Europe and the entire world resonates again through the dialogic double construction of the qedoshim and the shuhada (sing. shahid), the Arabic term for martyr.[4] The complexity of the lethal dialogue between those two concepts of martyrdom would need a much more thorough ethnography and especially a study of mass media than can be provided here. However, a theoretical insight that seems fruitful in this context is Homi Bhabha's concept of "mimicry," in his cultural analysis of colonialism inspired by Lacanian psychology:

> In mimicry, the representation of identity and meaning is rearticulated along the axis of metonymy. As Lacan reminds us, mimicry is like camouflage, not a harmonization of repression of difference, but a form of resemblance, that differs from or defends presence by displaying it in part, metonymically. Its threat, I would add, comes from the prodigious and strategic production of conflictual, fantastic, discriminatory "identity effects" in the play of a power that is elusive because it hides no essence, no "itself." (Bhabha 1994: 90)

The threat mentioned by Bhabha reminds us of the powerful effect of religious language when geared into the business of stereotyping the other in creating the fantasy of averting the threat. The discursive transformation is perceptively described by Paul Ricoeur:

> Defilement itself is scarcely a representation, and what representation there is is immersed in a specific sort of fear that blocks reflection. With defilement we enter into the reign of Terror. Thereupon the philosopher recalls Spinoza's nec spe nec metu: hope for nothing in order to fear nothing; and he learns from the psychoanalyst that this fear is akin to an obsessional neurosis. (Ricoeur 1969: 25)

The moral, religious interpretation of terror results then, according to Ricoeur, in a problematic apology: "If it is true that man suffers because he is impure, then God is innocent" (31–32). Ricoeur's dilemma, that has been reiterated by him numerous times, whether in dealing with Shoah or the biblical book of Job, sharpens the problematic arising between the canonized forms of religion and their potential for either interpreting the violence of the other religiously, or the worse case, in turning violence into a religious act.

This essay cannot be brought to its inconclusive end without mentioning a private nightmare of mine that was sharpened by the reactions on the Israeli raid in the Jenin refugee camp in 2001. Is it possible that by legitimizing the foundation of Israel on the martyrdom of the Shoah, Western consciousness may have set a challenge for the Palestinians to produce a martyrdom of the same magnitude in order to establish Palestine? If so, are the Jews again cast in the taboo-laden role of the Sacred Executioner traditionally allotted to them by European culture? (Maccoby 1982). The inflamed effect of the usage of martyr-shahid-qadosh on all sides of the Middle Eastern conflict, the Western, European and Third World "audiences" included, becomes thus a dangerous weapon. How will the Jews in Israel harness the moral traditions of Judaism in order to subvert and counteract this karma?

NOTES

1 Also see the following groundbreaking works: Frend, 1967, and Bowersock, 1995. Whereas Bowersock's historical approach situates the origin of the phenomenon strictly within early Christianity, Boyarin's cultural method opts for a dialogic, mutual emergence of the phenomenon in a way that breaks down the dichotomy between the two entities in their early phases of formation. See also Jan Willem van Henten and Friedrich Avemarie, *Martyrdom and Noble Death: Selected Texts from Graeco-Roman, Jewish, and Christian Antiquity. The Context of Early Christianity*, London: Routledge, 2002.

2 Glikl Memoires, 1691–1719. Edited and translated from the Yiddish by Chava Turniansky. Jeruslem: The Zalman Shazar Center for Jewish History and The Ben-Zion Dinur Center for Research in Jewish History, The Hebrew University of Jerusalem, 2006.

3 The centrality of sacrificial violence is the focus of discussion in Girard, 1977, especially relevant for our discussion is chapter 6, "From Mimetic Desire to the Monstrous Double".

4 Due to ignorance I cannot venture a similar reconstruction of the historical roots and associations of the Arabic term *shahid* as I have tried to provide for the Hebrew *qadosh*.

REFERENCES

Agamben, Giorgio 1998: *Homo Sacer: Sovereign Power and Bare Life*. Translated by Daniel Heller-Roazen. Stanford, Calif.

Bhabha, Homi 1994: *The Location of Culture*. London.

Bowersock, Glen 1995: *Martyrdom and Rome. The Wiles Lectures Given at the Queen's University of Belfast*. Cambridge.

Boyarin, Daniel 1999: *Dying for God: Martyrdom and the Making of Christianity and Judaism*. Stanford, Calif.

Davis, Natalie Zemon 1995: *Women on the Margins: Three Seventeenth-Century Lives*. Cambridge, Mass.

Diamond, Janes S. 1986: *Homeland or Holy Land? The "Canaanite" Critique of Israel*. Bloomington.

Einbinder, Susan 2002: *Beautiful Death: Jewish Poetry and Martyrdom in Medieval France*. Princeton.

Frend, W.H.C. 1967: *Martyrdom and Persecution in the Early Church: A Study of a Conflict from the Maccabees to Donatus*. Garden City, N.Y.

Girard, René 1977: *Violence and the Sacred*. Translated by Patrick Gregory. Baltimore.

Kellner, Menachem 1991: *Maimonides on Judaism and the Jewish People*. Albany.

Kuzar, Ron 2001: *Hebrew and Zionism: A Discourse Analytic Cultural Study*. Berlin.

Lowenthal, Marvin (ed. and translator) 1977: *The Memoirs of Glueckel of Hameln*. New introduction by Robert S. Rosen. New York: Schocken Books.

Maccoby, Hyam 1982: *Human Sacrifice and the Legacy of Guilt*. London.

Ricoeur, Paul 1969: *The Symbolism of Evil*. Translated by Emerson Buchanan. Boston.

Shavit, Yaacove 1987: *The Hebrew Nation: A Study in Israeli Heresy and Fantasy*. London.

Yuval, Israel Jacob 2000: *"Two Nations in Your Womb" – Perceptions of Jews and Christians*. Tel-Aviv. (Hebrew. The English Version is in press at the University of California Press 4.)

Afterword

46

Evidence and Presence, Spectral and Other

Stephan Palmié

Stephan Palmié is an anthropologist trained at the University of Munich. After teaching in the History Department at the University of Maryland, Palmié is currently a member of the Department of Anthropology at the University of Chicago.

This Afterword, which is actually the Prologue to Palmié's book *Wizards and Scientists*, brings together a number of themes encountered throughout the *Reader*. Here the subjects of the anthropologist speak back; they assert that his research is motivated by a spirit guardian. Appearance and reality, rationality and truth, and the power of representation are up for grabs. Palmié reminds us also of the importance of death and the dead. If Vico is right that human history begins with the intentional burial of the dead, then religion, funerary practices, history, and the very condition of human culture are closely intertwined. But what

happens to the "unburied," the unredeemed? If history has of late become the dominant mode of anthropological understanding, Palmié pushes us to consider the way that our very conceptualization of "history" is itself culturally, ethically, and politically shaped. Any authoritative form of knowledge, whether it be a religious orthodoxy or an anthropology of religion, leaves behind the unacknowledged. The margins can only return as ghostly traces. (For further work on historicity see Koselleck 2004, Lambek 2002a, b, 2004, and Mueggler 2001, among others.)

The message of the ghost is necessarily ambiguous. Whatever his meaning for Palmié's teachers, or for Palmié personally, one possibility is to take Tomás as an evocation of the anthropological impulse itself, an impulse born of modernity, disruption, and violence that seeks

From Stephan Palmié, "Evidence and Presence, Spectral and Other," in *Wizards and Scientists: Explorations in Afro-Cuban Modernity & Tradition* (Durham NC: Duke University Press, 2002), pp.1–14. Most footnotes removed.

redemption in representation and resuscitation, in knowledge that attempts to embrace the margins. And yet Tomás equally disturbs our comfortable privilege as researchers and students, writers and readers. Palmié reminds us that the very world in which we live was "erected, at least in part, on the unmarked graves of African slaves" and "drew its wealth and confidence in a ghastly dual movement of accumulating capital and knowledge." Ghostly and ghastly, we end thus on a note not yet of (religious) redemption but of (critical) disquiet.

When I first began doing ethnographic fieldwork in Miami in 1985, people whom I soon learned to think of as "my informants" repeatedly asked me why I had chosen Afro-Cuban religion as a topic of research. What did I want from them? Why had I come all the way from Europe to study their practices and beliefs? And to what end? I have always felt somewhat at a loss for an answer. My own rationalization of my increasingly frequent visits to their homes as part of a dissertation project seemed a rather weak argument even then, and I cannot say that I have come up with more convincing explanations during the subsequent research that I have conducted in Cuba since 1993. Back in Miami in 1985, at any rate, I was both puzzled and intrigued by an interpretation first ventured by a professional diviner and friend named Cecilia Laca and later – to my surprise – confirmed by another initiated priest of *regla ocha* whom I came to know only as Carlos. The question that both of them had tried to tackle was the following: Given that I steadfastly denied that either I or my personal forebears had any palpable connection with Africa, Cuba, or the Caribbean, how was it that I seemed so obviously compelled to seek information about matters connected with the history of these places? The answer that Cecilia and Carlos came up with was that I had been driven to their doorsteps by the spirit of a dead slave – a solution straightforwardly plausible within the world of Afro-Cuban religion but just about as utterly fantastic within the universe of meaning that I inhabit as the suggestion that a tempest magically unleashed by Shakespeare's exiled duke of Milan had blown me there.

Cecilia's and Carlos's theories explaining my unusual interest in Afro-Cuban religion had,

of course, nothing to do with wistful literary metaphorics. They recurred to the spiritist doctrines to which both of them, to varying degrees, subscribed. According to the popular versions of Kardecian spiritism, which, in the second half of the nineteenth century, began to merge with various African-derived conceptions of personalized mystical agents, the dead continue to be present among us as they undergo a spiritual progression from earthbound embodiment to increasing purity and detachment from the base world of matter. Individuals with "developed" spiritist faculties can experience their presence in the form of *videncias*, *audiencias*, or *sensaciones* – that is, visual, aural, or tactile perceptions. I cannot say that I discouraged these readings of *my* presence in my informants' lives, eager as I was to be introduced into a world in which such interpretations represented common sense. However, I vividly recall my surprise when both Cecilia and Carlos (who did not know each other) independently told me that they *saw* the presence of Tomás: the spirit of an elderly African slave who had lived and died in nineteenth-century Cuba and had come to attach himself to my person, hovering behind me, in the way the dead are wont to do.

Cecilia described him to me in considerable detail: the "muerto detras de mi" (the dead person behind me) was tall and slender and very dark-skinned. He wore a coarsely tailored pair of white pants and a white shirt girded at the waist with a red sash. Tomás's mission was to redeem himself in the spirit world by taking on the task of watching over me so that no harm would come to me as I made my way through a world saturated with both physical and mystical dangers. Miami, as Cecilia and many others had told me, was a dangerous place, and falling victim to a traffic accident or an accidental shooting might not be the worst that could happen. The city abounded with spirits of people who had lived evil lives or died bad deaths. Such "unevolved" spirits seek out the living in the hope that they will help them attain "peace and light." But their tormented state begins to rub off on those to whom they have attached themselves, affecting them with inexplicable sadness, or driving them to erratic and harmful forms of behavior. My spirit guardian was of a more benign nature. Yet had he not, Cecilia would ask, made his influence felt in nudging me toward research on Afro-Cuban religion? Carlos – whose mundane professions perhaps imparted to him a somewhat nonchalant attitude about such matters[1] – simply recommended that, on a day when I felt somewhat depressed, I should sit down in front of a mirror, drink a glass of rum, and smoke a cigar while reflecting on my deepest hopes and worries in life. Surely, I would then gradually see the contours of "my *muerto*" emerging in the mirror. "Try it out," he told me. "Then judge for yourself."

I admit that I tried. Yet, although I never saw Tomás, what I do see today is that the notion of such a presence in my life has levels of significance not exhausted in the literalism implied by such terms as *belief*, *plausibility*, or *rationality*. Of course, to borrow Françoise Meltzer's (1994, 44) handy phrase, nothing brings out positivism more quickly than what we are talking about here: ghosts. We cannot seem to resist transcribing spirits, gods, or the work of witchcraft into codes that satisfy our deeply held beliefs that stories in which they figure are really about something else: category mistakes, faulty reasoning, forms of ideological misrecognition, projections of mental states, and so on, figments of the individual or collective imagination that may be profitably analyzed in terms of their psychological or social functions but that cannot be taken literally as referents to a reality that is *really* "out there."[2] Yet what if we were to treat Cecilia's and Carlos's accounts, not as the charmingly exotic outgrowth of some sort of shared religious (and therefore irrational, or, at least, mistaken) belief, but as pertaining to a discourse on history merely encoded in an idiom

different from the one with which we feel at home?

Ghost Stories

In a very concrete sense, every form of historical knowledge involves propositions about the role of the dead in the world of the living, shaped as it invariably is by past human existence and agency. Such knowledge lay claims on the past in instantiating, maintaining, or contesting a present world. But it does so in ways not at all captured by objectivist conceptions of historical representation as mere retrieval or correspondence theories of historical truth. This is by no means a particularly novel insight. Histories, Carl Becker pointed out as early as 1932, are themselves historically situated cultural products, even if they do aspire to universal status. Hence, they differ, not just in content, but in respect to the no-less-historical criteria according to which some claims on the past are judged believable, while others are relegated to the realm of the implausible (Becker 1932, 1938). Writing from across the Atlantic, R. G. Collingwood and Michael Oakeshott put the matter in even stronger terms. For the former, historical thought was necessarily driven, not by the accumulation of data, but by the "historical imagination" that constructs empirical givens into evidence rendering varying hypotheses about past events and processes differentially plausible (Collingwood 1994, 231–49). In Oakeshott's (1933, 111ff.) view, knowledge of the historical past cannot be but "a special organization" of a present world of experience *sub specie praeteritorum*. Its object is a construction rather than an empirically ascertainable given, and its truth consists, not in a correspondence between "what the evidence obliges us to believe" and "a past course of events," but in the coherence of the judgments by which "facts" are inferentially constituted with the world constituted by other such judgments.

"Written history," Charles Beard (1934) famously suggested in his 1933 presidential address to the American Historical Association, consequently, cannot be but "an act of faith" – an expression of belief bolstered by evidence not principally different from that by which other interpretative communities (be they composed of Zande diviners, subatomic physicists, statisticians, or practitioners of Afro-Cuban religion) infer, assess, and debate the reality of phenomena and processes inaccessible to "normal" ranges of human sensory perception (cf. Sperber 1982; Danto 1985). Beard was eventually severely castigated by later generations of historians for these assertions (cf. Novick 1988). But he was right – if only because any form of plausibility expressed in a natural language must ultimately rest on horizons of experience and expectation that are historically as well as culturally contingent. Hence Becker's (1932, 235) argument that it should rather relieve than upset us to recognize that "every generation, our own included, will, must inevitably, understand the past and anticipate the future in light of its own restricted experience, must inevitably play on the dead whatever tricks it finds necessary for its own peace of mind." "The appropriate trick," Becker continues, "is not a malicious invention designed to take anyone in, but an unconscious and necessary effort on the part of 'society' to understand what it is doing in the light of what it has done and what it hopes to do," Durkheim (or Marx for that matter) could not have put it more succinctly. Sociologically speaking, no less than religion, history is, ultimately, an assemblage of collective representations positing realities that are – logically – beyond empirical proof.[3] Their consequences, of course, are hardly beyond direct experience. For socially effective constructions of the "historically real" – that is, versions of history that have attained the status of what Marx called *objectively necessary appearances* within specific social contexts – not only tend to underwrite formations of subjectivity, institutional arrangements, and routinized practices in the present, endowing them with a sense of self-evidence and transparency. Rather, the inherently narrative (and therefore inevitably teleological) structure of the historical imagination of particular collectivities can also come to motivate their members to write forward, at times in violent fashion, those unfinished stories that they perceive as their "history." To concede this is not to consign historiography to the status of "mere" discourse (Palmer 1990), a fanciful play of historicizing signifiers on a past the "reality" of which is, and must remain, fundamentally arbitrary. What is at issue instead is what makes certain claims on the past contextually negotiable and dispels others beyond thresholds of credibility that cannot be but historically and culturally specific (MacGaffey 1978; Appadurai 1981; Stoler 1992; Hamilton 1998).

Since at least the eighteenth century, Western historians have constructed their claims on the past on the basis of conceptions of a linear and irreversible growth of unbridgeable temporal distance between past and present realities (Koselleck 1985; Habermas 1987; Kemp 1991; Terdiman 1993). In Koselleck's terms, what this notion enables is the laying out of a *historical space of experience*, or *world* in Oakeshott's sense, in which the dead no longer enjoy the kind of agency that Cecilia and Carlos ascribed to my invisible spirit guide. They are denizens of a world that no longer exists, and, even though we may concede that our world reverberates with the consequences – intended or not – of the actions that the dead once took, the choice whether we want to see matters this way must remain ours. Paraphrasing Marx, one might say that, given this particular structuring of the past in the Western historical imagination, the dead have to be represented precisely because they can no longer represent themselves. We may choose to remember or forget, venerate or vilify them. But they themselves have no say in these matters. In a very real sense, we have to recall them into our present.

This is a proposition without which objectivist notions of truth or factuality in historical representation become tenuous, to say the least. For is not the assumption that the past is over, done with, and hence ontologically sealed off from the present the very foundation of both popular and disciplined quests for the "facts of history" in the contemporary Western world? And yet, not only have philosophers of history long pointed to the fundamental illogicality of such notions (Mink 1978; Danto 1985; Hayden 1973). Rather, as the current multidisciplinary flurry of interest in the phenomenon of memory and the conflictive politics of remembrance and commemoration shows, even within Western cultures there exists an awareness that "the past is not finished and done with, receding ever further into the distance," but remains "imperfect," not just in the grammatical, but also in the ontological sense (Lambek 1996, 246). Finite as the province of meaning of past causes may seem, its content nevertheless leaks into the realm of present effects that become knowable as such only on the basis of hindsight. More paradoxically even, such retrospection not only provides the only basis for discerning structures of past eventuation and causality, but inevitably realigns the past to fit present horizons of historical knowledge and configurations of historical interest (cf. Danto 1985, chap. 8). As soon, in other words, as we think about how to represent the past, we already begin to intervene in its content.

Viewed thus, what is at issue in judging different modalities of constructing what J. G. A. Pocock (1962) calls socially contingent *past relationships* obviously cannot be their relative accuracy or reality equivalence as measured against any putatively absolute or universal standard. It is rather their capacity for generating coherent worlds by rendering the act of establishing relations between past and present a moral endeavor: a "history taking" (*anamnesis*) that interrogates the present in order to reveal its condition as symptomatic of a past, regardless of whether we wish to see such a past as constitutive of our present order, happily superseded, or ultimately irrelevant and "done with." This is so not just because the past itself is available to us only in the form of present phenomena – objects, texts, social forms – whose evidentiary status needs to be recognized as such (Bloch 1953; cf. Ginzburg 1983a). This is so also because the credibility of the resulting diagnostics depends, minimally, on a social consensus about the moral and political consequences of the selection of particular types of evidence from which to spin narratives designed to establish, destabilize, or cancel out certain forms of past relationships.

If so, however, might not my informants' story about my being driven to Miami and

Cuba by the spirit of a dead slave simply register a type of past relationship that escapes certain historiographic criteria of facticity but is nevertheless morally all but unrealistic, implausible, or "untrue"? For once we admit ghosts like Tomás to the language game that we call history, does not the man whom Tomás might once have been – an African slave worked to death on a nineteenth-century Cuban plantation – belong to my past no less than to theirs? Might one not argue that thousands and thousands of similar ghosts populate the notionally "remote areas" (Ardener 1989) of the history of that curious entity often called *Western modernity*, an entity known as much through its negatives and absences as through any positively definable characteristics of its own (Gilroy 1992; Comaroff and Comaroff 1993; Felski 1995)? Indeed, might not their invisibility to most of us be more the product of a particular set of beliefs we have come to understand as "history" than a defensible proof of their nonexistence? Is it the proposition about Tomás's presence in our present that is unacceptable, or are we talking about the unlikeliness of his presence in our pasts?

The latter part of this question can be answered only in the negative. As most classical political economists from Locke and Postlethwayt to Smith, Wakefield, and Merivale understood only too well, the brutal exploitation of enslaved and forcefully transplanted African labor in the Americas formed the mainstay of some of the most profitable colonial economies emerging in the New World. At the same time, not only the resulting agricultural and commercial achievements, but also the violence and destruction attendant on them, were substantially entailed in the transformation of Europe into a world of nation-states: political entities increasingly conscious of their separate political-economic identities, their role as competitors within a globalizing theater of capital accumulation, and their agency in forging what by the eighteenth century became thinkable as world history and modern civilization. Despite ongoing historiographic debate about the particulars of the relations obtaining between these processes (e.g., Solow and Engerman 1987; Blackburn

1997), it is undeniable that the modern capitalist world system was erected, at least in part, on the unmarked graves of African slaves whose lives were systematically wasted in the service of what Marx identified as *primitive accumulation*.

Nor has the fate of the victims of these processes escaped scholarly attention. In recent decades, a burgeoning historiography of slavery has provided us with a truly stunning wealth of aggregate data on how human beings very much like Tomás lived and died in New World cane fields and slave barracks. Not only do we have an increasingly clear idea of how many enslaved Africans survived the horrors of the middle passage to be unloaded in regional New World slaving entrepôts. We can pinpoint, with relative precision, their average life expectancy in specific local contexts at certain times; we know their demographic profiles (age structures, sex ratios, birthrates, and mortality); we are aware of how different work regimes and changes in productive technology affected them, what their clothing and food rations consisted in, how they were housed, what diseases they tended to suffer from; we know how often slaves rebelled and how they were punished for it; in some instances we even know what average height they attained or the statistical frequency with which the average slave would have endured the whip. Still, regardless of whatever mixture of zeal, caution, and care went into the compilation and analysis of the sources from which such data were synthesized, regardless, also, of how important some of these findings may prove in correcting previous conceptions of New World slavery, there is an ultimately quite frightening sense of irrelevancy in all this.

For not only are we utterly incapable of disaggregating such data in a way that could illuminate what living through slavery might have meant for more than the minute fraction of its victims whose recollections of life under "the peculiar institution" were ever committed, in one way or the other, to writing. Rather, this mounting heap of abstract knowledge about the atrocities that the *esclave moyen* endured may well contribute to blocking from view what the image of the ghost of a named individual slave haunting the author of this book might be a vivid reminder of. For does not the very idea of the existence of "something" like Tomás (whatever ontological status we may accord him) indicate that there *also* exists a history that largely escapes – perhaps cannot be inscribed at all – into the narratives that we construct from the logs of slave ships, plantation account books, or the diaries of slaveholders? The problem with Tomás, in other words, is not that his existence – somewhere in the Cuban past – is inherently implausible or unrealistic. It is that the person he may once have been remains beyond historiographic recovery because the nature of the evidence we deem admissible simply erases his historical being and subjectivity.

Yet, if there is no place for Tomás within the realm of plausibilities constituted by academic historiographic consensus, might there not be something in the very idea of the spectral presence of dead slaves like him in our present that intrinsically militates against the histories that we have spun from the records his oppressors have left? And might it not be that such ghosts can be "seen" to haunt us precisely because all this writing has not just obliterated the historical reality of their lives, but artificially distanced or displaced it from ours? "The only written thing on slave ships," says Edouard Glissant (1997, 5n), "was the account book listing the exchange value of slaves. Within the ship's space the cry of those deported was stifled, as it would be in the realm of the Plantations." "This confrontation" between the documentary traces of the past and those aspects of it that can be only imagined, Glissant concludes, "continues to this day," and it is not easily resolved in the disciplines with which I myself have cast my academic lot. Elsewhere, Glissant (1989), thus, urges us to acknowledge that "history has its dimension of the unexplorable." And he is right. There exist pasts the reality of which we cannot deny but that we may never find ourselves able to evidence unless we "revalu[ate our] conventions of analytical thought." For the recognition of such systematically obliterated past realities – as well as the recovery of the historical subjectivities of those who lived through them – "has as much to do with the problematics of investigation as with a historical organization of things" (66, 65).

Perhaps echoing Foucault's (1970, 1972) notion of "thresholds of positivity" organizing the generation of what can count as knowledge within a particular "historical organization of things," Glissant's formulation not only opens the door to histories condensed in the image of the ghostly presence of Tomás that might not otherwise find expression. It also takes on critical significance in implying that – as Paul Gilroy (1992, 49) argues – such histories are, not the "special property" of the descendants of their victims, but "part of the ethical and intellectual heritage of the West as a whole." For, to recur once more to Glissant (1989, 66), the very least that a proposition about our being haunted by the spirits of dead slaves might achieve is to relieve us, in Carl Becker's sense, "of the linear, hierarchical vision of a single History," a vision that relegates the violence and dehumanization my "spirit guide" would have endured to a past distant in both space and time. It is not that "this History" has not "roared around the edge of the Caribbean," as Glissant puts it. It has. On the contrary, the Caribbean region provides perhaps clearer evidence of its tempestuous nature than any other site on which European colonization has unleashed Prospero's rationalizing magic. The question rather pertains to what Glissant calls a *subterranean convergence of our histories*. For, arguably, the global historical storm first conjured up in the Antilles in the sixteenth century continues to envelop us all.

In developing this argument, Glissant evokes the image of African slaves thrown overboard on the high seas – an image of human lives sacrificed, not to inescapable exigencies, but to the very ideas and forces that ruled the worlds of their captors and the merchant investors backing their ventures. Nothing, of course, is unrealistic about this, and we know it well. When in 1781 the captain of the HMS *Zong* threw 133 sick and dying African slaves overboard, he did so not merely to be able to collect the premium for which he had insured his human cargo (Fryer 1984, 127ff.). He also affirmed a particular "historical organization of things" in which instrumental rationality and the profit motive – imagined as conjoined

in the providential work of the market's invisible hand – had begun to circumscribe a cosmic order that we continue to inhabit. Hinging accountability on amoral (and, often enough, patently immoral) procedures of establishing facticity, this order, I will argue, is a haunted one. Marx clearly saw this when, in the opening paragraph of *Das Kapital*, he referred to his own social formation as an "uncanny" or "monstrous" world of commodities in which massive processes of historical displacement and organized forgetting, not only stabilized social fantasies ("objectively necessary appearances") of the agency of objects, but likewise reduced humans to the status of things. Glissant's image of the economically rational destruction of human commodities, however, points to yet another constitutive feature of this order: the externalization and displacement of the nightmarish excess of its operation beyond the boundaries of the conceptual space occupied by Western modernity. If, in that sense, the victims of the *Zong* left any imprint on this order, it was by involuntarily documenting what Kamau Brathwaite calls a *submarine unity* obtaining, not just within the Caribbean region itself, but between the self-consciously "modern" cores of the capitalist world system and the peripheral spaces of death from which the "West" drew its wealth and confidence in a ghastly dual movement of accumulating capital and knowledge.

"All objectification is a forgetting," Horkheimer and Adorno (1972, 230) once argued in their profoundly disquieting reflections on the immorality and unreason by means of which the West has represented, to itself, its global ascendancy as a "march of reason." And it is such forgetting that, to my idea, Cecilia's and Carlos's vision of a disembodied visitor from an unmarked grave dug in the distant past might help counteract. So let not the language I am using here distract you. Words like *spirit* or *ghost* are merely that: words, elements in a language game different from the one that I am playing as I write these lines. Suppose that we take them to signify a notion about relations between past and present that underlie a contemporary order but remain unacknowledged, unspoken, or even unthinkable within its reigning narrative conventions and definition of the *historically real*? "Haunting," Jacques Derrida (1994, 37) suggests, "belongs to the state of everyday hegemony." It occurs precisely at the moment when that state is thrown into doubt and reveals itself as ridden with "historical excess . . . resisting final codification" (Feldman 1995, 237); when historical "frames" (in Felman and Laub's [1992] sense) begin to fracture; and when an occluded dimension of the past becomes visible through a form of recognition that seizes on its fleeting image before it sinks into irretrievable oblivion, as Walter Benjamin (1968, 257) once phrased it. The feeling of being "haunted" arises when our everyday worlds suddenly appear uncannily bereft of their normalcy and reveal themselves as what they are: collectively instituted and maintained infrastructures of certainty (Castoriadis 1987) built on the systematic (and systemically necessary) forgetting, displacement, and disavowal in time and space of that of which propositions about the existence of spirits like Tomás provide powerfully estranging reminders.

Hence, perhaps, the value of introducing such anecdotal and decidedly flimsy "spectral evidence" as I have marshaled so far into a regime of knowledge that – since Michelet's times (Anderson 1991, 197ff.) – has pledged itself to "speaking on behalf of the dead" but that cannot face the full implications such disciplined forms of necromancy might entail. "Ghost stories," Graham Huggan (1998, 129) suggests, might be considered "as vehicles of historical revisionism, or as means by which repressed histories can be brought back to the surface." For what they render "uncanny" and thereby transform is "not the past itself, but our 'normal,' socialized perception of it." Huggan is concerned with the figure of the ghost or revenant as a trope allowing for the construction or release of versions of history that – irrespective of their moral plausibility – otherwise not just remain "unevidenced" but are actively rendered invisible (Feierman 1999) or unspeakable (Spivak 1988a; Sheriff 2000): not because their relation to the past is merely imaginary, but because such a relation goes beyond the limits of what is representable within the discursive formation that we call *history*.

But "ghosts" such as Tomás are not just figures of speech, and we know that all too well. I have no reason to believe that Cecilia and Carlos did "not really" see Tomás hovering behind my back or merely wanted to humor me. In fact, even to pose such a question may well be already to miss the point (cf. Appiah 1992, 107–36; Fabian 1996, 297–316). Nor is the problem, as David Scott (1991) and Luise White (2000) insist, adequately addressed by carving acceptable facts out of narratives encumbered by patently fantastic, improbable, or, at best, "symbolic" ballast. In his bitter reflections about the murder of twenty-eight black children in Atlanta between 1979 and 1981, James Baldwin (1985, xi), thus, angrily recalls how, in the face of experienced terror, even individual memory can turn into "something one imagines oneself to remember." Baldwin's emphasis on the evidentiary function of "things unseen" is echoed by Karen Fields (1994), who similarly speaks of the sheer moral weight of "things one cannot not remember correctly." What is at issue here is not simply the relativity of the processes and procedures by which knowledge of the past and the pastfulness of the contemporary world is established and expressed. For such "pastfulness" itself is a concession made by – or sometimes painfully wrested from – the present. As Michel-Rolph Trouillot (1995, 16) phrases the matter, the constitution of historical subjectivities is not predicated on an immutable factual storage house of events in various stages of retrievability. Rather, it "goes hand in hand with the continuous creation of the past" by those who aim to predicate their historical being on it. "As such," he adds, "they do not succeed the past: they are its contemporaries."

Afro-Cuban diviners might understand. For, although the majority of their clients tend not to see it that way – eager as they usually are to have their personal life crises resolved – the diviner's craft is an eminently historical one. Guided by the pronouncements of gods or the sprits of the dead who speak through specific oracular signs, they select ways in which the pithy sayings associated with each of them, the accompanying divination verses, and stories about mythological precedents can be applied to the client's present. Diviners in *regla ocha* take that responsibility seriously, and, even though my metier be different, I intend to do no less. Quite clearly, whatever "modernity" may be ascribed to our – or their – lives, unfolding as they are at the dawn of the twenty-first century, the very possibility of our perceiving it as such must build on pasts that we create. And all too often we do so in a manner that inflicts violence on what the spirit guide my informants saw hovering behind me should be a reminder of.

The question, thus, really is not whether Tomás looks over my shoulder as I write these lines. It is to what extent I will succeed in convincing the reader to follow me in instantiating the possibility of an intersection of my agency as an author with the thoughts and concerns, actions and experiences of people who – given the historical positioning that I enjoy and they endured – must irredeemably remain historical others for me. At a conference at which I presented parts of what became chapter 1 of this book, one of the participants – Timothy Burke – raised the question whether one could ever get the story of people such as the early-nineteenth-century free black Cuban artisan-visionary I talked about "right." Well, how *does* one get somebody's story right? What Burke suggested was that, at times, one is forced to relinquish the notion of being able to reconstruct historical subjectivities and

instead acknowledge that – irrespective of one's meticulousness or fidelity to the sources – bringing the past back into the present (i.e., re-presenting it) must involve allowing ourselves to become haunted by it: to turn it into a revenant that neither we nor anyone else can easily shake.

To do so is to estrange and render "uncanny" what Glissant (1989, 64) calls *a highly functional fantasy of the West*, to break the "all compelling frames" of normalized history (Felman and Laub 1992), to counteract the multifarious forms of "narrative fetishism" (Santner 1992, 153) that "exorcise from the body of the West – from its patterns and projects of modernization – the violence, destruction, and human suffering that have belonged to and continue to belong to its history." And, in this respect, the presence of a being like Tomás in my life makes sense to me – if only as a possibility that I feel I need to entertain. Taking Tomás's invisible presence seriously is a moral obligation that I have incurred in my work. If pasts such as his must remain, to varying degrees, "foreign countries" whose citizenship I neither possess nor must endure, they may still be places toward which the spirits of dead people – rather than a mere Shakespearean historical "tempest" – might well have driven me.

[. . .]

NOTES

1   At the time, Carlos was earning a living as the supervisor of several laundromats and a part-time private eye (or so he claimed). "Don't even question it," he used to say when talking about matters such as spiritual afflictions. "Most of my clients are far more crazy than you and me put together."

2   On epistemology, language, and "out-there-ness," cf. Rorty (1991), Rorty (1999, 175–89), Needham (1972), and Das (1998). For particularly lucid statements of the problems underlying the long-standing tendency of Western social science to insinuate its own categorial apparatus into life

worlds that these very categories cannot but represent as structured by "belief" or other forms of "irrationality," see also Hildred Geertz (1975), MacGaffey (1981), and Clark (1983).

3   It is for this reason that even staunchly secular, nonprovidentialist views of history somehow never quite escape analogies with those classic definitions of religion that do not feature the belief in personalized divinities as a necessary component. Who, e.g., could seriously disagree with a view of historiography as constituting "(1) a set of symbols which acts to (2) establish powerful, pervasive, and long lasting moods and motivations in men by (3) formulating conceptions of general order of existence and

(4) clothing these conceptions with such an aura of factuality that (5) the moods and motivations seem uniquely realistic" (Geertz 1973, 90). Geertz, of course, is not speaking about history here.

REFERENCES

Anderson, Benedict. 1991. *Imagined Communities*. London: Verso.

Appadurai, Arjun. 1981. "The Past as a Scarce Resource." *Man* 16: 201–19.

Appiah, Anthony Kwame. 1992. *In My Father's House*. New York: Oxford University Press.

Ardener, Edwin. 1989. *The Voice of Prophecy*. Oxford: Blackwell.

Baldwin, James. 1985. *The Evidence of Things Not Seen*. New York: Holt, Rinehart and Winston.

Beard, Charles A. 1934. "Written History as an Act of Faith." *American Historical Review* 39: 219–29.

Becker, Carl. 1932. "Everyman His Own Historian." *American Historical Review* 37: 221–36.

Benjamin, Walter. 1968. *Illuminations*. New York: Harcourt, Brace & World.

Blackburn, Robin. 1988. *The Overthrow of Colonial Slavery*. London: Verso.

——. 1997. *The Making of New World Slavery*. London: Verso.

Bloch, Marc. 1953. *The Historian's Craft*. New York: Knopf.

Castoriadis, Cornelius. 1987. *The Imaginary Institution of Society*. Trans. Kathleen Blamey. Cambridge, Eng.: Polity.

Clark, Stewart. 1983. "French Historians and Early Modern Popular Culture." *Past and Present* 100: 62–99.

Collingwood, R. G. 1994. *The Idea of History*. 1946. Reprint, Oxford: Oxford University Press.

Comaroff, John, and Jean Comaroff. 1993. Introduction to *Modernity and Its Malcontents*, ed. John Comaroff and Jean Comaroff, xi–xxxvii. Chicago: University of Chicago Press.

Dantas Gois, Beatriz. 1988. *Vovo Nagô e Papai Branco*. Rio de Janeiro: Graal.

Danto, Arthur C. 1985. *Narration and Knowledge*. New York: Columbia University Press.

Das, Veena. 1998. "Wittgenstein and Anthropology." *Annual Reviews of Anthropology* 27: 171–95.

Derrida, Jacques. 1994. *Specters of Marx*. London: Routledge.

Fabian, Johannes. 1996. *Remembering the Present*. Berkeley and Los Angeles: University of California Press.

Feierman, Steven. 1999. "Colonizers, Scholars, and the Creation of Invisible Histories." In *Beyond the Cultural Turn*, ed. Victoria E. Bonnell and Lynn Hunt, 182–216. Berkeley and Los Angeles: University of California Press.

Feldman, Allen. 1995. "Ethnographic States of Emergency." In *Fieldwork under Fire*, ed. Carolyn Nordstrom and Antonius C. G. M. Robben, 224–52. Berkeley and Los Angeles: University of California Press.

Felman, Shoshana, and Dori Laub. 1992. *Testimony: Crises of Witnessing in Literature, Psychoanalysis, and History*. London: Routledge.

Felski, Rita. 1995. *The Gender of Modernity*. Cambridge, Mass.: Harvard University Press.

Fields, Karen. 1994. "What One Cannot Remember Mistakenly." In *History and Memory in African-American Culture*, ed. Geneviève Fabre and Robert O'Mealley, 150–63. Oxford: Oxford University Press.

Foucault, Michel. 1970. *The Order of Things*. New York: Random House.

Fryer, Peter. 1984. *Staying Power: The History of Black People in Britain*. London: Pluto.

Geertz, Clifford. 1973. *The Interpretation of Cultures*. New York: Basic.

Geertz, Hildred. 1975. "An Anthropology of Religion and Magic, I." *Journal of Interdisciplinary History* 6: 71–89.

Gilroy, Paul. 1992. *The Black Atlantic: Modernity and Double Consciousness*. Cambridge, Mass.: Harvard University Press.

Ginzburg, Carlo. 1983a. "Clues: Morelli, Freud, and Sherlock Holmes." In *The Sign of Three*, ed. Umberto Eco and Thomas A. Sebeok, 81–118. Bloomington: Indiana University Press.

Glissant, Edouard. 1989. *Caribbean Discourse*. Charlottesville: University of Virginia Press.

——. 1997. *Poetics of Relation*. Ann Arbor: University of Michigan Press.

Habermas, Jürgen. 1987. *The Philosophical Discourse on Modernity*. Cambridge, Mass.: MIT Press.

Hamilton, Carolyn. 1998. *Terrific Majesty: The Powers of Shaka Zulu and the Limits of Historical Invention*. Cambridge, Mass.: Harvard University Press.

Hayden, Robert M. 1996. "Imagined Communities and Real Victims: Self-Determination and Ethnic Cleansing in Yugoslavia." *American Ethnologist* 23: 783–801.

Horkheimer, Max, and Theodor W. Adorno. 1972. *Dialectic of Enlightenment*. New York: Herder and Herder.

Huggan, Graham. 1998. "Ghost Stories, Bone Flute, Cannibal Countermemories." In *Cannibalism and the Colonial World*, ed. Francis Barker, Peter Hulme, and Margaret Iversen, 126–41. Cambridge: Cambridge University Press.

Kemp, Anthony. 1991. *Estrangement of the Past*. New York: Oxford University Press.

Koselleck, Reinhard. 1985. *Futures Past: On the Semantics of Historical Time*. Cambridge, Mass.: MIT Press.

Lambek, Michael. 1996. "The Past Imperfect: Remembering as Moral Practice." In *Tense Past*, ed. Paul Antze and Michael Lambek, 235–54. London: Routledge.

MacGaffey, Wyatt. 1978. "African History, Anthropology, and the Rationality of Natives." *History in Africa* 5: 101–20.

——. 1981. "African Ideology and Belief: A Survey." *African Studies Review* 24: 227–74.

Meltzer, Françoise. 1994. "For Your Eyes Only: Ghost Citing." In *Questions of Evidence*, ed. James Chandler, Arnold I. Davidson, and Harry Harootunian, 43–9. Chicago: University of Chicago Press.

Mink, Louis. 1978. "Narrative Form as a Cognitive Instrument." In *The Writing of History*, ed. Robert H. Canary and Henry Kozicki, 129–49. Madison: University of Wisconsin Press.

Needham, Rodney. 1972. *Belief, Language, and Experience*. Chicago: University of Chicago Press.

Novick, Peter. 1998. *That Noble Dream: The "Objectivity Question" and the American Historical Profession*. Cambridge: Cambridge University Press.

Oakeshott, Michael. 1933. *Experience and Its Modes*. Cambridge: Cambridge University Press.

Palmer, Bryan D. 1990. *Descent into Discourse*. Philadelphia: Temple University Press.

Pocock, J. G. A. 1962. "The Origins of Study of the Past: A Comparative Approach." *Comparative Studies in Society and History* 4: 209–46.

Rorty, Richard. 1991. *Objectivity, Relativism, and Truth*. Cambridge: Cambridge University Press.

——. 1999. *Philosophy and Social Hope*. London: Penguin.

Santner, Eric L. 1992. "History Beyond the Pleasure Principle: Some Thoughts on the Representation of Trauma." In *Probing the Limits of Representation: Nazism and the "Final Solution,"* ed. Saul Friedlander, 143–54. Cambridge, Mass.: Harvard University Press.

Scott, David. 1991. "That Event, This Memory: Notes on the Anthropology of African Diasporas in the New World." *Diasporas* 1: 261–84.

Sheriff, Robert E. 2000. "Exposing Silence as Cultural Censorship: A Brazilian Case." *American Anthropologist* 102: 114–32.

Solow, Barbara, and Stanley L. Engerman. 1987. *British Capitalism and Caribbean Slavery: The Legacy of Eric Williams*. Cambridge: Cambridge University Press.

Sperber, Dan. 1982. "Apparently Irrational Beliefs." In *Rationality and Relativism*, ed. Martin Hollis and Steven Lukes, 149–80. Cambridge, Mass.: MIT Press.

Spivak, Gayatri Chakravorti. 1988a. "Can the Subaltern Speak?" In *Marxism and the Interpretation of Culture*, ed. Cary Nelson and Lawrence Grossberg, 271–313. Urbana: University of Illinois Press.

Stoler, Ann Laura. 1992. "'In Cold Blood': Hierarchies of Credibility and the Politics of

Colonial Narratives." *Representations* 37: 151–89.

Terdiman, Richard. 1993. *Present Past*. Ithaca, N.Y.: Cornell University Press.

Trouillot, Michel-Rolph. 1995. *Silencing the Past*. Boston: Beacon.

White, Luise. 2000. *Speaking with Vampires: Rumor and History in Colonial Africa*. Berkeley and Los Angeles: University of California Press.

Part V

Research Tools

A Guide to the Literature

Michael Lambek and Shirley Yeung

This guide (and bibliography) is far from exhaustive. For reasons of space, it empha-sizes full-length books rather than journal articles or chapters. Among the best new books to appear on Christianity are Joel Robbins, *Becoming Sinners: Christianity and Moral Torment in a Papua New Guinea Society* (2004) and Fenella Cannell, ed., *The Anthropology of Christianity* (2006); see especially her introduction. Good, if some-what advanced, new books on Islam include Saba Mahmood, *Politics of Piety: The Islamic Revival and the Feminist Subject* (2004) and Charles Hirschkind, *The Ethics of Listening: Cassette Sermons and Islamic Counterpublics* (2006); Abdellah Ham-moudi, *A Season in Mecca: Narrative of a Pilgrimage* (Polity 2006) is a compelling personal account. An excellent introduction to Hinduism is C. J. Fuller, *The Camphor Flame: Popular Hinduism and Society and India* (new edition, 2004).

For additional articles, as well as book reviews, consult journals such as *American Ethnologist, Journal of the Royal Anthropological Institute* (formerly *Man*), as well as *American Anthropologist, Social Anthropology, Anthropologica, Ethnos, Social Analysis, Cultural Dynamics, Journal of Religion in Africa, Oceania, Anthropological Quarterly, Current Anthropology, Cultural Anthropology*, and so on.

The guide to the literature is constructed in index form. References are to authors listed in the main bibliography only; many more leads will be found in the biblio-graphies appended to individual articles. Often several works by an author will be relevant to a given topic; otherwise the title will suggest the most appropriate source. Dates are only given where the titles are ambiguous. The topical index is merely suggestive of the range of ideas to be found within the works cited.

Regional Index

The index is constructed roughly east to west, starting with Oceania. Countries and subregions are listed alphabetically.

Oceania

Australia
Bell, Berndt, Durkheim, Dussart, Hiatt, H. McDonald, McKnight, Morphy, Munn 1970, Myers, Poirier, Rumsey and Weiner, Stanner, Tonkinson, D. Turner.

Fiji
Arno, Kaplan, J. Kelly, Miyazaki, Tomlinson, Toren.

General
Barker, de Coppet and Iteanu, Lattas, Mageo and Howard.

Micronesia
Besnier, Parmentier, Spiro.

Papua New Guinea (and Melanesia more generally)
van Baal, Bamford, Barth, Bateson, Battaglia, Biersack, Bonnemère, Brunton, Burridge, Clifford 1992, Fortune, Frankel, Gell 1975, Gewertz, Gillison, Godelier, Harrison, Herdt, Iteanu, Jebens, Juillerat, Keesing, R. Kelly, Knauft, Lawrence, Leenhardt, Leroy, G. Lewis, Lindenbaum, Lindstrom, Lutkehaus and Roscoe, Malinowski, Meigs, Mimica, Munn, Rappaport, Robbins, Rumsey and Weiner, Schieffelin, Schwimmer, Stephen, Stewart and Strathern 2002, Strathern, Trompf, Tuzin, R. Wagner, Weiner, Whitehouse, Wiessner and Tumu, Worsley, Young.

Polynesia
Firth, Gell, Hocart, Sahlins, Valeri.

Asia

Burma
Leach, Spiro.

Central and northern Asia
Hamayon, Humphrey, Kwon, Privratsky, Vitebsky.

China (and Taiwan)
Ahern, Chau, Feuchtwang, Freedman, Gillette, Granet, Hsu, R. Hymes, Jing, Moskowitz, Mueggler, Sangren, Stafford, R. Watson, Watson and Rawski, Weller, Wheatley, A. Wolf, Yang.

Indonesia
Anderson, Aragon, Atkinson, Barnes, Barth, Beatty, Bowen, Errington, Forth, J. Fox, Geertz, George, Hefner, Hicks, Hoskins, Keane, Keeler, Kipp, Kuipers, Lansing, P. Metcalf, Peacock, Sears, Schrauwers, Siegel, Steedly, Traube, Volkman, M. Wiener, Woodward.

Japan
Bellah, Cox, Hardacre, Ivy, McFarland, Nakamaki, Nelson, Schattschneider, R. Smith, Traphagan, D. Williams.

Korea
Kendall, Kim.

Malaysia
Endicott, Howell, Nagata, Ong, Peletz.

Philippines
Barton, Cannell 1999, Claussen, Gibson, Raphael, M. Rosaldo, R. Rosaldo, Wiegele.

Southeast Asia
Becker and Yengoyan, H. Geertz, Headley, Hobart, Hoskins, Howe, Kershaw, Lukens-Bull, Metcalf, Sather, Tannenbaum and Kammerer, Watson and Ellen.

Thailand
Essen, Keyes, Klima, R. Morris, Symonds, Tambiah.

South Asia

India (and Hinduism)
Alter, Appadurai 1981, Babb, Babb and Wadley, Banerjee Dube, Basham, Beteille, Bhargava, Bhatt, Blank, Caldwell, Cohn, Daniel, Das, Dirks, Dumont, R. Fox, Froystad, Fuller, Gold, Hansen, Hussain and Ghosh, Langford, Madan, Marriott, Mosse, Nabokov, Nandy, Nicholas, Ostor, Parry, Peabody, Pocock, Raheja, Raj and Dempsey, Robinson and Clarke, Singer, Snow-Wadley, Srinivas, Srivastava, Trawick, van der Veer.

Jainism
Humphrey and Laidlaw, Laidlaw, Vallely.

Nepal and Tibet
Calkowski, Desjarlais, Gaenszle, Gellner, Goldstein and Kapstein, Holmberg, Huber, Levy, Maskarinec, Mills, Mumford, Ortner, Paul.

Pakistan and South Asian Muslims
Ahmed, Ewing, Hansen 2000, Hegland, P. Werbner, Werbner and Basu.

Sri Lanka
Carrithers, Daniel, Gombrich and Obeyesekere, Good, Kapferer, Obeyesekere, Tambiah, Weeratunge.

Tribal
Radcliffe-Brown, Vitebsky.

see also Topical Index: **Buddhism, Hinduism, caste**

Middle East and North Africa

Egypt
Abu-Lughod, Gaffney, Gilsenan, Haeri, Hirschkind, Mahmood, Mitchell.

Iran
Chehabi, Fischer, Fischer and Abedi.

Israel
Kahn.

Levant
Antoun, Gilsenan.

Mahgreb (especially Morocco)
Bahloul, Bourdieu, Combs-Schilling, Crapanzano, Eickelman, Geertz, Gellner, Mernissi, Messick, Munson, Pandolfo.

Sudan
Boddy, Buxton, Holy, Kenyon.

Turkey
Delaney, Mardin, Navaro-Yashin, Shankland, Tapper, Yalman.

Yemen
vom Bruck, Meneley, Messick.

see also Topical Index: **Islam**

Europe

Contemporary
Arextaga, Badone, Barthes, Bax, Bloul, Bowen 2006, Buckser, Bunzl, Carroll, Casanova, Chakrabarty, Christian, Cucchiari, Danforth, Douglass, Dubisch, Favret-Saada, Gilmore, Goluboff, Goody, H. Harris, Hecht, Hebdige, Heelas, Herzfeld, Kertzer, Ivakhiv, Lane, Lindquist, Luhrmann, B. Metcalf, Mitchell, Nye, Parsons, Pina-Cabral, Port, C. Prince and Riches, Seremetakis, C. Stewart, M. Stewart, van de Port, Verdery, P. Werbner 2002, E. Wolf.

Historical
Asad, Bakhtin, Bertelli, P. Brown, Bynum, Ginzburg, Kivelson, J. Schneider, Stallybrass and White, Tawney, Walzer, Weber 1958.

Africa (sub-Saharan)

Central Africa
van Binsbergen and Schofeleers, De Boeck, Devisch, van Dijk, Fabian, Fernandez, Gluckman, Janzen, Kopytoff, Long, Packard, Richards, E. Turner, V. Turner, R. Werbner.

East Africa
Beidelman, Evans-Pritchard, Giles, Green, G. Harris, Heald, Hoehler-Fatton, James, Johnson, Kratz, Lienhardt, J. Middleton, Middleton and Winter, Nisula, Parkin, Purpura, Rigby, Ruel, Sanders, Shipton, Thornton, Weiss, M. Wilson, el-Zein.

General
Behrend and Luig, van Binsbergen and Schofeleers, Ellis, Forde, Fortes and Dieterlin, R. Hackett, Herbert, de Heusch, Jacobson-Widding, Kramer, Moore, Moore and Sanders, Peek, R. Werbner, L. White.

Madagascar and Western Indian Ocean
Bloch, Cole, Feeley-Harnik, Keller, Lambek, K. Middleton, Sharp, Walsh.

Southern Africa
Ashforth, Comaroff(s), Fry, Garbett, Guenther, Junod, Krige, Lan, Lewis-Williams and Pearce, B. Morris, Ngubane, Ranger, Solway, Sundkler.

West Africa
A. Adler, Appiah, Apter, Barber, De Boeck and Plissart, Calame-Griaule, Dilley, Ellis, Fardon, Feldman-Savelsberg, Ferme, Fisiy and Geschiere, Forde, Fortes, Geschiere, Goody, Gottlieb, Griaule, Horton, Jackson, Launay, Lovell, MacGaffey, Masquelier, Matory, Meyer, Muller, Nadel, Peel, Piot, Roberts and Roberts, Rowlands and Warnier, Shaw, Soares, Stoller, Yamba, Zahan.

The Americas

Black New World (Colombia, Brazil, Caribbean, Surinam, USA)
Abrahams, D'Alisera, Austin-Broos, Bastide, David Brown, D. Brown, K. Brown, Da Matta, Hagedom, Hinson, Johnson, Leacocks, Littlewood, Matory 2005b, Metraux, Palmié, Pollard and Whelchel, Rouse, Taussig, P. Taylor, Thoden van Velzen and van Wettering, Wafer.

Mexico and Central America
Bricker, Cahn, Colby, Dow and Sandstrom, Falla, Gossen, Hanks, Harris, Hunt, Ingham, Kovic, Lester, Lewis, Merrill, Myerhoff 1974, Romberg, Rus and Wasserstrom, L. Sullivan, B. Tedlock, D. Tedlock, Trexler, Vogt, Wogan, E. Wolf, Wright.

North America (Euro-American, immigrant)
Bellah, K. Brown, M. Brown, Carnes and Yang, Chidester, Crapanzano 2000, Csordas, Cunningham, Denzler, Ginsburg, Greenhouse, Guest, Harding, Ivakhiv, Kneale-Gould, Kugelmass, E. Martin, B. Metcalf, Myerhoff, Ong, Orsi, Peacock and Tyson, Reynolds, Richardson, D. Schneider, Shokeid, K. Stewart, Trix, M. Wacker, Wagner, Warner, Weber 1946b, Wuthnow.

North America (native)
Aberle, K. Basso, Benedict, Bierwert, Boas, Bodenhorn, Brightman, Bringhurst, Dee Brown, Buckley, Dombrowski, Fowler, Gill, Goldman 1975, Goulet, Hallowell,

Topical Index

Buddhism Calkowski, Carrithers, Cox, Keyes and Daniel, Desjarlais, Essen, Gellner, Klima, Mills, Nelson, Ortner, Schattschneider, Silber, Spiro, Tambiah, D. Williams *see also* Regional Index: Nepal, Sri Lanka, etc.

Candomblé Johnson, Matory 2005b

capitalism Campbell, Comaroffs, Gillette, Marx, Nash, Ong, Romberg, Sharp, Solway, Taussig, Tawney

cargo cults Lattas, Lindstrom *see also* **movements**

carnival and play Bouissac, Da Matta, Gilmore, Gluckman, Huizinga, Kapferer, Kugelmass, Manning *see also* **inversion, taboo, trickster**

caste Beteille, Dilley, Dumont, Froystad, Lewis, Parry, Raheja, Srinivas

Catholics Badone, Burdick, Cannell, Carroll, Christian, Csordas, Ingham, Morrill et al, Orsini, Wiegele *see also* **Christianity**

charisma Coleman, Csordas, Dow and Sandstrom, Silber, Lindholm, D. Martin, Weber *see also* **prophets, saints**

Christianity Apolito, Aragon, Barker, Bax, Cahn, Cannell, Claussen, Coleman, Corten and Marshall-Fratani, Cucchiari, Cunningham, van Dijk, Douglas, Dow and Sandstrom, Eade and Sallnow, Feuerbach, Gilmore, Greenhouse, Harding, Hinson, James and Johnson, Kan, Keane 1998, Keller, Kertzer, Lester, D. Martin, McDonald, Merton, Meyer, Peacock and Tyson, Rafael, Raj and Dempsey, Reynolds, Richardson, Robbins, Ruel, Sharp, Silber, Stromberg, Sunkler, Trexler, Troeltsch, Wacker, Weber *see also* **Catholics, fundamentalism, missionaries**

civil society Hefner, Hirschkind, Mitchell, Palmié *see also* **community, nation, politics, state**

class Froystad, Gose, Gramsci, Kipp, Marx, Silverblatt, Stallybrass and White, Trexler, Wiegele, Williams *see also* **money, colonialism, resistance, state**

cognition Astuti, Atran, Berliner and Sarró, Bloch 1998 and 2005, Boyer, Sperber

colonialism Banerjee Dube, Chakrabarty, B. Cohn, Cole, Comaroffs, Dirks, Harris, Langford, L. Lewis, Mitchell, Pels, Rafael, Schrauwers, Sears, Silverblatt, Steedly, Stoller, Taussig, van der Veer, L. White, Wiener

commodity fetishism *see* **money**

communism Lane, M. Stewart, Verdery

education *see* **knowledge, initiation**

environment (ecology, landscape) Bamford, Descola and Pálsson, Forth, Huber, Lansing, Messer and Lambek, Philip and Gold, Rappaport, Vallely, Weeratunge

epistemology Berliner and Sarró, Fabian, Geertz, MacIntyre, Saler, Sanders 2006, Skorupski, J. Smith, Strathern

ethics Foucault *see also* **morality**

exchange *see* **gifts and exchange**

experience Gilsenan 1973, Jackson, James 1961, Lowie *see also* **phenomenology**

exploitation *see* **capitalism**

evil Meyer, Parkin, Ricoeur, C. Stewart *see also* **witchcraft and sorcery**

fantasy Gillison, Port, Thoden van Velzen and Van Wetering *see also* **dreams**

foundational texts and authors Aristotle, Durkheim (*see also* Durkheim 1973 intro. by Bellah, Lukes, O'Toole, Pickering), Feuerbach, Freud, Fustel de Coulanges, van Gennep, Hertz, Hobbes, Hubert and Mauss, Lukes, Marx, Mauss (*see also* Carrithers et al., James and Allen), Otto, Peirce, Pickering, Robertson, Sapir, Saussure, Robertson Smith (*see also* Beidelman), Steiner (*see also* Adler and Fardon), Weber (*see also* Bellah 1964, Giddens, Gerth and Mills, Koshul, Lehman and Roth, O'Toole, Peacock and Kirsch, Wrong)

fundamentalism Antoun, Harding, James, Jebens, Martin and Appleby, Marsden, Nagata, Peacock, M. Wagner

gender Ahern 1975, Ardener, Arextaga, Bamberger, Barber 1991, Beidelman, D. Bell, Boddy, Bonnemère, J. Brown, Bynum, Chodorow, Claussen, Collier and Yanagisako, Combs-Schilling, Delaney, Dubisch, Dussart, Feldman-Savelsberg, Gewertz, Giles, Gillison, Hegland, Herbert, Herdt, Herzfeld, Hicks, Hoehler-Fatton, Julé, R. Kelly, Kendall, Kenyon, Knauft, Kratz, Lutkehaus and Roscoe, Mahmood, E. Martin, Matory, McKnight, Meneley, Mernissi, Messick, H. Moore et al., Murphy and Murphy, Myerhoff 1978, Ortner, Ortner and Whitehead, Peletz, Perruchon, Reynolds, Richards, Rouse, Sanders, Schattschneider, Schwarz, Sered, Silverblatt, Strathern, Symonds, Tuzin, Vallely

gifts and exchange Holmberg, Hoskins, Iteanu, Kapferer, Keane, Klima, Malinowski, Marriott, Mauss, Munn, Parry, Schieffelin, Strathern, Traube, Vallely, Volkman, Wiessner and Tumu, Yang

globalization Ahmed and Donnan, Appadurai 1996, Babb and Wadley, Coleman, B. Metcalf, Meyer and Geschiere, van der Veer, Werbner

God/s (and other supernatural or transcendent beings) Babb, Boyer 2001, Evans-Pritchard, Hunt, Lambek 2001b, Luhrmann, Magneo and Howard, J. Middleton 1967b, Mosse, Obeyesekere, Spiro

grace Bateson, Peristiany and Pitt-Rivers

headhunting Barton, George, Hoskins, M. Rosaldo, R. Rosaldo

healing Atkinson, Boddy, K. Brown, M. Brown, Buxton, Cannell, Crapanzano, Csordas, Desjarlais 1992, Devisch, Fingarette, Frankel, Hobart, Kapferer, Lambek 1993, Lambek and Antze, Langford, Lévi-Strauss 1963a, b, Lindenbaum, Little-wood, Ngubane, Nisula, Obeyesekere, Orsi, Romberg, Sather, Stoller, Tambiah, Taussig, E. Turner, V. Turner, Ward

hierarchy Dumont, Gupta, Howe, R. Kelly, Rus and Wasserstrom *see also* **caste, political ritual, sacred kingship**

Hinduism Becker, Bhatt, Biardeau, Dumont, Froystad, Fuller, Geertz, Gellner, Hansen, Hefner, Howe 2001, Peabody, Pocock, Snow-Wadley, Suthren-Hirst and Thomas, Vertovec *see also* **caste**, Regional Index: South Asia

history, historicity Chakrabarty, B. Cohn, Daniel 1996, Ferme, Hobsbawm and Ranger, Hoehler-Fatton, Janzen, Jing, Kan, Kelly and Kaplan, Koselleck, Kwon, Lambek 1998 and 2003a, Lambek and Walsh, Ortner 1989, Parmentier, Sahlins, Shaw, Srinivas, Trigger, van der Veer, Walsh, H. White, Wiessner and Tumu, Wolf *see also* **colonialism, memory, space and time**

icon and image Gell, Turner and Turner 1978, Whitehouse

ideology *see* **popular culture**

individualism Burridge, Long, Mills, Parkin

initiation Barth, Beidelman, Berliner and Sarró, Bloch, J. Brown, van Gennep, Heald, Herdt, S. Hugh-Jones, Knauft, Kratz, Junod, La Fontaine, G. Lewis, Lowie, Lutkehaus and Roscoe, Piot, Richards, V. Turner, E. Turner, Tuzin

interpretation Bernstein, Crapanzano, Geertz, Ricoeur

inversion Babcock, Bakhtin 1968, Rigby, Stallybrass and White, V. Turner *see also* **carnival, taboo, trickster**

Islam Ahmed and Donnan, D'Alisera, Antoun, Asad, Beatty, Blank, Bloul, J. Bowen, vom Bruck, Chehabi, Combs-Schilling, Crapanzano, Dilley, Eickelman, Ewing, Fischer, Fischer and Abedi, Gaffney, Geertz, Gellner, Gillette, Gilsenan, Goody, Hefner, Hegland, Hirschkind, Holy, Kershaw, Korom, Lambek, Launay, Lukens-Bull, Mahmood, Malik and Hinnells, Mamdani, Mardin, Masquelier, Meneley,

nature *see* animals and animism, cosmos, environment, structuralism

New Age and New Religious Movements M. Brown, Denzler, Greenwood, Heelas, Ivakhiv, Lindquist, Nye, Prince and Riches

pentecostalism *see* Christianity, missionaries

performance Abrahams, Abu Lughod, Graham, Hagedom, Handelman, Kapferer 1983, Kapferer and Hobart, Kratz, Mendoza, Peacock 1978, Richardson, Sather, Schechner and Appel, Schieffelin, Singer, Snow-Wadley, Trexler, V. Turner, Werbner 2002, el-Zein shadow theater Becker, Keeler, Sears

performativeness Austin, Bloch, Lee, Rappaport, Searle, Tambiah

person Carrithers et al., Clifford 1992, Daniel, Geertz, G. Harris, Harrison, Mauss, Mauzé, Poirier, Watson *see also* body, self

perspectivism Viveiros de Castro

phenomenology Csordas, Jackson, Kapferer 1997, Munn 1990, Schutz, Weiner, Weiss

pilgrimage Banerjee Dube, Coleman and Eade, Danforth, Daniel 1984, Dubisch, Eade and Sallnow, Eickelman, Gold, Huber, Morinis, Myerhoff 1974, Sallnow, Sangren, V. Turner, V. Turner and E. Turner, van der Veer, Yamba

place K. Basso, Daniel, Gordillo, Mueggler, Myers, Poirier, Rumsey and Weiner, P. Werbner, R. Werbner *see also* space and time

play Turner *see also* carnival

pluralism *see* debate, state, syncretism

poetics Bauman and Briggs, Becker, Bruner, Culler, J. Fox, Guss, Herzfeld, D. Hymes, Jakobson, Leavitt, Norman, Pandolfo, Stallybrass and White, Steedly, K. Stewart, D. Tedlock, Trawick, Weiner, H. White, Williams *see also* art, language, myth

political ritual Abeles, Bertelli, Cannadine and Price, Gluckman, Matory, Packard, Verdery *see also* power, sacred kingship

politics Ahmed, Apter, Arendt, Ashforth, Bowen, Chau, Cunningham, Das, Dombrowski, Eickelman and Piscatori, Ellis, Essen, Firth, Fischer, R. Fox, Gaffney, Gauchet, Gilsenan, Hansen, Hefner, Johnson, Kertzer, Kovic, Lan, Mahmood, Marx, Mooney, Moore and Myerhoff, Parmentier, Peabody, Ranger, Ruel, Soares, Tannenbaum and Kammerer, V. Turner, West 2005, Whiteley *see also* colonialism,

ritual Bateson, Beattie, C. Bell, Bloch, J. Bowen 1989, de Coppet, van Gennep, Gluckman, Handelman and Lindquist, Humphrey and Laidlaw, James 2003, Kelly and Kaplan, Kreinath et al., La Fontaine, G. Lewis, Lienhardt, Mahmood, McCauley and Lawson, Mitchell, Moore and Myerhoff, Radcliffe-Brown, Rappaport, Ruel, Sahlins, Tambiah, V. Turner esp. 1967, 1969, R. Werbner, Whitehouse and Laidlaw 2004

sacred, sanctity Collier and Yanagisako, Durkheim, Messer and Lambek, Rappaport

sacred kingship Bertelli, Cannadine and Price, Dirks, Errington, Feeley-Harnik, Frazer, Geertz, Hocart, Munson, Parry 1998, Peabody, Sahlins, Shils, Valeri **African** Adler, De Boeck, Evans-Pritchard, Forde, de Heusch, Krige and Krige, Muller

sacrifice and offerings Baumgarten, Benson and Cook, Bloch, Bourdillon and Fortes, Cole, Combs-Schilling, Delaney, Dunnill, Fuller, Gibson, Girard, de Heusch, Howell, Hubert and Mauss, Lienhardt, Parry, Paul, Rappaport, Ruel, Robertson Smith, Valeri, Vogt

saints P. Brown, vom Bruck, Cannell, Eickelman, Ewing, Fabian, Gellner, Gilsenan, Orsi, Purpura, Werbner and Basu, R. Werbner 1977 *see also* **charisma, prophecy**

Santeria David Brown, Hagedom

science Bouquet and Porto, Hecht, Lambek, Merton

secularism Asad, Bhargava, Bowen, Casanova, Connolly, Navaro-Yashin, Shankland, W. Sullivan, C. Taylor

self Boddy, Fingarette, Gell, Heelas, Keeler, Myers, M. Rosaldo, Schwimmer, Stromberg, C. Taylor *see also* **body, person**

semiotics Bouissac, Daniel, B. Lee, Lee and Urban, Mertz and Parmentier, Peirce, Singer

senses Desjarlais, Hirschkind

sexuality *see* **gender**

shamans Atkinson, David Brown, Crocker, Firth, Hamayon, Humphrey, Humphrey and Thomas, Kehoe, Kendall, Kim, Kwon, Leavitt, Lévi-Strauss 1963a,b, I. Lewis, Lindquist, Maskarinec, Mumford, Perruchon, Sather, Taussig, Vitebsky *see also* **charisma, practitioners, spirit possession**

Sikhism Axel, Basran and Bolaria

sorcery *see* **witchcraft and sorcery**

tradition Asad, C.J. Fuller, MacIntyre, Palmié, Redfield, Singer, Spiro

tricksters Guenther, Hynes and Doty, Norman, Radin

truth Rappaport 1999

violence Ashforth 2005, Arextaga, Axel, Bax, Behrens and Luig, Bloch, Daniel, Das, Ellis 1999, Ferme, Girard, Heald, Kapferer, Klima, Knauft, Mamdani, Mueggler, van de Port, Tambiah, Taussig see also **movements, resistance, sacrifice, state**

virtue *see* **morality**

witchcraft and sorcery Ashforth, Bond and Ciekawy, Bongmba, E. Bowen, Comaroffs 1993, Douglas 1970, Evans-Pritchard 1937, Favret-Saada, Fisiy and Geschiere, Fortune, Geschiere, Ginzburg, Gluckman, Green, Handelman and Shulman 2004, Kapferer, R. Kelly, Knauft, La Fontaine, L. Lewis, Lindenbaum, Luhrmann, Mair, Marwick, McKnight, McLeod, Middleton and Winter, Moore and Sanders, Niehaus, Romberg, Rowlands and Warnier, J. Schneider, Shaw, Silverblatt, Solway, Stephen, Stewart and Strathern 2003, Stoller and Olkes, Thoden van Velzen and Van Wetering, V. Turner 1957, Watson and Ellen, Weiss, Whitehead and Wright, M. Wilson

Bibliography

ABBREVIATIONS

American Anthropologist	*AA*
American Ethnologist	*AE*
Comparative Studies in Society and History	*CSSH*
Journal of the Royal Anthropological Institute	*JRAI*

Abélès, Marc. 1988. Modern Political Ritual: Ethnography of an Inauguration and a Pilgrimage by President Mitterrand. *Current Anthropology* 29: 391–404.

Aberle, David. 1982. *The Peyote Religion among the Navaho*. Chicago.

Abrahams, R. D. 1983. *The Man-of-Words in the West Indies: Performance and the Emergence of Creole Culture*. Baltimore.

Abu-Lughod, Lila. 1986. *Veiled Sentiments: Honor and Poetry in a Bedouin Society*. Berkeley.

Adams, William Y. 2005. *Religion and Adaptation*. Stanford.

Adler, A. 1982. *La mort et le masque du roi: la royauté des Moundang de Tchad*. Paris.

Adler, Jeremy and Richard Fardon, eds. 1999. *Franz Baermann Steiner: Selected Writings*, 2 vols. New York.

Adler, Judith. 2006. Cultivating Wilderness: Environmentalism and Legacies of Early Christian Asceticism. *CSSH* 48(1): 4–37.

Aggarwal, Ravina. 2001. At the Margins of Death: Ritual Space and the Politics of Location in an Indo-Himalayan Border Village. *AE* 28(3): 549–73.

Ahern, Emily Martin. 1973. *The Cult of the Dead in a Chinese Village*. Stanford.

—— 1975. The Power and Pollution of Chinese Women. In M. Wolf and R. Witke, eds., *Women in Chinese Society*. Stanford.

—— and Hill Gates, eds. 1981. *The Anthropology of Taiwanese Society*. Stanford.

Ahmed, Akbar. 1983. *Religion and Politics in Muslim Society: Order and Conflict in Pakistan*. Cambridge.

—— and Hastings Donnan, eds. 1994. *Islam, Globalization and Postmodernity*. New York.

Allen, Brooke. 2005. Our Godless Constitution. *The Nation*, Feb. 6.

Allen, Nick. 2000. *Categories and Classifications: Maussian Reflections on the Social*. Oxford.

Alter, Joseph S. 2004. *Yoga in Modern India: The Body between Science and Philosophy*. Princeton.

Anderson, Benedict. 1983. *Imagined Communities: Reflections on the Origins and Spread of Nationalism*. London.

—— 1990 [1972]. The Idea of Power in Javanese Culture. In *Language and Power: Exploring Political Cultures in Indonesia*. Ithaca.

Andriolo, Karin. 1973. Old Testament World View and Genealogy. *AA* 75: 1657–69.

Angrosino, Michael. 2002. Civil Religion Redux. *Anthropological Quarterly* 75(2): 239–67.

Antoun, Richard. 1989. *Muslim Preacher in the Modern World*. Princeton.

—— 2002. *Understanding Fundamentalism: Christian, Muslim, and Jewish Movements*. New York.

—— 2006. Fundamentalism, Bureaucratization, and the State's Co-optation of Religion: A Jordanian Case Study. *The International Journal of Middle East Studies* 38(3).

Apolito, Paolo. 2005. *The Internet and the Madonna: Religious Visionary Experience on the Web*. Chicago.

—— and Anthony Shugaar. 2005. *The Internet and the Madonna: Religious Visionary Experience on the Web*.

Appadurai, Arjun. 1981. *Worship and Conflict under Colonial Rule: A South Indian Case*. Cambridge.

—— 1996. *Modernity at Large: Cultural Dimensions of Globalization*. Minneapolis.

Appiah, Kwame Anthony. 1992. *In My Father's House: Africa in the Philosophy of Culture*. New York.

Apter, Andrew. 1992. *Black Critics and Kings: The Hermeneutics of Power in Yoruba Society*. Chicago.

Aragon, Lorraine V. 2000. *Fields of the Lord: Animism, Christian Minorities, and State Development in Indonesia*. Honolulu.

Ardener, Edwin. 1975. Belief and the Problem of Women. In S. Ardener, ed., *Perceiving Women*. London.

Arendt, Hannah. 1999 [1958]. *The Human Condition*. Chicago.

Arens, W. and Ivan Karp, eds. 1989. *Creativity of Power*. Washington, DC.

Aretxaga, Begoña. 1997. *Shattering Silence: Women, Nationalism and Political Subjectivity in Northern Ireland*. Princeton.

Arno, Andrew. 2003. Aesthetics, Intuition, and Reference in Fijian Ritual Communication: Modularity in and out of Language. *AA* 105(4): 807–19.

Arnold, Philip P. and Ann Grodzins Gold, eds. 2001. *Sacred Landscapes and Cultural Politics: Planting a Tree*. Aldershot.

Asad, Talal. 1982. Anthropological Conceptions of Religion: Reflections on Geertz. *Man* 18: 237–59.

—— 1986. *The Idea of an Anthropology of Islam*. Washington, DC.

—— 1993. *Genealogies of Religion: Discipline and Reasons of Power In Christianity and Islam*. Baltimore.

—— 2003. *Formation of the Secular: Christianity, Islam, Modernity*. Stanford.

Ashforth, Adam. 2000. *Madumo: A Man Bewitched*. Chicago.

—— 2005. *Witchcraft, Violence and Democracy in South Africa*. Chicago.

Astuti, Rita. 2007. How Do We Know What They Believe? In H. Whitehouse and J. Laidlaw, eds., *Ritual and Cognition: Challenges for the Anthropology of Religion*. Chapel Hill.

Atkinson, Jane. 1989. *The Art and Politics of Wana Shamanship*. Berkeley.

—— 1992. Shamanism Today. *Annual Review of Anthropology* 21; 307–29.

Atran, Scott. 2004. *In Gods We Trust: The Evolutionary Landscape of Religion*. Oxford.

Austin, J. L. 1962. *How to Do Things with Words*. Oxford.

Austin-Broos, Diane. 1997. *Jamaica Genesis: Religion and the Politics of Moral Orders*. Chicago.

Axel, Brian. 2001. *The Nation's Tortured Body: Violence, Representation and the Formation of a Sikh Diaspora*. Durham.

Baal, Jan van. 1966. *Dema. Description and Analysis of Marind-Anim Culture (South New Guinea)*. The Hague.

Babb, Lawrence. 1975. *The Divine Hierarchy: Popular Hinduism in Central India*. New York.

—— and Susan Wadley, eds. 1995. *Media and the Transformation of Religion in South Asia*. Philadelphia.

Babcock, Barbara, ed. 1978. *The Reversible World: Symbolic Inversion in Art and Society*. Ithaca.

Bacigalupo, Ana Mariella. 2004. The Mapuche Man who Became a Woman Shaman: Selfhood, Gender Transgression, and Competing Cultural Norms. *AE* 31(3): 440–57.

Badone, Ellen, ed. 1990. *Religious Orthodoxy*

and Popular Faith in European Society. Princeton.

Bahloul, Joëlle. 1996. *The Architecture of Memory: A Jewish-Muslim Household in Colonial Algeria, 1937–1962.* New York.

Bakhtin, M. M. 1968. *Rabelais and His World.* Bloomington.

—— 1981. *The Dialogic Imagination: Four Essays.* Austin.

Bamberger, Joan. 1974. The Myth of Matriarchy: Why Men Rule in Primitive Society. In M. Rosaldo and L. Lamphere, eds., *Women, Culture, and Society.* Stanford.

Bamford, Sandra, ed. 1998. Environment and Sociality in Melanesia. *Social Analysis* 42(3). Special issue.

Banerjee Dube, Ishita. 2001. *Divine Affairs: Religion, Pilgrimage and the State in Colonial and Postcolonial India.* Shimla.

Barber, Elizabeth W. and Paul T. Barber. 2005. *When They Severed Earth from Sky: How the Human Mind Shapes Myth.* Princeton.

Barber, Karin. 1981. How Man Makes God in West Africa. Yoruba Attitudes Towards the Orisa. *Africa* 51: 724–45.

—— 1991. *I Could Speak Until Tomorrow: Oríkì, Women and the Past in a Yoruba Town.* Edinburgh.

Barker, John, ed. 1990. *Christianity in Oceania.* Langham, MD.

Barnes, R. 1974. *Kedang: A Study of the Collective Thought of an Eastern Indonesian People.* Oxford.

Barth, Fredrik. 1975. *Ritual and Knowledge among the Baktaman of New Guinea.* New Haven.

—— 1990. *Cosmologies in the Making: A Generative Approach to Cultural Variation in Inner New Guinea.* Cambridge.

—— 1993. *Balinese Worlds.* Chicago.

Barthes, Roland. 1972. *Mythologies.* New York.

Barton, R. F. 1946. *The Religion of the Ifugaos.* Menasha, WI.

Basham, A. L. 1963. *The Wonder that was India.* New York.

Basran, Gurcharn S. and B. Singh Bolaria. 2003. *The Sikhs in Canada: Migration, Race, Class, and Gender.* Oxford.

Basso, Ellen. 1985. *A Musical View of the Universe: Kalapalo Myth and Ritual Performances.* Philadelphia.

Basso, Keith. 1996. *Wisdom Sits in Places: Landscape and Language among the Western Apache.* Albuquerque.

—— and Henry Selby, eds. 1976. *Meaning in Anthropology.* Albuquerque.

Bastide, Roger. 1960. *The African Religions of Brazil.* Baltimore.

Bateson, Gregory. 1958. *Naven: A Survey of the Problems Suggested by a Composite Picture of the Culture of a New Guinea Tribe Drawn from Three Points of View.* Stanford.

—— 1972. *Steps to an Ecology of Mind.* New York.

Battaglia, D. 1990. *On the Bones of the Serpent: Person, Memory and Mortality in Sabarl Island Society.* Chicago.

Bauman, Richard. 1984 [1977]. *Verbal Art as Performance.* Prospect Heights, IL.

—— and Charles Briggs. 1990. Poetics and Performance as Critical Perspectives on Language and Social Life. *Annual Review of Anthropology* 19: 59–88.

Baumann, Gerd. 1999. *The Multicultural Riddle: Rethinking National, Ethnic, and Religious Identities.* New York.

Baumgarten, Albert I., ed. 2002. *Sacrifice in Religious Experience.* Leiden.

Bax, Max. 1995. *Medjugorge: Religion, Politics, and Violence in Rural Bosnia.* Amsterdam.

Beattie, John 1964. *Other Cultures.* London.

—— 1966. Ritual and Social Change. *Man,* n.s. 1: 60–74.

—— 1970. On Understanding Ritual. In B. Wilson, ed., *Rationality.* Evanston.

Beatty, Andrew. 1999. *Varieties of Javanese Religion.* Cambridge.

—— 2006. The Pope in Mexico: Syncretism in Public Ritual. *AA* 108(2): 324–35.

Becker, A. L. 1979. Text–Building, Epistemology, and Aesthetics in Javanese Shadow Theatre. In Becker and Yengoyan, eds., *The Imagination of Reality.*

—— 1995. *Beyond Translation: Essays toward a Modern Philology.* Ann Arbor.

—— and Aram A. Yengoyan, eds. 1979. *The Imagination of Reality: Essays in Southeast Asian Coherence Systems.* Norwood, NJ.

Behrend, Heike and Ute Luig, eds. 1999. *Spirit*

Possession, Modernity & Power in Africa. Oxford.

Beidelman, Tom. 1974. *William Robertson-Smith and the Sociological Study of Religion*. Chicago.

—— 1982. *Colonial Evangelism*. Bloomington.

—— 1986. *Moral Imagination in Kaguru Modes of Thought*. Bloomington.

—— 1997. *The Cool Knife: Imagery of Gender, Sexuality, and Moral Education in Kaguru Initiation Ritual*. Washington, DC.

Bell, Catherine. 1992. *Ritual Theory, Ritual Practice*. New York.

Bell, Diane. 1983. *Daughters of the Dreaming*. Melbourne.

Bellah, Robert. 1957. *Tokugawa Religion: The Values of Pre-Industrial Japan*. Boston.

—— 1964. Religious Evolution. *American Sociological Review* 29: 358–74.

—— 1970. *Beyond Belief: Essays on Religion in a Post-Traditional World*. New York.

—— 1975. *The Broken Covenant: American Civil Religion in Time of Trial*. New York.

—— and Phillip E. Hammond, eds. 1980. *Varieties of Civil Religion*. San Francisco.

—— R. Madsen, W. Sullivan, A. Swidler, and S. Tipton. 1985. *Habits of the Heart: Individualism and Commitment in American Life*. New York.

Benedict, Ruth. 1934. *Patterns of Culture*. Boston.

Benjamin, Walter. 1969 [1936]. The Work of Art in the Age of Mechanical Reproduction. In H. Arendt, ed., *Illuminations*. New York.

Benson, Elizabeth P. and Anita G. Cook, eds. 2001. *Ritual Sacrifice in Ancient Peru*. Austin.

Berger, Peter. 1967. *The Sacred Canopy: Elements of A Sociological Theory of Religion*. Garden City, NY.

—— and Thomas Luckmann. 1966. *The Social Construction of Reality*. Garden City, NY.

Berliner, David. 2005. An "Impossible" Transmission: Youth Religious Memories in Guinea–Conakry. *AE* 32(4): 576–92.

—— and Ramon Sarró, eds. 2007. *Learning Religion: Anthropological Approaches*. Oxford and New York.

Berndt, Ronald, ed. 1970. *Australian Aboriginal Anthropology*. Nedlands, Australia.

Bernstein, Richard J. 1988. *Beyond Objectivism and Relativism: Science, Hermeneutics, and Praxis*. Philadelphia.

Bertelli, Sergio. 2001. *The King's Body: Sacred Rituals of Power in Medieval and Early Modern Europe*. University Park.

Besnier, Niko. 1995. *Literacy, Emotion, and Authority: Reading and Writing on a Polynesian Atoll*. Cambridge.

Béteille, André. 1965. *Caste, Class and Power: Changing Patterns of Stratification in a Tanjore Village*. Berkeley.

—— 1969. Caste in a South Indian Village. In A. Béteille, ed., *Social Inequality*. Harmondsworth.

Bhargava, Rajeev, ed. 1998. *Secularism and Its Critics*. Delhi.

Bhatt, Chetan. 2001. *Hindu Nationalism: Origins, Ideologies, and Modern Myths*. Oxford.

Biardeau, Madeleine. 1994. *Hinduism: The Anthropology of a Civilization*. Oxford.

Biersack, Aletta. 1996. Word Made Flesh: Religion, the Economy, and the Body in the Papua New Guinea Highlands. *History of Religions* 36: 85–111.

Bierwert, Crisca. 1999. *Brushed By Cedar: Coast Salish Figures of Power*. Tucson.

Binsbergen, Wim van and M. Schofeleers, eds. 1985. *Theoretical Explorations in African Religion*. London.

Bird-David, Nurit. 2006. Animistic Epistemology: Why Do Some Hunter-Gatherers Not Depict Animals? *Ethnos* 71(1): 33–50.

Blanes, Ruy Llera. 2006. The Atheist Anthropologist: Believers and Non-Believers in Anthropological Fieldwork. *Social Anthropology* 14(2): 219–22.

Blank, Jonah. 2001. *Mullahs on the Mainframe: Islam and Modernity among the Daudi Bohras*. Chicago.

Bloch, Maurice. 1986. *From Blessing to Violence: History and Ideology in the Circumcision Ritual of the Merina of Madagascar*. Cambridge.

—— 1989a. *Ritual, History, and Power: Selected Papers in Anthropology*. London.

—— 1989b [1977]. The Past and the Present in the Present. In Bloch 1989a.

—— 1989c [1974]. Symbols, Song, Dance and Features of Articulation: Is Religion an Extreme Form of Traditional Authority? In Bloch 1989a.

Bloch, Maurice 1989d [1977]. The Disconnection between Power and Rank as a Process: An Outline of the Development of Kingdoms in Central Madagascar. In Bloch 1989a.

—— 1989e [1987]. The Ritual of the Royal Bath in Madagascar: The Dissolution of Death, Birth, and Fertility into Authority. In Bloch 1989a.

—— 1992. *Prey Into Hunter: The Politics of Religious Experience.* Cambridge.

—— 1998. *How We Think They Think: Anthropological Approaches to Cognition, Memory, Literacy.* Boulder.

—— 2005. *Essays on Cultural Transmission.* Oxford.

—— and Jonathan Parry, eds. 1982. *Death and the Regeneration of Life.* Cambridge.

Bloul, Rachel. 1996. Engendering Muslim Identities: Deterritorialization and the Ethnicization Process in France. In B. Metcalf, ed., *Making Muslim Space in North America and Europe.* Berkeley.

Boas, Franz. 1966. Religion of the Kwakiutl Indians. In H. Codere, ed., *Kwakiutl Ethnography.* Chicago.

Boddy, Janice. 1988. Spirits and Selves in Northern Sudan: The Cultural Therapeutics of Possession and Trance, *AE* 15 (1): 4–27.

—— 1989. *Wombs and Alien Spirits: Women, Men, and the Zar Cult in Northern Sudan.* Madison.

—— 1994a. *Aman: The Story of a Somali Girl.* Toronto.

—— 1994b. Spirit Possession Revisited: Beyond Instrumentality. *Annual Review of Anthropology* 23: 407–34.

—— 2007. *Civilizing Women: British Crusader in Colonial Sudan.* Princeton.

Bodenhorn, Barbara. 1990. "I'm Not the Great Hunter, My Wife Is." *Etudes/Inuit/ Studies* 14: 55–74.

Boellstorff, Tom. 2005. Between Religion and Desire: Being Muslim and Gay in Indonesia. *AA* 107(4): 575–85.

Bond, George C. and Diane M. Ciekawy, eds. 2002. *Witchcraft Dialogues: Anthropologi-* *cal and Philosophical Exchanges.* Athens, OH.

Bongmba, Elias Kifon. 2001. *African Witchcraft and Otherness: A Philosophical and Theological Critique of Intersubjective Relations.* Albany, NY.

Bonnemère, Pascale, ed. 2004. *Women as Unseen Characters: Male Ritual in Papua New Guinea.* Philadelphia.

Bornstein, Erica. 2001. Child Sponsorship, Evangelism, and Belonging in the Work of World Vision Zimbabwe. *AE* 28(3): 595–622.

—— 2005. *The Spirit of Development: Protestant NGOs, Morality and Economics in Zimbabwe.* Stanford.

Bouissac, Paul. 1976. *Circus and Culture: A Semiotic Approach.* Bloomington.

Bouquet, Mary and Nuno Porto, eds. 2004. *Science, Magic, and Religion: The Ritual Processes of Museum Magic.* New York.

Bourdieu, Pierre. 1977. *Outline of a Theory of Practice.* Cambridge.

—— 1990 [1980]. *The Logic of Practice.* Stanford.

—— 1991. Rites of Institution. In *Language and Symbolic Power.* Cambridge, MA.

Bourdillon, M. F. C. and M. Fortes, eds. 1980. *Sacrifice.* London.

Bourguignon, Erika, ed. 1973. *Religion, Altered States of Consciousness, and Social Change.* Columbia, OH.

—— 2005. Memory in an Amnesic World: Holocaust, Exile, and the Return of the Suppressed. *Anthropological Quarterly* 78(1): 89–123.

Bowen, Elenore Smith [Laura Bohannon]. 1964. *Return to Laughter.* Garden City, NY.

Bowen, John. 1983. *Muslims Through Discourse: Religion and Ritual in Gayo Society.* Princeton.

—— 1989. Salat in Indonesia. The Social Meaning of an Islamic Ritual. *Man* 24: 600–19.

—— 1998. *Religions in Practice.* Boston.

—— ed. 1998. *Religion, Culture, and Society.* Boston.

—— 2003. *Islam, Law and Equality in Indonesia: An Anthropology of Public Reasoning.* Cambridge.

—— 2004a. Does French Islam Have Borders? Dilemmas of Domestication in a Global Religious Field. *AA* 106(1): 43–55.

—— 2006. *Why the French Don't Like Headscarves*. Princeton.

Bowie, Fiona. 1999. *The Anthropology of Religion*. Oxford.

—— 2003. An Anthropology of Religious Experience: Spirituality, Gender and Cultural Transmission in the Focolare Movement. *Ethnos* 68(1): 49–72.

Boyer, P. 1994. *The Naturalness of Religious Ideas: A Cognitive Theory of Religion*. Berkeley.

—— 2001. *Religion Explained: The Human Instincts that Fashion Gods, Spirits and Ancestors*. London.

Brain, James. 1973. Ancestors and Elders in Africa. *Africa* 43(2): 122–33.

Bricker, Victoria. 1981. *The Indian Christ, the Indian King: The Historical Substrate of Maya Myth and Ritual*. Austin.

Brightman, Robert. 1993. *Grateful Prey: Rock Cree Human–Animal Relationships*. Berkeley.

Bringhurst, Robert. 2000. *A Story as Sharp as a Knife: The Classic Haida Mythtellers and their World*. Omaha.

Brodwin, Paul. 2003. Pentecostalism in Translation: Religion and the Production of Community in the Haitian Diaspora. *AE* 30(1): 85–101.

Brown, David H. 2003. *Santería Enthroned: Art, Ritual, and Innovation in an Afro-Cuban Religion*. Chicago.

Brown, Dee. 2001. *Bury My Heart at Wounded Knee: An Indian History of the American West*. New York.

Brown, Diana. 1986. *Umbanda. Religion and Politics in Urban Brazil*. Ann Arbor.

Brown, Judith K. 1963. A Cross Cultural Study of Female Initiation Rites. *AA* 65: 837–53.

Brown, Karen McCarthy. 1991. *Mama Lola. A Vodou Priestess in Brooklyn*. Berkeley.

Brown, Michael. 1985. *Tsewa's Gift: Magic and Meaning in an Amazonian Society*. Washington, DC.

—— 1997. *The Channeling Zone: American Spirituality in an Anxious Age*. Princeton.

Brown, Peter. 1981. *The Cult of the Saints: Its Rise and Function in Latin Christianity*. Chicago.

vom Bruck, Gabriele. 2005. *Islam, Memory and Morality in Yemen: Ruling Families in Transition*. New York.

Bruner, Edward, ed. 1983. *Text, Play, and Story: The Construction and Reconstruction of Self and Society*. Washington, DC.

Brunton, R. 1980. Misconstrued Order in Melanesian Religion. *Man* 15: 112–28.

Bubandt, Nils. 2006. Sorcery, Corruption, and the Dangers of Democracy in Indonesia. *JRAI* 12(2): 413–31.

Buckley, Thomas. 2002. *Standing Ground: Yurok Indian Spirituality, 1850–1990*. Berkeley.

Buckser, Andrew. 2003a. *After the Rescue: Jewish Identity and Community in Contemporary Denmark*. New York.

—— 2003b. Religious Practice and Cultural Politics in Jewish Copenhagen. *AE* 30(1): 102–17.

Bulmer, Ralph. 1967. Why is the Cassowary not a Bird? *Man* 2(1): 5–25.

Bunzl, Matti. 2004. *Symptoms of Modernity: Jews and Queers in Late-Twentieth-Century Vienna*. Berkeley.

—— 2005. Between Anti-Semitism and Islamophobia: Some Thoughts on the New Europe. *AE* 32(4): 499–508.

Burdick, John. 1993. *Looking for God in Brazil: The Progressive Catholic Church in Urban Brazil's Religious Arena*. Berkeley.

—— 1998. *Blessed Antastácia: Women, Race and Popular Christianity in Brazil*. New York.

Burghardt, Richard. 1983. Renunciation in the Religious Traditions of South Asia. *Man* 18(4): 635–53.

Burridge, Kenelm. 1960. *Mambu: A Melanesian Millennium*. London.

—— 1969. *New Heaven, New Earth: A Study of Millenarian Activities*. Oxford.

—— 1979. *Someone, No One: An Essay on Individuality*. Princeton.

—— 1991. *In the Way: A Study of Christian Mission Endeavors*. Vancouver.

Buxton, Jean. 1973. *Religion and Healing in Mandari*. Oxford.

Bynum, Caroline Walker. 1984. Women's

Stories, Women's Symbols: A Critique of Victor Turner's Theory of Liminality. In F. Reynolds and R. Moore, eds., *Anthropology and the Study of Religion*. Chicago.

—— 1991. *Fragmentation and Redemption: Essays on Gender and the Human Body in Medieval Religion*. New York.

Bynum, Caroline Walker S. Harell, and P. Richman, eds. 1986. *Gender and Religion: On the Complexity of Symbols*. Boston.

Cahn, Peter S. 2003. *All Religions are Good in Tzintzuntzan: Evangelicals in Catholic Mexico*. Austin, TX.

—— 2006. Building Down and Dreaming Up: Finding Faith in a Mexican Multilevel Marketer. *AE* 33(1): 126–42.

Cairns, David. 2000. The Object of Sectarianism: The Material Reality of Sectarianism in Ulster Loyalism. *JRAI* 6(3): 437–52.

Calame–Griaule, G. 1986 [1965]. *Words and the Dogon World*. Philadelphia.

Calavia Sáez, Oscar. 2004. In Search of Ritual: Tradition, Outer World and Bad Manners in the Amazon. *JRAI* 10(1): 157–73.

Caldwell, Sarah. 1999a. *Oh Terrifying Mother: Sexuality, Violence, and Worship of the Goddess Kali*. Delhi: Oxford University Press.

—— 1999b. Transcendence and Culture: Anthropologists Theorize Religion. *Religious Studies Review* 25(3): 227–32.

Calkowski, Marcia. 2000. Buddhism. In Scupin 2000.

Campbell, Colin. 1987. *The Romantic Ethic and the Spirit of Modern Consumerism*. Oxford.

Cannadine, David and Simon Price, eds. 1987. *Rituals of Royalty: Power and Ceremonial in Traditional Societies*. Cambridge.

Cannell, Fenella. 1999. *Power and Intimacy in the Christian Philippines*. Cambridge.

—— 2005. The Christianity of Anthropology. *JRAI* 11(2): 335–56.

—— ed. 2006. *The Anthropology of Christianity*. Durham.

Carnes, Tony and Fenggang Yang, eds. 2004. *Asian American Religions: The Making and Remaking of Borders and Boundaries*. New York.

Carrin, Marine and Harald-Tambs Lyche.

2003. "You Don't Joke With These Fellows": Power and Ritual in South Canara, India. *Social Anthropology* 11(1): 23–42.

Carrithers, Michael. 1983. *The Forest Monks of Sri Lanka: An Anthropological and Historical Study*. Oxford.

—— S. Collins, and S. Lukes. eds. 1985. *The Category of the Person*. Cambridge.

Carroll, Michael. 1986. *The Cult of the Virgin Mary*. Princeton.

—— 1996. *The Logic of Popular Catholicism in Italy*. Baltimore.

Casanova, José. 1994. *Public Religions in the Modern World*. Chicago.

Chakrabarty, Dipesh. 2000. *Provincializing Europe: Postcolonial Thought and Historical Difference*. Princeton.

Chau, Adam Yuet. 2005. *Doing Popular Religion in Contemporary China*. Stanford.

Chehabi, H. E. 1991. Religion and Politics in Iran: How Theocratic is the Islamic Republic? *Daedalus* 120(3): 69–91.

Chidester, David. 2005. *Authentic Fakes: Religion and American Popular Culture*. Berkeley.

Chodorow, Nancy. 1989. *Feminism and Psychoanalytic Theory*. New Haven.

—— 1999. *The Power of Feelings*. New Haven.

Christian, William. 1989. *Person and God in a Spanish Valley*. Princeton.

Clammer, John, Sylvie Poirier and Eric Schwimmer, eds. 2004. *Figured Worlds: Ontological Obstacles in Intercultural Relations*. Toronto.

Claussen, Heather L. 2001. *Unconventional Sisterhood: Feminist Catholic Nuns in the Philippines*. Ann Arbor.

Clifford, James. 1992. *Person and Myth: Maurice Leenhardt in the Melanesian World*. Durham, NC.

—— 1997. *Routes: Travel and Translation on the Late Twentieth Century*. Cambridge, MA.

Cohen, Abner. 1976. *Two-Dimensional Man: An Essay on the Anthropology of Power and Symbolism in Complex Society*. Berkeley.

Cohen, Anthony. 1985. *The Symbolic Construction of Community*. London.

—— and N. Rapport. 1995. *Questions of Consciousness*. London.

Cohen, Percy. 1969. Theories of Myth. *Man* 4: 337–53.

Cohn, Bernard. 1987. *An Anthropologist among the Historians*. Delhi.

Colby, Benjamin and Lore Colby. 1981. *The Daykeeper: The Life and Discourse of an Ixil Diviner*. Cambridge, MA.

Cole, Jennifer. 2001. *Forget Colonialism? Sacrifice and the Art of Memory in Madagascar*. Berkeley.

Coleman, Simon. 2000. *The Globalisation of Charismatic Christianity: Spreading the Gospel of Prosperity*. Cambridge.

—— 2004. The Charismatic Gift. *JRAI* 10(2): 421–42.

—— and John Eade, eds. 2004. *Reframing Pilgrimage: Cultures in Motion*. London.

Collier, Jane and Sylvia Yanagisako. 1989. Theory in Anthropology since Feminist Practice. *Critique of Anthropology*. 9(2): 27–37.

Comaroff, Jean. 1985. *Body of Power, Spirit of Resistance: The Culture and History of a South African People*. Chicago.

—— and John L. Comaroff. 1991. *Of Revelation and Revolution: Christianity, Colonialism, and Consciousness in South Africa*. Vol. 1. Chicago.

—— 1992. *Ethnography and the Historical Imagination*. Boulder.

—— eds. 1993. *Modernity and Its Malcontents: Ritual and Power in Postcolonial Africa*. Chicago.

Comaroff, John L. and Jean Comaroff. 1997. *Of Revelation and Revolution: The Dialetics of Modernity on a South African Frontier*. Vol. 2. Chicago.

—— 1999. Occult Economies and the Violence of Abstraction: Notes from the South African Postcolony. *AE* 26(2): 279–303.

—— eds. 2000a. *Millennial Capitalism and the Culture of Neoliberalism*. Durham, NC.

—— 2000b. Millennial Capitalism: First Thoughts on a Second Coming. *Public Culture* 12(2): 291–343.

—— 2002. Alien-Nation: Zombies, Immigrants, and Millennial Capitalism. *South Atlantic Quarterly* 101(4): 779–805.

Combs-Schilling, Elaine. 1989. *Sacred Performances: Islam, Sexuality, and Sacrifice*. New York.

Connolly, William E. 1999. *Why I am Not a Secularist*. Minneapolis.

Coombe, Rosemary. 1998. *The Cultural Life of Intellectual Properties*. Durham, NC.

Cooper, Barbara. 2006. *Evangelical Christians in the Muslim Sahel*. Indiana.

Coppet, Daniel de, ed. 1992. *Understanding Rituals*. London.

—— and André Iteanu, eds. 1995. *Cosmos and Society in Oceania*. Oxford.

Corten, André, and Ruth Marshall-Fratani, eds. 2001. *Between Babel and Pentecost: Transnational Pentecostalism in Africa and Latin America*. Bloomington, IN.

Cox, Rupert. 2003. *The Zen Arts: An Anthropological Study of the Culture of Aesthetic Form in Japan*. London.

Crapanzano, Vincent. 1973. *The Hamadsha. A Study in Moroccan Ethnopsychiatry*. Berkeley.

—— 1980. *Tuhami: Portrait of a Moroccan*. Chicago.

—— 1992. *Hermes' Dilemma and Hamlet's Desire: On the Epistemology of Interpretation*. Cambridge, MA.

—— 2000. *Serving the Word: Literalism in America from the Pulpit to the Bench*. New York.

—— 2003. *Imaginative Horizons: An Essay in Literary-Philosophical Anthropology*. Chicago.

—— and V. Garrison, eds. 1977. *Case Studies in Spirit Possession*. New York.

Creed, Gerald. 2004. Constituted through Conflict: Images of Community (and Nation) in Bulgarian Rural Ritual. *AA* 106(4): 56–70.

Crocker, Christopher. 1977. My Brother the Parrot. In Sapir and Crocker, eds., *The Social Use of Metaphor*. Philadelphia, PA.

—— 1983. Being and Essence: Totemic Representation among the Eastern Bororo. In Crumrine and Halpin, eds., *The Power of Symbols*.

—— 1985. *Vital Souls: Bororo Cosmology, Natural Symbolism, and Shamanism*. Tuscon.

Csordas, Thomas. 1994a. *The Sacred Self: A*

Cultural Phenomenology of Charismatic Healing. Berkeley.

—— ed. 1994b. *Embodiment and Experience: The Existential Ground of Culture and Self*. Cambridge.

—— 1997. *Language, Charisma, and Creativity*. Berkeley.

—— 2002. *Body/Meaning/Healing*. New York.

—— 2004. Asymptote of the Ineffable: Embodiment, Alterity, and the Theory of Religion. *Current Anthropology* 45(2): 163–85.

Cucchiari, Salvatore. 1990. Between Shame and Sanctification: Patriarchy and its Transformation in Sicilian Pentecostalism. *AE* 17: 687–707.

Culler, Jonathan. 1975. *Structuralist Poetics*. London.

Cunningham, Hilary. 1995. *God and Caesar at the Rio Grande: Sanctuary and the Politics of Religion*. Minneapolis.

—— 2000. The Ethnography of Transnational Social Activism. *AE* 26: 583–604.

D'Alisera, JoAnn. 2004. *An Imagined Geography: Sierra Leonean Muslims in America*. Philadelphia, PA.

Da Matta, Roberto. 1984. Carnival in Multiple Planes. In J. MacAloon, ed., *Rite, Drama, Festival, Spectacle: Rehearsals Toward a Theory of Cultural Performance*. Philadelphia.

Danforth, Loring. 1982. *The Death Rituals of Rural Greece*. Princeton.

Daniel, E. Valentine. 1984. *Fluid Signs: Being a Person the Tamil Way*. Berkeley.

—— 1996. *Charred Lullabies: Chapters in an Anthropography of Violence*. Princeton.

Daniels, Maria Inge. 2003. Scooping, Raking, Beckoning Luck: Luck, Agency and the Interdependence of People and Things in Japan. *JRAI* 9(4): 619–38.

Das, Veena, ed. 1990. *Mirrors of Violence: Communities, Riots and Survivors in South Asia*. New York.

—— 1995. *Critical Events: An Anthropological Perspective on Contemporary India*. New York.

—— ed. 2001. *Remaking a World: Violence, Social Suffering and Recovery*. Berkeley.

DeBernardi, Jean, 2006. *The Way that Lives in the Heart: Chinese Popular Religion and Spirit Mediums in Penang, Malaysia*. Stanford.

De Boeck, Filip. 1991. Therapeutic Efficacy and Consensus among the aLund of Southwestern Zaire. *Africa* 61: 37–71.

—— 1994. Of Trees and Kings: Politics and Metaphor among the aLund of Southwestern Zaire. *AE* 21: 451–73.

—— 1998. Beyond the Grave: History, Memory and Death in Postcolonial Congo/Zaire. In R. Werbner, ed., *Memory and the Postcolony*. London.

—— 1999. Domesticating Diamonds and Dollars: Identity, Expenditure and Sharing in Southwestern Zaire (1984–1997). In Meyer and Geschiere, eds., *Globalization and Identity*.

—— and Marie-Françoise Plissart. 2004. *Kinshasa: Tales of the Invisible City*. Ghent.

Declich, Francesca. 2000. Sufi Experience in Rural Somali: A Focus on Women. *Social Anthropology* 8(3): 295–318.

Delaney, Carol. 1986. The Meaning of Paternity and the Virgin Birth Debate. *Man*, n.s. 21: 494–513.

—— 1991. *The Seed and the Soil: Gender and Cosmology in Turkish Village Society*. Berkeley.

—— 1998. *Abraham on Trial: The Social Legacy of Biblical Myth*. Princeton.

De Neve, Geert. 2000. Patronage and "Community": The Role of a Tamil "Village" Festival in the Integration of a Town. *JRAI* 6(3): 501–19.

Denzler, Brenda. 2001. *The Lure of the Edge: Scientific Passions, Religious Beliefs, and the Pursuit of UFOs*. Berkeley.

Descola, Philippe. 1994. *In the Society of Nature: A Native Ecology in Amazonia*. Cambridge.

—— 1998. *Spears of Twilight: Life and Death in the Amazon Jungle*. New York.

—— and Gísli Pálsson, eds. 1996. *Nature and Society: Anthropological Perspectives*. London.

Desjarlais, Robert. 1992. *Body and Healing: The Aesthetics of Illness and Healing in the Nepal Himalayas*. Philadelphia.

—— 2003. *Sensory Biographies: Lives and*

Deaths among Nepal's Yolmo Buddhists. Berkeley.

Devisch, René. 1993. *Weaving the Threads of Life: The Khita Gyn-Eco-Logical Healing Cult among the Yaka.* Chicago.

De Vries, Hent, ed. 2007. *Religion: Beyond a Concept.* New York.

Diamond, Stanley. 1972. Introductory Essay: Job and the Trickster. In Radin, *The Trickster.*

—— 1974. *In Search of the Primitive: A Critique of Civilization.* New Brunswick, NJ.

Dilley, Roy. 2005. *Islamic and Caste Knowledge Practices among Haalpulaaren in Senegal.* Edinburgh.

Dirks, Nicholas. 1987. *The Hollow Crown: Ethohistory of an Indian Kingdom.* New York.

——, G. Eley, and S. Ortner, eds. 1994. *Culture/Power/History: A Reader in Contemporary Social Theory.* Princeton.

Dolgin, Janet, David Kemnitzer, and David Schneider, eds. 1977. *Symbolic Anthropology.* New York.

Dombrowski, Kirk. 2002. *Against Culture: Development, Politics and Religion in Indian Alaska.* Lincoln.

Douglas, Mary. 1966. *Purity and Danger: An Analysis of the Concepts of Pollution and Taboo.* London.

—— 1967. The Meaning of Myth, with Special Reference to "La Geste d'Asdiwal." In Leach, ed., *The Structural Analysis of Myth and Totemism.*

—— 1970. *Natural Symbols.* New York.

—— ed. 1970. *Witchcraft Confessions and Accusations.* London.

—— ed. 1973. *Rules and Meanings.* Harmondsworth.

—— 1975. Animals in Lele Religious Symbolism. In *Implicit Meanings.* London.

—— 1993. *The Wilderness: The Doctrine of Defilement in the Book of Numbers.* Sheffield.

—— 1996. *Thought Styles: Critical Essays on Good Taste.* London.

—— 1999. *Leviticus as Literature.* Oxford.

Douglass, W. A. 1969. *Death in Murelaga. Funerary Rituals in a Spanish Basque Village.* Seattle.

Dow, James. 2005. The Expansion of Protestantism in Mexico: An Anthropological View. *Anthropological Quarterly* 78(2): 794–827.

—— and Allen Sandstrom, eds. 2001. *Holy Saints and Fiery Preachers: The Anthropology of Protestantism in Mexico and Central America.* Westport.

Dransart, Penelope. 2002. Concepts of Spiritual Nourishment in the Andes and Europe: Rosaries in Cross-Cultural Contexts. *JRAI* 8(1): 1–21.

Dubisch, Jill. 1995. *In a Different Place: Pilgrimage, Gender, and Politics at a Greek Island Shrine.* Princeton.

Dumont, Louis. 1969. Caste, Racism, and Stratification. In A. Béteille, ed., *Social Inequality.* Harmondsworth.

—— 1970. *Homo Hierarchicus: The Caste System and its Implications.* Chicago.

—— 1986. *Essays on Individualism: Modern Ideology in Anthropological Perspective.* Chicago.

Dunnill, John. 2005. *Covenant and Sacrifice in the Letter to the Hebrews.* Cambridge.

Durkheim, Emile. 1915 [1912]. *The Elementary Forms of the Religious Life.* Joseph Ward Swain, trans. New York.

—— 1973. *Emile Durkheim on Morality and Society: Selected Writings.* R. Bellah, intro. Chicago.

—— 1974. *Sociology and Philosophy.* D. F. Pocock, trans. J. G. Peristiany, intro. New York.

—— 1992. *Professional Ethics and Civic Morals.* Preface by B. Turner. London.

—— 1995 [1912]. *The Elementary Forms of Religious Life*, Karen Fields ed. and trans. New York.

—— and Marcel Mauss. 1963 [1903]. *Primitive Classification.* Chicago.

Dussart, Françoise. 2000. *The Politics of Ritual in an Aboriginal Settlement: Kinship, Gender, and the Currency of Knowledge.* London.

Eade, John and Michael Sallnow, eds. 1991. *Contesting the Sacred: The Anthropology of Christian Pilgrimage.* London.

Eickelman, Dale. 1976. *Moroccan Islam: Tradition and Society in a Pilgrimage Center.* Austin.

—— 1982. The Study of Islam in Local Contexts. *Contributions to Asian Studies*, XVII: 1–18.

—— 1985. *Knowledge and Power in Morocco*. Princeton.

—— 1992. Mass Higher Education and the Religious Imagination in Contemporary Arab Societies. *AE* 19(4): 643–55.

—— and James Piscatori, eds. 1996. *Muslim Politics*. Princeton.

Eickelman, Dale and Jon W. Anderson. 2003. *New Media in the Muslim World: The Emerging Public Sphere*. Bloomington, IN.

Eilberg-Schwartz, Howard. 1990. *The Savage in Judaism*. Bloomington.

Eisenlohr, Patrick. 2006a. As Makkah is sweet and beloved, so is Madina: Islam, Devotional Genres, and Electronic Mediation in Mauritius. *AE* 33(2): 230–45.

—— 2006b. The Politics of Diaspora and the Morality of Secularism: Muslim Identities and Islamic Authority in Mauritius. *JRAI* 12(2): 395–412.

Eiss, Paul K. 2002. Hunting for the Virgin: Meat, Money, and Memory in Tetiz, Yucatán. *Cultural Anthropology* 17(3): 291–330.

Eliade, Mircea. 1959. *Cosmos and History: The Myth of the Eternal Return*. New York.

Ellis, Stephen. 1999. *The Mask of Anarchy: The Destruction of Liberia and the Religious Dimension of an African Civil War*. London.

—— 2001. Mystical Weapons: Some Evidence from the Liberian War. *Journal of Religion in Africa* 31(2): 222–36.

—— and Gerrie Ter Haar. 2004. *Worlds of Power: Religious Thought and Political Practice in Africa*. New York.

Endicott, Kirk. 1979. *Batek Negrito Religion: The World-View and Rituals of a Hunting and Gathering People of Peninsular Malaysia*. New York.

Engelke, Matthew. 2004. Text and Performance in an African Church: The Book, "Live and Direct". *AE* 31(1): 76–91.

—— 2005. The Early Days of Johane Masowe: Self-Doubt, Uncertainty, and Religious Transformation. *CSSH* 47(4): 781–808.

—— 2007. *A Problem of Presence: Beyond Scripture in an African Church*. Berkeley.

—— and Matt Tomlinson, eds 2007. *The Limits of Meaning: Case Studies in the Anthropology of Christianity*. New York.

Englund, Harri. 1996. Witchcraft, Modernity and the Person: The Morality of Accumulation in Central Malawi. *Critique of Anthropology* 16(3): 257–79.

Errington, S. 1989. *Meaning and Power in a Southeast Asian Realm*. Princeton.

Erzen, Tanya. 2006. *Straight to Jesus: Sexual and Christian Conversions in the Ex-Gay Movement*. California.

Essen, Juliana. 2005. *"Right Development": The Santi Asoke Buddhist Reform Movement of Thailand*. New York.

Evans-Pritchard, E. E. 1933. The Intellectualist (English) Interpretation of Magic. *Bulletin of the Faculty of Arts* (Alexandria) i.

—— 1934. Lévy–Bruhl's Theory of Primitive Mentality. *Bulletin of the Faculty of Arts* (Alexandria) ii.

—— 1937. *Witchcraft, Oracles, and Magic among the Azande*. Oxford.

—— 1940. *The Nuer*. Oxford.

—— 1956. *Nuer Religion*. Oxford.

—— 1964. The Divine Kingship of the Shilluk. In *Social Anthropology and Other Essays*.

—— 1965. *Theories of Primitive Religion*. Oxford.

—— 1976. *Witchcraft, Oracles and Magic among the Azande*. Abridged. E. Gillies, intro. Oxford.

Evens, T. M. S. 1982. On the Social Anthropology of Religion. *Journal of Religion* 62 (4): 376–91.

—— 1996. Witchcraft and Selfcraft. *Archives of European Sociology*.

Eves, Richard. 2000. Sorcery's the Curse: Modernity, Envy and the Flow of Sociality in a Melanesian Society. *JRAI* 6(3): 453–68.

Ewing, Katherine. 1994. Dreams from a Saint: Anthropological Atheism and the Temptation to Believe. *AA* 96: 571–83.

—— 1997. *Arguing Sainthood: Modernity, Psychoanalysis and Islam*. Durham, NC.

Fabian, Johannes. 1971. *Jamaa. A Charismatic Movement in Katanga*. Evanston.

—— ed. 1979. Beyond Charisma. Religious Movements as Discourse. *Social Research* 46(1): 1–203.

—— 1983. *Time and the Other: How Anthropology Makes its Object*. New York.

Falla, Ricardo. 2001. *Quich-Rebelde: Religious Conversion, Politics, and Ethnic Identity in Guatemala*. Austin, TX.

Fardon, Richard. 1991. *Between God, the Dead and the Wild: Chamba Interpretations of Ritual and Religion*. Edinburgh.

—— 1999. *Mary Douglas: An Intellectual Biography*. London.

Faubion, James D. 2003. Religion, Violence, and the Vitalistic Economy. *Anthropological Quarterly* 76(1): 71–85.

Favret-Saada, J. 1980. *Deadly Words: Witchcraft in the Bocage*. Cambridge.

Feeley-Harnik, Gillian. 1985. Issues in Divine Kinship. *Annual Review of Anthropology* 14: 73–313.

—— 1991. *A Green Estate: Restoring Independence in Madagascar*. Washington, DC.

—— 1994. *The Lord's Table: The Meaning of Food in Early Judaism and Christianity*. Washington, DC.

Feld, Steven and Keith Basso, eds. 1996. *Senses of Place*. Santa Fe.

Feldman, Jeffrey D. 2004. The Jewish Roots and Routes of Anthropology. *Anthropological Quarterly* 77(1): 107–25.

Feldman-Savelsberg, Pamela. 1999. *Plundered Kitchens, Empty Wombs: Threatened Reproduction and Identity in the Cameroon Grassfields*. Ann Arbor.

Ferme, Marianne. 2001. *The Underneath of Things: Violence, History and the Everyday in Sierra Leone*. Berkeley.

Fernandez, James W. 1974. The Mission of Metaphor in Expressive Culture. *Current Anthropology* 15(2): 119–45.

—— 1983. *Bwiti: An Ethnography of the Religious Imagination in Africa*. Princeton.

—— 1986a [1985]. Returning to the Whole. In Fernandez 1986.

—— 1986b. *Persuasions and Performances*. Bloomington.

—— ed. 1991. *Beyond Metaphor: The Theory of Tropes in Anthropology*. Stanford.

Feuchtwang, Stephan. 1975. Investigating Religion. In Maurice Bloch, ed., *Marxist Analyses and Social Anthropology*. London.

—— 1991. A Chinese Religion Exists. In H. Baker and S. Feuchtwang, eds., *An Old State in New Settings*. Oxford.

—— 1992. *The Imperial Metaphor: Popular Religion in China*. London.

Feuerbach, Ludwig. 1975. *The Essence of Christianity*. George Eliot, trans. New York.

Fingarette, Herbert. 1963. *The Self in Transformation*. New York.

Firth, Raymond. 1940. *The Work of the Gods in Tikopia*. London.

—— 1967. *Tikopia Ritual and Belief*. Boston.

—— 1973. *Symbols Public and Private*. London: Allen & Unwin.

—— 1981. *Spiritual Aroma. Religion and Politics. AA* 83: 582–601.

—— 1996. *Religion: A Humanist Interpretation*. London.

Fischer, Michael. 1980. *Iran: From Religious Dispute to Revolution*. Cambridge, MA.

—— and Mehdi Abedi. 1990. *Debating Muslims: Cultural Dialogues in Postmodernity and Tradition*. Madison.

Fisher, William H. 2003. Name Rituals and Acts of Feeling Among the Kayapó (Mebengokre). *JRAI* 9(1):117–35.

Fisiy, Cyprian and Peter Geschiere. 1990. Judges and Witches, Or How Is the State to Deal with Witchcraft? – Examples from Southeastern Cameroon. *Cahiers d'études Africaines* 118: 135–56.

—— 1991. Sorcery, Witchcraft and Accumulation – Regional Variation in South and West Cameroon. *Critique of Anthropology* 11: 251–78.

Flueckiger, Joyce. 2006. *In Ammas Healing Room: Gender and Vernacular Islam in South Asia*. Indiana.

Forde, Daryll, ed. 1954. *African Worlds: Studies in the Cosmological Ideas and Social Values of African Peoples*. Oxford.

Fortes, Meyer. 1983 [1959]. *Oedipus and Job in West African Religion*. Cambridge.

—— 1987. *Religion, Morality and the Person: Essays on Tallensi Religion*. Cambridge.

—— and Germaine Dieterlen, eds. 1965. *African Systems of Thought*. London.

Forth, Gregory. 2000. *Beneath the Volcano: Religion, Cosmology and Spirit Classifica-*

tion among the Nage of Eastern Indonesia. Leiden.

Fortune, Reo. 1932. *Sorcerers of Dobu*. New York.

—— 1934. *Manus Religion*. Lincoln.

Foucault, Michel. 1977. *Discipline and Punish: The Birth of the Prison*. London.

—— 1978. *The History of Sexuality*. Vol. 1. New York.

—— 1983. The Subject and Power and On the Genealogy of Ethics. In H. Dreyfus and P. Rabinow, eds., *Michel Foucault: Beyond Structuralism and Hermeneutics*. Chicago.

—— 1997. *Ethics: Subjectivity and Truth*, P. Rabinow, ed. New York.

Fowler, Loretta. 1987. *Shared Symbols, Contested Meanings: Gros Ventre Culture and History*. Ithaca.

Fox, James, ed. 1980. *The Flow of Life: Essays on Eastern Indonesia*. Cambridge, MA.

—— ed. 1988. *To Speak in Pairs: Essays on the Ritual Languages of Eastern Indonesia*. Cambridge.

Fox, Richard. 1989. *Gandhian Utopia. Experiments with Culture*. Boston.

Frankel, Stephen. 2005. *The Huli Response to Illness*. Cambridge.

Frazer, Sir James. 1890. *The Golden Bough*. London.

Freedman, Maurice. 1967. Ancestor Worship: Two Facets of the Chinese Case. In *Social Organisation*. London.

Freud, Sigmund. 1953 [1900–30]. *The Interpretation of Dreams*. Vols. 4 and 5 of *The Standard Edition of the Complete Psychological Works of Sigmund Freud* [hereafter *SE*]. Trans. James Strachey in collaboration with Anna Freud. London.

—— 1958 [1913]. Totem and Taboo: Some Points of Agreement between the Mental lives of Savages and Neurotics. In *SE*. Vol. 13, pp. ix–162.

—— 1961 [1927]. The Future of an Illusion. In *SE*. Vol. 21, pp. 1–56.

Frisbie, Charlotte. 1980. *Southwestern Indian Ritual Drama*. Albuquerque.

Froerer, Peggy. 2006. Emphasizing "Others": The Emergence of Hindu Nationalism in a Central Indian Tribal Community. *JRAI* 12(1): 39–59.

Froystad, Kathinka. 2005. *Blended Boundar-*

ies: Caste, Class and Shifting Faces of Hinduness in a North Indian City. Oxford.

Fry, Peter. 1976. *Spirits of Protest: Spirit-Mediums and the Articulation of Consensus among the Zezuru of Southern Rhodesia (Zimbabwe)*. Cambridge.

Fuller, Chris. 1984. *Servants of the Goddess: The Priests of a South Indian Temple*. Cambridge.

—— 1988. The Hindu Pantheon and the Legitimation of Hierarchy. *Man* 23: 19–39.

—— 1992. *The Camphor Flame: Popular Hinduism and Society in India*. Princeton.

—— 2003. *The Renewal of the Priesthood: Modernity and Traditionalism in a South Indian Temple*. Oxford.

Fürer-Haimendorf, Christoph von. 1974. The Sense of Sin in Cross-Cultural Perspective. *Man* 9: 539–56.

Fustel de Coulanges, Numa Denis. 1956 [1864]. *The Ancient City*. Garden City, NY.

Gaenszle, Martin. 2002. *Ancestral Voices: Oral Ritual Texts and their Social Contexts among the Mewahang Rai of East Nepal*. London.

Gaffney, Patrick 1994. *The Prophet's Pulpit: Islamic Preaching in Contemporary Egypt*. Berkeley.

Garber, James, Richard Warms and Jon McGee, eds. 2004. *Social Realms: Essays in Religion, Belief, and Society*. Oxford.

Garbett, Kingsley. 1969. Spirit Mediums as Mediators in Valley Korekore Society. In J. Beattie and J. Middleton, eds. *Spirit Mediumship and Society in Africa*. New York.

Gauchet, Marcel. 1997. *Disenchantment of the World: A Political History of Religion*. Princeton.

Geertz, Armin. 2003. Ethnohermeneutics and Worldview Analysis in the Study of Hopi Indian Religion. *Numen* 50(3): 308–48.

Geertz, Clifford. 1960. *The Religion of Java*. Glencoe, IL.

—— 1966a. *Person, Time, and Conduct in Bali: An Essay in Cultural Analysis*. New Haven. Reprinted in Geertz 1973a.

—— 1966b. Religion as a Cultural System. In Michael Banton, ed., *Anthropological*

Approaches to the Study of Religion. London. Reprinted in Geertz 1973a.

—— 1968. *Islam Observed: Religious Development in Morocco and Indonesia.* Chicago.

—— 1973a. *The Interpretation of Cultures.* New York.

—— 1973b. Thick Description: Toward an Interpretive Theory of Culture. In Geertz 1973a.

—— 1973c [1962]. The Growth of Culture and the Evolution of Mind. In Geertz 1973a.

—— 1973d [1964]. "Internal Conversion" in Contemporary Bali. In Geertz 1973a.

—— 1973e [1967]. The Cerebral Savage. In Geertz 1973a.

—— 1980. *Negara. The Theatre State in Nineteenth-Century Bali.* Princeton.

—— 1983. *Local Knowledge: Further Essays in Interpretive Anthropology.* New York.

—— 2000. *Available Light: Anthropological Reflections on Philosophical Topics.* Princeton.

—— 2005. Shifting Aims, Moving Targets: On the Anthropology of Religion. *JRAI* 11(1): 1–15.

Geertz, Hildred. 2004. *The Life of a Balinese Temple: Artistry, Imagination, and History in a Peasant Village.* Honolulu.

Gell, Alfred. 1975. *Metamorphosis of the Cassowaries: Umeda Society, Language and Ritual.* London.

—— 1979. Reflections on a Cut Finger: Taboo in the Umeda Conception of the Self. In R. Hook, ed. *Fantasy and Symbol.* London.

—— 1992a. *The Anthropology of Time.* Oxford.

—— 1992b. The Technology of Enchantment and the Enchantment of Technology. In J. Coote and A. Shelton, eds., *Anthropology, Art, and Aesthetics.* Oxford.

—— 1993. *Wrapping in Images: Tattooing in Polynesia.* Oxford.

—— 1995. Closure and Multiplication: An Essay on Polynesian Cosmology and Ritual. In Daniel de Coppet and André Iteanu, eds. *Understanding Rituals.* Oxford.

Gellner, David N. 1992. *Monk, Householder*

and Tantric Priest: Newar Buddhism and its Hierarchy of Ritual. Cambridge.

—— 1999. Anthropological Approaches. In P. Connolly, ed., *Approaches to the Study of Religion.* London.

—— 2001. *The Anthropology of Buddhism and Hinduism: Weberian Themes.* New Delhi.

—— 2005. The Emergence of Conversion in a Hindu-Buddhist Polytropy: The Kathmandu Valley, Nepal, c. 1600–1995. *CSSH* 47(4): 755–80.

Gellner, Ernest 1981. *Muslim Society.* Cambridge.

Gennep, Arnold van. 1904. *Tabou et totémisme à Madagascar.* Paris.

—— 1960 [1908]. *The Rites of Passage.* London.

George, Kenneth. 1996. *Showing Signs of Violence: The Cultural Politics of a Twentieth-Century Headhunting Ritual.* Berkeley.

Gerth, H. H. and C. Wright Mills, ed. and trans. 1946. *From Max Weber: Essays in Sociology.* New York.

Geschiere, Peter. 1997. *The Modernity of Witchcraft: Politics and the Occult in Post-colonial Africa.* Charlottesville, VA.

Gewertz, Deborah. ed. 1988. *Myths of Matriarchy Reconsidered.* Sydney.

Gibson, Thomas. 1986. *Sacrifice and Sharing in the Philippine Highlands.* London.

—— 2005. *And the Sun Pursued the Moon: Symbolic Knowledge and Traditional Authority among the Makassar.* New York.

Giddens, Anthony. 1971. Rationalisation, the World Religions, and Western Capitalism. In *Capitalism and Modern Social Theory.* Cambridge.

Giles, Linda. 1987. Possession Cults on the Swahili Coast. *Africa* 57: 234–57.

Gill, Sam. 1981. *Sacred Words: A Study of Navajo Religion and Prayer.* Westport, CT.

—— 1987. *Native American Religious Action: A Performance Approach to Religion.* Columbia, SC.

Gillette, Maris Boyd. 2000. *Between Mecca and Beijing: Modernization and Consumption among Urban Chinese Muslims.* Stanford.

Gillison, Gillian. 1993. *Between Culture and Fantasy: A New Guinea Highlands Mythology*. Chicago.

Gilmore, David. 1998. *Carnival and Culture: Sex, Symbol, and Status in Spain*. New Haven.

Gilsenan, Michael. 1973. *Saint and Sufi in Modern Egypt*. Oxford.

—— 1992 [1982]. *Recognizing Islam: Religion and Society in the Modern Middle East*. London.

—— 1996. *Lords of the Lebanese Marches*. Berkeley.

—— 2000. Signs of Truth: Enchantment, Modernity and the Dreams of Peasant Women. *JRAI* 6(4): 597–615.

Ginsburg, Faye. 1989. *Contested Lives: The Abortion Debate in an American Community*. Berkeley.

——, Lila Abu-Lughod, and Brian Larkin, eds. 2002. *Media Worlds: Anthropology on New Terrain*. Berkeley.

Ginzburg, Carlo. 1982. *The Cheese and the Worms: The Cosmos of a Sixteenth-Century Miller*. New York.

—— 1985. *The Night Battles: Witchcraft and Agrarian Cults in the 16th and 17th Centuries*. New York.

Girard, René. 1977. *Violence and the Sacred*. Baltimore.

Glaskin, Katie. 2005. Innovation and Ancestral Revelation: The Case of Dreams. *JRAI* 11(2): 297–314.

Glazier, Stephen, ed. 1999. *Anthropology of Religion A Handbook*. Westport, CT.

Glick-Schiller, Nina. 2005. Racialized Nations, Evangelizing Christianity, Police States, and Imperial Power. *AE* 32(4): 526–32.

Gluckman, Max, ed. 1962. *Essays on the Ritual of Social Relations*. Manchester.

—— 1965. The Licence in Ritual. In *Custom and Conflict in Africa*. Oxford.

—— 1970. The Logic of African Science and Witchcraft. In Marwick, ed., *Witchcraft and Sorcery*.

Godelier, Maurice. 1992. Corps, parenté, pouvoir(s) chez les Baruya de Nouvelle-Guinée. *Journal de la Société des Océanistes*.

Gold, Ann Grodzins. 1988. *Fruitful Journeys: The Ways of Rajasthani Pilgrims*. Berkeley.

Goldberg, Harvey, ed. 1987. *Judaism Viewed from Within and Without*. Albany.

—— 2003. *Jewish Passages: Cycles of Jewish Life*. Berkeley.

Goldman, Irving 1975. *The Mouth of Heaven: An Introduction to Kwakiutl Religious Thought*. New York.

—— 2004. *Cubeo Hehénewa Religious Thought: Metaphysics of a Northwestern Amazonian People*. New York.

Goldschmidt, Henry. 2006. *Race and Religion among the Chosen Peoples of Crown Heights*. New Jersey.

Goldstein, Melvin and Matthew Kapstein, eds. 1998. *Buddhism in Contemporary Tibet: Religious Revival and Cultural Identity*. Berkeley.

Goluboff, Sascha L. 2003. *Jewish Russians: Upheavals in a Moscow Synagogue*. Philadelphia.

Gombrich, Richard and Gananath Obeyesekere. 1988. *Buddhism Transformed: Religious Change in Sri Lanka*. Princeton.

Good, Anthony. 1991. *The Female Bridegroom: A Comparative Study of Life-Crisis Rituals in South India and Sri Lanka*. Oxford.

—— 2000. Congealing Divinity: Time, Worship, and Kinship in South Indian Hinduism. *JRAI* 6(2): 273–92.

Goodale, Mark. 2006. Ethical Theory as Social Practice. *AA* 108(1): 25–37.

Goody, Jack. 1962. *Death, Property and the Ancestors: A Study of the Mortuary Customs of the LoDagaa of West Africa*. Stanford.

—— 2003. *Islam in Europe*. Oxford.

Gordillo, Gaston. 2002. The Breath of the Devils: Memories and Places of an Experience of Terror. *AE* 29(1): 33–57.

—— 2004. *Landscapes of Devils: Tensions of Place and Memory in the Argentinean Chaco*. Durham, NC.

Gordon, David. 2004. The Cultural Politics of a Traditional Ceremony: Mutomboko and the Performance of History on the Luapula. *CSSH* 46(1): 63–83.

Gose, Peter. 1994. *Deathly Waters and Hungry Mountains: Agrarian Ritual and Class Formation in an Andean Town*. Toronto.

Gossen, Gary. 1974. *Chamulas in the World*

of the Sun: Time and Space in a Maya Oral Tradition. Cambridge, MA.

Gottlieb, Alma. 1992. *Under the Kapok Tree: Identity and Difference in Beng Thought*. Bloomington.

Goulet, Jean-Guy. 1998. *Ways of Knowing: Experience, Knowledge, and Power among the Dene Tha*. Lincoln.

Gow, Peter. 2001. *An Amazonian Myth and its History*. Oxford.

Graham, Laura. 1995. *Performing Dreams: Discourses of Immortality among the Xavante of Central Brazil*. Austin.

Gramsci, Antonio. 1971. *Selection from the Prison Notebooks*. Q. Hoare and G. Nowell Smith, eds. and trans. New York.

Granet, Marcel. 1975 [1922]. *The Religion of the Chinese People*. M. Freedman, ed. and trans. New York.

Green, Maia. 2003. *Priests, Witches and Power: Popular Christianity after Mission in Southern Tanzania*. Cambridge.

—— and Simeon Mesaki. 2005. The Birth of the "Salon": Poverty, "Modernization," and dealing with Witchcraft in Southern Tanzania. *AE* 32(3): 371–88.

Greenfield, Sidney M. and A. F. Droogers. 2001. *Reinventing Religions: Syncretism and Transformation in Africa and the Americas*. Lanham, MD.

Greenhouse, Carol. 1986. *Praying for Justice: Faith, Order, and Community in an American Town*. Ithaca.

Greenwood, Susan. 2005. *The Nature of Magic: An Anthropology of Consciousness*. Oxford.

Griaule, Marcel 1965. *Conversations with Ogotemmeli: An Introduction to Dogon Religious Ideas*. London.

—— and G. Dieterlin. 1954. The Dogon. In Forde, ed., *African Worlds*.

Grimes, Ronald. 1990. *Ritual Criticism*. Columbia, SC.

Guenther, Mathias. 1999. *Tricksters and Trancers*. Bloomington.

Guest, Kenneth. 2003. *God in Chinatown: Religion and Survival in New York's Evolving Immigrant Community*. New York.

Gupta, Akhil. 2002. Reliving Childhood? The Temporality of Childhood Narratives of Reincarnation. *Ethnos* 67(1): 33–56.

Gupta, Dipankar, ed. 2004. *Caste in Question: Identity or Hierarchy?* New Delhi.

Guss, David. 1989. *To Weave and to Sing: Art, Symbol, and Narrative in the South American Rainforest*. Berkeley.

Hackett, Rosalind I. J. 1996. *Art and Religion in Africa*. London.

—— 2001. Field Envy: Or, the Perils and Pleasures of Doing Fieldwork. *Method and Theory in the Study of Religion* 13(1): 98–109.

—— 2003. Discourses of Demonisation in Africa. *Diogenes* 50(3): 61–75.

—— 2005. Anthropology of Religion. In John Hinnells, ed., *The Routledge Companion to the Study of Religion*. London.

Haeri, Niloofar. 2003. *Sacred Language, Ordinary People*. New York.

Hage, Ghassan. 2003. "Comes a Time We Are All Enthusiasm": Understanding Palestinian Suicide Bombers in Times of Exighophobia. *Public Culture* 15(1): 55–64.

Hagedom, Katherine J. 2001. *Divine Utterances: The Performance of Afro-Cuban Santeria*. Washington.

Hallowell, A. Irving. 1960. Objiwa Ontology, Behavior and World View. In S. Diamond, ed., *Culture in History*. New York.

—— 1967 [1955]. *Culture and Experience*. New York.

Hallpike, C. R. 2004. *The Evolution of Moral Understanding*. Alton, UK.

Hamayon, Roberte. 1990. *La chasse à l'âme: esquisse d'une théorie du chamanisme Sibérien*. Nanterre.

Hammoudi, Abdellah. 2006. *A Season in Mecca: Narrative of a Pilgrimage*. Cambridge.

Handelman, Don. 1989. *Models and Mirrors*. New York.

—— and David Shulman. 1997. *God Inside Out: Siva's Game of Dice*. New York.

—— and David Shulman. 2004. *Siva in the Forest of Pines: An Essay on Sorcery and Self-Knowledge*. New York.

—— and Galina Lindquist, eds. 2005. *Ritual In Its Own Right: Exploring the Dynamics of Transformation*. New York.

Hanks, William. 1991. *Referential Practice: Language and Lived Space in a Maya Community*. Chicago.

Hann, C. M. 2003. Creeds, Cultures and the "Witchery of Music". *JRAI* 9(2): 223–39.

Hansen, Thomas Blom. 1999. *The Saffron Wave: Democracy and Hindu Nationalism in Modern India*. Princeton.

—— 2000. Predicaments of Secularism: Muslim Identities and Politics in Mumbai. *JRAI* 6(2): 255–72.

Hardacre, Helen. 1989. *Shinto and the State, 1868–1988*. Princeton.

Harding, Susan. 1987. Convicted by the Holy Spirit: The Rhetoric of Fundamental Baptist Conversion. *AE* 14: 167–81.

—— 1991. Representing Fundamentalism: The Problem of the Repugnant Cultural Other. *Social Research* 58(2): 373–93.

—— 2001. *The Book of Jerry Falwell: Fundamentalist Language and Politics*. Princeton.

Harris, Grace. 1978. *Casting Out Anger*. Cambridge.

Harris, Hermione. 2006. *Yoruba in Diaspora: An African Church in London*. New York.

Harris, Marvin. 1985. *The Sacred Cow and the Abominable Pig*. New York.

Harris, Max. 2000. *Aztecs, Moors, and Christians: Festivals of Reconquest in Mexico and Spain*. Austin, TX.

Harrison, Simon. 1990. *Stealing People's Names: History and Politics in a Sepik River Cosmology*. Cambridge.

—— 1993. *The Mask of War: Violence, Ritual, and the Self in Melanesia*. Manchester.

—— 2004. Emotional Climates: Ritual, Seasonality and Affective Disorders. *JRAI* 10(3): 583–602.

Harvey, Graham. 2006. *Animism: Respecting the Living World*. New York.

Hatfield, Donald J. 2002. Fate in the Narrativity and Experience of Selfhood, a Case from Taiwanese Chhiam Divination. *AE* 29(4): 857–77.

Hauser-Schäublin, Brigitta. 2005. Temple and King: Resource Management, Rituals and Redistribution in Early Bali. *JRAI* 11(4): 747–71.

Headley, Stephen. 2001. *From Cosmogony to Exorcism in a Javanese Genesis: The Split Seed*. Oxford.

Heady, Patrick. 2003. Conscripts and Christians: Representing Kinship and Affinity in the Carnian Alps. *JRAI* 9(1): 77–95.

Heald, Suzette. 1989. *Controlling Anger*. Manchester.

Hebdige, Dick. 1979. *Subculture: The Meaning of Style*. London.

Hecht, Jennifer. 2003. *The End of the Soul: Scientific Modernity, Atheism, and Anthropology in France*. New York.

Heelas, Paul. 1996. *The New Age Movement: The Celebration of the Self and the Sacralization of Modernity*. Oxford.

—— and David Martin. 1998. *Religion, Modernity and Postmodernity*. Oxford.

Hefner, Robert. 1985. *Hindu Javanese: Tengger Tradition and Islam*. Princeton.

—— ed. 1993. *Conversion to Christianity: Historical and Anthropological Perspectives on a Great Transformation*. Berkeley.

—— 1998. Multiple Modernities: Christianity, Islam, and Hinduism in a Globalizing Age. *Annual Review of Anthropology* 27: 83–104.

—— 2000. *Civil Islam: Muslims and Democratization in Indonesia*. Princeton.

—— 2002. Global Violence and Indonesian Muslim Politics. *AA* 104(3): 754–66.

—— 2005. *Remaking Muslim Politics: Pluralism, Contestation, Democratization*. Princeton.

—— and Patricia Horvatich, eds. 1997. *Islam in an Era of Nation States: Politics and Religious Renewal in Muslim Southeast Asia*. Honolulu.

—— and Muhammad Qasim Zaman, eds, 2006. *Schooling Islam*. Princeton.

Hegland, Mary. 1998. Flagellation and Fundamentalism: (Trans)forming Meaning, Identity and Gender through Pakistani Women's Rituals of Mourning. *AE* 25(2): 240–66.

—— 2003. Shi'a Women's Rituals in Northwestern Pakistan: The Shortcomings and Significance of Resistance. *Anthropological Quarterly* 76(3): 411–42.

Herbert, Eugenia. 1993. *Iron, Gender, and Power: Rituals of Transformation in African Societies*. Bloomington.

Herdt, Gilbert, ed. 1982. *Rituals of Manhood:*

Male Initiation in Papua New Guinea. Berkeley.

—— 1984. *Ritualized Homosexuality in Melanesia*. Berkeley.

—— 2003. *Secrecy and Cultural Reality: Utopian Ideologies of the New Guinea Men's House*. Ann Arbor.

—— and Michelle Stephen, eds. 1989. *The Religious Imagination in New Guinea*. New Brunswick, NJ.

Hertz, Robert. 1960 [1909]. *Death and the Right Hand*. London.

Herzfeld, Michael. 1985. *The Poetics of Manhood: Contest and Identity in a Cretan Mountain Village*. Princeton.

Heusch, Luc de. 1985. *Sacrifice in Africa. A Structuralist Approach*. Manchester.

—— 1997. The Symbolic Mechanisms of Sacred Kingship: Rediscovering Frazer. *JRAI*, n.s. 3: 213–32.

Hiatt, L. R. ed. 1975. *Australian Aboriginal Mythology*. Canberra.

Hicks, David. 2003. *Tetum Ghosts and Kin: Fertility and Gender in East Timor*. Long Grove, IL.

Hinson, Glenn. 2001. *Fire in my Bones: Transcendence and the Holy Spirit in African American Gospel*. Philadelphia.

Hirschkind, Charles. 2001a. Civic Virtue and Religious Reason: An Islamic Counter-Public. *Cultural Anthropology* 16(1): 3–34.

—— 2001b. Passional Preaching, Aural Sensibility, and the Islamic Revival in Cairo. *AE* 28(2): 536–54.

—— 2006. *The Ethics of Listening: Cassette Sermons and Islamic Counterpublics*. New York.

—— and Saba Mahmood. 2002. Feminism, the Taliban, and the Politics of Counter-Insurgency. *Anthropological Quarterly* 752: 339–54.

—— and David Scott. 2006. *Powers of the Secular Modern: Talal Asad And His Interlocutors*. Stanford.

Hobart, Angela. 2003. *Healing Performances of Bali: Between Darkness and Light*. Oxford.

Hobbes, Thomas. 1991 [1651]. *Leviathan*. Richard Tuck, ed. Cambridge.

Hobsbawm, E. J. and T. O. Ranger, eds. 1983. *The Invention of Tradition*. Cambridge.

Hocart, A. M. 1970 [1936]. *Kings and Councillors*. Chicago.

Hodgson, Dorothy. 2005. *The Church of Women: Gendered Encounters between Maasai and Missionaries*. Indiana.

Hoehler-Fatton, Cynthia. 1996. *Women of Fire and Spirit: History, Faith and Gender in Roho Religion in Western Kenya*. New York.

Holbraad, Martin. 2005. Expending Multiplicity: Money in Cuban Ifa Cults. *JRAI* 11(2): 231–54.

Hollis, Martin and Steven Lukes, eds. 1994 [1982]. *Rationality and Relativism*. Cambridge, MA.

Holmberg, David. 1989. *Order in Paradox: Myth, Ritual and Exchange among Nepal's Tamang*. Ithaca.

—— 2000. Derision, Exorcism, and the Ritual Production of Power. *AE* 27(4): 927–49.

Holy, Ladislav. 2006. *Religion and Custom in a Muslim Society: The Berti of Sudan*. Cambridge.

Hornborg, Alf. 2006. Animism, Fetishism, and Objectivism as Strategies for Knowing (or Not Knowing) the World. *Ethnos* 71(1): 21–32.

Horton, Robin. 1970 [1967]. African Traditional Thought and Western Science. In Wilson, ed., *Rationality*.

—— 1971. African Conversion. *Africa* 41: 85–108.

—— 1993. *Patterns of Thought in Africa and the West: Essays on Magic, Religion and Science*. Cambridge.

—— and R. Finnegan, eds. 1973. *Modes of Thought: Essays on Thinking in Western and Non-Western Societies*. London.

Hoskins, Janet. 1993. *The Play of Time: Kodi Perspectives on Calendars, History, and Exchange*. Berkeley.

—— ed. 1996. *Headhunting and the Social Imagination in Southeast Asia*. Stanford.

Howe, Leo. 2000. Risk, Ritual and Performance. *JRAI* 6(1): 63–80.

—— 2001. *Hinduism and Hierarchy in Bali*. Santa Fe.

—— 2005. *Changing World of Bali: Religion, Society and Tourism*. Oxford.

Howell, Signe. 1984. *Society and Cosmos: Chewong of Peninsular Malaysia*. New York.

—— ed. 1996. *For the Sake of Our Future: Sacrificing in Eastern Indonesia*. Leiden.

—— ed. 1997. *The Ethnography of Moralities*. London.

Howes, David, ed. 1991. *The Varieties of Sensory Experience*. Toronto.

—— 2003. *Sensual Relations: Engaging the Senses in Culture and Social Theory*. Ann Arbor, MI.

—— ed. 2005. *The Empire of the Senses: The Sensual Culture Reader*. Oxford.

Hoy, David. 1978. *The Critical Circle: Literature, History, and Philosophical Hermeneutics*. Berkeley.

Hsu, Francis. 1948. *Under the Ancestor's Shadow*. New York.

Huber, Toni. 1999. *The Cult of Pure Crystal Mountain: Popular Pilgrimage and Visionary Landscape in Southeast Tibet*. New York.

Hubert, Henri and Marcel Mauss. 1964 [1898]. *Sacrifice: Its Nature and Function*. London.

Hugh-Jones, Christine. 1979. *From the Milk River: Spatial and Temporal Processes in Northwest Amazonia*. Cambridge.

Hugh-Jones, Stephen. 1979. *The Palm and the Pleiades: Initiation and Cosmology in Northwest Amazonia*. Cambridge.

Huizinga, Johannes. 1955. *Homo Ludens: A Study of the Play-Element in Culture*. Boston.

Humphrey, Caroline. 2002. Rituals of Death as a Context for Understanding Personal Property in Socialist Mongolia. *JRAI* 8(1): 65–87.

—— and James Laidlaw. 1994. *The Archetypal Actions of Ritual: A Theory of Ritual Illustrated by the Jain Rite of Worship*. Oxford.

—— and Nicholas Thomas, eds. 1994. *Shamanism, History, and the State*. Ann Arbor.

—— and Urgunge Onon. 1996. *Shamans and Elders: Experience, Knowledge, and Power among the Daur Mongols*. Oxford.

Humphreys, S. C. and Helen King, eds. 1981. *Mortality and Immortality: The Anthropology and Archaeology of Death*. London.

Hunt, Eva 1977. *The Transformation of the Hummingbird: Cultural Roots of a Zinacantecan Mythical Poem*. Ithaca.

Huntington, Richard and Peter Metcalf. 1979. *Celebrations of Death: The Anthropology of Mortuary Ritual*. Cambridge.

Hussain, Monirul and Lipi Ghosh, eds. 2002. *Religious Minorities in South Asia: Selected Essays on Post-Colonial Situations*. New Delhi.

Hymes, Dell. 2003. *Now I Know Only So Far: Essays in Ethnopoetics*. Lincoln, Nebraska.

Hymes, Robert. 2002. *Way and Byway: Taoism, Local Religion, and Models of Divinity in Sung and Modern China*. Berkeley.

Hynes, W. J. and W. G. Doty, eds. 1993. *Mythical Trickster Figures*. Tuscaloosa.

Ikenga–Metuh, E. 1987. The Shattered Microcosm: A Critical Survey of Explanations of Conversion in Africa. In K. H. Petersen, ed., *Religion, Development, and African Identity*. Uppsala.

Ingham, John. 1986. *Mary, Michael, and Lucifer: Folk Catholicism in Central Mexico*. Austin.

Ingold, Tim. 2006. Rethinking the Animate, Re-Animating Thought. *Ethnos* 71(1): 9–20.

Iteanu, André. 1983. *La Ronde des Echanges: De la Circulation aux Valeurs chez les Orokaiva*. Paris.

Ivakhiv, Adrian J. 2001. *Claiming Sacred Ground: Pilgrim and Politics at Glastonbury and Sedona*. Bloomington.

Ivy, Marilyn. 1995. *Discourses of the Vanishing: Modernity, Phantasm, Japan*. Chicago.

Izard, Michel and Pierre Smith. 1982. *Between Belief and Transgression: Structuralist Essays in Religion, History, and Myth*. Chicago.

Jacka, Jerry. 2002. Cults and Christianity among the Enga and Ipili. *Oceania* 72(3): 196–214.

—— 2005. Emplacement and Millennial Expectations in an Era of Development and

Globalization: Heaven and the Appeal of Christianity for the Ipili. *AA* 107(4): 643–53.

Jackson, Michael. 1982. *Allegories of the Wilderness: Ethics and Ambiguity in Kuranko Narratives*. Bloomington.

—— 1989. *Paths Toward a Clearing*. Bloomington.

—— 1998. *Minima Ethnographica. Intersubjectivity and the Anthropological Project*. Chicago.

—— 2005. *Existential Anthropology: Events, Exigencies, and Effects*. New York.

Jacobson, Shari. 2006. Modernity, Conservative Religious Movements, and the Female Subject: Newly Ultraorthodox Sephardi Women in Buenos Aires. *AA* 108(2): 336–46.

Jacobson-Widding, Anita. 1991. *Body and Space: Symbolic Models of Unity and Division in African Cosmology and Experience*. Uppsala.

Jakobson, Roman. 1960. Linguistics and Poetics. In T. Sebeok, ed., *Style in Language*. Cambridge, MA.

James, Wendy. 1988. *The Listening Ebony: Moral Knowledge, Religion and Power among the Uduk of Sudan*. Oxford.

—— ed. 1995. *The Politics of Certainty: Religious and Cultural Formulations*. London.

—— 2004. *The Ceremonial Animal: A New Portrait of Anthropology*. Oxford.

—— and N. Allen, eds. 1998. *Marcel Mauss: A Centenary Tribute*. New York.

—— and Douglas Johnson, eds. 1988. *Vernacular Christianity*. Oxford.

James, William. 1961 [1902]. *The Varieties of Religious Experience*. New York.

Jameson, Fredric. 1991. *Postmodernism or, The Cultural Logic of Late Capitalism*. Durham, NC.

Janzen, John. 1982. *Lemba, 1650–1930: A Drum of Affliction in Africa and the New World*. New York.

—— 1992. *Ngoma. Discourses of Healing in Central and Southern Africa*. Berkeley.

Jarvis, Simon. 2000. Old Idolatry: Rethinking "Ideology" and "Materialism." In Rossington and Whitehead, eds., *Between the Psyche and the Polis*. Aldershot, UK.

Jebens, Holger. 2005. *Pathways to Heaven: Contesting Mainline and Fundamentalist Christianity in Papua New Guinea*. New York.

Jing, Jun. 1996. *The Temple of Memories: History, Power, and Morality in a Chinese Village*. Stanford.

Johnson, Douglas. 1994. *Nuer Prophets: A History of Prophecy from the Upper Nile*. Oxford.

Johnson, Paul C. 2005. *Secrets, Gossip and Gods: The Transformation of Brazilian Candomblé*. Oxford.

Juillerat, Bernard. 1992. *Shooting the Sun: Ritual and Meaning in West Sepik*. Washington, DC.

—— 1996. *Children of the Blood: Society, Reproduction and Cosmology in New Guinea*. Oxford.

Julé, Allyson, ed. 2005. *Gender and the Language of Religion*. New York.

Junod, Henri. 1962. *The Life of a South African Tribe*. 2 vols. London.

Kahn, Susan Martha. 2000. *Reproducing Jews: A Cultural Account of Assisted Conception in Israel*. Durham.

Kalmar, Ivan D. and Derek J. Penslar, eds. 2004. *Orientalism and the Jews*. Hanover.

Kan, Sergei. 1989. *Symbolic Immortality: The Tlingit Potlatch of the 19th Century*. Washington, DC.

—— 1999. *Memory Eternal: Tlingit Culture and Russian Orthodox Christianity through Two Centuries*. Seattle.

Kandiyoti, Deniz and Nadira Azimova. 2004. The Communal and the Sacred: Women's Worlds of Ritual in Uzbekistan. *JRAI* 10(2): 327–49.

Kaplan, Martha. 1995. *Neither Cargo Nor Cult: Ritual Politics and the Colonial Imagination in Fiji*. Durham.

Kapferer, Bruce, ed. 1976. *Transaction and Meaning: Directions in the Anthropology of Exchange and Symbolic Behavior*. Philadelphia.

—— 1983. *A Celebration of Demons: Exorcism and the Aesthetics of Healing in Sri Lanka*. Bloomington.

—— 1988. *Legends of People, Myths of State: Violence, Intolerance, and Political Culture in Sri Lanka and Australia*. Washington, DC.

—— 1997. *The Feast of the Sorcerer*. Chicago.

—— 2000a. Sexuality and the Art of Seduction in Sinhalese Exorcism. *Ethnos* 65(1): 5–32.

—— 2000b. The Sorcery of Consciousness: A Sinhala Buddhist Ritual Discourse on the Dynamics of Consciousness. In Mike Ball, ed., Accessing Aspects of Consciousness, *Communication & Cognition* 33(1/2): 97–120.

—— ed. 2003. *Beyond Rationalism: Rethinking Magic, Witchcraft and Sorcery*. New York.

—— and Angela Hobart, eds. 2005. *Aesthetics in Performance: Formations of Symbolic Construction and Experience*. New York.

Karp, Ivan, and Charles Bird, eds. 1980. *Explorations of African Systems of Thought*. Washington, DC.

Keane, Webb. 1997a. Religious Language. *Annual Review of Anthropology* 26: 47–71.

—— 1997b. *Signs of Recognition: Powers and Hazards of Representation in an Indonesian Society*. Berkeley.

—— 1998. Calvin in the Tropics: Objects and Subjects at the Religious Frontier. In Spyer, ed., *Border Fetishisms*.

—— 2002. Sincerity, "Modernity," and the Protestants. *Cultural Anthropology* 17(1): 65–92.

Keane, Webb. 2006. *Christian Moderns: Freedom and Fetish in the Mission Encounter*. Berkeley.

Keeler, Ward. 1987. *Javanese Shadow Plays, Javanese Selves*. Princeton.

Keesing, Roger. 1982. *Kwaio Religion*. New York.

Kehoe, Alice. 1989. *The Ghost Dance: Ethnohistory and Revitalization*. New York.

—— 2000. *Shamans and Religion: An Anthropological Exploration in Critical Thinking*. Long Grove.

Keller, Eva. 2004. Towards Complete Clarity: Bible Study among Seventh-Day Adventists in Madagascar. *Ethnos* 69(1): 89–112.

—— 2005. *The Road to Clarity: Seventh-Day Adventism in Madagascar*. New York.

—— 2006. Scriptural Study as Normal Science: Seventh-Day Adventist Practice on the East Coast of Madagascar. In F. Cannell, ed., *The Anthropology of Christianity*. Durham.

Kelly, John D. 1991. *A Politics of Virtue: Hinduism, Sexuality, and Countercolonial Discourse in Fiji*. Chicago.

—— and Martha Kaplan. 1990. History, Structure, and Ritual. *Annual Review of Anthropology*. 19: 119–50.

Kelly, Raymond C. 1976. Witchcraft and Sexual Relations: An Exploration in the Social and Semantic Implications of the Structure of Belief. In Paula Brown and Georgeda Buchbinder, eds., *Man and Woman in the New Guinea Highlands*. Washington, DC.

—— 1993. *Constructing Inequality: The Fabrication of a Hierarchy of Virtue among the Etoro*. Ann Arbor.

Kendall, Laurel. 1985. *Shamans, Housewives, and Other Restless Spirits: Women in Korean Ritual Life*. Honolulu.

Kent, Alexandra. 2004. Divinity, Miracles and Charity in the Sathya Sai Baba Movement of Malaysia. *Ethnos* 69(1): 43–62.

Kenyon, Susan. 1991. *Five Women of Sennar: Culture and Change in Central Sudan*. Oxford.

Kershaw, Eva Maria. 2000. *A Study of Brunei Dusun Religion: Ethnic Priesthood on a Frontier of Islam*. Phillips, ME.

Kertzer, David. 1980. *Comrades and Christians: Religion and Political Struggle in Communist Italy*. Cambridge.

—— 1988. *Ritual, Politics, and Power*. New Haven.

Keyes, Charles and V. Daniel, eds. 1983. *Karma*. Berkeley.

Keyes, Charles, Laurel Kendall, and Helen Hardacre, eds. 1995. *Asian Visions of Authority: Religion and the Modern States of East and Southeast Asia*. Honolulu.

Kim, Chongho. 2003. *Korean Shamanism: The Cultural Paradox*. Aldershot.

Kipp, Rita. 1990. *The Early Years of a Dutch Colonial Mission: The Karo Field*. Ann Arbor.

—— 1993. *Dissociated Identities: Ethnicity, Religion, and Class in an Indonesian Society*. Ann Arbor.

—— and Susan Rodgers, eds. 1987. *Indonesian Religions in Transition*. Tucson.

Kirsch, Thomas. 2004. Restaging the Will to Believe: Religious Pluralism, Anti Syncretism, and the Problem of Belief. *AA* 106(4): 699–709.

Kivelson, Valerie. 2003. Male Witches and Gendered Categories in Seventeenth Century Russia. *CSSH* 45(3): 606–31.

Khan, Naveeda. 2006. Of Children and Jinn: An Inquiry into an Unexpected Friendship during Uncertain Times. *Cultural Anthropology* 21(2): 234–65.

Klass, Morton. 1995. *Ordered Universes: Approaches to the Anthropology of Religion*. Boulder.

—— and Maxine Weisgrau, eds. 1999. *Across the Boundaries of Belief: Contemporary Issues in the Anthropology of Religion*. Boulder.

Klassen, Pamela. 2001. *Blessed Events: Religion and Home Birth in America*. Princeton.

Klima, Alan. 2002. *The Funeral Casino: Meditation, Massacre, and Exchange with the Dead in Thailand*. Princeton.

Knauft, Bruce. 1985. *Good Company and Violence: Sorcery and Social Action in a Lowland New Guinea Society*. Berkeley.

—— 1993. *South Coast New Guinea Cultures*. Cambridge.

Kneale-Gould, Rebecca. 2005. *At Home in Nature: Modern Homesteading and Spiritual Practice in America*. Berkeley.

Knobler, Adam. 2006. Holy Wars, Empires, and the Portability of the Past: The Modern Uses of Medieval Crusades. *CSSH* 48(2): 293–325.

Komlosy, Anouska. 2004. Procession and Water Splashing: Expressions of Locality and Nationality during Dai New Year in Xishuangbanna. *JRAI* 10(2): 351–73.

Kopytoff, Igor. 1971. Ancestors and Elders in Africa. *Africa* 43(2): 129–42.

Korom, Frank J. 2003. *Hosay Trinidad: Muharram Performances in an Indo-Caribbean Diaspora*. Philadelphia.

Koselleck, Reinhart. 1985. *Futures Past: On the Semantics of Historical Time*. Cambridge, MA.

Koshul, Basit Bilal. 2005. *The Postmodern Significance of Max Weber's Legacy*. New York.

Kovecses, Zoltan. 2005. *Metaphor in Culture: Universality and Variation*. Cambridge.

Kovic, Christine. 2005. *Mayan Voices for Human Rights: Displaced Catholics in Highland Chiapas*. Austin.

Kramer, Fritz. 1993. *The Red Fez: Art and Spirit Possession in Africa*. London.

Kratz, Corinne. 1994. *Affecting Performance: Meaning, Movement, and Experience in Okiek Women's Initiation*. Washington, DC.

Kreinath, Jens, Annette Deschner and Constance Hartung, eds. 2004. *The Dynamics of Changing Rituals: The Transformation of Religious Rituals within Their Social and Cultural Context*. New York.

Krige, E. J. and J. D. Krige. 1943. *The Realm of the Rain-Queen*. London.

Kroeber, Alfred A. 1979a [1920]. Totem and Taboo: An Ethnologic Psychoanalysis. In Lessa and Vogt, eds., *Reader in Comparative Religion*.

—— 1979b [1939]. Totem and Taboo in Retrospect. In Lessa and Vogt, eds., *Reader in Comparative Religion*.

Krohn-Hansen, Christian. 2001. A Tomb for Columbus in Santo Domingo: Political Cosmology, Population and Racial Frontiers. *Social Anthropology* 9(2): 165–92.

Kugelmass, Jack, ed. 1988. *Between Two Worlds: Ethnographic Essays on American Jewry*. Ithaca.

—— 1994. *Masked Culture: The Greenwich Village Halloween Parade*. New York.

—— 1996 [1986]. *The Miracle of Intervale Avenue: The Story of a Jewish Congregation in the South Bronx*. New York.

Kuhn, Thomas. 1970. *The Structure of Scientific Revolutions*, 2nd edn. Chicago.

Kuipers, Joel. 1990. *Power in Performance: The Creation of Textual Authority in Weyewa Ritual Speech*. Philadelphia.

Kwon, Heonik. 2000. To Hunt the Black Shaman: Memory of The Great Purge in East Siberia. *Etnofoor* XIII(1): 33–50.

—— 2006. *After the Massacre: Commemoration and Consolation in Ha My and My Lai*. Berkeley.

—— 2008. *Ghosts of War in Vietnam.* Cambridge.

LaBarre, Weston. 1970. *The Ghost Dance.* New York.

La Fontaine, Jean, ed. 1972. *The Interpretation of Ritual.* London.

—— 1985. *Initiation.* Harmondsworth.

—— 1998. *Speak of the Devil: Allegations of Satanic Child Abuse in Contemporary England.* Cambridge.

Laidlaw, James. 1995. *Riches and Renunciation: Religion, Society, and Economy among the Jains.* Oxford.

Lakoff, George and Mark Johnson. 1980. *Metaphors We Live By.* Chicago.

Lambek, Michael. 1981. *Human Spirits: A Cultural Account of Trance in Mayotte.* New York.

—— 1992. Taboo as Cultural Practice among Malagasy Speakers. *Man* 27: 245–66.

—— 1993a. *Knowledge and Practice in Mayotte: Local Discourses of Islam, Sorcery, and Spirit Possession.* Toronto.

—— 1993b. Cultivating Critical Distance: Oracles and the Politics of Voice, *PoLAR, Political and Legal Anthropology Review* 16(2): 9–18.

—— 1996. The Past Imperfect: Remembering as Moral Practice. In P. Antze and M. Lambek, eds., *Tense Past: Cultural Essays in Trauma and Memory.* New York.

—— 1998. The Sakalava Poiesis of History. *AE* 25: 106–27.

—— 2000a. The Anthropology of Religion and the Quarrel between Poetry and Philosophy. *Current Anthropology* 41: 309–20.

—— 2000b. Localising Islamic Performances in Mayotte. In Parkin and Headley, eds., *Islamic Prayer across the Indian Ocean.* New York.

—— 2001. The Value of Coins in a Sakalava Polity: Money, Death, and Historicity in Mahajanga, Madagascar. *CSSH* 43(4): 735–62.

—— 2002a. *The Weight of the Past: Living with History in Mahajanga, Madagascar.* New York.

—— 2002b. Nuriaty, the Saint and the Sultan: Virtuous Subject and Subjective Virtuoso of the Post-Modern Colony. In Richard Werbner, ed., *Post-Colonial Subjectivities.* London.

—— 2003a. Memory in a Maussian Universe. In Susannah Radstone and Katharine Hodgkin, eds., *Regimes of Memory.* London.

—— 2003b. Rheumatic Irony: Questions of Agency and Self-Deception as Refracted through the Art of Living with Spirits. In Lambek and Antze, pp. 40–59.

—— 2003c. Fantasy in Practice: Projection and Introjection, or the Witch and the Spirit-Medium. In Bruce Kapferer, ed., *Beyond Rationalism: Rethinking Magic, Witchcraft and Sorcery.* New York and Oxford.

—— 2004. The Saint, the Sea Monster, and an Invitation to a Dîner-Dansant: Ethnographic Reflections on the Edgy Passage – and the Double Edge – of Modernity, Mayotte 1975–2001. *Anthropologica* 46(1): 57–68.

—— 2006a. The Playful Side of Islam and Its Possible Fate in Mayotte. In R. Loimeier and R. Seesemann, eds., *Dini na Dunia: The Global Worlds of the Swahili.* Hamburg, pp. 161–86.

—— 2006b. Anthropology and Religion. In Philip Clayton, ed., *The Oxford Handbook of Religion and Science.* Oxford, pp. 271–89.

—— 2006c. What's In a Name? Name Bestowal and the Identity of Spirits in Mayotte and Northwest Madagascar. In B. Bodenhorn and G. vom Bruck, eds., *The Anthropology of Names and Naming.* Cambridge, pp. 116–38.

—— 2007a. Sacrifice and the Problem of Beginning: Reflections from Sakalava Mythopraxis. *JRAI* 13(1): 19–38.

—— 2007b. Provincializing God? Provocations, Post-Secular Apprehensions from an Anthropology of Religion. In H. de Vries, ed., *Religion: Beyond a Concept.* New York.

—— 2007c. On Catching Up with Oneself: Learning to Know that One Means What One Does. In D. Berliner and R. Sarró, eds., *Learning Religion.* Oxford.

—— and Paul Antze, eds. 2003. *Illness and Irony: On the Ambiguity of Suffering in Culture.* New York.

—— and Andrew Strathern, eds. 1998. *Bodies and Persons: Comparative Perspectives from Africa and Melanesia*. Cambridge.

—— and Andrew Walsh. 1999. The Imagined Community of the Antankarana. Identity, History, and Ritual in Northern Madagascar. In Middleton, ed., *Ancestors, Power & History in Madagascar*. Leiden.

Lan, David. 1985. *Guns and Rain: Guerrillas and Spirit Mediums in Zimbabwe*. Berkeley.

Lane, C. 1981. *The Rites of Rulers: Ritual in Industrial Society – The Soviet Case*. Cambridge.

Langer, Susanne K. 1963 [1942]. *Philosophy in a New Key*. New York.

Langford, Jean. 1999. Medical Mimesis: Healing Signs of a Cosmopolitan "Quack." *AE* 26(1): 24–46.

—— 2002. *Fluent Bodies: Ayurvedic Remedies for Postcolonial Imbalance*. Durham, NC.

—— 2005. Spirits of Dissent: Southeast Asian Memories and Disciplines of Death. *Comparative Studies of South Asia, Africa, and the Middle East* 25(1): 161–76.

Langhor, Vickie. 2005. Colonial Education Systems and the Spread of Local Religious Movements: The Cases of British Egypt and Punjab. *CSSH* 147(2): 161–89.

Lansing, J. Stephen. 1991. *Priests and Programmers: Technologies of Power in the Engineered Landscape of Bali*. Princeton.

Lantenari, Vittorio. 1963. *The Religions of the Oppressed*. New York.

Lattas, Andrew. 1998. *Cultures of Secrecy: Reinventing Race in Bush Kaliai Cargo Cults*. Madison, WI.

—— 2006. The Utopian Promise of Government. *JRAI* 12(1): 129–50.

Launay, Robert. 1992. *Beyond the Stream: Islam and Society in a West African Town*. Berkeley.

Lawrence, Peter. 1964. *Road Belong Cargo. A Study of the Cargo Cult in the Madang District, New Guinea*. New York.

Lawrence, Peter and Mervyn Meggitt, eds. 1965. *Gods, Ghosts, and Men in Melanesia*. Melbourne.

Leach, E. R. 1954. Myth as a Justification for Faction and Social Change. In *Political Systems of Highland Burma*. Boston.

—— 1961. Two Essays Concerning the Symbolic Representation of Time. In *Rethinking Anthropology*. London.

—— 1964. Anthropological Aspects of Language: Animal Categories and Verbal Abuse. In E. H. Lenneberg, ed., *New Directions in the Study of Language*. Cambridge, MA.

—— 1966. Ritualization in Man. *Philosophical Transactions of the Royal Society of London*, Series B 251(722): 403–8.

—— ed. 1967. *The Structural Study of Myth and Totemism*. London.

—— ed. 1968. *Dialectic in Practical Religion*. Cambridge.

—— 1969. *Genesis as Myth and Other Essays*. London.

—— 1970. *Claude Lévi–Strauss*. New York.

—— 1976. *Culture and Communication*. Cambridge.

Leacock, Seth and Ruth Leacock. 1972. *Spirits of the Deep: A Study of an Afro-Brazilian Cult*. Garden City, NY.

Leavitt, John, ed. 1997. *Poetry and Prophecy: The Anthropology of Inspiration*. Ann Arbor.

Lee, Benjamin. 1997. *Talking Heads: Language, Metalanguage, and the Semiotics of Subjectivity*. Durham, NC.

—— and Greg Urban, eds. 1989. *Signs, Self, and Society*. Berlin.

Lee, Dorothy. 1959. *Freedom and Culture*. Englewood Cliffs, NJ.

Leenhardt, Maurice. 1979 [1947]. *Do Kamo: Person and Myth in the Melanesian World*. Chicago.

Lehmann, Hartmut and G. Roth, eds. 1993 *Weber's "Protestant Ethic": Origin, Evidence, Contexts*. Cambridge.

Leroy, John. 1985. *Fabricated World: An Interpretation of Kewa Tales*. Vancouver.

Lessa, William and Evan Vogt, eds. 1979. *Reader in Comparative Religion: An Anthropological Approach*, 4th edn. New York.

Lester, Rebecca J. 2005. *Jesus in our Wombs: Embodying Modernity in a Mexican Convent*. Berkeley.

Levine, Sarah and David Gellner. 2005. *Rebuilding Buddhism: The Theravada Movement in Twentieth-Century Nepal*. Cambridge, Mass.

Lévi–Strauss, Claude. 1963a. *Structural Anthropology*. Vol. I. New York.

—— 1963b [1949]. The Sorcerer and His Magic. In Lévi-Strauss 1963a.

—— 1963c [1949]. The Effectiveness of Symbols. In Lévi-Strauss 1963a.

—— 1963d [1955]. The Structural Study of Myth. In Lévi-Strauss 1963a.

—— 1963e [1962]. *Totemism*, R. Needham, trans. Beacon.

—— 1964–71 *Mythologiques*. 4 vols. Paris.

—— 1966 [1962]. *The Savage Mind*. Chicago.

—— 1967. The Story of Asdiwal. In Leach ed., *The Structural Study of Myth and Totemism*.

—— 1969 [1964]. *The Raw and the Cooked: Introduction to a Science of Mythology*. Vol. 1. London.

—— 1970 [1955]. *Tristes Tropiques*. New York.

—— 1973. *From Honey to Ashes*. London.

—— 1988 [1985]. *The Jealous Potter*, Bénédicte Chorier, trans. Chicago.

Levy, Robert. 1990. *Mesocosm: Hinduism and the Organization of a Traditional Newar City in Nepal*. Stanford.

Lévy-Bruhl, Lucien. 1949. *Les Carnets de Lucien Lévy-Bruhl*. Paris.

—— 1966 [1923]. *Primitive Mentality*. Boston.

—— 1985 [1910]. *How Natives Think*. Trans. Lilian A. Clare. Princeton.

Lewis, Gilbert. 1980. *Day of Shining Red: An Essay on the Understanding of Ritual*. Cambridge.

—— 2002. Between Public Assertion and Private Doubts: A Sepik Ritual of Healing and Reflexivity. *Social Anthropology* 10(1): 11–21.

Lewis, I. M. 1971. *Ecstatic Religion: An Anthropological Study of Spirit Possession and Shamanism*. Harmondsworth.

—— 1986. *Religion in Context: Cults and Charisma*. Cambridge.

Lewis, Laura A. 2003. *Hall of Mirrors: Power, Witchcraft, and Caste in Colonial Mexico*. London.

Lewis-Williams, J. D. and D. G. Pearce. 2004. *San Spirituality: Roots, Expression, and Social Consequences*. Walnut Creek, CA.

Lienhardt, Godfrey. 1960: Religion. In H. Shapiro, ed., *Man, Culture, and Society*. New York.

—— 1961. *Divinity and Experience: The Religion of the Dinka*. Oxford.

Lightfoot, Kent. 2004. *Indians, Missionaries, and Merchants: The Legacy of Colonial Encounters on the California Frontiers*. Berkeley.

Lincoln, Bruce. 1989. *Discourse and the Construction of Society: Comparative Studies of Myth, Ritual, and Classification*. New York.

—— 2000. *Theorizing Myth: Narrative, Ideology, and Scholarship*. Chicago.

Lindenbaum, Shirley. 1979. *Kuru Sorcery: Disease and Danger in the New Guinea Highlands*. Palo Alto.

Lindholm, Charles. 1990. *Charisma*. Cambridge, MA.

—— 2002. Authenticity, Anthropology and the Sacred. *Anthropological Quarterly* 75(2): 331–8.

Lindquist, Galina. 1997. *Shamanic Performances on the Urban Scene: Neo-Shamanism in Contemporary Sweden*. Stockholm.

Lindstrom, Lamont. 1990. *Knowledge and Power in a South Pacific Society*. Washington, DC.

—— 1993. *Cargo Cults: Strange Stories of Desire from Melanesia and Beyond*. Honolulu.

Littlewood, Roland. 2001. *Religion, Agency, Restitution*. Oxford.

Loewe, Donald and Helene Hoffman. 2002. Building the New Zion: Unfinished Conversations between the Jews of Venta Prieta, Mexico, and Their Neighbors to the North. *AA* 104(4): 1135–48.

Long, Norman. 1968. *Social Change and the Individual: A Study of the Social and Religious Responses to Innovation in a Zambian Rural Community*. Manchester.

Lovell, Nadia. 2003. *Cord of Blood: Possession and the Making of Voodoo*. London.

Lowie, Robert. 1935. *The Crow Indians*. New York.

—— 1948. *Primitive Religion*. New York.

Luhrmann, Tanya. 1989. *Persuasions of the*

Witch's Craft: Ritual Magic in Contemporary England. Cambridge, MA.

—— 2004. Metakinesis: How God Becomes Intimate in Contemporary U.S. Christianity. *AA* 106(3): 518–28.

Lukens-Bull, Ronald. 2005. *A Peaceful Jihad: Negotiating Identity and Modernity in Muslim Java.* New York.

Lukes, Steven. 1973. *Emile Durkheim: His Life and Work.* New York.

Lutkehaus, Nancy and Paul Roscoe, eds. 1995. *Gender Ritual: Feminine Initiation in Melanesia.* New York.

MacGaffey, Wyatt. 1983. *Modern Kongo Prophets: Religion in a Plural Society.* Bloomington, IN.

MacIntyre, Alasdair. 1984. *After Virtue.* 2nd edn. Notre Dame.

—— 1990. *Three Rival Versions of Moral Enquiry.* London.

Madan, T. N. 1987. *Non–renunciation: Themes and Interpretations of Hindu Culture.* Delhi.

—— 1989. Religion in India. *Daedalus* 4: 115–46.

Mageo, Jeannette and Alan Howard, eds. 1996. *Spirits in Culture, History, and Mind.* New York.

Mahmood, Saba. 2001a. Feminist Theory, Embodiment, and the Docile Agent: Some Reflections on the Egyptian Islamic Revival. *Cultural Anthropology* 16(2): 202–36.

—— 2001b. Rehearsed Spontaneity and the Conventionality of Ritual: Disciplines of Salat. *AE* 28(4): 827–53.

—— 2001c. Terrorism, Myth, and the Power of Ethnographic Praxis. *Journal of Contemporary Ethnography* 30(5): 520–45.

—— 2004. *Politics of Piety: The Islamic Revival and the Feminist Subject.* Princeton.

—— 2006. Secularism, Hermeneutics and Empire: The Politics of Islamic Reformation. *Public Culture* 18(2): 323–47.

Mair, Lucy. 1969. *Witchcraft.* New York.

Malefijt, Annemarie de Waal. 1968. *Religion and Culture.* New York.

Malik, Jamal and John Hinnells, eds. 2006. *Sufism in the West.* Oxford.

Malinowski, Bronislaw. 1922. *Argonauts of the Western Pacific.* London.

—— 1935. *Coral Gardens and Their Magic.* London.

—— 1954 [1926]. Myth in Primitive Psychology. In *Magic, Science and Religion and Other Essays.* Garden City, NY.

Mamdani, Mahmood. 2002. Good Muslim, Bad Muslim: A Political Perspective on Culture and Terrorism. *AA* 104(3): 766–75.

—— 2005. *Good Muslim, Bad Muslim: America, the Cold War, and the Roots of Terror.* New York.

Manning, Frank, ed. 1983. *The Celebration of Society: Perspectives on Contemporary Cultural Performances.* Bowling Green, OH.

Maranda, Pierre, ed. 2001. *The Double Twist.* Toronto.

Mardin, S. 1989. *Religion and Social Change in Modern Turkey: The Case of Bediuzzaman Said Nursi.* Albany.

Marriott, McKim. 1955. *Village India. Studies in the Little Community.* Chicago.

—— 1976. Hindu Transactions: Diversity without Dualism. In B. Kapferer, ed., *Transaction and Meaning.* Philadelphia.

Marsden, George M. 2006. *Fundamentalism and American Culture: The Shaping of Twentieth-Century Evangelicalism, 1870–1825.* New York.

Martin, D. 1990. *Tongues of Fire: The Explosion of Protestantism in Latin America.* Oxford.

—— 2001. *Pentecostalism: The World Their Parish.* Oxford.

Martin, Emily. 1992. *The Woman in the Body.* Boston.

—— 1994. *Flexible Bodies: Tracking Immunity in American Culture from the Days of Polio to the Age of AIDS.* Boston.

Marty, Martin and Scott Appleby, eds. 1997. *Fundamentalisms and Society.* Chicago.

—— 2004. *Accounting for Fundamentalism: The Dynamic Character of Movements.* Chicago.

Marwick, Max, ed. 1970. *Witchcraft and Sorcery.* Harmondsworth.

Marx, Karl. 1961 [1887]. *Capital: A Critique of Political Economy.* Vol. I. Moscow. (Originally published in German, 1867.)

—— 1977. The Fetishism of Commodities and the Secret Thereof. Excerpt from *Capital.* In

Dolgin, Kemnitzer, and Schneider, eds., *Symbolic Anthropology*. New York.

—— and Friedrich Engels. 1964 [1841–95]. *Marx and Engels on Religion*. R. Niebuhr, intro. New York.

Maskarinec, Gregory. 1995. *The Rulings of the Night: An Ethnography of Nepalese Shaman Oral Texts*. Madison.

Masquelier, Adeline. 1994. Lightning, Death, and the Avenging Spirits: *Bori* Values in a Muslim World. *Journal of Religion in Africa* 24(1): 2–51.

—— 2001. *Prayer Has Spoiled Everything: Possession, Power, and Identity in an Islamic Town of Niger*. Durham, NC.

—— 2002. Road Mythographies: Space, Mobility, and the Historical Imagination in Postcolonial Niger. *AE* 29(4): 829–56.

—— 2002. From Hostage to Host: Confessions of a Spirit Medium in Niger. *Ethos* 30(1–2): 49–76.

Masuzawa, Tomoko. 2005. *The Invention of World Religions*. Chicago.

Matory, Lorand. 2005a. [1994] *Sex and the Empire that is No More: Gender and the Politics of Metaphor in Oyo Yoruba Religion*. New York.

—— 2005b. *Black Atlantic Religion: Tradition, Transnationalism, and Matriarchy in the Afro-Brazilian Candomblé*. Princeton.

Mauss, Marcel. 1973 [1935]. Techniques of the Body. *Economy and Society* 2: 70–88.

—— 1985 [1938]. A Category of the Human Mind: The Notion of Person, the Notion of Self. In M. Carrithers et al., eds., *The Concept of the Person*. Cambridge.

—— 1990 [1925]. *The Gift*. London.

Mauzé, Marie. 1994. The Concept of the Person and Reincarnation among the Kwakiutl Indians. In A. Mills and R. Slobodin, eds., *Amerindian Rebirth*. Toronto.

Maybury-Lewis, David. 1984. Name, Person, and Ideology in Central Brazil. In E. Tooker and H. Conklin, eds., *Naming Systems*. Washington, DC.

McCauley, Robert N. and E. Thomas Lawson, eds. 2002. *Bringing Ritual to Mind: Psychological Foundations of Cultural Forms*. New York.

McDonald, Heather. 2001. *Blood, Bones and Spirit: Aboriginal Christianity in an East Kimberley Town*. Melbourne.

McDonaugh, Christian. 2000. Spirit, Substance, Vehicle: Kinship and Cosmology among the Dangaura Tharu, Nepal. *Social Anthropology* 8(1): 19–32.

McFarland, H. Neil. 1967. *The Rush Hour of the Gods: A Study of the New Religious Movements of Japan*. New York.

McIntosh, Janet. 2004. Reluctant Muslims: Embodied Hegemony and Moral Resistance in a Giriama Spirit Possession Complex. *JRAI* 10(1): 91–112.

McKnight, David. 2005. *Of Marriage, Violence and Sorcery: The Quest for Power in Northern Queensland*. Aldershot.

McLeod, Malcolm. 1972. Oracles and Accusations among the Azande. In A. Singer and B. Street, eds., *Zande Themes*. Totowa, NJ.

Meigs, Anna. 1984. *Food, Sex, and Pollution: A New Guinea Religion*. New Brunswick, NJ.

Mendoza, Zoila S. 2000. *Shaping Society through Dance: Mestizo Ritual Performance in the Peruvian Andes*. Chicago.

Meneley, Anne. 1996. *Tournaments of Value: Sociability and Hierarchy in a Yemeni Town*. Toronto.

Mernissi, Fatima. 1991. *Women and Islam: An Historical and Theological Enquiry*. Oxford.

Merrill, William. 1988. *Rarámuri Souls: Knowledge and Social Process in Northern Mexico*. Washington, DC.

Merton, Robert. 1957. Puritanism, Pietism, and Science. In *Social Theory and Social Structure*. Glencoe, IL.

Mertz, Elizabeth and Richard Parmentier, eds. 1985. *Semiotic Mediation*. Orlando.

Messer, Ellen and M. Lambek, eds. 2001. *Ecology and the Sacred: Engaging the Anthropology of Roy A. Rappaport*. Ann Arbor.

Messick, Brinkley. 1987. Subordinate Discourse: Women, Weaving, and Gender Relations in North Africa. *AE* 14(2): 210–24.

—— 1993. *The Calligraphic State: Textual Domination and History in a Muslim Society*. Berkeley.

Metcalf, Barbara Daly, ed. 1996. *Making Muslim Space in North America and Europe*. Berkeley.

Metcalf, Peter. 1982. *A Borneo Journey into Death: Berawan Eschatology from its Rituals*. Philadelphia.

—— 1987. Wine of the Corpse: Endocannibalism and the Great Feast of the Dead in Borneo. *Representations* 17: 96–109.

—— 1989. *Where Are You Spirits? Style and Theme in Berawan Prayer*. Washington, DC.

Metraux, Alfred 1972 [1959]. *Voodoo in Haiti*. S. Mintz, intro. New York.

Meyer, Birgit. 1998. "Make a Complete Break with the Past": Memory and Postcolonial Modernity in Ghanaian Pentecostal Discourse. In R. Werbner, ed., *Memory and the Postcolony: African Anthropology and the Critique of Power*.

—— 1999. *Translating the Devil: Religion and Modernity among the Ewe in Ghana*. Edinburgh.

—— 2004. "Praise the Lord": Popular Cinema and Pentecostalite Style in Ghana's New Public Sphere. *AE* 31(1): 92–110.

—— and Peter Geschiere, eds. 1999. *Globalization and Identity: Dialectics of Flow and Closure*. Oxford.

—— and Annelies Moors, eds. 2005. *Religion, Media, and the Public Sphere*. Indiana.

—— and Peter Pels, eds. 2003. *Magic and Modernity: Interfaces of Revelation and Concealment*. Stanford.

Middleton, John. 1967 [1954]. Some Social Aspects of Lugbara Myth. In Middleton, ed., *Myth and Cosmos*.

—— ed. 1967a. *Magic, Witchcraft, & Curing*. Austin.

—— ed. 1967b. *Gods & Rituals*. Austin.

—— ed. 1967c. *Myth & Cosmos*. Austin.

——1987 [1960]. *Lugbara Religion: Ritual and Authority among an East African People*. Washington, DC.

—— and E. Winter, eds. 1963. *Witchcraft and Sorcery in East Africa*. London.

Middleton, Karen, ed. 1999. *Ancestors, Power and History in Madagascar*. Leiden.

Mills, Antonia and Richard Slobodin, eds. 1994. *Amerindian Rebirth: Reincarnation Belief among North American Indians and Inuit*. Toronto.

Mills, Martin A. 2000. Vajra Brother, Vajra Sister: Renunciation, Individualism and the Household in Tibetan Buddhist Monasticism. *JRAI* 6(1): 17–34.

—— 2003. *Identity, Ritual and State in Tibetan Buddhism: The Foundations of Authority in Gelukpa Monasticism*. London.

Mimica, Jadran. 1988. *Intimations of Infinity*. Oxford.

Mines, Diane P. 2002. Hindu Nationalism, Untouchable Reform, and the Ritual Production of a South Indian Village. *AE* 29(1): 58–85.

—— 2005. *Fierce Gods: Inequality, Ritual and the Politics of Dignity in a South Indian Village*. Indiana.

Mir, Farina. 2006. Genre and Devotion in Punjabi Popular Narratives: Rethinking Cultural and Religious Syncretism. *CSSH* 48(3): 727–58.

Mitchell, Jon. 2002. *Ambivalent Europeans: Ritual, Memory and the Public Sphere in Malta*. London.

—— 2004. Ritual Structure and Ritual Agency: "Rebounding Violence" and Maltese Festa. *Social Anthropology* 12(1): 57–75.

Mitchell, Timothy. 1988. *Colonising Egypt*. Cambridge.

Miyazaki, Hirokazu. 2000. Faith and its Fulfillment: Agency, Exchange, and the Fijian Aesthetics of Completion. *AE* 27(1): 31–51.

—— 2004. *The Method of Hope: Anthropology, Philosophy, and Fijian Knowledge*. Chicago.

Moisseef, Marika. 2005. La Procréation dans les Mythes Contemporains: Une Histoire de Science-Fiction. *Anthropologie et Sociétés* 29(2): 69–94.

Molendijk, Arie L. and Peter Pels, eds. 1998. *Religion in the Making: The Emergence of the Sciences of Religion*. Boston.

Mooney, James 1965 [1896]. *The Ghost-Dance Religion and the Sioux Outbreak of 1890*. Chicago.

Moore, Henrietta, Bwire Kaare, and Todd Sanders, eds. 1999. *Those Who Play with Fire: Gender, Fertility, and Transformation in East and Southern Africa*. London.

Moore, Henrietta and Todd Sanders, eds. 2001. *Magical Interpretations, Material Realities: Modernity, Witchcraft and the Occult in Postcolonial Africa*. London.

Moore, Sally Falk and Barbara Myerhoff, eds. 1975. *Symbol and Politics in Communal Ideology*. Ithaca.

—— 1977. *Secular Ritual*. Assen, NL.

Morgan, L. H. 1877. *Ancient Society*. New York.

Morinis, Alan, ed. 1992. *Sacred Journey: The Anthropology of Pilgrimage*. Westport, CT.

Morphy, Howard. 1991. *Ancestral Connections: Art and an Aboriginal System of Knowledge*. Chicago.

Morrill, Bruce T., Joanna E. Ziegler, and Susan Rodgers, eds. 2006. *Practicing Catholic: Ritual, Body, and Contestation in Catholic Faith*. New York.

Morris, Brian. 1987. *Anthropological Studies of Religion*. Cambridge.

—— 2000. *Animals and Ancestors: An Ethnography*. Oxford.

Morris, Rosalind. 2000. *In the Place of Origins: Modernity and Its Mediums in Northern Thailand*. Durham.

Moskowitz, Marc L. 2001. *The Haunting Fetus: Abortion, Sexuality, and the Spirit World in Taiwan*. Honolulu.

Mosse, David. 1994. Catholic Saints and the Hindu Village Pantheon in Rural Tamil Nadu. *Man* 29: 301–32.

Mueggler, Erik. 2001. *The Age of Wild Ghosts: Memory, Violence, and Place in Southwest China*. Princeton.

Muller, Jean-Claude. 1980. *Le roi bouc émissaire: pouvoirs et rituels chez les Rukuba du Nigeria Central*. Paris.

Mumford, S. R. 1989. *Himalayan Dialogue: Tibetan Lamas and Gurung Shamans in Nepal*. Madison.

Munn, Nancy. 1970. The Transformation of Subjects into Objects in Walbiri and Pitjantjatjara Myth. In R. M. Berndt, ed., *Australian Aboriginal Anthropology*. Nedlands, Australia.

—— 1973. Symbolism in a Ritual Context. In J. Honigmann, ed., *Handbook of Social and Cultural Anthropology*. Chicago.

Munn, Nancy 1986. *The Fame of Gawa. A Symbolic Study of Value Transformation in a Massim (PNG) Society*. Cambridge.

—— 1990. Constructing Regional Worlds in Experience: Kula Exchange, Witchcraft and Gawan Local Events. *Man* 25: 1–17.

—— 1992. The Cultural Anthropology of Time: A Critical Essay. *Annual Review of Anthropology* 21: 93–123.

Munson, Henry. 1993. *Religion and Power in Morocco*. New Haven.

Murphy, Robert and Yolanda Murphy. 1974. *Women of the Forest*. New York.

Myerhoff, Barbara. 1974. *The Peyote Hunt: The Sacred Journey of the Huichol Indians*. Ithaca.

—— 1978. *Number Our Days*. New York.

Myers, Fred. 1986. *Pintupi Country, Pintupi Self: Sentiment, Place and Politics among Western Desert Aborigines*. Washington, DC.

Myhre, Knut Christian. 2006. Divination and Experience: Explorations of a Chagga Epistemology. *JRAI* 12(2): 313–30.

Nabokov, Isabelle. 2000. *Religion against the Self: An Ethnography of Tamil Rituals*. Oxford.

—— 2000a. Deadly Power: A Funeral to Counter Sorcery in South India. *AE* 27(1): 147–68.

Nadel, S. F. 1954. *Nupe Religion*. London.

Nagata, Judith. 1984. *The Reflowering of Malaysian Islam: Modern Religious Radicals and Their Roots*. Vancouver.

—— 2001. Beyond Theology: Toward and Anthropology of "Fundamentalism." *AA* 103(2): 481–99.

Nakamaki, Hirochika. 2003. *Japanese Religions at Home and Abroad: Anthropological Perspectives*. Oxford.

Nandy, Ashis. 1989. The Political Culture of the Indian State. *Daedalus* 118: 1–26.

Nash, June. 1979. *We Eat the Mines and the Mines Eat Us: Dependency and Exploitation in Bolivian Tin Mines*. New York.

Navaro-Yashin, Yael. 2002. *Faces of the State: Secularism and Public Life in Turkey*. Princeton.

Needham, Rodney. 1967. Percussion and Transition. *Man*, n.s. 2: 606–14.

—— 1972. *Belief, Language, and Experience*. Chicago.

—— ed. 1973. *Right and Left: Essay on Dual Symbolic Classification*. Chicago.

—— 1975. Polythetic Classification: Convergence and Consequence. *Man*, n.s. 10: 349–69.

—— 1980. *Reconnaissances*. Toronto.

—— 1981. Characteristics of Religion. In *Circumstantial Deliveries*. Berkeley.

—— 1985. *Exemplars*. Berkeley.

Nelson, John K. 2000. *Enduring Identities: The Guise of Shinto in Contemporary Japan*. Honolulu.

Neylan, Susan. 2002. *The Heavens are Changing: Nineteenth-century Protestant Missions and Tsimshian Christianity*. Montreal.

Ngubane, H. 1977. *Body and Mind in Zulu Medicine*. London.

Nicholas, Ralph W. 2003. *Fruits of Worship: Practical Religion in Bengal*. New Delhi.

Niehaus, Isak. 2001. Witchcraft in the New South Africa. In I. Niehaus, E. Mohlala, and K. Shokane, eds., *Witchcraft, Power and Politics: Exploring the Occult in the South African Lowveld*. Sterling.

Niezen, Ronald. 2001. *Spirit Wars: Native North American Religions in the Age of Nation Building*. Berkeley.

Nisula, Tapio. 1999. Everyday Spirits and Medical Interventions. *Transactions of the Finnish Anthropological Society* NRO XLIII.

Norman, Howard. 1976. *The Wishing Bone Cycle: Narrative Poems from the Swampy Cree Indians*. New York.

Noys, Benjamin. 2005. *The Culture of Death*. Oxford.

Nye, Malory. 2001. *Multiculturalism and Minority Religions in Britain: Krishna Consciousness, Religious Freedom, and the Politics of Location*. Oxford.

Obeyesekere, Gananath. 1981. *Medusa's Hair: An Essay on Personal Symbols and Religious Experience*. Chicago.

—— 1984. *The Cult of the Goddess Pattini*. Chicago.

—— 1990. *The Work of Culture: Symbolic Transformation in Psychoanalysis and Anthropology*. Chicago.

—— 1992. *The Apotheosis of Captain Cook*. Princeton.

—— 2002. *Imagining Karma: Ethical Transformation in Amerindian, Buddhist and Greek Rebirth*. Berkeley.

Ong, Aihwa. 1987. *Spirits of Resistance and Capitalist Discipline: Factory Women in Malaysia*. Albany.

—— 2003. *Buddha is Hiding: Refugees, Citizenship, the New America*. Berkeley.

Orsi, Robert. 1985. *The Madonna of 115th Street: Faith and Community in Italian Harlem 1880–1950*. New Haven.

—— 1996. *Thank You, St. Jude: Women's Devotion to the Patron Saint of Hopeless Causes*. New Haven.

—— 2004. *Between Heaven and Earth: The Religious Worlds People Make and the Scholars Who Study Them*. Princeton.

Orta, Andrew. 2002. "Living the Past in Another Way": Reinstrumentalized Missionary Selves in Aymara Mission Fields. *Anthropological Quarterly* 75(4): 707–44.

—— 2005. *Catechizing Culture: Missionaries, Aymara and the "New Evangelization"*. New York.

Ortiz, Alfonso. 1969. *The Tewa World: Space, Time, Being, and Becoming in a Pueblo Society*. Chicago.

Ortner, Sherry B. 1973. On Key Symbols. *AA* 75: 1338–46.

—— 1974. Is Female to Male as Nature is to Culture? In M. Rosaldo and L. Lamphere, eds., *Woman, Culture, and Society*. Stanford.

—— 1978. *Sherpas through their Rituals*. Cambridge.

—— 1984. Theory in Anthropology since the Sixties. *CSSH* 26: 126–66.

—— 1989. *High Religion: A Cultural and Political History of Sherpa Buddhism*. Princeton.

—— 1995. Resistance and the Problem of Ethnographic Refusal. *CSSH* 37: 173–93.

—— 1996. *Making Gender: The Politics and Erotics of Culture*. Boston.

—— 1999a. Thick Resistance: Death and the Cultural Construction of Agency in Himalayan Mountaineering. In Ortner, ed., 1999c.

—— ed. 1999b. *The Fate of "Culture": Geertz and Beyond*. Berkeley.

—— 1999c. *Life and Death on Mt. Everest.* Princeton.

—— and Harriet Whitehead, eds. 1981. *Sexual Meanings: The Cultural Construction of Gender and Sexuality.* Cambridge.

Osanloo, Arzoo. 2006. Islamico-Civil "Rights Talk": Women, Subjectivity, and Law in Iranian Family Court. *AE* 33(2): 191–209.

Ostor, Akos. 1980. *The Play of the Gods: Festivals of a Bengali Town.* Chicago.

O'Toole, Roger. 1984. *Religion: Classic Sociological Approaches.* Toronto.

Otto, Rudolf. 1923 [1917]. *The Idea of the Holy.* Oxford.

Overing, Joanna, ed. 1985. *Reason and Morality.* London and New York.

Özyürek, Esra. 2005. The Politics of Cultural Unification, Secularism, and the Place of Islam in the New Europe. *AE* 32(4): 509–12.

Packard, Randall. 1981. *Chiefship and Cosmology.* Bloomington.

Palmié, Stephan. 2002. *Wizards and Scientists: Explorations in Afro-Cuban Modernity and Tradition.* London.

—— 2006. A View from Itia Ororó Kande. *Social Anthropology* 14(1): 99–118.

Palumbo, Bernardino. 2004. The War of the Saints: Religion, Politics and the Poetics of Time in a Sicilian town. *CSSH* 46(1): 4–34.

Pandolfo, Stefania. 1997. *Impasse of the Angels: Scenes from a Moroccan Space of Memory.* Chicago.

Parish, Jane. 2000. From the Body to the Wallet: Conceptualizing Akan Witchcraft at Home and Abroad. *JRAI* 6(3): 487–500.

Parkin, David. 1972. *Palms, Wine and Witnesses: Public Spirit and Private Gain in an African Farming Community.* San Francisco.

—— ed. 1982. *Semantic Anthropology.* London.

—— ed. 1985. *The Anthropology of Evil.* Oxford.

—— 1991. *Sacred Void: Spatial Images of Work and Ritual among the Giriama of Kenya.* Cambridge.

Parkin, David and Stephen Headley, eds. 2000. *Islamic Prayer across the Indian Ocean: Inside and Outside the Mosque.* Richmond, Surrey.

Parkin, Robert. 1996. *The Dark Side of Humanity: The Work of Robert Hertz and its Legacy.* Amsterdam.

Parmentier, Richard. 1987. *The Sacred Remains: Myth, History, and Polity in Belau.* Chicago.

Parry, Jonathan. 1986. The *Gift*, The Indian Gift, and the "Indian Gift". *Man* 21: 453–73.

—— 1994. *Death in Banaras.* Cambridge.

—— 1998. Mauss, Dumont and the Distinction between Status and Power. In James and Allen, eds., *Marcel Mauss: A Centenary Tribute.*

—— and Maurice Bloch, eds. 1989. *Money and the Morality of Exchange.* Cambridge.

Parsons, Anne. 1969. *Belief, Magic, and Anomie.* New York.

Paul, Robert A. 1983. *The Tibetan Symbolic World.* Chicago.

—— 1996. *Moses and Civilization: The Meaning Behind Freud's Myth.* New Haven.

Peabody, Norbert. 2003. *Hindu Kingship and Polity in Precolonial India.* Cambridge.

Peacock, James. 1968. *Rites of Modernization: Symbolic and Social Aspects of Indonesian Proletarian Drama.* Chicago.

—— 1978a. *Muslim Puritans: Reformist Psychology in Southeast Asian Islam.* Berkeley.

—— 1978b. *Purifying the Faith: The Muhammadijah Movement in Indonesian Islam.* Menlo Park, CA.

—— and Thomas Kirsch. 1980. *The Human Direction.* Englewood Cliffs, NJ.

—— and R. W. Tyson. 1989. *Pilgrims of Paradox: Calvinism and Experience among the Primitive Baptists of the Blue Ridge.* Washington, DC.

Pedersen, Morten A. 2001. Totemism, Animism and North Asian Indigenous Ontologies. *JRAI* 7(3): 411–27.

Peek, Philip, ed. 1991. *African Divination Systems.* Bloomington.

Peel, J. D. Y. 1968. *Aladura. A Religious Movement among the Yoruba.* London.

—— 2001. *Religious Encounter and the Making of the Yoruba.* Bloomington.

Peirce, C. S. 1960. *The Collected Papers of Charles Saunders Peirce*. C. Hartshorne and P. Weiss, eds. Cambridge, MA.

Peletz, Michael. 1993. Sacred Texts and Dangerous Words: The Politics of Law and Cultural Rationalization in Malaysia. *CSSH* 35: 66–109.

—— 1996. *Reason and Passion: Representations of Gender in a Malay Society*. Berkeley.

—— 2002. *Islamic Modern: Religious Courts and Cultural Politics in Malaysia*. Princeton.

Pels, Peter. 1999. *A Politics of Presence: Contacts Between Missionaries and Waluguru in Late Colonial Tanganyika*. Amsterdam.

Pepper, Stephen. 1942. *World Hypotheses*. Berkeley and Los Angeles: University of California Press.

Peristiany, J. G. and J. Pitt-Rivers, eds. 1992. *Honor and Grace in Anthropology*. Cambridge.

Perruchon, Marie. 2003. *I am Tsunki: Gender and Shamanism among the Shuar of Western Amazonia*. Uppsala.

Pessar, Patricia. 2004. *From Fanatics to Folk: Brazilian Millenarianism and Popular Culture*. Durham.

Pickering, W. 1975. *Durkheim on Religion*. London.

—— 1984. *Durkheim's Sociology of Religion*. London.

Pietz, William. 1985. The Problem of the Fetish. *Res* 9: 5–17.

—— 1987. The Problem of the Fetish, II. *Res* 13: 23–45.

—— 1988. The Problem of the Fetish, III a. *Res* 16: 105–23.

Pina-Cabral, João de. 1986. *Sons of Adam, Daughters of Eve: The Peasant Worldview of the Alto Minho*. Oxford.

Pirie, Fernanda. 2006. Secular Morality, Village Law, and Buddhism in Tibetan Societies. *JRAI* 12(1): 173–90.

Piot, Charles. 1999. *Remotely Global: Village Modernity in West Africa*. Chicago.

Placido, Barbara. 2001. "It's All To Do With Words": An Analysis of Spirit Possession in the Venezuelan Cult of Maria Lionza. *JRAI* 7(2): 207–24.

Pocock, David. 1973. *Mind, Body and Wealth: A Study of Belief and Practice in an Indian Village*. Oxford.

Poirier, Sylvie. 2005. *A World of Relationships: Itineraries, Dreams and Events in the Australian Western Desert*. Toronto.

Polanyi, Michael. 1970. The Stability of Scientific Theories against Experience. In Marwick, ed., *Witchcraft and Sorcery*.

Pollard, Alton B. III and Love Henry Whelchel Jr., eds. 2003. *"How Long This Road": Race, Religion, and the Legacy of C. Eric Lincoln*. New York.

Pouillon, Jean. 1982 [1979]. Remarks on the Verb "To Believe." In Izard and Smith, eds., *Between Belief and Transgression*.

Prince, Ruth and David Riches. 2002. *The New Age in Glastonbury: The Construction of Religious Movements*. Oxford.

Privratsky, Bruce G. 2001. *Muslim Turkistan: Kazak Religion and Collective Memory*. Richmond.

Purpura, Allyson. 2000. Portrait of Seyyid Silima from Zanzibar: Piety and Subversion in Islamic Prayer. In Parkin and Headley, eds., *Islamic Prayer Across the Indian Ocean*.

Radcliffe–Brown, A. R. 1964a [1922]. *The Andaman Islanders*. New York.

—— 1964b [1952]. *Structure and Function in Primitive Society*. New York.

Radin, Paul. 1957a [1927]. *Primitive Man as Philosopher*. New York.

—— 1957b [1937]. *Primitive Religion*. New York.

—— 1972 [1956]. *The Trickster: A Study in American Indian Mythology*. New York.

Rafael, Vincente. 1992 [1988]. *Contacting Colonialism: Translation and Christian Conversion in Tagalog Society under Early Christian Rule*. Durham, NC.

Raheja, Gloria. 1988. India. Caste, Kingship, and Dominance Reconsidered. *Annual Review of Anthropology* 17: 497–522.

Raj, Selva J. and Corinne G. Dempsey, eds. 2002. *Popular Christianity in India: Writing Between the Lines*. New York.

Ramanujan, A. K. 1990. Is There an Indian Way of Thinking? In M. Marriot, ed., *India Through Hindu Categories*. New Delhi and London.

Ramble, Charles. 1990. How Buddhist are Buddhist Communities? The Construction of Tradition in two Lamaist Villages. *Journal of the Anthropological Society of Oxford* 21(2): 185–97.

—— 2002. Temporal Disjunction and Collectivity in Mustang, Nepal. *Current Anthropology* 43: 75–84.

Ranger, Terence. 1991. Missionaries, Migrants, and the Manyika, In L. Vail, ed., *The Invention of Tribalism in Southern Africa*. Berkeley.

—— 1993a. The Local and the Global in Southern African Religious History. In Hefner, ed., *Conversion to Christianity*.

—— 1993b. Religious Movements and Politics in Sub-Saharan Africa. *African Studies Review* 29(2): 1–69.

Rappaport, Roy A. 1979a. *Ecology, Meaning, and Religion*. Richmond, CA.

—— 1979b. The Obvious Aspects of Ritual. In *Ecology, Meaning, and Religion*.

—— 1984 [1968]. *Pigs for the Ancestors*. New Haven.

—— 1999. *Ritual and Religion in the Making of Humanity*. Cambridge.

Rasanayagam, Johan. 2006. Healing with Spirits and the Formation of Muslim Selfhood in Post-Soviet Uzbekistan. *JRAI* 12(2): 377–93.

Ray, Reginald. 1995. Tibetan Buddhism as Shamanism? *The Journal of Religion* 75(1): 90–101.

Redfield, Robert. 1953. *The Primitive World and Its Transformations*. Ithaca.

—— 1956. The Social Organization of Tradition. In *Peasant Society and Culture*. Chicago.

Reichard, Gladys. 1950. *Navaho Religion: A Study of Symbolism*. 2 vols. New York.

Reichel-Dolmatoff, Gerardo. 1971. *Amazonian Cosmos: The Sexual and Religious Symbolism of the Tukano Indians*. Chicago.

Renne, Elisha P. 2002. The Fundamentals of Fertility: Cosmology and Conversion in a Southwestern Nigerian Town. *JRAI* 8(3): 551–69.

Reynolds, Margaret. 2001. *Plain Women: Gender and Ritual in the Old Order River Brethren*. University Park, PA.

Richards, Audrey. 1956. *Chisungu*. London.

Richardson, Miles. 2003. *Being-in-Christ and Putting Death in its Place: An Anthropologist's Account of Christian Performance in Spanish America and the American South*. Baton Rouge.

Ricoeur, Paul 1967. *The Symbolism of Evil*. New York.

—— 1971. The Model of the Text. *Social Research* 38: 529–62.

—— 1976. *Interpretation Theory*. Fort Worth.

—— and Claude Lévi-Strauss. 1970. A Confrontation. *New Left Review* 62: 57–74.

Ridington, Robin. 1988. *Trail to Heaven: Knowledge and Narrative in a Northern Native Community*. Vancouver.

—— and Dennis Hastings. 2000. *Blessing for a Long Time: The Sacred Pole of the Omaha Tribe*. Lincoln.

Rigby, Peter. 1968. Some Gogo Rituals of "Purification." In Leach, ed., *Dialectic in Practical Religion*.

Rival, Laura. 2005. The Attachment of the Soul to the Body among the Huaorani of Amazonian Ecuador. *Ethnos* 70(3): 285–310.

Robben, Antonius C. G. M., ed. 2004. *Death, Mourning, and Burial: A Cross-Cultural Reader*. Oxford.

Robbins, Joel. 1995. Dispossessing the Spirits: Christian Transformations of Desire and Ecology among the Urapmin of Papua New Guinea. *Ethnology* 34: 211–24.

—— 2001a. God is Nothing But Talk: Modernity, Language and Prayer in a Papua New Guinea Society. *AA* 103(4): 901–13.

—— 2001b. Ritual Communication and Linguistic Ideology: A Reading and Partial Reformulation of Rappaport's Theory of Ritual. *Current Anthropology* 42(5): 591–614.

—— 2003. What Is a Christian? Notes Toward an Anthropology of Christianity. *Religion* 33(3): 191–9.

—— 2004. *Becoming Sinners: Christianity and Moral Torment in a Papua New Guinea Society*. Berkeley.

—— 2006. Anthropology and Theology: An Awkward Relationship? *Anthropological Quarterly* 79(2): 262–85.

Roberts, Allen and Mary Roberts. 2003. *A Saint in the City: Sufi Arts of Urban Senegal.* Los Angeles.

Robertson, Roland, ed. 1969. *Sociology of Religion.* Baltimore.

Robinson, Rowena and Sathianathan Clarke, eds. 2003. *Religious Conversion in India: Modes, Motivations, and Meanings.* Delhi.

Rodseth, Lars and Jennifer Olsen. 2000. Mystics Against the Market: American Religions and the Autocritique of Capitalism. *Critique of Anthropology* 20(3): 265–88.

Romberg, Raquel. 2003. *Witchcraft and Welfare: Spiritual Capital and the Business of Magic in Modern Puerto Rico.* Austin.

Rosaldo, Michelle. 1980. *Knowledge and Passion: Ilongot Notions of Self and Social Life.* New York.

Rosaldo, Renato. 1980. *Ilongot Headhunting: 1883–1974.* Stanford.

—— 1989. Grief and a Headhunter's Rage. In *Culture and Truth.* Boston.

Rosen, Lawrence. 2003. *The Culture of Islam: Changing Aspects of Contemporary Muslim Life.* Chicago.

Rouse, Carolyn Moxley. 2004. *Engaged Surrender: African American Women and Islam.* Berkeley.

Rowlands, Michael and Jean–Pierre Warnier. 1988. Sorcery, Power and the Modern State in Cameroon. *Man,* n.s. 23: 118–32.

Royer, Patrick. 1999. Le Massa et L'Eau de Moussa: Cultes Régionaux, "Traditions" Locales et Sorcellerie en Afrique De L'Ouest. *Cahiers d'Études Africaines* 154: 337–66.

Rozenberg, Guillaume. 2004. How Giving Sanctifies: The Birthday of Thamanyan Hsayadaw in Burma. *JRAI* 10(3): 495–515.

Ruel, Malcolm. 1969. *Leopards and Leaders: Constitutional Politics among a Cross River People.* London.

—— 1982. Christians as Believers. In John Davis, ed., *Religious Organization and Religious Experience.* London.

—— 1990. Non–Sacrificial Ritual Killing. *Man* 25: 323–35.

—— 1997. *Belief, Ritual and the Securing of Life: Reflexive Essays on a Bantu Religion.* Leiden.

Rumsey, Alan and James F. Weiner, eds. 2001. *Emplaced Myth: Space, Narrative and Knowledge in Aboriginal Australia and Papua New Guinea.* Honolulu.

Rus, Jan and R. Wasserstrom. 1980. Civil–Religious Hierarchies in Central Chiapas: A Critical Perspective. *AE* 7: 466–78.

Sahlins, Marshall. 1976. *Culture and Practical Reason.* Chicago.

—— 1976. *The Use and Abuse of Biology: An Anthropological Critique of Sociobiology.* Ann Arbor.

—— 1985. *Islands of History.* Chicago.

—— 1995. *How "Natives" Think: About Captain Cook, For Example.* Chicago.

—— 1996. The Sadness of Sweetness: The Native Anthropology of Western Cosmology. *Current Anthropology* 37(3): 395–428.

—— 1999. Two or Three Things That I Know About Culture. *JRAI* 5(3): 399–419.

—— 2000. *Culture in Practice: Selected Essays.* New York.

—— 2004. *Apologies to Thucydides: Understanding History as Culture and Vice Versa.* Chicago.

Saler, Benson. 1993. *Conceptualizing Religion: Immanent Anthropologists, Transcendent Natives, and Unbounded Categories.* Leiden.

Sallnow, Michael. 1987. *Pilgrims of the Andes: Regional Cults in Cusco.* Washington, DC.

Samarin, William, ed. 1976. *Language in Religious Practice.* Rowley.

Sanders, Todd. 2000. Rains Gone Bad, Women Gone Mad: Rethinking Gender Rituals of Rebellion and Patriarchy. *JRAI* 6(3): 469–86.

—— 2001. Save Our Skins: Structural Adjustment, Morality and the Occult in Tanzania. In H. Moore and T. Sanders, eds., *Magical Interpretations, Material Realities: Modernity, Witchcraft and the Occult in Postcolonial Africa.* London.

—— 2003. Reconsidering Witchcraft: Postcolonial Africa and Analytic (Un)certainties. *AA* 105(2): 338–52.

—— 2006. *Anthropology in Theory: Issues in Epistemology.* Oxford.

—— In press. *Beyond Bodies: Rainmaking and Sense Making in Tanzania*. Toronto.

Sangren, Stephen. 1987. *History and Magical Power in a Chinese Community*. Stanford.

—— 1993. Power and Transcendence in the Matsu Pilgrimages of Taiwan. *AE* 20(3): 564–82.

Sapir, Edward. 1956 [1928]. The Meaning of Religion. In *Culture, Language and Personality: Selected Essays*. Berkeley.

Sapir, J. David and Christopher Crocker, eds. 1977. *The Social Use of Metaphor: Essays on the Anthropology of Rhetoric*. Philadelphia.

Sather, Clifford. 2001. *Seeds of Play, Words of Power: An Ethnographic Study of Iban Shamanic Chants*. Kuala Lumpur.

Saussure, Ferdinand de. 1959. *Course in General Linguistics*. New York.

Sawyer, John, ed. 1996. *Reading Leviticus: A Conversation with Mary Douglas*. Sheffield.

Schattschneider, Ellen. 2003. *Immortal Wishes: Labor and Transcendence on a Japanese Sacred Mountain*. London.

Schechner, Richard and W. Appel, eds. 1990. *By Means of Performance*. Cambridge.

Scheper-Hughes, Nancy. 2000. The Global Traffic in Human Organs. *Current Anthropology* 41(2): 191–224.

Schieffelin, Edward. 1976. *The Sorrow of the Lonely and the Burning of the Dancers*. New York.

—— 1985. Performance and the Cultural Construction of Reality. *AE* 12: 707–24.

Schmidt, Titti. 2007. *Morality as Practice: The Santo Daime, an Eco-Religious Movement in the Amazonian Rainforest*. Uppsala.

Schneider, David. 1977 [1969]. Kinship, Nationality and Religion in American Culture. In Dolgin, Kemnitzer, and Schneider, eds., *Symbolic Anthropology*.

—— 1980 [1968]. *American Kinship: A Cultural Account*. 2nd edn. Chicago.

Schneider, Jane. 1990. Spirits and the Spirit of Capitalism. In Badone, ed., *Religious Orthodoxy and Popular Faith in European Society*.

—— and Shirley Lindenbaum, eds. 1987.

Frontiers of Christian Evangelism. *AE* 14. Special issue.

Schrauwers, Albert. 2000. *Colonial "Reformation" in the Highlands of Central Sulawesi, Indonesia*. Toronto.

Schrempp, Gregory. 1992. *Magical Arrows: The Maori, the Greeks and the Folklore of the Universe*. Madison.

—— and William Hansen, eds. 2002. *Myth: A New Symposium*. Bloomington, IN.

Schulz, Dorothea. 2006. Promises of (Im)mediate Salvation: Islam, Broadcast Media, and the Remaking of Religious Experience in Mali. *AE* 33(2): 210–29.

Schutz, Alfred. 1964. *Collected Papers*. The Hague.

Schwarz, Maureen Trudelle. 2003. *Blood and Voice: Navajo Women Ceremonial Practitioners*. Tucson.

Schwimmer, Eric. 1979. The Self and the Product. In S. Wallman, ed., *Social Anthropology of Work*. London.

Scott, Colin. 2006. Spirit and Practical Knowledge in the Person of the Bear among Wemindji Cree Hunters. *Ethnos* 71(1): 51–66.

Scott, Michael. 2005a. "I was Like Abraham": Notes on the Anthropology of Christianity from the Solomon Islands. *Ethnos* 70(1): 101–25.

—— 2005b. Hybridity, Vacuity and Blockage: Visions of Chaos from Anthropological Theory, Island Melanesia, and Central Africa. *CSSH* 47(1): 190–216.

—— 2007. *The Severed Snake: Matrilineages, Making Place, and a Melanesian Christianity in Southeast Solomon Islands*. Carolina.

Scupin, Raymond, ed. 2000. *Religion and Culture: An Anthropological Focus*. Upper Saddle River, NJ.

Searle, John. 1969. *Speech Acts: An Essay in the Philosophy of Language*. Cambridge.

Sears, Laurie. 1996. *Shadows of Empire: Colonial Discourse and Javanese Tales*. Durham, NC.

Seguin, Margaret, ed. 1993 [1984]. *The Tsimshian*. Vancouver.

Sered, Susan. 1994. *Priestess, Mother, Sacred Sister: Religions Dominated by Women*. New York.

Seremetakis, Nadia. 1991. *The Last Word:*

Women, Death, and Divination in Inner Mani. Chicago.

Shankland, David. 2003. *The Alevis in Turkey: The Emergence of a Secular Islamic Tradition*. London.

Sharma, Ursula. 1973. Theodicy and the Doctrine of Karma. *Man* 8(3): 347–64.

Sharp, Lesley. 1993. *The Possessed and the Dispossessed: Spirits, Identity, and Power in a Madagascar Migrant Town*. Berkeley.

Shaw, Rosalind. 1997. The Production of Witchcraft/Witchcraft as Production: Memory, Modernity, and the Slave Trade in Sierra Leone. *AE* 24: 856–76.

—— 2002. *Memories of the Slave Trade: Ritual and the Historical Imagination in Sierra Leone*. Chicago.

Shils, Edward. 1975. *Center and Periphery: Essays in Macrosociology*. Chicago.

Shipton, Parker. 1989. *Bitter Money: Cultural Economy and Some African Meanings of Forbidden Commodities*. Washington, DC.

Shokeid, Moshe. 1995. *A Gay Synagogue in New York*. New York.

Shweder, Richard A. and Byron Good, eds. 2005. *Clifford Geertz by His Colleagues*. Chicago.

Siegel, James. 1969. *The Rope of God*. Berkeley.

Silber, Ilana. 2005. *Virtuosity, Charisma and Social Order: A Comparative Sociological Study of Monasticism in Theravada Buddhism and Medieval Catholicism*. Cambridge.

Silverblatt, Irene. 1987. *Moon, Sun, and Witches: Gender Ideologies and Class in Inca and Colonial Peru*. Princeton.

Silverstein, Brian. 2003. Islam and Modernity in Turkey: Power, Tradition and Historicity in the European Provinces of the Muslim World. *Anthropological Quarterly* 76(3): 497–518.

Simpson, Bob. 2004. Impossible Gifts: Bodies, Buddhism and Bioethics in Contemporary Sri Lanka. *JRAI* 10(4): 839–59.

Singer, Milton. 1972. *When a Great Tradition Modernizes: An Anthropological Approach to Indian Civilization*. New York.

—— 1984. *Man's Glassy Essence: Explorations in Semiotic Anthropology*. Bloomington.

Skorupski, John. 1976. *Symbol and Theory: A Philosophical Study of Theories of Religion in Social Anthropology*. Cambridge.

Smith, Daniel Jordan. 2001. Ritual Killing, 419, and Fast Wealth: Inequality and the Popular Imagination in Southeastern Nigeria. *AE* 28(4): 803–26.

Smith, Huston. 1958. *The Religions of Man*. New York.

Smith, James H. 2005. Buying a Better Witch Doctor: Witch-finding, Neoliberalism, and the Development Imagination in the Taita Hills, Kenya. *AE* 32(1): 141–58.

Smith, Jonathan Z. 1978. *Map Is Not Territory: Studies in the History of Religions*. Leiden.

—— 1998. Religion, Religions, Religious. In Taylor, ed., *Critical Terms for Religious Studies*.

Smith, Robert J. 1974. *Ancestor Worship in Contemporary Japan*. Stanford.

Smith, W. Robertson. 1894. *Lectures on the Religion of the Semites*. London.

Snodgrass, Jeffrey G. 2002. A Tale of Goddesses, Money, and Other Terribly Wonderful Things: Spirit Possession, Commodity Fetishism, and the Narrative of Capitalism in Rajasthan, India. *AE* 29(3): 602–36.

Snow-Wadley, Susan. 2004. *Raja Nal and the Goddess: The North Indian Epic Dhola in Performance*. Bloomington.

Soares, Benjamin F. 2004. Islam and Public Piety in Mali. In Armando Salvatore and Dale Eickelman, eds., *Public Islam and the Common Good*. Leiden.

—— 2005. *Islam and the Prayer Economy: History and Authority in a Malian Town*. Edinburgh.

Solway, Jacqueline. 1998. Taking Stock in the Kalahari: Accumulation and Resistance on the Southern African Periphery. *Journal of Southern African Studies* 24: 425–41.

Southwold, Martin. 1978. Buddhism and the Definition of Religion. *Man* 13: 362–79.

Sperber, Daniel. 1975. *Rethinking Symbolism*. Cambridge.

—— 1996. *Explaining Culture*. Cambridge, MA.

Spiro, Melford E. 1952. Ghosts, Ifaluk and Teleological Functionalism. *AA* 54: 497–503.

—— 1966. Religion: Problems of Definition and Explanation. In M. Banton, ed., *Anthropological Approaches to the Study of Religion*. London.

—— 1971a. *Kibbutz: Venture in Utopia*. New York.

—— 1971b. *Buddhism and Society: A Great Tradition and its Burmese Vicissitudes*. Berkeley.

—— 1978 [1967]. *Burmese Supernaturalism*. Philadelphia.

—— 1979. Whatever Happened to the Id? *AA* 81: 5–13.

—— 1982. *Oedipus in the Trobriands*. Chicago.

—— 1987. *Culture and Human Nature: Theoretical Papers of Melford E. Spiro*. B. Kilbourne and L. Langness, eds. Chicago.

—— 2004. Utopia and Its Discontents: The Kibbutz and Its Historical Vicissitudes. *AA* 106(3): 556–68.

Spyer, Patricia, ed. 1998. *Border Fetishisms: Material Objects in Unstable Places*. New York.

Srinivas, M. N. 1952. *Religion and Society among the Coorgs of South India*. Oxford.

—— 1969. The Caste System in India. In A. Béteille, ed., *Social Inequality*. Harmondsworth.

Srinivas, Smriti. 2001. *Landscapes of Urban Memory: The Sacred and the Civic in India's High-Tech City*. Minneapolis.

Srivastava, Vinay. 1998. *Religious Renunciation of a Pastoral People*. Oxford.

Stafford, Charles. 2000. *Separation and Reunion in Modern China*. Cambridge.

Stallybrass, Peter and Allon White. 1986. *The Politics and Poetics of Transgression*. Ithaca.

Stambach, Amy. 2004. Faith in Schools: Toward an Ethnography of Education, Religion, and the State. *Social Analysis* 48(3).

Stanner, W. E. H. 1963. *On Aboriginal Religion*. Sydney.

—— 1979 [1962]. Religion, Totemism and Symbolism. In *White Man Got No Dreaming, Essays 1938–1973*. Canberra.

Steedly, Mary. 1993. *Hanging Without a Rope: Narrative Experience in Colonial and Postcolonial Karoland*. Princeton.

Steiner, Franz. 1956. *Taboo*. Harmondsworth.

—— 1999. *Taboo, Truth, and Religion: Selected Writings*. Vol. I. J. Adler and R. Fardon, eds. New York.

Stephen, Michelle, ed. 1987. *Sorcerer and Witch in Melanesia*. New Brunswick, NJ.

Stewart, Charles. 1991. *Demons and the Devil: Moral Imagination in Modern Greek Culture*. Princeton.

—— and Rosalind Shaw, eds. 1994. *Syncretism/Anti–Syncretism: The Politics of Religious Synthesis*. London.

Stewart, Kathleen. 1996. *A Space on the Side of the Road*. Princeton.

Stewart, Michael. 1997. *The Time of the Gypsies*. Boulder.

Stewart, Pamela and Andrew Strathern. 2002. *Remaking the World: Myth, Mining, and Ritual Change among the Duna of Papua New Guinea*. London.

—— 2003. *Witchcraft, Rumours, Sorcery and Gossip*. Cambridge.

—— 2004. *Empowering the Past, Confronting the Future: The Duna People of Papua New Guinea*. New York.

Stoll, David. 1982. *Fishers of Men or Founders of Empire?* London.

—— 1990. *Is Latin America Turning Protestant? The Politics of Evangelical Growth*. Berkeley.

Stoller, Paul. 1989. *Fusion of the Worlds: An Ethnography of Possession among the Songhay of Niger*. Chicago.

—— 1995. *Embodying Colonial Memories: Spirit Possession, Power, and the Hauka in West Africa*. New York.

—— 2005. *Stranger in the Village of the Sick: A Memoir of Cancer, Sorcery and Healing*. Boston.

—— and C. Olkes. 1989. *In Sorcery's Shadow*. Chicago.

Straight, Bilinda. 2006. *Miracles and Extraordinary Experience in Northern Kenya*.

Strathern, Marilyn. 1988. *The Gender of the Gift: Problems with Women and Problems with Society in Melanesia*. Berkeley.

Stromberg, Peter. 1993. *Language and Self-Transformation: A Study of the Christian Conversion Narrative*. Cambridge.

Sullivan, Lawrence. 2002. *Native Religions and Cultures of Central and South America: Anthropology of the Sacred*. New York.

Sullivan, Winnifred. 2005. *The Impossibility of Religious Freedom*. Princeton.

Sundkler, Bengt. 1961. *Bantu Prophets in Southern Africa*. London.

—— and Christopher Steed. 2000. *A History of the Church in Africa*. Cambridge.

Suthren Hirst, Jacqueline and Lynn Thomas, eds. 2004. *Playing for Real: Hindu Role Models, Religion and Gender*. Oxford.

Symonds, Patricia V. 2005. *Calling in the Soul: Gender and the Cycle of Life in a Hmong Village*. Seattle.

Tambiah, Stanley J. 1970. *Buddhism and the Spirit Cults in Northeast Thailand*. Cambridge.

—— 1973. Form and Meaning of Magical Acts. In Horton and Finnegan, eds., *Modes of Thought*.

—— 1976. *World Conqueror and World Renouncer*. Cambridge.

—— 1979. A Performative Approach to Ritual. *Proceedings of the British Academy* LXV: 113–67. Reprinted in Tambiah 1985.

—— 1984. *The Buddhist Saints of the Forest and the Cult of Amulets*. Cambridge.

—— 1985. *Culture, Thought, and Social Action: An Anthropological Perspective*. Cambridge, MA.

—— 1990. *Magic, Science, Religion, and the Scope of Rationality*. Cambridge.

—— 1992. *Buddhism Betrayed? Religion, Politics, and Violence in Sri Lanka*. Chicago.

—— 1996. *Levelling Crowds: Ethnonationalist Conflicts and Collective Violence in South Asia*. Berkeley.

Tannenbaum, Nicola and Cornelia Ann Kammerer, eds. 2003. *Founders' Cults in Southeast Asia: Ancestors, Polity, and Identity*. New Haven.

Tanner, Adrian. 1979. *Bringing Home Animals: Religious Ideology and Mode of Production of the Mistassini Cree Hunters*. New York.

Tapper, Richard. 1991. *Islam in Modern Turkey: Religion, Politics and Literature in a Secular State*. New York.

Taussig, Michael. 1977. The Genesis of Capitalism among a South American Peasantry: Devil's Labor and the Baptism of Money. *CSSH* 19 (2): 130–55.

—— 1980. *The Devil and Commodity Fetishism in South America*. Chapel Hill.

—— 1987. *Shamanism, Colonialism, and the Wild Man: A Study in Terror and Healing*. Chicago.

—— 1993. *Mimesis and Alterity: A Particular History of the Senses*. London.

—— 1995. The Sun Gives Without Receiving: An Old Story. *CSSH* 35: 368–98.

—— 1997. *The Magic of the State*. London.

—— 1998. Transgression. In Taylor, ed., *Critical Terms for Religious Studies*.

—— 1999. *Defacement: Public Secrecy and the Labor of the Negative*. Stanford.

—— 2003. Viscerality, Faith, and Skepticism: Another Theory of Magic. In Birgit Meyer and Peter Pels, eds., *Magic and Modernity: Interfaces of Revelation and Concealment*. Stanford.

—— 2006. *Walter Benjamin's Grave*. Chicago.

Tawney, Richard H. 1998. *Religion and the Rise of Capitalism*. New Brunswick, NJ.

Taylor, Anne-Christine. 1993. Remembering to Forget: Identity, Mourning, and Memory among the Jivaro. *Man* 28: 653–78.

Taylor, Charles. 1989. *Sources of the Self: The Making of Modern Identity*. Cambridge, MA.

—— 2004. *Modern Social Imaginaries*. Durham, NC.

Taylor, Mark C. 1998. *Critical Terms for Religious Studies*. Chicago.

Taylor, Patrick, ed. 2001. *Religion, Identity, and Cultural Difference in the Caribbean*. Bloomington.

Taylor, William. 1987. The Virgin of Guadalupe in New Spain: An Inquiry into the Social History of Marian Devotion. *AE* 14(1): 9–33.

Tedlock, Barbara. 1992. *Time and the Highland Maya*. Albuquerque.

—— 2005. *The Woman in the Shaman's Body: Reclaiming the Feminine in Religion and Medicine*. New York.

Tedlock, Dennis. 1983. *The Spoken Word and the Work of Interpretation*. Philadelphia.

—— trans. and comm. 1985. *Popol Vuh*. New York.

—— 1990. *Days from a Dream Almanac.* Urbana.

—— 1997. The Poetics of Time in Mayan Divination. In Leavitt, ed., *Poetry and Prophecy.*

—— 2003. *Rabinal Achi: A Mayan Drama of War and Sacrifice.* Oxford.

Thoden van Velzen, H. U. E. and W. Van Wetering. 1988. *The Great Father and the Danger: Religious Cults, Material Forces, and Collective Fantasies in the World of the Surinamese Maroons.* Dordrecht.

Thornton, Robert. 1980. *Space, Time, and Culture among the Iraqw of Tanzania.* New York.

Thrupp, Sylvia, ed. 1970. *Millenial Dreams in Action: Studies in Revolutionary Religious Movements.* New York.

Tomlinson, Matt. 2004a. Ritual, Risk and Danger: Chain Prayers in Fiji. *AA* 106(1): 6–16.

—— 2004b. Perpetual Lament: Kava-Drinking, Christianity and Sensations of Historical Decline in Fiji. *JRAI* 10(3): 653–73.

Tonkin, Elizabeth. 2004. Consulting Ku Jlople: Some Histories of Oracles in West Africa. *JRAI* 10(3): 539–60.

Toren, Christina. 2003. Becoming a Christian in Fiji: An Ethnographic Study of Ontogeny. *JRAI* 9(4): 709–27.

Traphagan, John. 2004. *The Practice of Concern: Ritual, Well-being, and Aging in Rural Japan.* Durham, NC.

Traube, Elizabeth. 1986. *Cosmology and Social Life: Ritual Exchange among the Mambai of East Timor.* Chicago.

Trawick, Margaret. 1990. *Notes on Love in a Tamil Family.* Berkeley.

Trexler, Richard. 2003. *Reliving Golgotha: The Passion Play of Iztapalapa.* Cambridge.

Trigger, Bruce. 2003. *Understanding Early Civilizations.* Cambridge.

Trix, Frances. 1993. *Spiritual Discourse: Learning with an Islamic Master.* Philadelphia.

Troeltsch, Ernst. 1986. *Protestantism and Progress: The Significance of Protestantism for the Rise of the Modern World.* Philadelphia.

Trompf, G. W. 1991. *Melanesian Religion.* Cambridge.

Turner, David 1985. *Life Before Genesis.* New York.

Turner, Edith 1987. *The Spirit and the Drum: A Memoir of Africa.* Tucson.

—— 1992. *Experiencing Ritual: A New Interpretation of African Healing.* Philadelphia.

Turner, Terence. 1969. Oedipus: Time and Structure in Narrative Form. In R. Spencer, ed., *Forms of Symbolic Action.* Seattle.

Turner, Terence 1980. The Social Skin. In J. Cherfas and R. Lewin, eds., *Not Work Alone.* Beverly Hills.

Turner, Victor. 1957. *Schism and Continuity in an African Society.* Manchester.

—— 1962. *Chihamba, the White Spirit: A Ritual Drama of the Ndembu.* Manchester.

—— 1967. *The Forest of Symbols: Aspects of Ndembu Ritual.* Ithaca.

—— 1969. *The Ritual Process: Structure and Anti–Structure.* Chicago.

—— 1974. Pilgrimage as Social Process. In *Dramas, Fields, and Metaphors.* Ithaca.

—— 1975. *Revelation and Divination in Ndembu Ritual.* Ithaca.

—— 1979. *Process, Performance, and Pilgrimage.* New Delhi.

—— 1981 [1968]. *The Drums of Affliction.* Ithaca.

—— 1982. Acting in Everyday Life and Everyday Life in Acting. In *From Ritual to Theatre: The Human Seriousness of Play.* New York.

—— 1986. *The Anthropology of Performance.* New York.

—— and Edith Turner 1978. *Image and Pilgrimage in Christian Culture.* New York.

Tuzin, Donald. 1997. *The Cassowary's Revenge: The Life and Death of Masculinity in a New Guinea Society.* Chicago.

Tylor, E. B. 1958 [1871]. *Primitive Culture.* 2 vols. New York.

Urban, Greg. 1996. *Metaphysical Community: The Interplay of the Senses and the Intellect.* Austin.

Valentine, Lisa Philips and Regna Darnell, eds. 1999. *Theorizing the Americanist Tradition.* Toronto.

Valeri, Valerio. 1985. *Kingship and Sacrifice:*

Ritual and Society in Ancient Hawaii. Chicago.

Vallely, Anne. 2001. *Moral Landscapes: Ethical Discourses among Orthodox and Diaspora Jains.* Previously unpublished.

—— 2002. *Guardians of the Transcendent: An Ethnography of a Jain Ascetic Community.* Toronto.

van de Port, Mattijs. 1998. *Gypsies, Wars & Other Instances of the Wild: Civilisation and Its Discontents in a Serbian Town.* Amsterdam.

Van der Veer, Peter. 1988. *Gods on Earth: The Management of Religious Experience and Identity in a North Indian Pilgrimage Centre.* London.

—— 1994. *Religious Nationalism: Hindus and Muslims in India.* Berkeley.

—— ed. 1996. *Conversion to Modernities: The Globalization of Christianity.* New York.

—— 2001. *Imperial Encounters: Religion and Modernity in India and Britain.* Princeton.

—— 2002. Religion in South Asia. *Annual Review of Anthropology* 31(1): 173–87.

—— and Hartmut Lehmann, eds. 1999. *Nation and Religion: Perspectives on Europe and Asia.* Princeton.

Van Dijk, Rijk. 1998. Pentecostalism, Cultural Memory and the State: Contested Representations of Time in Postcolonial Malawi. In R. Werbner ed., *Memory and the Postcolony.* London.

—— 2001. "Voodoo" on the Doorstep: Young Nigerian Prostitutes and Magic Policing in the Netherlands. *Africa* 71(4): 558–86.

Varisco, Daniel. 2005. *Islam Obscured: The Rhetoric of Anthropological Representation.* New York.

Verdery, Katherine. 1999. *The Political Lives of Dead Bodies: Reburial and Postsocialist Change.* New York.

Vertovec, Steve. 2000. *The Hindu Diaspora: Comparative Patterns.* New York.

Villas Boas, Orlando and Claudio Villas Boas. 2004. *Xingu: The Indians, their Myths.* London.

Vitebsky, Piers. 1993. *Dialogues with the Dead: The Discussion of Mortality among the Sora of Eastern India.* Cambridge.

—— 1995. *The Shaman: Voyages of the Soul, Trance, Ecstasy and Healing from Siberia to the Amazon.* Boston.

—— 2005. *The Reindeer People: Living with Animals and Spirits in Siberia.* Boston, MA.

Viveiros de Castro, Eduardo. 1992. *From the Enemy's Point of View.* Chicago.

—— 1998. Cosmological Deixis and Amerindian Perspectivism. *JRAI,* n.s. 4(3): 469–88.

Vogt, Evon. 1976. *Tortillas for the Gods: A Symbolic Analysis of Zinacanteco Rituals.* Cambridge, MA.

Volkman, Toby. 1985. *Feasts of Honor: Ritual and Change in the Toraja Highlands.* Urbana.

Von Glahn, Richard. 2004. *The Sinister Way: The Divine and the Demonic in Chinese Religious Culture.* Berkeley.

Wacker, Grant. 2001. *Heaven Below: Early Pentecostals and American Culture.* Cambridge, MA.

Wafer, Jim. 1991. *The Taste of Blood: Spirit Possession in Brazilian Candomblé.* Philadelphia.

Wagner, Melinda B. 1990. *God's Schools: Choice and Compromise in American Society.* New Brunswick, NJ.

Wagner, Roy. 1978. *Lethal Speech: Daribi Myth as Symbolic Obviation.* Ithaca.

—— 1981 [1975]. *The Invention of Culture.* Chicago.

Wallace, Anthony F. C. 1956. Revitalization Movements. *AA* 58: 264–81.

—— 1966. *Religion: An Anthropological View.* New York.

—— 1972. *The Death and Rebirth of the Seneca.* New York.

Wallis, Robert J. 2002. The Bwili or "Flying Tricksters" of Malakula: A Critical Discussion of Recent Debates on Rock Art, Ethnography and Shamanisms. *JRAI* 8(4): 735–60.

Walsh, Andrew. 2001. When Origins Matter: The Politics of Commemoration in Northern Madagascar. *Ethnohistory* 48(1–2): 237–56.

—— 2002a. Saving Souls, Preserving Bodies: Religious Incongruity in a Northern Malagasy Mining Town. *Journal of Religion in Africa* 32(3): 366–92.

—— 2002b. Responsibility, Taboos and "The Freedom to do Otherwise" in Ankarana, Northern Madagascar. *JRAI* 8(3): 451–68.

Walzer, Michael. 1965. *The Revolution of the Saints: A Study in the Origins of Radical Politics*. Cambridge, MA.

—— 1997. *On Toleration*. New Haven.

Ward, Colleen, ed. 1989. *Altered States of Consciousness and Mental Health: A Cross-Cultural Perspective*. Newbury Park, CA.

Warner, W. Lloyd. 1959. *The Living and the Dead: A Study of the Symbolic Life of Americans*. New Haven.

Watson, C. W. 2005. A Popular Indonesian Preacher: The Significance of Aa Gymnastiar. *JRAI* 11(4): 773–92.

—— and R. Ellen, eds. 1993. *Understanding Witchcraft and Sorcery in Southeast Asia*. Honolulu.

Watson, James and E. Rawski, eds. 1988. *Death Ritual in Late Imperial and Modern China*. Berkeley.

Watson, Rubie. 1986. The Named and the Nameless. *AE* 13: 619–31.

Weber, Max. 1946a. *From Max Weber: Essays in Sociology*. H. H. Gerth and C. W. Mills, eds. and trans. New York.

—— 1946b [1915]. The Social Psychology of the World Religions. In Weber 1946a.

—— 1946c [1922–3]. The Protestant Sects and the Spirit of Capitalism. In Weber 1946a.

—— 1946d [1915]. Religious Rejections of the World and Their Directions. In Weber 1946a.

—— 1958 [1904–5]. *The Protestant Ethic and the Spirit of Capitalism*. T. Parsons, trans. New York. [Reprinted 1998, R. Collins, intro.]

—— 1963 [1922]. *The Sociology of Religion*. Ephraim Fischoff, trans. Boston.

Weeratunge-Starkloff, Nireka. 2000. Nature, Harmony and the Kaliyugaya. Global/Local Discourses on the Human-Environment Relationship. *Current Anthropology* 41(2): 249–28.

Weiner, James. 1988. *The Heart of the Pearl Shell: The Mythological Dimension of Foi Sociality*. Berkeley.

—— 1991. *The Empty Place: Poetry, Space,*

and Being among the Foi of Papua New Guinea. Bloomington.

Weiss, Brad. 1996. *The Making and Unmaking of the Haya Lived World: Consumption and Commoditization in Everyday Practice*. Durham, NC.

—— 1998. Electric Vampires: Haya Rumors of the Commodified Body. In M. Lambek and A. Strathern, eds., *Bodies and Persons*. Cambridge.

Weller, Robert. 1987. *Unities and Diversities in Chinese Religion*. Houndmills, Basingstoke.

—— and Meir Shahar, eds. 1996. *Unruly Gods: Divinity and Society in China*. Honolulu.

Werbner, Pnina, 1996a. Allegories of Sacred Imperfection: Magic, Hermeneutics, and Passion in the Satanic Verses. *Current Anthropology* 37 (Suppl.): S56–78.

—— 1996b. Stamping the Earth with the Name of Allah: Zikr and Sacralizing of Space among British Muslims. *Cultural Anthropology* 11: 309–38.

—— 2001. The Limits of Cultural Hybridity: On Ritual Monsters, Poetic License and Contested Postcolonial Purification. *JRAI* 7(1): 133–52.

—— 2002. *Imagined Diasporas among Manchester Muslims: The Public Performance of Pakistani Transnational Identity Politics*. Oxford.

—— 2003. *Pilgrims of Love: The Anthropology of a Global Sufi Cult*. London.

—— and Helene Basu, eds. 1998. *Embodying Charisma. Modernity, Locality, and the Performance of Emotion in Sufi Cults*. New York.

Werbner, Richard, ed. 1977. *Regional Cults*. New York.

—— 1989. *Ritual Passage, Sacred Journey: The Process and Organization of Religious Movement*. Washington, DC.

—— ed. 1998. *Memory and the Postcolony: African Anthropology and the Critique of Power*. London.

West, Harry. 2001. Sorcery of Construction and Socialist Modernization: Ways of Understanding Power in Postcolonial Mozambique. *AE* 28(1): 119–50.

—— 2005. *Kupilikula: Governance and*

the Invisible Realm in Mozambique. Chicago.

—— 2007. *Ethnographic Sorcery*. Chicago.

—— and Todd Sanders, eds. 2003. *Transparency and Conspiracy: Ethnographies of Suspicion in the New World Order*. Durham.

Wheatley, Paul. 1971. *The Pivot of the Four Quarters*. Chicago.

White, Allon. 1993. *Carnival, Hysteria, and Writing*. Oxford.

White, Hayden. 1973. *Metahistory: The Historical Imagination in 19th-Century Europe*. Baltimore.

White, Leslie. 1949. *The Science of Culture*. New York.

White, Luise. 2000. *Speaking with Vampires: Rumor and History in Colonial Africa*. Berkeley.

Whitehead, Neil L. and Robin Wright, eds. 2004. *In Darkness and Secrecy: The Anthropology of Assault Sorcery and Witchcraft in Amazonia*. Durham.

Whitehouse, Harvey. 1995. *Inside the Cult: Religious Innovation and Transmission in Papua New Guinea*. Oxford.

—— 2000. *Arguments and Icons: Divergent Modes of Religiosity*. Oxford.

—— 2004. *Modes of Religiosity: A Cognitive Theory of Religious Transmission*. Walnut Creek, CA.

—— and James Laidlaw. 2004. *Ritual and Memory: Toward a Cognitive Anthropology of Religion*. Walnut Creek, CA.

Whiteley, Peter. 1988. *Deliberate Acts: Changing Hopi Culture through the Oraibi Split*. Tucson.

—— 1998. *Rethinking Hopi Ethnography*. Washington, DC.

Wiegele, Katherine. 2004. *Investing in Miracles: El Shaddai and the Transformation of Popular Catholicism in the Philippines*. Honolulu.

Wiener, Marjorie. 1995. *Visible and Invisible Realms: Power, Magic, and Colonial Conquest in Bali*. Chicago.

Wiessner, Polly and Akii Tumu. 1998. *Historical Vines: Enga Networks of Exchange, Ritual, and Warfare in Papua New Guinea*. Washington, DC.

Williams, Duncan R. 2004. *The Other Side of Zen: A Social History of Soto Zen Buddhism in Tokugawa Japan*. Princeton.

Williams, Raymond. 1977. *Marxism and Literature*. Oxford.

Willis, Roy, ed. 1975. *The Interpretation of Symbolism*. New York.

—— 1990. *Signifying Animals: Human Meaning in the Natural World*. London.

Wilson, Bryan, ed. 1970. *Rationality*. Evanston.

—— 1975. The Debate over Secularization. *Encounter* 45(4): 77–83.

—— 1979. The Return of the Sacred. *Journal for the Scientific Study of Religion* 18(3): 268–80.

Wilson, Monica Hunter. 1957. *Rituals of Kinship among the Nyakyusa*. London.

—— 1970 [1951]. Witch–Beliefs and Social Structure. In Max Marwick, ed., *Witchcraft and Sorcery*.

Winch, Peter. 1970 [1964]. On Understanding a Primitive Society. In Wilson, ed., *Rationality*.

Witherspoon, Gary. 1977. *Language and Art in the Navajo Universe*. Ann Arbor.

Wittgenstein, Ludwig. 1979 [written 1931]. *Remarks on Frazer's Golden Bough*. A. Miles, trans., Rush Rhees, ed. Retford, UK.

Wolf, Arthur, ed. 1974. *Religion and Ritual in Chinese Society*. Stanford.

Wolf, Eric R. 1958. The Virgin of Guadalupe: A Mexican National Symbol. *Journal of American Folklore* LXXI: 34–9.

—— 1964. Santa Claus: Notes on a Collective Representation. In R. Manners, ed., *Process and Pattern in Culture*. Chicago.

—— 1982. *Europe and the People Without History*. Berkeley.

—— ed. 1984. *Religion, Power, and Protest in Local Communities: The Northern Shore of the Mediterranean*. Berlin.

—— ed. 1991. *Religious Regimes and State Formation: Perspectives from European Ethnology*. Albany.

—— 1999. *Envisioning Power: Ideologies of Dominance and Crisis*. Berkeley.

Wolf, Richard K. 2006. The Poetics of "Sufi" Practice: Drumming, Dancing and Complex

Agency at Madho Lal Husain (and beyond). *AE* 33(2): 246–68.

Woodward, Mark 1989. *Islam in Java. Normative Piety and Mysticism in the Sultanate of Yogyakarta.* Tucson.

Worsley, Peter. 1957. *The Trumpet Shall Sound: A Study of "Cargo" Cults in Melanesia.* London.

Wright, Ronald. 1990. *Time Among the Maya.* Markham, ON.

—— 1992. *Stolen Continents: The Indian Story.* London.

Wrong, Dennis, ed. 1970. *Max Weber.* Englewood Cliffs, NJ.

Wuthnow, Robert. 1988. *The Restructuring of American Religion.* Princeton.

Yalman, Nur. 1991. On Secularism and Its Critics: Notes on Turkey, India and Iran. *Contributions to Indian Sociology* 25(2): 237–67.

Yamba, Bawa. 1991. *Permanent Pilgrims: The Role of Pilgrimage in the Lives of West African Muslims in Sudan.* Washington, DC.

Yang, Mayfair Mei-hui. 1994. *Gifts, Favors, and Banquets: The Art of Social Relationships in China.* Ithaca.

Young, Michael. 1983. *Magicians of Manumanua. Living Myth in Kalauna.* Berkeley.

Zahan, Dominique. 1979. *The Religion, Spirituality, and Thought of Traditional Africa.* Chicago.

el–Zein, Abdul Hamid. 1974. *The Sacred Meadows.* Evanston.

Zeitlyn, David. 2001. Finding Meaning in the Text: The Process of Interpretation in Text-Based Divination. *JRAI* 7(2): 225–40.

Zubrzycki, Genevieve. 2006. *The Crosses of Auschwitz: Nationalism and Religion in Post-Communist Poland.* Chicago.

Index